Misshapes

The Making of Tatty Devine

Tatty Devine®

Tatty Devine

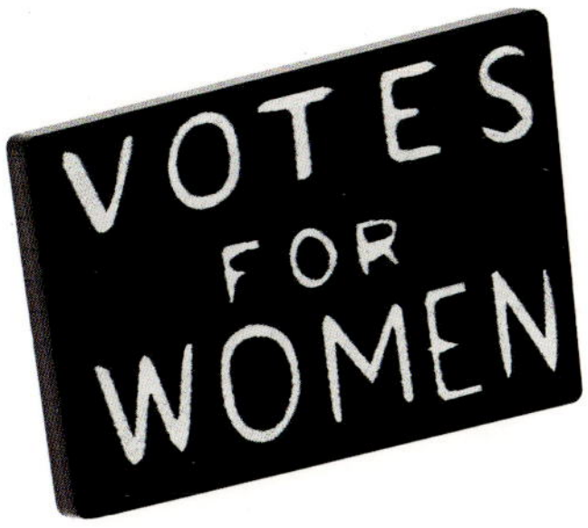
VOTES
FOR
WOMEN

CRAFT POWER

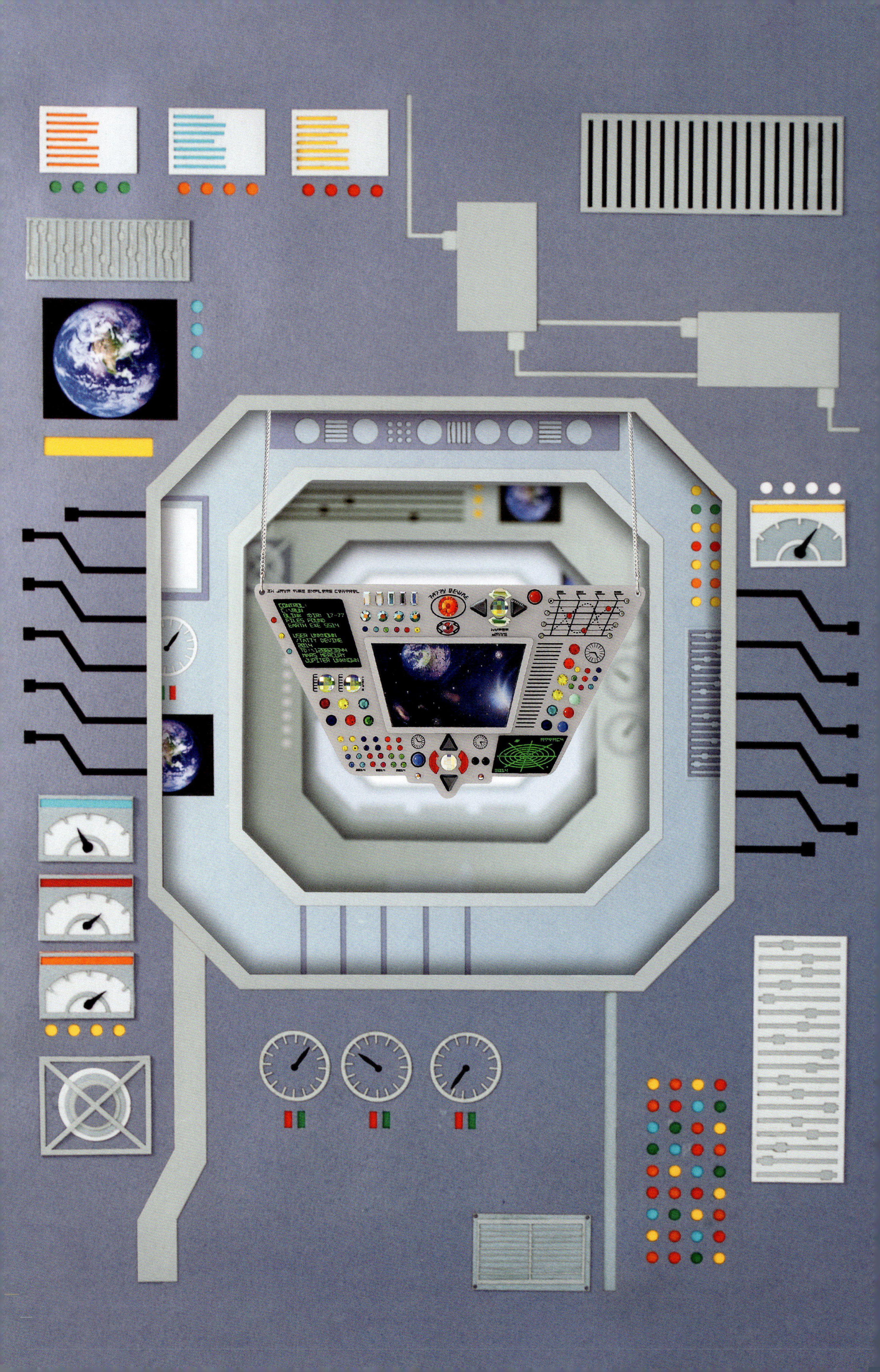

Tatty Devine at 20

When Rosie Wolfenden met Harriet Vine at Chelsea College of Art and Design in 1996, the UK was on the brink of electing its first Labour government in 18 years. Just as *Time* magazine had declared London 'Swinging' in a cover story in 1966, thirty years later *Newsweek* pronounced London the 'World's Coolest City', illustrated with a model on the cover wearing a plumed Philip Treacy headpiece resembling a Union Jack flag. British fashion was again in the global spotlight. The same year, Alexander McQueen and John Galliano – the *enfants terribles* of British fashion, who both trained at London's Central Saint Martins – were appointed to Givenchy and Christian Dior respectively, leading soon to be ex-Prime Minister John Major to declare: 'our country has taken over the fashion catwalks of Paris.'[1]

Two years later, while Rosie and Harriet were still at art school, Chris Smith, the then Secretary of State for Culture, Media and Sport, published a book called *Creative Britain* which argued for wider access to the arts, and for the economic importance of the creative industries. These ideas formed the backbone of the cultural policy of the New Labour government, which included increased public investment, as well as funding from initiatives like the recent National Lottery. Culture and creativity were given a prominent place in political discussions, in an era which Tony Blair later called a 'golden age' of the arts.[2]

This political emphasis on creativity built on the spirit of regeneration that was spreading across the capital, giving new life to former industrial spaces, especially in the East End. *Vanity Fair* encapsulated this excitement just two months before the Labour election victory in 1997, claiming: 'Every rotting wharf, every disused factory, every seedy locale where Ronnie Kray once nailed someone's head to the floor, is a restaurant or arts complex waiting to happen.... virtually every aspect of the city's culture has experienced a defining moment of revival.'[3] The Eurostar had launched earlier in the decade. London was open to the world, and 'Cool Britannia' was on the rise.

The East End had been home to the fashion industry for centuries. Waves of immigration into the area contributed to the patchwork of sartorial trades and industries around the borough of Tower Hamlets. From the late 17th century, persecuted French Protestant Huguenots fled Catholic France and brought silk weaving to Spitalfields. In the second half of the 19th century, Jewish immigration from Eastern Europe (again due to fleeing persecution) had a profound impact on the tailoring trades and manufacturing in the East End.[4] The industry of the area was vital to the functioning success of the retail revival of 'swinging' west and central London in the 1950s and 1960s.[5] In the 1960s and 1970s the rag trade tradition was continued by the Bengali community, centred around the aptly-named Fashion Street.[6]

The art-fashion mix that came to define the regeneration of the area can be traced to 1988's Freeze exhibition in London's Docklands. Organised by Damien Hirst while he was still at Goldsmiths College, the show heralded the ascendance of the Young British Artists (YBAs, as they became known) in the London art scene. Assemblage, found objects and readymades were central to the early ethos of Tatty Devine jewellery, a thread that can also be found in the work of some prominent YBAs. In 1999, after finding bin bags of leather sample books in the street, Harriet designed a leather cuff with an arrow head fastening. Objects such as guitar plectrums were turned into jewellery. Pieces were picked up from markets, skips and charity shops, and reconfigured to become works of wearable art, as

1. Anthony Bevins, 'Cool Britannia: Major claims the credit' *The Independent*, 12 November 1996
2. For more, see David Lee, David Hesmondhalgh, Kate Oakley and Melissa Nisbett (2014) 'Regional creative industries policy-making under New Labour', *Cultural Trends*, 23:4, 217–231; and, Philip Schlesinger (2017) 'The creative economy: invention of a global orthodoxy', *Innovation: The European Journal of Social Science Research*, 30:1, 73–90
3. David Kamp, 'London Swings Again!' *Vanity Fair*, March 1997
4. See, for example, Anne J. Kershen (1997) 'Morris Cohen and the Origins of the Women's Wholesale Clothing Industry in the East End', *Textile History*, 28:1, 39–46
5. Christopher Breward (2006) 'Fashion's Front and Back: 'Rag trade' Cultures and Cultures of Consumption in Post-war London c. 1945–1970', *The London Journal*, 31:1, 15–40
6. James Maitland Gard'ner (2004) 'Heritage Protection and Social Inclusion: A Case Study from the Bangladeshi Community of East London', *International Journal of Heritage Studies*, 10:1, 75–92

Harriet has noted, it was less about jewellery than about, 'attaching things to your body so you could go out wearing them.' These early pieces were featured in magazines from *Vogue* to *Sleazenation* and stocked in exclusive department stores, experimental boutiques and vintage stores alike.

At the dawn of the new millennium, arts and culture were embedded into the national agenda. The Tate Modern opened in the former Bankside Power Station, emphasising the post-industrial focus on the arts. Jay Jopling opened his White Cube gallery in Hoxton Square. Having cut their teeth on the market stalls of Portobello, Camden and Spitalfields, and having secured their first orders, Rosie Wolfenden and Harriet Vine signed the lease on their Brick Lane shop.

> **In the space of nine months, they have transformed themselves from debt-ridden fine art graduates into fashion designers whose unique products have not only appeared in the millennium issue of *Vogue*, worn by Erin O'Connor, but are also stocked at Harvey Nichols, Fenwick, Whistles and Steinberg & Tolkien.**
> Melanie Rickey, *The Telegraph*, 21 April 2000

The Tatty Devine store took inspiration from YBAs Tracey Emin and Sarah Lucas, who for six months in 1993 sold their artwork from a Bethnal Green location known simply as The Shop. The Shop functioned as both retail hub and social space, as well as a calling card to international art dealers keen to capitalise on the moment. Tracey Emin's 30th birthday party marked The Shop's close, with a night called, 'Fuckin' Fantastic at 30 and She's Just About Old Enough to Do Whatever She Wants'. Harriet and Rosie, on the hunt for a studio, had been making jewellery and conducting sales meetings from their bedrooms. Getting a shop not only provided room for making and selling their jewellery, but allowed space for events and ideas to flourish.

The rise of the internet ensured small businesses could grow beyond bricks and mortar. The digital revolution was spearheaded in the fashion industry with the launch of Nick Knight's SHOWstudio in 2000 – the company continues to innovate across fashion imagery and communication. The internet would reshape the shopping experience through e-commerce and social media, allowing designs to reach a global audience. Technology, too, plays a vital role in the Tatty Devine story. In 2001, on a research trip to New York, Harriet and Rosie found laser-cut acrylic on Canal Street, in the heart of Chinatown. The relatively recent technology of laser cutting was only developed in the 1960s, and would transform the aesthetic of Tatty Devine. The following year, in 2002, Harriet taught herself to use a laser-cutter, and future Tatty Devine classics such as the Glasses and Lobster necklaces soon followed.

Experimental retail thrived around the turn of the millennium. Vintage clothing was on the rise, sold across the city from Beyond Retro just off Brick Lane, to Rosie's former employer Steinberg & Tolkien in Chelsea. Another inspiration was The Pineal Eye, on Broadwick Street in Soho. Stocking young designers next to established names, the store acted as a breeding ground for fashion talent, including creative director and fashion editor Nicola Formichetti who has credited his time there with starting his career.[7] This tradition is kept alive in the city, despite increasingly high rents and rates, by Tatty Devine, alongside more recent stores such as Dover Street Market, MACHINE-A and LN-CC.

> **They are adept at sparking trends and they're pop-culture catalysts.**
> *Vogue*, 2003

The mid-2000s saw a boom in nightlife across the capital, forming the perfect theatre for unconventional and playful jewellery. Hoxton Square had been home to Metalheadz at Blue Note in the 1990s, a regular haunt for Harriet and Rosie. The electroclash scene at the turn of the millennium was fuel for midweek club nights such as Trash, Kash Point and Nag Nag Nag, while an interest in early jazz, jive and cabaret ignited vintage glamour at Lady Luck and Rakehell's Revels – the latter held at the decadent Grill Room at the Cafe Royal. By the time the Tatty Devine store on Soho's Brewer Street opened in 2004, the geography of shopping and clubbing had merged across the East and West End. Hoxton Square, just a stone's throw from the alt-drag Radio Egypt parties at the George & Dragon pub, was now home to Richard Mortimer's flamboyant BoomBox on a Sunday night, featuring guests from Kylie Minogue to Princess Julia, Bjork and Naomi Campbell. Continuing the legacy of forerunners such as Blitz, Taboo and Kinky Gerlinky, London was the stage for a revival of spectacular nightlife, and extravagant dressing was essential for entry.

With the financial crisis of 2008, the economic and political landscape shifted. A general election in 2010 saw a coalition government take the helm, and usher in a policy of austerity and cuts. Fractures became clear across the country in August 2011 when riots broke out in Tottenham after the police killing of local man Mark Duggan. Violence and unrest spread across the country. The 2012 Olympics took place in East London, promising much-needed regeneration, but also faced criticism for exacerbating social division and gentrification.[8] By the time of the 2016 EU referendum, the political was both personal and public, and a desire to show allegiances saw slogan clothing at the forefront of protest marches in this new era of political engagement. Designer Katharine Hamnett, whose anti-nuclear T-shirt made headlines in 1984 when she met the then Prime Minister Margaret Thatcher at a Downing Street reception, created 'Cancel Brexit' T-shirts in reaction to the result. Meanwhile, Harriet and Rosie, both avid collectors of pin badges, channelled their political messages through their designs.

The 2018 centenary of the Representation of the People Act celebrated the success of suffrage campaigners who had waged long and sometimes bloody campaigns in the fight to give women a political voice. As female entrepreneurs, collections celebrating women had always been a part of Rosie and Harriet's ethos. The art collective and electroclash band Chicks on Speed were early collaborators, as was the musician and performance artist Peaches. For the centenary, Tatty Devine created designs for the Fawcett Society campaigning for gender equality and women's rights, and made a Suffragette collection for the Museum of London inspired by original protest banners in the museum's collection.

A government press release in 2018 celebrated the value of the creative industries for the UK economy, which had smashed through the £100 billion mark.[9] Despite this, Rosie and Harriet have been vocal about the impact of rates and rent rises on businesses in East London.[10] In a TEDx Talk delivered at Tate Liverpool as part of the Formby Point Women event, they made their concerns clear about the current lack of investment in arts education. To counteract this, in 2019 they began their own awareness-raising campaign for creativity, building on their success over the last two decades to encourage other young businesses to follow in their footsteps. Despite adversity, Tatty Devine remains a thriving female-run independent British company whose longevity and innovation is an inspiration for future generations.

Amber Butchart
May 2019

7. Stuart Brumfitt, 'London's Legendary Stores' *iD*, 9 November 2015

8. See Paul Watt (2013) '"It's not for us": Regeneration, the 2012 Olympics and the gentrification of East London', *City: analysis of urban trends, culture, theory, policy, action*, 17:1, 99–118, and Jen Harvie (2013) 'Brand London 2012 and 'The Heart of East London': Competing Urban Agendas at the 2012 Games', *Contemporary Theatre Review*, 23:4, 486–501

9. Department for Digital, Culture, Media & Sport and The Rt Hon Jeremy Wright MP, 'Britain's creative industries break the £100 billion barrier' press release, 28 November 2018

10. Julia Kollewe, 'East End artists and businesses driven out as railway rents spiral' *The Guardian*, 7 April 2018

Introduction

Was it really only £8 for our first market stall? Did we really only earn £45 for time-and-a-half waitressing on New Year's Day in 1997? These were some of the questions we asked ourselves as we looked back on 20 years of Tatty Devine. The reason for our reminiscing? In 2018 we were offered a touring exhibition by the Crafts Council to celebrate the making of Tatty Devine from our beginnings as art students to where we are now. As we looked through boxes and boxes of ephemera, filled with bits of paper, gig tickets, party invites, fan mail, faxes, sketchbooks and notebooks, we realised it would make a brilliant book. All the bits and pieces told our story, and showed how much had changed over the years, but also how much had stayed the same.

During our 20 years we have switched from analogue to digital, moved from a market stall to shops, learned how to use a laser-cutter – and how to run a business. We have constantly tried out new things, but what hasn't changed is our amazing friendship, and how much we value creativity in all its forms.

Amber's introduction wonderfully sets the scene, describing how exciting London was when we started making jewellery. There was so much going on, with art and creativity of all kinds taking centre stage, and we were constantly inspired by London and all that was happening in it – there was a real sense that anything was possible. But it was our friendship and shared sense of values that really made things happen. Everything we've designed has started with a conversation: we're always chatting about things we've seen, and the odd things that inspire us. It could be a band, a piece of embroidery, a colour, or a concept, and as we talk, Harriet makes notes, or draws in her sketchbook, and between the two of us we work out how to make it, and how to make it work in the world of Tatty Devine.

This book celebrates our friendship and partnership and the 6000 pieces of jewellery we've made. The first half is a fast-paced flurry of events – everything seemed to happen at top speed as we got to grips with what we were doing, who we were and what we wanted Tatty Devine to be. The second half is all about the jewellery, and the inspiration behind it.

We don't see Tatty Devine as a job – for us, it's a way of life, and we are so lucky that we get to share it together. After all this time we still believe in and value exactly the same things: individuality, originality, creativity, happiness and the sharing of ideas. We hope you enjoy reading our story.

Rosie Wolfenden and Harriet Vine
May 2019

24.
9.
7.

1A
2
ILFORD HP5 PLUS
2A
3
9 6 5 0
3A
4
ILFORD HP5 PLUS
7
7A
ILFORD HP5 PLUS
8
8A
9
ILFORD HP5 PLUS
9A
10
9 6 5 0
13
13A
9 6 5 0
14
14A
ILFORD HP5 PLUS
15
15A
16
ILFORD HP5
19
19A
ILFORD HP5 PLUS
20
20A
9 6 5 0
21
21A
ILFORD HP5 PLUS
22
25
ORD HP5 PLUS
25A
26
26A
ILFORD HP5 PLUS
27
27A
9 6 5 0
28

Picture This

The Big Bang *1996–2001*

When we look back at the first few months of Tatty Devine, it's hard to believe that so much happened in such a short space of time. One minute we were carefree students wondering about our future, and the next we were making jewellery and appearing in *Vogue* – and all because of a simple leather cuff. It was a whirlwind, but also totally exhilarating and we loved every minute of it.

Even before we met at Chelsea College of Art and Design in 1996, we'd always made things. We were the sort of girls who painted scenery for the school play or backdrops for the local bands. We even rustled up hair scrunchies and friendship bracelets to sell on the local market when we were little. At college we cut up our jeans and turned them into skirts, made clothes from old patterns salvaged from charity shops and customised everything we went out in. And we went out a lot. We loved music so we'd go and see bands, and then head out dancing. And because we had inspiring art teachers, like Martin Creed and Chris Ofili, we went to as many art events as we could. We'd spend the early evenings in busy East London – that was where everything seemed to happen – at Cantaloupe, 333, Vibe Bar, Flowers East. But then it transformed into a ghost town late at night, and we'd rummage through the printers' bins looking for paper and card off-cuts to make work out of. When we weren't in East London we'd hang out at the ICA, where they put on events like Typical Girls and Little Stabs at Happiness.

The Event 111 flyer, ICA, 1997

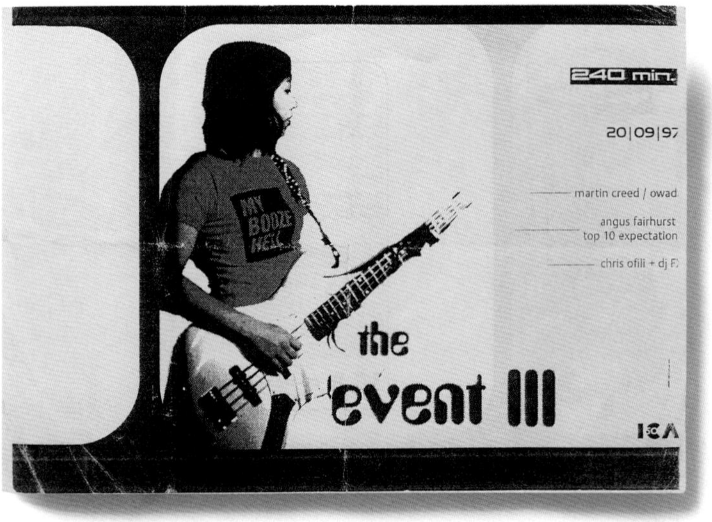

Typical Girls programme, ICA, 1997

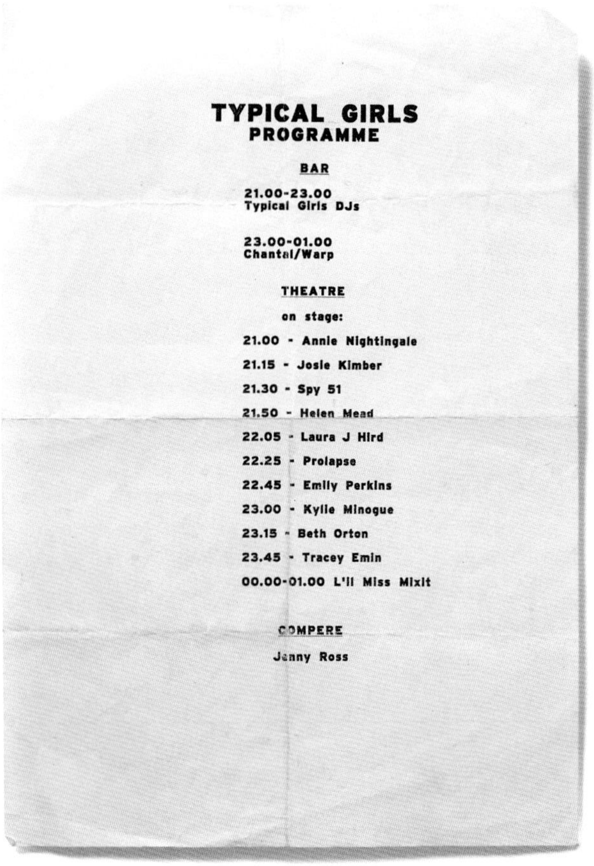

TYPICAL GIRLS
PROGRAMME

BAR

21.00-23.00
Typical Girls DJs

23.00-01.00
Chantal/Warp

THEATRE

on stage:

21.00 - Annie Nightingale
21.15 - Josie Kimber
21.30 - Spy 51
21.50 - Helen Mead
22.05 - Laura J Hird
22.25 - Prolapse
22.45 - Emily Perkins
23.00 - Kylie Minogue
23.15 - Beth Orton
23.45 - Tracey Emin
00.00-01.00 L'il Miss Mixit

COMPERE

Jenny Ross

Omsk flyer, 333 Old Street, 1997

2000 Troubled Teenagers flyer, Paradise Bar, 1998

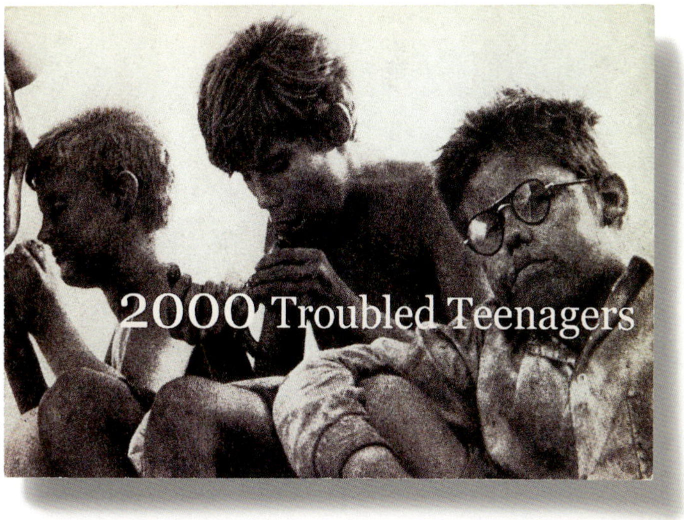

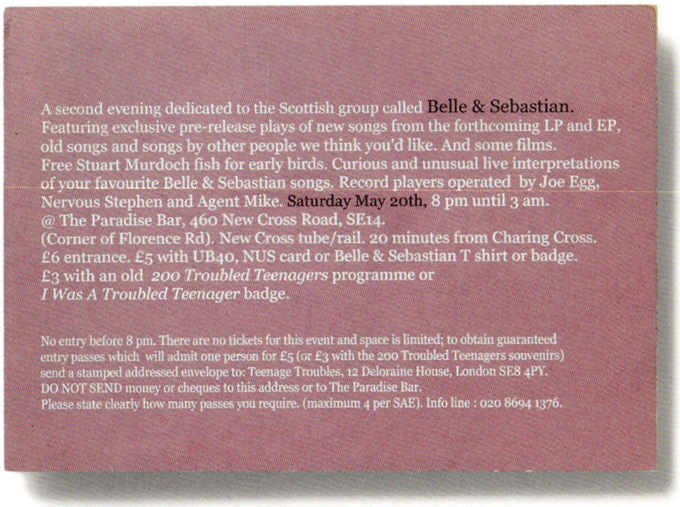

A second evening dedicated to the Scottish group called Belle & Sebastian.
Featuring exclusive pre-release plays of new songs from the forthcoming LP and EP,
old songs and songs by other people we think you'd like. And some films.
Free Stuart Murdoch fish for early birds. Curious and unusual live interpretations
of your favourite Belle & Sebastian songs. Record players operated by Joe Egg,
Nervous Stephen and Agent Mike. Saturday May 20th, 8 pm until 3 am.
@ The Paradise Bar, 460 New Cross Road, SE14.
(Corner of Florence Rd). New Cross tube/rail. 20 minutes from Charing Cross.
£6 entrance. £5 with UB40, NUS card or Belle & Sebastian T shirt or badge.
£3 with an old *200 Troubled Teenagers* programme or
I Was A Troubled Teenager badge.
No entry before 8 pm. There are no tickets for this event and space is limited; to obtain guaranteed
entry passes which will admit one person for £5 (or £3 with the 200 Troubled Teenagers souvenirs)
send a stamped addressed envelope to: Teenage Troubles, 12 Deloraine House, London SE8 4PY.
DO NOT SEND money or cheques to this address or to The Paradise Bar.
Please state clearly how many passes you require. (maximum 4 per SAE). Info line : 020 8694 1376.

Chelsea College of Art and Design Private View invite, Manresa Road, 1998

THE LONDON INSTITUTE
Chelsea College of Art & Design
BA HONOURS FINE ART DEGREE SHOWS
Private View: 7.00pm - 9.00pm 'Students and Guests'
Friday 12th June 1998.
Manresa Road, London SW3 6LS. Telephone 0171 514 7750
PUBLIC EXHIBITION (open entry)
Sunday 14th June, 10.00am to 5.00pm
Monday 15th June, 10.00am to 8.00pm
Tuesday 16th June, 10.00am to 8.00pm
Wednesday 17th June, 10.00am to 8.00pm
Thursday 18th June, 10.00am to 12.00 noon
Sponsored by
THE FREEDOM BREWING CO.
FREEDOM
FULHAM LONDON
Smoking is not permitted within this building
This card admits 1 person to the Private View. It must be shown at the door to gain entry.

We had three wonderful years at college, and although we knew we wanted to make stuff for a living, we weren't exactly sure what – or how – to go about it. While we were pondering our future we set about organising a degree show party, as no one else had. We chose Eve's nightclub on Regent Street because we knew Pulp had filmed the video for Common People on the light-up dance floor there. We designed and printed the invites, negotiated a free drink for everyone, and sold the tickets in a mad flurry. It was brilliant, and the first time we realised how well we worked together as a team.

Chelsea Degree Show party invite, Eve's, 1999

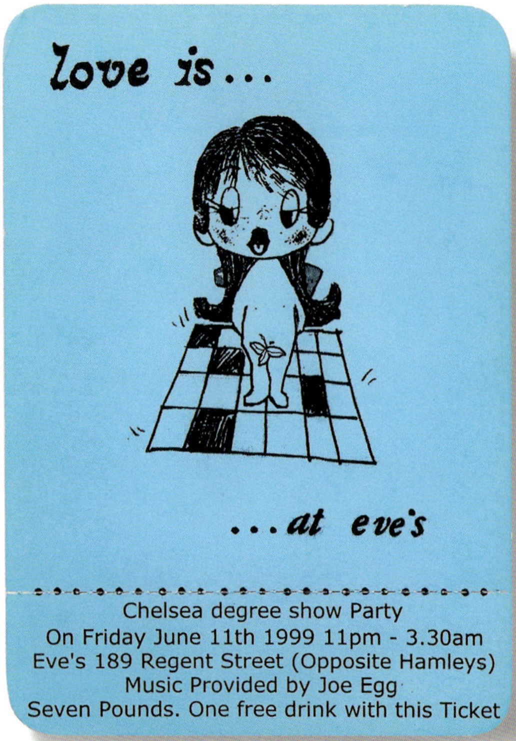

Harriet and Rosie on their graduation day, 1999

Here's us graduating at Central Hall Westminster in July 1999. We wore flip-flops with our graduation robes.

Arrow Head Cuffs, 1999
Leather

A chance find of a bundle of leather sample books abandoned outside a fancy upholstery shop set us on the path to becoming Tatty Devine. Harriet stumbled across them on the way back from the pub, smuggled them home in the dead of night, and left them under her bed, where they languished for months. She'd been wearing a leather cuff that had been sliced off a white belt and was held together with a hair grip. It was very Morten Harket from A-ha and Harriet had been getting lots of compliments for her lo-fi accessory. So, armed with craft knives and a lot of enthusiasm we set about making some similar ones to sell. We cut up the sample books – they were a treasure trove of brightly coloured leather, suede and snake skin in every shade of the rainbow – and abandoned the hair grip for a more secure fastening invented by Harriet's dad, Roger. And then we queued at dawn to get a pitch on a market.

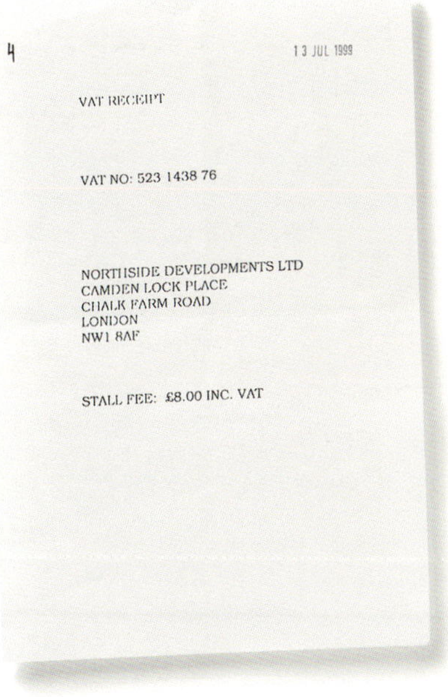

4 13 JUL 1999

VAT RECEIPT

VAT NO: 523 1438 76

NORTHSIDE DEVELOPMENTS LTD
CAMDEN LOCK PLACE
CHALK FARM ROAD
LONDON
NW1 8AF

STALL FEE: £8.00 INC. VAT

Camden market VAT receipt, 1999

Our first foray was in Camden on Tuesday 13 July 1999. We sold five cuffs and made £50; a boy bought one to put in a time capsule, and that felt like a lucky sign. The next week we tried out Portobello market on a Saturday and Spitalfields on a Sunday. It was cold and damp, and we had to put cardboard insoles into our shoes to keep our feet warm, but we loved it. It was so exciting; you never knew who was going to walk up to the stall – stylists, boutique owners, and people who would become friends and collaborators. We loved the camaraderie, and we worked every weekend up until the week before Christmas 1999.

We weren't the only ones selling cuffs, there was lots of competition, but thanks to the sample books, we had the best colours and styles. To make us stand out even more, we decided we needed a name. Harriet had been called 'Miss de Vine' at college, and we both loved finding old, tattered stuff in junk shops and car boot sales – and so in August 1999 we became Tatty Devine.

Stall book, 1999

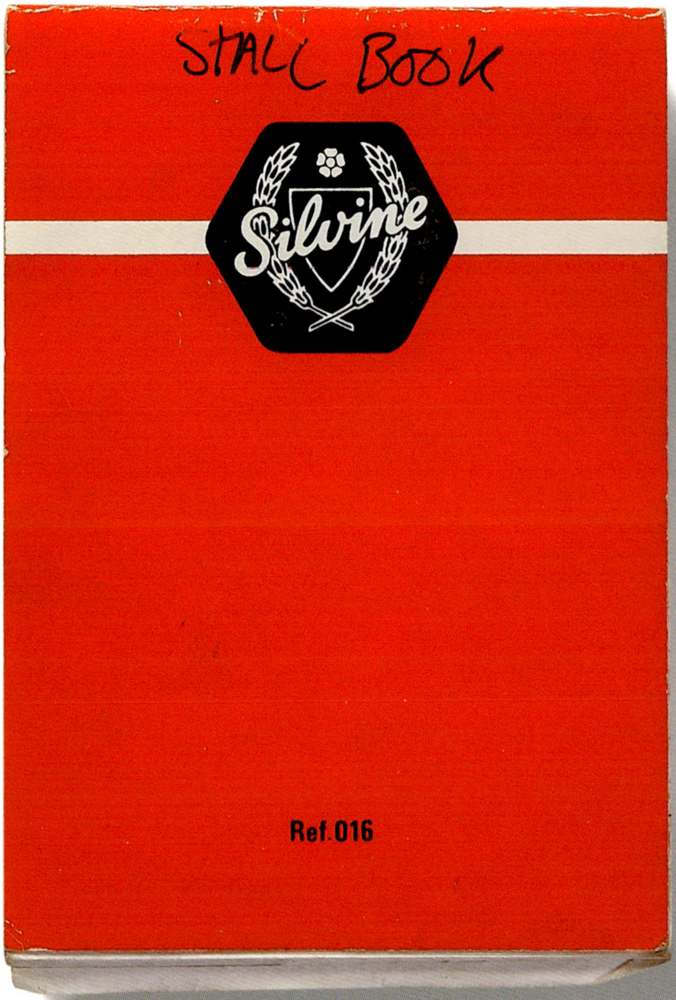

Harriet, Spitalfields market, 1999

The sun shone on us in more ways than one that summer. On a bright day in August Rosie headed to her part time job at vintage emporium Steinberg & Tolkien wearing a gem headpiece we'd refashioned from a 1980s cummerbund. A *Vogue* stylist was smitten by it, and before we knew it we had an invitation to take our collection to Vogue House to show Fashion Director Lucinda Chambers. We didn't actually have a collection, so we spent a mad-cap weekend creating gemmed belts and cuffs, with the help of Harriet's mum, Ann and her trusty sewing machine. Here we are on the following Monday, just about to go up to the *Vogue* offices.

Rosie and Harriet, Hanover Square, 1999

***Vogue* carrier bag**, 1999

Vogue borrowed many items from our impromptu, made-in-a-weekend collection and they returned the jewellery in a branded plastic bag, which we've never been able to throw away.

Zebra Skinny Cuff, 1999
Leather, suede, plastic gems

Zebra Wide Belt, 1999
Leather, suede

We loved putting our stamp on things. We printed 'Tatty Devine' on the inside of some belts using a kit that came with a tiny alphabet and tweezers to help arrange the letters. It was fiddly work, so much so that we forgot to punch holes in the belts we'd sold to a Japanese store, so they couldn't actually be fastened. We were mortified.

Whistles remittance advice, 1999

Whistles ordered dozens of zebra print cuffs in pink suede and we had to keep pinching ourselves that it was all really happening.

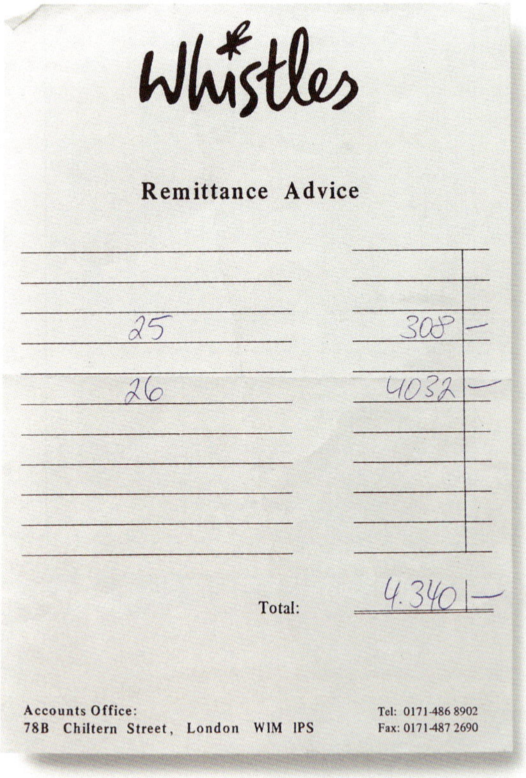

Whistles

Remittance Advice

25	308 —
26	4032 —

Total: 4.340 —

Accounts Office:
78B Chiltern Street, London W1M IPS

Tel: 0171-486 8902
Fax: 0171-487 2690

Print of Tatty Devine sign, 1999

Keen to get some advice we went along to the East London Small Business Centre who suggested we try The Clothes Show at the NEC in Birmingham. In December 1999, we loaded up Rosie's trusty Mini with a boot-load of jewellery and a giant fake neon sign. We couldn't afford the real thing so we made a DIY version out of colour photocopies and foam board.

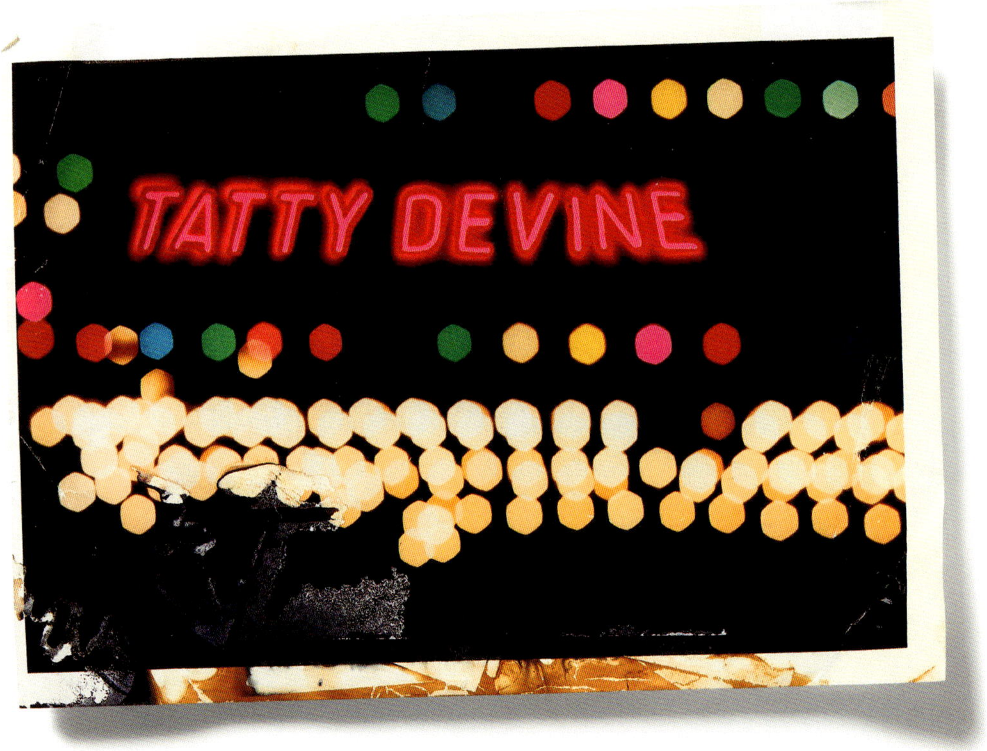

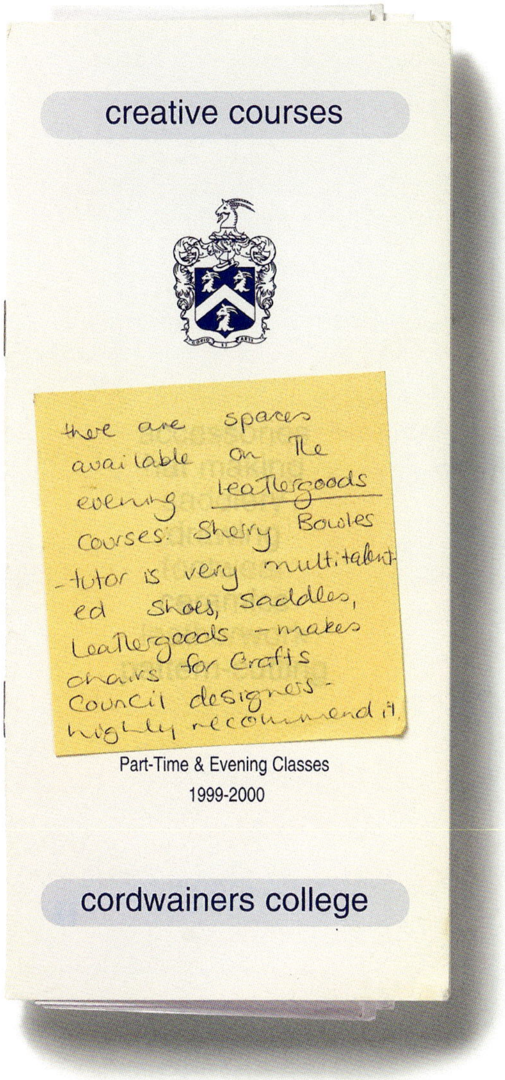
creative courses
there are spaces available on the evening leathergoods courses. Sherry Bowles - tutor is very multitalented shoes, saddles, leathergoods - makes chairs for Crafts Council designers - highly recommend it.
Part-Time & Evening Classes
1999-2000
cordwainers college

Cordwainers College Creative Courses leaflet, 1999

At one point we thought we should take an evening course at Cordwainers to learn how to work with leather properly. We got the leaflet, but never actually made it to a class – we were too relentlessly busy making things.

***Vogue* goods returns form**, 1999

Erin O'Connor wore the 'Chocolate Leather Two Pink Stripe Cuff' in *Vogue's* millennium issue. She was photographed by Mario Testino, alongside Jane and Louise Wilson, Beth Orton and David Collins – whom we later worked with on an interiors project.

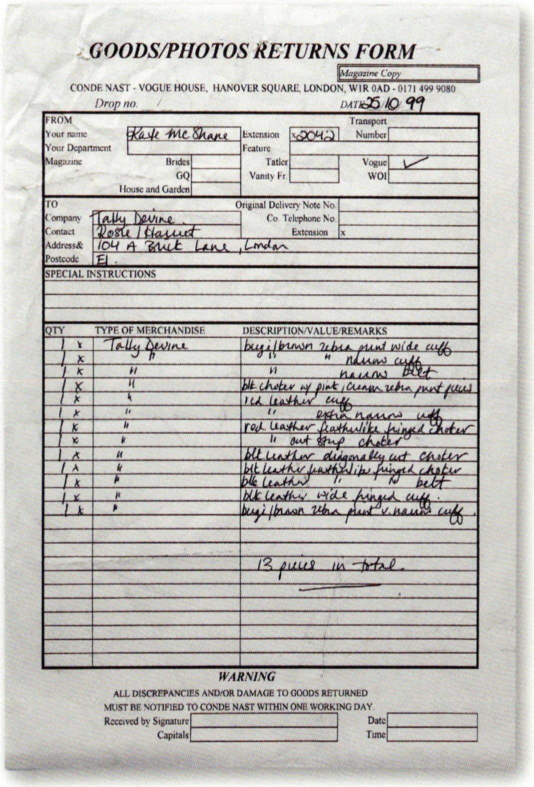

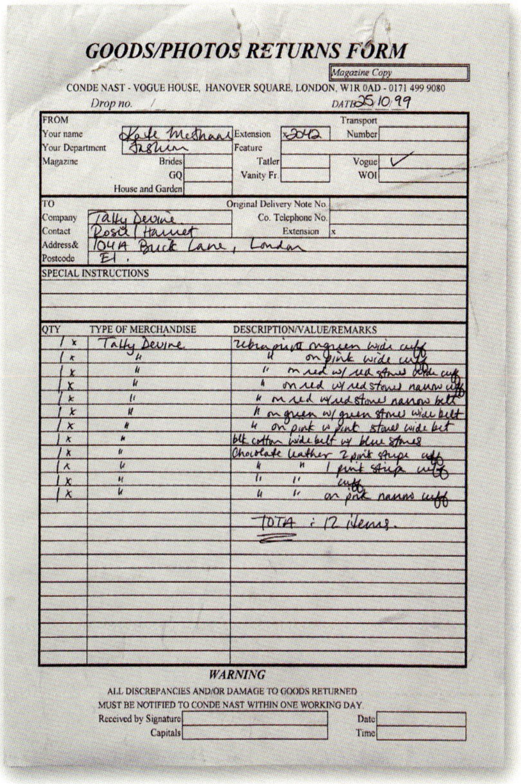

Notebook and Brogue Cuff, 1999
Leather, press studs

This early sketchbook entry shows how we went about making and producing the Brogue Cuff. We had invested in a press stud machine. Sketchbooks have always been among our prized possessions, and we never leave the house without one. There are stacks in our archive. We sketch out ideas, scribble out new ways of making things, and ways of experimenting with materials. Here we're working out how you could transform shiny black leather: Burn it, sand it, carve it, score it, peel it, nail varnish remover it, solvent it, caustic soda it, angle grind it, grate it, bleach it, glue on it, soldering iron it. We were determined to find new ways of doing things.

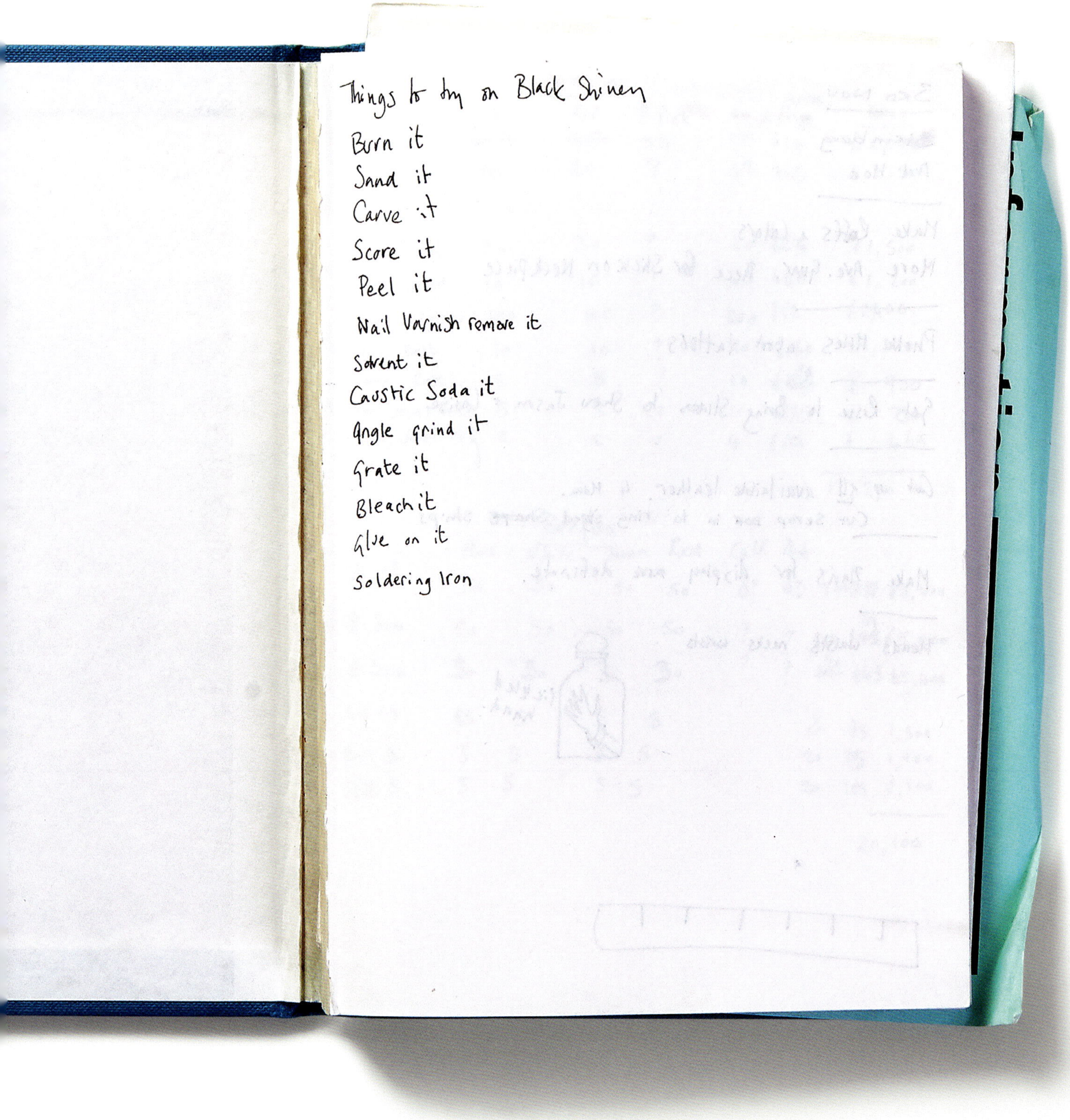

Things to try on Black Shiney
Burn it
Sand it
Carve it
Score it
Peel it
Nail Varnish remove it
Solvent it
Caustic Soda it
Angle grind it
Grate it
Bleach it
Glue on it
Soldering Iron

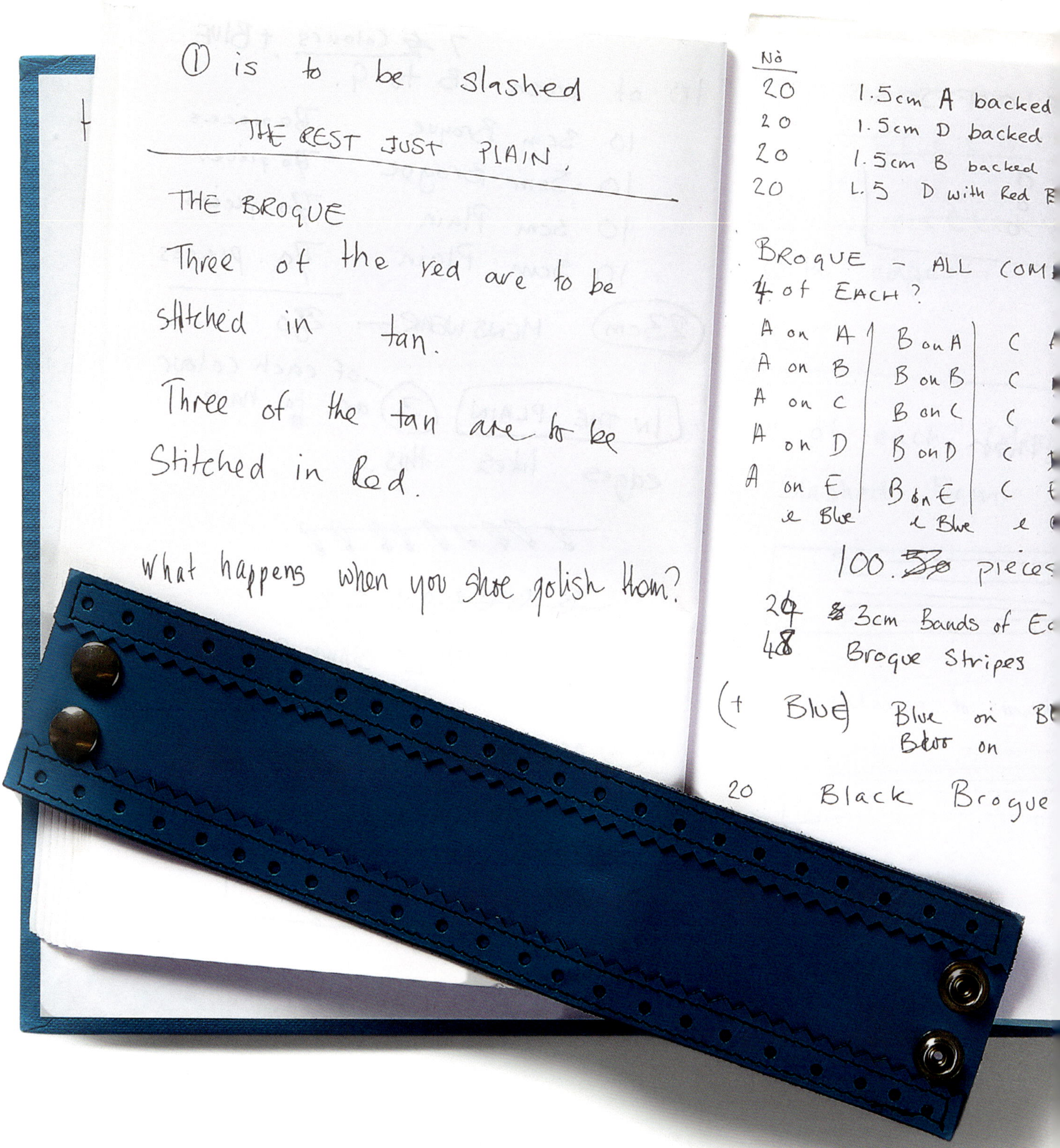
① is to be slashed
THE REST JUST PLAIN.
THE BROQUE
Three of the red are to be
stitched in tan.
Three of the tan are to be
Stitched in Red.
What happens when you shoe polish them?
No
20 1.5cm A backed
20 1.5cm D backed
20 1.5cm B backed
20 1.5 D with Red
BROQUE - ALL
4 of EACH ?
A on A
A on B
A on C
A on D
A on E
B on A
B on B
B on C
B on D
B on E
100. pieces
24 3cm Bands of
48 Broque Stripes
(+ Blue)
20 Black Brogue

Faxed Order from Harvey Nichols, 1999

We got an order from Harvey Nichols after they'd read a piece about us in the *Evening Standard*.

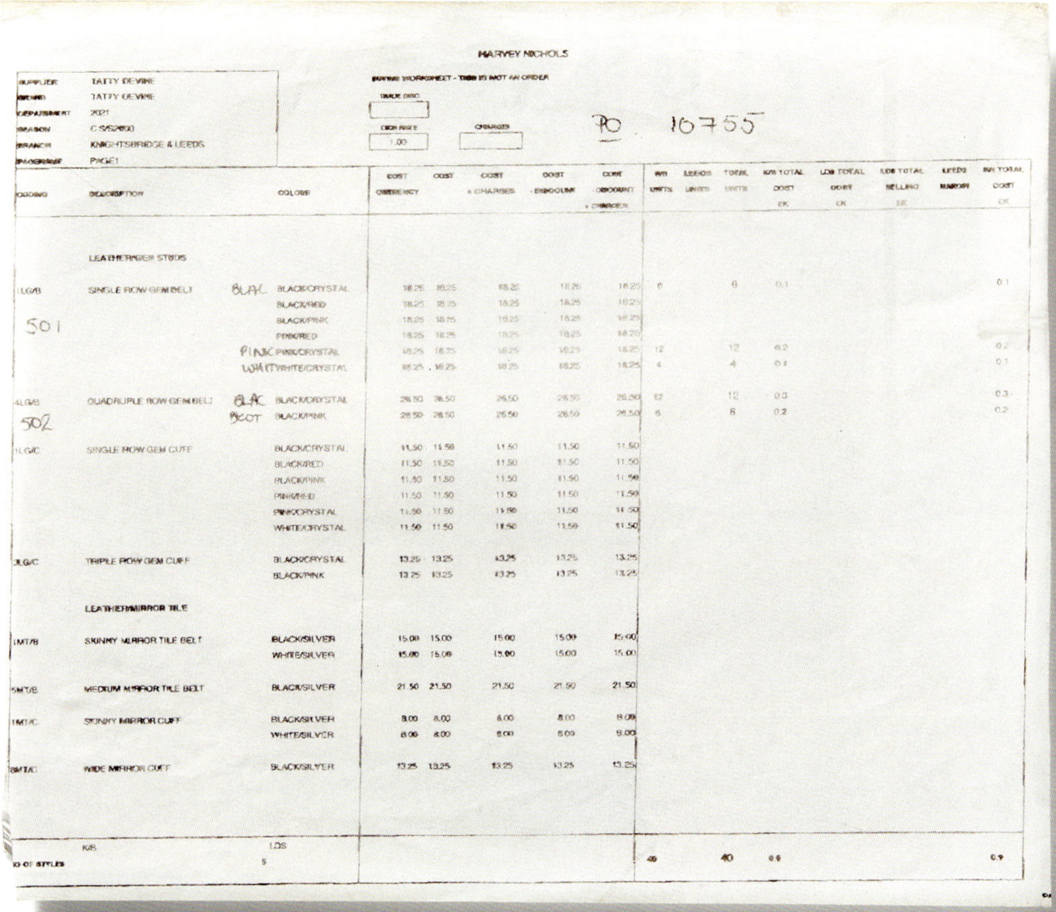

HARVEY NICHOLS

BUYING WORKSHEET - THIS IS NOT AN ORDER

SUPPLIER	TATTY DEVINE
BRAND	TATTY DEVINE
DEPARTMENT	2021
SEASON	C S/S2000
BRANCH	KNIGHTSBRIDGE & LEEDS
PAGE	PAGE1

TRADE DISC

EXCH RATE 1.00

CHARGES

PO 16755

CODING	DESCRIPTION		COLOURS	COST CURRENCY	COST	COST + CHARGES	COST - DISCOUNT	COST DISCOUNT + CHARGES	KB UNITS	LEEDS UNITS	TOTAL UNITS	KB TOTAL COST £K	LDS TOTAL COST £K	LDS TOTAL SELLING £K	LEEDS MARGIN	HN TOTAL COST £K
	LEATHER/GEM STUDS															
1LG/B	SINGLE ROW GEM BELT	BLAK	BLACK/CRYSTAL	18.25	18.25	18.25	18.25	18.25	6		6	0.1				0.1
			BLACK/RED	18.25	18.25	18.25	18.25	18.25								
501			BLACK/PINK	18.25	18.25	18.25	18.25	18.25								
			PINK/RED	18.25	18.25	18.25	18.25	18.25								
		PINK	PINK/CRYSTAL	18.25	18.25	18.25	18.25	18.25	12		12	0.2				0.2
		WHIT	WHITE/CRYSTAL	18.25	18.25	18.25	18.25	18.25	4		4	0.1				0.1
4LG/B	QUADRUPLE ROW GEM BELT	BLAC	BLACK/CRYSTAL	28.50	28.50	28.50	28.50	28.50	12		12	0.3				0.3
502		BCOT	BLACK/PINK	28.50	28.50	28.50	28.50	28.50	6		6	0.2				0.2
1LG/C	SINGLE ROW GEM CUFF		BLACK/CRYSTAL	11.50	11.50	11.50	11.50	11.50								
			BLACK/RED	11.50	11.50	11.50	11.50	11.50								
			BLACK/PINK	11.50	11.50	11.50	11.50	11.50								
			PINK/RED	11.50	11.50	11.50	11.50	11.50								
			PINK/CRYSTAL	11.50	11.50	11.50	11.50	11.50								
			WHITE/CRYSTAL	11.50	11.50	11.50	11.50	11.50								
3LG/C	TRIPLE ROW GEM CUFF		BLACK/CRYSTAL	13.25	13.25	13.25	13.25	13.25								
			BLACK/PINK	13.25	13.25	13.25	13.25	13.25								
	LEATHER/MIRROR TILE															
1MT/B	SKINNY MIRROR TILE BELT		BLACK/SILVER	15.00	15.00	15.00	15.00	15.00								
			WHITE/SILVER	15.00	15.00	15.00	15.00	15.00								
5MT/B	MEDIUM MIRROR TILE BELT		BLACK/SILVER	21.50	21.50	21.50	21.50	21.50								
1MT/C	SKINNY MIRROR CUFF		BLACK/SILVER	8.00	8.00	8.00	8.00	8.00								
			WHITE/SILVER	8.00	8.00	8.00	8.00	8.00								
8MT/C	WIDE MIRROR CUFF		BLACK/SILVER	13.25	13.25	13.25	13.25	13.25								
NO OF STYLES	KB		LDS 5						45		40	0.8				0.9

Single Row Gem Belt, 1999
Leather, suede, plastic gems, ribbon

We made the initial Harvey Nichols order with the help of a group of friends – there was just too much work for just the two of us. We camped out in Rosie's room and the table was piled high with coloured gems, leather and ribbon bought from our local shop, Frankle Trimmings on Bethnal Green Road. We sat around trying not to gossip, get distracted or prick our fingers onto the white leather and thread as we stitched all the gems on by hand.

Colouring Book collection, 2000

In February 2000, we showed a collection at a trade show in Olympia. We hadn't named the collection, but we did have a catalogue. It was a colouring book and came with a set of crayons so you could fill in Harriet's drawings of us wearing the jewellery.

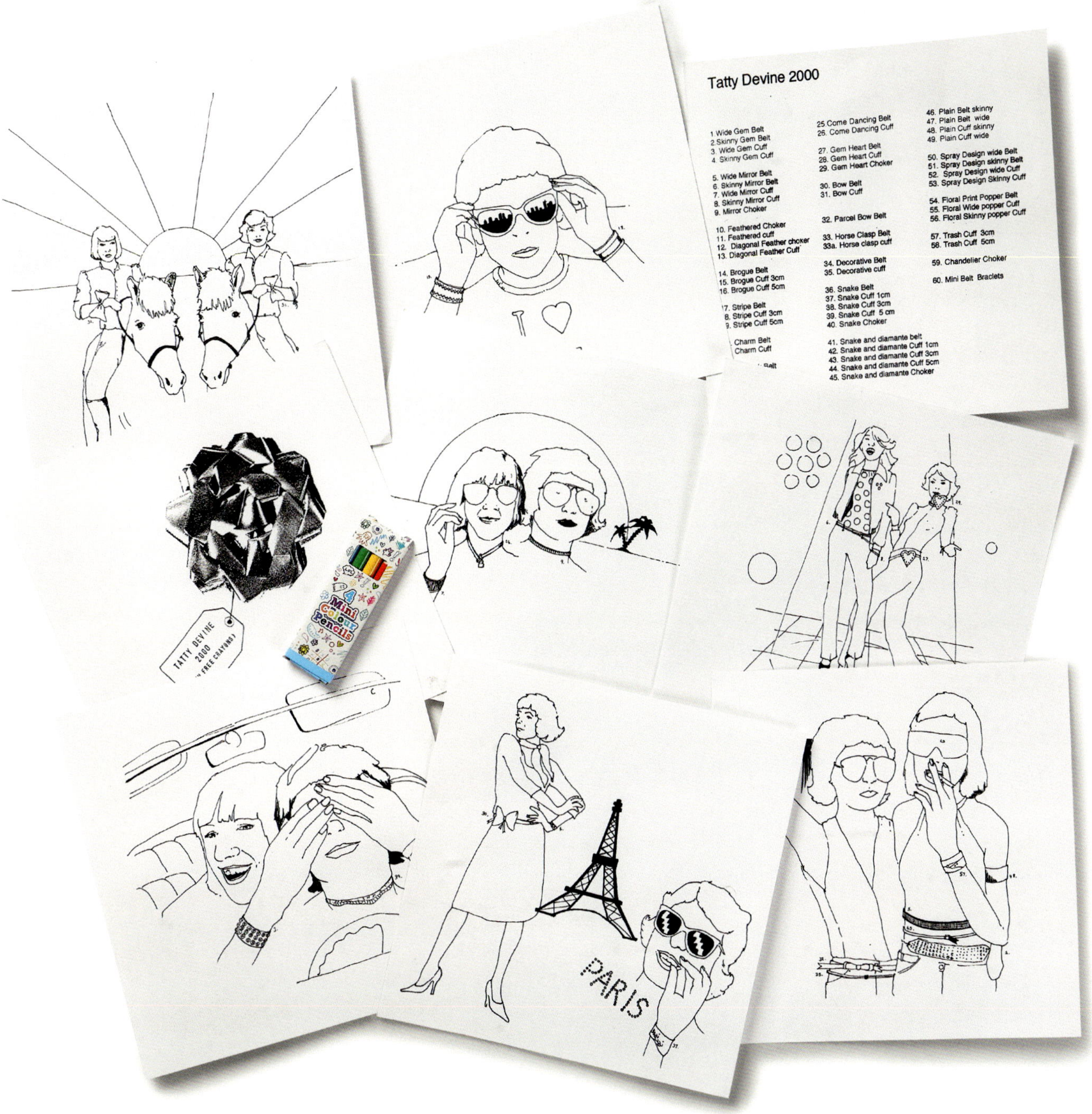

Tatty Devine 2000
1 Wide Gem Belt
2 Skinny Gem Belt
3. Wide Gem Cuff
4. Skinny Gem Cuff
5. Wide Mirror Belt
6. Skinny Mirror Belt
7. Wide Mirror Cuff
8. Skinny Mirror Cuff
9. Mirror Choker
10. Feathered Choker
11. Feathered cuff
12. Diagonal Feather choker
13. Diagonal Feather Cuff
14. Brogue Belt
15. Brogue Cuff 3cm
16. Brogue Cuff 5cm
7. Stripe Belt
8. Stripe Cuff 3cm
9. Stripe Cuff 5cm
Charm Belt
Charm Cuff
25.Come Dancing Belt
26. Come Dancing Cuff
27. Gem Heart Belt
28. Gem Heart Cuff
29. Gem Heart Choker
30. Bow Belt
31. Bow Cuff
32. Parcel Bow Belt
33. Horse Clasp Belt
33a. Horse clasp cuff
34. Decorative Belt
35. Decorative cuff
36. Snake Belt
37. Snake Cuff 1cm
38. Snake Cuff 3cm
39. Snake Cuff 5 cm
40. Snake Choker
41. Snake and diamante belt
42. Snake and diamante Cuff 1cm
43. Snake and diamante Cuff 3cm
44. Snake and diamante Cuff 5cm
45. Snake and diamante Choker
46. Plain Belt skinny
47. Plain Belt wide
48. Plain Cuff skinny
49. Plain Cuff wide
50. Spray Design wide Belt
51. Spray Design skinny Belt
52. Spray Design wide Cuff
53. Spray Design Skinny Cuff
54. Floral Print Popper Belt
55. Floral Wide popper Cuff
56. Floral Skinny popper Cuff
57. Trash Cuff 3cm
58. Trash Cuff 5cm
59. Chandelier Choker
60. Mini Belt Braclets
TATTY DEVINE 2000
4 Mini Colour Pencils
PARIS

Watch Out order form, 2000

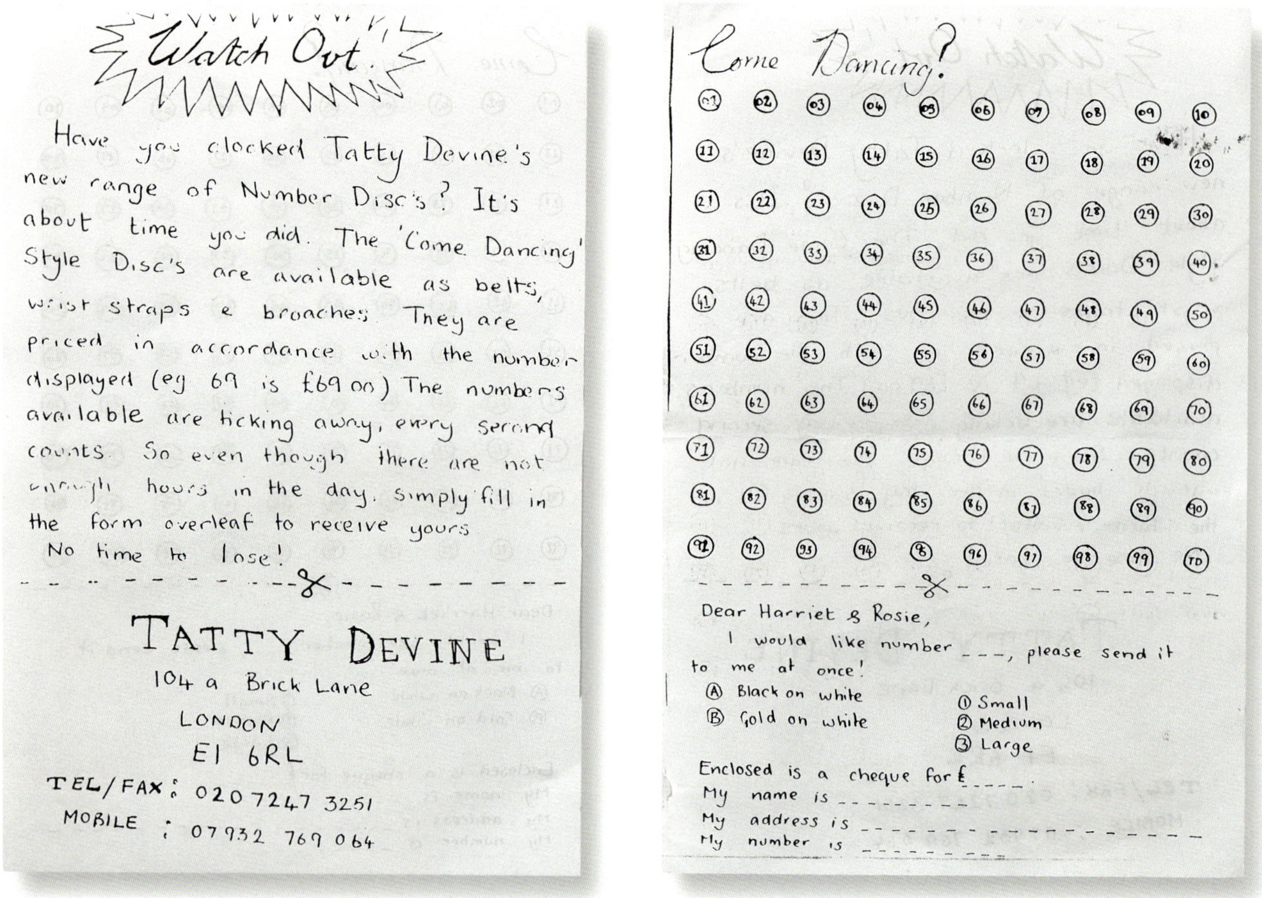

Watch Out!

Have you clocked Tatty Devine's new range of Number Disc's? It's about time you did. The 'Come Dancing' Style Disc's are available as belts, wrist straps & brooches. They are priced in accordance with the number displayed (eg 69 is £69.00) The numbers available are ticking away, every second counts. So even though there are not enough hours in the day. Simply fill in the form overleaf to receive yours

No time to lose!

TATTY DEVINE
104 a Brick Lane
LONDON
E1 6RL

TEL/FAX: 020 7247 3251
MOBILE: 07932 769 064

Come Dancing?

01 02 03 04 05 06 07 08 09 10
11 12 13 14 15 16 17 18 19 20
21 22 23 24 25 26 27 28 29 30
31 32 33 34 35 36 37 38 39 40
41 42 43 44 45 46 47 48 49 50
51 52 53 54 55 56 57 58 59 60
61 62 63 64 65 66 67 68 69 70
71 72 73 74 75 76 77 78 79 80
81 82 83 84 85 86 87 88 89 90
91 92 93 94 95 96 97 98 99 TD

Dear Harriet & Rosie,

I would like number ___, please send it to me at once!

Ⓐ Black on white
Ⓑ Gold on white

① Small
② Medium
③ Large

Enclosed is a cheque for £ ____
My name is ____
My address is ____
My number is ____

Come Dancing Number Disc Cuff, 2000
Leather, metal buckle

The Come Dancing Number Disc Cuffs were part of the collection. We've always been fascinated by ballroom dancing, gymkhanas and parades; there's something so celebratory about them. The price of each piece was linked to the number on it, so one to 20 sold quickly, and 69 did not, which is why we still have it.

Harriet covered in Come Dancing Cuffs, Choker and Brooches, 2000

Flyer for All Tomorrow's Parties,
Camber Sands, 2000

On 7 April 2000 we piled into a hired minibus with a load of friends and headed down the A2 to Camber Sands for the All Tomorrow's Parties festival. It was one of those times when everything comes together – we were doing what we loved, we were bursting with ideas for making more jewellery, we were listening to the music that became the soundtrack to our lives and we were in the company of likeminded people. It was perfect.

Sweetie Bracelet, 2000
Porcelain, elastic

We found a ceramicist in the Yellow Pages (We didn't have the internet yet) because we were keen to make a porcelain version of the childhood sweetie bracelets. He offered Rosie a flat next to his studio space and it became her home and our office. It was a magical place, with a greenhouse full of cacti and a shared courtyard occupied by a family of tortoises, who occasionally mistook our varnished nails for cherry tomatoes as we glued gems onto belts for our next batch of orders.

Promotional Finger Puppets, 2000

With a new workspace and office we got a new fax machine. We felt-tipped the new number onto the bosoms of our T-shirts, took pictures, made finger puppets from the images and sent them out as our calling cards.

T-shirt used in the Finger Puppet campaign, 2000

The Telegraph, Melanie Rickey, 31 April 2000

We were interviewed by Melanie Rickey from *The Telegraph*, and photographed wearing matching outfits.

STYLE

Rags meant riches for two go-ahead young designers. **Melanie Rickey** meets them

Tat is where it's at

YOU'D be hard pushed to find another design duo like Harriet Vine and Rosie Wolfenden, the creative minds behind hot new accessories line Tatty Devine. They dress alike, think alike and talk alike, to the point where they could be taken for female versions of Gilbert and George — they even live in G and G's stamping ground in the East End of London.

In the space of nine months, they have transformed themselves from debt-ridden fine art graduates into fashion designers whose unique products have not only appeared in the millennium issue of *Vogue*, worn by Erin O'Connor, but are also stocked at Harvey Nichols, Fenwick, Whistles and Steinberg & Tolkien.

Their career began on a London street while the pair were still completing their fine art degrees at Chelsea College of Art and Design.

"I saw a pile of black bags stuffed with amazing swatches of leather, suede, brocade, snake-print, chintz and flocked fabric dumped on the pavement," says Harriet, 23. "So I thought: Ooh, I know, I'll make a few wristbands and belts out of that." She dragged the bags home and, with flat-mate Rosie, set to work.

Before you could say "mine's a fronded diamanté wristband with matching belt" — their first products — every magpie fashion stylist in London had "discovered" their quirky little creations.

Their stall at Portobello Road market was overflowing with one-off goodies, such as hip-slinger belts, slashed suede neck-pieces and the all important wrist-cuffs, all randomly covered with studs or twinkling crystals.

"At that time, everyone wanted to wear funky belts and unusual things around their wrists and there was no one doing anything like it," says Rosie, 22.

"I was always looking for unusual pieces, too," says Harriet, "so it was natural for us to make our own."

Soon, their products began to pop up on MTV, both on the presenters and in the videos, then in numerous fashion shoots and finally in *Vogue*, whose support gave the girls the impetus to take their fledgling business seriously.

Now Tatty Devine don't "do" market stalls. They have also moved on from making accessories from materials found in rubbish bags. "Top Shop, for example, were so quick at producing wrist-cuffs that were similar in spirit to ours, it forced us to be more inventive and adventurous," says Rosie.

The result is that Tatty Devine has just produced its first seasonal collection of handmade belts, brooches and wrist-cuffs with a difference. The collection is inspired by equestrian activities, such as gymkhanas and pony clubs and horsy bits and bobs such as saddles, horseshoes and even horse heads. Del Boy from *Only Fools and Horses*, brass pub fittings, *Come Dancing*, Blondie, children's sweetie necklaces and men's brogue detailing are also influences.

There are red leather bow belts and cuffs, and a matching limited edition of 1-100 *Come Dancing* number belts and cuffs, as well as saddle inspired bracelets and the almost ridiculous themed "sporty", "love" and "horsy" charm hip-belts — prices range from £30 to £100.

Their best innovations, however, are perfect for girls who never want to grow up. The Tatty Devine girls are currently producing a ceramic version of the multi-coloured sweetie bracelets we all used to gnaw on as children, and "Dolly belts" that could encircle a Barbie doll's hips three times but are designed for a grown-up girl's wrist, complete with a tiny buckle.

"We are not 'proper' fashion people, so we are not immersed in what people say *is* fashion," says Rosie.

"We've got our own style. We like artificial things like fake gold wedding cake decorations or pretend leather Seventies key-rings.

"We also like brooches, pink and red, we especially love red and gold, and we *adore* glamour in the best and worst way. Essentially, we just make things that we want to wear."

When designers express those sentiments, you know they must be on to a winner: if they want it enough to make it for themselves, soon everyone else will feel the same way.

☐ *Tatty Devine, available from Harvey Nichols, London SW1; Whistles, St Christopher's Place, London W1; Fenwick, Bond Street, London W1. Inquiries: 020 7247 3251.*

Picture: JIMMY GASTON

Creative: Vine, left, and Wolfenden launched Tatty Devine

Outtake from *The Telegraph* shoot, 2000
Photography by Jimmy Gaston

Proof Print Of	PD*2217533	Library Reference	
Created on	18/04/2000 at 18:03:36	Last Published on	
Copyright	Jimmy Gaston	No. Times Published	0
Provider			
Caption	BELT, BROOCH AND BRACLET ACCESSORY DESIGNERS, ROSIE WOLFENDEN AND HARRIET VINE		

A FASTFOTO system report printed by colour1 at 10:27 on 19/04/2000 - Proof 1 of 1

Sleazenation, Namalee Bolle, July 2000

Namalee Bolle, the Fashion Editor of *Sleazenation*, came to interview us in Rosie's office/bedroom.

'Bringing DIY wit to the banality of humourless fashion post by mailing out finger puppets of themselves and cunning mail order forms where you decide how much you want to pay for a 'Come Dancing' brooch (ie. £1 for No.1 - £99 for 99). Genius.'

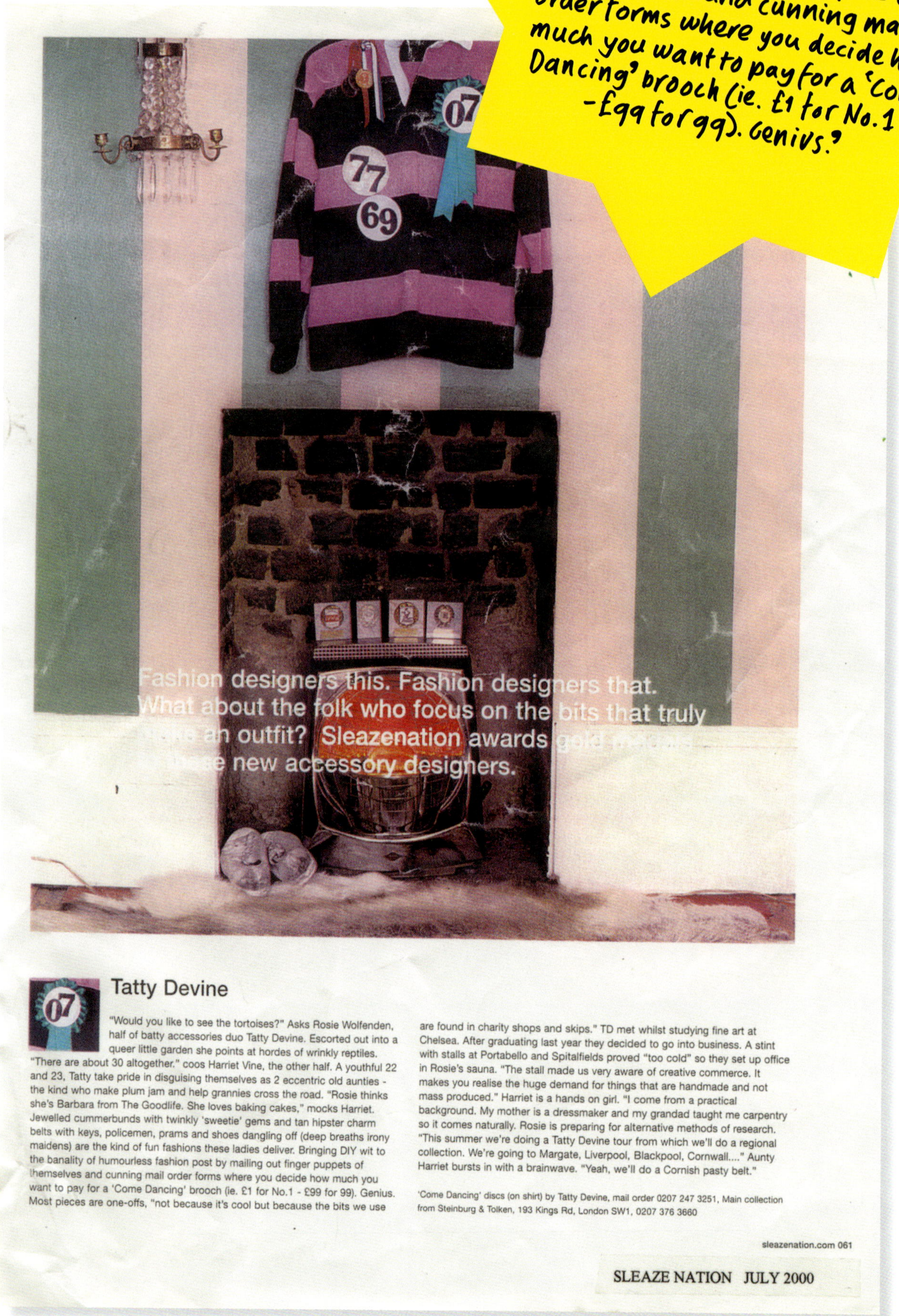

Fashion designers this. Fashion designers that. What about the folk who focus on the bits that truly [illegible] an outfit? Sleazenation awards [illegible] new accessory designers.

Tatty Devine

"Would you like to see the tortoises?" Asks Rosie Wolfenden, half of batty accessories duo Tatty Devine. Escorted out into a queer little garden she points at hordes of wrinkly reptiles. "There are about 30 altogether." coos Harriet Vine, the other half. A youthful 22 and 23, Tatty take pride in disguising themselves as 2 eccentric old aunties - the kind who make plum jam and help grannies cross the road. "Rosie thinks she's Barbara from The Goodlife. She loves baking cakes," mocks Harriet. Jewelled cummerbunds with twinkly 'sweetie' gems and tan hipster charm belts with keys, policemen, prams and shoes dangling off (deep breaths irony maidens) are the kind of fun fashions these ladies deliver. Bringing DIY wit to the banality of humourless fashion post by mailing out finger puppets of themselves and cunning mail order forms where you decide how much you want to pay for a 'Come Dancing' brooch (ie. £1 for No.1 - £99 for 99). Genius. Most pieces are one-offs, "not because it's cool but because the bits we use are found in charity shops and skips." TD met whilst studying fine art at Chelsea. After graduating last year they decided to go into business. A stint with stalls at Portabello and Spitalfields proved "too cold" so they set up office in Rosie's sauna. "The stall made us very aware of creative commerce. It makes you realise the huge demand for things that are handmade and not mass produced." Harriet is a hands on girl. "I come from a practical background. My mother is a dressmaker and my grandad taught me carpentry so it comes naturally. Rosie is preparing for alternative methods of research. "This summer we're doing a Tatty Devine tour from which we'll do a regional collection. We're going to Margate, Liverpool, Blackpool, Cornwall...." Aunty Harriet bursts in with a brainwave. "Yeah, we'll do a Cornish pasty belt."

'Come Dancing' discs (on shirt) by Tatty Devine, mail order 0207 247 3251, Main collection from Steinburg & Tolken, 193 Kings Rd, London SW1, 0207 376 3660

sleazenation.com 061

SLEAZE NATION JULY 2000

Faxed order from Browns Focus, 2000

A flatmate's friend introduced Rosie to the buyer at Browns Focus, who loved our Charm Belts and Heart Brooches. This is our first order from them, sent by fax.

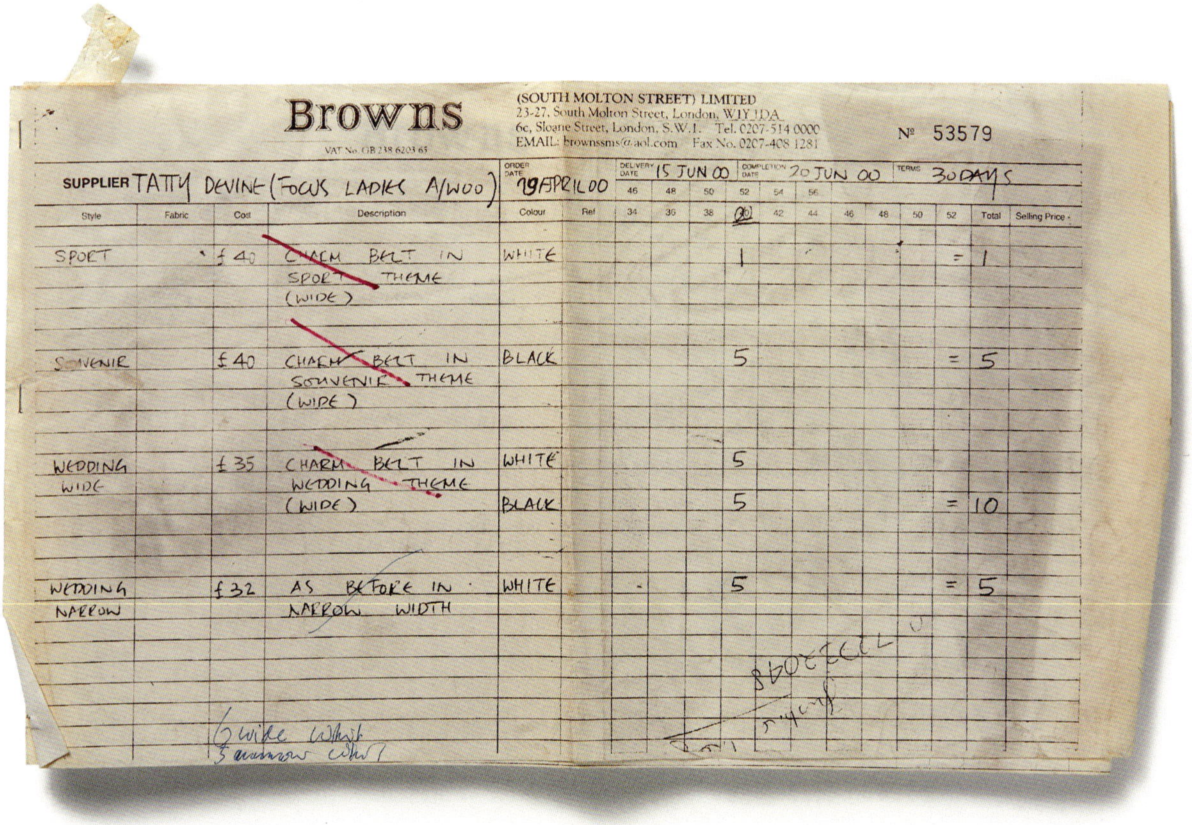

Browns

VAT No. GB 238 6203 65

(SOUTH MOLTON STREET) LIMITED
23-27, South Molton Street, London, W1Y 1DA
6c, Sloane Street, London, S.W.1. Tel. 0207-514 0000
EMAIL: brownssms@aol.com Fax No. 0207-408 1281

№ 53579

SUPPLIER TATTY DEVINE (FOCUS LADIES A/W00) ORDER DATE 19 APRIL 00 DELIVERY DATE 15 JUN 00 COMPLETION DATE 20 JUN 00 TERMS 30 DAYS

Style	Fabric	Cost	Description	Colour	Ref	34	36	38	40	42	44	46	48	50	52	Total	Selling Price
SPORT		£40	CHARM BELT IN SPORT THEME (WIDE)	WHITE					1						=	1	
SOUVENIR		£40	CHARM BELT IN SOUVENIR THEME (WIDE)	BLACK					5						=	5	
WEDDING WIDE		£35	CHARM BELT IN WEDDING THEME (WIDE)	WHITE					5								
				BLACK					5						=	10	
WEDDING NARROW		£32	AS BEFORE IN NARROW WIDTH	WHITE					5						=	5	

6 wide white
5 narrow white

Gem Heart Brooch, 2000
Leather, plastic gems

Diary, 2000

On 25 May 2000 we took a selection of jewellery in a giant handmade Pearl Necklace Box to the British Fashion Council. Harriet's dad helped us make it – we clad it in leatherette and embossed it with decorative gold leaf. The lid was lined with fabric and printed with a crest, which read: 'Tatty Devine est. 1999'. We like to think it helped us get a place at London Fashion Week.

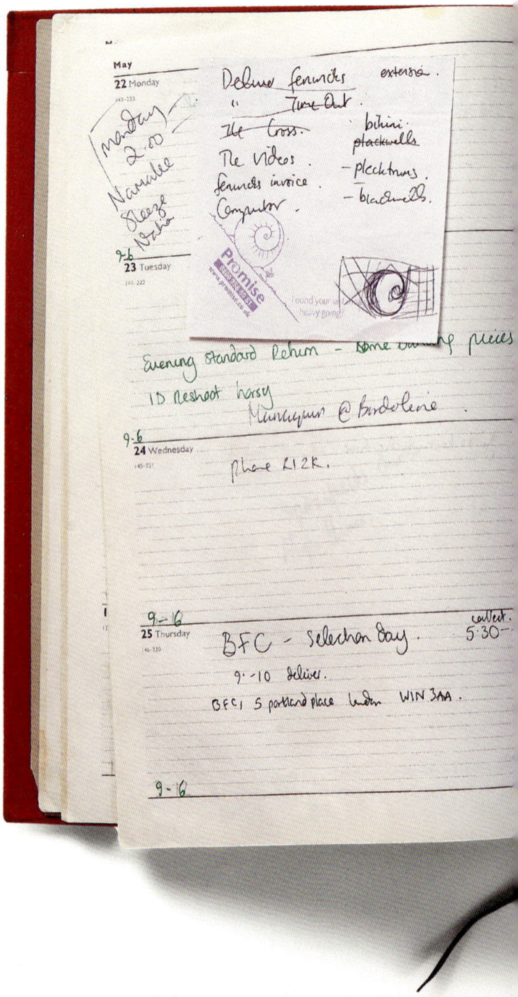

Giant Pearl Box, 2000
Made by Roger Vine
Wood, leatherette, fabric

Rainbow Gem Belt, 2000
Leather, plastic gems, press studs

Harriet recently bought this belt on eBay, as all the ones we made sold out at the Hoxton Boutique.

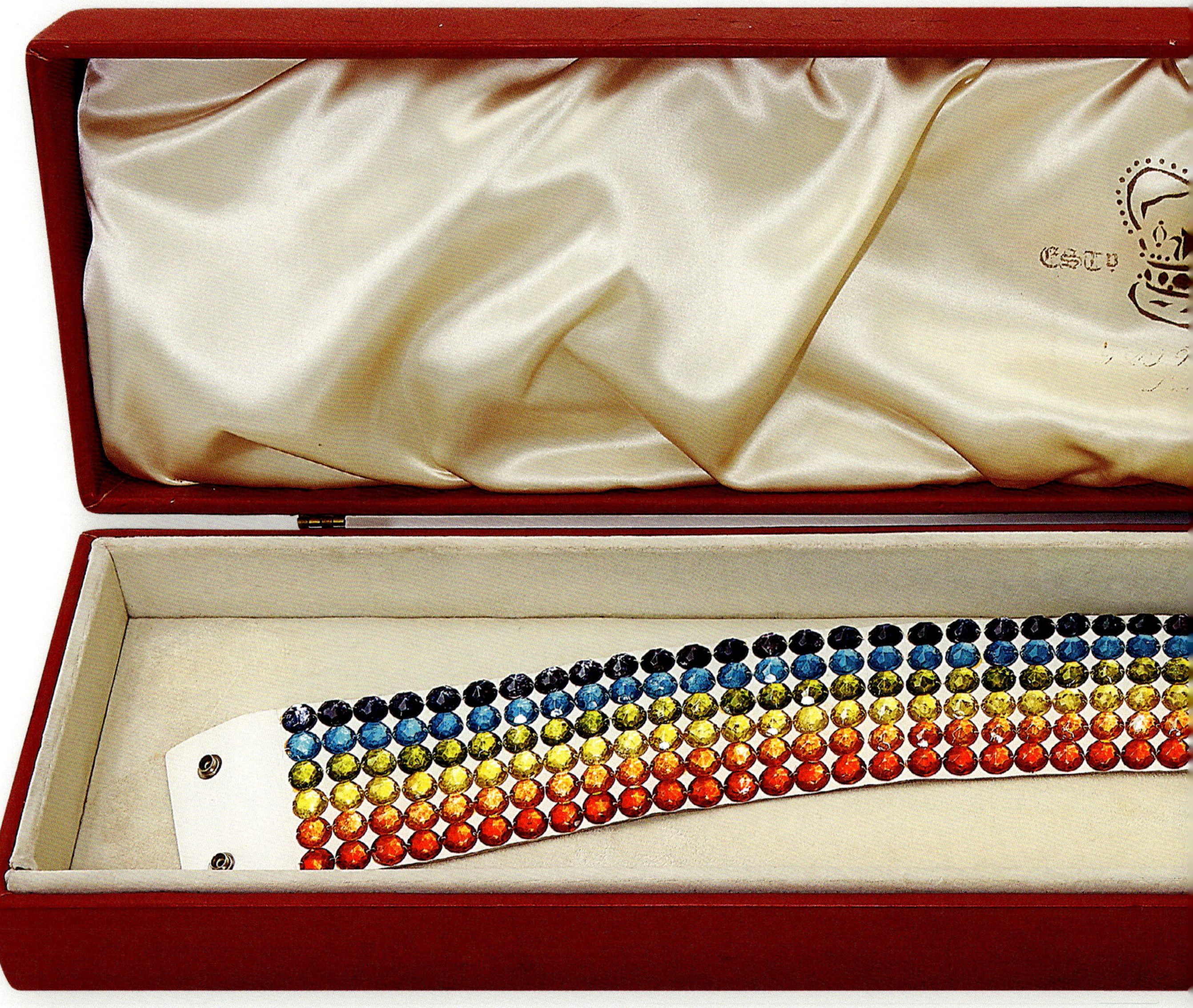

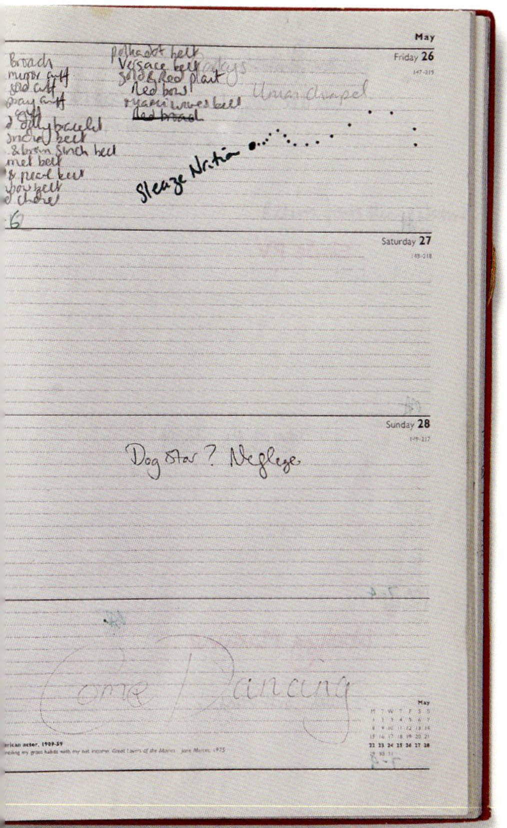

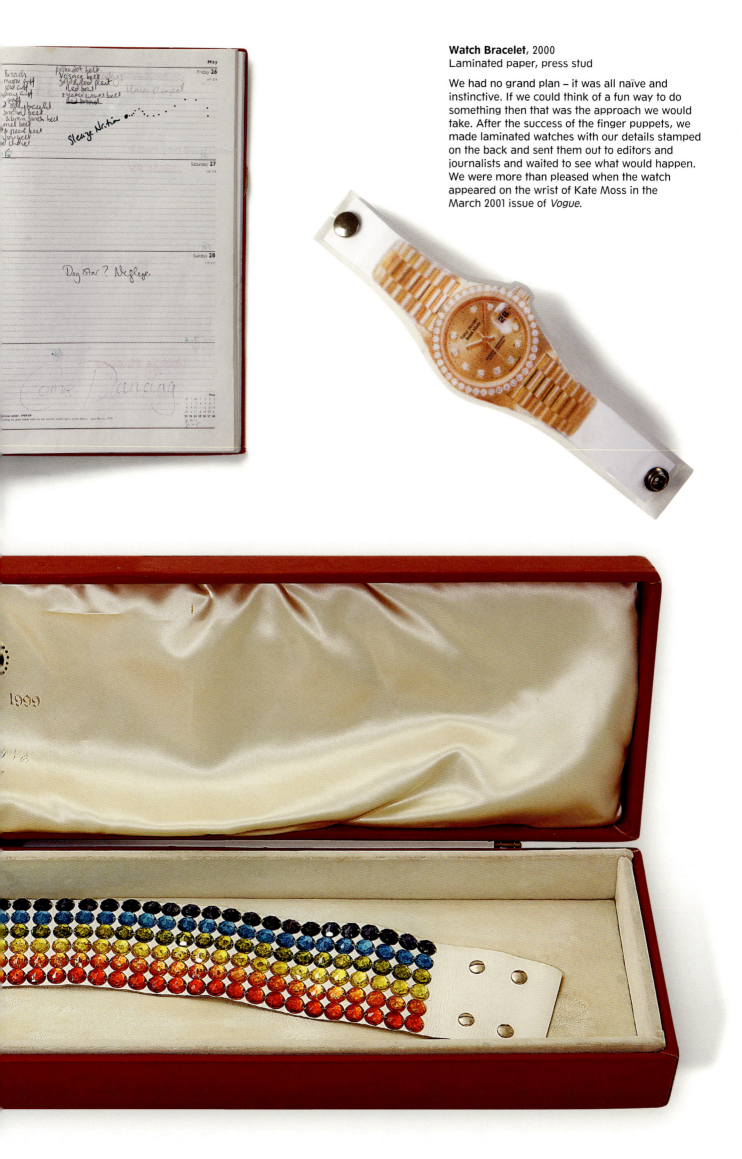

Watch Bracelet, 2000
Laminated paper, press stud

We had no grand plan – it was all naïve and instinctive. If we could think of a fun way to do something then that was the approach we would take. After the success of the finger puppets, we made laminated watches with our details stamped on the back and sent them out to editors and journalists and waited to see what would happen. We were more than pleased when the watch appeared on the wrist of Kate Moss in the March 2001 issue of *Vogue*.

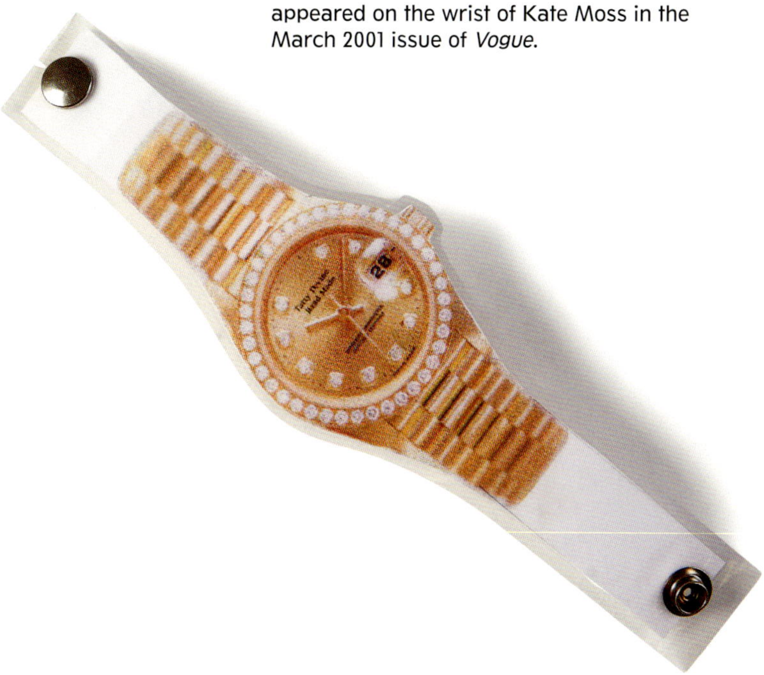

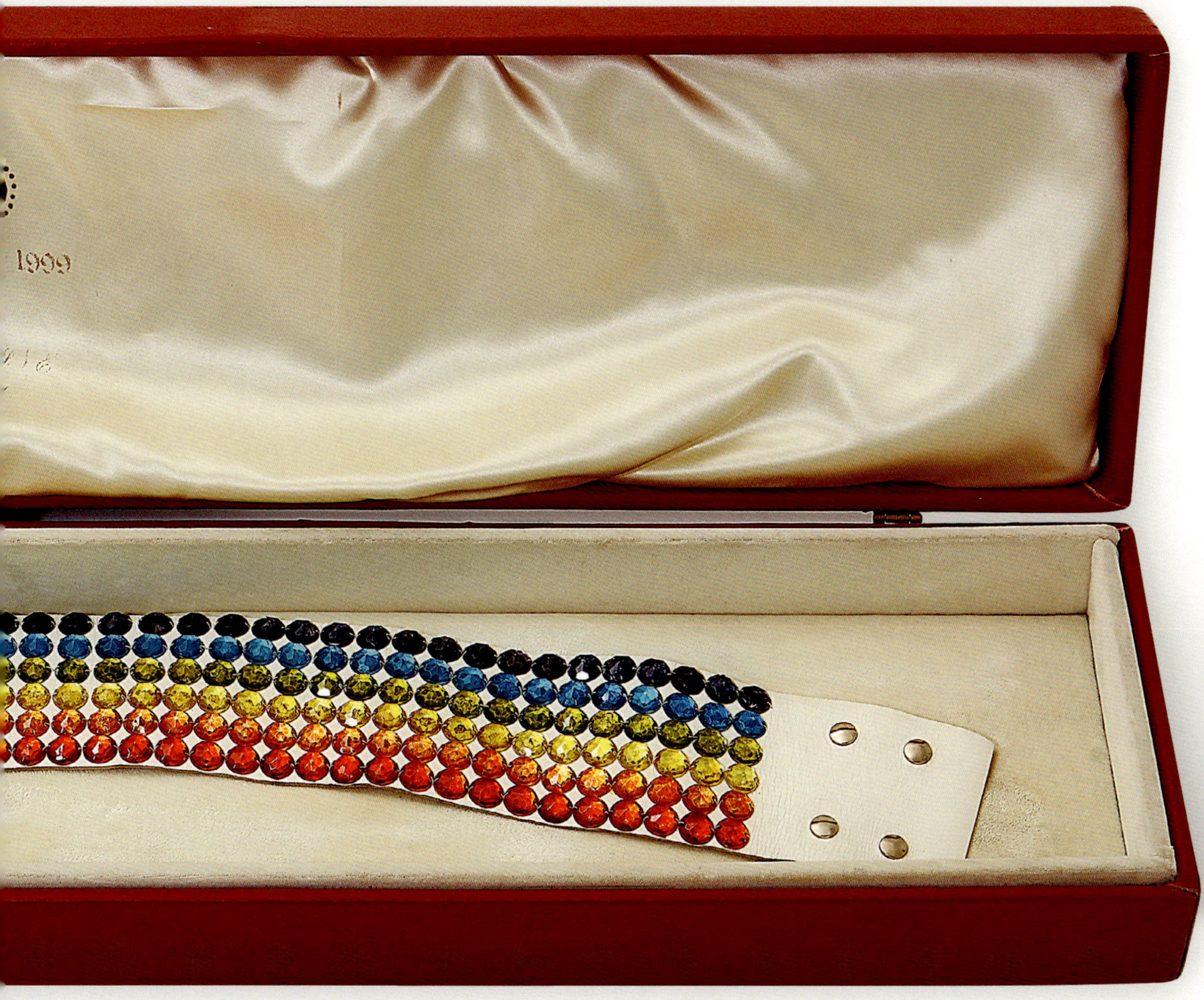

Flyer and invite to Blue Boy Shop,
Oval Mansions, 2000

We spent a lot of time south of the river, at artists' space City Racing, the Bonnington Café and the renowned squat and art hang out at Oval Mansions. Our friend Rachel Ortas invited us to be part of an exhibition at the Blue Boy Shop in July 2000, where we showed a giant photocopied version of our laminated watch to be worn as a belt.

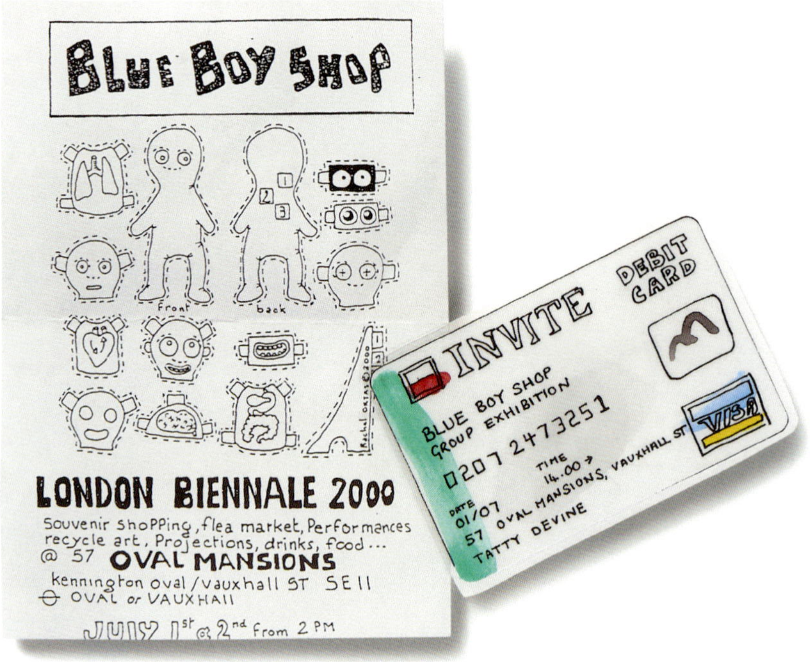

Wish You Were Here catalogue, SS01

On a night out we met a 'Lomo Ambassador', who was on a mission to introduce the Soviet-style camera to the UK. He lent us a camera and the super saturated picture were perfect for our Wish You Were Here collection, as they looked just like the holiday snaps from our childhood.

Wish You Were Here catalogue, SS01

Wish You Were Here zine, SS01

Wish You Were Here postcard, SS01

We channelled a nostalgic mood when we celebrated the launch of this jewellery. We held a tea party on 28 September 2000 at Coffee@ on Brick Lane, with cakes made by Harriet's mum, and invites that were laminated photocopies of a pearl bracelet. In keeping with our DIY ethos we handed out a zine, with features written by friends, and a pin badge designed to look like a medal

Pearl Bracelet tea party invite, SS01
Laminated paper, press stud

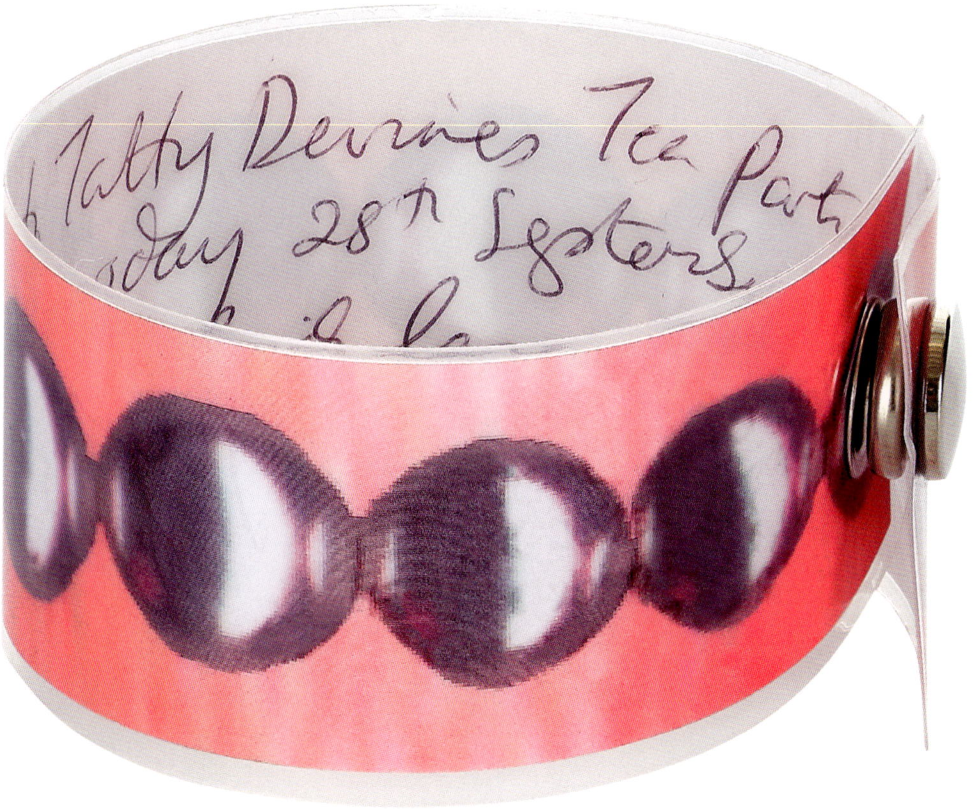

Ice Cream Cone Brooch, SS01
Leather, sequins, beads, metal alloy

Brick Lane was a constant source of inspiration to us. We still didn't have the internet so we headed out to the local shops to look for ribbons, trimming and sequins. It was an adventure, because we never knew what we might find, or what it could be turned into.

Bunting Necklace, SS01
Fabric, plastic beads

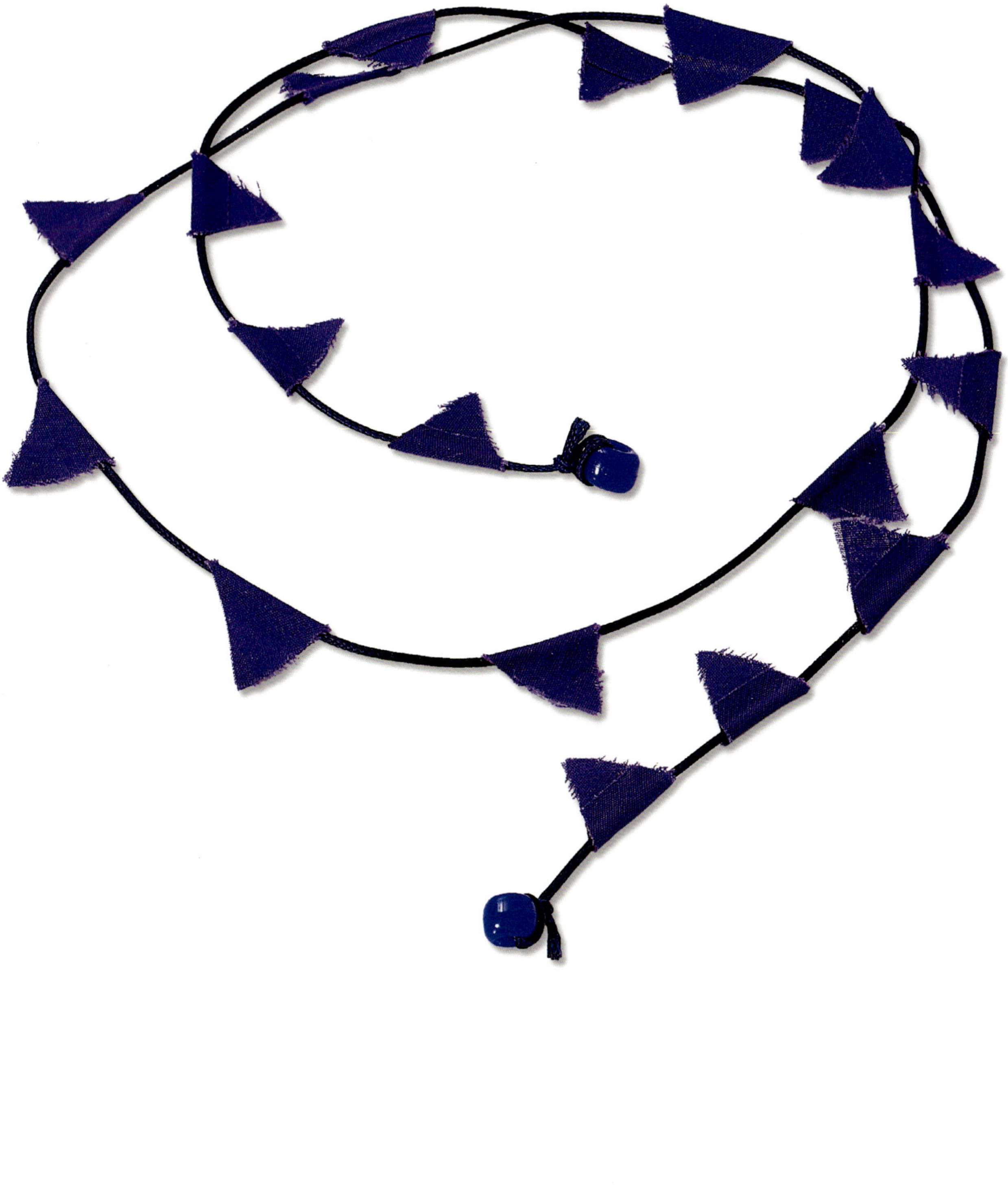

Plectrum Kilt Pin, SS01
Plastic plectrum, metal alloy

Keyboard Belt, SS01
Leather, metal press studs

This Keyboard Belt was a hand-stitched one-off, which took ages to make. So we ended up screen printing them, onto eye-catching white, pink and yellow leather. The artist Cindy Sherman took a shine to them and draped them over herself in her Clown photographs, commissioned by *Vogue*. The fashion cupboards were a treasure trove of Tatty belts, which had been called into for shoots.

Dog Sticker Rosettes, SS01
Ribbon, stickers, metal alloy

Dart Flight Earring, SS01
Dart flight, metal alloy

We were hooked on making things by now, and anything we came across we'd transform into jewellery. We made one-off pieces from the bits and bobs we discovered in boot sales and charity shops, and we'd pounce on anything unusual. On a rainy day trip to Whitstable in the summer of 2000 we ended up in a trophy shop, where we bought a stash of dart flights, medals and pet stickers and made them into earrings, bracelets and rosettes. Plectrums were another 'found object' that got the Tatty treatment. Harriet shared a Brick Lane flat with a band, and the boys left guitar plectrums everywhere. We'd drill a hole in the brightly-coloured plastic and attach them to kilt pins for a bit of punk-rock glamour.

Diary, 2000

Charm belts were another obsession, and we'd pop on puzzle pieces, cake decorations and souvenir keyrings. Rosie headed off to Paris for the day to stock up on Eiffel Tower keyrings, and after haggling in her imperfect French, came home with 130 keyrings for 1390 francs.

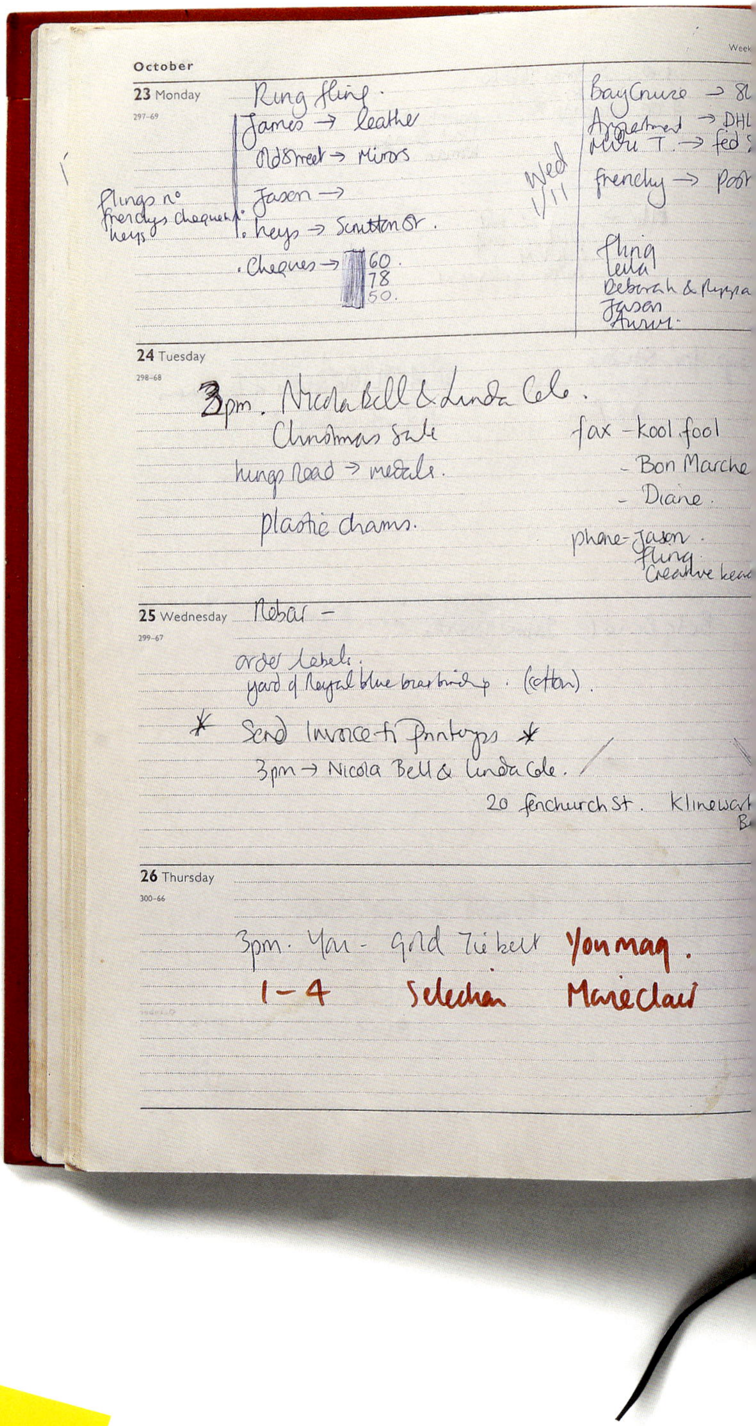

'We know belts are super-trendy, but some are taking it too far, like the duo behind accessories label Tatty Devine.'

Nicky Haslam, *Sunday Times Style*, 30 July 2000

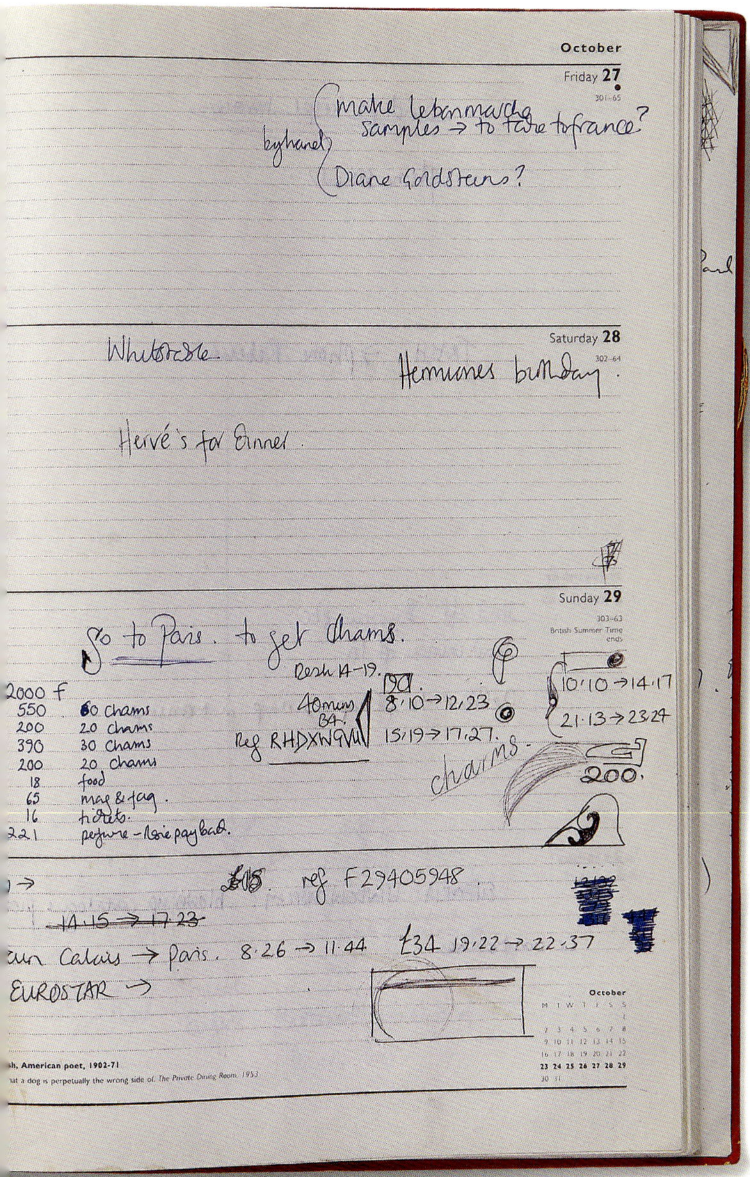

Charm Belt London, SS01
Souvenir keyrings, leather

Harriet in Paris, 2000

We were offered so many opportunities, and everything happened at such a fast pace that we didn't have time to think, we just felt lucky to be doing something we loved. We were invited to Paris to discuss designing accessories for Emanuel Ungaro and we headed off to France with matching red suitcases. We didn't get the job, but it made us realise that starting Tatty Devine gave us the freedom to not get real jobs and remain outside the mainstream – we could do whatever we wanted. With that in mind we decided we needed a new workspace. Our flats were too crammed full of stuff – we'd go to bed surrounded by piles of material, and fall asleep with the smell of contact adhesive and suede creeping into our noses.

Advent Calendar, 2000

One of our favourite pastimes is scouring second hand clothes shops for outfits and then dressing up in the purchases. For December 2000 we produced an advent calendar with a different look for every day of the month.

Bangla Town Carpet & Furniture flyer, 2000

On a wander around East London we came across a 'To Let' sign outside an old carpet shop at 236 Brick Lane. We took the plunge and signed a five-year lease, and nineteen years later we're still here.

Bangla Town Carpet & Furniture
236 Brick Lane, London E2 7EB
(Near to Bethnal Green Road)
Tel: 0171 729 8910
Mobile: 0961 300813
আমাদের দোকানে সবধরনের কার্পেট, রাগস, বিভিন্ন রকমের ফার্নিচার যেমন চেয়ার, টেবিল, বেড, সোফা, সোফাবেড, সোকেইস, ওয়ারড্রবস পাওয়া যায়'।
All Types of Carpets are Available
We sell Wilton & Exminister Carpet
WE ALSO SELL BEDS, DINING TABLES AND CUPBOARDS
WEDDING FURNITURE'S ARE AVAILABLE
FREE DELIVERY
FREE CARPET FITTING
বাংগালী মালিক দ্বারা পরিচালিত

The Day the World Turned Day Glo

Rebelling *2001–2007*

It's difficult to describe how exciting it was getting the keys to the shop in early 2001 – it seemed a long way from the cold market stall days when we dreamed about warm baths and hot whiskies, and it was the start of whole new brightly-hued adventure. The shop was a wreck – the basement had an old dirt floor, complete with the carcass of a dead rat and the toilet was blocked up with cement. But we rolled up our sleeves and got stuck in. We painted the walls white, stored our bits and pieces in old cigar boxes and first-aid tins salvaged from charity shops, made shelves and lined them with recycled jars and hung whatever we were making on the walls. We hadn't planned on opening a shop – we were using it as a studio space – but passers-by kept dropping in, curious to see what we were creating and before long we opened the doors to Tatty Devine on Brick Lane.

Rosette Brooches, 2001
Ribbon, tape measures, metal alloy

'Among the grey urban mayhem of London's Brick Lane, there is a little haven of all things fun and colourful – Tatty Devine's new shop and showroom is a window into the accessory duo Harriet Vine and Rosie Wolfenden's creative, if not slightly batty, minds.'

Observer, 18 March 2001

Gift token and envelope, 2001

Anyone we met went straight onto our mailing list. This is the £5 gift token we sent out in April 2001. On the reverse it says: 'Do come to visit Tatty Devine on a Sunday between 10–4. Appointments can be made for any time'.

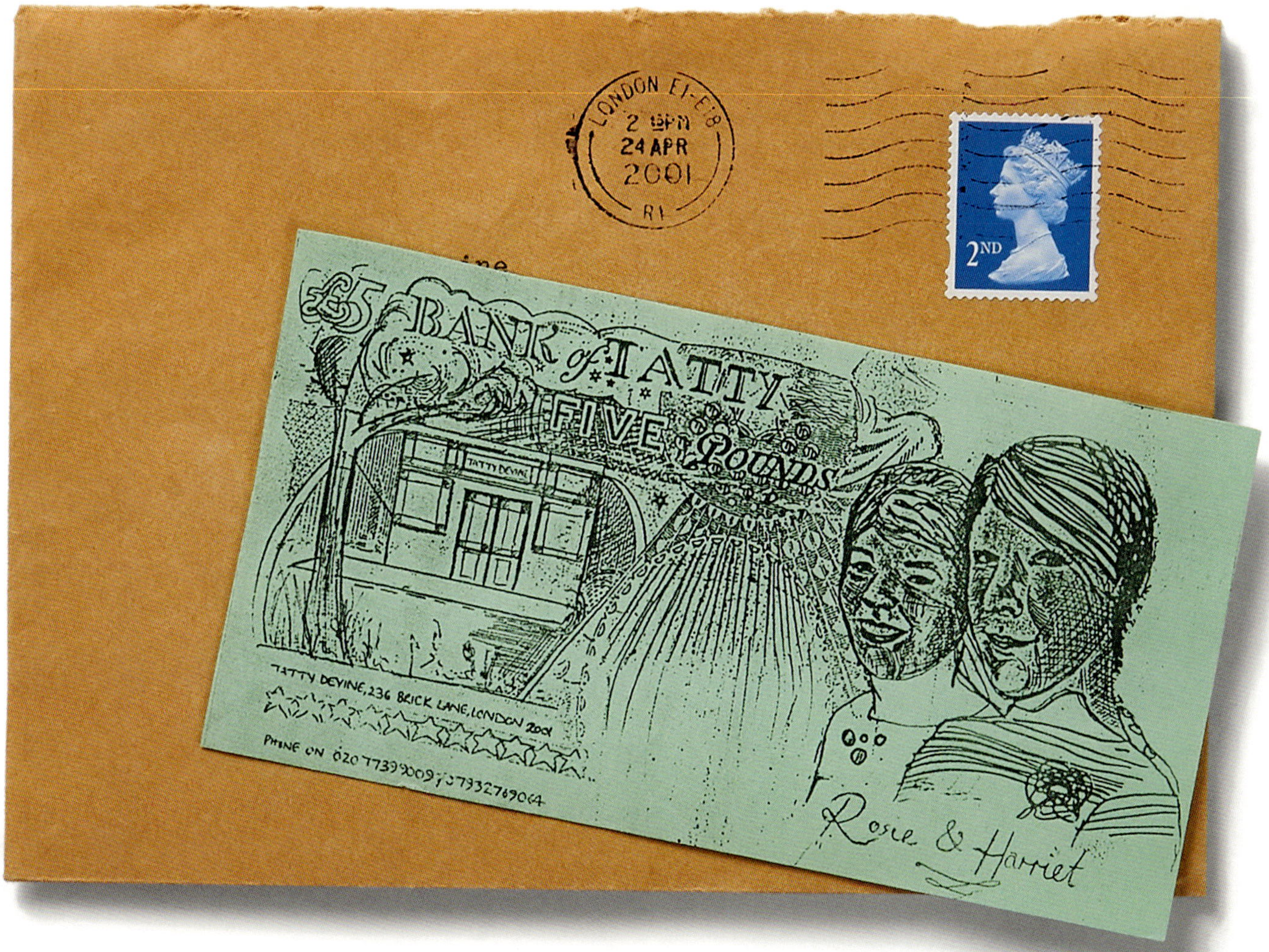

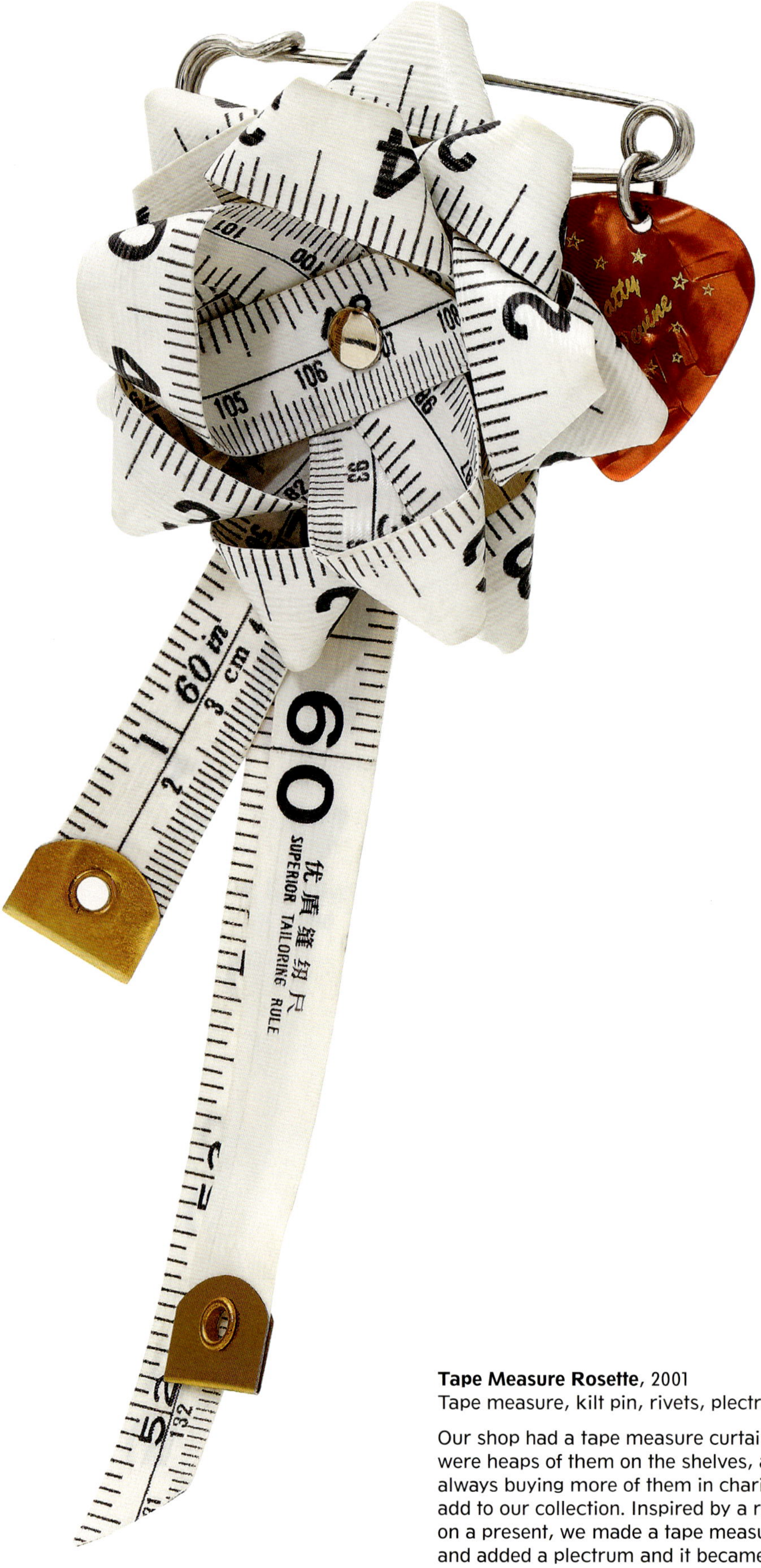

Tape Measure Rosette, 2001
Tape measure, kilt pin, rivets, plectrum

Our shop had a tape measure curtain, and there were heaps of them on the shelves, as we were always buying more of them in charity shops to add to our collection. Inspired by a ribbon rosette on a present, we made a tape measure rosette and added a plectrum and it became one of our bestselling accessories.

Nick Abrahams private view, Brick Lane, 2001

In June of 2001 we started hosting exhibitions at the Brick Lane shop. We handed over the white walls of our space to our friends and friends-of-friends and it had a real community feel. We showed work by Nick Abrahams, Mark Pawson and met Mike Gabel and Jennifer Earle, who ran Hot Breath Karaoke. Every Tuesday night we'd head to the Legion on Old Street and sing everything from Ça Plane Pour Moi to Total Eclipse of the Heart. We went on to sell Mike's handmade Toothbrush Bracelets.

Toothbrush Bracelet, 2001

Posters of forthcoming exhibitions and an afterparty, 2001

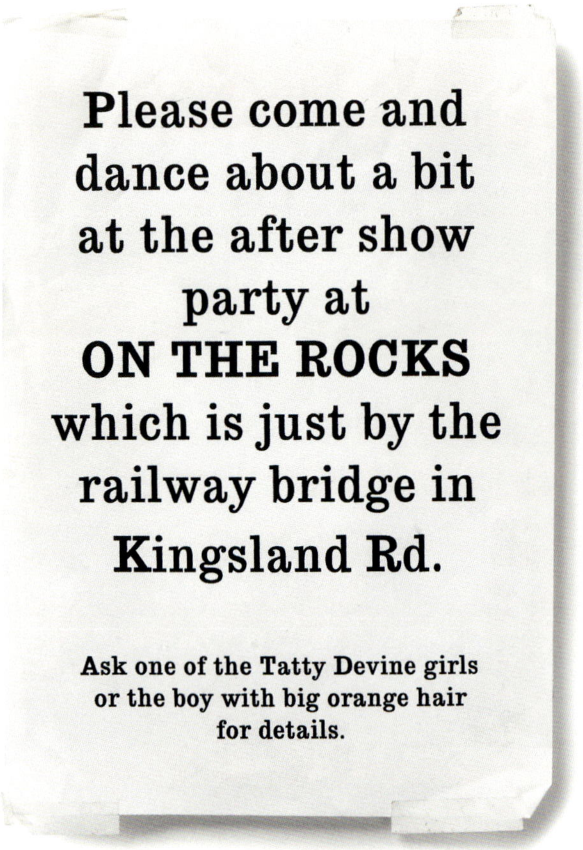
Please come and dance about a bit at the after show party at **ON THE ROCKS** which is just by the railway bridge in Kingsland Rd.

Ask one of the Tatty Devine girls or the boy with big orange hair for details.

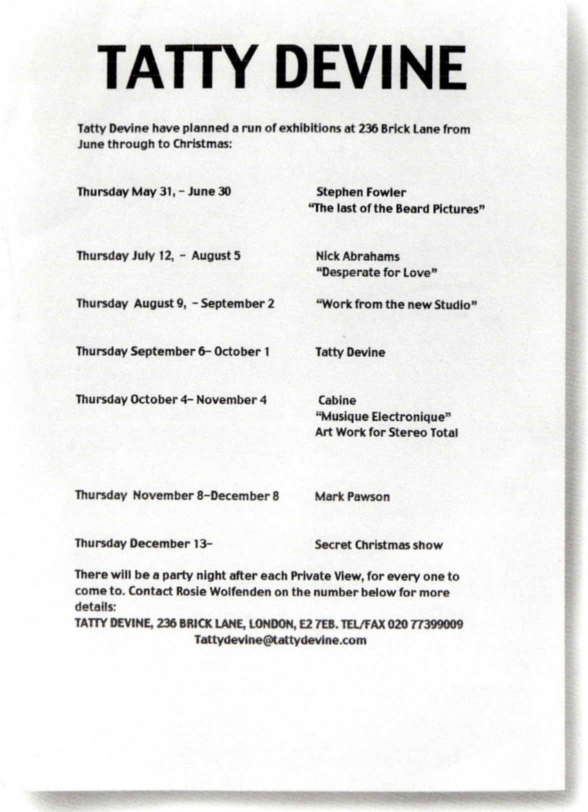
TATTY DEVINE

Tatty Devine have planned a run of exhibitions at 236 Brick Lane from June through to Christmas:

Thursday May 31, – June 30	Stephen Fowler "The last of the Beard Pictures"
Thursday July 12, – August 5	Nick Abrahams "Desperate for Love"
Thursday August 9, – September 2	"Work from the new Studio"
Thursday September 6– October 1	Tatty Devine
Thursday October 4– November 4	Cabine "Musique Electronique" Art Work for Stereo Total
Thursday November 8–December 8	Mark Pawson
Thursday December 13–	Secret Christmas show

There will be a party night after each Private View, for every one to come to. Contact Rosie Wolfenden on the number below for more details:
TATTY DEVINE, 236 BRICK LANE, LONDON, E2 7EB. TEL/FAX 020 77399009
Tattydevine@tattydevine.com

Thank you card, 2001

Our private views were a hotbed of friendship formations – we met new people all the time. This is a thank you note from Bev and Kim who had come along as friends-of-friends. It was such a special time.

Chicks on Speed Record Earring, 2001
Acrylic, metal alloy

We were obsessed by the band Chicks on Speed. We first saw them at the Notting Hill Arts Club, where they tore off their paper dresses and threw them into the audience – Rosie managed to grab one. We met them in 2001 and started making merch for them to take on tour to the USA and Japan. We made Record Single Earrings and Plectrum Earrings saying 'We Don't Play Guitar'.

Harriet and Rosie, Brick Lane, 2001

Harriet and Rosie wearing
Chicks on Speed Dresses, 2001

We also stocked the Chicks' clothing in the shop. The printing was rough and ready, and we loved the punky aesthetic of it.

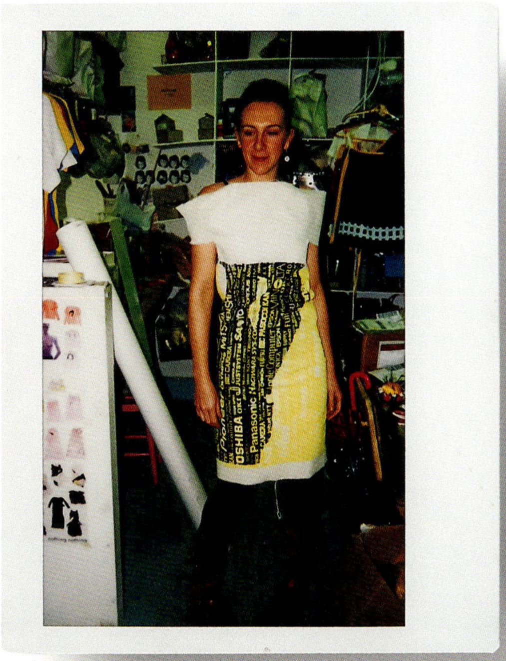

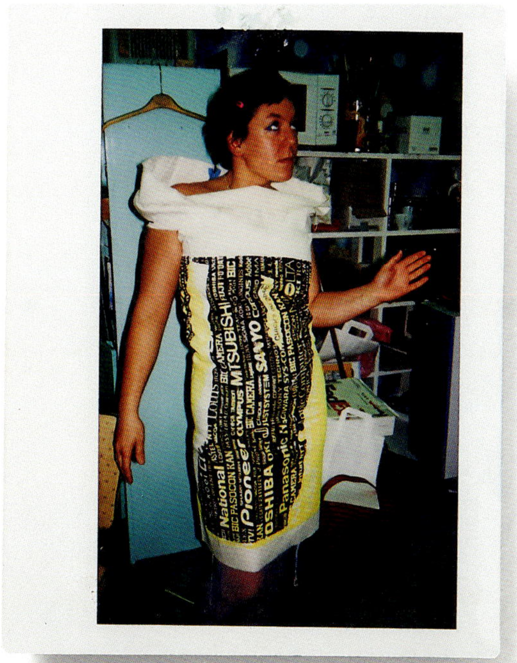

Exhibition invites, 2001–2010

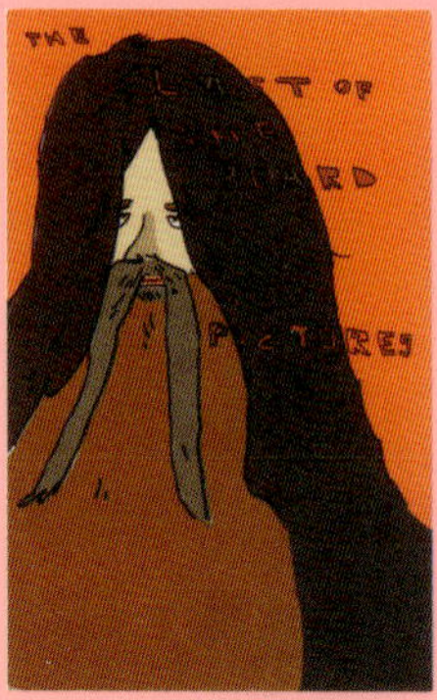

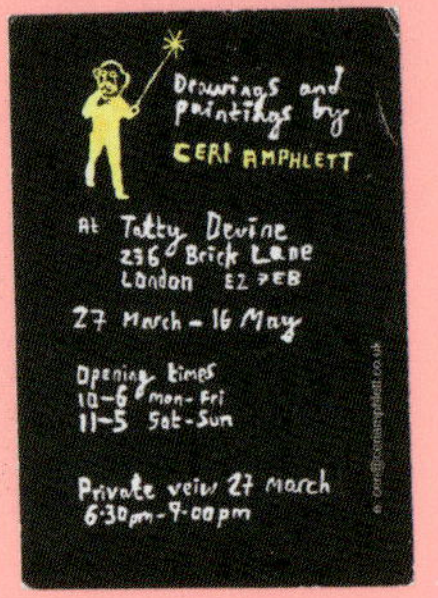

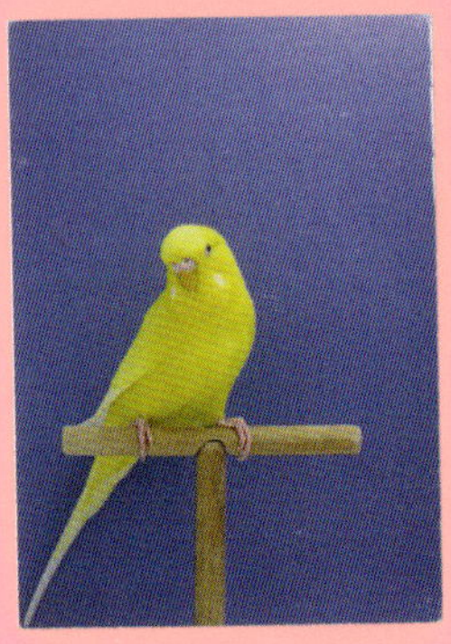

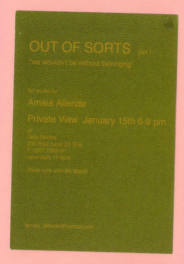

SIGNS by Mark Pawson
at Tatty Devine
For SIGNS at Tatty Devine, Mark has designed 12 new limited edition Perspex signs, following on from the success of his 'Open/Closed' signs (which can be seen in the windows of several stylish boutiques around London). Themes range from practical and useful to whimsical and provocative. Some of the pieces will be based on themes from previous works, such as 'Wear More Badges' and 'Never Throw Anything Away Ever'.
The signs will be in editions of 15-60 and there will also be a small collection of necklaces and brooches being sold alongside the signs. Each piece will be packaged in a screen-printed cotton bag and sold as a numbered edition, with a certificate and signature. They will all be available to buy from Tatty Devine's Brick Lane store for the duration of the show.
www.mpawson.demon.co.uk
www.tattydevine.com
Tatty Devine
CHICKS ON SPEED
IT'S A PROJECT
Published by Booth-Clibborn Editions
BOOK LAUNCH
25thFEBRUARY 2004
5-8 pm
Tatty Devine
57b Brewer St.
London W1F 9UR
0207 4342257
info@tattydevine.com
ALEX, MELISSA AND KIKI WILL BE SIGNING THEIR BOOK AND MAKING
AN INSTALLATION AT THE NEW TATTY DEVINE IN SOHO
Work From The NEW Studio
At Tatty Devine, 236 Bricklane London E2 7EB
Private View Thursday 9 August 6.30pm - 8.30pm
Exhibition continues to Saturday 6 September
Gallery opening times Sunday to Friday 10am - 6pm
HIGHLIGHTS & LOWLIGHTS
An exhibition of work by Sarah Doyle
Sarah Doyle
Dark Places
An Exhibition by Nick Phillips
Also featuring The Vagina Montages
Opening: Thurs 2nd Sept, 2004. 6 - 9pm
Enquiries: 020 7739 9009
info@tattydevine.com
Mon - Fri: 10am - 6pm
Sat & Sun: 11am - 5pm
Tatty Devine
236 Brick Lane
London
E2 7EB
www.tattydevine.com
ROCKY'S CUPBOARDS
an exhibition at
TATTY DEVINE
236 Brick Lane
London E2 7EB
opening 20th November 6pm - 9pm
Little Miss Lazlo
"Show me where the bad man touched you"
OPENING: SUN MAY 9TH 2004: 6-9PM
Tatty Devine
236 Brick Lane
London E2 7EB
This is an Analogue Amnesty. Do not throw away tape cassettes. Bring them to Tatty Devine, or your local haberdashery shop Prick Your Finger. They will be spun into a chunky/aran weight yarn to protect you against the elements.
Choose your colours a bit like this...
Girly Gather
Nature's Splendour
Sci Fi Ply
Tarantino Tweed
Tension Tight Horror
Weddings from Hell
Spaghetti Western
Dusty Heads
Classic Flicks
Bible Adventures
Spent Porn
Old Family Dog
Spinning schedule and crap video viewings
Exhibition and participation free, spun yarn prices on request.
25th November & 13th January
VHS TDK Amnesty Day
Drop in your old videos or cassettes, watch and listen for the final time, and place your order for them to be spun by the Miller's Daughter.
17th January
Party!
Rumpelstiltskins disappear through the floor to collect the yarns and the finest wines to distribute throughout the entire kingdom! A big party with competition prizes, knitted displays, and the secrets of the midnight miracles. The final dance with the Miller's Daughter.
7th November - 17th January
at Tatty Devine
236 Brick Lane, London E2 7EB
and Prick Your Finger
260 Globe Rd, London E2 0JD
To join in, email
rumpelstiltskin@tattydevine.com
www.tattydevine.com
www.prickyourfinger.com
Prick Your Finger
Tatty Devine
An Exhibition of work by
MISTER MINISTECK
at TATTY DEVINE
236 BRICK LANE, LONDON, E2 7EB
T/F 020 7739 9009
PRIVATE VIEW: 4TH JULY, 6-9pm
Music provided by LILY ROSE MELODY
Show continues to 29th AUGUST
Opening Times: Mon-Fri 10-6pm, Sundays 11-5pm
Enquiries contact:
tattydevine@tattydevine.com
www.misterministeck.com
Dainippon Type Organization
TYPO WORLD EXPO
TATTY DEVINE
236 BRICK LANE, LONDON, E2 7EB
SHOW CONTINUES TO 14TH MAY 2002
OPENING TIMES:
MON- FRI 10- 6PM/ SUN 11-5PM
CONTACT: ROSIE WOLFENDEN ON
+44 (0)20 77399009
tattydevine@tattydevine.com
CABINE
ILLUSTRATION & DESIGN

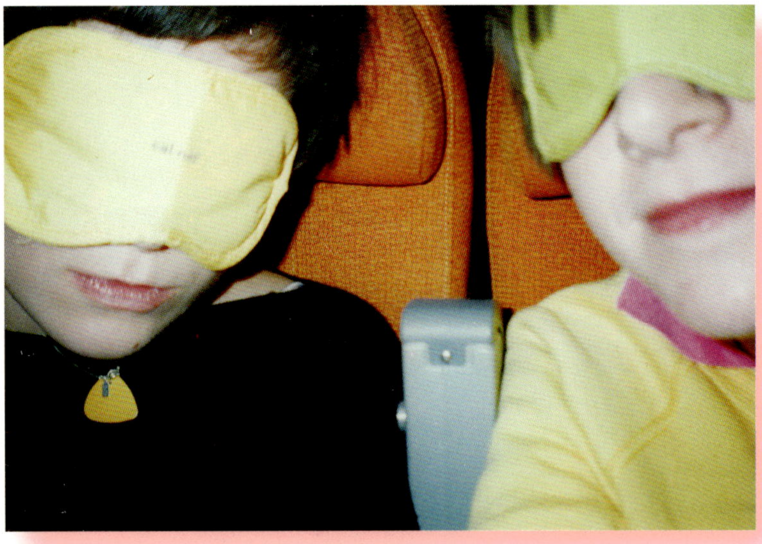

Rosie and Harriet on their flight, 2001

We headed on a research trip to New York in 2001, funded by a grant from the European Commission. We were meant to be looking for shops to sell to, but instead we found a shop that would change Tatty Devine forever and set us on the path to making our own acrylic jewellery. We stumbled across Canal Plastics by accident. They made shop signage, but also stocked pre-cut plastic shapes of poodles and champagne glasses and we bought loads, and turned them into necklaces and brooches. We were inundated with so many orders at London Fashion Week that we could barely keep up. We had to ring Canal Plastics and order hundreds of the laser-cut shapes at a time, trying to remember the time difference and only call after lunch.

Canal Plastics, New York, 2001

Poodle Brooch, 2001

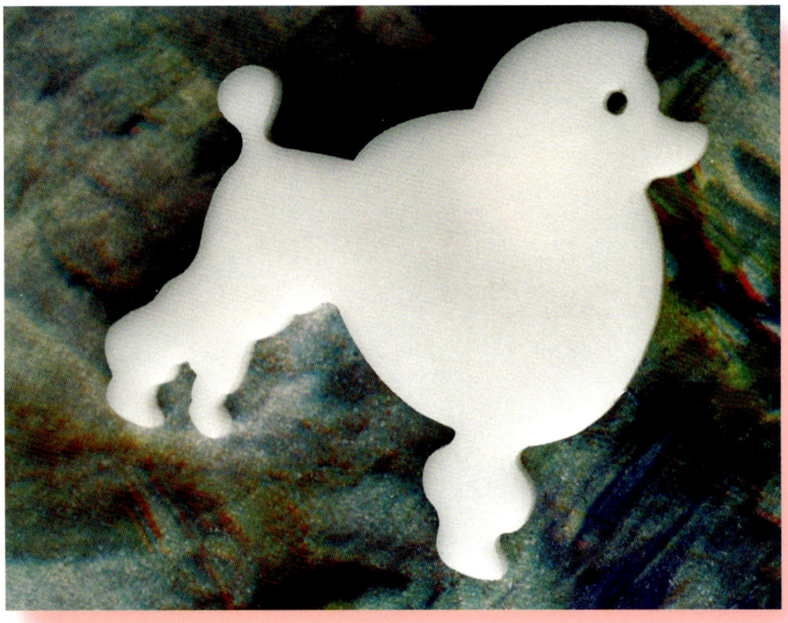

Amy Higgins, Brick Lane, 2001

On the 10 September 2001 we took on our first intern, Amy Higgins. She was studying jewellery design at Middlesex University and was as obsessed by pop culture as we were. We'll never forget her first day at work. We left her to mind the shop while we headed out to buy more leather but we were away for hours, glued to the TV at the suppliers watching 9/11 unfold. Amy became our first full-time employee in 2003, and worked with us as Production Manager until 2012.

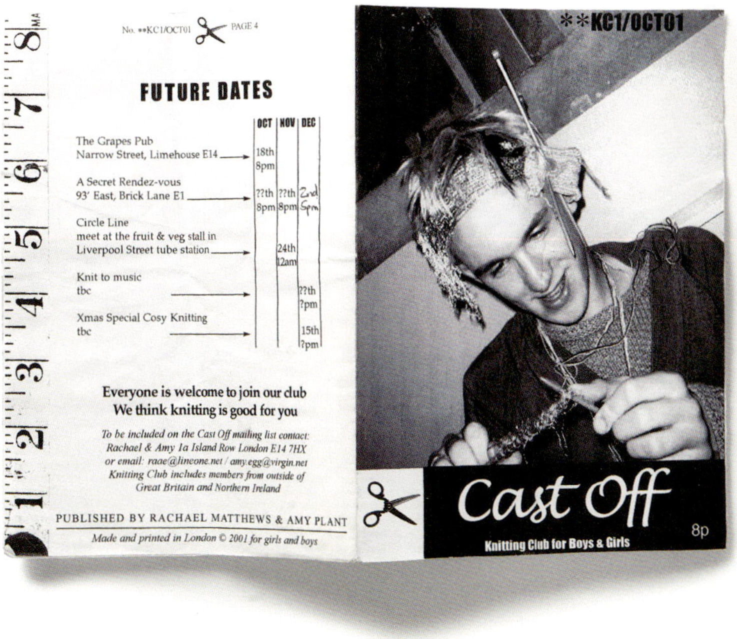

Knitting Club Zine, 2001

We've always loved knitting so it seemed inevitable that we'd be part of Cast Off, 'the knitting club for boys and girls' set up by Rachael Matthews and Amy Plant. We'd meet up and knit in pubs and gigs, and on one memorable occasion, on the Circle Line. At the time knitting and crochet seemed like forgotten arts and it felt subversive to be out and about with needles and wool in unexpected places. It definitely influenced our work – we made and displayed the Knitted Crown Jewels, and sold Knitting Needle Bracelets (we had to bend the charity shop knitting needles round tins of tomatoes to shape them). Blanket Scarves and Earmuffs were also part of our AW02 collection.

Knitted Crown Jewels Headband, 2001
Rowan Lurex Shimmer wool

Harriet and Rosie Rag Dolls, 2001
Made by Rachael Matthews

In 2001, artist Rachael Matthews made rag dolls of us. Her previous collection of dolls had sold out at legendary shop The Pineal Eye. Her new collection modelled outfits from top fashion houses, including the latest Versace, Prada and Chanel, and were featured in issue two of *Nova* magazine. She created replicas of our favourite outfits and brilliantly captured our likenesses in cloth and wool.

Tombola collection catalogue, AW01

We presented our AW01 collection at London Fashion Week, tombola style. Journalists and buyers wrote their details on the back of a raffle ticket and the winners were drawn on the last day.

Rubik's Cube Bracelet, AW01
Acrylic, sticky back plastic

There something very pleasing about sticky back plastic. We used it to make window signs for the shop, and on the Rubik's Cube Bracelet. The plain cubes were cut from acrylic at local specialist, Hamar Acrylic, and then we painstakingly put coloured sticky back plastic on each side of every cube. It was all worthwhile when Joan Collins picked up one of the Rubik's Cube Clip On Earrings and admired it. A London Fashion Week highlight for us.

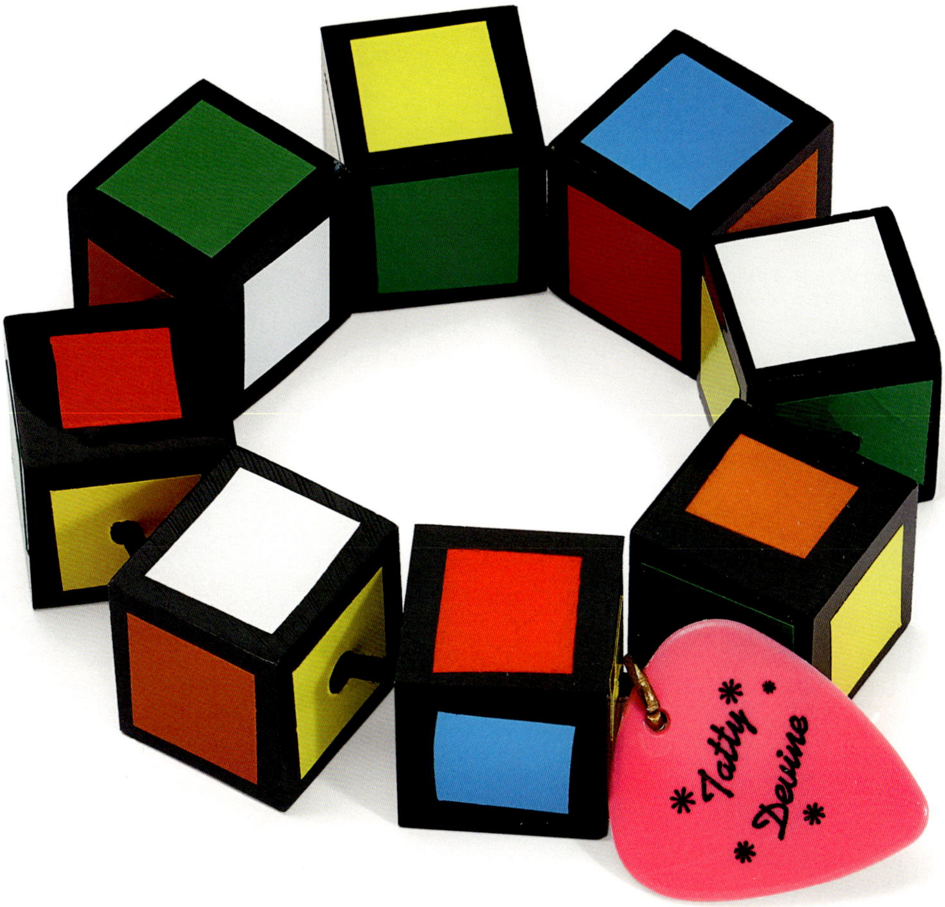

'Remember the Rubik's Cube? The maddening toy, invented by Professor Erno Rubik in 1974, is the unlikely inspiration behind the most sought-after – and impossible to find – accessory of the season.'

Julia Robson, *The Telegraph*, 3 November 2001

Tape Cassette Purse, SS02
Cotton drill, zip fastening

We soon realised that we needed help to print the Tape Cassette Purse, Tape Measure Belt, Keyboard Belt and Record Bag. We met our friend and artist Rob Ryan at Mangle, a studio off Hackney Road. Rob had never screenprinted onto leather before, but he shared our 'go for it' experimental approach and ended up printing belts, T-shirts and purses for us over the coming years.

Dressing Table collection, SS02

For SS02 we raided Harriet's bedroom. We were always looking for interesting ways to display our jewellery and Harriet's lovely, old-fashioned dressing table was perfect.

Record Bag, SS02
Leather, zip fastening

Here's what our first logo looked like. We put it on the Record Bag, and we designed it to look like a 1950s record. The first record bag was embossed, but the later versions are screenprinted by Rob Ryan.

Budgie Brooch, 2001
Paper, hardboard

Our Budgie Brooch for AW01 was a lo-fi forerunner of our laser-cut jewellery. We photocopied a 1960s technicolour pet book that we'd found in a charity shop, pasted it to hardboard and then carefully cut round it with a jigsaw. The brooch was 30cm long and fastened with a kilt pin.

Master document for Rose Brooches, 2001

For SS02 we made Rose Brooches and Chocolate Éclairs using the same technique, but with images found in horticulture and recipe books. We took photocopies from this, stuck the cut-out image to hardboard and then added layer upon layer of varnish to protect the brooches from wear and tear.

Chewing Gum Cuffs, 2002

Chewing Gum Cuffs were also part of the SS02 collection. The paper sleeves slid off to reveal a silver cuff, made of thin pinking-sheared silver foil leather and thicker leather, so that the whole thing looked like a giant stick of chewing gum. We sprinkled it with peppermint oil to make it even more authentic.

Collection, AW02

At this stage in our history, we weren't very computer-savvy. There'd been just a handful of computers at Chelsea – a couple in the library and a few in the Combined Media room, and this was years before smartphones and mass ownership of technology changed everything. In the early 2000s, we would literally cut and paste photographs to compile our catalogues and to put images onto our website. We took the snaps on an old Olympus camera, cut out each image individually, stuck them onto paper and then photocopied them.

3 14
8 9
MADEIN
1

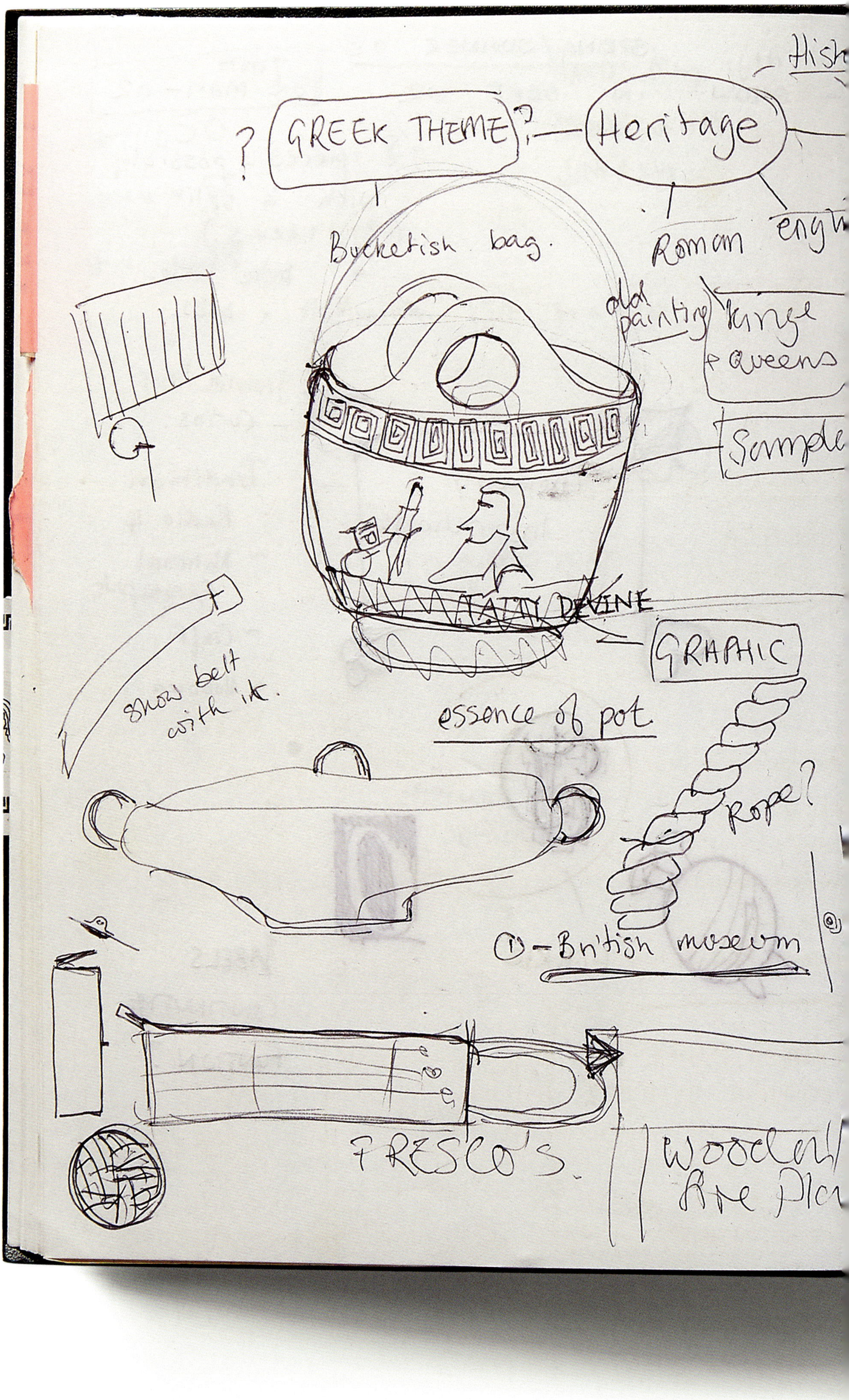
GREEK THEME
Heritage
Bucketish bag.
Roman
old painting
Kings + Queens
Sample
TATTY DEVINE
GRAPHIC
show belt with it.
essence of pot
Rope?
1 – British museum
FRESCO'S.

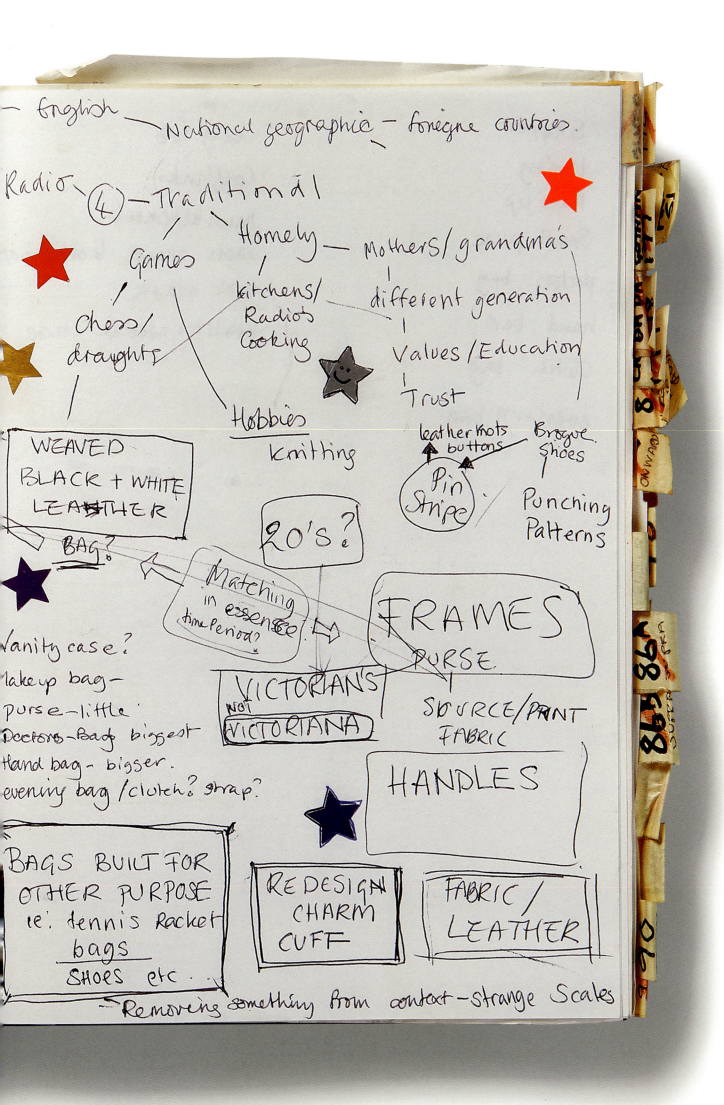

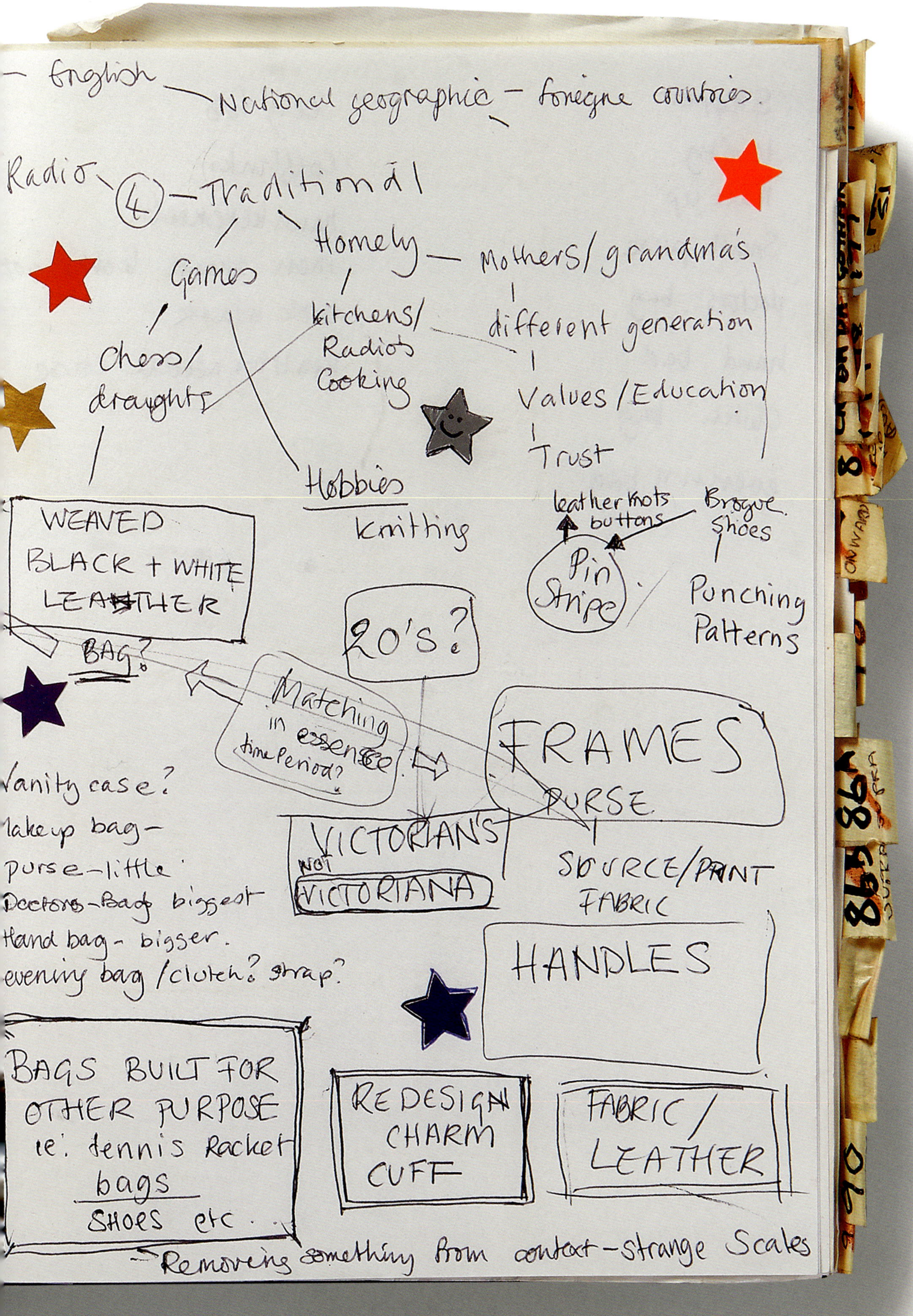
English
National geographic - foreigne countries
Radio 4 - Traditional
Homely - Mothers/grandma's
Games
Kitchens/ Radio's Cooking
different generation
Chess/ draughts
Values/Education
Trust
Hobbies
Knitting
leather knots buttons
Brogue shoes
Pin Stripe
Punching Patterns
WEAVED BLACK + WHITE LEATHER
BAG?
20'S?
Matching in essence time Period?
FRAMES
PURSE
Vanity case?
Makeup bag-
purse-little
Doctors-Bag biggest
Hand bag- bigger.
evening bag /clutch? strap?
VICTORIAN'S
NOT VICTORIANA
SOURCE/PRINT FABRIC
HANDLES
BAGS BUILT FOR OTHER PURPOSE ie: tennis Racket bags
SHOES etc.
REDESIGN CHARM CUFF
FABRIC / LEATHER
Removing something from context - strange Scales

Sketchbook, 2002

Harriet's 2002 sketchbook showing all the acrylic shapes we found in New York, plus a selection of plectrums and beads, and an early drawing of the Tape Cassette Purse and our logo.

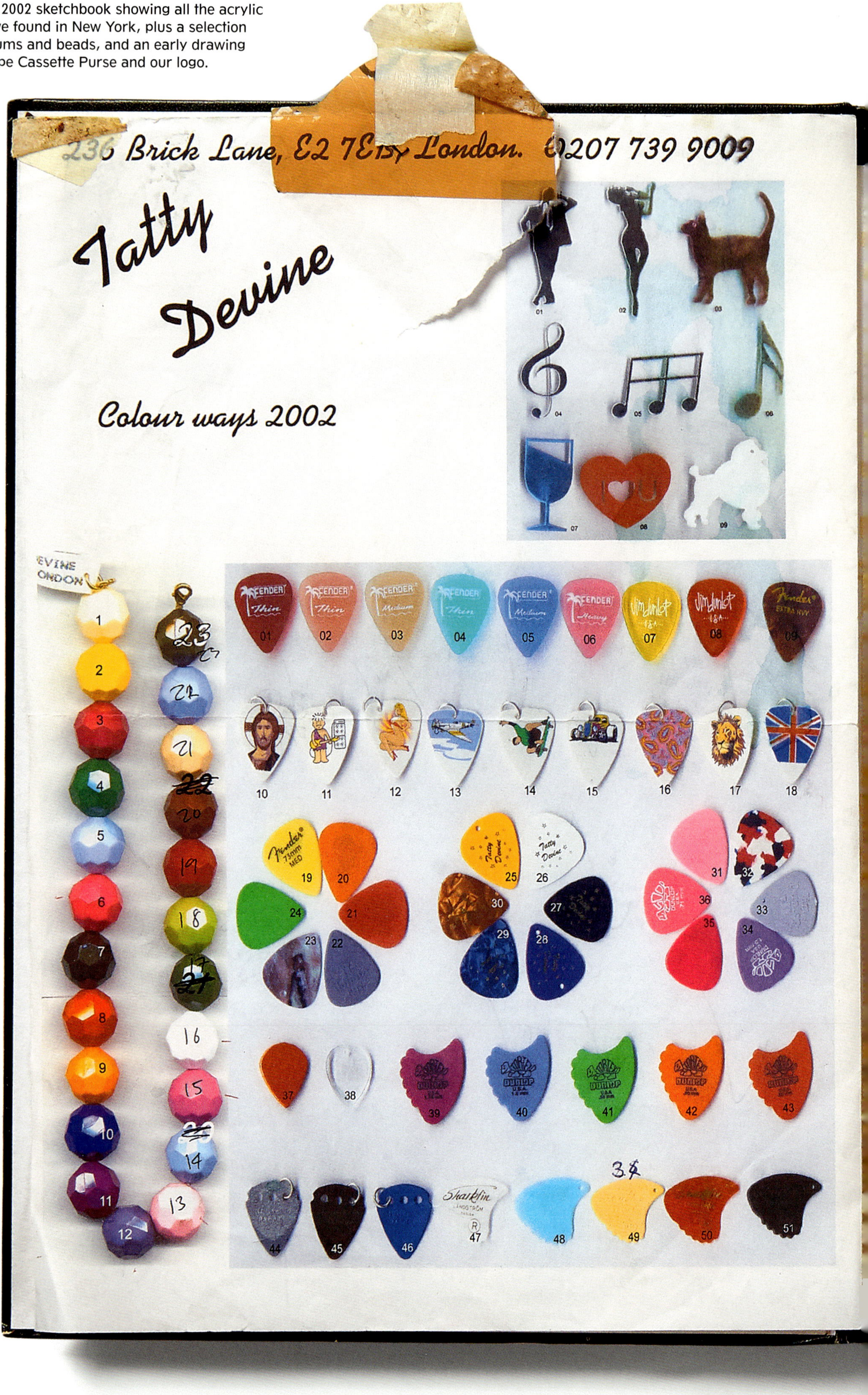

Tatty Devine

presents...

Faxed drawings from Cabine, 2002

In 2002 we made the momentous decision to design our own acrylic collection from scratch. We'd loved the bright, bold shapes of Fuzzy-Felts when we were young, and thought they'd be a brilliant starting point, but we didn't know how to draw on a computer. We turned to our friends Hervé and Paul, who ran design partnership Cabine for help. We swapped ideas and drawings by fax, until we'd come up with the basis for our first laser-cut collection, which was cut by a local model-maker.

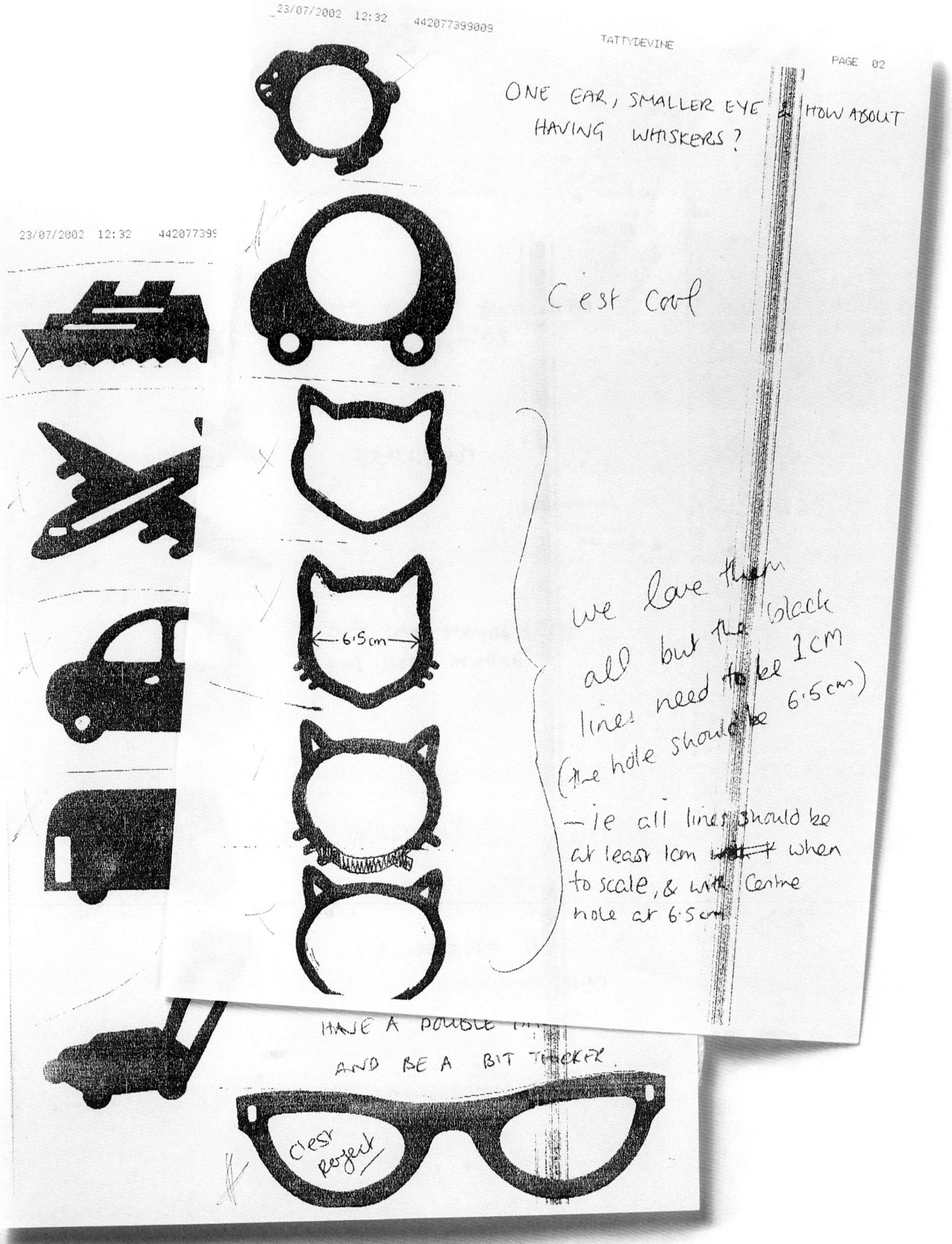

Cat Bangle, SS03
Acrylic

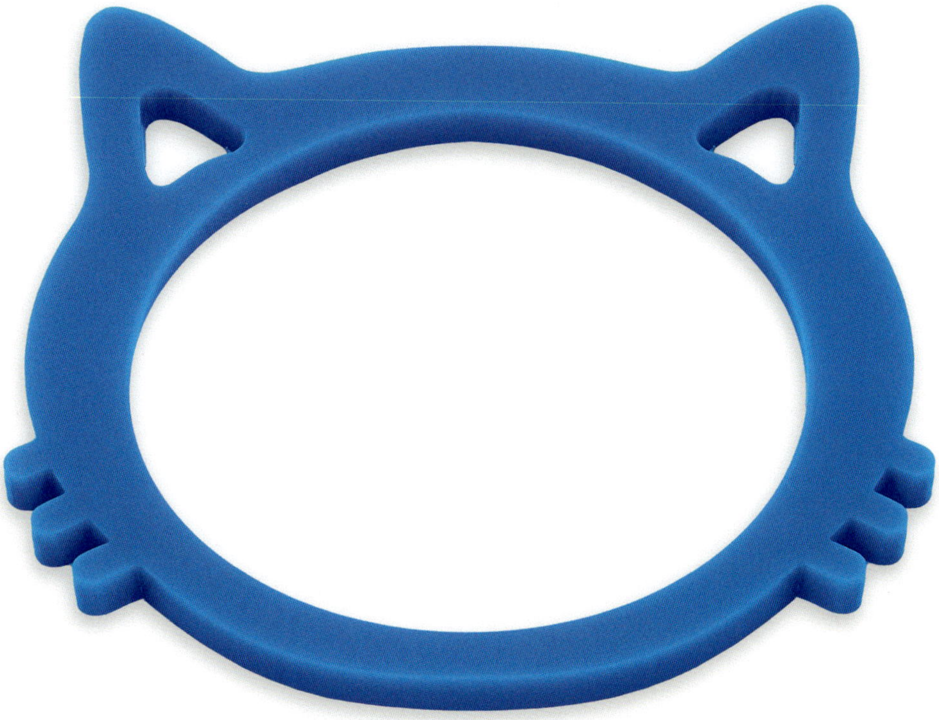

Glasses Necklace, SS03
Acrylic, plug chain

The Glasses Necklace made an appearance on the fifth series of TV's Absolutely Fabulous, worn by our favourite character, Bubbles, played by Jane Horrocks.

Telephone Bag, SS03
Cotton drill, acrylic

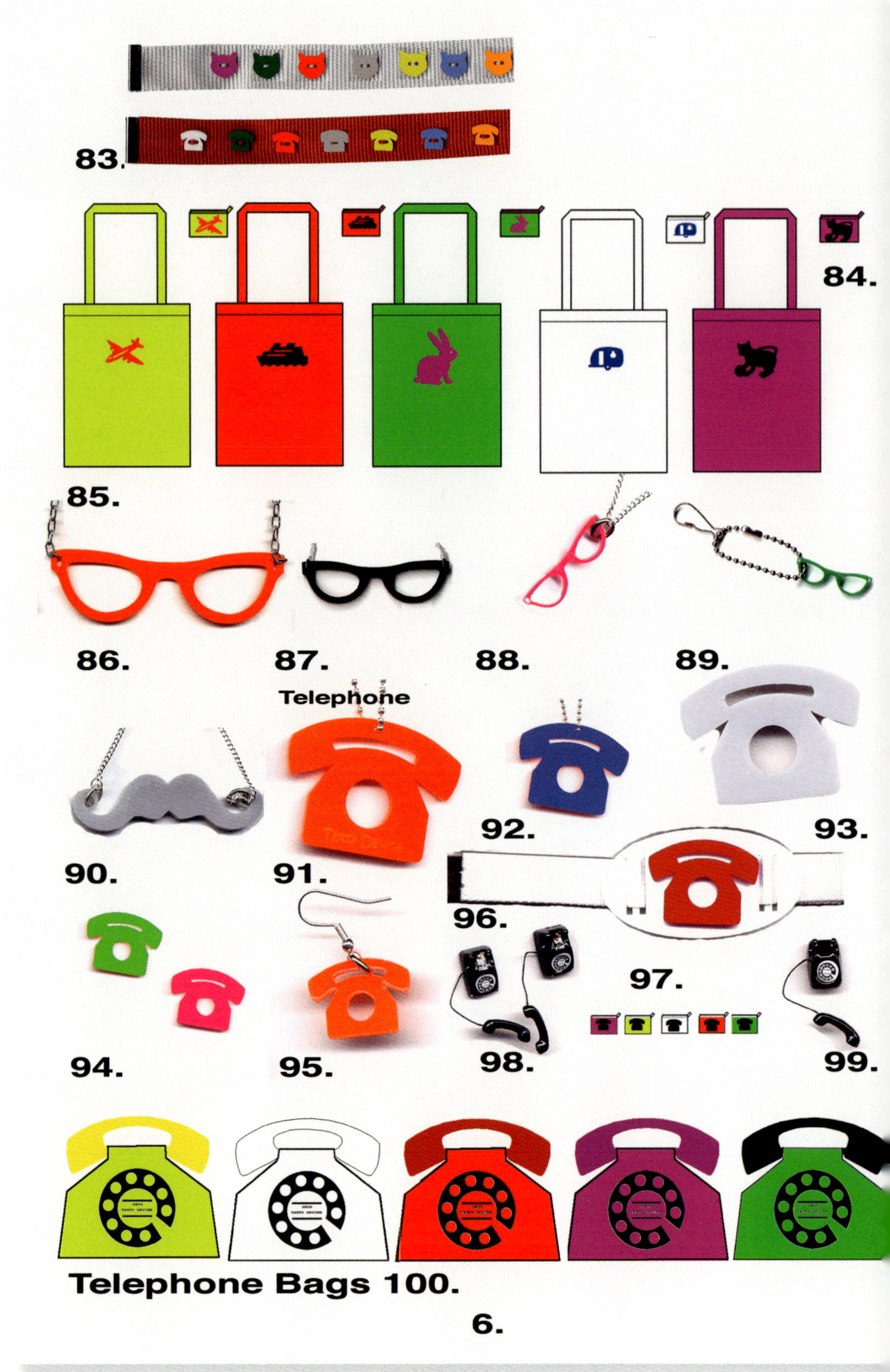
83.
84.
85.
86.
87.
88.
89.
Telephone
90.
91.
92.
93.
96.
94.
95.
98.
97.
99.
Telephone Bags 100.
6.

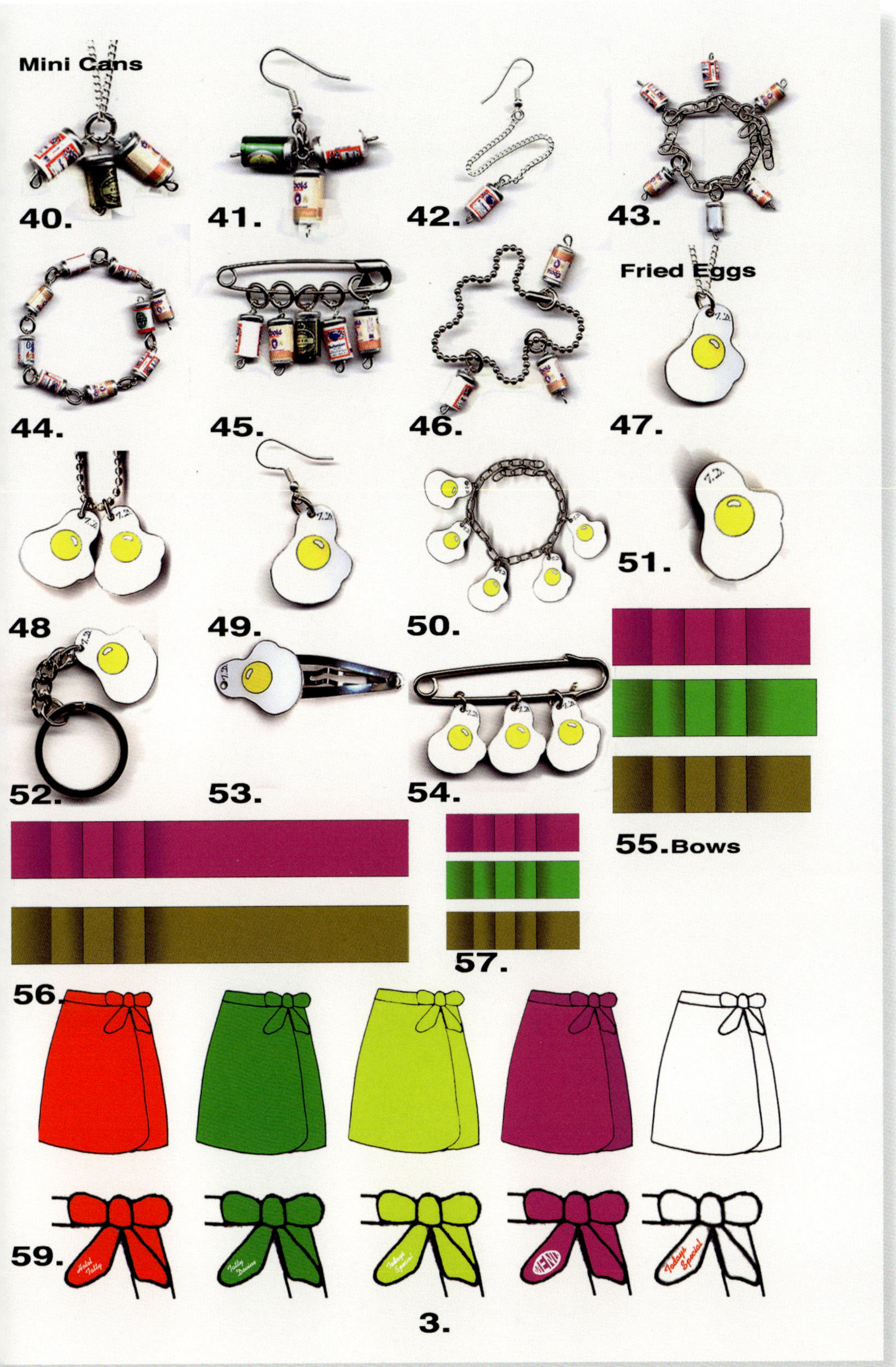

Mini Cans
40.
41.
42.
43.
44.
45.
46.
Fried Eggs
47.
48
49.
50.
51.
52.
53.
54.
55.Bows
56.
57.
59.
3.

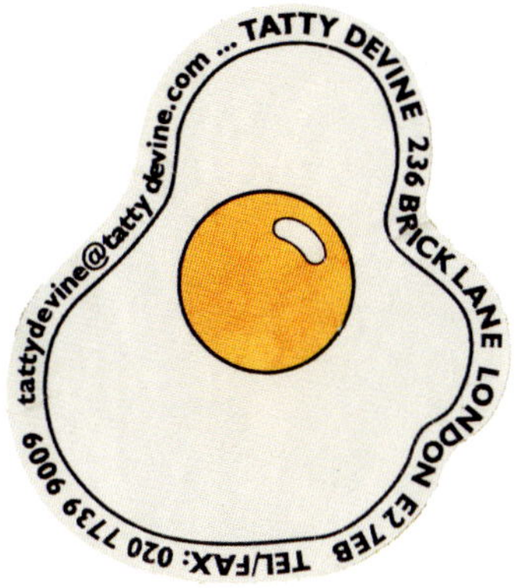

tattydevine@tattydevine.com ... TATTY DEVINE 236 BRICK LANE LONDON E2 7EB TEL/FAX: 020 7739 9009

Gekko print of Fuzzy-Felt shapes, 2002
Mark Pawson

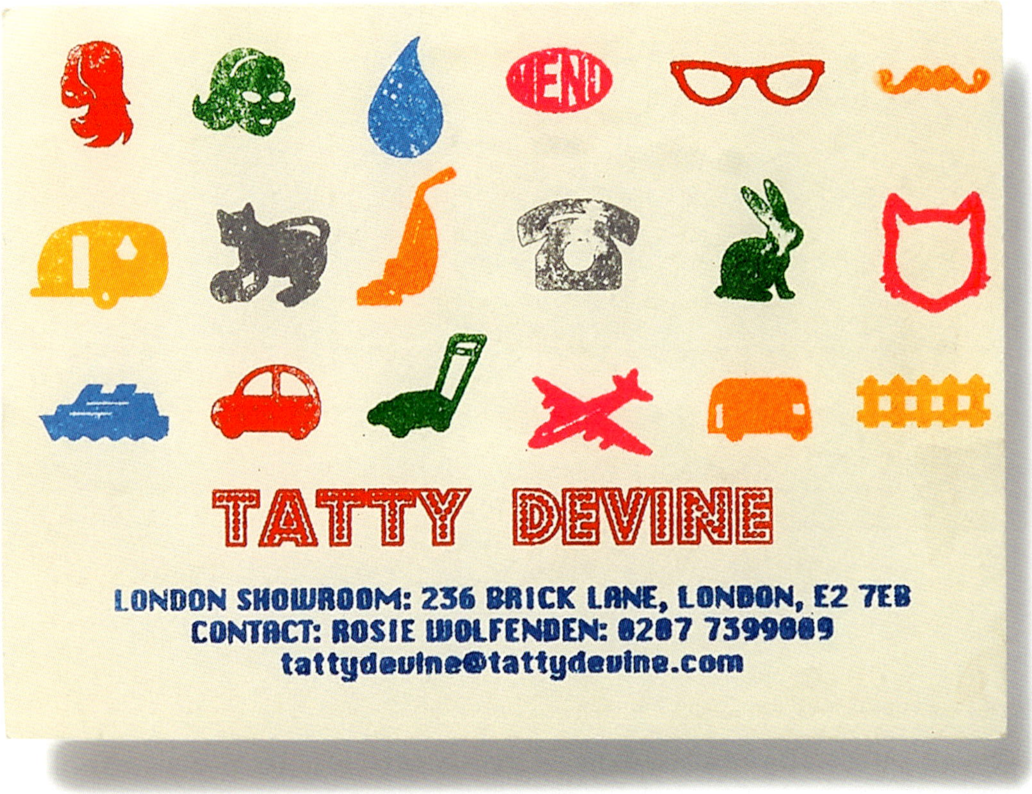

Gomez, 2002

We headed to Paris with the Fuzzy-Felt collection, and met this lovely dog called Gomez. He was a bit accident prone and he sat in chewing gum, so most of the night was spent trying to pick it out of his fur. This photo was on our studio wall for years and he's always felt like part of the team.

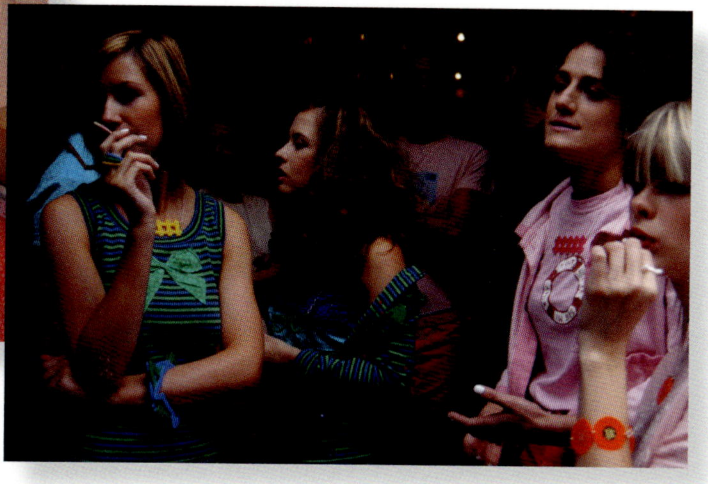

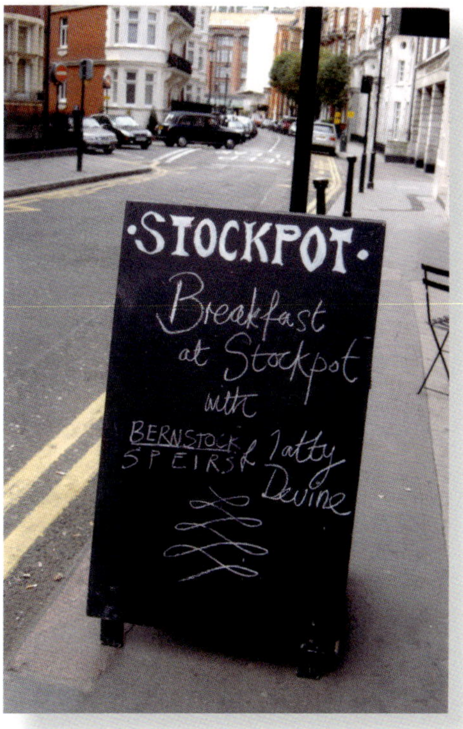

Stockpot presentation, September 2002

We presented the Fuzzy-Felt collection at London Fashion Week in September 2002, at The Stockpot in Knightsbridge, alongside our shop-neighbours and friends, Bernstock Speirs. The models wore Bernstock Speirs clothing and our jewellery, and the gathered journalists, friends and photographers were served a full English breakfasts by a waitress who wore outfits that matched the Fuzzy-Felt collection.

Fashion East show, February 2003

Our AW03 collection was selected to be part of Fashion East, a non-profit initiative set up to encourage the careers of young designers. Feeling ambitious, we decided to make 16 dresses, which had the feel of our jewellery. We temporarily transformed the shop into a sewing room, and under the guidance of Harriet's mum, a couture seamstress, we managed to get everything finished in one intense week. The models all wore pixie ears and knee-length socks as they walked to a soundtrack of birdsong.

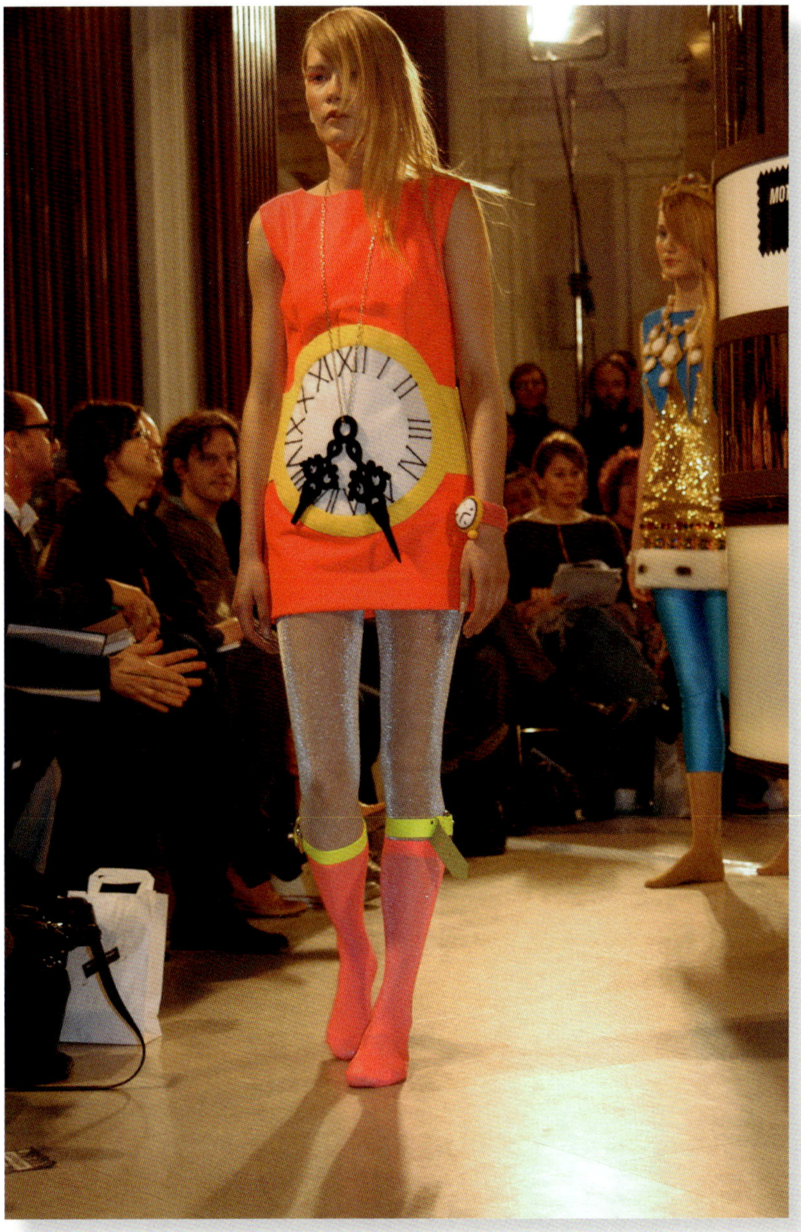

Motorola booklet, AW03

Motorola sponsored the show and produced a booklet using images from an early camera phone. We loved the grainy, lo-fi look of the images, even this picture of Harriet leaning on her kitchen table has a black-and-white-French-film feel.

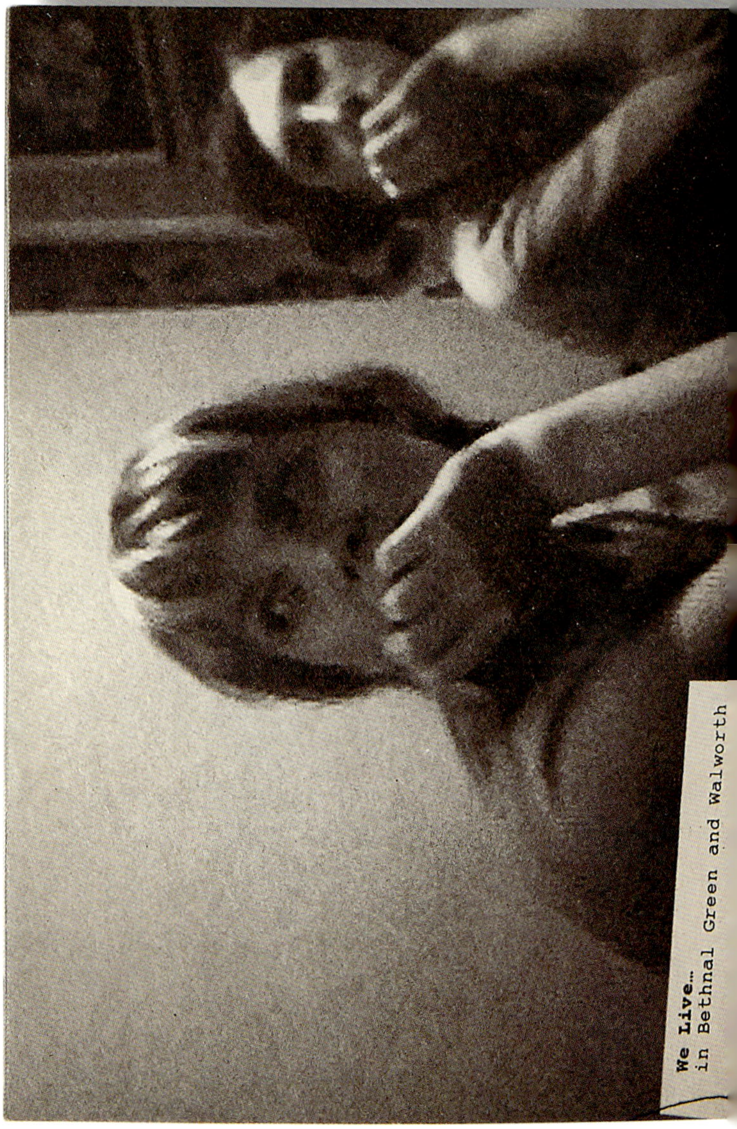

MotoFashionEast invitation, AW03

MOTOFASHIONEAST
A PROGRAMME TO SUPPORT
NEW TALENT IN BRITISH FASHION DESIGN
TATTY DEVINE
ROKSANDA ILINCIC
JONATHAN SAUNDERS
3PM SUNDAY 16TH FEBRUARY 2003
AURORA, THE GREAT EASTERN HOTEL
LIVERPOOL STREET, LONDON EC2
CONTACT LULU 0044(0)207 7706150
LULU@FASHIONEAST.CO.UK
MOTOROLA
intelligence everywhere
THE OLD TRUMAN BREWERY
GEH
Business Link
sew-east
PHOTOGRAPH FOUND, AUTHOR UNKNOWN

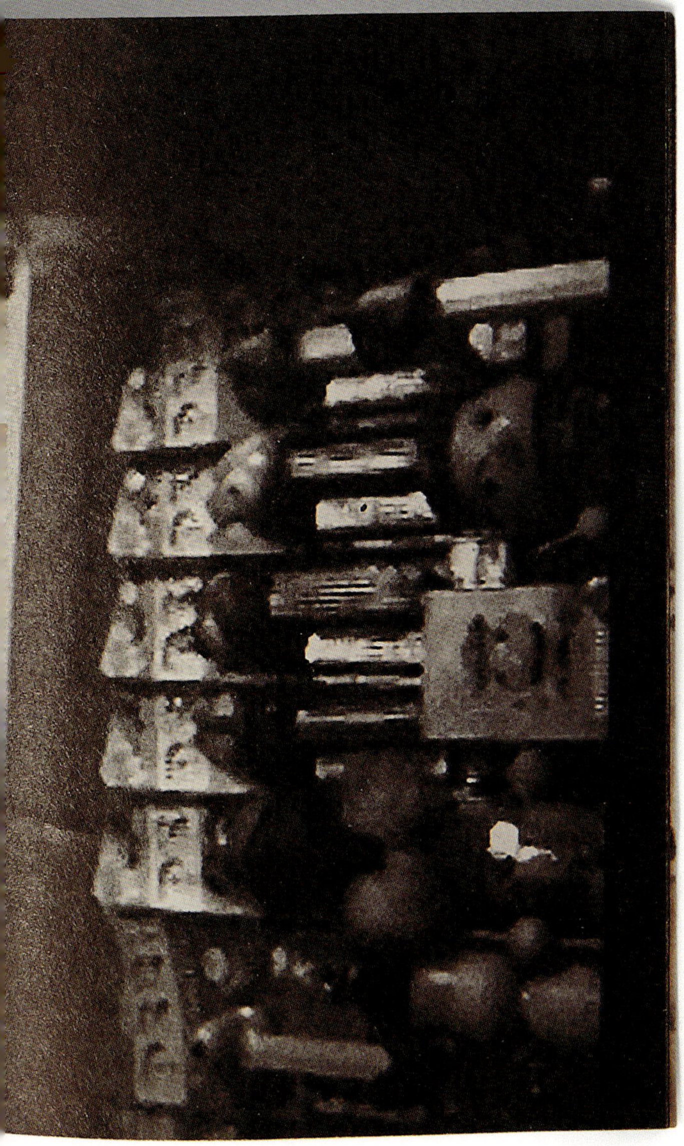

Song Bird Dress, AW03
Cotton drill, felt, feathers

Bird Brooches, AW03
Hand-painted plywood, feather,
Swarovski crystals, metal alloy

Crown Dress, AW03
Cotton drill, lurex, acrylic gems, fun fur, marker pen

Crown Jewels Necklace, AW03
Rowan Lurex Shimmer wool

Purse Dress, AW03
PVC, felt, cotton drill

Sing a Song of Sixpence Dress, AW03
Cotton drill, satin ribbon

Music Note Necklace, AW03
Acrylic, chain

Knitted Bird Brooch, AW03
Wool, metal alloy

The Knitted Bird Brooch came in black or white and was inspired by the nursery rhyme, Sing a Song of Sixpence. It was pinned to the Music Note Dress, along with the Bell Bracelet.

Midnight Owl Dress, AW03
Cotton drill, fabric, felt

Speech Bubble Dress, AW03
Printed cotton

Speech Bubble Brooches, AW03
Acrylic, metal alloy

Toadstool Dress with cape, AW03
Corduroy, felt, cotton drill, wool

Toadstool Brooches, AW03
Hand-painted plywood, metal alloy

Singing Ringing Tree Dress, AW03
Corduroy, felt, piping cord

Wooden Bird Brooches, AW03
Hand-painted wood, feather, metal alloy

Tatty Devine

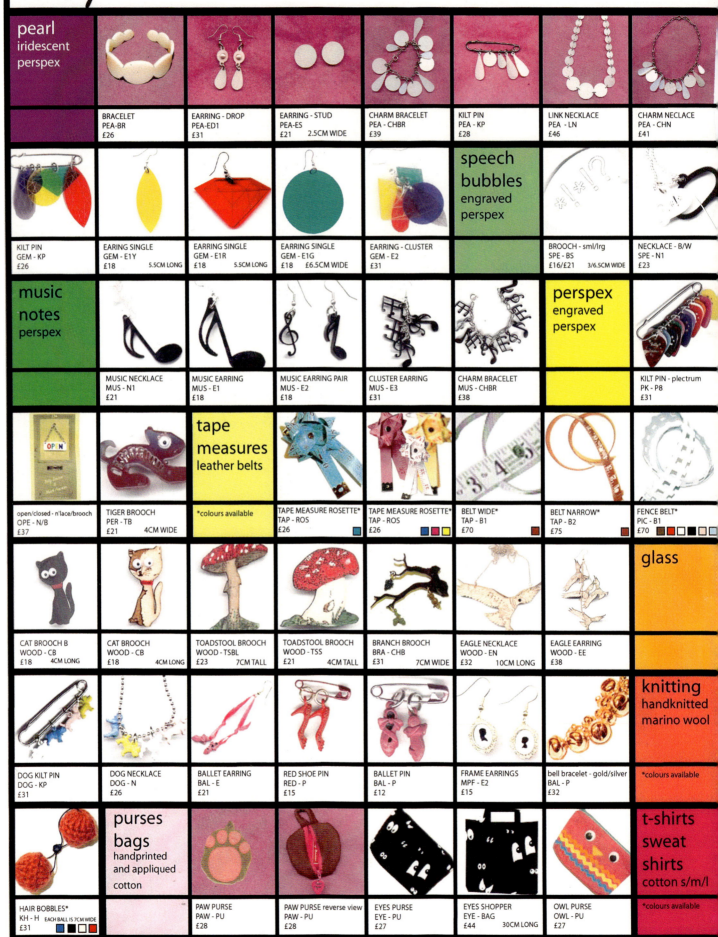

236 Brick Lane, London, E2 7EB. TEL 0207 7399009, E-mail: tat

pearl iridescent perspex	BRACELET PEA-BR £26	EARRING - DROP PEA-ED1 £31	EARRING - STUD PEA-ES £21 2.5CM WIDE	CHARM BRACELET PEA - CHBR £39	KILT PIN PEA - KP £28	LINK NECKLACE PEA - LN £46	CHARM NECLACE PEA - CHN £41

KILT PIN GEM - KP £26	EARING SINGLE GEM - E1Y £18 5.5CM LONG	EARRING SINGLE GEM - E1R £18 5.5CM LONG	EARRING SINGLE GEM - E1G £18 £6.5CM WIDE	EARRING - CLUSTER GEM - E2 £31	speech bubbles engraved perspex	BROOCH - sml/lrg SPE - BS £16/£21 3/6.5CM WIDE	NECKLACE - B/W SPE - N1 £23

music notes perspex	MUSIC NECKLACE MUS - N1 £21	MUSIC EARRING MUS - E1 £18	MUSIC EARRING PAIR MUS - E2 £18	CLUSTER EARRING MUS - E3 £31	CHARM BRACELET MUS - CHBR £38	perspex engraved perspex	KILT PIN - plectrum PK - P8 £31

open/closed - n'lace/brooch OPE - N/B £37	TIGER BROOCH PER - TB £21 4CM WIDE	tape measures leather belts *colours available	TAPE MEASURE ROSETTE* TAP - ROS £26	TAPE MEASURE ROSETTE* TAP - ROS £26	BELT WIDE* TAP - B1 £70	BELT NARROW* TAP - B2 £75	FENCE BELT* PIC - B1 £70

CAT BROOCH B WOOD - CB £18 4CM LONG	CAT BROOCH WOOD - CB £18 4CM LONG	TOADSTOOL BROOCH WOOD - TSBL £23 7CM TALL	TOADSTOOL BROOCH WOOD - TSS £21 4CM TALL	BRANCH BROOCH BRA - CHB £31 7CM WIDE	EAGLE NECKLACE WOOD - EN £32 10CM LONG	EAGLE EARRING WOOD - EE £38	glass

DOG KILT PIN DOG - KP £31	DOG NECKLACE DOG - N £26	BALLET EARRING BAL - E £21	RED SHOE PIN RED - P £15	BALLET PIN BAL - P £12	FRAME EARRINGS MPF - E2 £15	bell bracelet - gold/silver BAL - P £32	knitting handknitted marino wool *colours available

HAIR BOBBLES* KH - H EACH BALL IS 7CM WIDE £31	purses bags handprinted and appliqued cotton	PAW PURSE PAW - PU £28	PAW PURSE reverse view PAW - PU £28	EYES PURSE EYE - PU £27	EYES SHOPPER EYE - BAG £44 30CM LONG	OWL PURSE OWL - PU £27	t-shirts sweat shirts cotton s/m/l *colours available

PLEASE NOTE THAT ALL SIZES ARE APPROXIMATE

ydevine@tattydevine.com Press: 0207 7298762 Autumn/Winter 03

diamonds transparent fluorescent perspex *colours available	NECKLACE* DIA - N £36	EARRING* DIA - E £31	KILT PIN DIA - KP £28	CHARM BRACELET DIA - CHBR £38	**gem** transparent perspex	NECKLACE GEM - N £21	CHARM BRACELET GEM - CHBR £36

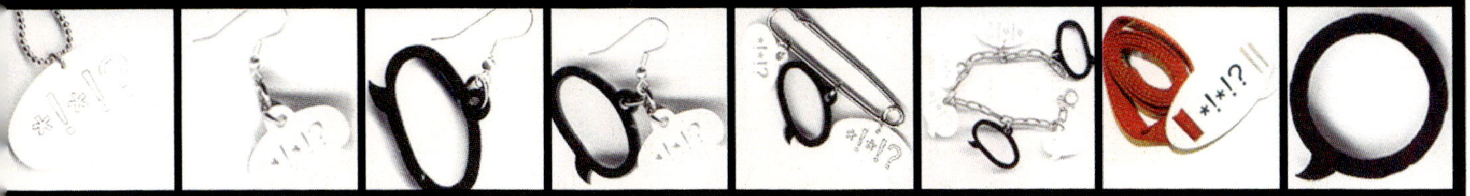

NECKLACE - W SPE - N2 £21	EARRING - W SPE - EW £12	EARRING - B SPE - EB £12	EARRING - B/W SPE - EBW £21	KILT PIN SPE - KP £26	CHARM BRACELET SPE - CHBR £38	WEBBING BELT SPE - WB1 £40	RING SPE - R £10

NECKLACE - plectrum PN - 8 £38	CHARM BRACELET - plec PCH - BR8 £47	CHARM BRACELET REC - CHBR £31	PERSPEX BRACELET V - CHBR £38	BIRD CHARM BRACELET B - CHBR £38	LADY AND DOG LD - B £32 10CM WIDE	PUPPET MAN EARRING PUP - E £31	SWALLOW NECKLACE SWA - N £27 13CM LONG

wooden handpainted wood	WOODEN BIRD BROOCH WOOD - BB £31 9CM LONG	WOODEN BIRD BROOCH WOOD - BB £31 9CM LONG	WOODEN BIRD BROOCH WOOD - BB £31 9CM LONG	WOODEN BIRD BROOCH WOOD - BB £31 9CM LONG	PINE CONE EARRING WOOD - PCE £23	PINE CONE NECKLACE WOOD - PCN £26	SCOUT BROOCH WOOD - SB £21 3CM WIDE

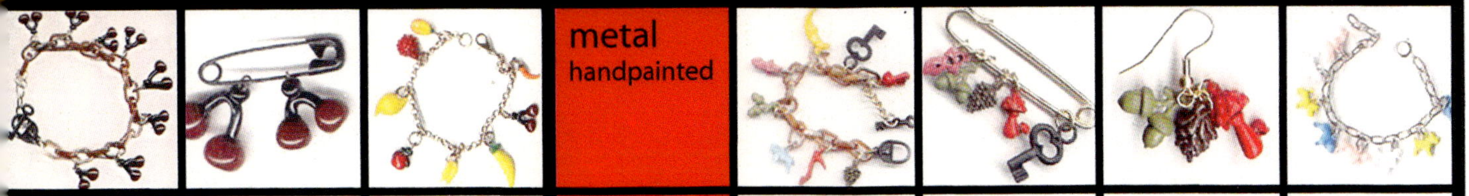

CHERRY BRACELET CHEO - CHBR £41	CHERRY PIN CHE - P £12	FRUIT BRACELET FRU - CHBR £26	**metal** handpainted	FAIRY TALE BRACELET FT - CHBR £41	FAIRY KILT PIN FT - KP £26	FAIRY EARRING FT - E1 £21	DOG BRACELET DOG - CHBR £38

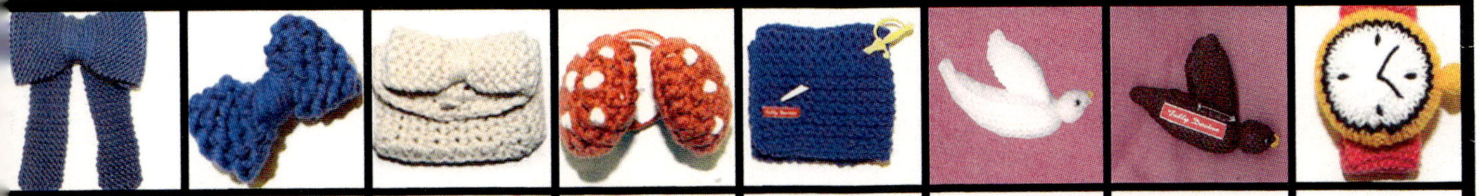

BOW SCARF* BOW - SC £83	BOW BADGE* BOW - B 9CM WIDE £23	BOW PURSE* BOW - PU 16CM WIDE £38	TOADSTOOL EARMUFF TS - EARM £40	SWORD SCARF* SWO - SC £75	BIRD HAIR CLIP b/w* KB - H 15CM LONG £46	BIRD BROOCH b/w KB - B 15CM LONG £46	KNITTED WATCH KW - BR £46

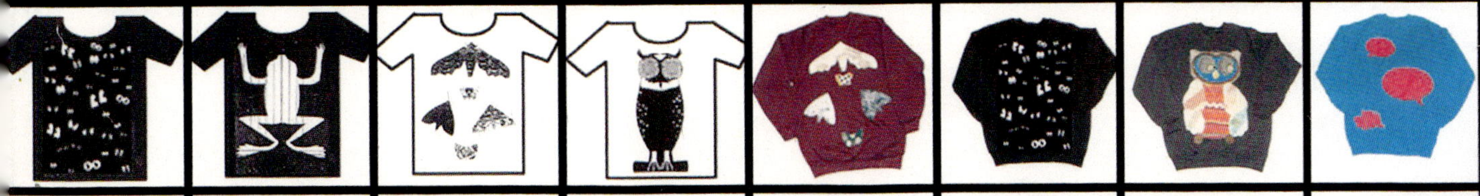

EYES T-SHIRT* EYE - T £30	KISS ME1 T-SHIRT* KISS1 - T £30	MOTH T-SHIRT* MOT - T £30	OWL T-SHIRT* OWL - T £30	MOTH SWEATSHIRT MOT - SWE £78 HAND APPLIQUED	EYES SWEATSHIRT EYE - SWE £52	OWL SWEATSHIRT OWL - SWE £90 HAND APPLIQUED	SPEECH SWEATSHIRT SPE - SWE £78 HAND APPLIQUED

Knitted Watch Bracelet, AW03
Wool

Bell Bracelet, AW03
Metal bells, plug chain, plectrum

We were still making jewellery from found objects – like this Bell Bracelet. It was incredibly noisy to wear, a constant jingle jangle of sound, but people seemed to like that.

Gem Charm Bracelet, AW03
Acrylic, plug chain

Mini Can Single Earring, AW03
Dolls' house can, metal alloy

All of our earrings were designed to be worn singly and never as a pair. Rosie often had to reassure people that she hadn't lost an earring – there was meant to be only one of them.

Shop Opens Soon poster, 2003

Late 2003 heralded the opening of another Tatty Devine shop. Tucked away in a little alleyway off Brewer Street, Soho, it was tiny – a small kiosk really – but we were excited to be in the centre of the city. It took us a while to get it ship-shape. In its previous incarnation it had been a sex shop, with a mosaic floor decorated with penises. We opened on Valentine's Day 2004 with a big party in the yard behind the shop, and served heart-shaped pizzas from the local Domino's. Alongside our jewellery we sold records, comics, zines and artworks by Mark Pawson, Zeel, Little Miss Lucifer, Rachael Matthews and Chicks on Speed.

Open party invitation, 2004

Soho shop, 2004

Sticky back plastic logo on Soho shop door, 2004

Rubber stamps, 1999–2005

Favourite sketchbooks

Harriet has been using the Daler Rowney A4 sketchbooks since college – nothing else will do.

Sketchbook, AW03

The Name Necklaces are one of our best-loved pieces of jewellery. Harriet was thinking about Christmas presents in 2003 and began doodling friends' names in her sketchbook, and realised that if they were cut out in acrylic they'd make perfect personalised gifts. They were so popular with our friends that we started making them to order in all the colours of the rainbow.

Olukemi
Olukemi
tessa
Vicki
Kate
SJ
Cat
Bree
Mimi
Manami
Tatty

STEREO
TATTY DEVINE, 236 BRICK LANE, LONDON E2 7EB. T/F 0207 739 9008. TATTYDEVINE@TATTYDEVINE.COM
Tatty Devine
33

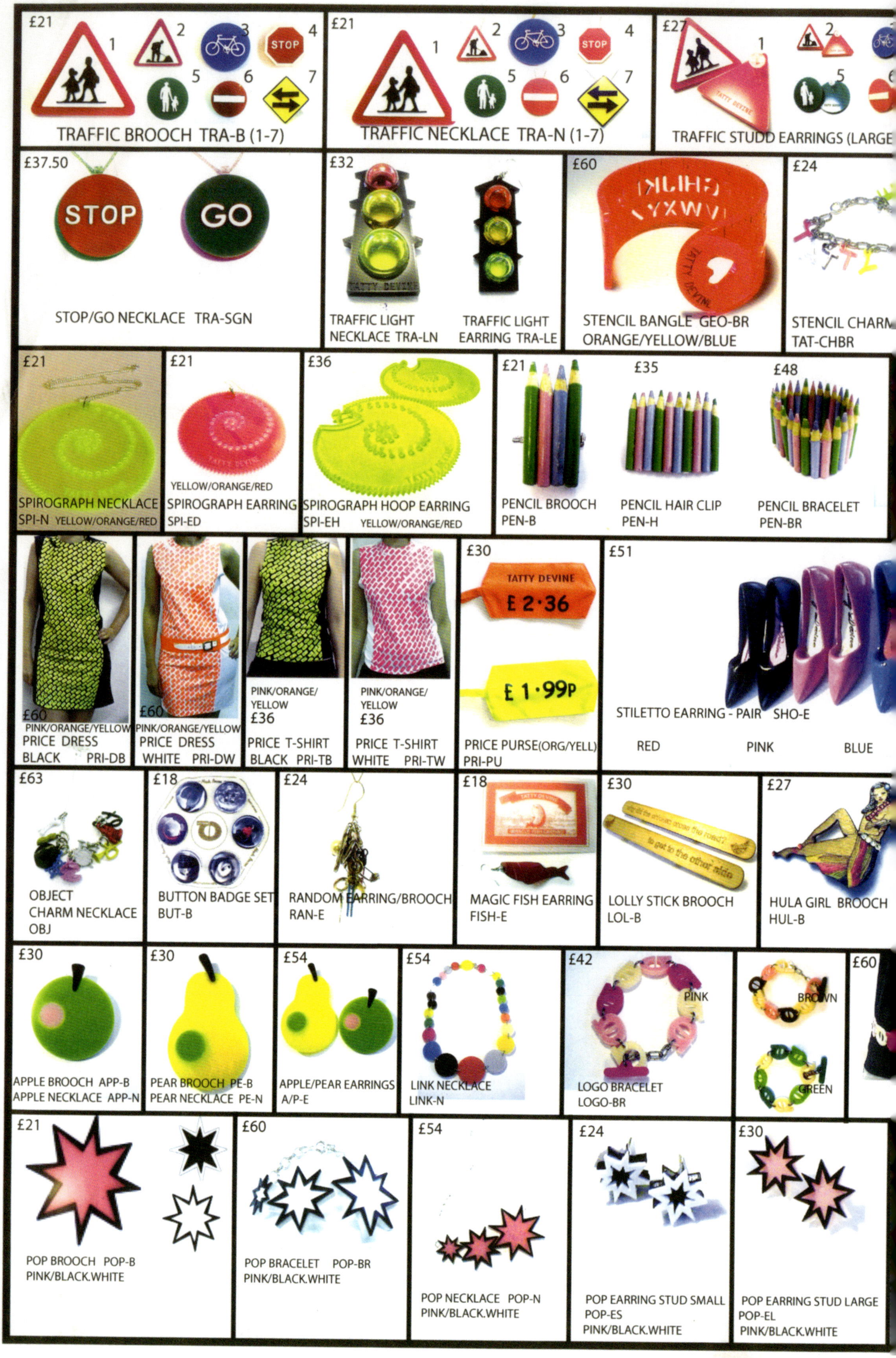
£21
TRAFFIC BROOCH TRA-B (1-7)
£21
TRAFFIC NECKLACE TRA-N (1-7)
£27
TRAFFIC STUDD EARRINGS (LARGE
£37.50
STOP
GO
STOP/GO NECKLACE TRA-SGN
£32
TRAFFIC LIGHT NECKLACE TRA-LN
TRAFFIC LIGHT EARRING TRA-LE
£60
STENCIL BANGLE GEO-BR ORANGE/YELLOW/BLUE
£24
STENCIL CHARM TAT-CHBR
£21
SPIROGRAPH NECKLACE SPI-N YELLOW/ORANGE/RED
£21
YELLOW/ORANGE/RED
SPIROGRAPH EARRING SPI-ED
£36
SPIROGRAPH HOOP EARRING SPI-EH YELLOW/ORANGE/RED
£21
PENCIL BROOCH PEN-B
£35
PENCIL HAIR CLIP PEN-H
£48
PENCIL BRACELET PEN-BR
£60
PINK/ORANGE/YELLOW
PRICE DRESS BLACK PRI-DB
£60
PINK/ORANGE/YELLOW
PRICE DRESS WHITE PRI-DW
PINK/ORANGE/ YELLOW
£36
PRICE T-SHIRT BLACK PRI-TB
PINK/ORANGE/ YELLOW
£36
PRICE T-SHIRT WHITE PRI-TW
£30
TATTY DEVINE
£ 2·36
£ 1·99P
PRICE PURSE(ORG/YELL) PRI-PU
£51
STILETTO EARRING - PAIR SHO-E
RED PINK BLUE
£63
OBJECT CHARM NECKLACE OBJ
£18
BUTTON BADGE SET BUT-B
£24
RANDOM EARRING/BROOCH RAN-E
£18
MAGIC FISH EARRING FISH-E
£30
LOLLY STICK BROOCH LOL-B
£27
HULA GIRL BROOCH HUL-B
£30
APPLE BROOCH APP-B
APPLE NECKLACE APP-N
£30
PEAR BROOCH PE-B
PEAR NECKLACE PE-N
£54
APPLE/PEAR EARRINGS A/P-E
£54
LINK NECKLACE LINK-N
£42
PINK
LOGO BRACELET LOGO-BR
BROWN
GREEN
£60
£21
POP BROOCH POP-B
PINK/BLACK.WHITE
£60
POP BRACELET POP-BR
PINK/BLACK.WHITE
£54
POP NECKLACE POP-N
PINK/BLACK.WHITE
£24
POP EARRING STUD SMALL POP-ES
PINK/BLACK.WHITE
£30
POP EARRING STUD LARGE POP-EL
PINK/BLACK.WHITE

£25
TRAFFIC HAIR BOBBLES TRA-H (1-5)
£78
TRIANGLE BRACELET TRA-BR
STUD EARRINGS (SMALL) TRA-ES (1-2)
£24
£18
TRIANGLE HOOPS TRA-HE
£50
RULER BANGLE GEO-BR2
ORANGE/YELLOW/BLUE
£90
360 BANGLE-360-BR
YELLOW/ORANGE/BLUE/WHITE
£25
SET SQUARE EARRING
ORANGE/BLUE GEO-E1
£25
SET SQUARE NECKLACE
ORANGE/BLUE GEO-N
£54
SET SQUARE CHARM BRACELET
GEO-CHBR
NECKLACE BON-N
/GREEN/WHITE
£29
FISH EARRING BON-E
BLACK/GREEN/WHITE
£12
PRICE TICKET
BROOCH PRI-B
£45
PRICE TICKET BAG 3
PRI-BAG3
£45
PINK/ORANGE/YELLOW
PRICE TICKET D RING BAG
BLACK PRI-BAGDB
£45
PINK/ORANGE/YELLOW
PRICE TICKET BAG
GREY PRI-BAGDG
ACK WHITE
£66
OBJECT
CHARM BRACELET
OBJ-CHBR
£66
PEOPLE
CHARM BRACELET
PEO-CHBR
£21
PEOPLE
EARRING SET OF 3
PEO-E3
£21
OBJECT
EARRING SET OF 3
OBJ-E3
£63
PEOPLE CHARM NECKLACE
PEO-CHN
ONKEY
CH FEZ-B
£21
SAIL OCH
SAIL-B
£36
PERCHED BIRD
BROOCH PERCH-B
£54
JEANETTE
LADY BROOCH
LAD-BJ
£54
MATILDA
LADY BROOCH
LAD-BM
£54
DOROTHY
LADY BROOCH
LAD-BD
LOGO-B1
GREEN
£21
BROWN
PINK
GREEN
LOGO NECKLACE
LOGO-N
£18
LOGO EARRINGS- PAIR- SMALL
LOGO-ES PINK/BROWN/GREEN
£24
LOGO EARRING LARGE
LOGO-EL
PINK/BROWN/GREEN
S DANGLE
WHITE
£21
POP HAIR BOBBLE
POP-H
PINK/BLACK.WHITE
£25
POP HAIR SLIDE
POP-S
PINK/BLACK.WHITE
£105
POP BELT
POP-B1
PINK/BLACK.WHITE
Tatty Devine
SPRING/SUMMER 2004

Price Ticket Cufflinks, SS04
Hard enamel

We used to walk past a park bench that was covered in fluorescent price tickets. An old man sat there every day drinking a can of Special Brew and adding the sticker from his can to the bench. We designed a price ticket print and made it into brooches cufflinks, purses, T-shirts, dresses and tote bags. All the Tatty team wore a Price Ticket Dress for the opening of the Soho store.

Dinosaur Necklace, SS04
Acrylic, beads, metal alloy

On a trip to the National History Museum we noticed that the dinosaur skeletons looked like giant necklaces threaded onto string, and we immediately set about trying to recreate that effect. It was technically challenging, as each individual bone had to be laser-cut and then turned on its side to be drilled. We'd have 'dino days', where all the bones would be laid in a circle on a table and we'd all walk around it, making up the necklace as we went. Initially the Dinosaur Necklaces were made in black, white or lime green – this one was a sample which Rosie kept, she being a fan of all things orange.

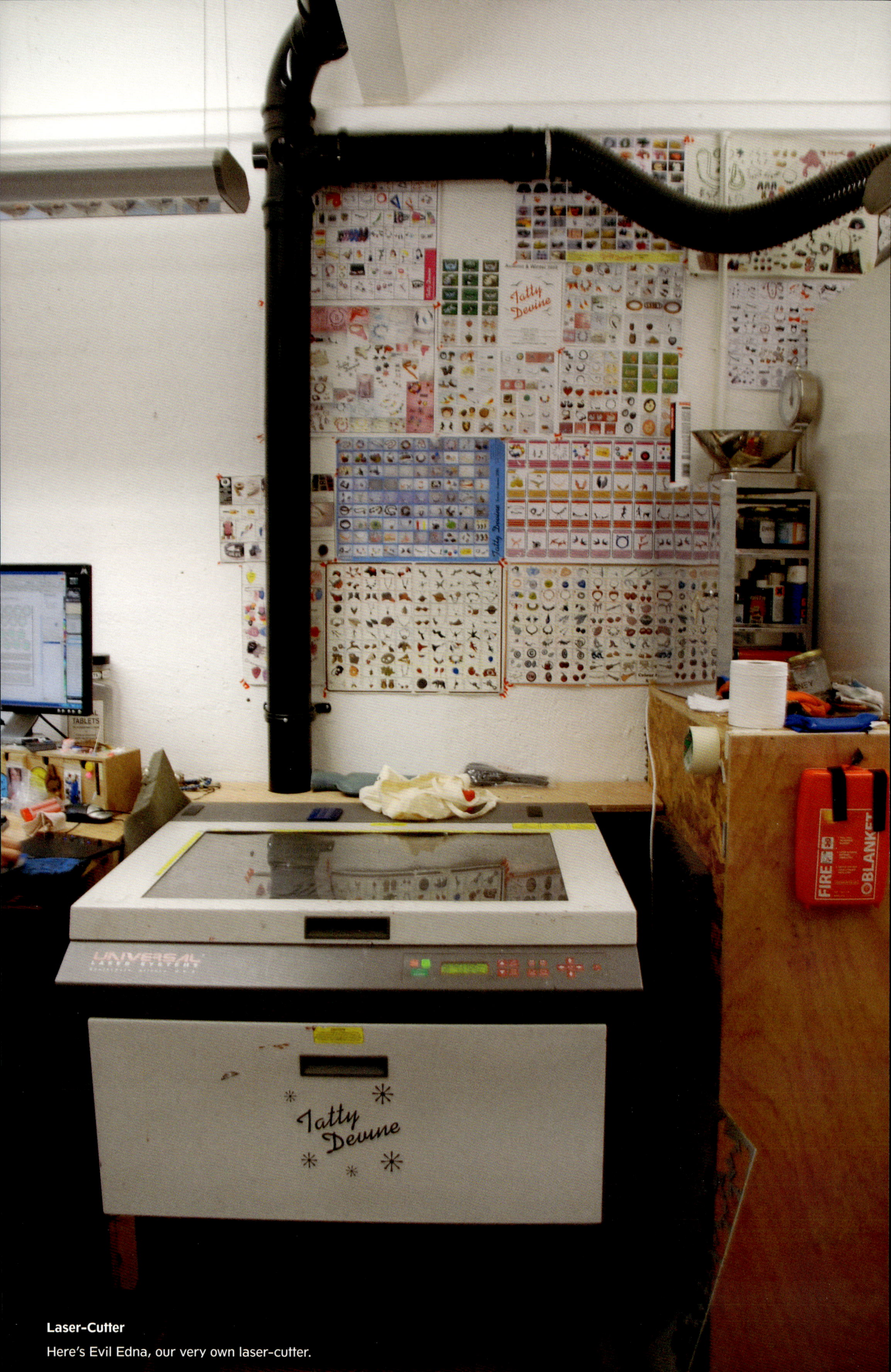

Laser-Cutter

Here's Evil Edna, our very own laser-cutter.

Lobster Necklace, AW04
Acrylic, metal alloy

Getting our own laser-cutter opened up
a whole new world of creativity for us. We
could experiment with all kinds of techniques.
It allowed us to develop our signature style,
and design jewellery like the Lobster Necklace,
which we still produce today.

Swallow Brooches, AW04
Hand-painted plywood, metal alloy

Tattoos were still relatively unusual and alternative in 2004 when we designed these tattoo brooches. Rosie's flatmate had found a flashbook of Sailor Jerry's drawings in a charity shop, and we made these for people who didn't want to commit to the real thing.

Volume Brooch, SS04 & AW04
Moulded plastic, metal alloy

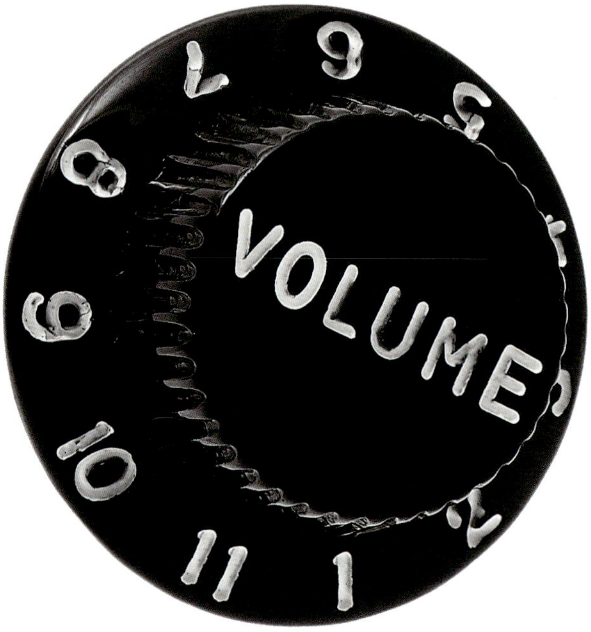

Catalogue, AW04

This is a worn and torn copy of our A3-size AW04 catalogue, which showcased the Sweetie Necklace, Lobster, the Horse and Carriage Necklace and our ongoing obsession with hearts.

1. £103
1
2. £49
2
12.
9. £22
8. £27
4. £21
3. £21
6. £32
10.
11.
BONES
4.
3.
6.
11.
10
13a
13b.
15
16.
28.
29.
27.
ALPINE
30.
31.
32.
33.
34.
17.
56.
TATTY RAG
TATTY RAG
DALSTON
68.
69.
66.
67.
62.
GLASSES
NEWSPAPER
70.
71.
ALSO IN PINK
60.
63.
61.
79.
80.
82.
81.
ALSO IN CREAM
58.
PAGE
73.
75.
76.
74.
77.
72.
78.
BEADS
ALSO IN BLACK
85.
55.
84.
83.
88.
86.
87.
96.
FRUIT STICKERS

ALSO IN BROWN
FISH
25.
24.
23.
18.
19.
20.
21.
22.
26.
36.
39.
51.
38.
35.
COWBOY
50
44.
ine
41.
43.
45.
44.
45.
64.
40.
42.
RUBIX
92.
91.
57.
48.
59.
53.
46.
47.
49.
93.
54.
52.
Logo
97.
99.
98.
FLOWERS
86.
87.
90.
88.
88.
90.
87.
86.
89.
87.

Felicity Hayward in the Fishbone Necklace, AW04
Photography by Saga Sig

Newsprint Jazz Shoes, SS05
Canvas upper, man-made sole

In 2005 we were asked by Poste Mistress to design some shoes. We took traditional shoe shapes, like these jazz pumps, and gave them a Tatty twist. We created the newspaper in letterpress using articles we'd written. We also made court shoes with a sheriff's badge and wooden mules with an appliquéd alpine design.

Autumn & Winter 2005

Tatty Devine

Buyers/ Inquiries
236 Brick Lane, London E2 7EB Phone/Fax: +44(0)20 7739 9009
info@tattydevine.com
Soho Shop
57 b Brewer Street, London W1F 9UL Phone/Fax: +44(0)20 7434 2257
Press Office:
Blow PR +44(0)207 287 0041
WWW.TATTYDEVINE.COM

DOMINOES

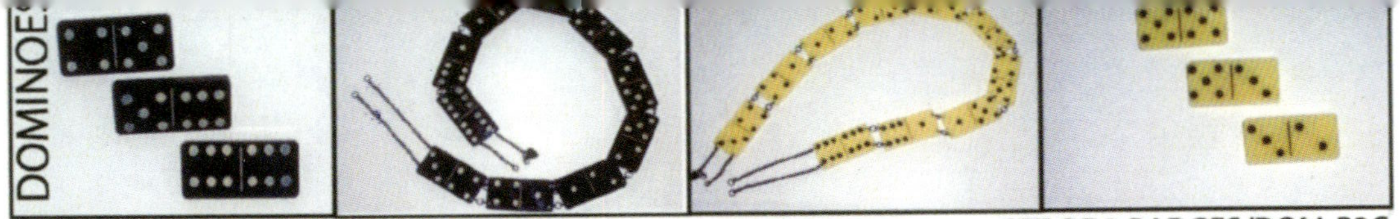

SET OF 3 BADGES/DOM-B3B | BELT/DOM-B1B | BELT/DOM-B1C | SET OF 3 BADGES/DOM-B3C

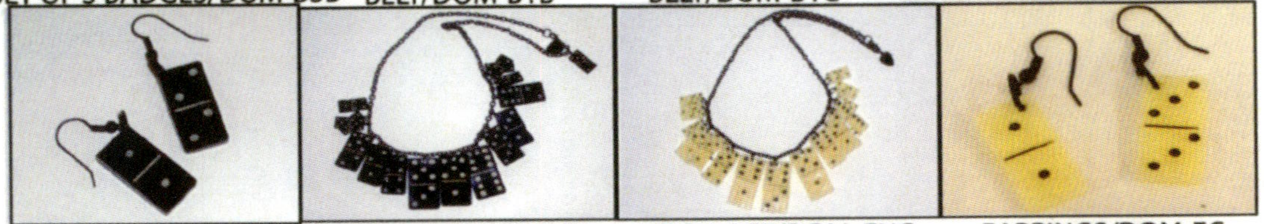

EARRINGS/DOM-EB | NECKLACE/DOM-CNB | NECKLACE/DOM-CNC | EARRINGS/DOM-EC

NECKLACE/ DOM-N3B | BRACELET/DOM-LBRB | BRACELET/DOM-LBRC | NECKLACE/ DOM-N3C

HEARTS

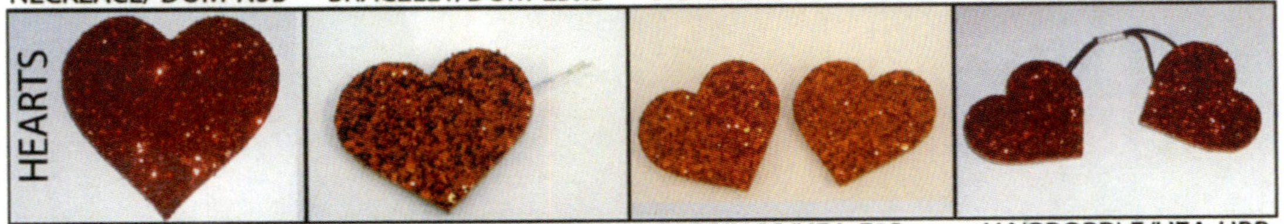

BROOCH/HEA-BR | HAIRGRIP/HEA-HR | EARRINGS/HEA-E2R | HAIRBOBBLE/HEA-HBR

SWANS

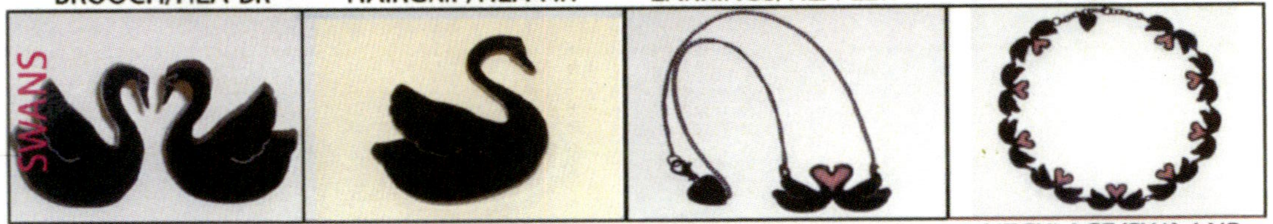

EARRINGS/SWA-E2B | BROOCH/SWA-BB | NECKLACE/SWA-N3B | NECKLACE/SWA-LNB

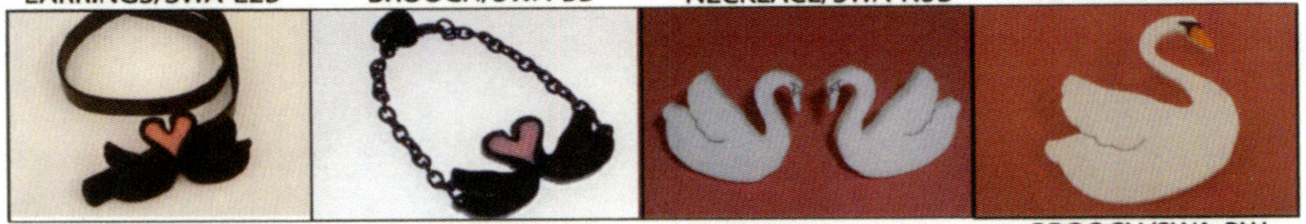

BELT/SWA-B1B | BRACELET/SWA-BRB | EARRINGS/SWA-E2W | BROOCH/SWA-BW

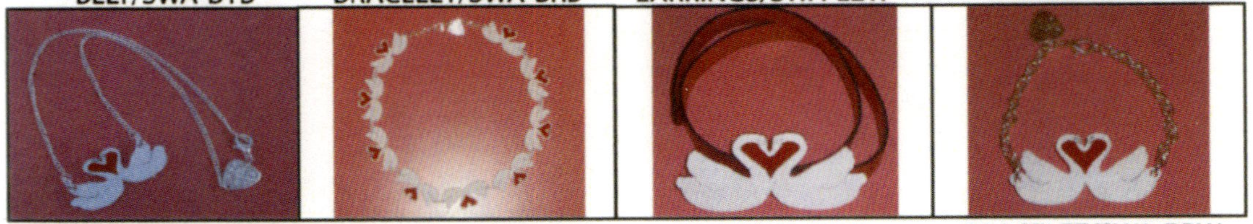

NECKLACE/SWA-N3W | NECKLACE/SWA-LNW | BELT/SWA-B1W | BRACELET/SWA-BRW

SEWING BOX

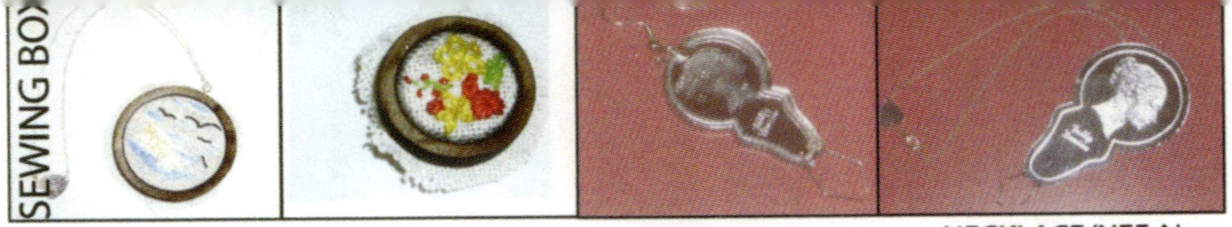

NECKLACE/TAP-N | BROOCH-TAP-B | EARRING-S/NEE-E1 | NECKLACE/NEE-N

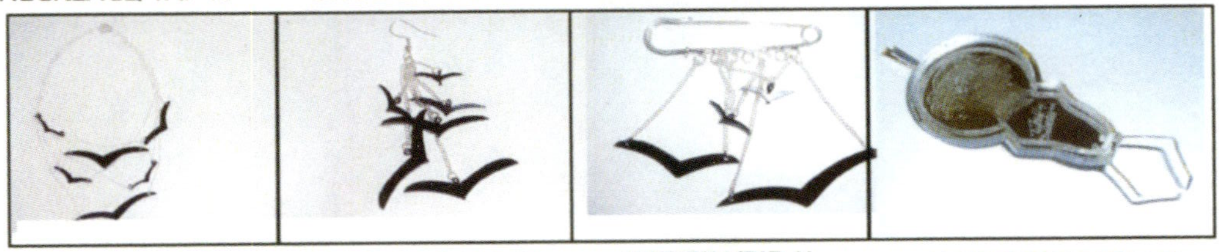

NECKLACE/BIR-N | EARRING-S/BIR-E3 | KILT PIN/BIR-K | HAIRSLIDE/NEE-HS

BROOCH/FAC-B | PURSE/FAC-PU | BROOCH/ICE-B | KILT PIJN & NECKLACE/FAI-K&FAI-N

OLD FAVORITES

NECKLACE/BON-N | BROOCH/GUI-B | BRACELET/PCHBR8

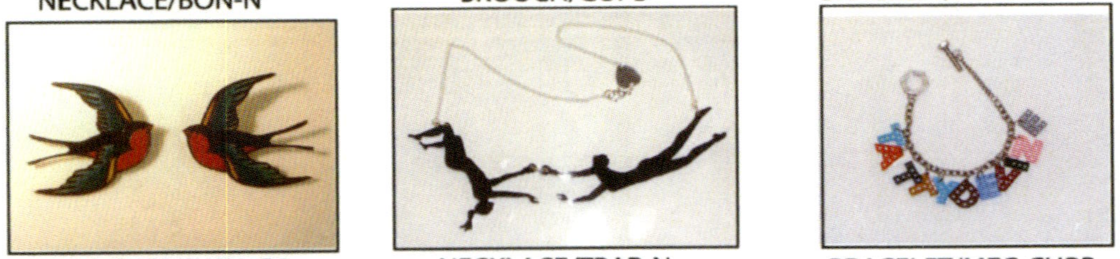

BROOCHES/SWAL-B2 | NECKLACE/TRAP-N | BRACELET/MEC-CHBR

BRACELET/RCHBR | NECKLACE/PN3 | PIN/PRI-B

RAFFIA NECKLACE RAF-N | RAFFIA BRACELET RAF-BR | RAFFIA BELT RAF-B1 | WOODEN BEAD NECKLACE BEA-N | WOODEN BEAD BRACELET BEA-BR | BEAD

SHELL RING SHE-R | SHELL STUD EARRINGS SHE-SE | SHELL BROOCH SHE-B | SHELL BRACELET SHE-BR | SHELL PENDENT SHE-P | SH

SEAWEED NECKLACE SEA-N | SEAWEED EARRING SEA-E1 | SEAWEED VEIL SEA-V | L FLAG NECKLACE FLA-LN | S FLAG NECKLACE FLA-SN | FLAG CI

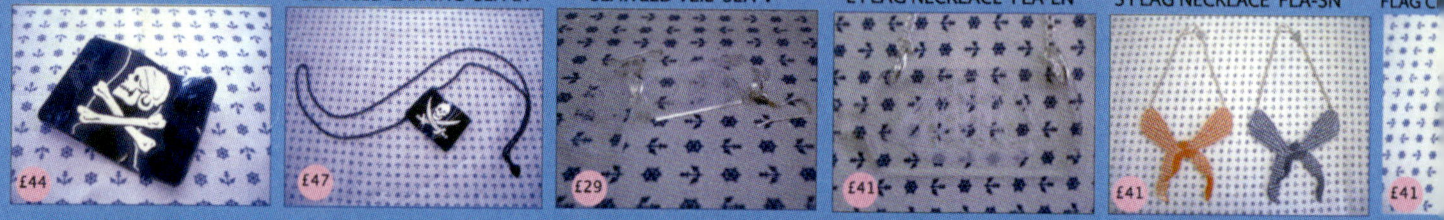

PIRATE FLAG BROOCH PIRF-B | PIRATE FLAG NECKLACE PIRF-N | SHIP IN BOTTLE EARRINGS BOT-E2 | SHIP IN BOTTLE NECKLACE BOT-N | NECKERCHIEF NECKLACE NECK-N | LIFE

PIRATE FLAG CUFFLINKS PIRF-CL | CRYSTAL RIGGING NECKLACE C/RIG-N | CUTLASNECKLACE CUT-N | CUTLAS EARRRING- CUT-E1 | CUTLAS PENDENT- CUT-P | CUT

TREASURE CHEST BELT- CHE-B1 | BLOCK KEY CHAIN RIG-KR | BLOCK CHAIN BELT RIG/C-B 1 | BLOCK CHAIN NECKLACE RIG/C-N | BLOCK CHAIN BRACELET RIG/C-BR | BLOCK

TREASURE CHEST CUFF CHE-C | COMPASS NECKLACEE COM-N | COMPASS BROOCH COM-B | COMPASS WOOD NECKLACE COM-WN | COMPASS WOOD KEYCHAIN COM-WKR | OCTOPU

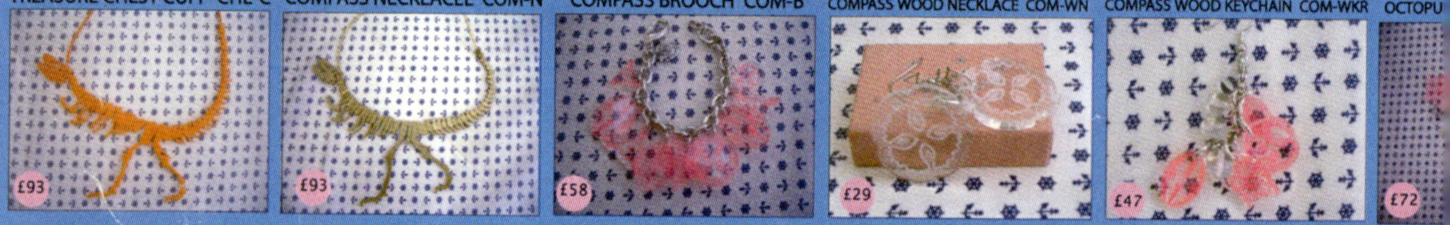

ORANGE DINOSAUR NECKLACE O/DINO-N | GOLD DINOSAUR N ECKLACE G/DINO-N | SEA CREATURE CHARM BRACELET SCRE-CHBR | SEA CREATURE EARRINGS SCRE-E2 | SEA CREATURE EARRING SCRE-E3 | SEA CR

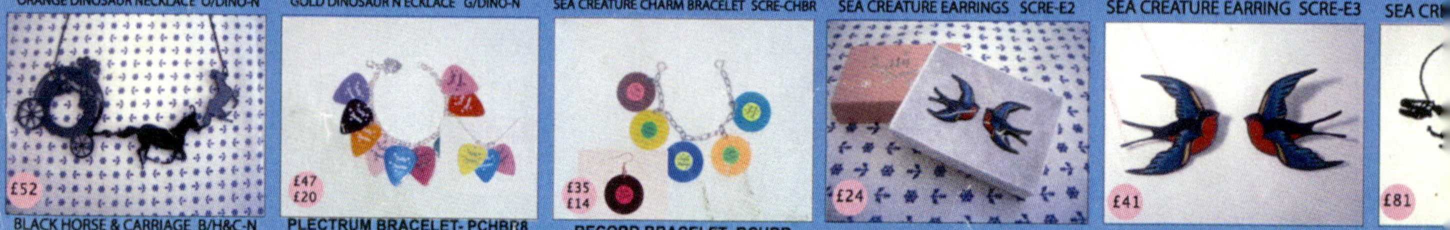

BLACK HORSE & CARRIAGE B/H&C-N | PLECTRUM BRACELET- PCHBR8 PLECTRUM NECKLACE- PN3 | RECORD BRACELET- RCHBR RECORD EARRING- RE1 | SWALLOW EARRINGS SWA-E2 | SWALLOW BROOCHES SWA-B2 | DINOSA

RRP

0cm 1cm 2cm 3cm 4cm

Tatty Devine Spring - Summer 2006

236 BRICK LANE,
LONDON, E2 7EB.
TEL/FAX: 0044(0)2077399009
e.mail: info@tattydevine.com
www.tattydevine.com
PR : BLOW 02074369449
soho shop- 57b Brewer st, W1

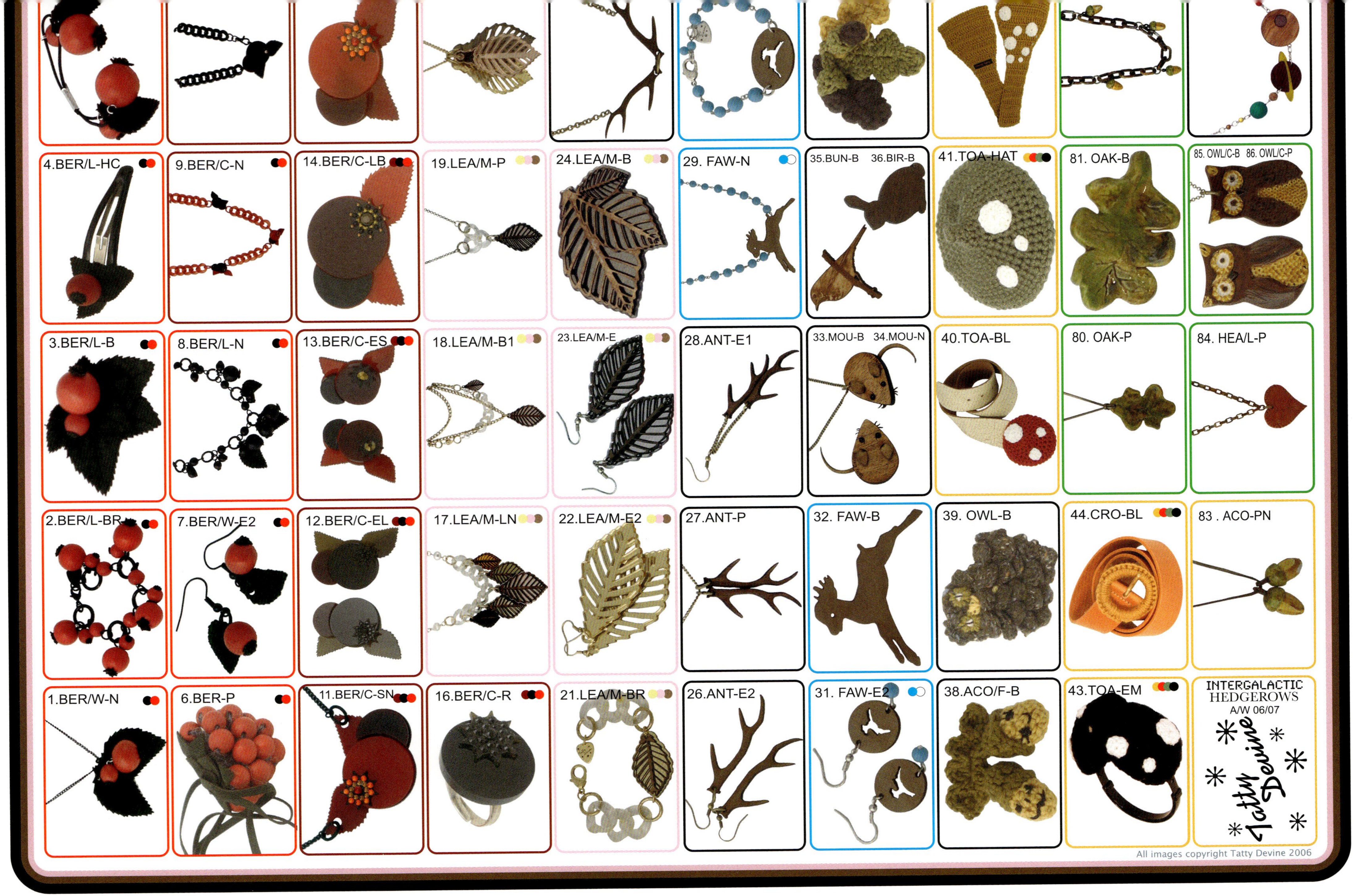
INTERGALACTIC
HEDGEROWS
A/W 06/07
Tatty Devine
1.BER/W-N
2.BER/L-BR
3.BER/L-B
4.BER/L-HC
6.BER-P
7.BER/W-E2
8.BER/L-N
9.BER/C-N
11.BER/C-SN
12.BER/C-EL
13.BER/C-ES
14.BER/C-LB
16.BER/C-R
17.LEA/M-LN
18.LEA/M-B1
19.LEA/M-P
21.LEA/M-BR
22.LEA/M-E2
23.LEA/M-E
24.LEA/M-B
26.ANT-E2
27.ANT-P
28.ANT-E1
29. FAW-N
31. FAW-E2
32. FAW-B
33.MOU-B
34.MOU-N
35.BUN-B
36.BIR-B
38.ACO/F-B
39. OWL-B
40.TOA-BL
41.TOA-HAT
43.TOA-EM
44.CRO-BL
80. OAK-P
81. OAK-B
83 . ACO-PN
84. HEA/L-P
85. OWL/C-B
86. OWL/C-P

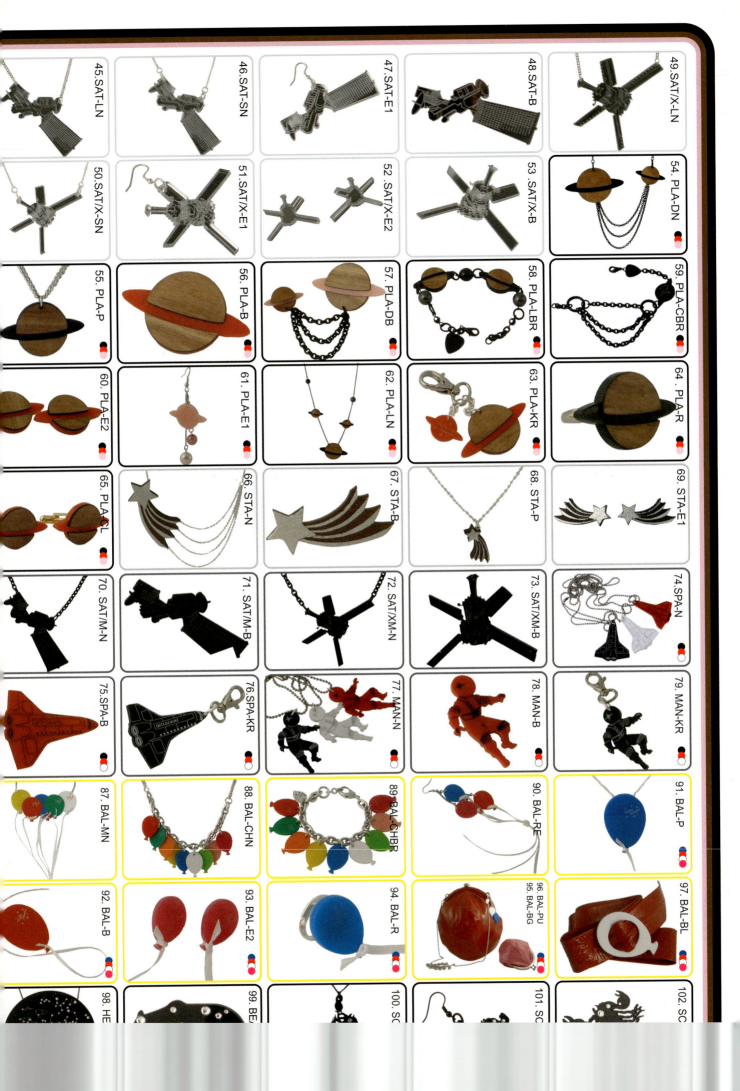

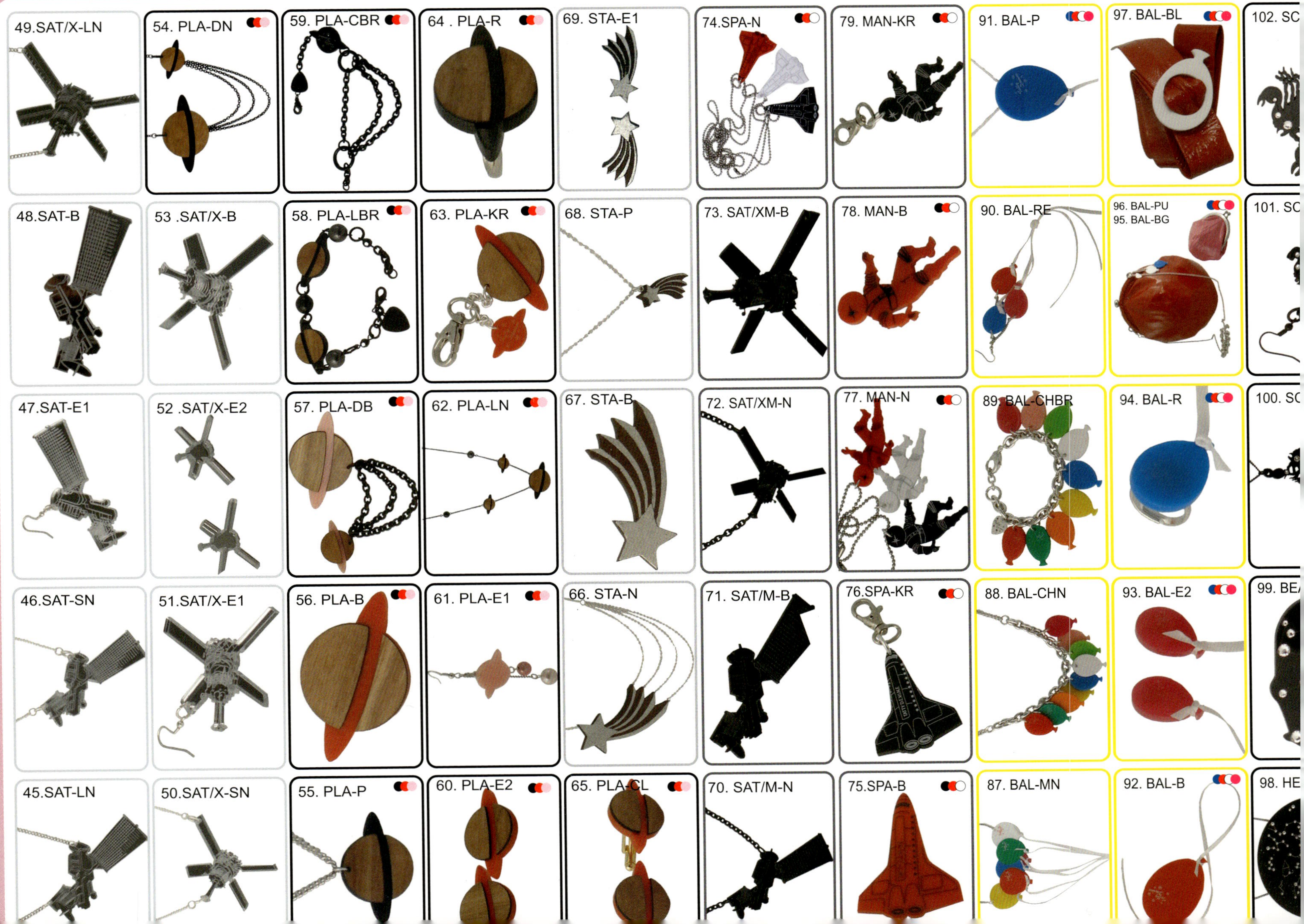
49.SAT/X-LN
54. PLA-DN
59. PLA-CBR
64 . PLA-R
69. STA-E1
74.SPA-N
79. MAN-KR
91. BAL-P
97. BAL-BL
48.SAT-B
53 .SAT/X-B
58. PLA-LBR
63. PLA-KR
68. STA-P
73. SAT/XM-B
78. MAN-B
90. BAL-RE
96. BAL-PU
95. BAL-BG
47.SAT-E1
52 .SAT/X-E2
57. PLA-DB
62. PLA-LN
67. STA-B
72. SAT/XM-N
77. MAN-N
89. BAL-CHBR
94. BAL-R
46.SAT-SN
51.SAT/X-E1
56. PLA-B
61. PLA-E1
66. STA-N
71. SAT/M-B
76.SPA-KR
88. BAL-CHN
93. BAL-E2
45.SAT-LN
50.SAT/X-SN
55. PLA-P
60. PLA-E2
65. PLA-CL
70. SAT/M-N
75.SPA-B
87. BAL-MN
92. BAL-B

Oh My God! I Miss You model the Moustache Necklace, 2006

In 2006 we created the Best Of collection after realising that some of our designs should stay around longer than a season.

THE

Tat

Horse & Carriage

£52

Total length - 52cm

Black or Silver

Cat Bangle

£30

Blue, Black,

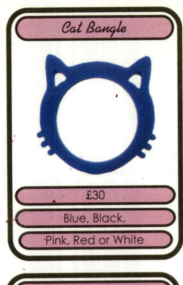

Pink, Red or White

Cube Bracelet

£36

St-t-r-r-r-etches to fit

It's hip to be square

Crisp Triple Necklace

£32

Snack on plastic

Chain - 42cm

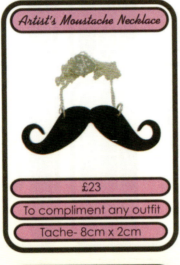

Artist's Moustache Necklace

£23

To compliment any outfit

Tache- 8cm x 2cm

Dinosaur Necklace

£96

Prehistoric pop

In Black, Gold or White

Glasses Necklace

£22

Chain - 45cm

Glasses - 6cm

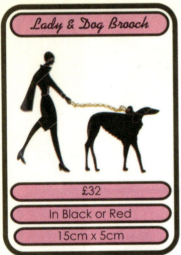

Lady & Dog Brooch

£32

In Black or Red

15cm x 5cm

Price Ticket Brooch

£12

Enamel

2.5cm x 1cm

Price Ticket Cufflinks

£24

The price is right

Enamel

Swallow Necklace

£34

Black or Red

Chain - 38cm, Birds - 12c

Ghost Necklace

£25

He's a friendly ghost

Chain - 60cm

Disco Honeycomb Necklace

£52

Black or Silver

Biggest hexagon 5x5 cm

Heart Ring

£12

A real sweetheart

Heart 2.3x2.3 cm

Gold Crown Necklace

£21

Fit for a queen!

Crown 4cm wide

BEST OF..

Devine

Record Charm Bracelet

£45
Disco discs
18cm long

Record Earring

£15
Pink, Yellow or Green
Single earring

ctrum Triple Necklace

£18
Choose your colours
Chain - 44cm

Plectrum Charm Bracelet

£36
Easy pickings
18cm long

Plectrum Earring

£7
Pick from 12 colours
Single earring

Plectrum Single Necklace

£12
Pick from 12 colours
Chain - 42cm

Music Note Bracelet

£45
Just add bars
Black or Red

Music Note Earrings

£15
Tune in!
Black or Red

Music Note Pendant

£21
Hit the high note
Black or Red

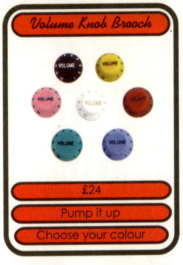

Volume Knob Brooch

£24
Pump it up
Choose your colour

Pegasus Wing Earrings

£25
Black Gold or Silver
4cm long

Pegasus Wing Necklace

£37
Black Gold or Silver
Wings - 12cm across

Wooden Wing Necklace

£44
Walnut wood
Wings - 16cm across

Wood Wing Charm Necklace

£37
Walnut wood, gold leaf
Chain - 60cm

Hit The Deck!

Number One Hit — A finely tuned collection for all you musical folk out there.

Woodland Notebook — Turn over a new leaf with some of nature's finest little helpers.

Pegasus Wings — A legendary Tatty Devine collection - look fly or just wing it.

Sailors 'n' Showgirls — Pieces to take you from the sea to the stage.

Antlers Petite Pendant

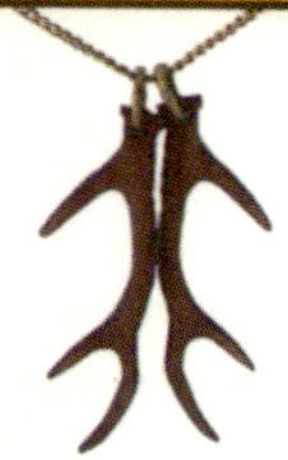

£23
Walnut wood
Chain - 42cm

Fawn Brooch

£21
For your deerest
5cm

Eagle Necklace

£33
Wood
Chain - 36cm

Swallow Brooches

£42
Hand-painted
6cm each

Swallow Cufflinks

£24
For fly guys
Enamel, 2cm

Swallow Earrings

£24
Pink or Red
Enamel, 2cm

Birdie Brooch

£23
Etched leather
5cm

Mouse Brooch

£23
Pounce on this
Wood, leather & crystal

Mouse Necklace

£23
Swarovski crystal eyes
Chain - 44cm

Fishbone Necklace

£36
Bone to be wild
Fish - 17cm, Chain - 30cm

Swing Girl Necklace

£33
Swinging silhouette
Chain - 46cm

Trapeze Necklace

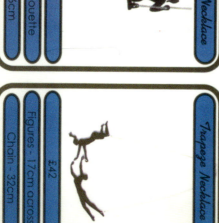

£42
Figures - 17cm across
Chain - 32cm

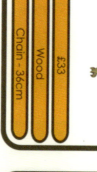

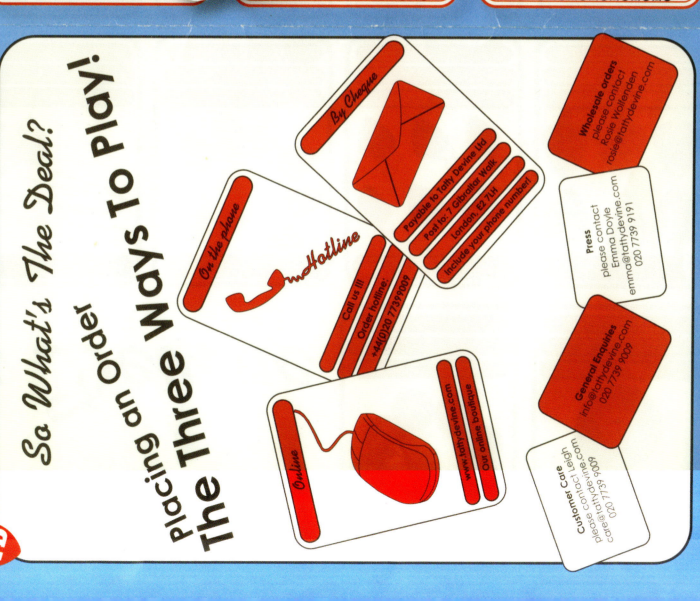

So What's The Deal?

Placing an Order
The Three Ways To Play!

Online
www.tattydevine.com
Our online boutique

On the phone
Hotline
Call us !!!
Order hotline:
+44(0)20 77399009

By Cheque
Payable to Tatty Devine Ltd
Post to: 7 Gibraltar Walk
London, E2 7LH
Include your phone number!

Customer Care
please contact Leigh
care@tattydevine.com
020 7739 9009

General Enquiries
info@tattydevine.com
020 7739 9009

Press
please contact
Emma Doyle
emma@tattydevine.com
020 7739 9191

Wholesale orders
please contact
Rosie Wolfenden
rosie@tattydevine.com

Colour Me In....

"It is late summer in the late 70's and the heat is rising. Sitting in your garden, passing the time with comics and puzzles, you watch the bees feed from the bright audacious flowers, and you fall into a deep . . . Disco Daydream . . ."

Tatty Devine's Spring/Summer 2007 collection is a bright cohesive collection reminiscent of growing up with colour, games, rollercoasters, patchwork, kisses and many other distractions. With the usual use of bright acrylic and colourful beads *Tatty Devine* transform the ordinary into the extrordinary.

The OOOOOHH and AARRGHH necklaces are the ultimate word necklaces to wear on rollercoasters and the petal necklace is the perfect finishing touch to a pretty dress.

Protect your self-identity with the copyright range. Choose from the oversized necklace that hangs from logo cord and is a massive statement or from the more elegant earrings. You could also trademark your look with the Trademark range in striking red or subtle pink.

With so many styles and colours, *Tatty Devine* are ready to colour you in.

Tatty Devine

For more information and to order please call +44(0)20 7739 9009 or visit our shops:
Tatty Devine, 236 Brick Lane, London E2 7EB Tel/Fax +44(0)20 7739 9191
Tatty Devine, 57b Brewer Street, London W1F 9UL Tel/Fax +44(0)20 77434 2257
info@tattydevine.com www.tattydevine.com

Tatty Devine
Spring Summer 2007
LOVE
Tatty Devine

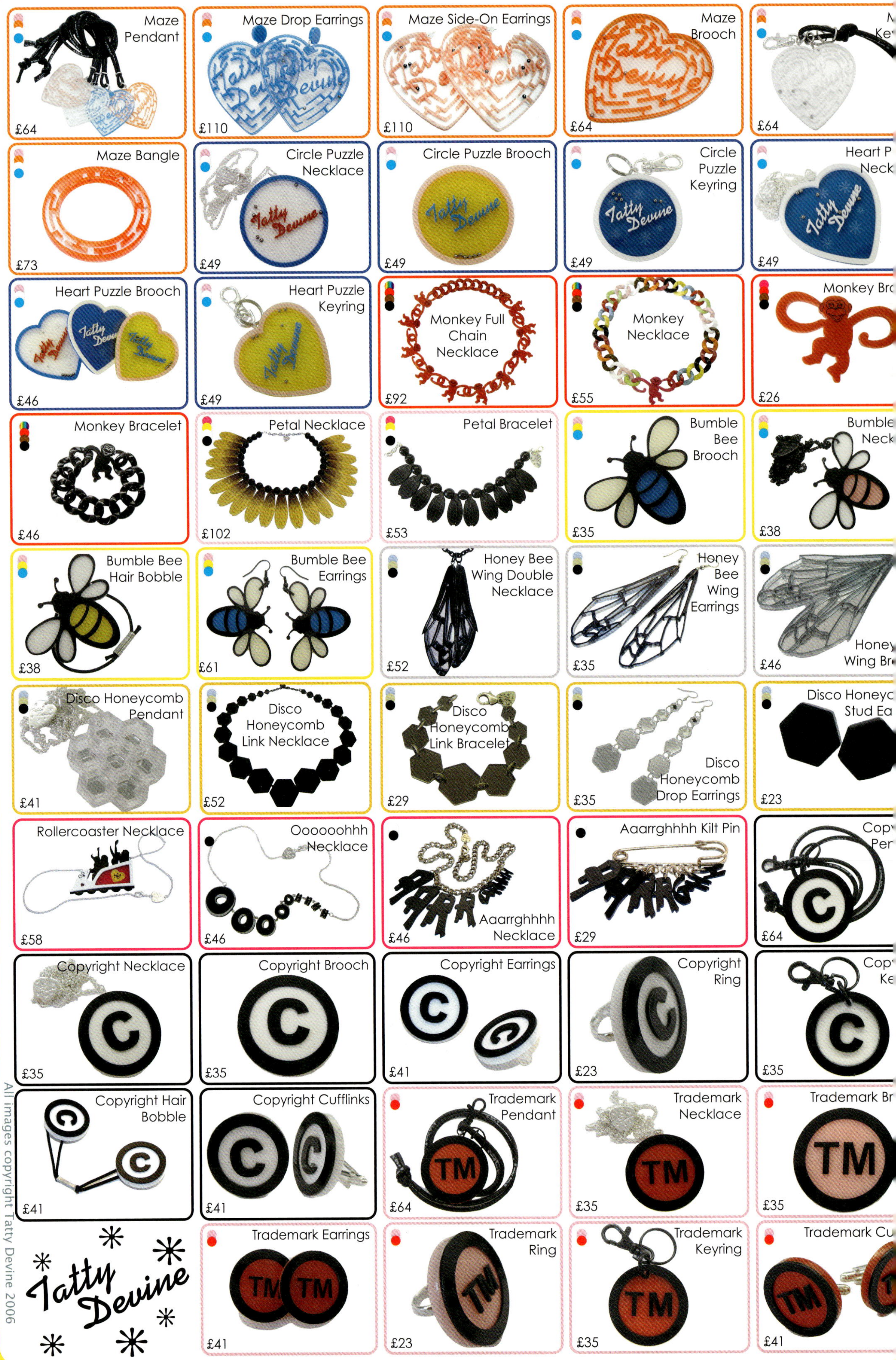

Maze Pendant £64
Maze Drop Earrings £110
Maze Side-On Earrings £110
Maze Brooch £64
£64
Maze Bangle £73
Circle Puzzle Necklace £49
Circle Puzzle Brooch £49
Circle Puzzle Keyring £49
£49
Heart Puzzle Brooch £46
Heart Puzzle Keyring £49
Monkey Full Chain Necklace £92
Monkey Necklace £55
Monkey £26
Monkey Bracelet £46
Petal Necklace £102
Petal Bracelet £53
Bumble Bee Brooch £35
£38
Bumble Bee Hair Bobble £38
Bumble Bee Earrings £61
Honey Bee Wing Double Necklace £52
Honey Bee Wing Earrings £35
£46
Disco Honeycomb Pendant £41
Disco Honeycomb Link Necklace £52
Disco Honeycomb Link Bracelet £29
Disco Honeycomb Drop Earrings £35
£23
Rollercoaster Necklace £58
Ooooohhh Necklace £46
Aaarrghhhh Necklace £46
Aaarrghhhh Kilt Pin £29
£64
Copyright Necklace £35
Copyright Brooch £35
Copyright Earrings £41
Copyright Ring £23
£35
Copyright Hair Bobble £41
Copyright Cufflinks £41
Trademark Pendant £64
Trademark Necklace £35
£35
Trademark Earrings £41
Trademark Ring £23
Trademark Keyring £35
£41
Tatty Devine

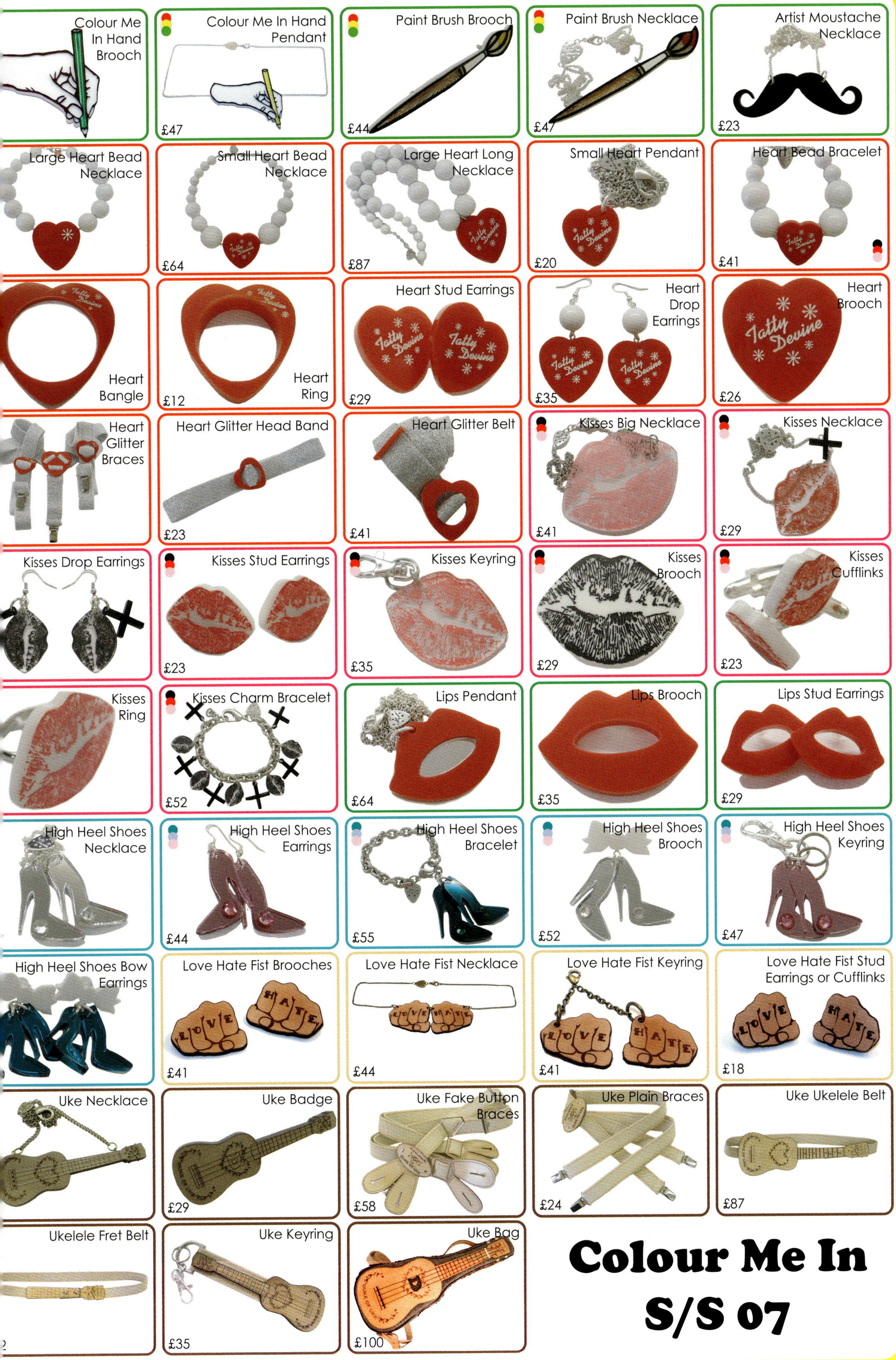
Colour Me In Hand Brooch
Colour Me In Hand Pendant £47
Paint Brush Brooch £44
Paint Brush Necklace £47
Artist Moustache Necklace £23
Large Heart Bead Necklace
Small Heart Bead Necklace £64
Large Heart Long Necklace £87
Small Heart Pendant £20
Heart Bead Bracelet £41
Heart Bangle
Heart Ring £12
Heart Stud Earrings £29
Heart Drop Earrings £35
Heart Brooch £26
Heart Glitter Braces
Heart Glitter Head Band £23
Heart Glitter Belt £41
Kisses Big Necklace £41
Kisses Necklace £29
Kisses Drop Earrings
Kisses Stud Earrings £23
Kisses Keyring £35
Kisses Brooch £29
Kisses Cufflinks £23
Kisses Ring
Kisses Charm Bracelet £52
Lips Pendant £64
Lips Brooch £35
Lips Stud Earrings £29
High Heel Shoes Necklace
High Heel Shoes Earrings £44
High Heel Shoes Bracelet £55
High Heel Shoes Brooch £52
High Heel Shoes Keyring £47
High Heel Shoes Bow Earrings
Love Hate Fist Brooches £41
Love Hate Fist Necklace £44
Love Hate Fist Keyring £41
Love Hate Fist Stud Earrings or Cufflinks £18
Uke Necklace
Uke Badge £29
Uke Fake Button Braces £58
Uke Plain Braces £24
Uke Ukelele Belt £87
Ukelele Fret Belt
Uke Keyring £35
Uke Bag £100

Colour Me In S/S 07

Moustache Necklace, SS07
Acrylic, metal alloy

The Moustache was one of the very first things we cut out in acrylic in the Fuzzy-Felt collection, and when we redesigned it as part of the SS07 collection it became a hit. There was a wave of moustache madness at the time; they were appearing on everything from mugs to pens, and even tattooed onto forefingers. There was a bar in Dalston called the Moustache Bar and people would hang out there wearing this necklace.

Colour Me In collection, SS07

Brick Lane shop, 2006

By 2006 the Brick Lane shop was beginning to feel a little bit cramped. We had six employees by now, and we were designing, making, packing, doing admin, accounting and running all aspects of the business from this tiny room. We knew we needed somewhere bigger. Luckily a studio space came up just around the corner and we were able to de-camp.

Rosie and Harriet carrying mannequin parts, 2006

Once we moved the office and the studio away from 236 Brick Lane, the shop suddenly seemed huge and we went on the hunt for second-hand shop fittings. We found these mannequin legs on the Holloway Road, and they were perfect to display the Eley Kishimoto and Antoni & Alison tights and leggings we were selling at the time.

Hot Topic

Obsessing *2007–2013*

In 2007 we got a Twitter account. Nowadays everyone has one, but back then it was a whole new thing. It was set up by Sonja Todd, who had just joined our team, and who was a visionary when it came to social media. She designed and built our website, and set up Mailchimp so we could email our customers and start a conversation with them. It was just like being back on the market stall – there was a real sense of community and we got immediate feedback from the people who bought our jewellery. We really embraced the immediacy of it, and it spurred us on to become bigger and better. We set up a larger production team and a new studio in Kent. And then we were ready to explore some of our favourite themes – craft, food, magic and tradition.

Magic

Harriet's grandfather was a magician and so is her brother Ben. We've always been fascinated by the wonder of magic, and intrigued by the craft and skills involved in making the magic happen. Ben was Rosie's flatmate for a while and he would practice magic on her at every available moment. Their kitchen ceiling was covered in signed playing cards, as Ben practised his tricks. Trickery, witchcraft and fortune-telling have always featured in our jewellery and more recently we've fully embraced witchcraft's association with feminism. The figure of a witch represents such enviable independent female power.

Dora Diamant wearing Crown Headband and Mayor's Chain, AW07

Tiger Necklace, AW07
Acrylic, metal alloy

The Tiger Necklace and Knight Necklace come from the Dark Stages AW07 collection, which was all about medieval times and magic of all kinds. The necklace was a nod to magicians and 'masters of the impossible', Siegfried & Roy, who were famous for appearing with fearsome white tigers.

MAGIC
6390
T.D.
LOCKS
CHAINS
KEYS

Knight Necklace, AW07
Acrylic, metal alloy

Gloves and Doves Brooch, AW07
Acrylic, Swarovski crystals, metal alloy

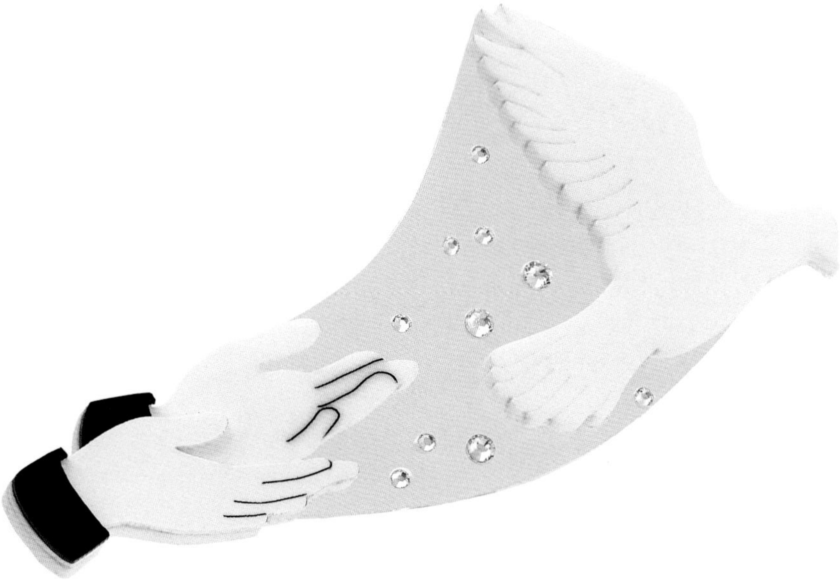

Rabbit in a Hat Necklace fan letter, 2007

Dear Tatty Devine,

Your jewlery is sooo awesome!!!!
Me and my friend Georgia have loads of your jewlery!

I have your red, ruby slippers necklace, plectrum braclet, rabbit in a hat, necklace, name necklace, Ace and

THE Dark Stages

A/W 07

Tatty Devine

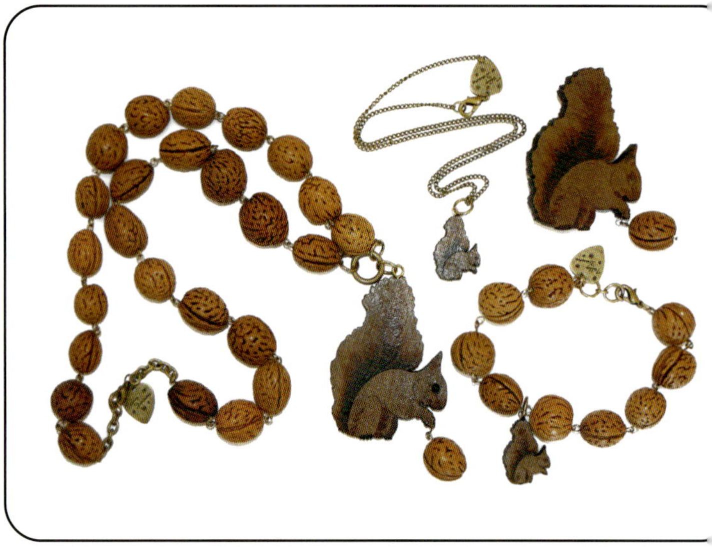

92

Feather Tip Necklace

93

Feather Tip Brooch

96

Red Squirrel Necklace

97

Red Squirrel Bracelet

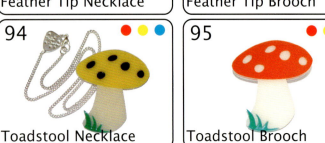

94

Toadstool Necklace

95

Toadstool Brooch

98

Red Squirrel Pendant

99

Red Squirrel Brooch

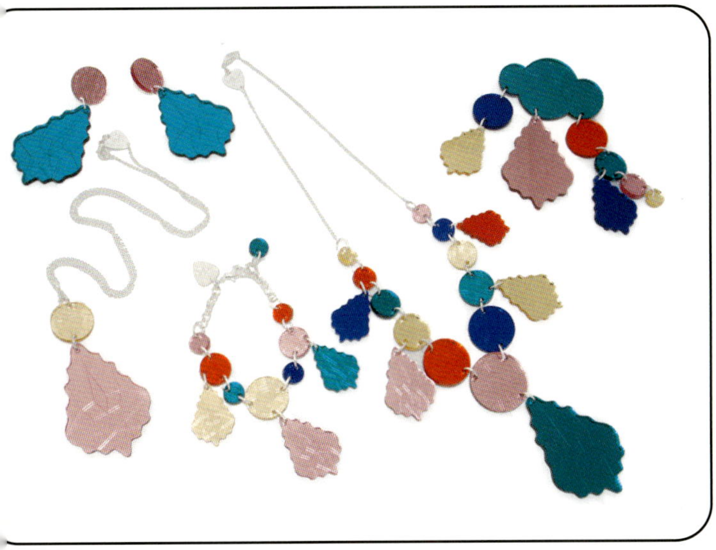

0

handelier Necklace

71

Chandelier Pendant

80

Velvet Bow Necklace

81

Velvet Bow Bead Necklace

82

Velvet Bow Bracelet

2

handelier Earrings

73

Chandelier Brooch

83

The Mayor's Chain N/Lace

84

The Mayor's Chain Belt/Sash

85

Arrow of Love Pendant

ck Lane Shop
6 Brick Lane
DON, E2 7EB
0)20 7739 9191

Soho Shop
57b Brewer Street
SOHO, W1F 9UL
+44(0)20 7434 2257

Online Shop
www.tattydevine.com
info@tattydevine.com
+44(0)20 7739 9009

Studio/ H.Q
7 Gibraltar Walk
LONDON, E2 7LH
+44(0)20 7739 9009

Tatty Devine

86
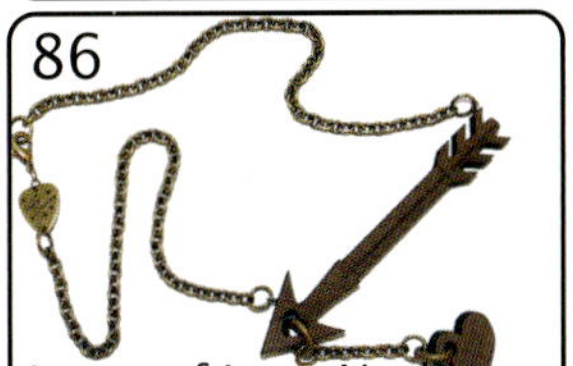
Arrow of Love Necklace

87

Arrow of Love Sm.Necklace

4

night Necklace

75

Helmet Brooch

76

Gloves Necklace

88
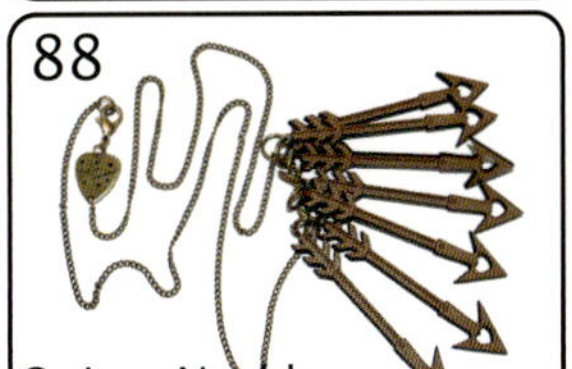
Quiver Necklace

89

Arrow Earrings

7

umage Necklace

78
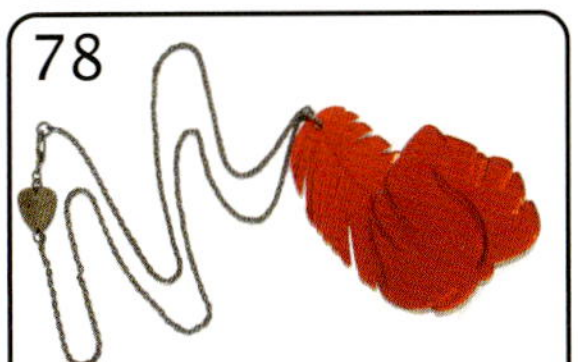
Plumage Pendant

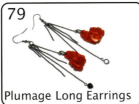

79
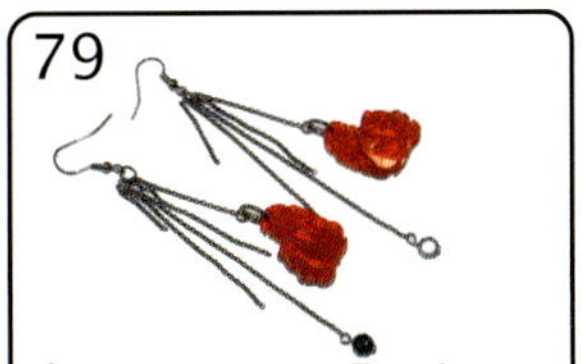
Plumage Long Earrings

90
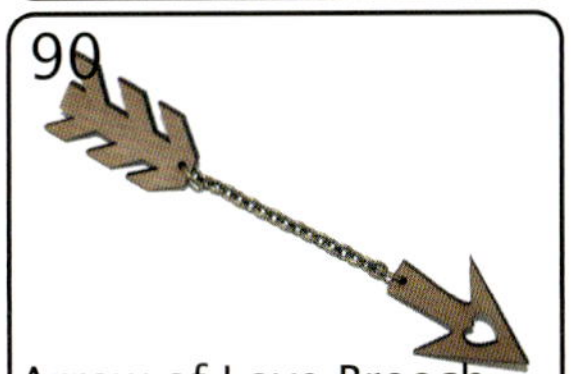
Arrow of Love Brooch

91

Shot in the Heart Brooch

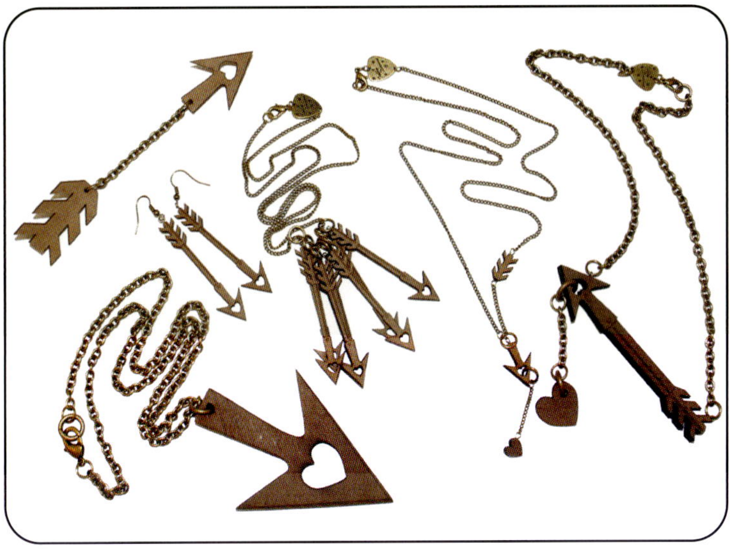

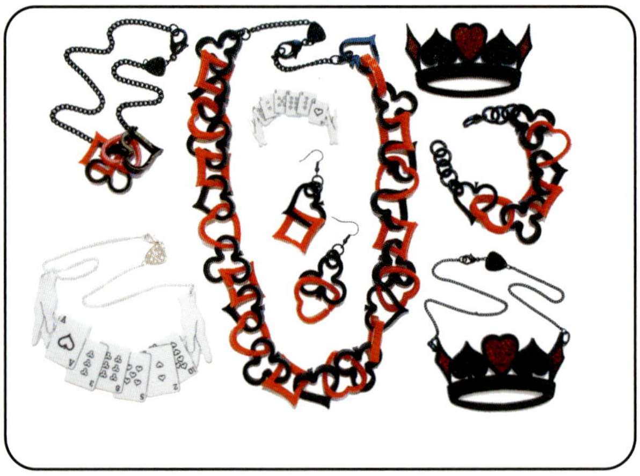

1

Magic Necklace

2

Rabbit in a Hat Necklace

3

Rabbit in a Hat Brooch

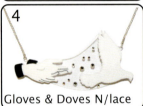

4
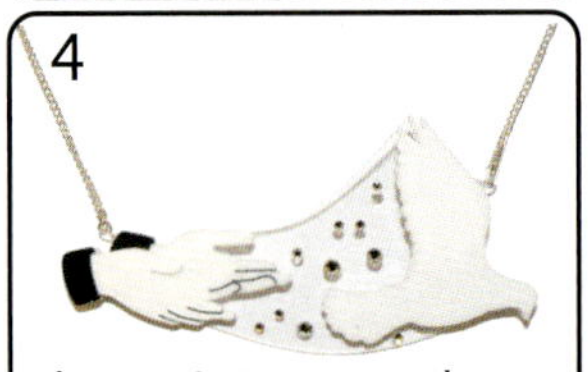
Gloves & Doves N/lace

5
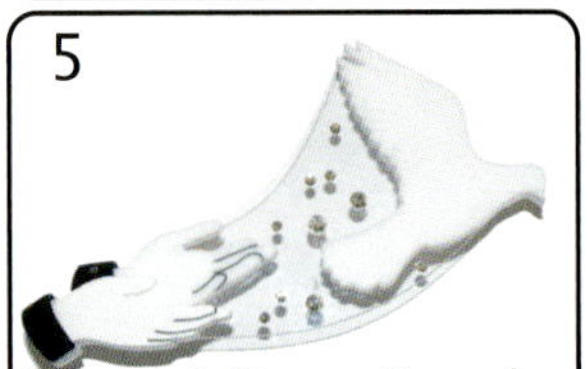
Gloves & Doves Brooch

6

Magic Wand Necklace

7

Magic Wand Brooch

8

Magic Stars Necklace

9

Magic Stars Brooch

10

Magic Stars Drop E/ring

11

Magic Stars Stud E/ring

12

Magic Stars Pendant

13
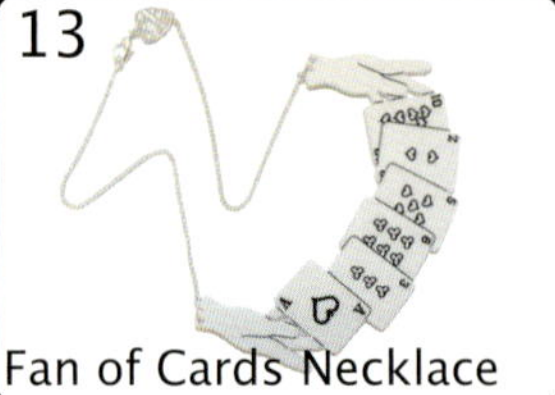
Fan of Cards Necklace

14

Fan of Cards Brooch

15

The 4 Suits Necklace

16

The 4 Suits Pendant

17

The 4 Suits Drop E/ring

18

The 4 Suits Bracelet

19

Queen of Hearts Crown N/lace

20

Queen of Hearts Crown N/lace

21

Bow Tie Necklace

22
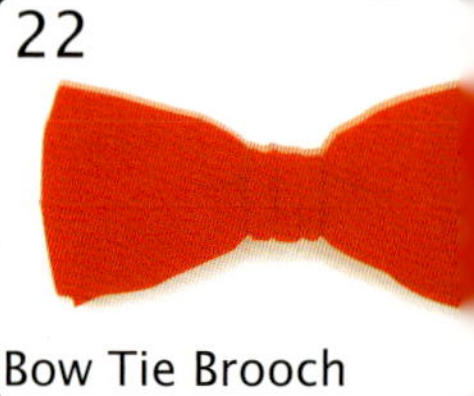
Bow Tie Brooch

23
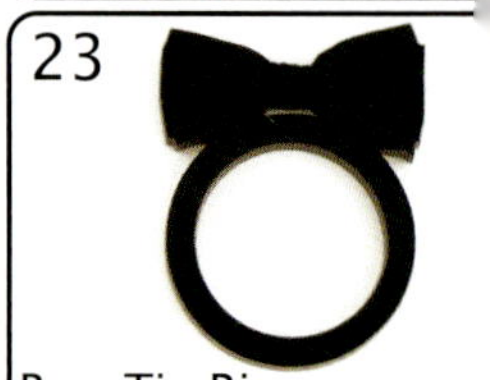
Bow Tie Ring

24

Bow Tie Bracelet

37

Tiger Necklace

41

Escapology Bracelet

57

Disco Necklace

58

Mirror Ball Pendant

59
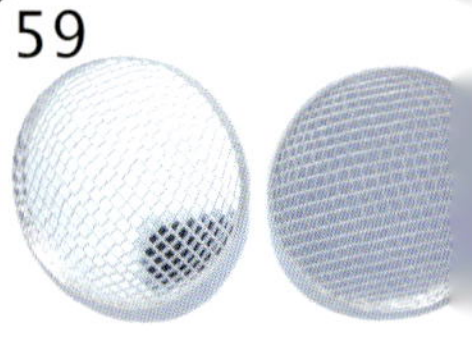
Mirror Ball Stud E/ri

61

Mirror Ball Brooch

62

Mirror Ball Ring

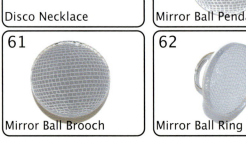

63
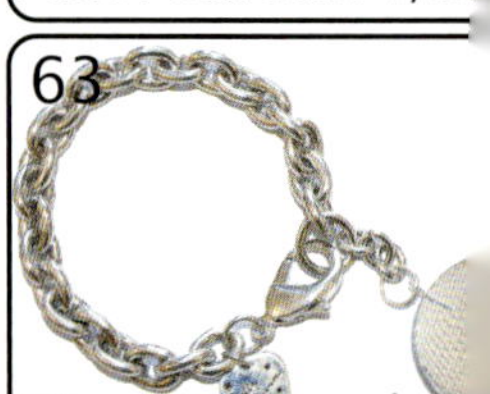
Mirror Ball Bracelet

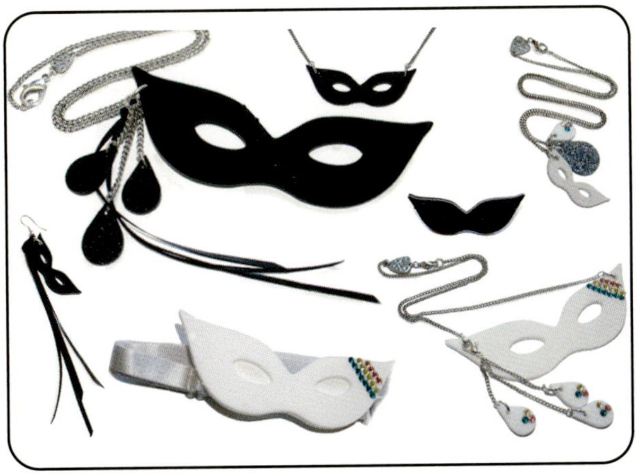

Tie Hair Band

29

Masquerade Lrg. N/lace

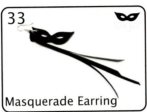

33

Masquerade Earring

45

Baby Grand Sm. N/lace

51

Baby Grand Cufflinks

Tie Earrings

30

Masquerade Necklace

34

Masquerade Brooch

46

Baby Grand Pendant

52

Crystal Baby Grand N/lace

Tie Cufflinks

31

Masquerade Sm. N/lace

35
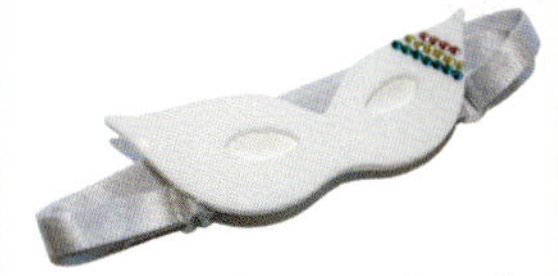
Masquerade Hair Band

47

Baby Grand Sm. Brooch

53

Crystal Baby Grand Brooch

Tie Undone N/lace

32

Masquerade Charm N/lace

36

Specs Necklace

48

Baby Grand Lrg. Brooch

54

Piano Keys Necklace

er Brooch

39

Escapology Necklace

40

Escapology Keychain

49
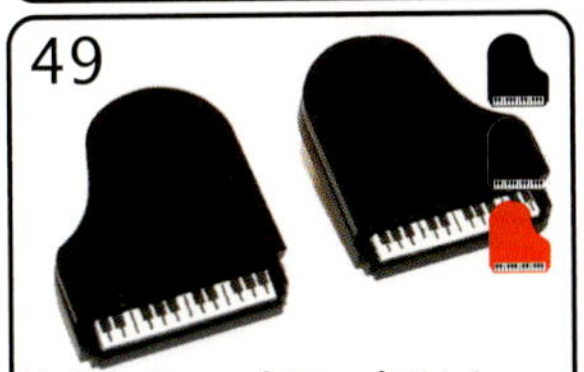
Baby Grand Stud E/ring

55

Piano Keys Sm.Necklace

apology Brooch

43

Escapology Pendant

44

Escapology Keyring

50

Baby Grand Ring

56

Piano Keys Bracelet

or Ball Drop Earrings

66

Velvet Crown Head Band

67

Velvet Crown Belt

4 & 65

or Ball Key/R & Cufflinks

68

Velvet Crown Bracelet

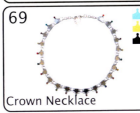

69

Crown Necklace

Sabrina Tabuchi and Cléo Ferin Mercury model the Dark Stages collection, 2007

Zodiac Power Bangle, SS11
Acrylic, metal alloy, plastic gems

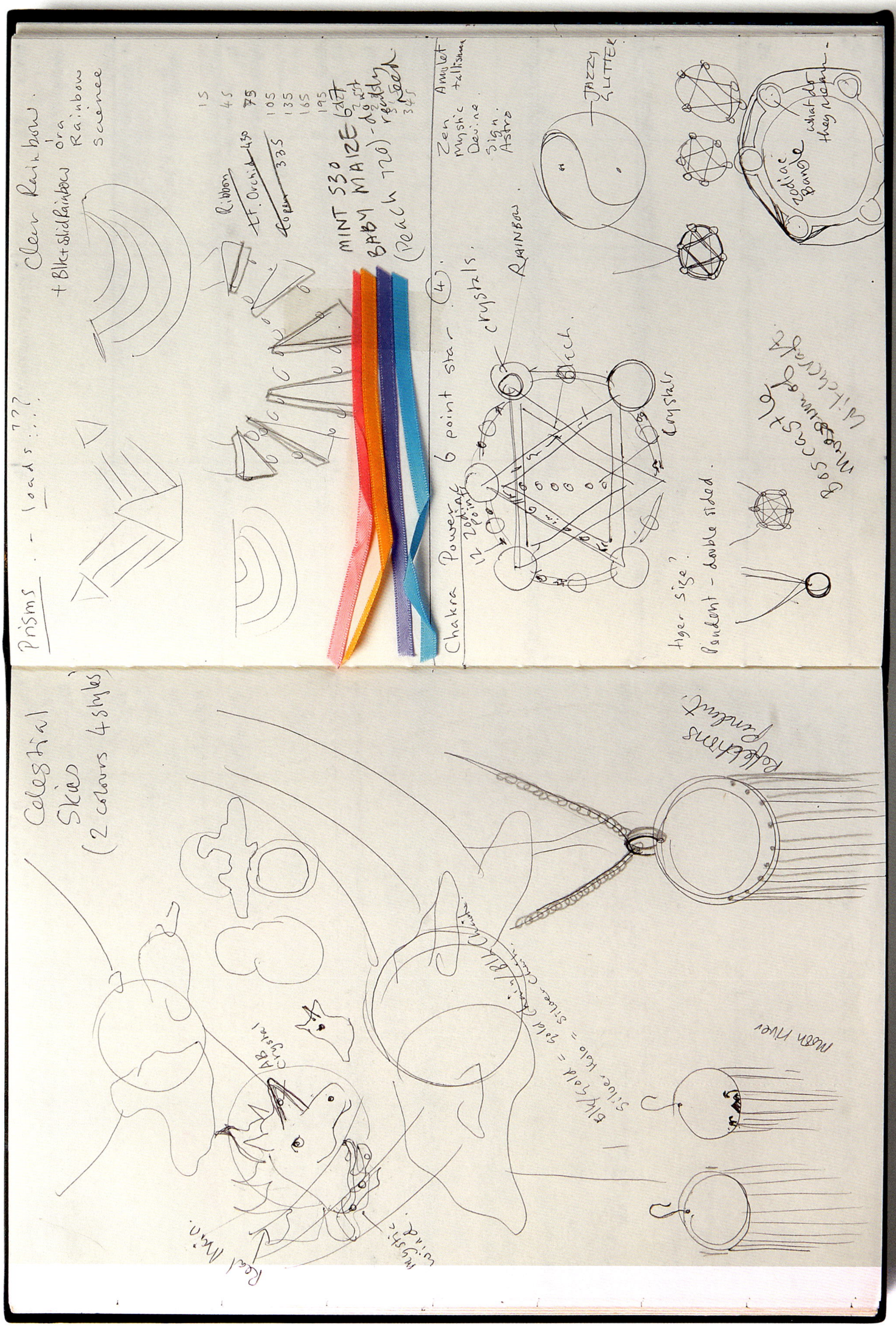
Prisms
Clear Rainbow
Chakra Power
6 point star
Celestial Skies (2 colours 4 styles)
MINT 530
BABY MAIZE

House of Cards Necklace, AW14
Acrylic, metal alloy

Miscellany

We've always loved trawling through charity shops, car boot sales and flea markets on the hunt for treasure. We love the look of all kinds of everyday things: games, old technology, vintage graphics, records and throwaway ornaments, and have always thought that the ordinary can be transformed into the extraordinary. There's something very inspiring about re-discovering things from the past that have been discarded by someone from the present, and making them into something new.

Cockatiel Bead Necklace, SS09

For years we had old toys from a birdcage hanging in our studio. Eventually after years of looking at them, we made the Cockatiel Necklace and Canary Ring for the Leisure Pursuits SS09 collection.

3D Glasses Necklace, SS08
Acrylic, metal alloy

3D glasses! We've always been obsessed by Americana and the sort of films where teenagers drive around in big cars, head to a drive-in movie and then end up sitting in diners all night talking about how they're going to take on the world. The acrylic glasses had a starring role in our SS08 collection, Movie Mayhem, and we also made a giveaway paper version to hand out at our launch party at Madame Jojo's in Soho, during London Fashion Week.

Rosie and Harriet wearing the 3D Glasses, 2008

Promotional paper 3D Glasses, 2008

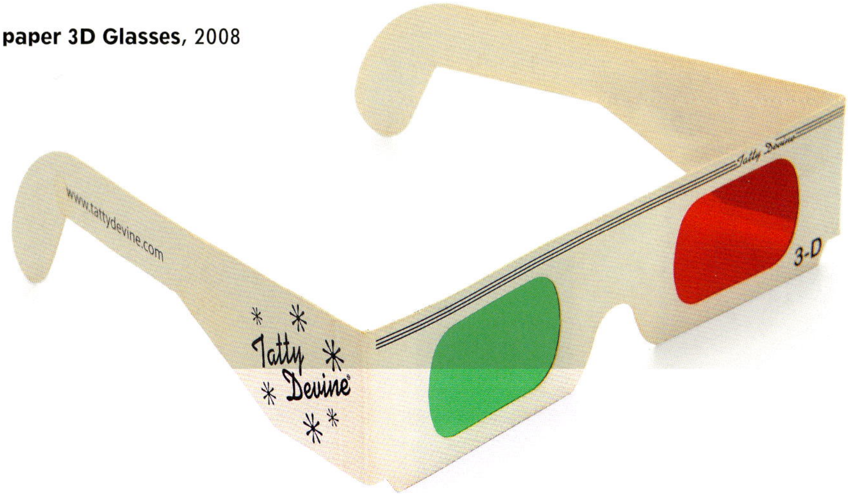

SS08

At The Movies

1

£78 Film Reel Necklace

2
Film Reel Brooch

£84

3
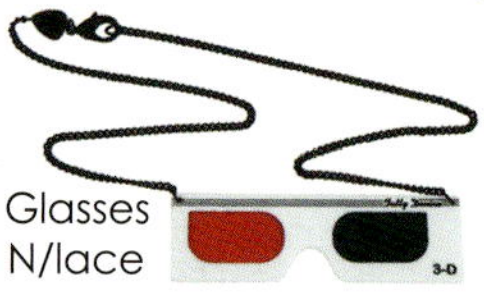
3-D Glasses Lrg. N/lace
£35

4
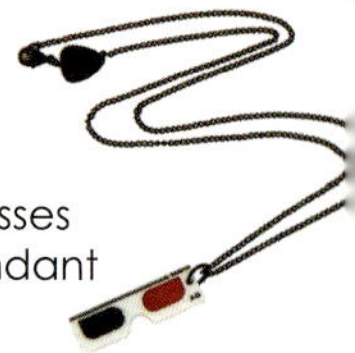
3-D Glasses Sm. Pendant
£26

Popcorn

10
Popcorn Packet Brooch

£43

11
Popcorn Packet N/lace

£43

12
Popcorn Packet Sm. Pendant

£29

13
Popc
Pack
Earrir
£43

Lolita

16
Heart Glasses N/lace

£41

17

£41 Heart Glasses Brooch

18

Heart Glasses Cutout Pendant
£35

The Lollipop

19
Heart Shaped Lolly N/lace

£29

Layered Hearts

25

Layered Love Heart N/lace
£20

26
Layered Love Heart Brooch

£20

Music Notes

27

Music Score N/lace
£52

28

Music Score Brooch
£52

29
Double Heart No
Big N/lac
£32

Cocktail Party

39
Champagne Cocktail Party N/lace

£44

40
Champagne Cocktail Party Earrings

£35

41
Neon Cocktail N/lace

£41

Paisley Goes Pop!

45
Paisley Gem N/lace

£93

46
Paisley Gem Brooch
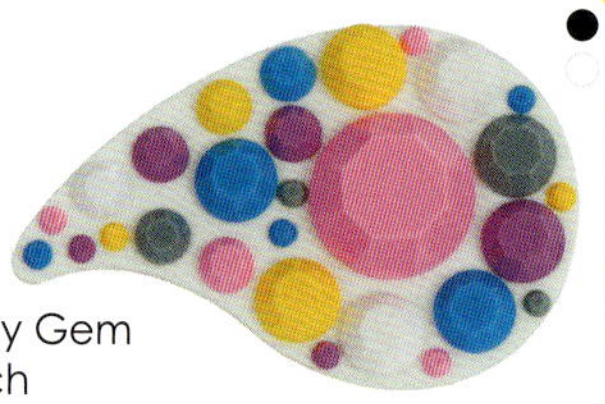
£53

47

Paisley Gem Studs
£27

Studded Mirror

52

Studded Mirror N/lace
£73

53

Studded Mirror Ribbon Belt
£70

54
Studded Mirror Hairband

£58

Teeth Necklace

58
Large Set of Teeth N/lace

£159

59
Large Mirror Set of Teeth N/lace

£174

60
Smaller Set o
Teeth N/lace
£116

Lovely Lady Leigh

63
Lovely Lady Leigh Brooch

£53

64
Lovely Lady Leigh N/lace

£66

65

Lovely Lady Leigh Brooch
£26

66
Lovely Lady Leigh Brooch
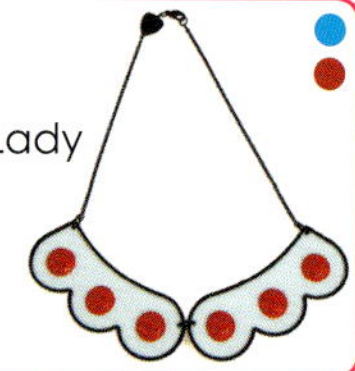
£41

67
Lovely Lady Leigh Flower Studs

£29

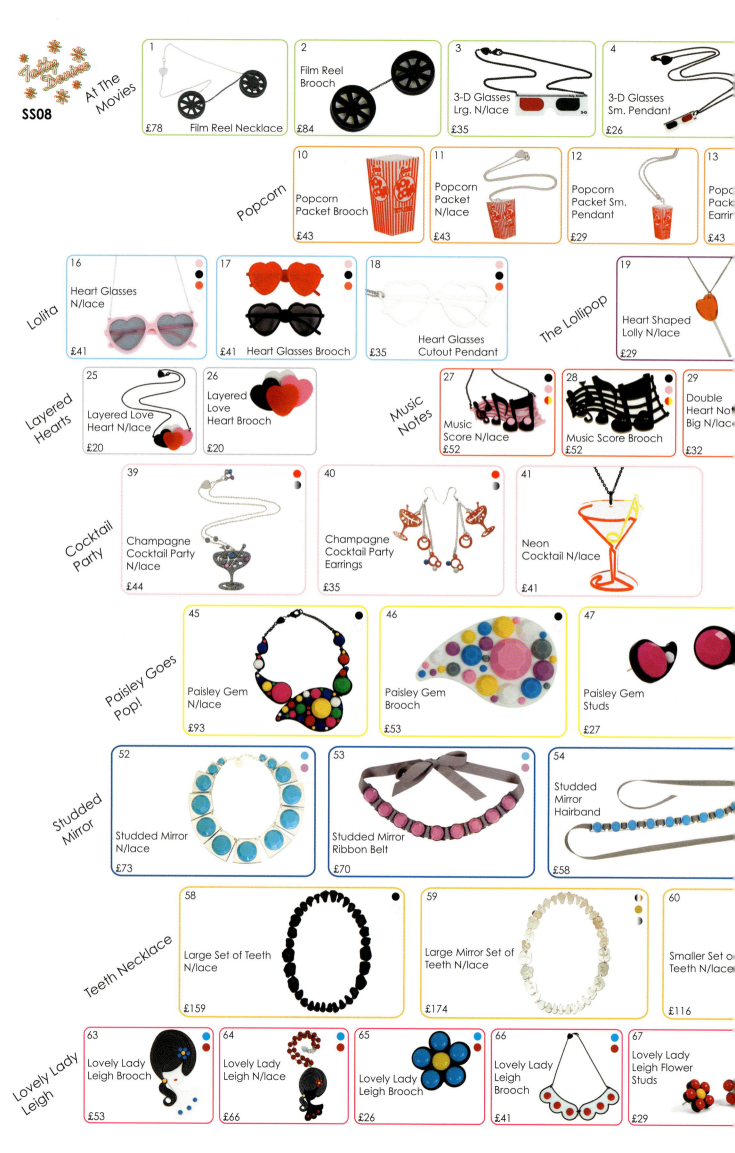

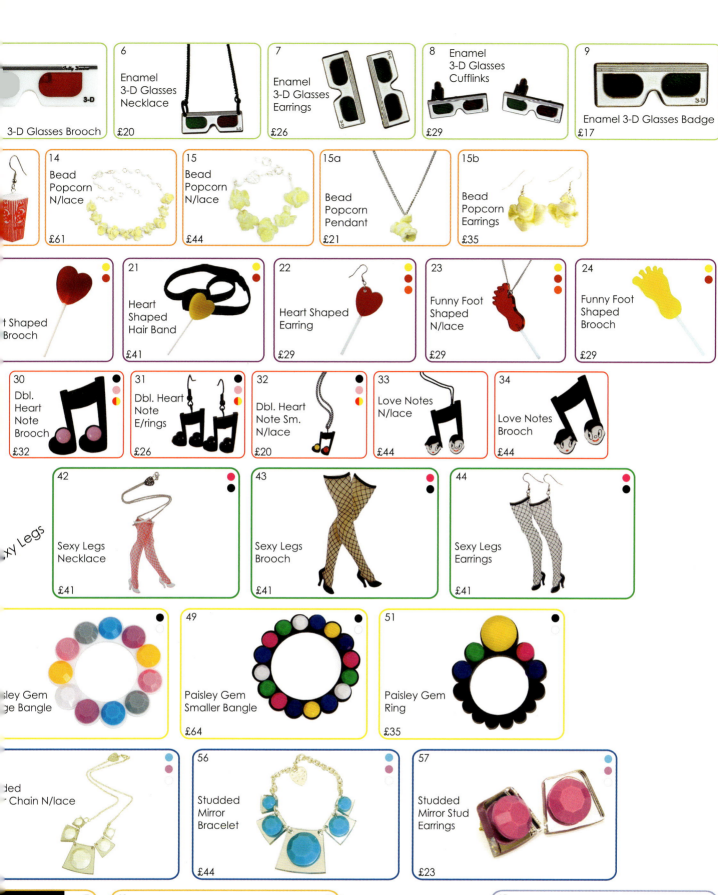

3-D Glasses Brooch

6
Enamel 3-D Glasses Necklace
£20

7
Enamel 3-D Glasses Earrings
£26

8
Enamel 3-D Glasses Cufflinks
£29

9
Enamel 3-D Glasses Badge
£17

14
Bead Popcorn N/lace
£61

15
Bead Popcorn N/lace
£44

15a
Bead Popcorn Pendant
£21

15b
Bead Popcorn Earrings
£35

t Shaped Brooch

21
Heart Shaped Hair Band
£41

22
Heart Shaped Earring
£29

23
Funny Foot Shaped N/lace
£29

24
Funny Foot Shaped Brooch
£29

30
Dbl. Heart Note Brooch
£32

31
Dbl. Heart Note E/rings
£26

32
Dbl. Heart Note Sm. N/lace
£20

33
Love Notes N/lace
£44

34
Love Notes Brooch
£44

xy Legs

42
Sexy Legs Necklace
£41

43
Sexy Legs Brooch
£41

44
Sexy Legs Earrings
£41

sley Gem
ge Bangle

49
Paisley Gem Smaller Bangle
£64

51
Paisley Gem Ring
£35

ded
Chain N/lace

56
Studded Mirror Bracelet
£44

57
Studded Mirror Stud Earrings
£23

61
Smaller Mirror Set of Teeth N/lace
£131

Wishbone Necklace

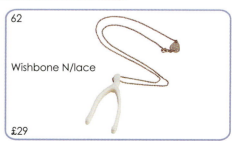

62
Wishbone N/lace
£29

Lady Flower Hairband

69
Stinky Skunk Brooch
£35

Water Pistol

70
Water Pistol N/lace
£46

71
Water Pistol Earrings
£43

72
Water Pistol Keyring
£41

Telephone Pendant, SS09
Acrylic, metal alloy

We were both brought up with rotary phones – it took ages to dial a number and the ring would ping around the house when you put the receiver down, so secret late-night calls to friends and boyfriends were hard. Our necklace had a rotating dial and the receiver had a brooch back, so you could pin it wherever you wanted. The cord is made from a spiral keychain.

Cocktail Umbrella Necklace, SS10
Acrylic, metal alloy

We've always loved popping cocktail umbrellas in our hair, so we were determined to try and replicate them in acrylic. We made a hair barrette, and a necklace, and the traditional flower design was etched onto the parasol. It really captured the vintage vibe that was in fashion at the time. The collection was called Sundae Best and the campaign shoot was by our friend, the artist Tai Shani.

Firework Brooches, AW10
Acrylic, Swarovski crystals

We both love fireworks, and marvel at their beauty and at the chemistry that creates them.

Octopus Ribbon Brooch, SS06
Acrylic, ribbon

Telephone Brooch, SS09
Acrylic, metal alloy

Lips Pendant, SS07
Acrylic, metal alloy

Set of Teeth Necklace, AW08
Acrylic, metal alloy

Lovely Lady Leigh Necklace, SS08
Acrylic, glass beads, plastic cabochon

Ping Pong Tiny Necklace, SS09
Plywood, Formica, plastic cabochon, metal alloy

We discovered a Formica laminate in exactly the same shades of red and blue as ping-pong bats, and we already knew that we could laser cut plywood to make it look like a bat handle, and that was how the Ping Pong Necklace came about.

Zip Giant Necklace, AW08
Acrylic, metal alloy

Sometimes an object already reminds us of a piece of jewellery, and the trick is to re-create it anew. Zips have always looked like necklaces to us, and so it was an easy leap to make a Zip Necklace in acrylic. By linking each 'tooth' with a jump ring, the necklace hangs perfectly.

Peaches wearing the Gold Zip Giant Necklace, 2008

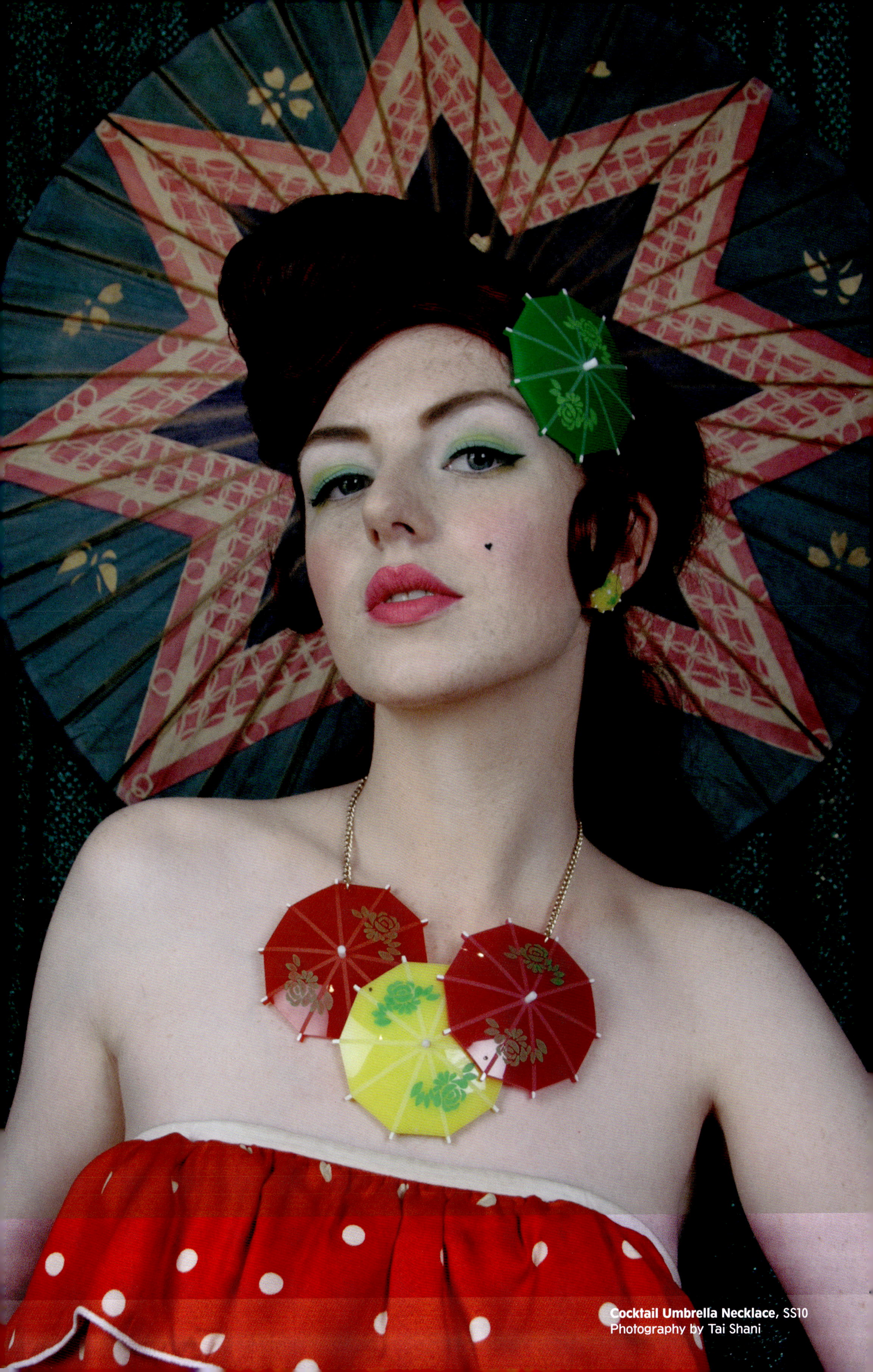

Cocktail Umbrella Necklace, SS10
Photography by Tai Shani

All styles available in glow-in-the-dark or white
Ready
A vision in white
Cartoon Eyes Necklace £54
Cartoon Eyes Earrings £36
Cartoon Eyes Cufflinks £36
Cartoon Eyes Brooches £51
Cartoon Eyes Rings £36
Steady
Go goggle-eyed for glow-in-the-dark
Looks almost white...
Cartoon Eyes Necklace £54
Cartoon Eyes Earrings £36
Cartoon Eyes Cufflinks £36
brand new colour!
Glow!
...till you turn out the light!
Night of a thousand eyes
X-ray Specs Necklace £66
X RAY VISION
SPECS APPEAL
X-ray Specs Brooch £51
Party Pop Star Charm Bracelet £48
It's my party
Make your outfit go with a bang!
Party Pop Brooch £54
Party Pop Necklace £54
Party Pop Star Charm Necklace £54
Party Pop Pendant £45
actual size
green shown at actual size
Parcel Bow Necklace £33
Get yourself gift-wrapped!!!
Parcel Bow Earrings £33
Parcel Bow Hairband £66
Pretty Parcel Bo
Parcel Bo Ring £24
Parcel Bow Brooch £36
actual size
All Parcel Bow styles available in green, red or silver

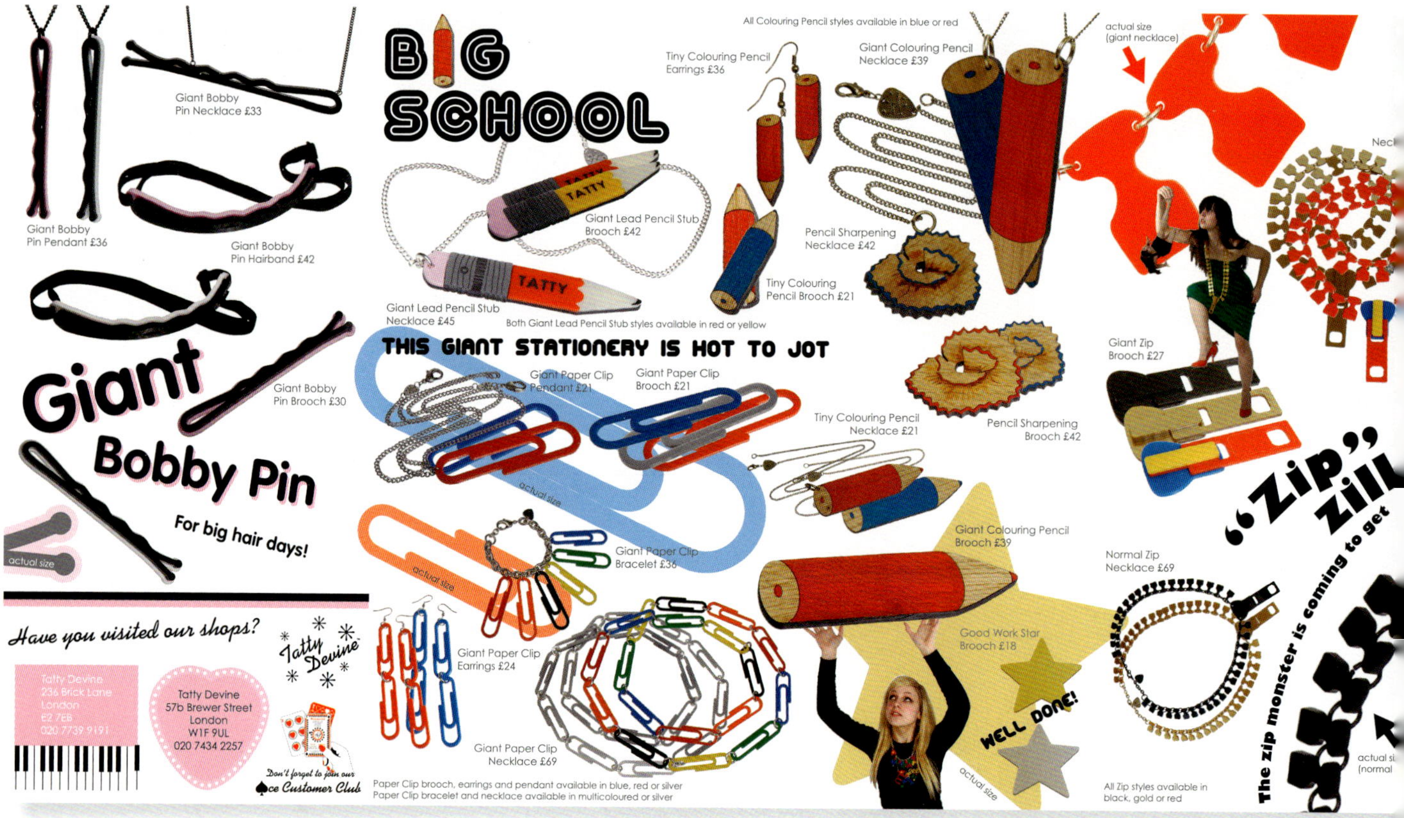

Giant Bobby Pin Necklace £33
Giant Bobby Pin Pendant £36
Giant Bobby Pin Hairband £42
Giant Bobby Pin Brooch £30
Giant Bobby Pin
For big hair days!
actual size
Have you visited our shops?
Tatty Devine 236 Brick Lane London E2 7EB 020 7739 9191
Tatty Devine 57b Brewer Street London W1F 9UL 020 7434 2257
Tatty Devine
Don't forget to join our Ace Customer Club
BIG SCHOOL
All Colouring Pencil styles available in blue or red
Tiny Colouring Pencil Earrings £36
Giant Colouring Pencil Necklace £39
Giant Lead Pencil Stub Brooch £42
Pencil Sharpening Necklace £42
Tiny Colouring Pencil Brooch £21
Giant Lead Pencil Stub Necklace £45
Both Giant Lead Pencil Stub styles available in red or yellow
THIS GIANT STATIONERY IS HOT TO JOT
Giant Paper Clip Pendant £21
Giant Paper Clip Brooch £21
actual size
Tiny Colouring Pencil Necklace £21
Pencil Sharpening Brooch £42
Giant Paper Clip Bracelet £36
Giant Paper Clip Earrings £24
Giant Paper Clip Necklace £69
Paper Clip brooch, earrings and pendant available in blue, red or silver
Paper Clip bracelet and necklace available in multicoloured or silver
Giant Colouring Pencil Brooch £39
Good Work Star Brooch £18
WELL DONE!
actual size
actual size (giant necklace)
Giant Zip Brooch £27
Normal Zip Necklace £69
"Zip" Zill
The zip monster is coming to get
All Zip styles available in black, gold or red

LIGHT UP
HE NIGHT
Fairy Light
Star Necklace £87
sparkling stars
and fairy lights
Fairy Light
Fawn
Necklace
£87
Star Single
£33
Fairy Light
Fawn Brooch £87
airy Light Star
tud Earrings £42
able in multicoloured or silver
Flying Fawns
Necklace £66
Flying Fawns
Flying Fawns
Earrings £36
actual size
Jewellery to fawn over
actual size
(largest)
Flying Fawns
Brooches Set £66
All styles available in black or red
NOW SHOWING
ATTACK OF THE 50FT JEWELLERY
YOU'RE LOST IN A STRANGE LANDSCAPE, DODGING OBJECTS FALLING FROM THE SKY... EVERYTHING FROM BOBBY PINS TO PAPER CLIPS, ZIPS TO EARRING BACKS... STRANGER STILL, EVERYTHING IS GIANT! IT'S THE ATTACK OF THE 50FT JEWELLERY!
How to order
www.tattydevine.com
Hotline 020 7739 9009
£2.50
UK first class
£5.00
UK next day
or Europe
£7.00
Worldwide
Tatty Devine Bank
Tatty Devine Ltd
Please include your contact details
Tatty Devine
7 Gibraltar Walk
London
E2 7LH
Customer Care 020 7739 9009 care@tattydevine.com
Wholesale 020 7739 9009 wholesale@tattydevine.com
Press 020 7739 9191 press@tattydevine.com
all images and designs in this catalogue ©2008 Tatty Devine™
Tatty Devine
7 Gibraltar Walk
London
E2 7LH
ROYAL MAIL
POSTAGE PAID GB
2
Tatty Devine
TATTY DEVINE PICTURES presents
ATTACK
OF THE 50FT.
JEWELLERY
AW08
STARRING GIANT NECKLACES • JUMBO JEWELS • BIG STUFF
DIRECTED BY WWW.TATTYDEVINE.COM WRITTEN BY TATTY DEVINE

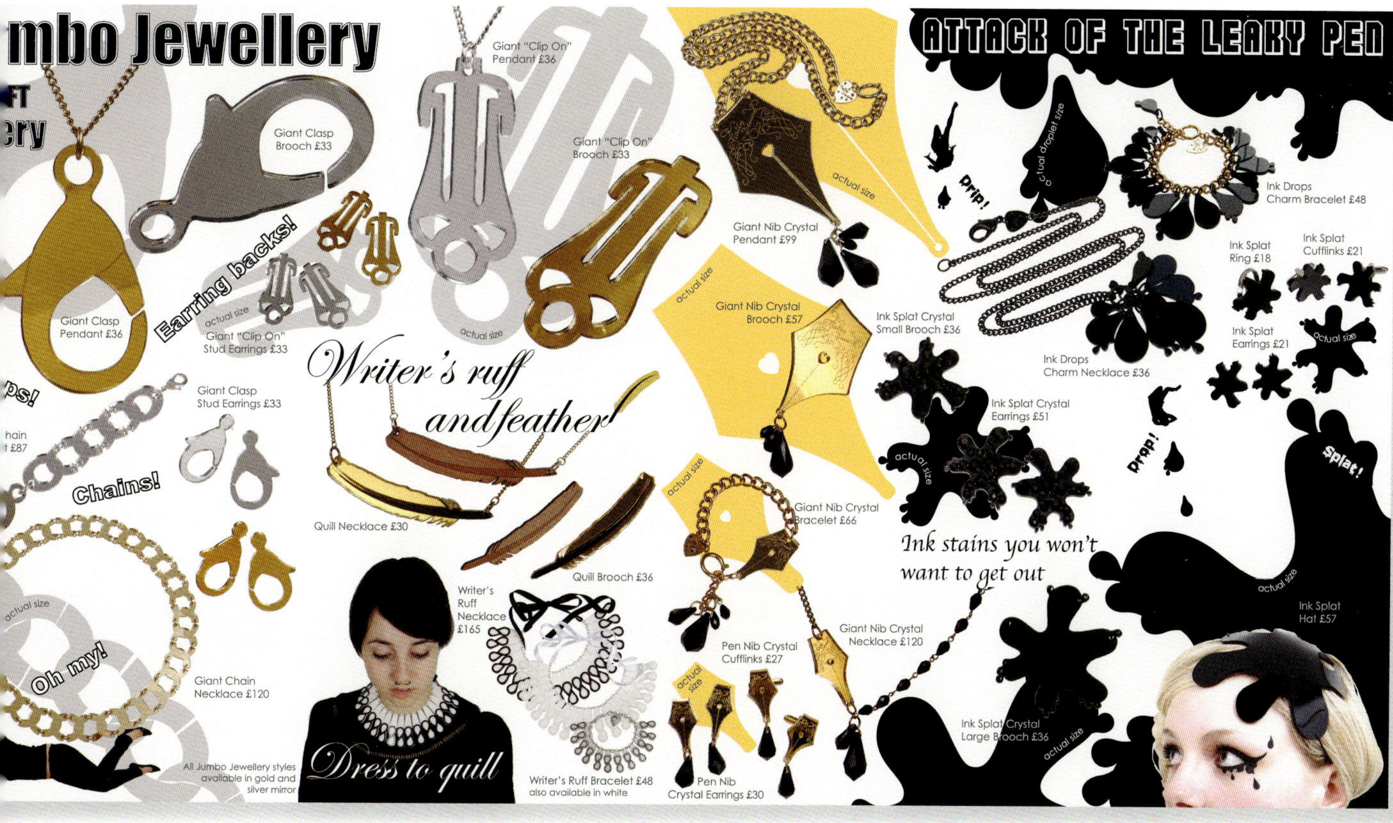

mbo Jewellery
Giant "Clip On"
Pendant £36
Giant Clasp
Brooch £33
Giant "Clip On"
Brooch £33
Earring backs!
Giant Clasp
Pendant £36
actual size
Giant "Clip On"
Stud Earrings £33
actual size
Giant Clasp
Stud Earrings £33
Chains!
Writer's ruff
and feather
Quill Necklace £30
Quill Brooch £36
Oh my!
Giant Chain
Necklace £120
All Jumbo Jewellery styles available in gold and silver mirror
Writer's
Ruff
Necklace
£165
Dress to quill
Writer's Ruff Bracelet £48
also available in white
actual size
Giant Nib Crystal
Pendant £99
actual size
Giant Nib Crystal
Brooch £57
actual size
Giant Nib Crystal
Bracelet £66
Pen Nib Crystal
Cufflinks £27
Giant Nib Crystal
Necklace £120
Pen Nib
Crystal Earrings £30
ATTACK OF THE LEAKY PEN
actual droplet size
Drip!
Ink Drops
Charm Bracelet £48
Ink Splat
Ring £18
Ink Splat
Cufflinks £21
Ink Splat Crystal
Small Brooch £36
Ink Splat
Earrings £21
actual size
Ink Drops
Charm Necklace £36
Ink Splat Crystal
Earrings £51
actual size
Drop!
Splat!
Ink stains you won't
want to get out
actual size
Ink Splat
Hat £57
Ink Splat Crystal
Large Brooch £36
actual size

Cockatiels & Canaries

There's plenty here to line your nest. The Cockatiel Bead Necklace flips around to reveal its feet peeping over a branch, or let the Cockatiel Ring alight on your little finger for cocktail party chic. Canary bells add a finishing touch to our beautiful birds.

Cockatiel Bead Necklace £68
cck-bn

front

back

Cockatiel Necklace £27
cck-n

Cockatiel Brooch £32
cck-b

Cockatiel Ring £18
cck-r

Canary Earrings £21
can-e2

Canary Brooch £24
can-b

Canary Ring £9
can-r

Canary Bell Necklace £26
can-n

Canary Mirror Pendant £55
can-p

MAGPIES

Magpie Pair of Brooches £61
mag-b2

Magpie Crystal Necklace £48
mag-n

Magpie Earrings £24
mag-e2

Magpie Pair of Rings £12
mag-r2

Swoop down on our magpie pairs, always in two-for-joy sets. The rings perch in so many ways across your fingers, or share them with a friend!

Plimsoll

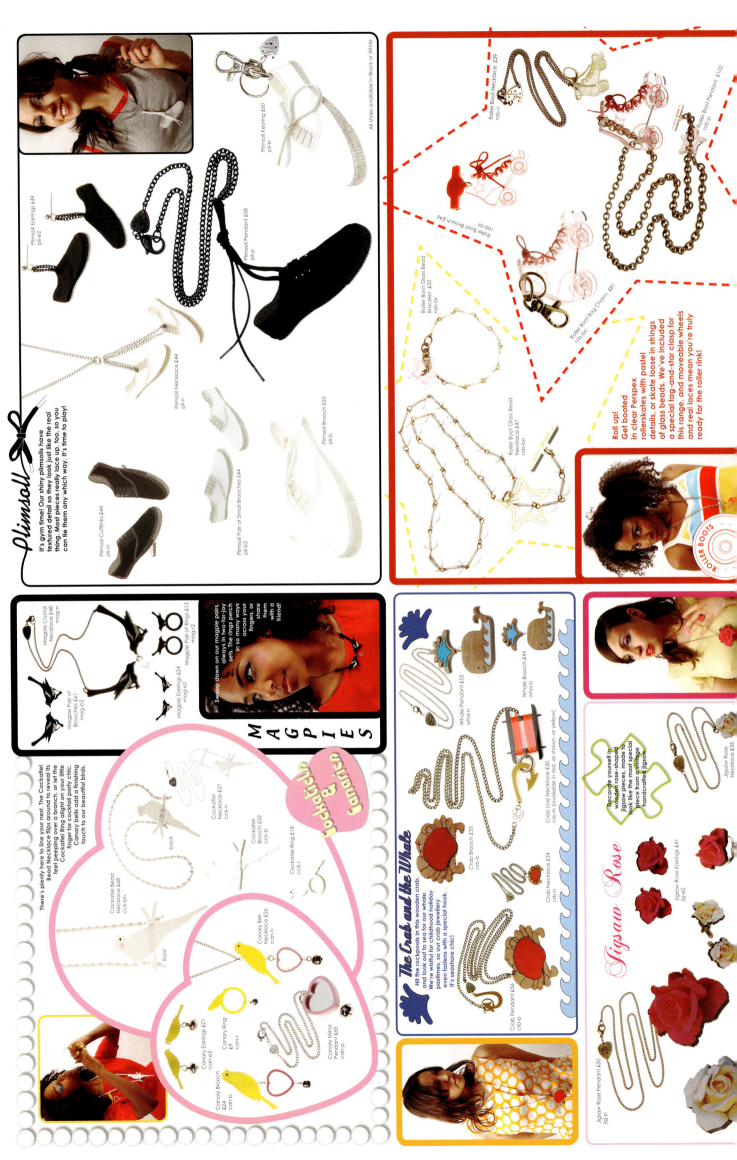

It's gym time! Our shiny plimsolls have textured detail so they look just like the real thing. Most pieces really lace up, too, so you can tie them any which way. It's time to play!

Plimsoll Cufflinks £44
pli-cl

Plimsoll Necklace £44
pli-n

Plimsoll Earrings £49
pli-e2

Plimsoll Pair of Small Brooches £44
pli-b2

Plimsoll Pendant £58
pli-p

Plimsoll Keyring £60
pli-kr

Plimsoll Brooch £55
pli-b

All styles available in Black or White

The Crab and the Whale

Hit the rockpools in this wooden crab, and look out to sea for our whale. We're wistful for childhood holiday pastimes, so our crab jewellery even fastens with a special hook. It's seashore chic!

Crab Brooch £35
crb-b

Whale Pendant £55
wha-n

Crab Pendant £56
crb-p

Crab Necklace £24
crb-n

Crab Line Necklace £30
crb-ln (available in red, as shown, or yellow)

Whale Brooch £44
wha-b

Jigsaw Rose

Jigsaw Rose Pendant £50
jig-p

Jigsaw Rose Earrings £41
jig-e2

Decorate yourself in wooden rose-shaped jigsaw pieces, made to look like the most special piece from a vintage handcrafted jigsaw.

Jigsaw Rose Necklace £35

Roller Boots

Roller Boot Glass Bead Necklace £47
rob-bn

Roller Boot Glass Bead Bracelet £35
rob-br

Roller Boot Brooch £46
rob-br

Roller Boot Necklace £29
rob-n

Roller Boot Bag Charm £81
rob-bc

Roller Boot Pendant £102
rob-p

Roll up! Get booted in clear Perspex rollerskates with pastel details, or skate loose in strings of glass beads. We've included a special tag-and-star clasp for this range, and moveable wheels and real laces mean you're truly ready for the roller rink!

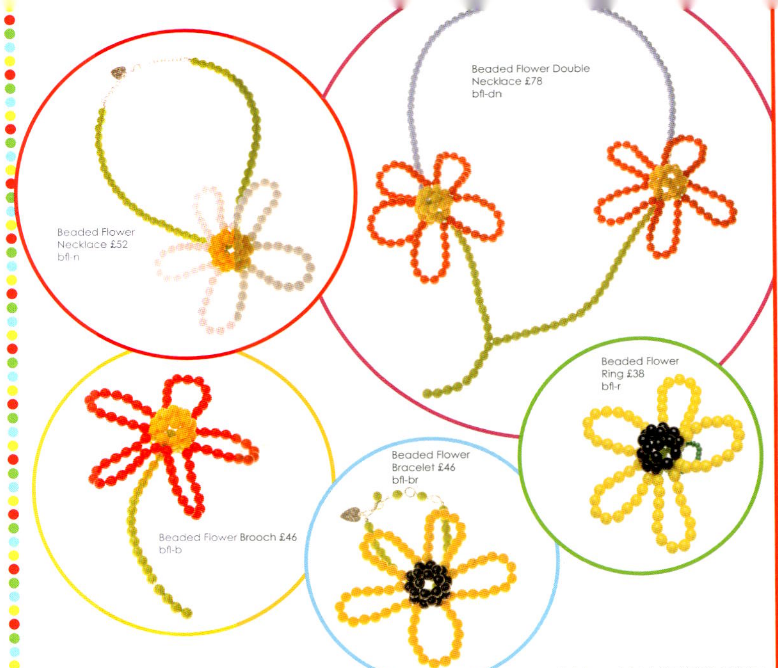

All styles available in Red, White or Yellow

Go table-tennis-tastic in realistic Ping Pong jewellery. These mini wooden bats have a tactile surface and ball-like beads, and the pendant and keyring are even reversible – blue on one side, red on the other. It's your serve...

Ping Pong Pendant and Bag Charm are reversible (blue one side, red the other). All other styles available in Blue or Red

Telephone!
Bring! Bring! Hello, Tatty calling. Did you hear the news about our vintage-style telephone jewellery? The necklace fastens with a magnetic receiver and some of the dials even move around! Gotta hang up now, speak soon!
Telephone Earrings £21
tel-e2
Telephone Necklace £49
tel-n
Telephone Magnet Bead Necklace £75
tel-mbn
Telephone Small Brooch £47
tel-sb
Telephone Ring £9
tel-r
Telephone Receiver Keyring £35
tel-kr
Telephone Bangle £32
tel-br
moving dial!
Telephone Large Pendant £96
tel-p
Telephone Double Brooch £90
tel-db
moving dial!

All styles available in Black, Cream or Red

Tatty Devine

Get ready to play – this season is all about hobbies and leisure, so we've included lots of real, moveable pieces for you to play with! Rollerskate wheels go round, telephone receivers click into place, plimsolls really lace up, and our ping pong necklaces even come complete with a ball!

We're playing with the idea of jewellery too – many of our rings come in pairs, so you can perch them on different fingers for different looks. Many brooches come two by two too, so position them either side of a jacket or together on your jumper. Our crab necklaces even fasten with a fishing line hook!

We've added new materials to the Tatty mix – formica, fishing line, decoupage, magnets and soft plastic all play their part to make this collection really textured and tactile. Even our customary acrylic has been transformed to look just like rubber soles or telephone receivers.

Are you ready to play?

www.tattydevine.com

How-to-order

www.tattydevine.com

Hotline 020 7739 9009

Customer Care/Ordering	020 7739 9009	care@tattydevine.com
General Enquiries	020 7739 9009	info@tattydevine.com
Press	020 7739 9191	press@tattydevine.com
Wholesale Orders	020 7739 9009	wholesale@tattydevine.com

Visit our shops

Tatty Devine
236 Brick Lane
London
E2 7EB
020 7739 9191

Tatty Devine
57b Brewer Street
London
W1F 9UL
020 7434 2257

Models Pinky and Elaine
Model Images by Flashgun and Gloss

Button Up

AW 2009

This season is all about pom poms, pearlies, brass and buttons! Get into unusual uniforms inspired by fun folk traditions - we're dressing up as clowns, majorettes, pearly kings and queens, and members of the marching band. There's a whole orchestra of accessories, so create your own uniform, put it on, and button up!

Tatty Devine™

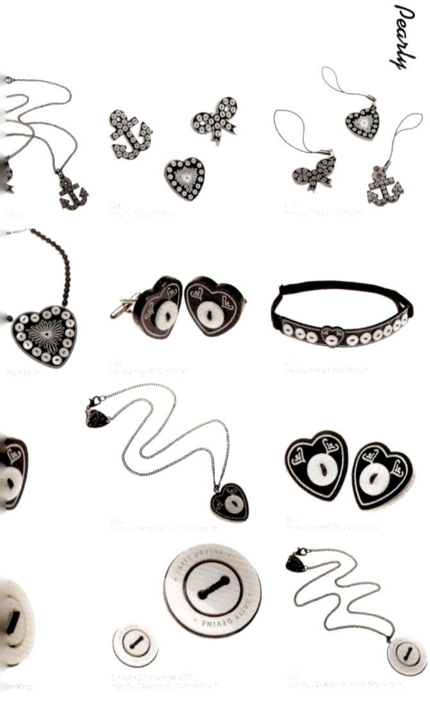

Sewing Box

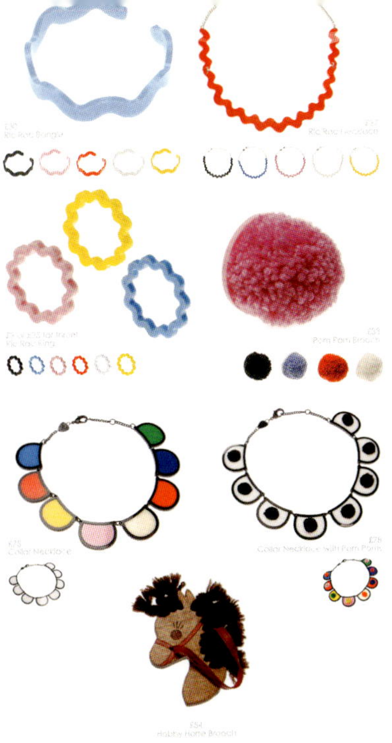

ing Box

Harlequin

Marching Band

www.tattydevine.

Tatty Devine

SUNDAE BEST

SPRING '10

LAUNCHING 29TH JANUARY

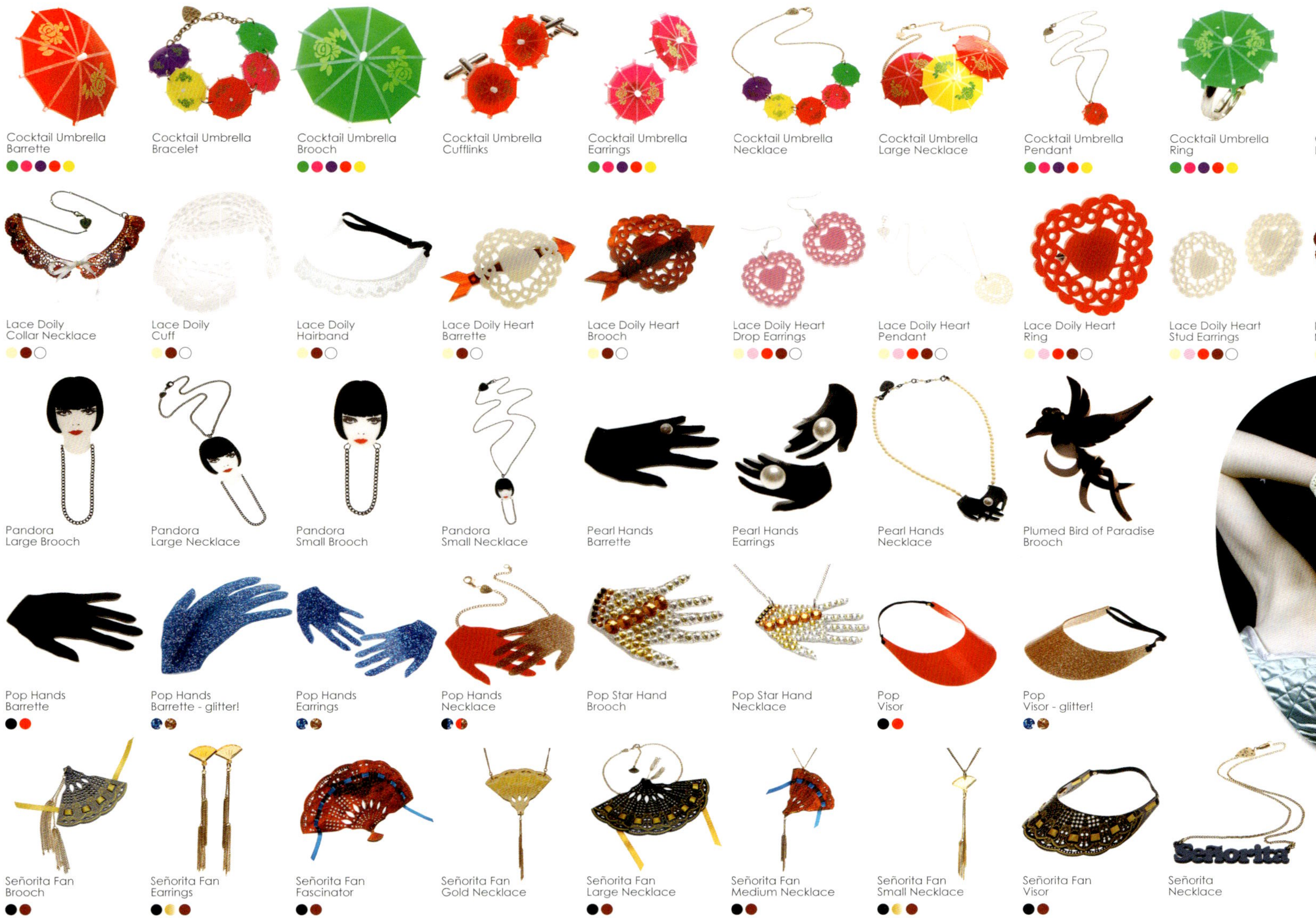

What to wear for spring and summer? It's simple - put on your sundae best! Tatty Devine are serving up everything you need to look ice cream delicious.

Top off your outfit with wafers, cocktail umbrellas, splats of ice cream, and a glossy glacé cherry on top!

This season comes with a twist - instead of launching all at once, Tatty Devine release a Spring collection in February, followed by the Summer collection in May...

it's double the fun!

Tatty Devine
SUNDAE BEST
SUMMER '10
LAUNCHING 30TH APRIL
Ice Cream Splat Barrette
Ice Cream Splat Brooch
Ice Cream Splat Earrings
Ice Cream Sundae Brooch
Ice Cream Sundae Necklace
Ice Cream Wafer Barrette
Ice Cream Wafer Brooch
Ice Lolly Brooch
Ice Lolly Necklace
Iced Party Ring Brooch
Iced Party Ring Necklace
Salty Pup Brooch
Salty Pup Necklace
Seabed Anchor'n'Chain Brooch
Seabed Anchor'n'Chain Earrings
Seabed Anchor'n'Chain Large Pendant
Seabed Anchor'n'Chain Tiny Necklace
Seagull with Anchor Barrette
Seagull with Anchor Brooch
Seagull with Anchor Large Necklace
Seagull with Anchor Small Necklace
Seagull with Heart Barrette
Seagull with Heart Brooch
Seagull with Heart Large Necklace
Seagull with Heart Small Necklace
Seaside Bunting Necklace
Seaside Bunting Extravaganza Necklace
Seaside Chip Fork Barrette
Seaside Chip Fork Brooch
Seaside Chip Fork Necklace
Seaside Chip Fork Tiny Necklace
Silk Flowers Barrette
Silk Flowers Brooch
Silk Flowers Cuff
Silk Flowers Necklace
Silk Flowers Posy Earrings
Silk Flowers Ribbon Hairband
Silk Flowers Ribbon Necklace
Silk Flowers Small Earrings
Sales
Amy Louth wholesale@tattydevine.com +44 (0)20 7739 9009
www.tattydevine.com/wholesale (request your password!)
Press
Amy Durrant press@tattydevine.com +44 (0)20 7739 9191
Head Office
info@tattydevine.com +44 (0)20 7739 9009
7 Gibraltar Walk, London, E2 7LH
In Japan...
Sales: Mr Hasegawa Press: Ms Miura
mach55-japan@nifty.com +81 3 5784 3555
MACH 55, 3F Kyuseigun Bldg,
1-20-5 EbisuNishi, Shibuya-Ku, Tokyo,150-0021
In France...
Dress Code
13 Rue de Turbigo, 75002, Paris
+33 (1) 42 33 36 33
www.dresscodepress.com
www.tattydevine.com

Tatty Devine™
AUTUMN/WINTER 2010
Ready to break new ground? Pioneering jewellery designers Tatty Devine turn ten this year, and they're taking inspiration from women who set the world alight.
Are you an aviatrix navigating new gender roles in goggles and lipstick, a flapper winning the vote in pearls and crystals, a cowgirl breaking wild horses in a western shirt and gingham neckerchief, or a lady striding defiantly into the gentlemen's club with a pipe and pocket watch?
It's time to blaze your own trail.

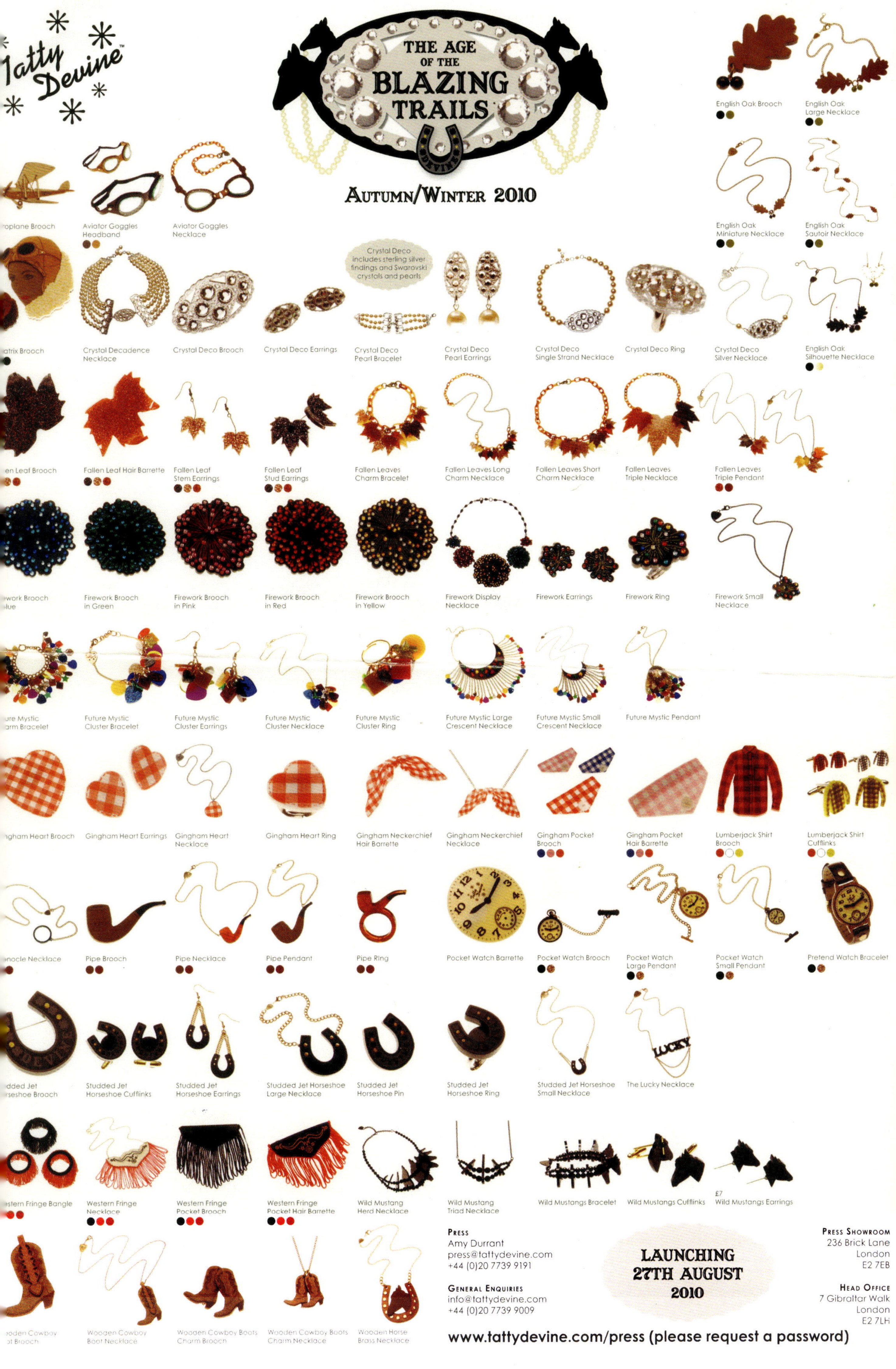
Tatty Devine
THE AGE OF THE BLAZING TRAILS
Autumn/Winter 2010
English Oak Brooch
English Oak Large Necklace
oplane Brooch
Aviator Goggles Headband
Aviator Goggles Necklace
English Oak Miniature Necklace
English Oak Sautoir Necklace
Crystal Deco includes sterling silver findings and Swarovski crystals and pearls
atrix Brooch
Crystal Decadence Necklace
Crystal Deco Brooch
Crystal Deco Earrings
Crystal Deco Pearl Bracelet
Crystal Deco Pearl Earrings
Crystal Deco Single Strand Necklace
Crystal Deco Ring
Crystal Deco Silver Necklace
English Oak Silhouette Necklace
en Leaf Brooch
Fallen Leaf Hair Barrette
Fallen Leaf Stem Earrings
Fallen Leaf Stud Earrings
Fallen Leaves Charm Bracelet
Fallen Leaves Long Charm Necklace
Fallen Leaves Short Charm Necklace
Fallen Leaves Triple Necklace
Fallen Leaves Triple Pendant
work Brooch lue
Firework Brooch in Green
Firework Brooch in Pink
Firework Brooch in Red
Firework Brooch in Yellow
Firework Display Necklace
Firework Earrings
Firework Ring
Firework Small Necklace
ure Mystic arm Bracelet
Future Mystic Cluster Bracelet
Future Mystic Cluster Earrings
Future Mystic Cluster Necklace
Future Mystic Cluster Ring
Future Mystic Large Crescent Necklace
Future Mystic Small Crescent Necklace
Future Mystic Pendant
ngham Heart Brooch
Gingham Heart Earrings
Gingham Heart Necklace
Gingham Heart Ring
Gingham Neckerchief Hair Barrette
Gingham Neckerchief Necklace
Gingham Pocket Brooch
Gingham Pocket Hair Barrette
Lumberjack Shirt Brooch
Lumberjack Shirt Cufflinks
nocle Necklace
Pipe Brooch
Pipe Necklace
Pipe Pendant
Pipe Ring
Pocket Watch Barrette
Pocket Watch Brooch
Pocket Watch Large Pendant
Pocket Watch Small Pendant
Pretend Watch Bracelet
dded Jet rseshoe Brooch
Studded Jet Horseshoe Cufflinks
Studded Jet Horseshoe Earrings
Studded Jet Horseshoe Large Necklace
Studded Jet Horseshoe Pin
Studded Jet Horseshoe Ring
Studded Jet Horseshoe Small Necklace
The Lucky Necklace
stern Fringe Bangle
Western Fringe Necklace
Western Fringe Pocket Brooch
Western Fringe Pocket Hair Barrette
Wild Mustang Herd Necklace
Wild Mustang Triad Necklace
Wild Mustangs Bracelet
Wild Mustangs Cufflinks
£7
Wild Mustangs Earrings
oden Cowboy ot Brooch
Wooden Cowboy Boot Necklace
Wooden Cowboy Boots Charm Brooch
Wooden Cowboy Boots Charm Necklace
Wooden Horse Brass Necklace
Press
Amy Durrant
press@tattydevine.com
+44 (0)20 7739 9191
General Enquiries
info@tattydevine.com
+44 (0)20 7739 9009
LAUNCHING 27TH AUGUST 2010
Press Showroom
236 Brick Lane
London
E2 7EB
Head Office
7 Gibraltar Walk
London
E2 7LH
www.tattydevine.com/press (please request a password)

Tatty Devine™
Spring/Summer 2011
Light, legend and luxury... Pile on layers of rich gold and deep turquoise to become a fierce Cairo Queen. The all-seeing eye watches over you, hidden in money, pyramids and ancient beetles. Spectrums of light burst through pastel-hued shards of rainbow and 3-D prisms that jut out from the body.
Light saturates glitter and crystals in celestial Moons and the cryptic signs of the Zodiac and Yin-Yang. Finally, fluttering tropic hummingbirds, mystical unicorns and chunks of quartz crystal come together in a collection that is all about pure fantasy.

Tatty Devine™

ASTRAL HAZE

Spring/Summer 2011

Press
Amy Durrant
press@tattydevine.com
+44 (0)20 7739 9191

www.tattydevine.com/press
(please request a password)

Press Showroom
236 Brick Lane
London
E2 7EB

ncient Pyramid arrings

Ancient Pyramid Inverted Necklace

Ancient Pyramid Long Pendant

Ancient Pyramid Necklace

Ancient Pyramid Small Necklace

Cleopatra Belt

Cleopatra Bracelet

Cleopatra Necklace

Chamber of the Sun Bracelet

Chamber of the Sun Drop Earrings

Chamber of the Sun Hair Barrette

Chamber of the Sun Link Necklace

Chamber of the Sun Long Necklace

Chamber of the Sun Ring

Chamber of the Sun Stud Earrings

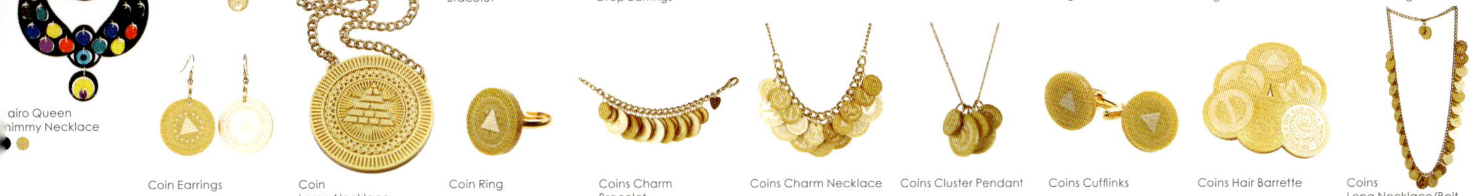

airo Queen himmy Necklace

Coin Earrings

Coin Large Necklace

Coin Ring

Coins Charm Bracelet

Coins Charm Necklace

Coins Cluster Pendant

Coins Cufflinks

Coins Hair Barrette

Coins Long Necklace/Belt

ollar Eye Pendant

Dollar Eye Ring

Dollar Note Brooch

Dollar Note Collar

Dollar Note Hair Barrette

Dollar Note Pendant - Large

Dollar Note Pendant - Small

Eye Large Necklace

gyptian Pharoah elt

Egyptian Pharaoh Brooch

Egyptian Pharaoh Necklace

Egyptian Pharaoh Earrings

Egyptian Pharaoh Ring

Egyptian Pharaoh Small Mirror Necklace

Egyptian Pharaoh Large Mirror Necklace

Eye Small Necklace

litter Hummingbird eadpiece

Glitter Hummingbird Necklace

Glitter Hummingbird Wing Earrings

Glitter Humingbird Winged Necklace

Halcyon Moon Earrings

Halcyon Moon Pendant

Halcyon Skies Brooch

Halcyon Skies Large Necklace

Halcyon Skies Small Necklace

ism Light Cluster ecklace: Brights

Prism Light Cluster Ring: Brights

Prism Light Earrings: Brights

Prism Light Necklace: Brights

Prism Light Pendant: Brights

Prism Light Cluster Necklace: Clear

Prism Light Cluster Ring: Clear

Prism Light Earrings: Clear

Prism Light Necklace: Clear

Prism Light Pendant: Clear

uartz Crystal eadpiece (Clear only)

Quartz Crystal Keyring (Clear only)

Quartz Crystal Large Cluster Pendant (Clear only)

Quartz Crystal Bangle

Quartz Crystal Bib Necklace

Quartz Crystal Charm Bracelet

Rainbow Hearts Necklace

Rainbow Hearts Pendant

Rainbow Heart Ring

Rainbow Spectrum Bracelet

uartz Crystal arrings

Quartz Crystal Mini Cluster Pendant

Quartz Crystal Multi Shard Necklace

Quartz Crystal Charm Cluster Ring

Quartz Crystal Shards Ring

Quartz Crystal Single Shard Ring

Unicorn Beaded Necklace

Unicorn Brooch

Unicorn Necklace

ng Yang Belt

Ying Yang Large Necklace

Ying Yang Ring

Ying Yang Small Pendant

Zodiac Power Belt

Zodiac Power Bangle

Zodiac Power Large Pendant

Zodiac Power Small Pendant

Zodiac Power Ring

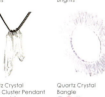

UNITED DEVINE BANK LONDON
TATTY
DEVINE

GOLD

Haberdashery

We both had crafty upbringings – there was a sense in both of our homes that creativity was as natural as breathing. We both got into cross-stitch in the 1980s and vividly remember sewing on brightly-coloured Binca fabric. We felt like we were following in a family tradition – Rosie's granny wrote a book called *The Satisfaction of Stitchery*, and Harriet's mum was a couture seamstress. The making wasn't confined to small things; both families were up for taking on bigger DIY endeavours. Rosie's granny headed up vast craft projects, like making a replica of a Roman mosaic as carpet for her living room. Harriet's parents were constantly sketching out ideas on the back on envelopes, working out how to create all the costumes for the local panto or how to build a 24ft skate ramp in the family garden (it helped that Harriet's dad was a carpenter). The message was the same for both of us – if you could imagine it, you could find a way to make it.

Needle Threader Necklace, AW05
Acrylic, metal alloy

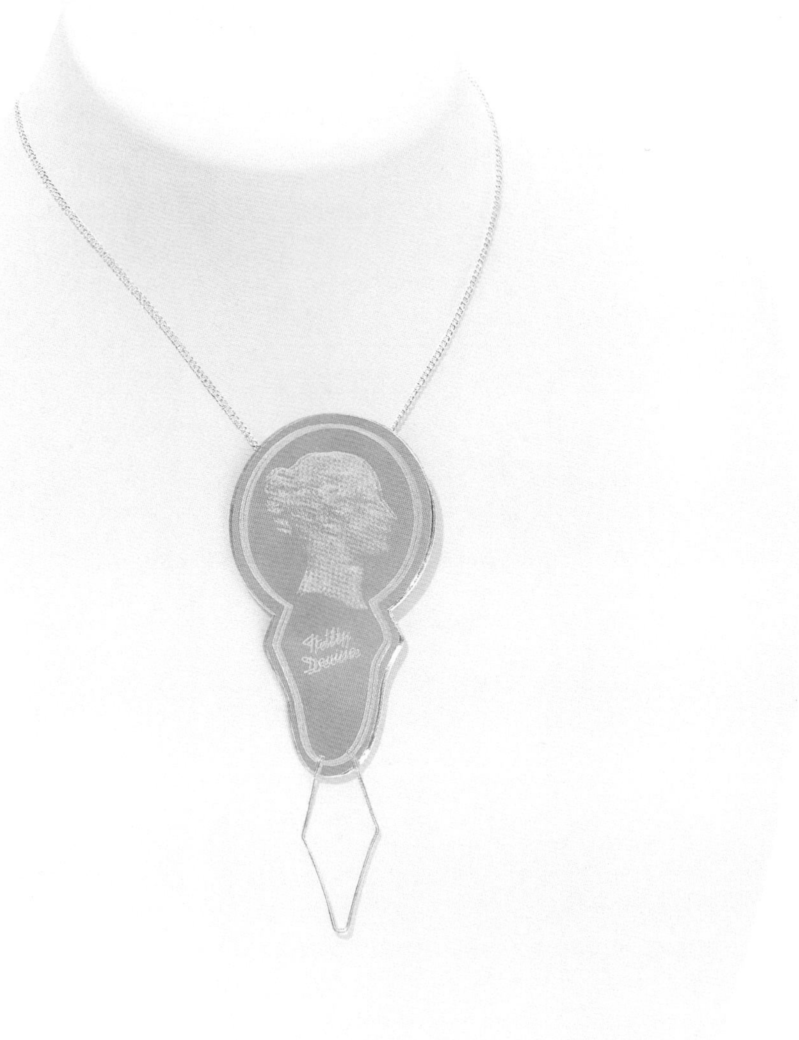

Writer's Ruff Necklace, AW08
Acrylic, ribbon, metal alloy

We love costumes and historical dress, and it often finds its way into our jewellery. We'll look at everything, from historical pattern books, the ruffs in Elizabethan paintings or an episode of Blackadder.

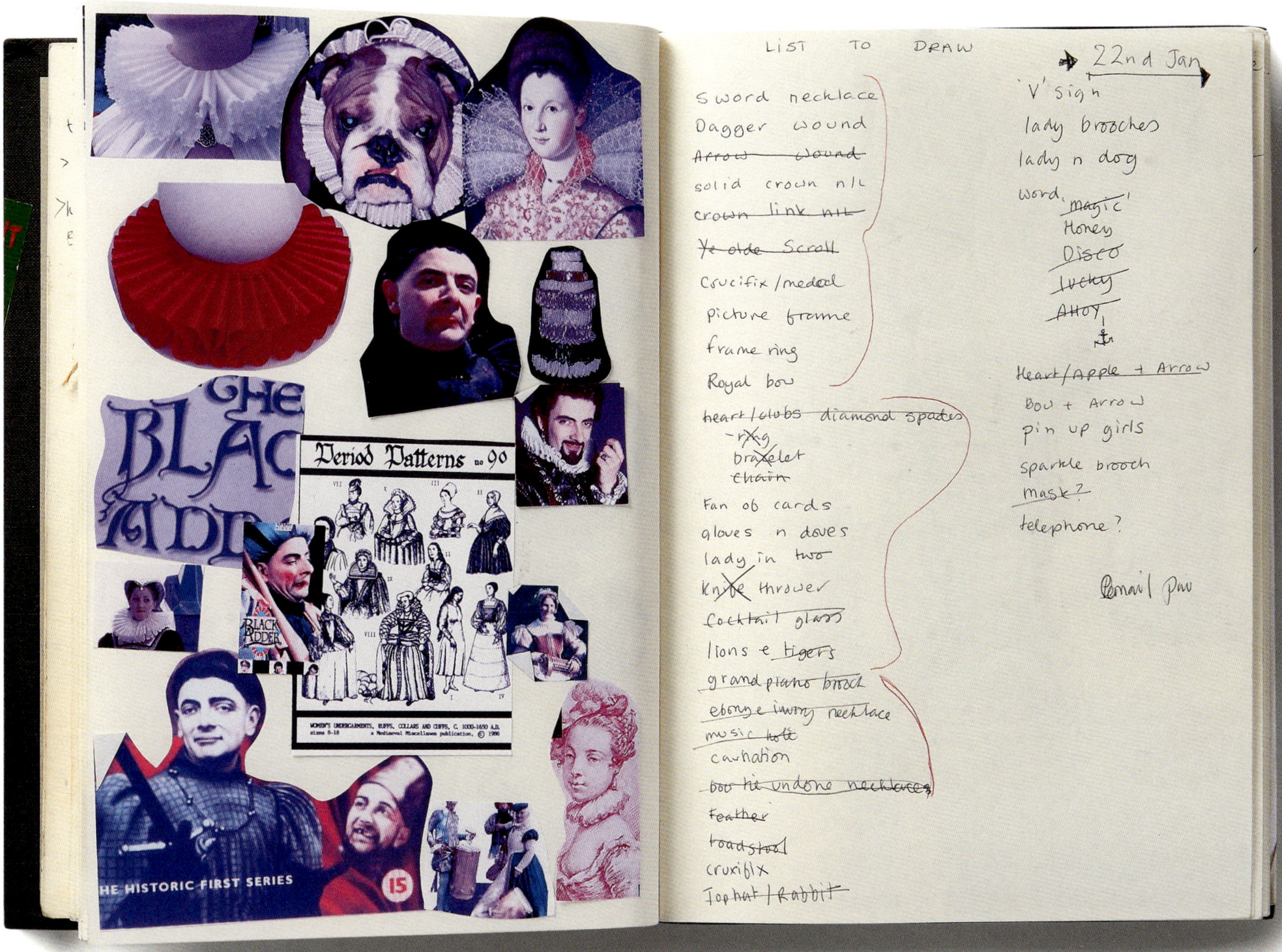
Period Patterns no 90
HE HISTORIC FIRST SERIES
15
LIST TO DRAW
Sword necklace
Dagger wound
Arrow wound
solid crown n/l
crown link n/l
Ye olde Scroll
Crucifix/medal
picture frame
frame ring
Royal bow
heart/clubs diamond spades
- ring
bracelet
chain
Fan of cards
gloves n doves
lady in two
knife thrower
Cocktail glass
lions & tigers
grand piano brooch
ebony & ivory necklace
music note
carnation
bow tie undone necklaces
Feather
toadstool
crucifix
Top hat / Rabbit
22nd Jan
'V' sign
lady brooches
lady n dog
word. 'magic'
Honey
Disco
lucky
AHOY
Heart/Apple + Arrow
Bow + Arrow
pin up girls
sparkle brooch
mask?
telephone?

Frogging Necklace 5 Tiers, AW09
Acrylic, metal alloy

Pearly collection, AW09
Photography by Mae Finlayson

Sketchbook, AW09

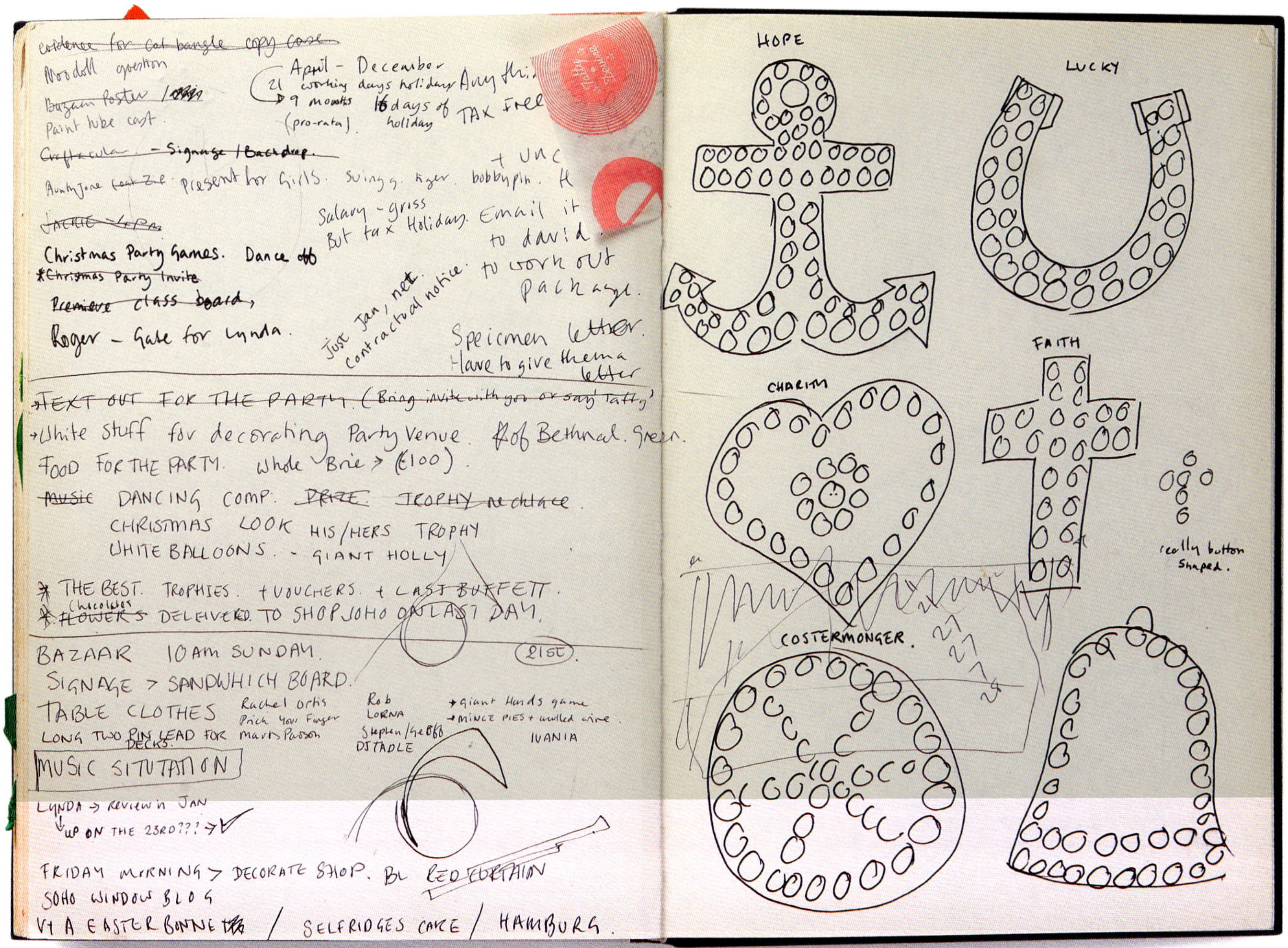

Pearly Queen Heart Bead Necklace, AW09
Acrylic, mother of pearl buttons,
glass beads, metal alloy

The Pearly Queen Heart Bead Necklace is a homage to the Pearly Kings and Queens, who raise money for charity and cut a stylish dash by wearing suits and dresses embellished with of mother of pearl buttons in all kinds of patterns. Our Pearly Necklace is decorated with hand-sewn buttons on a shape that represents charity. We launched the AW09 collection Button Up alongside a photographic exhibition with a knees-up celebration in the Brick Lane shop, which was attended by the Pearly Queen and King of Islington.

Song sheet for Harry Dutton private view at the Brick Lane shop, 2009

Pearly King Brooch, AW09
Acrylic, metal alloy

Mittens Necklace, AW09
Acrylic, metal alloy

Creating the artwork for this piece was like creating a knitting pattern: we worked out the stitches on the computer and the end result looks like knitting in acrylic.

Seaside Bunting Extravaganza, SS10
Acrylic, metal alloy

Aviatrix Brooch, AW10
Leather, acrylic, metal alloy headpin

Taken from The Age of the Blazing Trails collection, this brooch depicts the famous pioneering female aviator Amy Johnson. This collection showcased the textures of textiles and fabrics, including Western shirt fringing, gingham and the shearling and goggles of Amy Johnson's getup.

Aviator Goggles Headband, AW10
Leather, acrylic, metal alloy headpins

Statements

Between 2007 and 2013 our designs were getting bigger, bolder and more complex. It felt like mass design was taking over the world, leaving no place for individualism, and we really wanted to kick against that. We loved the idea that a necklace could be a conversation starter, and that the wearer would be the centre of attention, so we began experimenting and manipulating the acrylic to make work that was startling, striking and original.

Tatty Devine®

Tatty Devine®

Autumn/Winter 2011

Finders keepers... Come foraging with Tatty Devine. The forest is rich with acorns, blackberries and seeds, all transformed into jewellery in our new matt frosted perspex. Crown yourself with ivy wreaths in translucent green, glittering gold or charcoal black. Spot a fox slipping through the undergrowth, or an owl disappearing through the trees. Go exploring dressed in colourful perspex patchwork in oranges and creams, or dazzling peacock shades of mirror. Our haul of texture and pattern is completed by tartan ribbons on strings of oversized beads, and leather belts with a hand-punched brogue pattern made locally in East London, in step with our matching wooden brogue jewellery. What will you find?

rogue Belt - black patent | brown | maroon | tan | yellow

Brogue Brooch

Brogue Large Pendant

Brogue Small Pendant

orest Charm Earrings - acorn | blackberry | dandelion seed

Forest Charm Necklace - acorn | blackberry | dandelion seed

Forest Cluster Bracelet

Forest Cluster Necklace

orest Large Cluster Bracelet

Forest Large Cluster Necklace

Fox Brooch - black glitter | tortoiseshell | white

Fox Necklace - tortoiseshell

em Owl Heart Necklace - black | yellow

Gem Owl Mask Large Necklace - black | yellow

Gem Owl Mask Ring - black | yellow

Gem Owl Mask Small Necklace - black | yellow

Gem Owl Super Necklace - black | yellow

Honesty Seed Pod Earrings

Honesty Seed Pod Link Necklace

Honesty Seed Pod Stem Necklace £17

Ivy Five Leaves Necklace - green | gold glitter | matt black

Ivy Leaves Bracelet - green | gold glitter | matt black

Ivy Leaves Earrings - green | gold glitter | matt black

y Leaves Long Necklace - green | old glitter | matt black

Ivy Vines Necklace - green | gold glitter | matt black

Ivy Wreath Hair Ribbon - green | gold mirror | black mirror

Ivy Wreath Necklace - green | gold mirror | black mirror

wl Brooch - blue | orange

Owl Large Pendant - blue | orange | tortoiseshell

Owl Small Pendant - blue | orange | tortoiseshell

Patchwork Bib Ribbon Necklace - colourblock | peacock

Patchwork Bracelet - colourblock | peacock

atchwork Brooch - colourblock | peacock

Patchwork Flowers Necklace - colourblock | peacock

Patchwork Hair Ribbon - colourblock | peacock

Patchwork Hexagon Earrings - cream | green | red | yellow | blue mir | green mir | purple mir | turquoise mir

atchwork Pendant - colourblock | peacock

Patchwork Ribbon Belt - colourblock | peacock

Patchwork Ring - colourblock | peacock

Patchwork Single Flower Necklace - colourblock | peacock

Patchwork Single Strand Necklace - colourblock | peacock

ycamore Seed harm Necklace

Sycamore Seed Earrings

Sycamore Seed Helicopter Necklace

Tartan Bead Necklace - black | red

Wooden Owl Mask Large Necklace

Wooden Owl Mask Ring

Wooden Owl Mask Small Necklace

Wooden Owl Super Necklace

FKA Twigs wearing the Watermelon Necklace and Earrings, SS12
Photography by Saga Sig

Tatty Devine®

Spring/Summer 2012

Say 'hola' to a really juicy jewellery collection. Colour zings from watermelons, marigolds, sweetcorn and parakeets. Fiesta flowers come in bright perspex, and Mexican embroidery is recreated as beautiful linked silhouettes. Frida Kahlo's iconic face is etched into leather, and her famous floral hair is done in pretty beads which spill over into 'junk memory' jewellery, strung with Tatty Devine icons. Skulls and skeletons nod to the Day of the Dead, but look closely and you'll find them decorated with symbols from the rest of the collection. Hot news, too: we've created eyelash sunglasses for summer 2012. You might just need them.

Eyelash Sunglasses

Conical Pom Pom Hat
Corn Dolly Necklace
Corn on the Cob Necklace
Floral Eye Earrings
Floral Eye Large Triple Necklace
Floral Eye Pendant
Floral Eye Ring
Frida Brooch
Frida Flower Necklace
Frida Large Necklace
Frida Small Necklace
Junk Memory Bead Necklace
Junk Memory Bead Bracelet
Junk Memory Bib Necklace / Headpiece
Junk Memory Charm Necklace
Junk Memory Heart Necklace
Maracas Brooch
Maracas Necklace
Marigold Bib Necklace / Headpiece
Marigold Brooch
Marigold Earrings - orange | yellow
Marigold Pendant - orange | yellow
Marigold Ring - orange | yellow
Marigold Triple Necklace
Melon Earrings - cantaloupe | watermelon
Melon Hat - cantaloupe | watermelon
Melon Large Necklace - cantaloupe | watermelon
Melon Small Necklace - cantaloupe | watermelon
Mexican Embroidery Bluebird Earrings
Mexican Embroidery Bracelet
Mexican Embroidery Large Necklace - multicoloured | white
Mexican Embroidery Medium Necklace - multicoloured | white
Mexican Embroidery Small Necklace
Mexican Flower Drop Earrings
Mexican Flower Hair Barrette
Mexican Flower Necklace
Mexican Flower Ring
Mexican Flower Stud Earrings
Parakeet Brooch
Parakeet Earrings - black | gold | green
Parakeet Small Necklace - black | gold | green
Parakeet Medium Necklace - black | gold | green | white
Parakeet Large Necklace - gold | green | white
Posie Ribbon - dusk | brights | white
Posie Bracelet - dusk | brights | white
Posie Chain Necklace - dusk | brights | white
Posie Necklace - blue | dusk | pink | purple | red | white | yellow
Posie Ring - blue | dusk | pink | purple | red | white | yellow
Skeleton Small Necklace
Sugar Skull Brooch - black | white
Sugar Skull Ring - black | white
Skeleton Large Necklace
Sugar Skull Earrings - black | white
Sugar Skull Mini Necklace - black | white
Sugar Skull Large Necklace - black | white
Sugar Skull Pendant - black | white
Sugar Skull Link Necklace

Cantaloupe Melon Hat, SS12
Acrylic, acrylic gems, elastic

Posie Chain Necklace, SS12
Acrylic, pressed glass beads, metal alloy

Parakeet Large Necklace, SS12
Acrylic, metal alloy

30
13cm
3o
5cm
8cm

Tatty Devine®

Autumn/Winter 2012

Digital prints land on jewellery, as Tatty Devine pioneer the technique on wood and perspex. Imagine a neglected Bloomsbury mansion, with willow pattern plates straight out of the dining room recreated as digitally printed jewellery. From dark corners come art deco moths, printed directly onto birch. Town and country mice nibble on acorns and cheese, and there are bunches of musty grapes to be found in the overgrown garden. There's a grown-up twist to florals as semi-precious stones make their debut at Tatty Devine, with agate and jade at the heart of poisonous plants. The dressing room delivers crystal-encrusted paisley, and nature meets artifice as the classic leopard motif gets the Tatty Devine treatment. The collection is topped off with lavish headpieces.

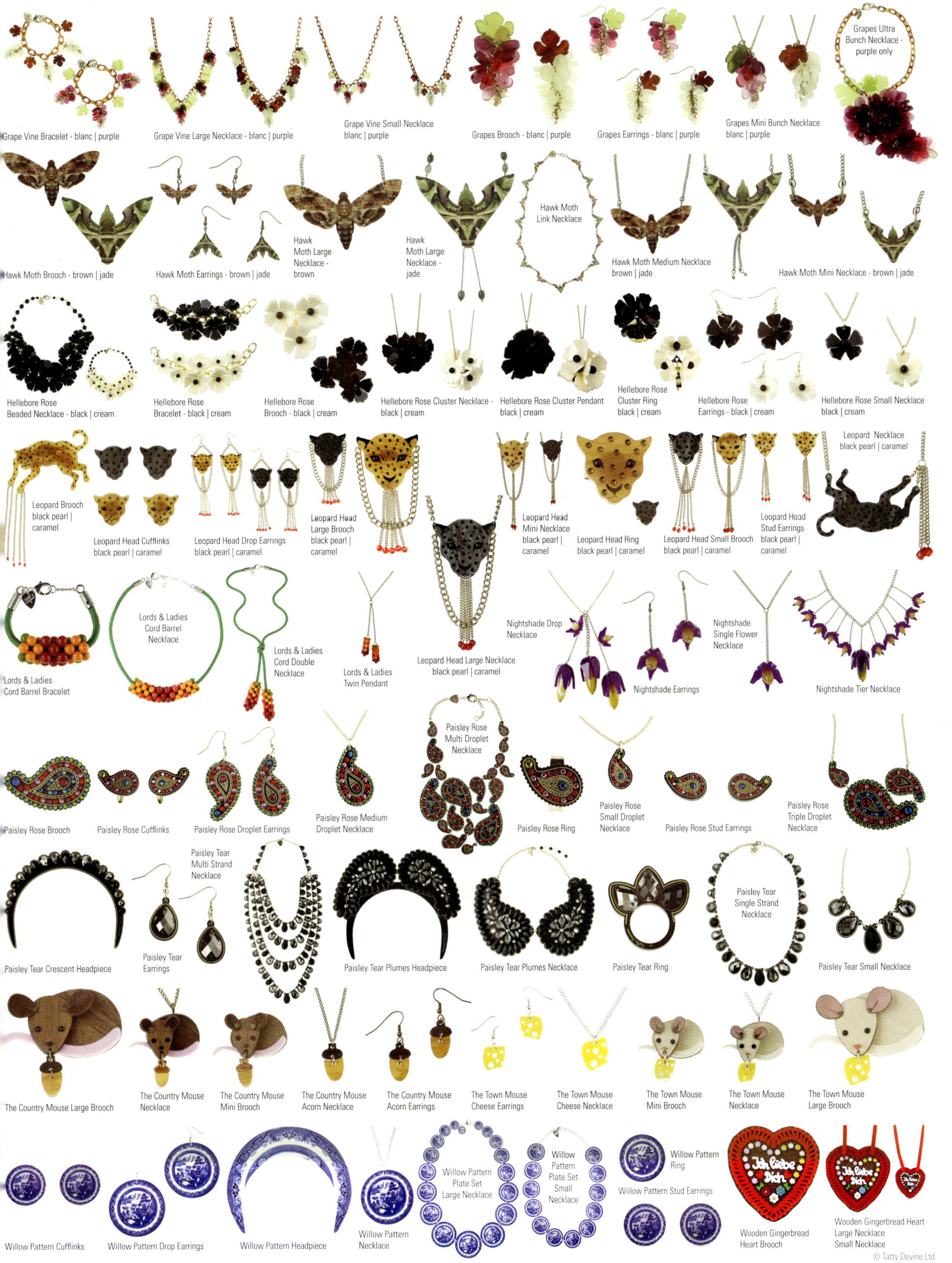

Grape Vine Bracelet - blanc | purple

Grape Vine Large Necklace - blanc | purple

Grape Vine Small Necklace blanc | purple

Grapes Brooch - blanc | purple

Grapes Earrings - blanc | purple

Grapes Mini Bunch Necklace blanc | purple

Grapes Ultra Bunch Necklace - purple only

Hawk Moth Brooch - brown | jade

Hawk Moth Earrings - brown | jade

Hawk Moth Large Necklace - brown

Hawk Moth Large Necklace - jade

Hawk Moth Link Necklace

Hawk Moth Medium Necklace brown | jade

Hawk Moth Mini Necklace - brown | jade

Hellebore Rose Beaded Necklace - black | cream

Hellebore Rose Bracelet - black | cream

Hellebore Rose Brooch - black | cream

Hellebore Rose Cluster Necklace - black | cream

Hellebore Rose Cluster Pendant black | cream

Hellebore Rose Cluster Ring black | cream

Hellebore Rose Earrings - black | cream

Hellebore Rose Small Necklace black | cream

Leopard Brooch black pearl | caramel

Leopard Head Cufflinks black pearl | caramel

Leopard Head Drop Earrings black pearl | caramel

Leopard Head Large Brooch black pearl | caramel

Leopard Head Large Necklace black pearl | caramel

Leopard Head Mini Necklace black pearl | caramel

Leopard Head Ring black pearl | caramel

Leopard Head Small Brooch black pearl | caramel

Leopard Head Stud Earrings black pearl | caramel

Leopard Necklace black pearl | caramel

Lords & Ladies Cord Barrel Bracelet

Lords & Ladies Cord Barrel Necklace

Lords & Ladies Cord Double Necklace

Lords & Ladies Twin Pendant

Nightshade Drop Necklace

Nightshade Earrings

Nightshade Single Flower Necklace

Nightshade Tier Necklace

Paisley Rose Brooch

Paisley Rose Cufflinks

Paisley Rose Droplet Earrings

Paisley Rose Medium Droplet Necklace

Paisley Rose Multi Droplet Necklace

Paisley Rose Ring

Paisley Rose Small Droplet Necklace

Paisley Rose Stud Earrings

Paisley Rose Triple Droplet Necklace

Paisley Tear Crescent Headpiece

Paisley Tear Earrings

Paisley Tear Multi Strand Necklace

Paisley Tear Plumes Headpiece

Paisley Tear Plumes Necklace

Paisley Tear Ring

Paisley Tear Single Strand Necklace

Paisley Tear Small Necklace

The Country Mouse Large Brooch

The Country Mouse Necklace

The Country Mouse Mini Brooch

The Country Mouse Acorn Necklace

The Country Mouse Acorn Earrings

The Town Mouse Cheese Earrings

The Town Mouse Cheese Necklace

The Town Mouse Mini Brooch

The Town Mouse Necklace

The Town Mouse Large Brooch

Willow Pattern Cufflinks

Willow Pattern Drop Earrings

Willow Pattern Headpiece

Willow Pattern Necklace

Willow Pattern Plate Set Large Necklace

Willow Pattern Plate Set Small Necklace

Willow Pattern Ring

Willow Pattern Stud Earrings

Wooden Gingerbread Heart Brooch

Wooden Gingerbread Heart Large Necklace Small Necklace

Tatty Devine®

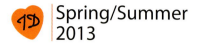

Spring/Summer 2013

Warmth, light and power radiate from Tatty Devine's latest collection. Designers Rosie Wolfenden and Harriet Vine continue to recreate the real world in perspex, this time adding new colours and techniques. Radiant Goddess celebrates colour with fantastic sunrise ombres & new shimmering rainbow perspex and the Goddess Kali's elegant arms are recreated in colbalt blue perspex. Hot House centres around a wreath of tropical leaves, glistening with resin dew and decorated with butterflies, ladybirds & tortoises. Painted Elephant combines beautiful elephants with striking geometric patterns and garlands of lotus flowers. Acid Blossom juxtaposes the delicateness of paper cherry blossoms with a fresh neon colour palette and glossy marbled perspex.

Radiant Goddess

Goddess Arm Ultra Necklace

Goddess Hand Earrings

Goddess Hand Bracelet

Goddess Hand Strand Necklace

Goddess Hand Ring

Goddess Hand Multi Strand Necklace

Goddess Hand Necklace

Goddess Sunrise Necklace

Radiance Earrings - shimmer | sunrise

Radiance Necklace - shimmer | sunrise

Radiance Link Necklace - shimmer | sunrise

Radiance Ultra Necklace - shimmer | sunrise

Painted Elephant

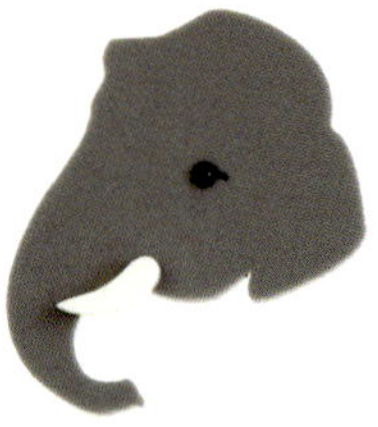

Elephant Head Brooch

Elephant Head Necklace

Elephant Necklace

Geometric Bracelet

Geometric Necklace

Lotus Bud Earrings

Lotus Bud Link Necklace

Lotus Bud Garland Necklace

Lotus Bud Necklace

Lotus Flower Necklace

Lotus Flower Celebration Necklace

ot House

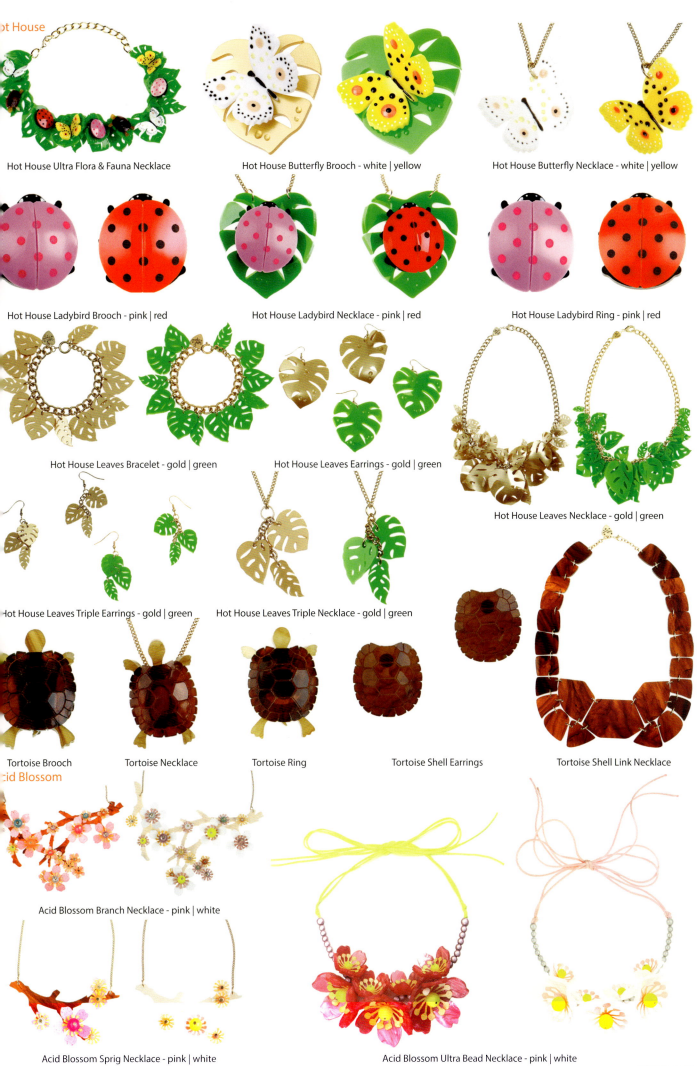

Hot House Ultra Flora & Fauna Necklace

Hot House Butterfly Brooch - white | yellow

Hot House Butterfly Necklace - white | yellow

Hot House Ladybird Brooch - pink | red

Hot House Ladybird Necklace - pink | red

Hot House Ladybird Ring - pink | red

Hot House Leaves Bracelet - gold | green

Hot House Leaves Earrings - gold | green

Hot House Leaves Necklace - gold | green

Hot House Leaves Triple Earrings - gold | green

Hot House Leaves Triple Necklace - gold | green

Tortoise Brooch

Tortoise Necklace

Tortoise Ring

Tortoise Shell Earrings

Tortoise Shell Link Necklace

cid Blossom

Acid Blossom Branch Necklace - pink | white

Acid Blossom Sprig Necklace - pink | white

Acid Blossom Ultra Bead Necklace - pink | white

Acid Blossom Bead Ultra Necklace, SS13
Acrylic, Tyvek, paint, Swarovski crystals, miracle beads, metal alloy

Another discovery was Tyvek, a tough kind of unbreakable paper, which we used to create the delicate stamens on the Acid Blossom piece. Acrylic was too thick and lighter fabrics would have frayed.

Flora and Fauna Ultra Necklace, SS13
Acrylic, thixotropic resin, paint, metal alloy

The Hot House Necklace evokes tropical heat, Indian festivals and glistening summer mornings. We popped on our favourite reptile, which we made in tortoiseshell-effect acrylic. We used resin for the water droplets, a recent discovery of ours that was also perfect for gluing together the ladybird's wings and the tortoise's shell.

Leopard Head collection, AW12
Photography by Jeff Hahn

Jewel Print Earrings, AW13
Acrylic, metal alloy

Food

We've always loved the idea that food and art can go together. We're fascinated by fake food – and the notion that you can recreate something perishable in materials that won't spoil – like the set of four bangles that make up a sandwich and the necklace of rubber olives. The Chip Fork Necklace, Fried Egg Brooch and Crisp Necklace are a result of our trips to the seaside, visits to the local café and the corner shop.

Giant Lobster Necklace
Photography by Jeff Hahn

Letter from Hunx, 2005

In 2003 we were listening a lot to the band Gravy Train!!!! Singer Seth Bogart a.k.a Hunx ran a hair salon called Down at Lulu's in Oakland, California, which we visited in 2007. If you wanted to look like you were in the Ramones, this was the place to go.

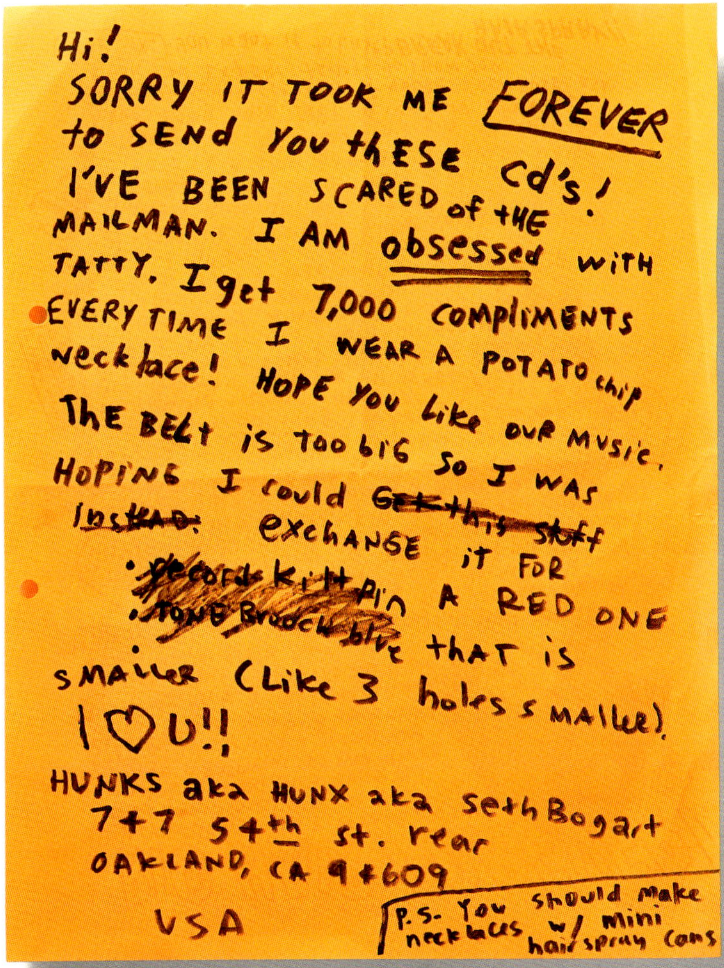
Hi!
SORRY IT TOOK ME FOREVER to SEND YOU tHESE Cd's! I'VE BEEN SCARED of tHE MAILMAN. I AM obsessed with TATTY. I get 7,000 compliments EVERY TIME I WEAR A POTATO chip necklace! HOPE YOU Like OUR MUSIC. THE BELt is too big SO I WAS HOPING I could ~~Get this stuff instead:~~ exchange it FOR ~~• … • … Brooch blue~~ A RED ONE that is smaller (Like 3 holes smaller).
I ♥ U!!
HUNKS aka HUNX aka seth Bogart
7+7 54th st. rear
OAKLAND, CA 9+609
USA

P.S. You should make necklaces w/ mini hairspray cans

BIG HAIR FOREVER!
ALTHOUGH NOT FOR EVERYONE, BIG HAIR WILL NEVER DIE. HERE ARE SOME TIPS on how to MAKE YOUR GORGEOUS MANE BIGGER than you EVER HOPED.
STEP ONE: BEGIN WITH A VOLUMIZING OR thickENING SHAMPOO & CONDITIONER.
STEP TWO: Apply a thickENING/voLUMIZING/ texTURE SPRAY + BLAST The ROOTS ON damp, towel dried hair.
STEP THREE: (This one is especially handy for those who aren't talented at brush-work). TURN YOUR head upside down & BLOWDRY YOUR hair, blasting the ROOTS. Don't stop till it's dry. At the very end for 20-30 seconds set your dryer to "COOL" and lightly blow hair. This helps to seal the cuticle.
STEP FOUR: This is an optional step. A good way to add wave to straight hair & build volume ARE HOT ROLLERS.
STEP FIVE: *CRITICAL* Steps 1 thru 4 set you on the right track to big hairdom but if you've Been asleep 'till now - WAKE UP! This is the best & funnest STEP. The lost ART of teasing. A lot of hairdressers dismiss this technique as being "too fifties" but hair hoppers had it right. Being a master is easy, you just have to practice. Start at the back of the crown of the head where it curves. Hold ¼" section of hair straight up and tease in a circular motion (not just up + down.) After each section is teased, spray w/ a strong hold laquer. Move toward the face but stop before the section where you want fullness to begin so that you'll have some hair left to smooth over the nest you just created. If you're confused ask me or an expert tease to show you.
STEP SIX: You want it to Last? BREAK OUT THE HAIRSPRAY!!

Olive Necklace, AW04
Plastic, glass beads, metal alloy

Sandwich Stack Bangle, 2016
Acrylic

BUON APPETITO III
BUON APPETITO
BUON APPETITO
BUON APPETITO
BUON APPETITO
BUON APPETITO
HOT
Pizza
FRESH

BUON APPETITO !!!

Banana Necklace, 2011
Acrylic, metal alloy

Corn on the Cob Necklace, SS12
Acrylic, Swarovski crystals, metal alloy

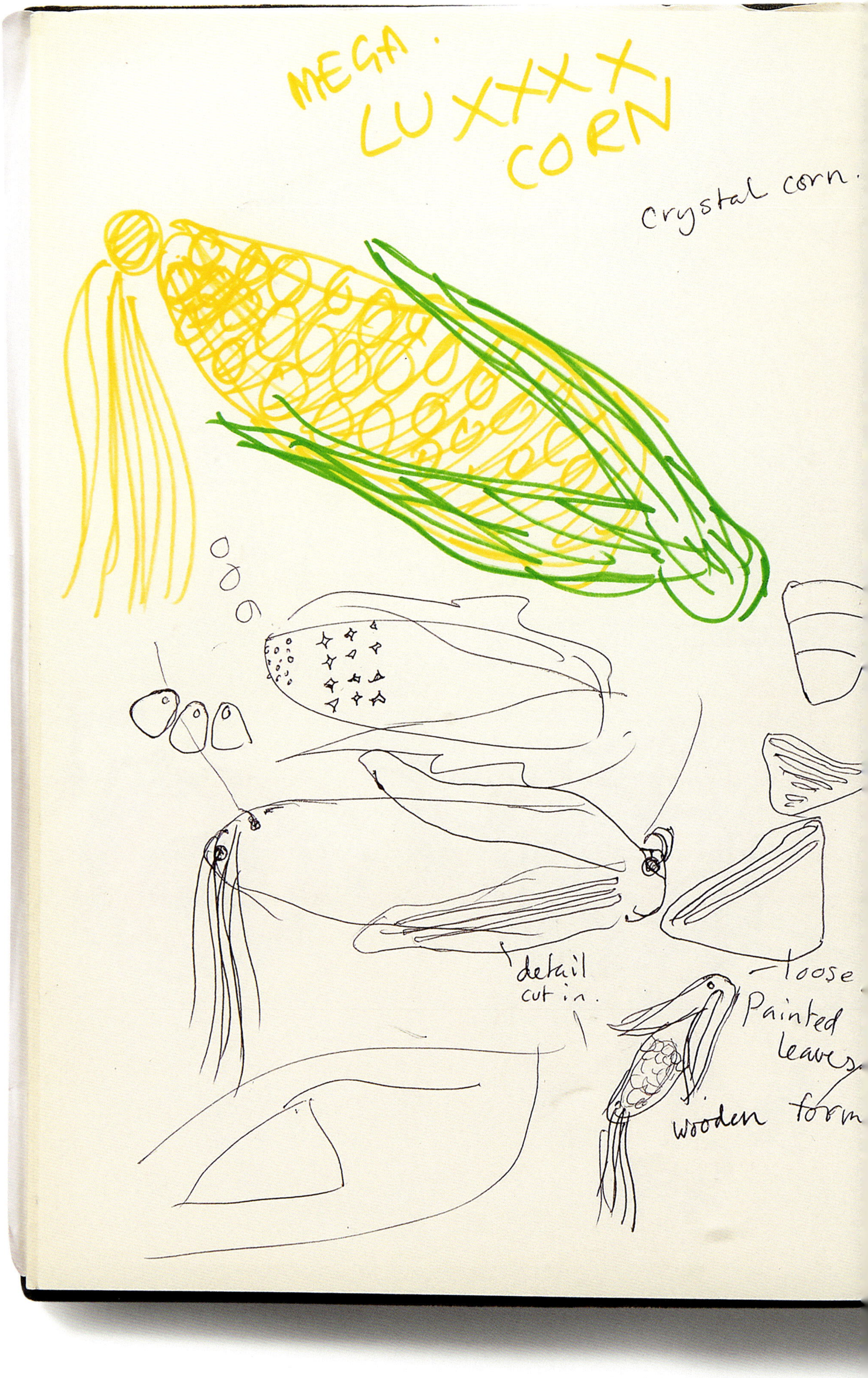
MEGA
LUXXXX
CORN
crystal corn.
detail
cut in.
loose
Painted
leaves
wooden form

3 x 30
crazy crystals
magic eyes.
Clear acrylics or crazy?
double sided Pendent + Big earrings.
Draw:
onkey
orn
kull

Cinco de Mayo
cut outs like paper picado/grids scallops
googley eyes.
Yellow
green multi coloured.
pinking shears/scallo
+CROWN
Heart gem in centre
Yellow
MAGENTA.
8x4 stick ons?
Metal Roses
Crystals
green yellow etch.
Rose stick
pressed glass beads to match colour of Plastic Flower Beads.

dham kirchof
embroidery
etching.
painting
on frost?
white
orange
black
Red/
orange.

Felicity Hayward wearing Squeezy Mustard Necklace and Cheeseburger Necklace, 2014
Photography by Marc Sethi

Cheeseburger Necklace, 2014
Wood, acrylic, Swarovski crystals, metal alloy

Chip Fork Barrette, SS10
Plywood, metal alloy

Harriet and Rosie as Chips and Ketchup, shot for our 2011 book *How to Make Jewellery with Tatty Devine*. Photography by Saga Sig

Harriet at her food-themed 30th birthday party, 2007

Ich liebe
Dich

Fabric invites for shop opening, 2007

We celebrated the move from the Soho shop to our new Seven Dials store with a ceremonial parade. Our friends, relatives and team gathered at the old shop to lock it one last time, then we walked in procession to the new store, accompanied by a small band playing accordion, snare drum and tuba. We carried a specially-designed banner made in laser-cut lining fabric bonded on to yellow satin. We also made mini screenprinted versions and sent them out as invites.

Rosie and Harriet carrying the banner at the parade, 2007

Harriet Vine MBE and Rosie Wolfenden MBE, 2013

In 2012 we received a letter from David Cameron asking if we were happy to be presented with an MBE by the Queen. At first we thought it was a prank, as the paper was so ordinary and unofficial-looking. But it was real and we headed to Buckingham Palace to collect our medals on the 7 June 2013, happily wearing our current favourite pieces of Tatty Devine jewellery, the Emerald Gem Cut Statement Necklace and a Giant Dinosaur Necklace in yellow.

All is Full of Love

Collections *2013–2018*

As time has gone on we have evolved and adapted to Tatty Devine's needs. In 2013 we decided it was time for Harriet to start art directing the campaign shoots, to give them a more holistic feel and carry through the storytelling from conception to customer. With this shift, the subject matter of the seasonal collections became more idiosyncratic and Harriet started exploring ideas and fascinations in great detail meaning that the jewellery got more detailed too. In 2016 we took the further step of making each piece from the seasonal collections in a limited edition. They became more valued by the customer and more sought-after. Our obsession with collecting had finally rubbed off on our customers! We were starting to design several collections a year and more and more collaborations, bringing the number of annual designs up to 350 in 2014. The team was at its peak of 60 people when we 'popped up' with our Name Necklace concessions in Selfridges, making on-the-spot necklaces in London, Manchester and Birmingham. People were going crazy for personalisation and everyone had to have a Name Necklace.

FIELD
EQUATION
SEROTONIN

Head in the Clouds, AW13
Photography by Jonny Storey

The Head in the Clouds collection saw Harriet art directing her first campaign shoot. She inveigled her way into a classroom and laboratory at Imperial College London and as this email shows, she had a very eclectic vision for the photographs.

I have chosen to focus on the "Skylab/Solar storm" jewellery from the collection. The premise of the shoot is a cute 1967 English groupie-type girl (Pattie Boyd-esque), in her other life as an astronomer/physicist, looking at the stars from her lab with her bright red telescope. Old reference textbooks help her to find the meeting point between science and romance. Think science labs, statement jewellery, chair-stacking like in Poltergeist and odd school room furniture arrangements, telescopes, oversized glamorous glasses looking like safety eyewear, beautiful leather gloves taking the place of rubber ones... She is listening to Silver Machine by Hawkwind, Disraeli Gears by Cream and the Bonzo Dog Doo-Dah Band. She loves the illustration of Peter Max, and her heros are Bruce Lacey and Vivienne Stanshall but really she fancies George Harrison.

Saturn Statement Necklace, AW13
Photography by Jonny Storey

Astronomy Bangle, AW13
Acrylic, Swarovski crystals

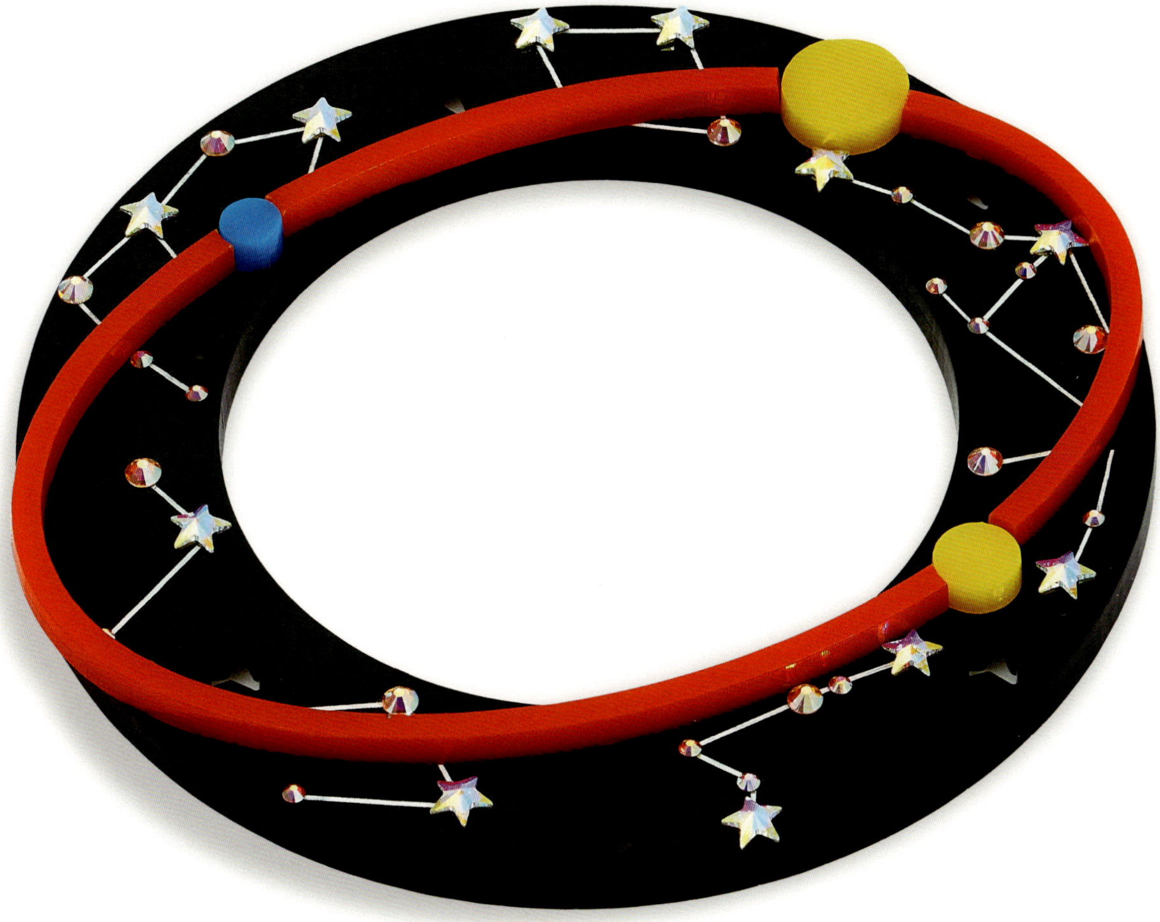

Autumn / Winter 2013

Avant Garde Robot Bib Necklace

Avant Garde Robot Brooch

Jewel Print Brooch

Jewel Print Earrings

Jewel Print Necklace

Jewel Print Triple Necklace

Jewel Print Statement Necklac

Gem Cut Statement Necklace - green | gold | ruby

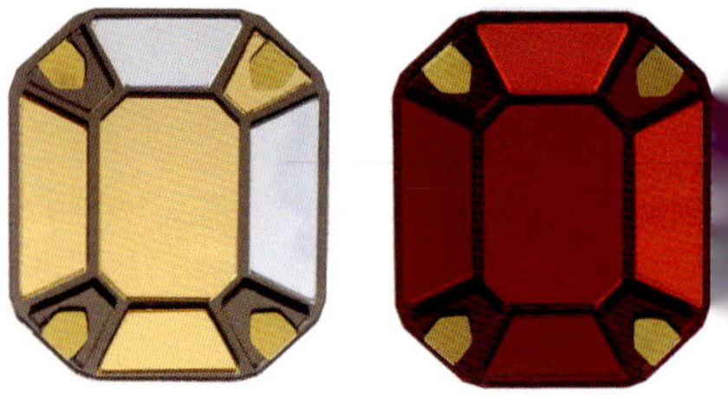

Gem Cut Brooch - green | gold | ruby

Gem Cut Pendant - green | gold | ruby

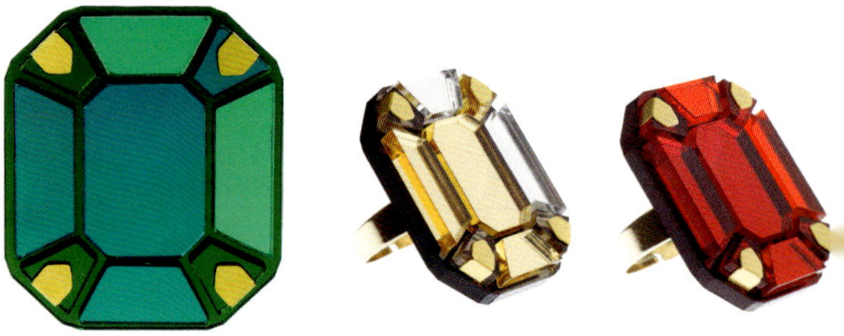

Gem Cut Ring - green | gold | ruby

Head In The Clouds Brooch

Head In The Clouds Collar Necklace

Head In The Clouds Earrings

Head In The Clouds Headband

Head In The Clouds Rainbow Neck

una Moon Brooch

La Luna Moon Earrings - gold | opal

La Luna Moon Large Necklace - gold | opal

La Luna Moon Small Necklace - gold | opal

hedelic Heart Brooch

Psychedelic Heart Earrings

Psychedelic Heart Large Necklace

Psychedelic Heart Ring

Psychedelic Heart Small Necklace

Psychedelic Link Necklace

Psychedelic Love Necklace

Planet Brooch - amber | red

Planet Necklace - amber | red

Planet Ring - amber | red

Planetary System Necklace

Saturn Charm Bracelet

Saturn Solar System Beaded Necklace

Saturn Orbit Earrings

Saturn Planet Earrings

Saturn Planet Necklace

Saturn Statement Necklace

y Lab Astronomy Bangle

Sky Lab Astronomy Earrings

Sky Lab Astronomy Necklace

Sky Lab Bear Brooch

Sky Lab Rabbit Brooch

Sky Lab Rabbit Necklace

Avant Garde Robot Face Necklace, AW13
Acrylic, metal alloy

Our friends Nick Abrahams and Jeremy Deller had made such an intriguing film about the great eccentric artist and performer Bruce Lacey that we immediately went away and studied his work. We were so taken with Lacey's robot, Rosa Bosom, that we made the Avant Garde Robot Face Necklace as a tribute to her being entered into the Alternative Miss World competition.

Gem Cut Statement Necklace, AW13
Acrylic, metal alloy, brass

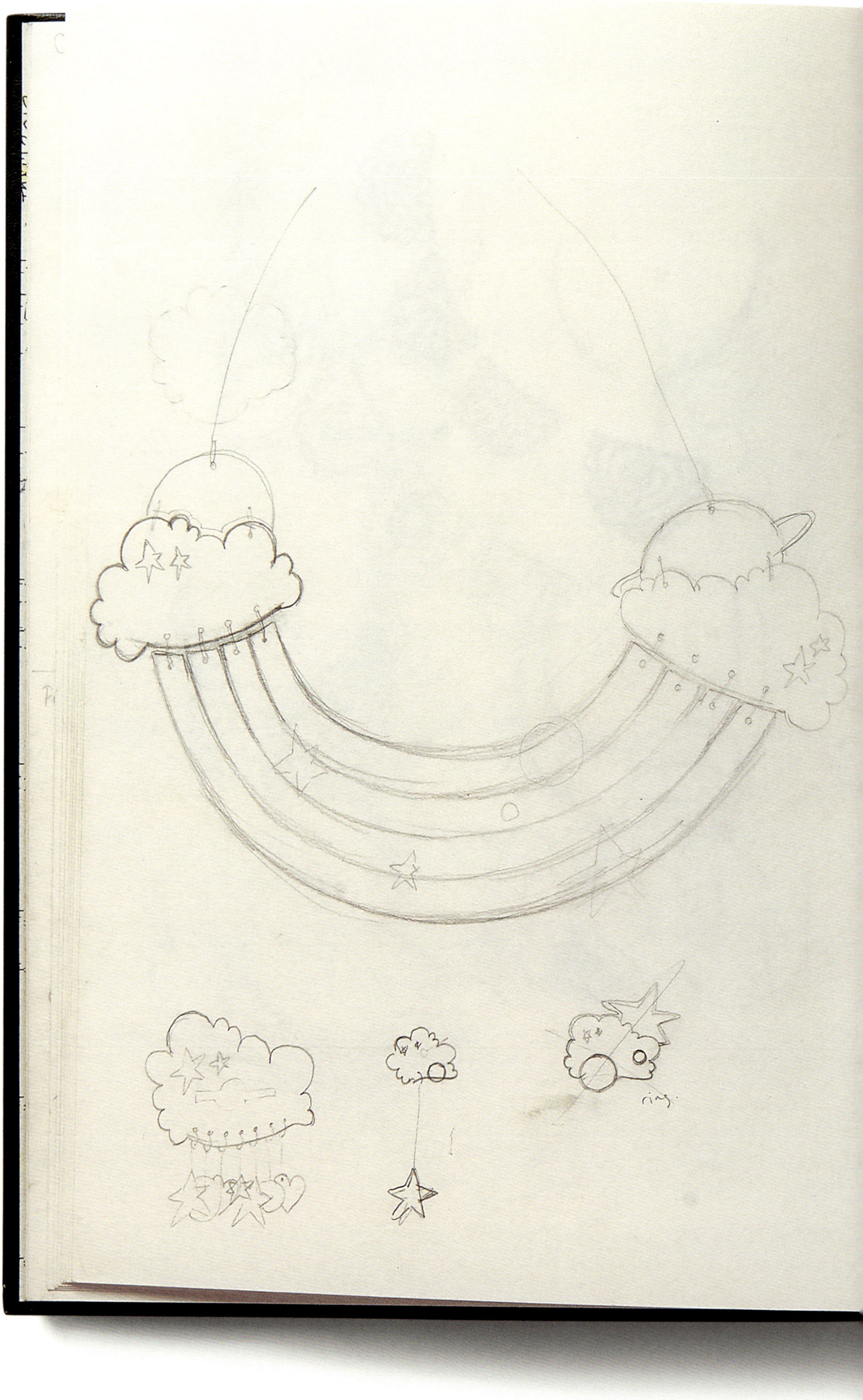
ring.

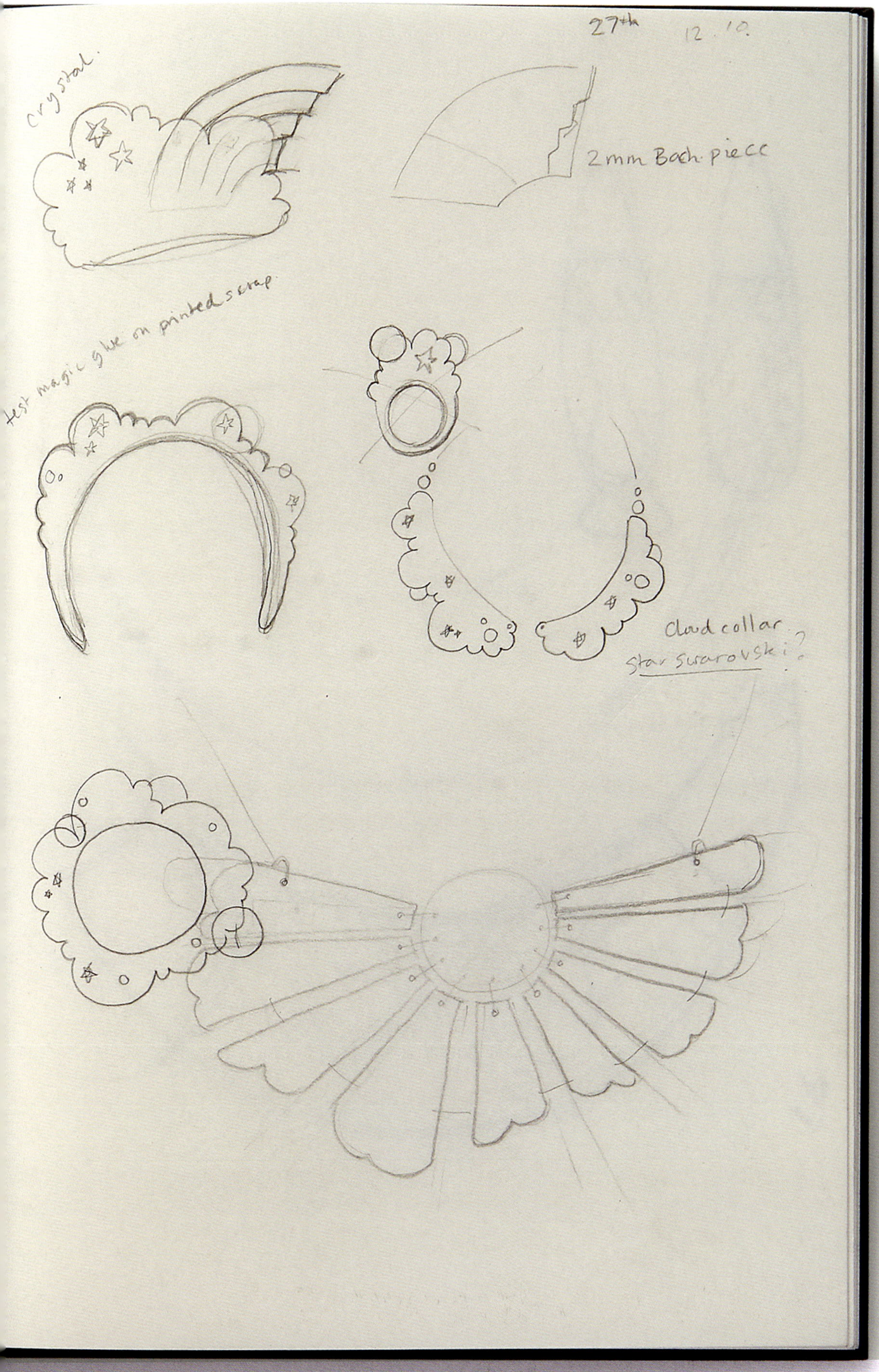
27th 12.10.
crystal.
2mm Bach piece
test magic glue on printed scrap
Cloud collar.
star swarovski?

Impossible Spaces, SS14
Photography by Catherine Laura

The SS14 collection celebrated the spirit of exploration and captured the magical depths of oceans and outer space – places we've always been drawn to. The lenticular card at the centre of the Mission Control Necklace was made with the help of the last lenticular-maker in England, who helped us to create the illusion of travelling through the galaxy towards Earth. The Ruffle Waves Necklace was a feat of acrylic engineering – we made a custom mould to bend the flat sheet of acrylic into a delicate curve without splitting or smudging the sheen of the material.

Mission Control Necklace, AW14
Acrylic, metal alloy, Swarovski crystals,
lenticular card

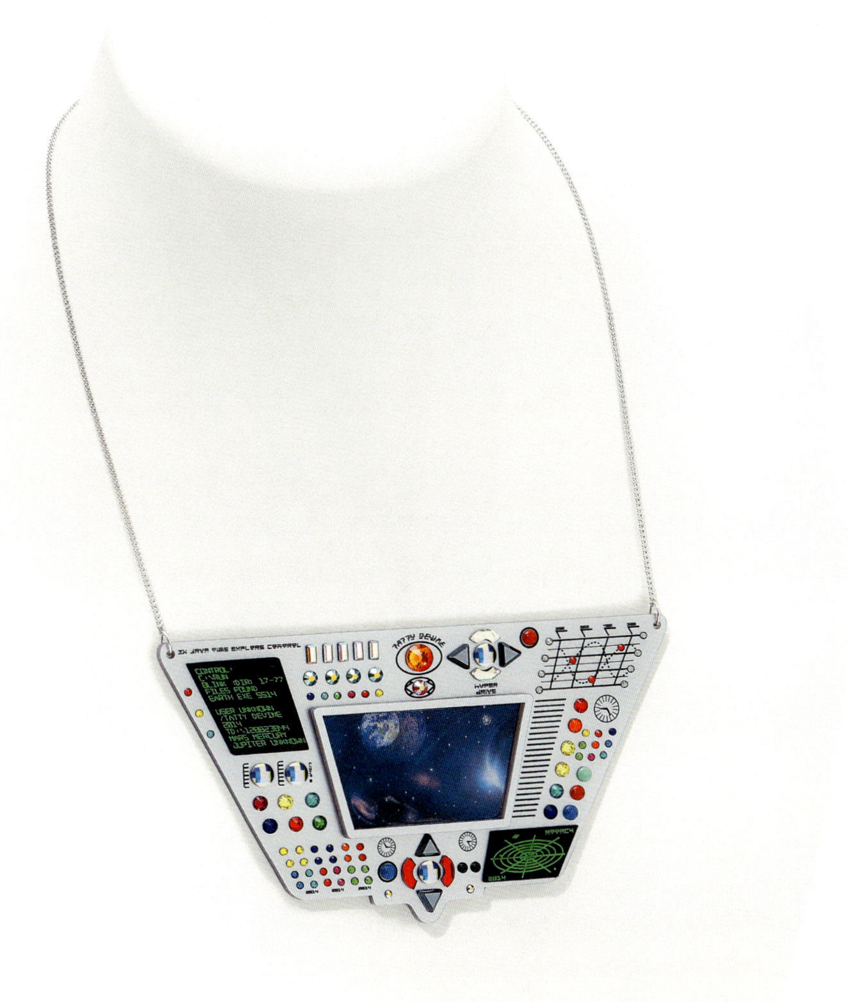

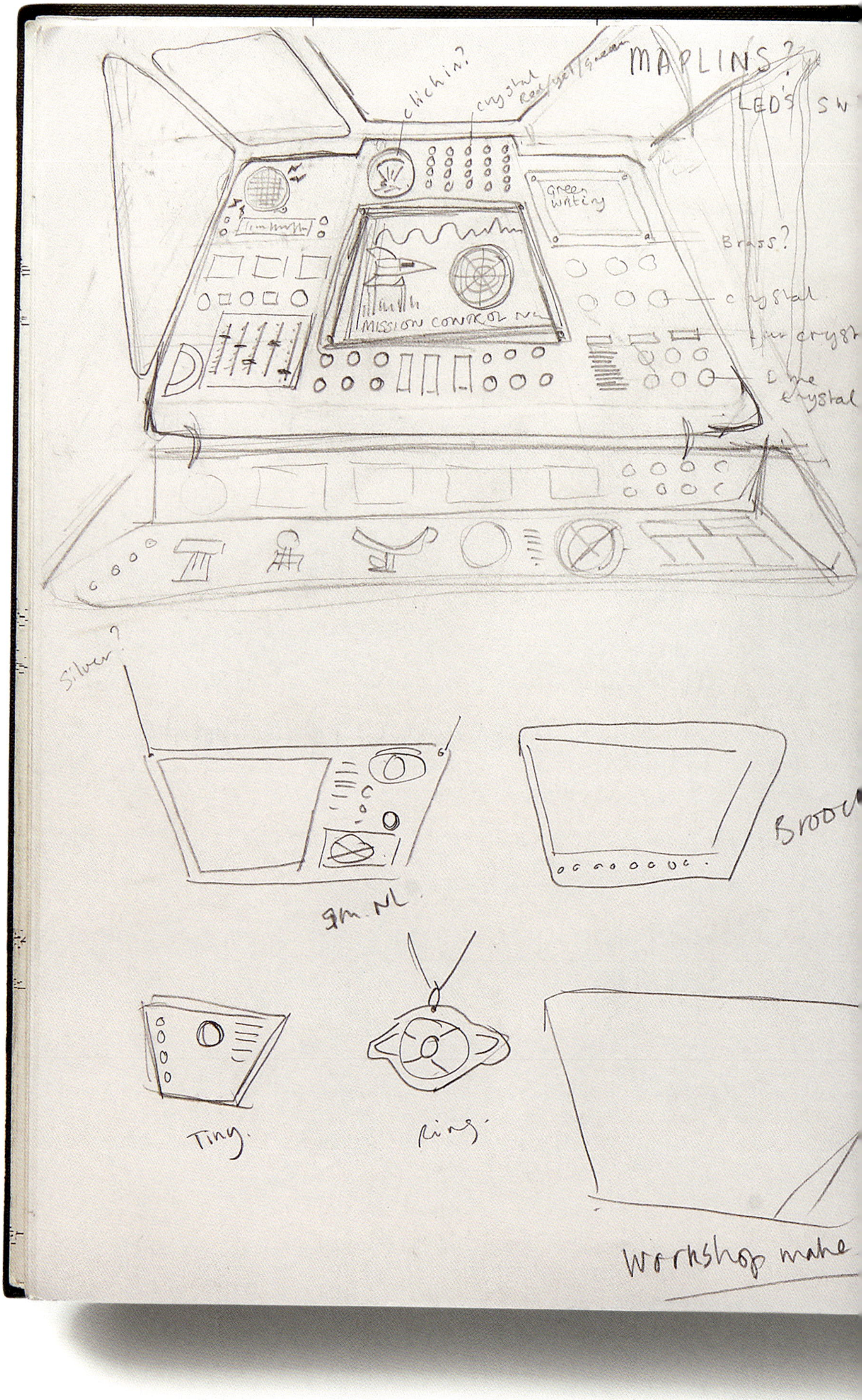
MAPLINS?
LED's
clickin?
crystal
green writing
Brass?
crystal
MISSION CONTROL NL
Silver?
Ting.
Ring.
Workshop make

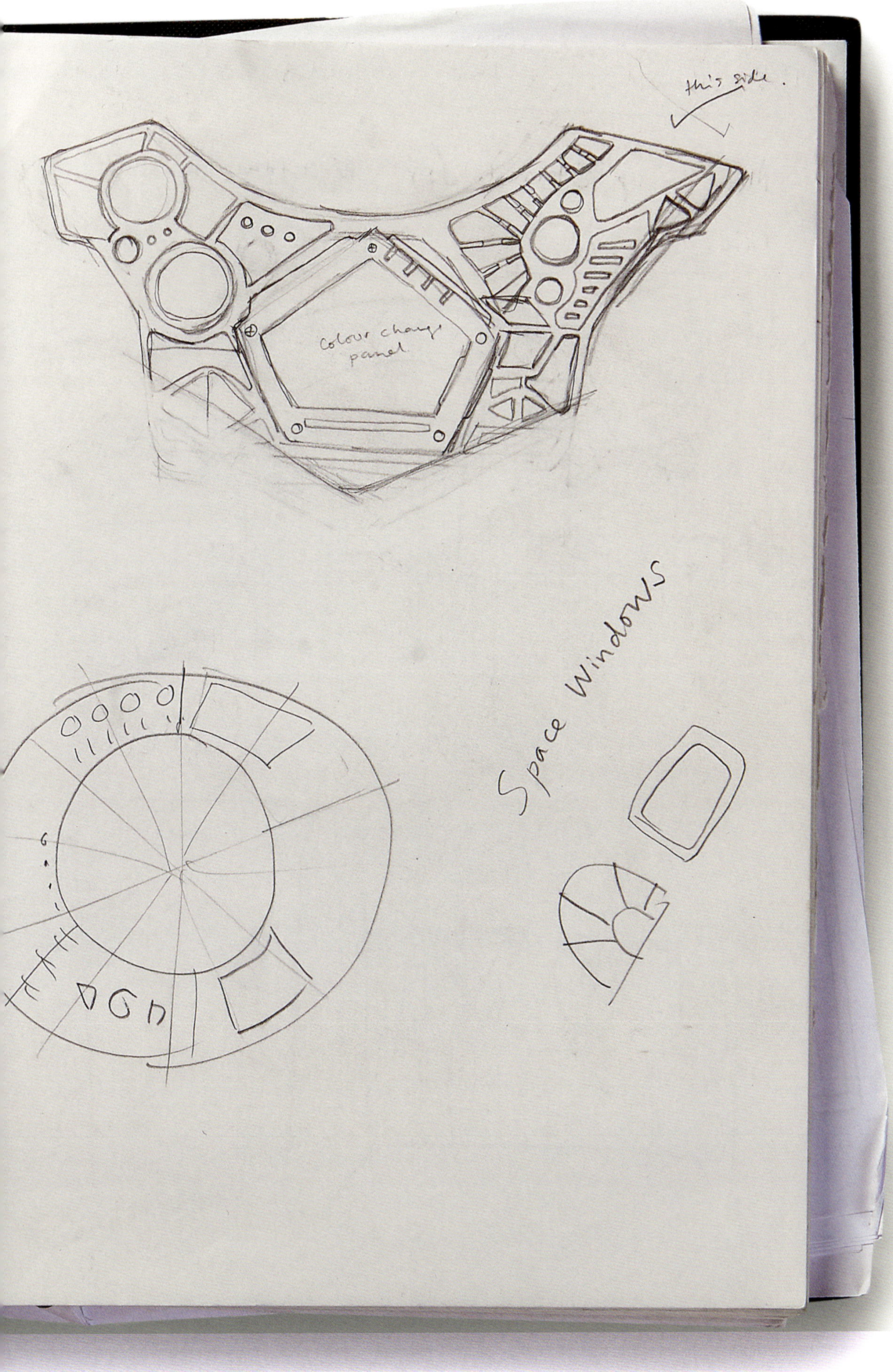
this side.
Colour change panel
Space Windows

Ruffle Necklace, SS14
Photography by Catherine Laura

This was such an ambitious and challenging underwater shoot – the water was freezing in the swimming pool, the make-up had to be waterproof and the jewellery behaved in an entirely unexpected way. It ended up looking beautiful.

Shell Grotto Statement Necklace, SS14

Psychokinetic Gypsy collection, AW14

There are times when the concept for a collection can be a little hard to pin-point. We'll have an inkling of an idea, but we have to give it time to develop. We'd been thinking about magic of all kinds for the Psychokinetic Gypsy collection, but it was watching Ghostbusters over the Christmas holiday, and the brilliance of the mind-reading scene in the film, that made everything click into place. It made us remember that we both thought we had magical powers as children and so the jewellery celebrated the mystic arts of fortune-telling, divination and female power.

Alpine Statement Necklace, AW14
Photographer Rebecca Miller

We were fascinated by the elaborate decorations on Eastern European folk costume, and were determined to capture its delicacy in jewellery form.

Séance Hands Necklace, AW13

Mock Tudor collection, SS15
Photography by Jonathan West

We'd been on a trip to Hever Castle and the Weald and Downland Living Museum to research the Tudor era. Just by chance, we happened to drive down a cul-de-sac where all the houses were 1970s mock Tudor. We liked the playfulness of the two very different ideas existing side by side in the jewellery.

Knot Garden Statement Necklace, SS15
Acrylic, metal alloy

The Knot Garden Necklace tested our mettle on the making front. Knot gardens are meant to look like the over and under threads used in needlework patterns, like outdoor tapestries. Plants and thread are much easier to work with than hot acrylic, which has to be heated in the oven until it's malleable enough to weave into this intricate design.

FRENCH WITHOUT TEARS

Tudor Manor Statement Necklace, SS15
Walnut wood, metal alloy

Memphis Dream collection, AW15
Photography by Holly Falconer

We were thinking about the Memphis Group when we designed the Memphis Dream collection. The Italian designers revelled in references to art deco, pop art and 1950s kitsch, and we adopted their riotous attitude and combined it with our love for the graphics from music magazine *Smash Hits*, Pee-wee Herman and the patterns on ceramics. We used a studio for the shoot, and piled it high with props, including set designer Kerry Hughes' paper house plants and a TV – a surreal backdrop for the models, who are lookalikes of the women in Robert Palmer's Addicted to Love video.

spider plant
necklace
domed

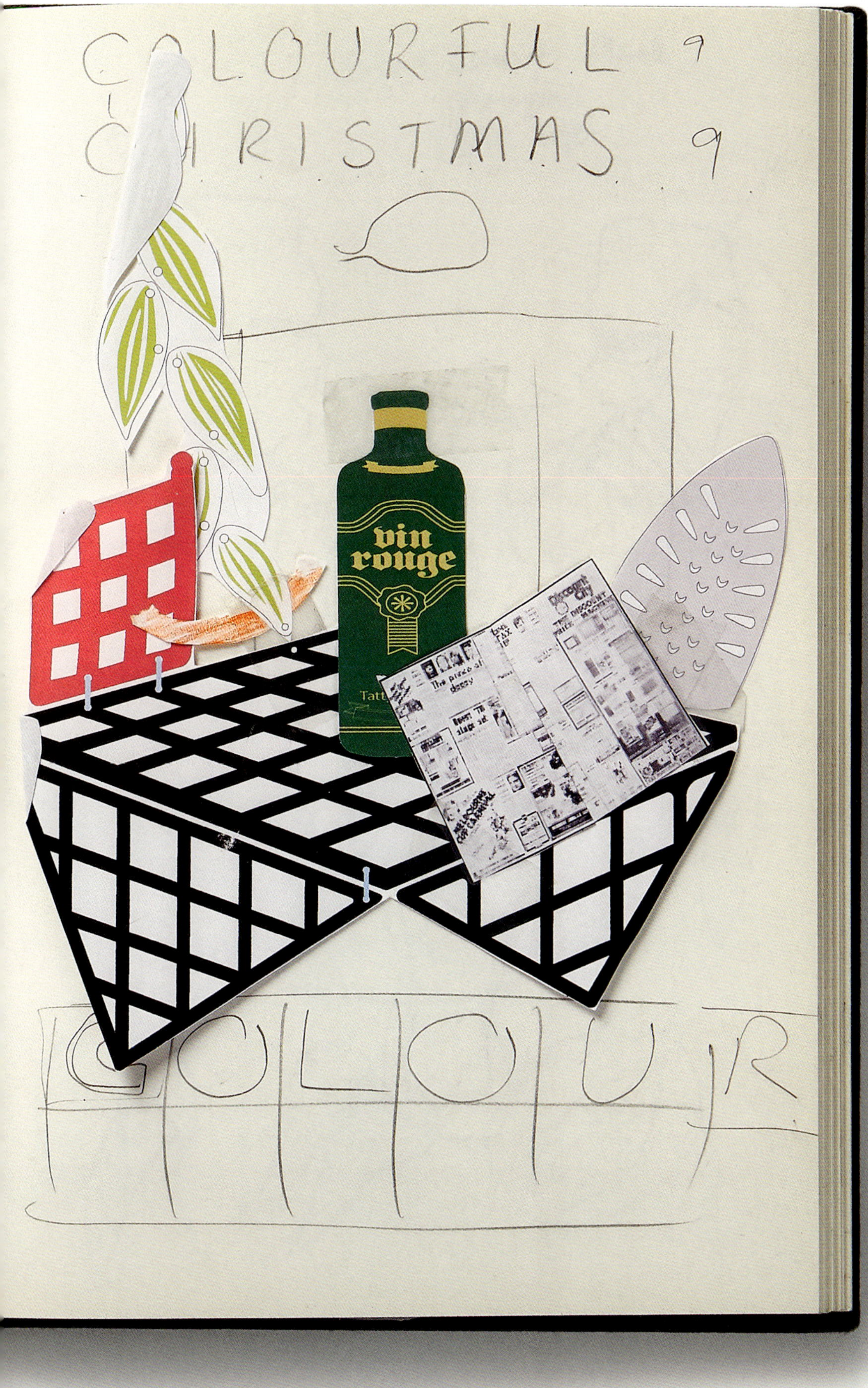
COLOURFUL
CHRISTMAS
vin rouge
COLOUR

Eighties Phone Necklace, SS15
Acrylic, metal alloy

Magazine Collage Necklace, AW15
Photography by Holly Falconer

Skies of Antiquity collection, SS16
Photography by Holly Falconer

Skies of Antiquity was our first limited edition seasonal collection; each piece of jewellery came with a certificate of authenticity. Harriet went to Rome for a speedy 24 hours to shoot the imagery for a collection that headed off on a Grand European Tour, with nature, Roman architecture and trompe l'oeil as stopping-off points. Rain was promised, but luckily there wasn't a cloud in the sky.

NEW PENCE
10

Fountain Statement Necklace, SS16, edition of 50
Acrylic, Swarovski crystals

Play the Part collection, AW16

Pollack's Toy Museum in London is one of our favourite places. We've spent hours trawling through the vast collection of vintage toys housed there. There are three floors, steep narrow stairs and dimly-lit rooms packed with folk dolls, puppets and toy theatres. We also have a shared history with the museum – their address in the early 1960s up until the late 1980s was 44 Monmouth Street in Covent Garden, and that's where you'll find a Tatty Devine shop today.

Scenery Statement Necklace, AW16, edition of 50
Acrylic, printed acrylic, metal alloy,
Swarovski crystals

Harriet hand-drew the scenery and then it was screenprinted onto the acrylic. Each section is held together with headpins.

Textiles Stitch Necklace, AW16
Photography by Holly Falconer

The Textiles Stitch Necklace is laser-cut with a pinking shear edge, and curved by hand to mimic gathered fabric. Then it's 'sewn' together with chain, and finished off with a laser-cut pin and needle. We made the pin by sewing in half a double ended knitting needle and gluing a bead to the top.

The Art of Wasting Time collection, SS17
Photography by Yeon You

Things were hectic in 2016, and the idea of spare time seemed like an impossible dream as we juggled running a business with family life. Just the idea of doing the crossword entirely uninterrupted was beyond reach, so we began to imagine what it would be like to have the time to take up a hobby – and Japanese flower arranging came to mind. It seemed so elegant and serene, and so we mixed elements of kimono prints and sprays of flowers in the Kimono Bloom Statement Necklace.

Kimono Bloom Statement, SS17, edition of 25
Acrylic, metal alloy

Pills Statement Necklace, SS17, edition of 50
Acrylic, metal alloy

We both devoured the iconic 1966 book *Valley of the Dolls* by Jacqueline Susann. It's the inspiration for the Pills Statement Necklace, with its oversized capsules and pills laser-cut in colourful acrylic. A variation of this was sold at the Wellcome Collection for their Can Graphic Design Save Your Life? exhibition.

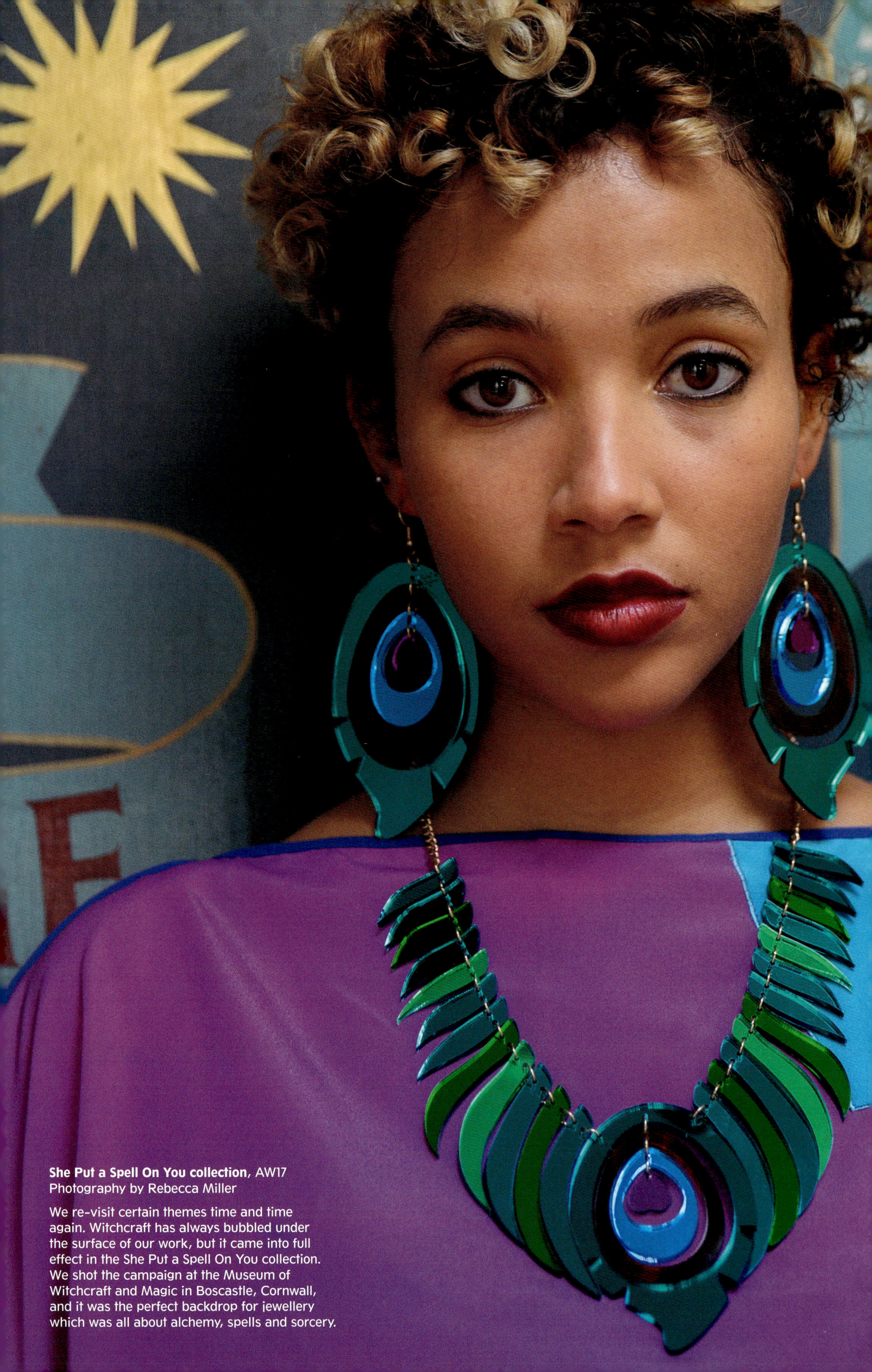

She Put a Spell On You collection, AW17
Photography by Rebecca Miller

We re-visit certain themes time and time again. Witchcraft has always bubbled under the surface of our work, but it came into full effect in the She Put a Spell On You collection. We shot the campaign at the Museum of Witchcraft and Magic in Boscastle, Cornwall, and it was the perfect backdrop for jewellery which was all about alchemy, spells and sorcery.

STAR

The Alchemist Necklace, AW17, edition of 50
Acrylic, metal alloy, leather

Secret Spell Statement Necklace, AW17, edition of 25
Acrylic, Swarovski crystals, metal alloy

Sketchbook, 2017

Here's the initial drawing for the Secret Spell Statement Necklace. We made a test version in paper to see how the necklace would sit on the body. We try things out on paper first: it's the easiest way to discover if a piece needs adjustment, needs to be re-shaped or re-sized.

crystal
Rose
Patina
Opels?
enough
perspex?
purple?
amethysts
Lorem ipsum dolor sit amet.
Lorem ipsum dolor sit amet.
Lorem ipsum dolor sit amet.
Forever for everyone
who believes in themselves
and forever

Spring Forth and Break Through collection, SS18
Photography by Xanthe Hutchinson

Harriet went to a performance of Stravinsky's The Rite of Spring in a car park in Peckham, and enjoyed the combination of wild nature and an urban environment. The fact that the original production caused a riot made it an even more impressive achievement. We like the idea that art, music and jewellery can be beautiful and provocative.

Orchestra Statement Necklace, SS18, edition of 25
Acrylic, metal alloy

Bluebell Statement Necklace prototype, SS18
Paper, metal alloy

EMMA
RICHARDS
AROUND ALONE
BOBBY SCHENK
ACROSS THE WESTERN
Sailing Ships
Then We Sailed Away
Mike Peyton
QUALITY TIME?
Roland Denk
Goodenough

Liminal Fantasy collection, AW18
Photography by Xanthe Hutchinson

Twilight, dusk and near dark are the best time to tell stories. As Liminal Fantasy took in fantasy fiction, fairytales and folklore, a photoshoot in the country's second largest bookshop seemed the perfect setting. The Milky Way Necklace pays homage to the Egyptian Goddess, Nut, a nude, blue, star-sprinkled woman who arched over the Earth as the personification of the sky and the heavens. Her breast milk is said to have created the Milky Way. Sometimes stories are more believable than science.

Calla Lily Statement Necklace, AW18, edition of 50
Acrylic, metal alloy

Two For Joy

Collaborations

Our friendship is at the heart of everything we do. From the first moment we met we've shared ideas and obsessions, and as soon as we started Tatty Devine we talked non-stop about all the things we wanted do or make, and that conversation has continued down the years. We know each other so well that we can finish each other's sentences. We look at the world in the same way, with our heads slightly tilted, so that our view is slightly skewed – a perspective that influences the way we work and the work we make. It's always great to collaborate with artists, musicians, institutions and causes who approach their world in a similar way.

Art

We have always surrounded ourselves with art and artists so its not surprising that we have collaborated with quite a few.

Mark Pawson

Before we met Mark Pawson, we'd read about him. He was 'a self-confessed image junkie, photocopier fetishist and Print Gocco fiend' and was known for his DIY mail art, books, postcards, badges, multiples and other essential ephemera. Mark loves badges so much he has created a Tatty Devine badge for every significant Tatty Devine moment over the last twenty years.

Free Stuff party invite, 2000

We met Mark in 2000 at his Free Stuff party, a rooftop frenzy of stuff-swapping. Mark had written a piece on encouraging people to swap stuff for Bay Garnett's zine, *Cheap Date*, and was putting his words into action.

FREE STUFF PARTY & BBQ Sat 23rd June

You are invited to the long awaited second FREE STUFF PARTY !
For this occasion we have secured a glamorous outdoor rooftop location, which will allow us to combine the FREE STUFF PARTY with a Barbecue.

Arrive from 2pm onwards, and get ready to climb the mountain of FREE STUFF at 4pm!

Bring your unwanted Junk, Bring a friend, Bring something to BBQ.

Saturday 23rd June, 2pm-6pm
6a Silesia Buildings, Hackney E8 3PX
(just by London Fields)
Tube; Bethnal Green
Buses; 26,48,55,106,236,253,276,277.

What the heck is this all about?? Call Mark Pawson
020 8983 1738

Open and Closed Necklace, 2003
Acrylic, metal alloy

In 2003 we made the Open and Closed Necklace with Mark, followed by full sized Open and Closed shop signs, which grace shop doors around Britain, including our own.

After finding a 1970s Open and Closed handmade sign in a north London car boot sale I envisaged the necklace version that I could make with Tatty Devine, so a meeting was arranged. In the studio the worktable was covered with a large sheet of paper covered with drawings of the forthcoming collection. Fortuitously I'd come at just the right time. I showed Harriet and Rosie a couple of drawings and explained the concept of the necklace, we discussed some practical questions about size, Perspex colours and chain length and then there was a pause. Harriet and Rosie silently exchanged glances, then smiled and said: 'Great, can we have the finished artwork in two days' time please?' A perfect collaboration.
Mark Pawson

Rob Ryan

We first met Rob Ryan in 2001 when he helped us print bags and belts. He's now a highly-acclaimed artist specialising in papercuts and limited-edition screenprints. His work is romantic, and his poetic prose expresses his thoughts in a way that's entirely his own.

Everything in My Heart, 2008
Papercut and brooch

Rob's next exhibition was in 2008 with four specially-made papercuts. Each papercut housed a piece of jewellery, which completed the piece. The brooch shows everything in Rob's heart and the papercut went on to show what was in our hearts.

Love Rules invite, 2004

In 2004 Rob held an exhibition in our Brick Lane shop called Love Rules, which was a series of hand-painted giant rulers.

Every Beat of My Heart Necklace, 2013
18-carat gold

We collaborated with Rob Ryan again in 2013 on a very special project. Always struggling to depict paper in acrylic, we decided to create the effect of a sculpted paper necklace using silver and gold.

Whether we like it or not, we do live in a world of instant cultural, artistic and visual gratification. It doesn't take much effort these days to find the things that you relate to and then remake your own versions of them, while still retaining the effrontery to call your endeavours "creative". Not so Rosie and Harriet of Tatty Devine. Their joyful work comes from somewhere deep inside themselves, it literally shines out of them in their smiles. Their love of life and fun and their genuine interest in our world is inextricably woven into what they create – it is all one great wonderful thing. They are both original and the originators, they lead where others follow. They are the real deal and as the great Ashford and Simpson wrote: "Ain't nothing like the real thing!"
Rob Ryan

Gilbert and George

On a trip to San Francisco in 2007 we were invited to the de Young Museum to discuss making jewellery for their forthcoming major retrospective of Gilbert and George, which Tate Modern was touring. We had always been fans of the artists and their work and were always spotting them walk up and down Brick Lane. We loved their 1972 art film Gordon's Makes Us Drunk, in which they drank gin and tonics to a soundtrack of classical music. As part of the collaboration we used the iconic Gordon's gin bottle to create a necklace and brooch: in a nod to their favourite tipple, we used their silhouettes and signature, and borrowed words from their work to make Fear and Hope necklaces. When we asked if we could use their signature, they insisted we put it on everything.

Gilbert and George Gin Necklace, 2008
Photography by Gabriella Antunes

Gilbert and George Silhouette Necklace, 2008
Acrylic, metal alloy

Angel of the North Necklace, 2008
Acrylic, metal alloy

The Baltic Centre for Contemporary Art commissioned us to make a piece of jewellery to celebrate Antony Gormley's sculpture Angel of the North.

Toilet Flush Earrings, 2011
Acrylic, Swarovski crystal, metal alloy

These earrings were one-offs made for the artist Silvia Ziranek, who performed as part of the Dirt exhibition at the Wellcome Collection. Her performance, Not Undirty, was 'a dirty performance (by a clean artist) presenting foul habits, leaking aspirations, fetid humour, and fermenting imagination.'

Warhol Cameo Brooch and Morris Cameo Brooch, 2014
Acrylic, metal alloy

In 2014 we were invited to collaborate with Jeremy Deller. He was curating the Love is Enough exhibition at Modern Art Oxford, which looked at the artistic parallels between Andy Warhol and William Morris. We used their iconic profiles on cameo brooches, with their silhouettes laser-cut in acrylic.

Flamboyant Necklace, 2012
Acrylic, Swarovski crystals,
leather, glass beads, metal alloy

Sue Kreitzman is a London-based New York-born outsider artist who creates amazing paintings and assemblages using bold colour and unwanted objects. This necklace was exhibited at Dare to Wear, an exhibition that was held at the The Crypt Gallery in October 2012 and celebrated flamboyant style.

Magic
Jeremy Deller

Ida Necklace, 2016
Printed acrylic, metal alloy

We first came across illustrator Laura Callaghan's female-centric drawings on Instagram and later at her exhibition at the KK Outlet Gallery in Hoxton and Pick Me Up at Somerset House. We just love the details in her work, and her bold colours and patterns.

Fashion

From the beginning we quickly fell into the rhythm of the fashion world, showing collections at London and Paris Fashion Weeks. We met designers, both established and emerging, and created pieces for their catwalk shows.

Basso & Brooke Weapon Necklace, AW05
Wood, metal alloy

Our first catwalk jewellery was for digital-print pioneers Basso & Brooke in 2005. The collection of hand-painted and varnished brooches and necklaces was based on the drawings and prints in Basso & Brooke's collection. We made hundreds of pieces, sourcing the chain from a furnishing hardware store in Paris.

The Rodnik Band Chips Headband, SS12
Acrylic, elastic

Eley Kishimoto Batmosphere Necklace, 2011
Acrylic, metal alloy

Louise Gray collaboration, 2013
Photography by Fashion East

Pink Lobster Giant Necklace, for Isabella Blow:
Fashion Galore! exhibition at Somerset House, 2013
Acrylic, Swarovski crystals, metal alloy

Clio Peppiatt Hotel Clio Mini Suitcase, AW16
Acrylic, Swarovski crystals, brass

Kit Neale Little Monster Necklace, SS15
Acrylic, Swarovski beads, marabou feather, wood, metal alloy

Matty Bovan Shape Earrings, SS17
Acrylic, glitter, metal alloy

Culture

We often make work that comments on contemporary culture, or make more politically-orientated pieces which champion the need for grassroots action.

100
Happy 100th! This special tiered cake was created exclusively by Tatty Devine in celebration of Selfridges' centenary
PHOTOGRAPHY: LACEY
CAKE: TATTY DEVINE
SET DESIGN: HANA AL-SAYED

100th Birthday Cake, for Selfridges & Co 100, 2009

In 2009, Selfridges asked us to make a Tatty Devine cake to celebrate their 100th birthday, which was displayed at the party and printed in their magazine. It was covered in lots of iconic Tatty Devine shapes including music notes, stars and hearts.

Sushi Bag, for Nintendo Wii, 2007
Acrylic, metal alloy, Swarovski crystals

In 2007, Nintendo commissioned us to create a bag for a new Wii remote controller, based on the new MySims game. We made the Sushi Bag, which is based on Chef Watanabe, a character in the game, who dedicates his life to the art of sushi.

Stonehenge Necklace, for English Heritage, 2017
Acrylic, metal alloy

This necklace is a replica of Stonehenge. We used black glitter acrylic to conjure up the spellbinding way the sun rises over the famous landmark during the summer solstice.

Dog On Wheels Brooch, for Belle and Sebastian, 2010
Acrylic, wood, leather, metal alloy

Ever since we first heard Belle and Sebastian's debut EP Dog on Wheels in 1997 we've been hooked on their music, so we were beyond delighted to make this brooch for them to sell on tour.

Peaches Necklace and signed box, for Peaches, 2009
Acrylic, metal alloy

We saw Peaches perform her first album, The Teaches of Peaches, at 93 Feet East in 2000 which blew our minds – she invited all the ladies to dance on stage with her and the album became part of the soundtrack to our early years. We went on to create a giant version of her name for her to wear when she played at London's Koko in December 2009. She also did a signing at our Brick Lane shop.

Comb, in collaboration with Charlie Le Mindu, 2009
Acrylic

We were introduced to Charlie by our friends from Cabine, and when he moved to London he set up a residency in the Brick Lane shop. You could make an appointment to see Charlie and have your hair transformed. He's gone on to be haute coiffure designer for Lady Gaga, and his work now appears on the heads of catwalk models the world over.

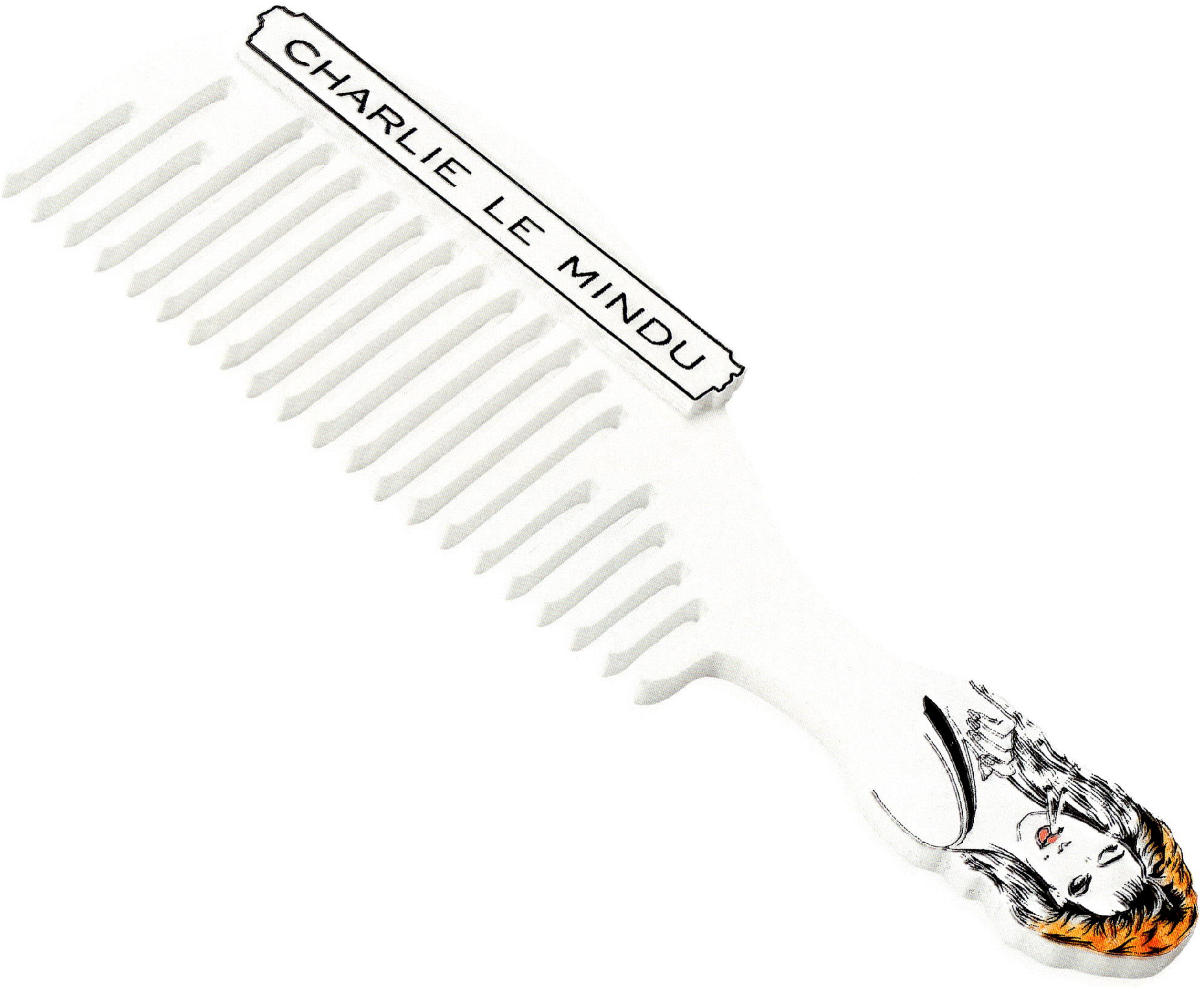

Snoopy Love Heart Necklace, for the Good Grief
Charlie Brown! exhibition at Somerset House, 2018
Acrylic, metal alloy

No More Page Three Necklace,
for No More Page Three campaign, 2013
Acrylic, metal alloy

In 2013 we noticed many customers were ordering Name Necklaces that said 'Feminist', and we realised that they were as passionate about these issues as we were. So when No More Page Three approached us to get involved in their campaign to ban topless photos from *The Sun* newspaper, we made these necklaces. We were ecstatic when *The Sun* withdrew Page Three from the paper. What a result!

Feminist Necklace
Photography by Xanthe Hutchinson

Queer Boy! Brooch, Fucking Faggots! Brooch, Fucking Dyke! Brooch, all in collaboration with The Pansy Project, 2011
Wood, metal alloy

We met artist Paul Harfleet in 2011 at a party and when he told us the story of his work, we felt drawn to collaborate with him. Paul plants pansies on sites of homophobic abuse and then photographs and names the flowers after the horrific words that were said, then posts the images on his website. Paul chose the words and we created three wooden brooches that Paul hand-painted. To date Paul has planted over 300 pansies around the world.

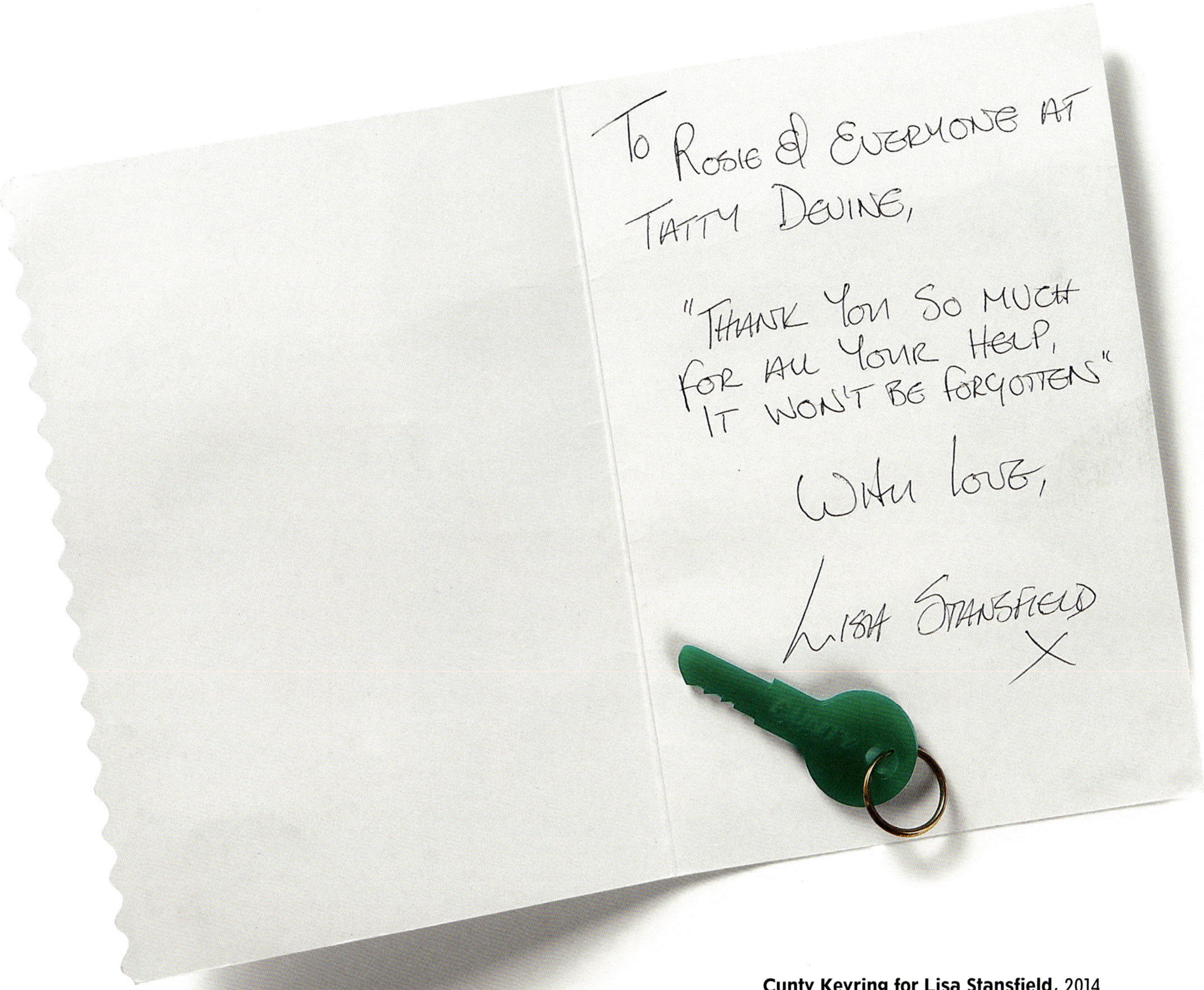
To Rosie & Everyone at
Tatty Devine,
"Thank you so much
for all your help,
it won't be forgotten"
With love,
Lisa Stansfield
X

Cunty Keyring for Lisa Stansfield, 2014
Acrylic, metal alloy

Tatty Devine were asked by singer and actress Lisa Stansfield to create a Cunty Keyring and Necklace to raise awareness of the threat of closure of the Colony Room Club, described by Sebastian Horsley as 'a vibrant, unique and historical drinking den for artists, writers, musicians, actors and their acolytes...' Muriel Belcher ran the Colony Room until the late 1970s, and she used 'cunty' as a term of endearment to her rackety clientele.

EETG Brooch for East End Trades Guild members, 2016
Wood, metal alloy

We are founding members of the East End Trades Guild. The EETG is an alliance of over 300 small independent businesses in East London, all of whom are vital to the local economy and community. We're proud to be part of an organisation that helps protect and promote their rights.

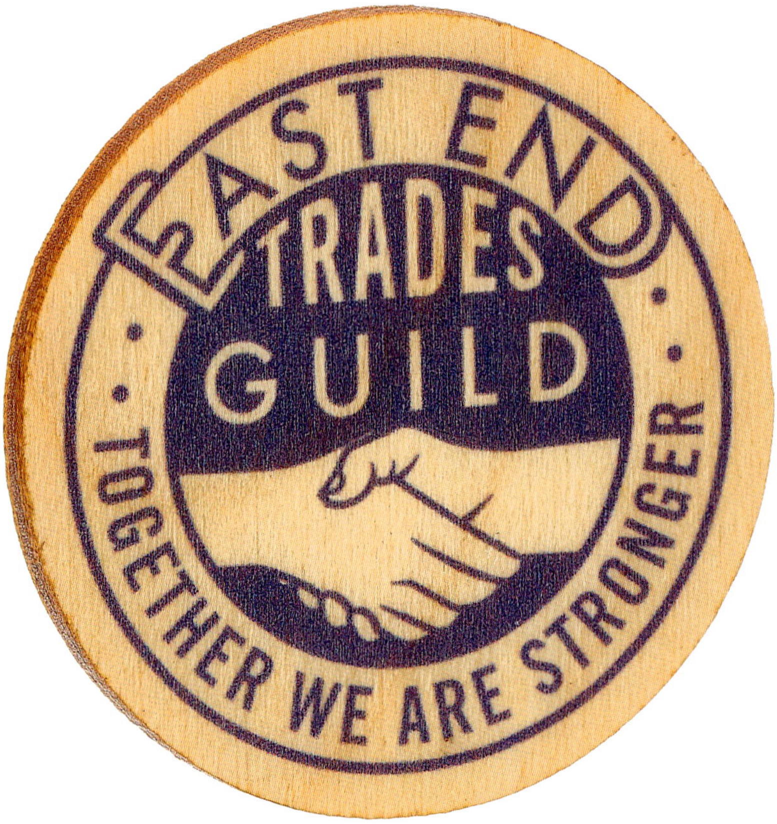

Votes for Women Brooch,
for Museum of London, 2018
Acrylic, metal alloy

Made in partnership with Museum of London as part of Vote 100, celebrating the centenary of women getting the right to vote in the UK.

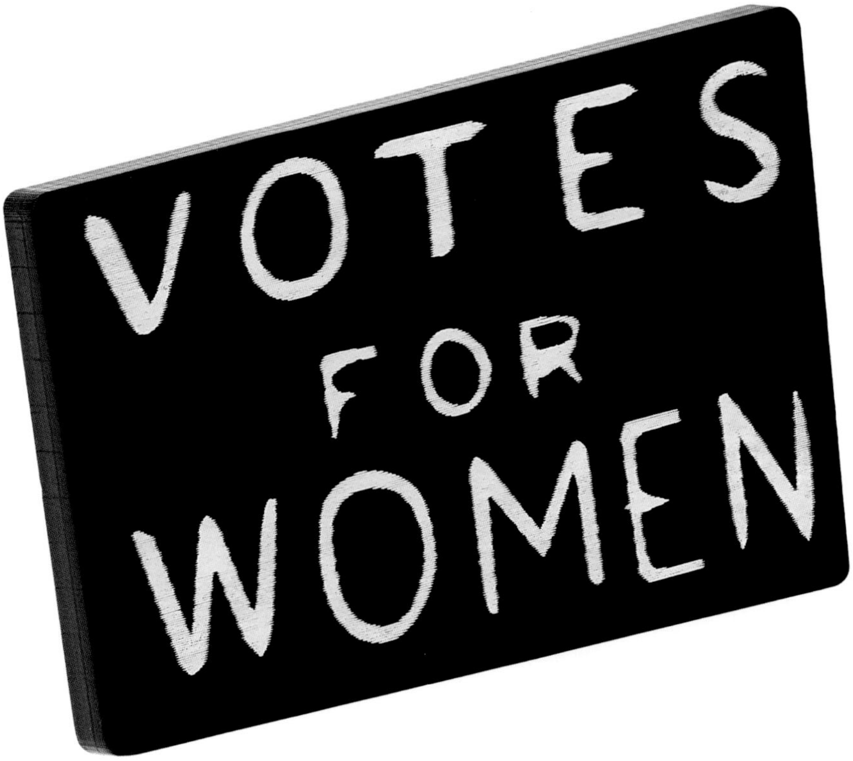

Courage Calls Brooch,
for the Fawcett Society, 2018
Acrylic, metal alloy

In April 2018, we headed down to Parliament Square for the unveiling of Millicent Fawcett's statue – Millicent was a suffragist who made securing women the right to vote her life's work. In celebration of this event, we made a collection of jewellery in partnership with the Mayor of London's office and the Fawcett Society, who are the UK's leading charity campaigning for gender equality and women's rights. The jewellery covered issues from equal pay to anatomy not being a destiny. This is the first ever sculpture of a woman to grace Parliament Square and it's also the first in the square to be created by a woman, artist Gillian Wearing.

I am so excited about Tatty Devine's exclusive collection. The pieces are both fun as well as having deeper political messages. It's great that a donation from each sale will go to the Fawcett Society. I am a huge fan and cannot wait to wear this new jewellery.
Gillian Wearing

Do Your Bit Brooch, in collaboration with Poppy Chancellor, 2018
Acrylic, metal alloy

To mark International Women's Day, we collaborated with artist Poppy Chancellor to produce jewellery relating to six remarkable contemporary women from the creative sector. This brooch celebrates writer, Bwalya Newton, who was inspired by an Angela Davies talk which explained how the world could change if everyone did their bit. We displayed the collection in the month of March at the Southbank alongside the Women of the World festival.

Smashing Stereotypes Necklace,
in partnership with the Fawcett Society, 2019
Acrylic, metal alloy

Creativity for Joy Necklace, 2019
Acrylic, metal alloy

Public Art

In more recent years we've been commissioned to make work for public spaces. These installations have proven to be unique opportunities to bring our ideas to life on a huge scale and tell our story to a wider, public audience.

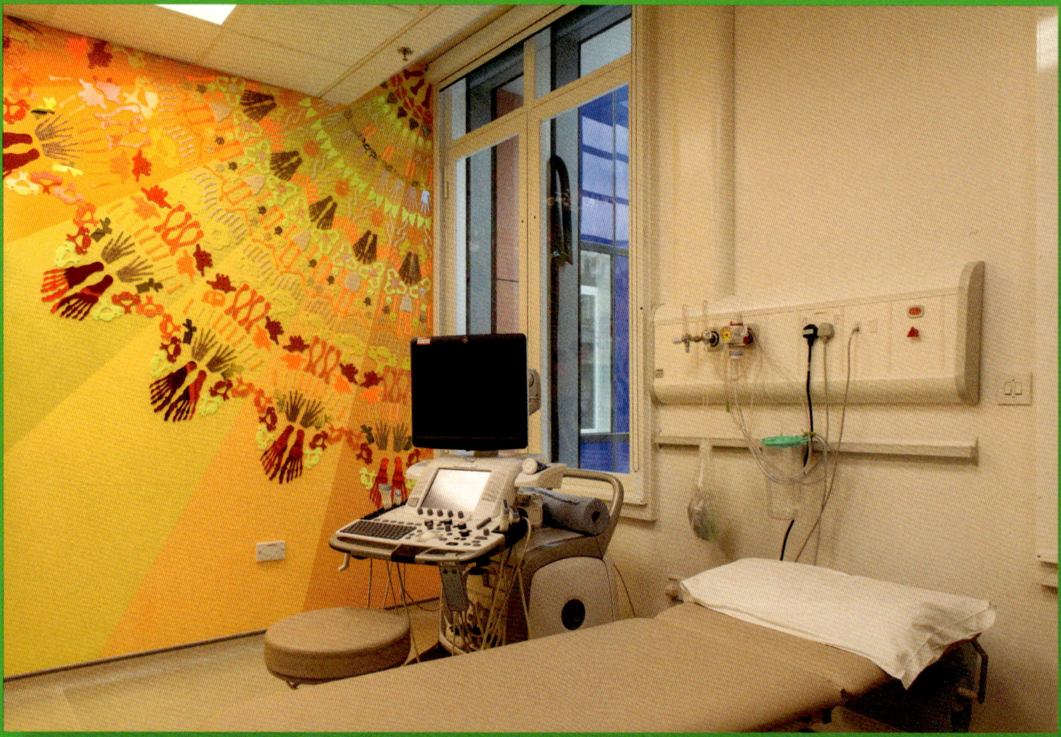

Kaleidoscopic Reflections,
commissioned by Vital Arts, 2016

This installation was created for the children's imaging department at the Royal London hospital, with the intention of helping to make hospital visits a better experience for children and the adults with them. Amongst shapes of bones, Tatty Devine shapes are intermittently placed, giving families a game to play while waiting – can you spot the umbrella?

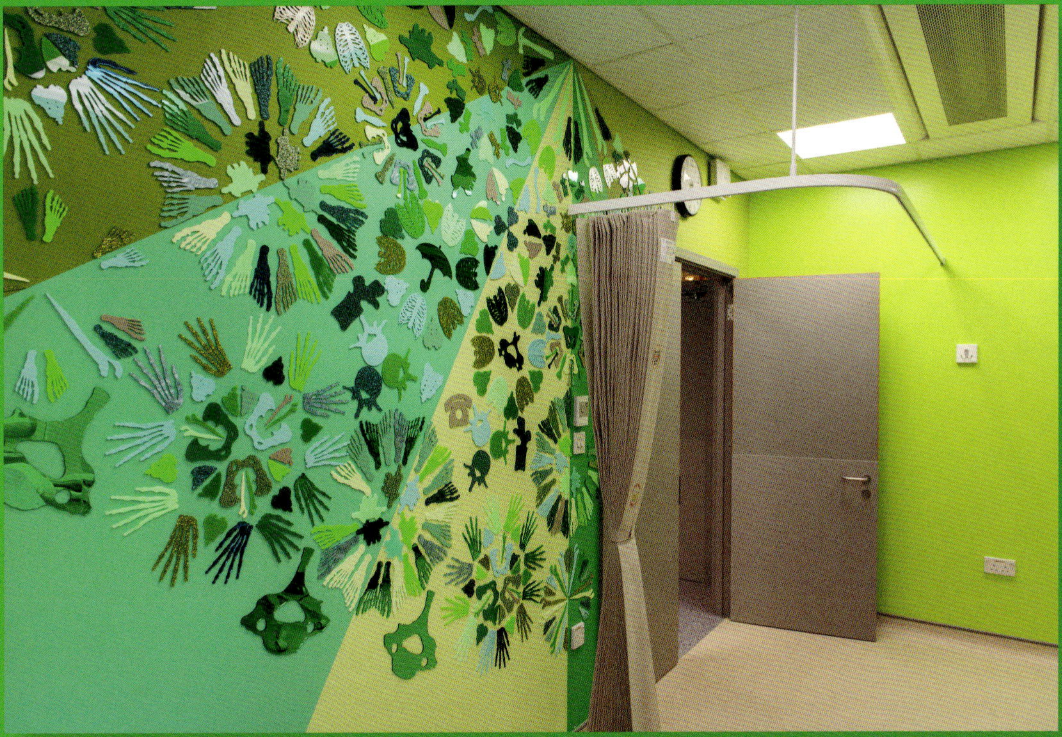

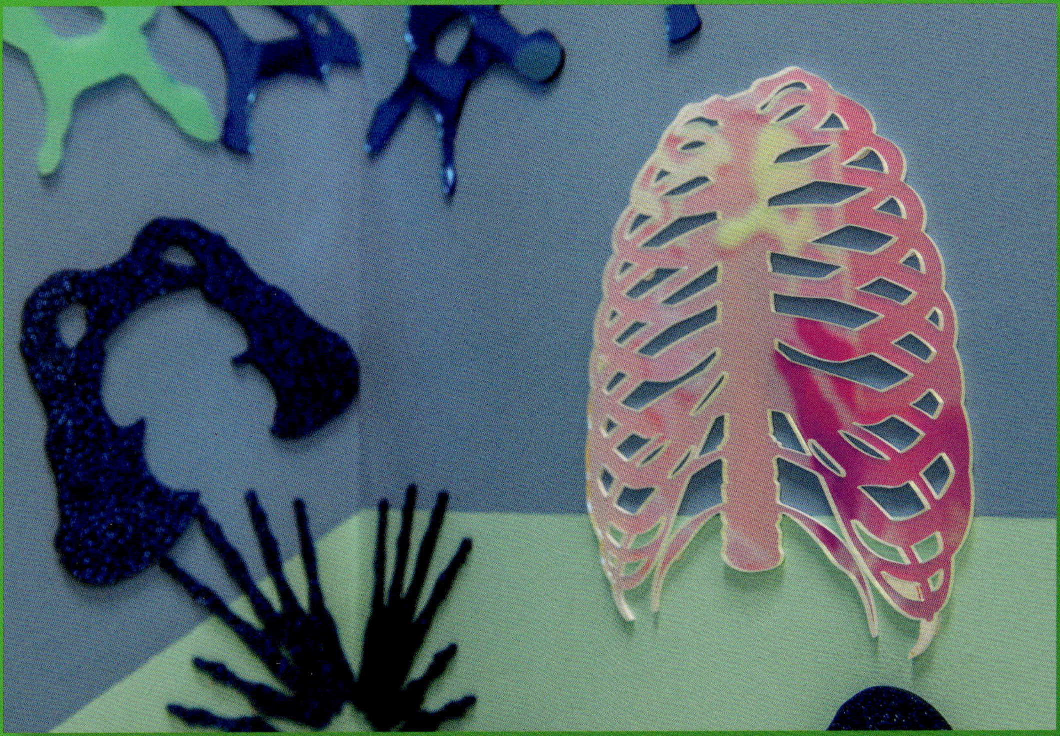

Rainbow Halo, Greenwich Peninsula, London, commissioned by Now Gallery, 2018

The Rainbow Halo was a transformation of our Shooting Star Rainbow Statement Necklace. Each glowing star represented the gifts of love, peace, unity, luck, magic and joy, all in cosmic harmony.

Tatty Devine

Make Your Future

We've absolutely loved writing *Misshapes: The Making of Tatty Devine*, and it's really reminded us how important creativity is – it can be easy to forget that it is a privilege to be cherished. We were brought up in families where making was all around us: our parents and grandparents taught us to sew, knit, do woodwork, cook, draw, think and dream. School and college taught us to think creatively; to take risks.

Reading through our interviews, articles, sketchbooks and diaries in our archive, it's clear that individuality, originality, self-expression and invention have been at the heart of all we do. So it's been shocking to discover the countless ways that creativity is being undermined and undervalued in Britain. The recent years of austerity, plus a change in education policy has meant that the arts have been sidelined. If this continues there will be a generation that won't have had first-hand experience of making and crafting, with all the benefits they bring. And it's not just the arts that will suffer.

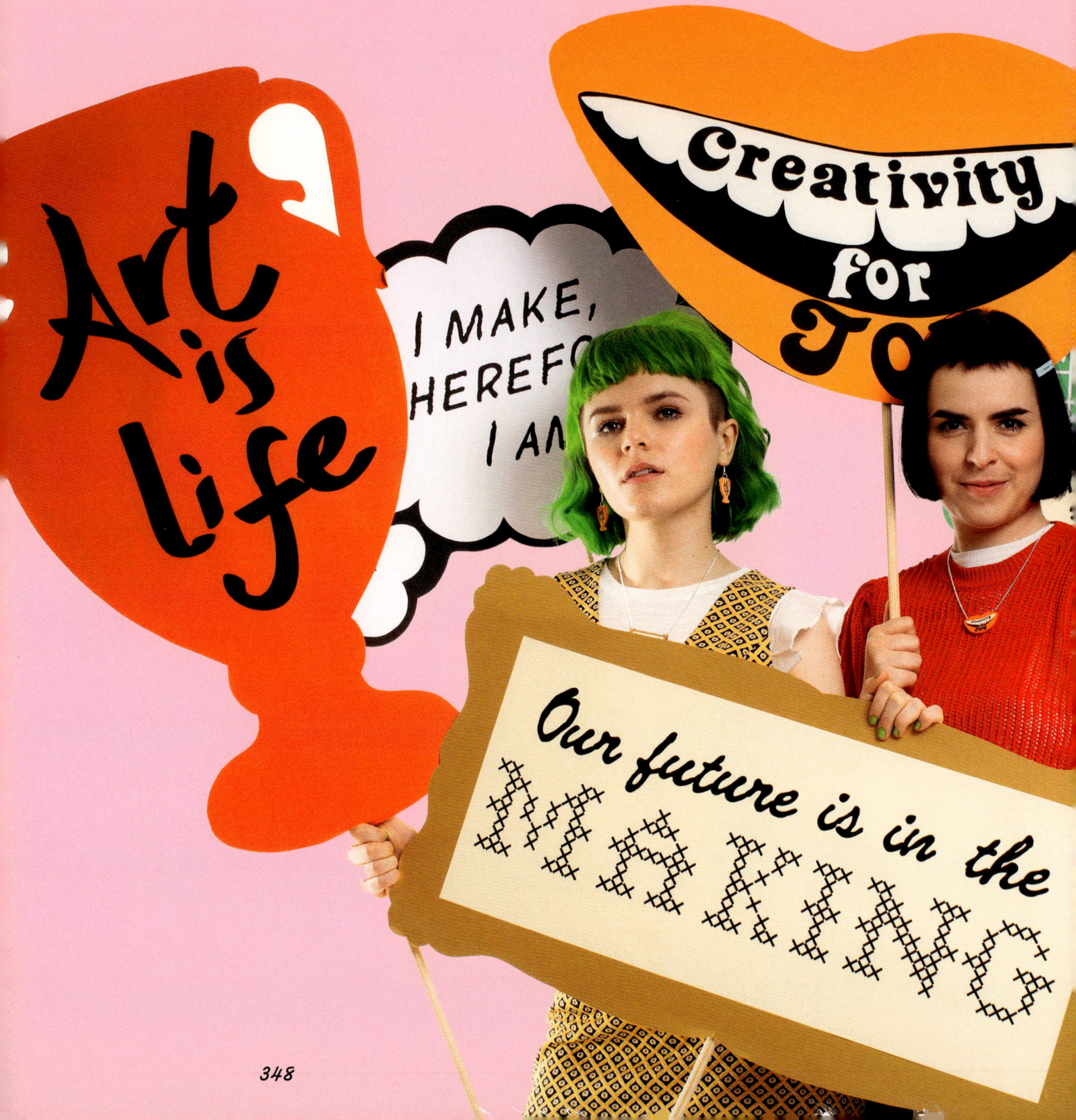

With the focus on academic achievement, the number of students enrolling in creative subjects has fallen by 35% since 2010, including a 57% fall in Design and Technology GCSE.[1] And this is despite the fact that the creative industries are contributing more to the economy than ever before – £101.5 billion in 2017.[2]

Working with the Crafts Council has shown us how schools are no longer necessarily equipped with the tools and craft skills to inspire future makers from an early age.

Professor Roger Kneebone, Professor of Surgical Education and Engagement Science at Imperial College London gives a fantastically clear example of what happens when art and craft isn't taught.[3] New medical students don't have the practical skills that are essential to surgery – they don't have the confidence or dexterity to wield a scalpel, or the ability to successfully stitch a wound. Architects are confronted with graduates who've never handled wood or a brick, and many employers are struggling to find people with the right skill-sets.

It could all be so different. We know from our own experiences that art has enriched our lives; that it's vital to our wellbeing and brings much needed joy. Without a creative education, there wouldn't have been a Tatty Devine, and that's a mind-boggling thought. So we urge you to take action, to embrace and value creativity in your own lives and encourage and support it in the community and in the business world. Together we can help reverse this trend.

We'd like to dedicate this book to all of the inspiring teachers, tutors, friends and family who have encouraged and helped us. Thank you.

Rosie Wolfenden and Harriet Vine
May 2019

1. Cultural Learning Alliance, August 2018
2. Creative Industries Federation, 7 December 2018
3. Telegraph.co.uk, 30 October 2018

£ 1·99p

Acknowledgements

To list everyone who helped to make Tatty what it is would fill up another 352 pages; we are so lucky to have met, worked with and hung out with such amazing people. We would like to acknowledge the following people who have contributed directly into this book in one way or another:

Tony Collins, Artie Collins, Francis Collins, Bebe Higgins, Roger Vine, Ann Vine, Eithne Farry, Nicholas Pankhurst, Stephen Fowler, Joe Egg, Rachel Ortas, Melanie Rickey, Namalee Bolle, Anna-Marie Crowhurst, Amber Butchart, Camilla Simson, Sue Krietzman, Mark Pawson, Rob Ryan, Silvia Ziranek, Alex Murray, Amy Newman, Rachael Matthews, Paul Ioannidis and Hervé Lecouffe, Thelma Speirs and Paul Bernstock, Martial Ramage, Lulu Kennedy, Ivania Caeiro, Rhyannon Styles, Kirsty Merrett, Caroline Breen Thorn, Becky Forknall, Stuart Thorn, Natalie Hall, Dora Diamant, Felicity Hayward, Sabrina Tabuchi, Cléo Ferin Mercury, Leigh Milsom Fowler, Sonja Todd, Peaches, John William, Xanthe Hutchinson, FKA Twigs, Rebecca Swift, Gilbert and George, Jeremy Deller, Laura Callaghan, Philip Colbert, Louise Gray, Clio Peppiatt, Kit Neale, Matty Bovan, Belle and Sebastian, Charlie Le Mindu, Claire Catterall, Paul Harfleet, Lisa Stansfield, Lucy-Anne Holmes, Rita Rooney, Gillian Wearing, Kirsten Dunne, Jo Baxendale, Justine Simons, Poppy Chancellor, Bwalya Newton, Rosy Nicholas, Gemma Shiel, Lakwena Maciver, Marawa the Amazing, Catsou Roberts, Jemima Burrill, Kaia Charles, Susanna Edwards, Jarvis Cocker, Paul Creavin, Robert Danton-Rees, Jenny Lewis, Jimmy Gaston, Saga Sig, Barry Newman, Suzie Winsor, Tai Shani, Mae Finlayson, Matthew Brindle, Holly Falconer, Jeff Hahn, Gabriela Antunes, Harry Dutton, Yeon You, Marc Sethi, Jonny Storey, Catherine Laura, Rebecca Miller, Jonathan West.

Fraser Muggeridge, Joe Nava and all at Fraser Muggeridge studio for all their help in making this book and realising our vision.

Annabelle Campbell, Justine Boussard, Uli Gamper and all at the Crafts Council for their help in curating and organising the exhibition which has inspired the selection of objects in this book. Thank you for believing in us.

Hollie Melding and Megan Shipton who created the paper backgrounds and props for this book and for assisting Harriet on set.

Lisa Osborne for helping us organise the archive and for digitally logging over 6,000 items.

Richard Bostock, Tim Spiers and Nicola Rundle at Glassmint photography for their patience and for producing such a beautiful set of photographs used for the book.

Art Workers' Guild and The Old Bank Vault for the use of their spaces in sorting through the archive.

Team Tatty present: Alice Barnes, Amy Durrant, Anna Ingliss-Hall, Cerys Healy, Charlotte Gowing, Charlotte Middleton, Charlotte Prichard, Charlotte Smith, Chris Davies, Eleanor Rowlands, Liz Hughes, Elizabeth Law, Flo Mooring, Hannah Gouldsmith, Hollie Melding, Isabelle Hennessy, Julie MacKey, Katie Vickers, Kristy Burch, Lynda Philips, Lyndsay Krelle, Megan Shipton, Melissa Flynn, Niamh Smith, Nicole George, Rachel Spencer-Smith, Rebecca Coombs, Rebecca Smith, Samantha Martin-Harper and Team Tatty both past and future...

Published on the occasion of Tatty Devine's 20th anniversary, to coincide with the Crafts Council touring exhibition

Misshapes: The Making of Tatty Devine

Lethaby Gallery, Central Saint Martins, University of the Arts London
20 July – 11 August 2019

The Wilson, Cheltenham
7 September – 9 November 2019

De Montfort University Gallery, Leicester
16 November 2019 – 1 February 2020

Stephen Lawrence Gallery, University of Greenwich, London, 24 February – 3 April 2020

Ty Pawb, Wrexham
10 July – 13 September 2020

Hove Museum and Art Gallery, Brighton and Hove
3 October 2020 – 26 January 2021

New Brewery Arts, Cirencester
21 June – 10 September 2021

Exhibition curated by Rosie Wolfenden MBE and Harriet Vine MBE in partnership with The Crafts Council

First published in 2019 by Tatty Devine Ltd
236 Brick Lane, London, E2 7EB
www.tattydevine.com

ISBN 978-1-5272-4116-9

Graphic Design: Fraser Muggeridge studio
Photography: Richard Bostock, Glassmint
Printed in Belgium

Deformation of the Continental Crust: The Legacy of Mike Coward

Geological Society books refereeing procedures

The Society makes every effort to ensure that the scientific and production quality of its books matches that of its journals. Since 1997, all book proposals have been refereed by specialist reviewers as well as by the Society's Books Editorial Committee. If the referees identify weaknesses in the proposal, these must be addressed before the proposal is accepted.

Once the book is accepted, the Society Book Editors ensure that the volume editors follow strict guidelines on refereeing and quality control. We insist that individual papers can only be accepted after satisfactory review by two independent referees. The questions on the review forms are similar to those for *Journal of the Geological Society*. The referees' forms and comments must be available to the Society's Book Editors on request.

Although many of the books result from meetings, the editors are expected to commission papers that were not presented at the meeting to ensure that the book provides a balanced coverage of the subject. Being accepted for presentation at the meeting does not guarantee inclusion in the book.

More information about submitting a proposal and producing a book for the Society can be found on its web site: www.geolsoc.org.uk.

It is recommended that reference to all or part of this book should be made in one of the following ways:

Ries, A. C., Butler, R. W. H. & Graham, R. H. (eds) 2007. *Deformation of the Continental Crust: The Legacy of Mike Coward.* Geological Society, London, Special Publications, **272**.

Holdsworth, R. E., Alsop, G. I. & Strachan, R. A. 2007. Tectonic stratigraphy and structural continuity of the northernmost Moine Thrust Zone and Moine Nappe, Scottish Caledonides. *In*: Ries, A. C., Butler, R. W. H. & Graham, R. H. (eds) *Deformation of the Continental Crust: The Legacy of Mike Coward.* Geological Society, London, Special Publications, **272**, 121–142.

GEOLOGICAL SOCIETY SPECIAL PUBLICATION NO. 272

Deformation of the Continental Crust: The Legacy of Mike Coward

EDITED BY

A. C. RIES
Ries–Coward Associates Limited, UK

R. W. H. BUTLER
University of Leeds, UK

and

R. H. GRAHAM
Amerada Hess, UK

2007
Published by
The Geological Society
London

THE GEOLOGICAL SOCIETY

The Geological Society of London (GSL) was founded in 1807. It is the oldest national geological society in the world and the largest in Europe. It was incorporated under Royal Charter in 1825 and is Registered Charity 210161.

The Society is the UK national learned and professional society for geology with a worldwide Fellowship (FGS) of over 9000. The Society has the power to confer Chartered status on suitably qualified Fellows, and about 2000 of the Fellowship carry the title (CGeol). Chartered Geologists may also obtain the equivalent European title, European Geologist (EurGeol). One fifth of the Society's fellowship resides outside the UK. To find out more about the Society, log on to www.geolsoc.org.uk.

The Geological Society Publishing House (Bath, UK) produces the Society's international journals and books, and acts as European distributor for selected publications of the American Association of Petroleum Geologists (AAPG), the Indonesian Petroleum Association (IPA), the Geological Society of America (GSA), the Society for Sedimentary Geology (SEPM) and the Geologists' Association (GA). Joint marketing agreements ensure that GSL Fellows may purchase these societies' publications at a discount. The Society's online bookshop (accessible from www.geolsoc.org.uk) offers secure book purchasing with your credit or debit card.

To find out about joining the Society and benefiting from substantial discounts on publications of GSL and other societies worldwide, consult www.geolsoc.org.uk, or contact the Fellowship Department at: The Geological Society, Burlington House, Piccadilly, London W1J 0BG: Tel. +44 (0)20 7434 9944; Fax +44 (0)20 7439 8975; E-mail: enquiries@geolsoc.org.uk.

For information about the Society's meetings, consult *Events* on www.geolsoc.org.uk. To find out more about the Society's Corporate Affiliates Scheme, write to enquiries@geolsoc.org.uk

Published by The Geological Society from:
The Geological Society Publishing House, Unit 7, Brassmill Enterprise Centre, Brassmill Lane, Bath BA1 3JN, UK

(*Orders*: Tel. +44 (0)1225 445046
Fax +44 (0)1225 442836)
Online bookshop: www.geolsoc.org.uk/bookshop

British Library Cataloguing in Publication Data

A catalogue record for this book is available from the British Library.

ISBN 978-1-86239-215-1

Typeset by The Charlesworth Group

Printed by MPG Books Ltd, Bodmin, UK

Distributors

North America
For trade and institutional orders:
The Geological Society, c/o AIDC, 82 Winter Sport Lane, Williston, VT 05495, USA
Orders: Tel +1 800-972-9892
Fax +1 802-864-7626
Email gsl.orders@aidcvt.com
For individual and corporate orders:
AAPG Bookstore, PO Box 979, Tulsa, OK 74101-0979, USA
Orders: Tel +1 918-584-2555
Fax +1 918-560-2652
Email bookstore@aapg.org
Website http://bookstore.aapg.org

India
Affiliated East-West Press Private Ltd, Marketing Division, G-1/16 Ansari Road, Darya Ganj, New Delhi 110 002, India
Orders: Tel. +91 11 2327-9113/2326-4180
Fax +91 11 2326-0538
E-mail affiliat@vsnl.com

CONTENTS

Mike Coward (1945–2003): portrait of a structural geologist

This Special Publication celebrates the life and times of one of the late 20th century's most influential structural geologists, Mike Coward. At various times Mike was H H Read Professor of Geology at Imperial College, Chair of the UK Tectonic Studies Group and Council Member of the Geological Society of London; but these official titles belie a deeply unconventional man who loved to challenge accepted wisdom and dogma. Mike's career was an eclectic mix of pure and applied research in structural geology that straddled continents and geological time. Normal chronological narratives can hardly do justice to a man who could step from theme to theme at times, seemingly to colleagues, almost on a daily basis. This brief biography attempts to draw together some of the strands, in rather the same way as the Special Publication itself, to offer a glimpse of a character who could be very much larger than life.

Student days

Michael Peter Coward was born in Bolton, Lancashire, on 26 June 1945 and grew up as an only child in neighbouring Farnworth. Through a great sacrifice on the part of his parents, he attended Bolton School, an institution he held in great esteem throughout his life. In 1963 he passed the scholarship examination in physics and chemistry for Imperial College. When he arrived there that autumn he changed to geology, entering what was at the time one of the greatest departments in the world. The geology course

From: RIES, A. C., BUTLER, R. W. H. & GRAHAM, R. H. (eds) 2007. *Deformation of the Continental Crust: The Legacy of Mike Coward*. Geological Society, London, Special Publications, **272**, vii–xii.
0305-8719/07/$15

involved a great deal of fieldwork, an activity Mike would love for the rest of his life. But it was not structural geology that attracted him at the beginning. At the end of his first year he did a mapping project in Iceland, supervised by George Walker, against the backdrop of erupting Surtsey, and thus almost became a volcanologist. It was John Ramsay, leading a field class to the Scottish Highlands, who later took Mike into the world of structural geology.

In 1966, having graduated with first class honours, Mike stayed on at Imperial College to do a PhD. A fanciful notion of doing structural geology among elephants led him towards making early efforts to set up a project in either what was then Ceylon, or in southern Africa. Janet Watson, his future supervisor, had other ideas and sent him to the Outer Hebridean island of South Uist where the only big game were sheep and deer. John Myers was already one year into his thesis on neighbouring Harris and Janet thought they would make a good team. The team soon grew. Pete Francis took on Barra, Rod Graham worked on North Uist, the islands in the Sound of Harris and much of South Harris, while John Myers mapped the rest of Harris. Later, Rick Sibson worked in detail on the Outer Isles thrust zone and Richard Lisle mapped northern Lewis. Mike's area was South Uist and Benbecula. He fell in love with the wide white strands, the moorland, the mountains and perhaps most of all, the way of life in the Western Isles. He stayed in Bornish, South Uist with an elderly spinster called Morag Macmillan, whom he looked upon as his adoptive mother. The magic of Uist was always to remain very special to Mike. These early researches are described in more detail elsewhere (Graham this volume).

The early career: South America and Australia

But Mike still felt the pull of dramatic volcanic landforms, and after finishing his PhD in 1969, he decided to abandon deep crustal structures for a while. With Pete Francis, he organized an expedition to northern Chile to study the volcanology, structure and geochemistry of the highest volcanoes in South America. John (Taff) Roobol, Pete Cobbold and George Walker joined them. Mike was quartermaster for the trip and very successfully managed to scrounge the necessary food and money, including a crate of whisky. The Royal Society paid their air fares and the Natural Environment Research Council (NERC) provided a Land Rover. They flew to Santiago in July 1969 and established base camps for fieldwork in the mining towns of Calimo and Chuquicamata, in the High Andes. When the work was completed, they travelled by bus through Ecuador, Colombia and Central America, and returned from Mexico City to the UK in 1970.

The South American trip failed to quell Mike's wanderlust and shortly after returning to England, he emigrated to Adelaide, having accepted a job with a small mining company exploring for nickel in the Northern Territories and Western Australia. When the company ran out of funds, Mike went travelling again, this time through South Africa and Mozambique.

Structural geology in Africa

Mike's return to the UK in 1971 coincided with yet another field trip to the Hebrides. In the kitchen of the Rodel Hotel on South Harris, Robert Shackleton, then Professor of Geology and Director of the Research Institute of African Geology at the University of Leeds, offered Mike a job as his research assistant. Within a month, Mike was dispatched to collect a Land Rover from Malawi and drive it to Salisbury to begin the long-lasting project in the Limpopo Belt.

The Limpopo study marked the first of a series of significant African projects that continued throughout Mike's life. It led to innovative reinterpretations of the Archaean greenstone belts of what was then Rhodesia and gave him early experience of gold mineralization, a topic he would return to in later life. His growing attraction to Africa was encouraged by Robert Shackleton, who continued his own studies at the same time on the Pan-African belts of East Africa. A major structural and geochronological study of the Pan-African Damaran fold belt in Namibia came in the mid-1970s. Sponsored by NERC and RTZ, this was the first time Mike found himself leading a significant, multi-disciplined research project. Working with a series of students and the geochronologists from the University of Leeds (notably Chris Hawkesworth) a modern geometric, kinematic and geochemical analysis revealed new perspectives on Pan-African evolution.

The Damaran work led Mike along the postulated former plate boundary to Central Africa. In the early 1980s he worked with Mike Daly, then a field geologist with the Geological Survey of Zambia, and later a postgraduate student in Leeds. Around a camp fire, towards the end of a 10 day foot-safari in the Muchinga Mountains of northern Zambia, Mike reflected ruefully to Daly: 'I don't know why, but my students always believe that crucial exposures are only found at the top of the highest mountain or, in your case, in the most remote part of Africa imaginable.' That day he had walked past huge herds of elephants, crossed rivers full of watching crocodiles and settled down to a dinner of fresh impala and Scotch whisky.

Not only did Mike exude his own tireless passion for field research, he required, and inspired, it in the people he worked with. Together with Mike Daly he set up a number of structural field classes in Africa known as 'Geotraverses'. Run by UNESCO, in co-operation with the Musée Royal de l'Afrique Centrale in Belgium, this laudable initiative brought modern field geology to the African universities. The students loved the enthusiasm and fun that came with Mike.

The Leeds and Moine thrust years

In 1975, Mike was appointed Lecturer in the University of Leeds. Together with Andrew Siddans and then Rob Knipe, the later part of the decade saw Mike build on the foundations laid by John Ramsay during his time at Leeds, to reorganize and expand the undergraduate courses in structural geology. Students either loved or hated the 'work hard—play hard' philosophy and the occasionally outrageous field classes, complete with Hebridean singing. The extra-curricular geology trips live longest in the memory. Mike would set up spontaneous mid-week, mid-semester trips to see structures, sometimes heading off to Pembrokeshire or even Brittany, with a minibus of undergraduates and PhD students. This did create certain antagonism among some of his colleagues. In the modern micro-managed world of 'teaching and learning outcomes', universities do not offer undergraduate experiences like that any more. Perhaps it is no coincidence that well over half of the graduates from those years went on to become professional geoscientists.

Mike's main research during his time at Leeds was on the structural evolution of the Moine thrust belt, a major NERC funded project that provided the springboard for a dozen PhD projects. It was initiated at about the same time as deep seismic reflection profiles were beginning to be shot through the continents, timing that added much to the interpretation of the profiles and led to Mike playing a leading role in the steering group of the NERC-sponsored BIRPS seismic programme in the early 1980s. This period was probably one of the happiest times of his life, doing fieldwork in surroundings he loved with new ideas emerging all the time.

One of the attractions of NW Scotland was its long tradition of structural investigation, exemplified particularly in the classic North-West Highland Memoir of 1907. Indeed, Mike Coward could be compared with Ben Peach in the rapidity with which he could map ground. Each field season in Scotland generated some new insight and a string of papers, challenging both the rules of thrust system development and the accepted wisdom for classic outcrops. Sometimes these reinterpretations were of his own papers from a couple of seasons earlier. Keeping up with this creativity could be challenging for the expanding group of PhD students, some of whom characterized each new discovery as the 'whim of the week'. But the work has stood the test of time, with many of his papers retaining fundamental importance for understanding thrust systems and their relationship to larger orogenic processes. All this fieldwork did not do his teeth any good, for Mike was always a great chewer of pencils and crayons. On rainy days the colour would run and you could tell where Mike had been mapping by the rainbow on his face.

Like Peach and his contemporaries, Mike often stayed at the Inchnadamph Hotel, and at his request, his ashes were scattered on a hillside near the hotel, with views of the Ben More range.

The Greater Ranges

In the mid-1970s, after years of construction, the Karakoram Highway was finally opened, linking Pakistan to western Tibet and providing one of the world's great geological transects. Like many other geologists, Mike felt compelled to go and investigate it. In 1979 he started work, initially with Brian Windley, in northern Pakistan, supported by a string of NERC grants. Fieldwork in the NW Himalayas, then as now, was always an adventure. The basic provisions were often supplemented by smuggled parmesan cheese, ham and saucisson, munched with relish on some dusty track each day. Suitably nourished, Mike was in his element, able to draw cross-sections through vast tracts of barely known geology in an astonishingly short time. Almost all of this work was carried out in collaboration with the University of Peshawar, and similar cooperation with UK geoscientists continues to this day.

It also saved his life. Disaster struck in the late summer of 1981 when, high above the northern town of Skardu, the vehicle containing Mike, Brian Windley, Carol Pudsey and Asif Khan rolled off a narrow road. Such events are commonly fatal, because in many places the roads lie hundreds of metres up steep hillsides. The only member of the group to escape without major injury was Asif Khan, at the time a PhD student of Mike's from the University of Peshawar. Asif walked 40 km back to an army outpost to raise the alarm, but it was many hours before help arrived and, as night came, so did the snow. Mike knew that if he went to sleep he might never wake up, and kept going with endless renditions of Hebridean and Irish songs. They were rescued at four in the morning and bumped back down the road to the Skardu military hospital. Before they could operate on Mike's badly damaged leg, an earthquake struck. Days later, with the roads blocked by landslips, the team was flown out of Skardu on the floor of a small plane. Despite the dire circumstances, Mike managed to get some spectacular photographs of Nanga Parbat from the plane, snaps he showed at meetings for years afterwards. Back in Leeds, Mike enlisted the whole group of PhD students in gastronomic smuggling to ensure he was sustained during his hospitalization and kept threatening to write a paper on the balanced cross-section and structural restoration of his lower leg, which was perfectly imaged in the X-rays.

In 1985 he was asked by Robert Shackleton to join a research project, funded by the Royal Society and the Academica Sinica, which involved a traverse across Tibet. Robert organized 14 leading western geoscientists to form a team with Chinese counterparts. The cost was well over £1 million and involved reconnaissance trips to China, plus training and 'group bonding' visits to geological sites in Europe. Mike celebrated his 40th birthday on the traverse with donkey and chips, washed down with some local wine and followed by a sing-song. A year later, during a medical check prior to a follow-up trip to Beijing and Lhasa, his heart problem was diagnosed. After a triple bypass operation, he was able to go as far as Beijing but did not attempt another high-altitude Tibetan trip, though it did not affect travel elsewhere.

Imperial College, basins and the European ranges

In 1983 Mike was appointed Reader at Leeds, but soon after was offered the prestigious H. H. Read Chair of Geology at Imperial College and moved there in 1984. His Moine thrust studies continued for a while and he became interested in tracing the system offshore. As he gained access to industrial seismic data from the West Orkney basin, his attention turned from the thrust itself to the sedimentary basins on top of it. One especially damp afternoon he was discovered by some of his students with several tens of metres of paper seismic lines, completely covering the floors of the residents' lounge and corridors of Ceilidh Place Hotel, Ullapool. This heralded a period of research on the structure of the British sedimentary basins, which would take him closer to the oil industry and further away from academic geology. The North Sea became an important focus, with an industrial incentive of course. Yet there was a significant academic component to the new ideas that were developed, such as with Simon Stewart on the salt tectonics of the southern North Sea. The culmination of all this work was a major contribution to the *Millennium Atlas* (2003). These three chapters were Mike's last major publications.

The loss of the Tibetan research led Mike to discover European geology and use his experience of inversion, gained from looking at seismic profiles from the southern North Sea and elsewhere on the UK continental shelf, to look at the external zones of the Alps, where Gidon, Lemoine, Graciansky and others had described deformed Mesozoic half-graben. His first research students at Imperial College mostly worked on one or more of these graben and, of course, were expected to do a great deal by themselves. Jean-Pierre Gratier, Professor of Geology at Grenoble, once remarked that he always knew when summer was coming because it was invariably heralded by an English student knocking on his door, explaining that he was a Mike Coward student, and asking if Professor Gratier knew where his field area was.

It is easy to be cynical about Mike's relatively brief encounter with the Alps; but anyone tempted to say it was more about good food and great wine than geology should read the major Alpine review that he wrote with Dorothée Dietrich in the Geological Society's Special Publication on *Alpine Tectonics* in 1989.

The European and offshore inversion themes continued into the 1990s. Involvement with British Gas offered the Mike the chance to move east along the Alpine chain into the Carpathians. Not only was the orogenic belt seen at this time as an area of interest for hydrocarbons, it also offered some exciting regional structural problems and led to the collaboration with Michal Nemčok and colleagues at Bratislava.

Minerals and oil

After his work on African mobile belts and greenstone belts, Mike became increasingly involved in the mid-1980s with the mining houses of South Africa, and was a frequent visitor to the copper mines of Zambia. He revelled in the 3D geometrical data available from the mines, quarries and drilling, a precursor of his passion for good seismic data. While working on the structural setting of the gold deposits, initially with BP Mining then with its successor, Gencor and Iamgold, he met Richard Spencer, with whom he was associated for many years. The focus of attention was the Witwatersrand basin, with its sequence of four stacked basins ranging in age from Archaean to Jurassic. Undoubtedly its geographical proximity to his beloved Limpopo belt made it too much to resist. His interpretation of 2500 line km of Gencor's seismic data from the Witwatersrand basin was done at a characteristically frenetic pace and, although he often appeared to be doing something else like tying his shoe laces or staring out of the window while someone was talking to him, his conclusions would always faithfully draw on ideas and snippets of field evidence that had been presented to him. His 'gold' colleagues speak of working with Mike as a wonderful, often humbling experience where the greater significance of something that they had been working on for months frequently occurred to him in a flash.

Richard Spencer notes that Mike's ability to visualize structure in three dimensions was extraordinary. He had an amazing ability to sketch sections and maps, almost to scale, on the fly. He would ask to go back to a road-cut that had been passed at speed on the way to the outcrop of principal interest saying 'I think I saw something like this' and he would haul out his notebook and produce the cross-section from memory. From a stop at the road-cut on the return journey, Mike would casually fill in the details on his sketch, rounded off with a few structural measurements or confirmation as to what stratigraphy was involved.

At this time, Mike seemed to distrust work-stations and insisted that interpretations be done on paper, possibly a throwback to the Ceilidh Place Hotel. Consequently, mining company meeting rooms were converted into vaguely controlled chaos with all working surfaces pushed together to accommodate the base maps, and the walls draped with various layers of seismic sections. Mike's consulting trips to the Witwatersrand basin were always rounded off by a presentation to management, held on Friday afternoon, and as the week progressed towards this deadline, pencil consumption would increase and his teeth would become ever more encrusted with paint chips. He made a fundamental contribution to the understanding of the tectonics and development of the Witwatersrand basin and helped to put the structural controls of gold mineralization into that context. It was a key to the development of exploration targets. Mike left his contacts in Gencor and Iamgold the gift of being able to think differently. One wonders whether he ever realized the extent of his positive influence on the people with whom he worked.

Through the 1990s and until his death in 2003, Mike experienced ever-increasing involvement in both mining and oil industries; for by now, large numbers of his ex-students had become a powerful network through which to access ideas and data. He consulted for almost all of the active companies in the North Sea, notably (in his last years) for Statoil on North Sea fault block structure and evolution. He worked for both the oil and mining industry in many parts of the world, on major interpretation projects; with BP in Venezuela exploring the Monagas thrust belt, with Ecopetrol in Colombia, and with Placerdome in North America and Australia. The list is endless, but although working closely with industry, Mike rarely expressed appreciation for the challenge of commercializing geological insight, preferring to see conversations about commercial risk as an equivocation about a particular interpretation rather than a quantification of imperfect sight. As 3D seismic data became commonplace, Mike eventually became a proficient user of seismic work-stations; but he never lost the use of crayons and paper, or the fundamental belief that if you hadn't seen things in the field you would struggle to see them in seismic profiles.

As the 1990s progressed, Mike found academic life increasingly frustrating and life as a consultant more fulfilling. His health also deteriorated so that in 1997 he took early retirement on medical grounds from Imperial College and moved full time into his consulting company. He still maintained an aggressive pace of work, travelling widely to new areas, yet at the same time revisiting problems he had studied years before and reappraising them in the light of new experience and knowledge. He kept up this frenetic pace into the last weeks of his life.

Legacy

Mike married a fellow geologist, Alison Ries, in 1987. Their daughter Sarah was born in 1989, when they moved to Reading, and Charlie was adopted from Paraguay in 1994. Alison had been a friend since his postgraduate days and had been very much a part of his life during his years in Leeds. Now, though the creation of Ries–Coward Associates Ltd, they were able to work closely together once again.

Mike Coward leaves a huge collection of published articles, edited books, notebooks, maps, manuscripts and independent reports. Some of these are listed in this Special Publication and many are cited by the papers that follow. Yet perhaps Mike's most significant achievement was his capacity to pass on his enthusiasm and passion for geology to his numerous colleagues and co-workers, his postgraduate and graduate students, and of course to the hundreds of geologists who have listened to his infectious talks and read his papers. Many of his doctorate students are today professors and lecturers, exploration executives in oil and mining companies, or geoscientists in government and non-governmental institutions around the world. More than anything else, they are Mike Coward's legacy.

With contributions from Rob Butler, Mike Daly, Rod Graham, Alison Ries and Richard Spencer

Introduction: the deformation of continental crust and Mike Coward's impact on its understanding

R. W. H. BUTLER[1], R. H. GRAHAM[2] & A. C. RIES[3]

[1]*Institute of Geophysics and Tectonics, School of Earth and Environment, University of Leeds, Leeds LS2 9JT, UK (e-mail: butler@earth.leeds.ac.uk)*

[2]*Amerada Hess, The Adelphi Building, 1–11 John Adam Street, London WC2N 6AG, UK*

[3]*Ries-Coward Associates Ltd, 70 Grosvenor Road, Caversham, Reading RG4 5ES, UK*

Understanding geological structure and structural evolution requires imagination, and the ability to see simple patterns in complex data and make the simplicity evident. It requires the transfer of insight and approach from one area of discipline (geographical or scientific) to another. To Mike Coward it was second nature to do these things, and he stood out as one of the most innovative structural geologists of recent years. He was a great exponent of what is currently referred to as 'up-scaling': understanding the significance of small-scale, local observations and datasets then using them to elucidate geological evolution on a crustal scale.

This introductory paper is a brief review of some key themes in the study of the deformation of the continental crust, and how Coward influenced them. It focuses particularly on thinking in structural geology during the past 50 years or so, but does not cover such topics as seismicity, geodetic data or microstructural approaches in deformation studies. The emphasis is on the importance of understanding medium- to large-scale structural geometry. This was Mike Coward's forté, for it emphasizes the key role of field geology. The discipline of field mapping is a great aid in the interpretation of 3D relationships in seismic data volumes. It is no coincidence that this account begins in the field but leads into seismic data. It is a journey followed not only by Mike Coward but also by many of the authors contributing to this volume.

Crustal-scale shear zone models

Field geologists have long been aware that structures seen in outcrops of high-grade metamorphic rocks may be used as analogues for the deformation *in situ* in the deep crust. Argand (1924) used structural styles seen in the Alps to support his models of crustal deformation beneath the Himalayas and Tibet. Sutton & Watson (1951) recognized that tracts of deformed gneisses in the Lewisian represented the roots to Proterozoic orogens. These deformed gneiss terrains formed obvious places to test and develop quantitative methods of strain and kinematic analysis, especially applying the methods of Ramsay (1967). Later the shear zone model of Ramsay & Graham (1970) was used to understand the kinematic evolution of these regions, and by inference, the deep continental crust. Escher & Watterson (1974) were the first to upscale the model to understand crustal-scale deformation, using the Nagssugtoquidian structures in southern Greenland. Coward used the model qualitatively, first to explain the 3D nature of crustal-scale shear zones and networks of shear zones that define areas of deformed and less-deformed crust of the Lewisian (reviewed elsewhere in this volume), then more widely and at continental scale in, for example, the Limpopo mobile belt and adjacent Archaean cratons, and the Damaran and Zambezi belts. Rather than attempting to understand ductile deformation in terms of correlating fold phases and tightly defined sequences of deformation, he applied models from linked fault systems. He recognized that there is a continuum from ductile shear at deep crustal levels to thrusting or extension at higher levels. This was clearly illustrated in a number of Coward's papers through the 1970s and 1980s (e.g. Coward 1984) and, although self evident now, they represented the cutting edge thinking at the time.

Thrust belts

The external parts of mountain belts are commonly marked by zones of thrusting and tectonic imbrication. Many also contain basement slices of variable thickness and deformation state. Pioneering research in the Moine thrust belt in the 1880s by Peach *et al.* (1907) and their contemporaries was revisited by Elliott & Johnson (1980). They employed an approach that was influenced by trans-Atlantic ideas on thin-skinned tectonics and section balancing

From: RIES, A. C., BUTLER, R. W. H. & GRAHAM, R. H. (eds) 2007. *Deformation of the Continental Crust: The Legacy of Mike Coward*. Geological Society, London, Special Publications, **272**, 1–8.
0305-8719/07/$15

developed in the external zones of the Rocky Mountains and Appalachians. Coward realized the importance of the approach but questioned many of the strict 'thrust belt rules'. He developed a new understanding of thrust sequences that required more complex structural evolution than previously envisaged and there was a new emphasis on the interpretation of strain patterns in thrust sheets (chiefly reviewed by Coward *et al.* 1992). In the late 1970s accepted wisdom related strain patterns to mechanisms of thrust sheet emplacement, such as gravity gliding and gravity spreading (e.g. Elliott 1976). Coward and his students (e.g. Coward & Kim 1981; Fischer & Coward 1982) introduced a matrix approach to describe the 3D finite strain state using data from deformed *Skolithos* in the Cambrian Pipe Rock Formation. They showed that the strains related to distributed shearing that in turn reflected partitioning of deformation away from simple thrust displacements. The benchmark description of 3D strain patterns by Coward & Potts (1983) provided a framework for many of the general strain studies associated with transpression or transtension (e.g. Fossen & Tikoff 1998). The key to these strain papers in the Moine thrust belt lay in relating the outcrop-scale deformation to the larger-scale geometric evolution of the system, especially to possible displacement gradients that originated from thrust zone propagation.

Fieldwork in the north Assynt district revealed a series of structural relationships that Coward (1982) interpreted as reflecting extensional faulting within the thrust belt. His mapping showed that these faults linked onto thrusts, indicating that they were associated with thrust sheet translation. His surge zone hypothesis, although controversial, formed the basis of larger-scale geodynamic interpretations of thrusting in NW Scotland (e.g. Coward 1983) that continue in some analyses today (Holdsworth *et al.* 2007).

Crustal-scale thrusting models

The research in the Moine thrust belt coincided with imaging the subsurface continuity of thrusts in the Appalachians (Cook *et al.* 1979) and the early applications of deep seismic reflection soundings in Britain (the BIRPS programme; e.g. Brewer & Smythe 1984). Coward was not alone in understanding the importance of deep seismic data. Soper & Barber (1982) were the first to apply structural restoration concepts to crustal-scale interpretations of the Moine thrust. They proposed a crustal duplex model, with steeply rooting thrust trajectories. However, Coward (1980; Butler & Coward 1984) used field data, which indicated large displacements in the thrust belt, to propose that the Moine thrust followed a shallow trajectory in the upper crust and that the NW Highlands were underlain by Lewisian basement of the Caledonian foreland. He went on to apply these methods to the Himalayas (Coward & Butler 1985; Butler & Coward 1989), well ahead of the acquisition of the crustal geophysics datasets by the INDEPTH team (e.g. Zhao & Nelson 1993). In essence these researches were a natural continuation from looking at deformed gneiss terrains but show the importance of up-scaling field observations in the interpretation of deep seismic reflection profiles. Subsequently, these approaches have been followed with modifications, closely associated with deep seismic acquisition programmes, such as the NRP20 project in the Swiss Alps (Pfiffner *et al.* 1997) and CROP in the Italian Apennines (Scrocca *et al.* 2003).

Orogenic systems: Himalayas–Tibet

One of the key advantages of studying modern orogenic systems is the precision gained from geochronological and stratigraphic studies. In this regard, the Himalayan–Tibetan system has been a fundamental test track for tectonic models. Research in this area received a great impetus in the mid-1970s with the opening of the Karakoram Highway and consequently much of the early work focused on the NW Himalayas of Pakistan, building on the recognition that much of Kohistan represented a Cretaceous island arc, caught up in the collision zone (Tahirkheli & Jan 1979). Structural studies in the exhumed lower arc (e.g. Coward *et al.* 1987) provided the platform for subsequent research, establishing the section as an important outcrop analogue for lower crustal processes (e.g. Treloar *et al.* 1990). There are also seductive similarities in the patterns of strain localization and kinematics to basement gneiss terrains, such as parts of the Lewisian complex, that Coward was not slow to recognize.

An important finding from the research in NW Pakistan was the recognition that the Indian continental crust beneath the Kohistan arc had experienced subhorizontal extension and thrusting. Coward *et al.* (1987) informally termed this 'hedgehog tectonics', famously likening the process to that of road-kill, harking back to Termier's (1904) 'crushing sledge' model for Alpine orogenesis. This kinematic relationship is now embraced by the protagonists of 'channel flow' (e.g. Beaumont *et al.* 2001).

Although suggested by seismicity and remote sensing, the fundamental differences between the tectonics of Tibet and the Himalayas were firmly established only after the fieldwork conducted on the 1985 Tibetan Geotraverse expedition (Coward *et al.* 1988). Although there are structures that indicate subhorizontal shortening, in general these date from early in the history of collision tectonics in the region. The younger structures are largely strike-slip and normal faults. There has been much refinement of these findings in the past 20 years, especially linking the active surface deformation detected from geodetic data (e.g. Zhang *et al.* 2004) to seismological results (e.g. Ozacar & Zandt 2004). These results illustrate the importance of different strain states down through the crust. The importance of low-angle thrusting within the Himalayas, suggested by Argand (1924) and developed by Coward & Butler (1985) and others since (DeCelles *et al.* 2001), is apparently confirmed by modern seismological studies (Schulte-Pelkum *et al.* 2005).

Inversion

Models for thrust system evolution, derived and modified from those developed in the Rocky Mountains, were applied to NW Scotland (e.g. Elliott & Johnson 1980) and to Tethyan orogens, such as the Alps (e.g. Boyer & Elliott 1982). However, these applications were not especially successful because the pre-orogenic stratigraphic template was not simple. The Mesozoic inheritance in the western Alps was brought vividly into modern context by Lemoine *et al.* (1986), who described tilted fault blocks and half-graben analogous to those on present-day continental margins. Some of these are barely deformed but simply elevated. Others, as recognized by Gidon (1981), were significantly shortened during Cenozoic mountain building. Coward took these models and developed them, initially in the Alps (Gillcrist *et al.* 1987) and then more generally (e.g. Coward 1994). His reappraisal of thrust geometry in the Kirthar Range of Pakistan shows how a 'thin-skinned' interpretation (e.g. Banks & Warburton 1986) requires very large (and very unlikely) net displacements. Inverted normal faults, without much displacement, are a more realistic alternative. These types of reappraisal were extended to other settings, such as the Apennines (Coward *et al.* 1999*a*), where they continue to have an impact on the understanding of orogenic belts (e.g. Tavarnelli *et al.* 2004). Clearly, in the orogens of the western Tethys, where pre-existing basin-controlling faults can be readily inferred from the lateral variations in Mesozoic stratigraphy (e.g. Bosellini 2004), some form of structural inheritance is likely. This general recognition is well established (e.g. Jackson 1980). The implications for crustal balancing are recognized in the region (e.g. Coward & Dietrich 1989). However, the lessons have barely been applied to the restacked continental margin in the Himalayas, notwithstanding many attempts at crustal-scale thrust interpretations (discussed above). In this light, the existing interpretations of crustal structure are likely to be highly non-unique.

Basin evolution

The late 1980s saw a shift in the focus of structural geology as commercial seismic reflection data became routinely available for academic research. Coward was quick to recognize the opportunities for fundamental structural research and essentially reframed his paper on crustal deformation styles for contraction (Coward 1983) in terms of extensional tectonics (Coward 1986). Like others (e.g. Watson 1985), he realized that many of the basin structures around the British Isles owed their trends to earlier structures. Thus Enfield & Coward (1987) showed that the West Orkney basin preferentially reactivated the Caledonian deformation fabric, as imaged in the MOIST deep seismic data (e.g. Brewer & Smythe 1984). This was not simply reactivation of pre-existing faults. Rather it was the penetrative anisotropy that controlled the orientation of normal faults. Coward's work on the Caledonian controls of rifting, off the north coast of Scotland and in Orkney, led to a wider interest in the influence of Caledonian structures in the Mesozoic rifting around Britain. Much of this was reviewed in a series of contributions to the *Millennium Atlas* (Coward *et al.* 2003; Zanella & Coward 2003; Zanella *et al.* 2003). These basement-reactivation ideas have been developed and expanded by several groups (reviewed, for example, by Butler *et al.* 1997).

Halokinesis is commonly a key factor in the structural evolution of sedimentary basins, including the southern North Sea. Classically salt movement in intracratonic basins, such as the North Sea, is viewed in vertical terms alone so that structures are expressed solely in terms of salt pillars, walls and diapirs (reviewed by Jackson & Talbot 1994). However, work on passive continental margins, such as the northern Gulf of Mexico (e.g. Humphris 1978; Wu *et al.* 1990), showed that salt migration can be strongly asymmetrical, leading to down-slope migration both of the salt and the overlying sedimentary prism. Stewart & Coward (1995) were amongst the first to show that similar asymmetrical processes also occur, albeit on a smaller scale, on extensional tilt blocks within the southern North Sea.

Basic structural concepts have long been important in the exploration for natural resources and there has been significant exchange of ideas between the research and industrial sectors. Famously, the impetus for the re-examination of many thrust belts, especially in Europe (e.g. Boyer & Elliott 1982), came from oil exploration in the Canadian Rocky Mountains (Bally *et al.* 1966). Although it has much older origins, section balancing, developed in the Rockies (Dahlstrom 1969), was applied first to the Moine thrust belt (Elliott & Johnson 1980) and then to the Pyrenees (e.g. Williams & Fischer 1984), the Alps (Beach 1981) and beyond. Coward's research forms part of this tradition, especially in the use of regional-scale tectonic understanding to inform knowledge of specific development prospects. As hydrocarbon exploration reaches out into regions of increasing technological challenge and geological complexity, the demands on structural geology continue. Similar challenges face the minerals sector. In a typical piece of innovation towards the end of his career, Coward took the oil industry's approach to basin evolution into mining through his consultancy in gold exploration (Coward *et al.* 1995). Such applications remain in their infancy; indeed, they are highly controversial and challenge existing thinking.

About this volume

The papers in this volume all build on Coward's legacy. Some offer distinctly personal commentaries and reviews. Others present the results of structural studies from settings that he researched extensively to those that he never visited but that nevertheless follow the tradition. They are arranged so as to track, in broadly chronological order, the research themes that Coward developed through his career.

Coward's early work in the Precambrian basement of NW Scotland is summarized by **Graham**. This paper outlines his structural studies in the Lewisian and the development of models of strain and fabric histories in broad zones of ductile deformation. Coward's work significantly advanced the understanding of the large-scale structural evolution of the continental crust through the application of shear zone models. With the development of new geophysical imaging techniques, there is a renewed interest in the ductile deformation of deep continental crust. Consequently, kinematic models based on simple shear for deformation zones in crystalline basement are being re-examined. Like Coward before him, **Wheeler** uses the Lewisian of NW Scotland as an outcrop analogue for deep crustal deformation processes but presents data from the little-known Torridon area. Detailed field studies are used to assess the applicability of ideal simple shear zone models in describing kinematics on a variety of scales. Although ideal simple shear may explain local structures, it is less applicable to broader zones of deformation and on the scale of the crust. The tradition of detailed kinematic studies in the Lewisian is also continued by **Tatham & Casey**, who re-examine the Badcall shear zone, described by Coward & Potts (1983). The paper accepts the geometric challenge of deciphering spatially varying lineation patterns, invoking variable shear directions rather than heterogeneous combinations of pure shear and simple shear. Similar scaling issues are addressed by **Cosgrove**, who examines shear zone development in a brittle–ductile setting. Here the perennial problem of relating finite structures to deduce the orientation of regional stress axes from outcrop data is addressed.

The next group of papers retains a focus on structural geometry and draws on examples from the Caledonian thrust and shear systems of NW Scotland. As with the papers on Lewisian kinematics and structure, **Alsop & Holdsworth** build on the pioneering strain models of Coward & Potts (1983). They examine fold patterns in the mylonites of the Moine thrust belt, drawing comparisons with other 3D folding systems, such as slumps. The patterns of folding are used to deduce zones of differential movement in ductile thrust complexes. Coward's work on thrust systems in the NW Highlands in the 1980s continues to influence research on the structural evolution in the region together with the outer parts of mountain belts in general. **Butler *et al.*** examine the southern part of the Moine thrust belt, an area long overlooked in favour of the better known Assynt and Eriboll districts. They describe the structural relationships between relatively minor imbricate thrust systems and the major thrusts. A key conclusion is that end-member thrust-sequence models are not applicable in detail and that displacements in thrust arrays may have been synchronous rather than sequential. **Holdsworth *et al.*** revisit the northern part of the Moine thrust belt, developing the classic notion that folds and other minor structures have only local rather than regional significance in mylonite zones, and reassess the relationships between these structures and the major thrust surfaces. The internal deformation state of thrust sheets is a theme also addressed by **Vitale *et al.*** Coward's conclusion that deformation processes in the higher parts of the Moine thrust belt involved important components of quasi-coaxial stretching is mirrored in this study, although the example here is from the Southern Apennines of Italy. Partitioning of different degrees of simple shear and stretching are related to alternating competency contrasts in the carbonates of the thrust sheet.

Coward's work on the larger-scale significance of structures in the Moine thrust belt identified a series of faults and shear zones that appeared to accommodate regional extension (e.g. Coward 1983). He saw the same phenomenon in younger systems with his recognition of large-scale extensional relationships within the otherwise contractional orogenic belt of the NW Himalayas (Coward *et al.* 1987). Presenting a range of kinematic data derived from linked field and petrological studies, **Treloar *et al.*** discuss ductile extensional flow in the NW Himalayas. Rather than invoke the currently popular channel flow models (e.g. Beaumont *et al.* 2001), these workers suggest that extension has been polyphase in nature, in part resulting from re-equilibration of the orogen following inferred slab break-off. The theme of extensional tectonics and the coeval exhumation of deeply buried crust is continued in the following two papers. **Al-Wardi & Butler** present new field data from the northern Oman Mountains, where extension in the weakly buried Arabian continental crust at shallow levels in the orogen can be traced down a palaeo-subduction zone into ductile shear in adjacent metamorphic terrains. Complex interactions between folding and extension on a variety of scales can be explained by the differential shear model of Coward & Potts (1983). **Bond *et al.*** address the kinematics of ductile extension within the Cyclades, drawing on field studies on the island of Syros. Harking back to Coward's (1986) discussion of continental extensional tectonics, these researchers provide a field study that documents heterogeneous quasi-coaxial stretching associated with the exhumation of blueschists and eclogites. The theme links back to discussions of the kinematics of distributed deformation in basement terrains, such as the Lewisian.

In the next group of papers, which deal with regional tectonic problems, **Daly** revisits the Irumide belt of central Africa, drawing inspiration from Coward's regional shear zone models (e.g. Coward 1984). He shows the importance of the basic framework of structural geometry for the integration of diverse geological data. A synthesis of field geology and geochronology is used to develop a history of arc accretion in the assembly of continental crust. The study makes an interesting counterpoint to case histories of Tertiary orogenesis, such as the account by **Robertson *et al.*** of the eastern Taurus Mountains of Turkey where the history of distinct crustal blocks can be deduced from stratigraphic data. Relating local structures, such as fault systems, to plate kinematics was one of Coward's central research themes. **Nemčok *et al.*** look at the regional evolution of the Carpathians, using vein arrays to estimate the orientation of palaeostress fields. **Acosta *et al.*** continue the tradition in their study of the Colombian cordillera. For these researchers, the large-scale convergence associated with the subduction of the Nazca Plate is differentially partitioned at different lithospheric levels and is manifested by a complex history of strike-slip and thrust faulting. An analogous theme is developed for the whole of the South American continent by **Cobbold *et al.*** A series of scaled physical models are presented as analogues for this deformation, showing how varying plate kinematics acting on the edge of the continent drove faulting in the orogenic interior over the past 100 Ma.

During the 1980s, Coward began to see the importance of commercial seismic data in structural geology, beginning a series of investigations of sedimentary basins that continued for the rest of his career. Commonly, complex structure in sedimentary basins is associated with the presence (and mobility) of salt. Building on regional studies, such as appraisal of the South Atlantic continental margins by Coward *et al.* (1999*b*), **Davison** presents a review of salt mobility and basin evolution in offshore Brazil. He demonstrates the importance of regional tilts, governed both by tectonics and sediment loading, in influencing salt mobility and the consequent large-scale gravity collapse structures. This style of salt tectonics on a continental margin is different from that of more symmetrical intracontinental basins, and Davison's paper provides an interesting counterpoint to **Stewart**'s review of salt tectonics in the North Sea. This is a 'users' guide' to seismic interpretation using growth strata to deduce the development of salt structures. The modern concepts of salt tectonics, especially the role of differential loading and subtle tilting, are well illustrated here, as is the role of fundamental basement structures in governing the pattern of salt structures across the basin.

The role of basement structures in controlling the geological history of sedimentary basins was one of the great themes for much of Coward's work through the 1990s. In this volume several papers take many of the classic inversion tectonic concepts (e.g. Coward 1994, 1996) and apply them to unusual settings. The oblique reactivation of pre-existing rift structures is explored through a series of physical models presented by **Mattioni *et al.***. They show that under a constant far-field stress regime, complex polyphase structural histories may be generated in transpressional settings. **Casini *et al.*** apply ideas of inversion to an outcrop-scale linked system of net-contractional faults, arguing that they represent a microcosm of structural evolution in the northern Apennines. **Sepehr & Cosgrove** also discuss the role of structural inheritance, but apply the notion to parts of the Zagros fold belt.

The later papers in the volume are what might be called 'applied', and remind us that much of Mike Coward's later work was for the oil and gas and mining industries. **Cooper** undertakes a major review of hydrocarbon prospectivity in foreland fold and thrust belts, a study incorporating information from over 2900 fields worldwide. He shows that there is no single structural factor that makes hydrocarbon systems work in thrust belts; rather, it is a combination of attributes unique to each example that governs prospectivity. He makes it clear that the lessons drawn from case studies must be applied with care. A critical risk in many thrust belts is the relative timing of structural development and hydrocarbon migration. This issue is directly addressed by **Sassi *et al.*** in the Magdalena foreland fold and thrust belt of Colombia, through integrated modelling of structural evolution and petroleum systems. They show that whereas one geological history predicts that the target structure is prospective, in another the source rock is over-mature and the reservoir is destroyed. In many structurally complex settings, small-scale structures, such as fracture networks, play a major role in reservoir performance. Too often, however, reservoir modelling studies are based on theoretical considerations alone. There remains a paucity of field-based analogue studies, such as those presented here by **Belayneh *et al.***, which constrain the fracture patterns. Those workers use chalk outcrops of SE England to populate a reservoir model, to investigate structural controls on fluid flow, especially zones of concentrating fracturing (fracture corridors), linking these to larger-scale structural evolution.

The geometry and evolution of structures influences fluid flow in settings other than those associated with hydrocarbon migration. **Sibson** examines hydrothermal systems and related gold mineralization within the context of earthquake models. He recognizes that most of the world's hydrothermal gold deposits are associated with greenschist-facies metamorphism and therefore developed in the vicinity of the 'brittle–ductile transition'. He speculates that it is the undulations in the depth of the brittle–ductile transition that exert control on the migration of overpressured metamorphically derived fluids in the crust, especially during the development of major brittle thrust faults.

During his later career, Coward did much to promote the application of large-scale structural geology and basin evolution in mineral exploration, an area where such an approach was not previously the norm. It is therefore appropriate that the volume concludes with case studies associated with mineral exploration. The first two of these deal with the Witwatersrand basin of South Africa, building directly upon Coward's work. **Beach & Smith** present a series of cross-sections that document the structural relationships and evolution of the basin, explicitly presenting their conclusions in terms inherited from the world oil industry, straddling processes and scale. **Jolley *et al.*** also emphasize the importance of fault reactivation in the Witwatersrand basin and discuss the impact on the architecture of individual fault zones. The fact that the region has experienced contraction, followed by extension, means that individual fault zones commonly record a composite history, arguably controlling the distribution of gold mineralization. **Muntean *et al.*** use models for inversion tectonics to understand the evolution of faults and folds, associated with the Palaeozoic Antler Orogeny of central Nevada; the faults subsequently served to focus gold mineralization in Tertiary times.

Muntean directly acknowledges the role of his co-author, Mike Coward, for 'opening his eyes to the forest as well as the trees'. It is a sentiment that we know will be shared both by the contributors to this Special Publication and by the geological community at large.

This collection of papers written by Mike Coward's former students, friends and colleagues arises from a conference held in his memory at the Geological Society in May 2004 and an associated field trip to the Highlands and Islands of NW Scotland. We thank all those who participated in these activities.

References

ARGAND, E. 1924. *La tectonique de l'asie*. Brussels, 13th International Geological Congress, **1**, 170–372.

BALLY, A. W., GORDY, P. L. & STEWART, G. A. 1966. Structure, seismic data and orogenic evolution of Southern Canadian Rocky Mountains. *Bulletin of Canadian Petroleum Geology*, **14**, 337–381.

BANKS, C. J. & WARBURTON, J. 1986. Passive roof duplex geometry in the frontal structures of the Kirthar and Sulaiman mountain belts, Pakistan. *Journal of Structural Geology*, **8**, 229–237.

BEACH, A. 1981. Thrust tectonics and crustal shortening in the external French Alps based on a seismic cross-section. *Tectonophysics*, **79**, T1–T6.

BEAUMONT, C., JAMIESON, R. A., NGUYEN, M. H. & LEE, B. 2001. Himalayan tectonics explained by extrusion of a low-viscosity crustal channel coupled to focused surface denudation. *Nature*, **414**, 738–742.

BOSELLINI, A. 2004. The western passive margin of Adria and its carbonate platforms. *In*: CRESCENTI,

U., D'Offizi, S., Merlini, S. & Sacchi, R. (eds) *The Geology of Italy*. Società Geologica Italiana, Special Volume, 79–92.

Boyer, S. & Elliott, D. 1982. Thrust systems. *AAPG Bulletin*, **66**, 1196–1230.

Brewer, J. & Smythe, D. K. 1984. MOIST and the continuity of crustal reflector geometry along the Caledonian–Appalachian orogen. *Journal of the Geological Society, London*, **141**, 105–120.

Butler, R. W. H. & Coward, M. P. 1984. Geological constraints, structural evolution and deep geology of the Northwest Scottish Caledonides. *Tectonics*, **3**, 347–365.

Butler, R. W. H. & Coward, M. P. 1989. Crustal scale thrusting and continental subduction during Himalayan collision tectonics on the NW Indian plate. *In*: Şengör, A. M. C. (ed.) *Tectonic Evolution of Tethyan Regions*. Proceedings, NATO ASI, **C259**, 387–413.

Butler, R. W. H., Lloyd, G. E. & Holdsworth, R. E. 1997. The role of basement reactivation in continental deformation. *Journal of the Geological Society, London*, **154**, 69–71.

Cook, F. A., Albaugh, D. S., Brown, L. D., Kaufman, S., Oliver, J. E. & Hatcher, R. D. Jr 1979. Thin-skinned tectonics in the crystalline southern Appalachians: COCORP seismic-reflection profiling of the Blue Ridge and Piedmont. *Geology*, **7**, 563–567.

Coward, M. P. 1980. The Caledonian thrust and shear zones of NW Scotland. *Journal of Structural Geology*, **2**, 11–17.

Coward, M. P. 1982. Surge zones in the Moine thrust zone of N.W. Scotland. *Journal of Structural Geology*, **4**, 247–256.

Coward, M. P. 1983. The thrust and shear zones of the Moine Thrust zone and the NW Scottish Caledonides. *Journal of the Geological Society, London*, **140**, 795–811.

Coward, M. P. 1984. Major shear zones in the Precambrian crust; examples from NW Scotland and southern Africa and their significance. *In*: Kröner, A. & Greiling, R. (eds) *Precambrian Tectonics Illustrated*. Schweizerbart, Stuttgart, 207–235.

Coward, M. P. 1986. Heterogeneous stretching, simple shear and basin development. *Earth and Planetary Science Letters*, **80**, 325–336.

Coward, M. P. 1994. Inversion tectonics. *In*: Hancock, P. L. (ed.) *Continental Deformation*. Pergamon, Oxford, 289–304.

Coward, M. P. 1996. Balancing sections through inverted basins. *In*: Buchanan, P. G. & Nieuwland, D. A. (eds) *Modern Developments in Structural Interpretation, Validation and Modelling*. Geological Society, London, Special Publications, **99**, 51–77.

Coward, M. P. & Butler, R. W. H. 1985. Thrust tectonics and the deep structure of the Pakistan Himalaya. *Geology*, **13**, 417–420.

Coward, M. P. & Dietrich, D. 1989. Alpine tectonics: an overview. *In*: Coward, M. P. & Dietrich, D. (eds) *Alpine Tectonics*. Geological Society, London, Special Publications, **45**, 1–29.

Coward, M. P. & Kim, J. H. 1981. Strain within thrust sheets. *In*: McClay, K. R. & Price, N. J. (eds) *Thrust and Nappe Tectonics*. Geological Society, London, Special Publications, **9**, 275–292.

Coward, M. P. & Potts, G. J. 1983. Complex strain patterns at the frontal and lateral tips to shear zones and thrust zones. *Journal of Structural Geology*, **5**, 383–399.

Coward, M. P., Nell, P. R. & Talbot, J. 1992. An analysis of the strains associated with the Moine Thrust zone, Assynt, Northwest Scotland. *In*: Mitra, S. & Fisher, G. W. (eds) *Structural Geology of Fold and Thrust Belts*. John Hopkins University Press, Baltimore, MD, 105–22.

Coward, M. P., Spencer, R. M. & Spencer, C. E. 1995. Development of the Witwatersrand Basin, South Africa. *In*: Coward, M. P. & Ries, A. C. (eds) *Early Precambrian Processes*. Geological Society, London, Special Publications, **95**, 243–269.

Coward, M. P., Dewey, J. F., Hempton, M. & Holroyd, J. 2003. Regional tectonics. *In*: Evans, D., Graham, C., Armour, A. & Bathurst, P. (eds) *The Millennium Atlas: Petroleum Geology of the Central and Northern North Sea*. Geological Society of London, 17–33.

Coward, M. P., Butler, R. W. H., Asif Khan, M. & Knipe, R. J. 1987. The tectonic history of Kohistan and its implications for Himalayan structure. *Journal of the Geological Society, London*, **144**, 377–391.

Coward, M. P., De Donatis, M., Mazzoli, S., Paltrinieri, W. & Wezel, F.-C. 1999*a*. The frontal part of the northern Apennines foreland fold and thrust belt in the Romagna–Marche area (Italy): shallow and deep structural styles. *Tectonics*, **18**, 559–574.

Coward, M. P., Purdy, E. G., Ries, A.C. & Smith, D. G. 1999*b*. The distribution of petroleum reserves in basins of the South Atlantic margins. *In*: Cameron, N. R., Bate, R. H. & Clure, V. S. (eds) *The Oil and Gas Habitats of the South Atlantic*. Geological Society, London, Special Publications, **53**, 101–131.

Coward, M. P., Kidd, W. S. F., Pan Yun, Shackleton, R. M. & Zhang Hu 1988. The structure of the 1985 Tibet Geotraverse, Lhasa to Golmud. *Philosophical Transactions of the Royal Society of London, Series A*, **327**, 307–336.

Dahlstrom, C. D. A. 1969. Balanced cross-sections. *Canadian Journal of Earth Sciences*, **6**, 743–757.

DeCelles, P. G., Robinson, D. M., Quade, J., Ojha, T. P., Garzione, C. N., Copeland, P. & Upreti, B. M. 2001. Stratigraphy, structure and tectonic evolution of the Himalayan fold–thrust belt in western Nepal. *Tectonics*, **23**, 487–509.

Elliott, D. 1976. The energy balance and deformation mechanisms of thrust sheets. *Philosophical Transactions of the Royal Society of London, Series A*, **283**, 289–312.

Elliott, D. & Johnson, M. R. W. 1980. Structural evolution in the northern part of the Moine thrust belt, NW Scotland. *Transactions of the Royal Society of Edinburgh*, **71**, 69–96.

Enfield, M. A. & Coward, M. P. 1987. The structure of the West Orkney Basin, Northern Scotland. *Journal of the Geological Society, London*, **144**, 871–884.

Escher, A. & Watterson, J. 1974. Stretching fabrics, folds and crustal shortening. *Tectonophysics*, **22**, 223–231.

Fischer, M. W. & Coward, M. P. 1982. Strains and folds within thrust sheets: the Heilam sheet Northwest Scotland. *Tectonophysics*, **88**, 291–312.

Fossen, H. & Tikoff, B. 1998. Extended models of transpression and transtension, and application to tectonic settings. *In*: Holdsworth, R. E., Strachan, R. A. & Dewey, J. F. (eds) *Continental Transpressional and Transtensional Tectonics*. Geological Society, London, Special Publications, **135**, 15–33.

Gidon, M. 1981. Les déformations de la couverture des Alpes occidentals externes dans le région de Grenoble: leurs rapports avec celles du socle. *Comptes Rendus de l'Académie des Sciences*, **292**, 1057–1060.

Gillcrist, R., Coward, M. P. & Mugnier, J. L. 1987. Structural inversion and its controls: examples from the Alpine foreland and the French Alps. *Geodinamica Acta*, **1**, 5–34.

Holdsworth, R. E., Alsop, G. I. & Strachan, R. A. 2007. Tectonic stratigraphy and structural continuity of the northernmost Moine Thrust Zone and Moine Nappe, Scottish Caledonides. *In*: Ries, A. C., Butler, R. W. H. & Graham, R. H. (eds) *Deformation of the Continental Crust: The Legacy of Mike Coward.* Geological Society, London, Special Publications, **272**, 121–142.

Humphris, C. C., Jr 1978. Salt motion of continental slope, northern Gulf of Mexico. *In*: Bouma, A. H., Moore, G. T. & Coleman, J. M. (eds) *Framework, Facies and Old-trapping Characteristics of the Upper Continental Margin.* American Association of Pctrolcum Gcologists, Studics in Gcology, **7**, 69–85.

Jackson, J. A. 1980. Reactivation of basement faults and crustal shortening in orogenic belts. *Nature*, **283**, 343–346.

Jackson, M. P. A. & Talbot, C. J. 1994. Advances in salt tectonics. *In*: Hancock, P. L. (ed.) *Continental Deformation.* Pergamon, Oxford, 159–179.

Lemoine, M., Bas, T., Arnaud-Vanneau, A. *et al.* 1986. The continental margin of the Mesozoic Tethys in the western Alps. *Marine and Petroleum Geology*, **3**, 179–199.

Ozacar, A. A. & Zandt, G. 2004. Crustal seismic anisotropy in central Tibet: Implications for deformation style and flow in the crust: *Geophysical Research Letters*, **31**, doi: 10.1029/2004GL021096.

Peach, B. N., Horne, J., Gunn, W., Clough, C. T., Hinxman, L. W. & Teall, J. J. H. 1907. *The Geological Structure of the North-West Highlands of Scotland.* Memoirs of the Geological Survey of Great Britain.

Pfiffner, O. A., Lehner, P., Heitzmann, P., Mueller, S. & Steck, A. (eds) 1997. *Results of NRP20: Deep Structure of the Swiss Alps.* Birkhäuser, Basel.

Ramsay, J. G. 1967. *Folding and Fracturing of Rocks.* McGraw–Hill, New York.

Ramsay, J.G. & Graham, R.H. 1970. Strain variation in shear belts. *Canadian Journal of Earth Sciences*, **7**, 786–813.

Schulte-Pelkum, V., Monsalve, G., Sheehan, A., Pandey, M. R., Sapkota, S., Bilham, R. & Wu, F. 2005. Imaging the Indian subcontinent beneath the Himalaya. *Nature*, **435**, 1222–1225.

Scrocca, D., Doglioni, C., Innocenti, F. *et al.* (eds) 2003. *CROP Atlas: Seismic Reflection Profiles of the Italian Crust.* Memorie Descrittive della Carta Geologica d'Italia, **62**.

Soper, N. J. & Barber, A. J. 1982. A model for the deep structure of the Moine thrust zone. *Journal of the Geological Society, London*, **139**, 127–138.

Stewart, S. A. & Coward, M. P. 1995. A synthesis of salt tectonics in the southern North Sea, U.K. *Marine and Petroleum Geology*, **12**, 457–475.

Sutton, J. & Watson, J. V. 1951. The pre-Torridonian metamorphic history of the Loch Torridon and Scourie areas in the North-West Highlands and its bearing on the chronological classification of the Lewisian. *Quarterly Journal of the Geological Society of London*, **106**, 241–307.

Tahirkheli, R. A. K. & Jan, M. Q. (eds) 1979. *The Geology of Kohistan, Karakoram Himalaya, Northern Pakistan.* Geological Bulletin of the University of Peshawar, Special Issue, **11**.

Tavarnelli, E., Butler, R. W. H., Decandia, F. A., Calamita, F., Grasso, M., Alvarez, W. & Renda, P. 2004. Implications of fault reactivation and structural inheritance in the Cenozoic tectonic evolution of Italy. *In*: Crescenti, U., D'Offizi, S., Merlini, S. & Sacchi, R. (eds) *The Geology of Italy.* Societa Geologica Italiana, Special Volume, 209–222.

Termier, P. 1904. Les nappes des Alpes Orientales et la synthèse des Alpes. *Bulletin de la Société Géologique de France*, **4**, 711–765.

Treloar, P. J., Brodie, K. H., Coward, M. P. *et al.* 1990. The evolution of the Kamila shear zone, Kohistan, Pakistan. *In*: Salisbury, M. H. & Fountain, D. M. (eds) *Exposed Cross Sections of the Continental Crust.* Kluwer, Dordrecht, 175–214.

Watson, J. V. 1985. Northern Scotland as an Atlantic–North Sea divide. *Journal of the Geological Society, London*, **142**, 221–243.

Williams, G. D. & Fischer, M. W. 1984. A balanced cross-section across the Pyrenean orogenic belt. *Tectonics*, **3**, 773–780.

Wu, S., Bally, A. W. & Cramez, C. 1990. Allochthonous salt, structure and stratigraphy of the northeastern Gulf of Mexico, Part II: structure. *Marine and Petroleum Geology*, **7**, 334–370.

Zanella, E. & Coward, M. P. 2003. Structural framework. *In*: Evans, D., Graham, C., Armour, A. & Bathurst, P. (eds) *The Millennium Atlas: Petroleum Geology of the Central and Northern North Sea.* Geological Society of London, 45–59.

Zanella, E., Coward, M. P. & McGrandle, A. 2003. Crustal structure. *In*: Evans, D., Graham, C., Armour, A. & Bathurst, P. (eds) *The Millennium Atlas: Petroleum Geology of the Central and Northern North Sea.* Geological Society of London, 35–42.

Zhang, P.-Z., Shen, Z., Wang, M. *et al.* 2004. Continuous deformation of the Tibetan plateau from global positioning system data. *Geology*, **32**, 809–812.

Zhao, W. & Nelson, K. D. 1993. Deep seismic reflection evidence for continental underthrusting beneath southern Tibet. *Nature*, **366**, 557–559.

Mike Coward's early days: the Lewisian, and what he made of it

RODNEY H. GRAHAM

Amerada Hess Ltd, The Adelphi Building, 1–11 John Adam Street, London WC2N 6AG, UK
(e-mail: rod.graham@hess.com)

Abstract: Mike Coward began his career working on Lewisian rocks and readdressed the problems they pose several times during his life. His ability to extrapolate ideas from one area of geology to another and to straddle geological time scale enabled him to reappraise the regional Lewisian structure and evolution in the light of ideas evolving elsewhere, whether that was in his own head or in the geology of the wider world. It was done through an understanding of theoretical structural geology and small-scale example, yet at the same time it extrapolated to large scale and was significant not only in terms of the Lewisian and the Precambrian in general, but also in understanding the way in which the Earth's crust deforms. Coward's work rarely stayed within conventional bounds; and when it did, it pushed the limits. Our understanding of the world progresses through that sort of approach. It is seen too rarely nowadays.

Mike Coward ranged wide across the discipline of structural geology. He worked everywhere: the Caledonides, Africa, the Alps, the Himalaya, South America, North America, China. He worked on academic strain problems, with mining companies on crystalline rocks, and on sedimentary basins with oil companies. Whenever he did anything, he instinctively looked for something new, developed an alternative interpretation, or could see a possibility to apply and develop 'state-of-the-art' ideas.

But it started in the Lewisian. Coward did his PhD thesis on South Uist between 1966 and 1969, with Janet Watson as supervisor and Peter Francis, John Myers and myself as fellow students on adjacent islands.

At first sight, the 'stirred porridge' of the Lewisian gneiss might seem an unrewarding place to do structural geology, especially at a time when (under the influence of John Ramsay) there was a significant drive towards quantification. Almost certainly, this difficult and unconventional challenge was exactly what attracted Mike. The Alps were 'old hat'. This was new.

Historically, the first breakthrough in the interpretation of the Lewisian came with the publication of the great *North-West Highlands Memoir* in 1907 (Peach *et al.* 1907), and in it the recognition of a 'fundamental complex' (Fig. 1a), cut by a set of later cross-cutting dykes (Fig. 1b and c), which were then deformed together during later earth movements (Fig. 1d and e). Sutton & Watson (Fig. 1f) developed and enhanced this idea in their 1951 paper, a study that became classic in Precambrian geology. The 'fundamental complex' became the Scourian complex and the dykes the 'Scourie dykes' (after the township in Sutherland where Janet Watson was known as 'tapping Jenny'). The redeformation and remetamorphism ('reworking') of the Scourian and the dykes was called the 'Laxfordian', the name derived from Laxford Bridge where, at the 'Laxford Front' a profound change in the state of deformation and metamorphism of the Lewisian is starkly apparent and marked by a wide zone of amalgamated sheets of granite and pegmatite (Fig. 1g).

Dearnley (1962) applied the concept of Scourian–Laxfordian evolution to the Western Isles and defined a central Scourian block (Fig. 2), bounded by areas of more intense Laxfordian reworking (as in Fig. 1e). He mapped the southern boundary of the central zone through South Uist (Fig. 2a), and argued for the displacement of Hebridean and Mainland zones on a transcurrent fault (like the Great Glen Fault) in the Minch (Fig. 2b).

This was what Coward wanted to work on in detail. The introduction to his PhD thesis tells us, 'My original idea was to study the structural and metamorphic variations which occurred at the edge of an orogenic belt. Dearnley (1962) had described such a boundary running through the centre of South Uist, so this seemed an ideal place for such an investigation. I [Coward] found, however, that the geology was by no means as simple as Dearnley had suggested and there was no actual boundary between Scourian and Laxfordian zones.'

Note: Given the nature of this paper, most of the figures have deliberately been taken without modification from Coward's original publications. On some, detail may not always be clear. Where this is the case, interested readers should refer to the original publications.

From: Ries, A. C., Butler, R. W. H. & Graham, R. H. (eds) 2007. *Deformation of the Continental Crust: The Legacy of Mike Coward.* Geological Society, London, Special Publications, **272**, 9–25.
0305-8719/07/$15

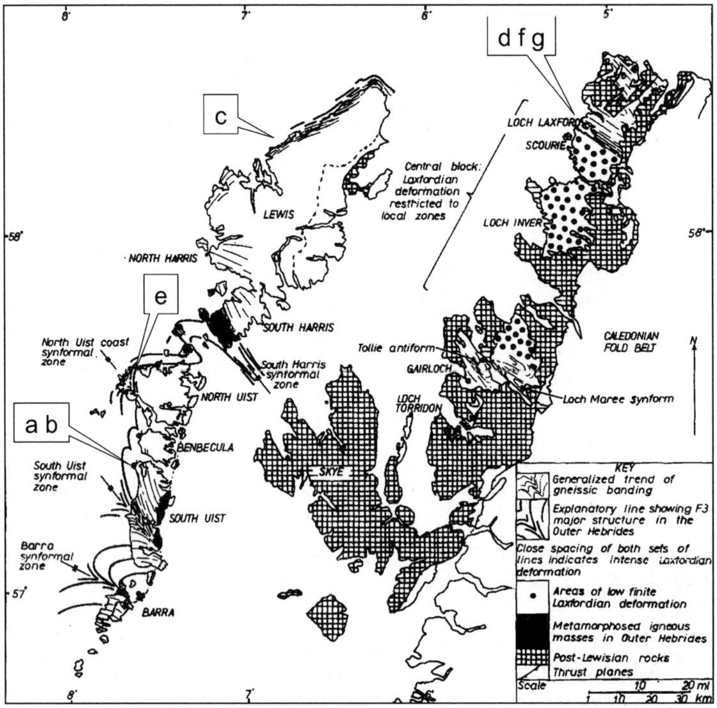

Fig. 1. Scourie: Laxford, the theme, the place and the inventors of the terminology. The map above shows the location of the pictures opposite.

Instead Coward discovered a series of small-scale 'Scourie–Laxfords' through his field area (Coward 1973*b*). The intense granitization of Laxford is not visible in South Uist and Benbecula, but analogous deformation variations are, and it was these that he analysed. He was not the first to look at them. Dearnley & Dunning (1968) had already recognized areas of low finite Laxfordian deformation at Ardivachar Point in South Uist and Garry a Siar on Benbecula, but they did not describe them as such, and assumed them to be typical exposures of their larger Scourian block.

The first step in understanding the context of these strain variations was, of course, to establish the regional structure and deformation sequence of South Uist in particular and the Southern Hebrides in general. It was done by mapping, tracing foliation and banding, mapping minor fold vergence and detailed age relationships. This was a major achievement, necessary to change the mindset that the Lewisian was a geometrically impenetrable mass of flowed material. Even in the absence of stratigraphy, the common-sense techniques of structural mapping could be shown to work. Coward's map of South Uist (Coward 1973*a*) is shown in Figure 3a. Putting South Uist into the concept of the major structure of the Hebrides (Fig. 4) was a joint effort (Coward *et al.* 1970), with Coward not just alphabetically the first author.

The overall architecture was given by a set of northwesterly plunging upright folds, broad box-shaped anticlines, separated by 'nipped in' synclines. The foliation, deformed around the folds, was interpreted as a penetrative strain fabric of gneissic banding and Scourie dyke-derived amphibolite bodies that had been dragged into parallelism with the banding. The amphibolites were seen to be folded or boudinaged (depending on the orientation of the structures in the strain ellipsoid), and the old Scourian agmatite streaked out into the ubiquitous banded 'grey gneiss' of the Hebrides.

Scourie dyke-derived amphibolites, deformed in this way, show internally folded or modified earlier fabrics, which suggested that this intense deformation was the second episode of Laxfordian strain (F_2), commonly obliterating evidence of the earlier one (F_1).

On the scale of the islands, the original orientations of the fabrics, associated with these deformation events, were approximately reconstructed. The gentle dip of the enveloping surface of the youngest structures, the box-shaped upright anticlines with intervening tighter

Fig. 1. Continued

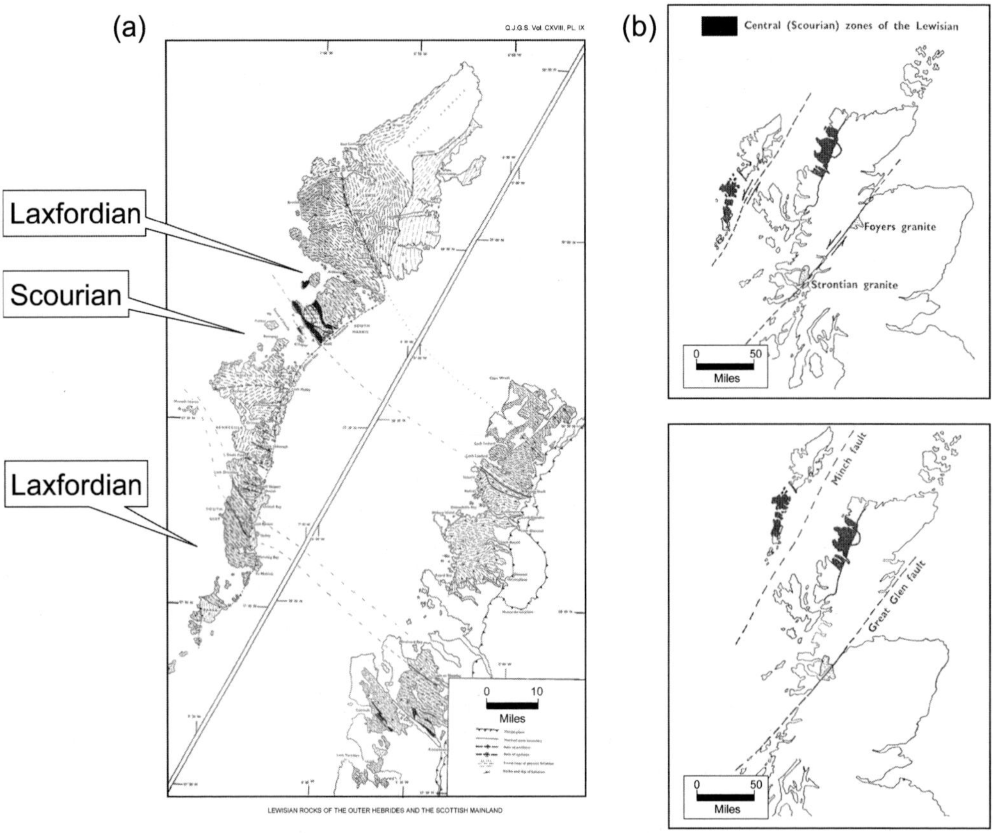

Fig. 2. Dearnley's view of the Lewisian; status quo before Coward's work. (**a**) Lewisian rocks of the Outer Hebrides and the Scottish mainland, showing foliation trends and zone boundaries. The Outer Hebrides are shown in their approximate relative positions before the postulated displacement along the Minch Fault (Dearnley 1962, plate IX). (**b**) The Minch Fault and the Great Glen Fault showing the positions of the Outer Hebrides and mainland Lewisian central zones and the Strontian and Foyers granites (above) and the postulated original positions before displacement along the Minch and Great Glen faults (Dearnley 1962, p. 163).

synclines ('F_3' in the sequence), suggests that the F_2 fabric, which they deform, was originally born with a gentle dip; an important observation that Coward alluded to again and again in later publications. The areas of low deformation were perceived to be pods of less deformed rock within this overall pervasive fabric, analogous perhaps to less strained pods visible in the smaller-scale ductile shear zones (Fig. 5) that were being described and analysed at about this time (Ramsay & Graham 1970).

The location of the less deformed pods close to, or within, the broad hinge zones of the anticlines (Fig. 6d) was probably related to the fact that these are also areas of lowest F_3 strain. As it might be expected (and taken for granted now, though we did not necessarily then), thoroughly amphibolitized deformed rocks, with a pervasive planar fabric, are weaker than less deformed agmatitic, more isotropic gneisses with the relic of a granulite-facies assemblage. Strain variations persist through deformation history. Coward described them in a structural language that had been derived from John Ramsay, and he quantified the Laxfordian strain intensity based on careful measurement of the angular relationships between the Scourie dykes and the older Scourian agmatite or gneissic banding into which they were originally intruded (Fig. 6b).

Coward also analysed the variations in intensity and symmetry of the internal fabric of the Scourie dyke-derived amphibolites, more linear where they are less deformed, yet becoming LS tectonites (i.e. with both linear and planar fabric components) where dragged parallel to deformed gneissic banding. Recognizing that the dyke fabric would originally have been isotropic, he deduced that the superimposition of strains in the Hebridean gneisses was effectively orthogonal, therefore avoiding more complex rotational

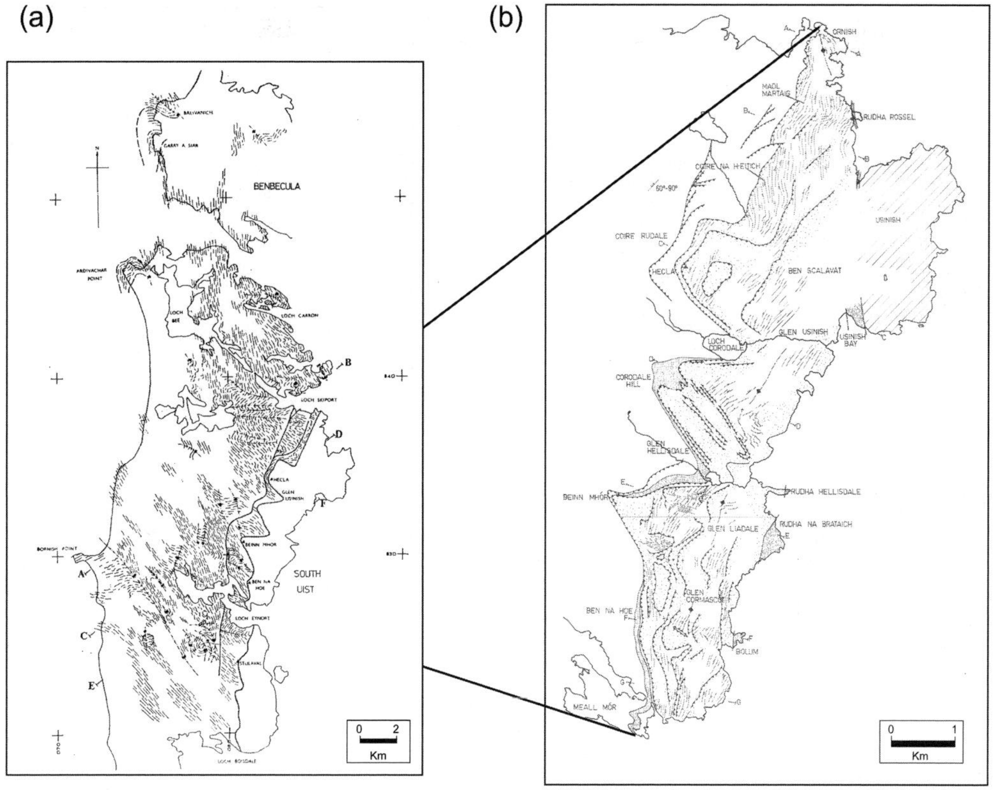

Fig. 3. Coward's maps of South Uist, Western and Eastern Gneisses. (**a**) Geological map of South Uist and Benbecula showing the trend of the gneissose foliation round structures of F_3 and F_4 age, west of the Outer Isles thrust (Coward 1973*a*, p. 145). (**b**) The structure of the Eastern Gneisses of South Uist, between Ornish and Loch Eynort (Coward 1972, fig. 2).

strain, to allow the co-axial multiplication of the strains, employing the principles of the optical indicatrix (Fig. 6a). The approach was made possible by Flinn's classic theoretical work (Flinn 1965) and Ramsay's (1967) analyses of deformed conglomerates, but in this context it was a piece of brilliant original, simplifying thinking, also applicable (though less generally and more cautiously) to the gross shape fabrics of the gneisses themselves (Fig. 6c). Of course, it might seem common sense now that the mineral aggregates in metamorphic rocks are not necessarily that much different from deformable objects in sedimentary rocks, but Mike Coward saw the power of it and applied it to great effect where no-one else had previously thought to. The fabric evolution of the deformed dykes was plotted as a series of strain paths on a Flinn diagram (Fig. 6a) and thus became both deductive and predictive in terms of analysing the regional variations in Laxfordian strain intensity. It was an early taste of Coward's genius for applying ideas and principles from one area of discipline to another. Very simple in retrospect, at the time it was a major step forward in thinking about the strain state of crystalline rocks.

On a completely different scale, Coward noticed the similarity of the shape of the large-scale third folds of the Hebrides (Fig. 4) to Ramsay's illustrations of the cuspate shape of a shortened interface between more ductile and less ductile media. He associated it with the change from lower crustal granulite-facies rocks on the eastern side of the Uists with more granitic amphibolite-facies rocks in the west. It was a far-reaching extrapolation of scale, an early sign of another intuitive Coward flair and indicative of what was to come in much of his later work. No-one used 'Pumpelly's rule' (that small-scale structures reflect large-scale structures) more

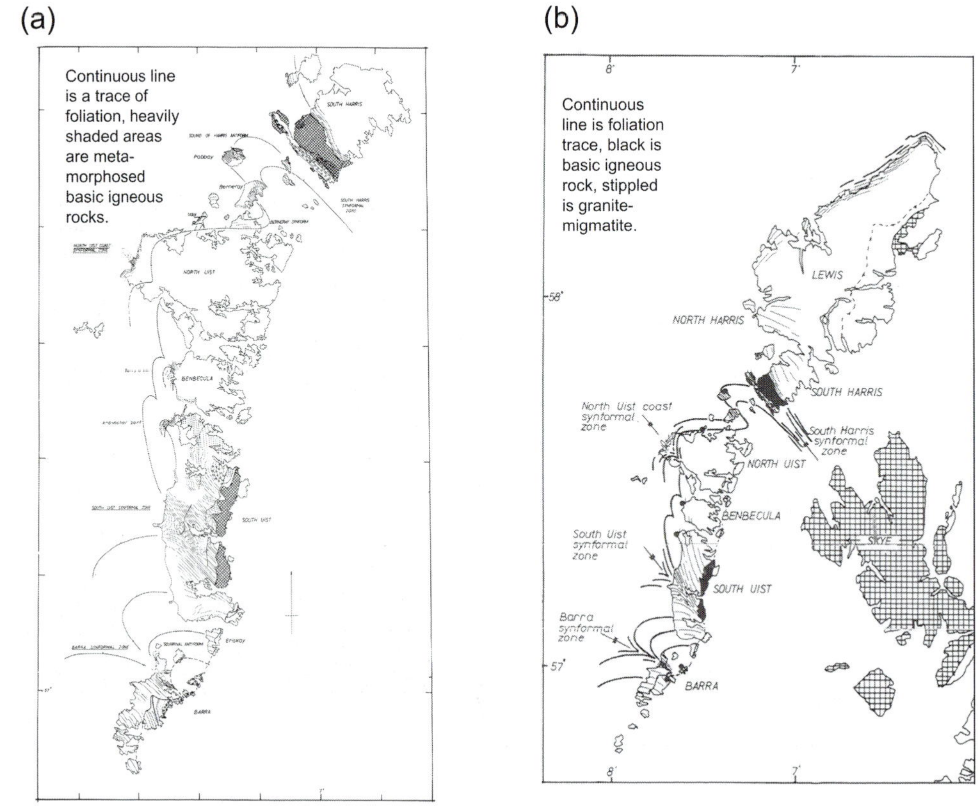

Fig. 4. Hebridean structural synthesis. (**a**) Schematic map of parts of the southern islands, Outer Hebrides illustrating the arrangement of Laxfordian F_3 antiforms and synforms in relation to other tectonic and metamorphic features (Coward *et al.* 1970, fig. 1). (**b**) Schematic map showing the arrangement of Laxfordian F_3 structures in the Outer Hebrides in relation to variations in the Lewisian outcrop of the Scottish mainland (Coward *et al.* 1970, fig. 2).

Fig. 5. Ductile simple shear zones at their simplest, North Uist.

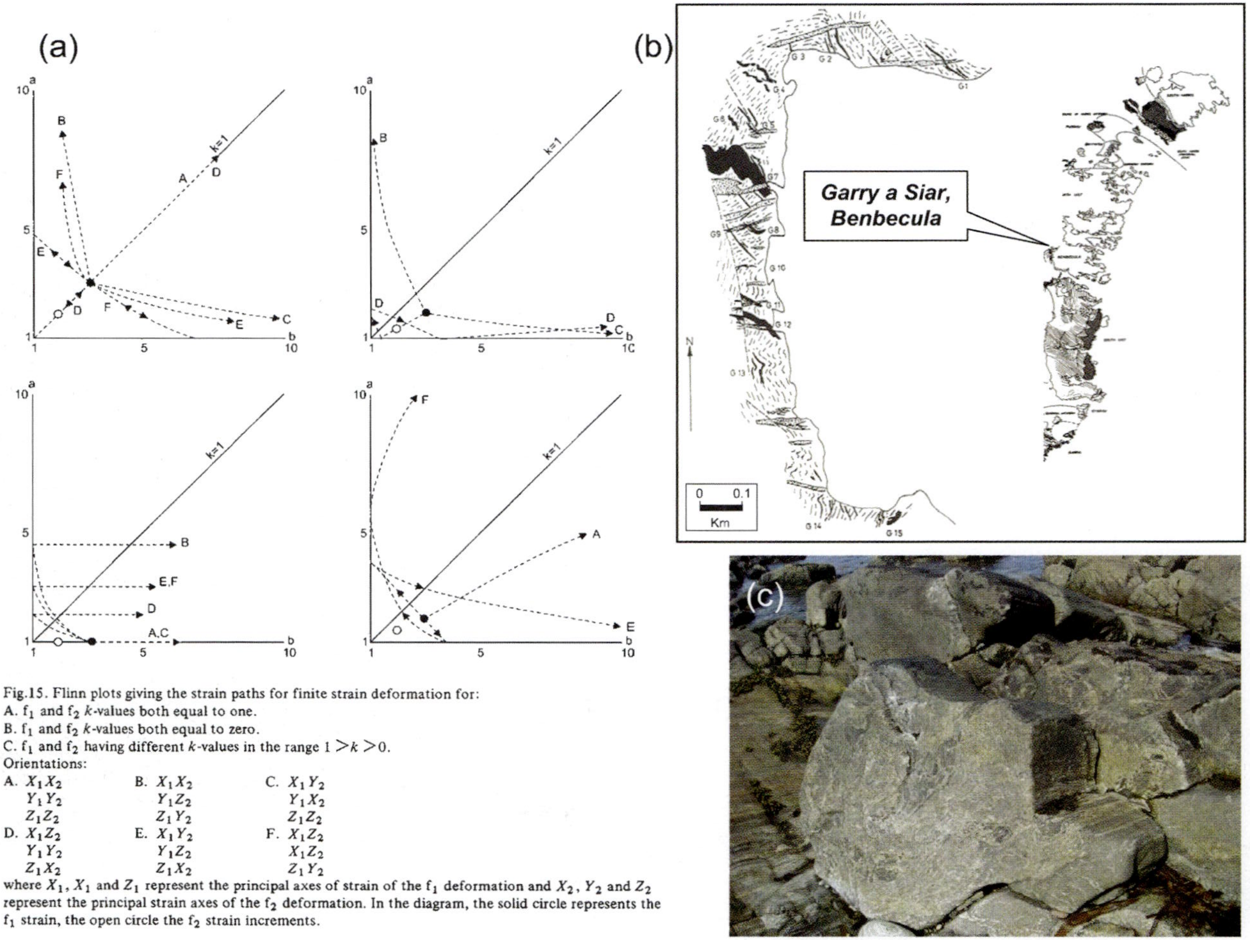

(a)
(b)
(c)
k=1
Garry a Siar, Benbecula
0 0.1 Km
N
Fig.15. Flinn plots giving the strain paths for finite strain deformation for:
A. f_1 and f_2 k-values both equal to one.
B. f_1 and f_2 k-values both equal to zero.
C. f_1 and f_2 having different k-values in the range $1 > k > 0$.
Orientations:
A. X_1X_2 Y_1Y_2 Z_1Z_2
B. X_1X_2 Y_1Z_2 Z_1Y_2
C. X_1Y_2 Y_1X_2 Z_1Z_2
D. X_1Z_2 Y_1Y_2 Z_1X_2
E. X_1Y_2 Y_1Z_2 Z_1X_2
F. X_1Z_2 X_1Z_2 Z_1Y_2
where X_1, X_1 and Z_1 represent the principal axes of strain of the f_1 deformation and X_2, Y_2 and Z_2 represent the principal strain axes of the f_2 deformation. In the diagram, the solid circle represents the f_1 strain, the open circle the f_2 strain increments.

Fig. 6. Coward's innovative geometrical approaches in the areas of low finite Laxfordian strain in South Uist. (**a**) Flinn plots giving the strain paths for finite strain deformations (Coward 1973*b*, fig. 15). (**b**) Map of the coastline round Garry-a-Siar, Benbecula (Coward 1973*b*, fig. 3). (**c**) Linear fabric in Scourian grey gneisses.

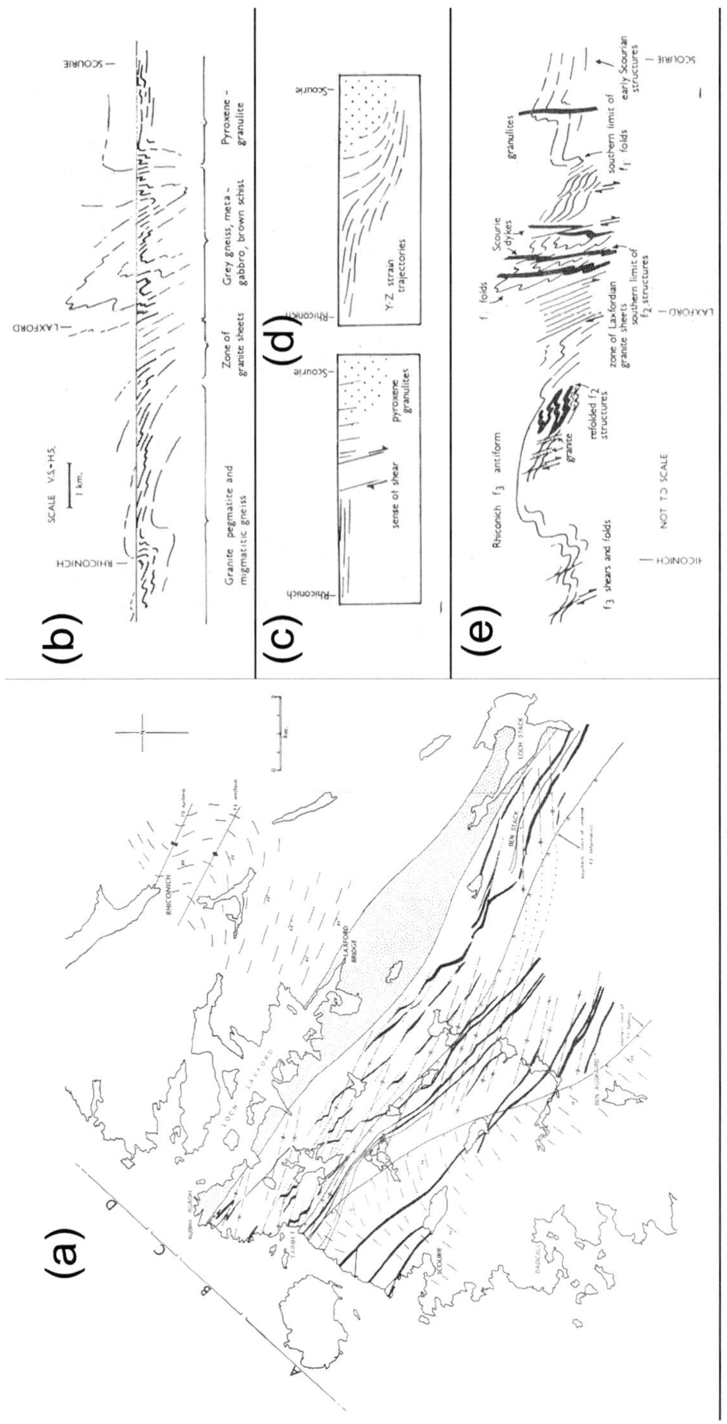
(a)
(b)
SCALE V.S.=H.S.
1 km.
RHICONICH
LAXFORD
SCOURIE
Granite pegmatite and migmatitic gneiss
Zone of granite sheets
Grey gneiss, meta-gabbro, brown schist
Pyroxene-granulite
(c)
Rhiconich
Scourie
sense of shear
pyroxene granulites
(d)
Y-Z strain trajectories
(e)
f3 shears and folds
Rhiconich f3 antiform
granite
refolded f2 structures
zone of Laxfordian granite sheets
southern limit of f2 structures
Scourie dykes
southern limit of f1 folds
granulites
early Scourian structures
NOT TO SCALE
(f)
Rhiconich Antiform
Zone of Laxfordian Granite sheets

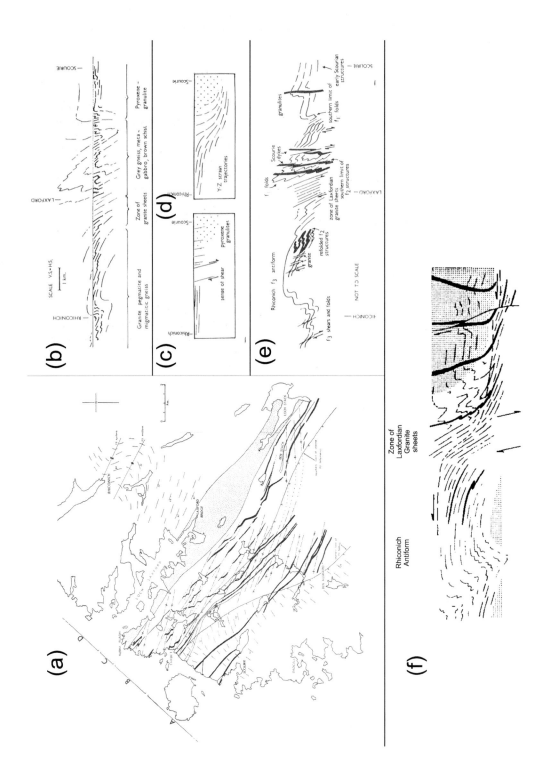

naturally or more innovatively. The issue of the lower crust and its deformation became a recurrent theme of Coward's work. Even at the time of the regional Hebridean paper, it was clearly in his mind that what he was seeing in South Uist might have significance on a far larger scale than that of the Hebrides.

Scourie–Laxford, the Scottish mainland and the Lewisian generality

The Laxford Front on the Scottish mainland was the place where, along with Alastair Beach and myself, Coward tackled the Lewisian for a second time. The central 'Scourie block' of the mainland was interpreted as a less deformed pod, analogous to those of the Hebrides but on a much grander scale, with the Laxford Front a complex shear zone at its northern boundary (Figs 7 and 8). Here granulite-facies rocks sit in the hanging wall of the south-dipping ductile shear zone with granitic, amphibolite facies in the footwall, the latter presumably having originated at a higher crustal level. The fundamental difference in metamorphic grade between the two units, and the clear evidence of the migration of water and potassium through shear zones within the originally dry and sodic Scourie gneisses (Beach & Fyfe 1976; Beach 1976), suggests the tectonic emplacement of the Scourie zone over the Laxford zone. So too does the large-scale dextral deflection of the foliation on a large scale, but in the shear zones the sinistral sense of displacement of dykes, together with the southeasterly plunging stretching fabric in the shear zone, indicates oblique normal displacement rather than the thrusting. Minor structures (sheared pods, minor folds) share the perversity of sheared dykes.

Two models were proposed by Beach *et al.* (1974) to explain this (Fig. 8). One has the Laxford shear zone as the underside margin of a less deformed pod surrounded by gneisses deformed by regional pure shear or flattening (the sense of shear being a function of the position with respect to the pod). The other has the Scourie zone as a pod in a horizontal shear zone with 'top-towards-the-north' sense.

A little later than, and deriving from but outreaching Beach *et al.* (1974), Mike Coward published a short paper of real genius, which attacked the problem of lower crustal deformation head on (Coward 1974). This was 'Flat lying structures within the Lewisian basement gneiss complex of NW Scotland' and in it is the realization that the early Laxfordian strain generated flat-lying or gently dipping foliation, throughout the Lewisian complex (Fig. 9). It is another great example of the Coward art of up-scaling geological observation. He argued, 'If, over large areas the flat foliation was produced by pure shear involving vertical compression, and hence extension in a horizontal direction, then there is a space problem' (Fig. 9a). Indeed there is, but no-one had spelled it out like this before. His answer, *the* answer, to the problem is, of course, that the flat-lying fabric was created by deep crustal simple shear, with the consequent lateral translation of the upper crust or, as Coward put it in 1973, 'The onset of Laxfordian deformation is best interpreted as a flat shear zone'.

The displacement within this horizontal shear zone could be generated by contractional strain, thrusting or collision in the upper crust. Equally, upper crustal extension could also be accommodated at depth in a gently dipping shear fabric. In the 1960s and 1970s, no-one thought very much about extension; it came later, requiring the Mackenzie model on the one hand and the early geometrical thinking of oil company structural geologists on the other. This was the early 1980s era of the 'Chevron construction', North Sea seismic data, and listric faults that needed to 'sole out' somewhere. If this 'soling out' were to occur in the ductile lower crust, then ductile strain fabrics would have to develop to accommodate the deformation, and they would, of course, be gently dipping (Fig. 10).

At about this time a number of deep seismic lines were shot in Britain. MOIST (Fig. 11) was shot off the north coast of Scotland and identified major thrust zones, reactivated as normal faults, which 'flatten or terminate at 17–20 km deep'; deeper (actually in the mantle) in the case of the Flannan thrust (Brewer & Smythe 1984). The nature of subhorizontal reflectors deep in the

Fig. 7. The Laxford Front as seen by Beach *et al.* (1974). (**a**) The principal tectonic structures of the Scourie–Laxford region, based on detailed mapping in the Scourie–Rubha Ruadh–Ben Stack–Ben Auskaird region, and reconnaissance mapping elsewhere. (**b**) Section across the Laxford Front from Rhiconich and Scourie. (**c**) Sketch section showing the variation in orientation of F_2 axial surfaces between Rhiconich and Scourie. (**d**) Suggested model for the F_2 XY strain trajectories between Rhiconich and Scourie. The stipple marks the Scourian pyroxene granulites. (**e**) Schematic section between Rhiconich and Scourie to show the form and age of fold structures and the sense of shear movement. Not to scale. (**f**) Schematic section through the Laxford Front showing the granulites carried over by later, steep shear zones with north side upwards sense of movement. Dykes are shown by bold lines (Coward 1974, fig. 5c).

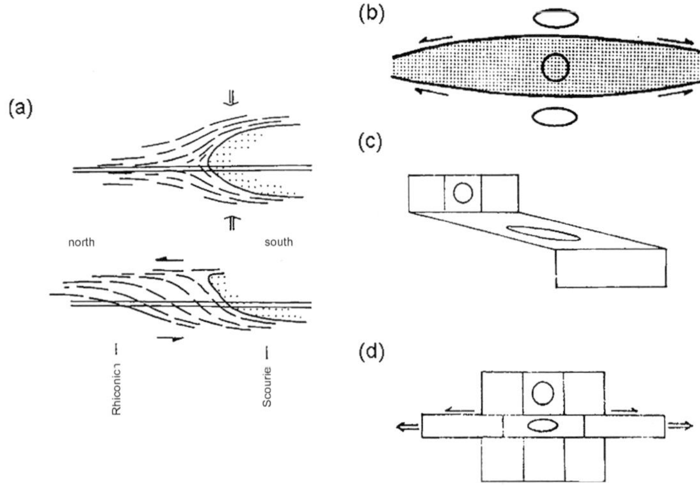

Fig. 8. Coward's analysis of the flat-lying structures of the Hebrides. (**a**) Model to explain the form of the F_2 strain trajectories assuming heterogeneous regional vertical compression (top) and horizontal simple shear (bottom) (Beach *et al.* 1974, fig. 4a). (**b**) Model to show the variation in shear sense to maintain compatibility between a zone of low-intensity deformation and surrounding regions of more intense flattening strains (Coward 1974, fig. 7a). (**c**) Simple shear model (Coward 1974, fig. 2b). (**d**) Pure shear deformation model (Coward 1974, fig. 2a).

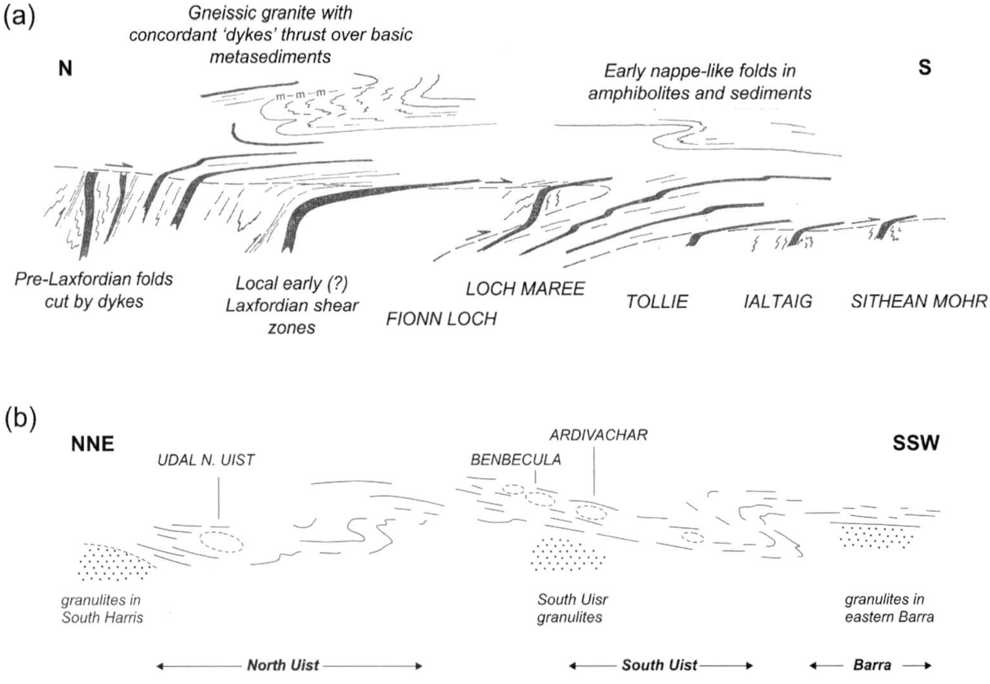

Fig. 9. MOIST (Brewer & Smythe 1984). (**a**) Schematic section through the area between Gruinard Bay and Sithean Mhor after the removal of the upright structures, late folds and faults (Coward 1974, fig. 4). (**b**) Schematic section through the southern Hebrides from the Sound of Harris in the north to Barra in the south, showing the form of the F_2 folds (Coward 1974, fig. 6).

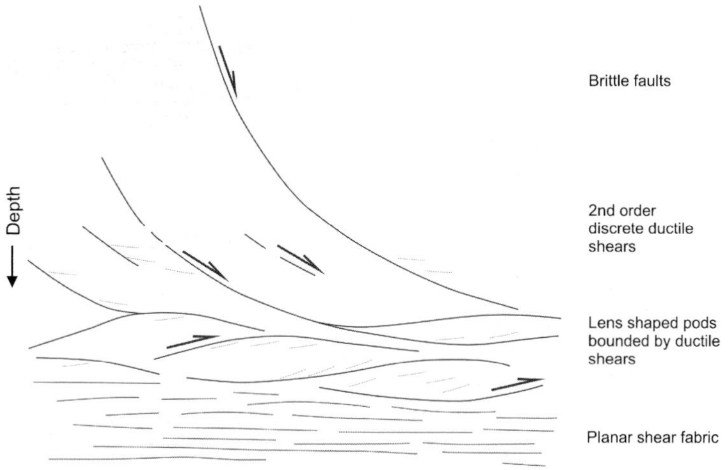

Fig. 10. Simplified model for crustal extension with zones 1–4 (Coward 1990).

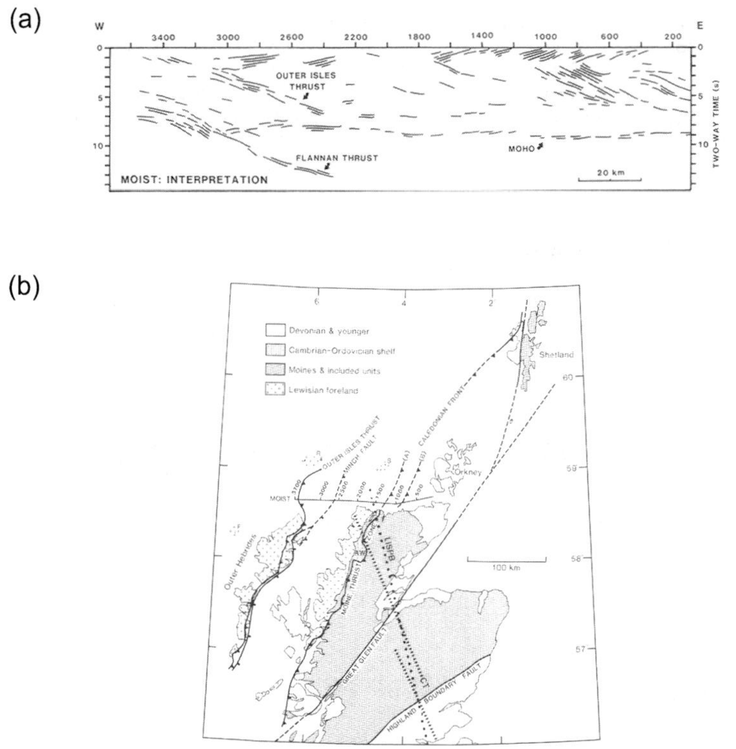

Fig. 11. (**a**) Interpretation of principal reflectors on MOIST, prepared from unmigrated and migrated sections (Brewer & Smythe 1984, fig. 4). (**b**) Simplified geological map of northern Scotland with the location of MOIST (Brewer & Smythe 1984, fig. 2).

crust was debated. After his Lewisian experience, Coward knew what they were by reference to outcrop, and later, having become involved with seismic interpretation in the North Sea and elsewhere, he used this knowledge in his ideas on the formation of extensional basins.

The Outer Isles Thrust and the Eastern Gneisses

Relevant in this context of lower crustal deformation is a separate aspect of Coward's thesis work on South Uist: his analysis of the Outer

Fig. 12. The wild and rugged eastern side of South Uist.

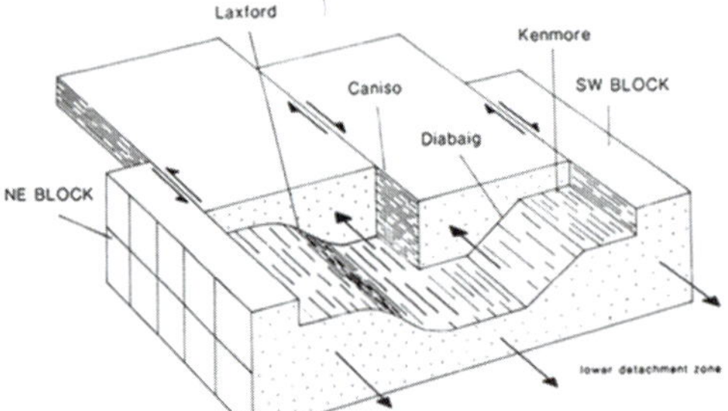

Fig. 13. Block diagrams illustrating overthrust model for the Lewisian (Coward & Park 1987, fig. 6).

Isles Thrust Zone and the 'Eastern Gneisses' that lie in its hanging wall. These rocks had been described by Jehu & Craig (1926) in their geological equivalent of Johnson and Boswell. Dearnley (1962) had also made important observations on the igneous nature and granulite-facies assemblage in one of the major units of the Eastern Gneisses, but Coward made the first real map (Fig. 3b). Apart from being a major physical achievement, Coward's mapping of this wild and remote area (Fig. 12) put it into modern context, and along with his work and that of his co-workers, some of it eventually became incorporated in the British Geological Survey maps of the Hebrides.

Much of the Eastern Gneiss is a layered basic complex in granulite facies; analogous rocks exist in Harris, and were being described by Windley, and others in Greenland. Coward recognized granulite-facies assemblages in these rocks, indicating that they had originally belonged in the lower crust. He anticipated that rocks, like the Eastern Gneisses, are the less ductile material at deeper levels in the eastern part of the islands, those predicted in the cuspate model for the F_3 folds of the Western Gneisses, but now at a high tectonic level in the hanging wall of the Outer Isles Thrust. The fault rocks of the thrust zone were described and mapped, and their time relationships and mechanical significance established. The pseudotachylite (glass) that is so spectacularly developed along the Outer Isles Thrust Zone, on the hills of South Uist, was seen to have developed in response to brittle seismogenic deformation in dry rocks at

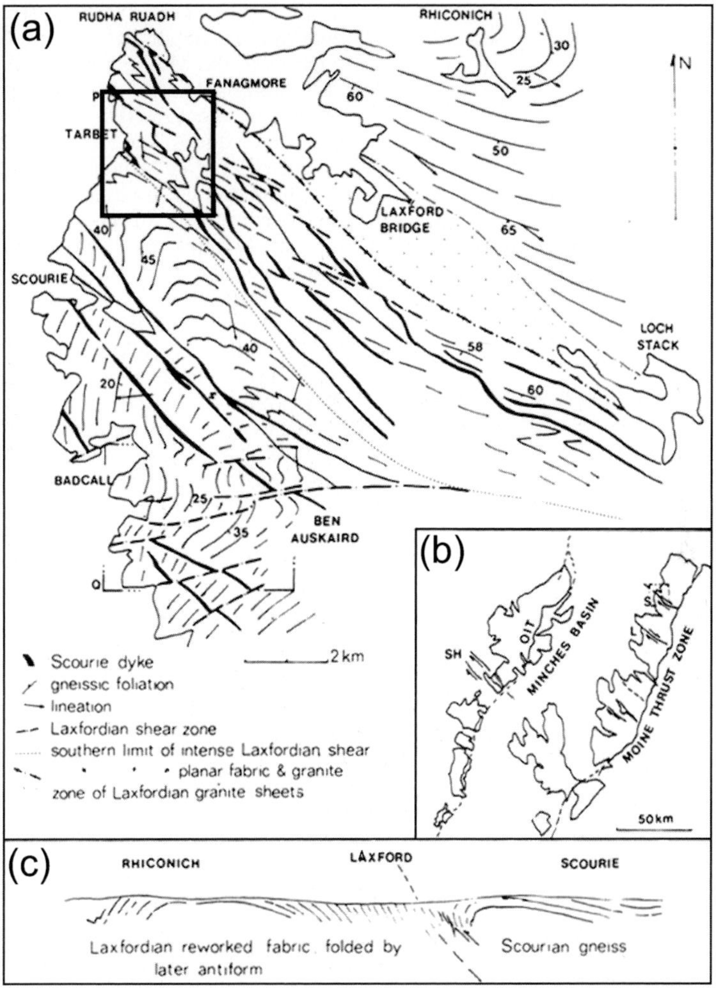

Fig. 14. (**a**) Simplified map of the Scourie–Laxford region showing the main structures and localities. (**b**) Location map for (**a**): L, Lochinver Shear; S, Scourie; SH, South Harris Shear. From Coward (1990).

depth and was associated with brittle failure. Small-scale geometrical observations suggested that pseudotachylite developed at jogs on displacement surfaces, and had become mobile and intrusive. Large-scale accumulations of pseudotachylite, like that on the Outer Isles Thrust Zone, were therefore deduced be the product of multiple earthquakes. Sibson's later work in the Hebrides (Sibson 1977) substantiated all of this and put it in the context of a general classification of fault rocks, a study that became known far beyond the context of the Hebrides.

The Outer Isles Thrust Zone is more or less parallel to the Moine Thrust system. At the time Coward worked on it, there was much discussion about the age of the structure and the various fault rocks associated with it: was it Caledonian like the Moine Thrust Zone, or was it older? (Coward always thought it older.) The debate may have been an additional prompt for him to begin his extensive work on the Moine Thrust system itself, work that, along with research on the Precambrian in various parts of southern Africa, replaced the Lewisian as the main focus of Coward's attention through the late 1970s and 1980s.

Lewisian revisited

Fourteen years after the 'Flat-lying structures' paper, Coward returned to Lewisian problems in 1987 in a joint paper with Graham Park (Coward

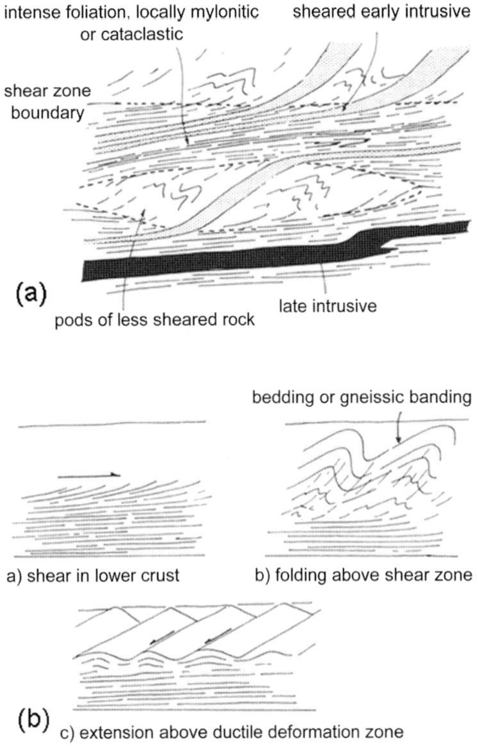

Fig. 15. (**a**) Development of structures in the crust that produce seismic fabrics. (**b**) Models for the development of a layered crust, with an upper crust that appears non-reflective seismically above a reflective lower crust (Coward 1990, fig. 5).

& Park 1987). It was written after he had started working in detail at higher-level thrust geometries in the Moine Thrust Zone, the Western Alps and other areas of 'thin-skinned' tectonics. Although the Lewisian fundamentals remain, much is added. The simplicity and generality of the 'Flat-lying structures' paper is no longer apparent and we are in a world of extrapolation pushing towards an all-embracing model. It is the sort of approach that typified much of Mike Coward's later work and it is augmented here by Park's own lifelong knowledge of the Lewisian. It is accepted here that some of the steep NW–SE-trending deformation belts are essentially transcurrent shear zones and they are made to link at depth to the gently dipping pervasive fabric as ductile lateral ramps (Fig. 13).

The Hebrides are believed to lie structurally lower than most of the mainland, the footwall of a northwesterly-directed ductile overthrust with the mainland as the southeasterly hanging wall. The Coward & Park paper puts the Lewisian outcrop as part of the Nagsugtoqidian deformation zone of Greenland, the product of proposed oblique collisions of the Archaean cratons of North and South Greenland. The word 'plate' is actually used to describe the Greenland Archaean blocks, the first time it had appeared in Coward's Lewisian papers. It is proposed that the Lewisian strains and their orientation are determined by the convergence directions of the plates in Greenland.

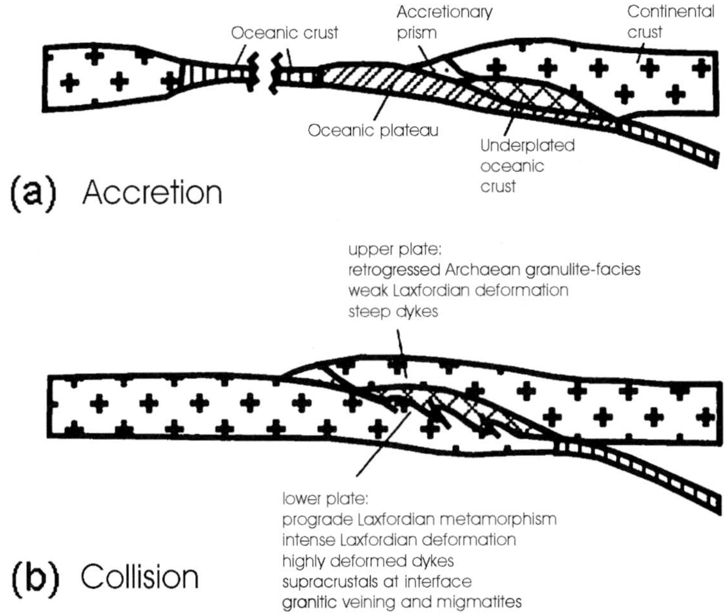

Fig. 16. Graham Park's schematic model of an idealized subduction–accretion–collision sequence (Park 2005, fig. 1). (**a**) Accretion stage; (**b**) collision stage.

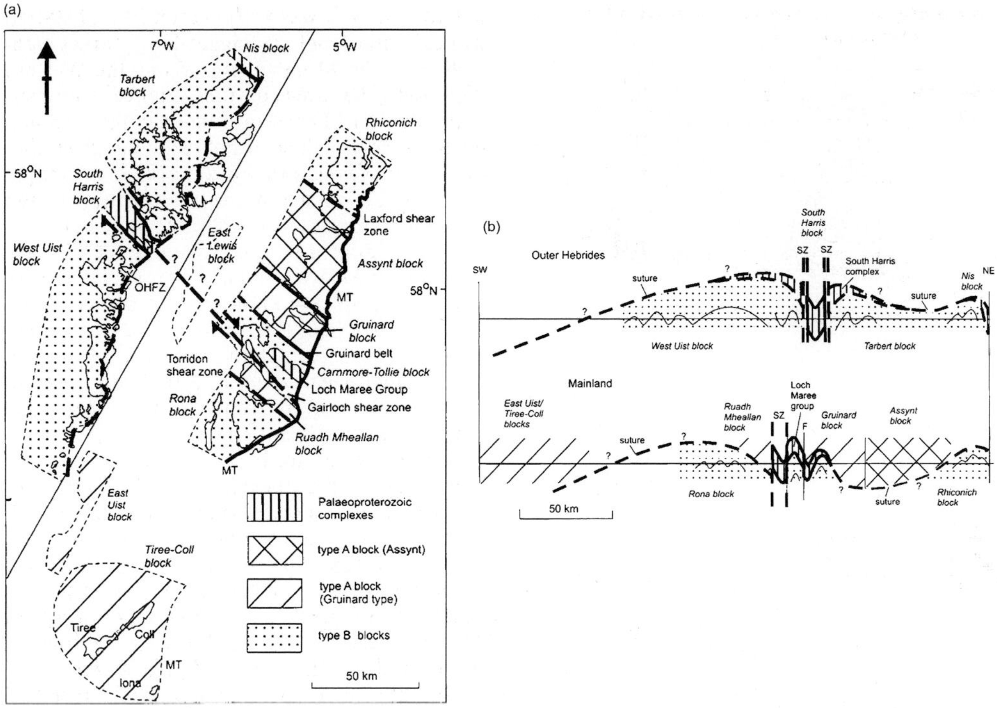

Fig. 17. Kinney & Friend's fundamentally different members of the Lewisian complex put into geological context by Park (2005, fig. 2). (**a**) The Outer Hebrides is shown displaced by 50 km dextrally along a NE–SW line to align the dextral strike-slip shear zones of Gairloch and South Harris (MT, Moine Thrust; OHFZ, Outer Hebrides Fault Zone). (**b**) Two schematic cross-sections illustrate the present interpretation in terms of upper- and lower-plate terranes separated by a suture zone locally containing Palaeoproterozoic accretionary complexes (SZ, shear zones; F, fault).

Mike Coward's latest work on the Lewisian (Coward 1990) was his remapping and rethink of the Laxford Front. This paper makes two points, one local, one of more general significance. Locally, his re-mapping highlights the large-scale swing of the Scourian foliation, SE of Tarbet (Fig. 14) and makes a clear case for dextral thrusting at the Laxford Front. This early displacement had been pointed to by Beach *et al.* (1974), but the main subject matter of that paper was the sinistral/normal sense of shear, judged from the displaced dykes between Tarbet and Laxford. In the 1990 paper this was seen as a younger modification of the fundamental structure, and new field evidence for the earlier structuration was presented. The general point of this paper, however, was to describe the likely structural appearance of lower crustal reflectors in more detail than before (Fig. 15). Coward's thinking had been heading here ever since the Brewer & Smythe paper. It is spelled out here. In this paper he incorporated concepts such as heat flow, crustal strength, seismic impedance contrasts, fluids, deformation mechanisms, shear zone geometry and crustal thickening. They are wound up with field observation, to reach a hypothesis of crustal configuration and the nature of the brittle–ductile transition. It is a great example of how those who have seen, in H. H. Read's words 'the most rocks' are well placed to understand the significance of more indirect pieces of geological data and scale extrapolation. It is also a good example of how an imaginative scientist modifies and adapts on the basis of his own widening knowledge.

Terranes

So, had he lived, what would Coward have made of the changes that have taken place in Lewisian geology since he wrote that paper in 1990? The recognition of juvenile arc material (and therefore collision) of Proterozoic age by Park *et al.* (2001) and Whitehouse & Bridgewater (2001) would certainly have interested him. He would also have been intrigued by the new U–Pb

Fig. 18. South Uist and Mike Coward.

dating by Kinney & Friend (1997) and Friend & Kinney (2001), which leads to a 'terrane-based nomenclature' for the Lewisian. This isotope geochemistry suggests that the Lewisian complex is assembled from bodies of gneiss that have fundamentally different ages and origins.

Coward was sometimes sceptical of 'black boxes', but he would almost certainly have wanted to put the geochronologically defined blocks (which as they stand pay scant regard to Lewisian structure) into a structural context that made sense.

He had worked on accreted terranes. In Peru in the 1970s, along with Peter Cobbold, Alison Ries and Robert Shackleton (Shackleton *et al.* 1979), he was involved in one of the earliest attempts to test terrane accretion models outside western North America. And in any case, it is not a great step from the models of Coward & Park (1987) to the concept of terrane accretion.

Park (2005) has already gone down the road that Coward might have taken, accommodating the new data into regional geological understanding. Some of Park's diagrams (Figs 16 and 17) would have struck a chord, and indeed, they do represent a stimulating model to which future Lewisian research will doubtless refer. It is a great pity that Mike Coward was never able to see them.

Postscript

Figure 18 is a photograph taken from the west coast of South Uist looking across the machair to Ben Mhor (right) and Hecla (left) and the Outer Isles Thrust. It is a reminder that to Mike Coward, the Hebrides, the Lewisian, and South Uist were not just academic problems to solve. There was the magic of the Western Isles, the landscape, the hilarity of many aspects of life there, and most of all, perhaps, the great good fortune to be close to local people, who, shorn of frills, cut their laconic way to the heart of things. I think that Mike Coward would have been pleased if he thought his science reflected Hebridean wisdom, irreverence and fun. It nearly always did.

We should be glad that his life's work began there.

A. Beach and G. Park reviewed the manuscript, and (I hope) it has been much improved because of that. G. Park also generously made his latest (at that time unpublished) work available and allowed me to include his diagrams. He also acted as wise counsel to someone who has not looked at a crystalline rock seriously for 30 years. Thank you.

References

BEACH, A. 1976. The inter relationships of fluid transport, deformation, geochemistry and heat-flow in early Proterozoic shear zones in the Lewisian complex. *Philosophical Transactions of the Royal Society of London, Series A*, **280**, 569–604.

BEACH, A. & FYTE, W. S. 1976. Fluid transport and shear zones at Scourie, Sutherland: Evidence of overthrusting? *Contributions to Mineralogy and Petrology*, **36**, 175–180.

BEACH, A., COWARD, M. P. & GRAHAM, R. H. 1974. An interpretation of the structural evolution of the Laxford Front, north west Scotland. *Scottish Journal of Geology*, **9**, 297–308.

BREWER, J. A. & SMYTHE, D. K. 1984. MOIST and the continuity of crustal reflector geometry along the Caledonian–Appalachian orogen. *Journal of the Geological Society, London*, **141**,105–120.

COWARD, M. P. 1972. The Eastern Gneisses of South Uist. *Scottish Journal of Geology*, **8**, 1–22.

COWARD, M. P. 1973*a*. Heterogeneous deformation in the development of the Lewisian complex of South Uist, Outer Hebrides. *Journal of the Geological Society, London*, **129**, 139–160.

COWARD, M. P. 1973*b*. The structure and origin of areas of anomalously low intensity deformation in the basement gneiss complex of the Outer Hebrides. *Tectonophysics*, **16**, 117–140.

COWARD, M. P. 1974. Flat lying structures within the Lewisian basement gneiss complex of NW Scotland. *Proceedings of the Geologists' Association*, **85**, 459–472.

COWARD, M. P. 1990. Shear zones at the Laxford Front, NW Scotland and their significance in the interpretation of lower crustal structure. *Journal of the Geological Society, London*, **147**, 279–286.

COWARD, M. P. & PARK, R. G. 1987. The role of mid crustal shear zones in the Early Proterozoic evolution of the Lewisian. *In*: PARK, R. G. & TARNEY, J. (eds) *Evolution of the Lewisian and Comparable Precambrian High Grade Terrains.* Geological Society, London, Special Publications, **27**, 127–138.

COWARD, M. P., FRANCIS, P. W., GRAHAM, R. H. & WATSON, J. V. 1970. Large Scale Laxfordian structures of the Outer Hebrides in relation to those of the Scottish Mainland. *Tectonophysics*, **10**, 425–435.

DEARNLEY, R. 1962. An outline of the Lewisian Complex of the Outer Hebrides in relation to that of the Scottish mainland. *Journal of the Geological Society, London*, **118**, 143–176.

DEARNLEY, R. & DUNNING, F. W. 1968. Metamorphosed and deformed pegmatites and basic dykes in the Lewisian complex of the Outer Hebrides and their geological significance. *Quarterly Journal of the Geological Society of London*, **123**, 335–378.

FLINN, D. 1965. On folding during three dimensional finite strain. *Geological Magazine*, **102**, 36–45.

FRIEND, C. R. L. & KINNEY, P. D. 2001. A reappraisal of the Lewisian Gneiss complex: geochronological evidence for its tectonic assembly from disparate terranes in the Proterozoic. *Contributions to Mineralogy and Petrology*, **142**,198–218.

KINNEY, P. D. & FRIEND, C. R. L. 1997. U–Pb isotopic evidence for the accretion of different crustal blocks to form the Lewisian Complex of northwest Scotland. *Contributions to Mineralogy and Petrology*, **129**, 326–340.

JEHU, T. J. & Craig, J. M. 1926. Geology of the Outer Hebrides. *Transactions of the Royal Society of Edinburgh*, **54**, 467–89.

PARK, R. G. 2005. The Lewisian terrane model: a review. *Scottish Journal of Geology*, **41**(2), 105–118.

PARK, R. G., TARNEY, J. & CONNELLY, J. N. 2001. The Loch Maree Group: Palaeoproterzoic subduction – accretion complex in the Lewisian of N.W. Scotland. *Precambrian Research*, **105**, 2–4, 205–226.

PEACH, B. N., HORNE, J., GUNN, W., CLOUGH, C. T. & HINXMAN, L. W. 1907. *The Geological Structure of the North-West Highlands of Scotland.* Memoirs of the Geological Survey of Great Britain.

RAMSAY, J. G. 1967. *Folding and Fracturing of Rocks.* McGraw–Hill, New York.

RAMSAY, J. G. & GRAHAM, R. H. 1970. Strain variations in shear belts. *Canadian Journal of Earth Sciences*, **7**, 786–813.

SHACKLETON, R. M., RIES, A. C., COWARD, M. P. & COBBOLD, P. R. 1979. Structure, metamorphism, geochronology and palaeomagnetism of the Arequipa Massif of coastal Peru. *Journal of the Geological Society, London*, **136**(2), 195–214.

SIBSON, R. H. 1977. Fault rocks and fault mechanisms. *Journal of the Geological Society, London*, **133**, 191–213.

SUTTON, J. & WATSON, J. V. 1951. The Pre-Torridonian metamorphic history of the Loch Torridon and Scourie areas in the North-West Highlands of Scotland. *Quarterly Journal of the Geological Society of London*, **106**, 214–307.

A major high-strain zone in the Lewisian Complex in the Loch Torridon area, NW Scotland: insights into deep crustal deformation

JOHN WHEELER

Department of Earth and Ocean Sciences, Liverpool University, Brownlow Street, Liverpool L69 3GP, UK (e-mail: johnwh@liv.ac.uk)

Abstract: The Lewisian Complex is an Archaean–Proterozoic high-grade gneiss region with widespread amphibolite-facies fabrics. These fabrics have, on the 100 km scale, a subhorizontal enveloping surface and are interpreted as forming in gently dipping crustal-scale shear zones and steeper lateral ramp structures. The Scourie dyke swarm, of Proterozoic age, runs NW–SE subvertically outside such zones, but is transformed into subhorizontal concordant amphibolite sheets within them. The terms 'Scourian' and 'Laxfordian' are used to describe pre-dyke and post-dyke fabrics and events. In the southern mainland Lewisian at Loch Torridon, unmodified Scourian gneisses in the north pass southwards into lozenges bounded by anastomosing zones of Laxfordian deformation, and eventually to a region consisting entirely of Laxfordian fabrics. This geometry is compatible with a major Laxfordian shear zone that dips northeastwards beneath a Scourian hanging wall. Detailed maps show that structures on the metre to kilometre scale do not relate in a simple way to the crustal shear zone model for four reasons. First, many amphibolite-facies fabrics in the quartzo-feldspathic gneisses predate the dykes (they relate to a late Scourian or 'Inverian' event), so the dykes cannot be used to infer overall geometry and movement sense. A few structures along the Loch Roag Line, the most northeasterly high-strain belt in the Loch Torridon inliers, may indicate syntectonic dyke emplacement. Second, local shear with opposing senses is present in both the pre-dyke and post-dyke (Laxfordian) deformation. Third, foliation deflections on a variety of scales relate more to varying shear planes than to the deflection caused by increasing simple shear strain, and cannot be used to infer shear sense. Fourth, there is pure-shear stretching within the gneisses that masks the effects of simple shear. These structures can be incorporated into a crustal-scale shear zone model, but are not diagnostic of it. The scatter of foliation planes with a relatively constant lineation is a feature of other crustal-scale high-strain zones (e.g. Canisp, Nordre Strømfjord), although different explanations are available. Other high-strain zones (e.g. the Laxford Front) show a spatially varying lineation pattern, but this could relate more to a varying shear direction than to deflections of linear features into a single movement direction. The geometry of classic simple shear is not versatile enough to explain the kilometre-scale geometry of such high-strain zone, although it may work well in local subareas.

Structural information on all scales is essential for understanding continental tectonics. Pervasive deformation in collisional orogens on scales of 100–1000 km demonstrates that the rigid plate paradigm does not apply during collision or, in regions such as the Basin and Range province, in extension. This raises the question of what is the overall deformation style, and whether it can be interpreted, at the broadest level, in terms of mainly pure shear or simple shear.

The Lewisian Complex of NW Scotland is a region of Archaean and Proterozoic quartzo-feldspathic gneisses, cut by variably deformed Proterozoic dykes (the Scourie dykes). A significant part of the deformation and metamorphism in the Lewisian post-dates the Scourie dyke swarm, and is called Laxfordian; the pre-dyke history is Scourian (Fig. 1). The Lewisian is notable for being one of the first places where the history of basement was unravelled in terms of multiple structural and igneous events (Sutton & Watson 1951), for providing a 'type locality' for shear zones (Ramsay & Graham 1970), and for provoking influential models for crustal deformation that postulate large-scale simple shear (Beach *et al.* 1974; Sibson 1977; Coward 1984). Arguments for large-scale simple shear in the Lewisian and other basement regions include the following.

(1) The heterogeneity of strain, which is not possible in pure shear (Coward 1984). Heterogeneities on one scale, however, may still relate to pure shear on a larger scale; for example, pervasive conjugate shear zones might be accommodating pure shear.

(2) The identification of small shear zones within larger structures (Beach *et al.* 1974); although timing and kinematic equivalence of small and large structures should be demonstrated.

From: RIES, A. C., BUTLER, R. W. H. & GRAHAM, R. H. (eds) 2007. *Deformation of the Continental Crust: The Legacy of Mike Coward.* Geological Society, London, Special Publications, **272**, 27–45.

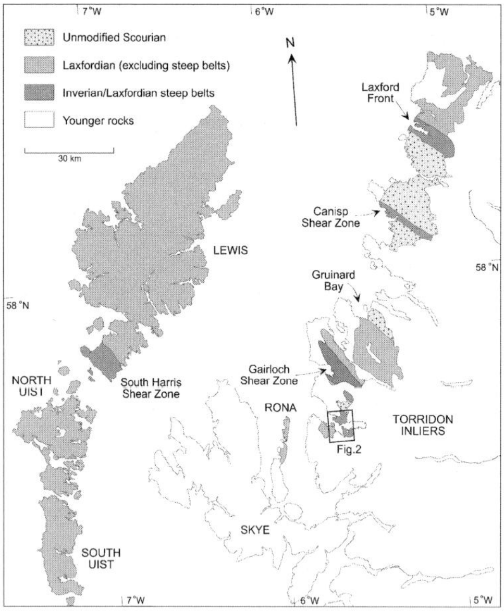

Fig. 1. The main outcrops of the Lewisian Complex in NW Scotland.

(3) Rotations of pre-existing markers, such as dykes, at the margins of high-strain zones. Rotations are a consequence of any imposed strain, but become more diagnostic of simple shear when more than one set of markers is available; for example, two sets of dykes (Escher *et al.* 1975).

(4) Offsets of pre-existing markers, such as igneous associations (Sørensen 1983).

(5) The persuasive, although sometimes indirect, argument is that fault zones in the upper crust are kinematically equivalent to simple shear at lower levels where plastic deformation is prevalent, so it is to be expected that fault zones pass downwards into shear zones. This can be directly demonstrated where brittle and plastic structures with the same kinematics are associated in, for example, the Outer Hebrides (Sibson 1977), the Liachar thrust in the Himalayas (Butler & Prior 1988) and the Alpine fault of New Zealand (Norris & Cooper 2003). In the Lewisian, however, any brittle features are much younger than the plastic deformation discussed here.

(6) Kinematic indicators are extremely useful to constrain non-coaxiality. They may be abundant in greenschist-facies crustal-scale shear zones such as the Gressoney Shear Zone in the Alps (Reddy *et al.* 1999). In this author's experience they are not common in amphibolite-facies rocks even when other criteria suggest a strong component of shear. In the Nanga Parbat syntaxis of the Pakistan Himalayas, gneisses, which were intensely strained at amphibolite facies beneath the south-directed Main Mantle Thrust, are exposed over a 30 km transect, yet shear sense indicators are almost completely absent (Wheeler *et al.* 1995). In the whole Lewisian Complex, asymmetric augen are too rare to be used with confidence to deduce non-coaxiality; features with the appearance of shear bands are rare and cannot be used to deduce shear sense (see below). Criteria (2)–(4) are what remain as applicable in the Lewisian, in relation to structural observations.

Models for Laxfordian deformation on the scale of the whole outcrop (Fig. 1) include top-to-the-NW shear with crustal thickening (Coward 1984), strike-slip with some transtension followed by dextral transpression (Coward & Park 1987), and top-to-the-SE shear (Park 2005). This diversity of interpretations illustrates that first-order aspects of the structural evolution of the Lewisian Complex remain ambiguous, for reasons outlined now. First, we may consider relationships on the metre to 10 metre scale. Strain heterogeneity is obvious in the Scourie dykes, where recrystallized plagioclase and mafic mineral aggregates indicate shape change. At intermediate levels of Laxfordian strain, metre-scale shear zones may be used to deduce an overall shear sense. At high strains dykes may show pervasive fabrics subparallel to their margins, with shear sense consequently more difficult to deduce. In the gneisses, banding and fabrics defined by elongate quartz and plagioclase aggregates are variably developed. Some fabrics are cut at high angles by Scourie dykes, proving they are Scourian. Fabrics parallel to dyke contacts were inferred to be Laxfordian (Sutton & Watson 1951), and this together with the strain intensity in the dykes themselves provided a framework for mapping Laxfordian strain across the mainland (Fig. 1). A central region showing generally low Laxfordian strain has regions of higher Laxfordian strain to the north and south. The northern transition zone is called the Laxford Front (Fig. 1); the southern transition zone is more diffuse. In principle, mapping of Scourian fabrics into Laxfordian high-strain zones should reveal shear sense. In practice this is not straightforward because Scourian fabrics were variably oriented on all scales. On the regional scale Laxfordian fabrics are folded (Coward 1984) so not all orientation variations are due to heterogeneous shear.

In the central region the Scourie dykes are of fairly consistent NW–SE orientation, suggesting they could be used as strain markers. For example, near the Laxford Front they dip

SW at shallower angles. This could indicate a component of top-to-the-NE shear. However, the Laxfordian stretching lineation is NW–SE; simple shear in this direction could not, if exactly parallel to the dykes, reorient them. Linear fabrics may not be consistent with simple shear models, but it is essential to incorporate them into the wider structural context (Robin & Cruden 1994; Passchier 1998).

At present levels of exposure the Laxfordian deformation was in amphibolite facies, except in South Harris (Cliff *et al.* 1983), where it was granulite facies. The classic Scourian is granulite facies in the central region, but amphibolite facies south of Gruinard Bay in the southern region. Even in the central region, some amphibolite-facies deformation predates dyke intrusion and this is referred to as 'Inverian' (Evans 1965). It is characterized by a more consistent structural trend than that of the higher-grade deformation. In the southern region, almost all pre-dyke fabrics are associated with amphibolite-facies mineral assemblages. The term 'Inverian' has been applied to some of the younger structures that pre-date the Scourie dykes in the southern region, the criterion being their NW–SE trend and their relationship to the dykes. Park & Cresswell (1973) have argued that Scourie dyke emplacement was controlled in places by these pre-existing structures so that dykes can be subparallel to pre-existing fabrics in their surroundings, although showing local discordances. Other work argues against this (Beach *et al.* 1974) and it is still not established how widespread the Inverian event or events were in the Lewisian. This is partly because of the potential ambiguity in interpreting field relationships, and partly because absolute dating of deformation remains difficult.

Recently geochronological work has been used to identify 'terrane boundaries' in the Lewisian. It was argued (Kinny *et al.* 2005) that disparate formation and metamorphic ages from different parts of the Lewisian imply that these parts were once widely separated. By implication, the boundaries between these terranes are major shear zones with large displacements, so these arguments are relevant to the theme of this paper. The nearest terrane boundary to the Loch Torridon area was proposed to run along the south side of the Gairloch Shear Zone (Fig. 1). Rocks to the north include a Palaeoproterozoic cover sequence and quartzo-feldspathic gneiss basement with protolith ages of 2860 Ma and 2820 Ma. Rocks to the south include quartzo-feldspathic gneisses with protolith ages of 3135 Ma and 2880 Ma. This author is in agreement with the general claim made by Park (2005) that such age differences do not necessitate a terrane boundary; the disparate ages could instead represent the long complex history of a relatively coherent piece of crust. Despite this, Park evolved a model involving two terranes, with a complex boundary, one segment of which runs through the north part of the Diabaig inlier (Fig. 2).

In this contribution I aim to illustrate the applicability of simple shear models in the southern transition zone, using detailed maps to show structures on the metre to 100 m scale. The maps are intended to be an objective representation of the geology. They are open to more than one interpretation, so should illustrate why some aspects of Lewisian geology remain controversial. In the next section of the paper the geology of the Lewisian inlier at Loch Torridon is outlined; then the nature of the structural problems is addressed using detailed maps. Finally, the Torridon area is discussed in relation to continental tectonics in general.

Lewisian Complex in the Loch Torridon area

The Loch Torridon region was one of the two classic areas mapped by Sutton & Watson (1951), in which they demonstrated the importance of dykes as time markers in unravelling structural events. The Lewisian Complex crops out as inliers beneath the late Proterozoic Torridonian sandstone (Fig. 2). These inliers form high ground, up to 300 m, because they are partly fault bounded and the basal Torridonian unconformity had considerable relief that is reflected in the present-day topography.

The main rock types are as follows.

(1) Quartzo-feldspathic pale grey gneisses, which appear as homogeneous, isotropic, banded (with segregations, perhaps migmatitic, of quartz, feldspar and biotite), flaggy (with L and/or S defined by elongate mineral aggregates) or both banded and flaggy. The term 'grey gneiss' is used here to encompass all varieties. The homogeneous gneiss, with or without a faint shape fabric, is referred to here as smooth gneiss. The texture is almost igneous, either original or as a result of extensive migmatization. The smooth gneiss shows gradations and blurred contacts with the banded gneiss, or occasionally an intrusive relationship (Fig. 3a). The banded and smooth gneisses were formed during early Scourian intrusion, deformation and metamorphism. The presence of strong shape fabrics gives rise to distinctive flaggy gneisses that do not generally show renewed migmatization (although that was

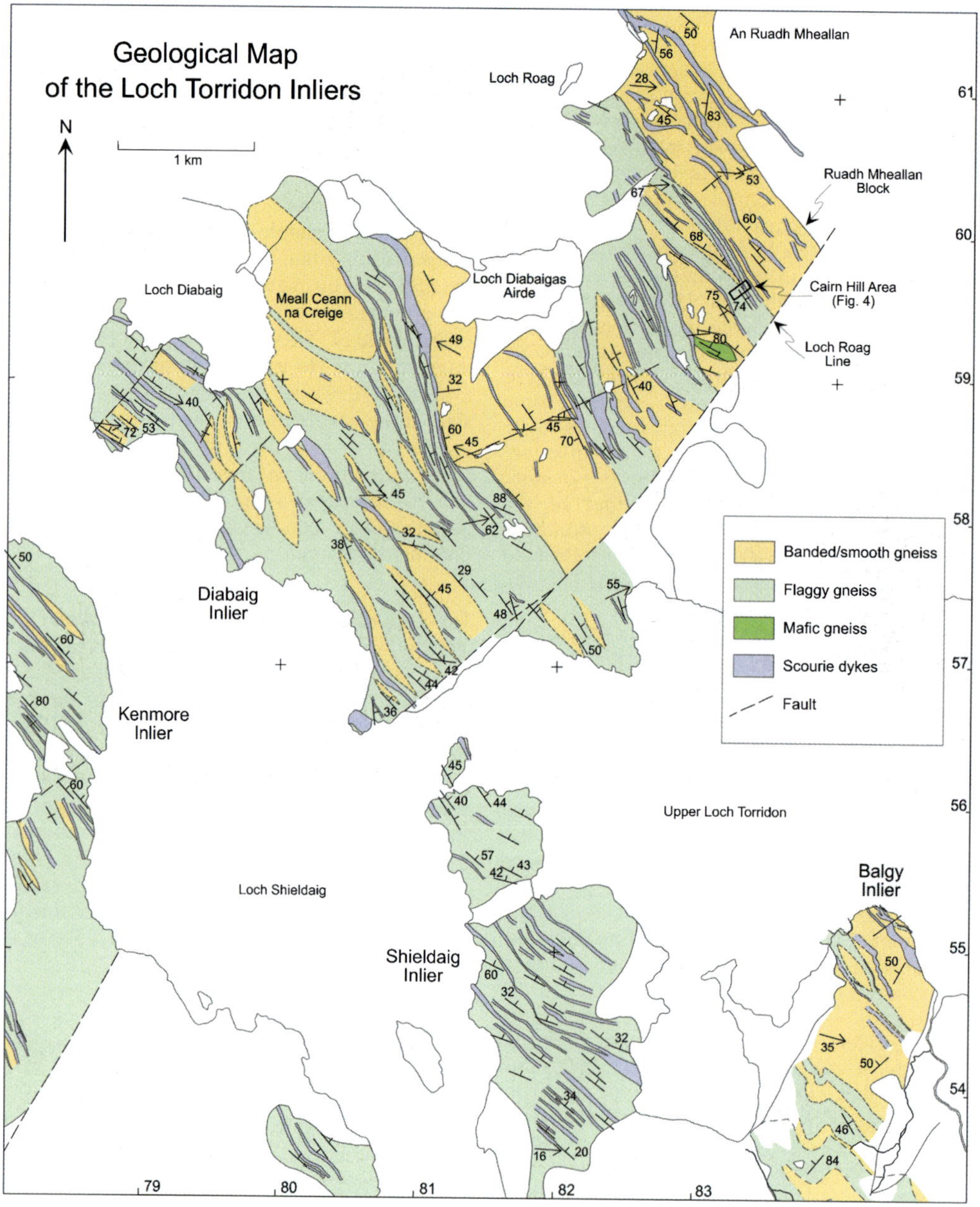

Fig. 2. General features of the Lewisian inliers at Loch Torridon, showing thickest Scourie dykes and schematic strain variations in gneisses. Gneisses are classified as banded/smooth gneiss (with no fabric, or banding at high angle to dykes) and flaggy gneiss with strong LS shape fabric and/or attenuated banding fabrics, often subparallel to dykes. Modified from Wheeler *et al.* (1987).

recorded by Cresswell (1972)), and tend to show less complex decimetre-scale folding. Flaggy gneiss is interpreted to be derived by deformation of banded and/or smooth gneiss throughout the area (Fig. 3b).

(2) Dark grey amphibolite sheets, from <1 m to >30 m thick, isotropic or schistose with sharp boundaries, identified as metamorphosed Scourie dykes based on the fact that they occasionally show relict igneous pyroxene and are

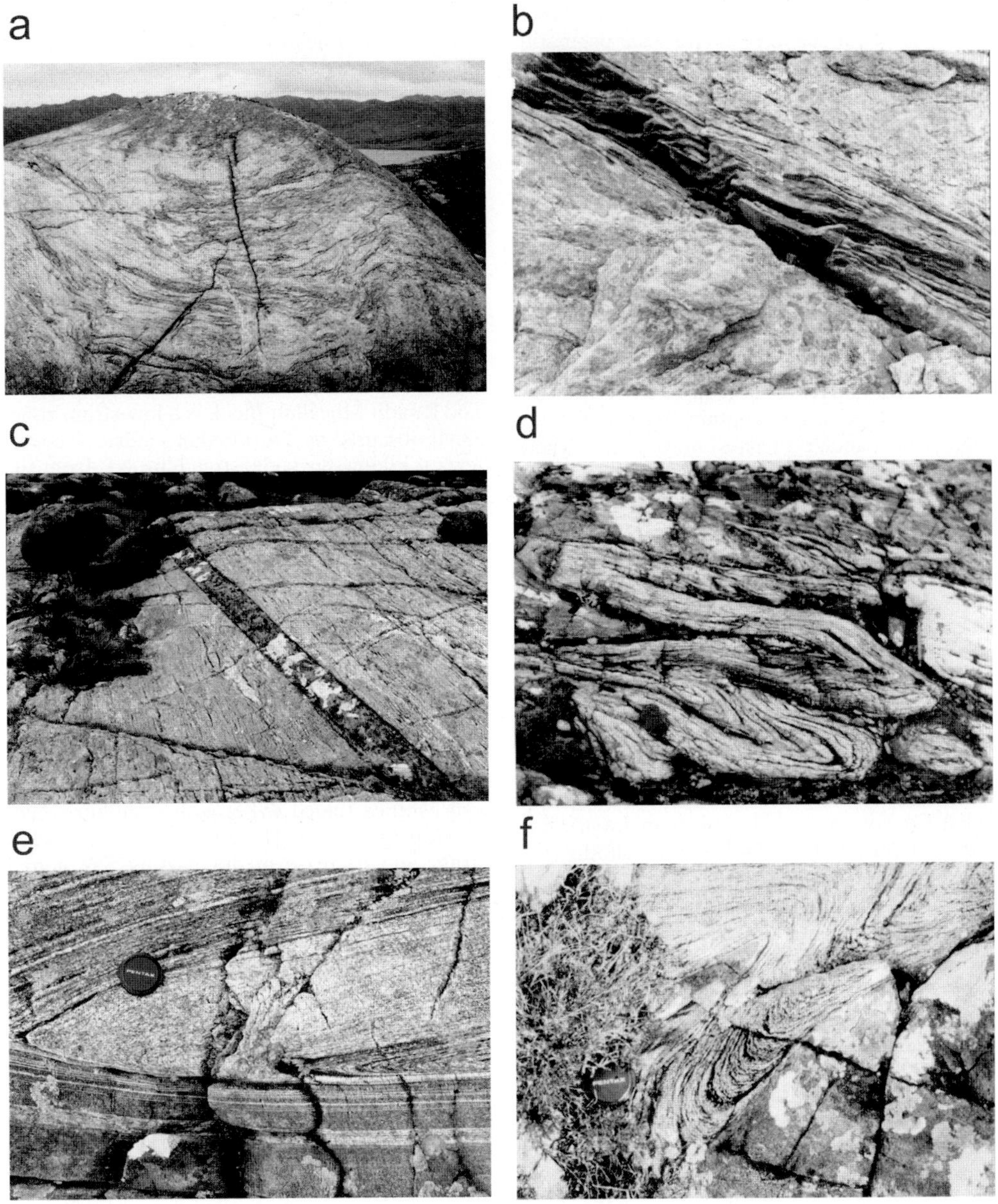

Fig. 3. (**a**) Junction between smooth gneiss (left) and banded gneiss (right) from the Balgy inlier [842545]. (**b**) Zone of flaggy gneiss in smooth gneiss, shoreline in Diabaig inlier [826571]. (**c**) Scourie dyke at low angle to platy fabric in country rock, [834598], in the Loch Roag Line just NE of the map in Figure 4. It should be noted that the dyke is darker than country rock but decorated with white lichen, as in other photographs. (**d**) View E, of isoclinally folded gneiss screen in deformed Scourie dyke [823589]. Lineation is parallel to fold hinges. (**e**) Tight fold in gneiss immediately adjacent to highly deformed Scourie dyke at E in Figures 4 and 6. (**f**) Fold affecting dyke and margin at H in Figure 5. Dyke shows almost no fabric within fold.

usually continuous sheets. They cut all other rock types except for scattered metre-scale pegmatite sheets.

(3) Banded amphibolites, often veined by migmatitic leucosomes that resemble the smooth gneisses, plus isolated, sometimes isotropic, mafic pods, inferred to predate the bulk of the quartzo-feldspathic grey gneisses, and are referred to as 'early basics'.

Since the work of Sutton & Watson (1951) it has been recognized that strain at Loch Torridon is highly heterogeneous on scales of kilometres to centimetres. This is best documented by the heterogeneous strain in the Scourie dykes, which overall increases towards the SW. Locally the smooth gneisses contain intensely platy zones; the banded gneisses show zones where banding is thinner and more planar than usual. These high-strain zones in the gneisses may be parallel to, and at the margins of, Scourie dykes, leading to the conclusion that they are Laxfordian (Sutton & Watson 1951). However, dyke–country rock relationships have also been interpreted as implying that, in places, dykes intruded along pre-existing foliations (Park & Cresswell 1973). These foliations, which strike NW–SE parallel to Laxfordian foliations but pre-date dykes, were correlated with the Inverian event. The most detailed structural work on the Diabaig inlier is that of Cresswell (1972), who identified five Scourian and four Laxfordian stages of deformation. This detailed subdivision relied to an extent on the correlation of folds based on style and orientation. This approach has more recently been regarded as limited insofar as one deformation event can produce a variety of folds and foliations (Sanderson 1972; Coward 1984), so that nine stages of deformation is likely to be an overestimate. More recent structural work in the 1970s was strongly influenced by the vision that the deformation in the Lewisian was dominated by simple shear (Beach *et al.* 1974; Coward 1975). Beach (1976) identified some of the high-strain zones at Torridon as sinistral shear zones which, in Cresswell's model, would have been fold limbs. Coward (1984) postulated regional subhorizontal shearing in the Laxfordian, with lateral ramps and/or later folding giving the present-day geometry, although he did not consider the Torridon area in detail. Wheeler et al. (1987) identified pre- and post-dyke shearing, but both episodes involved both sinistral and dextral shearing. Park *et al.* (1987) agreed that there is evidence for different shear senses. They described multiple Laxfordian events, but shear sense is variable even within some of these subdivisions. Main aspects are a north-side up dextral-reverse Inverian deformation, and a dextral-normal early Laxfordian shear sense.

There are two structural problems at Torridon, which are symptoms of unresolved issues in the Lewisian and other basement regions: (1) the age of the deformation, given that pre- and post-dyke deformation in the gneisses may have common features; (2) the extent of simple shear deformation, and the shear sense.

The larger areas of low and high Inverian or Laxfordian strain are shown in Figure 2. There is an increase in average strain passing SW, as shown by the lower proportion of low-strain zones ('banded/smooth gneiss' in the figure). The Ruadh Mheallan Block is a low-strain zone, albeit obscured by Torridonian sandstone cover, several kilometres wide, stretching NE from the study area towards the Gairloch schist belt, and is regarded as the margin to the Torridon structures (Park *et al.* 1987). The most northeasterly high-strain zone in the Diabaig inlier is exposed along a line 200–300 m wide running SE from Loch Roag, which was named the Loch Roag Line by Wheeler (1986). The Diabaig inlier shows steep dips of dykes and fabrics in the NE but these become more gently inclined passing SW. The Shieldaig inlier is similar to the SW part of the Diabaig inlier, but is entirely high strain. The Kenmore inlier is almost entirely high strain, and exhibits folded dykes with a subhorizontal enveloping surface. There is thus an increase in strain and decrease in dip passing SW across these three inliers. The Balgy inlier resembles the SW Diabaig inlier insofar as it has some substantial low-strain zones; it may be offset by later faulting so as to appear along strike from the Shieldaig inlier, which has somewhat different character.

Two study areas are used to illustrate structural features. In addition to 1:10 000 mapping, more detailed study is essential to give insight into the structural evolution of the Torridon Lewisian. Figure 4 shows a map made at 1:100 scale across part of the Loch Roag Line near its SE end [between grid references 832596 and 834597]. To the SW of this transect is *c.* 300 m of smooth gneiss with faint shape fabrics, interpreted as fairly low strain. To the NE is a further 100 m of banded gneiss with evidence of strain, before the Ruadh Mheallan Block is reached (Fig. 2). Figures 5 and 6 show details from this map (see also Fig. 7). Larger versions of these maps are available from the author on request.

The detailed map from the Loch Roag Line illustrates the main structural issues to be addressed, so is described first. The other study area is the Balgy inlier (Figs 2 and 9), mapped

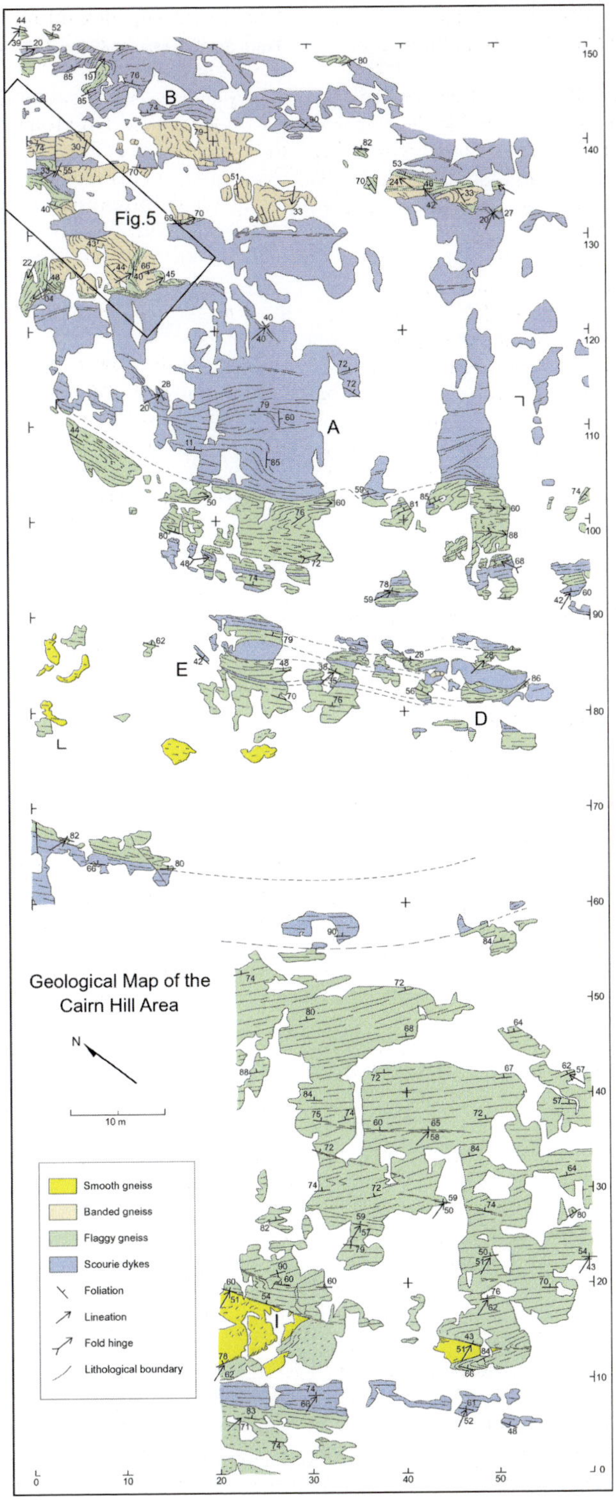

Fig. 4. Detailed map of part of a high-strain zone in the NE part of the Diabaig inlier (Loch Roag Line).

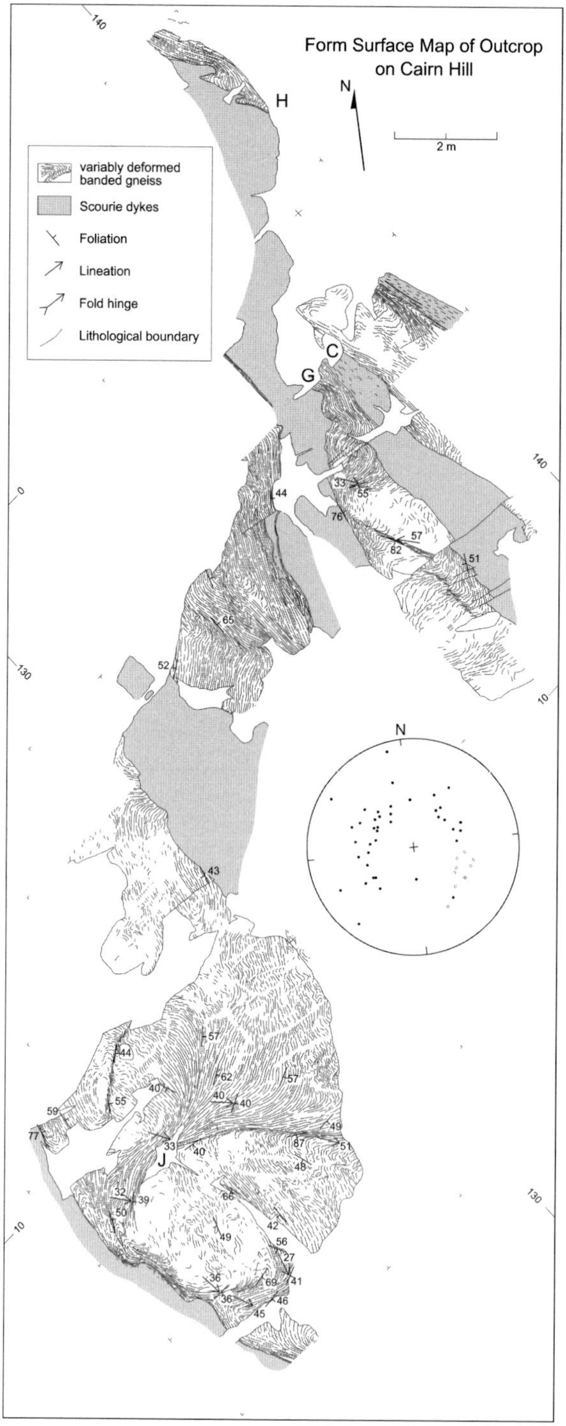

Fig. 5. Detail of outcrop-scale structure in northern part of Figure 4 (using same coordinate system) showing concordant and discordant dyke margins and banding in gneisses. The white stripes cutting the banding in the southern part are small pegmatite veins with diffuse margins. Inset stereonet shows data from the southern part of this map; ●, poles to foliation; ○, lineations.

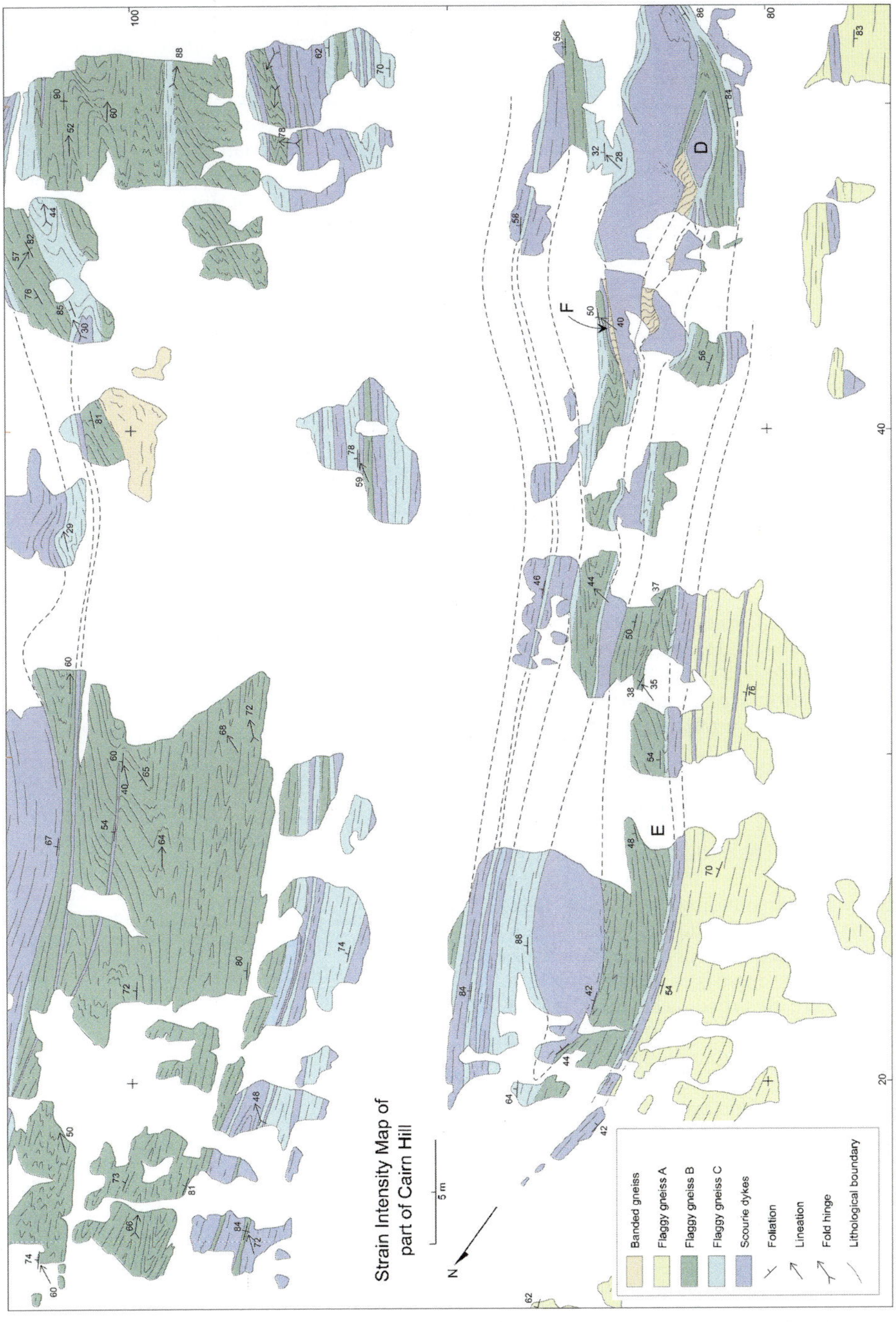

Fig. 6. Detail of outcrop-scale structure in part of Figure 4 showing boudinaged dyke geometries. The flaggy gneiss is here subdivided into three types: type A, relatively homogeneous with a strong shape fabric, derived from smooth gneiss; type **B**, tightly folded and/or attenuated banding, derived from banded gneiss; type C, relatively fine-grained with no earlier structures preserved, probably derived from smooth gneiss.

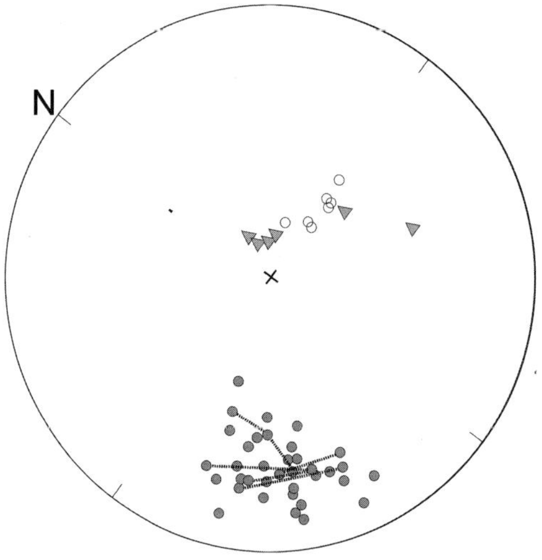

Fig. 7. Stereonet shows data from the southern part of map in Figure 4, aligned to be parallel to the orientation of that map. ●, poles to foliation; ○, lineations; grey triangles, intersection directions for foliations inside and immediately outside 'shear band' structures.

at 1:5000. Before addressing specific areas the arguments that can be used to diagnose the age of NW-trending structures in the gneisses are listed, based upon work from Torridon and elsewhere: these are then discussed in relation to the specific study areas.

Criteria to identify Laxfordian structures

Direct evidence for Laxfordian deformation in the Lewisian grey gneisses includes: (1) folded dykes, implying surrounding rocks are also folded; (2) axial-planar fabrics in gneisses that pass into axial surfaces of folds affecting dykes; (3) shear zones offsetting dykes and passing into gneisses; these are recorded near the Laxford Front (Coward & Park 1987; Tatham & Casey 2007), but there are few unambiguous examples of these at Torridon. Indirect (less reliable) arguments for the Laxfordian age of fabrics in the gneisses include: (1) parallelism with the dykes; (2) stronger fabrics where dykes show stronger fabrics.

Criteria to identify Inverian structures

The identification of Inverian structures is subjective. A structural definition could be 'structures and fabrics which are pre-Scourie dyke but are quite high strain, consistently oriented NW–SE and formed at amphibolite facies'. Direct evidence for Inverian deformation includes: (1) undeformed dyke apophyses cutting NW–SE fabrics; (2) low-angle cross-cutting relationships of dykes and gneisses (e.g. Fig. 3c), with no increase in strain in gneisses adjacent to dykes; (3) NW–SE dyke-parallel fabrics traceable into discordant fabrics that match up (crudely) on either side of small dykes. Indirect (less reliable) arguments for Inverian fabrics include: (1) fabrics identified as Inverian in one place mapped out, or correlated on basis of fabric style and orientation; (2) belts of Inverian deformation are characterized by Scourie dykes that were originally thinner and more numerous than those emplaced elsewhere (Park & Cresswell 1973); (3) evidence that dykes were less competent than country rock could be extrapolated to argue that most deformation in the gneisses was Inverian.

Loch Roag Line

Laxfordian structures

The main map (Fig. 4) shows a large Scourie dyke with irregular masses of gneiss within it in the north, and some thinner dykes in the south. The large dyke at location A shows localized shear zones with variable foliation strike; these variations arc not related to shear sense but to a variable shear plane. Where foliation bends are seen, as in nearby dykes, both shear senses may be seen. For example, Figure 8 (from the Loch Roag Line, Fig. 2) shows shear zones at a low angle to one another showing different apparent shear senses. The geometry is suggestive of a conjugate set, accommodating NE–SW shortening. The lineation, although likely to be plunging east, cannot be seen in this smooth 2D exposure, so the geometry cannot be interpreted fully in three dimensions. At B a small dyke, possibly connected to the largest dyke in three dimensions, shows foliation parallel to the contact with gneiss. Although there is a gap in exposure of a few centimetres, the gneisses are completely unaffected as their banding is at right angles to the dyke contact. This suggests that the dykes were less competent than country rock during the Laxfordian (Wheeler *et al.* 1987). The metre-wide dyke at C shown in Figure 5 shows a faint fabric, with a stronger fabric in the gneisses parallel to the dyke contact. This could, in isolation, be interpreted to imply strong Laxfordian deformation in the gneiss, with less deformation in the dyke. However, the fabric in the gneiss on the SW side of the dyke bends away from the contact and a metre to the east is discordant. This fabric is interpreted to be Inverian and the local

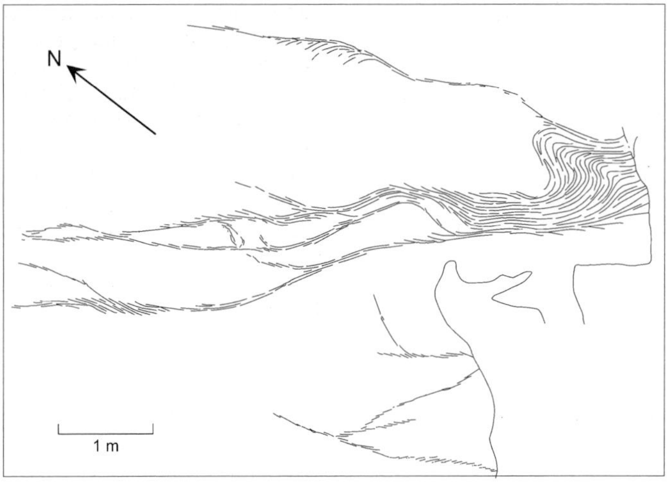

Fig. 8. Foliation in a set of shear zones in a Scourie dyke [831601] in the Loch Roag Line.

parallelism is due to the foliation facilitating brittle failure during dyke emplacement (Park & Cresswell 1973). It should be noted that the fabrics on the other side of this narrow dyke do, broadly, match up supporting the Inverian hypothesis. In the south of the region shown in Figure 4 the narrow dykes are pervasively deformed and do not yield a shear sense. They are parallel to the foliation in the gneisses which is interpreted to be Inverian (see below).

The central part of the area shown in Figure 4 (enlarged in Fig. 6 with added detail) shows some unusual features that are found only along the Loch Roag Line. Dykes show pronounced thickness variations and are boudinaged in places (e.g. the isolated lens at D). Unusually fine-grained, platy fabrics in the country rock surround portions of the dykes, which themselves have weak or no fabrics. In this case, the country rock fabrics appear to be truly Laxfordian. First, there are highly localized but intense folds adjacent to the dykes (e.g. at E, Fig. 6; see also Fig. 3e). Second, fabrics can differ greatly on either side of even small apophyses, as shown by that, only a few centimetres across, in Figure 6 at F. On its NE side are intense platy fabrics parallel to the contact, but on the SW side the migmatitic banding is at right angles to the contact. This large strain difference is best explained if the apophysis were present and acting as a less competent zone across which deformation was decoupled. However, the dykes have little or no fabric. One way to reconcile these apparently contradictory structures is to postulate that the deformation occurred partly during dyke emplacement. So, for example, deformation could decouple across the molten apophysis, which later crystallized with an isotropic texture. This could also explain the tapered shapes of the boudin ends, rather than the blunt ends to be expected when a strong layer is boudinaged. Watterson (1974) documented pinch and swell geometry in dykes from West Greenland that show little internal deformation. He hypothesized that such 'primary pinch and swell' could result from dyke intrusion into hot country rocks, so that the latter could deform while the dyke was still molten. Bons *et al.* (2004) discussed similar possibilities. The precise driving force for such deformation during dyke emplacement remains unclear, although partial collapse of an initially wide feeder dyke could play a role. An extreme result of 'primary pinch and swell' could be the boudinage of the molten sheet into lens-shaped pockets, even while still molten, and this may explain the geometries seen today (Fig. 6). It should be noted that the large dyke has a sinuous southern boundary which may also be a gentle pinch and swell structure. Small folds in dyke margins (G and H in Fig. 5; see also Fig. 3f) may also have formed while the dykes were molten, because they show no fabric even though the NW pair are tight. Intense folds in the gneisses localized along dyke margins (e.g. at E, and Fig. 3e) could have formed when the dykes were solid but hot with the original pyroxene–plagioclase mineralogy being stronger than the quartzo–feldspathic grey gneisses at that stage.

Inverian structures

It was argued above that some NW–SE fabrics in the northeastern part of Figure 4 (e.g. around the dyke at C) are Inverian. Figure 3c shows a dyke cutting flaggy gneiss fabrics at a low angle (Fig. 8), from just NE of the mapped area. There is no deflection of the gneissic fabric near the dyke, which is to be expected if there was a competence contrast, so it is likely that the fabric was there before the dyke was emplaced. A consequence of this hypothesis is that the dyke, when it acquired its own foliation, was actually less competent than the country rock. Figure 3d shows an isoclinally folded screen of grey gneiss within a Scourie dyke. Although the folds are tight, dyke material is almost pinched out of fold cores, suggesting the gneisses were more competent than the dyke. This competence contrast is regarded as a general feature of the Laxfordian deformation in the southern mainland Lewisian (Park *et al.* 1987; Wheeler *et al.* 1987).

The fabric in the gneiss at E (Fig. 3e) is also inclined to the dyke to its immediate SW, except in the 3 cm wide zone adjacent to the dyke where it is deflected. Again the main fabric is interpreted as Inverian (significant Laxfordian strain being restricted to the 3 cm wide border region). This suggests that the fabric in the SW part of Figure 4 is mainly Inverian, even though it is parallel to the foliated dykes.

The Inverian NW–SE fabrics in the SW of Figure 4 are heterogeneous on a metre scale. There is a low-strain lens at I, similar to structures on a kilometre scale (Fig. 2); the strain heterogeneity proves there must be a component of simple shear. The belt of fabrics shows what look like dextral shear bands. The stereonet (Fig. 7) shows fabrics measured from outside and inside these structures. It can be seen that the intersection of fabrics inside and outside is, within error, parallel to the mineral aggregate elongation lineation. Therefore the apparent dextral sense is illusory; the fabric obliquity is not diagnostic of shear sense. These minor structures can be thought of as small lateral ramps; that is, they have the same movement direction as the 'main' shear zone forming the fabrics in Figure 4. A sample, M2 (Wheeler 1986), from adjacent to low-strain lozenge I, cut parallel to foliation and perpendicular to lineation to show the profile plane, contains oblique microstructures indicating sinistral-reverse shear. The low-strain lens at I shows two rather sharp boundaries at a high angle to each other, but having the same lineation and movement direction. Figure 5 shows a low-strain pod with migmatitic banding at J. This is again bounded by shear zones in various orientations but the one on the north side shows unambiguous dextral shear sense.

These structures provide small-scale analogues for larger-scale structures in the Torridon Lewisian. The low-strain lens is analogous to those mapped on the kilometre scale (Fig. 2). Wheeler *et al.* (1987), using Cresswell's data, noted that the foliations in the Diabaig inlier are more variable than the lineations. To a first approximation, the anastomosing shear zones have the same movement direction in the inlier. So, as in the outcrop-scale example in Figure 4, the foliation patterns in the area should be interpreted with care, in that the bending associated with strain variations does not necessarily relate to shear sense.

Summary of Loch Roag Line

The early Scourian in the vicinity of the Loch Roag Line consists of banded gneiss immediately to the north and smooth gneiss to the south. The contact is now marked by a zone of intense strain which probably juxtaposed the two rock types. Inverian deformation consisted of overall simple shear in the south with local shear planes at a variety of angles and sharing a common lineation. In the north, where shear planes are highly variable (e.g. the south part of Fig. 5), the lineation is again much more consistent. Tight folds, with hinges parallel to lineation, resulted when earlier banding lay in the shortening field of the Inverian strain. Scourie dykes intruded parallel or subparallel (e.g. Fig. 3c) to Inverian fabrics and discordant to earlier banding. In the centre of Figure 5 (enlarged in Fig. 6) there is evidence for deformation in the country rocks while dykes were molten. Subsequent Laxfordian deformation caused localized or pervasive foliation in the dykes and some very localized high-strain deformation in the gneisses. Inverian and Laxfordian structures both show both shear senses; there is no clear overall pattern.

Park (2005) proposed a terrane boundary along the north side of the Diabaig inlier, which is apparently coincident with the Loch Roag Line (although his fig. 2 is not detailed). This implies movement of tens or hundreds of kilometres. Although there are certainly some high strains on the Loch Roag Line, it is difficult to envisage such displacements. Gneisses to the north and south cannot be distinguished on field criteria. Although the Scourian protolith was banded to the north and smooth to the south of the Line in the detailed study of Figure 4, both rock types occur throughout the Torridon inliers, both north and south of the proposed boundary. A displacement of less than 1 km could juxtapose the two rock types. Further structural and geochronological investigations are required to address the existence of a terrane boundary here.

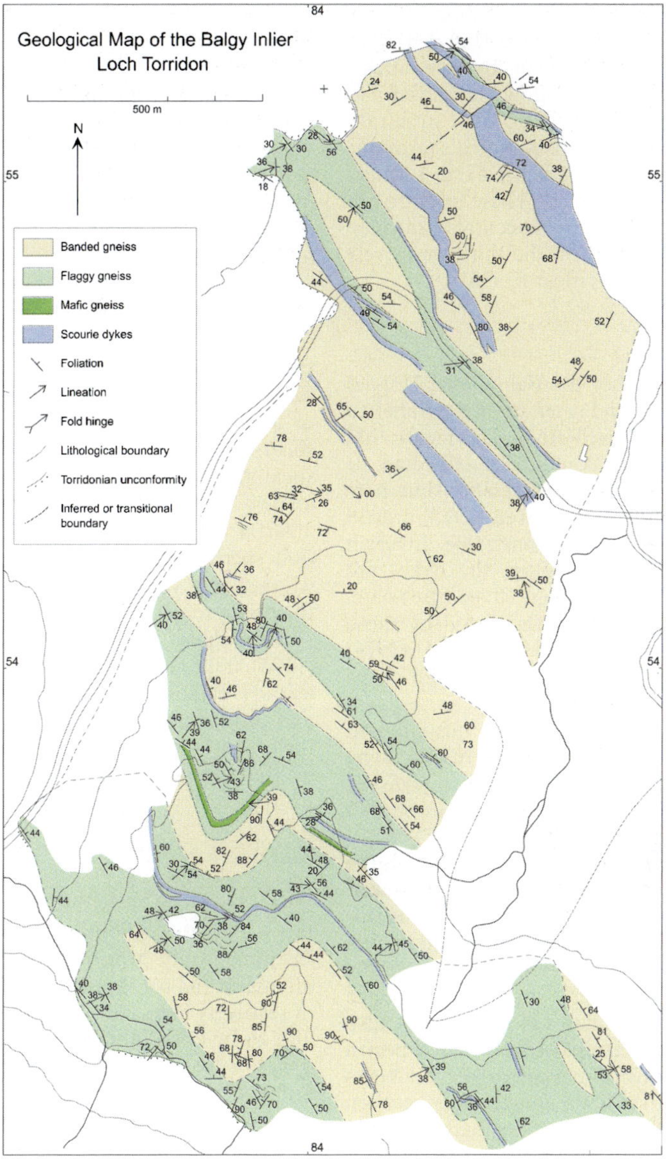

Fig. 9. Map of the Lewisian inlier at Balgy, south side of Loch Torridon. Coastline shown is high water mark, with some geology being exposed intertidally in the NW of map.

Balgy inlier

Laxfordian structure

The Balgy area (SE part of Fig. 2; Fig. 9) shows discrete shears within dykes in its northern part; for instance, the dyke exposed on the northern headland [843553] contains a dextral-normal shear. Thinner dykes in the south of the inlier are pervasively deformed and therefore do not indicate shear sense. A low-strain zone of banded gneiss shows apparent dextral reorientation at the margins of two dykes, *c.* 300 m south of the headland [843548 and 844550, Fig. 9]. No lineation is visible in the gneisses, which means that, in general, true sense should be deduced with care

(Wheeler 1987); however, the banding is fairly steep so there is likely to be a true dextral component. This might be Laxfordian. In the southern half of the map, thin dykes show pervasive foliation. The only other clear Laxfordian structures at Balgy are the major and minor disharmonic folds with north–south-striking axial surfaces seen in the south of the inlier. These folds do not affect the low-strain zone in the centre of the map and may have detached on the thin pervasively deformed Scourie dykes [near 839541].

Inverian structure

In the southern part of the Balgy inlier (Fig. 9) foliations in dykes and gneisses are parallel to dyke margins and to each other. This means that the gneissic foliation could be Laxfordian or Inverian but there are no direct relationships here to help decide. Park & Cresswell (1973) argued that, where there are demonstrable Inverian fabrics in the southern region, the dykes are thinner and more numerous than elsewhere, because their emplacement was aided by those pre-existing steep fabrics. Beach *et al.* (1974) pointed out that thinner more deformed dykes in more highly deformed gneisses are equally explicable by strong Laxfordian strains imposed on all rock types, reducing dyke thickness by strain and imposing strong foliations in gneisses. How can one discriminate between these two very different hypotheses?

The southern part of the Balgy inlier shows thinner dykes than the northern part. However, ignoring the late fold, there is no systematic difference in dip between the thin dykes and thicker dykes present in the north. This is true generally in the Diabaig inlier. Simple shear cannot change the thickness of a planar object unless it also rotates it, and in principle one would expect a systematic relationship between dyke thickness and orientation. If α is the initial angle between a dyke and the shear plane, α' the final angle and γ the shear strain, then from equation (2.3) of Ramsay & Huber (1983),

$$\cot \alpha' = \cot \alpha' - \gamma$$

and the ratio of initial to final dyke thickness is given by

$$\sin \alpha / \sin \alpha'.$$

The thickest dykes at Torridon are 50 m or more across, whereas thin sheared ones may be 5 m or less (see Fig. 4 for typical examples), so we require thinning by a factor of, say, 10. Shear is most efficient at thinning if $\alpha = 90°$, in which case $\gamma = 10$ is sufficient. However, the final α' value is less than 6°, so we require the dyke to be deflected through almost a right angle. Such deflections are not present in the Torridon Lewisian. If the dyke initially lay at a low angle of 10° to the shear plane, then $\gamma = 52$ is required, and now the deflection is just 9°. This angle is within the range of dyke dips observed. However, the shear strain X/Z ratio is 2706 from equation (2.7) of Ramsay & Huber (1983). Such a huge strain is not in accord with the general nature of the flaggy gneisses where, although mineral aggregates record 'high' strains, they are far less strained than this number indicates. In summary, the differences in dyke thicknesses from one area to another are difficult to explain in terms of shear-related deformation. High initial dyke/shear angles imply unrealistically large deflection angles; low initial dyke/shear angles imply unrealistically large strains. Other types of deformation, such as differential pure shear parallel to the dykes, could explain thickness changes but lead to space problems.

In summary, the idea of Park & Cresswell (1973) that the NW–SE gneiss foliations were already established before dyke emplacement, and influenced dyke thickness, is supported by the present study. Hence the flaggy gneiss fabrics in the southern part of the Balgy inlier are Inverian.

Summary of Balgy inlier

Early Scourian rocks were banded gneisses in the north and smooth gneisses in the south. Inverian strain was heterogeneous and more intense in the south, isolating 100 m wide lenses of relatively low strain. Dykes were intruded parallel to Inverian fabrics where they were present; dykes were originally thinner in such areas. Subsequent Laxfordian strain induced discrete shears within thick dykes and pervasive foliation in thinner ones. Later Laxfordian deformation involved disharmonic folding on all scales in the south of the area.

Other Loch Torridon inliers

The Balgy inlier (except for the Laxfordian folds) and, on the small scale, the Loch Roag Line (except for the pinch and swell structures) illustrate the main structural features found throughout the Diabaig inlier: heterogeneous strain in the gneisses, thick dykes in the low-strain lenses; thinner dykes elsewhere; Laxfordian strain localized in thinner dykes; no clear overall shear sense.

Laxfordian structure

The Kenmore and Shieldaig inliers show pervasive foliation development in dykes. The Kenmore inlier is characterized by NW–SE-trending folds that affect strongly foliated dykes (Park *et al.* 1987). There is no doubt that the dykes show intense Laxfordian strain, and that the folds affecting them are Laxfordian. Niamatullah & Park (1990) diagnosed intense deformation in the gneisses as Laxfordian as well, and this area is identified as the 'Kenmore Shear Zone'

Inverian structure

Although there is no ambiguity about the high strain in the dykes at Kenmore and at Shieldaig, there is evidence that the fabrics in the surrounding gneisses are composite, and were initiated in the Inverian (Niamatullah & Park 1990). In a discussion of the Laxfordian D_1 deformation, those authors stated: 'It is not possible to differentiate this [Laxfordian] fabric in the gneisses from the previous Inverian fabric in general, because the two are sub-parallel.' The relative contributions of Inverian and Laxfordian strains in the gneisses therefore remain uncertain.

Conceptual model for the Lewisian deformation at Loch Torridon

At Torridon and elsewhere in the Lewisian, Inverian deformation was significant (Coward & Park 1987). On all scales, Inverian shear sense is not easy to establish. Variations in foliation orientation relate to a single lineation direction, and thus are likely to relate to varying shear planes. Where shear sense can be established on a metre scale, there are examples of both dextral-normal and sinistral-reverse shears. Laxfordian shear zones within Scourie dykes also show examples of both movement senses, or show foliation curvature that does not relate to shear sense.

Arguments for overall shear sense are, as a result, based on large-scale structures. Figure 10a shows a block diagram of the Torridon area, based on the surface geology (that of the Diabaig inlier being shown in perspective) extrapolated to depth. Structural styles equivalent to the other inliers are marked. Diabaig shows large low-strain lozenges in the north bounded by steep shear zones, with a gradual increase in strain and decrease in dip passing southwards. Balgy has thick and thin low-strain lozenges, the latter being folded together with foliated dykes. Shieldaig has no low-strain zones and shows significant NE dip. These three inliers all have an east-plunging lineation, so the main cross-section cut is east–west. Kenmore has upright folds affecting almost entirely high-strain gneisses and dykes; the enveloping surface can be thought of as subhorizontal, and the lineation runs NW–SE parallel to fold hinges. The two section cuts here emphasize the folding (on a NE–SW cut) and hinges parallel to lineation (so the structure looks simple on the NW–SE cut). The transition from Kenmore to Shieldaig resembles a ductile flat to ramp, the latter being extrapolated northwards beneath the Diabaig inlier, hypothesizing that dips decrease downwards as well as southwards.

The large arrow indicates a top-to-the-NW movement sense for the whole area. The general bending of low-strain lozenges is consistent with this. Figure 10b–e shows how a set of lozenges separated by initially steep dykes (Fig. 10b) could evolve as a consequence of dykes being less competent than surrounding gneisses. Let us suppose that during top-to-the-west or top-to-the-NW shear the vertical height of the large shear zone remains constant. The gneisses will undergo dyke-parallel stretching as the lozenges, shown as rectangles for simplicity, rotate and there will be top-SE normal-sense shear in the dykes, opposite to the overall movement (Fig. 10c). Strain in the lozenges need not be intense, even if the localized strain in dykes is large, and this accords with the faint but roughly NE-dipping foliations in the low-strain lozenges (Wheeler *et al.* 1987). As the lineation at Diabaig is oblique, the shear sense here at this stage of evolution would be dextral-normal and top-to-the-east. More intense strain (Fig. 10d) would rotate dykes close to the shear plane, where a reversal in shear can be envisaged (Fig. 10e). This reversal could propagate out from the main shear zone, along the easy-slip dykes, to cause local movement reversals even in the north of the Diabaig inlier. This model is proposed as being consistent with the observed data, but is not unique.

Discussion

The Kenmore area resembles much of the Outer Hebrides insofar as it consists of deformed metabasic sheets interpreted as transposed dykes parallel to intense fabrics in the gneisses with a NW–SE lineation. The Torridon area is therefore important as marking the boundary of this crustal-scale high-strain zone against the central part of the Lewisian, which is only locally affected by Inverian and Laxfordian strain. Globally, there is a variety of structural styles in such boundaries, which is discussed below.

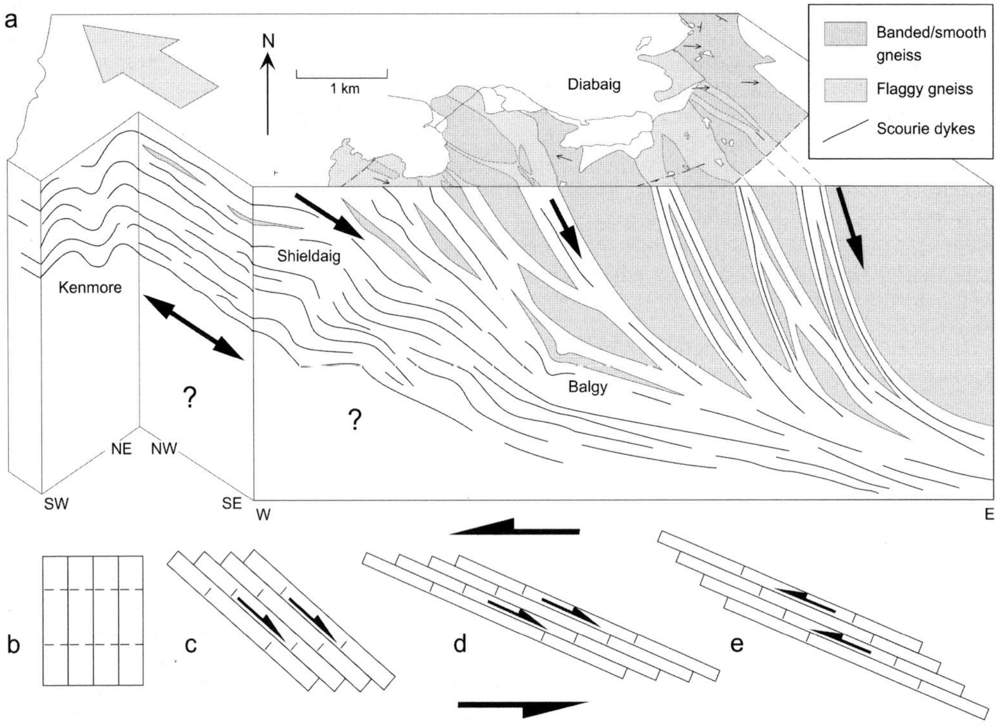

Fig. 10. (**a**) Schematic block diagram showing structure of the Loch Torridon inliers (see text for details). (**b**)–(**d**) Illustration of how overall top-to-the-west shear can induce top-to-the-east shear in dykes if they are less competent and form easy slip horizons. Increasing displacement on the large scale causes increasing pure shear strain in grey gneisses between dykes. Dashed lines indicate notional marker levels. Laxfordian strain in the country rock could then be pure shear, and not necessarily very intense. (**e**) When dykes are rotated to be subparallel to the shear plane as in (**d**), the movement sense may reverse.

Boundaries through which pre-existing planar markers can be mapped, and their reorientation traced, provide the clearest indication of strain. Thus, the Southern Nagssugtoqidian front in Greenland (Escher *et al.* 1975; van Gool *et al.* 2002) is clearly a south-up thrust sense shear; the base of the Sarv thrust sheet, Scandinavian Caledonides (Gilotti & Kumpulainen 1986), is clearly an ESE-directed shear. Both areas have dykes that can be traced from low to high strain. Of all the major Lewisian shear zones, only South Harris (Fig. 1) shows a very clear pattern of foliations indicating its overall (dextral) movement sense (Graham & Coward 1973; Graham 1980). The Canisp Shear Zone does show a deflection of fabrics with a north side down movement sense in the Inverian, but the large-scale Laxfordian pattern does not show such obvious deflections. Other than these examples, the Lewisian lacks large-scale unambiguous offsets of dykes; in addition, the behaviour of foliations and lineations at high-strain boundaries is not what simple shear models would predict.

In the Lewisian, the northern boundary of the central Archaean region is the Laxford Front, but this is marked by an increase in tightness of folding passing northwards, rather than by the heterogeneous anastomosing shear zones seen at Torridon. Discrete sinistral shears are present to the south of the Front (Coward 1984) but do not anastomose. These could be used to infer a sinistral movement in the area as a whole. The overall lineation pattern in the area also seems to show a sinistral lineation deflection passing northwards towards higher-strain areas (Coward *et al.* 1980) but this pattern could reflect a varying shear direction within a single shear plane (Wheeler 1987), a geometry documented on the small scale nearby (Tatham & Casey 2007).

The Canisp Shear Zone does display deflection of fabrics consistent with north side down Inverian displacement. However, the overall Laxfordian lineation is rather constant in orientation both inside and outside the shear zone (see stereonets of Jensen (1984). The deflections in fabric, even if they are partly Laxfordian, cannot then be used to deduce shear sense. The evidence for this comes instead from local dextral shears in dykes within the 500 m wide shear zone (Attfield 1987) and a slight bend in foliation over a transition zone less than 5m wide at its edges (Jensen 1984).

The Diabaig inlier is characterized by anastomosing shear zones, increasing in abundance southwards and structurally downwards until they coalesce. The dip decrease in lozenges is interpreted as relating to top-to-the-NW shear, which could in turn relate to crustal shortening, although local shearing can be extensional (Fig. 10). It should be noted that the Laxfordian deformation duplicates a Palaeoproterozoic basement–cover interface north of Loch Maree (Park *et al.* 2001), evidence for crustal shortening. Low-strain lozenges separated by anastomosing shears are recorded from other compressional settings such as the Grenville orogen (Davidson 1984). However, the geometry is similar to that proposed for the Basin and Range (Hamilton 1987), an extensional setting. There the anastomosing shears with both shear senses pass structurally down into more homogeneous pure shear fabrics. This seems very similar to the Torridon geometry, especially as both shear senses are present. At Torridon, however, the movement direction parallels the long axes of the lozenges, whereas in the Hamilton model the implication is that it anastomoses around the lozenges, in a plane strain framework.

These three examples illustrate that the Lewisian high-strain zones do not have the characteristics of simple shear on the kilometre scale; this is true of structures from basement regions elsewhere. The Nordre Strømfjord steep belt, Greenland, contains high-strain amphibolite-facies fabrics and was described as a major sinistral shear with more than 100 km of displacement (Sørensen 1983). However, fabrics south of the steep belt are also high strain and carry an ENE–WSW lineation roughly parallel to that in the steep belt. No 'bending-in' of the lineation is seen as the steep belt is approached. The steep structure is therefore better interpreted as a zone of NNW–SSE-directed shortening acting on a subhorizontal ENE-directed shear (Passchier *et al.* 1997).

Some generalizations about high-strain zones in deep crustal deformation can be made from this brief survey.

(1) Deflections of planar features may indicate shear, as at the Southern Nagssugtoqidian front and South Harris. Alternatively, they may indicate folding of a shear fabric (e.g. folds in the Outer Hebrides (Coward 1984); Nordre Strømfjord steep belt). The Torridon area shows that, as a third possibility, deflections can relate to a variety of shear planes anastomosing round low-strain lozenges.

(2) Lineation data must form part of structural synthesis. Pre-existing lineations are expected to bend in to shear zones; new lineations are expected to initiate at 45° to the shear plane and track into it. In fact, the spatial pattern of lineations does not fit with these ideas for any large high-strain zone this author is aware of. In the Laxford Front shallow ESE-plunging lineations are rotated anticlockwise from steep south-plunging lineations at lower strains, but all lineations lie approximately in the same shear plane. The spatial distribution may relate to varying shear directions but cannot relate to accumulating shear strain in a single kinematic framework. In Nordre Strømfjord the lineations in the steep belt are parallel to those outside; a result of local NNW–SSE shortening being perpendicular to lineation. In the Canisp Shear Zone Laxfordian lineations in the steep belt are (similarly) parallel to those outside, although the cause of this may be different. At Torridon, in the Diabaig inlier it is the shear planes that vary and the lineation that is relatively fixed in direction. Even in the low-strain lozenges, some stretching has given rise to the same lineation direction (Fig. 10; Wheeler 1987).

Future directions

In the introduction two key problems in the Lewisian are mentioned, which also apply to other high-grade regions: the lack of 'pervasive' shear sense indicators, and difficulties of dating.

Shear sense indicators are not always abundant in high-grade rocks, but new investigation techniques may be used. Jensen (1984) measured quartz *c*-axis fabrics in the Canisp Shear Zone so as to infer dextral shear sense. More recently, new techniques have allowed rapid analysis of lattice preferred orientations (LPOs) in other minerals. These have produced surprising results; for example, plagioclase in the amphibolite-facies Lewisian rocks may have no LPO, even though it is interspersed with hornblende that has a strong LPO (Lapworth *et al.* 2002; Thurston 2003). A better understanding of how such microstructures evolve would help to clarify the large-scale story. There are very few studies of quartz fabrics in basement regions, but the technique has considerable potential.

In the evolution of the Lewisian complex, the role of the Inverian remains to be quantified. Field data yield constraints on age but direct dating of fabrics could play a major role as there have been many advances in the last three decades. Many new dates from the Lewisian have been obtained, particularly by U/Pb analyses on zircon by conventional (Mason *et al.* 2004) and spot analysis (sensitive high-resolution ion microprobe) techniques (Kinny *et al.* 2005). Some of these ages have been interpreted in terms of protolith formation and therefore do not directly date deformation; however, they have given rise to new and divergent hypotheses about Lewisian tectonics (Kinny *et al.* 2005; Park 2005). A boundary close to or coincident with the Loch Roag Line is proposed to separate terranes that, from a database of ages scattered on the scale of tens of kilometres (Kinny *et al.* 2005), are deduced to be of different ages (Park 2005). Maps on the scale of hundreds of metres to kilometres presented here do not provide ready support for such a proposal. However, the terrane boundary may be hypothesized to be a wider strip of anastomosing shear zones, whose total displacement was large. One would expect the lozenges within such a strip to record complex and diverse histories, related to (or possibly independent of) one or other of the terranes on either side. None of this is obvious from field data from the Loch Torridon inliers, which underlines the importance of tying geochronological investigation to field observations on all scales. This contribution illustrates the complex heterogeneity of deformation in the Lewisian, which must be characterized through field-based structural study to allow proper interpretation of radiometric ages and provide context for microstructural and metamorphic investigations.

Mike Coward's vision of the Lewisian Complex and tectonics in general has had a great influence on my thinking. I thank R. Knipe, J. Watterson and B. Windley for discussion in the field, R. Butler and K. McCaffrey for reviewing, and A. Ries for editing the manuscript. K. Lancaster redrafted the diagrams. This work was funded by a Natural Environment Research Council PhD studentship (1982–1985).

References

Attfield, P. 1987. The structural history of the Canisp Shear Zone. *In*: Park, R. G. & Tarney, J. (eds) *Evolution of the Lewisian and Comparable Precambrian High Grade Terrains*. Geological Society, London, Special Publications, **27**, 165–173.

Beach, A. 1976. The interrelations of fluid transport, deformation, geochemistry and heat flow in early Proterozoic shear zones in the Lewisian complex. *Philosophical Transactions of the Royal Society of London, Series A*, **280**, 569–604.

Beach, A., Coward, M. P. & Graham, R. H. 1974. An interpretation of the structural evolution of the Laxford front, north-west Scotland. *Scottish Journal of Geology*, **9**, 297–308.

Bons, P. D., Druguet, E., Hamann, I., Carreras, J. & Passchier, C. W. 2004. Apparent boudinage in dykes. *Journal of Structural Geology*, **26**, 625–636.

Butler, R. W. H. & Prior, D. J. 1988. Tectonic controls on the uplift of the Nanga Parbat massif, Pakistan Himalayas. *Nature*, **333**, 247–250.

Cliff, R. A., Gray, C. M. & Huhma, H. 1983. A Sm–Nd isotopic study of the South Harris Igneous Complex, the Outer Hebrides. *Contributions to Mineralogy and Petrology*, **82**, 91–98.

Coward, M. P. 1975. Flat-lying structures within the Lewisian basement gneiss complex of NW Scotland. *Proceedings of the Geologists' Association*, **85**, 459–472.

Coward, M. P. 1984. Major shear zones in the Precambrian crust; examples from NW Scotland and southern Africa and their significance. *In*: Kröner, A. & Greiling, R. (eds) *Precambrian Tectonics Illustrated*. Schweizerbart, Stuttgart, 207–235.

Coward, M. P. & Park, R. G. 1987. The role of mid-crustal shear zones in the Early Proterozoic evolution of the Lewisian. *In*: Park, R. G. & Tarney, J. (eds) *Evolution of the Lewisian and Comparable Precambrian High Grade Terrains*. Geological Society, London, Special Publications, **27**, 127–138.

Coward, M. P., Kim, J. H. & Parke, J. 1980. A correlation of Lewisian structures and their displacement across the Moine thrust zone. *Proceedings of the Geologists' Association*, **91**, 327–337.

Cresswell, D. 1972. The structural development of the Lewisian rocks on the north shore of Loch Torridon, Ross-shire. *Scottish Journal of Geology*, **8**, 293–308.

Davidson, A. 1984. Identification of ductile shear zones in the southwest Grenville Province of the Canadian Shield. *In*: Kröner, A. & Greiling, R. (eds) *Precambrian Tectonics Illustrated*. Schweizerbart, Stuttgart, 263–279.

Escher, A., Escher, J. C. & Watterson, J. 1975. The reorientation of the Kangamiut dyke swarm, West Greenland. *Canadian Journal of Earth Sciences*, **12**, 158–173.

Evans, C. R. 1965. Geochronology of the Lewisian basement near Lochinver, Sutherland. *Nature*, **207**, 54–55.

Gilotti, J. A. & Kumpulainen, R. 1986. Strain softening induced ductile flow in the Sarv Thrust Sheet, Scandinavian Caledonides. *Journal of Structural Geology*, **8**, 441–455.

Graham, R. H. 1980. The role of shear belts in the structural evolution of the South Harris Igneous Complex. *Journal of Structural Geology*, **2**, 29–37.

Graham, R. H. & Coward, M. P. 1973. The Laxfordian of the Outer Hebrides. *In*: Park, R. G. & Tarney, J. (eds) *The Early Precambrian of Scotland and Related Rocks of Greenland*. University of Keele, Keele, 85–93.

HAMILTON, W. 1987. Crustal extension in the Basin and Range Province, southwestern United States. *In*: COWARD, M. P., DEWEY, J. F. & HANCOCK, P. F. (eds) *Continental Extensional Tectonics*. Geological Society, London, Special Publications, **28**, 155–176.

JENSEN, L. N. 1984. Quartz microfabric of the Laxfordian Canisp Shear Zone, NW Scotland. *Journal of Structural Geology*, **6**, 293–302.

KINNY, P. D., FRIEND, C. R. L. & LOVE, G. J. 2005. Proposal for a terrane-based nomenclature for the Lewisian Gneiss Complex of NW Scotland. *Journal of the Geological Society, London*, **162**, 175–186.

LAPWORTH, T., WHEELER, J. & PRIOR, D. J. 2002. The deformation of plagioclase investigated using electron backscatter diffraction crystallographic preferred orientation data. *Journal of Structural Geology*, **24**, 387–399.

MASON, A. J., PARRISH, R. R. & BREWER, T. S. 2004. U–Pb geochronology of Lewisian orthogneisses in the Outer Hebrides, Scotland: implications for the tectonic setting and correlation of the South Harris Complex. *Journal of the Geological Society, London*, **161**, 45–54.

NIAMATULLAH, M. & PARK, R. G. 1990. Laxfordian structure, strain distribution and kinematic interpretation of the Kenmore Inlier, Loch Torridon — anatomy of a major Lewisian shear zone. *Transactions of the Royal Society of Edinburgh, Earth Sciences*, **81**, 195–207.

NORRIS, R. J. & COOPER, A. F. 2003. Very high strains recorded in mylonites along the Alpine Fault, New Zealand: implications for the deep structure of plate boundary faults. *Journal of Structural Geology*, **25**, 2141–2157.

PARK, R. G. 2005. The Lewisian terrane model: a review. *Scottish Journal of Geology*, **41**, 105–118.

PARK, R. G. & CRESSWELL, D. 1973. The dykes of the Laxfordian belt. *In*: PARK, R. G. & TARNEY, J. (eds) *The Early Precambrian of Scotland and Related Rocks of Greenland.* University of Keele, Keele, 119–130.

PARK, R. G., CRANE, A. & NIAMATULLAH, M. 1987. Early Proterozoic structure and kinematic evolution of the southern mainland Lewisian. *In*: PARK, R. G. & TARNEY, J. (eds) *Evolution of the Lewisian and Comparable Precambrian High Grade Terrains.* Geological Society, London, Special Publications, **27**, 139–152.

PARK, R. G., TARNEY, J. & CONNELLY, J. N. 2001. The Loch Maree Group: Palaeoproterozoic subduction–accretion complex in the Lewisian of NW Scotland. *Precambrian Research*, **105**, 205–226.

PASSCHIER, C. W. 1998. Monoclinic model shear zones. *Journal of Structural Geology*, **20**, 1121–1137.

PASSCHIER, C. W., DEN BROK, S. W. J., VAN GOOL, J. A. M., MARKER, M. & MANATSCHAL, G. 1997. Laterally constricted shear zone system — the Nordre Stromfjord steep belt, Nagssugtoqidian Orogen, W Greenland. *Terra Nova*, **9**, 199–202.

RAMSAY, J. G. & GRAHAM, R. H. 1970. Strain variation in shear belts. *Canadian Journal of Earth Sciences*, **7**, 786–813.

RAMSAY, J. G. & HUBER, M. I. 1983. *The Techniques of Modern Structural Geology. Volume 1: Strain Analysis*. Academic Press, London.

REDDY, S. M., WHEELER, J. & CLIFF, R. A. 1999. The geometry and timing of orogenic extension: an example from the western Italian Alps. *Journal of Metamorphic Geology*, **17**, 573–589.

ROBIN, P. Y. F. & CRUDEN, A. R. 1994. Strain and vorticity patterns in ideally ductile transpression zones. *Journal of Structural Geology*, **16**, 447–466.

SANDERSON, D. J. 1972. The development of fold axes oblique to the regional trend. *Tectonophysics*, **16**, 55–70.

SIBSON, R. H. 1977. Fault rocks and fault mechanisms. *Journal of the Geological Society, London*, **133**, 191–213.

SØRENSEN, K. 1983. Growth dynamics of the Nordre Strømfjord shear zone. *Journal of Geophysical Research*, **88**, 3419–3437.

SUTTON, J. & WATSON, J. V. 1951. The pre-Torridonian metamorphic history of the Loch Torridon and Scourie areas in the NW Highlands and its bearing on the chronological classification of the Lewisian. *Journal of the Geological Society, London*, **106**, 241–308.

TATHAM, D. & Casey, M. 2007. Testing kinematic inferences: the Laxfordian shear zone at Upper Badcall, NW Scotland. *In*: RIES, A. C., BUTLER, R. W. H. & GRAHAM, R. H. (eds) *Deformation of the Continental Crust: The Legacy of Mike Coward.* Geological Society, London, Special Publications, **272**, 47–57.

THURSTON, A. C. 2003. *Deformation–metamorphism interrelationships in metabasic rocks: a case study of some amphibolite grade shear zones in NW Scotland.* PhD thesis, Manchester University.

VAN GOOL, J. A. M., CONNELLY, J. N., MARKER, M. & MENGEL, F. C. 2002. The Nagssugtoqidian Orogen of West Greenland: tectonic evolution and regional correlations from a West Greenland perspective. *Canadian Journal of Earth Sciences*, **39**, 665–686.

WATTERSON, J. 1974. Investigations on the Nagssugtoqidian boundary in the Holsteinborg district, central West Greenland. *Rapport Grønlands Geologiske Undersøgelse*, **65**, 33–37.

WHEELER, J. 1986. *Physical and chemical processes in ductile shear zones.* PhD thesis, Leeds University.

WHEELER, J. 1987. The determination of true shear senses from the deflection of passive markers in shear zones. *Journal of the Geological Society, London*, **144**, 73–77.

WHEELER, J., WINDLEY, B. F. & DAVIES, F. B. 1987. Internal evolution of the major Precambrian shear belt at Torridon, NW Scotland. *In*: PARK, R. G. & TARNEY, J. (eds) *Evolution of the Lewisian and Comparable Precambrian High Grade Terrains.* Geological Society, London, Special Publications, **27**, 153–164.

WHEELER, J., TRELOAR, P. J. & POTTS, G. J. 1995. Structural and metamorphic evolution of the Nanga Parbat syntaxis, Pakistan Himalayas, on the Indus gorge transect: the importance of early events. *Geological Journal*, **30**, 349–371.

Inferences from shear zone geometry: an example from the Laxfordian shear zone at Upper Badcall, Lewisian Complex, NW Scotland

DANIEL J. TATHAM & MARTIN CASEY

Earth Sciences, School of Earth and Environment, Leeds University, Leeds LS2 9JT, UK
(e-mail: tatham@earth.leeds.ac.uk)

Abstract: This contribution presents a Laxfordian age shear zone near Upper Badcall, NW Scotland, as an example of using field data and theory to assess the kinematics and nature of deformation in a shear zone. The deformation zone includes quartzofeldspathic background gneiss and a dolerite dyke that cuts the gneissic banding at a high angle. A detailed field description of the deformation zone, which is critically discussed in terms of pure and simple shear, is presented. Analysis of gneissic banding and mineral lineation data, together with a consideration of the outcrop pattern, shows that the deformation zone is best described in terms of a simple shear zone with varying finite stretching direction. To analyse this deformation we introduce the concept of local plane strain. Although the deformation of the zone as a whole is 3D, at each point there is a direction in which it does not change its length. This direction is perpendicular to the local shear direction and so varies in orientation across the shear zone. In a reference frame defined at a point, the deformation can thus be understood in terms of conventional simple shear. Details of strain are hence determined according to this conclusion. A stereographic method for the determination of the reorientation of lines is used to calculate shear strain. The shear strain values across the shear zone are then used to restore the sheared dolerite dyke to its undeformed geometry. The success of the restoration provides supports for the strain calculation and also the conclusion of simple shear deformation.

To evaluate tests of kinematic inferences requires a field area that has undergone an extended period of successive phases of deformation separated by marker intrusions. This allows the worker to assess the nature of deformation through time in terms of its magnitude, orientation and coaxiality.

The Archaean to Proterozoic Lewisian gneiss complex of NW Scotland shows evidence of a protracted and complex history including multiple phases of deformation and intrusion (e.g. Sutton & Watson 1951). This makes it a particularly useful resource for identifying and studying the relative importance of deformation styles (pure or simple shear) in the mid- to lower crust. The Lewisian gneiss is broadly divided into the Scourian granulites (*c*. 2800 Ma, Chapman & Moorbath 1977; Hamilton *et al.* 1979) and the Laxfordian amphibolites (*c*. 1750 Ma, Moorbath *et al.* 1969; Kinny & Friend 1997), two tectonothermal events separated by a period of intrusion (2400–2000 Ma, Chapman 1979; Waters *et al.* 1990) of an approximately east–west- to NW–SE-trending suite of tabular and laterally extensive, dominantly dolerite dykes (Scourie dyke suite, Sutton & Watson 1951; Park & Tarney 1987). The Scourie dykes are locally undeformed and unaltered in the Scourian granulites and are then cut and deformed by discrete local- and regional-scale Laxfordian shear zones. The Laxfordian shear zone at Farhead Point near Upper Badcall, NW Scotland (Fig. 1), has been described by previous workers (e.g. Beach 1974) and is one that has been used to demonstrate the style or nature of shear in Laxfordian shear zones (Coward & Potts 1983) owing to interesting geometries of well-exposed deformed Scourie dykes. This contribution reassesses these early thoughts with the advantage of new and detailed field data collected by the authors. Field data analyses (including gneissic banding, lineations and outcrop geometry), together with tectonic movement directions measured from collected samples, are used in the discussion of the nature of deformation across the shear zone. The shear zone is then qualitatively and quantitatively described, based on this revised understanding of the shear.

The compatibility argument of Ramsay & Graham (1970) is reinforced with a mathematical proof of the allowable states of strain in a generalized deformation zone that permits a varying shear direction across the zone, presented in Appendix 2. Mathematical proof that the line of intersection of a plane and a generalized shear zone remains unchanged, whatever the orientation of the movement direction in the shear zone is also presented.

From: Ries, A. C., Butler, R. W. H. & Graham, R. H. (eds) 2007. *Deformation of the Continental Crust: The Legacy of Mike Coward*. Geological Society, London, Special Publications, **272**, 47–57.

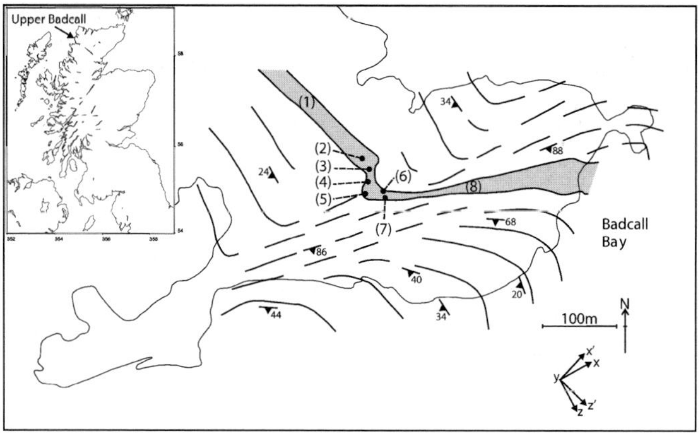

Fig. 1. Simplified structural map of Farhead Point, Upper Badcall, NW Scotland. The Scourie dyke and the orientation and formed surface gneissic banding are shown. Numbers in parentheses refer to sample locations. Both the shear zone (*xyz*) and undeformed dyke (*x′yz′*) reference frames are illustrated. This inset map of Scotland shows the location of Upper Badcall.

Field data

Gneissic banding

The poles to gneissic banding, plotted in Figure 2a, show a steady migration from the undeformed wall rock orientation at the southern coast of Farhead Point (e.g. 145/27W) to a zone of intense and subvertical fabric development (e.g. 075/84S) shown in Figure 1.

Mineral lineations

Figure 2c shows a plot of mineral lineations measured in the quartzofeldspathic gneiss between the central band of intense shear fabric development and the southern coast of Farhead Point (Fig. 1). Dyke lineations, defined by the shape fabric of plagioclase clots, are shown only for samples collected between the northern boundary of the shear zone and the band of intense shear fabric development (Fig. 2b). Poor exposure of the dyke towards the southern boundary of the shear zone prevented sample collection there.

It can be seen from Figure 2b and c that quartzofeldspathic gneiss and dyke mineral lineations can be broadly contained within a girdle that intuitively approximates the shear zone. This is most clearly developed in the dyke lineations (Fig. 2b), where the undeformed dyke material outside the shear zone is isotropic. Therefore, all mineral lineations plotted from within the dyke are the result of Laxfordian deformation. This is in contrast to mineral lineations from the quartzofeldspathic gneiss country rock, where a pre-existing mineral lineation is observed outside the shear zone; a remnant from some earlier tectonothermal event. Mineral lineations caused by the shear zone strain within the quartzofeldspathic gneiss may have some memory of an earlier orientation and progressively rotate to the orientation of the new deformation field. Hence, these data have significantly more scatter, especially away from the band of highest shear fabric development. Most of the west-plunging lineations in the gneiss refer to locations south of the zone of intense shear fabric development, including pre-existing linear fabrics and the early stages of those rotating into the shear zone orientation. East-dipping plunges mark mineral lineations from within the zone of intense fabric development, although there is scant correlation between the plunge of east-dipping lineations and the location of those data transversely across the zone. In contrast, dyke mineral lineations migrate from a subvertical plunge near the northern boundary of the shear zone to a subhorizontal plunge in the zone of intense fabric development.

Outcrop geometry

The NW–SE-trending steeply dipping dyke intersects the northern boundary of the shear zone at a high angle (Fig. 1). From this point southwards, the dyke is deflected left-laterally through the high-strain zone, in which it is offset by *c.* 190 m, before returning to an undeformed state at its most southeastern outcrop in Badcall Bay. The ‘kink’ in the deflection of the dyke at

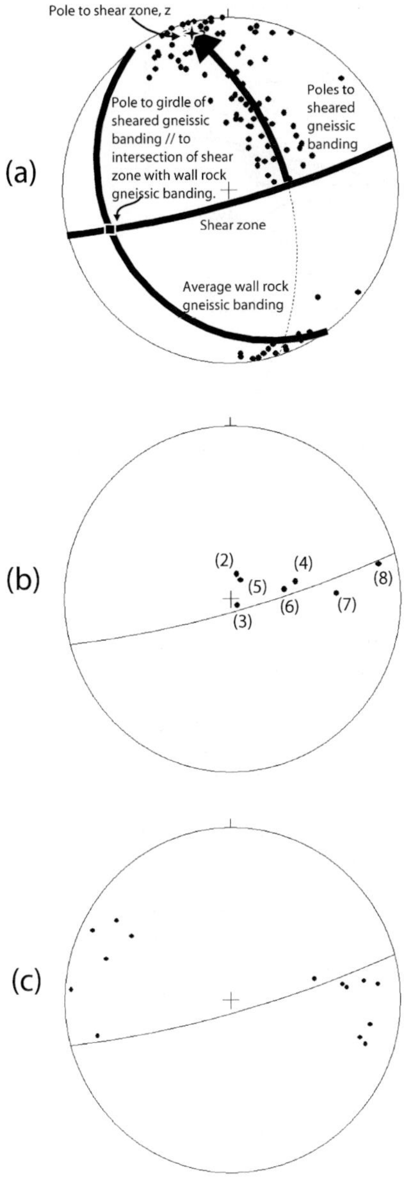

Fig. 2. Gneissic banding and lineation data. (**a**) Stereogram illustrating the parallelism of the point of intersection between the average shear zone orientation and the average wall rock gneissic banding orientation, and the pole to the girdle of sheared gneissic banding. This is used to indicate deformation under simple shear. The trace of the arrow indicates the migration of poles to gneissic banding with increasing deformation. (**b**) Lineations in the Scourie dyke. Numerical annotations refer to the sample number from which they were derived. Sample 1 is not included because of its undeformed state and therefore lack of tectonic lineation. (**c**) Lineations in the quartzofeldspathic gneiss.

the northern boundary of the shear zone should be noted. This is a real feature and not an artefact of topographic interference.

Discussion of field data

Although the heterogeneous strain field of a shear zone undisputedly is the result of mechanical effects, the reorientation of linear and planar features in shear zones can be studied as a consequence of the heterogeneous deformation field alone. Thus the distinction of the active or passive nature of linear or planar fabric elements is not relevant. The left-lateral sense of shear, inferred from the deflection of the dyke, is supported by the apparent deflection of gneissic banding as shown in Figure 1. According to the method of determining true shear sense from the deflection of passive markers, described by Wheeler (1987), this inference of left-lateral shear from the gneissic fabric is a correct one.

According to Ramsay (1967), hinge lines and fold axes in a simple shear zone are always parallel to the line of intersection of the shear plane with the surface being folded. Hence, the line of intersection between the undeformed gneissic banding in the wall rock and the simple shear zone itself should remain constant in spatial orientation during deformation. As shown in Figure 2a, the pole to the girdle containing poles to gneissic banding lies parallel to the line of intersection between the undeformed gneissic banding orientation and the shear zone. It should be noted also that during simple shear, poles to marker planes are deformed along a great circle that contains the pole to the shear plane (z), and they eventually approach that pole, as illustrated in Figure 2a. The field data thus support both of these tests for simple shear.

It has been shown that the behaviour of linear fabrics, such as mineral lineations, can be used to infer the kinematics of deformation prevalent in a shear zone. Wheeler (1987) suggested that passive linear markers, when deformed under simple shear, deform along great circles that contain the movement direction and ultimately approach a trend parallel to that direction. Figure 2b and c shows that to some degree of accuracy this rule can be upheld. Scatter in the data may be due to a number of factors. For example, the varying mineral lineation directions from the dyke, within a fixed foliation orientation, suggest that the tectonic movement direction across the shear zone is not constant. Undeformed dyke material in the wall rock is isotropic and shows no fabric development; however, dyke mineral lineations migrate from subvertical at the northern boundary of the shear zone to subhorizontal in

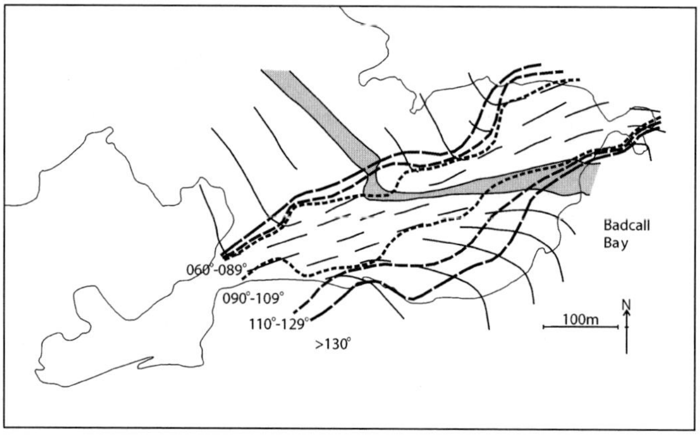

Fig. 3. Isogons of strike of gneissic banding. Isogons are parallel and laterally continuous.

the zone of intense shear fabric development. This may indicate either spatial partitioning of the strain field or temporal variations in the movement direction and magnitude of strain.

Parallelism of gneissic banding strike isogons (as measured in the field) supports the quality of the approximation of a concentrated zone deforming by simple shear (Fig. 3). This satisfies the condition that deformation is constant at each successive level transversely across the dyke, normal to the shear zone boundary.

The inference of a variable tectonic movement direction is supported by the apparently antithetic 'kink' in the deflection of the dyke at the northern boundary of the shear zone. This can be explained by a number of mechanisms. The most simple explanation is that the entire shear zone is deforming under simple shear with the tectonic movement direction spatially partitioned or temporal variation in the strain field transversely across the shear zone. The exact 3D orientation of the undeformed dyke could not be measured, although it was clear that it dipped steeply to the NE. The dyke could hence develop this kinked geometry at its northern margin under the condition that it dipped more shallowly than the mineral lineations or movement directions in, for example, Sample 5. This concept is shown schematically in Figure 4. It should be noted that the anomalously shallower plunge of Sample 4 (Fig. 2b) amongst the steep plunges of Samples 3 and 5 close to its location in the shear zone (Fig. 1) suggests that the sample may not be representative.

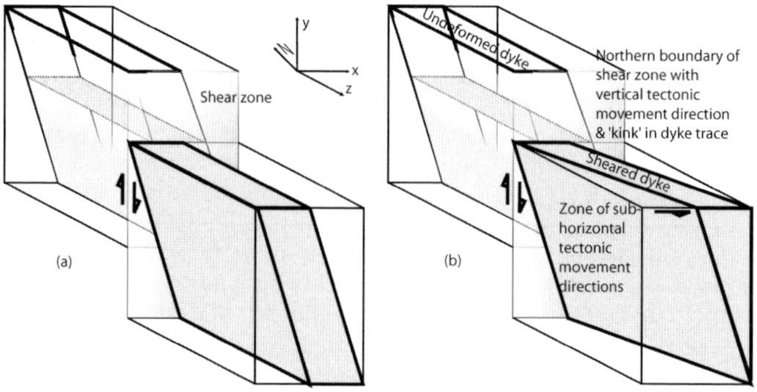

Fig. 4. (**a**) A diagram to illustrate how a steeply dipping dyke can be sheared to generate a kink in its outcrop trace. A vertical shear zone with a vertical shear direction can create an apparently right-lateral outcrop trace. (**b**) Model for the shear zone at Upper Badcall. Vertical shear on a vertical shear zone at the northern boundary of the shear zone provides the subvertical linear fabric and kink in the dyke trace observed. Simple shear with a horizontal displacement vector in the southern block gives a left-lateral offset geometry of the dyke and subhorizontal linear fabric.

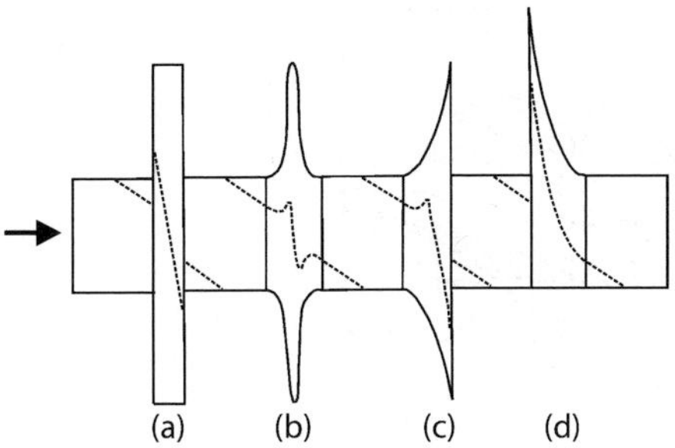

Fig. 5. Expected geometries under pure shear deformation as described by Escher *et al.* (1975). Geometries **(a)**–**(d)** refer to situations with different boundary conditions where the shear zone–wall rock interface switches between no slip and free slip.

It could be suggested that the dyke outcrop geometry developed under pure shear. Escher *et al.* (1975) depicted a selection of outcrop geometries that can prevail when a unit of rock, cross-cut by a subvertical marker, is deformed by a pure shear zone, each with different boundary conditions (Fig. 5). Upon initial inspection there is an almost convincing similarity between the unusual geometry, mapped at the northern boundary of the shear zone at Upper Badcall, and the patterns depicted in Figure 5b and c. However, there are a number of factors that invalidate this theory. The variation in lineation directions across the shear zone from subhorizontal to subvertical suggests that a single pure shear plane strain field does not exist. To generate the observed map-view outcrop pattern from the spatially consistent pure shear strain field indicated in Figure 5b and c, all mineral lineations would have to plunge horizontally; a condition that is clearly not observed. Alternatively, to a first approximation, the field outcrop and mineral lineation data can be satisfied with a model of combined and spatially partitioned pure and simple shear (Fig. 6). This model provides the subvertical finite movement directions and the apparently antithetic kink in the dyke outcrop trace in the block of pure shear towards the northern boundary of the shear zone, and subhorizontal finite movement directions in the southern region of simple shear. Any pure shear, however, would change the orientation of the line of intersection between the undeformed gneissic banding in the wall rock and the shear zone. This is not observed (Fig. 2a), and hence suggests that pure shear deformation, in any orientation, does not occur in this shear zone.

Furthermore, pure shear necessitates that the displacement and strain in the shear zone varies along its length. That is, about some centre point of the shear zone, strain and displacement increase cumulatively longitudinally outwards. Figure 7 illustrates transverse material lines deforming in a pure shear zone. This prediction is not supported by field observations. In addition, Figure 5b and Figure 5c suggest respectively, an equivalent and opposite kink in the outcrop geometry or a discrete discontinuity on the southern boundary of the shear zone. Again, these are not observed.

The problem of strain compatibility and increasing differential shear parallel to the shear zone highlights a further problem in pure shear deformation, one of space. A shear zone of finite length must show evidence for the extrusion of the 'filling' at its lateral terminations if it is to be modelled by pure shear. The main high-strain segment of the shear at Upper Badcall is considered to be of relatively finite length parallel to the zone boundary, although Beach (1974), Barber

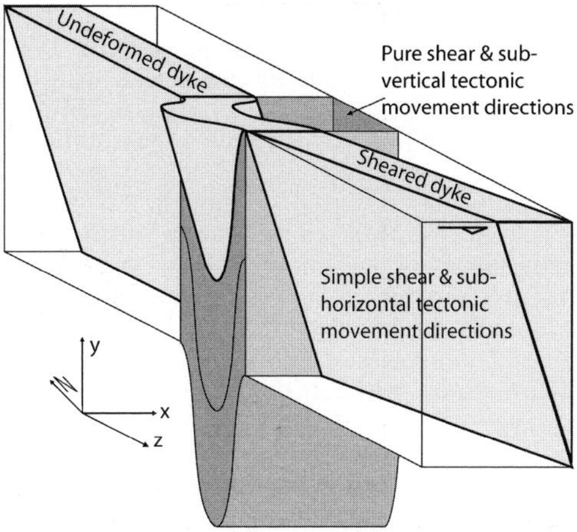

Fig. 6. An alternative hypothesis of deformation in the dyke including pure shear near the northern boundary of the shear zone.

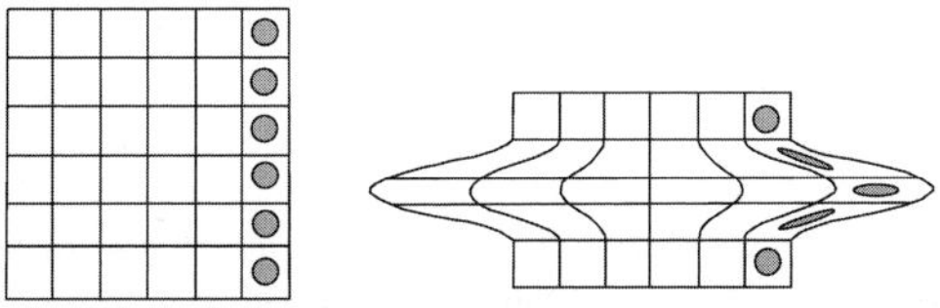

Fig. 7. Material lines deforming in a pure shear zone. The cumulative increase in displacement parallel to the shear zone walls outward from the centre-point of the deformation zone should be noted. Modified from Ramsay & Huber (1987).

et al. (1978) and the original survey field maps of the area (Geological Survey of Scotland 1892) linked the zone to one or two shears with less apparent offset to the east of Badcall Bay. At neither end of the mapped zone is there sufficient evidence to suggest that this lateral extrusion of filling has occurred. Although this feature would not be observed in outcrop for the vertically extruding pure shear zone of Figure 6, it is difficult to conceive how this space problem is overcome at deep tectonic levels, such as the amphibolite-facies conditions of Laxfordian deformation, without the presence of a free surface such as the Earth's surface (Escher *et al.* 1975).

These limitations support the inference that pure shear deformation is not prevalent in the deformation zone at Upper Badcall, which is best approximated as a simple shear zone with a transversely varying tectonic movement direction.

Shear zone with varying finite stretching direction

Ramsay & Graham (1970) demonstrated that a band of high deformation between wall rocks with no deformation can only have a heterogeneous simple shear or heterogeneous uniaxial volume change. It is simple to show with a deck of cards that this can be generalized to combinations of spatially partitioned simple shear in orthogonal directions (e.g. Treagus & Lisle 1997). Further, the finite displacement direction of the shear may vary across the shear zone. A mathematical proof of this is given in Appendix 2. The card deck thought-experiment also shows clearly that there is no deformation in the shear plane, so that the orientation of any line in this plane does not change (see also Appendix 2). An example of such a direction relevant to the current analysis is the intersection line of the gneissic banding and the plane of the shear zone. The constant orientation of this line means that it is a generator of the folded surface of gneissic banding across the shear zone and is the explanation of the observation that the poles to gneissic banding (Fig. 2a) lie on a great circle, normal to this direction.

Any general pure shear strain in the high-strain band would change the orientation of the intersection lineation and the pole to banding would no longer lie on a great circle.

Determining shear strain

A coordinate system is established with the x-axis parallel to the strike of the average orientation of the shear zone (positive to the east), y-axis positive up, and z-axis transversely across the shear zone (positive to the south). The origin lies at the northern shear zone boundary, on the western margin of the dyke.

Data points, where the finite stretching direction and the orientation of the pole to gneissic banding are known, can be used to determine the magnitude of the finite shear strain, γ, using the method of the reorientation of marker lines, as described by Ramsay (1967). The procedure is as follows:

(1) Plot shear zone boundary orientation as a plane and pole.

(2) Plot gneissic banding outside the shear zone.

(3) For each lineation (shear) direction:

(a) plot the direction;

(b) plot the great circle containing shear direction and shear zone pole;

(c) plot the gneissic banding inside the shear zone for this level;

(d) read off α and α' as the intersections of the gneissic banding and the plane constructed in (b) (see Ramsay 1967, fig. 3.23 for definition).

(e) Calculate γ.

An example is shown in Figure 8 and the results are shown in Table 1. The equation (from Ramsay 1967, equation (3–71), p. 88) is

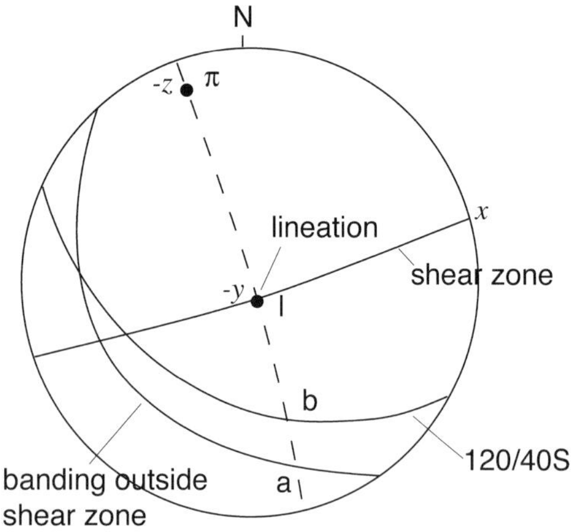

Fig. 8. Example of the stereonet determination of α and α'. Angle *a–l* measured in the great circle is α and angle *b–l* is α'. Also marked on the plot are the coordinate directions x and y. The angle x–l is θ, in this case negative because on this lower hemisphere plot the lineation is pointing downwards and $+\theta$ is defined as the anticlockwise angle from positive x to the lineation.

Table 1. *Kinematic data from points distributed across a transect transversely from north to south over the Laxfordian shear zone at Upper Badcall*

Lineation (azimuth/plunge and corresponding sample number)	Gneissic banding (dip/strike)	α (deg)	α′ (deg)	γ	θ (deg)	Δz (m)	Cumulative displacement in x (m, W to E)	Cumulative displacement in y (m, vertically downwards)
135/86 (3)	120/40S	73	54	0.42	−88	23.75	0.3	10.0
080/64 (6)	100/86S	74	9	6.03	−64.1	16.25	43.1	98.1
087/38 (7)	082/84S	76	5	11.18	−39.2	11.25	140.6	177.6
087/38 (7)	078/90	76	0	15.0	−39.2	15	315.0	319.8
077/12 (8)	078/76S	65	4	13.83	−12.1	25	653.1	392.3
077/12 (8)	098/52S	65	28	1.41	−12.1	20	680.8	398.2
077/12 (8)	098/44S	65	30	1.27	−12.1	21.25	707.1	403.9
077/12 (8)	108/32S	65	38	0.81	−12.1	22.5	725.0	407.7
077/12 (8)	110/32S	65	40	0.73	−12.1	20	739.2	410.8

Each data line refers to a location transversely across the shear zone. Table lines include lineation data taken from the dyke sample closest to the shear fabric measured in the quartzofeldspathic gneiss country rock at that location, α, α′, γ, Δz, and the resolved cumulative displacements in x and y. The average orientation of the gneissic banding outside the shear zone is 145/27W and the average orientation of the shear zone is 075/84SW.

$$\gamma = \cot \alpha' - \cot \alpha. \quad (1)$$

The x and y components of γ can be calculated from

$$\gamma_x = \gamma \cos \theta \quad (2)$$

$$\gamma_x = \gamma \cos \theta \quad (3)$$

where θ is the angle from positive x to the lineation measured in the x,y plane (Figure 8).

A series of points, each including a measurement of gneissic banding and an associated lineation direction related to a sample point, were taken across a transverse section of the shear zone. At each of these points γ_x and γ_y were determined according to equations (1)–(3) and considered constant across a finite width of the shear zone. The relative displacements (ΔU_x, ΔU_y) across each segment of shear zone (Δz) are calculated from

$$\Delta U_x = \gamma_x \Delta z \quad (4)$$

$$\Delta U_y = \gamma_y \Delta z. \quad (5)$$

The cumulative displacements are then obtained by summing the contributions of each segment across the shear zone from north to south (Table 1).

Restoration of the dyke

To test the method of determining shear strain, sheared dyke coordinates as seen in outcrop are restored to their pre-deformation geometry. This procedure has two purposes. First, it tests the method of γ and offset calculation via simple observation of continuity with the unsheared wall rock dyke and the restored dyke coordinates. Second, it estimates the orientation of the undeformed dyke where direct field measurements were unreliable.

Coordinates of points selected along the dyke within the shear zone were restored by removing the cumulative displacement, as calculated above, from the coordinate values at the point under consideration. In general, points moved to the west and upwards on restoration. The cumulative displacements across the shear zone totalled 739.2 m left-lateral in x and 410.8 m north-side upwards in y (Table 1). To determine the geometry of the undeformed dyke the restored coordinates were viewed in a new reference frame with the x'-axis perpendicular to the trace of the undeformed dyke outside the shear zone, the z'-axis parallel to the strike of the undeformed dyke, and y-axis up. Coordinate points were found by simple trigonometry:

$$x' = x \cos \phi + z \sin \phi \quad (6)$$

where ϕ is the angle of rotation of the x- and z-axes about the y-axis between the old (shear zone, xyz) and the new (undeformed dyke, $x'yz'$) reference frames. Restored coordinates projected onto the undeformed dyke profile plane ($x'y$) suggest a dip of *c.* 56° to the NE for the undeformed dyke outside of the shear zone (see Fig. 9). This value compares well with field data

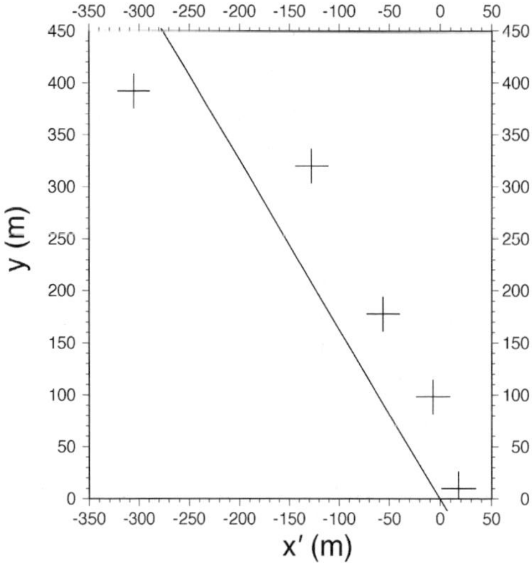

Fig. 9. Restored points on the west margin of the dyke in the section containing its dip direction. The coordinate *x*′ is horizontal and trending perpendicular to the trace of the dyke (increasing to 044). The coordinate *y* is vertical, increasing upwards. The symbols are restored coordinates of points on the dyke, and the line is the best fit to these points.

of the undeformed dyke orientation, although sparse. The best-fit line of Figure 9 represents the trace of the planar dyke in the section plane that has the strike direction of the undeformed dyke as its pole. The minor deviations of the points from the lines shows that the hypothesis of simple shear with a varying shear direction is reasonable, considering the irregularity of the shear zone (see Figs 2a and 3). Furthermore, it gives support to inferences made above on the origin of the kink in the trace of the dyke, near the northern boundary of the shear zone.

Discussion and conclusions

The model of simple shear with a varying shear direction within a constant shear plane is capable of explaining the complex geometry and field data of the Badcall shear zone without recourse to varying amounts of heterogeneous pure shear. In particular, the apparently antithetic kink or fold in the dyke near the northern margin of the shear zone is seen to be an artefact of the interaction of subvertical movement direction of the shear zone in that region, as recorded in the finite stretching lineation, and the shallower dip of the dyke. Although a model of spatially partitioned pure and simple shear across the shear zone can superficially explain the observed field data and outcrop geometries, further thought regarding the geometry of pure shear and interactions of planar fabrics shows that this scenario is not possible here.

Hence, the kinematics of the Laxfordian shear zone at Upper Badcall, NW Scotland, is best modelled as a zone of local plane strain simple shear through which the finite movement direction varies from subhorizontal near its southern boundary to subvertical near its northern boundary. The temporal variation in the magnitude and direction of strain is not clear and may present an issue for future study.

The cumulative displacements across the shear zone can be compared with those calculated by Beach (1974). Parallel to x (left-lateral) and y (north-side up), respectively, the displacements of 739.2 m and 410.8 m, calculated here, are noticeably larger than the values of 250 m and 91 m, calculated by Beach (1974), in a simple geometrical problem based on a single movement direction within the shear zone, the orientation of the shear zone and a marker, and the horizontal offset of that marker. Clearly, and as discussed by Beach (1974), significant errors are introduced where shear zones have a varying movement direction.

In its simplest sense, this study supports decades of research in the Lewisian complex (e.g. Beach *et al.* 1974; Coward 1990), which suggests that the Laxfordian deformation in some part proceeded by north-block up and left-lateral shear deformation. To place this research in the wider context of regional Laxfordian deformation, a full description and re-evaluation of the tectonics and kinematics of the tectonothermal event would be necessary. Moreover, it would undoubtedly require significant fieldwork to interpret the plethora of Laxfordian shears in the Lewisian complex in accordance with the routine outlined here. This is beyond the scope of this paper, although is a very interesting project for future research.

The work was supported by NERC PhD Studentship NER/S/A/2002/10477. The authors thank J. Balfour and Scottish Natural Heritage for sample collection licence. J. Wheeler and J. Watkinson are thanked for their helpful manuscript reviews. Further details including field data or calculations included herein can be obtained from the corresponding author.

Appendix 1: Sample numbers

Scourie Dyke samples 1–8 described herein refer to the following University of Leeds, School of Earth Sciences sample catalogue numbers.

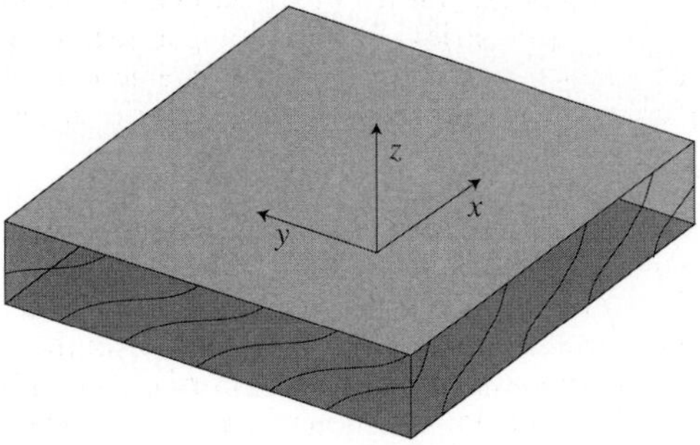

Fig. A1. General shear zone with varying strain profiles in x and y. The state of deformation is identical at points an equal height above the base of the shear zone in both the x and y directions.

1: 62485
2: 62483
3: 62484
4: 62482
5: 62481
6: 62480
7: 62479
8: 62478

Appendix 2: General shear zone

A generalized 3D shear zone is shown in Figure A1. The state of deformation is constant in x and y, but varies with position in z.

The deformation from the undeformed state to the deformed state can be defined by three functions of position giving the x, y and z components of the finite displacement, u, v, w, to the position after deformation:

$$u = u(x, y, z) \quad \text{(A1)}$$

$$v = v(x, y, z) \quad \text{(A2)}$$

$$w = w(x, y, z). \quad \text{(A3)}$$

The strains and rotations can be derived from the gradients of the displacement with respect to x, y and z, the displacement gradient matrix:

$$\begin{pmatrix} \frac{\partial u}{\partial x} & \frac{\partial u}{\partial y} & \frac{\partial u}{\partial z} \\ \frac{\partial v}{\partial x} & \frac{\partial v}{\partial y} & \frac{\partial v}{\partial z} \\ \frac{\partial w}{\partial x} & \frac{\partial w}{\partial y} & \frac{\partial w}{\partial z} \end{pmatrix}. \quad \text{(A4)}$$

Taking the term $\partial u/\partial z$ and differentiating with respect to x gives a result that can be set equal to zero because there is no variation of strain state in the x direction:

$$\frac{\partial^2 u}{\partial x \partial z} = 0. \quad \text{(A5)}$$

The order of partial differentiation does not influence the result:

$$\frac{\partial^2 u}{\partial z \partial x} = 0 \quad \text{(A6)}$$

which means that $\partial u/\partial x$ does not vary in z; that is, it is constant across the shear zone. The same argument can be applied to the terms $\partial v/\partial z$ and $\partial w/\partial z$ to show that $\partial v/\partial x$ and $\partial w/\partial x$ are constant across the shear zone. Repeating the procedure for differentiation of the terms in the third column of the displacement gradient matrix with respect to y shows that $\partial u/\partial y$, $\partial v/\partial y$ and $\partial w/\partial y$ are also constant across the shear zone, so the displacement gradient matrix becomes

$$\begin{pmatrix} c_1 & c_4 & \frac{\partial u}{\partial z} \\ c_2 & c_5 & \frac{\partial v}{\partial z} \\ c_3 & c_6 & \frac{\partial w}{\partial z} \end{pmatrix}. \quad \text{(A7)}$$

There is no condition that can be applied to the terms in the third column, so these can be functions of z, but not of x and y because of the constancy of deformation state in these directions. Further identifying that $\partial u/\partial z$ is the shear strain in x, γ_x, $\partial v/\partial z$ is the shear strain in y, γ_y, and $\partial w/\partial z$ is a uniaxial volume change in the z direction, Δ, the displacement gradient matrix becomes

$$\begin{pmatrix} c_1 & c_4 & \gamma_x(z) \\ c_2 & c_5 & \gamma_y(z) \\ c_3 & c_6 & \Delta(z) \end{pmatrix}. \quad \text{(A8)}$$

Thus the state of strain in a general shear zone can be variable shear in the x and y directions varying across the zone and a volume change, achieved by uniaxial shortening in the z direction also varying in z. No other state of strain is possible except that homogeneous strain can be added by matrix multiplication. The constant terms in equation (A4) can be subsumed into this homogeneous strain leaving zeros and the deformation gradient matrix can be formed by adding one to the diagonal terms.

$$\begin{pmatrix} 1 & 0 & \gamma_x(z) \\ 0 & 1 & \gamma_y(z) \\ 0 & 0 & 1+\Delta(z) \end{pmatrix}. \quad \text{(A9)}$$

Treagus & Lisle (1997) considered this kind of shear zone and demonstrated that there are no continuous principal planes of finite strain, but it is still possible to see continuous planes on the local scale.

Reorientation of planes

Flinn (1979) gave the following equation for the reorientation of normals to planes under the deformation described by the deformation gradient matrix:

$$\left(n_x'\ n_y'\ n_z'\right)=\left(n_x\ n_y\ n_z\right)\begin{pmatrix} D_{11}^{-1} & D_{12}^{-1} & D_{13}^{-1} \\ D_{21}^{-1} & D_{22}^{-1} & D_{23}^{-1} \\ D_{31}^{-1} & D_{32}^{-1} & D_{33}^{-1} \end{pmatrix} \quad \text{(A10)}$$

where ($n_x'\ n_y'\ n_z'$) are the direction cosines of the plane normal in the deformed state, ($n_x\ n_y\ n_z$) are the direction cosines of the plane normal in the undeformed state and the matrix in D_{ij}^{-1} is the inverse of the deformation gradient matrix.

For a constant-volume shear zone the deformation gradient matrix is

$$\begin{pmatrix} 1 & 0 & \gamma_x(z) \\ 0 & 1 & \gamma_y(z) \\ 0 & 0 & 1 \end{pmatrix} \quad \text{(A11)}$$

which has the inverse

$$\begin{pmatrix} 1 & 0 & -\gamma_x(z) \\ 0 & 1 & -\gamma_y(z) \\ 0 & 0 & 1 \end{pmatrix}. \quad \text{(A12)}$$

Thus, equation (A6) becomes

$$\left(n_x'\ n_y'\ n_z'\right)=\left(n_x\ n_y\ n_z\right)\begin{pmatrix} 1 & 0 & -\gamma_x(z) \\ 0 & 1 & -\gamma_y(z) \\ 0 & 0 & 1 \end{pmatrix} \quad \text{(A13)}$$

or

$$(n_x'\ n_y'\ n_z')=[n_x\ n_y\ (-n_x\gamma_x-n_y\gamma_y+n_z)]. \quad \text{(A14)}$$

At any point in the shear zone the movement direction will be oriented at an angle θ to the x axis. If the amount of finite shear strain is given the symbol γ, components of shear in the x and y directions will be

$$\gamma_x=\gamma\cos\theta \quad \text{(A15)}$$

$$\gamma_y=\gamma\sin\theta. \quad \text{(A16)}$$

Hence we may write

$$(n_x'\ n_y'\ n_z')=[n_x\ n_y\ n_z-\gamma(n_x\cos\theta+n_y\sin\theta)]. \quad \text{(A17)}$$

The fact that the x and y components of the unit vector in the direction of the plane normal do not change is a consequence of there being no strain on the shear plane. If there were a varying pure shear component in the shear zone, then x and y components would vary with position in the shear zone and the intersection line of gneissic banding and the zone boundary would vary.

Normalizing equation (A13) gives the following for n_z':

$$n_z'=\frac{n_z-\gamma\left(n_x\cos\theta+n_y\sin\theta\right)}{\left\{n_x^2+n_y^2+\left[n_z-\gamma\left(n_x\cos\theta+n_y\sin\theta\right)\right]^2\right\}^{\frac{1}{2}}}. \quad \text{(A18)}$$

This equation can be rearranged to give an expression for γ, but the stereonet and the use of equation 1 is more practical.

References

BARBER, A. J., BEACH, A., PARK, R. G., TARNEY, J. & STEWART, A. D. 1978. *The Lewisian and Torridonian Rocks of NW Scotland.* Geologists' Association Guides, **21**.

BEACH, A. 1974. The measurement and significance of displacements on Laxford Shear Zones, Northwest Scotland. *Proceedings of the Geologists' Association*, **85**, 13–21.

BEACH, A., COWARD, M. P. & GRAHAM, R. H. 1974. An interpretation of the structural evolution of the Laxford Front, north-west Scotland. *Scottish Journal of Geology*, **9**, 297–308.

CHAPMAN, H. J. 1979. 2390 Myr Rb–Sr whole-rock age for the Scourie dykes of north-west Scotland. *Nature*, **277**, 642–643.

CHAPMAN, H. J. & MOORBATH, S. 1977. Lead isotope measurements from the oldest recognised Lewisian gneisses of north-west Scotland. *Nature*, **268**, 41–42.

COWARD, M. P. 1990. Shear zones at the Laxford front, NW Scotland and their significance in the interpretation of lower crustal structure. *Journal of the Geological Society, London*, **147**, 279–286.

COWARD, M. P. & POTTS, G. J. 1983. Complex strain patterns developed at the frontal and lateral tips to shear zones and thrust zones. *Journal of Structural Geology*, **5**, 383–399.

ESCHER, A., ESCHER, J. C. & WATTERSON, J. 1975. The reorientation of the Kangamiut Dike Swarm, West Greenland. *Canadian Journal of Earth Sciences*, **12**, 158–173.

FLINN, D. 1979. The computation of deformations. *Geological Journal*, 87–98.

GEOLOGICAL SURVEY OF SCOTLAND 1892. *Lochinver Sheet 107*, 1 inch to a mile.

HAMILTON, P. J., EVENSEN, N. M., O'NIONS, R. K. & TARNEY, J. 1979. Sm–Nd systematics of the Lewisian gneisses: implications for the origin of the granulites. *Nature*, **277**, 25–28.

KINNY, P. D. & FRIEND, C. R. L. 1997. U–Pb isotopic evidence for the accretion of different crustal blocks to form the Lewisian Complex of northwest Scotland. *Contributions to Mineralogy and Petrology*, **129**, 326–340.

MOORBATH, S., WELKE, H. & GALE, N. H. 1969. The significance of lead isotope studies in ancient, high-grade metamorphic basement complexes, as exemplified by the Lewisian rocks of northwest Scotland. *Earth and Planetary Science Letters*, **6**, 245–256.

PARK, R. G. & TARNEY, J. 1987. The Lewisian complex: a typical Precambrian high-grade terrain? *In*: PARK, R. G. & TARNEY, J. (eds) *Evolution of the Lewisian and Comparable Precambrian High Grade Terrains*. Geological Society, London, Special Publications, **27**, 13–25.

RAMSAY, J. G. 1967. *Folding and Fracturing of Rocks*. McGraw–Hill, London.

RAMSAY, J. G. & GRAHAM, R. H. 1970. Strain variation on shear belts. *Canadian Journal of Earth Sciences*, **7**, 786–813.

RAMSAY, J. G. & HUBER, M. I. 1987. *The Techniques of Modern Structural Geology: Folds and Fractures*. Academic Press, London.

SUTTON, J. & WATSON, J. 1951. The pre-Torridonian metamorphic history of the Loch Torridon and Scourie areas in the North-West Highlands, and its bearing on the chronological classification of the Lewisian. *Quarterly Journal of the Geological Society, London*, **106**, 241–308.

TREAGUS, S. H. & LISLE, R. J. 1997. Do principal surfaces of stress and strain always exist? *Journal of Structural Geology*, **19**, 997–1010.

WATERS, F. G., COHEN, A. S., O'NIONS, R. K. & O'HARA, M. J. 1990. Development of Archaean lithosphere deduced from chronology and isotope chemistry of Scourie Dykes. *Earth and Planetary Science Letters*, **97**, 241–255.

WHEELER, J. 1987. The determination of true shear senses from the deflection of passive markers in shear zones. *Journal of the Geological Society, London*, **144**, 73–77.

The use of shear zones and related structures as kinematic indicators: a review

J. W. COSGROVE

Department of Earth Science & Engineering, Royal School of Mines, Imperial College, London SW7 2BP, UK (e-mail: j.cosgrove@imperial.ac.uk)

Abstract: Shear zones (i.e. locally developed planar zones of ductile deformation that contain a tectonically induced fabric) are one of the most commonly used kinematic indicators (i.e. asymmetric structures that can be used to determine the sense of movement and the orientation of the stress field operating at the time of their formation). This is because of the abundant occurrence of these structures, and the assumption that there is a unique relationship between them and their causative stress field. However, there is a range of structures that, when viewed in two dimensions on an outcrop surface, display the geometry of shear zones but are formed in a variety of different ways and are oriented at various angles to the maximum principal compression. These include shear zones that form at angles between 25° and 45° to σ_1 and that have the same relationship to σ_1 as brittle shear fractures, shear zones linked to the deformation of anisotropic materials that form at angles between 45° and almost 90° to σ_1, and structures with the geometry of a shear zone that can be inclined at angles between *c.* 10° and 80° to σ_1 and that appear on certain sections though folded mineral fabrics. Unless the mechanisms of formation of these structures are understood, there is a strong possibility that their kinematic implications will be misinterpreted.

The deformation of the crust varies between a uniform distribution of strain, associated with ductile behaviour and homogeneous flattening, and the highly localized deformation associated with brittle failure. The mode of deformation is controlled by the rheology of the rock, which is determined by several factors including lithology, pressure, temperature and strain rate. Between the two end-members of homogeneous deformation, such as occurs in a slate belt where a pervasive flattening is achieved by recrystallization and reorientation of platy minerals, and the highly localized planes of intense deformation, represented by fractures (either extensional or shear), lies a large and complex array of structures and associated deformation patterns. It is the task of the structural geologist to understand the mechanical principles behind the generation of these patterns so that they can be used to (1) determine the rheological state of the rocks during their deformation and (2) assess the kinematic implications of the individual structures. Armed with this understanding many of the ambiguities relating to the use of kinematic indicators can be avoided and a more complete picture of the pattern of deformation and its implications obtained.

This paper presents a brief discussion of the various processes by which features with the appearance of shear zones can be generated. The aim is to provide a clearer understanding of their relationship to their causative stress fields and thus allow a more accurate and focused use of these structures as kinematic indicators. The discussion is divided into seven sections. In the first, the mechanical reasons for the formation of localized structures, such as folds and shear zones, in place of a uniform, homogeneous flattening are considered, and, in the second, the way in which the orientation of the principal stresses with respect to the layering or fabric of a rock (i.e. its mechanical anisotropy) controls the geometry of the resulting structures is discussed. In the third section, the mechanical reason for the formation of localized structures such as folds or shear zones in place of homogeneous flattening is reviewed, and, in the fourth, the related problem of the relationship between shear and extensional brittle failure is examined. In the fifth section, the effect of scale of observation on the deformation pattern is noted, and, in the sixth, the development of shear zones in isotropic materials is explained. In the final section, the impact of section orientation through micro-folds on the geometry of the outcrop pattern is illustrated. These processes and effects are discussed to a greater or lesser extent depending on the insight they provide into the use of the resulting structures as kinematic indicators.

The key point in resolving the problem of the misuse of shear zones as 'kinematic' indicators (i.e. deformation structures whose asymmetry can be used to deduce the sense of shear linked to their formation) is the recognition that features

From: Ries, A. C., Butler, R. W. H. & Graham, R. H. (eds) 2007. *Deformation of the Continental Crust: The Legacy of Mike Coward*. Geological Society, London, Special Publications, **272**, 59–74.

with the geometry of a shear zone can be formed as a result of different processes and can have a wide range of orientations with respect to the principal stresses. Unless the mechanisms of formation of the structures are understood it is likely that their kinematic implications will be misinterpreted (see e.g. Behrmann 1987).

Pervasive and localized deformation during the ductile deformation of anisotropic materials

One of the most important contributions to the understanding of ductile deformation of rocks was made by Biot (1961, 1964, 1965). In describing the ductile deformation behaviour of mechanically anisotropic materials, such as sedimentary successions and mineral fabrics, Biot provided an insight into the factors that control the partitioning of the deformation within the deforming material. He showed that, just as there is an increase in strain localization as deformation changes from ductile to brittle, so there is a similar change as the mechanical anisotropy of a material increases.

Biot (1965) considered the response of a homogeneous anisotropic material being compressed, parallel to one of the axes of symmetry (e.g. parallel or normal to a fabric or layering; Fig. 1a). It has been argued that layered systems (e.g. sedimentary successions and mineral fabrics such as a slaty cleavage) approximate well to such materials (Biot 1961; Cobbold *et al.* 1971; Price & Cosgrove 1990). Biot (1961) showed that, under such stress conditions, two possible deformation patterns can form depending on the magnitude of the mechanical anisotropy of the material, a measure of which is given by the ratio of the resistance to compression (M') and shear (L') in the direction of the applied compression. The deformation is expressed as sinusoidal buckles with axial planes normal to the causative principal compressive stress if the anisotropy is low (Fig. 1b), whereas the deformation is more localized and is represented by the formation of kink-bands if the anisotropy is high (Fig. 1c). These kink-bands form oblique to the applied compression and may occur in conjugate sets to produce box folds. The latter are referred to as reverse kink-bands because the sense of shear along them when viewed in profile section is the same as that along a reverse fault.

The two mathematical solutions to this problem of the buckling of anisotropic materials are of different types. The first is an analytical solution which allows the displacements to be determined at all points in the material. This deformation pervades the whole of the material (Fig. 1b). In contrast, the second solution is non-analytical and gives the orientation of directions within the material along which deformation will occur most easily. These directions are referred to as characteristic directions and are fundamental symmetry planes of the deformation field. They have important mathematical properties and physical significance. For example, Nádai (1950, p. 555) pointed out that local disturbances within a material tend to propagate along characteristic directions and that the displacement vectors along these directions are all parallel. The deformation along them approximates to heterogeneous simple shear.

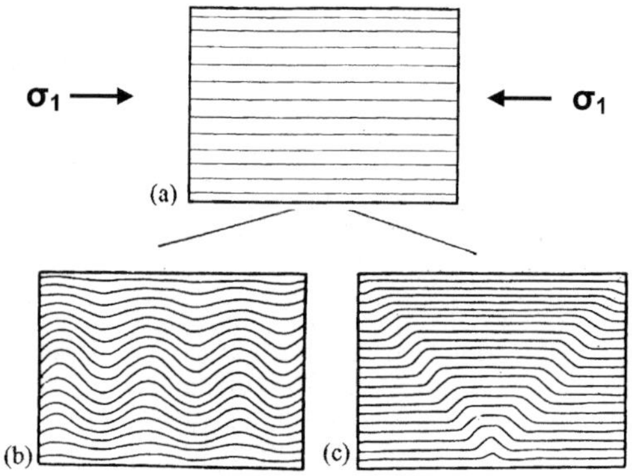

Fig. 1. Two modes of deformation (**b**) and (**c**) that can develop when an anisotropic material (**a**) is compressed parallel to the layering or fabric. The conjugate kink-bands in (**c**) form parallel to the two characteristic directions in the deforming material and the displacements along them are those of dextral and sinistral simple shear, parallel to these directions. Biot showed that the conjugate kink-bands are the result of the juxtaposition of the two characteristic directions, and the formation of the upright buckles (**b**) is the result of the superposition of the two simple shear deformations.

Despite the very different expression of the two styles of buckling of these materials (compare Fig. 1b and c), the displacements linked to their formation shows that the two are more closely related than their different geometries might indicate. The displacements associated with box folds (Fig. 1c) result from the juxtaposition of two simple shears of opposite sense, parallel to the conjugate characteristic directions, and those associated with the upright buckles (Fig. 1b) result from the superposition of two simple shears of opposite sense, parallel to these directions.

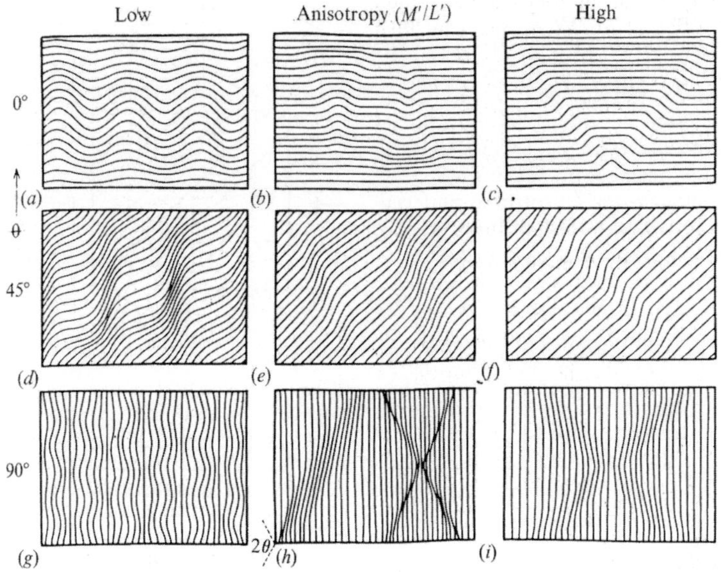

Fig. 2. Some possible modes of expression of stress-induced instabilities in materials with different anisotropy and oriented with the axes of symmetry of the anisotropy parallel to, at 45° to, or normal to the direction of maximum compression. After Cosgrove (1976).

The role of the stress orientation, with respect to the layering or fabric of a rock, on the geometry of the resulting structures

There is a gradual change from the pervasive deformation, when a material is compressed parallel to the layering or fabric (Fig. 2a), to localized deformation (Fig. 2c) as the mechanical anisotropy changes from low to high. In addition, it is important to remember that Biot's analysis is valid for all situations where the principal stresses are symmetrically oriented with respect to the axes of symmetry of the anisotropy; that is, parallel, at 45° or normal to the layering or fabric. Thus the displacements shown in Figure 2a–c can also be applied to models where the layering is at 45° (Fig. 2d–f) and normal to the maximum principal compression direction (Fig. 2g–i). When the maximum principal compression (σ_1) is normal to the layering or fabric, a transition between internal pinch-and-swell structures (Fig. 2g) and conjugate normal kink-bands (Fig. 2i) occurs with increasing anisotropy. The combined effect of the two solutions and the different orientations of the stress axes, with respect to the axes of symmetry of the anisotropy, leads to the formation of structures with a range of geometries, many of which are likely to be classified as 'shear zones' when observed in the field.

The geometric relationship between the maximum principal compressive stress, σ_1, and the conjugate planar zones of deformation (the kink-bands) is shown in Fig. 2c, h and i. The angle (2θ) between the conjugate kink-bands, which is bisected by σ_1, ranges from 180° to 90° depending on the anisotropy of the material; that is, it is the obtuse angle between the zones of deformation. This is in contrast to brittle deformation, where σ_1 bisects the acute angle between the conjugate brittle shear planes.

The mechanical reasons for the formation of localized structures, such as folds and shear zones, in place of a uniform homogeneous flattening

To appreciate the rheological and mechanical significance of the type and distribution of deformational structures in a rock, it is important to understand the principles behind their formation. The formation of localized structures, such as folds, shear zones and faults, is preceded by a period of homogeneous flattening during which time the stresses build up to a 'yield' stress above which the mode of deformation changes dramatically (e.g. from homogeneous flattening to buckling; Cobbold 1976). It is useful to consider the reasons for the change from flattening to the more localized deformation of buckling, which takes place when the yield stress (critical buckling stress) is reached, in, for example, the folding of a homogeneous anisotropic material (Fig. 1), as this provides an insight into the reason for such localization. Rocks that possess a pervasive mineral fabric, such as a slate or schist, approximate to such a material and it can be argued that well-bedded successions, such as turbidites with their rapid alternations of sandstones and shales, are also good analogues (Cobbold *et al.* 1971).

As noted above, Biot (1965) argued that a material is anisotropic if its resistance to compression (defined by a modulus M') and shear (defined by a modulus L') are not the same, and a useful measure of the anisotropy of the material can be obtained from the ratio of these two resistances; the greater the difference between them, the greater the mechanical anisotropy.

Such a material can deform either by slip between the layering or by deformation of the layers (Cobbold *et al.* 1971; Price & Cosgrove 1990). Deformation will tend to occur by the former because this mechanism uses the lower of the two moduli and requires less energy (Fig. 3a). However, when σ_1 is either parallel or normal to the layering, the lower modulus cannot be utilized to achieve the required shortening (Fig. 3b). Consequently, deformation does not involve slip between the layers and occurs only by layer-parallel (or normal) contraction; that is, the deformation is resisted by the higher of the two moduli.

If, however, rearrangement of the layering can occur so that in some locations within the multilayer the layering becomes oblique to σ_1, then, at these localities, shortening in the σ_1 direction can occur by slip between the layers. It is for this reason that a state of homogeneous flattening (Fig. 3c) gives way to one of buckling (Fig. 3d). On the limbs of the folds, shortening in the σ_1 direction occurs by slip between the layers. In the multilayer under consideration, before the change from flattening to buckling can take place, the applied stress must be of sufficient magnitude to overcome the internal resistance of the layering to flexing. This stress is termed the 'critical buckling stress', and the essential element of the instability is the local flexing of the layering into an orientation in which shortening, in the σ_1 direction, can occur by slip between the layering; that is, by utilizing the lower of the two moduli (Fig. 3e and f). This instability can be organized in such a way as to generate folds as shown in Figure 4a.

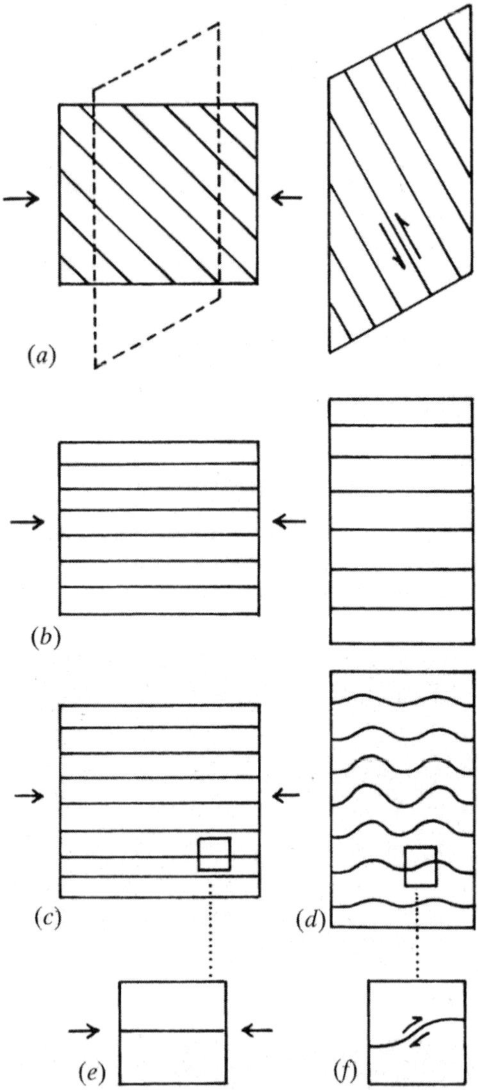

Fig. 3. Deformation of a layered material by (**a**) slip between the layers and (**b**) contraction of the layers. (**c**) Contraction followed by (**d**) slip between the layers. The change-over is facilitated by flexing (buckling) of the layer (**e**) and (**f**). From Price & Cosgrove (1990).

It was noted above that Biot's (1961) theory of the deformation of a mechanically anisotropic material predicts the formation of structures with a large range of geometries, many of which are likely to be classified as 'shear zones' (Fig. 2). In addition to the relationship between these structures summarized in Figure 2, the identification

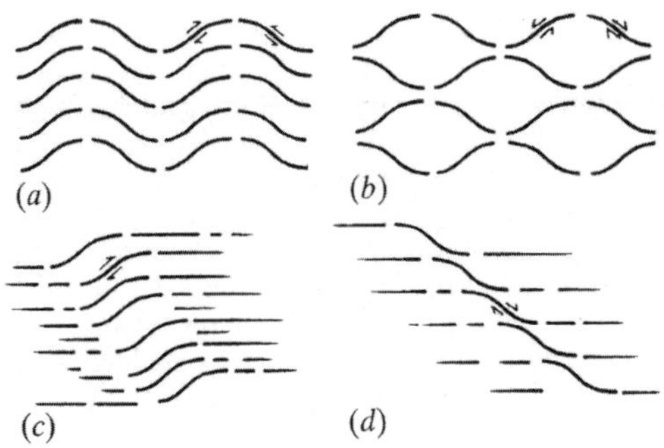

Fig. 4. Various arrangements of the basic instability (see Fig. 3f) to generate (**a**) folds, (**b**) internal pinch-and-swell structures, (**c**) reverse kink-bands and (**d**) normal kink-bands.

of the fundamental instability associated with this deformation (Fig. 3f) allows a further link between these apparently disparate structures to be recognized. Figure 4 shows how this instability can be arranged in a variety of ways to achieve the required bulk shape change imposed by the applied stress. For example, when σ_1 is parallel to the layering, the instabilities are arranged either into buckles (Figs 2a and 4a) or, if the conditions are such that the deformation occurs more locally, into reverse kink-bands (Figs 2c and 4c). When the contraction is normal to the layering, the bulk shape changes are achieved by arranging the instabilities in such a way as to form interlocking pinch-and-swell structures (Figs 2g and 4b), or normal kink-bands (Figs 2h, i and 4d).

The relationship between shear zones and brittle failure, and shear and extensional brittle failure

The generation of structures with geometries similar to shear zones discussed above relates to the ductile deflection of a pre-existing layering or fabric. Many shear zones with almost identical geometries, however, are linked mechanically to the process of brittle failure (Fig. 5); that is, they

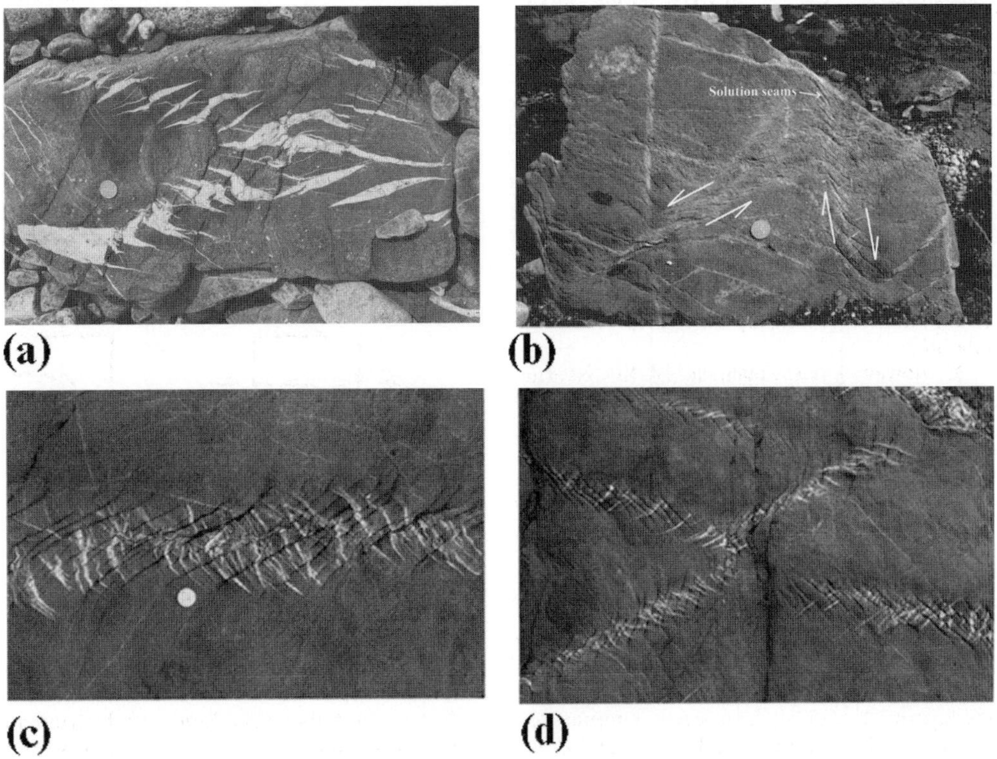

Fig. 5. (**a**) Conjugate shear zones represented by two sets of en echelon veins (see Fig. 7b); (**b**) conjugate shear zones defined by solution seams (see Fig. 7c). (**c**) En echelon veins and solution seams developed synchronously. (**d**) A conjugate set of shears containing both en echelon veins and a solution seams. Marloes Sands, Pembrokeshire, South Wales.

form in the same orientation with respect to the principal axes of stress as discrete brittle faults. Because of this link with brittle deformation it is relevant and instructive to consider briefly certain aspects of brittle failure theory.

Brittle failure represents the extreme example of strain localization and falls at one end of the spectrum of strain distribution patterns, the other end of which is represented by a pervasive ductile deformation that leads to homogeneous flattening. Theoretically, during brittle deformation, failure occurs along an infinitely thin plane that separates blocks of rock that are undeformed.

Two types of brittle failure have been recognized, namely, shear and extensional failure, and these two types have different relationships to their causative stress fields, have different failure criteria and form under different conditions of differential stress. Nevertheless, it is argued below that these apparently very different types of instabilities are in fact intimately related on a microscopic scale.

Figure 6a shows the combined failure criteria for brittle materials together with two stress fields, represented by the two Mohr circles, which satisfy the criteria of shear and extensional failure. The two failure criteria that are combined to form the complete brittle failure envelope are the Navier–Coulomb criterion of shear failure (e.g. Anderson 1951) and the Griffith criterion of extensional failure (Anderson 1951). These criteria are fundamentally different. The former is based on the assumption that shear failure occurs along a plane in the material when the component of shear stress (τ), acting along the potential fracture plane, is large enough to overcome the cohesive strength of the material, C (i.e. a measure of the material's ability to resist a shear stress), and the resistance to slip on the plane once it has been formed (i.e. the resistance to sliding (τ_s) which is given by Amonton's law $\tau_s = \mu\sigma_n$, where μ is the coefficient of sliding friction and σ_n the component of normal stress acting on the plane). The failure criterion can be expressed as follows

$$\tau = C + \mu\sigma_n \qquad (1)$$

and is represented by the straight portion of the failure envelope (Fig. 6a), which occupies the stress regime where all the principal stresses are compressive.

The criterion of extensional failure, developed by Griffith, is based on a completely different model. He argued that the theoretical tensile strength of a material should be related to its inter-atomic bond strength. The fact that it is generally several orders of magnitude lower than this led Griffith to suggest that this type of failure was facilitated by the existence of microfractures. He argued that stress magnification, at the fracture tips, allows a relatively small applied tensile stress to be locally magnified to a magnitude that approaches the inter-atomic bond strength of the material. In this way, tensile failure can be brought about by a relatively small applied tensile stress. The failure criterion developed by Griffith can be expressed as

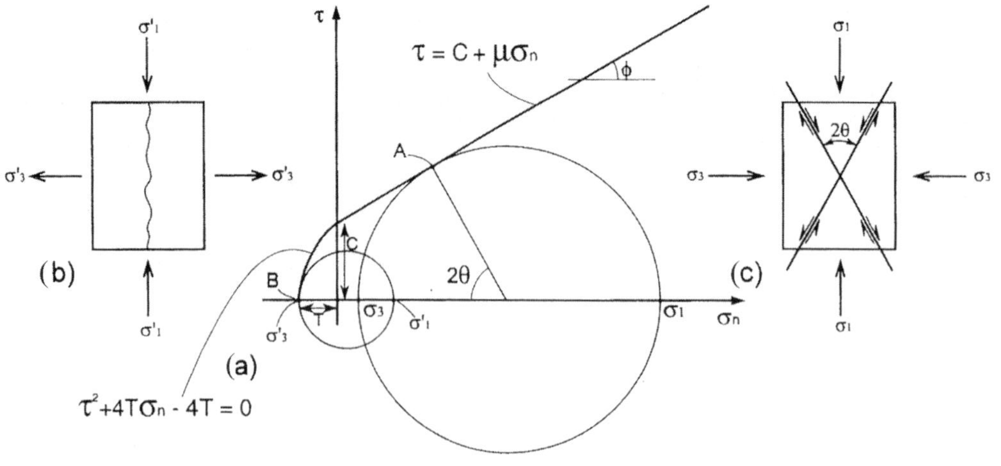

Fig. 6. (**a**) Navier–Coulomb and Griffith brittle failure envelope. The two Mohr circles represent stress states that would give rise to extensional failure (the small circle) and shear failure. The spatial relationship between the fractures and the stress under which they are generated is shown in (**b**) and (**c**) for extensional failure and shear failure, respectively. From Cosgrove (1995).

$$\tau^2 + 4T\sigma_n - 4T = 0 \qquad (2)$$

where T is the tensile strength of the material. It is represented by the parabolic part of the combined failure criteria shown in Figure 6a and is drawn in the stress regime where the principal stresses are tensile.

It can be seen that the two criteria are fundamentally different, one being based on generating a critical shear stress along a potential failure plane and the other on the development of a critical tensile normal stress across the potential fracture plane. In addition to these differences, there are three other important differences between the two fracture types, which drive home the point that the two modes of failure are related to two separate processes. These are the orientation of the fracture planes, the sense of movement on them and the stress conditions necessary for their formation.

Shear fractures form symmetrically about the maximum principal compression, σ_1, as a conjugate set of fractures (Fig. 6c) and their orientation with respect to the principal compression is determined by φ, the angle of sliding friction (Anderson 1951), which, for many rocks, is *c.* 30°:

$$\theta = \pm(45° - \varphi/2) \qquad (3)$$

It follows from this that, in contrast to the conjugate shear structures formed during ductile deformation (e.g. Fig. 2c, h and i), where σ_1 bisects the obtuse angle between them, during brittle failure σ_1 bisects the acute angle between the conjugate shear fractures. The sense of movement of the two sides of the fracture is parallel to the fracture, whereas movement on extensional fractures occurs normal to the fracture (Fig. 6b). In addition, the stress conditions necessary for the formation of the two fracture types is different (Fig. 6a). For shear failure to occur the stress state (represented by the Mohr circles in this figure) must satisfy the shear failure criterion; that is, the Mohr circle must touch the shear failure part of the failure envelope. Similarly, for extensional failure to occur, the stress state must satisfy the tensile failure criterion; (that is, the Mohr circle must touch the extensional failure part of the failure envelope e.g. circle B in Fig. 6a). Inspection of these two Mohr circles shows that shear failure requires a large circle (i.e. a large differential stress; $\sigma_1 - \sigma_3 > 4T$) and extensional failure a relatively small differential stress ($\sigma_1 - \sigma_3 < 4T$). However, despite these fundamental differences there is evidence that, on a microscopic scale, these two failure modes are closely related. The link between shear failure and extensional failure becomes apparent when the second order structures associated with this deformation are examined. These structures are discussed in the next section.

The formation of second-order structures within shear zones; their geometry and kinematic implications

The rheology of a rock is determined not only by its intrinsic properties but also by the physical conditions (e.g. pressure, temperature and strain rate) operating during deformation. As the physical conditions change, so the response of the material to deformation may also change. For example, as the temperature increases or the strain rate decreases, material behaving in a brittle manner may behave in a more ductile manner. The strain becomes less localized and the fracture planes become planar zones of relatively intense deformation (i.e. a shear zone; Fig. 7), across which shear displacement occurs but which does not necessarily involve loss of continuity of the material, the essential criterion of brittle failure. The type of deformation within these shear zones is determined by the lithology and physical conditions. It may be dominantly brittle (Fig. 7a) dominantly ductile (Fig. 7c) or some mixture of the two (Fig. 7b).

Brittle deformation inside a shear zone

The long established association of localized extensional failure within a shear zone (Figs 5 and 7b) makes arrays of en echelon veins one of the most reliable kinematic indicators. However, it also indicates a fundamental link between the two modes of brittle failure as indicated in Figure 8. Examples of extensional failure and shear failure are shown in Figure 8b and c, respectively. Both are achieved by the formation of extensional veins. In Figure 8b, the veins are uniformly distributed throughout the rock and in Figure 8c

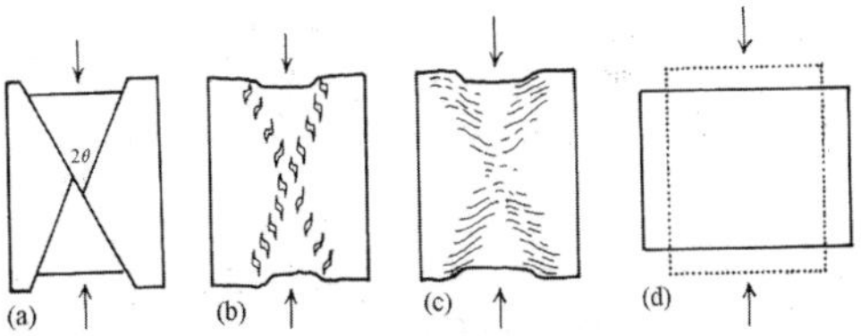

Fig. 7. (**a**) Brittle, (**b**) semi-brittle and (**c**) ductile expression of Andersonian shear failure.
(**d**) Homogeneous flattening. The arrows indicate the orientation of the maximum principal compression, σ_1, and it bisects the acute angle between the conjugate shears (i.e. $2\theta < 90°$).

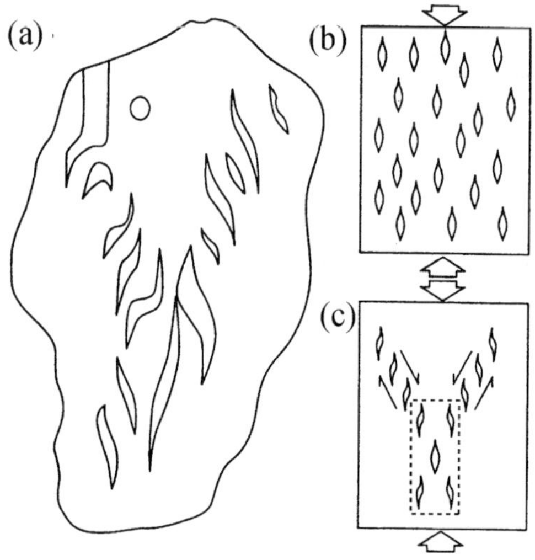

Fig. 8. (**a**) Field sketch of a conjugate set of en echelon veins (see Fig. 5a). (**b**) A uniform distribution of veins representing extensional failure. (**c**) The organization of veins to produce localized shear failure. After Kidan & Cosgrove (1996).

they are arranged in conjugate, en echelon arrays to form shear zones. There seems in these examples to be no difference in the mechanics of deformation (i.e. the formation of extension fractures) associated with the formation of both extensional and shear failure. The only difference is in the organization of the mode I fractures. It can be concluded from these observations that under conditions of low differential stress ($\sigma_1 - \sigma_3 < 4T$), deformation is achieved more efficiently by the uniform distribution of tension gashes, whereas under relatively high differential stress conditions ($\sigma_1 - \sigma_3 < 4T$), the organization of the gashes into en-echelon arrays is more efficient.

Thus despite the differences between the two modes of failure, it is apparent that the two modes of failure are related (Fig. 8). Detailed studies of the incipient stages of shear fracture formation in rocks show that the initial microfractures are small extension fractures that form along grain contacts, subparallel to the maximum principal stress. The formation of the macroscopic shear fracture occurs by the subsequent linking of appropriately positioned, grain-scale, extension fractures (Main *et al.* 1993)

Before continuing this discussion of the formation of small-scale structures within a shear zone and their use as kinematic indicators, it is instructive to compare the two modes of ductile deformation (pervasive buckles and localized kink-bands, Fig. 2a and c) with the two modes of brittle deformation (Fig. 8b and c). It has been demonstrated above that, although these two types of ductile structures are the result of two different solutions to the problem of the buckling of anisotropic materials addressed by Biot (1965), they are both the result of the same basic instability (Fig. 4). This linking of two apparently fundamentally different modes of failure by showing that they form by the development of the same instability, is directly comparable with the observations made above that the two modes of brittle failure are also related by the same basic instability, namely, the formation of an extensional fracture oriented normal to the least principal compression (Fig. 8).

Other similarities between the two ductile structures also find parallels in the two brittle structures. As noted above, in the section on 'pervasive and localized deformation during the ductile deformation of anisotropic materials', conjugate kink-bands (Fig. 2c and 2i) represent the juxtaposition of two simple shear deformations with opposite senses of shear, and pervasive buckling (Fig. 2a) the superposition of two conjugate simple shears. In a similar way, it can be argued that the semi-brittle expression of shear and extensional failure shown in Figure 8 represents, respectively, the juxtaposition of the conjugate arrays of tension fractures shown in Figure 8a and c and the superposition of these arrays (Fig. 8b). It can be seen that the cross-over region of the conjugate arrays of en-echelon arrays of tension gashes (dotted box in Fig. 8c) is indistinguishable from the random, but statistically uniform, distribution of tension gashes that represent extensional failure (Fig. 8b).

Ductile deformation within a shear zone

In the previous section the formation of brittle structures within a shear zone and the use of these structures as kinematic indicators were discussed. However, deformation within the shear zone may occur by ductile processes (Figs 5b, 7c and 9). The formation of a deformation fabric within the shear zone has been discussed extensively in the literature (e.g. Ramsay & Graham 1970; Coward, 1976; Ramsay 1980; Ramsay & Lisle 2000). Initially, a planar fabric forms normal to σ_1 (Fig. 9a and b). With progressive deformation, shear movement along the shear zone causes the fabric to rotate. However, as the zone of fabric development widens, the newly formed fabric at the shear-zone margins continues to form normal to σ_1 (Fig. 9c). Consequently, the fabric within the shear zone becomes curved, generating the classical geometry of a shear zone

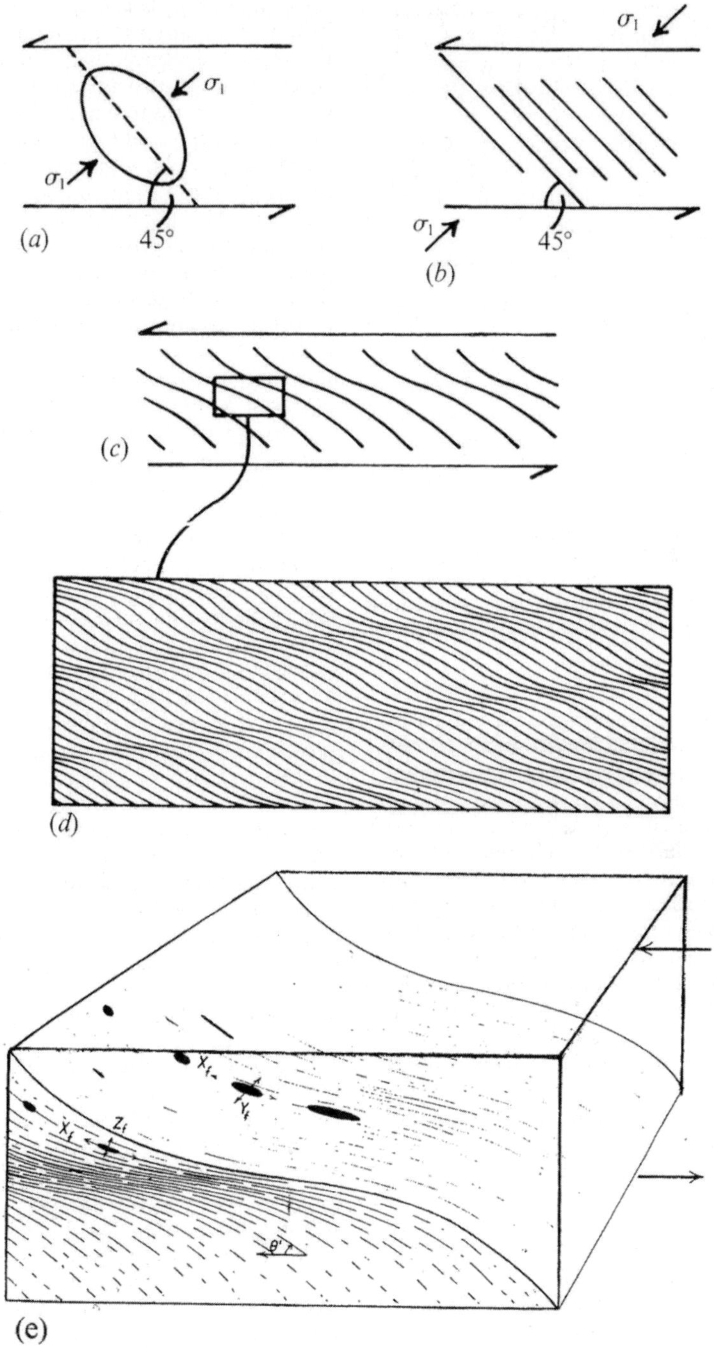

Fig. 9. (**a**) Orientation of the maximum principal compressive stress associated with the first increment of simple shear deformation. (**b**) Tectonic flattening fabric (S fabric) induced by this compression. (**c**) Rotation of the shear-zone fabric as a result of continued deformation. (**d**) After rotation, the early formed fabric is no longer normal to the compression and as a result only one of the possible conjugate sets of normal kink-bands (C fabric) is formed. (**e**) Variation of orientation and strain associated with a simple shear-zone fabric. (**e**) is after Ramsay (1980); (**a**)–(**d**) are after Price & Cosgrove (1990).

(Fig. 9c and e). The fabric is known as an S fabric, indicating that it was generated within a shear zone, and its asymmetry with respect to the shear zone makes it a excellent kinematic indicator. As noted above and indicated in Figs 5 and 7, despite the various expressions of the shear zones, they all form in the same orientation as that of an ideal shear fracture; that is, at $\pm(45° - \varphi/2)$ to σ_1 (equation (3)).

The formation of more than one shear zone during a single deformation (C/S bands)

As illustrated in Figure 2h and i, the orientation (θ) of normal kink-bands, with respect to σ_1, is determined by the magnitude of the mechanical anisotropy of the material. It ranges from a theoretical minimum of 45°, when there is an infinitely high anisotropy, to 90° as the anisotropy decreases to two. Normal kink-bands have been generated experimentally (Fig. 10b; Cobbold *et al.* 1971; Kidan & Cosgrove 1996). The original orientation (θ) of the bands in the experiments was *c.* 60° and by the end of the experiment, it had increased to 65°. The angle in many rock fabrics is found to be around 60°. When the anisotropy is high and σ_1 acts oblique to the layering or fabric (Fig. 2e and f), only one of the conjugate kink-bands will form. One of the most common examples of this occurs during the progressive development of a fabric within a shear zone (Fig. 9d). As noted above, the shear-zone fabric initially forms normal to σ_1 (Fig. 9b) but, as deformation continues, it increases in intensity and rotates towards parallelism with the shear zone, with the result that it is no longer normal to σ_1. Because the intensity of the shear-zone fabric increases as deformation proceeds, it is likely that the anisotropy of the fabric will become high and that, as a consequence, localized normal kink-bands will develop (Fig. 2i). However, as σ_1 is oblique to the fabric, only one set of normal kink-bands will develop; that is, the set whose orientation and sense of shear is closest to that being achieved by the shear zone (Figs 2e, f and 9d). These normal kink-bands cutting across the S fabric are known as C bands (Passchier & Trouw 2005).

Thus the evolution of the S fabric and C bands within a shear zone is the result of two different processes occurring at different stages in the progressive evolution of a shear zone. The S fabric is the local planar fabric that forms inside the zone (Fig. 9b), which increases in intensity and rotates as the shear zone develops, generating conditions conducive for the formation of a single set of normal kink-bands (C bands). These bands represent one of the most commonly used kinematic indicators (e.g. Lister & Snoke 1984; Passchier & Trouw 2005).

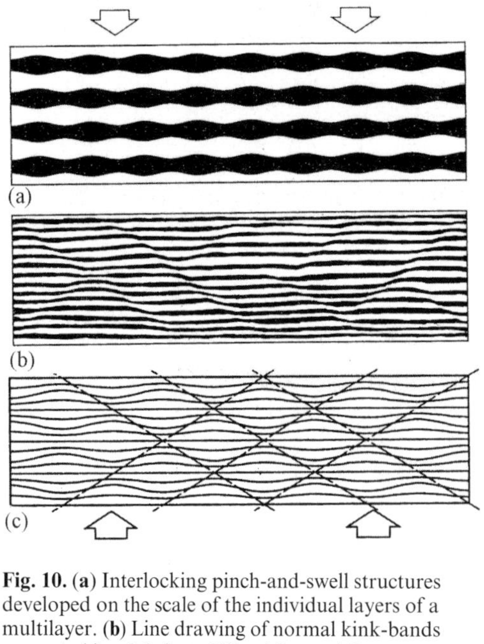

Fig. 10. (**a**) Interlocking pinch-and-swell structures developed on the scale of the individual layers of a multilayer. (**b**) Line drawing of normal kink-bands generated in a lubricated Plasticine multilayer as a result of compression normal to the layering. (**c**) Interlocking pinch-and-swell structures developed on a larger scale than in (**a**); that is, involving four layers. It should be noted that the geometry of the pinch-and-swell structures is equivalent to a network of conjugate normal kink-bands parallel to the dashed lines. (**a**) and (**c**) are after Kidan & Cosgrove (1996); (**b**) is after Cobbold *et al.* (1971).

Impact of scale of observation on the symmetry of the deformation pattern recorded

Figure 2g–i shows a spectrum of structures between the pervasively developed internal pinch-and-swell structures (Fig. 2g) and the localized deformation represented by the conjugate normal kink-bands (Fig. 2i). The wavelength of the internal pinch-and-swell structures will be as small as possible and is determined by the strength and thickness of the layering or fabric elements making up the material. Thus in Figure 10a, which shows a hypothetical multilayer made up of alternating black and white layers with identical properties and with low cohesion between them, each layer forms the smallest possible pinch-and-swell structure and the structures pervade the material. As can be seen from this figure, the swell regions in one layer are next to the pinched regions in the adjacent layers so that the structures interlock. All parts of the layers are affected by the structures and there are no relatively undeformed areas in the material.

In contrast, the structures shown in Figure 10b are localized normal kink-bands formed by the layer-normal compression of a Plasticine multilayer. The Plasticine layers have similar properties and are lubricated by Vaseline. The structures are separated by relatively undeformed regions of the multilayer. Structures intermediate between those shown in Figure 10a and b are shown in Figure 10c. Here the formation of internal pinch-and-swell structures has occurred on a larger scale than in Figure 10a. The individual units, deforming into pinch-and-swell structures, are made up of four layers. Inspection of this geometry shows that, as well as defining a series of interlocking pinch-and-swell structures, it can also be regarded as a network of conjugate normal kink-bands, parallel to the dashed lines.

In more complex layered systems, such as that shown in Figure 11, several types of layer-normal compression structures can form during the same deformation, and observations of experiments on such multilayers provide important insights into their temporal and spatial relationships (see Kidan & Cosgrove (1996) for a more detailed discussion). The first structures to form in this model were the rectangular boudins in the competent (black) layers, which failed by the

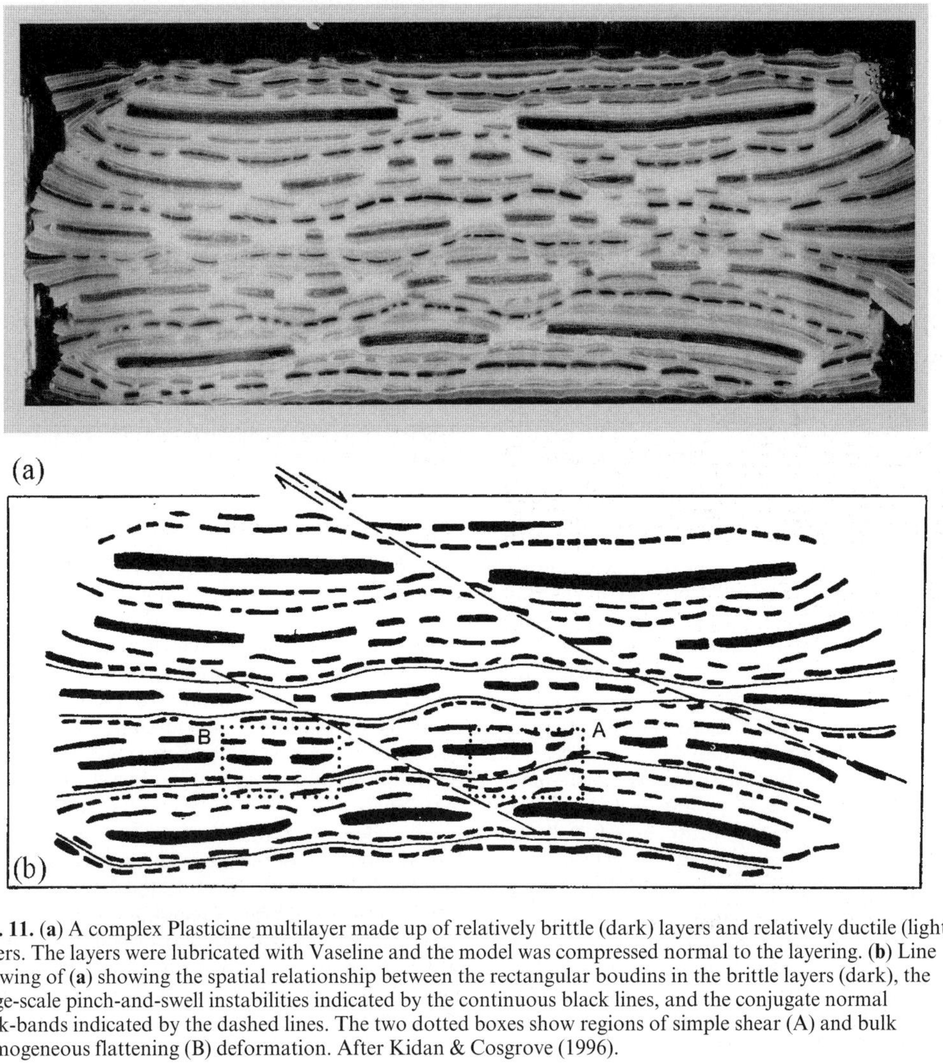

Fig. 11. (**a**) A complex Plasticine multilayer made up of relatively brittle (dark) layers and relatively ductile (light) layers. The layers were lubricated with Vaseline and the model was compressed normal to the layering. (**b**) Line drawing of (**a**) showing the spatial relationship between the rectangular boudins in the brittle layers (dark), the large-scale pinch-and-swell instabilities indicated by the continuous black lines, and the conjugate normal kink-bands indicated by the dashed lines. The two dotted boxes show regions of simple shear (A) and bulk homogeneous flattening (B) deformation. After Kidan & Cosgrove (1996).

formation of extensional fractures. With progressive deformation, deflection of the layered matrix into the neck region between separating boudins generated a series of interlocking pinch-and-swell structures shown by the continuous black lines in Figure 11b. With continued deformation, these pinch-and-swell structures amplified, and normal kink-bands, which are highlighted by the dashed lines cutting across Figure 11b formed by the linking of various neck regions of the pinch-and-swell array, became apparent. The experiment shows that the structures develop sequentially and that the formation and amplification of one structure initiates the next.

Figure 11 illustrates that the symmetry of the deformation pattern will be determined by the scale at which the observations are made. The bulk deformation of the model is flattening in the direction of the layer-normal maximum, principal compression. However, if the field of observation is smaller (e.g. sub-area 'A' in Fig. 11b) then the local deformation field may have a strong asymmetry and the kinematic indicators will yield, in this example, a consistent sinistral sense of shear. Other sub-areas (e.g. 'B' in Fig. 11b), would appear to have experienced bulk pure shear deformation and would have equal numbers of sinistral and dextral small-scale shear zones. Thus, depending on the scale of observation, the deformation will appear statistically pervasive and symmetric or localized and asymmetric.

Development of shear zones in isotropic materials

It follows from the above discussion that structures that have the geometry of a shear zone can be generated by several different processes. Some represent the diffuse expression of brittle failure as declared by their relationship to the causative principal stresses (i.e. *c.* 30°; Figs 5 and 8). However, when similar structures are observed in anisotropic materials (Figs 9d and 10b), they may occur at angles greater than 45° to σ_1, according to the analysis of the deformation of such materials presented by Biot (1965) and represented diagrammatically in Figure 2h and i. It is difficult to differentiate between the two unless they occur in conjugate sets because the structures have such similar geometries. It might be argued that the two can be differentiated in the field on the basis of the rocks in which they form. 'Brittle' shear zones, which form at *c.* 30° to σ_1, form in isotropic rocks and the normal kink-band shear zones in anisotropic materials. However, work by Latham (1983, 1985*a*,*b*) discussed below shows that these criteria are unreliable.

In the theory of ductile deformation of mechanically anisotropic materials presented by Biot (1965), it is assumed that the material has a linear stress–strain or stress–strain rate relationship. Latham (1985*a*,*b*) considered this assumption to be geologically unrealistic and incorporated the effect of non-linear material properties into this work. By doing so he added substantially to our understanding of the geological implications of the theory as well as resolving some of the problems regarding the mechanical significance of shear zones and kink-bands. It is only possible to give a brief outline of this work here, and the interested reader is directed to the original publications and the summary presented by Price & Cosgrove (1990).

The type of non-linearity selected by Latham (1985*a*,*b*) was that of a power-law material, represented by the graph in Figure 12a. At a particular strain (point X on the curve) it is possible to define two moduli, the tangent modulus given by the slope of the curve at point X and the secant modulus given by the slope of line OX. In the unstrained state (i.e. at the origin) these two moduli have the same value, but with progressive deformation their values change so that the difference between them progressively increases. In a linear material the two moduli are the same at any state of strain. The secant modulus is that which relates the stress to the total strain. For example, a bulk strain e_B in Figure 12a occurs when a stress σ_B is applied, and the relationship between e_B and σ_B is given by the secant modulus. The tangent modulus relates incremental stresses and strains; for example, if an increment of stress $\delta\sigma$ is added to the stress state, σ_B, it induces an increment of strain (δe) (Fig. 12a). The difference between the two moduli during the deformation of a non-linear material results in an anisotropy being induced in the material. The greater the difference between the two moduli, the greater will be the induced anisotropy. Thus, even if a non-linear material is intrinsically isotropic, it will become anisotropic as deformation proceeds and this induced anisotropy will increase with the deformation.

It follows that the total anisotropy of a rock will be made up of the intrinsic anisotropy, which the material possesses prior to the deformation as a result of any fabric or layering, plus a component of induced anisotropy, introduced during deformation as a consequence of any non-linear material properties.

Latham (1985*a*,*b*) pointed out that, because most rocks are non-linear, the process of

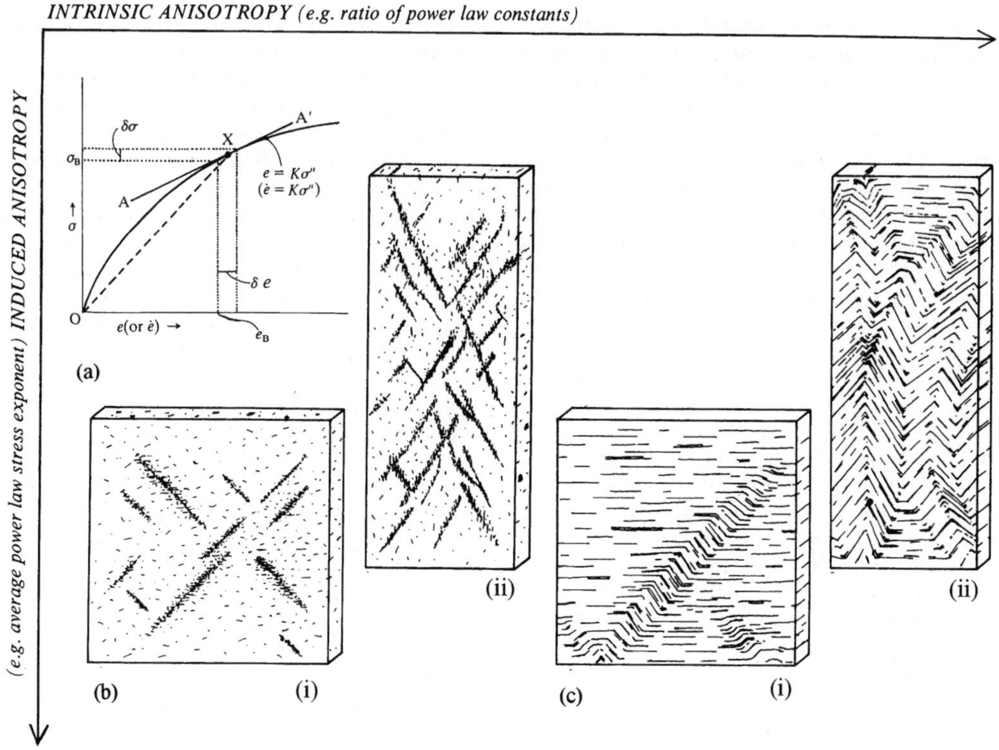

Fig. 12. (**a**) The stress–strain or stress–strain rate curve for a power-law material. The slopes of the lines OX and AX relate to two moduli (see text). (**b**) and (**c**) show the deformation of two materials, one with a low intrinsic anisotropy and high induced anisotropy, and the other with a high intrinsic anisotropy and high induced anisotropy, respectively. (The diagrams are based on analogue models and theoretical analysis.) Deformation will induce an anisotropy in both because they are non-linear. The square sections (**a**) (i) and (**b**) (i) represent the form of the first expression of instability. The effect of further shortening is shown in the rectangular sections (**a**) (ii) and (**b**) (ii). After Latham (1985*b*).

deformation will induce an anisotropy, even in isotropic rocks such as massive sandstones and granites, and that as a result it is likely that instabilities of the type predicted by Biot's theory of ductile deformation of mechanically anisotropic materials will develop. Thus the occurrence of shear zones in intrinsically isotropic rocks does not necessarily imply that they are linked to 'brittle failure' and are related to the principal stresses as indicated in Figures 5–8.

Some possible structures that can form in two types of non-linear materials, one with a low or no intrinsic anisotropy and the other with a well-developed intrinsic anisotropy, are shown in Figure 12b and c, respectively. In the former the development of an anisotropy, as the stress builds up within the material allows structures, such as the conjugate normal kink-bands, which require a high anisotropy, to form (Fig. 12b). The latter material has an even greater total anisotropy as it is both non-linear and intrinsically anisotropic (Fig. 12c). Not surprisingly, structures characteristic of such materials (e.g. kink-bands) will form, either conjugate reverse kink-bands (Fig. 2c) or conjugate normal kink-bands (Fig 2h and i) depending on the orientation of the fabric or layering with respect to the principal stress.

The possibility of the formation of normal kink-band shear zones in intrinsically isotropic rocks means that the suggested criteria for differentiating between the two different shear zones (i.e. that shear zones in isotropic rocks are linked to the processes of brittle failure and those in anisotropic materials linked to a 'buckling' instability) are invalid.

Impact of section orientation through micro-folds on the geometry of the outcrop pattern

In the preceding sections a variety of mechanisms have been discussed that can give rise to structures with a shear-zone-like geometry. In addition, it is possible to generate structures that have shear-zone geometries when viewed on 2D exposed surfaces, but that are not shear zones. This potential problem, which relates directly to the use of shear zones as kinematic indicators, has been addressed by Lexa *et al.* (2004), who showed how different structures (shear bands and folds) can generate identical geometries when viewed on a 2D exposed surface. Unless this is fully appreciated there is a likelihood of misinterpreting structures as kinematic indicators, leading to an erroneous structural analysis.

The ambiguity is the result of oblique sections through small-scale folds in anisotropic materials, such as mineral fabrics. Some of these sections have geometries identical to profile sections through shear-bands. The example shown in Figure 13a shows both the true geometry of the folds, which is found on the profile section (i.e. the section normal to the fold axis), and an oblique section displaying the geometry of shear zones. For folds with horizontal axes and subvertical axial planes, it is found that sections with outcrop patterns comparable with shear zones are those that are steeply inclined and striking at a small angle to the fold axis (Fig. 13b). Lexa *et al.* (2004) determined the orientations of the sections that have shear-zone-like geometries and presented the range of these orientations on stereographic projections. The range of orientations and the geometry of the outcrop patterns on these sections are determined by both the amplitude (interlimb angle) and symmetry of the folds. Figure 13c and d show the influence of amplitude, and Figure 13e and f the influence of asymmetry on the geometry of the outcrop pattern. The apparent sections on the left-hand side are those with the orientation shown in Figure 13a and b (i.e. steeply dipping and trending NNW–SSE). The apparent sections on the right-hand side are steeply dipping and trending NNE–SSW.

The mechanical anisotropy folded by these folds is usually a secondary (i.e. tectonically induced fabric (cleavage or schistosity)), rather than a primary fabric. It follows therefore that these misinterpretations are most likely to occur in areas of multiple deformation when earlier, tectonically generated fabrics are folded by a later deformation.

Thus, to be confident that the geometry displayed on a 2D exposed surface is related to a true shear band and can therefore be used as a valid kinematic indicator, it is essential to know the 3D geometry of the structure and the orientation of the exposure surface with respect to it.

Conclusions

A variety of different mechanisms have been considered that can give rise to structures with the geometry of a shear zone and that consequently might be used as a kinematic indicator. The detailed geometry of these structures, their relationship to the stress field in which they were generated and the mechanical reason for their development has been discussed in an attempt to (1) understand the mode of behaviour of the rock during their formation (i.e. whether its behaviour can be understood in terms of brittle failure, even though the localized planes of deformation that the structures represent may not always lead to loss of continuity (Fig. 7)) or (2) determine whether they are linked to other processes such as kink-band formation.

In the analysis of both ductile and brittle deformation it is found that a range of structures can form, many of which have shear-zone-like geometries. Although the structures that define the limits of these ranges appear to be fundamentally different (e.g. they may be the result of different failure criteria, may have a different relationship with their causative stress field and may have distinctly different geometries), there are nevertheless very close links between them when they are considered in terms of their basic instabilities (e.g. the flexing of a fabric or the formation of small-scale extensional fractures).

The better the understanding of the modes of origin of kinematic indicators and structures with similar geometries, and the greater the appreciation of their fundamental differences and similarities, the less likely it is that they will be misused. The problem of correctly identifying structures that can be used as kinematic indicators is compounded by the fact that structures with the geometries of shear zones can be generated on certain 2D sections through structures that are perfectly symmetrical and therefore have no kinematic implications.

As the deformation of a complex anisotropic material progresses, a series of different structures are likely to develop through time and early formed structures (e.g. boudins in relatively competent layers) may generate the perturbation necessary for the formation of other structures

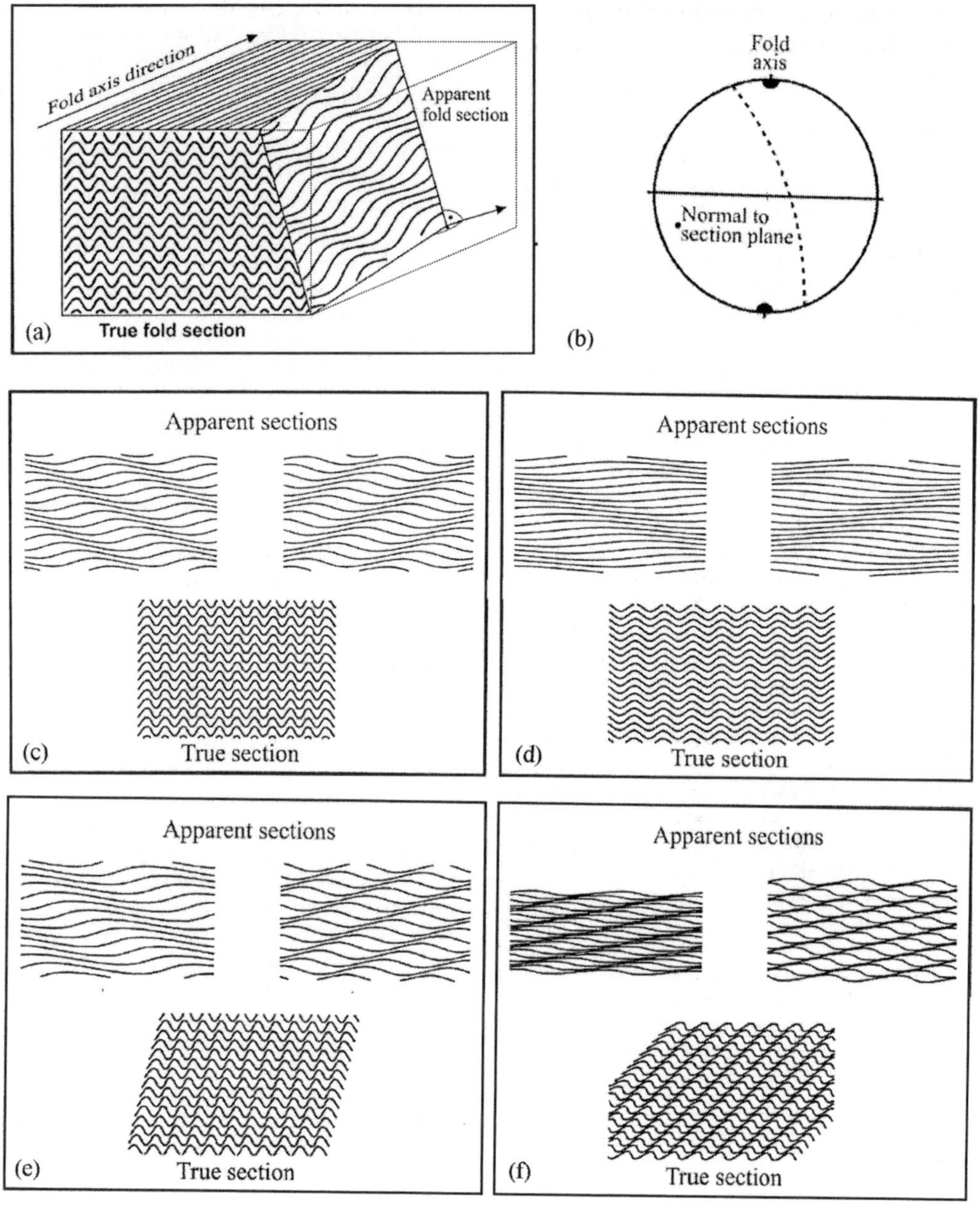

Fig. 13. Oblique sections through folds formed by the buckling of mineral fabrics. (**a**) The true (profile section) geometry of folds and their geometry on a section oblique to the profile plane. Although the folds are symmetric, their geometry on the oblique section is asymmetric and may be used mistakenly as a kinematic indicator. (**b**) Relative orientation of the horizontal fold axis (the axial plane is vertical and strikes north–south), the profile section (vertical and striking east–west) and the plane of section (dashed line) shown on a stereographic projection. (**c**) and (**d**) show the effect of fold amplitude on the geometry of the folds as they appear on oblique sections. (**e**) and (**f**) show the effect of fold asymmetry on the geometry of the folds as they appear on an oblique section. From Lexa *et al.* (2004).

(e.g. conjugate normal kink-bands). The distribution of deformation in such a multilayer is both complex and varied. In areas where the deformation approximates to homogeneous flattening, equal numbers of sinistral and dextral kinematic indicators are found. Deformation in other areas may be dominated by simple shear, and kinematic indicators with one sense of shear will prevail. It follows that when considering the implications of a kinematic analysis, in addition to ensuring that the kinematic indicators being used are valid indicators, it is important to remember the impact that the scale of observation can have on the perceived geometry and style of the deformation.

The author is grateful to the two referees for their helpful advice and constructive criticism of the original manuscript.

References

ANDERSON, E. M. 1951. *The Dynamics of Faulting and Dyke Formation with Applications to Britain.* Oliver & Boyd, Edinburgh.

BEHRMANN, J. H. 1987. A precautionary note on shear bands as kinematic indicators. *Journal of Structural Geology*, **9**(5–6), 659–666.

BIOT, M. A. 1961. Theory of folding of stratified viscoelastic media and its implication in tectonics and orogenesis. *Geological Society of America Bulletin*, **72**, 1595–1620.

BIOT, M. A. 1964. Theory of internal buckling of a confined multilayer sequence. *Geological Society of America Bulletin*, **75**, 563–568.

BIOT, M. A. 1965. *Mechanics of Incremental Deformation*. Wiley, New York.

COBBOLD, P. R. 1976. Fold shapes as a function of progressive strain. *Philosophical Transactions of the Royal Society of London, Series A*, **283**, 129–138.

COBBOLD, P. R., COSGROVE, J. W. & SUMMERS, J. M. 1971. The development of internal structures in deformed anisotropic rocks. *Tectonophysics*, **12**, 23–53.

COSGROVE, J. W. 1976. The formation of crenulation cleavage. *Journal of the Geological Society, London*, **262**, 153–176

COSGROVE, J. W. 1995. The expression of hydraulic fracturing in rocks and sediments. *In*: AMEEN, M. S. (ed.) *Fractography: Fracture Topography as a Tool in Fracture Mechanics and Stress Analysis*. Geological Society, London, Special Publications, **92**, 187–196.

COWARD, M. P. 1976. Strain within ductile shear zones. *Tectonophysics*, **34**, 181–197.

KIDAN, T. W. & COSGROVE, J. W. 1996. The deformation of multilayers by layer normal compression; an experimental investigation. *Journal of Structural Geology*, **18**(4), 461–474.

LATHAM, J.-P. 1983. *The influence of mechnical anisotropy on the development of geological structures.* PhD thesis, University of London.

LATHAM, J.-P. 1985*a*. The influence of non-linear material properties and resistance to bending on the development of internal structures. *Journal of Structural Geology*, **7**(2), 225–236.

LATHAM, J.-P. 1985*b*. A numerical investigation and geological discussion of the relationship between folding, kinking and faulting. *Journal of Structural Geology*, **7**(2), 237–249.

LEXA, O., COSGROVE, J. W. & SCHULMANN, K. 2004. Problems related to the role of shear bands as kinematic indicators. *Journal of Structural Geology*, **26**, 155–161.

LISTER, G. S. & SNOKE, A. W. 1984. S–C mylonites. *Journal of Structural Geology*, **6**(6), 617–638.

MAIN, I. G., SAMMONDS, P. R. & MEREDITH, P. G. 1993. Application of a modified Griffith criterion to the evolution of fractal damage during compressional rock failure. *Geophysical Journal International*, **115**(2), 367–380.

NÁDAI, A. 1950. *Theory of Flow and Fracture of Solids. Vol. 1*. McGraw–Hill, New York.

PASSCHIER, C. W. & TROUW, R. A. J. 2005. *Microtectonics*. Springer, Berlin.

PRICE, N. J. & COSGROVE, J. W. 1990. *The Analysis of Geological Structures*. Cambridge University Press, Cambridge.

RAMSAY, J. G. 1980. Shear zone geometry: a review. *Journal of Structural Geology*, **2**(1–2), 83–99.

RAMSAY, J. G. & GRAHAM, R. H. 1970. Strain variation in shear belts. *Canadian Journal of Earth Sciences*, **7**, 786–813.

RAMSAY, J. G. & LISLE, R. J. 2000. *The Techniques of Modern Structural Geology, Vol 3. Application of Continuum Mechanics in Structural Geology*. Academic Press, New York, 701–1061.

Flow perturbation folding in shear zones

G. I. ALSOP[1] & R. E. HOLDSWORTH[2]

[1]*Crustal Geodynamics Group, School of Geography & Geosciences, University of St. Andrew, St. Andrews KY16 9AL, UK (e-mail: gia@st-andrews.ac.uk)*

[2]*Reactivation Research Group, Department of Earth Sciences, University of Durham, Durham DH1 3LE, UK*

Abstract: Variable patterns of displacement in shear zones may result in arcuate fold and fault traces as recognized by Mike Coward and co-workers in the early 1980s. Within such deformation zones, localized perturbations in flow may undergo acceleration (surging flow) or deceleration (slackening flow) with respect to the adjacent regions. Such flow cells may govern the orientation and geometries of folds and fabrics and thereby provide evidence of the scale and nature of deformation associated with heterogeneous flow in the high-strain zones. The length/width ratio of individual flow cells (measured in the direction of flow) may vary from <1 to >1 for situations when flow cells are, respectively, dominated by layer-parallel shear (LPS) or layer-normal shear (LNS). Folds initiating at high angles to transport are associated with LPS, whereas LNS may generate folds with slight clockwise (sinistral LNS) or anticlockwise (dextral LNS) trends relative to flow. Continued progressive deformation may subsequently modify and reduce angular relationships between folds and fabrics, but these geometric obliquities are generally preserved. Using examples from the Moine metasediments of northern Scotland, we show that folding displays predictable geometric patterns that can be related to the development of flow perturbation cells associated with Caledonian ductile thrusting under mid-crustal conditions. The differing relative timing of folds and individual ductile thrusts reflects the complexity of flow cells within ductile imbricates and additionally highlights the progressive foreland-directed propagation of ductile thrusting. These geometric relationships developed during contractional shear are compared with those generated in extensional systems, to provide an overall framework for the study of perturbation patterns. The geometric arrangement of mean fold axial planes about the flow direction results in their intersection forming parallel to the transport direction. This relationship permits transport directions to be calculated via the axial-planar intersection method (AIM), and also allows comparison with other techniques devised primarily for the study of soft-sediment deformation and palaeoslope analysis.

Shear zones may be defined as zones of relatively high strain across which significant displacement has taken place. They develop in a broad range of geological environments and therefore the study of structures associated with their development has widespread applications and implications (see Ramsay 1980; Alsop & Holdsworth 2004*a*, for a review). Folds are a particularly important field of study as they are relatively resilient to subsequent deformation and, once created, are difficult to destroy (unlike fabrics, which are more readily transposed). In addition, folds may be generated in a broad range of both materials and environments in which coherent ductile flow may operate. Folds are also readily subjected to systematic and rigorous geometric analysis and may therefore provide a unique and reliable record of deformation.

Variably oriented folds may be created by a number of mechanisms broadly categorized into two major types. Fold hinges displaying primary curvature occur where sinuous fold patterns reflect an original variation during active fold initiation and growth (e.g. Ghosh & Ramberg 1968; Dubey & Cobbold 1977). This group includes synshearing folds associated with flow perturbations (Coward & Potts 1983; Ridley 1986; Holdsworth 1990). Fold hinges displaying secondary curvature are generated when original hinge-lines are subsequently passively rotated during progressive deformation (Bryant & Reed 1969; Sanderson 1973; Escher & Watterson 1974; Rhodes & Gayer 1977; Bell 1978; Williams 1978; Ghosh & Sengupta 1984, 1987; Fossen & Rykkelid 1990; Mies 1991; Alsop 1992). Such secondary curvature may be imposed on fold hinges that may or may not display a degree of primary curvature, and may ultimately result in highly curvilinear sheath fold geometries (Carreras *et al.* 1977; Quinquis *et al.* 1978;

From: RIES, A. C., BUTLER, R. W. H. & GRAHAM, R. H. (eds) 2007. *Deformation of the Continental Crust: The Legacy of Mike Coward.* Geological Society, London, Special Publications, **272**, 75–101.
0305-8719/07/$15

Minnigh 1979; Berthé & Brun 1980; Cobbold & Quiquis 1980; Skjernaa 1980, 1989; Holdsworth & Roberts 1984; Lacassin & Mattauer 1985; Goscombe 1991; Alsop 1994; Alsop & Holdsworth 1999, 2004*c*; Alsop & Holdsworth 2006).

In this study, the primary curvature of fold patterns related to surge zones within thrust belts, directly analogous to those originally studied in the early 1980s by Coward and co-workers in the Moine Thrust Zone of NW Scotland, is discussed (Coward & Kim 1981; Coward 1982, 1983, 1984; Coward & Potts 1983). The effects of differential shear on fold hinges within the more internal portions of orogenic belts were also discussed by Downing & Coward (1981) in the Damaran belt of Namibia. Following the proposals made by Elliott (1976), Coward & Potts (1983) demonstrated that intense shear strains (γ_1) may develop at the frontal tips to thrusts and shear zones, where layer-parallel shortening will lead to folding at a high angle to transport (Fig. 1a and 2). Coward & Potts (1983) also demonstrated that lateral tips are marked by additional differential shear strains (γ_2), resulting in asymmetric buckle folds with axes oblique or even subparallel to the direction of flow (Fig. 1b). Differential shear in mylonite zones may thus generate variable fold patterns in adjacent rocks (Fig. 1c); (e.g. Evans & White 1984, fig. 11) and may be related to transient flow perturbations that develop at different scales. The resulting folds and associated structures may therefore also display differing scales, differing relative timing relationships, differing orientations in terms of fold trend, and differing geometries in terms of fold shape and vergence. Many of these criteria have in the past been used to separate fold 'phases' in a rigorous framework (i.e. F_1, F_2, F_3, etc). Flow perturbations models cast doubt on the validity and correlation of fold sequences within high-strain zones on geometric grounds and without recourse to independent methods of testing, such as isotopic dating.

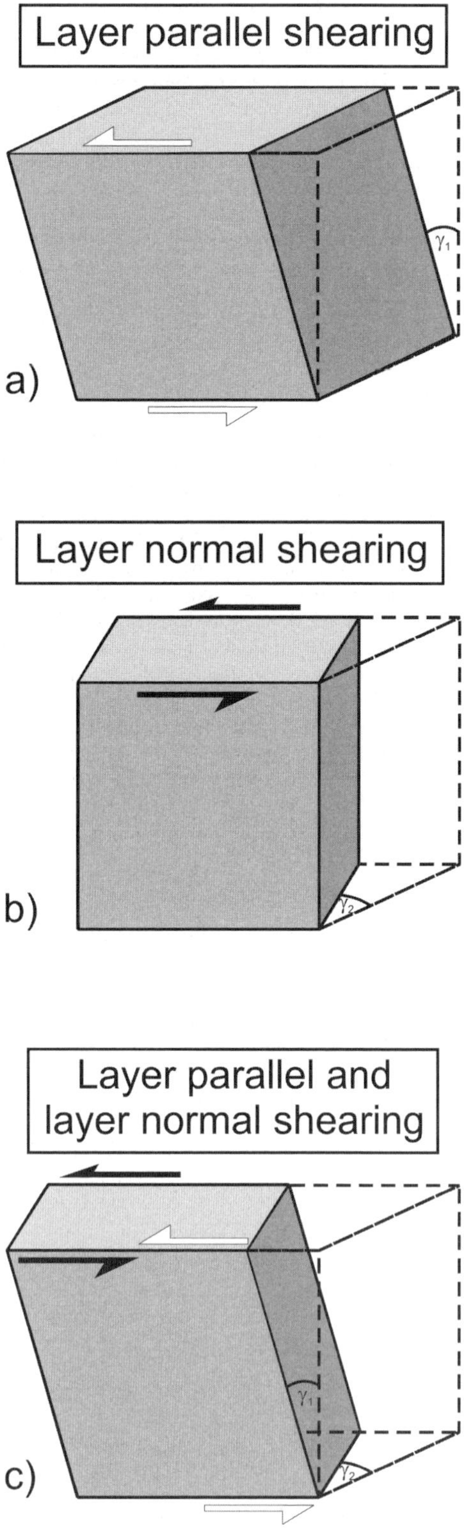

Fig. 1. (**a**) Shear strains (γ_1) associated with layer-parallel shearing may develop at the frontal tips to thrusts and shear zones, resulting in folding at a high angle to transport. Layering lies approximately parallel to the base of the cube. (**b**) Differential shear strains (γ_2) associated with layer-normal shearing may develop at lateral tips to thrusts and shears, resulting in asymmetric buckle folds with axes oblique or even subparallel to the direction of flow. (**c**) Combinations of layer-parallel (γ_1) and layer-normal (γ_2) shearing may develop in mylonite zones, resulting in variable fold patterns in adjacent rocks. Modified from Coward & Kim (1981) and Coward & Potts (1983).

This paper reviews the concept of flow perturbations, and in particular the role of differential shear in the generation of flow cells with different shapes. These models are then tested using a case study from the Caledonides of northern Scotland, where flow perturbation folds display markedly different geometric relationships with hinge trends varying through more than 90°. Various distinguishing criteria and geometric consequences are highlighted from flow perturbations in both contractional and extensional settings, followed by a discussion of flow folding and its relationship to the transport direction.

Synshearing flow folds

Localized perturbations in flow within a shear zone may result in a relative acceleration (surging flow) or deceleration (slackening flow) when compared with the 'background' velocity of the adjacent flow (Fig. 2). Fold culminations are associated with surging flow, with an arc of hinge-line curvature that closes in the direction of transport (Fig. 2a). Depressions are marked by slackening flow, with an arc of hinge-line curvature that opens in the transport direction (Fig. 2b). Within each type of flow cell, localized areas of relative deceleration will generate folds, whereas locally accelerating flow results in extensional shear bands dipping in the flow direction and describing convex and concave arcs in surging and slackening flow cells, respectively. The leading edge of surging flow cells is marked by decelerating flow, whereas the trailing edge is associated with accelerating flow. The reverse pattern occurs in slackening flow cells (Fig. 2b).

The flanks of the flow cells are associated with differential (sinistral or dextral) shear. In both surging and slackening flow cells, sinistral shear generates fold traces clockwise of the flow direction, whereas dextral shear creates anticlockwise-trending folds. The resulting arcuate folds display a concave fold trace in surging flow and convex trace in slackening flow, both of which are bisected by the flow direction. In both surging and slackening flow, folds developed at a high angle to transport will verge in the flow direction. However, transport-subparallel folds developed on the flanks may verge towards the outer edges (surging flow), or towards the inner centre (slackening flow), resulting in markedly different vergence patterns around culmination or depression traces (Fig. 2a and b). Associated fold facing shows a distinct convex arc towards the outer edge of the cell in surging flow, and a concave facing arc towards the centre of slackening flow cells. Thus, culmination or depression surfaces are marked by reversals in the polarity of structural facing, minor fold limb vergence, and fold hinge–transport lineation obliquity (Fig. 2a and b). Fold hinges trending clockwise of transport represent sinistral shear and those trending anticlockwise result from dextral shear. A general description of the regional geological setting of the case study area is provided below, prior to a detailed analysis and interpretation of the highly variable fold patterns.

Regional setting: Caledonian Moine Nappe, Sutherland

The regional geology of NW Scotland is dominated by structures generated during the Early Palaeozoic Scandian phase of the Caledonian Orogeny (*c.* 430 Ma). The most important of these structures is the ESE-dipping Moine Thrust and associated ductile thrusts, such as the Sgurr Beag–Naver Thrust (Fig. 3); (see Strachan *et al.* 2002, for a review). The case study area, centred on the Kyle of Tongue on the north coast of Sutherland, comprises Late Archaean acidic orthogneiss (Lewisian) that forms a basement to Neoproterozoic Moine psammites and subordinate pelites that contain S_1 fabrics and minor F_1 folds, although major D_1 structures are absent (Fig. 3; see Holdsworth *et al.* 2001 for a full review). Structurally, the area is dominated by a D_2 Caledonian ductile thrust stack comprising the Achininver, Ben Hope and Dherue thrusts, together with numerous subordinate ductile thrust imbricates, all containing abundant top-to-the-WNW shear criteria (Fig. 3; Holdsworth *et al.* 2001). Throughout the area, the gently east-dipping regional foliation (S_n) is a bedding-subparallel fabric that intensifies into broad zones of platy mylonite, marking (D_2) ductile thrusts formed at mid-crustal depths (greenschist–amphibolite facies) (Holdsworth 1989; Holdsworth & Grant 1990; Holdsworth *et al.* 2001; Fig. 3). Within the plane of the foliation, a pronounced mineral lineation (L_n), defined by mica together with elongate quartz and feldspar aggregates, plunges gently towards the east directly down the dip of the foliation and is considered to define the trend of tectonic transport (Fig. 4a). Associated (F_2) folds are typically rotated into near parallelism with L_n and define highly curvilinear sheath fold geometries on all scales (Holdsworth 1989; Alsop & Holdsworth 1999, 2004*c*).

The ductile thrusts and associated foliation (S_n) have, during progressive deformation, been folded by kilometre-scale open (F_3) folds that form either subparallel to or at a high angle to the trend of tectonic transport. These major upright

	a) Antiformal Culmination	b) Synformal Depression
Plan View	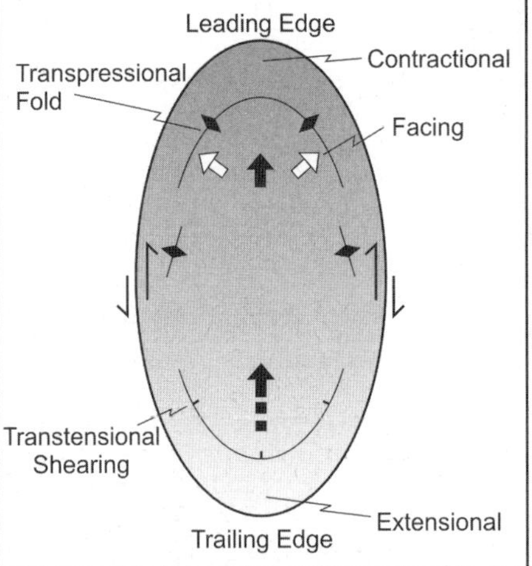	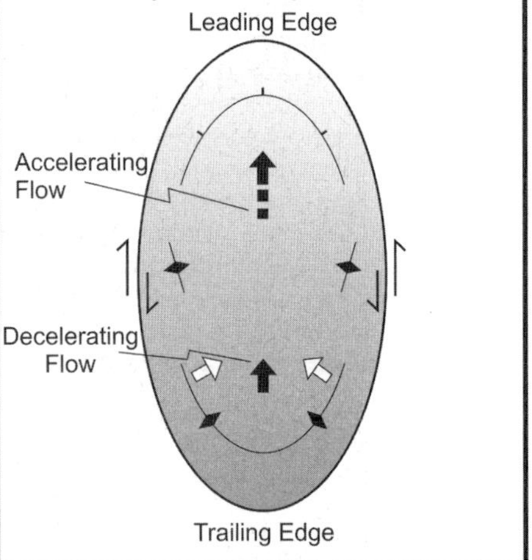
Flow Type	**Surging Flow**	**Slackening Flow**
Flow Pattern	Leading edge - Decelerating flow Trailing edge - Accelerating flow	Leading edge - Accelerating flow Trailing edge - Decelerating flow
Deformation Pattern	Leading edge - Contractional folds Trailing edge - Extensional shears	Leading edge - Extensional shears Trailing edge - Contractional folds
Fold Trace Pattern	Concave fold trace bisected by decelerating flow at leading edge	Convex fold trace bisected by decelerating flow at trailing edge
Fold Trace Pattern - Flanks	Fold traces clockwise of flow related to differential sinistral shear Fold traces anticlockwise of flow related to differential dextral shear	Fold traces clockwise of flow related to differential sinistral shear Fold traces anticlockwise of flow related to differential dextral shear
Fold Vergence Pattern	Folds verge in flow direction at leading edge and towards outer edges on flanks	Folds verge in flow direction at trailing edge and towards inner centre on flanks
Fold Facing Pattern	Convex fold facing arc towards outer edge of flow cell	Concave fold facing arc towards inner centre of flow cell
Shear Pattern	Convex extensional shears dipping in flow direction and bisected by accelerating flow	Concave extensional shears dipping in flow direction and bisected by accelerating flow

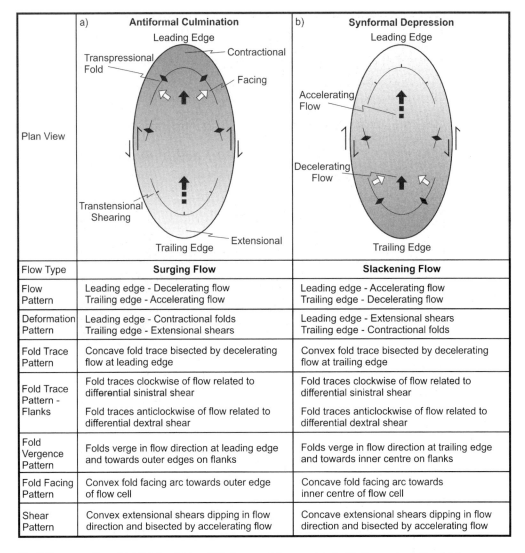

Fig. 2. Summary figure highlighting fold and fabric geometries associated with flow perturbation folding. Antiformal culminations are associated with surging flow (left-hand column) whereas synformal depressions are marked by slackening flow (right-hand column). Locally decelerating flow (solid black arrows) results in contractional flow-normal folding, whereas layer-parallel extension associated with locally accelerating flow (broken black arrows) generates extensional shear bands. The flanks of the flow cells are marked by sinistral or dextral layer-normal shear, which results in folds initiating clockwise or anticlockwise to flow, respectively. Arcuate fold trace patterns are marked by variable fold-facing directions (open arrows). (See text for further discussion).

folds define culmination or depression surfaces that root downwards onto underlying thrusts, and have previously been attributed to perturbations in ductile flow within underlying mylonite zones (Holdsworth 1990; Alsop & Holdsworth 1993, 2002, 2004*b*; Alsop *et al.* 1996; Holdsworth *et al.* 2007; Fig. 3).

Major medial (culmination or depression) surfaces typically form orthogonal to the foliation surface and are parallel to transport. Associated (F_3) fold hinges define arcuate traces that may vary from largely transport-parallel to transport-normal. F_3 fold traces, developed subparallel to the transport direction (marked by

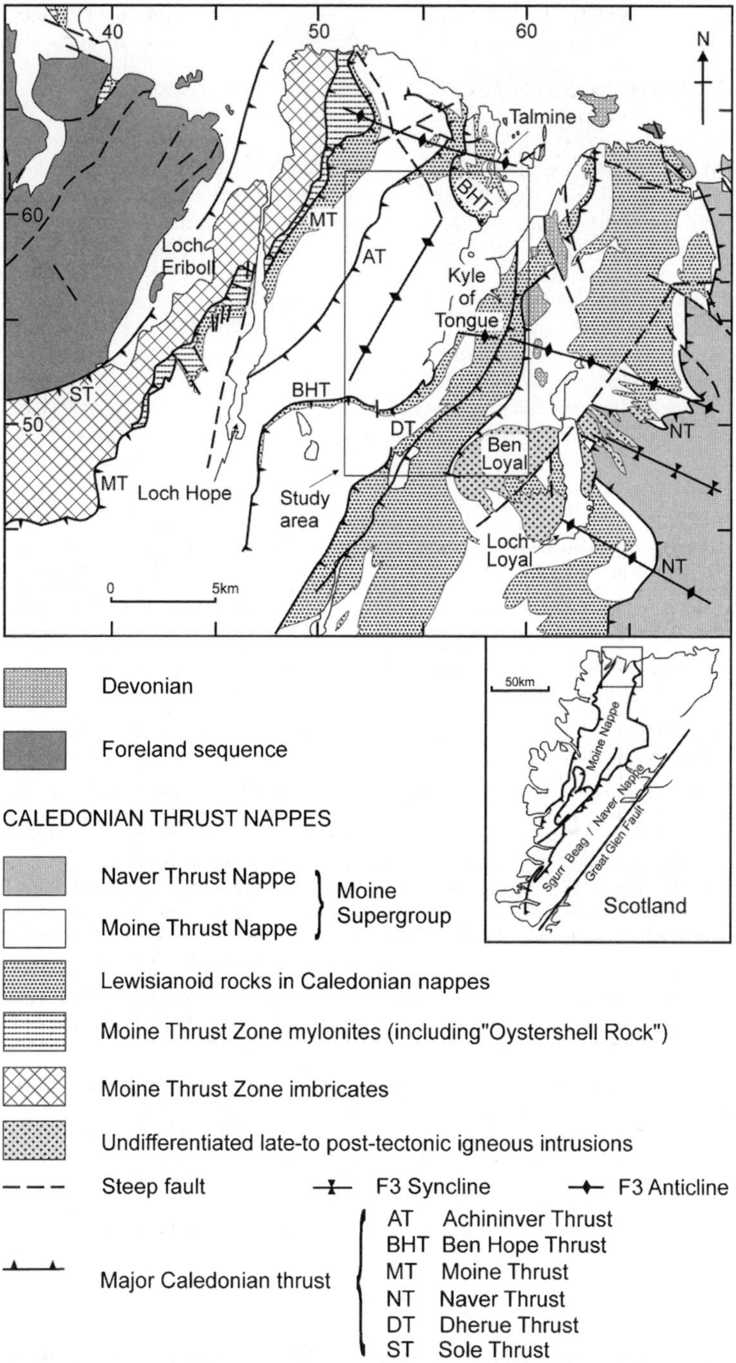

Fig. 3. Simplified geological map of the Moine and Naver nappes in the Kyle of Tongue area, highlighting the location of the study area (see also British Geological Survey 1997, 2002). Major NW- to WNW-directed Caledonian ductile thrusts that carry reworked Lewisian in the hanging wall are shown with solid barbs. These thrusts are subsequently folded by major upright folds, trending either subparallel or at high angles to tectonic transport. The reference grid relates to the UK National Grid, with the map area falling within the NC prefix quadrangle. The inset shows the location of the map in relation to Scotland, with the Moine and Naver nappes being carried on Caledonian thrusts.

the mineral lineation), are observed to the east of the Kyle of Tongue, where the Naver Thrust is markedly deflected by SE-trending folds that root downwards onto the underlying Ben Blandy Shear Zone and Dherue Thrust (Figs 3 and 4a; Alsop *et al.* 1996; Holdsworth *et al.* 2001). In the Talmine area, at the northern end of the Kyle of Tongue, transport-parallel F_3 folding arches the Ben Hope and Achininver thrusts, together with the underlying Moine Thrust, resulting in a marked thickening of the associated mylonites (Alsop & Holdsworth 1993, 2002, 2004*b*; Figs 3 and 4a). The planar geometry of the structure underlying the mylonites in the hinge of the culmination suggests that it has not been affected by the flow perturbation folding and may have acted as the local basal décollement to the deformation (Alsop *et al.* 1996; Holdsworth *et al.* 2001; Alsop & Holdsworth 2002).

F_3 fold traces, developed at a high angle to transport and trending NE–SW, are observed immediately to the west of the Kyle of Tongue (Fig. 3). The trace of the Ben Hope Thrust is markedly deflected by this folding, resulting in a pronounced swing in strike where it arches around the gentle culmination. The overall arching and folding of the Ben Hope Thrust and associated contacts results in the orientation of the mean regional foliation (S_n) and lineation (L_n) varying around the closures at the northern and southern terminations of the major transport-normal fold (Fig. 4a–d). This major eye-shaped closure thus governs the trend of the regional foliation (S_n) and mineral extension lineation (L_n)

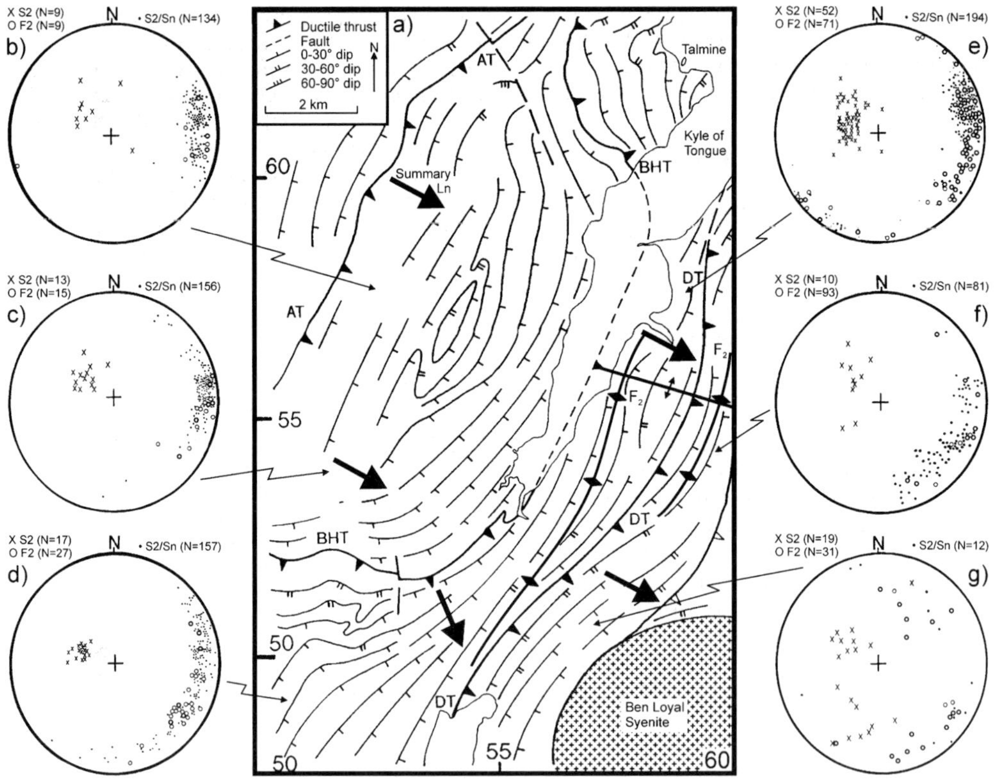

Fig. 4. (**a**) Simplified structural map of the Kyle of Tongue area, highlighting the location of the Achininver (AT), Ben Hope (BHT) and Dherue (DT) thrusts. The trace of the regional foliation (S_n) is marked and typically dips gently to moderately towards the SE. Summary lineation (L_n) arrows are also shown and plunge gently to the SE. Major F_2 antiforms, on either side of the Dherue Thrust, are marked on the eastern side of the map. Equal area lower hemisphere stereographic projections of F_2 fold hinges, S_2–S_n intersection lineations and poles to axial-planar S_2 are shown from the western (**b–d**), and eastern sides (**e–g**) of the Kyle of Tongue. F_2 fold hinges and S_2–S_n intersection lineations define stereographic girdle patterns that are consistent with large-scale curvilinear folding. (See text for further discussion.)

developed immediately to the west of the Kyle of Tongue, and has previously been attributed to F_3 folding in the area (Alsop & Holdsworth 1993). The underlying Achininver Thrust appears to maintain a constant NE–SW strike and is unaffected by these transport-normal folds, which are therefore considered to root downwards onto this planar structure (Fig. 3). Thus, the Achininver Thrust appears to act as a basal décollement for the transport-normal folding west of the Kyle of Tongue, but is itself folded by the transport subparallel folding of the Talmine area, which roots downward into the Moine Thrust Zone mylonites (Fig. 3). The folding in both areas deforms the main foliation (S_n) and lineation (L_n) and is therefore considered to be of broadly similar (F_3) age. The differing relative timing of F_3 folds and individual ductile thrusts reflects the complexity of flow cells within ductile imbricates and additionally highlights the progressive propagation of thrusting and associated deformation towards the foreland (WNW), so that folds rooting down into structurally lower thrusts generally formed later in the sequence.

Patterns of folding in the Moine Nappe

It is important to assess whether the differing trends of F_3 folds can be attributed to the influence of earlier F_2 structures. A detailed geometric analysis of the (F_2) sheath folds and (F_3) syn-shearing flow perturbation folds on either side of the Kyle of Tongue is therefore presented below.

F_2 folding

Throughout the Kyle of Tongue study area, the axes of tight to isoclinal F_2 folds generally plunge gently towards the east, and define incomplete stereographic girdle patterns (Fig. 4). An intense fabric (S_2), developed axial-planar to F_2 folds, typically dips gently towards the ESE and forms an S_2–S_n intersection lineation with the regional foliation (S_n). In the northern part of the area to the west of the Kyle of Tongue, S_2–S_n plunges gently towards the east and is typically developed anticlockwise of the associated F_2 fold hinges (Fig. 4a–c). Such relationships are consistent with clockwise rotating fold hinges (see Alsop & Holdsworth 1999, 2004*c*, for reviews). In the southern part of this area, F_2 hinges and S_2–S_n intersections display greater variability of trends with increased SE- and south-directed plunges, resulting in a pronounced stereographic girdle (Fig. 4d). Increasing south- and SE-directed plunges (which are also displayed by L_n) may be a consequence of the subsequent overall arching on the southern flank of the F_3 culmination that dominates the area.

The pronounced transport-normal F_3 folding is largely absent in the region east of the Kyle of Tongue, as shown in Fig. 4, and this provides an opportunity to study F_2 fold patterns that are little affected by subsequent arching. In the north, both F_2 hinges and S_2–S_n generally plunge gently towards the ENE and define incomplete gently east-dipping stereographic girdles, subparallel to the axial-planar S_2 fabric (Fig. 4e). Similar patterns are observed farther south, although with a greater variability in trends, which typically become more SE plunging (Fig. 4f and g). This F_2 folding is associated with a major curvilinear antiform, cored by Lewisian gneiss, which is developed immediately to the east of the Kyle of Tongue (Fig. 4a; Holdsworth 1989; Holdsworth *et al.* 2001). The WNW-trending culmination of this F_2 fold broadly corresponds to the variation in F_2 fold patterns noted above and is also clearly marked by the outcrop of a ‘core region’ of more acidic Lewisian orthogneiss mapped within the basement inlier (British Geological Survey 1997; Holdsworth *et al.* 2001). It is notable that this culmination also coincides with the continuation along-transport of the major F_3 culmination described from the western side of the Kyle of Tongue (Fig. 4a). This may suggest a degree of ‘inheritance’ across the intervening Ben Hope Thrust.

F_3 folding

Although F_3 folds and fabrics clearly deform the earlier F_2 structures, they may be considered as being related to progressive deformation during D_2 thrusting because of their similar top-to-the-west kinematics and close association with D_2 thrusts (for further details see Holdsworth 1990; Alsop & Holdsworth 2004*b*). Throughout the study area, F_3 folds typically form close to tight buckles, which deform the main regional foliation (S_n) and associated extension lineation (L_n). A crenulation cleavage (S_3) is axial-planar to F_3 folds and typically is more steeply dipping than the adjacent foliation.

To the west of the Kyle of Tongue, F_3 folds display close to tight geometries, display overall west-directed vergence and, in the northern part of the area, plunge gently towards both the NNE and SSW (Fig. 5a and b). The associated axial-planar S_3 fabric is NNE-striking and dips moderately towards the ESE, steeper than S_n. Farther south, F_3 folds increasingly display SSE-directed plunges off the southern flanks of the regional F_3 whaleback, whereas the axial-planar S_3 fabric consistently dips moderately towards the ESE

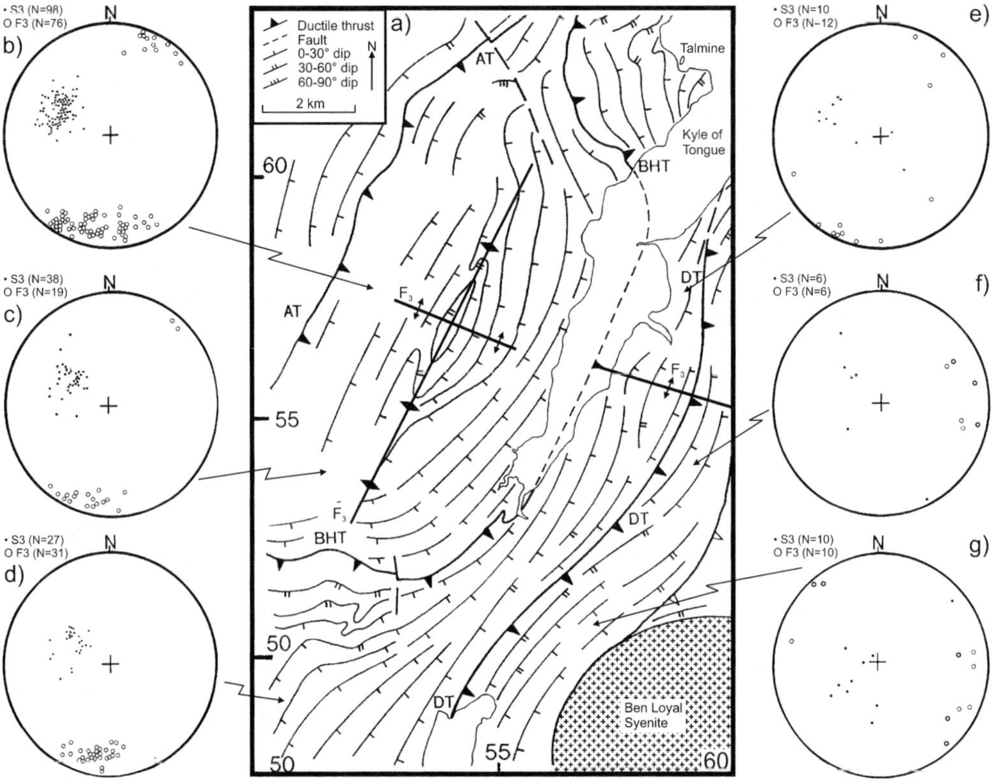

Fig. 5. (**a**) Simplified structural map of the Kyle of Tongue area, highlighting the location of the Achininver (AT), Ben Hope (BHT) and Dherue (DT) thrusts. The trace of the regional foliation (S_n) and Ben Hope Thrust displays a pronounced swing in strike where it arches around the gentle NE-trending F_3 antiform to the west of the Kyle of Tongue. Major F_3 culminations on either side of the Kyle of Tongue are aligned parallel to tectonic transport. Equal area lower hemisphere stereographic projections of F_3 fold hinges and poles to axial-planar S_3 are shown from the western (**b–d**), and eastern sides (**e–g**) of the Kyle of Tongue. (See text for further discussion.)

(Fig. 5c and d). Overall, to the west of the Kyle of Tongue, there is an absence of measured F_3 hinge trends along a 106° arc, centred about the ESE-plunging extension lineation defining tectonic transport. As this arc is precisely and symmetrically bisected by mean L_n, it suggests that the pattern of F_3 folds represents an actual distribution, rather than a coincidental artefact of sampling and exposure.

To the east of the Kyle of Tongue, close to tight F_3 folds display ESE trends, subparallel to L_n, and no distinct arc lacking F_3 folds is observed (Fig. 5e–g). F_3 folds display variably oriented axial planes that define an imprecise stereographic girdle pattern rather than the clustered distribution observed to the west of the Kyle of Tongue (Fig. 5e–g). It is notable that the pole to this best-fit axial-planar girdle broadly corresponds to the transport lineation (L_n) (see below and Alsop & Holdsworth 2002).

F_2 and F_3 topological relationships

A further analysis of F_2 and F_3 data is presented on fabric topology plots (FTPs) that directly compare angles between sets of planar and linear data (see Alsop & Holdsworth 2004*c*, for a review). In dip-slip thrust systems, the asymmetry of minor F_2 and F_3 folds may be described as Z, S or neutral verging M when viewed down-plunge. In addition, the obliquity of minor F_2 fold hinges to the mineral lineation (L_n), defining tectonic transport, may be described as clockwise or anticlockwise when viewed from above. This distinction is less meaningful in F_3 folds that are typically transport-normal and are therefore described as Z or S folds that are broadly west- or east-verging.

The angle between F_2 hinges and L_n displays a strong positive relationship with the trend of F_2 hinges, reflecting the variability of F_2 hinges about the relatively constant mineral lineation (L_n; Fig. 6a, b and e). The trend of F_2 hinges strongly correlates with the F_2 pitch on associated axial planes, with most hinges pitching between 30° and 120° (Fig. 6c and f). The pitch of F_2 hinges is also seen to vary in relation to the strike of F_2 axial planes, with hinges trending clockwise of L_n typically pitching at greater angles (Fig. 6d and g). Thus, the development of Z and S minor F_2 fold hinges both clockwise and anticlockwise of L_n suggests that both the upper and lower limbs of larger-scale F_2 sheath folds have been sampled (see Alsop & Holdsworth 2004*c*). In addition, F_2 data from both the west and east of the Kyle of Tongue display similar overall patterns on the FTPs, indicating that no consistent geometric differences exist in F_2 folds and fabrics across the Kyle of Tongue.

In contrast, analysis of F_3 folds on FTPs reveals distinctly different patterns on either side of the Kyle of Tongue. On both the eastern and western side, the angle between F_3 hinges and L_n displays a strong positive relationship with the trend of F_3 hinges, reflecting the variability of F_3 hinges about the relatively constant mineral lineation (L_n; Fig. 7a, b and e). However, the data from the western side typically display angles of $>60°$ between fold hinges and the lineation, whereas the eastern side is marked by angles of $<60°$. These distinct differences in the trend of F_3 fold hinges across the Kyle of Tongue are also clearly reflected in the values of F_3 hinge pitch on axial planes (Fig. 7c and f). The pitch of F_3 fold hinges on associated axial planes is less clearly related to the strike of axial planes than that of the F_2 folds (Fig. 7d and g). This weaker F_3 correlation reflects the wide range of hinge trends that are developed within the variably oriented axial planes. Thus, the F_3 topological patterns observed from the east of the Kyle of Tongue are similar to those described for F_2 folds from this same area. However, in the region to the west, very different F_3 and F_2 patterns emerge, with NE–SW-trending westerly verging F_3 folds forming a transport-normal whaleback. The relative constancy of F_2 structures on either side of the Kyle of Tongue may suggest that the siting of the major transport-normal F_3 folding is not significantly influenced by any variability or location of pre-existing F_2 structures. These distinct F_2 and F_3 fold patterns across the Kyle of Tongue are now interpreted in terms of flow perturbation models that are briefly reviewed below.

Flow perturbation folding

Folds generated by variations in flow within underlying mylonitic high-strain zones (flow perturbation folds) may define a variety of arcuate fold trace patterns about the transport direction. Velocity (and hence shear strain) gradients parallel to the direction of flow will generate layer-parallel shear (LPS) with the fold hinges initiating at a high angle to transport, whereas gradients in velocity normal to the direction of flow will generate differential layer-normal shear (LNS) with fold hinges oblique or subparallel to transport (Alsop & Holdsworth 2002). Variable combinations of LPS and LNS components will thus generate a variety of distinct arcuate fold patterns described below.

Layer-normal shearing

Flow in which differential LNS is dominant over LPS will generate folds with hinges initiating oblique or even subparallel to flow (Figs 8a and 9a). Culmination or depression surfaces will correspond to reversals in the sense of differential LNS. Differential sinistral LNS will generate anticlockwise vorticity, with Z fold hinges (looking down transport) preserved clockwise of the transport direction, whereas differential dextral LNS will create clockwise vorticity, with anticlockwise-trending S fold hinges (Figs 8a and 9a). Histograms of fold hinge trends will define an oblique bimodal distribution pattern on either margin of the transport (X) direction. The obliquity of fold hinge trends about the culmination surface is marked by reversals in the sense of fold facing, which will also define an oblique bimodal pattern on histograms considered typical of flow perturbation folding (e.g. Alsop & Holdsworth 2002, fig. 9) (Figs 8a and 9a). Hinge rotation can be precluded from generating such transport-subparallel cylindrical folds as they possess open–close interlimb angles that would be severely tightened if progressive shear had produced significant rotation of originally transport-normal hinges (see Alsop & Holdsworth 1999, 2004*c*, 2005). The length/width ratio of individual flow cells (measured parallel to flow) within LNS-dominated deformation will typically be >1, with flow cells elongate in the direction of flow.

Layer-parallel shearing

Flow in which LPS is dominant over differential LNS will generate folds that verge in the direction of shear, and initiate with hinges lying at high angles to the flow direction. The transport-subnormal attitude of such folds means they may be susceptible to significant hinge rotations during continued progressive LPS deformation to define parabolic traces about the flow

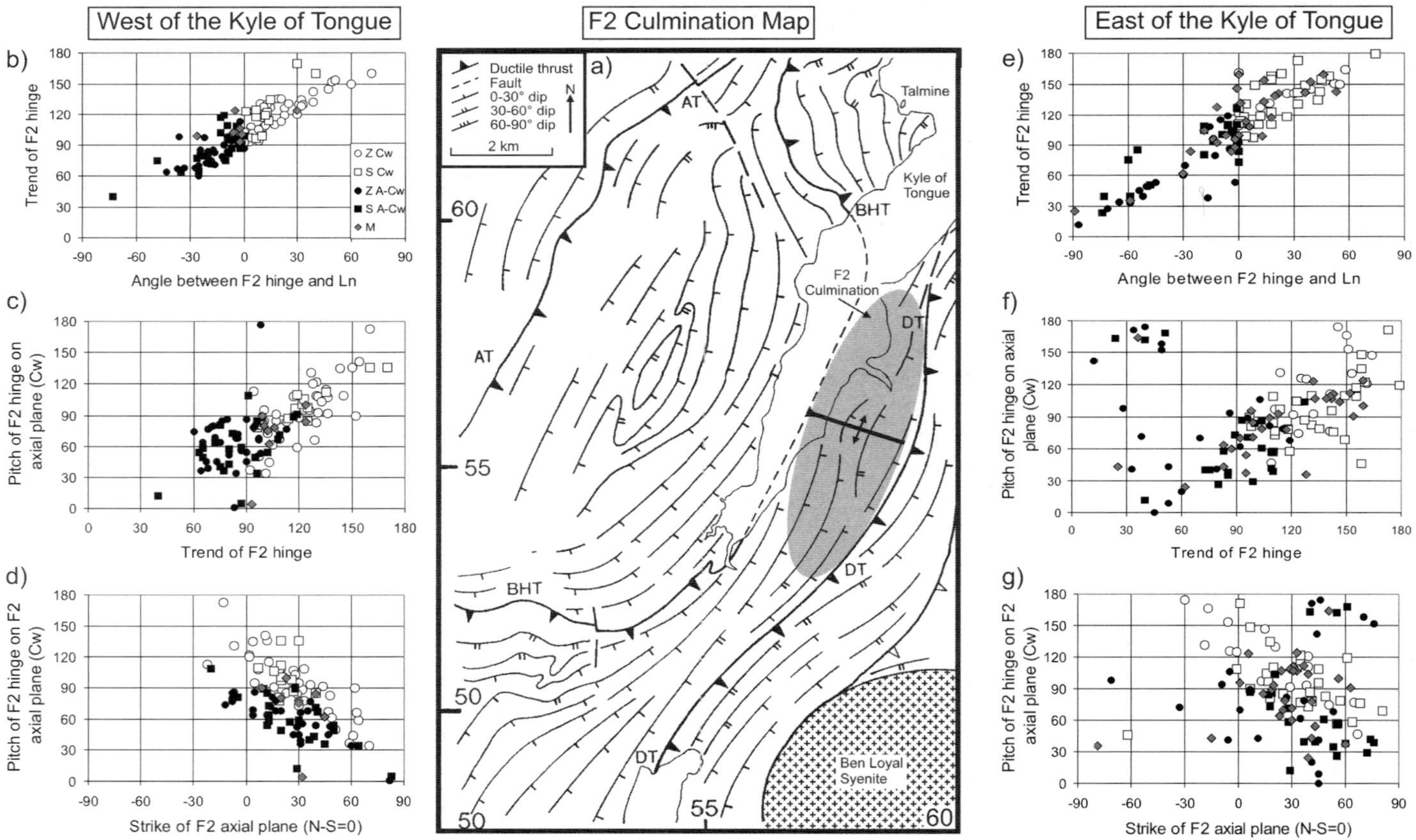

Fig. 6. (**a**) F_2 culmination map showing the location of the major transport-parallel culmination trace to the east of the Kyle of Tongue. The elliptical geometry of the flow cell is schematically shown (tone) and notably corresponds to an F_2 antiform cored by Lewisian gneiss. Fabric topology plots (FTPs) display F_2 fold data, which may be clockwise (open symbols) or anticlockwise (filled symbols) of the adjacent transport lineation from the west (**b**,**c**,**e**) and east (**e**,**f**,**g**) of the Kyle of Tongue. Structures associated with F_2 Z folds (circles), S folds (squares) or M folds (diamonds) may be clockwise or anticlockwise (negative) of L_n (**b**,**e**), whereas the pitch of F_2 fold hinges (**c**,**d**,**f**,**g**) is measured clockwise from axial-planar strike. Whereas F_2 fold trend values are given between 0° and 180°, values of axial-planar strike are displayed for 90° either side of 0° strike, to illustrate more clearly the continuation of geometric trends across the north–south direction. (Refer to text for further details.)

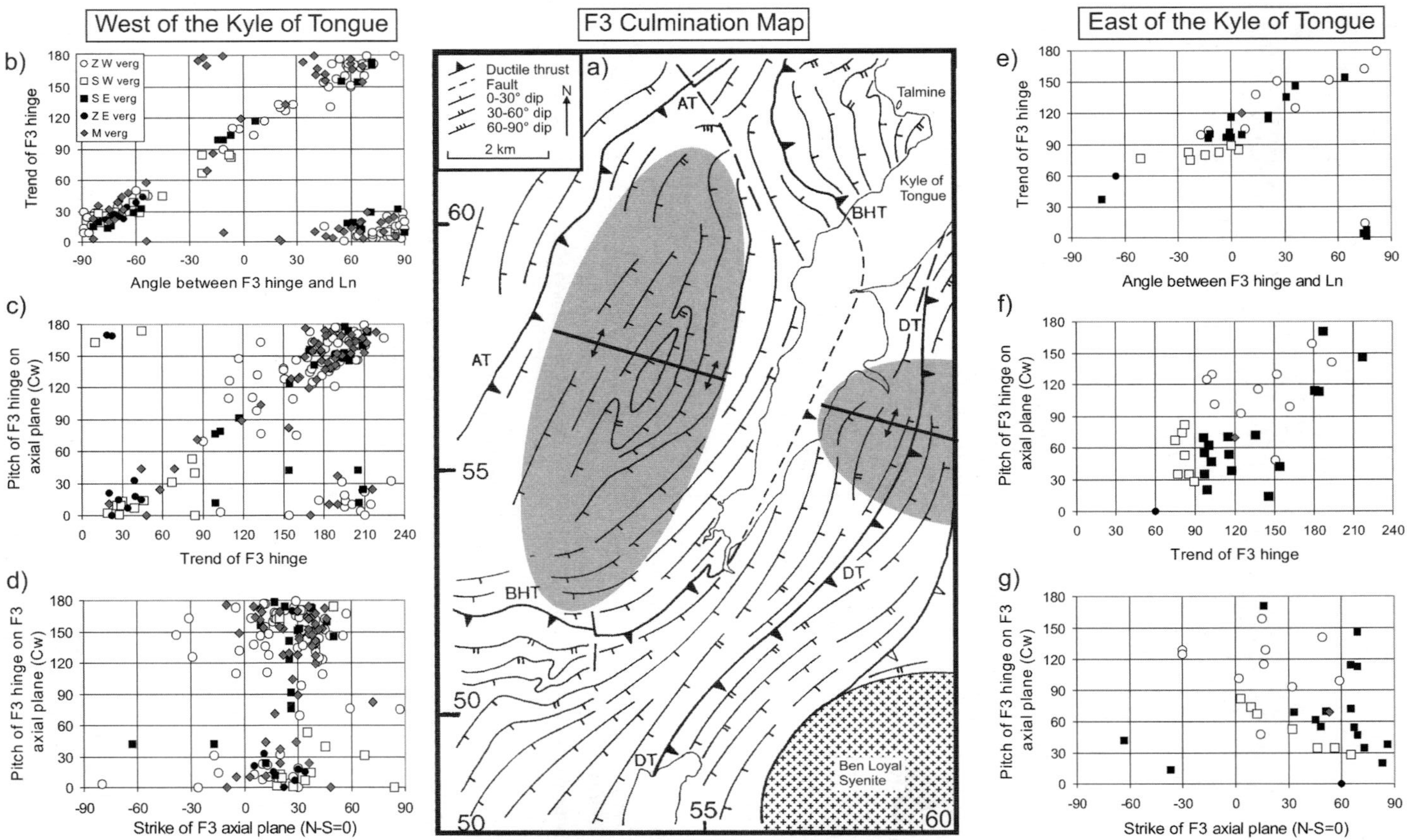

Fig. 7. (**a**) F_3 culmination map showing the location of the major transport-parallel culmination traces to the west and east of the Kyle of Tongue. The elliptical geometry of the flow cells is schematically shown (tone) and displays markedly different trends. Fabric topology plots (FTPs) display F_3 fold data, which may be north- and west-vergent (open symbols), south- and east-vergent (filled symbols) or neutral-vergent (tone) from the west (**b,c,e**) and east (**e,f,g**) of the Kyle of Tongue. Structures associated with F_3 Z folds (circles), S folds (squares) or M folds (diamonds) may be clockwise or anticlockwise (negative) of L_n (**b,e**), whereas the pitch of F_3 fold hinges (**c,d,f,g**) is measured clockwise from axial-planar strike. Whereas F_3 fold trend values are given between 0° and 240°, values of axial-planar strike are displayed for 90° either side of 0° strike, to illustrate more clearly the continuation of geometric trends across the north–south direction. (Refer to text for further details.)

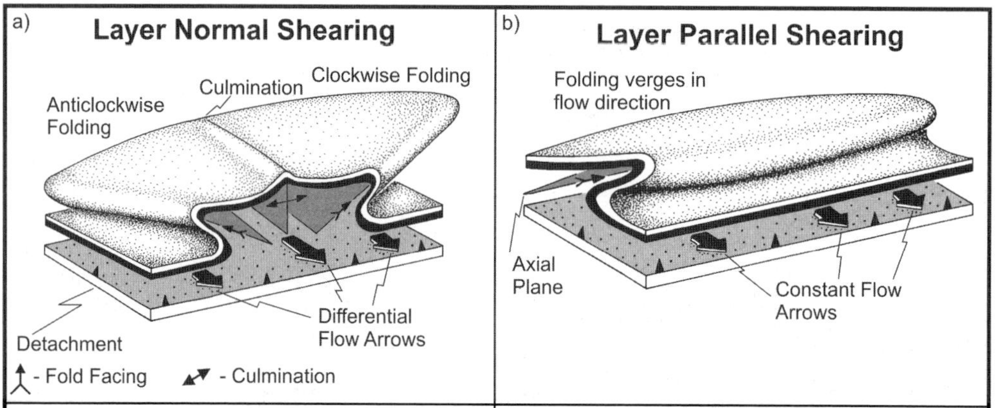

General LNS relationships	**General LPS relationships**
Flow cell ratio >1	Flow cell ratio <1
Ductile equivalent to lateral ramps	Ductile equivalent to frontal ramps
With progressive deformation, folds may evolve into oblique asymmetric folds	With progressive deformation, folds may evolve into curvilinear sheath folds
Arching produces major deflections in strike of overlying layers	Arching produces limited deflections in strike of overlying layers
Fold hinge orientation, vergence and facing	**Fold hinge orientation, vergence and facing**
Cylindrical folds <45° to flow direction	Non-cylindrical folds >45° to flow direction
Reverse asymmetry vergence about flow direction	Normal asymmetry vergence about normal to flow direction
Overall fold vergence at a high angle to flow direction	Overall fold vergence sub-parallel to flow direction
Bimodal fold facing pattern at a high angle to flow direction	Unimodal fold facing pattern sub-parallel to flow direction
Axial-planar orientations	**Axial-planar orientations**
Systematic steepening of axial planes as strike becomes transport-parallel	Systematic steepening of axial planes as strike becomes transport-normal
Z and S fold axial planes intersect parallel to flow direction	Z and S fold axial planes intersect normal to flow direction
M fold hinges and axial planes are sub-parallel to flow direction	M fold hinges and axial planes are sub-normal to flow direction

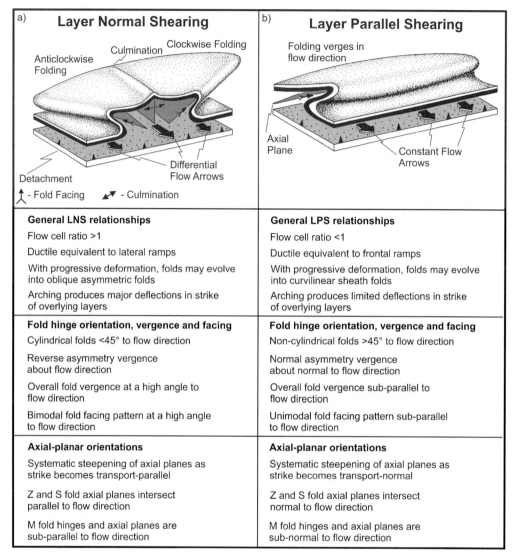

Fig. 8. Summary figure highlighting fold, fabric and facing geometries associated with flow perturbation folding. Flow perturbation folding dominated by layer-normal shearing (LNS) is shown in the left-hand column, and layer-parallel shearing (LPS) is displayed in the right-hand column. Within LNS, the size of the flow arrow represents the velocity of flow, with dextral shear generating anticlockwise trending folds, whereas sinistral shear is associated with folds trending clockwise of flow. The sense of differential LNS reverses across the culmination surface. The general relationships and geometric consequences of each type of flow pattern are discussed further in the text.

direction (Figs 8b and 9b). The sense of hinge rotation reverses across the medial (culmination or depression) surface, with incomplete anticlockwise rotation preserving fold hinge trends clockwise of the transport lineation and partial clockwise rotation leading to anticlockwise hinge trends (Figs 8b and 9b). Clockwise and anticlockwise fold hinge trends are also marked by reversals in the polarity of fold facing about the culmination surface (Figs 8b and 9b). Histograms of fold hinge trends will define a normalized distribution pattern, centred about the normal to the flow direction, whereas associated fold facing defines a unimodal pattern about the

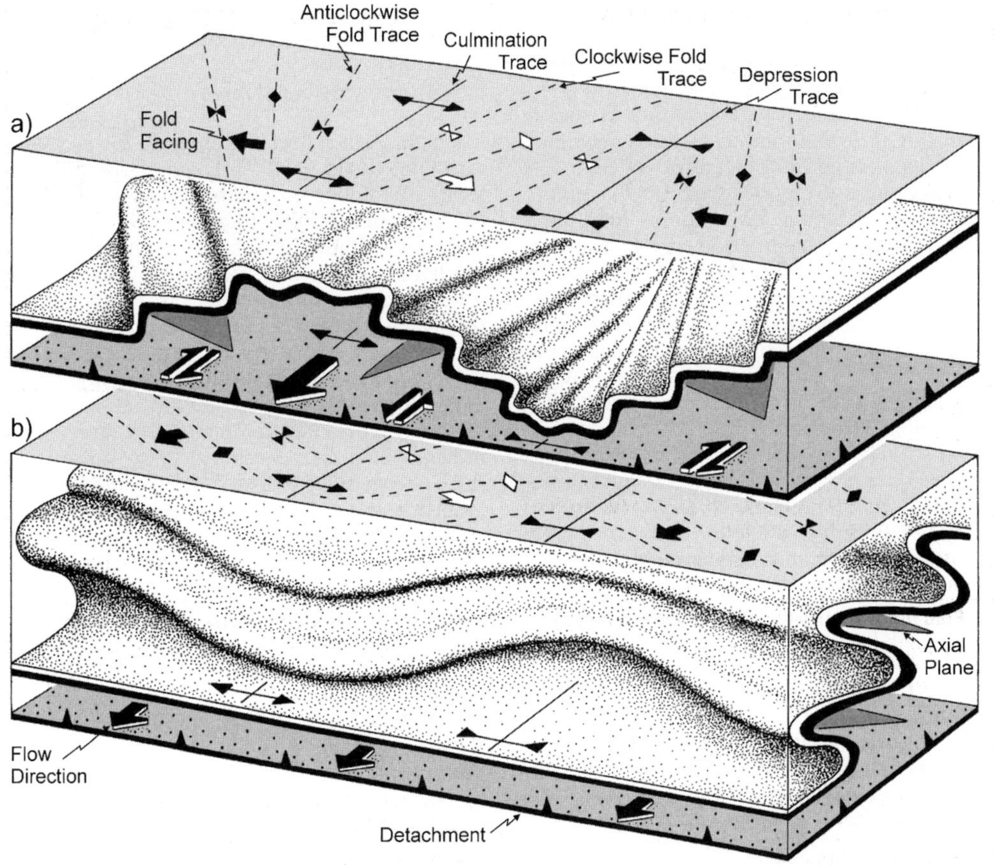

Fig. 9. Schematic 3D illustration of the geometry and orientation of minor structures associated with culmination and depression surfaces in layer-normal shearing (**a**) and layer-parallel shearing (**b**). Culmination surfaces mark regions of surging flow (towards the observer) along the underlying detachment, whereas depression surfaces relate to slackening flow. In (**a**), culminations or depressions separate regions of layer-normal differential dextral shear (shown by half arrows) associated with S folds trending anticlockwise of transport from layer-normal differential sinistral shear relating to Z folds developed clockwise of transport. This results in markedly bimodal facing directions, together with a reversal in the direction of dip of minor axial planes across the culmination or depression surfaces. In (**b**), fold vergence is in the direction of flow, resulting in gentle curvilinear fold traces that typically define facing arcs about the flow direction. (See text for further details.)

flow direction (Figs 8b and 9b). The length/width ratio of individual flow cells within LPS-dominated deformation will typically be <1, with flow cells elongate at high angles to flow.

Summary

During flow perturbation folding, fold traces that define arcuate patterns about the transport direction may be generated by variable components of LPS and LNS, with folding within flow cells balanced by extensional shear bands developed at high angles to transport (Coward & Potts 1983). Flow in which the LPS component dominates will generate flow perturbation folds with fold hinges initiating at high angles to flow, whereas the LNS-dominated flow initiates folding oblique to flow. Thus, close to tight non-cylindrical folds (with hinges typically $>30°$ to flow) reflect LPS whereas close to open cylindrical folds (typically $<30°$ to flow) reflect LNS. Culmination or depression surfaces will correspond to reversals in the sense of differential LNS, with sinistral shear generating Z fold hinges preserved clockwise of the transport direction (looking down plunge) whereas differential dextral LNS will create anticlockwise-trending S fold hinges (Figs 8a,b and 9a,b). The scale and shape of the resultant arcuate fold traces is thus dependent on the degree of partitioning of the two LPS and LNS components and on spatial and temporal variations in rheological parameters, governed by a variety of factors such as strain rate, deformation mechanisms, metamorphic reactions and fluid pressures, together with mechanical anisotropy (see Platt 1983).

Flow perturbation fold patterns may themselves be severely modified and accentuated by continued progressive deformation, resulting in a range of skewed crescentric hinge-lines. Potentially, the parabolic hinge-lines of highly curvilinear folds, previously interpreted as classical sheath folds, could in reality represent one end-member in the continuously evolving hinge morphologies generated by combinations of progressive deformation and (LPS/LNS) perturbations during flow. Progressive deformation (especially that dominated by LPS) will amplify the pre-existing fold arcuate shape and thereby accentuate fabric and facing patterns related to hinge curvature. Increasing components of LNS-dominated flow encourage folds to initiate oblique to transport and to show apparently greater degrees of hinge rotation towards the transport direction for any total shear strain (Coward & Potts 1983). Such LNS-dominated folds will rotate in the same sense for any given differential shear and thereby generate folds that display a consistent sense of obliquity to transport rather than the more variable geometries characteristic of true sheath folds (Alsop & Holdsworth 1999). The exact distribution and frequency of the two transport-parallel and transport-normal fold components is thus governed by (1) the geometry of the flow cell and (2) the role of any subsequent hinge rotation during progressive deformation.

Controls on fold patterns in the Moine Nappe

F_3 fold patterns on either side of the Kyle of Tongue may be interpreted in terms of LPS- and LNS-dominated flow cells described above. To the east of the Kyle of Tongue, F_3 folds are typically developed within 30° of the transport lineation (L_n), suggesting that the area may be dominated by LNS (Fig. 5). Conversely, on the western side of the Kyle of Tongue, the typically high angle (>45°) between L_n and F_3 hinges may reflect a greater component of LPS (see Alsop & Holdsworth 1993). The underlying Achininver Thrust remains unfolded by the major transportnormal folds, suggesting that they may root downwards onto this thrust (Fig. 5). The difference in the LPS and LNS F_3 flow cells on either side of the Kyle of Tongue may reflect a variety of controls, which are discussed below.

Control by structural inheritance

Minor F_2 data collected from both the west and east sides of the Kyle of Tongue are similar in terms of fold hinge trends, axial-planar orientations or mineral lineation trends (L_n; Fig. 4). In both areas, minor F_2 fold hinges define girdles centred about the ESE-plunging L_n. The consistency of minor F_2 folding suggests that it has not significantly influenced subsequent F_3 structures, which display considerable variability across the Kyle of Tongue. In the western area, F_3 folds may have been constrained to develop subparallel to transport with LNS-dominated flow due to the presence of a well-developed linear anisotropy (L_n + near-parallel F_2 axes), which could strongly influence the orientation of subsequent folds and linear fabrics (Watkinson & Cobbold 1981). Interestingly, F_2 hinges are generally more variable in orientation within the F_2 culmination zone to the east of the Kyle of Tongue, whereas the L_n lineation is absent or weak (Holdsworth *et al.* 2001, p. 23).

Control by structural heterogeneity

Major differences in the lithological heterogeneity occur on either side of the Kyle of Tongue. The eastern side displays both acid and mixed Lewisian gneiss, numerous amphibolite sheets and interbanded Moine pelite and psammite, which have been thrust and interfolded at a range of scales. This contrasts starkly with the relatively homogeneous Moine psammites exposed to the west, which lack distinct markers and ductile thrusts (British Geological Survey 1997; Holdsworth *et al.* 2001). In the Talmine and Loch Loyal areas, immediately to the north and east, respectively, a varied and heterogeneous sequence is marked by LNS-dominated deformation (see Alsop *et al.* 1996; Alsop & Holdsworth 2002). This suggests that overall heterogeneity of the system may strongly influence the ability of LNS-dominated flow cells to develop within mylonites and overlying rocks. Heterogeneity (along with fluids and strain rates) may strongly influence the partitioning processes, which will encourage components of LNS flow to develop in the more viscous layers whereas LPS deformation is focused into thinner, less viscous layers (Ridley 1986; Holdsworth 1990; Alsop & Holdsworth 2002). Continued progessive deformation within these weaker units will encourage sheath folds to develop from the originally high-angle LPS folds. The relative heterogeneity of the mixed Lewisian and Moine sequence to the east of the Kyle of Tongue may thus favour LNS-dominated deformation, whereas LPS is encouraged by the relatively homogeneous Moine psammites to the west.

Summary of controls

Unfortunately, the contact between the LPS- and LNS-dominated F_3 flow cells is largely concealed by the Kyle of Tongue. However, at the southern end of the sea loch, south-plunging F_3 folds, suggesting LPS-dominated flow, are developed in both the footwall and hanging wall of the Ben Hope Thrust, which is itself folded on a regional scale by these folds (see Holdsworth 1989, 1990). In this immediate region, the switch from LNS to LPS flow appears to occur across the structurally higher Dherue Thrust (Fig. 7). However, the LNS flow cell to the east of the Kyle of Tongue produces an arching of the Dherue Thrust, and is therefore considered to possibly root downwards onto the underlying Ben Hope Thrust. Thus, LNS- and LPS-dominated F_3 flow cells appear to have different structural relationships to the D_2 Dherue and underlying Ben Hope thrusts.

The relationships described above are to be expected in a foreland-propagating ductile thrust system where 'younger' flow cells, rooting onto structurally lower thrusts, will deform the overlying (older) structures. Complexities concerning the relative ages of flow perturbation folds and ductile thrusts are thus developed both across-strike in the Kyle of Tongue area, and along-strike when thrusts are traced farther north into the Talmine area (see section on Regional setting above, Fig. 3). Some general remarks and observations on flow perturbations are presented below, prior to a wider consideration of folding relationships and their applications in contractional and extensional settings.

Geometric fold patterns about flow perturbations

Around flow perturbations there are ordered, scale-independent geometric relationships between fold hinges, fold vergence, fold facing, and fold axial-planar patterns. The exact nature of these relationships will depend on the relative components of LNS- and LPS-dominated flow. The geometric patterns essential to the interpretation of flow perturbation cells are now described in detail and summarized in Table 1.

Fold hinge patterns about flow perturbations

Fold hinges within flow perturbations may form arcuate traces about the flow direction, with sinistral shear on the flanks of the cell generating folds clockwise of transport, whereas dextral shear on the opposing flank will create folds anticlockwise of transport. Within individual perturbations, fold patterns may vary not only in plan view (X–Y plane) on the surface or zone of detachment, but also within the flowing cell itself. For example, folds often display the greatest obliquity to transport on the upper flanks of the perturbation, with the angle of obliquity gradually reducing towards the underlying detachment (e.g. Alsop & Holdsworth 2002). This results in fold trace patterns converging towards the flow direction, both across-strike towards the basal detachment and along-strike towards the culmination or depression surface. This pattern is a consequence of variable strain gradients associated with differential (LNS) shear, possibly coupled with a component of progressive shearing and associated fold-hinge rotation towards the flow direction of the underlying detachment.

Fold vergence patterns about flow perturbations

Flow perturbation folds are marked by minor fold limb vergence, which reflects the sense of short-limb–long-limb asymmetry and may be described in dip-slip systems in terms of down-plunge S, Z and neutral verging M/W folds. The sense of minor fold limb vergence will reverse across-strike when crossing major fold axial planes, and also along-strike when crossing culmination or depression surfaces (for examples, see Alsop & Holdsworth 2002). In most 'classical' folds, normal asymmetry vergence is developed in which the short limbs of minor folds rotate in an opposite (antithetic) sense to the major fold limb, which then reverses across the axial plane. Reversals in minor fold asymmetry are observed across-strike when crossing axial planes associated with LPS-dominated folds (Figs 8b and 9b). Such normal asymmetry vergence (i.e. towards antiformal structures) is the exact opposite to that observed in LNS, folds, where short limbs of minor folds rotate in a synthetic sense to the major fold limb (Figs 8a and 9a; Alsop & Holdsworth 2002). Major antiformal culminations and synformal depressions generated during LNS are thus marked by reverse asymmetry vergence, which switches across the culmination or depression surface.

Statistically similar attitudes of pre-existing foliations around major LNS culmination or depression surfaces is simply a consequence of reverse asymmetry vergence where the long limbs of minor folds (with opposing vergence) remain

Table 1. *Summary of topological relationships associated with layer-parallel shearing (LPS) and layer-normal shearing (LNS) in both contractional and extensional settings*

Topological parameter	Observation	Cause	Contractional sense of rotations	Contractional topological relationships	Extensional sense of rotations	Extensional topological relationships	LPS > LNS patterns	LNS > LPS patterns	Effect of progressive deformation on LPS or LNS
(a) *Angle between trend of fold hinge and L_n*	**(a)** reduces with greater deformation	Rotation of fold hinge towards *X*	S hinges rotate Cw Z hinges rotate A-Cw	S hinges trend A-Cw of L_n Z hinges trend Cw of L_n	S hinges rotate A-Cw Z hinges rotate Cw	S hinges trend Cw of L_n Z hinges trend A-Cw of L_n	Broad arc of hinge trends (>45°) to L_n	Cluster of hinge trends subparallel (<45°) to L_n	Greater reduction in (a) in LPS setting
(b) *Angle of pitch of fold hinge on axial plane*	**(b)** increases with greater deformation	Rotation of fold hinge and axial plane towards *X* and *X–Y*, respectively	Z hinges and S axial planes rotate A-Cw S hinges and Z axial planes rotate Cw	S axial plane = Cw hinge pitch Z axial plane = A-Cw hinge pitch	S hinges and S axial planes rotate A-Cw Z hinges and Z axial planes rotate Cw	S axial plane = A-Cw hinge pitch Z axial plane = Cw hinge pitchs	Low values (<45°) of hinge pitch	High values (<60°) of hinge pitch	Greater increase in (b) in LPS settings
(c) *Angle of L_n pitch on axial plane*	**(c)** increases with greater deformation	Rotation of axial plane towards *X–Y* plane	S axial planes rotate A-Cw Z axial planes rotate Cw	S axial plane = Cw L_n pitch Z axial plane = A-Cw L_n pitch	S axial planes rotate A-Cw Z axial planes rotate Cw	S axial plane = Cw L_n pitch Z axial plane = A-Cw L_n pitch	High values (>60°) of L_n pitch	Low values (<45°) of L_n pitch	Greater increase in (c) in LNS settings
(d) *Angle between pitch of fold hinge and L_n*	**(d)** reduces with greater deformation	Rotation of fold hinge and axial plane towards *X* and *X–Y*, respectively	Z hinges and S axial planes rotate A-Cw S hinges & Z axial planes rotate Cw	S hinges pitch A-Cw of L_n Z hinges pitch Cw of L_n	S hinges and S axial planes rotate A-Cw Z hinges and Z axial planes rotate Cw	S hinges pitch Cw of L_n Z hinges pitch A-Cw of L_n	Large differences (>60°) in fold hinge and L_n pitch values	Small differences (<30°) in fold hinge and L_n pitch values	Greater reduction in (d) in LPS setting
(e) *Angle between strike of axial plane and L_n trend*	**(e)** increases with greater deformation	Rotation of axial plane towards *X–Y* plane	S axial planes rotate A-Cw Z axial planes rotate Cw	S axial plane strikes A-Cw of L_n Z axial plane strikes Cw of L_n	S axial planes rotate A-Cw Z axial planes rotate Cw	S axial plane strikes A-Cw of L_n Z axial plane strikes Cw of L_n	Axial planes strike subnormal (>60°) to L_n trend	Axial planes strike oblique (<60°) to L_n trend	Greater increase in (e) in LNS settings
(f) *Angle between strikes of axial plane and S_n*	**(f)** reduces with greater deformation	Rotation of axial plane towards *X–Y* plane	S axial planes rotate A-Cw Z axial planes rotate Cw	S axial plane strikes Cw of S_n Z axial plane strikes A-Cw of S_n	S axial planes rotate A-Cw Z axial planes rotate Cw	S axial plane strikes Cw of S_n Z axial plane strikes A-Cw of S_n	Axial planes strike subparallel (<30°) to S_n trend	Axial planes strike oblique (<60°) to S_n trend	Greater reduction in (f) in LNS setting

Table 1. *Continued*

Topological parameter	Observation	Cause	Contractional sense of rotations	Contractional topological relationships	Extensional sense of rotations	Extensional topological relationships	LPS > LNS patterns	LNS > LPS patterns	Effect of progressive deformation on LPS or LNS
(g) *Acute angle between axial plane and S_n*	**(g)** reduces with greater deformation	Rotation of axial plane towards *X–Y* plane	S axial planes rotate A-Cw Z axial planes rotate Cw	S axial plane = Cw of S_n Z axial plane = A-Cw of S_n	S axial planes rotate A-Cw Z axial planes rotate Cw	S axial plane = Cw of S_n Z axial plane = A-Cw of S_n	Axial planes oblique (< 30°) to S_n	Axial planes oblique (< 45°) to S_n	Greater reduction in (g) in LNS setting

When viewed from above, fold hinges and axial planes may trend clockwise (CW) or anticlockwise (A-Cw) of the adjacent mineral lineation (L_n) or foliation (S_n). The effects of continued progressive deformation on fold and fabric relationships are also highlighted in the right-hand column. (Refer to text for further details.)

parallel to one another across the culmination surface (see Fig. 9; Alsop & Holdsworth 2002). Clearly, this is the opposite to, and may be used to discriminate from, normal asymmetry vergence patterns, where the long limbs of minor folds are typically rotated, thus resulting in statistically different attitudes on either side of a major fold.

Fold facing patterns about flow perturbations

Fold facing may be defined as 'the direction, normal to the fold hinge, along the fold axial plane, and towards the younger beds' (Shackleton 1958; Holdsworth 1988). In LNS-dominated systems, fold hinges may develop oblique or subparallel to the flow direction, resulting in pronounced bimodal facing patterns at a high angle to transport (Fig. 9a). Minor folds associated with LPS fold limb vergence will typically develop unimodal facing patterns defining gentle arcs, subparallel to the flow direction (Fig. 9b). In both LPS- and LNS-dominated flow cells, the sense of fold facing (measured relative to the constant flow direction) reverses when crossing the culmination or depression surface. Facing patterns may appear highly skewed if the flow cell itself is asymmetric, or if only one flank of the flow cell is sampled. Culminations will be associated with fold facing-arcs directed outwards towards the margins of the perturbation, whereas depressions will be marked by facing directed inwards towards the centre of the cell (Fig. 9, Table 1).

Axial-planar patterns about flow perturbations

Minor fold axial planes display arcuate traces about the flow direction varying from contractional folds developed at high angles to transport, to fold axial planes associated with differential shear striking subparallel to flow on the flanks of the cells. Within LNS-dominated flow cells associated with thrusting, Z fold axial planes strike clockwise of transport and reflect differential sinistral shear, whereas S fold axial planes will strike anticlockwise of transport, indicating differential dextral shear. Neutral verging M/W fold axial planes typically strike at high angles to the flow direction in LPS settings, whereas in LNS-dominated regimes they typically trend subparallel to the flow direction (for examples, see Alsop & Holdsworth 2002). Within such LNS systems, S, Z and M/W axial planes display a systematic steepening as the axial-planar strike becomes transport-parallel. This

3D axial-planar fanning geometry is thus developed about the flow direction (see below), whereas in LPS settings it will occur about the transport-normal direction (Figs 8 and 9).

Axial-planar patterns also vary within the flow cells. Axial planes display the greatest obliquity to the adjacent folation (S_n) on upper flanks of perturbations, whereas the least obliquity to S_n occurs on the lower flanks of the perturbation (Alsop & Holdsworth 2002). Within LNS systems, this results in a convergent axial-planar trace both across-strike towards the underlying basal detachment zone and along-strike across the culmination or depression surface. The rotation of the axial-planar strike towards the trend of the foliation (S_n) is considered to be a consequence of increasing strain towards the underlying detachment zone and thus reflects deformation gradients within the flow cell.

Flow perturbation folds in different environments

The recognition that variable patterns of displacement in thrusts may result in arcuate fold and fault traces was developed in the Canadian Rockies (Elliott 1976) and Moine Thrust Zone (Fig. 10a) (Coward & Potts 1983). This concept has subsequently been widely applied to other thrust belts in which folds apparently root downwards onto detachments (e.g. Allen *et al.* 2001). These techniques and concepts of flow perturbation may, however, also be used in a variety of other settings in which kinematically coherent systems of flow may develop, such as soft-sediment slumps and mud flows. These near-surface settings are gravity-driven and as such will generate dip-slip-dominated systems of deformation related to extensional tectonics.

Soft-sediment slump sheets are an obvious application of the flow perturbation concept (e.g. Woodcock 1979; Farrell 1984; Strachan 2002; Strachan & Alsop 2006) and even display progressive deformation structures reminiscent of mid-crustal curvilinear sheath folds (e.g. Roberts 1989; Fig. 10b). Hansen (1971) applied many of the detailed concepts of flow perturbations to a landslip in which the top 15 cm of tundra sod had moved downslope in Trollheimen, Norway. Similar arcuate fold patterns developed by differential layer-normal shear about the downslope direction are observed in tundra landslips of West Greenland (Fig. 10c). The slipping of material on a shallow detachment surface has also been recognized in snow slides (e.g. Lajoie 1972), where the variability of fold hinge and axial planar orientations was considered a direct consequence of the amount of slide translation. Flow perturbation fold patterns are also developed on a variety of scales in mud flows stemming from mud volcanoes (Fig. 10d). Channelized flow displays drag on either margin, with the degree of finite differential shear (and hence fold trace curvature) therefore increasing down the individual flow (Fig. 10d). Surges within glacial flow have been considered to produce broadly similar features (e.g. Lawson *et al.* 1994; Hambray & Lawson 2000), and salt glaciers and diapirs also display characteristics of variable flow, which may reflect episodic surges associated with variable precipitation (Talbot 1979; Talbot & Jarvis 1984; Talbot & Aftabi 2004). Fold patterns observed in volcanic lava flows (e.g. Fink 1980) may be complicated by the surface cooling of lava, resulting in a thick chilled skin to the flow. This increasingly results in longer-wavelength folds that refold the earlier lava crenulations, resulting in the classic ropy lava with consistent senses of 'twisting' about the flow direction (e.g. Ramsay & Lisle 2000, p. 939).

Many of the above applications of flow perturbation theory are developed in the near surface and are essentially gravity-driven. As such, the deforming material is typically therefore within an extensional system in which downslope (dip-slip) movement predominates. We shall now examine and compare the geometric relationships of flow perturbations developed in such extensional settings with those previously described from contractional settings.

Geometric comparison of flow perturbations in contractional and extensional settings

The sense of hanging-wall movement relative to the flow perturbation detachment has a number of important implications and geometric consequences that will now be briefly reviewed. Folds and fabrics in both contractional and extensional dip-slip systems of deformation are traditionally described by viewing the geometry of such structures in a down-plunge orientation (e.g. McClay 1987). A direct consequence of this is that folds and fabrics are described when looking down-plunge and in the same direction as transport in extensional settings, whereas in contractional settings the down-plunge construction is viewed in a direction exactly opposite to the transport azimuth.

Fold hinge patterns in contraction and extension

A component of fold hinge rotation towards the flow direction is typically demonstrated by

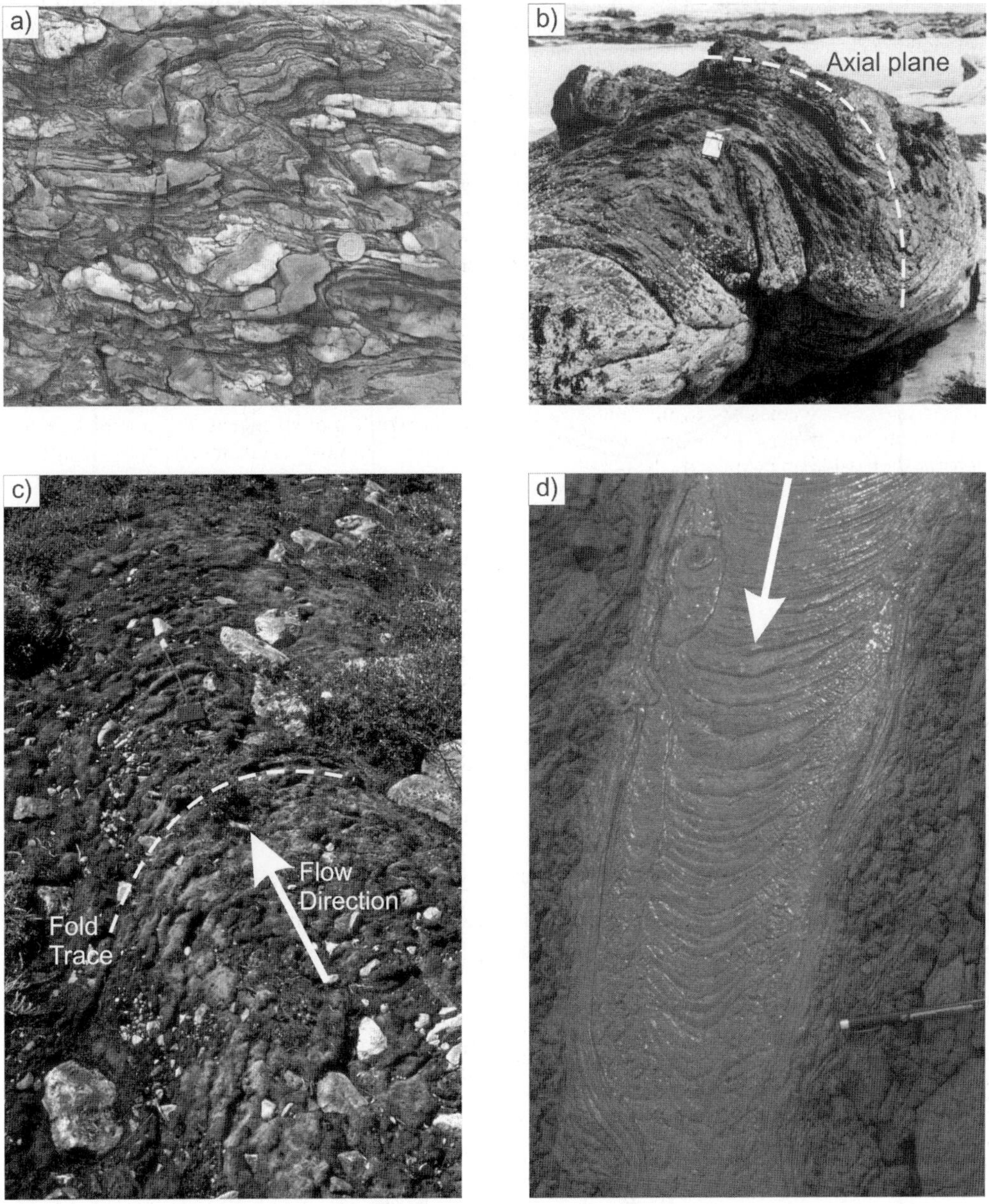

Fig. 10. (**a**) Typical 'F_3' flow perturbation folds refolding the mylonitic foliation (S_n) and mineral lineation (L_n) in mylonitized quartzite of the Moine Thrust Zone, Eriboll. (**b**) Gravity-driven near-surface flow perturbations observed in soft-sediment slump sheets in the Jurassic of northern Scotland. These slumps display curvilinear folding and refold patterns, reminiscent of progressive deformation in mid-crustal settings. (**c**) Arcuate fold patterns form in tundra landslips of West Greenland. Differential layer normal shear (away from the observer) occurs about the downslope direction (marked by the compass chord). (**d**) Mud flows stemming from mud volcanoes in Azerbaijan. Channelized flow (towards the observer) displays drag on either margin, with the degree of finite differential shear (and hence fold trace curvature) therefore increasing down the individual flow.

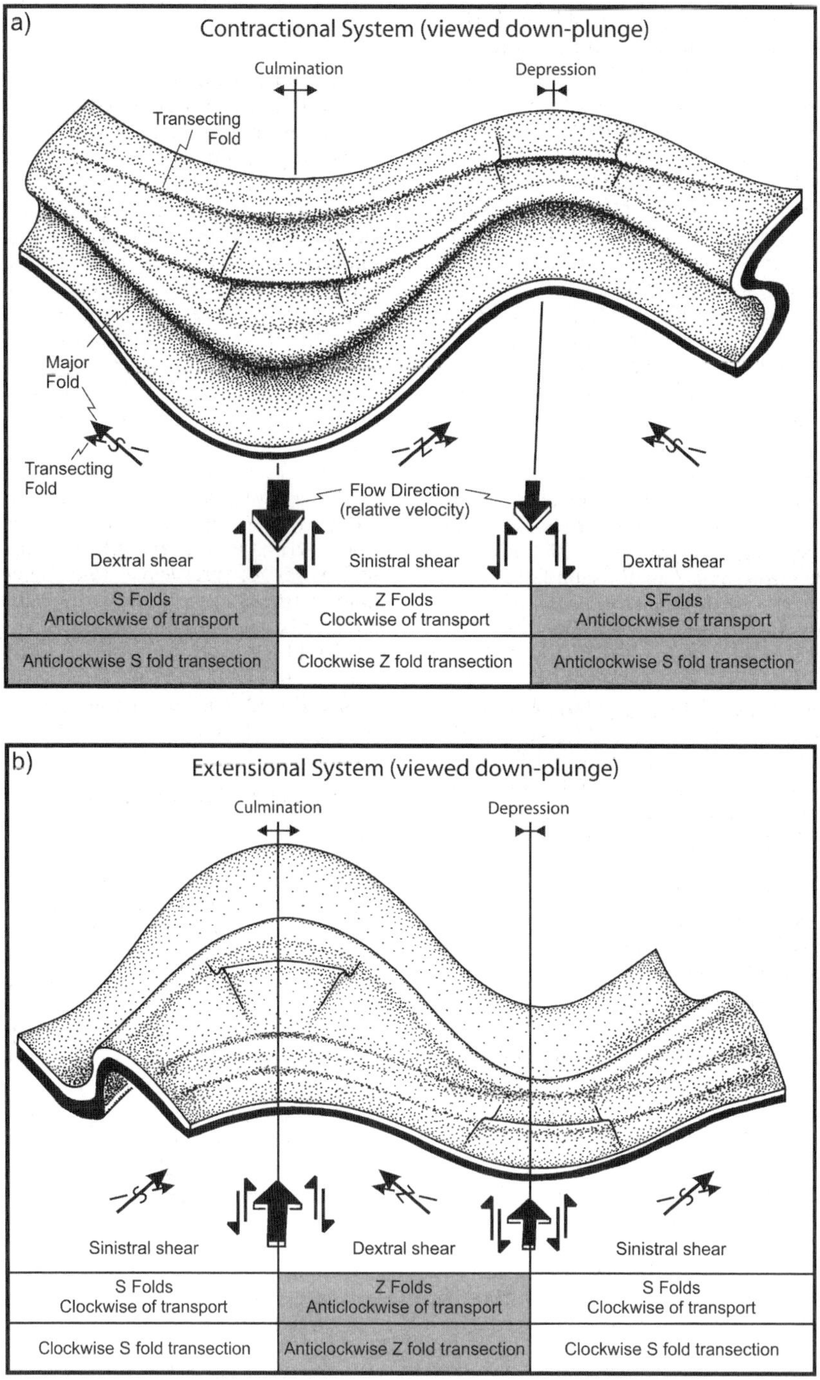

Fig. 11. In both contractional (**a**) and extensional (**b**) systems, differential dextral shear will consistently generate fold hinges anticlockwise of flow (boxes with grey tone), whereas sinistral shear forms folds with a clockwise obliquity. Subsequent folds may overprint older, rotated folds, with the younger folds transecting the older structures with a consistent clockwise or anticlockwise obliquity. Flow directions (and relative velocities) are shown by the black arrows pointing towards the observer in the contractional system (**a**) and away from the viewer in (**b**). (Refer to the text for further details.)

overprinting minor folds on the upper flanks of flow perturbation folds (e.g. Alsop & Holdsworth 2002). These minor folds are considered to relate to the continuing development of the flow perturbation cell, as they consistently display the same sense of asymmetry and obliquity to L_n as the earlier flow folds. However, the overprinting folds make greater angles of obliquity to L_n, such that they display anticlockwise transection of anticlockwise fold hinges and clockwise transection of clockwise fold hinges (Fig. 11). This consistent sense of transection is considered to reflect a degree of hinge rotation during fold amplification and flow cell development.

Differential dextral shear will consistently generate fold hinges anticlockwise of flow in both contractional and extensional settings (Fig. 11a and b). They will, however, display an apparent down-plunge S asymmetry in contractional settings and Z asymmetry in extensional settings. Similarly, differential sinistral shear will consistently generate folds clockwise of flow, which will display apparent Z or S asymmetry in contractional and extensional settings, respectively (Fig. 11a and b). As flow continues, fold hinges may undergo rotation towards the transport direction. The sense of rotation will be governed by the sense of obliquity, with folds generated during dextral and sinistral differential shear undergoing clockwise and anticlockwise rotations, respectively. Subsequent folds may overprint the older rotated folds and will continue to initiate at higher angles to flow. This geometric relationship results in the younger folds consistently transecting the older structures with either a clockwise sense in sinistral shear or anticlockwise sense in dextral shear. These transecting relationships also provide a potential mechanism to determine shear sense.

Fold axial-planar patterns in contraction and extension

The strike of fold axial planes also displays distinct relationships to the trend of flow. Despite the sense of obliquity of S and Z fold hinges reversing from contractional to extensional settings (see Fig. 9a), the sense of axial-planar obliquity relative to the flow direction remains constant (Fig. 12a and b). The strikes of S fold axial planes are consistently anticlockwise of transport, whereas those of Z fold axial planes are clockwise. A consequence of the reversal in fold hinge obliquity and consistency of axial-planar orientations is that the sense in which Z or S fold hinges pitch on their axial planes will reverse from contractional to extensional settings (Fig. 12).

Summary of fabric patterns in contraction and extension

The relationships described above highlight the geometric patterns developed in contractional and extensional systems. Thus, sinistral shear consistently generates fold hinges clockwise of the flow direction, whereas dextral shear generates anticlockwise-trending folds in both contraction and extension. Similarly, the sense of obliquity between the flow direction and the axial-planar strike of Z folds (clockwise) or S folds (anticlockwise) also remains constant in both settings. However, an inherent consequence of the traditional down-plunge view of Z and S fold asymmetry is that S folds appear to be Z folds when viewed from the opposing direction (and vice versa). This geometric artefact results, for example, in the kinematic association of Z fold hinges apparently switching from sinistral to dextral shear in contraction and extension, respectively (Fig. 11a and b). To help alleviate these types of problems, fold hinges whose plunge varies about the horizontal datum may therefore be best described using down-plunge Z and S fold asymmetry coupled where necessary with an additional vergence direction (e.g. west-verging Z fold, etc) as demonstrated by the F_3 folds in the case study area (Fig. 7).

Calculation of flow direction via fold analysis

A variety of techniques have been established, principally in sedimentary environments, that utilize the development of folds to determine the direction of movement. The two existing principal methods for the determination of directions of slumping and hence palaeoslope have been discussed in detail by Woodcock (1979). These are described briefly below prior to a consideration of a recent technique that utilizes the geometric consistency of flow perturbation folds to determine transport.

The mean axis method (MAM)

The mean axis method (MAM) was pioneered by Jones (1940) and takes the (downslope) transport direction as the perpendicular to the calculated mean slump fold axis (which is assumed to verge downslope) (Fig. 13a). Although this technique is simple and easy to apply, the disadvantage is that it fails to allow for differential downslope movements that will result in folds being generated oblique to the palaeoslope. In addition, folds that initiate at high angles to the palaeoslope may subsequently undergo hinge rotation towards

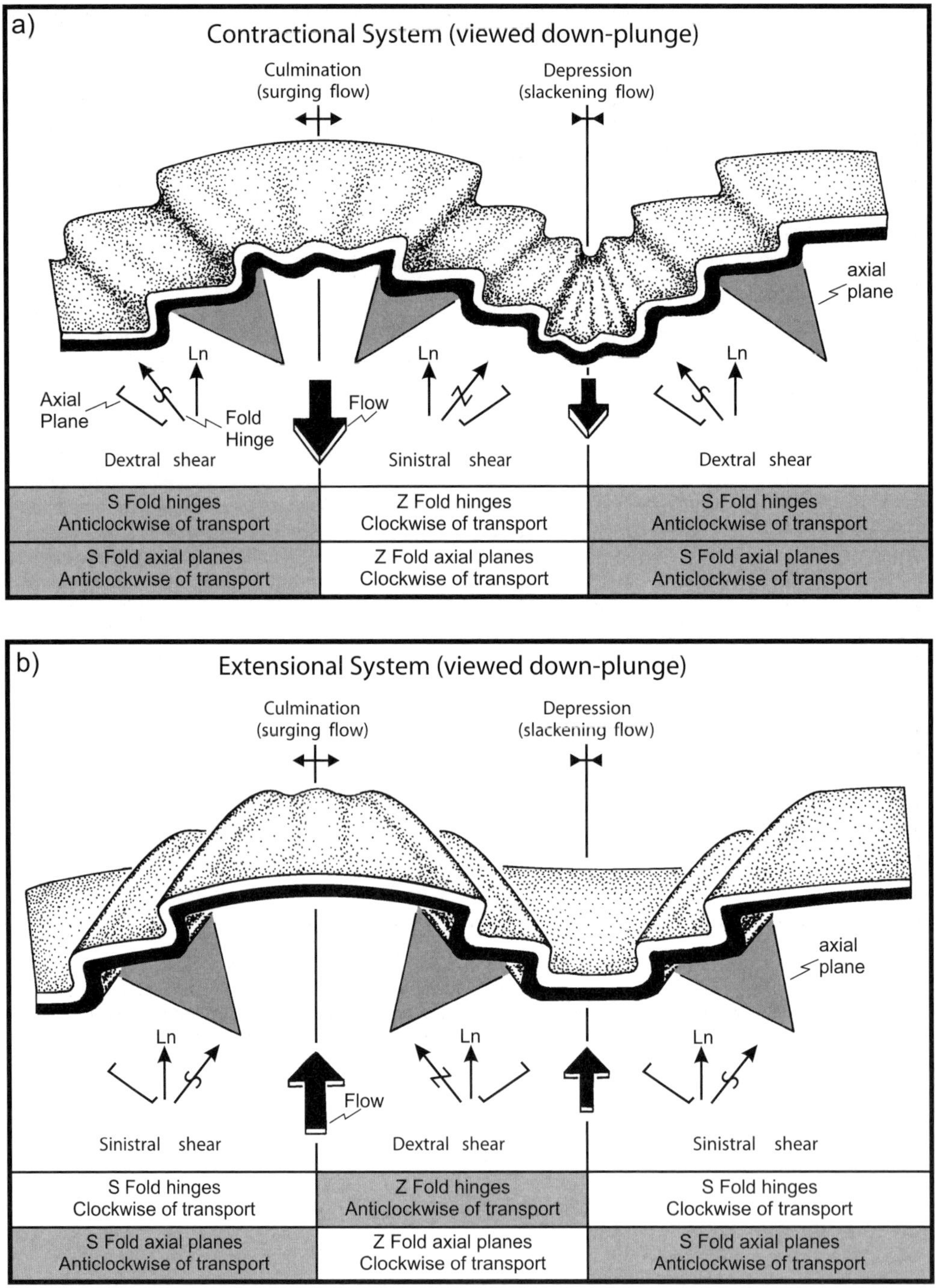

Fig. 12. In both contractional (**a**) and extensional (**b**) systems, the sense of axial planar obliquity remains constant with Z axial planes striking clockwise of transport, whereas S axial planes trend anticlockwise of transport (boxes with grey tone). The sense in which Z or S fold hinges pitch on their axial planes will, however, reverse (relative to L_n) from contractional to extensional systems. Flow directions (and relative velocities) are shown by the black arrows pointing towards the observer in the contractional system in (**a**) and away from the viewer in (**b**). (Refer to the text for further details.)

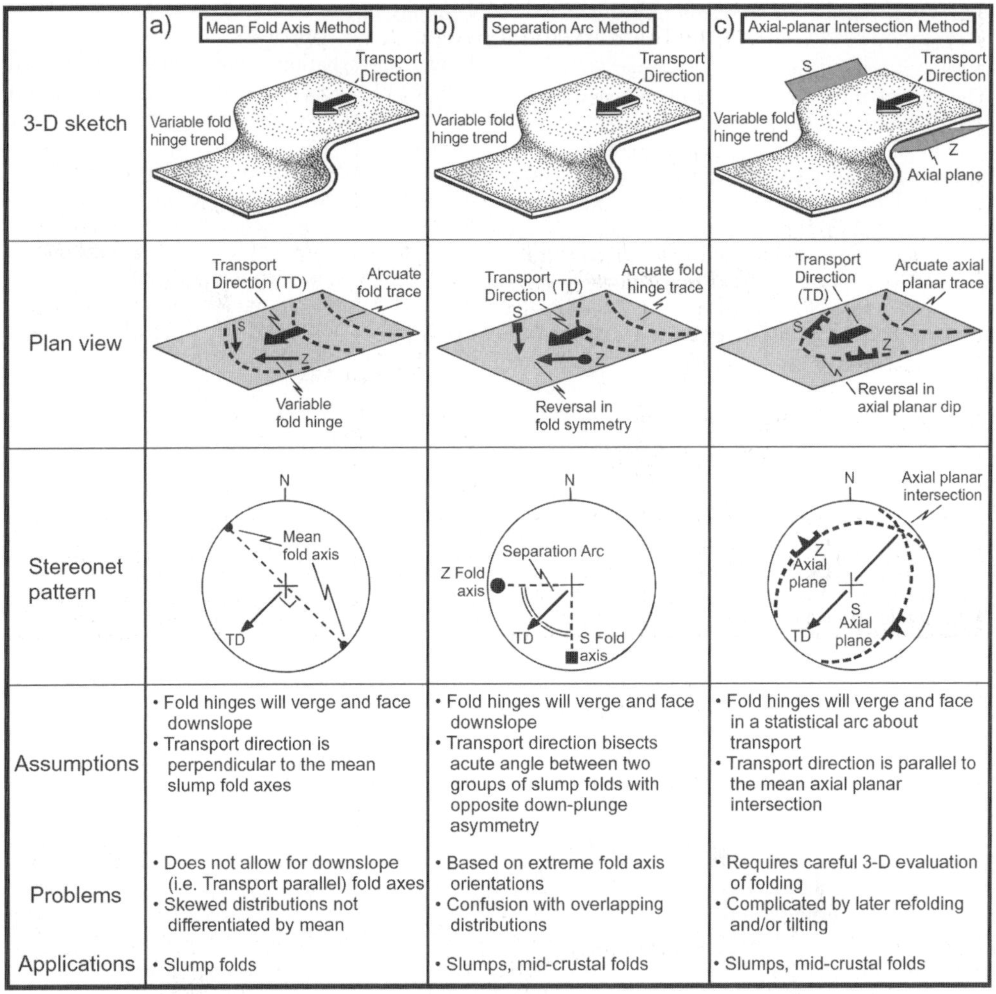

Fig. 13. Summary figure highlighting the principal methods for the determination of transport directions (TD) in a range of settings. The two existing principal techniques are the mean axis method (MAM) and the separation arc method (SAM). The axial-planar intersection method (AIM) utilizes the geometric fanning of mean Z and S fold axial planes about the flow direction to determine transport. (Refer to text for further details.)

the transport direction as the slump translates downslope. This will result in highly curvilinear sheath fold geometries in which the mean fold axis may be oblique (or even subparallel) to the flow direction, thereby resulting in highly inaccurate estimates of palaeoslope.

The separation arc method (SAM)

The second widely employed technique to determine the palaeoslope is the separation arc method (SAM) of Hansen (1965, 1967, 1971), who recognized that folds may display highly variable hinge orientations about the palaeoslope direction. This method assumes that the flow direction will bisect the acute angle between two groups of slump folds that display opposing down-plunge asymmetry (i.e. Z and S vergence; Fig. 13b). The problem with this approach, however, is the over-reliance on extreme fold hinge orientations to effectively constrain the bisecting transport direction. Further confusion may arise if the distribution of the two groups of asymmetric folds is overlapping thus negating any ‘separation arc’ with which to define the transport direction.

The axial-planar intersection method (AIM)

The dip of minor fold axial planes, associated with LNS-dominated flow perturbations, systematically increases as their strike becomes transport-parallel (Alsop & Holdsworth 2002, 2004*b*). This overall fanning arrangement also reflects S fold axial planes striking anticlockwise of transport, whereas Z fold axial planes strike clockwise. Typical flow patterns, incorporating both LPS and LNS components, will thus result in axial planes dipping in a listric arc about the transport direction. This relationship permits the trend and direction of tectonic transport to be reliably defined via the axial-planar intersection method (AIM). This technique involves simply calculating the mean axial planes of Z and S minor folds and then plotting these as great circles on a stereographic projection (Fig. 13c). The point of intersection of the mean Z and S great circles parallels the trend of tectonic transport. Within LPS-dominated settings, variably oriented minor folds, verging in the direction of transport, are marked by a listric arc of axial planes that dip into the flow direction. This sense of asymmetry thus provides the potential means of determining the direction of tectonic transport, which, in this (LPS) case, will form normal to the stereographic intersection of axial planes.

The AIM relies on mean axial-planar orientations for folds with opposing downslope vergence and is therefore statistically more robust than the SAM, which is dependent on extreme 'end-member' orientations to constrain transport. In addition, the AIM utilizes the inherent variability in hinge and axial-planar orientations that develop within a deforming mass undergoing differential shear at the margins. Consequently, it may be more reliable than the MAM, which will become highly inaccurate if folds are initiated during differential shear or are subjected to progressive deformation and rotation during translation.

Thus, the geometric arrangement of mean fold axial planes about the flow direction results in their intersection forming parallel to the transport direction. This relationship permits transport directions to be calculated via the AIM, and also allows comparison with the MAM and SAM, which were devised primarily for the study of soft-sediment deformation and palaeoslope analysis. This variability and fanning of minor fold axial planes allows the AIM to be used to determine transport directions in both contractional and extensional settings, and may also be applicable to a range of other environments in which material may flow and fold.

Conclusions

Flow perturbations are long-lived features capable of generating a range of primary sinuous fold patterns. Systematic analysis of such folds demonstrates that original fabric obliquities may be modified but not reversed during progressive deformation. As a consequence, they are extremely resilient to subsequent shearing and therefore may act as a reliable record of deformation. Fold hinge trends converge both along-strike, when crossing culmination or depression surfaces, and across-strike towards underlying higher strain detachments reflecting 3D variations in deformation within flow cells. Similar patterns are also shown by the strike of associated axial planes. The consistent senses of minor fold transection within flow perturbation folds reflect a component of progressive deformation and allow the sense of layer-normal differential shear to be determined. Such zones of layer-normal shear are also marked by patterns of reverse asymmetry vergence around the culmination, together with reversals in the polarity of structural facing, which is directed outwards from the culmination. In addition, the repeatability of the geometric relationships we have described allows these techniques to act as a reliable and predictive methodology in both contractional and extensional settings. In particular, the statistical fanning of minor fold axial planes within flow perturbations allows the transport direction to be determined by the axial-planar intersection method (AIM).

The (F_2) sheath folds and (F_3) synshearing flow folds in the Kyle of Tongue area share many geometric properties as both are related to the same top-to-the-WNW kinematic regime. Careful analysis of structural data on fabric topology plots demonstrates that curvilinear F_2 folding shows no distinct difference across the Kyle of Tongue marking the Ben Hope Thrust. However, F_3 folds are typically transport-subparallel to the east in the hanging wall of the Ben Hope Thrust and become transport-normal in its footwall. This pattern may be interpreted in terms of a switch from layer-normal shearing (LNS) in the hanging wall to layer-parallel shearing (LPS) in the footwall. The transport-parallel alignment of LPS and LNS culminations across the Ben Hope Thrust, together with the superposition of F_3 on F_2 culminations, indicates a component of structural inheritance on the location of successive perturbations, possibly with its origins in the underlying Lewisian basement rocks (Alsop *et al.* 1996).

The Ben Hope Thrust is folded and arched up by the transport-normal (LPS-dominated) F_3

folds in its footwall, whereas overlying transport-parallel (LNS-dominated) F_3 folds apparently root downwards onto it. These relationships are to be expected in a simple foreland-propagating system of ductile deformation. However, our analysis also shows that folds of similar 'F_3' generation may show variable relationships to underlying detachments both across- and along-strike. Thus, major transport-normal F_3 folds, west of the Kyle of Tongue, root into the underlying Achinver Thrust, which is itself folded farther north along-strike by transport-parallel F_3 folds in the Talmine area that root downwards into the Moine Thrust Zone mylonites. LNS appears to develop most readily in multilayer sequences such as the hanging wall of the Ben Hope Thrust and Talmine Imbricate Zone, whereas LPS typically forms in more homogeneous systems such as developed in psammites to the west of the Kyle of Tongue. Flow perturbation events therefore appear to be spatially recurrent features with long-lived control possible, related to material anisotropy. These relationships serve to highlight the complex interaction between flow cells associated with (1) broadly foreland-propagating deformation, (2) along-strike interplay between adjacent cells, and (3) homogeneous and heterogeneous multilayer sequences associated with LPS- and LNS-dominated flow, respectively.

Fieldwork for this paper was funded under the NERC–BGS Academic Mapping Programme awarded to the University of Durham (Grant F60/G2/36). Subsequent additional funding was provided from the Edinburgh Geological Society and the Irving and Welch bequests of the University of St. Andrews. The authors would especially like to thank R. Strachan and D. Cheer, together with the field trip participants of the 2002 shear zones meeting and the 2003 Highland workshop, for many interesting discussions concerning folding patterns in the Moine Nappe. Finally, we would like to thank H. Fossen and G. Lloyd for careful and constructive reviews of the manuscript.

References

ALLEN, M. B., ALSOP, G. I. & ZHEMCHUZHNIKOV, V. G. 2001. Dome and basin refolding associated with transpressive inversion along the Karatau Fault System, southern Kazakstan. *Journal of the Geological Society, London*, **158**, 83–95.

ALSOP, G. I. 1992. Progressive deformation and the rotation of contemporary fold axes in the Ballybofey Nappe, northwest Ireland. *Geological Journal*, **27**, 271–283.

ALSOP, G. I. 1994. Relationships between distributed and localised shear in the tectonic evolution of a Caledonian fold and thrust zone, northwest Ireland. *Geological Magazine*, **131**, 123–136.

ALSOP, G. I. & HOLDSWORTH, R. E. 1993. The distribution, geometry and kinematic significance of Caledonian buckle folds in the western Moine Nappe, northwestern Scotland. *Geological Magazine*, **130**, 353–362.

ALSOP, G. I. & HOLDSWORTH, R. E. 1999. Vergence and facing patterns in large-scale sheath folds. *Journal of Structural Geology*, **21**, 1335–1349.

ALSOP, G. I. & HOLDSWORTH, R. E. 2002. The geometry and kinematics of flow perturbation folds. *Tectonophysics*, **350**, 99–125.

ALSOP, G. I. & HOLDSWORTH, R. E. 2004*a*. Shear zones — an introduction and overview. *In*: ALSOP, G. I., HOLDSWORTH, R. E., MCCAFFREY, K. J. W. & HAND, M. (eds) *Flow Processes in Faults and Shear Zones*. Geological Society, London, Special Publications, **224**, 1–9.

ALSOP, G. I. & HOLDSWORTH, R. E. 2004*b*. Shear zone folds: records of flow perturbation or structural inheritance? *In*: ALSOP, G. I., HOLDSWORTH, R. E., MCCAFFREY, K. J. W. & HAND, M. (eds) *Flow Processes in Faults and Shear Zones*. Geological Society, London, Special Publications, **224**, 177–199.

ALSOP, G. I. & HOLDSWORTH, R. E. 2004*c*. The geometry and topology of natural sheath folds: a new tool for structural analysis. *Journal of Structural Geology*, **26**, 1561–1589.

ALSOP, G. I. & HOLDSWORTH, R. E. 2005. Discussion on evidence for non-plane strain flattening along the Moine Thrust, Loch Strath nan Aisinnin, North-West Scotland by Strine & Wojtal. *Journal of Structural Geology*, **27**, 781–784.

ALSOP, G. I. & HOLDSWORTH, R. E. 2006. Sheath folds as discriminators of bulk strain type. *Journal of Structural Geology*, **28**, 1588–1606.

ALSOP, G. I., HOLDSWORTH, R. E. & STRACHAN, R. A. 1996. Transport-parallel cross folds within a mid-crustal Caledonian thrust stack, northern Scotland. *Journal of Structural Geology*, **18**, 783–790.

BELL, T. H. 1978. Progressive deformation and reorientation of fold axes in a ductile mylonite zone: the Woodroffe thrust. *Tectonophysics*, **44**, 285–321.

BERTHÉ, D. & BRUN, J. P. 1980. Evolution of folds during progressive shear in the South Amorican Shear Zone, France. *Journal of Structural Geology*, **2**, 127–133.

BRITISH GEOLOGICAL SURVEY 1997. *Tongue, Scotland 114E.* Solid Geology, 1:50 000.

BRITISH GEOLOGICAL SURVEY 2002. *Loch Eriboll, Scotland 114W.* Solid Geology, 1:50 000.

BRYANT, B. & REED, J. C. 1969. Significance of lineation and minor folds near major thrust faults in the southern Appalachians and the British and Norwegian Caledonides. *Geological Magazine*, **106**, 412–429.

CARRERAS, J., ESTRADA, A. & WHITE, S. 1977. The effect of folding on the *c*-axis fabrics of a quartz mylonite. *Tectonophysics*, **39**, 3–24.

COBBOLD, P. R. & QUINQUIS, H. 1980. Development of sheath folds in shear regimes. *Journal of Structural Geology*, **2**, 119–126.

COWARD, M. P. 1982. Surge zones in the Moine thrust zone of NW Scotland. *Journal of Structural Geology*, **4**, 247–256.

COWARD, M. P. 1983. The thrust and shear zones of the Moine thrust zone and the NW Scottish Caledonides. *Journal of the Geological Society, London*, **140**, 795–811.

COWARD, M. P. 1984. The strain and textural history of thin-skinned tectonic zones: examples from the Assynt region of the Moine Thrust zone, NW Scotland. *Journal of Structural Geology*, **6**, 89–99.

COWARD, M. P. & KIM, J. H. 1981. Strain within thrust sheets. *In*: MCCLAY, K. R. & PRICE, N. J. (eds) *Thrust and Nappe Tectonics.* Geological Society, London, Special Publications, **9**, 275–292.

COWARD, M. P. & POTTS, G. J. 1983. Complex strain patterns developed at the frontal and lateral tips to shear zones and thrust zones. *Journal of Structural Geology*, **5**, 383–399.

DOWNING, K. N. & COWARD, M. P. 1981. The Okahandja Lineament and its significance for Damaran tectonics in Namibia. *Geologische Rundshau*, **70**, 972–1000.

DUBEY, A. K. & COBBOLD, P. R. 1977. Noncylindrical flexural slip folds in nature and experiment. *Tectonophysics*, **38**, 223–239.

ELLIOT, D. 1976. The energy balance and deformation mechanisms of thrust sheets. *Philosophical Transactions of the Royal Society of London*, **283**, 289–312.

ESCHER, A. & WATTERSON, J. 1974. Stretching fabrics, folds and crustal shortening. *Tectonophysics*, **22**, 223–231.

EVANS, D. J. & WHITE, S. H. 1984. Microstructural and fabric studies from the rocks of the Moine Nappe, Eriboll, NW Scotland. *Journal of Structural Geology*, **6**, 369–389.

FARRELL, S. G. 1984. A dislocation model applied to slump structures, Ainsa Basin, South Central Pyrenees. *Journal of Structural Geology*, **6**, 727–736.

FINK, J. 1980. Surface folding and viscosity of rhyolite flows. *Geology*, **8**, 250–254.

FOSSEN, H. & RYKKELID, E. 1990. Shear zone structures in the Øygarden area, West Norway. *Tectonophysics*, **174**, 385–397.

GHOSH, S. K. & RAMBERG, H. 1968. Buckling experiments on intersecting fold patterns. *Tectonophysics*, **5**, 89–105.

GHOSH, S. K. & SENGUPTA, S. 1984. Successive development of plane noncylindrical folds in progressive deformation. *Journal of Structural Geology*, **6**, 703–709.

GHOSH, S. K. & SENGUPTA, S. 1987. Progressive development of structures in a ductile shear zone. *Journal of Structural Geology*, **9**, 277–287.

GOSCOMBE, B. 1991. Intense non-coaxial shear and the development of mega-scale sheath folds in the Arunta Block, Central Australia. *Journal of Structural Geology*, **13**, 299–318.

HAMBREY, M. J. & LAWSON, W. 2000. Structural styles and deformation fields in glaciers: a review. *In*: MALTMAN, A. J., HUBBARD, B. & HAMBREY, M. J. (eds) *Deformation of Glacial Materials.* Geological Society, London, Special Publications, **176**, 59–83.

HANSEN, E. 1965. Methods of deducing slip-line orientations from the geometry of folds. *Carnegie Institution of Washington Yearbook*, **65**, 387–405.

HANSEN, E. 1967. Natural slip folds in which the fold axes nearly parallel the slip lines. *Carnegie Institution of Washington Yearbook*, **66**, 536–538.

HANSEN, E. 1971. *Strain Facies.* Springer, New York.

HOLDSWORTH, R. E. 1988. The stereographic analysis of facing. *Journal of Structural Geology*, **10**, 219–223.

HOLDSWORTH, R. E. 1989. The geology and structural evolution of a Caledonian fold and ductile thrust zone, Kyle of Tongue region, Sutherland, N. Scotland. *Journal of the Geological Society, London*, **146**, 809–823.

HOLDSWORTH, R. E. 1990. Progressive deformation structures associated with ductile thrusts in the Moine Nappe, Sutherland, N. Scotland. *Journal of Structural Geology*, **12**, 443–452.

HOLDSWORTH, R. E. & GRANT, C. J. 1990. Convergence-related 'dynamic spreading' in a mid-crustal ductile thrust zone: a possible orogenic wedge model. *In*: KNIPE, R. J. & RUTTER, E. H. (eds) *Deformation Mechanisms, Rheology and Tectonics.* Geological Society, London, Special Publications, **54**, 491–500.

HOLDSWORTH, R. E. & ROBERTS, A. M. 1984. A study of early curvilinear fold structures and strain in the Moine of the Glen Garry region, Inverness-shire. *Journal of the Geological Society, London*, **141**, 327–338.

HOLDSWORTH, R. E., STRACHAN, R. A. & ALSOP, G. I. 2001. *Geology of the Tongue District.* Memoirs of the British Geological Survey, Sheet 114E (Scotland).

HOLDSWORTH, R. E., ALSOP, G. I. & STRACHAN, R. A. 2007. Tectonic stratigraphy and structural continuity of the northernmost Moine Thrust Zone and Moine Nappe, Scottish Caledonides. *In*: RIES, A. C., BUTLER, R. W. H. & GRAHAM, R. H. (eds) *Deformation of the Continental Crust: The Legacy of Mike Coward.* Geological Society, London, Special Publications, **272**, 121–142.

JONES, O. T. 1940. The geology of the Colwyn Bay district: study of submarine slumping during the Salopian Period. *Quarterly Journal of the Geological Society of London*, **95**, 335–382.

LACASSIN, R. & MATTAUER, M. 1985. Kilometre-scale sheath fold at Mattmark and implications for transport directions in the Alps. *Nature*, **315**, 739–742.

LAJOIE, J. 1972. Slump fold axis orientations: an indication of paleoslope? *Journal of Sedimentary Petrology*, **42**, 584–586.

LAWSON, W. J., SHARP, M. J. & HAMBRAY, M. J. 1994. The structural geology of a surge-type glacier. *Journal of Structural Geology*, **16**, 1447–1462.

MCCLAY, K. R. 1987. *The Mapping of Geological Structures.* Geological Society, London, Handbook.

MIES, J. W. 1991. Planar dispersion of folds in ductile shear zones and kinematic interpretation of fold hinge girdles. *Journal of Structural Geology*, **13**, 281–297.

MINNIGH, L. D. 1979. Structural analysis of sheath-folds in a meta-chert from the Western Italian Alps. *Journal of Structural Geology*, **1**, 275–282.

PLATT, J. P. 1983. Progressive refolding in ductile shear zones. *Journal of Structural Geology*, **5**, 619–622.

QUINQUIS, H., AUDREN, C., BRUN, J. P. & COBBOLD, P. R. 1978. Intense progressive shear in Ile de Groix blueschists and compatibility with subduction or obduction. *Nature*, **273**, 43–45.

RAMSAY, J. G. 1980. Shear zone geometry: a review. *Journal of Structural Geology*, **2**, 83–99.

RAMSAY, J. G. & LISLE, R. 2000. *The Techniques of Modern Structural Geology. Volume 3: Applications of continuum Mechanics in Structural Geology*. Academic Press, London.

RHODES, S. & GAYER, R. A. 1977. Non-cylindrical folds, linear structures in the X-direction and mylonite developed during translation of the Caledonian Kalak Nappe Complex of Finnmark. *Geological Magazine*, **114**, 329–341.

RIDLEY, J. 1986. Parallel stretching lineations and fold axes oblique to displacement direction — a model and observations. *Journal of Structural Geology*, **8**, 647–654.

ROBERTS, A. 1989. Fold and thrust structures in the Kintradwell 'Boulder beds', Moray Firth. *Scottish Journal of Geology*, **25**, 173–186.

SANDERSON, D. J. 1973. The development of fold axes oblique to the regional trend. *Tectonophysics*, **16**, 55–70.

SHACKLETON, R. M. 1958. Downward-facing structures of the Highland Border. *Quarterly Journal of the Geological Society of London*, **113**, 361–392.

SKJERNAA, L. 1980. Rotation and deformation of randomly oriented planar and linear structures in progressive simple shear. *Journal of Structural Geology*, **2**, 101–109.

SKJERNAA, L. 1989. Tubular folds and sheath folds: definitions and conceptual models for their development with examples from the Grapesvare area, northern Sweden. *Journal of Structural Geology*, **11**, 689–703.

STRACHAN, L. J. 2002. Slump-initiated and controlled syndepositional sandstone remobilization: an example from the Namurian of County Clare, Ireland. *Sedimentology*, **49**, 25–41.

STRACHAN, R. A., SMITH, M., HARRIS, A. L. & FETTES, D. J. 2002. The Northern Highland and Grampian Terranes. *In*: TREWIN, N. (ed.) *Geology of Scotland.* Geological Society, London, 81–147.

STRACHAN, L. J. & ALSOP, G. I. 2006. Slump folds as estimators of palaeoslope: a case study from the Fisherstreet slump of County Clare, Ireland. *Basin Research*, **18**, 451–470.

TALBOT, C. J. 1979. Fold trains in a glacier of salt in southern Iran. *Journal of Structural Geology*, **1**, 5–18.

TALBOT, C. J. & AFTABI, P. 2004. Geology and models of salt extrusion at Qum Kuh, central Iran. *Journal of the Geological Society, London*, **161**, 321–334.

TALBOT, C. J. & JARVIS, R. J. 1984. Age, budget and dynamics of an active salt extrusion in Iran. *Journal of Structural Geology*, **6**, 521–533.

WATKINSON, A. J. & COBBOLD, P. R. 1981. Axial directions of folds in rocks with linear/planar fabrics. *Journal of Structural Geology*, **3**, 211–217.

WILLIAMS, G. D. 1978. Rotation of contemporary folds into the X direction during overthrust processes in Laksefjord, Finnmark. *Tectonophysics*, **48**, 29–40.

WOODCOCK, N. H. 1979. The use of slump structures as palaeoslope orientation estimators. *Sedimentology*, **26**, 83–99.

Structural evolution of the Achnashellach Culmination, southern Moine Thrust Belt: testing the duplex model

R. W. H. BUTLER[1], S. J. MATTHEWS[2] & R. K. MORGAN[3]

[1]*Institute of Geophysics and Tectonics, University of Leeds, Leeds LS2 9JT, UK (e-mail: butler@earth.leeds.ac.uk)*

[2]*BP Exploration plc, Chertsey Road, Sunbury on Thames TW16 7LN, UK*

[3]*Veritas DGC Ltd., Crompton Way, Crawley RH10 9QN, UK*

Abstract: The Achnashellach Culmination is one of the major structures of the Moine Thrust Belt. As with other culminations in the belt, it is formed by a stack of imbricate thrusts. Up to 1 km of Torridon Group sediments, together with a further 200–250 m of Cambrian strata, are repeated up to 10 times, but with ramp-on-ramp thrust geometries. Thus structural thickening was chiefly achieved by thick thrust sheets with individually and aggregated displacements that are substantially lower than elsewhere in the thrust belt. The culmination is limited on its flanks by lateral ramps that climb section out of Torridon Group and up into Cambrian strata. To the north the imbricate thrusts may be deduced to branch onto the major Kinlochewe Thrust. To the south the imbricates are represented only by stacked Durness Limestone. The northward-climbing lateral ramp coincides with a major Precambrian structure, the Loch Maree Fault, which controls the thickness of Torridonian strata preserved beneath the sub-Cambrian unconformity, a rare example of basement influence on thrust system geometry within the Moine Thrust Belt. The imbricates of the Achnashellach Culmination show back-steepening and have bulged up the overriding Kishorn and Kinlochewe thrust sheets. However, these structurally higher level tectonic units slice across imbricate structures in their footwalls. Elsewhere high-level thrusts are folded by some parts of underlying imbricates. Collectively these relationships are not compatible with classical duplex models. They are explained better by models of quasi-synchronous slip on imbricate thrusts. Discordant relationships beneath major thrust sheets, including those that cut down stratigraphic section in the transport direction, can be explained by such models without necessitating low-angle extensional faulting within the thrust belt.

The duplex model has been widely used to explain and predict thrust system structure since the term was first coined by Dahlstrom (1970). The model was formalized by Boyer & Elliott (1982), who proposed a strict array of geometric attributes and a precise structural evolution. Since then, the model has been widely used to explore the geometry of thrust belts worldwide. Much of this application has been uncritical, commonly because the structural geometries are not well enough exposed to provide tests or because the settings themselves demand substantial simplifying approximations in the structural geometry. The purpose of this paper is to test the duplex model and propose modifications where necessary, using a particularly well-exposed, but since the work of Peach *et al.* (1907) undescribed, thrust system. First, however, it is appropriate to examine the model itself.

Boyer & Elliott's (1982) duplex model (Fig. 1) consists of an array of imbricate thrusts bounded upwards by a roof thrust and downwards by a floor thrust. The whole structure is considered to develop through sequential imbrication of the previously undeformed footwall to a major thrust sheet. The process effectively transfers rocks from what was in the foreland into the thrust belt. Each imbricate thrust grows in undeformed strata, cutting a new segment of floor thrust and branching onto the roof. Consequently each thrust cuts up-section in both hanging wall and footwall. The roof thrust glides on the youngest strata involved in the imbricates whereas the floor thrust glides in the oldest. During the evolution of the structure, only the lowest thrust surface is actively accumulating slip, so earlier thrusts are folded and the intervening imbricate slices bulged up as new imbricate slices are accreted onto the growing thrust complex. Consequently, the duplex model makes clear predictions of structural geometry, the distribution of displacements and evolution of thrust arrays.

The study area comes from the Moine Thrust Belt (Fig. 2), long a testing ground for models of thrust system geometry. Elliott & Johnson (1980)

From: RIES, A. C., BUTLER, R. W. H. & GRAHAM, R. H. (eds) 2007. *Deformation of the Continental Crust: The Legacy of Mike Coward.* Geological Society, London, Special Publications, **272**, 103–120.

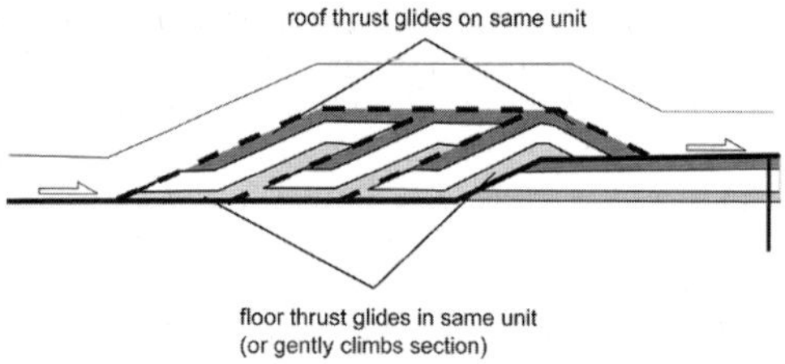

Fig. 1. Structural attributes of the duplex model of Boyer & Elliott (1982), seen in profile. In this model the inactive thrust segments are shown by dashed lines and the active thrust by a continuous line. It should be noted that the roof thrust is bulged up, although significant segments of it are subhorizontal.

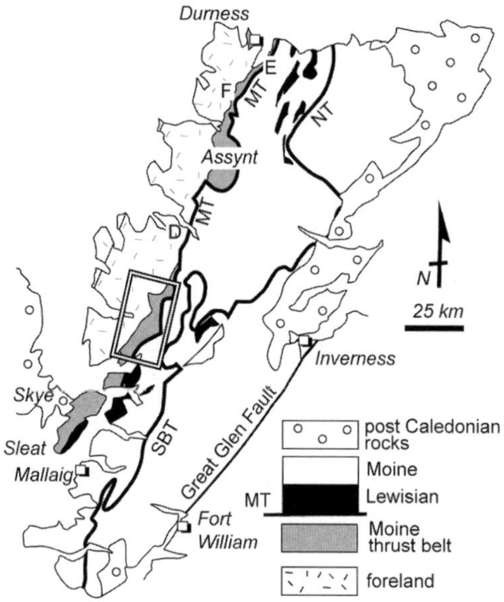

Fig. 2. Simplified map of the Moine Thrust Belt in NW Scotland, showing the location of the Achnashellach Culmination (boxed area). MT, Moine Thrust; major Caledonian thrusts within the Moine Thrust Sheet are indicated (NT, Naver Thrust; SBT, Sgurr Beag Thrust), as are key locations within the thrust belt (D, Dundonnel; E, Eriboll; F, Foinaven).

applied the duplex model widely through this system, and subsequently the Foinaven area (Fig. 2) was cited as the type area for duplex structures (Boyer & Elliott 1982). However, since then other studies have shown that many of the imbricate systems of the Moine Thrust Belt do not conform simply to the duplex model. Coward (1984) showed that many roof thrusts are commonly cut by other thrusts that climb from their footwalls (a geometric process termed 'breaching'; Butler 1987). Elsewhere, the footwalls to thrusts considered by Elliott & Johnson (1980) as forming duplex roofs can be demonstrated to truncate the underlying imbricates (e.g. in southern Assynt, Coward 1985). These 'overstep' geometries have also been interpreted in terms of late-stage, low-angle extensional faults, parts of 'surge zones' (Coward 1982). Recently, some of these architectures have been reappraised and interpreted in terms of synchronous, rather than sequential, thrust activity within imbricate fans (Butler 2004), where roof thrusts both truncate and are folded by imbricates in their footwalls.

Although the Moine Thrust Belt has inspired many of the developments and modifications of the duplex model, all these researches have focused on just the northern half of the system. Descriptions of structural geometry are provided here that are then used to deduce the geometric evolution of folds and thrusts from part of the southern Moine Thrust Belt, the Achnashellach Culmination (Fig. 2).

Background and setting

The Moine Thrust Belt defines the NW limit of penetrative Caledonian deformation in NW Scotland. Following the approach of Elliott & Johnson (1980), the Moine Thrust is considered here to be the structure that carries Moine metasediments and their Lewisianoid basement onto rocks of the former Caledonian foreland, namely Lewisian, Torridonian and Cambro-Ordovician strata (together with any minor intrusions these units may host). This structure was mapped from Cape Wrath to Skye (Fig. 2) by Peach *et al.* (1907), who considered it to be a near-continuous structure, albeit locally offset by what are now known to be late- to post-Caledonian faults (e.g. the Strathcarron Fault). Regionally, thrusting is generally assumed to have been towards the WNW, parallel to shear directions determined from deflected *Skolithos*, and the axis of stretching lineations in mylonites.

One of the principal reasons for successful descriptions of structural geometry in the Moine Thrust Belt is the simplicity of the rock units involved in the deformation (Fig. 3). For the most part, the structures are developed in a well-differentiated succession of Cambrian sediments that generally show remarkable lateral persistence in facies and thickness. Regrettably, the terminology of these units has changed over the years. Here we follow current usage (Park *et al.* 2002). The oldest Cambrian strata in NW Scotland are quartzites of the Eriboll Formation. This divides into two members of approximately equal thickness totalling about 200 m. The oldest are shallow-marine tidal sandstones with

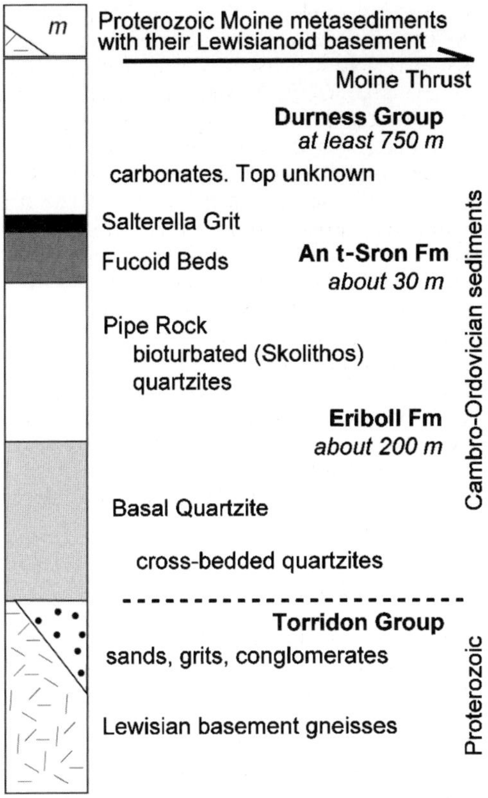

Fig. 3. Simplified stratigraphy for the Moine Thrust Belt, modified after Park *et al.* (2002), with thicknesses of An t-Sron and Eriboll Formation rocks appropriate to the Achnashellach area.

prominent cross-bedding (the Basal Quartzite Member) whereas the upper half is intensely bioturbated with extensive *Skolithos* and rare *Monocraterion* (the Pipe Rock Member). Above lies a more varied sequence of brown-weathering sands, shales and thin dolostones (the Fucoid Beds, *c.* 20 m thick) and a capping quartzite (the Salterella Grit, *c.* 8 m thick; collectively the An t-Sron Formation). Above lies a near-exclusively carbonate sequence (the Durness Group, colloquially termed the 'Durness Limestone') that is divided into five formations. Only the lower two are of concern here: the Ghrudaidh and Eilean Dubh formations. The total thickness of the Durness Limestone is believed to have exceeded 750 m (Park *et al.* 2002) but in general only a few metres of its basal part, the Ghrudaidh Formation, are preserved within the thrust belt. Younger strata are believed to have been cut and translated westwards by Caledonide thrusts (e.g. Elliott & Johnson 1980).

In the foreland of the southern part of the Moine Thrust Belt, the Cambro-Ordovician strata overlie two distinct Precambrian units, the Lewisian complex of amphibolite–granulite-facies gneisses, and a Late Proterozoic clastic sequence termed the Torridon Group (Park *et al.* 2002; Stewart 2002). This succession, of up to 6 km thickness, consists of a basal unit, the Diabaig Formation, followed by the dominant succession of sands, gravels and subordinate shales, the Applecross Formation. After about 3–4 km of section, the Applecross Formation passes up into younger but similar units, but these do not concern us here. Close to the thrust belt the Applecross Formation is unconformably overlain by the Cambrian quartzites and a thickness of less than 2 km of Torridon Group is preserved.

Previous work in the southern Moine Thrust Belt

In contrast to its outcrops between Loch Eriboll and Assynt, the Moine Thrust Belt between Ullapool and Kishorn has received remarkably little attention since the work of Peach *et al.* (1907). Ramsay (1969) used the offset of Lewisian structures in the Kinlochewe thrust sheet to estimate thrust displacements (*c.* 45 km). The Dundonnel structure, just south of Ullapool (Fig. 1), was important for Elliott & Johnson (1980) in their analysis of the relative timing of thrusts. They deduced a piggy-back sequence for these structures. McClay & Coward (1981) offered a cross-section through the Kinlochewe district (Fig. 1), a section subsequently used to support the notion of surge zones, late-stage, gravity-driven rotational lenses that disrupt the thrust stack (Coward 1982). More detailed work is restricted to unpublished PhD theses (Matthews 1984; Morgan 1985). There have been sporadic studies of structural evolution on Lochalsh and Sleat, Isle of Skye (Fig. 2), but the geometries here, dominated by regional-scale recumbent folds, are radically different from the rest of the thrust belt (e.g. Coward & Whalley 1979).

The Achnashellach Culmination

Our study focuses on structural evolution in the Achnashellach area, between the villages of Kinlochewe and Kishorn (Fig. 4). Being the most mountainous part of the entire thrust belt, there are unparalleled vertical sections of thrust structures that are arguably the best exposed in the British Isles. In common with the main imbricate

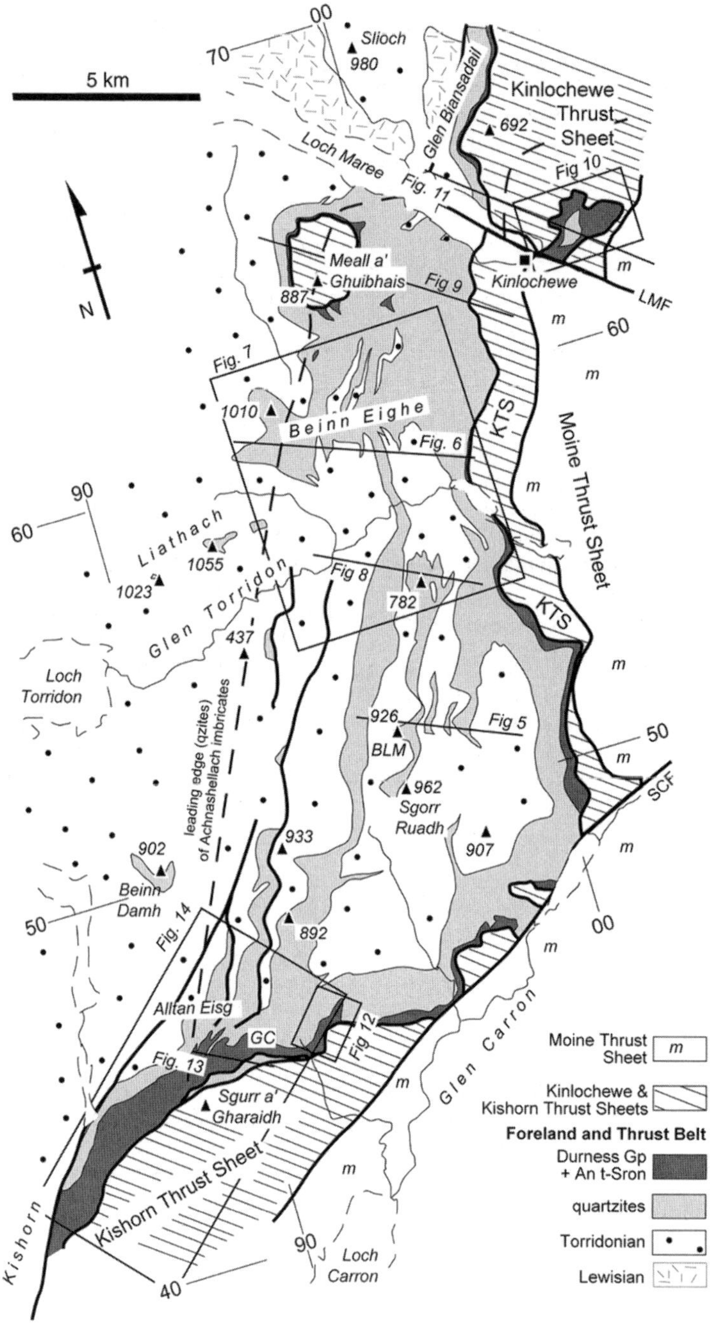

Fig. 4. Simplified geological map of the Moine Thrust Belt at the Achnashellach Culmination (location shown in Fig. 2; modified after Peach *et al.* 1907, and mapping by the authors). KTS, Kinlochewe Thrust Sheet; LMF, Loch Maree Fault; SCF, Strathcarron Fault; GC, Glas Cnoc; BLM, Beinn Liath Mhor. The grid lines in this and other figures are UK National Grid.

systems of Assynt, the imbricated Cambrian strata of the southern Moine Thrust Belt (Fig. 4) are not capped by the Moine Thrust itself. Rather, an allochthonous sheet or sheets of Lewisian and Torridonian rocks form the roof. In the north of the study area the upper allochthon is termed the Kinlochewe Thrust Sheet. In its type area, north of the eponymous village, the thrust sheet consists largely of Lewisian rocks. Ramsay (1969) used offsets of Precambrian structures within the Lewisian rocks, correlated between the thrust sheet and the neighbouring foreland, to deduce a slip of *c*. 45 km on the Kinlochewe Thrust. Immediately north of Kinlochewe, the thrust sheet contains Torridonian and Cambrian strata, these becoming increasingly important towards the south. To the south of the study area, the structural position of the Kinlochewe Thrust Sheet is taken by the Kishorn Thrust Sheet (Coward & Whalley 1979). Prior to erosion and slip along the Strathcarron Fault (Fig. 4), these two allochthonous Precambrian units may have been continuous. It should be noted that the Torridonian rocks of the Kishorn sheet include a distinct sequence of sandstones and shales (termed the Sleat Group, Stewart 2002) believed to be slightly older than the Torridon Group. These issues and structural evolution are beyond the scope of this paper; the Kishorn–Kinlochewe Thrust Sheet(s) is considered as a single tectonic unit for the purposes of this paper.

Whereas the upper boundary of the Achnashellach Culmination is defined by the composite Kishorn–Kinlochewe Thrust Sheet, its lower boundary is the foreland. Consequently, we are concerned with the frontal structures of the thrust belt. According to the sequential model of Elliott & Johnson (1980), the imbricates of the Achnashellach Culmination should have formed relatively late in the structural evolution of this part of the thrust belt. These imbricate systems are discussed now.

Structural style

The Achnashellach Culmination is characterized by a map pattern of alternating Cambrian quartzites and Torridonian rocks (Fig. 4). Peach *et al.* (1907) interpreted the structure in terms of imbricate thrusting with associated folding. The finest section through the structure lies along the summit ridge of Beinn Liath Mhor (Fig. 5). The flanks of the ridge provide 300–400 m of relief that expose an array of antiforms cored by Torridon Group sediments. At the level of the ridge the outcrop is dominated by repetitions of the Cambrian Basal Quartzite. Cross-bedding in both units clearly indicates that the folds are upward facing.

Thrusts on Beinn Liath Mohr ubiquitously cut up-section towards WNW, in some cases demonstrably in both hanging wall and footwall (Fig. 5). However, the fold geometries are more

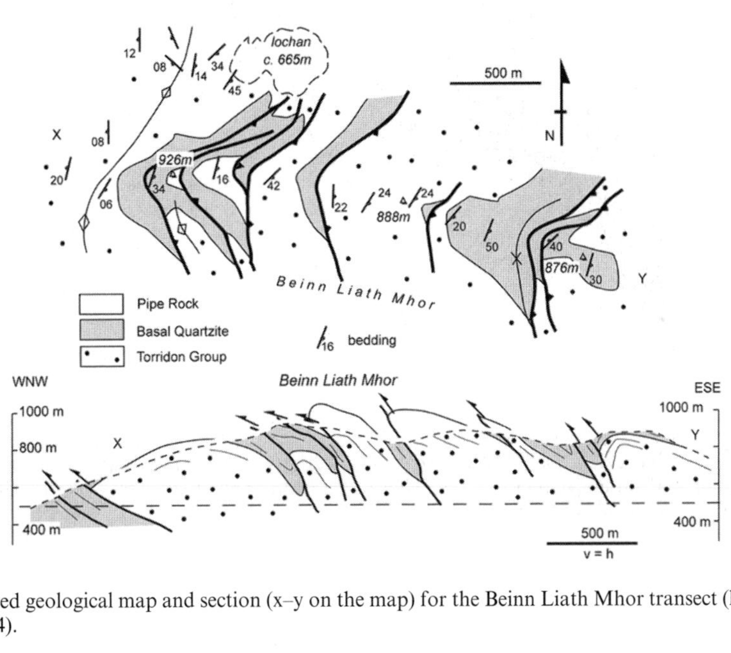

Fig. 5. Simplified geological map and section (x–y on the map) for the Beinn Liath Mhor transect (location shown in Fig. 4).

complex than being simple fault-bend folds. Cut-off angles are commonly steep and several thrusts show footwall synclines at the level of the quartzites. These observations are borne out on various scales within the Achnashellach Culmination, indicating that thrusting was accompanied by significant components of buckling.

Folding within the quartzites is found throughout the Achnashellach Culmination. Studies by one of us (R.K.M.) established that beds generally retain thickness around fold structures, and, at the level of the Pipe Rock, *Skolithos* burrows retain near-circular sections on bedding planes and remain orthogonal to bedding. However, the quartzites are extensively fractured, especially close to fold hinges, with the dominant fracture orientations both parallel and perpendicular to local fold hinge lines (Morgan 1985). The fractures have generally very little displacement and are unlikely to accommodate significant distributed strain within units. Interlimb angles at the level of the Basal Quartzite typically are around 90°. At some locations [e.g. grid reference NH 894464] the folds and associated small-scale imbricate thrusts are truncated by the map-scale thrusts. This may suggest that minor folding and thrusting occurred throughout the sequence prior to the development of the main imbricate structure that juxtaposed different parts of the stratigraphy. In general, however, the major fold structures are spatially related to the major thrusts in the culmination (as shown in Fig. 5).

Balanced section

The Beinn Liath Mhor transect provides a clear insight into the geometry of the imbricates within the culmination at the level of the sub-Cambrian unconformity. For most of the imbricate thrusts it is possible to match the hanging wall with corresponding footwall cut-offs for this stratigraphic surface, indicating that displacements are rather small. The same, relatively low displacements are seen on another major ridge section, Beinn Eighe (Fig. 6). This section has been used to quantify the shortening across the imbricate system. To estimate distributed shortening in the section, extensive strain studies were carried out by one of us (S.J.M.) using distorted *Skolithos* burrows within the Pipe Rock. On this transect (Fig. 6) the bed-parallel strains are virtually undetectable, with strain ellipse axial ratios commonly 1.1:1 or less. Only in the uppermost slice of Pipe Rock, beneath the Kinlochewe Thrust, do strains increase to 1.2:1. Consequently, it was deduced that layer-parallel shortening played a very minor role in accommodating the bulk shortening on this transect. To quantify the bulk displacement, a balanced and restored section through the culmination along the Beinn Eighe transect is presented (Fig. 6). The southern

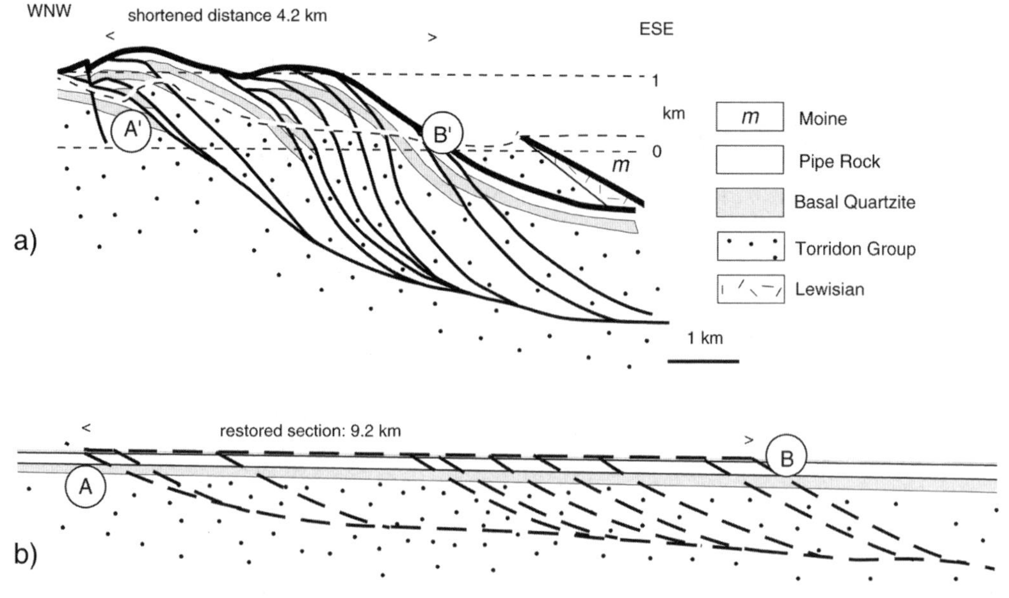

Fig. 6. (**a**) Balanced and (**b**) restored section through the Beinn Eighe transect (location shown in Fig. 4).

slopes of this ridge (running down into Glen Torridon) show thrusts cutting upwards from the Torridon Group into the overlying quartzites. The section has been constructed to balance the bed length within the Pipe Rock and the Basal Quartzites. A line-length restoration is justified because of the very low measured strains within this section. The restored length of Cambrian strata is 9.2 km (distance A–B in Fig. 6b). As the present section length is just 4.2 km, the total shortening across this part of the Achnashellach Culmination is 5 km.

The distance between thrusts at the level of the Torridon Group is generally less than 400 m. If these slices of Torridon Group were laid end to end, restored with a 400 m stratigraphic thickness involved in thrusting, the restored length would exceed 20 km. This length is not compatible with the restored length of the Cambrian strata. Consequently, we propose that there is almost 1 km of Torridonian stratigraphy involved in the imbricates (Fig. 6b). With the measured offsets on imbricate thrusts generally less than 1 km, the effect is for the slices of Torridon Group to be stacked 'ramp-on-ramp'. Using this rationale, the restored section illustrates that the floor thrust to the imbricate fan climbs towards the WNW at just a few degrees until it eventually climbs a steep ramp into the Cambrian quartzites at its leading edge. Ramp angles within the imbricate fan originated at about 20°, relative to the sub-Cambrian unconformity.

Lateral variation within the culmination

The thrust slices on Beinn Eighe can be mapped southwards across Glen Torridon to the neighbouring hill, Sgurr Dubh (Fig. 7). Here there are dramatic thrusts and thrust-related folds, chiefly within the Cambrian quartzites. The lower thrust slice carries a panel of Torridonian rocks, thicker

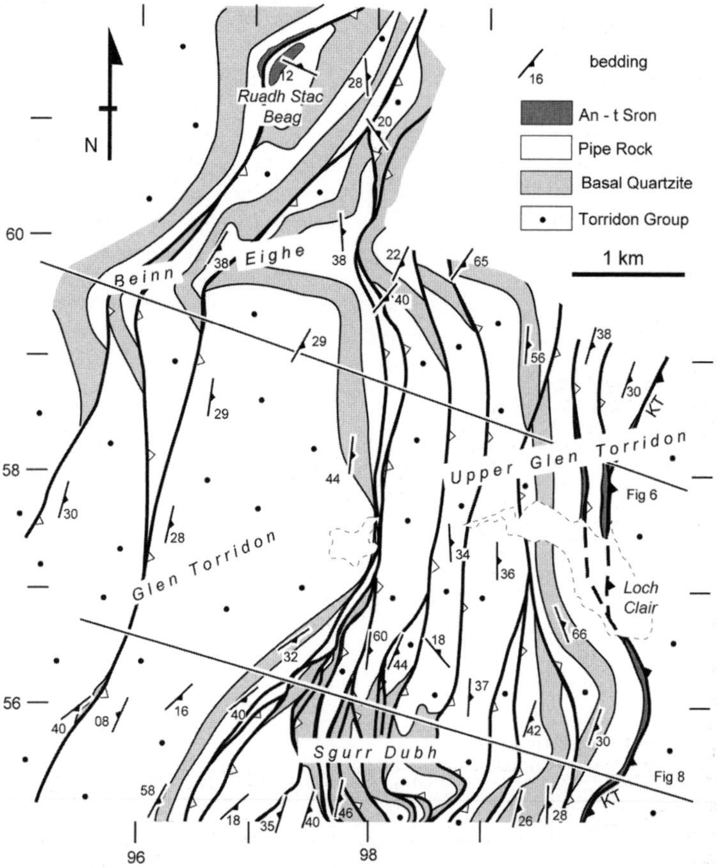

Fig. 7. Geological map of the thrust belt between Beinn Eighe and Sgurr Dubh (location shown in Fig. 4). KT, Kinlochewe Thrust.

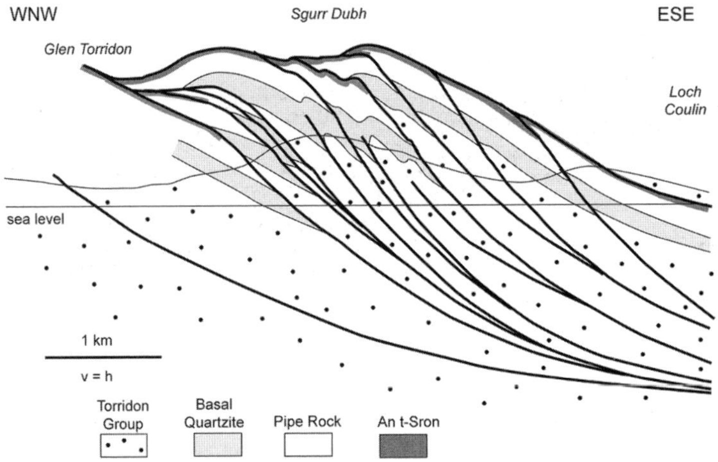

Fig. 8. Cross-section section through the Sgurr Dubh segment of the Achnashellach Culmination (location shown in Figs 4 and 7).

than 800 m (Fig. 8), indicating that the floor thrust lies at least this stratigraphic distance below the Cambrian quartzites further ESE. However, as at Beinn Eighe, the thickness of the slices of Torridon Group strata, as measured between the thrusts is small (<300 m). Therefore the imbricate stack here has developed by splays of closely spaced ramps. Structural elevation of the quartzites is achieved with rather little displacement (7.3 km; Matthews 1984).

Boyer & Elliott (1982) pointed out that, as the trailing branch lines in an imbricate fan bunch up, higher thrust slices are increasingly back-steepened. On the Sgurr Dudh transect this behaviour is evident: indeed, imbricate fans that grow from closely spaced ramps are likely to be particularly prone to such back-steepening. Bedding dips in the Torridon Group reach 60°, despite original ramp angles being about 20°. This form of back-steepening has been considered diagnostic of foreland-propagating (piggy-back) thrusting (Butler 1987). However, the geometry critical for such a deduction is the folding of higher thrusts over the hanging-wall ramp anticlines of underlying imbricate thrusts (Boyer & Elliott 1982; Butler 2004). Although such geometries are shown above the current erosion surface on the cross-section (Fig. 8), they may be deduced from the map pattern (Fig. 7) around the summit area of Sgurr Dudh. The geometry of the roof (Kinlochewe) thrust has been constructed to conform to this model. It may be concluded that, on this transect and the adjacent one through Beinn Eighe, the main imbricate slices within the Achnashellach culmination chiefly formed in a foreland-directed sequence, consistent with the Boyer & Elliott (1982) duplex model.

Roof thrust geometry

An outlier of Torridon Group rocks, resting on Pipe Rock and locally An t-Sron Group, famously crops out at Meall a'Ghiubhais (Fig. 4). Peach *et al.* (1907), and others since, interpreted this as a klippe of the Kinlochewe Sheet, a model followed here. The leading edge of the Beinn Eighe imbricate stack can be mapped beneath the NW margin of the Meall a'Ghiubhais klippe. Ahead lies intact stratigraphy of the foreland. The klippe rests directly on unthrusted An t-Sron Group rocks. On the southern side of the klippe the footwall includes Durness Limestone. However, the Cambrian strata on the SE side of the klippe are deformed (Fig. 9). This area is characterized at outcrop by imbricates carrying Pipe Rock that pass upwards into an imbricated tract of An t-Sron and Durness Limestone rocks. Collectively these units are interpreted to have bulged up the Kinlochewe Thrust Sheet. Consequently, on a large scale the behaviour of the Beinn Eighe imbricates is that of a classic duplex (in the sense of Boyer & Elliott 1982). The floor thrust is presumed to glide within Applecross Formation sandstones. Its depth beneath the sub-Cambrian unconformity can be inferred from the maximum thickness of Applecross Formation within the imbricate system, some 300 m.

The klippe at Meall a'Ghiubhais covers the leading edge of this part of the Achnashellach imbricate system (Fig. 9), as defined by the most

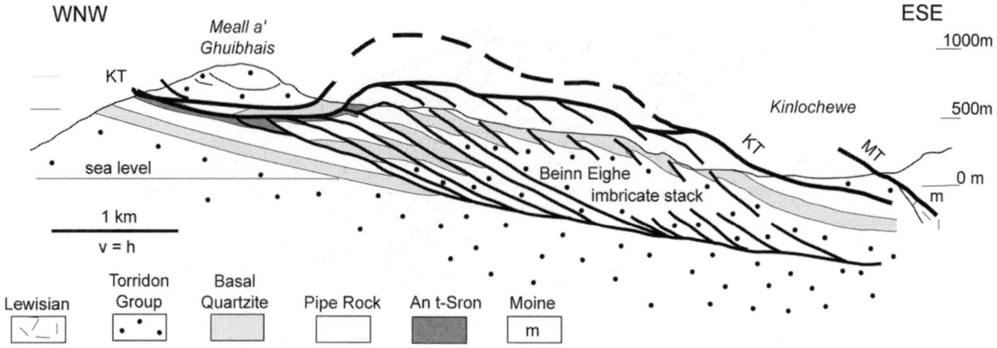

Fig. 9. Cross-section through the northern part of the Achnashellach Culmination, through the Meall a'Ghuibhais klippe of the Kinlochewe Thrust (KT). MT, Moine thrust. Location shown in Fig. 4.

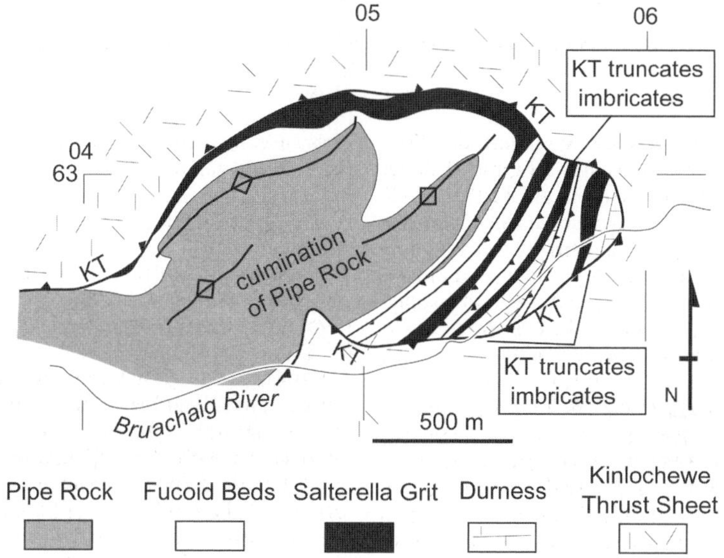

Fig. 10. Simplified geological sketch map of the Bruachaig window (location shown in Fig. 4) showing the relationships between the Kinlochewe Thrust (KT) and the imbricated Cambrian strata in its footwall that form the window.

western hanging-wall ramp of Cambrian quartzites rocks. This leading edge can also be inferred further SW to lie just ahead of Ruadh Stac Beag (Fig. 7), where Fucoid Beds are encountered on either side of the leading imbricate thrusts, separated by only a few metres of Pipe Rock. The further extent of the leading edge of the Achnashellach imbricates will be traced as other parts of the system are considered. Ahead of this leading edge, the Kinlochewe Thrust Sheet lies directly on Cambrian strata of the foreland.

The Bruachaig window

Glen Bruachaig, to the NE of Kinlochewe (Fig. 4) is classic ground in Highland geology for the early recognition of allochthonous Lewisian sheets (see Oldroyd 1990, for an account). Since the mapping of Peach *et al.* (1907), these units have been assigned to the Kinlochewe Thrust Sheet. Within its outcrop is a window into imbricated Cambrian strata in its footwall, a rare example of such a structure within the thrust belt as a whole. The centre of the window consists of Pipe Rock, rimmed by imbricates composed chiefly of Fucoid Beds and Salterella Grit. It is these An t-Sron rocks that dominate the outcrop of the window (Fig. 10). The SW edge of the window is controlled by the late Loch Maree Fault, which here downthrows to the SW. Otherwise, the edge of the window is defined by the Kinlochewe Thrust. On the eastern side of the

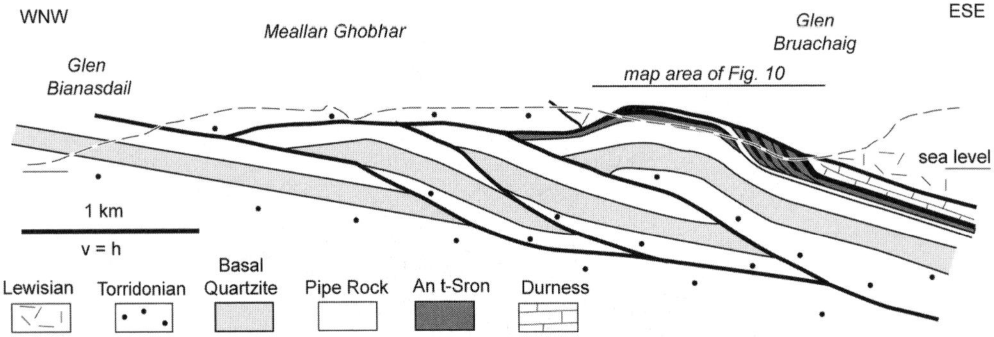

Fig. 11. Cross-section through the thrust belt on the NE side of the Loch Maree Fault, passing through the Bruachaig window (location shown in Fig. 4).

window (exposed in Bruachaig river) the footwall to the thrust lies in Durness Limestone. On the western side of the window the Kinlochewe Thrust glides on Salterella Grit. Slices of Pipe Rock and Fucoid Beds decorate the thrust plane around the window. However, the thrust must cut down section in its footwall from east to west (Durness Limestone down to Salterella Grit; Fig. 11). The main outcrop trace of the Kinlochewe Thrust, above Glen Bianasdail, glides on a footwall of Pipe Rock (cutting up into Fucoid Beds to the north), cutting out about 30 m of stratigraphy over a distance of 3 km (Fig. 11).

The Kinlochewe Thrust not only cuts across stratigraphy in its footwall but also truncates thrusts. Thus the northern outcrop of the Kinlochewe Thrust, around the window, lies on first Durness Limestone, then Salterella Grit, then Fucoid Beds (i.e. cutting down stratigraphic section). It then cuts across two more slices of Salterella Grit and Fucoid Beds. The dip of bedding is generally between 30° and 50° to the ESE. The discordance between the Kinlochewe Thrust and its footwall is therefore far greater than implied by simple consideration of the stratigraphic content.

The above description might be explained by a late, low-angle fault truncating previously imbricated strata (e.g. Coward 1982). However, the Kinlochewe Thrust has been bulged to create the Bruachaig window. Pipe Rock in its core is some 500 m above its projected position from the foreland (Fig. 11). We infer that this structural elevation has been generated by imbrication of the Cambrian quartzites, together with about 200 m of Torridonian rocks. This represents the northern margin of the Achnashellach imbricates. The shortening implied by this model is about 2 km. The structural elevation on the Kinlochewe Thrust Sheet here is depressed by more than 1 km, compared with that for the Sgurr Dudh section (Fig. 8), presumably because of two factors: the low aggregrate displacement for the imbricate thrusts and the reduced thickness of stratigraphy (chiefly of the Torridon Group) in the imbricate slices. It should be noted that the leading edge of these imbricates, the limit to the Achnashellach system, lies buried in this section (Fig. 11).

The geometry of the window is not consistent with the duplex model of Boyer & Elliott (1982; Fig. 1). For this model to be valid the footwall to the Kinlochewe Thrust should remain in Durness Limestone once it has climbed to this stratigraphic level. The overstep model favoured by Peach *et al.* (1907) for thrust sequences or other interpretations of late, low-angle faults (Coward 1982) are not valid either because the Kinlochewe Thrust is bulged up.

Roof thrust geometries: Torr na h-Iolaire

As in the Bruachaig window, on a large scale the roof of the Achnashellach imbricates presumably has been bulged up, as indicated by the outcrop pattern of the culmination (Fig. 4). For much of the northern part of the Achnashellach Culmination, away from the Bruachaig window, it is difficult to establish detailed relationships between the Kinlochewe Thrust and structures in its footwall. However, the footwall units are well exposed against the Kishorn Thrust, towards the SE side of the culmination, at Torr na h-Iolaire (Fig. 12). The thrust dips consistently SSE and has a hanging wall of Lewisian gneisses. The footwall is more varied. In the valley of Coire Mhic Fhearghais (Fig. 12), the footwall lies in Durness Limestone. However, on the slopes of Torr na h-Iolaire the Kishorn Thrust lies alternately on steeply dipping Fucoid Beds and Salterella Grit. The alternations represent

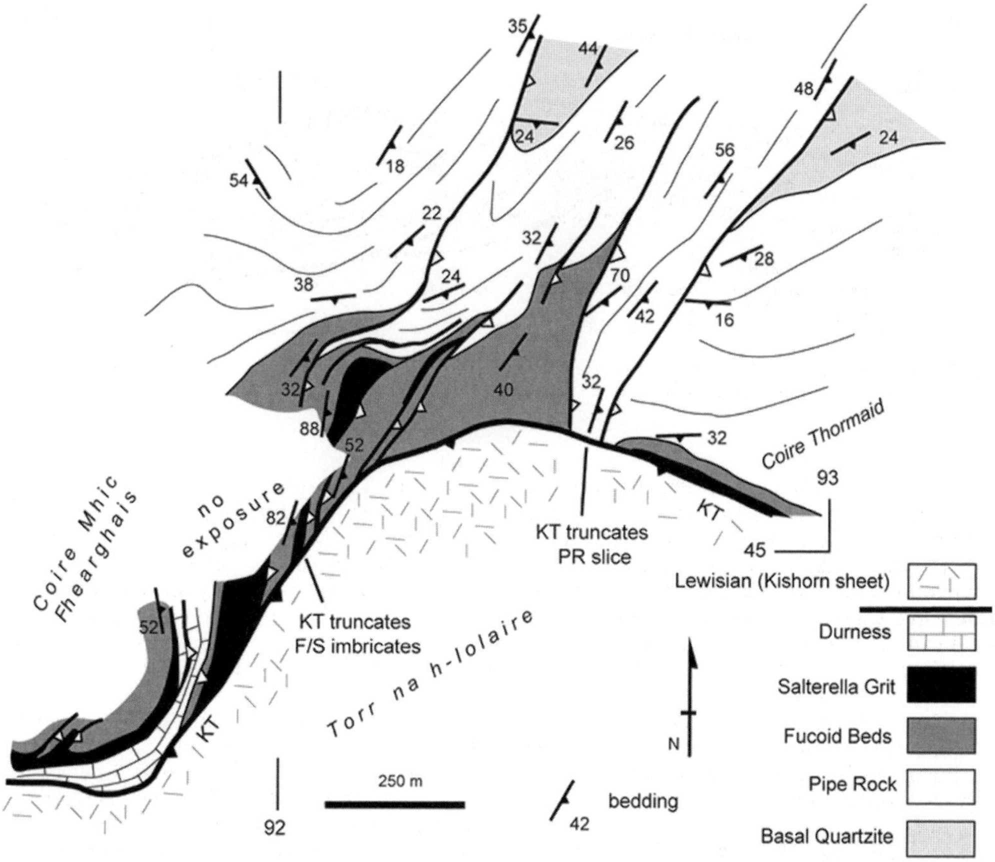

Fig. 12. Geological map of the field relationships between the Kishorn Thrust (KT) and the underlying imbricated Cambrian strata at Torr na h-Iolaire (location shown in Fig. 4). (See text for discussion.)

imbricate thrust slices that have been truncated in the footwall to the Kishorn Thrust.

The imbricated An t-Sron Group rocks pass northwards laterally into thrust slices carrying Pipe Rock and, in turn, the Basal Quartzite (Fig. 12). The quartzite slices show clear hanging-wall ramp geometries, and higher imbricate slices in the An t-Sron are folded by these structures. These relationships are consistent with simple foreland-directed thrust sequences, as deduced for the Sgurr Dudh section (Fig. 8). However, unlike the Sgurr Dudh section, where erosion has cut deeply into the structure, and in the Bruachaig window (Fig. 11), where only An t-Sron–Durness-bearing imbricate slices are truncated, here the main quartzite slices are truncated by the Kishorn Thrust. In upper Coire Thormaid (Fig. 12), Pipe Rock lies directly in the footwall to the Kishorn thrust. Bedding, dipping at 30° ESE in the Pipe Rock, is truncated and the Kishorn thrust cuts down-section towards the WNW. Consequently, at this location, it may be deduced that the Kishorn Thrust has moved after at least some of the imbrication in its footwall, truncating the top part of the underlying imbricates.

Imbricate geometries at Glas Cnoc

The Kishorn Thrust can be mapped continuously from Torr na h-Iolare to the northern slopes of Sgurr a'Gharaidh (Fig. 4). Here a slice of Cambrian quartzites, together with their Torridon Group substrate, has been carried as a 3 km long lens-like body in the footwall to the Kishorn Thrust (Fig. 13). The quartzites are folded, as is their basal thrust contact, yet the Kishorn Thrust is sub-planar. Consequently, we deduce that the Kishorn Thrust here too has moved relatively late in the structural sequence.

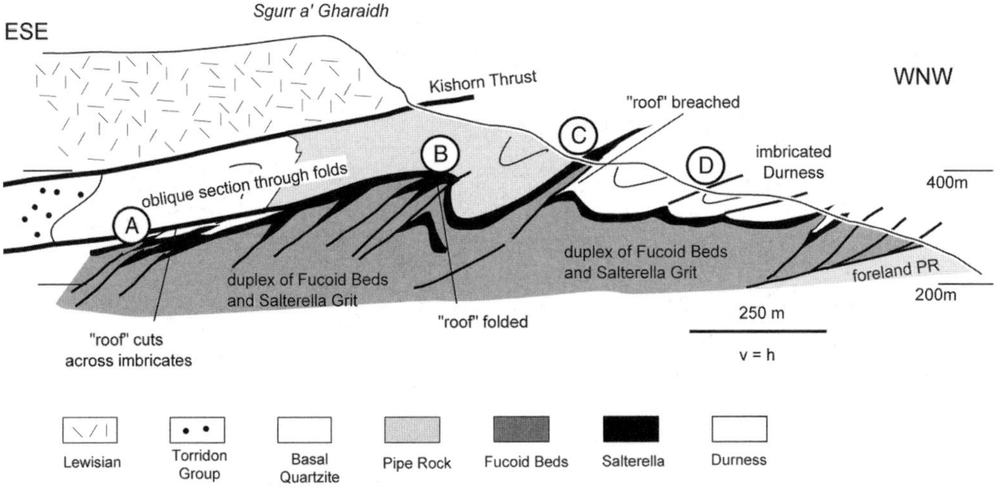

Fig. 13. Cross-section through the thrust belt at Glas Cnoc (GC in Fig. 4) illustrating the relationship between imbricated An t-Sron Formation and Durness Group rocks and the overlying thrust sheets. Geometric relationships at various sites (A–D) are discussed in the text. It should be noted that the sheet of folded Torridon Group, Basal Quartzite and Pipe Rock directly beneath the Kishorn Thrust pinches out laterally, but outside this section (see Fig. 14).

It is possible that the large lens of quartzite carried in the thrust zone is part of a previously decapitated imbricate slice that originated from further to the ESE.

Below the quartzite slice lies a tract of imbricated An t-Sron and Durness Group strata. Approximately 20 individual slices of Salterella Grit can be recognized in this section. These form part of a major imbricate fan. Towards the trailing edge of this system, near the pass of Glas Cnoc, the imbricates involve a few metres of Durness Limestone. However, beneath the central part of the thrust-bounded lens of quartzites, the imbricates contain only An t-Sron rocks. The thrust at the base of the lens truncates some of the imbricates in its footwall (A in Fig. 13). However, further west this upper thrust has been bulged, folded and locally breached by the underlying structures (e.g. B in Fig. 13). The leading edge of the quartzite lens is defined by a thrust that roots down into the An t-Sron imbricates. A thin slice of Fucoid Beds and Salterella Grit (C in Fig. 13) separate Pipe Rock from Durness carbonates. These too have been imbricated, with repetition of the Ghrudaidh and Eilean Dubh formations of the Durness Group (D in Fig. 13). The floor thrust to the thrusts in the limestone forms the roof to the imbricates of An t-Sron rocks below. Presumably displacements within the An t-Sron rocks transferred up into the overlying limestones rather than simply running out to form a duplex roof. Towards the preserved leading edge of these structures both the An t-Sron Formation and Durness Limestones are imbricated together. The Pipe Rock beneath is undeformed.

The sequence of structural development within the Glas Cnoc section is interesting. The thrust carrying the quartzites, apparently forming the roof to the imbricates of An t-Sron strata (and small amounts of Durness Limestone), cuts gently across these imbricates. However, it has also been folded and locally breached by them. This suggests that the imbricates of An t-Sron rocks did not form in a simple sequence. Furthermore, it suggests that the 'roof' thrust has a multiphase movement history. These deductions are in conflict with the simple thrust sequences implicit in the Boyer & Elliott (1982; Fig 1) duplex model.

The lateral terminations of the Achnashellach Culmination

The imbricates of Torridon Group and Cambrian quartzites that form the Achnashellach Culmination do not persist along the entire thrust belt. To the south of the main study area, the footwall to the Kishorn Thrust lies directly on Durness Limestone that, although imbricated, lies on undeformed Salterella Grit (Fig. 14). The imbricate systems therefore involve only the

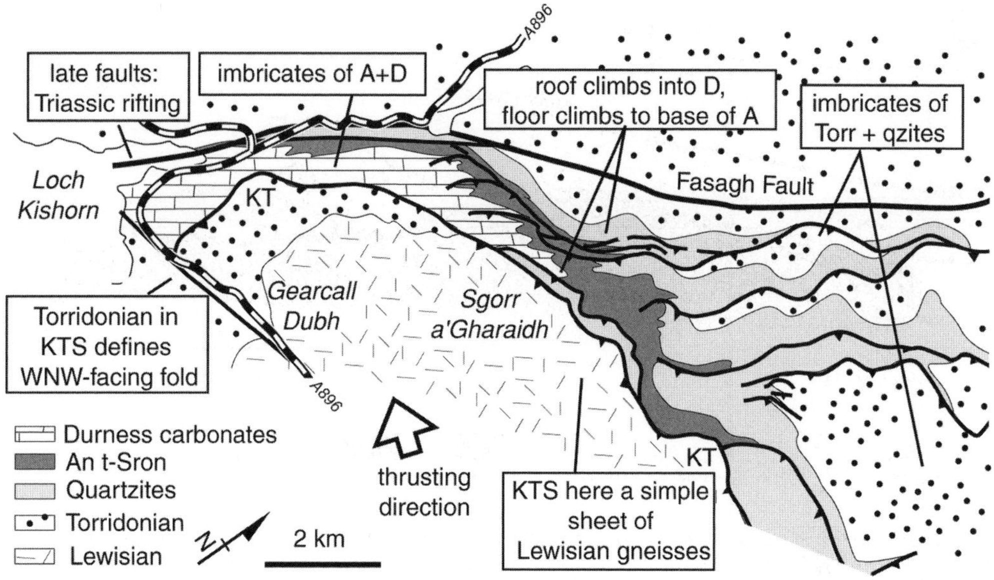

Fig. 14. Lateral variations in thrust belt structure in the Kishorn area (location shown in Fig. 4), shown in map view. KT, Kishorn Thrust; KTS, Kishorn Thrust Sheet.

upper parts of the Cambrian stratigraphy in the south; substantially less material than within the Achnashellach district. Consequently, the SW edge of the Achnashellach Culmination can be interpreted as being caused by the systematic southward climb in thrust trajectory, out of the Torridon Group and up into the Durness Group. The lateral terminations of two major slices of Torridon Group rocks exist in the upper Alltan Eisg valley (Fig. 4). The thrusts climb section laterally at *c.* 30° relative to the sub-Cambrian unconformity, which is the estimate here of the original ramp angle. These lateral to oblique hanging-wall ramps generate folds with hinge lines trending SSE, oblique to the NNE–SSW trend of hinges lines for folds associated with frontal ramps. Where the hanging wall still contains Torridonian rocks, the thrust footwalls lie in Pipe Rock. However, the footwalls also climb section towards the SSW to incorporate strata of the An t-Sron Formation. These pass laterally into the An t-Sron imbricates of the Glas Cnoc valley (Fig. 13). This strongly suggests that displacement on the thrusts, which carry Torridonian rocks in the main part of the Achnashellach Culmination, transfers onto the An t-Sron imbricates and then up onto the Kishorn Thrust; yet the present mapping at Glas Cnoc (Fig. 13) suggests a more complex pattern, perhaps with re-imbrication of an existing thrust stack within the An t-Sron rocks. Nevertheless, on a large scale the southward termination of the Achnashellach culmination is defined by systematic SW climb of thrusts up out of the Torridonian rocks, across the Cambrian quartzites and An t-Sron Group and into the Durness Limestone. The southern limit of the lowest Pipe Rock slice, in the lower Glas Cnoc valley (Fig. 14), provides the southern control on the location of the leading edge of the Achnashellach imbricate stack. These relationships are illustrated on a regional stratigraphic separation diagram for the culmination (Fig. 15; see Elliott & Johnson 1980, for early use of these diagrams in the northern thrust belt).

The lateral climb of imbricate thrusts deduced for the southern termination of the culmination is less apparent in the north. To the north of the present study area, in upper Glen Bianasdail (Fig. 4), the Kinlochewe Thrust Sheet rests on a footwall of undeformed Cambrian strata, up to the Salterella Grit. Presumably displacements within the Achnashellach Culmination are accommodated by slip on the Kinlochewe Thrust. The thickness of Torridonian units, inferred to be involved in thrust slices on the north side of Kinlochewe (Fig. 11), is just 200 m, compared with over 1000 m on the Beinn Eighe transect (Fig. 6) and over 300 m from Meall a Ghuibhais (Fig. 9) Therefore the floor thrust to the imbricate system climbs section towards the north, although less dramatically than inferred for the

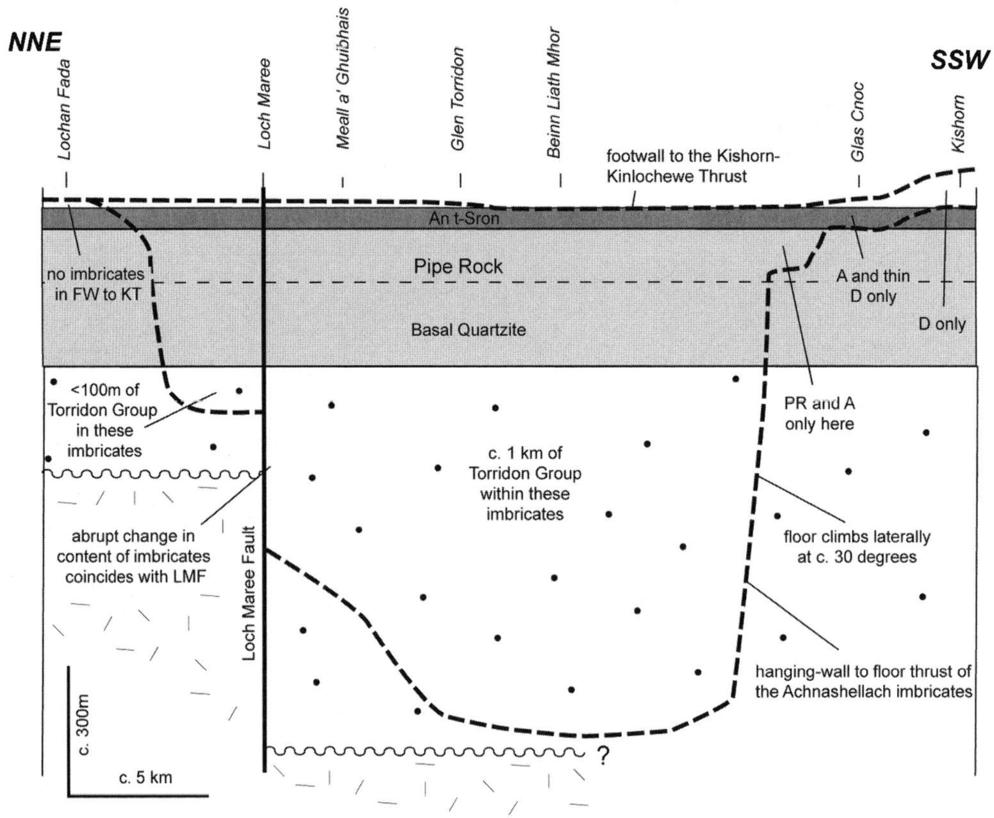

Fig. 15. Stratigraphic separation diagram for imbricate thrusts in the Achnashellach Culmination, showing lateral variation in the content of imbricate slices. A, An t-Sron Formation; D, Durness Group.

Kishorn area. There are, however, other lateral changes in this northern area.

The role of the Loch Maree Fault

The thrust belt abruptly changes character from north to south across Loch Maree (contrast section lines of Figs 9 and 11). Both the displacement and the thickness of Torridonian units involved in the thrust slices decrease markedly to the north. The loch lies along the trend of a significant Precambrian structure, the Loch Maree Fault. The structure of the Lewisian rocks within the foreland shows significant changes across this structure (e.g. Peach *et al.* 1907). Additionally, there is a significant change in thickness of the Torridonian rocks, preserved beneath the sub-Cambrian unconformity. The fault has also moved after thrusting, as all thrust structures are offset (Fig. 4). However, it also appears that the fault has influenced thrust development, perhaps because of the different thicknesses of Torridonian rocks preserved beneath the sub-Cambrian unconformity.

Discussion

Elsewhere in the thrust belt the Sole Thrust glides in Cambrian strata, so that the sub-Cambrian unconformity of the foreland can be traced beneath the thrust system. In Achnashellach, Precambrian and Cambrian strata are involved in the thrust belt. Consequently, the deep geometry of the thrust system is a matter of inference rather than observation. Peach *et al.* (1907) proposed that imbricate thrusts in the Torridonian rocks passed downwards into folds. The present interpretation follows the Boyer & Elliott (1982) duplex model, showing imbricate thrusts combining downwards onto a common floor thrust. This geometry is consistent with map patterns (e.g. Fig. 7) that illustrate laterally branching imbricate thrusts. The present studies have not identified trailing tip-line folds implicit in the

Peach *et al.* (1907) model. However, buckle folding is a feature of thrust ramps, especially through the sub-Cambrian unconformity and within the Cambrian quartzites. Such features are common in the northern part of the thrust belt, where they are inferred to represent tip-line folds generated during the early stages of thrust growth (Fischer & Coward 1982). Thrusts subsequently break through these folds, separating hanging-wall antiform from footwall synform. In the northern part of the thrust belt such folding is commonly accompanied by distributed strains, identified from distorted bed-sections of burrows in the Pipe Rock (e.g. Fischer & Coward 1982). These layer-parallel shortening strains, although developed in the Achnashellach Culmination, are very weak. Deformation is also accompanied by micro-fracturing rather than crystal plastic deformation, which is common in the Eriboll district. This may suggest that the Achnashellach imbricates developed under cooler ambient conditions or at higher strain rates than the structures further north in the thrust belt.

There are many culminations within the Moine Thrust Belt. The majority of these are formed of thrust sheets that individually involve < 100 m of stratigraphy (in some cases < 10 m), repeated many times on thrusts with large displacements. The structure in these examples is commonly dominated by 'flat-on-flat' geometries, where displacements on individual imbricate thrusts greatly exceed the stratigraphic thickness (ramp height) of the beds involved. In these systems the aggregated estimates of stratal shortening can exceed 40 (Butler & Coward 1984; Coward 1985). In Achnashellach, imbricate slices involve *c.* 1 km of Torridonian, plus 200–250 m of Cambrian strata. Individual displacements on thrusts are generally only a few hundred metres, with the structure chiefly showing ramp-on-ramp geometries. Aggregated displacements across the entire imbricate system are just 5–10 km. Thus, the Achnashellach Culmination is built from thick imbricate slices and rather little stratal shortening.

Although the thickness of Torridonian strata involved in the central transect of the Achnashellach Culmination exceeds 1 km, the imbricates do not retain this thickness along strike. To the south the thrusts climb section, presumably along lateral to oblique ramps at about 30°, then glide in the Durness Limestone. The reason for this southward climb in thrust profiles is unclear. However, the northern limit of the culmination is closely associated with the Precambrian Loch Maree Fault. Therefore it is possible that the architecture of the culmination is influenced by the distribution of Torridonian strata beneath the sub-Cambrian unconformity, which in turn was controlled by Precambrian faults. Basement controls such as this, although widely recognized in other thrust belts, are not well described from the Moine Thrust Belt.

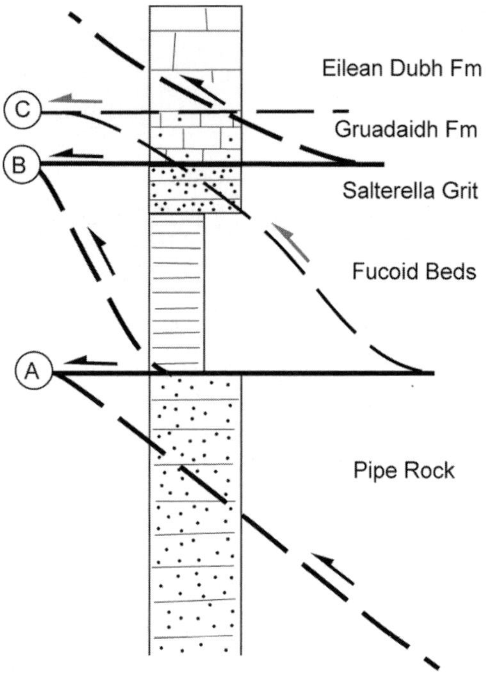

Fig. 16. Levels of important detachments (A, B, and C) and the linking ramps for imbricate thrusts of the Achnashellach Culmination within the Cambrian stratigraphy.

The internal structure of the Achnashellach imbricate system is apparently much more simple than for other parts of the thrust belt. Large-scale thrust flats are rarely developed within the Cambrian quartzites. The major thrusts of the system cut ramps that pass directly through the Torridon Group strata and Cambrian quartzites. This behaviour contrasts with much of the northern Moine Thrust Belt, where different parts of the quartzites are stacked preferentially by imbricates, with bed-parallel thrust surfaces developed extensively. However, horizons at higher stratigraphic levels are used as thrust flats at Achnashellach, as elsewhere in the thrust belt (Fig. 16). The hindward (eastern) outcrop of the Achnashellach Culmination shows variable imbricate stacks that involve the Fucoid Beds and Salterella Grit with subordinate inclusion of thin strips of the lowest part (Ghrudaidh Formation) of the Durness Group. This implies a

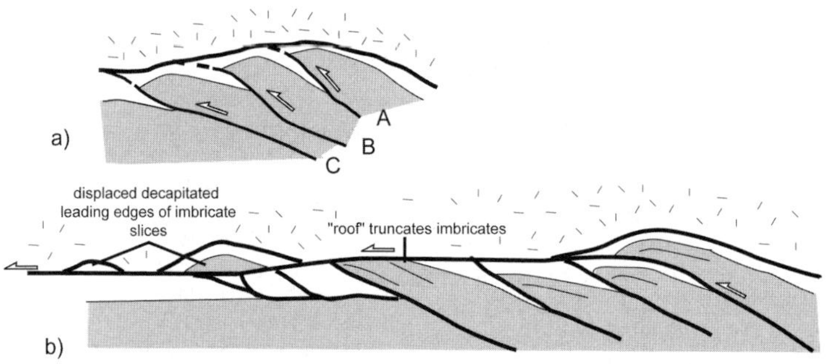

Fig. 17. Idealized models, seen in profile, of thrust geometry and structural relationships in the thrust belt at Achnashellach. (**a**) A simple imbricate fan with roof thrust. Conventional (Boyer & Elliott 1982) explanations infer a strict sequence of thrust activity (A–B–C in time). (**b**) Geometries that might result from hindward thrusts moving after forelandward thrusts in a roofed imbricate system. (See text for discussion.)

major detachment along the base of the Fucoid Beds (A in Fig. 16). For the thrust systems that contain just Salterella Grit and Fucoids Beds, the upper detachment (roof) must glide at the top of the Salterella Grit (B in Fig. 16). The local occurrence of Durness Limestone in the systems suggests that a further, if only sporadically activated, detachment horizon lies a few metres up into the limestones (C in Fig. 16). South of Achnashellach this geometry changes. As the imbricates in the Kishorn area include only limestones, the chief thrust flat must lie at the top of the Salterella Grit (B in Fig. 16), with older strata remaining undeformed below. Presumably there were further horizons of preferential thrust-flat activity at higher stratigraphic levels in the Durness Group, but these levels are not well preserved.

Given the known or inferred positions of the principal detachment horizons within the stratigraphic column from which the Achnashellach imbricates have been built, the Boyer & Elliott (1982) duplex model makes clear predictions of the stratigraphic relationships that can develop along the main thrusts (Fig. 1). On a large scale the Achnashellach Culmination shows similarities with the duplex model. Where thrusts bunch up, they and their imbricate slices show progressive back-steepening, a feature commonly used to infer simple foreland-directed thrust propagation (e.g. Butler 1987). The outcrop geometry of the Kishorn–Kinlochewe Thrust, which would define a roof thrust in the Boyer & Elliott (1982) model, or indeed the outcrop geometry of the Achnashellach Culmination itself, is consistent with the duplex model. Strict foreland propagation (e.g. sequence A–B–C in time in Fig. 17a) generates a folded roof thrust and back-steepening. However, the studies presented here from the footwall to the Kishorn–Kinlochewe Thrust yield geometries that are not compatible with the duplex model. At many sites, imbricate slices are truncated (e.g. Figs 10 and 12) so that the footwall to the Kishorn–Kinlochewe Thrust cuts up and down stratigraphic section in its transport direction (e.g. Fig. 11). These relationships are consistent with overstep thrust geometries (e.g. Butler 1987) that develop when the upper thrust in an array moves after the thrusts that lie foreland-ward of it. The same geometry can be achieved by an imbricate thrust towards the rear of the thrust system moving after those thrusts towards the foreland have already formed (e.g. Fig. 17b), transferring up onto part of the roof system. Although late movements could simply reactivate those parts of the original roof thrust that were near planar, minor culminations in it may, however, have been planed off. Such a process would have isolated small, far-travelled lenses of previously imbricated Cambrian units, such as the lens of quartzites at Glas Cnoc (Fig. 13), leaving truncated imbricates in the footwall to the roof thrust (e.g. at Torr na h-Iolaire, Fig. 12). Yet the roof and other thrusts at high structural levels are folded by underlying structures. This suggests that within the thrust array, slip did not simply transfer from imbricate to imbricate in a simple sequence. The geometries described here are better explained by displacements alternating between different imbricate thrusts. In the context of Figure 17a, increments of slip may have accumulated cyclically on the imbricate thrusts so that, over time, thrusts A, B and C appear to be active simultaneously.

Rather than adopting a simply contractional explanation, Coward (1982) and Butler & Coward (1984) proposed that discordant relationships throughout the Moine Thrust Belt reflected low-angle extensional faulting at a late stage in thrust belt evolution. In the north Assynt district, Coward (1982) further suggested that some of these putative extensional structures formed during the thrusting so that they were carried within thrust sheets. Although the status of the Assynt structures remains debatable, it is not believed here that such kinematic complexity is required for the Achnashellach Culmination. Apart from along the footwall of the Kinlochewe–Kishorn Thrust, there is no evidence for stratal extension. The constituent imbricate faults within the culmination all cut up-section in their transport direction. The overlying thrust sheets show no evidence of having experienced extension. The debate between horizontal contractional and extensional geometries within the Moine Thrust Belt is likely to continue. However, it may be pertinent to note that the only structural relationships that are candidates for extensional explanations are found cutting previously deformed (principally folded and thrust) units. In these settings it is difficult to demonstrate true horizontal extension (or contraction) as the synkinematic datum is difficult to resolve (Wheeler & Butler 1994). Extensional faulting might be easier to resolve for the lowest structures in the thrust belt such as the 'sole thrust'. However, such geometries have yet to be described. Given these observations, it is preferable to continue to explain structural relationships, certainly within the southern Moine Thrust Belt and especially around the Achashellach Culmination, in terms of contractional faulting, albeit with complex thrust activity.

Synchronous or simultaneous thrusting has been established for various emergent thrust systems, on the basis of growth strata patterns (e.g. Butler & Lickorish 1997; Meigs 1997). Recently synchronous thrusting has been proposed for parts of the northern Moine Thrust Belt (Butler 2004), including Boyer & Elliott's (1982) type duplex at Foinaven, on the basis of similar structural relationships as described here. It remains to be seen whether similar geometries exist in other thrust systems.

The fieldwork that underpins this description was originally carried out in the early 1980s when the three of us were PhD students supervised by Mike Coward. We are indebted to him for his enthusiasm and support at that time and on many subsequent occasions. R.W.H.B. carried out work more recently as part of the Geological Conservation Review and thanks J. Mendum for his involvement in this project. We also thank C. Bond, T. Needham and J. Wheeler for accompanying us on the 'long walk'. M. Krabbendam and R. Holdsworth are thanked for constructive reviews.

References

BOYER, S. & ELLIOTT, D. 1982. Thrust systems. *AAPG Bulletin*, **66**, 1196–1230.

BUTLER, R. W. H. 1987. Thrust sequences. *Journal of the Geological Society, London*, **144**, 619–634.

BUTLER, R. W. H. 2004. The nature of 'roof thrusts' in the Moine Thrust Belt, NW Scotland: implications for the structural evolution of thrust belts. *Journal of the Geological Society, London*, **161**, 849–859.

BUTLER, R.W.H. & COWARD, M. P. 1984. Geological constraints, structural evolution and the deep geology of the NW Scottish Caledonides. *Tectonics*, **3**, 347–365.

BUTLER, R. W. H. & LICKORISH, W. H. 1997. Using high resolution stratigraphy to date fold and thrust activity: examples from the Neogene of south–central Sicily. *Journal of the Geological Society, London*, **154**, 633–643.

COWARD, M. P. 1982. Surge zones in the Moine thrust zone of NW Scotland. *Journal of Structural Geology*, **4**, 247–256.

COWARD, M. P. 1984. A geometric study of the Amaboll and Heilam thrust sheets, NW of Ben Amaboll, Sutherland. *Scottish Journal of Geology*, **20**, 87–106.

COWARD, M. P. 1985. The thrust structures of southern Assynt, Moine thrust zone. *Geological Magazine*, **122**, 1–13.

COWARD, M. P. & WHALLEY, J. S. 1979. Texture and fabric studies across the Kishorn Nappe, near Kyle of Lochalsh, Western Scotland. *Journal of Structural Geology*, **1**, 259–273.

DAHLSTROM, C. D. A. 1970. Structural geology in the eastern margin of the Canadian Rocky Mountains. *Bulletin of Canadian Petroleum Geologists*, **18**, 332–406.

ELLIOTT, D. & JOHNSON, M. R. W. 1980. Structural evolution in the northern part of the Moine thrust belt, NW Scotland. *Transactions of the Royal Society of Edinburgh*, **71**, 69–96.

FISCHER, M. W. & COWARD, M. P. 1982. Strains and folds within thrust sheets: the Heilam sheet, NW Scotland. *Tectonophysics*, **88**, 291–312.

MATTHEWS, S. J. 1984. *Thrust sheet evolution in the Kinlochewe region of the Moine Thrust Zone, NW Scotland, and the Pelvoux–Brianconnais, French Alps.* PhD thesis, University of Leeds.

MCCLAY, K. R. & COWARD, M. P. 1981. The Moine Thrust zone: an overview. *In*: MCCLAY, K. R. & PRICE, N. J. (eds) *Thrust and Nappe Tectonics*. Geological Society, London, Special Publications, **9**, 241–260.

MEIGS, A. J. 1997. Sequential development of selected Pyrenean thrust faults. *Journal of Structural Geology*, **19**, 481–502.

MORGAN, R. K. 1985. *Comparison of strain and microstructure in deformed quartzites.* PhD thesis, University of Leeds.

OLDROYD, D. R. 1990. *The Highlands Controversy*. Chicago University Press, Chicago, IL.

Park, R. G., Stewart, A. D. & Wright, D. T. 2002. The Hebridean terrane. *In*: Trewin, N. H. (ed.) *The Geology of Scotland*, 4th edn. Geological Society, London, 45–80.

Peach, B. N., Horne, J., Gunn, W., Clough, C. T., Hinxman, L. W. & Teall, J. J. H. 1907. *The Geological Structure of the North-West Highlands of Scotland.* Memoirs of the Geological Survey of Great Britain.

Ramsay, J. G. 1969. The measurement of strain and displacement in orogenic belts. *In*: Kent, P. E., Satterthwaite, G. E. & Spencer, A. M. (eds) *Time and Place in Orogeny*. Geological Society, London, Special Publications, **3**, 43–79.

Stewart, A. D. (ed.) 2002. *The Later Proterozoic Torridonian Rocks of Scotland: their Sedimentology, Geochemistry and Origin*. Geological Society, London Memoirs, **24**.

Wheeler, J. & Butler, R. W. H. 1994. Criteria for identifying structures related to true extension in orogens. *Journal of Structural Geology*, **16**, 1023–1027.

Tectonic stratigraphy and structural continuity of the northernmost Moine Thrust Zone and Moine Nappe, Scottish Caledonides

R. E. HOLDSWORTH[1], G. I. ALSOP[2] & R. A. STRACHAN[3]

[1]*Reactivation Research Group, Department of Earth Sciences, University of Durham, Durham(e-mail: r.e.holdsworth@durham.ac.uk) DH1 3LE, UK*

[2]*Crustal Dynamics Group, School of Geography & Geosciences, University of St Andrews, St. Andrews KY16 9ST, UK*

[3]*School of Earth & Environmental Sciences, University of Portsmouth, Burnaby Road, Portsmouth PO1 3QL, UK*

Abstract: The Moine Thrust Zone and overlying Moine Nappe represent classic ground in Scottish geology in which Neoproterozoic Moine metasedimentary rocks were translated towards the WNW over the Laurentian foreland comprising Lewisian basement gneisses and a Cambrian cover succession during Caledonian orogenesis at *c*. 430 Ma. Systematic mapping of both the Moine Nappe and underlying Moine Thrust Zone in the Loch Hope to Whiten Head region of Sutherland extends the tectonic stratigraphy developed in other parts of the thrust zone to the little-studied north coast section. An apparent continuum of deformation is recognized from the Moine Nappe down into the underlying thrust zone with a consistent gently ESE-dipping foliation associated with down-dip mineral and extension lineations. The polyphase fold history present within the Moine Nappe and the thrust zone results from progressive deformation during thrusting. Thrust-related fold axes and bedding–cleavage intersections are typically subparallel to the transport direction in high-strain zones, whereas gently north- or south-plunging attitudes are common in lower strain portions of the thrust zone. Thrusts are commonly deformed by folds developed within their footwalls, consistent with a foreland-propagating sequence of deformation. The newly defined Lochan Riabhach Thrust is interpreted as an 'out-of-sequence' structure that sliced at low angles across the thrust zone and toward the WNW after initial thrust stacking. Comparison with the downfaulted segment of the Moine Nappe and thrust zone exposed on the foreland at Faraid Head demonstrates cross-strike continuity of the thrust sheet template and structural history for at least 15 km to the NW.

The Moine Thrust Zone and overlying western parts of the Moine Nappe form the NW margin of the Caledonian orogen in Scotland (Fig. 1). Its most northerly exposed part, around Loch Eriboll on the north coast of Sutherland, is classic ground in Highland geology (e.g. Lapworth 1885; Peach *et al.* 1907; Soper & Wilkinson 1975; Elliott & Johnson 1980) and featured prominently in the life and work of Mike Coward (e.g. Coward 1980, 1982, 1983, 1984*a*,*b*, 1985, 1988; Coward *et al.* 1980; McClay & Coward 1981; Fischer & Coward 1982; Coward & Potts 1983; Rathbone *et al.* 1983; Butler & Coward 1984). The original Geological Survey map, published in 1888, has been out of print for many years, but new maps of the area between Tongue and Durness have been published recently (British Geological Survey 1997, 2000); some of this remapping forms the basis of the present paper.

Previous papers have largely focused on three main structural levels of the thrust zone: the lowermost imbricated foreland sequences (e.g. McClay & Coward 1981; Butler 1982; Coward 1984*a*; Ramsay 1997), the overlying mylonite belt of the Moine Thrust Zone (e.g. Soper & Wilkinson 1975; Evans & White 1984; Law *et al.* 1984, 1986) and the uppermost Moine Nappe (Soper & Brown 1971; Soper & Wilkinson 1975; Holdsworth 1987, 1989*a*,*b*, 1990; Alsop & Holdsworth 1993; Holdsworth *et al.* 2001). Here we present for the first time a unified kinematic interpretation of all three levels in the little-studied northernmost part of the Moine Thrust Zone and overlying Moine Nappe, south of Whiten Head and at Faraid Head (Fig. 1).

Regional setting

The Laurentian Foreland to the Caledonian orogenic belt lies west of Loch Eriboll (Fig. 1). The oldest rocks are the Archaean–Palaeoproterozoic basement gneisses of the Lewisian Complex (Park *et al.* 1994, 2002) with

From: RIES, A. C., BUTLER, R. W. H. & GRAHAM, R. H. (eds) 2007. *Deformation of the Continental Crust: The Legacy of Mike Coward*. Geological Society, London, Special Publications, **272**, 121–142.

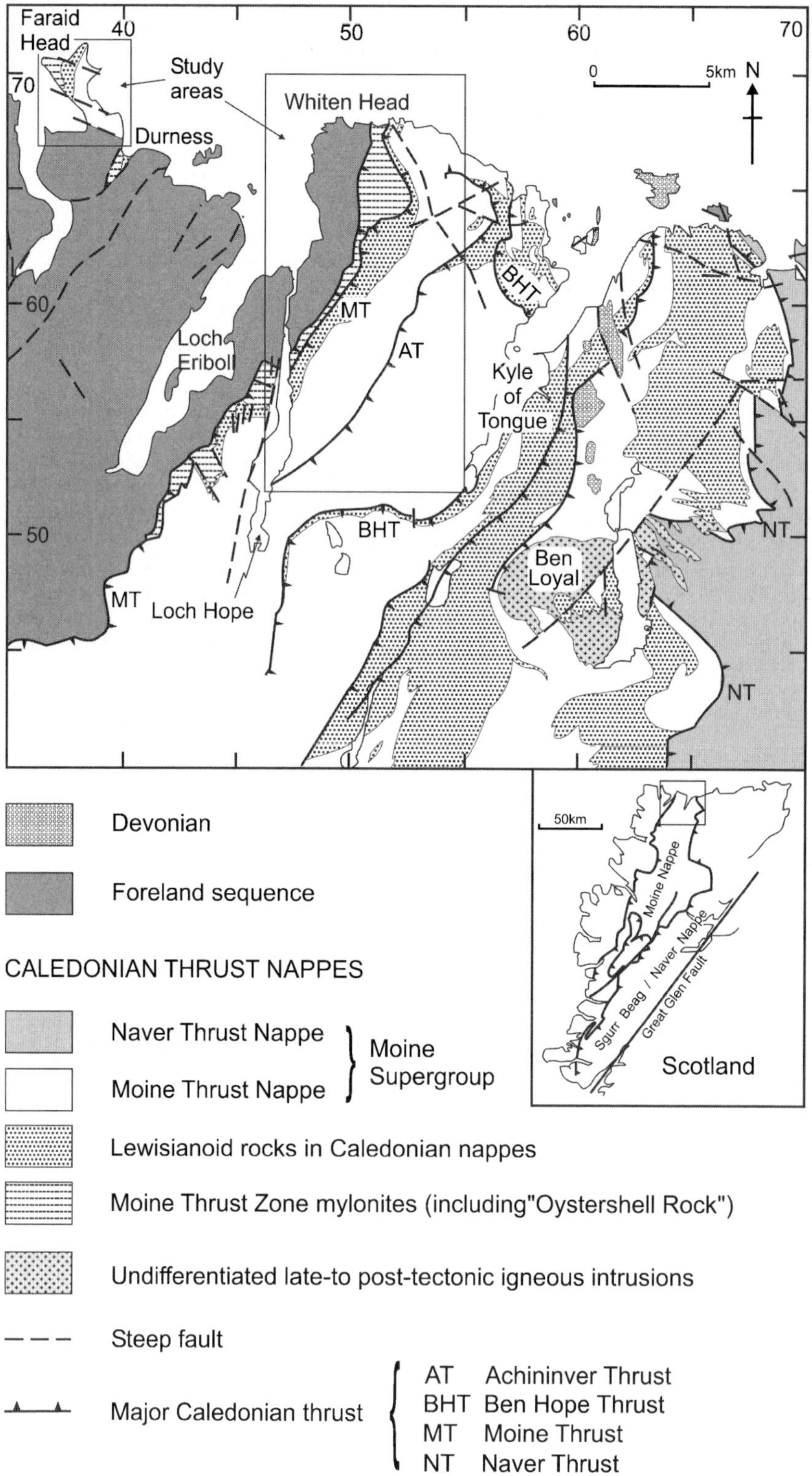
Faraid Head
40
50
60
70
70
60
50
Study areas
Whiten Head
Durness
0
5km
N
MT
AT
BHT
Loch Eriboll
Kyle of Tongue
BHT
Ben Loyal
NT
NT
MT
Loch Hope
50km
Moine Nappe
Sgurr Beag / Naver Nappe
Great Glen Fault
Scotland
Devonian
Foreland sequence
CALEDONIAN THRUST NAPPES
Naver Thrust Nappe
Moine Thrust Nappe
Moine Supergroup
Lewisianoid rocks in Caledonian nappes
Moine Thrust Zone mylonites (including"Oystershell Rock")
Undifferentiated late-to post-tectonic igneous intrusions
Steep fault
Major Caledonian thrust
AT Achininver Thrust
BHT Ben Hope Thrust
MT Moine Thrust
NT Naver Thrust

steeply dipping foliations trending approximately WNW–ESE (British Geological Survey 2000). They incorporate intrusive metabasic sheets (possibly deformed Scourie dykes) and numerous sheets of granite and pegmatite that were emplaced during Laxfordian deformation and metamorphism at *c*.1.8–1.7 Ga. The gneisses are overlain unconformably by Cambro-Ordovician sedimentary rocks (Peach *et al.* 1907). The Cambrian succession commences with the Eriboll Sandstone Formation, comprising the lower 75–125 m thick Basal Quartzite, followed by 75–100 m of *Skolithos*-bearing Pipe Rock quartzite (Swett *et al.* 1971; McKie 1990). This is overlain by the An t-Sron Formation comprising the calcareous shales of the Fucoid Beds (12–27 m thick) and the succeeding quartzites of the Salterella Grit (up to 20 m thick). The Durness Group carbonates (up to *c*. 750 m thick) form the top of the succession.

To the south and east of Loch Eriboll, the Lewisian and Cambro-Ordovician units are repeated tectonically in a series of thrust imbricate slices that collectively form the Moine Thrust Zone (MTZ; e.g. Fig. 2). In general, the structurally lowest thrust sheets cropping out to the WNW are characterized by brittle thrusting, whereas structurally overlying slices were heterogeneously to pervasively mylonitized during ductile thrusting (Soper & Wilkinson 1975; Butler 1982; Coward 1984*a*; Evans & White 1984; Law *et al.* 1984). The Moine Thrust itself defines the tectonic base of the Moine Nappe (British Geological Survey 1997, 2000), which comprises mainly Neoproterozoic metasedimentary rocks of the Moine Supergroup that were also deformed strongly during Caledonian ductile thrusting. The Moine rocks belong the Morar Group (Holdsworth *et al.* 1994) and are mainly psammites that regionally record a significant pre-Caledonian tectonic history involving garnet grade metamorphism at *c*. 800 Ma (Vance *et al.* 1998). The Moine rocks are interfolded and intersliced with strongly reworked, high-grade orthogneisses that are thought to represent fragments of the Lewisianoid basement (hereafter referred to as 'Lewisian' in the present paper) on which the Moine sedimentary protoliths were deposited unconformably (Holdsworth 1989*a*; Holdsworth *et al.* 1994, 2001; Soper *et al.* 1998).

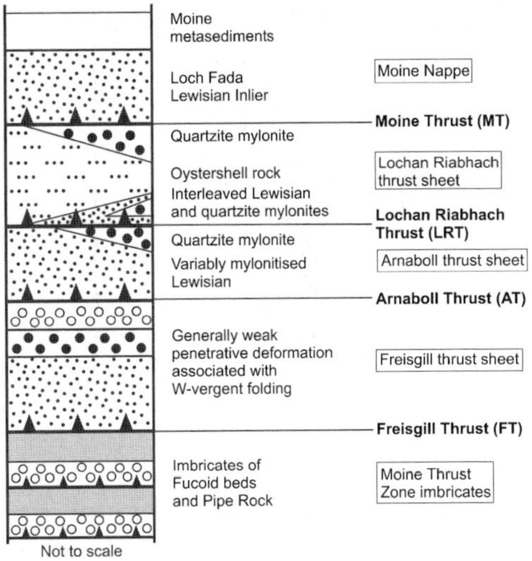

Fig. 2. Highly simplified tectonic stratigraphy of the Moine Thrust Zone and overlying Moine Nappe showing major thrusts and structural units. Ornaments are as in Figure 3.

A variety of displacement estimates have been reported for different levels and segments of the northernmost MTZ. Outliers of the thrust zone occur in the foreland near Durness and at Faraid Head (Fig. 1) and indicate a minimum displacement on the Moine Thrust of 11 km (Peach *et al.* 1907). The construction of balanced sections drawn parallel to the transport direction has shown that rather larger minimum horizontal displacements are likely. For example, Butler (1982) and Butler & Coward (1984) have suggested that the Cambrian–Ordovician succession can be restored for *c*. 54 km to the ESE. It is difficult to estimate the displacement along the Moine Thrust itself, but its association with a belt of mylonites, several hundred metres thick, suggests that it is a major displacement zone with a minimum offset of several tens of kilometres. A total displacement for the Moine Thrust and MTZ of well over 100 km is therefore commonly accepted. Isotopic evidence suggests that the bulk of Caledonian deformation within the Moine Thrust Zone and overlying Moine Nappe occurred during the Silurian at *c*. 435–425 Ma (van Breemen *et al.* 1979; Freeman *et al.* 1998; Dallmeyer *et al.* 2001; Kinny *et al.* 2003). Silurian orogenic activity in Northern Scotland is attributed to the 'Scandian' collision of Laurentia and Baltica during final stages of the closure of the

Fig. 1. Generalized geological map of the Moine and Naver nappes, Moine Thrust Zone and Foreland region in northern Sutherland. Boxes indicate locations of Figures 3 and 11. Inset map shows location map of Scottish Highlands, with major Caledonian–Scandian faults; box indicates study area shown in main part of figure.

Iapetus Ocean (Coward 1990; Dallmeyer *et al.* 2001; Dewey & Strachan 2003; Kinny *et al.* 2003).

The aims of this paper are threefold. First, we extend the classical thrust sheet template erected in the Loch Eriboll area (McClay & Coward 1981; Coward 1984*a*; British Geological Survey 2000), along strike to the north coast of Sutherland near Whiten Head. Second, we demonstrate within this area the continuity of thrust-related deformation within the Moine Nappe and the underlying Moine Thrust Zone. Finally, we establish linkages between the tectonostratigraphy and sequential structural evolution of this area and that of the outlier of the Moine Thrust Zone exposed on the Caledonian foreland at Faraid Head.

Tectonic stratigraphy of the Moine Nappe and MTZ in the Loch Hope–Whiten Head area

Remapping of the Moine Nappe and underlying MTZ in the area between Loch Hope and Whiten Head (Figs 2–4) reveals five main structural units. From east (structurally highest) to west (structurally lowest) these are: (1) the Moine Nappe, formed of medium-grade Moine psammites with strongly reworked slices and infolds of basement; (2) the Lochan Riabhach thrust sheet ('Eriboll nappe' of Ramsay 1997), formed of intensely mylonitized Lewisian lithologies and Cambrian Basal Quartzite; (3) the Arnaboll thrust sheet, comprising variably deformed Lewisian basement gneisses and Cambrian Basal Quartzite; (4) the Freisgill thrust sheet formed of weakly reworked Lewisian basement and Cambrian quartzites (both Basal Quartzite and Pipe Rock); (5) the imbricate zone involving interthrust slices of the Cambrian Pipe Rock and Fucoid Beds. The intensity of synthrusting metamorphism decreases progressively downwards through the thrust stack, and the associated dominant deformation mechanisms change from pervasive crystal plasticity, through semi-brittle deformation to brittle cataclasis and faulting.

Exposure in the study area is variable. The coastlines and immediately inland regions are generally well exposed. Spectacular sections are preserved in many cliff sections, although these are often inaccessible for detailed study. Large parts of the Moine Nappe and Lochan Riabhach thrust sheet occur inland and are poorly exposed in the Loch Hope–Faraid Head area because of thick accumulations of peat. However, the Moine Thrust and its associated hanging wall and footwall mylonite sequences are spectacularly exposed at Faraid Head.

Moine Nappe

This tectonic unit forms the hanging wall to the Moine Thrust and comprises reworked orthogneisses of the Loch Fada basement inlier that are overlain by psammites of the Moine Supergroup (Holdsworth *et al.* 2001; Fig. 3). The basement rocks of the Loch Fada inlier are mainly strongly banded, mafic to intermediate, variably mylonitic gneisses, composed of hornblende, biotite, quartz, plagioclase and secondary epidote, with accessory titanite, zircon and opaque minerals. Concordant sheets of amphibolite and strongly deformed granite may correlate, respectively, with the Scourie dykes and Laxfordian granites and pegmatites recognized within the Lewisian basement of the foreland. However, unequivocal linkage with the foreland basement remains to be proven. The Loch Fada inlier attains a maximum structural thickness of 950 m, SW of Ben Hutig (Fig. 3). The marked thinning of the inlier to the north and south is assumed to result from the Moine Thrust cutting laterally up section in its hanging wall. The overlying A'Mhoine Psammite Formation dominates the lower part of the Moine Nappe and consists mainly of pink–grey arkosic psammites with local pebbly bands and detrital seams of heavy minerals (Holdsworth *et al.* 2001). Cross-bedding and cross-lamination are preserved occasionally in areas of low tectonic strain. In the Ben Hutig region [NC 5390 6525], micaceous, banded psammites are interlayered with horizons of garnetiferous pelite up to 5 m thick. The boundary between the Loch Fada basement inlier and the overlying Moine rocks is exposed only in the inaccessible cliffs of the north coast, where it appears to be sharp and concordant [e.g. at NC 5223 6832]. It is interpreted as a tectonically modified unconformity across which ductile deformation has obliterated any signs of angular discordance (Holdsworth *et al.* 2001).

Lochan Riabhach thrust sheet

This tectonic unit lies between the Lochan Riabhach Thrust and the Moine Thrust, and comprises strongly mylonitized Lewisian gneisses and Cambrian quartzites as well as an extensive belt of chlorite–muscovite phyllonites of uncertain origin, the so-called 'Oystershell Rock' (Figs 2 and 3).

Fig. 3. Geological map of the Moine Nappe and Moine Thrust Zone between Loch Hope and Whiten Head showing the main geological units and thrusts. Boxes indicate location of Figures 5, 6 and 9.

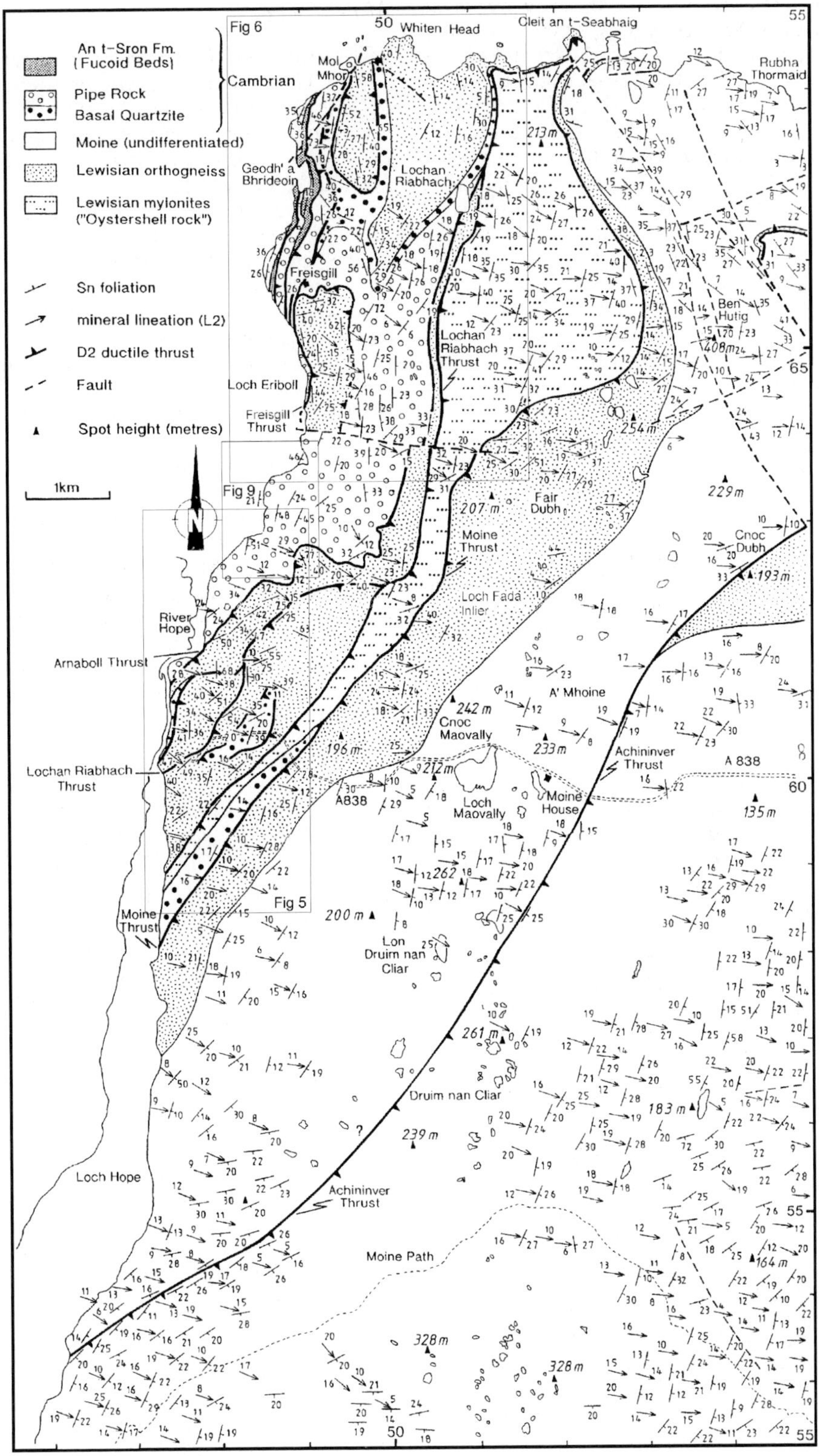
An t-Sron Fm.
(Fucoid Beds)
Pipe Rock
Basal Quartzite
Cambrian
Moine (undifferentiated)
Lewisian orthogneiss
Lewisian mylonites
("Oystershell rock")
Sn foliation
mineral lineation (L2)
D2 ductile thrust
Fault
Spot height (metres)
1km
N
Fig 6
Fig 9
Fig 5
Whiten Head
Cleit an t-Seabhaig
Rubha Thormaid
Mol Mhor
Geodh' a Bhrideoin
Lochan Riabhach
Freisgill
Ben Hutig
Lochan Riabhach Thrust
Loch Eriboll
Freisgill Thrust
Fair Dubh
Moine Thrust
Loch Fada Inlier
Cnoc Dubh
River Hope
Arnaboll Thrust
A' Mhoine
Cnoc Maovally
Achininver Thrust
A 838
A838
Lochan Riabhach Thrust
Loch Maovally
Moine House
Moine Thrust
Lon Druim nan Cliar
Druim nan Cliar
Loch Hope
Achininver Thrust
Moine Path
213m
254m
229m
193m
207m
242m
233m
196m
212m
135m
200m
261m
239m
183m
164m
328m
408m
50
55
65
60

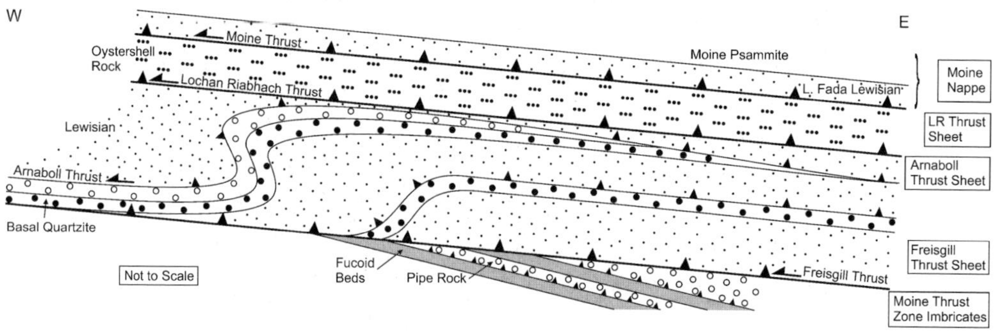

Fig. 4. Simplified ESE–WNW composite geological cross section through the Moine Nappe and Moine Thrust Zone in the Whiten Head area. (Note that the vertical scale is exaggerated.) The fold pair represent the Whiten Head Antiform and Synform shown in Figure 6 and both are believed to be truncated by the overlying Lochan Riabhach Thrust, which represents an 'out-of-sequence' or overstep structure. Ornaments are as in Figures 2 and 3.

The mylonitized Lewisian gneisses exposed immediately east of Loch Hope (Figs 3 and 5) are strongly banded on a millimetre to centimetre scale, with orange–pink quartzofeldspathic layers alternating with dark green, mafic layers dominated by actinolite and/or chlorite. Concordant, metre-scale, mafic sheets and pods may represent highly deformed Scourie dykes, and centimetre to metre-scale pink, granitic mylonites are thought to represent highly deformed Laxfordian pegmatites within the gneissic protolith. East of Loch Hope [NC 4800 6060], the mylonitic gneisses are tectonically interleaved with slices of strongly deformed Cambrian Basal Quartzite (Figs 3 and 5). These quartzites carry a penetrative mylonitic foliation and no traces of bedding or sedimentary structures are preserved.

The phyllonites correspond to the unit referred to as the 'Oystershell Rock' by previous workers (Peach *et al.* 1907; Soper & Wilkinson 1975). This distinctive unit can be traced along strike continuously as far as the western flanks of An Lean Charn, some 17 km to the SW (Soper & Wilkinson 1975; British Geological Survey 2000). The most common lithology is a fine- to medium-grained, dark green chlorite–muscovite phyllonite characterized by numerous thin, lunate, concordant lenses of quartz that correspond to the 'oystershells' first referred to by Peach *et al.* (1907). The phyllonites display textures typical of a low-grade mylonite (see below) with widespread evidence for dynamic recrystallization. At a few locations [e.g. NC 5283 6595, NC 5159 6444], small (1–2 mm) garnets are wrapped by the phyllonitic foliation. Grey–brown carbonate (?calcite) horizons are present a few metres below the Moine Thrust on the west side of Geodha nan Aigheann [NC 5322 6836].

Soper & Wilkinson (1975) suggested that the protolith of the 'Oystershell Rock' was a Cambrian sedimentary rock, based on the recognition of supposed detrital clasts in thin section. They proposed that it represents an off-shelf pelitic facies equivalent to the Durness Limestone. More recently, Holdsworth *et al.* (2001) suggested that a metamorphic origin (either Lewisian or Moine) is more likely because the quartz 'oystershells' are tectonically dismembered remnants of a metamorphic segregation fabric. Furthermore, the preservation of relict garnet porphyroclasts [e.g. at NC 5283 6595 and 5159 6444] suggests that the protolith had attained at least garnet grade during regional metamorphism prior to phyllonitization. A Lewisian origin is favoured by the presence within the phyllonite of millimetre- to metre-scale orange–pink lenses and layers of quartzofeldspathic mylonite derived probably from granite and pegmatite veins and/or leucosomes. Similar features are not found within the highly deformed Moine psammites of the Moine Nappe, but are widely preserved elsewhere within undisputed mylonites derived from Lewisian basement lithologies. In the north coast section [at NC 5240 6830], at least one 10 m thick unit of undoubted Lewisian-derived mylonite occurs interlayered with the phyllonite. Layers of brightly coloured orange and pink quartzofeldspathic mylonite, probably derived from granite or pegmatite veins, are prominent and

Fig. 5. Detailed geological map of part of the Moine Thrust Zone, immediately to the east of Loch Hope, illustrating the interleaving of mylonitized units of Cambrian quartzite and Lewisian gneiss in the hanging wall of the Lochan Riabhach Thrust [e.g. NC 4800 6060]. Refer to Figure 3 for location.

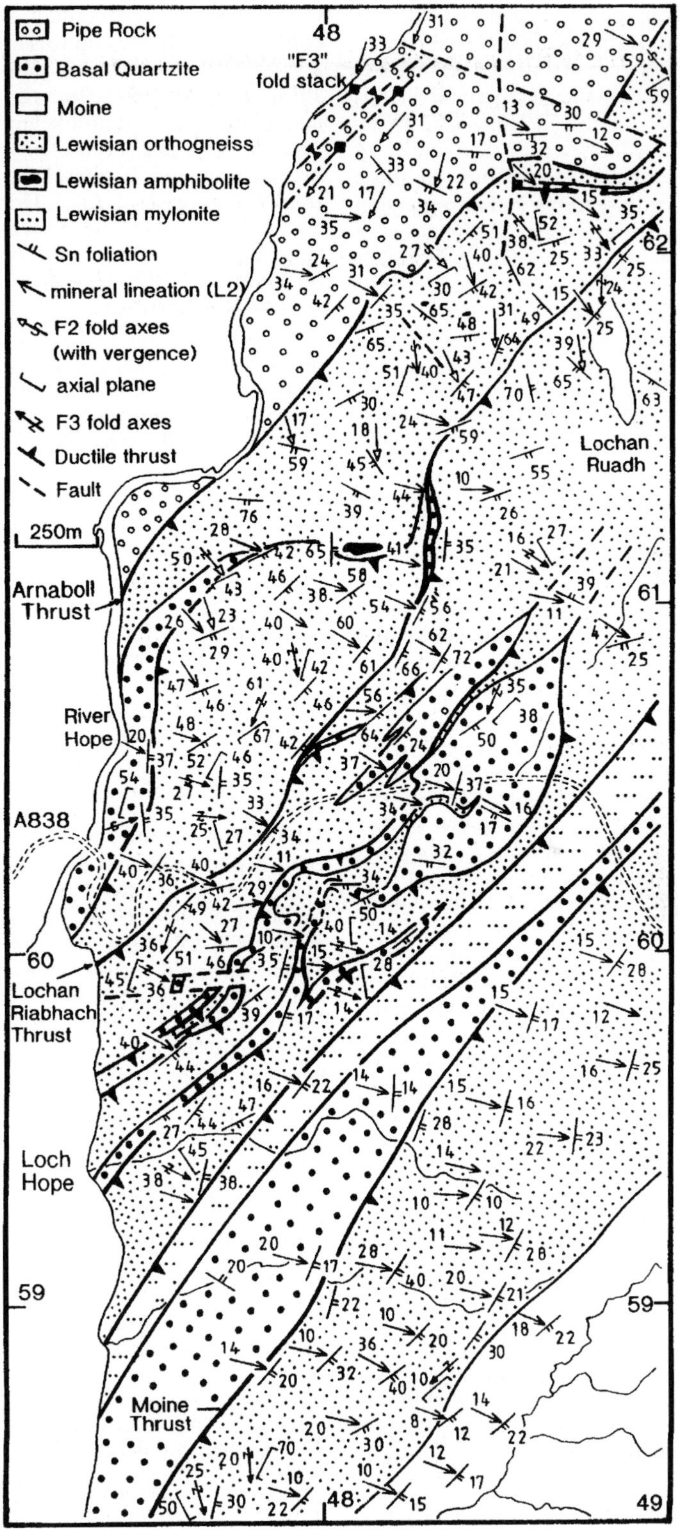

Pipe Rock
Basal Quartzite
Moine
Lewisian orthogneiss
Lewisian amphibolite
Lewisian mylonite
Sn foliation
mineral lineation (L2)
F2 fold axes
(with vergence)
axial plane
F3 fold axes
Ductile thrust
Fault
250m
48
"F3"
fold stack
62
Lochan
Ruadh
Arnaboll
Thrust
61
River
Hope
A838
60
Lochan
Riabhach
Thrust
Loch
Hope
59
Moine
Thrust
48
49

a 15 cm thick basic pod is also preserved. The occurrence of rare carbonate layers is also comparable with the presence of marbles within basement inliers elsewhere in the Northern Highlands (e.g. Winchester & Lambert 1970; Soper 1971). In general, the phyllonites are very similar in appearance, mineralogy and texture to those found associated with shearing and retrogression of Lewisian gneisses elsewhere in the Scottish Caledonides, notably in the Outer Hebrides Fault Zone (Sibson 1977; Butler *et al.* 1995; MacInnes *et al.* 2000; Imber *et al.* 2001).

A prominent sheet of quartz mylonite overlies the phyllonites in the southern part of the Whiten Head–Loch Hope area, east of Loch Hope (Figs 3 and 5). The quartz mylonite is much less feldspathic than any of the Moine psammites and mineralogically compares closely with the Cambrian quartzites. For this reason, this unit is assigned to the Cambrian. If the underlying phyllonites were derived from the mylonitization of a Lewisian protolith, as argued above, the contact between the two units probably represents a highly tectonized basement–cover unconformity. Butler (1988) interpreted the structure defined here as the Lochan Riabhach Thrust to be the Moine Thrust and thus assigned the overlying 'Oystershell' phyllonites and the quartzites described above to the Moine Nappe. However, because our preferred intepretation is that the quartzites correlate with the Cambrian succession, it seems clear that both they and the 'Oystershell' phyllonites must lie below the Moine Thrust (Figs 2 and 3).

Arnaboll thrust sheet

The Arnaboll Thrust, identified previously to the west of Loch Hope (e.g. Peach *et al.* 1907; McClay & Coward 1981; Coward 1984*a*), can be traced from close to the River Hope northeastwards over well-exposed ground as far north as Lochan Riabhach (Fig. 3). Two synformal outliers of the Arnaboll thrust sheet are also present south of Whiten Head (Fig. 6). The Arnaboll thrust sheet mainly comprises Lewisian gneisses that are unconformably overlain by, and locally tectonically interleaved with Cambrian Basal Quartzite immediately east of the River Hope (Fig. 5). The intensity of Caledonian tectonic strain within the Arnaboll thrust sheet is substantially lower than that in the overlying Lochan Riabhach thrust sheet. Most of the Lewisian gneisses are characterized by coarse-grained, gneissose fabrics; they commonly retain an original centimetre-scale colour banding defined by alternations of mafic and quartzofeldspathic layers. Foliated, concordant to shallowly discordant amphibolites up to several metres thick are correlated with the Scourie dykes (Coward 1984*a*; Ramsay 1997). Both the gneisses and the amphibolites are cut at low angles by numerous variably deformed sheets of coarse-grained granite and pegmatite of presumed Laxfordian age. Immediately east of Loch Hope, the foliation within the gneisses dips mainly to the east or ESE (Fig. 5; see also Ramsay 1997, figs 12 and 13) and the fabric becomes locally mylonitic. Caledonian strain has apparently modified the steep, ESE–WSW regional trend of the gneissose foliation on the foreland into broad parallelism with the dominant NNE structural grain of the Moine Thrust Zone. However, in certain areas [e.g. NC 4816 6142], the Lewisian gneisses strike ESE and have a moderate to steep south to SW dip, significantly oblique to the nearby Arnaboll Thrust. It is therefore possible that the original tectonic trends of the foreland are preserved in this part of the thrust sheet (Coward 1984*a*; Ramsay 1997). Where the Caledonian structural overprint is strong, the gneisses show abundant development of quartz, chlorite, epidote, zoisite and albite, often defining a prominent ESE-plunging mineral elongation lineation that is parallel to that recorded in the overlying thrust sheets (Figs 5–7).

Freisgill thrust sheet

The Freisgill thrust sheet comprises Lewisian gneisses and unconformably overlying Cambrian quartzites (Basal Quartzite and Pipe Rock) that, south of Whiten Head, are deformed into a mesoscopic, west-vergent fold-pair (Figs 3, 4 and 6). The Lewisian gneisses are exposed in the core of the Whiten Head Antiform. The two outliers of the overlying Arnaboll thrust sheet occupy the core of the complementary Whiten Head Synform. Two features show that the level of Caledonian penetrative strain in the Freisgill thrust sheet is appreciably less than that described from the overlying thrust sheets. First, bedding and sedimentary structures are commonly preserved within the Cambrian rocks. The Basal Quartzite also contains thin pebbly layers defined by equant clasts of quartz and feldspar, and original angles of *c.* 90° are often preserved between bedding and *Skolithos* worm tubes within the Pipe Rock. Second, the gneisses of

Fig. 6. Detailed geological map of part of the Moine Thrust Zone in the Whiten Head – Freisgill area, illustrating the main thrusts and folding of the Arnaboll Thrust in the core of the Whiten Head Synform (see text for discussion). The location of the views, shown in Figure 8a and b, are also shown.

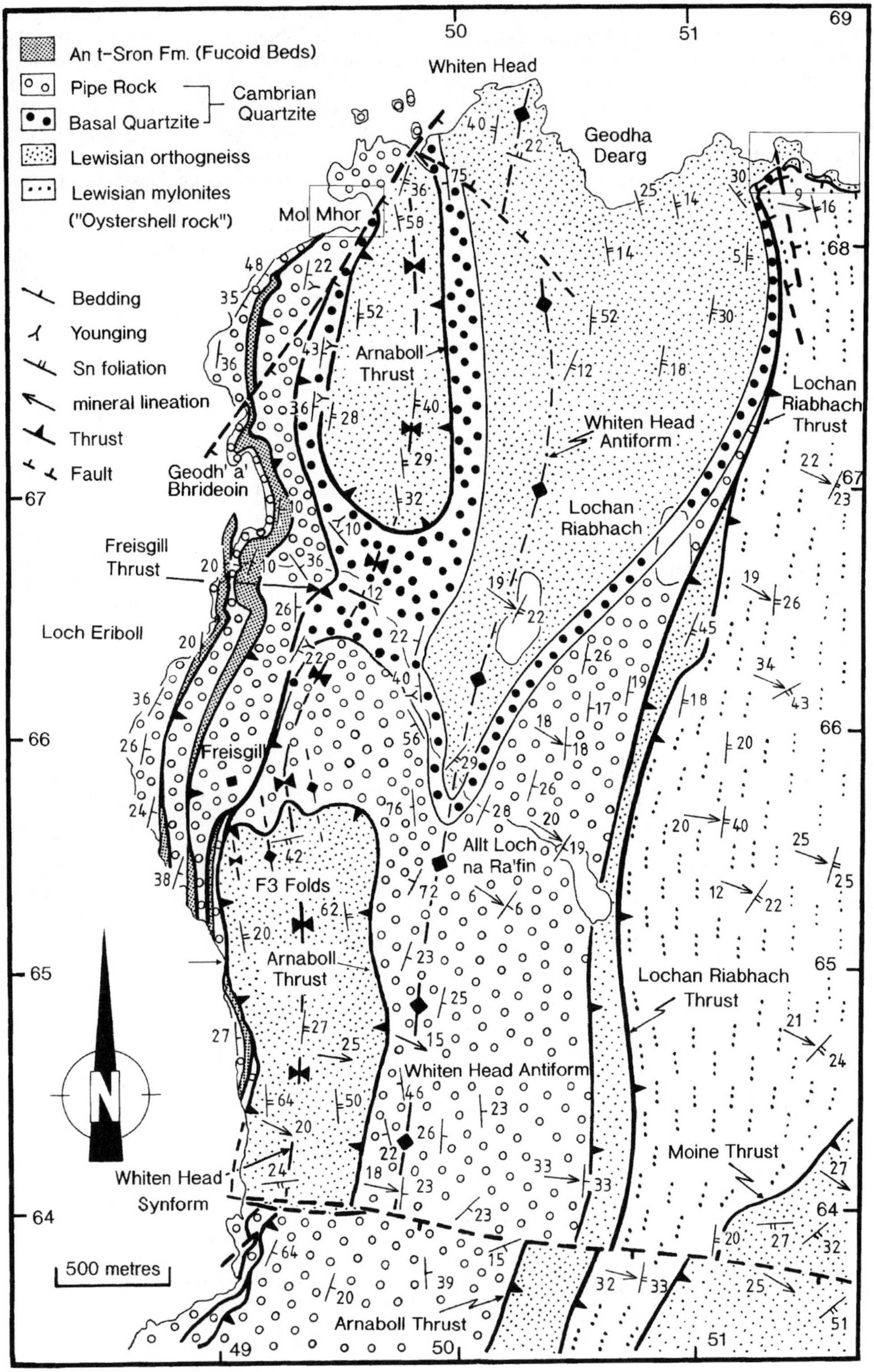

An t-Sron Fm. (Fucoid Beds)
Pipe Rock
Basal Quartzite
Cambrian Quartzite
Lewisian orthogneiss
Lewisian mylonites ("Oystershell rock")
Bedding
Younging
Sn foliation
mineral lineation
Thrust
Fault
Whiten Head
Geodha Dearg
Mol Mhor
Arnaboll Thrust
Whiten Head Antiform
Lochan Riabhach
Lochan Riabhach Thrust
Geodh' a' Bhrideoin
Freisgill Thrust
Loch Eriboll
Freisgill
Allt Loch na Ra'fin
F3 Folds
Moine Thrust
Whiten Head Synform
500 metres
N
50
51
69
68
67
66
65
64
49

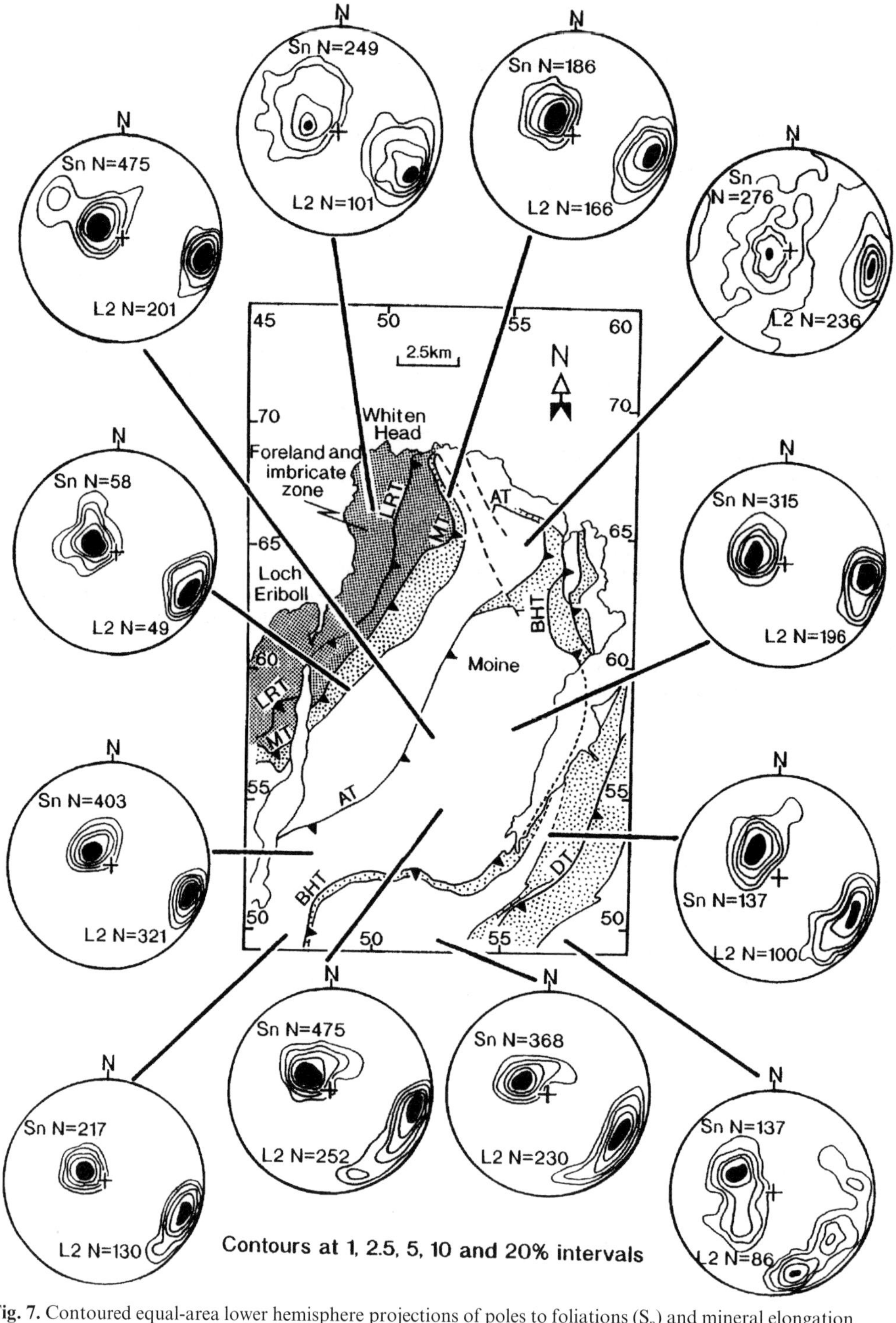

Fig. 7. Contoured equal-area lower hemisphere projections of poles to foliations (S_n) and mineral elongation lineation (L_2) orientations from the Moine Thrust Zone and overlying Moine Nappe. The consistency in fabric and lineation orientations across the thrust zone and Moine Nappe should be noted. Major basement inliers in the Moine are stippled. LRT, Lochan Riabhach Thrust; MT, Moine Thrust; AT, Achininver Thrust; BHT, Ben Hope Thrust; DT, Dherue Thrust.

Whiten Head are cut by ramifying networks of Laxfordian granite and pegmatite veins that are essentially undeformed, largely retaining their original highly discordant orientations. Caledonian penetrative strain was low overall, but narrow zones of intense deformation were localized along lithological boundaries and thrusts. The Basal Quartzite on the eastern limb of the Whiten Head Antiform is underlain by a 10 m thick zone of mylonitic Lewisian gneiss. The quartzites in the immediate footwall of the Lochan Riabhach Thrust are also strongly mylonitic. It is assumed that the Freisgill Thrust probably extends farther to the SW into the Loch Eriboll area, although its precise identification within the thrusted quartzites of Ben Heilam is uncertain because of lack of exposure (British Geological Survey 2000).

Significant parts of the Freisgill thrust sheet are highly imbricated by thrusts (e.g. Fig. 8a) and associated WNW-verging folds (Figs 4 and 6), which are particularly well displayed in Pipe Rock exposures on the northern and western flanks of Cnoc nan Gobhar (Fig. 9). Here, numerous examples occur of thrusts being refolded by folds detached along lower, later thrusts (e.g. Sections A and B in Fig. 9), illustrating the predominance of foreland-directed, piggyback thrusting in the MTZ (e.g. Elliott & Johnson 1980; Butler 1982, 2004). In the far north of the area, near to the base of the cliffs at Geodha Dearg (Fig. 8a), the Lewisian gneisses that crop out around Whiten Head are unconformably overlain by a thin unit of Basal Quartzite that is succeeded by a further thrust sheet of Lewisian gneiss (e.g. see Holdsworth *et al.* 2001, Fig. 15a and b). This unit of quartzite has not been detected in the poorly exposed inland region to the south, and both it and the large unit of Lewisian in the core of the Whiten Head Antiform must be cut out by the Freisgill Thrust up-transport as they do not crop out west of the Whiten Head Synform (Figs 4 and 6).

Moine Thrust Zone imbricates

The rocks structurally beneath the Freisgill Thrust comprise an imbricate stack of Cambrian Pipe Rock and Fucoid Beds (Figs 4 and 6; see also Bowler 1987). The cliff sections, north and south of Mol Mhor [NC 4950 6810], provide superb strike-parallel and strike-normal exposure through the imbricates (Fig. 8b). The degree of internal strain is generally low as sedimentary structures and original 90° angles between worm tubes and bedding in the Pipe Rock are commonly preserved. This sequence of imbricates appears to be the extension of the imbricate zone exposed along the west side of Ben Heilam in the Loch Eriboll area to the SW (British Geological Survey 2000).

Microstructures and syntectonic temperatures in the Moine Nappe and MTZ

Numerous detailed papers have been published on the deformation processes associated with the formation of the Moine Thrust Zone mylonites (e.g. Christie 1960; White 1979; White *et al.* 1982; Evans & White 1984; Law *et al.* 1984, 1986; Coward *et al.* 1992), and a smaller number have focused on the Moine Nappe (e.g. Phillips 1937; Evans & White 1984; Holdsworth & Grant 1990; Holdsworth *et al.* 2001). It is not the intention to replicate these comprehensive descriptions, but to summarize the most important microstructures and information pertaining to the temperatures at which deformation occurred.

Moine Nappe

In the Moine Nappe, the dominant foliation ('S_2') dips towards the ESE with a quartz mineral lineation ('L_2') plunging approximately downdip (Figs 3, 7 and 8c). This lineation is interpreted to represent the *X*-direction of the finite strain ellipsoid and to define the direction of tectonic transport. Shear bands in pelitic rocks [e.g. at NC 5808 6547] and occasional mica fish and asymmetric wrapping textures in other mylonite units [e.g. at NC 5931 6144] indicate a top-to-the-WNW sense of shear. Quartz *c*-axis fabrics also mainly display asymmetrical patterns consistent with a top-to-the-WNW sense of shear (e.g. Grant 1989; Holdsworth & Grant 1990).

The rocks of the Moine Nappe mainly contain upper greenschist- to mid-amphibolite-facies mineral assemblages that appear to result from superimposed Neoproterozoic (*c.* 820–730 Ma) and Early Palaeozoic (Caledonian) (*c.* 435–425 Ma) metamorphic events (Holdsworth *et al.* 2001; Strachan *et al.* 2002). Petrologically, these events are often difficult to separate, but a thrust-related metamorphic inversion is recognized regionally within the Moine Nappe, with a general west to east increase in metamorphic grade (Fig. 1; Soper & Brown 1971; Barr *et al.* 1986; Holdsworth *et al.* 2001).

In western Sutherland, the Moine rocks of the Moine Nappe are mostly fine- to medium-grained (0.1–1 mm) and do not carry gneissic fabrics. Pelitic and semi-pelitic rocks (Moine units and semi-pelitic basement schists) contain an assemblage of quartz + muscovite + biotite + plagioclase + garnet ± rare staurolite ± K-feldspar ± rare kyanite. Garnets mainly occur as idioblastic grains, up to 15 mm in diameter, with straight

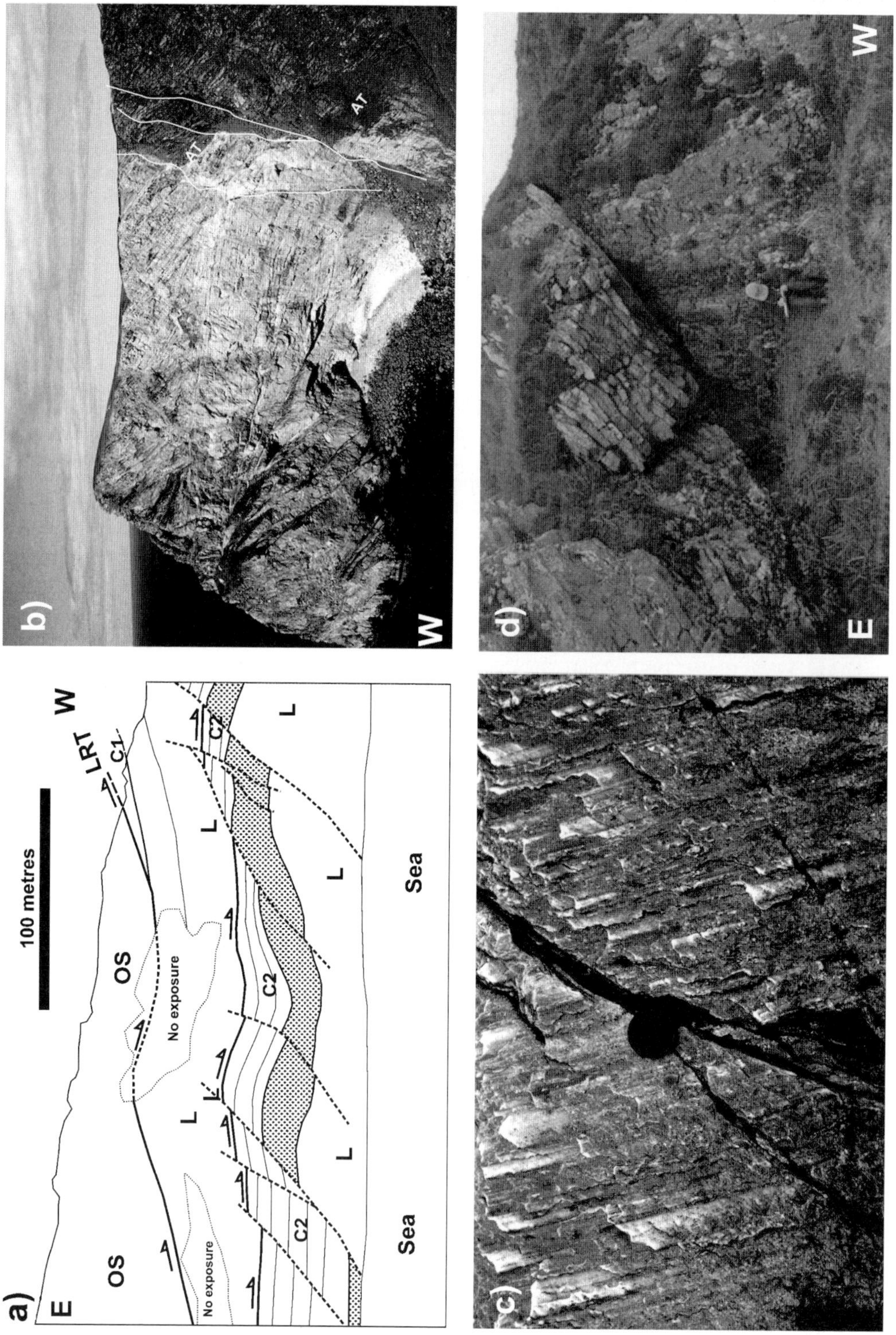

a)
E
W
100 metres
OS
No exposure
LRT
C1
C2
L
Sea
b)
AT
W
c)
d)
E
W

to curved inclusion trails of quartz [e.g. at NC 5808 6547]. A westward decrease in metamorphic grade within the Moine Nappe is indicated by the change in plagioclase composition in pelitic, calc-silicate and basic rocks from An_{10-30} (oligoclase) in the east to An_{0-10} (albite) in the west. There is also a east to west decrease in average quartz and feldspar grain size from *c.* 0.5–1 mm to *c.* 0.1–0.5 mm.

West of the Kyle of Tongue, mylonitic textures are preserved in zones of high strain, adjacent to ductile thrusts. Platy quartzofeldspathic units carry numerous strongly aligned flakes of white mica and small, rounded grains of epidote, sphene, ore and allanite, arranged in layers or trails separating highly elongate, recrystallized domains of quartz. The distribution and grain size of these minerals strongly controls the shape and grain size of recrystallized quartz as a result of grain boundary pinning (Vernon 2004). This secondary grain growth effect results in the formation of distinct planar domains of varying grain size and mica content that enhances strongly the platy aspect of the fabric (Holdsworth & Grant 1990). Basement inliers, present in the hanging walls of ductile thrusts in the Moine Nappe, are intensely deformed with extensive retrogression to form platy mylonitic schists rich in white mica, biotite, green amphibole, plagioclase (albite), epidote and quartz. The basement origin of such rocks is often not immediately obvious, although small lower-strain augen may preserve a relict gneissose fabric. Relict feldspar porphyroclasts, preserved in acid Lewisian gneisses and arkosic, pebbly Moine psammites, are wrapped by mantles and tails of small recrystallized feldspar grains. Internally, many of these relict grains preserve annealed shear and tensile fractures.

In the rocks of the Moine Nappe, east of the Kyle of Tongue, the effects of secondary recrystallization (annealing) are strong in both quartz and feldspar, such that few recognizable mylonitic fabrics are preserved and textures indicative of shear sense are generally absent. The apparently annealed character of these rocks, together with their coarser grain size and the more anorthitic composition of plagioclase, suggests that these rocks record Caledonian amphibolite-facies metamorphic conditions (>450 °C). The preservation of mylonitic fabrics, finer grain size and more albitic plagioclase compositions in rocks west of the Kyle of Tongue suggest metamorphic conditions transitional with the upper part of the greenschist facies (<450 °C), at least during later Caledonian metamorphism (Holdsworth *et al.* 2001). A zone of retrogression, first recognized by Read (1931, 1934), is developed in the Moine rocks in the immediate hanging wall of the Moine Thrust Zone. This is well illustrated on the western flanks of Ben Hutig [e.g. at NC 536 655], where biotite and garnet in the pelite bands are extensively altered to chlorite, giving the rocks a distinctive green tinge (e.g. Wilson 1953). The dominant S_2 foliation in this westernmost part of the Moine Nappe is more noticeably mylonitic (e.g. Evans & White 1984). This zone of retrogression and lower-temperature (250–350 °C) mylonitization is here considered to mark the transition into the underlying Moine Thrust Zone mylonites.

Moine Thrust Zone

The most widespread structure associated with the thrust zone is the ESE-dipping mylonitic foliation that is generally pervasive above the Arnaboll Thrust and heterogeneously developed in the underlying imbricate zone. The associated ESE-plunging mineral elongation lineation is interpreted to represent the *X*-direction of the finite strain ellipsoid and to define the direction of tectonic transport. Various shear criteria, including S–C fabrics, mica fish, extensional

Fig. 8. (**a**) Line drawing from photograph of view looking south towards the cliffs 0.5 km west of Cleit an t-Seabhaig (see Figs 3 and 6 for location) showing (from top to base) 'Oystershell' phyllonites (OS), the Lochan Riabhach Thrust (LRT), Cambrian Basal Quartzite (C1), and the upper part of the Freisgill thrust sheet comprising two units of Lewisian basement (L) separated by a thin slice of Cambrian Basal Quartzite (C2); the ornamented zone below the quartzite is a prominent sheet of Lewisian granite–pegmatite. It should be noted that the thrust pile is cross-cut by numerous post-Caledonian steeply east-dipping normal faults. The LRT cuts down section in its footwall northwards so that the Arnaboll thrust sheet sliver shown in Figure 4 is cut out. (**b**) View looking north of spectacular stacked sequences of imbricated Cambrian quartzites (Pipe Rock) on the north side of Mol Mhor (for location see Fig. 6). Note the steep post-Caledonian normal fault zone (highlighted in white), which down-faults the Arnaboll Thrust (AT) and its hanging wall of dark Lewisian basement. (**c**) Plan view of ESE-plunging mineral stretching lineation in platy Moine psammites. (**d**) Brittle out-of-sequence or overstep thrust emplacing previously mylonitized Cambrian quartzite over a footwall of mylonitic Lewisian basement. Slickenlines on this fault are parallel to its dip and it clearly cuts down section up-dip in its hanging wall: hence it exhibits an apparently extensional character typical of many out-of-sequence or overstep faults in the Moine Thrust Zone (e.g. see Butler 2004; Butler *et al.* 2006).

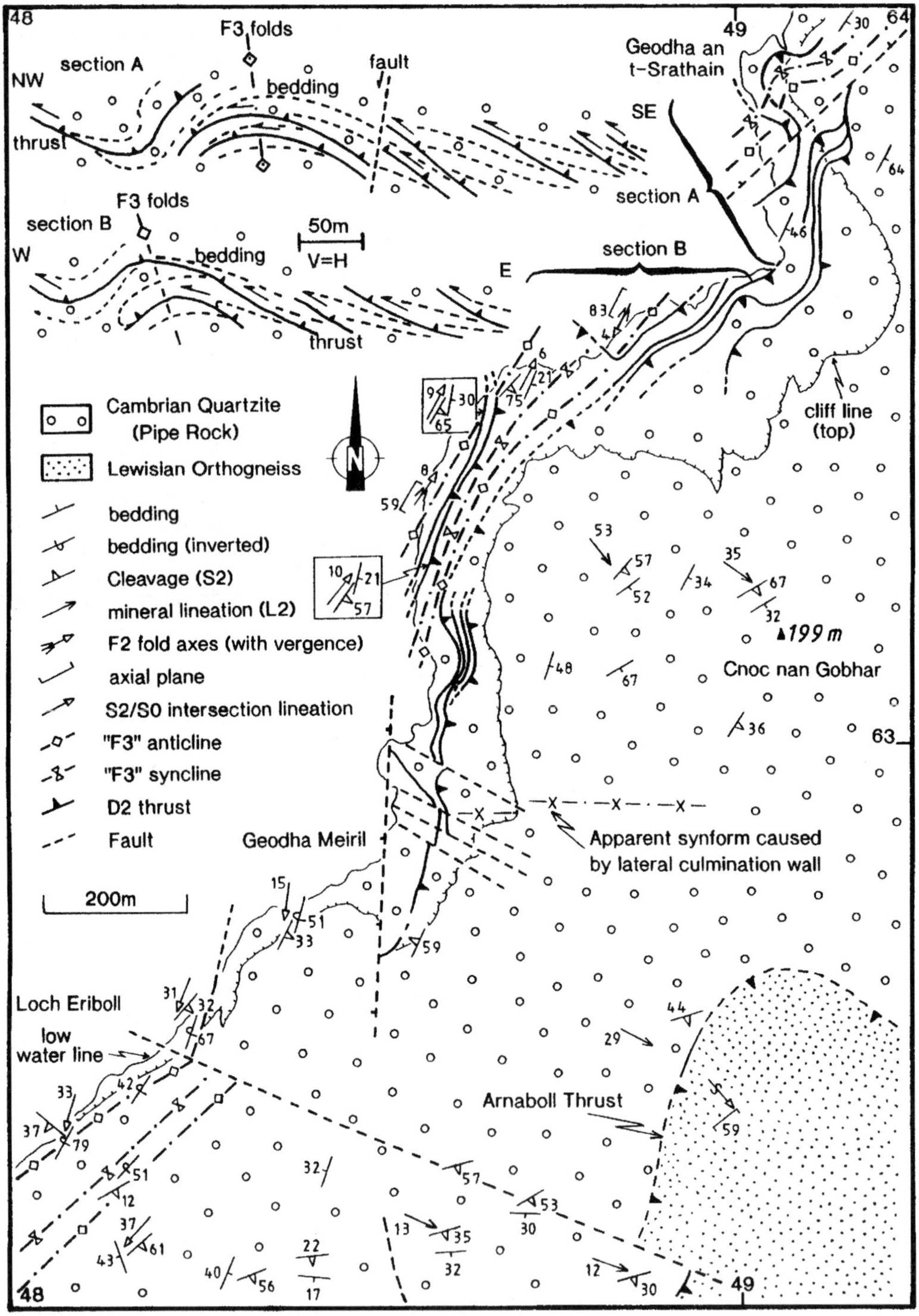

Fig. 9. Detailed geological map of part of the Moine Thrust Zone in the cliffs to the north, west and SW of Cnoc nan Gobhar (see Fig. 3 for location). Note the westward-verging folds of thrust imbricates that are considered to relate to underlying displacements reflecting a piggyback sequence of thrust propagation.

shear bands, and asymmetrically sheared porphyroclasts and *Skolithos* worm tubes, indicate a consistent top-to-the-WNW sense of thrusting, parallel to this lineation in all parts of the thrust zone.

Mineralogical and textural observations indicate that the temperatures associated with mylonitization were broadly equivalent to those of the greenschist facies (*c.* 250–350 °C). Within basement protoliths, the mylonitic foliation is defined by muscovite, chlorite, epidote and plagioclase (albite) that have resulted from the pervasive retrogression of earlier amphibolite- or upper greenschist-facies assemblages such as hornblende, biotite and anorthitic plagioclase (Holdsworth *et al.* 2001). The mylonitic foliation within the 'Oystershell' phyllonite is similarly defined by a greenschist-facies mineralogy of white mica, chlorite, quartz, plagioclase (albite), biotite and carbonate with accessory magnetite, pyrite, apatite and K-feldspar. Biotite, chlorite and white mica commonly form fibrous aggregates overgrowing porphyroclasts of quartz and feldspar in pressure shadows. Chlorite widely replaces biotite and rare early garnets. The white mica and epidote may have been derived, at least in part, from the breakdown of calcic feldspar, as the larger plagioclase grains are often sieved with numerous tiny flakes of white mica and epidote. At a few localities [e.g. NC 5283 6595; NC 5159 6444], the mica fabric wraps around small (1–2 mm) garnets that are thought to be relics of a previous higher-grade metamorphic event, but are now commonly partially altered to fine-grained aggregates of chlorite. Within most of the thrust zone feldspars, mostly deformed by brittle fracturing and kinking of grains, indicate that syntectonic temperatures were below *c.* 450–500 °C (e.g. Tullis & Yund 1987). In contrast, quartz underwent widespread dynamic recrystallization to form elongate ribbons that wrap around isolated feldspar porphyroclasts as documented elsewhere in the Moine thrust zone (White *et al.* 1982; Evans & White 1984; Law *et al.* 1984, 1986). This implies that syntectonic temperatures exceeded *c.* 300 °C (e.g. Hirth & Tullis 1992).

In detail, several lines of evidence indicate that a thrust-related metamorphic inversion has occurred within the MTZ. In the Loch Fada basement sheet, hornblende is sometimes replaced by actinolite, and feldspar porphyroclasts show signs of marginal recrystallization; these features suggest that syntectonic temperatures at this high structural level were probably equivalent to the mid- to upper greenschist facies (*c.* 300–400 °C). This contrasts with the heterogeneous replacement of hornblende by chlorite, as well as the entirely brittle deformation and cataclasis of feldspar porphyroclasts in structurally lower thrust sheets. The unmylonitized Lewisian gneisses, which occupy the core of the Whiten Head Antiform, are only weakly retrogressed, further showing how the grade of syntectonic metamorphism decreased structurally downwards through the thrust zone. The acid gneisses contain biotite, quartz and altered plagioclase (albite). Amphibolite pods still retain fresh green hornblende that is locally replaced by epidote.

Regional structure and deformation patterns within the Moine Thrust Zone and Moine Nappe

In the following section, we propose that the complex structure of this part of the Moine Thrust Zone and Moine Nappe results from foreland propagation of thrusts and related folds followed by out-of-sequence WNW-directed thrusting, principally along the Lochan Riabhach Thrust. Finally, the thrust sheet template described above is modified by steep normal faults in various orientations (Fig. 3).

Foreland-propagating thrusting and folding

The structures that indicate that deformation propagated towards the foreland are best discussed by addressing first of all the thrust-related structures within the Moine Nappe and then progressing westwards (and structurally downwards). Within the Moine Nappe, regional deformation related to ductile Caledonian thrusting (D_2) has resulted in two generations of folds referred to as F_2 and F_3 (Holdsworth 1990; Alsop & Holdsworth 1993, 1999, 2002, 2004*a*; Alsop *et al.* 1996; Holdsworth *et al.* 2001). F_2 folds of bedding and an early bedding-parallel S_1 fabric display an axial-planar, often penetrative (S_2) fabric and are marked by fold hinges that are highly curvilinear about the ESE-plunging mineral elongation lineation (L_2). F_2 sheath fold geometries are developed widely on all scales and are clearly associated with top-to-the-WNW ductile thrusting based on their patterns of vergence, facing and associated shear-sense criteria (Holdsworth 1989*a*; Alsop & Holdsworth 2004*b*). F_3 folds deform the existing foliation and L_2 lineation and are spatially associated with D_2 high-strain zones. Open–close F_3 folds are variably oriented about the mineral elongation lineation and are typically modelled as reflecting continued flow perturbations in the adjacent D_2 high-strain zones (Coward & Potts 1983; Ridley 1986; Alsop & Holdsworth 2004*a*), rather than resulting from distinct, separate deformation events at a regional scale as proposed by previous workers (e.g. Soper 1971; Soper & Brown 1971; Soper & Wilkinson 1975; Mendum 1979). Once again, the vergence patterns and associated shear-sense criteria suggest an association with top-to-the-WNW thrusting (Holdsworth 1990; Alsop & Holdsworth 1993, 2004*a*).

Within the underlying 'Oystershell' phyllonites, a comparable pattern of minor folding is developed, with at least two fold phases being preserved. Rare intrafolial 'F_2' isoclinal folds of the mylonitic foliation are present in some of the more quartzofeldspathic horizons [e.g. NC 5105 6629] and plunge ESE, at low angles to the mineral lineation. They are coaxially refolded by open-to-tight minor 'F_3' folds that are ubiquitously developed throughout the phyllonites. These folds are millimetre- to centimetre-scale buckles that are often markedly irregular and disharmonic in form. They cause widespread crenulation of the phyllonitic foliation, but as axial surfaces are typically curviplanar, well-defined crenulation cleavages are rare. The mineral lineation is seen to pass around the hinges of these folds in many exposures [e.g. NC 5173 6630; NC 5160 6450], although fold axes often lie at low angles or subparallel to the linear fabric (Alsop & Holdsworth 1993, 2002; Holdsworth *et al.* 2001). Changes in the plunge and fold vergence on either side of the area where the phyllonite zone reaches its greatest thickness correspond to a broad antiformal structure (Fig. 3). East-plunging 'S' vergent minor folds with a SSE-dipping axial plane are dominant on the north side of the culmination, whereas SE-plunging 'Z'-vergent minor folds with ENE-dipping axial planes dominate on the south side of the structure (Fig. 10). The style and vergence of these folds are similar to those of the 'F_3' folds in the overlying Moine Nappe. The passive upwarping of the earlier-formed Moine Thrust during development of the culmination within the phyllonites (Fig. 3) indicates that deformation propagated towards the foreland.

Further evidence for the foreland-propagating nature of deformation is provided by the tight folding of the Arnaboll Thrust in the core of the Whiten Head Synform (Figs 4 and 6). It is clear that west-directed emplacement of the Arnaboll thrust sheet must have predated development of the major fold pair in its footwall. The dominant foliation and accompanying mineral extension lineation with the gneisses above the Arnaboll Thrust are equated, respectively, with the composite S_0–S_1–S_2 fabric and associated L_2 in the overlying Lochan Riabhach thrust sheet and the Moine Nappe (Fig. 7). Because

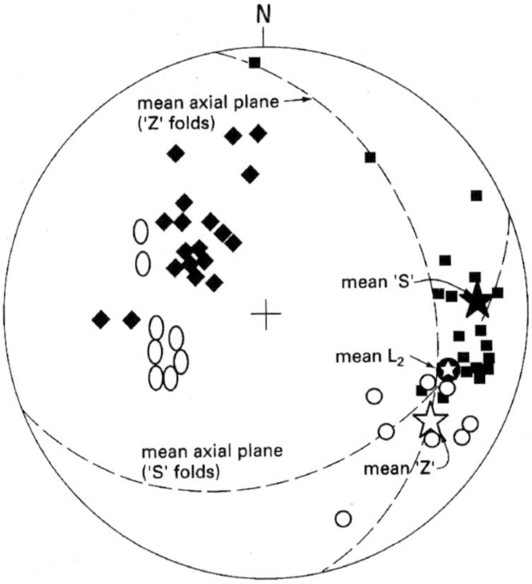

Fig. 10. Equal area stereoplot showing minor fold structures from the 'Oystershell' phyllonites and their relationship to the mean mineral lineation (after Holdsworth *et al.* 2001). Fold hinges are open circles (Z folds; $n = 8$) and filled squares (S folds; $n = 19$), with mean hinge orientations labelled; poles to fold axial planes are ellipses (Z folds; $n = 8$) and filled diamonds (S folds; $n = 19$), with mean planes plotted.

these fabrics are deformed by the mesoscopic fold pair associated with folding of the Arnaboll Thrust, these folds are thought to be analogous to the 'F_3' folds described in the overlying thrust sheets, most notably the NNE–SSW-trending folds recognized in the region west of the Kyle of Tongue by Alsop & Holdsworth (1993, fig 1). The Whiten Head fold pair are also structurally analogous to structures that deform the Arnaboll Thrust further SW in the Loch Eriboll area, such as the Kempie Bay Syncline (Coward 1984*a*).

In coastal sections through the imbricate zone SSW of Whiten Head, field relations show clearly that displacement along the Freisgill Thrust predated development of the underlying imbricate zone. Imbricated sequences of Cambrian quartzite and Fucoid Beds exposed north and south of Geodh'a Bhrideoin (Fig. 6) form a culmination zone that is aligned in the transport direction with that developed at higher structural levels within the 'Oystershell' phyllonites and the Moine Nappe (Fig. 3). These imbricates are overlain by the Friesgill Thrust, which is locally folded by buckle folds that are considered to reflect underlying displacements on thrusts within the imbricated zone; for example, south of Freisgill [NC 655 495] (Fig. 6). Thrust-related fold axes and bedding–S_2 cleavage intersections typically plunge gently towards the south. Further south, between Geodha Meiril [NC 4850 6290] and Geodha an t-Srathain [NC 4900 6390], Cambrian quartzite within the Freisgill thrust sheet is imbricated and repeated by WNW-directed thrusts with localized inversion of bedding on the overturned limbs of NNE–SSW-trending upright, mesoscopic folds (Fig. 9). This asymmetric folding is considered to develop in response to displacements on underlying thrusts within an overall 'piggyback' system of thrust propagation.

'Out-of-sequence' WNW-directed thrusting

The Lochan Riabhach Thrust (LRT) marks the basal contact of the 'Oystershell' phyllonites in the north of the study area and, to the south, of a pervasively deformed sequence of interleaved Lewisian- and quartzite-derived mylonites (Figs 2–4). It is exposed only on the north coast section west of Cleit an t-Seabhaig [e.g. NC 5120 6820], where it is marked by a brittle detachment fault dipping shallowly to the east (Fig. 8a). The rocks in the footwall of the LRT are always significantly less pervasively mylonitized compared with those in the hanging wall. The brittle detachment exposed on the north coast was interpreted by Holdsworth *et al.* (2001) to correlate with a series of top-to-the-ESE extensional detachments recognized further east in the Moine Nappe (Holdsworth 1989*a*). However, recent mapping to the SW in the Loch Eriboll area and around Durness (Holdsworth *et al.* 2006) has recognized the brittle LRT as an 'out-of-sequence' top-to-the-WNW low-angle structure that separates intensely mylonitized rocks in its hanging wall from generally less deformed rocks in its footwall. The apparently out-of-sequence nature of the LRT is evident in the area NE of Loch Hope, as the fault plane is clearly unaffected by, and therefore post-dates, the Whiten Head Antiform and Synform in its footwall. It is also unaffected by the major culmination that is associated with the passive upwarping of the Moine Thrust west of Ben Hutig. It is therefore suggested that the LRT sliced across the thrust zone at low angles after initial thrust stacking (Fig. 4). Further evidence for smaller-scale 'out-of-sequence' thrusting is identified in the hanging wall of the Lochan Riabhach Thrust, NE of Hope Bridge, where brittle thrusts are associated with re-imbrication of the ductile mylonites [NC 4800 6060]. Here, westerly directed thrusts associated with brittle fabrics and epidote veining cut the ductile mylonitic foliation and put Cambrian quartzites onto Lewisian gneisses (Fig 8d). At least one other fault of this kind occurs within the Oystershell phyllonite belt exposed on the north coast [NC 5160 6810] (Holdsworth *et al.* 2001, Fig. 15b).

Given the rather poor exposure in the present study area, it is difficult to shed much light on the underlying significance of the out-of-sequence structures. Clearly, they are comparable with late, apparently extensional detachments recognized elsewhere in the Moine Thrust Zone by Coward (1982, 1984*b*, 1985), in which case they may be related to gravity-driven collapse of the Moine Nappe and thrust zone during final stages of the Caledonian Orogeny. More recently, however, Butler (2004) and Butler *et al.* (2007) have suggested that such features are localized overstep thrusts resulting from synchronous and heterogeneous thrust movements.

Tectonic stratigraphy and structural history of the Moine Thrust Zone at Faraid Head

Small outliers of the Moine Thrust Zone are preserved in down-faulted blocks on the Caledonian Foreland at Durness and Faraid Head (Fig. 1; Peach *et al.* 1907). The age of the normal faults that bound the outliers is unknown but a Devonian (Old Red Sandstone) or Permo-Triassic age seems likely given the timing of sedimentary basin formation in the West Orkney Basin that lies immediately offshore and to the north (Coward & Enfield 1987; Enfield & Coward 1987; Stoker *et al.* 1993). The steep normal faults that are present within the thrust zone near Whiten Head (Figs 3 and 8a) are assumed to be of the same age. The Durness outlier has been described by Hippler & Knipe (1990) and Holdsworth *et al.* (2006); here we focus on the geology of the poorly known Faraid Head outlier, to assess whether or not the tectonic stratigraphy described above from the Whiten Head area can be continued in a direction parallel to thrust transport and up-dip.

The Faraid Head outlier exposes three lithotectonic units that dip mainly at a shallow angle to the ESE (Fig. 11a and b). An upper unit of Moine psammites overlies a unit of variably mylonitized Lewisian orthogneisses that include thin, subordinate layers of marble and schistose metasediment. The Lewisian rocks in turn overlie a unit of white mica–chlorite-rich phyllonite that is identical to the 'Oystershell Rock' described above. The Moine rocks comprise at least 500 m of fine- to medium-grained, grey–brown bedded psammites with occasional thin (<1 cm) layers of garnetiferous semi-pelite and pelite. The Lewisian rocks comprise units of variably

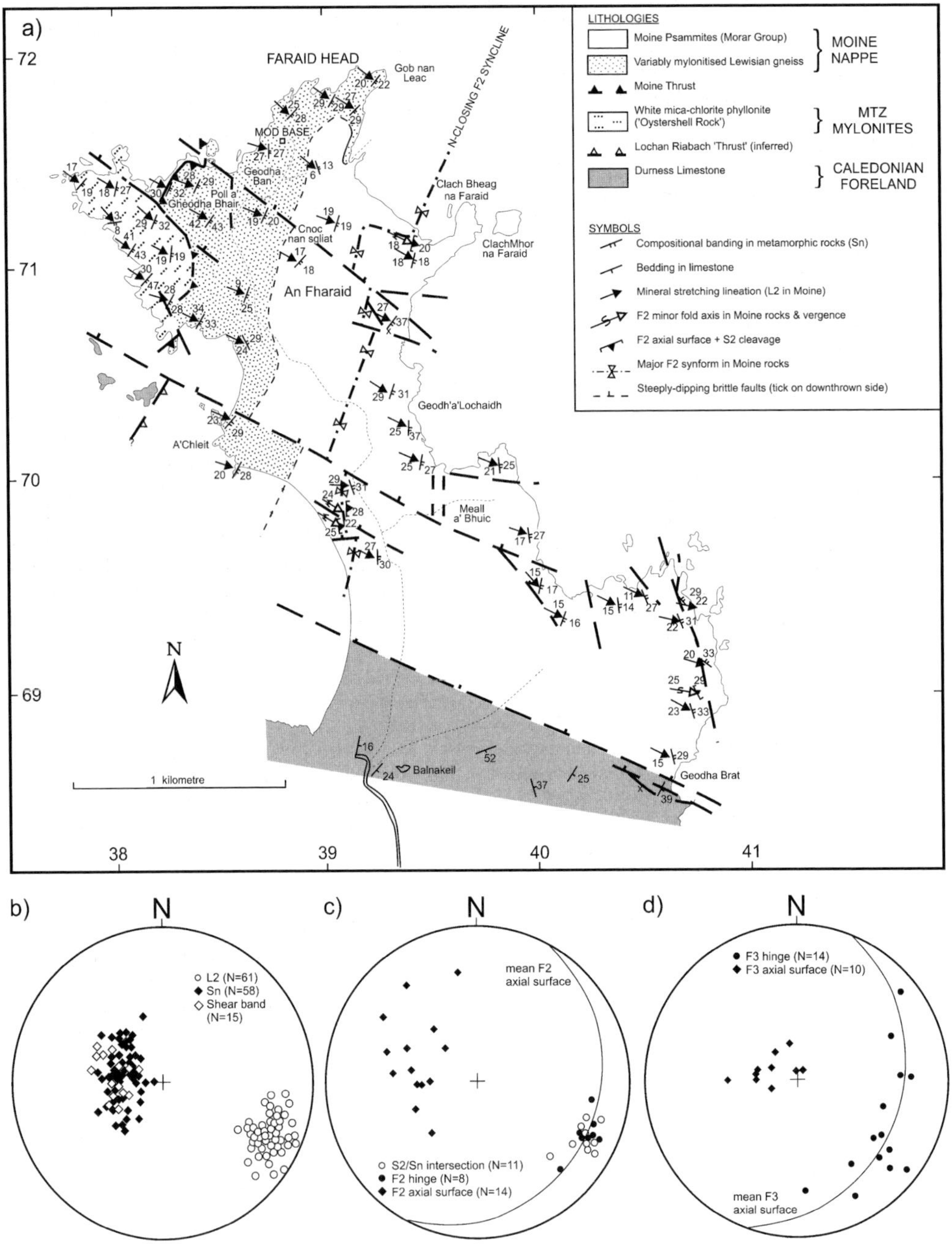

Fig. 11. (**a**) Simplified geological map of the Faraid Head outlier. (**b–d**) Equal-area, lower hemisphere stereoplots of minor structures including: (**b**) poles to foliation or layering, poles to shear bands and mineral stretching lineations; (**c**) poles to F_2 axial planes, S_2–S_n intersection lineations and F_2 minor fold hinges; (**d**) poles to F_3 axial planes and F_3 minor fold hinges.

mylonitic, pink acid to dark grey–green basic gneiss interbanded on all scales from millimetres to metres. Minor lenticular intercalations of grey–brown marble, dark brown biotite schist and concordant green amphibolites are also present locally. The concordant contact between Moine and Lewisian rocks is exposed only in steep cliff faces 300 m SSW of Gob nan Leac [NC 391 715]. The concordant contact between the Lewisian-derived mylonites above and the underlying 'Oystershell Rock' is exposed halfway up the steep cliffs west of Poll a' Gheodha Bhain [NC 382 713] and on the shore 500 m NNW of A'Chleit [NC 382 708] (Fig. 11) The 'Oystershell Rock' incorporates several layers of grey quartzofeldspathic rock up to several metres thick and narrow (<1 cm) seams of fine-grained grey–brown marble. The base of the phyllonites is not exposed on the peninsula.

The Moine rocks are folded on a large scale by a northward-closing, isoclinal reclined fold with a shallowly ESE-dipping axial planar fabric of local F_2 age (Fig. 11a and c). Remnants of cross-laminations, which are preserved only in low-strain psammites adjacent to F_2 fold hinges, indicate that the western limb of the major fold is right-way-up and that it faces SSW. Minor F_2 folds deform an earlier bedding-parallel foliation (S_1) and, in semi-pelitic units, fold a S_1-parallel quartz segregation fabric. Minor F_2 folds are well developed only in the hinge region of the major fold on the coast, west of Clach Bheag na Faraid and Meall a'Bhuic. F_2 fold axes and intersections plunge subparallel to a ubiquitous down-dip mineral stretching lineation (Fig. 11b and c). The S_2 fabrics are mylonitic but are mostly annealed with the quartz microstructure dominated by secondary recrystallization textures that coarsen slightly to the east. These fabrics pass downwards without any break into finer-grained, subparallel, mylonitic LS fabrics affecting the underlying gneissose Lewisian and Oystershell units. The observed continuity between fabrics in the Moine and the mylonitic fabrics in the underlying units suggests that these structures are broadly the same age. Shear-sense criteria (e.g. shear bands, asymmetrical porphyroclasts) consistently indicate top-to-the-WNW displacements, parallel to mineral stretching lineations in all three units. Secondary minor 'F_3-type' folds of the mylonitic foliation occur locally on centimetre- to metre-scale only in the two lower units, where they display variable plunges (e.g. Fig 11d) and vergence patterns typical of high-strain zones (see Alsop & Holdsworth 2002). The central part of the Lewisian unit is the least deformed and preserves the most obviously gneissose rock types with locally discordant pegmatite veins.

Within the Moine rocks, post-S_1 garnets are altered to biotite which, with white mica and quartz, defines the S_2 fabric. Syn-D_2 metamorphism was therefore probably a retrograde mid- to low-greenschist facies event. Greenschist-facies retrogression is pervasive in the underlying, originally gneissose Lewisian rocks, with hornblendes replaced extensively by actinolite–tremolite, biotite and chlorite, and calcic plagioclase by albite. Fibrous overgrowths around relict porphyroclasts (feldspar, amphibole and epidote) and along top-to-the-WNW shear bands are typically quartz, biotite, chlorite and white mica.

To summarize, lithologically and structurally the three lithotectonic units are directly comparable with units recognized in the uppermost parts of the Moine Thrust Zone at Whiten Head. The Moine Thrust is similarly placed along the upper contact of the Oystershell Rock (Fig. 11a). The contact between the basement gneisses and overlying, apparently right-way-up Moine rocks at Faraid Head is therefore interpreted as a highly sheared unconformity. The thrust sheet template and structural history established in the Whiten Head–Loch Eriboll area thus extends for at least 15 km northwestwards onto the foreland.

Conclusions

Systematic mapping of both the Moine Nappe and underlying Moine Thrust Zone in the Loch Hope to Whiten Head region of Sutherland has extended the tectonic stratigraphy developed in the thrust zone further south to the hitherto little-studied north coast section. The geometric and kinematic consistency of the dominant folds, thrusts and fabrics of this part of the Moine Nappe and Moine Thrust Zone demonstrates a progressive, foreland-propagating structural evolution across the region. Earlier ductile thrusts in the east are superseded by increasingly brittle thrusts to the west during a single, protracted phase of Caledonian movement, suggesting that foreland propagation of deformation occurred synchronously with exhumation (Barr *et al.* 1986). Recent isotopic ages of *c.* 435–425 Ma from syntectonic mineral assemblages in the Moine Thrust Zone (Freeman *et al.* 1998; Dallmeyer *et al.* 2001) and syntectonic granites in central Sutherland (Kinny *et al.* 2003) support a model of continuous structural evolution from the internal tectonic zones of the orogen to the external thrust belt. In this setting, we draw attention to the existence of persistent culmination zones marked by differential shear within the lower part of the Moine Nappe and the underlying Moine Thrust Zone south of Whiten Head (see also Alsop & Holdsworth 2002, 2004*a*). The development of such culminations, from mid- to upper crustal levels, reflects the protracted nature of such differential shearing features during thrust stacking sequences. Finally, the newly defined Lochan Riabhach Thrust is here interpreted as an 'out-of-sequence' or overstep structure that sliced at low angles across the thrust zone after initial thrust stacking.

Comparison with the downfaulted segment of the Moine Nappe and thrust zone exposed on the foreland at Faraid Head demonstrates the up-dip, across-strike continuity of the thrust sheet template and structural history for at least 15 km to the NW.

Fieldwork for this paper formed part of the remapping of British Geological Survey sheet 114E (Tongue) and part of 114W (Loch Eriboll) and was funded under the NERC–BGS Academic Mapping Programme (Grant F60/G2/36). R.E.H. would like to sincerely thank Mike Coward for introducing him to the joys of the Sutherland Moine and Moine Thrust Zone as his PhD supervisor: it all started with a bag of Maltesers and a sheep... We would all like to thank M. McErlean, C. Butler and I. Burns for many discussions and assistance in the field during the mapping of this region. M. Krabbendam, S. Matthews and A. Ries provided constructive reviews and comments on an earlier version of this paper. Mrs J. F. Mackay once again provided invaluable accommodation and logistical support. We would like to dedicate this paper to the memory of J. F. Mackay of Talmine for his friendship, good humour and piloting skills: we miss him, and Mike, greatly.

References

ALSOP, G. I. & HOLDSWORTH, R. E. 1993. The distribution, geometry and kinematic significance of Caledonian buckle folds in the western Moine Nappe, northwestern Scotland. *Geological Magazine*, **130**, 353–362.

ALSOP, G. I. & HOLDSWORTH, R. E. 1999. Vergence and facing patterns in large-scale sheath folds. *Journal of Structural Geology*, **21**, 1335–1349.

ALSOP, G. I. & HOLDSWORTH, R. E. 2002. The geometry and kinematics of flow perturbation folds. *Tectonophysics*, **350**, 99–125.

ALSOP, G. I. & HOLDSWORTH, R. E. 2004*a*. Shear zone folds: records of flow perturbation or structural inheritance? *In*: ALSOP, G. I., HOLDSWORTH, R. E., MCCAFFREY, K. J. W. & HAND, M. (eds) *Flow Processes in Faults and Shear Zones*. Geological Society, London, Special Publications, **224**, 177–199.

ALSOP, G. I. & HOLDSWORTH, R. E. 2004*b*. The geometry and topology of natural sheath folds: a new tool for structural analysis. *Journal of Structural Geology*, **26**, 1561–1589.

ALSOP, G. I., HOLDSWORTH, R. E., & STRACHAN, R. A. 1996. Transport-parallel cross folds within a mid-crustal Caledonian thrust stack, northern Scotland. *Journal of Structural Geology*, **18**, 783–790.

BARR, D., HOLDSWORTH, R. E. & ROBERTS, A. M. 1986. Caledonian ductile thrusting in a Precambrian metamorphic complex: the Moine of north-western Scotland. *Geological Society of America Bulletin*, **97**, 754–764.

BOWLER, S. 1987. Duplex geometry: an example from the Moine Thrust Belt. *Tectonophysics*, **135**, 25–35.

BRITISH GEOLOGICAL SURVEY 1997. *Tongue. Scotland Sheet 114E. Solid Geology. 1:50 000*. British Geological Survey, Keyworth.

BRITISH GEOLOGICAL SURVEY 2000. *Loch Eriboll. Scotland Sheet 114W. 1:50 000.* Solid Geology. British Geological Survey, Keyworth.

BUTLER, C. A., HOLDSWORTH, R. E. & STRACHAN, R. A. 1995. Evidence for Caledonian sinistral strike-slip motion and associated fault zone weakening, Outer Hebrides Fault Zone, NW Scotland. *Journal of the Geological Society, London*, **152**, 743–746.

BUTLER, R. W. H. 1982. A structural analysis of the Moine Thrust zone between Loch Eriboll and Foinaven, NW Scotland. *Journal of Structural Geology*, **4**, 19–29.

BUTLER, R. W. H. 1988. Excursion 11: The Moine Thrust Belt at Loch Eriboll. *In*: ALLISON, I., MAY, F. & STRACHAN, R. A. (eds) *An Excursion Guide to the Moine Geology of the Scottish Highlands*. Scottish Academic Press, Edinburgh, 195–215.

BUTLER, R. W. H. 2004. The nature of 'roof thrusts' in the Moine Thrust Belt, NW Scotland: implications for the structural evolution of thrust belts. *Journal of the Geological Society, London*, **161**, 849–859.

BUTLER, R. W. H. & COWARD, M. P. 1984. Geological constraints, structural evolution and the deep geology of the NW Scottish Caledonides. *Tectonics*, **3**, 347–365.

BUTLER, R. W. H., MATTHEWS, S. J. & MORGAN, R. 2007. Structural evolution of the Achnashellach Culmination, Southern Moine Thrust Belt: testing the duplex model. *In*: RIES, A. C., BUTLER, R. W. H. & GRAHAM, R. H. (eds) *Deformation of the Continental Crust: The Legacy of Mike Coward*. Geological Society, London, Special Publications, **272**, 103–120.

CHRISTIE, J. M. 1960. Mylonitic rocks of the Moine thrust zone in the Assynt region. *Transactions of the Edinburgh Geological Society*, **18**, 79–93.

COWARD, M. P. 1980. The Caledonian thrust and shear zones of NW Scotland. *Journal of Structural Geology*, **2**, 11–17.

COWARD, M. P. 1982. Surge zones in the Moine thrust zone of NW Scotland. *Journal of Structural Geology*, **4**, 247–256.

COWARD, M. P. 1983. The thrust and shear zones of the Moine thrust zone and the NW Scottish Caledonides. *Journal of the Geological Society of London*, **140**, 795–811.

COWARD, M. P. 1984*a*. A geometrical study of the Arnaboll and Heilam thrust sheets, NW of Ben Arnaboll, Sutherland. *Scottish Journal of Geology*, **20**, 87–106.

COWARD, M. P. 1984*b*. The strain and textural history of thin-skinned tectonic zones: examples from the Assynt region of the Moine Thrust zone, NW Scotland. *Journal of Structural Geology* **6**, 89–99.

COWARD, M. P. 1985. The thrust structures of southern Assynt, Moine Thrust Zone. *Geological Magazine*, **122**, 595–607.

COWARD, M. P. 1988. The Moine thrust and the Scottish Caledonides. *Geological Society of America, Special Paper*, **222**, 116.

COWARD, M. P. 1990. The Precambrian, Caledonian and Variscan framework to NW Europe. *In*: HARDMAN, R. F. P. & BROOKS, J. (eds) *Tectonic Events Responsible for Britains Oil and Gas Reserves*. Geological Society, London, Special Publications, **55**, 1–34.

COWARD, M. P. & ENFIELD, M.A. 1987. The structure of the West Orkney and adjacent basins. *In*: BROOKS, J. & GLENNIE, K. (eds) *The Petroleum Geology of North-west Europe*. Graham & Trotman, London, 687–696.

COWARD, M. P. & POTTS, G. J. 1983. Complex strain patterns developed at the frontal and lateral tips to shear zones and thrust zones. *Journal of Structural Geology*, **5**, 383–399.

COWARD, M. P., KIM, J. H. & PARKE, J. 1980. The Lewisian structures within the Moine thrust zone. *Proceedings of the Geologists' Association*, **91**, 327–337.

COWARD, M. P., NELL, P. R. & TALBOT, J. 1992. An analysis of the strains associated with the Moine Thrust Zone, Assynt, Northwest Scotland. *In:* MITRA, S. & FISHER, G. W. (eds) *Structural Geology of Fold and Thrust Belts*. Johns Hopkins University Press, Baltimore, MD, 105–122.

DALLMEYER, R. D., STRACHAN, R. A., ROGERS, G., WATT, G. R. & FRIEND, C. R. L. 2001. Dating deformation and cooling in the Caledonian thrust nappes of north Sutherland, Scotland: insights from $^{40}Ar/^{39}Ar$ and Rb–Sr chronology. *Journal of the Geological Society, London*, **158**, 501–512.

DEWEY, J. F. & STRACHAN, R. A. 2003. Changing Silurian–Devonian relative plate motion in the Caledonides: sinistral transpression to sinistral transtension. *Journal of the Geological Society, London*, **160**, 219–229.

ELLIOTT, D. & JOHNSON, M. R. W. 1980. Structural evolution in the northern part of the Moine thrust belt, NW Scotland. *Transactions of the Royal Society of Edinburgh: Earth Sciences*, **71**, 69–96.

ENFIELD, M. A. & COWARD, M. P. 1987. The structure of the West Orkney Basin, northern Scotland. *Journal of the Geological Society, London*, **144**, 871–884.

EVANS, D. J. & WHITE, S. H. 1984. Microstructural and fabric studies from the Moine rocks of the Moine Nappe, Eriboll, NW Scotland. *Journal of Structural Geology*, **6**, 369–389.

FISCHER, M. W. & COWARD, M. P. 1982. Strains and folds within thrust sheets: an analysis of the Heilam sheet, Northwest Scotland. *Tectonophysics*, **88**, 291–312.

FREEMAN, S. R., BUTLER, R. W. H., CLIFF, R. A. & REX, D. C. 1998. Dating mylonite evolution: an Rb–Sr and K–Ar study of the Moine mylonites, NW Scotland. *Journal of the Geological Society, London*, **155**, 745–758.

GRANT, C. J. 1989. *The kinematics and tectonic significance of ductile shear zones within the Northern Highland Moine*. PhD thesis, University of Liverpool.

HIPPLER, S. J. & KNIPE, R. J. 1990. The evolution of cataclastic fault rocks from a pre-existing mylonite. *In*: KNIPE, R. J. & RUTTER, E. H. (eds) *Deformation Mechanisms, Rheology and Tectonics*. Geological Society, London, Special Publications, **54**, 71–79.

HIRTH, G. & TULLIS, J. 1992. Dislocation creep regimes in quartz aggregates. *Journal of Structural Geology*, **14**, 145–160.

HOLDSWORTH, R. E. 1987. *Basement/cover relationships, reworking and Caledonian ductile thrust tectonics of the Northern Moine, NW Scotland*. PhD thesis, University of Leeds.

HOLDSWORTH, R. E. 1989*a*. The geology and structural evolution of a Caledonian fold and ductile thrust zone, Kyle of Tongue region, Sutherland, N. Scotland. *Journal of the Geological Society, London*, **146**, 809–823.

HOLDSWORTH, R. E. 1989*b*. Late brittle deformation in a Caledonian ductile thrust wedge: new evidence for gravitational collapse in the Moine Thrust sheet, Sutherland, Scotland. *Tectonophysics*, **170**, 17–28.

HOLDSWORTH, R. E. 1990. Progressive deformation structures associated with ductile thrusts in the Moine Nappe, Sutherland, N. Scotland. *Journal of Structural Geology*, **12**, 443–452.

HOLDSWORTH, R. E. & GRANT, C. J. 1990. Convergence-related 'dynamic spreading' in a mid-crustal ductile thrust zone: a possible orogenic wedge model. *In*: KNIPE, R. J. & RUTTER, E. H. (eds) *Deformation Mechanisms, Rheology and Tectonics*. Geological Society, London, Special Publications, **54**, 491–500.

HOLDSWORTH, R. E., STRACHAN, R. A. & HARRIS, A. L. 1994. Precambrian rocks in northern Scotland east of the Moine Thrust: the Moine Supergroup. *In*: GIBBONS, W. & HARRIS, A. L. (eds) *A Revised Correlation of Precambrian rocks in the British Isles*. Geological Society, London, Special Reports, **22**, 23–32.

HOLDSWORTH, R. E., STRACHAN, R. A. & ALSOP, G. I. 2001. *Geology of the Tongue District*. Memoir of the British Geological Survey. HMSO, London.

HOLDSWORTH, R. E., STRACHAN, R. A., ALSOP, G. I., GRANT, C. J. & WILSON, R. W. 2006. Thrust sequences and their significance of low-angle, out-of-sequence faults in the northernmost Moine Nappe and Moine Thrust Zone, NW Scotland. *Journal of the Geological Society, London*, **163**, 801–819.

IMBER, J., HOLDSWORTH, R. E., BUTLER, C. A. & STRACHAN, R. A. 2001. A reappraisal of the Sibson–Scholz fault zone model: The nature of the frictional to viscous ('brittle–ductile') transition along a long-lived, crustal-scale fault, Outer Hebrides, Scotland. *Tectonics*, **18**, 326–342.

KINNY, P. D., STRACHAN, R. A., ROGERS, G. R., FRIEND, C. R. L. & KOCKS, H. 2003. U–Pb geochronology of deformed meta-granites in central Sutherland, Scotland: evidence for widespread Silurian metamorphism and ductile deformation of the Moine Supergroup during the Caledonian orogeny. *Journal of the Geological Society, London*, **160**, 259–269.

LAPWORTH, C. 1885. The Highland controversy in British geology. *Nature*, 32, 558–559.

LAW, R. D., KNIPE, R. J. & DAYAN, H. 1984. Strain path partitioning within thrust sheets: microstructural and petrofabric evidence from the Moine Thrust zone at Loch Eriboll, northwest Scotland. *Journal of Structural Geology*, **6**, 477–497.

LAW, R. D., CASEY, M. & KNIPE, R. J. 1986. Kinematic and tectonic significance of microstructures and crystallographic fabrics within quartz mylonites from the Assynt and Eriboll regions of the Moine Thrust Zone, NW Scotland. *Transactions of the Royal Society of Edinburgh, Earth Sciences*, **77**, 99–126.

MACINNES, E. A., ALSOP, G. I. & OLIVER, G. J. H. 2000. Contrasting modes of reactivation in the Outer Hebrides Fault Zone, northern Barra, Scotland. *Journal of the Geological Society, London*, **157**, 1009–1017.

MCCLAY, K. R. & COWARD, M. P. 1981. The Moine Thrust zone: an overview. *In*: MCCLAY, K. R. & PRICE, N. J. (eds) *Thrust and Nappe Tectonics*. Geological Society, London, Special Publications, **9**, 241–260.

MCKIE, T. 1990. Tidal and storm influenced sedimentation from a Cambrian transgressive passive margin sequence. *Journal of the Geological Society, London*, **147**, 785–794.

MENDUM, J. R. 1979. Caledonide thrusting in NW Scotland. *In*: HARRIS, A. L., HOLLAND, C. H. & LEAKE, B. E. (eds) *The Caledonides of the British Isles — Reviewed*. Geological Society, London, Special Publications, **8**, 291–297.

PARK, R. G., CLIFF, R. A., FETTES, D. G. & STEWART, A. D. 1994. Lewisian and Torridonian. *In*: GIBBONS, F. C. & HARRIS, A. L. (eds) *A Revised Correlation of Precambrian Rocks in the British Isles*. Geological Society, London, Special Reports, **22**, 6–22.

PARK, R. G., STEWART, A. D. & WRIGHT, D. T. 2002. Geology of Scotland. The Hebridean terrane. *In*: Trewin, N. H. (ed.) *The Geology of Scotland*. Geological Society, London, 45–80.

PEACH, B. N., HORNE, J., GUNN, W., CLOUGH, C. T. & HINXMAN, L. W. 1907. *The Geological Structure of the Northwest Highlands of Scotland*. Memoirs of the Geological Survey of Great Britain.

PHILLIPS, F. C. 1937. A fabric study of some Moine Schists and associated rocks. *Quarterly Journal of the Geological Society, London*, **93**, 581–616.

RAMSAY, J. G. 1997. The geometry of a deformed unconformity in the Caledonides of NW Scotland. *In*: SENGUPTA, S. (ed.) *Evolution of Geological Structures in Micro- to Macro-scales*. Chapman & Hall, London, 445–472.

RATHBONE, P. A., COWARD, M. P. & HARRIS, A. L. 1983. Cover and basement: a contrast in style and fabrics. *In*: HARRIS, L. D. & WILLIAMS, H. (eds) *Tectonics and Geophysics of Mountain Chains*. Geological Society of America, Memoirs, **158**, 213–223.

READ, H. H. 1931. The Geology of Central Sutherland. Memoir of the Geological Survey of Great Britain. Sheets 108 and 109 (Scotland).

READ, H. H. 1934. Age problems in the Moine Series of Scotland. *Geology Magazine*, **71**, 302–317.

RIDLEY, J. 1986. Parallel stretching lineations and fold axes oblique to displacement direction—a model and observations. *Journal of Structural Geology*, **8**, 647–654.

SIBSON, R. H. 1977. Fault rocks and fault mechanisms. *Journal of the Geological Society, London*, **133**, 191–213.

SOPER, N. J. 1971. The earliest Caledonian structures in the Moine Thrust belt. *Scottish Journal of Geology*, **7**, 241–247.

SOPER, N. J. & BROWN, P. E. 1971. Relationship between metamorphism and migmatisation in the northern part of the Moine Nappe. *Scottish Journal of Geology*, **11**, 239–259.

SOPER, N. J. & WILKINSON, P. 1975. The Moine Thrust and Moine Nappe at Loch Eriboll, Scotland. *Scottish Journal of Geology*, **11**, 239–259.

SOPER, N. J., HARRIS, A. L. & STRACHAN, R. A. 1998. Tectonostratigraphy of the Moine Supergroup: a synthesis. *Journal of the Geological Society, London*, **155**, 13–24.

STOKER, M. S., HITCHIN, K. & GRAHAM, C. C. 1993. *The Geology of the Hebrides and West Shetland Shelves, and Djacent Deep-Water Basins*. British Geological Survey Offshore Regional Report. HMSO, London.

STRACHAN, R. A., SMITH, M., HARRIS, A. L. & FETTES, D. J. 2002. The Northern Highland and Grampian Terranes. *In*: TREWIN, N. (ed.) *Geology of Scotland*. Geological Society, London, 81–147.

SWETT, K., KLEIN, G. D. & SMIT, D. E. 1971. A Cambrian tidal sand body—the Eriboll Sandstone of NW Scotland: an ancient–recent analog. *Journal of Geology*, **79**, 400–415.

TULLIS, J. & YUND, R. A. 1987. Transition from cataclastic flow to dislocation creep of feldspar: Mechanisms and microstructures. *Geology*, **15**, 606–609.

VANCE, D., STRACHAN, R. A. & JONES, K. A. 1998. Extensional versus compressional settings for metamorphism: garnet chronometry and pressure–temperature–time histories in the Moine Supergroup, northwest Scotland. *Geology*, **26**, 927–930.

VAN BREEMEN, O., AFTALION, M. & JOHNSON, M. R. W. 1979. Age of the Loch Borrolan complex, Assynt, and late movements along the Moine Thrust zone. *Journal of the Geological Society, London*, **136**, 489–496.

VERNON, R. H. 2004. *A Practical Guide to Rock Microstructure*. Cambridge University Press, Cambridge.

WHITE, S. H. 1979. Grain size and sub-grain size variation across a mylonite zone. *Contributions to Mineralogy and Petrology*, **70**, 193–202.

WHITE, S. H., EVANS, D. J. & ZHONG, D. L. 1982. Fault rocks of the Moine Thrust Zone: microstructures and textures of selected mylonites. *Textures and Microstructures*, **5**, 33–61.

WILSON, G. 1953. Mullion and rodding structures in the Moine Series of Scotland. *Proceedings of the Geologists' Association*, **64**, 118–151.

WINCHESTER, J. A. & LAMBERT, R.ST.J. 1970. Geochemical distinctions between the Lewisian of Cassley, Durcha and Loch Shin, Sutherland and the surrounding Moinian. *Proceedings of the Geologists' Association*, **81**, 275–301.

Strain variations within a major carbonate thrust sheet of the Apennine collisional belt, northern Calabria, southern Italy

S. VITALE, A. IANNACE & S. MAZZOLI

Dipartimento di Scienze della Terra, Università di Napoli 'Federico II', Largo San Marcellino 10, 80138 Napoli (NA), Italy (e-mail: stvitale@unina.it)

Abstract: Mike Coward's seminal work on strain within thrust sheets clearly showed how understanding crustal scale deformation associated with orogenesis requires a knowledge of both: (1) deformation associated with major thrusts and/or high-strain shear zones, and (2) finite strain states within the (usually large) surrounding rock volumes. In this study, the strain variations within a major, far-travelled thrust sheet internally deformed at very low-temperature, sub-metamorphic conditions, are analysed. The studied rocks belong to the thick carbonate succession of the Apennine Platform, which constitutes a major tectonostratigraphic unit of the southern Apennines. Finite strain analysis, besides quantifying the relative importance of different deformation mechanisms and the role of matrix and object strain, points to the existence of both vertical and horizontal strain gradients. These are probably controlled by both heterogeneous shear deformation associated with NE-directed tectonic transport and sedimentary carbonate facies distribution. The relative position with respect to the main overlying tectonic contact and the occurrence of a barrier to fluid flow, represented by siliciclastic beds located at the top of the carbonate succession, are also likely to have played an important role in the development of the observed regional strain gradients. On the metre scale, deformation appears to be partitioned into domains of quasi-coaxial and dominantly non-coaxial strain, controlled by different degrees of strain localization in texturally different stratigraphic layers.

Deformation and crustal shortening in collisional orogens (e.g. Coward 1994) are commonly related to the activity of major shear zones and/or thrusts; that is, zones of highly localized, non-coaxial strain. However, it should be noted that: (1) deformation in such shear zones can migrate both spatially and temporally, giving rise to domains of older shear zone fabrics intercalated with zones of localized reworking (e.g. Reddy *et al.* 2003); (2) substantial deformation between major shear zones may also occur. Although this is a critical observation in the tectonic understanding of orogens, the relative importance of distributed (bulk) strain with respect to the localized, non-coaxial strain components associated with the narrow shear zones (or thrust displacement in the non-metamorphic, outer zones of collisional orogens) is rarely assessed. However, already back in the 1980s, Mike Coward clearly realized that understanding crustal-scale deformation associated with orogenesis requires a knowledge of the record of strain localization and partitioning within both high-strain shear zones and their surrounding, relatively low-strain neighbours. Addressing this problem led him and other researchers towards a thorough analysis of strain within thrust sheets (e.g. Coward & Kim 1981; Fisher & Coward 1982; Coward & Potts 1983; Coward 1984; Law *et al.* 1984; Evans & Dunne 1991; Coward *et al.* 1992).

Understanding the complexities of strain localization and 3D variations requires detailed kinematic analysis. This, in turn, involves the definition of the basic parameters of finite deformation (finite strain, volume change, and the degree of non-coaxiality; e.g. Ramsay 1967, 1980; Ghosh & Ramberg 1976; Gratier 1983; Ramsay & Huber 1983; Law *et al.* 1984; Passchier 1986, 1988, 1990; Ghosh 1987; Law 1990; Butler *et al.* 2002; Mancktelow *et al.* 2002), as well as a quantitative assessment of the relative importance of different strain components. The latter issue involves the analysis of strain factorization and partitioning (*sensu* Ramsay & Huber 1983), often requiring the integration of different techniques of strain analysis (e.g. Mitra 1976; Groshong et *al.* 1984; Evans & Dunne 1991; Mazzoli 1995).

Since the seminal studies of Ramsay (1967) and Dunnet (1969), numerous papers have been published on the evaluation of finite strain, based on the geometric changes undergone by rock components of known initial shape. Most of these studies make the more or less implicit assumption that whole-rock finite strain is equal to that calculated for their components, such as clasts in conglomerates or oolites and fossils in

From: Ries, A. C., Butler, R. W. H. & Graham, R. H. (eds) 2007. *Deformation of the Continental Crust: The Legacy of Mike Coward.* Geological Society, London, Special Publications, **272**, 143–154.

carbonate rocks. However, recently, Treagus & Treagus (2002), based on the pioneering papers by Gay (1968) and Bilby *et al.* (1975), emphasized the role of the matrix as an active component during deformation, pointing to the competence contrast between components and matrix as a critical element for a complete finite strain characterization. As a consequence, any accurate strain analysis should be based on the evaluation of the rheology of all the constituents of a deformed rock.

Carbonate successions cropping out in northern Calabria (southern Italy) offer a good opportunity to apply such an approach and to examine the lithological control on strain localization and finite strain development. In fact, the study rocks, which consist of both calcareous conglomerates and bioclastic–oncoidal packstones, have been affected by ductile deformation localized along narrow deformation zones (Iannace & Vitale 2004). These rocks form part of the 4 km thick shallow-water to slope carbonate succession of the so-called Apennine (or Internal, or Western) Platform, which crops out for hundreds of square kilometres in the axial zone of the southern Apennines fold–thrust belt of peninsular Italy (e.g Mostardini & Merlini 1986; Cello & Mazzoli 1999, and references therein). The aim of this paper is to document the different modes of deformation and states of internal strain (including its partitioning into different deformation mechanisms and various rock components such as matrix and objects) in these rocks, which form part of a major structural–stratigraphic unit within an important segment of the Alpine orogen.

Geological setting

The studied successions crop out in the southernmost part of the southern Apennines fold–thrust belt, close to the area where this is overthrust by the Calabrian Arc units (Fig. 1). Whereas the latter consist of NE-transported metamorphic crystalline and ophiolitic units (e.g. Amodio-Morelli *et al.* 1976; Dietrich 1988; Knott 1994; see Bonardi *et al.* 2001, for a recent synthesis), the southern Apennines are dominated by non-metamorphic successions representing remnants of the sedimentary cover of the continental margin of the Afro-Adriatic plate (e.g. Dewey *et al.* 1989; Mazzoli & Helman, 1994, and references therein). These comprise both shallow-water carbonates and deep-water pelagic and siliciclastic sediments that were affected by NE-directed thrusting during the Neogene (see Butler *et al.* 2004, for a recent synthesis).

The occurrence of ductile deformation and metamorphism in remnants of the telescoped Afro-Adriatic continental palaeomargin make the northern Calabria area a noteworthy sector within the Apennine belt. The general tectonic grain of this region has been recently reassessed by Iannace *et al.* (2005). They recognized two main tectonic units in northern Calabria: the Lungro–Verbicaro and the Pollino–Ciagola units. The first unit comprises a Middle Triassic to Lower Miocene slope to basin succession affected by early HP–LT metamorphism and deformation, and by a greenschist facies re-equilibration (Iannace *et al.* 2005; Perrone *et al.* 2006). The tectonically underlying Pollino–Ciagola Unit consists of platform carbonates to the north and NE (Monti di Lauria and Pollino Chain), which are replaced by coarse slope carbonates to the SW (Campotenese area, Monte Ciagola, Cozzo Petrara) and are covered by Langhian siliciclastic deposits (Bifurto Formation; Selli 1957; Patacca *et al.* 1992). Ductile deformation of the Pollino–Ciagola Unit occurred under non-metamorphic conditions in the footwall to the (previously metamorphosed) Lungro–Verbicaro Unit. Geological relationships, stratigraphic constraints and available geochronological data indicate that these events occurred between the Burdigalian and the Tortonian (Iannace & Vitale 2004; Vitale *et al.* 2004; Iannace *et al.* 2005).

Materials and methods

Large specimens were collected from some of the zones of localized strain characterizing, at different stratigraphic levels, the Pollino–Ciagola Unit. The samples, which consist of deformed oncoidal–bioclastic packstones and lithoclastic clast-supported conglomerates, show a well-developed foliation, essentially defined by flattened clasts. In some instances, a stretching lineation is also recognized as the preferential orientation of the maximum elongation axis of the components on the foliation plane.

The samples were cut along three planes corresponding to the principal sections of the finite strain ellipsoid, and the resulting surfaces were polished. Thin sections were made for some of the same surfaces, mainly in the packstones. Digital images of all the surfaces and thin sections were used for the analysis.

As an aim of the research was to discriminate between the relative role of components and matrix strain in the deformation, the first step was to evaluate the finite strain separately for the whole rock and for the components. The bulk

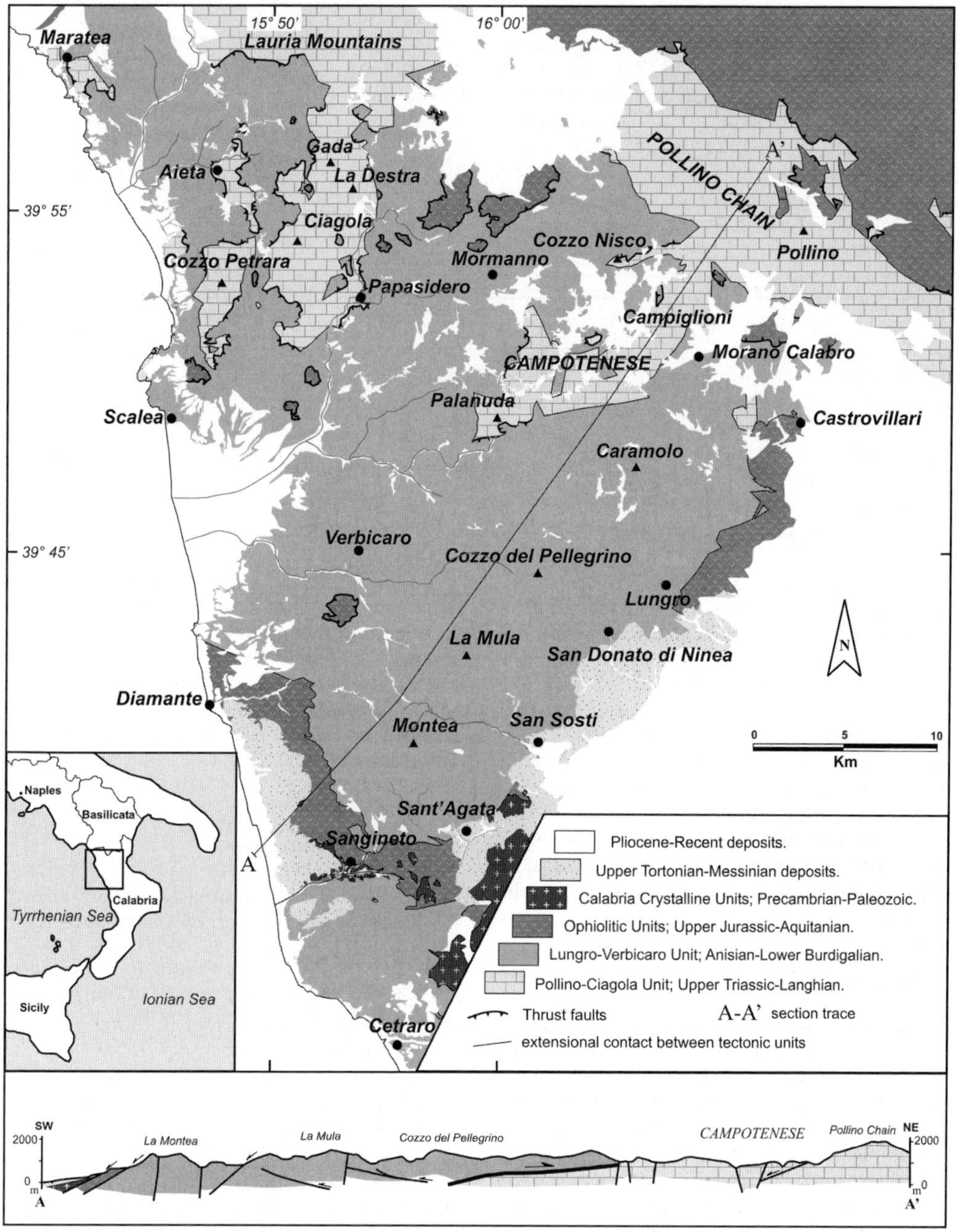

Fig. 1. Schematic tectonic map and cross-section of field study area.

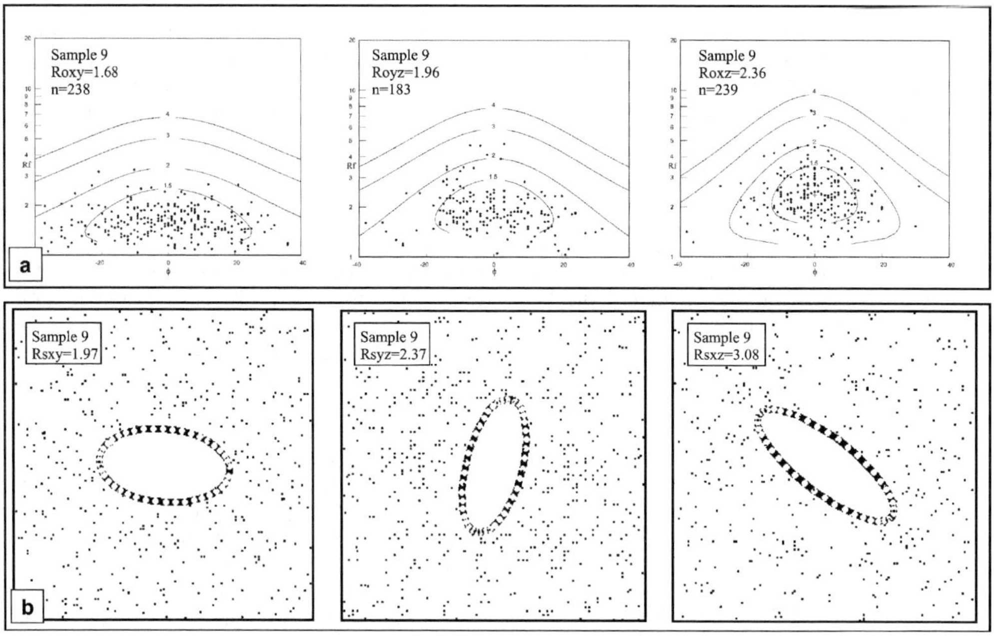

Fig. 2. Examples of strain analysis (sample 9, oncoidal packstone). *xy*, *yz* and *xz* principal sections of the measured finite strain ellipsoid are shown from left to right. (**a**) R_f/ϕ diagrams. (**b**) Fry diagrams.

strain has been calculated using the Fry analysis (Fry 1979), whereas for the components the well-established R_f/ϕ analysis has been applied (Dunnet 1969; Ramsay & Huber 1983; Lisle 1985). Both methods assume that no original (i.e. sedimentary) preferential orientation of the grains was present in the undeformed rock; that is, all components had randomly oriented long axes.

The ellipticity of single components and the angle that each component forms with a fixed orientation, necessary for the construction of the R_f/ϕ diagrams, have been calculated by digital image analysis using the ImageJ software. Intensity curves of the R_f/ϕ diagram have been constructed to evaluate the mean value of object strain. R_f/ϕ diagrams also show original object ellipticity curves *Ri* (*Ri* = 1.5, 2, 3, 4). The Fry analysis has been performed using the software GeoFryPlots 3.0 applied to images of polished slabs on which the centres of each object were determined.

The viscosity ratio has been obtained from the previous analysis using the following equation (Bilby *et al.* 1975; Gay 1976):

$$r = \ln\left(\frac{R_s}{R_o}\right)\frac{(R_o+1)}{(R_o-1)}+1 \qquad (1)$$

where R_s is the finite bulk strain and R_o is the object finite strain.

3D finite strain and viscosity ratio analysis

The distribution of strain within the Pollino–Ciagola Unit in northern Calabria is extremely inhomogeneous (Figs 2–4) reflecting facies variations and, hence, mechanical stratigraphy, as well as relative position with respect to the Miocene siliciclastic beds. The latter occur at the top of the stratigraphic succession of the Pollino–Ciagola Unit, and probably acted as a hydrological barrier (Iannace & Vitale 2004). In fact, the more massive platform successions to the NE do not show significant ductile deformation, whereas the margin to slope facies occurring to the SW, consisting of both lagoonal bioclastic oncolithic packstones and coarse rudites, show localized, intense ductile deformation. Higher in the stratigraphic succession, where resedimented carbonate material and siliciclastic components are dominant, the strain reaches the highest values.

Table 1 shows the results of strain analysis and the main features of the collected samples. The oncoidal packstones belonging to the Jurassic platform succession gave R_oxz and R_sxz maximum values of 3.60 and 4.78, respectively, and viscosity ratios ranging from 1.25 and 2.00 (examples are shown in Figs 2 and 3).

Sample 12 provided the opportunity to study the finite strain of different components such as oncoids, consisting of micrite, and echinoderm grains, consisting of sparry calcite. The R_f/ϕ analysis indicates a $R_{oncoid}xz$ of 3.31 whereas the $R_{echinoderm}xz$ is 1.20. As the finite strain for the whole rock is $R_sxz = 5.30$, the viscosity ratio r is 1.88 for oncoids and 14.56 for echinid fragments.

In the higher part of the succession, where clastic facies occur, R_oxz and R_sxz may be as high as 13.83 and 16.44, respectively. To evaluate the amount of deformation we calculated the two parameters (Ramsay & Huber 1983)

$$D = \sqrt{\ln(R_{xy})^2 + \ln(R_{yz})^2} \quad (2)$$

and

$$\varepsilon = \frac{1}{\sqrt{3}}\sqrt{\ln(R_{xy})^2 + \ln(R_{yz})^2 + \ln(R_{xz})^2}\,. \quad (3)$$

Both values are systematically higher for the whole rock than for the components alone. In the Campiglioni area, near Campotenese (refer to Fig. 1), it has been possible to observe the transition from almost undeformed Palaeogene conglomerates (sample 18, $R_oxz = 1.48$), to moderately deformed (sample 19, $R_oxz = 3.1$), up to intensely deformed ones (sample 20, $R_oxz =$ 13.83).

The finite strain ellipsoids for all the analysed samples have been plotted in the Ramsay logarithmic diagram and have been grouped according to texture and facies (Fig. 4). This shows that both platform packstone and conglomerate strain ellipsoids, calculated for the whole rock and the components, plot in the apparent flattening field (i.e. display an oblate shape). D values range from 0.59 and 0.91 for the components, and from 0.79 to 1.22 for the whole rock; ε is between 0.57 and 0.91 for the components and between 0.92 and 1.57 for the whole rock.

In the map shown in Figure 5, the maximum values of the natural logarithmic strain are shown, together with the isograds and trend of the stretching lineations.

Structural observations

SEM observations show that most oncoidal packstones consist of micritic calcite (Fig. 6). Sparry calcite is rare and generally is affected by internal deformation, such as sharp, undulose and patchy twinning (Fig. 6b, e, g and h). These crystals are slightly elongated and define a further foliation, which is oblique with respect to the main one (Fig. 6d). Porphyroclasts commonly display symmetric recrystallized pressure shadows (ϕ structures; Fig. 6e). Locally, however, asymmetric features such as δ structures (Fig. 6f) and bookshelf sliding (Fig. 6h) are well developed. Finer (micrite) grains do not show internal deformation structures and show a low ellipticity even when they are deformed as macroscopic aggregates such as oncoids (Fig. 6a).

Two sets of stylolites occur along the clast boundaries within the conglomerates. One of them is at a high angle, whereas the other is parallel to the main foliation. The former set of stylolites is deformed, whereas the latter cuts across calcite veins that formed essentially after the ductile deformation. Conjugate sets of en echelon vein arrays also occur (Fig. 3e). These conjugate 'brittle–ductile' shear zones (as defined by Ramsay & Huber 1987) are characterized by an acute bisector that is roughly perpendicular to the main foliation, therefore consistent with a maximum shortening oriented normal to the foliation. However, the obtuse bisector, which lies within the foliation plane, is normal to the stretching lineation. In summary, the two strain ellipsoids have the shortest (z) axis in common, whereas the intermediate (y) and maximum (x) axes are mutually exchanged, therefore resulting in an enhanced oblate shape of the total finite strain ellipsoid.

Most conglomerate clasts consist of wackestone fragments including components (e.g. oncoids) floating in a micritic matrix. This provides the opportunity to compare the strain obtained from such components with that of the whole clast containing them, and also with bulk rock strain (obtained by the Fry technique applied to the clasts). Because the stylolites affect only clast boundaries and not their interior, the relative contribution of pressure solution to the total deformation can be evaluated by comparing the finite strain of the bulk rock (R_s) with that obtained from the internal components of the clasts ($R_{internal}$). For sample 15, the $R_{internal}xz$ value, obtained by the Fry analysis performed on the components (e.g. oncoids) contained within each conglomerate clast, is 6.63, whereas that of the whole rock, R_sxz is 10.94. To evaluate the contribution of the pressure-solution (PS) component to the total finite strain, the following equation has been used:

$$\mathrm{PS}\% = \frac{\left[\ln(R_s) - \ln(R_{internal})\right]}{\ln(R_s)} \times 100. \quad (4)$$

For sample 15, a value of PS% = 21% has been obtained.

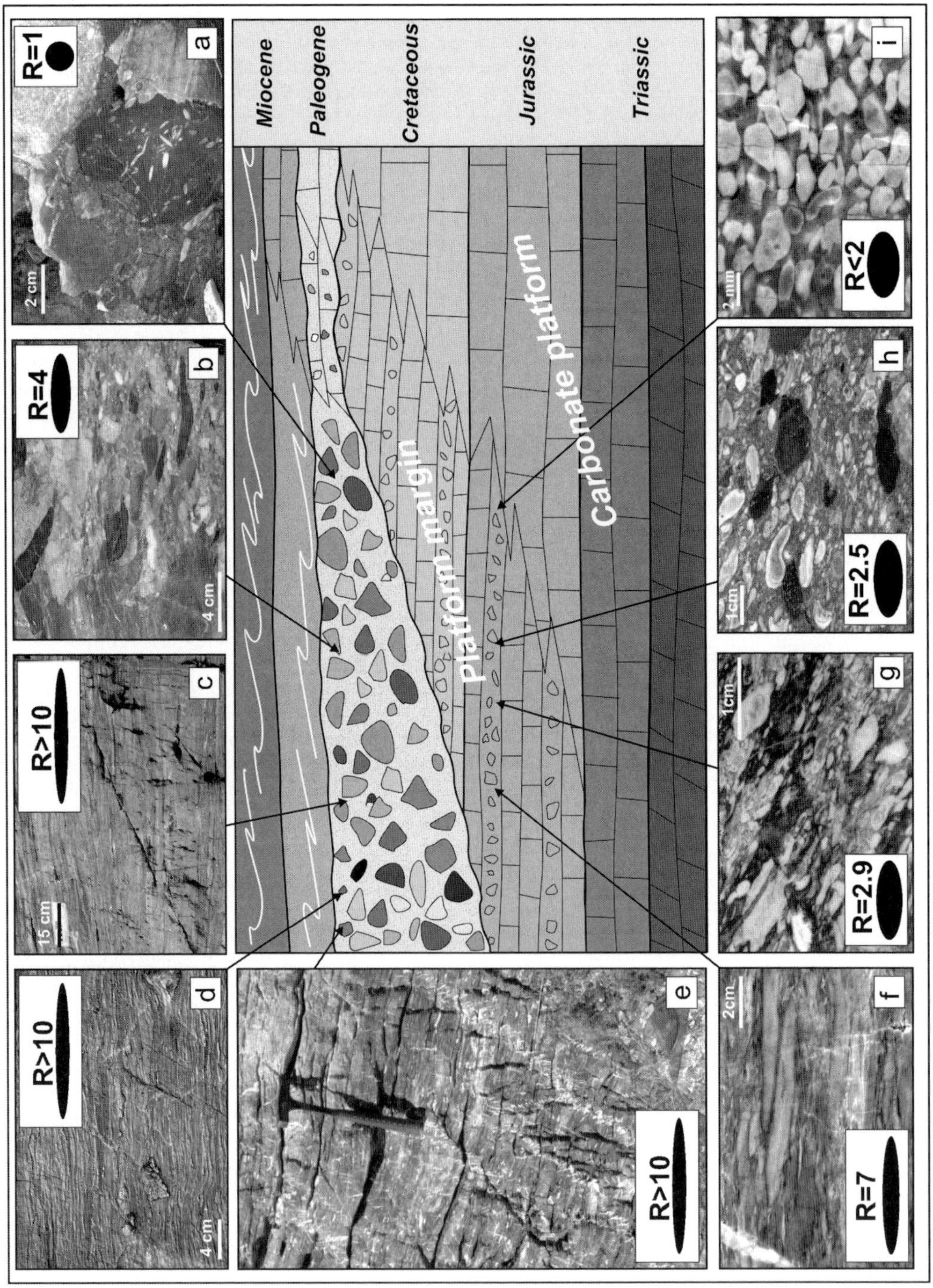
R=1
2 cm
a
R=4
4 cm
b
R>10
15 cm
c
R>10
4 cm
d
R>10
e
R=7
2cm
f
R=2.9
1cm
g
R=2.5
1cm
h
R<2
2 mm
i
Miocene
Paleogene
Cretaceous
Jurassic
Triassic
Platform margin
Carbonate platform

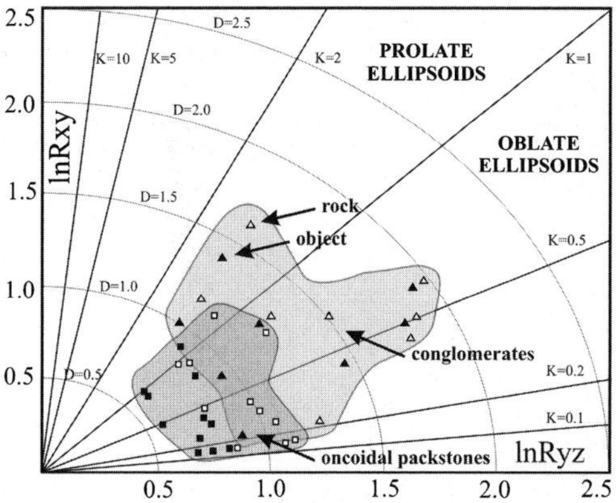

Fig. 4. Ramsay logarithmic diagram for all samples, grouped according to textural facies. Squares: packstones; triangles: conglomerates. Filled symbols refer to objects (oncoids, clasts); open symbols to bulk rock.

Discussion

The rocks of the Pollino–Ciagola Unit analysed in this study form part of the Apennine Platform, a major, far-travelled structural–stratigraphic unit of the southern Apennines. Minimum NE-directed thrust displacement along the base of this unit is several tens of kilometres (Mazzoli *et al.* 2001*a*). The tectonic contact with the overlying Lungro–Verbicaro Unit, marked by a significant metamorphic break (Iannace & Vitale 2004; Vitale *et al.* 2004; Iannace *et al.* 2005; Perrone *et al.* 2006), implies a displacement of the same order. Therefore, large translational deformation took place along the tectonic contacts at the top and base of the unit. Data from this study suggest that internal strain, localized in different areas and at different stratigraphic levels within the fault-bounded rock volume, is also significant.

Table 1. *Strain analysis data*

Sample	Locality	Object					Rock					Facies	*r*
		Roxz	Royz	Roxy	D	ε	Rsxz	Rsyz	Rsxy	D	ε		
1	**P-G**	2.60	2.30	1.13	0.84	0.74	3.39	2.91	1.17	1.08	1.33	P	1.60
2	**P-G**	2.70	2.10	1.29	0.78	0.73	3.56	2.60	1.39	1.01	1.33	P	1.60
3	**P-G**	2.40	2.00	1.20	0.72	0.65	3.62	2.79	1.31	1.06	1.36	P	2.00
4	**P-G**	2.37	2.12	1.12	0.76	0.66	3.56	3.04	1.18	1.12	1.38	P	2.00
5	**P-G**	2.90	2.40	1.21	0.90	0.80	4.37	3.39	1.31	1.25	1.58	C	1.84
6	**P-G**	2.20	1.99	1.11	0.70	0.61	2.65	2.35	1.13	0.86	1.06	P	1.50
7	**P-G**	2.20	1.70	1.29	0.59	0.57	2.86	2.04	1.42	0.79	1.07	P	1.70
8	**P-G**	2.41	2.03	1.34	0.62	0.62	3.03	2.37	1.47	0.84	1.17	P	1.70
9	**P-G**	2.36	1.96	1.68	0.85	0.85	3.08	2.37	1.97	1.12	1.30	P	1.66
10	**P-G**	2.41	2.03	1.34	0.77	0.73	2.90	2.37	1.43	0.93	1.16	P	1.45
11	**P-G**	1.86	1.58	1.51	0.62	0.62	2.18	1.67	1.80	0.69	0.80	P	1.25
12	**P-G**	3.31					5.30					P, oncoids	1.88
		1.20										P, echinoderm	14.56
13	**A**	6.77	3.79	1.79	1.45	1.39	9.81	5.07	2.06	1.78	2.36	C	1.50
14	**A**	3.60	1.83	1.97	0.91	0.91	4.78	2.12	2.32	1.13	1.57	P	1.50
15	**C**	10.94	4.94	2.23	1.79	1.73	11.69	5.21	2.30	1.85	2.51	C	1.08
16	**C**	13.80	5.10	2.71	1.91	1.87	14.79	5.38	2.81	1.97	2.73	C	1.08
17	**C**	3.70	2.20	1.68	0.94	0.93	7.63	3.53	2.32	1.52	2.07	C	2.26
18	**C**	1.48					1.51					C	1.10
19	**C**	3.10					4.11					C	1.55
20	**C**	13.83					16.44					C	1.20
21	**M**	7.00	2.20	3.18	1.40	1.38	9.03	2.50	3.80	1.62	2.23	C	1.34
22	**M**	4.08	1.82	2.24	1.01	1.00	5.01	2.01	2.55	1.17	1.63	C	1.34
23	**M**	5.76	2.60	2.22	1.24	1.24	6.22	2.73	2.31	1.31	1.84	C	1.11

Localities (refer to Fig. 1): P-G, Cozzo Petrara–Monte Gada; A, Aieta village; C, Campotenese; M, Maratea village. Facies: P, oncoidal packstones; C, conglomerates.

Fig. 3. Sketch stratigraphic log showing position of finite strain data (*xz* principal plane of the finite strain ellipsoid shown). (**a**) Undeformed Palaeogene conglomerate. (**b**) Moderately deformed conglomerate. (**c**) and (**d**) Highly strained conglomerates. (**e**) Highly strained Palaeogene conglomerate showing conjugate en echelon vein arrays superimposed onto the foliation. (**f**) Sample 4 (oncoidal packstone, Maratea, Lower Cretaceous). (**g**) Sample 1 (oncoidal packstone, Monte La Destra, Jurassic). (**h**) Sample 2 (oncoidal packstone, Monte La Destra, Jurassic). (**i**) Sample 3 (intrabioclastic packstone, Monte La Destra, Upper Jurassic).

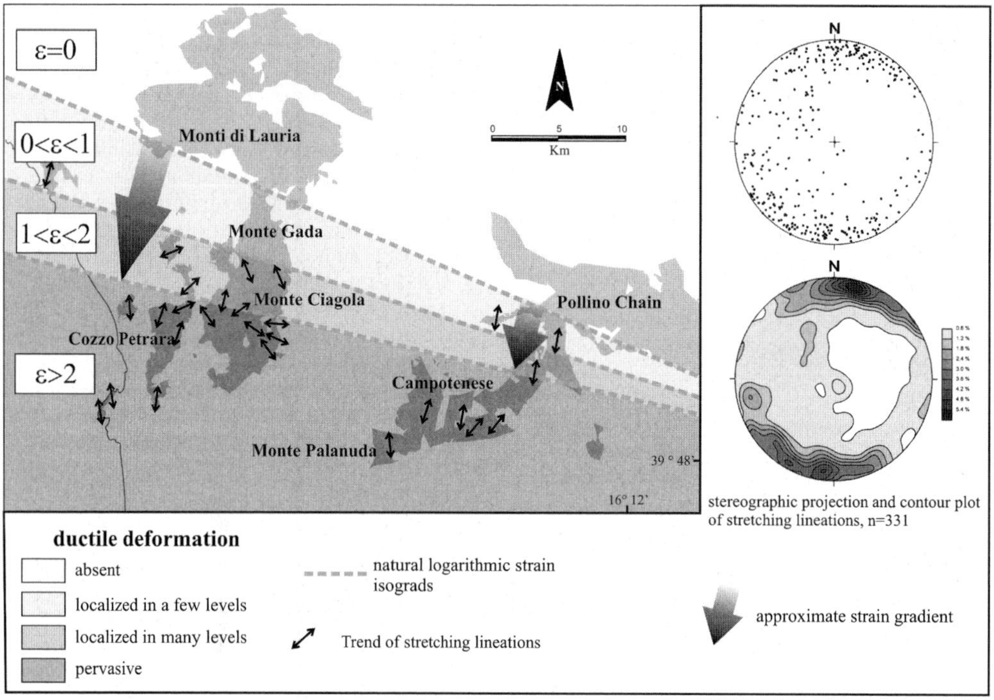

Fig. 5. Map showing the distribution of maximum values of natural logarithmic strain (ε) and trend of stretching lineations. Orientation data (right) are shown on lower hemisphere, Schmidt projection.

The presence of deformed stylolites in the conglomerates suggests that pressure solution has been active since the early stages of deformation. A second generation of stylolites, parallel to the main foliation, follows the main ductile deformation and is best related to conjugate arrays of en echelon veins. In both cases, the components occurring within conglomerate clasts are not affected by pressure solution. Thus, the difference between bulk-rock strain and the finite strain, calculated from these components, yields the net contribution of pressure solution to the deformation (21% of the total strain for sample 15).

The similarity of size and spacing of veins belonging to each conjugate en echelon array indicates that the associated deformation, involving a maximum shortening normal to the main foliation, was coaxial as a whole. On the other hand, rotated porphyroclasts, oblique foliation and asymmetric boudins all indicate that ductile deformation within the Tertiary conglomerates was dominated by non-coaxial strain. In contrast, only symmetrical structures occur in the stratigraphically underlying, deformed platform carbonates. A different rheology is indicated for the two sedimentary facies also by the Ramsay diagrams for the different textural facies (Fig. 4). The Tertiary conglomerates show generally higher *D* values with respect to those relative to platform carbonates. This could result from two factors: (1) the vicinity of the conglomerates to the stratigraphically overlying siliciclastic Miocene beds, which probably acted as a barrier for fluid flow, leading to the concentration of fluids during deformation; (2) a higher permeability of the conglomerates.

Finally, calculation of the isograds of the maximum value of the logarithmic natural strain indicates a SW–NE gradient (Fig. 5). This, coupled with the previous data, may be interpreted as a result of heterogeneous shear associated with the NE-directed tectonic transport of the unit, which was also roughly normal to the sedimentary isopic lines.

The microstructural analysis confirms the well-known control of grain size on the deformation mechanisms at the micro-scale. Micrite grains do not show evidence of intragranular deformation, even when the whole aggregate is heavily strained. This suggests a substantial contribution of grain boundary sliding (Raj & Ashby 1971) by which the grains slide one past another without substantial change in shape (although

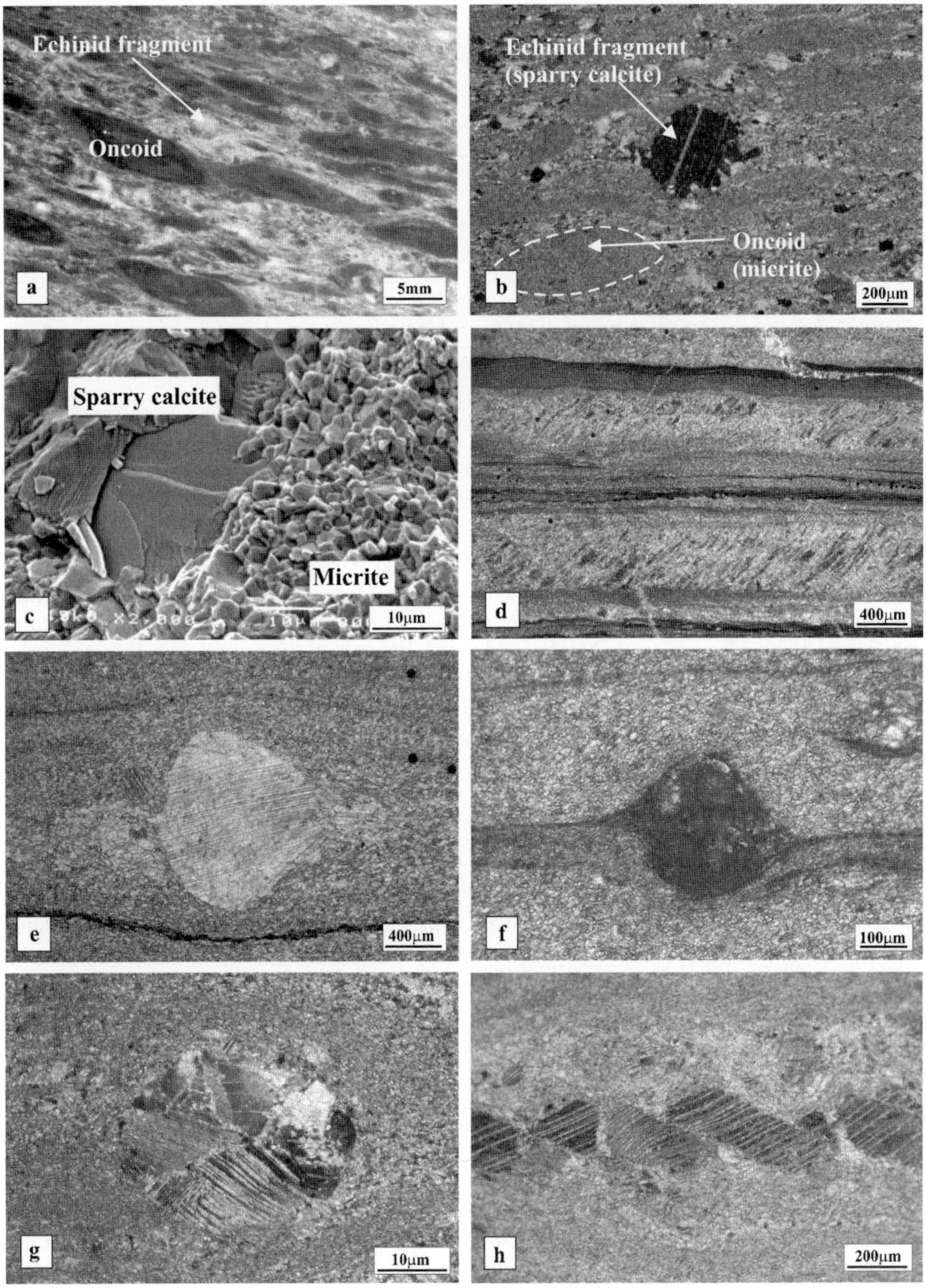

Fig. 6. Examples of microstructures. (**a**) Polished slab (parallel to the *xz* principal plane of the finite strain ellipsoid) from sample 8. (**b**) Microphotograph of thin section (parallel to the *xz* principal plane of the strain ellipsoid; crossed polars) from sample 8. (**c**) SEM image of etched surface of sample 8. (**d**) Microphotograph (crossed polars) of section (parallel to the *xz* principal plane of the finite strain ellipsoid) from sample 15 (note oblique foliation at a high angle to main foliation). (**e**) Microphotograph (crossed polars) of calcite porphyroclast showing ϕ structure and straight twins. (**f**) Microphotograph of dolomitized porphyroclast showing δ structure. (**g**) Microphotograph (crossed polars) of calcite porphyroclast showing undulose and patchy extinction and twinning. (**h**) Microphotograph (crossed polars) of 'bookshelf structure' in calcite, also showing undulose extinction and twinning.

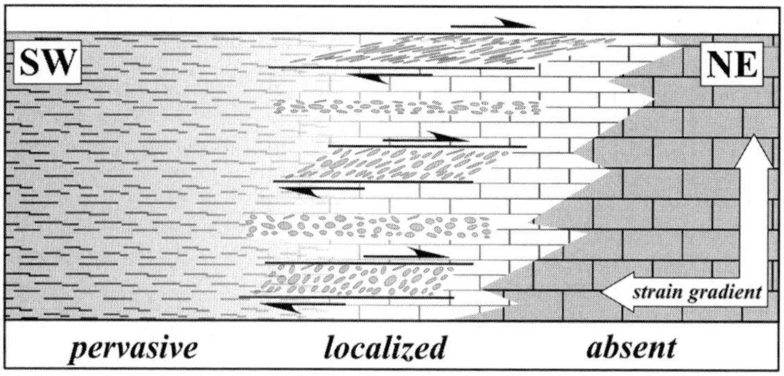

Fig. 7. Schematic diagram illustrating reconstructed deformation pattern in the Pollino–Ciagola Unit.

minor intracrystalline slip and/or dissolution–crystallization are likely to occur in the grain boundary region, to accommodate grain boundary misfits). Several studies suggest that this mechanism may be dominant in moderately deformed micritic limestones under low-temperature natural conditions (160–280 °C) (e.g. Burkhard 1990; Mazzoli *et al.* 2001*b*). The sparry calcite grains appear instead to have been deformed by intracrystalline mechanisms such as mechanical twinning, dislocation creep and subgrain rotation recrystallization. The presence of folded and patchy twins would indicate, according to Burkhard (1993), temperatures higher than 250 °C. On the other hand, the absence of metamorphic index minerals, even in siliciclastic beds, rules out temperatures in excess of 300 °C. For this approximate temperature range and geological strain rates of 10^{-13}–10^{-15} s^{-1} (Pfiffner & Ramsay 1982), the deformation features observed for different grain sizes in the study limestones are compatible with the prediction of experimentally–derived flow laws for calcite (e.g. Rutter 1974, 1976; Schmid *et al.* 1977, 1980; Schmid 1982).

Conclusions

The thrust-bounded Pollino–Ciagola Unit, which forms part of the Apennine Platform tectonostratigraphic unit that crops out extensively in the southern Apennines, is well exposed in the northern Calabria region of southern Italy and provides the opportunity to analyse the state of strain within a major thrust sheet characterized by displacement of tens of kilometres.

The studied carbonate rocks show evidence of substantial internal strain as a result of ductile deformation in sub-metamorphic conditions.

Significant variability of sedimentary facies within the Pollino–Ciagola Unit provided the opportunity to test several methods aimed at the evaluation of the relative contributions of different deformation mechanisms, and of components and matrix strain during deformation.

Finite strain analysis performed separately for the whole rock and for the components indicates that the latter have to be considered mechanically active during deformation, even though the competence contrast is low. This means that the chosen approach was actually necessary for the correct evaluation of finite strains.

Integration of the strain analysis into the regional geological picture suggests that strain intensity and distribution during the main ductile phase were controlled by heterogeneous shear deformation associated with NE-directed tectonic transport and by sedimentary carbonate facies distribution (refer to Fig. 3), as well as by the relative position with respect to the main overlying tectonic contact and the occurrence of a hydrological barrier represented by siliciclastic beds at the top of the carbonate succession (Iannace & Vitale 2004). Deformation appears to have been partitioned into domains of quasi-coaxial and dominantly non-coaxial strain, essentially controlled by mechanical stratigraphy (Fig. 7).

On the micro-scale, the mechanism of grain boundary sliding is likely to have played a primary role in the deformation of (prevailing) micrite aggregates. In contrast, intracrystalline deformation affected the sparry bioclastic grains. The process of dissolution–crystallization also played a very important role in the very low-temperature deformation of the studied rocks, as indicated by the occurrence of geometrically consistent stylolites and conjugate arrays of en echelon calcite veins.

Mike Coward's highly influential work has been of great inspiration to us. The time spent with Mike, both in the field and at Imperial College in the early 1990s, besides being always highly enjoyable, has been really illuminating for S.M. Thorough and constructive reviews by G. Cello and an anonymous referee helped to improve the paper. Financial support from the Italian MIUR Cofin 2001 (Resp. V. Perrone) is gratefully acknowledged.

References

Amodio-Morelli, L., Bonardi, G., Colonna, V. *et al.* 1976. L'arco Calabro–Peloritano nell'orogene Appenninico–Maghrebide. *Bollettino della Società Geologica Italiana*, **17**, 1–60.

Bilby, B. A., Eshelby, J. D. & Kundu, A. K. 1975. The change of shape of a viscous ellipsoidal region embedded in a slowly deforming matrix having a different viscosity. *Tectonophysics*, **28**, 265–274.

Bonardi, G., Cavazza, W., Perrone, V. & Rossi, S. 2001. Calabria–Peloritani terrane and northern Ionian Sea. *In*: Vai, G. B. & Martini, I. P. (eds) *Anatomy of an Orogen: the Apennines and Adjacent Mediterranean Basin*. Kluwer Academic, Dordrecht, 287–306.

Burkhard, M. 1990. Ductile deformation mechanisms in micritic limestones naturally deformed at low temperatures (150–350 °C). *In*: Knipe, R. J. & Rutter, E. H. (eds) *Deformation Mechanisms, Rheology and Tectonics*. Geological Society, London, Special Publications, **54**, 241–257.

Burkhard, M. 1993. Calcite twins, their geometry, appearance, and significance as stress–strain markers and indicators of tectonic regime: a review. *Journal of Structural Geology*, **15**, 351–368.

Butler, R. W. H., Casey, M., Lloyd, G. E., Bond, C. E., McDade, P., Shipton, Z. & Jones, R. 2002. Vertical stretching and crustal thickening at Nanga Parbat, Pakistan Himalaya: a model for distributed continental deformation during mountain building. *Tectonics*, **21**, 1–17.

Butler, R. W. H., Mazzoli, S. & Corrado, S. *et al.* 2004. Applying thick-skinned tectonic models to the Apennine thrust belt of Italy: limitations and implications. *In*: McClay, K. R. (ed.) *Thrust Tectonics and Hydrocarbon Systems*. American Association of Petroleum Geologists, Memoirs, **82**, 647–667.

Cello, G. & Mazzoli, S. 1999. Apennine tectonics in southern Italy: a review. *Journal of Geodynamics*, **27**, 191–211.

Coward, M. P. 1984. The strain and textural history of thin skinned tectonic zones: examples from the Assynt region of the Moine thrust zone, NW Scotland. *Journal of Structural Geology*, **6**, 89–100.

Coward, M. P. 1994. Continental collision. *In*: Hancock, P. L. (ed.) *Continental Deformation*. Pergamon, New York, 264–288.

Coward, M. P. & Kim, J. H. 1981. Strain within thrust sheets. *In*: McClay, K. R. & Price, N. J. (eds) *Thrust and Nappe Tectonics*. Geological Society, London, Special Publications, **9**, 275–292.

Coward, M. P. & Potts, G. J. 1983. Complex strain patterns at the frontal and lateral tips to shear zones and thrust zones. *Journal of Structural Geology*, **5**, 383–399.

Coward, M. P., Nell, P. R. & Talbot, J. 1992. An analysis of the strain associated with the Moine thrust zone, Assynt, northwest Scotland. *In*: Mitra, S. & Fisher, M. W. (eds) *Structural Geology of Fold and Thrust Belts*. Johns Hopkins University Press, Baltimore, MD, 105–122.

Dewey, J. F., Helman, M. L., Turco, E., Hutton, D. H. W. & Knott, S. D. 1989. Kinematics of the western Mediterranean. *In*: Coward, M. P., Dietrich, D., & Park, R. G. (eds) *Alpine Tectonics*. Geological Society, London, Special Publications, **45**, 265–283.

Dietrich, D. 1988. Sense of overthrust shear in the Alpine nappes of Calabria (Southern Italy). *Journal of Structural Geology*, **10**, 373–381.

Dunnet D. 1969. A technique of finite strain analysis using elliptical particles. *Tectonophysics*, **7**, 117–136.

Evans, M. A. & Dunne, W. M. 1991. Strain factorization and partitioning in the North Mountain thrust sheet, central Appalachians, U.S.A. *Journal of Structural Geology*, **13**, 21–35.

Fisher, M. W. & Coward, M. P. 1982. Strains and folds within thrust sheets: the Heilam sheet, NW Scotland. *Tectonophysics*, **88**, 291–312.

Fry, N. 1979. Random point distributions and strain measurement in rocks. *Tectonophysics*, **60**, 89–105.

Gay, N. C. 1968. Pure shear and simple shear deformation of inhomogeneous viscous fluids. 1. Theory. *Tectonophysics*, **5**, 211–234.

Gay, N. C. 1976. The change of shape of a viscous ellipsoidal region embedded in a slowly deforming matrix having a different viscosity—a discussion. *Tectonophysics*, **35**, 403–407.

Ghosh, S. K. 1987. Measure of non-coaxiality. *Journal of Structural Geology*, **9**, 111–113.

Ghosh, S. K. & Ramberg, H. 1976. Reorientation of inclusions by combination of pure and simple shear. *Tectonophysics*, **34**, 1–70.

Gratier, J. P. 1983. Estimation of volume changes by comparative chemical analyses in heterogeneously deformed rocks (folds with mass transfer). *Journal of Structural Geology*, **5**, 329–339.

Groshong, R. H., Pfiffner, O. A. & Pringle, L. R. 1984. Strain partitioning in the Helvetic thrust belt of eastern Switzerland from the leading edge to the internal zone. *Journal of Structural Geology*, **6**, 5–18.

Iannace, A. & Vitale, S. 2004. Ductile shear zones on carbonates: the calcaires plaquettés of northern Calabria (Italy). *Comptes Rendus Geoscience*, **336**, 227–234.

Iannace, A., Bonardi, G., D'Errico, M., Mazzoli, S., Messina, A., Perrone, V. & Vitale, S. 2005. Structural setting and tectonic evolution of the Apennine Units of northern Calabria. *Comptes Rendus Geoscience*, **337**, 1541–1550.

Knott, S. D. 1994. Structure, kinematics and metamorphism in Liguride Complex, southern Apennines, Italy. *Journal of Structural Geology*, **16**, 1107–1120.

Law, R. D. 1990. Crystallographic fabrics: a selective review of their applications to research in structural geology. *In*: Knipe, R. J. & Rutter, E. H. (eds) *Deformation Mechanisms, Rheology and Tectonics*. Geological Society, London, Special Publications, **54**, 241–257.

Law, R. D., Knipe, R. J. & Dayan, H. 1984. Strain path partitioning within thrust sheets: microstructural and petrofabric evidence from the Moine Thrust, Loch Eriboll. *Journal of Structural Geology*, **6**, 477–497.

Lisle, R. J. 1985. *Geological Strain Analysis. A Manual for the R_f/φ Technique*. Pergamon, Oxford.

Mancktelow, N. S., Arbaret, L. & Pennacchioni, G. 2002. Experimental observations on the effect of interface slip on rotation and stabilization of rigid particles in simple shear and a comparison with natural mylonites. *Journal of Structural Geology*, **24**, 567–585.

Mazzoli, S. 1995. Strain analysis in Jurassic argillites of the Monte Sirino area (Lagonegro Zone, southern Apennines, Italy) and implications for deformation paths in pelitic rocks. *Geologische Rundschau*, **84**, 781–793.

Mazzoli, S. & Helman, M. 1994. Neogene patterns of relative motion for Africa–Europe: some implications for recent central Mediterranean tectonics. *Geologische Rundschau*, **83**, 464–468.

Mazzoli, S., Barkham, S., Cello, G., Gambini, R., Mattioni, L., Shiner, P. & Tondi, E. 2001*a*. Reconstruction of continental margin architecture deformed by the contraction of the Lagonegro Basin, southern Apennines, Italy. *Journal of the Geological Society, London*, **158**, 309–319.

Mazzoli, S., Zampetti, V. & Zuppetta, A. 2001*b*. Very low-temperature, natural deformation of fine grained limestone: a case-study from the Lucania region, southern Apennines, Italy. *Geodinamica Acta*, **14**, 213–230.

Mitra, S. 1976. A quantitative study of deformation mechanisms and finite strain in quartzites. *Contributions to Mineralogy and Petrology*, **59**, 203–226.

Mostardini, F. & Merlini, S. 1986. Appennino centro-meridionale. Sezioni geologiche e proposta di modello strutturale. *Memorie della Società Geologica Italiana*, **35**, 177–202.

Passchier, C. W. 1986. Flow in natural shear zones—the consequences of spinning flow regimes. *Earth and Planetary Science Letters*, **77**, 70–80.

Passchier, C. W. 1988. Analysis of deformation paths in shear zones. *Geologische Rundschau*, **77**, 309–318.

Passchier, C. W. 1990. Reconstruction of deformation and flow parameters from deformed vein sets. *Tectonophysics*, **180**, 185–199.

Patacca, E., Scandone, P., Bellatalla, M., Perilli, N. & Santini, U. 1992. The Numidian-sand event in the Southern Apennines. *Memorie di Science Geologische, Universita de Padova*, **43**, 297–337.

Perrone, V., Martín-Algarra, A. & Critelli, S. *et al.* 2006. 'Verrucano' and 'Pseudoverrucano' in the central western Mediterranean Alpine Chains: palaeogeographical evolution and geodynamic significance. *In*: Moretti, G. & Chalouan, A. (eds) *Tectonics of the western Mediterranean and North Africa*. Geological Society, London, Special Publications, **262**, 1–43.

Pfiffner, O. A. & Ramsay, J. G. 1982. Constraints on geological strain rates: arguments from finite strain states of naturally deformed rocks. *Journal of Geophysical Research*, **87**(B1), 311–321.

Raj, R. & Ashby, M. F. 1971. Grain boundary sliding and diffusional creep. *Metallurgical Transactions*, **2**, 1113–1127.

Ramsay, J. G. 1967. *Folding and Fracturing of Rocks*. McGraw–Hill, New York.

Ramsay, J. G. 1980. Shear zone geometry: a review. *Journal of Structural Geology*, **2**, 83–89.

Ramsay, J. G. & Huber, M. I. 1983. *The Techniques of Modern Structural Geology. Volume 1: Strain Analysis*. Academic Press, London.

Ramsay, J. G. & Huber, M. I. 1987. *The Techniques of Modern Structural Geology. Volume 2: Folds and Fractures*. Academic Press, London.

Reddy, S. M., Wheeler, J., Butler, R. W. H. *et al.* 2003. Kinematic reworking and exhumation within the convergent Alpine Orogen. *Tectonophysics*, **365**, 77–102.

Rutter, E. H. 1974. The influence of temperature, strain rate and interstitial water in the experimental deformation of calcite rocks. *Tectonophysics*, **22**, 311–334.

Rutter, E. H. 1976. The kinetics of rock deformation by pressure solution. *Philosophical Transactions of the Royal Society of London, Series A*, **283**, 203–219.

Schmid, S. M. 1982. Laboratory experiments on rheology and deformation mechanisms in calcite rocks and their application to studies in the field. *Mitteilungen Geologisches Institut ETH und Universität Zürich*, **241**, 1–62.

Schmid, S. M., Boland, J. N. & Paterson, M. S. 1977. Superplastic flow in fine-grained limestone. *Tectonophysics*, **43**, 257–291.

Schmid, S. M., Paterson, M. S. & Boland, J. N. 1980. High temperature flow and dynamic recrystallization in Carrara marble. *Tectonophysics*, **65**, 245–280.

Selli, R. 1957. Sulla trasgressione del Miocene nell'Italia Meridionale. *Giornale di Geologia, Seria 2*, **26**, 1–54.

Treagus, S. H. & Treagus, J. E. 2002. Studies of strain and rheology of conglomerates. *Journal of Structural Geology*, **24**, 1541–1567.

Vitale, S., Bonardi, G., Compagnoni, R., D'Errico, M., Iannace, A., Mazzoli, S. & Messina, A. 2004. Deformation and HP/LT metamorphism in the metasedimentary units at the Apennines – Calabrian Arc boundary. Abstract presented at Gruppo Informale di Geologia Strutturale Annual Meeting, Prato, 28–30 January 2004.

Two-phase exhumation of ultra high-pressure and medium-pressure Indian Plate rocks from the Pakistan Himalaya

PETER J. TRELOAR[1], KATHRYN J. VINCE[1,2] & RICHARD D. LAW[3]

[1]*Centre for Earth and Environmental Sciences Research, Kingston University, Penrhyn Road, Kingston-upon-Thames KT1 2EE, UK (e-mail: P.Treloar@kingston.ac.uk)*

[2]*Present address: Landmark EAME Ltd, Hill Park South, Springfield Drive, Leatherhead KT22 7NL, UK*

[3]*Department of Geosciences, Virginia Tech, Blacksburg, VA 24061, USA*

Abstract: The Indian Plate rocks of NW Pakistan contain evidence for both Eocene and Miocene phases of post peak metamorphic exhumation. The Eocene phase shortly followed peak synchronous ultra high-pressure (UHP) and Barrovian metamorphism and was driven by the rapid return towards the surface of deeply buried, positively buoyant coesite-bearing UHP rocks, flanked by thrusts below and extensional shears above. Uplift of the UHP rocks contributed to crustal thickening and resulted in internal imbrication of the Barrovian metamorphic rocks onto which they were thrust. The Eocene and Miocene events were separated by a phase of large-amplitude and -wavelength folding. Upright folds related to this event have shallow WNW or ESE plunges. Quartz *c*-axis data suggest that the maximum stretching direction paralleled the fold axes. During the Miocene the Main Mantle Thrust was reactivated as a major top-side-north extensional fault zone. Cascading folds on its hanging wall and cascading folds and a variety of ductile to brittle top-side-north meso- and micro-structures on its footwall document significant top-side-north movement. The driving force for Miocene extension is unlikely to be channel flow as suggested for the central Himalaya. Instead, rapid shortening of the overriding plate following Late Oligocene slab break-off could have destabilized the wedge and driven extension in its upper parts.

Many orogenic belts contain evidence for extension synchronous with continuing lithospheric shortening. Coeval normal faulting at high structural levels and thrust faulting at deeper levels is recognized in many orogens including the Caledonides (Fossen 2000), the Alps (Reddy *et al.* 1999, 2003) and the Himalaya (Burg *et al.* 1984; Burchfiel & Royden 1985; Burchfiel *et al.* 1992; Searle 1999, 2003; Searle *et al.* 2003). A consequence of synconvergent extension is the exhumation of medium- to high-pressure rocks metamorphosed earlier in the orogenic event. Exhumation is accommodated through movement along hinterland-directed normal faults that operate synchronously with foreland-directed thrusts. Such exhumation implies bulk horizontal stretching of the upper crust, but not necessarily of the whole lithosphere.

Care must be taken to confirm that major, hinterland-directed faults are extensional structures (Wheeler & Butler 1994). In a south-vergent orogenic pile, fault zones that dip south with a top-side-north displacement sense could be back thrusts whereas fault zones that dip northward with a top-side-north displacement could be back thrusts rotated through the horizontal. More evidence than just a north-vergent sense of displacement is needed to confirm that such structures accommodate extension. In addition, fault zones with a top-side-north displacement (regardless of dip direction) could be associated with some form of wedge extrusion or channel flow, with the fault zone marking the top of the wedge or channel.

What drives synconvergent extension remains a matter of debate (e.g. Ring *et al.* 1999). It might be lithospheric or crustal in scale. Extension in both Tibet and the Betic Cordillera is interpreted as a result of gravitational potential following crustal uplift driven by lithospheric delamination (England & Houseman 1988; Platt & Vissers 1989; Vissers *et al.* 1995). In contrast, in the Alps and the Himalaya extension is on a crustal scale and is accommodated by extensional structures on the hanging wall of a major, foreland-propagating thrust system.

There are a number of possible mechanisms to account for synconvergent extension within a Himalayan-type system. It may be a simple function of over-steepening of the critical taper of the thrust wedge (Platt 1993). If material continues to be added to the base, or rear, of the wedge at a rate greater than that at which rock is removed by erosion from the top, or front, of the wedge, then the critical taper can only be maintained by horizontal stretching of the upper part of the

From: RIES, A. C., BUTLER, R. W. H. & GRAHAM, R. H. (eds) 2007. *Deformation of the Continental Crust: The Legacy of Mike Coward.* Geological Society, London, Special Publications, **272**, 155–185.
0305-8719/07/$15

wedge. In this case, extension along the top of the wedge will commence once sufficient thickening has occurred and should continue for as long as shortening persists. Collapse of the wedge may be encouraged by changes in the constitutive relation between stress and strain rate of material within the belt (including an increase in pore pressure, presence of melt and the brittle–ductile transition), and changes in the distribution of shear traction on the base of the wedge (England & Molnar 1993). Extension may also result from a reduction in the horizontal normal stresses applied to the belt (England & Molnar 1993). These could be driven by changes in far-field stresses, possibly the result of slab break-off (Davies & Von Blankenburg 1995) and/or a change from a retreating to a converging character of the plate boundary (see Royden 1993*a*,*b*). In the event of collapse, material movement within the wedge may follow paths similar to those predicted by corner flow models (i.e. Platt 1993, 2000). However, kinematic indicators and flow vortices in the crystalline slab of the High Himalaya in Nepal and NW India (Vannay & Grasemann 2001) are not readily reconcilable with such a model. Instead, they may be consistent with a channel flow model (Grujic *et al.* 1996; Beaumont *et al.* 2001, 2004; Jamieson *et al.* 2004) in which ductile material is forced through a narrow channel with a thrust sense below and an apparent extensional sense above.

Synconvergent extension is capable of bringing rocks metamorphosed at medium pressures back toward the surface during later stages of continuing convergence. However, the exhumation of UHP metamorphic rocks, metamorphosed early in an orogenic cycle, poses a different problem. UHP rocks probably return to surface through more than one phase of exhumation, with initial stages of exhumation of many high-pressure (HP) to UHP terranes occurring before thermal relaxation of the thickened crust (e.g. Chemenda *et al.* 1996, 2000). Data from both the western Alps and the western Himalaya show that exhumation of UHP rocks was coeval with early stages of crustal shortening. In these regions, exhumation from depths of *c*. 100 km to within 15–20 km of the surface occurred within a few million years (Desmons *et al.* 1999; Gebauer 1999; Rubatto & Hermann 2001; Treloar *et al.* 2003). The rapid loss of >80 km of vertical section requires some form of extensional tectonics, which was clearly synorogenic as it was followed by further crustal stacking. In contrast to late orogenic extension, modelling by Chemenda *et al.* (1996) suggested that early orogenic extension implies bulk horizontal shortening of the lithosphere and the incorporation of the UHP rocks into a developing thrust stack. 'Extension' is probably the wrong term to use here as rapid unroofing of a UHP sequence cannot be due solely to orogenic collapse but, instead, requires buoyant, upward transport of a segment of crust. UHP rocks unroofed in this way should be bounded by stacks of fault and shear zones, each marked by metamorphic breaks, with a normal sense above and a reverse, or thrust, sense below. The distinction of shears associated with deep-level differential uplift of UHP rocks from shallow-level faults associated with orogenic collapse is a major problem in collisional orogens.

Geochronological and structural data from the Indian Plate in North Pakistan (Fig. 1), to the west of the Nanga Parbat Syntaxis, as well as from the structurally overlying Kohistan Arc, permit construction of a model for Indian Plate exhumation that demands two discrete, short-lived phases of rapid exhumation separated by a long period of erosive exhumation with low unroofing rates. Evidence for this is summarized below and mechanical implications are assessed.

Deformation and metamorphism in the internal zones of the Indian Plate to the west of the Nanga Parbat Syntaxis

Collision in the NW Himalaya was between the leading edge of continental India and the Kohistan Arc (Fig. 1). During collision the arc was thrust onto continental India along the Main Mantle Thrust (MMT). The best constraints on the timing of collision are from palaeomagnetic (Patriat & Achache 1984) and sedimentological (Garzanti *et al.* 1996; Pivnik & Wells 1996; Rowley 1996; Najman *et al.* 2001; Zhu *et al.* 2005) data. These data indicate collision at *c*. 50 Ma or shortly thereafter. The structurally highest Indian Plate rocks contain strongly transposed, planar shear fabrics that show evidence, marked by L–S to L-tectonites (Fig. 2a), for high constrictional strains. Thrusting rather than recumbent folding was the dominant mechanism of crustal thickening. Planar foliations parallel the major thrust surfaces. Linear fabrics (Fig. 3) indicate a southward transport direction, varying from SW-directed, in the Kaghan Valley, to SSE-directed in the Hazara region (Treloar *et al.* 1991).

Much of the metamorphism in the internal zones of the Indian Plate in northern Pakistan was along a chlorite- to sillimanite-grade Barrovian-type metamorphic gradient at 9 ± 2 kbar (Treloar *et al.* 1989*a*,*b*; DiPietro 1991; DiPietro & Lawrence 1991; Treloar 1997; Foster

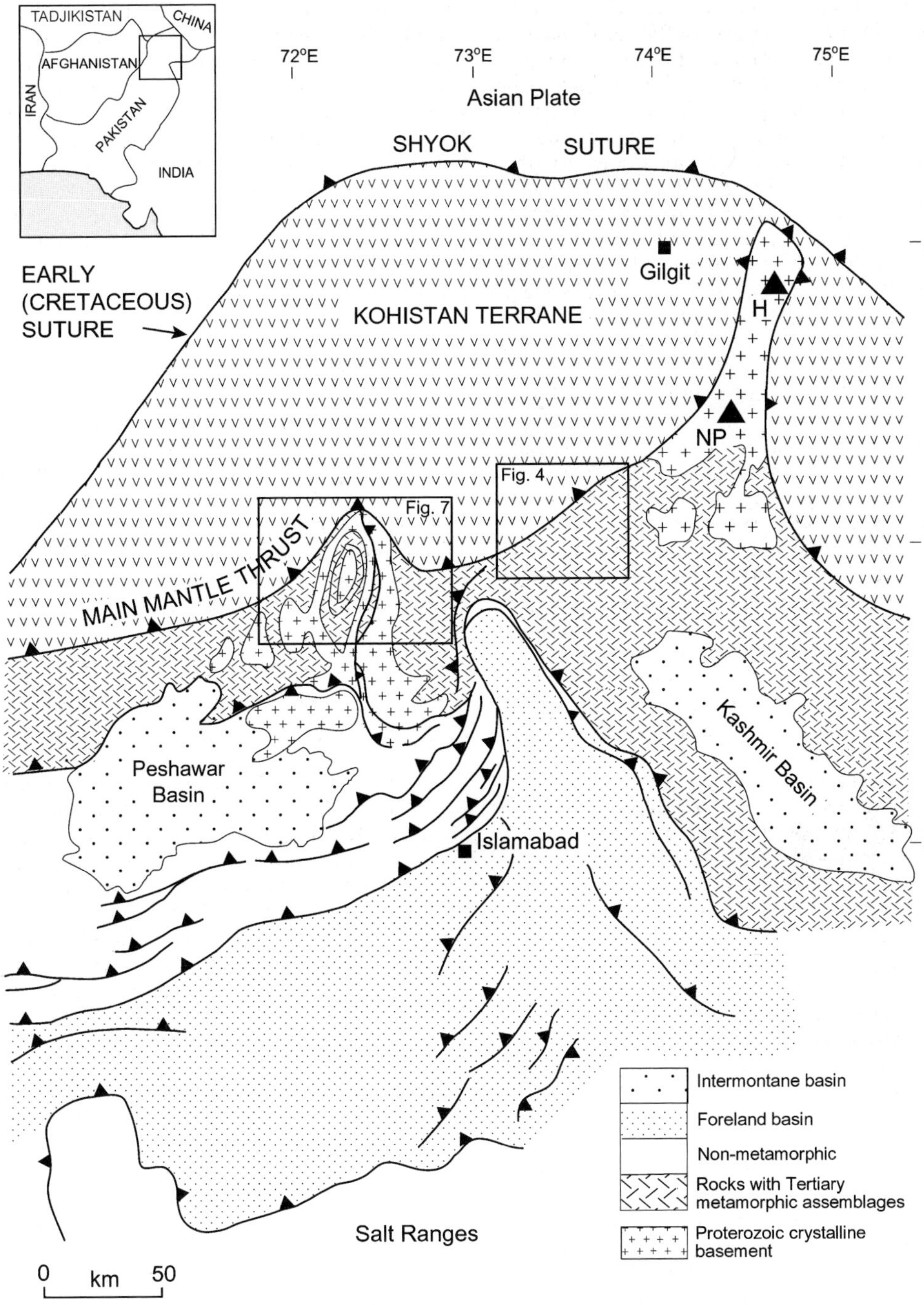

Fig. 1. Geological map of North Pakistan showing the separation of the Indian and Asian plates by the Kohistan Island Arc, the position of the Main Mantle Thrust and the locations of Figures 4 and 7.

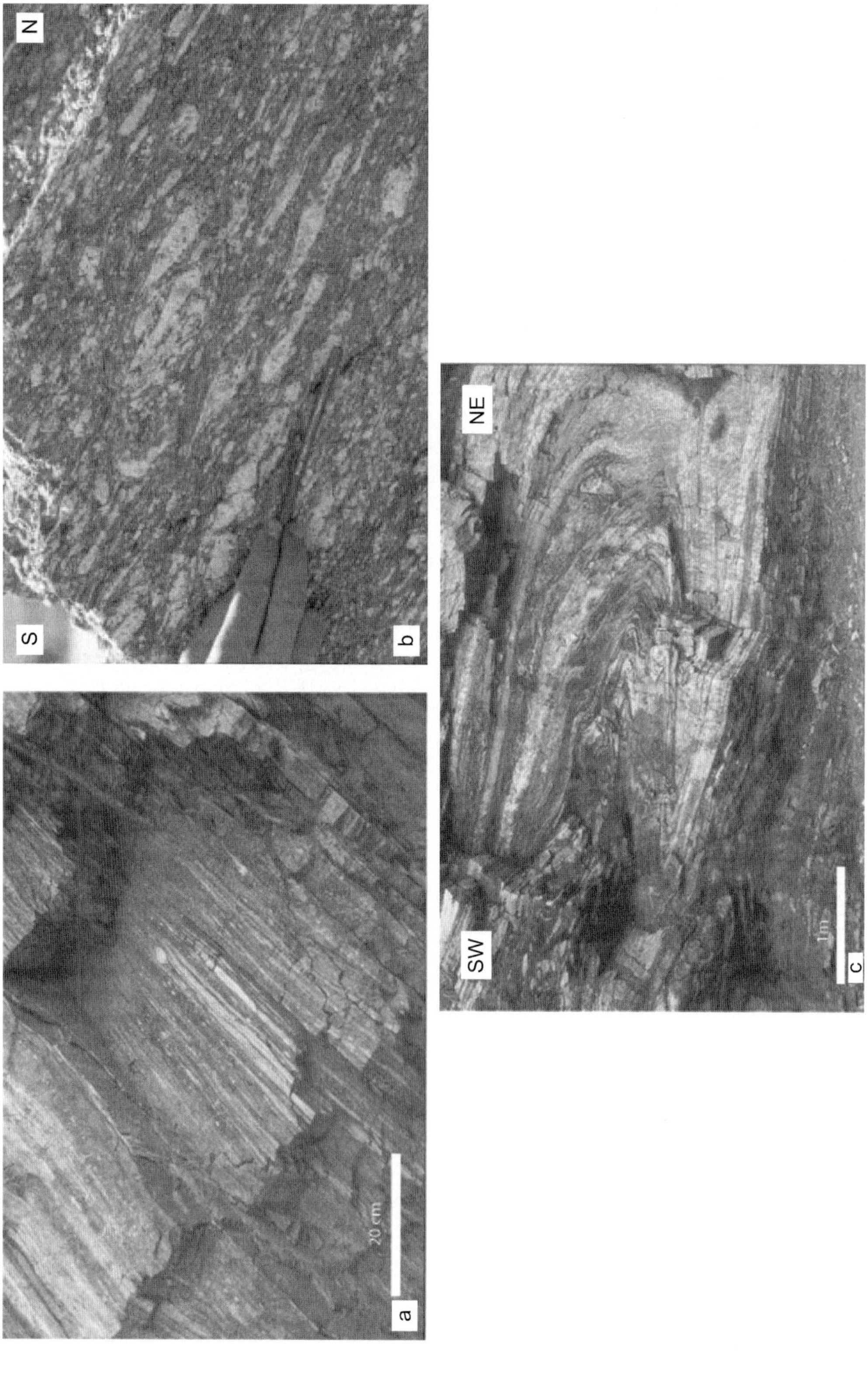
S
N
b
20 cm
a
SW
NE
1m
c

et al. 2002). Peak temperatures barely reached those of anatexis, with a probable maximum of 650 °C (Treloar *et al.* 1989*a*; DiPietro & Lawrence 1991; Treloar 1997; Foster *et al.* 2002). Although Treloar (1997) suggested that temperatures of 750 °C were attained in sillimanite-grade, garnet-bearing migmatitic gneisses of the Upper Kaghan Valley, re-examination of these rocks shows them to be poly-metamorphic with anatectic fabrics being pre-Tertiary, probably Proterozoic, in age. Only those Indian Plate rocks that remained at depth until recently, as at Nanga Parbat, had a sufficiently long time scale over which to attain temperatures high enough for anatexis (Winslow *et al.* 1995). Porphyroblast–matrix relationships and *P–T–t* modelling suggest that metamorphism followed a path of increasing pressure and temperature and was synchronous with tectonic burial of the leading edge of continental India beneath the Kohistan arc (Treloar *et al.* 1989*c*; Treloar 1997; Foster *et al.* 2002). Peak Barrovian metamorphism is dated at *c.* 47 ± 3 Ma (Smith *et al.* 1994; Foster *et al.* 2002). Hornblende Ar–Ar data date post peak metamorphic cooling at *c.* 41 Ma (42.6 ± 1.6 Ma, Chamberlain *et al.* 1991; 41 ± 2 Ma, Smith *et al.* 1994; 39.8 ± 1.6 Ma, Hubbard *et al.* 1995; 40 ± 1 Ma, Treloar & Rex 1990*a*,*b*).

UHP coesite-bearing eclogites, metamorphosed at > 20 kbar, crop out in the most internal zones of the Indian Plate metamorphic stack in the Kaghan Valley (Fig. 4; O'Brien *et al.* 2001; Kaneko *et al.* 2003; Treloar *et al.* 2003). A number of thermochronometers date peak UHP metamorphism at about 47 Ma (Tonarini *et al.* 1993; Kaneko *et al.* 2003; Parrish *et al.* 2003) and show that post-peak metamorphic cooling was well advanced by 44 Ma (Treloar *et al.* 2003). As initial India–Asia collision was at *c.* 50 Ma, burial of upper crustal Indian Plate rocks to *c.* 100 km must have been rapid, residence time there short, and exhumation to mid-crustal regions at rates as high as *c.* 20 km per million years.

Late Eocene exhumation and related deformation

There are three main lines of evidence for a mid- to Late Eocene exhumation event. These relate to the timing of events, the structures that accommodated rapid exhumation of the UHP coesite-bearing eclogites and the structures that accommodated metamorphic inversion in the Barrovian rocks within the MMT footwall.

Age data from the Pakistan Himalaya suggest that both Barrovian facies and UHP metamorphism were rapid. A combination of initial India–Asia collision at *c.* 50 Ma, peak metamorphism at *c.* 47 Ma and cooling back through 500 °C by 40 Ma suggest rapid post-peak metamorphic cooling. These data constrain the amphibolite- to greenschist-facies transition to about 40 Ma, and suggest that residence times at peak metamorphic conditions were short and that post-peak cooling was rapid and accommodated by Eocene unroofing and exhumation.

During the Eocene the UHP coesite-bearing eclogites were brought back to mid-crustal levels and thrust on top of the Barrovian sequences of the Kaghan Valley. Field relationships summarized by Treloar *et al.* (2003) show the UHP eclogite-bearing sequence to be flanked by south-vergent thrusts below and extensional, top-side-north shears above, and that thrusting, extension and the transition from amphibolite- to greenschist-facies metamorphism were synchronous. Part of the exhumation was accommodated by uplift along a south-vergent thrust, mapped near Besal (Fig. 4), which places UHP rocks on top of Permo-Triassic cover rocks metamorphosed to eclogite facies. Rather than being south-vergent, the dominant microstructures on the hanging wall of the thrust are penetratively developed S–C′ shear bands with top-side-north displacement sense, which document a phase of pervasive top-side-north extensional shearing (Treloar *et al.* 2003). Hornblendic amphiboles parallel a down-dip stretching lineation, which plunges at 32° toward 180°.

Initial exhumation of the Barrovian rocks was synchronous with that of the UHP rocks. Metamorphic grade within the Barrovian sequence decreases structurally downward (Treloar *et al.* 1989*a*; Treloar 1997). Rather than resulting from an originally inverted metamorphic gradient, inversion is due to imbrication by post-metamorphic ductile shear zones, each of which have higher grade rocks on the hanging wall than on the footwall. The ductile shear zones are S–L tectonites (Fig. 2b) with shear fabrics that anastomose around garnet, kyanite and K-feldspar porphyroclasts. Kinematic criteria indicate transport toward the SSE. Hornblendes from the

Fig. 2. Field photographs of: (**a**) strongly transposed shear fabrics developed in the uppermost part of the Indian Plate footwall of the MMT (photography taken on the Thakot to Besham road near Thakot (see Fig. 7 for location); (**b**) *x–y* section through S–L tectonites in shear zones that stack the Barrovian metamorphic sequence (photograph taken from just south of Batagram); (**c**) sheath fold developed in Indian Plate basement gneisses on the immediate footwall of the MMT, south of Jijal in the Indus Valley.

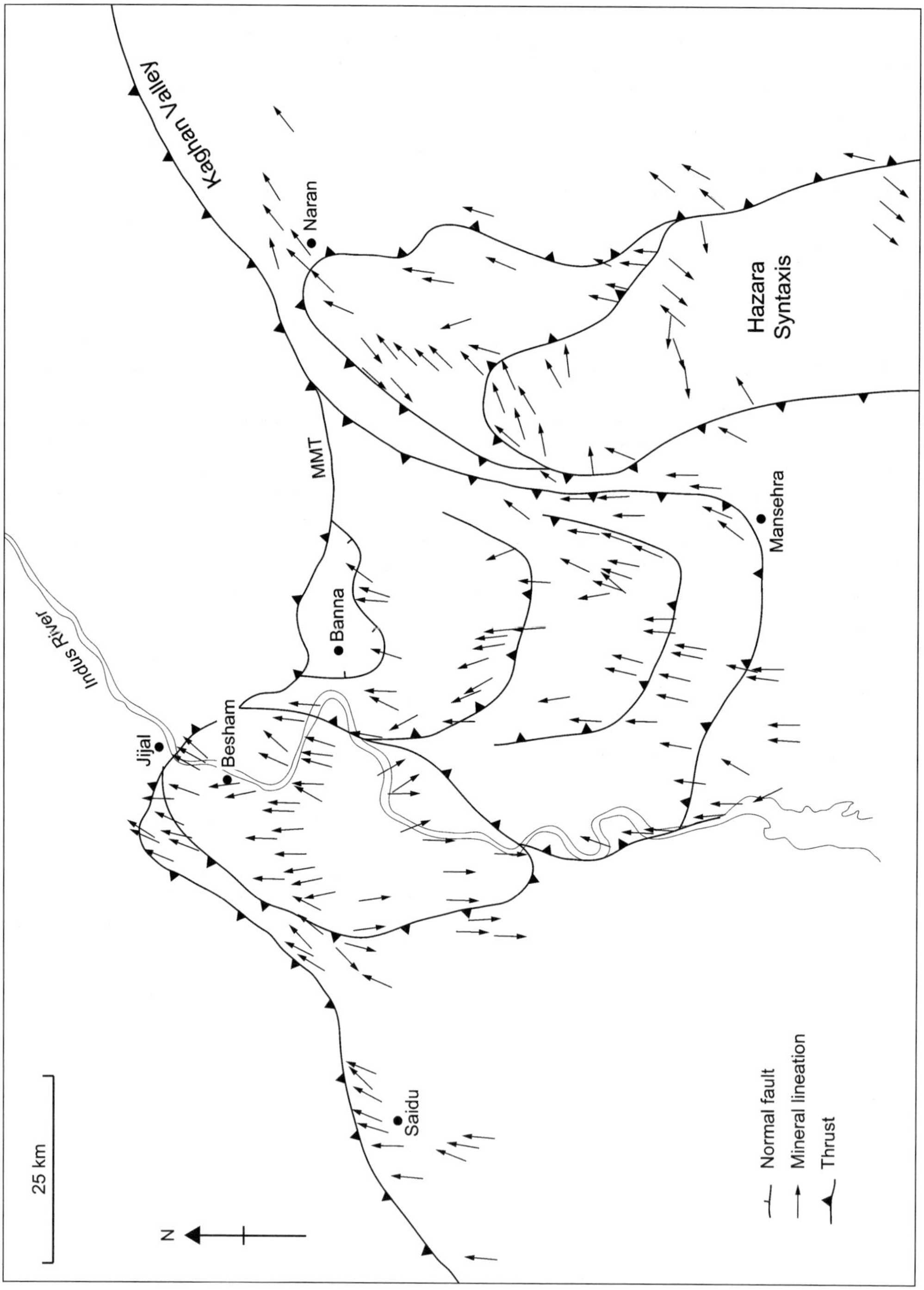
Kaghan Valley
Naran
Hazara
Syntaxis
MMT
Mansehra
Banna
Indus River
Jijal
Besham
Saidu
25 km
N
Normal fault
Mineral lineation
Thrust

shear zones have Ar–Ar ages of *c.* 40 Ma, similar to those outside the shear zones, suggesting that stacking predated cooling through 500 °C (Treloar & Rex 1990*a*,*b*). Imbrication occurred on the footwall of the major south-vergent thrusts that brought the UHP rocks rapidly from depth to mid-crustal levels and placed them on top of the Barrovian rocks. The UHP rocks in the Kaghan Valley carry pervasive top-side-north shear bands suggesting that they are flanked above by major extensional zones (Treloar *et al.* 2003). They are thus flanked by top-side-north extensional shears above and south-vergent thrusts below, both of which operated together. Cooling through the amphibolite–greenschist facies transition in both the UHP and Barrovian sequences was synchronous with thrusting. This suggests that the Barrovian rocks were themselves being uplifted on the hanging wall structurally lower south-vergent thrusts at the same time as they were being overthrust by the UHP rocks.

Although the Eocene shear zones that lie structurally above the UHP rocks have a top-side-north extensional geometry, they did not develop within an extensional regime. Lithospheric and crustal shortening was continuing and the apparently extensional structures are a result of buoyancy driven uplift of the UHP rocks, which contributed to continuing thickening of the developing orogenic pile.

Early Miocene upper crustal stretching

The second top-side-north stretching event that affected the metamorphic rocks of the internal zones of the Pakistan Himalaya was Miocene in age and is defined by structural data, major metamorphic breaks and cooling histories. Vince & Treloar (1996) showed that amphibolite-facies Indian Plate rocks on the immediate footwall of both the MMT and the Banna Fault carry ductile S–C′ fabrics with a top-side-north displacement sense. The ductile fabrics are locally cut by brittle fractures with a top-side-north displacement sense. Both fabrics are related to the same event (Vince & Treloar 1996). That the structures spanned the ductile to brittle transition implies that the sequence cooled during exhumation. This argument is supported by age data as well as metamorphic discontinuities within the upper part of the Indian Plate and across the MMT. A period of slow cooling from 500 °C to >400 °C in the upper Indian Plate (Fig. 5) followed the Eocene until *c.* 22 Ma when a period of rapid cooling started. MMT hanging wall rocks have a very different cooling history from the footwall rocks. The two sequences share a common cooling history only after both cooled through the apatite fission-track annealing temperature. These data are consistent with the MMT acting as a top-side-north normal fault zone during the Early Miocene. Major metamorphic breaks are recognized within the upper Indian Plate and along the MMT (Fig. 6). The MMT zone itself is marked by blueschist- and greenschist-facies rocks, which lie structurally above mid- to upper amphibolite-facies, sillimanite- to kyanite-grade Indian Plate rocks. These data suggest reactivation of the MMT as an extensional fault zone during both the Eocene and the Miocene.

Fig. 3. Map of mineral and stretching lineations developed in the approximately south-vergent shear zones of the internal, crystalline zones of the Indian Plate. Linear fabrics vary from SW-directed in the Kaghan Valley to SSE-directed in the Indus Valley.

This paper documents new data for the Miocene event from three sections through the MMT footwall (Fig. 7) and from the Kaghan Valley (Fig. 4). Two of the sections through the MMT footwall traverse muscovite-free, biotite-bearing gneisses of the Besham Group. The third traverses hanging-wall and footwall rocks of the Banna Fault.

Traverses through the Besham Group gneisses on the MMT footwall

Indian Plate Besham Group gneisses are biotite-bearing quartzo-feldspathic gneisses with a Palaeo- to Meso-Proterozoic deformational and metamorphic history but little evidence for a Tertiary thermal overprint (Baig *et al.* 1989; Treloar *et al.* 1989*d*; Treloar & Rex 1990*a*: DiPietro & Isachsen 2001). The sequence includes amphibolite-facies metabasic layers with hornblende Ar–Ar ages of *c.* 1850 Ma (Baig *et al.* 1989; Treloar *et al.* 1989*d*). Fabrics are cut by undeformed granitoids with Proterozoic ages. The Shang Granite is dated at 1864 ± 4 Ma (DiPietro & Isachsen 2001) and the Dubhair Granite at 1858 ± 7.2 Ma (Zeilinger 2002).

The dominant meso- and micro-structures present in the intensely deformed Besham Group gneisses on the immediate footwall of the MMT date from emplacement of the Kohistan Arc onto the Indian Plate during early stages of orogeny. On the Karakoram Highway, south of Jijal, the mylonitic fabrics are folded by recumbent, isoclinal folds with apparent SE vergence (Fig. 2c). These folds, described as sheath folds by Williams (1989), plunge at 040°/26°, subparallel to the locally developed stretching lineation (Fig. 8).

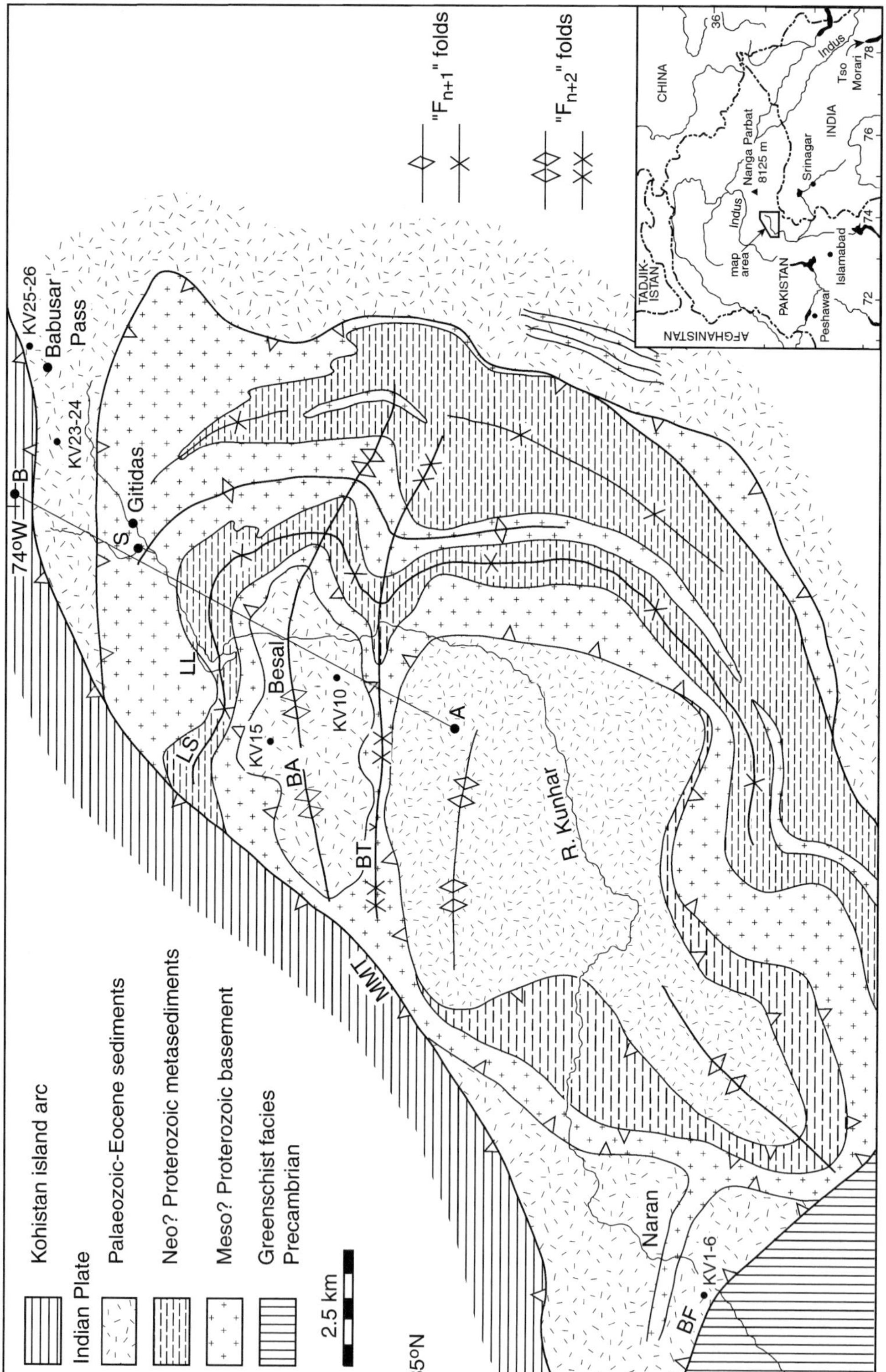
Kohistan island arc
Indian Plate
Palaeozoic-Eocene sediments
Neo? Proterozoic metasediments
Meso? Proterozoic basement
Greenschist facies Precambrian
2.5 km
35°N
74°W
"Fn+1" folds
"Fn+2" folds
KV25-26
Babusar Pass
KV23-24
B
S
Gitidas
LL
LS
Besal
KV15
KV10
BA
A
BT
MMT
R. Kunhar
Naran
KV1-6
BF
CHINA
TADJIKISTAN
AFGHANISTAN
PAKISTAN
INDIA
Indus
Nanga Parbat 8125 m
map area
Srinagar
Islamabad
Peshawar
Tso Morari
36
72
74
76
78

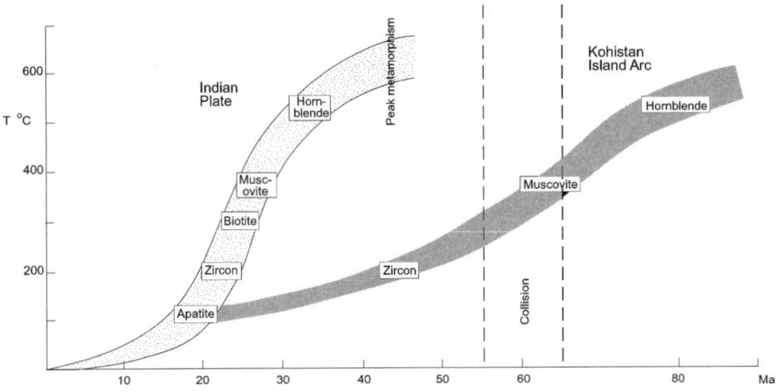

Fig. 5. Temperature–time path for post-metamorphic cooling in both the internal zones of the Indian Plate and the Kohistan Arc. Modified from Treloar & Rex (1990*a*,*b*) and Vince & Treloar (1996).

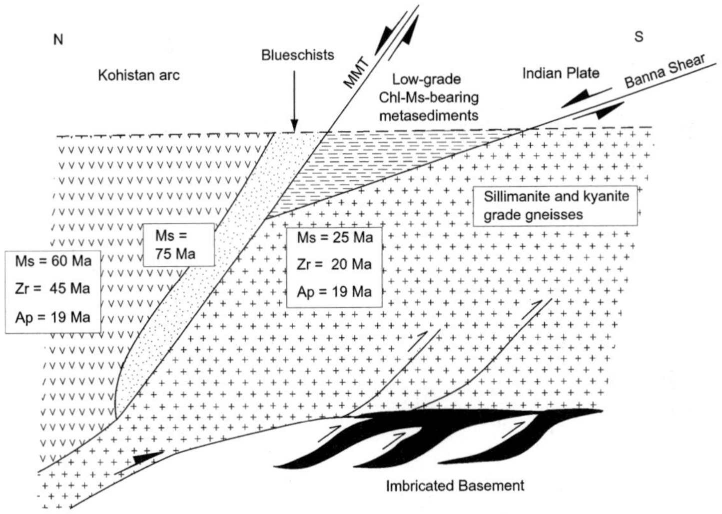

Fig. 6. Schematic illustration (modified from Vince & Treloar 1996) showing the main metamorphic breaks across the margin between the northern part of the Indian Plate and the Kohistan Arc, together with relevant age data (Zeitler 1985; Treloar & Rex 1990*a*,*b*).

The mylonites are strongly foliated and moderately lineated, with a foliation defined by planar, quartz-rich domains and elongate trails on feldspar grains. Matrix quartz grains are intensely flattened and quartz ribbons display preferred alignment of elongate recrystallized grains (Sb) oblique to foliation (S_a). A top-side-SW or WSW shear sense is indicated by deformation features in samples KV.29 and KV.30 (Fig. 9). These features include strongly asymmetric quartz *c*-axis fabrics, obliquity between macroscopic foliation and elongate dynamically recrystallized quartz grains, shear bands and delta-shaped tails on feldspar porphyroblasts. Quartz grains were deformed and recrystallized under regime II, possibly regime III, conditions of Hirth & Tullis (1992). Quartz *c*-axis opening angles for samples KV.29 and 30 are 54° and 57°, respectively. By correlation with the data of Kruhl (1998, fig. 2), combined with additional data reported by Law

Fig. 4. Geological map of the Kaghan Valley (from Treloar *et al.* 2003) showing the location of the Besal and Batal thrusts and of the UHP rocks, sample locations mentioned in the text, and the line of section (A–B) shown in Figure 22. BF, Batal Thrust; BT, Besal Thrust; BA, Besal Antiform; LS, Lalusar Synform; LL, Lalusar Lake; S, Saleh-de-Baihk coesite eclogite locality; MMT, Main Mantle Thrust.

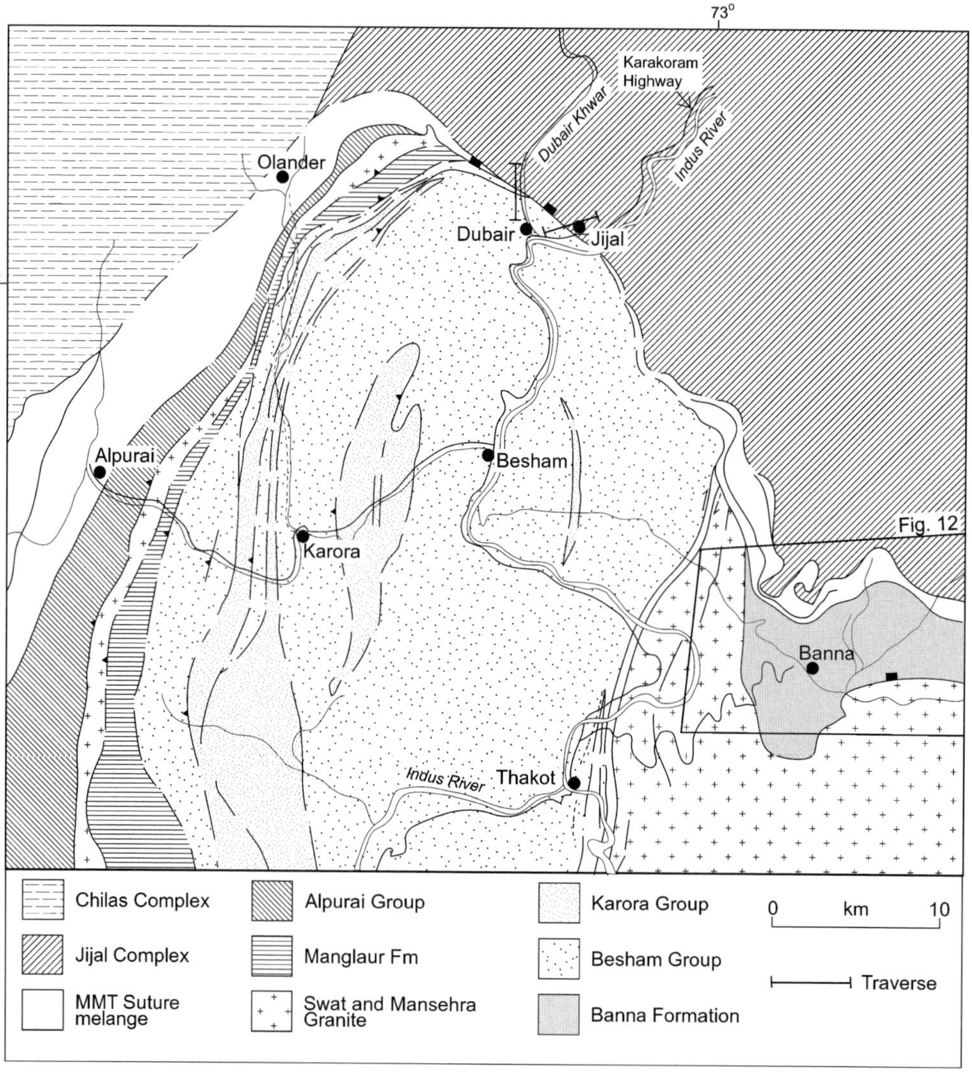

Fig. 7. Geological map of the northernmost part of the Indian Plate in the Indus valley section (from Vince 1997). The locations of Fig. 12 and of the Dubair Khwar and Karakoram Highway traverses through the MMT footwall are shown.

et al. (2004, fig. 7) and Morgan & Law (2004), these fabric opening angles suggest deformation temperatures of 415–460 ± 50 °C. These temperature estimates are in good agreement with deformation temperatures inferred from the well-developed quartz subgrain rotation microstructures (regime II recrystallization) and weakly developed grain boundary migration microstructures (see Stipp *et al.* 2002, figs 2 and 4).

Subsequent top-side-north deformation of the Besham Group gneisses along the Dubhair Khwar traverse (Fig. 7) was accommodated by a variety of ductile to brittle structures. Although some top-side-north structures are common throughout the traverse, others are developed locally at discrete levels within the MMT footwall. Immediately beneath the MMT, the gneisses contain abundant, NNE-dipping ductile shear surfaces that extensionally displace the Tertiary mylonites down to the north. The shear surfaces dip *c.* 20° more steeply toward the NNE than the mylonite fabrics that they displace.

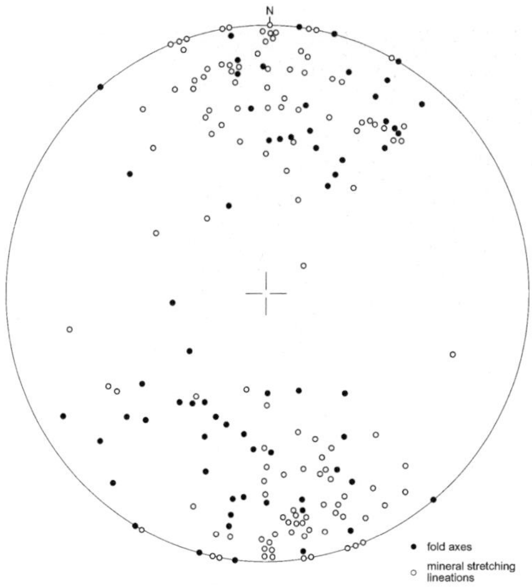

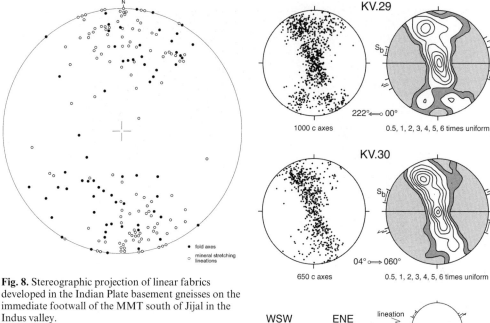

Fig. 8. Stereographic projection of linear fabrics developed in the Indian Plate basement gneisses on the immediate footwall of the MMT south of Jijal in the Indus valley.

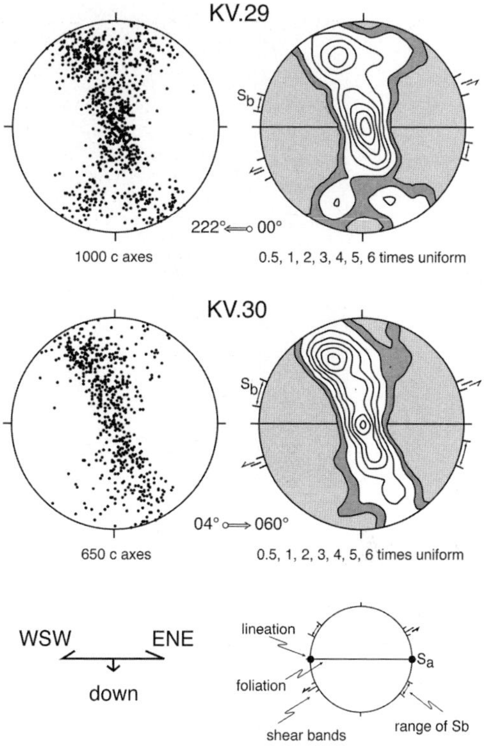

Fig. 9. Quartz *c*-axis fabrics from intensely deformed Indian Plate granitic basement rocks on the immediate footwall to the Main Mantle Thrust, south of Jijal (see Fig. 7 for location). Equal area projections on *xz* surfaces viewed towards the NW and NNW. S_a, macroscopic foliation; S_b, alignment of elongate recrystallized grains in quartz-rich domains. Plunge and trend of lineation are indicated. Data were derived using optical universal stage analysis.

Most shears are <5 cm long and curve onto, and crenulate, the mylonitic surfaces that date from the earlier SW-vergent shearing. Other than the ductile shears, the majority of the top-side-north structures along the Dubair Khwar traverse are brittle. Small-scale, north- to NE-dipping brittle shear fractures, between 4 and 20 cm long, crop out along the entire length of the traverse. Steeply north-dipping, brittle normal faults are common and are associated with secondary shears that dip steeply to either north or south. Synthetic Reidel shears form repetitive, north-dipping secondary fractures developed at angles of 21–35° to the main extensional fault planes. Infrequent, south-dipping extensional faults and associated synthetic Reidel shears may be conjugate to the dominant north-dipping shear zones. Small-scale synthetic and antithetic Reidel shears, <10 cm long with displacement of <1 cm, which developed in response to north-directed normal displacements along brittle shear surfaces, are oriented parallel or subparallel to the mylonitic fabric and occur dominantly within phyllosilicate-rich layers. About 100 m south of the MMT, south-vergent mylonitic fabrics within the basement gneiss are cut by tension gashes *c.* 5 cm long, which dip to the north or NE at an angle of 35–40° to the plane of the mylonitic fabric. The tension gashes are occasionally filled by quartz fibres that grew parallel to the minimum principal stress direction and indicate formation during a late, brittle stage of top-side-north to-NE shearing. Between 400 and 700 m south of the MMT, the mylonitized Indian Plate rocks contain a few north-dipping brittle shear surfaces up to 1 m in length, which offset the mylonitic fabrics by up to 8 cm. Both these shears and the ductile shears, seen at structurally higher levels, resemble C′ shear planes (Berthe *et al.* 1979).

Immediately below the MMT at Jijal (Fig. 7), and generally within the upper 30–35 m of the MMT footwall, Besham Group gneisses along the Karakoram Highway contain abundant north-dipping ductile normal shear planes. The shear planes are predominantly defined by biotite, are generally <5 cm long and curve onto, and crenulate, the mylonitic surfaces, which they extensionally displace down to the north. They

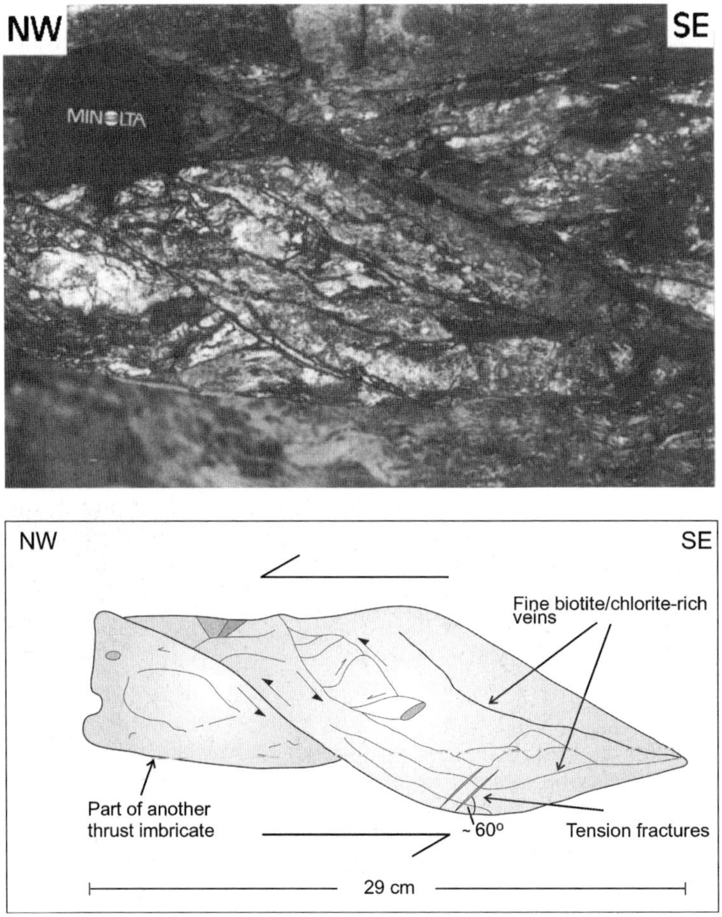

Fig. 10. Field photograph and sketch of a NW-vergent small-scale thrust duplex in the Besham basement gneisses on the KKH section through the MMT footwall.

have an S–C geometry and dip 22° more steeply to the NE than the mylonitic fabrics. Their frequency decreases abruptly downward with few present more than 60 m below the MMT. Mylonitic fabrics in the uppermost 5 m of the MMT footwall are deformed within a zone of north- to NNW-vergent thrust duplexes and NW-vergent folds with wavelengths of 5–10 cm. South-vergent, sheath folds that date from the thrusting of Kohistan onto India crop out above and below this zone of northerly-directed deformation (Fig. 10). North-dipping, top-side-north fractures, *c.* 30 cm long, and smaller north-vergent thrust duplexes occur within the imbricates (Fig. 10). Mineral lineations and chrysotile slickenfibres occur on 20–30% of the NE- to east-dipping mylonitic fabric surfaces in the uppermost 10 m of the MMT footwall. After removing the effects of later folding, these indicate reactivation of the fabric planes as north-vergent brittle normal faults with dip-slip displacement toward the north. At greater depths, ENE-striking NNW-dipping tension fractures 1–4 cm long are abundant. The majority of these opened within quartzo-feldspathic domains. The walls of some of the fractures are lined by biotite and, locally, chlorite and fracture tips coincide with the termination of north-dipping normal shear planes. This may indicate progression from ductile to semi-brittle conditions of deformation during late-stage, top-side-north stretching. At depths of >95 m into the MMT footwall north- and NNE-striking, planar and curviplanar faults, which dip at *c.* 60° to the north, cut the mylonitic fabrics. Striae on several of the fault planes indicate oblique, NE-directed displacements along the faults. There is a clear similarity between the orientation and movement direction of these faults and the reactivated mylonitic fabric surfaces that crop out within the top 10 m of the MMT footwall. Gouge fabrics within some of the fault zones show that the faults accommodated north-directed normal displacements (Zeilinger *et al.* 2000).

Extensional microstructures from the MMT footwall. Basement gneisses from the Dubhair Khwar and MMT traverses contain identical microstructures. Mylonitic fabrics associated with Early Tertiary SSW-vergent thrusting are characterized by feldspar-rich, quartz-rich and biotite-rich domains. Feldspar domains are composed of *c.* 18% antiperthitic feldspar porphyroclasts (0.5–4 mm) set in a matrix of albite and orthoclase with minor amounts of mica, quartz, epidote and titanite. Quartz domains are composed of *c.* 95% quartz and <5% white mica. The micas typically occur as fine-grained, intradomainal zones with rare grains of sodic plagioclase typically aligned in the bulk foliation plane. Biotite domains are <100 μm thick and contain biotite grains <500 μm long with remnant amphibole and epidote set in a fine-grained biotite-rich matrix.

Top-side-north fabrics that displace the main top-side-SSW fabrics down to the north to NE

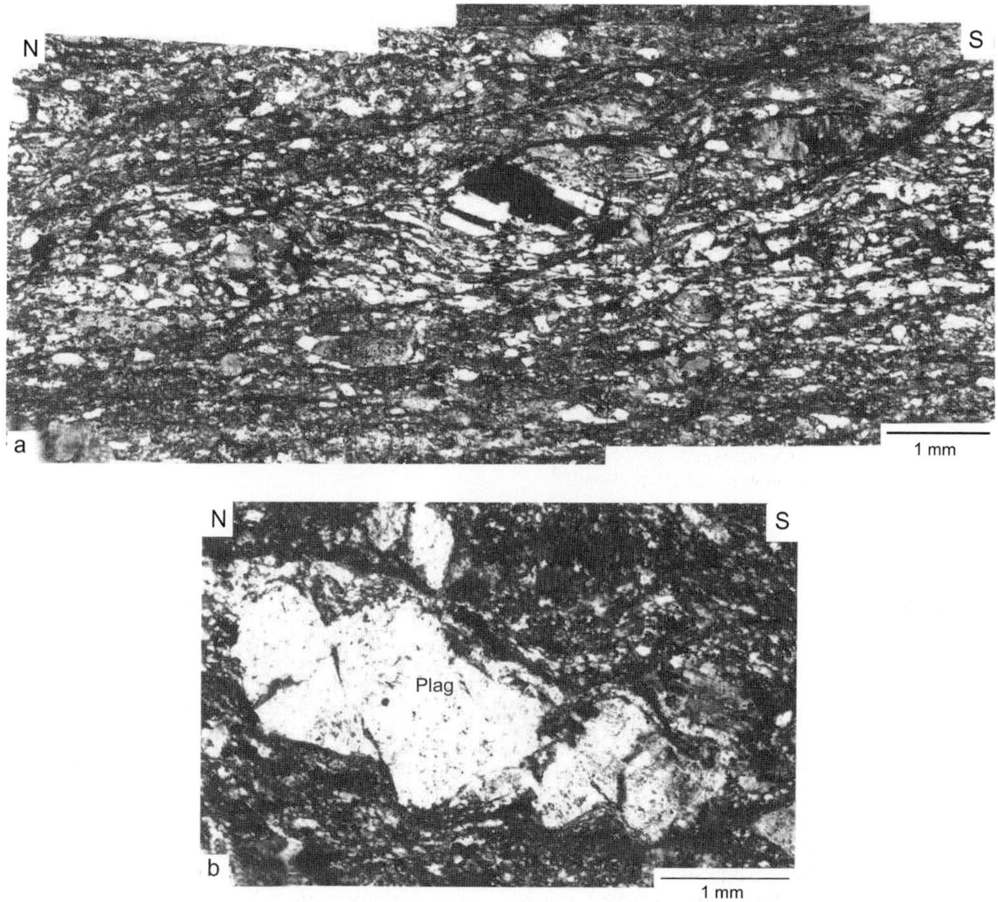

Fig. 11. Micrographs of top-side-north structures in the Besham basement gneisses on the immediate footwall of the MMT: (**a**) extensional biotite-rich shear bands displace the main top-to-the-SSW fabrics down to the north; (**b**) plagioclase porphyroblasts deformed by cataclastic micro-cracking and micro-faulting during extension produced disaggregated feldspar clasts with rotated domino fault blocks, jagged grain boundaries and extensional cleavage fractures.

are defined by phyllosilicate-rich shear bands, quartz *c*-axis fabrics and shear fractures within feldspar porphyroclasts (Fig. 11a). The shear bands are biotite-rich, ≤ 1 mm long and < 100 µm wide and dip 20° more steeply to the north than the main mylonitic fabrics. They contain very fine-grained biotite together with chlorite and transect and extend the older foliation. Asymmetry across the shear bands gives a top-side-north sense of displacement. Chlorite nucleation and growth occurred within the shear bands as a result of breakdown of amphibole and biotite. Plagioclase porphyroblasts were deformed by cataclastic micro-cracking and micro-faulting during extension. This produced disaggregated feldspar clasts with rotated domino fault blocks, indicating top-side-NE sense of shear, jagged grain boundaries and extensional cleavage fractures (Fig. 11b). Aggregates of small elongate quartz grains within Q-domains define a shape fabric oblique to the main SSW-vergent foliation, the sense of obliquity on which is consistent with a top-side-north to -NE sense of shear. Quartz fabrics are ductile and suggest deformation temperatures > 350 °C.

Traverses across the Banna Shear

The Banna Shear (Fig. 12) is a low-angle, north-dipping fault developed within Indian Plate rocks on the MMT footwall. The shear zone carries sillimanite-grade gneisses on its footwall and chlorite-grade metasediments on its hanging wall. Early fabrics on both footwall and hanging wall of the Banna Shear are consistent with south-directed shearing. Later north-vergent structures cut, and deform, the south-vergent fabrics on both the hanging wall and the footwall.

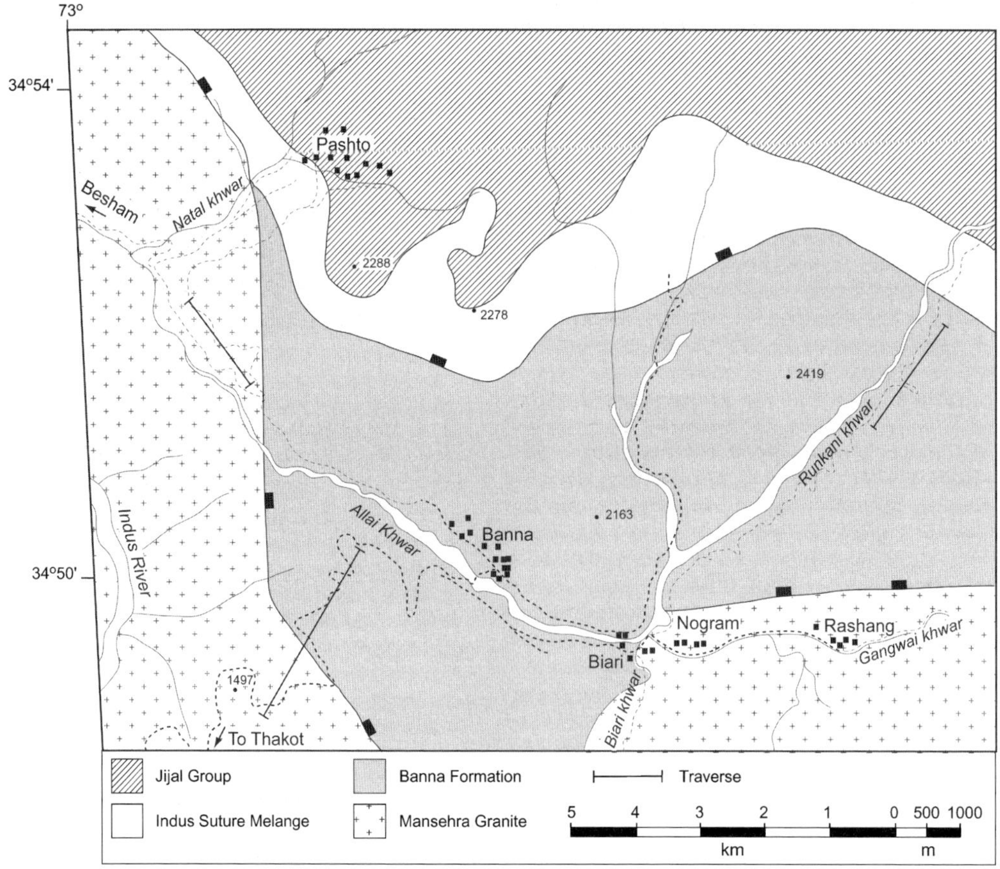

Fig. 12. Geological map of the MMT zone east of the Indus Valley, showing the location of the Banna Shear and the traverses described in the text.

Along the road section from Thakot to Banna (Fig. 12), the hanging wall of the Banna Shear is characterized by fine-grained, greenschist-facies, graphitic and non-graphitic pelites, calc-pelites and marbles of the Banna Formation. Quartz and muscovite are ubiquitous and biotite is locally present in small amounts, often with chlorite. Microstructural relationships imply that both biotite and chlorite were stable during greenschist-facies development of the main south-vergent tectonic fabrics. The S_1 fabric is a weakly developed, ENE-striking cleavage oriented subparallel to bedding. S_1 was crenulated during D_2 producing an S_2 fabric co-planar to S_1. Both F_1 and F_2 folds are south-vergent and relate to south-vergent deformation during the Early Tertiary. A series of folds and faults disrupt the greenschist-facies fabrics. Within the lowest 30 m of the hanging wall, chlorite-rich meta-sediments are crenulated by tight, north-vergent folds with axial planes that strike at *c.* 100° and dip at 45–50° towards the south. Between 10 and 80 m above the Banna Shear, 10–100 cm long, north-dipping normal faults displace layering in graphitic phyllites (Fig. 13a), typically by a few centimetres, or reactivate earlier fabrics as brittle extensional surfaces. Between 90 and 130 m into the hanging wall, a series of south-dipping, north-vergent back-thrusts deform the metasediments (Fig. 13b). These brittle faults displace graphitic phyllite layers northwards by ≤3 cm. At 130 m into the hanging wall, marble layers are folded by north-vergent folds with amplitudes of <15 cm and axial planes that dip at *c.* 45° to the south. At 145 m above the Banna Shear marble layers exhibit ductile deformation across minor north-vergent extensional shear zones (Fig. 13c). Adjacent phyllite layers show brittle failure across similar north-dipping faults. A few metres structurally higher in the sequence, conjugate sets of north- and south-dipping faults displace marble horizons by about 1 cm. Of the two, the north-dipping faults are dominant suggesting evolution during top-side-north shearing.

A second traverse across the hanging wall of the Banna Shear follows the Rupkani khwar. Within this section, quartz-filled, brittle shear surfaces <1 m long cut the pelites of the Banna Formation. The shear surfaces dip at *c.* 30° to the NW and carry striae that plunge at 20° to the NNE, consistent with oblique, dip-slip normal faulting towards the NNE.

The footwall of the Banna Shear is formed of medium- to coarse-grained quartz–feldspar–biotite–muscovite-bearing gneisses of the deformed Mansehra Granite. A strong, sub-horizontal S–C fabric is defined by aligned mica grains, elongate ribbon-like quartz domains and the aligned growth of recrystallized tails to feldspar megacrysts. Mineral lineations trend north–south. Muscovite S–C fabrics and asymmetry of feldspar tails both indicate a top-side-south shear sense for this fabric. Along the Banna–Thakot

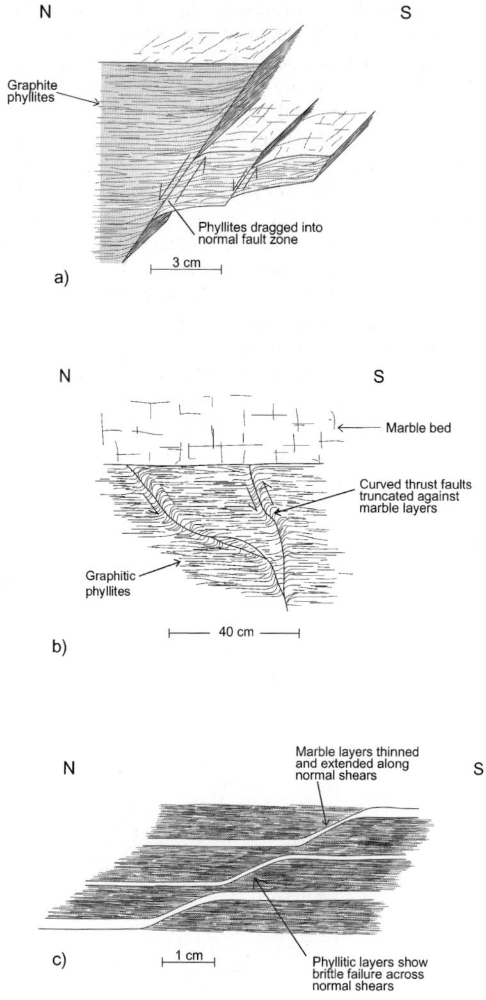

Fig. 13. Field sketches drawn from photographs of meso-scale north-vergent extensional structures developed in low-grade, chlorite-bearing metasediments on the hanging wall of the Banna Fault: (**a**) 10–100 cm long, north-dipping normal faults displace layering in graphitic phyllites typically by 1–2 cm; (**b**) south-dipping, north-vergent back-thrusts up to 100 cm long displace graphitic phyllite layers northwards by ≤3 cm; (**c**) marble layers exhibit ductile shearing across minor north-vergent extensional shear zones.

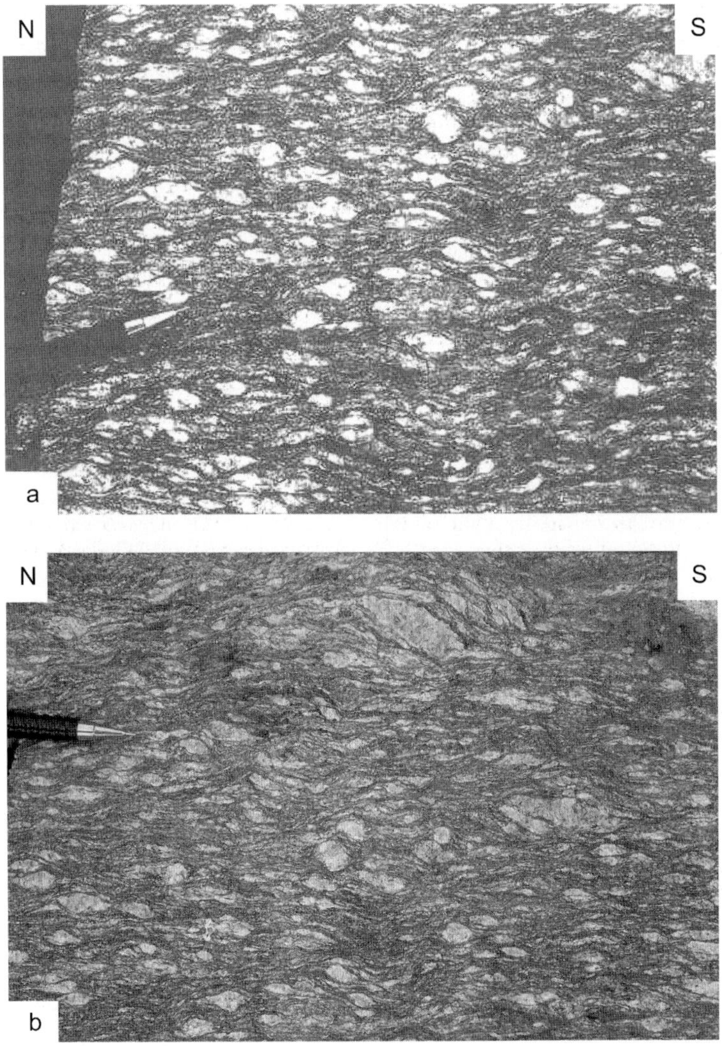

Fig. 14. (**a**, **b**) Field photographs of north-vergent ductile shears that cut earlier south-vergent shear fabrics in sillimanite-grade gneisses on the footwall of the Banna Shear.

traverse (Fig. 12), the granite gneiss on the immediate footwall of the Banna Shear contains abundant ductile north-vergent normal shears that cut the south-vergent fabrics (Fig. 14). As a consequence of its mica content, the shears developed within the gneiss are more prominent and numerous than those developed in the mica-poor basement gneisses on the MMT footwall. The ductile shears have an S–C′ geometry. Common within the top 30 m of the footwall their abundance decreases downwards. Few north-dipping shears are preserved within the granite gneiss at >80 m into the footwall. Along the Banna to Besham road section (Fig. 12) ductile, north-vergent shears are concentrated within the upper 100 m of the footwall. They measure a few centimetres long and displace the older fabrics by a few millimetres. With increasing depth the north-vergent extensional features become more brittle. Phyllosilicate-rich bands within the granite gneiss exhibit brittle failure across normal shears.

Along both traverses a variety of shear criteria and crystallographic fabrics within the gneiss document late-stage top-side-north- to NE-vergent stretching. Phyllosilicate-rich domains, less than 4 mm long and 300 μm wide, carry fine-grained biotite and chlorite with minor muscovite and cross-cut the primary gneissic foliation. They define a shear band fabric with a top-side-north or -NE displacement sense. Within the granite gneiss extensional shear deformation was partitioned heterogeneously into zones of varying deformation intensity. Within many of these zones the early south-vergent fabrics are largely overprinted by an S–C fabric defined by oblique fine-grained biotite domains. Trails of aligned mica fish, $\leq$4 mm long, occur within zones of intense shearing (Fig. 15a). In places cataclasis and boudinage of muscovite, with subsequent migration recrystallization, resulted in formation of neoblastic biotite and chlorite (Fig. 15b). Elsewhere, intense cataclasis of muscovite, originally aligned parallel to south-vergent thrust fabrics, followed by migration recrystallization was accompanied by growth of fine-grained biotite and chlorite in north-dipping extensional C′ shear bands (Fig. 15c).

The Upper Kaghan Valley

The Upper Kaghan Valley (Fig. 4) lies north of Naran. The rocks crop out on the hanging wall of the north-dipping Batal Fault (Chaudhry & Ghazanfar 1987), which separates greenschist-facies rocks on its footwall from kyanite- and sillimanite-grade amphibolite-facies rocks on its hanging wall. Further north, the Barrovian sequence is structurally overlain by coesite-bearing UHP eclogites (O'Brien *et al.* 2001; Treloar *et al.* 2003).

The Batal Fault is a south-vergent thrust zone (Chaudhry & Ghazanfar 1987; Greco 1989; Greco & Spencer 1993) operative during early stages of India–Asia collision. Our data show the thrust zone to be a steeply dipping sequence of mylonitic to sub-mylonitic rocks. The fault has been folded around a NNE-trending antiformal structure. Near Naran, the mylonitic fabrics strike NW, have a steep NE dip and carry a down-dip stretching lineation with an average trend and plunge of 054°/37° (Fig. 16). Although Greco & Spencer (1993) described the mylonitic protoliths as granitic, their mineral content (quartz–feldspar–biotite–muscovite $\pm$ chlorite $\pm$ garnet $\pm$ sillimanite or kyanite) suggests that they had a metasedimentary protolith.

Six samples have been analysed from the Batal Fault zone. KV.01 and KV.02 are dynamically recrystallized quartz veins that lie parallel to foliation in the quartz mica schists. KV.03, KV.04 and KV.05 are mylonitic quartz–feldspar–biotite–muscovite pelites and psammites with skeletal garnet grains. KV.06 is a quartz–chlorite–muscovite rock with much of the quartz in ribbons. Quartz microstructures in all six samples indicate high-temperature regime 3 crystallization conditions (Hirth & Tullis 1992) with ubiquitous evidence for quartz grain boundary migration. This is also indicated in KV.04 by plastic deformation of plagioclase grains and grain boundary bulging of feldspars. On the basis of feldspar plasticity an absolute minimum deformation temperature of 450 °C is indicated. All quartz *c*-axis fabrics from samples KV.01–KV.06 are Type II (Lister 1977) cross-girdle fabrics (Fig. 17) indicating approximately plane strain conditions (see review by Schmid & Casey 1986). Similar quartz *c*-axis fabrics, also measured by standard universal stage techniques, have previously been described by Greco (1989, fig. 4.26) 45 km along strike to the south of the Naran section in traverses across what could be regarded as the mapped extension of the Batal Fault zone (Greco 1989, fig. 4.24). Sense of fabric asymmetry in all our samples from the Naran section indicates top-side-SW sense of displacement during mylonite formation. Quartz *c*-axis fabric opening angles measured in the x–z plane range from 58 to 71°. By correlation with the quartz *c*-axis thermometry data of Kruhl (1998, fig. 2), combined with additional data reported by Law *et al.* (2004, fig. 7) and Morgan & Law (2004), this would indicate deformation temperatures of 460–560° $\pm$ 50 °C. The highest opening angles, and hence highest deformation temperature, are from sample KV.04, which also shows the most abundant microstructural evidence for plastic deformation of feldspar. These temperature estimates are in good agreement with deformation temperatures inferred from the quartz grain boundary migration microstructures (see Stipp *et al.* 2002, figs 2 and 4).

NE-dipping fabrics within the Batal Fault zone are deformed by centimetre-scale folds with SE-trending axes and SW-dipping axial planes. These NE-vergent folds are consistent with a top-side-NE shear sense and are interpreted as representing reactivation of the SW-vergent thrust-related shear surfaces of the Batal Fault. In this respect they are similar to the cascading top-to-the-NE folds described by Burg *et al.* (1996) on the footwall of the MMT to the NW of Naran. Burg *et al.* (1996) suggested the cascading folds to be located not just in the suture zone sequence that separates the Indian Plate rocks from the Kohistan arc sequence (their Bimbhal Valley traverse), but also in Indian Plate rocks on the hanging wall of the Batal Fault. They also identified NW-vergent folds within the Batal Fault Zone and stated that these could be traced downward to structural levels below that of the

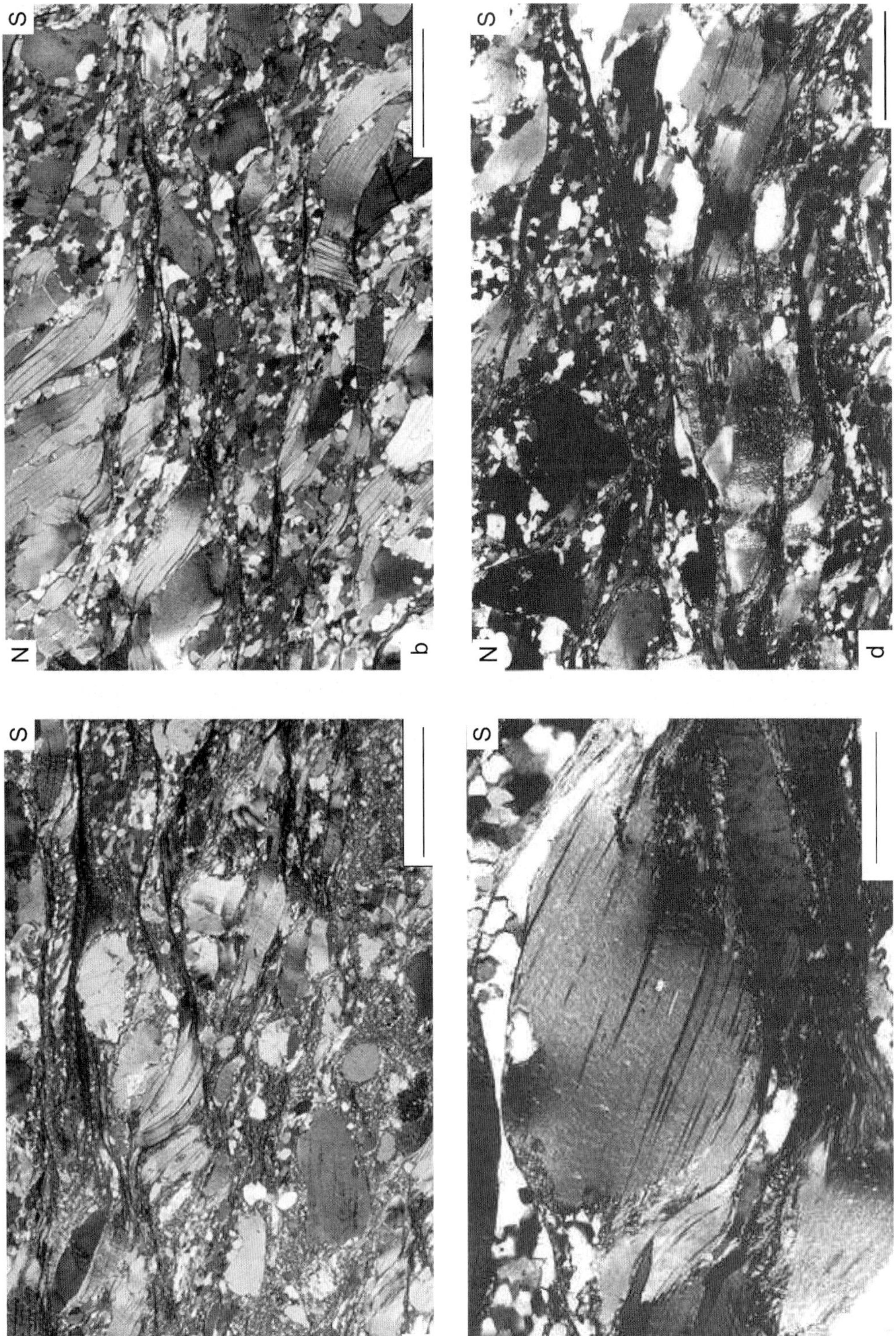
N
S
a
N
S
b
N
S
c
N
S
d

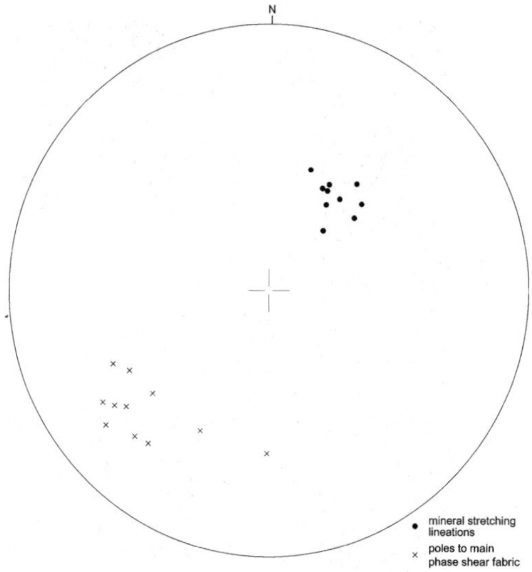

Fig. 16. Stereographic projections of S- and L-fabric orientations in the Batal Fault zone, SE of Naran in the Kaghan valley (see Fig. 4 for location).

fault. Our field data support the presence of a zone of distributed, late-stage, top-side-NE deformation throughout the area between the Batal Fault and the structurally overlying MMT and suggest that the early south-vergent structures were reactivated as top-side-north structures at greenschist-facies conditions.

The northernmost part of the Kaghan Valley contains evidence for both Eocene and Miocene top-side-north stretching. A field photograph from a road cut south of Besal (Treloar *et al.* 2003, fig. 2F) shows macroscopic evidence for top-side-north displacement. Treloar *et al.* (2003) argued that this top-side-north stretching occurred during mid- to Late Eocene cooling from UHP to greenschist-facies conditions and is related to the earliest stages of UHP eclogite exhumation during the Early Eocene.

The geology between Besal and the Babusar Pass has been described by Chaudhry & Ghazanfar (1987), Greco (1989) and Greco *et al.* (1989). The dominant structures are large-wavelength and -amplitude, approximately east–west-trending, folds (here termed F_{n+1}), folded by north- to NNE-trending folds (here termed F_{n+2}). Fold interference yields Ramsay Type One patterns characterized by domal features as around Besal. The F_{n+1} folds deform the extensionally reactivated, south-vergent Early Eocene thrusts. Hornblende chronometers date cooling through the amphibolite-greenschist facies transition here at *c.* 41 Ma. The F_{n+1} deformation thus postdates 41 Ma. Numerous macro- and microscopic parasitic folds are co-planar and co-axial to the macroscopic F_{n+1} folds. Mineral lineations and quartz rods parallel the fold axes (Fig. 18). Originally oblate albite porphyroblasts near Lake Lalusar, which grew during breakdown of UHP phengite crystals at greenschist-facies conditions (Treloar *et al.* 2003), are folded around mesoscopic F_{n+1} fold hinges that plunge to the WNW.

Sample KV.10 is from a dynamically recrystallized, 1 m wide quartz vein aligned parallel to foliation in a marble layer 3.5 km south of Besal (Fig. 4). Lineations on the vein margins plunge at 55° toward 170°. Although the plunge is a function of later folding, the azimuthal direction, which is close to that of hornblende stretching lineations (Fig. 18) described by Treloar *et al.* (2003), documents the primary south-vergent thrust sense. Quartz vein microstructures indicate Regime 3 recrystallization conditions of Hirth & Tullis (1992). However, highly lobate grain boundaries and deformation bands within quartz grains may indicate later deformation under lower-temperature Regime 1 conditions. Temperature of deformation was probably lower than that along the Batal Thrust. No convincing microstructural shear-sense indicators are preserved within the plastically deformed quartz vein. Quartz *c*-axes define a partially developed cross-girdle fabric (Fig. 19a). Although the fabric asymmetry could indicate a top-side-north shear sense, all that can be safely deduced from the *c*-axis fabric is that the fabric indicates approximately plane strain conditions and that the mineral lineation is a principal extension direction and may document the primary south-vergent shear sense.

Sample KV.15, from a quartzite layer within crenulated garnet–mica–kyanite schists, was collected from crags 150 m above the valley floor, 4.5 km WNW of Besal (Fig. 4). Lineations on the margins of the layer plunge at 26° towards 115°,

Fig. 15. Micrographs of north-vergent shear fabrics developed in the Mansehra granite gneiss on the footwall of the Banna Shear. (**a**, **b**) S–C fabric defined by oblique foliations within quartz aggregates, fine-grained biotite domains and mica 'fish' domains. (**c**) Cataclasis and boudinage of muscovite in mica fish, which, with subsequent migration recrystallization, resulted in formation of neoblastic biotite and chlorite. (**d**) Intense cataclasis of muscovite, followed by migration recrystallization, led to growth of fine-grained biotite and chlorite in north-dipping extensional C′ shear bands. Scale bars represent 1 mm.

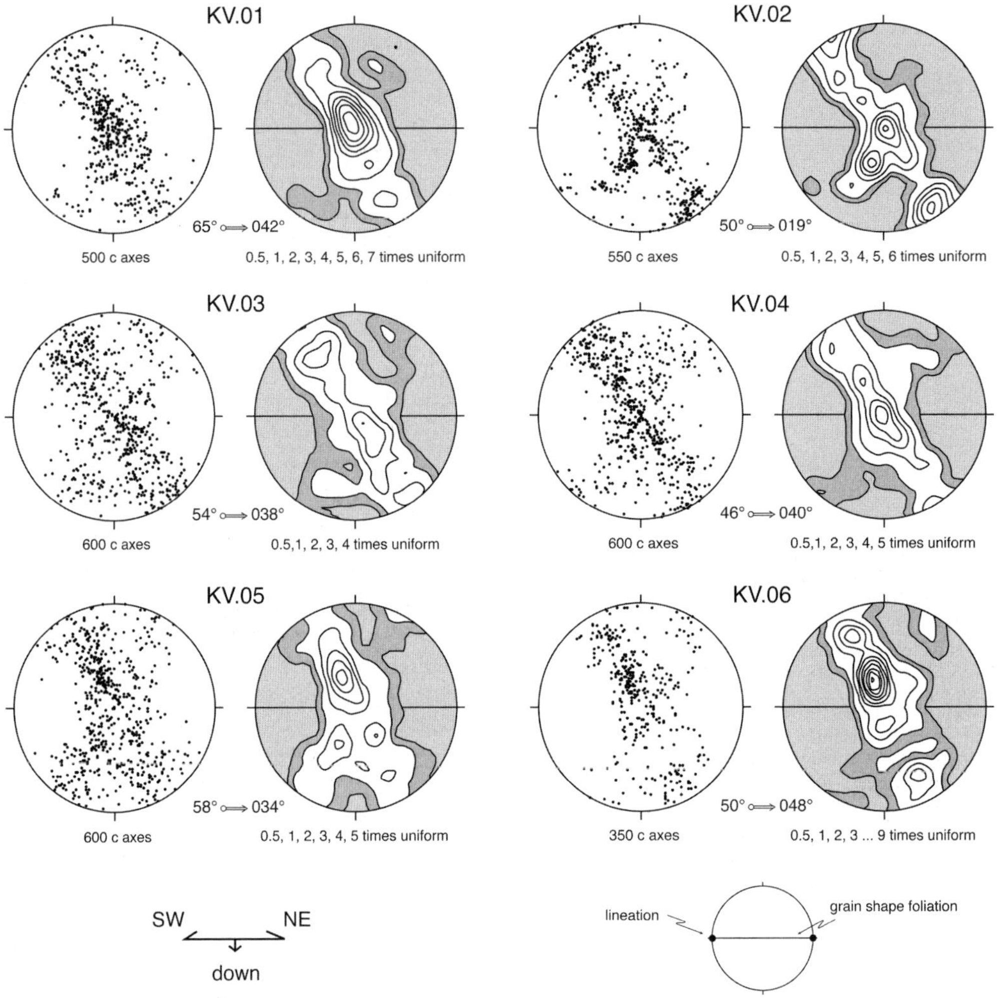

Fig. 17. Quartz *c*-axis fabrics from roadside exposures of plastically deformed and dynamically recrystallized metasedimentary rocks in the Batal Thrust Zone (see Fig. 4 for location). All fabrics are equal area projections on *xz* surfaces cut perpendicular to foliation and parallel to lineation. All fabrics are viewed towards the NW. Plunge and trend of lineation are indicated. Data were derived using optical universal stage analysis.

parallel to the crenulation lineation in the enveloping schists. Muscovite laths define a banding parallel to the compositional layering. There are no convincing microstructural shear-sense indicators in either the quartzite or the schist. Quartz microstructures indicate Regime 3 recrystallization conditions (Hirth & Tullis 1992), but with superposition of deformation bands at a very high angle to foliation. The sample shows a very strong crystallographic preferred orientation. Quartz *c*-axes define a fabric transitional between a Type II cross girdle fabric intersecting in the sample *y* direction and a small circle fabric of large opening angle centred about the lineation (Fig. 19b). This fabric pattern indicates plane strain with a slightly constrictional deformation (Schmid & Casey 1986). There is no fabric asymmetry that can be used as a shear-sense indicator, although the fabric pattern shows that both the mineral lineation and the crenulation hinges parallel the principle extension direction of 115°. This is parallel to the plunge direction of refolded, oblate albite porphyroblasts from near Lalusar Lake. These directions parallel the axial trends of the F_{n+1} folds and are probably related to their evolution.

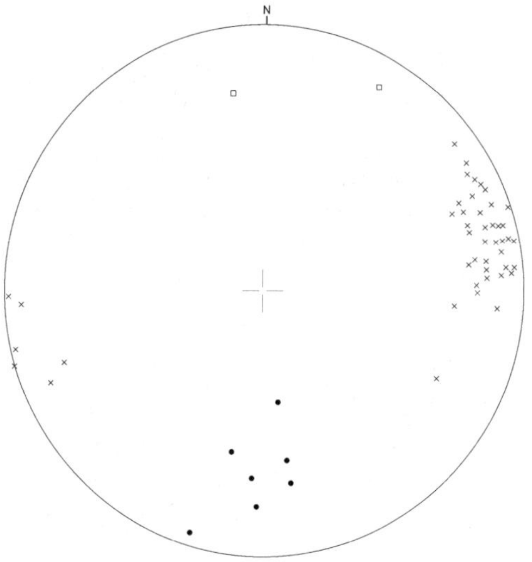

Fig. 18. Stereographic projections of linear fabrics from the northern Kaghan Valley. • mineral stretching lineations from S of Besal; × mineral stretching lineations and axes from between Besal and Babusar Pass; □ mineral stretching lineations associated with late stage N-directed slip on calcite veins.

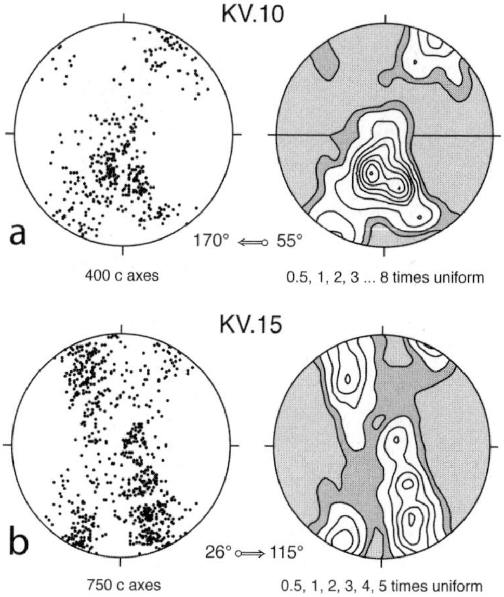

Fig. 19. Quartz *c*-axis fabrics from the Besal area, northern Kagan Valley (see Fig. 4 for location details): (**a**) *c*-axis fabric from coarse-grained dynamically recrystallized quartz vein (KV.10) in road cut south of Besal; equal area projection on *xz* surface viewed towards the west; (**b**) *c*-axis fabric from quartzite (KV.15) located *c*. 4.5 km WNW of 'Highway Lodge' at Besal; equal area projection on *xz* face viewed towards the NNE. Plunge and trend of lineation for each sample are indicated. Data were derived using optical universal stage analysis.

The Babusar Pass marks the north end of the Kaghan Valley. The MMT crops out just north of the Pass. A sequence of strongly foliated Indian Plate quartz–feldspar–mica–graphite schists and marbles are exposed at the Pass and along the ridge crest to the west. Marble units are intercalated with garnet–chlorite-bearing schists and metamorphosed mafic volcanic tuffs that contain hornblende, retrogressed to actinolite, and garnet. An early foliation is preserved in mafic boudins within marbles. The foliation in the schists and marbles is folded about ENE–WSW-trending subhorizontal fold hinges. Pervasive mineral lineations on foliation surfaces in schists and marble parallel the local fold hinges. Two sets of co-axial folds and crenulations are present. The first set has steep, NNW-dipping axial planes and is probably synchronous with the folds described from near Besal further south. The second has hinge planes that dip at 20–30° to the SSE. Inter-limb angles for the latter are typically 45–90°. Folds verge toward the NNW with long limbs dipping gently (20–30°) to the NNW, and short limbs dipping more steeply (40–70°) to the SSE. The geometry of the second set of folds is similar to that of the cascading folds described near Naran by Burg *et al.* (1996) and is consistent with top-side-north stretching. Calcite veins separate foliation surfaces on the NNW-dipping fold limbs. Mineral lineations on these plunge at 26° towards 350° and post-date the pervasive subhorizontal ENE–WSW-trending lineation developed in the schists. A top-down-to-NNW shear sense is indicated in the calcite veins by: obliquity between elongate calcite grains and vein margins; bending of calcite grains lamellae adjacent to planar zones of fine-grained calcite (<5 μm), which presumably represent zones of localized shear within veins; asymmetric trails of fine-grained calcite and graphite surrounding quartz clasts in fine-grained zones; and shear bands in fine-grained zones.

Samples KV.18 to KV.24 were collected from folded schists along the ridge crest at Babusar Pass. Axial planes dip shallowly to the SSE. Quartz *c*-axis fabrics from KV.23 and KV.24 (Fig. 20) confirm the subhorizontal ENE–WSW-trending lineation to be a true stretching lineation oriented parallel to the principal extension direction associated with penetrative deformation. Few unequivocal microstructural shear-sense indicators were found within the schists. Weakly developed shear bands in KV.23 (S: 052°/44°NW, L: 246°/12°) indicate a dextral sense of

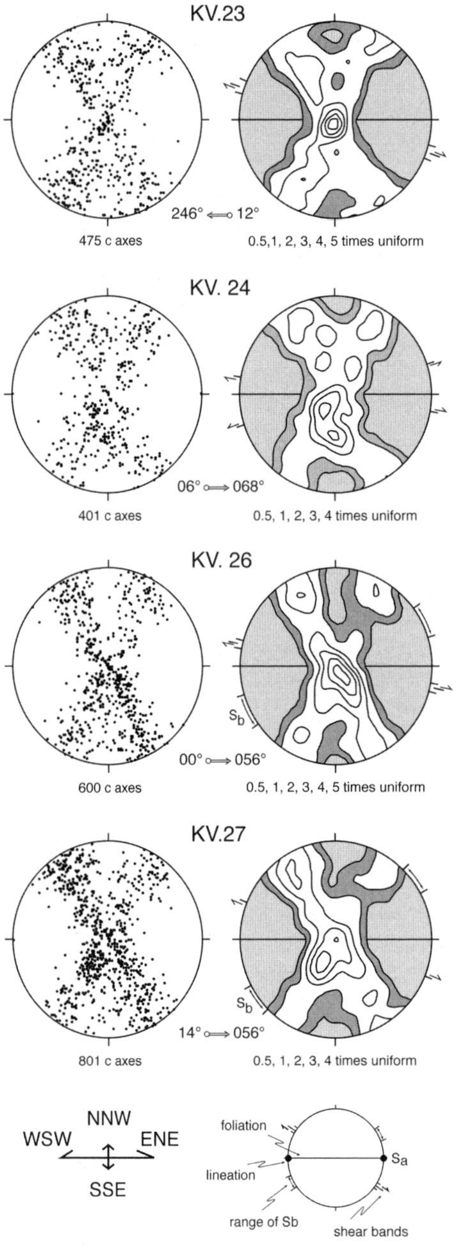

Fig. 20. Quartz *c*-axis fabrics from Babusar Pass area. Samples KV.23 and KV.24 were collected from the ridge crest due west of the summit of Babusar Pass; samples KV.26 and KV.27 were collected 2 km due north of Babusar Pass (see Fig. 4 for location details). All fabrics are equal area projections viewed geographically downwards onto *xz* surfaces. S_a, macroscopic foliation; S_b, alignment of elongate recrystallized grains in quartz-rich domains. Plunge and trend of lineation are indicated for each sample. Data were derived using optical universal stage analysis.

relative motion between the Indian Plate and Kohistan rocks when viewed geographically downward. This shear sense is compatible with the asymmetry in the quartz *c*-axis fabric data for KV.23, but the degree of fabric asymmetry is small. The skeletal asymmetry of the *c*-axis fabric from KV.24 (S: 060°/46°SE; L 068°/06°) also indicates a dextral sense of relative motion between the Indian Plate and Kohistan viewed geographically downward. Weakly developed shear bands in KV.24 locally indicate both dextral and sinistral shear senses. Weakly developed shear bands and asymmetric amphibole tails on garnet grains in KV.19 (a mafic boudin within a marble unit; S: 070°/20°NNW; L: 070°/00°) also indicate a dominant dextral shear sense, although some asymmetric tails indicate the opposite shear sense.

Hubbard & Spencer (1990) and Hubbard *et al.* (1995) suggested that meso- and micro-scale structures in rocks of both the Indian Plate and the Kohistan arc at Babusar Pass, together with the preferred crystallographic orientation of quartz, indicate a top-side-WSW shear sense associated with the pervasive WSW–ENE-trending mineral lineation. These structures include asymmetric pressure shadows, shear bands and preferred quartz grain shape orientations. The quartz *c*-axis fabric data described here (Fig. 20) are not consistent with the data of Hubbard & Spencer (1990). There are two possible reasons for this. First is a reference frame problem with reporting shear senses at Babusar Pass. This is because the main fabrics are folded about the WSW–ENE-trending co-axial stretching lineation, and may thus dip to the NNW, the SSE or be vertical. Descriptions of shear senses in terms of top-to-the-ENE or -WSW thus become meaningless when traced across a fold axis. When traced from one limb to an adjacent one, and always viewed from above onto the *xz* plane, a single original shear sense (Fig. 21a) after folding of foliation about a gently dipping hinge surface may appear to be sinistral (top-side-WSW) on the NNW-dipping limb, sinistral where foliation is vertical, and sinistral (but now top-side-ESE) on the SSE-dipping limb (Fig. 21b). At Babusar Pass, where folding has occurred about gently to moderately, SSE-dipping hinge surfaces, it is more useful to express shear senses in terms of either a dextral or sinistral sense of relative motion between the Indian Plate and Kohistan rocks when viewed geographically downward. That the primary fabrics are refolded around the meso-scale late folds at Babusar Pass suggests a further complication. The regional-scale, upright, large-amplitude ENE–WSW-trending F_{n+1} folds described above have fold axes and

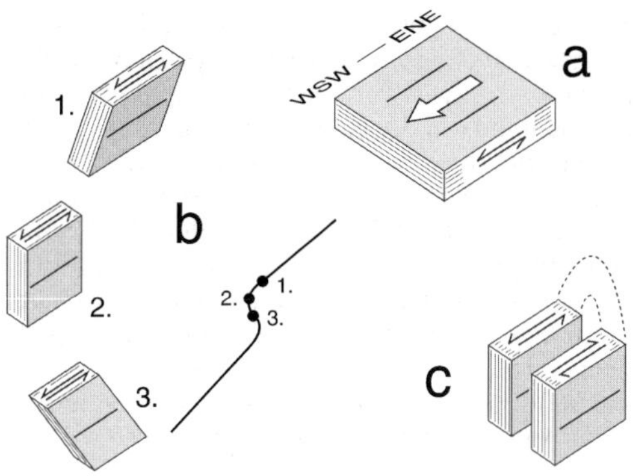

Fig. 21. Schematic diagrams illustrating the effects of folding about WSW–ENE-trending lineation on shear senses reported on *xz* surfaces. (**a**) Original planar foliation with top-to-the-WSW sense of shear on lineation as reported by Hubbard & Spencer (1990) and Hubbard *et al.* (1995) for the Babusar Pass area. (**b**) Folding about a hinge surface dipping gently to the SSE results in change in top-to-the-WSW 'upper over lower' shear sense (Hubbard & Spencer 1990; Hubbard *et al.* 1995) from top-to-the-WSW on NW-dipping fold limb (case 1) to top-to-the-ENE on the SE-dipping limb (case 3). Viewed geographically downwards onto the *xz* surface, however, a constant sinistral shear sense is observed. (**c**) Isoclinal folding about a hinge surface dipping steeply to the NNW results in opposite shear senses being observed on *xz* surfaces from adjacent fold limbs when viewed geographically downwards. However, results from our study (Fig. 20, sample KV.27) indicate the same (dextral) shear sense on both limbs, indicating that penetrative shearing outlasted isoclinal folding.

axis-parallel lineations subparallel to those of the late-stage, cascading folds at Babusar Pass. Quartz *c*-axis data reviewed above show that the F_{n+1} folds were not plane strain structures, as there was significant extension along their axes. The Hubbard & Spencer data would suggest that these major folds, which postdate the Eocene but predate extension along the MMT, had a sinistral sense of transpressive shear.

Samples KV.26 and KV.27 were collected 200 m east of the road, 2 km north of Babusar Pass. According to Chamberlain *et al.* (1991, fig. 2) these samples should be part of the Kohistan sequence. However, the samples are quartz–biotite–muscovite schists with euhedral garnet and are instead retrogressed, greenschist-facies Indian Plate rocks. Both samples are strongly foliated and lineated. Foliation is tightly to isoclinally folded on a centimetre to millimetre scale about gently plunging WSW–ENE-trending fold hinges with hinge surfaces dipping steeply to the NNW. A strong linear fabric is produced by quartz rods oriented parallel to fold hinges. A spaced (*c.* 10 cm) crenulation cleavage, oriented parallel to hinge surfaces, locally overprints the main foliation. Both the vergence of the folded main foliation and the sense of down-dip offset along spaced crenulation cleavage planes indicate a top-down-to-NNW shear sense. The presence of chlorite on the cleavage planes indicates a low metamorphic grade during crenulation development. The main foliation and the crenulation cleavage are locally cross-cut by NNE-dipping listric faults or shear bands which can be traced for over 1 m down dip and have a typical spacing of 10–30 cm. The sense of foliation deflection into these structures indicates a top-down-to-NNE shear sense. Mean strike and dip of five of these metre-scale extensional structures is 117°/46°NE. These structures, together with the lineated calcite veins described above, document a phase of north-directed extension that post-dates development of the crenulation cleavage and its associated WSW–ENE-trending lineation.

Sections from samples KV.26 and KV.27 were cut perpendicular to the main foliation and parallel to a lineation defined by quartz rods (i.e. the *xz* section). The section from KV.26 is from a domain of NNW-dipping foliation. That from KV.27 cuts across both limbs of an isoclinal, centimetre-scale antiform. The lineation developed on a foliation surface on KV.26 that dips 056°/70°NE is horizontal and trends towards 056°. The lineation on KV.27 plunges at 14° towards 056° on a vertical foliation surface that strikes 056°. When viewed downward onto xz surfaces, both shear bands and recrystallized quartz grain shape alignment (S_b) oriented oblique to main foliation (S_a) indicate an unequivocal dextral shear sense (Fig. 20). This is the same as that recorded in samples KV.23 and KV.24 to the west of Babusar Pass. Quartz *c*-axis fabrics from KV.26 and KV.27 are fairly symmetric in terms of skeletal outline, although the asymmetry of density distribution in both these fabrics could be interpreted to indicate a sinistral shear sense (Fig. 20). The difference in shear sense between the microstructures and the *c*-axis fabrics is unusual but could indicate a flip in shear sense with the *c*-axis fabric asymmetry probably recording the most recent motion. Quartz *c*-axis fabrics from samples KV.26 and KV.27 (Fig. 20) confirm the subhorizontal ENE–WSW-trending rodding lineation to be a true stretching lineation oriented parallel to the principal extension direction associated with penetrative deformation. As at Babusar Pass, and further south at Besal and Lake Lalusar, fold hinges are oriented parallel to this extension direction. To the north of the Pass folding is much tighter and generally associated with steeply dipping hinge surfaces. If isoclinal folding about subhorizontal hinges and steeply dipping hinge surfaces post-dated penetrative deformation, then opposite shear senses should be observed in *xz* sections on adjacent fold limbs (Fig. 21c). However, the same shear sense is indicated by both shear bands and oblique recrystallized grain shape alignment on adjacent fold limbs in KV.27, suggesting that along fold hinge straining outlasted isoclinal folding. The microstructural and *c*-axis data from small-scale east–west-trending structures implies that the large-wavelength and -amplitude east–west-trending folds are characterized by along-axis stretching. This is an important observation as it implies that regionally developed large-wavelength and -amplitude folds that deform the Early Eocene fabrics are not plane strain structures but exhibit evidence for pre-Miocene orogen-parallel stretching.

In the Upper Kaghan Valley the MMT zone crops out just north of Babusar Pass as a moderately north-dipping structure. Here, it separates two distinct sets of structures. On the footwall the main structures in the Indian Plate are a series of approximately east–west-trending upright folds with wavelength and amplitudes measurable in terms of tens of kilometres. These upright folds deform early Eocene thrusts and shear fabrics that accommodated exhumation to mid-crustal levels of the coesite eclogites (O'Brien *et al.* 2001; Treloar *et al.* 2003). The crenulations described from Besal and the Babusar Pass are co-planar to, and co-axial with, these large-scale structures and probably developed synchronously with them. The upright Eocene folds are characterized by along-axis stretching. Such folds are not found in the rocks of the Kohistan Arc that crop out on the hanging wall of the MMT. Large-amplitude folds in the Indian Plate rocks are truncated by the MMT north of Saleh de Bainkh (Fig. 22). Here Indian Plate rocks and bedding parallel fabrics dip steeply south and are cut by the north-dipping MMT (Treloar *et al.* 2003). In contrast, the MMT hanging wall just north of Babusar Pass carries hillside-sized, mesoscopic to macroscopic flat-lying northward-cascading folds (Fig. 23). These folds have sub-horizontal axial planes that dip gently towards the SE or SSE and axes that trend approximately east–west.

Summary of the structural and thermal evolution of the internal zones of the Indian Plate of North Pakistan

Data presented here, and elsewhere, allow construction of a structural history for the northern part of the Indian Plate during Eocene to Miocene collision with the Kohistan Island Arc. (1) South-vergent thrusts accommodated subduction of the leading edge of the Indian Plate beneath Kohistan along the Main Mantle Thrust. This was accompanied by prograde metamorphism along a path of increasing pressure. Both the UHP coesite-bearing eclogites and the Barrovian sequences reached metamorphic peaks at about 47 Ma. (2) Buoyancy forces caused rebound of the UHP rocks, bringing them back to mid-crustal levels, where they are flanked by normal faults above and thrust faults below. Imbrication of the Barrovian sequence occurred on the footwall of the thrusts that accommodated uplift of the UHP rocks. (3) Eocene fabrics were folded about large-wavelength and -amplitude, WSW–ENE-trending folds characterized by along-axis stretching. (4) Early Miocene upper

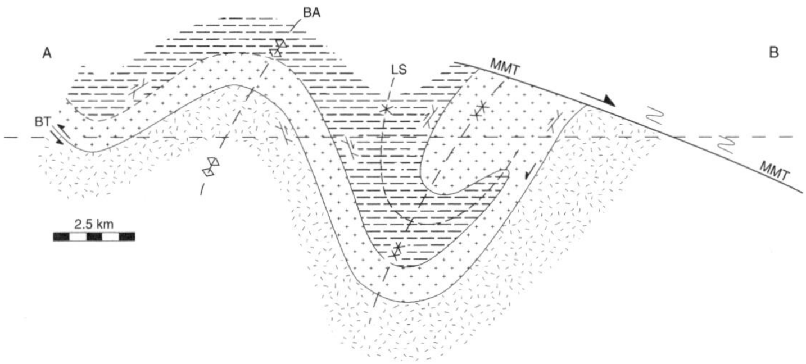

Fig. 22. Structural section, viewed towards the WNW, across the northern part of the Indian Plate and the MMT in the upper Kaghan Valley; line of section is indicated in Figure 4.

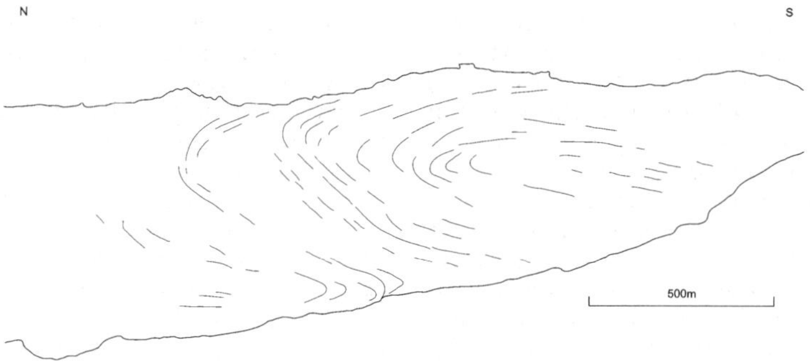

Fig. 23. Large-scale cascading folds developed on the MMT hanging wall at Babusar Pass. (Sketch drawn from a mosaic of field photographs.)

crustal stretching caused reactivation of the MMT zone as a top-side-north ductile to brittle shear zone. This brought rocks metamorphosed at UHP and mid-crustal conditions back to near the surface. In the Indus Valley, Early Miocene stretching is documented by a range of north-vergent ductile structures overprinted by north-vergent brittle structures. In the Kaghan Valley it is documented dominantly by north-vergent cascading folds and by excision of upright, large-wavelength folds in the Indian Plate by reactivation of the MMT. Thermo-chronological data show that cooling on the MMT footwall was much more rapid than that on the hanging wall, suggesting that differential uplift across the MMT zone during the early Miocene can be measured in terms of up to 10 km. The MMT zone is thus best described as a complicated, long-lived structure (originally with a thrust sense and latterly with a top-side-north extensional sense) that separates the Kohistan arc to the north, on its hanging wall, from the Indian Plate to the south on its footwall.

Principal stretch direction parallel to east–west trending fold hinges

The Upper Kaghan Valley (Fig. 4) is marked by a series of gently plunging east–west trending folds (with amplitudes varying from metre to kilometre scale) in which quartz petrofabric analysis indicates the principal stretching direction to be oriented parallel to fold hinges (Figs 19 and 20). This parallelism between east–west trending fold hinges and the principal extension direction is recorded only at relatively high structural levels of the Indian Plate sequence, above the Batal Thrust and below the MMT. In the Batal Thrust zone itself, the principal stretching direction plunges down-dip towards the NNE, and is perpendicular to the hinges of the cascading folds. This suggests that the relationship between the principal stretching direction and fold hinges is likely to be due to structural position within the orogenic wedge. Similar relationships between structural position and the orientation of principal stretching directions relative to orogenic strike have been identified in other collisional orogens, and have also been predicted on the basis of analogue and numerical modelling studies. For example, in the European Alps Ramsay (1981) identified a vertical distribution between stretching perpendicular to the orogenic strike at deeper structural levels and stretching parallel to orogenic strike at higher structural level. A similar geometry was reported from analogue models by Merle (1998, pp. 96–102).

One potential explanation for this domainal distribution of principal stretching directions was suggested by Platt (2000, fig. 10), who argued that during oblique plate convergence involving a viscous wedge, strike-parallel motion is concentrated near the rear of the wedge, or adjacent to the backstop, whereas motion in the frontal part of the wedge is essentially perpendicular to orogenic strike. In this numerical model, the strike-parallel component of flow increases upward from the base of the wedge. In the case of the Himalayan arc, it is clear from earthquake first motion fault-plane data, GPS-derived velocity fields and stretching lineations in the frontal parts of the arc that transport directions are perpendicular to strike (e.g. Bouchez & Pêcher 1981; Baranowski *et al.* 1984; Brunel 1986; Molnar & Lyon-Caen 1989; Grasemann *et al.* 1999; Larson *et al.* 1999; Bendick & Bilham 2001; Jade *et al.* 2004). However, within the orogenic hinterland of the Himalaya there is much evidence for the presence of along-arc strike-parallel extension (e.g. Pêcher 1991; Pêcher *et al.* 1991; Coleman 1996; McCaffrey & Nabelek 1998; Seeber & Pêcher 1999; Murphy & Copeland 2005). This close geometric relationship between arc curvature and the observed distribution of arc-perpendicular (radial) and arc-parallel stretching suggests a more direct relationship between degree of orogenic curvature and local stretching directions than that implied in models involving oblique plate convergence. Murphy & Copeland (2005, fig. 10) have suggested a mechanism for western Nepal that explains arc-normal contraction in the foreland and arc-parallel extension in the hinterland that is directly linked to degree of orogenic curvature. Their model predicts that with foreland-directed growth of the orogenic wedge, parts of the orogen pass with time from being located in domains undergoing arc-normal contraction to domains undergoing arc-parallel extension. Together, the two work to maintain the arcuate shape of the orogen.

By analogy, for northern Pakistan we can identify a temporal sequence from thrust-directed crustal thickening in the Early Eocene in what is now the hinterland, to a period, probably during the Oligocene, when the hinterland was being internally deformed by upright east–west trending folds with along-axis stretching, while simultaneously being carried southward along underlying south- to SW-vergent thrusts characterized by strike-normal (i.e. thrust transport-parallel) stretching. Our kinematic data (Fig. 20) suggest a dextral sense of shear along these fold axes. This period of crustal thickening came to an end during the early Miocene, when the upper part of the system went into overall extension and the upright folds were truncated by normal faults developed within the Main Mantle Thrust zone.

Exhumation: causes and mechanisms

Two phases of exhumation, separated by a long standstill with minimal apparent exhumation, are indicated for the metamorphic rocks, including the UHP rocks, of the northern part of the Indian Plate in Pakistan. Although both the Late Eocene and Early Miocene phases of extension are synchronous with continued convergence, the driving force for each is different although there are similarities in the structures that accommodate extension. Eocene exhumation was the result of buoyancy driven uplift of felsic UHP rocks. Structures that accommodated this uplift have been described by Treloar *et al.* (2003) and a mechanism for it by Chemenda *et al.* (1996, 2000). Although the north-dipping Eocene structures that structurally overlie the UHP rocks have a top-side-north extensional geometry, they did not develop within a regime of lithospheric extension. Lithospheric shortening was continuing and the structures with extensional senses are the result of vertical thickening driven by buoyant uplift of the UHP rocks which contributed to thickening of the developing orogenic pile.

Here we assess potential causes and mechanisms of Miocene upper crustal, orogen-perpendicular stretching. In the NW Himalaya such stretching could be a function of one of three possible processes: (1) over-steepening of the thrust wedge driven by changes in rate of accumulation to the base of the wedge; (2) slab break-off, which could cause over-steepening of the thrust wedge; (3) extrusion driven by channel flow. Because top-side-north stretching in the NW Himalaya occurred at the same time in the main Himalayan chain, there is no reason to invoke driving mechanisms in the central Himalaya that are different from those proposed for the NW Himalaya. For instance, if channel flow models that apparently explain upper crustal extension in the central Himalaya (Beaumont *et al.* 2001, 2004; Jamieson *et al.* 2004) do not obviously work for the rest of the Himalaya they are probably fundamentally flawed. Some models are assessed below although the assessment is based on the assumption that processes in the NW Himalaya are at least as important as those in the main Himalaya.

A large amount of published data relate to the concept of the thrust wedge. The Coulomb wedge model, outlined by Platt (1993), is a scenario that may be applicable to the Himalaya. In this model the taper of the wedge is a function of the angle of internal friction of the material within the wedge and the coefficient of friction along the base of the wedge. Features that affect the internal angle of friction include changes in pore pressure and the presence of melt. A stable orogenic wedge will not deform unless the balance between tractional forces at its base and gravitational forces related to wedge thickening is disturbed for some reason. The underplating of material to the base of the wedge is a consequence of continental collision and, unless compensated for elsewhere, will cause an increase in the angle of taper of the wedge. One way of maintaining the taper in such a situation would be by initiating extension at the rear of the wedge. The Coulomb model thus provides a mechanism through which underplating can occur synchonously with exhumation at higher structural levels. Harris & Massey (1994) suggested that weakening of the wedge through crustal anatexis might yield a similar result. The Coulomb wedge model is an attractive one to use to explain Early Miocene extension along the entire Himalayan chain. England & Molnar (1993) explored various scenarios in which extension along the Himalayan chain might be explained by changes within the wedge or along its base. The main problem with this analysis is that there is no real continuity along the length of the chain from Nepal to Pakistan. Hence, changes in the internal constitutive force in the Nepalese Himalaya, largely driven by melting, are not apparent in the NW Himalaya. Similarly, although abrupt reductions in the tractive strength of the basal detachment can be documented in the NW Himalaya where the basal thrusts cut down into salt horizons (Coward *et al.* 1988), the same cannot be shown in the central Himalayan chain. Hence, it is unlikely that simple thickening of the thrust wedge along the entire length of the Himalayan chain could have driven extension that was synchronous from Bhutan to Pakistan.

The second possibility is that exhumation of high-grade metamorphic rocks occurred as a result of channel flow. Beaumont *et al.* (2001, 2004) used numerical modelling to show that synconvergent extension in the main Himalayan chain could be the result of a form of toothpaste tectonics in which a ductile, melt-rich layer is squeezed out to the south. The South Tibetan Detachment Zone, with high-grade rocks below and low-grade rocks above, has a north-side down sense of normal displacement. Key elements of the model are a high plateau in the hinterland, a steep mountain front and elevated mid-crustal temperatures with rocks in the channel rheologically weakened by the presence of melt. Although the requirements might be met in the central Himalaya they are not in the NW Himalaya in North Pakistan. None of the key elements used to model channel flow in the central Himalaya are recognized in the NW Himalaya, where there is no evidence that a high plateau existed in the hinterland or that a steep mountain front was present during the early Miocene and where, unlike in the central Himalaya, no Himalayan age migmatites have been brought to surface. As synconvergent extension was operative synchronously in both the NW Himalaya and the central Himalayan, this suggests that the channel flow model may not be the ultimate solution. We note that the high Moho temperatures of 704 °C used in the models of Beaumont *et al.* (2001, 2004) are unreasonable and probably imply the model to be invalid even in the central Himalaya.

A third possibility is that upper crustal stretching at the top of the Himalayan thrust stack in Pakistan was driven by slab delamination and associated rollback. Maheo *et al.* (2001) argued the case for slab break-off north of the Indus suture on the basis of enhanced heat flows recorded in metamorphic rocks and the emplacement of alkaline mafic rocks and lamprophyres into the Asian crust. They suggested that slab break-off commenced at 25 Ma, or just before initiation of Miocene exhumation along the length of the Himalayan chain. Royden's (1993*a*) analysis of the mechanics of retreating and advancing subduction boundaries is relevant here. Orogenic belts that form at retreating boundaries are generally characterized by low mountains and the development of extensional back-arc basins. However, as subduction boundaries may switch from retreating to advancing and back again the characters of their suprastructure may change with time. In the case of the Himalaya, it is clear that the partitioning of shortening between thrusting in the main Himalayan chain, thickening of Tibet and lateral extrusion of Tibet has not been constant. The main effect of slab break-off will be to change the balance between slab pull and overall plate convergence. High slab pull will encourage retreating subduction boundaries and upper plate extension (Royden 1993*a*,*b*). In contrast, slab break-off will decrease the negative buoyancy, and hence tractive force, of the subducting slab, thus reducing the force exerted by the slab, and encourage subduction advance and hence increase shortening in the upper plate. Theoretically, this should lead an increase in the height of the mountain chain. However, feedbacks within the system are obvious. If the Late Oligocene–Early Miocene Himalayan mountain front can be viewed as a Coulomb wedge, increasing the shortening across the wedge would have a dramatic effect, regardless of the presence or otherwise of melt within it. Initiating addition of material to the base of the wedge, as a result of instigating activity along new, foreland-directed thrusts on the wedge base, will cause over-steepening of the wedge, which will drive extension in its upper parts. Hence, reducing the tractive force on the base of the system as a result of slab break-off may initiate wedge collapse simply as a result of the increased compression that results.

Since the Miocene the Pakistani Himalayan topographic high has been reduced by erosion rather than extension. Although thrusting has continued at the base of the wedge, growth of high mountains has been stopped by the presence of the Eocambrian salt layer within which the basal thrusts are now located. As a result, critical taper of the wedge is now maintained by out-of-sequence thrusting at the rear of the wedge, rather than thickening at its frontal base.

Conclusions

Two main phases (Eocene and Miocene) of exhumation of UHP and medium-pressure rocks are evident in the Pakistan Himalaya. The Eocene event is the function of buoyant uplift of upper crustal material rapidly buried to >100 km depth. Although flanked above by top-side-north ductile shears this uplift involved no real extension but instead contributed to the overall thickening of the subducting Indian Plate.

Top-side-north shear zones, developed in the upper part of the Indian Plate in North Pakistan during the Early Miocene, document a major phase of upper crustal, orogen-perpendicular, stretching. This occurred synchronously with upper crustal stretching in the central Himalaya. The structures described here are documented by clear metamorphic breaks (greenschist- or blueschist-facies rocks structurally overlying sillimanite-grade rocks) and by distinct breaks in cooling history across the major structures. In addition, they cause significant structural discontinuities best documented by the way that upright large-amplitude and -wavelength folds are cut by the north-dipping MMT. The combination of macro-, meso- and microscopic structures with a general top-side-north (hinterland-directed) sense of motion, metamorphic breaks and *P–T–t* data suggest that the top-side-north shear zones within the Pakistan Himalaya have a true extensional sense and support the notion that the thrust wedge was collapsing northward. They are not hinterland-directed back-thrusts.

It is unlikely that channel flow, as described from the central Himalaya, caused Early Miocene upper crustal stretching, as the boundary conditions for channel flow are not present in the NW Himalaya. The structures present would, however, be consistent with upper crustal stretching caused by collapse of the south-vergent Pakistani thrust wedge. Collapse would be encouraged by overthickening of the wedge as a result of the Indian Plate going into overall compression as the tractive force on the base of the wedge reduced during slab break-off.

P.J.T. says: Mike Coward introduced me to the NW Himalaya and I will always be grateful to him for that. Working with Mike was exciting, stimulating and always a pleasure. Our initial work was funded by an NERC Research Grant (GR3/6113). Subsequent fieldwork was supported by Royal Society grants. K.V. acknowledges an NERC research studentship tenable at Kingston University. R.D.L. acknowledges National Science Foundation Grants EAR 950625 and 0207524 that supported field and laboratory work. We thank J.-P. Burg and M. P. Searle for their reviews of an earlier version of this manuscript, and R. W. H. Butler for editing.

References

BAIG, M. S., SNEE, L. W. & LAFORTUNE, R. J. 1989. Timing of pre-Himalayan orogenic events in the northwest Himalaya. *Kashmir Journal of Geology*, **6–7**, 29–39.

BARANOWSKI, J., ARMBRUSTER, J. G., SEEBER, L. & MOLNAR, P. 1984. Focal depths and fault-plane solutions of earthquakes and active tectonics of the Himalaya. *Journal of Geophysical Research*, **89**, 6918–6928.

BEAUMONT, C., JAMIESON, R. A., NGUYEN, M. H. & LEE, B. 2001. Himalayan tectonics explained by extrusion of a low-viscosity crustal channel coupled to focused surface denudation. *Nature*, **414**, 738–742.

BEAUMONT, C., JAMIESON, R. A., NGUYEN, M. H. & MEDVEDEV, S. 2004. Crustal channel flows: 1. Numerical models with applications to the tectonics of the Himalayan orogen. *Journal of Geophysical Research B: Solid Earth*, **109**(B06406), 1–29.

BENDICK, R. & BILHAM, R. 2001. How perfect is the Himalayan arc? *Geology*, **29**, 791–794.

BERTHE, D., CHOUKROUNE, P. & JEGOUZO, P. 1979. Orthogneiss, mylonites and non-co-axial deformation of granites: the example of the South Armorican Shear Zone. *Journal of Structural Geology*, **1**, 31–42.

BOUCHEZ, J.-L. & PÊCHER, A. 1981. Himalayan Main Central Thrust pile and its quartz-rich tectonites in central Nepal. *Tectonophysics*, **78**, 23–50.

BRUNEL, M. 1986. Ductile thrusting in the Himalayas: shear sense criteria and stretching lineations. *Tectonics*, **5**, 247–265.

BURCHFIEL, B. C. & ROYDEN, L. H. 1985. North–south extension within the convergent Himalayan region. *Geology*, **13**, 679–682.

BURCHFIEL, B. C., ZHILIANG, C., HODGES, K. V., YUPING, L., ROYDEN, L., CHANGRONG, D. & JIENE, X. 1992. *The South Tibetan Detachment System, Himalayan Orogen: Extension Contemporaneous with and Parallel to Shortening in a Collisional Mountain Belt.* Geological Society of America, Special Papers, **269**.

BURG, J. P., BRUNEL, M., GAPAIS, D., CHEN, G. M. & LIU, G. H. 1984. Deformation of leucogranites of the crystalline Main Central sheet in southern Tibet (China). *Journal of Structural Geology*, **6**, 535–542.

BURG, J.-P., CHAUDHRY, M. N., GHAZANFAR, M., ANCZKIEWICZ, R. & SPENER, D. A. 1996. Structural evidence for backsliding of the Kohistan arc in the collisional system of NW Pakistan. *Geology*, **24**, 739–742.

CHAMBERLAIN, C. P., ZEITLER, P. K. & ERIKSON, E. 1991. Constraints on the tectonic evolution of the northwestern Himalaya from geochronologic and petrologic studies of Babusar Pass. *Journal of Geology*, **99**, 829–849.

CHAUDHRY, M. N. & GHAZANFAR, M. 1987. Geology, structure and geomorphology of upper Kaghan Valley, NW Himalaya, Pakistan. *Geological Bulletin, Punjab University*, **22**, 13–57.

CHEMENDA, A. I., MATTAUER, M. & BOKUM, A. N. 1996. Continental subduction and a mechanism for exhumation of high-pressure metamorphic rocks: new modelling and field data from Oman. *Earth and Planetary Science Letters*, **143**, 173–182.

CHEMENDA, A. I., BURG, J.-P. & MATTAUER, M. 2000. Evolutionary model of the Himalaya–Tibet system: geopoem based on new modelling, geological and geophysical data. *Earth and Planetary Science Letters*, **174**, 397–409.

COLEMAN, M. E. 1996. Orogen-parallel and orogen-perpendicular extension in the central Nepalese Himalayas. *Geological Society of America Bulletin*, **108**, 1594–1607.

COWARD, M. P., BUTLER, R. W. H., CHAMBERS, A. F. *et al.* 1988. Folding and imbrication of the Indian crust during Himalayan collision. *Philosophical Transactions of the Royal Society of London, Series A*, **326**, 89–116.

DAVIES, J. H. & VON BLANKENBURG, F. 1995. Slab break off: a model of lithosphere detachment and its test in the magmatism and deformation of collisional orogens. *Earth and Planetary Science Letters*, **129**, 85–102.

DESMONS, J., COMPAGNONI, R. & CORTESOGNO, L. 1999. Alpine metamorphism of the western Alps: II. High-*P/T* and related pre-greenschist metamorphism. *Schweizerische Mineralogische und Petrographische Mitteilungen*, **79**, 111–134.

DIPIETRO, J. A. 1991. Metamorphic pressure–temperature conditions of Indian plate rocks south of the Main Mantle Thrust, Lower Swat, Pakistan. *Tectonics*, **10**, 742–757.

DIPIETRO, J. A. & ISACHSEN, C. E. 2001. U–Pb zircon ages from the Indian Plate in northwest Pakistan and their significance to Himalayan and pre-Himalayan geologic history. *Tectonics*, **20**, 510–525.

DIPIETRO, J. A. & LAWRENCE, R. D. 1991. Himalayan structure and metamorphism south of the Main Mantle Thrust, Lower Swat, Pakistan. *Journal of Metamorphic Geology*, **9**, 481–495.

ENGLAND, P. C. & HOUSEMAN, G. A. 1988. The mechanics of the Tibetan Plateau. *Philosophical Transactions of the Royal Society of London, Series A*, **326**, 301–319.

ENGLAND, P. & MOLNAR, P. 1993. Cause and effect among thrust and normal faulting, anatectic melting and exhumation in the Himalaya. *In*: TRELOAR, P. J. & SEARLE, M. P. (eds) *Himalayan Tectonics*. Geological Society, London, Special Publications, **74**, 401–411.

FOSSEN, H. 2000. Extensional tectonics in the Caledonides: synorogenic or postorogenic. *Tectonics*, **19**, 213–224.

FOSTER, G. L., VANCE, D., ARGLES, T. W. & Harris, N. B. W. 2002. The Tertiary collision-related thermal history of the NW Himalaya. *Journal of Metamorphic Geology*, **20**, 827–844.

GARZANTI, E., CRITELLI, S. & INGERSOLL, R. V. 1996. Paleogeographic and paleotectonic evolution of the Himalayan Range as reflected by detrital modes of Tertiary sandstones and modern sands (Indus transect, India and Pakistan). *Geological Society of America Bulletin*, **108**, 631–642.

GEBAUER, D. 1999. Alpine geochronology of the Central and Western Alps: new constraints for a complex geodynamic evolution. *Schweizerische Mineralogische und Petrographische Mitteilungen*, **79**, 191–208.

GRASEMANN, B., FRITZ, H. & VANNAY, J. C. 1999. Quantitative kinematic flow analysis from the Main Central Thrust Zone (NW Himalaya, India); implications for a decelerating strain path and the extrusion of orogenic wedges. *Journal of Structural Geology*, **21**, 837–853.

GRECO, A. 1989. *Tectonics and Metamorphism in the Western Himalayan Syntaxis Area (Azad Kashmir, NE-Pakistan)*. Mitteilungen aus dem Geologischen Institut der Eidgenössisch Technische Hochschule und der Universität Zürich, Neue Folge, **274**.

GRECO, A. & SPENCER, D. A. 1993. A section through the Indian Plate, Kaghan Valley, NW Himalaya, Pakistan. *In*: TRELOAR, P. J. & SEARLE, M. P. (eds) *Himalayan Tectonics*. Geological Society, London, Special Publications, **74**, 221–236.

GRECO, A., MARTONITTI, G., PAPRITZ, K., RAMSAY, J. G. & REY, R. 1989. The crystalline rocks of the Kaghan Valley (NE Pakistan). *Eclogae Geologicae Helvetiae*, **82**, 629–653.

GRUJIC, D., CASEY, M., DAVIDSON, C., HOLLISTER, L., KUNDIG, K., PAVLIS, T. & SCHMID, S. 1996. Ductile extrusion of the Higher Himalayan crystalline in Bhutan: evidence from quartz microfabrics. *Tectonophysics*, **260**, 21–43.

HARRIS, N. B. W. & MASSEY, J. 1994. Decompression and anatexis of Himalayan metapelites. *Tectonics*, **13**, 1537–1546.

HIRTH, G. & TULLIS, J. 1992. Dislocation creep regimes in quartz aggregates. *Journal of Structural Geology*, **14**, 145–160.

HUBBARD, M. S. & SPENCER, D. A. 1990. WSW-trending deformation between Babusar Pass and Toshe Gali area, northern Pakistan. *Geological Bulletin, University of Peshawar*, **23**, 101–110.

HUBBARD, M. S., SPENCER, D. A. & WEST, D. P. 1995. Tectonic exhumation of the Nanga Parbat massif, northern Pakistan. *Earth and Planetary Science Letters*, **133**, 213–225.

JADE, S., BHATT, B. C., YANG, Z. *et al.* 2004. GPS measurements from the Ladakh Himalaya, India: preliminary tests of plate-like or continuous deformation in Tibet. *Geological Society of America Bulletin*, **116**, 1385–1391.

JAMIESON, R. A., BEAUMONT, C., MEDVEDEV, S. & NGUYEN, M. H. 2004. Crustal channel flows: 2. Numerical models with implications for metamorphism in the Himalayan–Tibetan orogen. *Journal of Geophysical Research B: Solid Earth*, **109**(B06407), 1–24.

KANEKO, Y., KATAYAMA, I., YAMAMOTO, H. *et al.* 2003. Timing of Himalayan, ultrahigh-pressure metamorphism: sinking rate and subduction angle of the Indian continental crust beneath Asia. *Journal of Metamorphic Geology*, **21**, 589–599.

KRUHL, J. H. 1998. Reply: Prism- and basal-plane parallel subgrain boundaries in quartz: a microstructural geothermobarometer. *Journal of Metamorphic Petrology*, **16**, 142–146.

LARSON, K., BÜRGMANN, R., BILHAM, R. & FREYMUELLER, J. 1999. Kinematics of the India–Asia collision zone from GPS measurements. *Journal of Geophysical Research*, **104**, 1077–1093.

LAW, R. D., SEARLE, M. P. & SIMPSON, R. L. 2004. Strain, deformation temperatures and vorticity of flow at the top of the Greater Himalayan Slab, Everest massif, Tibet. *Journal of the Geological Society, London*, **161**, 305–320.

LISTER, G. S. 1977. Crossed-girdle *c*-axis fabrics in quartzites plastically deformed by plane strain and progressive simple shear. *Tectonophysics*, **39**, 51–54.

MAHEO, G., ROLLAND, Y., GUILLOT, S. & PÊCHER, A. 2001. Metamorphic and magmatic evidences for slab break-off process below NW Himalaya. *Journal of Asian Earth Sciences*, **19**, 43–44.

MCCAFFREY, R. & NABELEK, J. 1998. Role of oblique convergence in the active deformation of the Himalayas and southern Tibet plateau. *Geology*, **26**, 691–694.

MERLE, O. 1998. *Emplacement Mechanisms of Nappes and Thrust Sheets.* Kluwer, Dordrecht.

MOLNAR, P. & LYON-CAEN, H. 1989. Fault plane solutions of earthquakes and active tectonics of the Tibetan Plateau and its margins. *Geophysical Journal International*, **99**, 123–155.

MORGAN, S. S. & LAW, R. D. 2004. Unusual transition in quartzite dislocation creep regimes and crystal slip systems in the aureole of the EJB pluton, California: a case for anhydrous conditions created by decarbonation of adjacent marbles. *Tectonophysics*, **384**, 209–231.

MURPHY, M. A. & COPELAND, P. 2005. Transtensional deformation in the central Himalaya and its role in accommodating growth of the Himalayan orogen. *Tectonics*, **24**(TC4012), doi:10.1029/2004TC001659.

NAJMAN, Y., PRINGLE, M., GODIN, L. & OLIVER, G. 2001. Dating of the oldest continental sediments from the Himalayan foreland basins. *Nature*, **410**, 194–197.

O'BRIEN, P. J., ZOTOV, N. LAW, R. D., KHAN, M. A. & JAN, M. Q. 2001. Coesite in Himalayan eclogite and implications for models of India–Asia collision. *Geology*, **29**, 435–438.

PARRISH, R. R., GOUGH, S., SEARLE, M. P. & WATERS, D. 2003. Extremely rapid exhumation of the Kaghan UHP terrane, Pakistan from U–Th–Pb measurements on accessory minerals. *Geological Society of America, Annual Meeting, Seattle, Abstracts*, **229–7**.

PATRIAT, P. & ACHACHE, J. 1984. India–Eurasia collision chronology and its implications for crustal shortening and driving mechanisms of plates. *Nature*, **311**, 615–621.

PÊCHER, A. 1991. The contact between the Higher Himalaya crystallines and the Tibetan sedimentary series—Miocene large-scale dextral shearing. *Tectonics*, **10**, 587–598.

PÊCHER, A., BOUCHEZ, J. L. & LE FORT, P. 1991. Miocene dextral shearing between Himalaya and Tibet. *Geology*, **19**, 683–685.

PIVNIK, D. A. & WELLS, N. A. 1996. The transition from Tethys to the Himalaya as recorded in NW Pakistan. *Geological Society of America Bulletin*, **108**, 1295–1313.

PLATT, J. P. 1993. Exhumation of high pressure rocks: a review of concepts and processes. *Terra Nova*, **5**, 119–133.

PLATT, J. P. 2000. Calibrating the bulk rheology of active obliquely convergent thrust belts and forearc wedges from surface profiles and velocity distributions. *Tectonics*, **19**, 529–548.

PLATT, J. & VISSERS, R. L. M. 1989. Extensional collapse of thickened continental lithosphere: a working hypothesis for the Alboran Sea and Gibraltar arc. *Geology*, **17**, 540–545.

RAMSAY, J. G. 1981. Tectonics of the Helvetic Nappes. *In*: MCCLAY, K. R. & PRICE, N. J. (eds) *Thrust and Nappe Tectonics.* Geological Society, London, Special Publications, **9**, 293–310.

REDDY, S. M., WHEELER, J. & CLIFF, R. A. 1999. The geometry and timing of orogenic extension: an example from the western Italian Alps. *Journal of Metamorphic Geology*, **17**, 573–589.

REDDY, S. M., WHEELER, J., BUTLER, R. W. H. *et al.* 2003. Kinematic reworking and exhumation within the convergent Alpine Orogen. *Tectonophysics*, **365**, 77–102

RING, U., BRANDON, M. T., WILLETT, S. D. & LISTER, G. S. 1999. Exhumation processes. *In*: RING, U., BRANDON, M. T., WILLETT, S. D. & LISTER, G. S. (eds) *Exhumation Processes: Normal Faulting, Ductile Flow and Erosion.* Geological Society, London, Special Publications, **154**, 1–27.

ROWLEY, D. B. 1996. Age of initiation of collision between India and Asia: a review of the stratigraphic data. *Earth and Planetary Science Letters*, **145**, 1–13.

ROYDEN, L. H. 1993*a*. The tectonic expression of slab pull at continental convergent boundaries. *Tectonics*, **12**, 303–325.

ROYDEN, L. H. 1993*b*. Evolution of retreating subduction boundaries formed during continental collision. *Tectonics*, **12**, 629–638.

RUBATTO, D. & HERMANN, J. 2001. Exhumation as fast as subduction? *Geology*, **29**, 3–6.

SCHMID, S. M. & CASEY, M. 1986. Complete fabric analysis of some commonly observed quartz *c*-axis patterns. *In*: HOBBS, B. E. & HEARD, H. C. (eds) *Mineral and Rock Deformation Laboratory Studies: the Paterson Volume.* American Geophysical Union, Geophysical Monographs, **36**, 263–286.

SEARLE, M. P. 1999. Extensional and compressional faults in the Everest–Lhotse massif, Khumbu Himalaya, Nepal. *Journal of the Geological Society, London*, **156**, 227–40.

SEARLE, M. P. 2003. *Geological map of the Everest massif, Nepal and South Tibet, Scale 1:100 000.* Department of Earth Sciences, Oxford University.

SEARLE, M. P., SIMPSON, R. L., LAW, R. D., PARRISH, R. R. & WATERS, D. J. 2003. The structural geometry, metamorphic and magmatic evolution of the Everest massif, High Himalaya of Nepal–south Tibet. *Journal of the Geological Society, London*, **160**, 345–366.

SEEBER, L. & PÊCHER, A. 1999. Strain partitioning along the Himalayan arc and the Nanga Parbat antiform. *Geology*, **26**, 791–794.

SMITH, H. A., CHAMBERLAIN, C. P. & ZEITLER, P. K. 1994. Timing and duration of Himalayan metamorphism within the Indian Plate, Northwest Himalaya, Pakistan. *Journal of Geology*, **102**, 493–508.

STIPP, M., STÜNITZ, H., HEILBRONNER, R. & SCHMID, S. M. 2002. Dynamic recrystallization of quartz: correlation between natural and experimental conditions. *In*: DE MEER, S., DRURY, M. R., DE BRESSER, J. H. P. & PENNOCK, G. M. (eds) *Deformation Mechanisms, Rheology and Tectonics: Current Status and Future Perspectives*. Geological Society, London, Special Publications, **200**, 171–190.

TONARINI, S., VILLA, I., OBERLI, F., MEIER, M., SPENCER, D. A., POGNANTE, U. & RAMSAY, J. G. 1993. Eocene age of eclogite metamorphism in the Pakistan Himalaya: implications for India–Eurasian collision. *Terra Nova*, **5**, 13–20.

TRELOAR, P. J. 1997. Thermal controls on early-Tertiary, short-lived, rapid regional metamorphism in the NW Himalaya, Pakistan. *Tectonophysics*, **273**, 77–104.

TRELOAR, P. J. & O'BRIEN, P. 2003. What do coesite eclogites tell us about the earliest stages of India–Asia collision? *Geological Society of America, Abstracts with Programs*, **35**(6), 95.

TRELOAR, P. J. & REX, D. C. 1990*a*. Cooling, uplift and exhumation rates in the crystalline thrust stack of the North Indian Plate, west of the Nanga Parbat syntaxis. *Tectonophysics*, **180**, 323–349.

TRELOAR, P. J. & REX, D. C. 1990*b*. Post-metamorphic cooling history of the Indian Plate crystalline thrust stack, Pakistan Himalaya. *Journal of the Geological Society, London*, **147**, 735–738.

TRELOAR, P. J., BROUGHTON, R. D., WILLIAMS, M. P., COWARD, M. P. & WINDLEY, B. F. 1989*a*. Deformation, metamorphism and imbrication of the Indian Plate, south of the Main Mantle Thrust, North Pakistan. *Journal of Metamorphic Geology*, **7**, 111–125.

TRELOAR, P. J., COWARD, M. P. & WILLIAMS, M. P. 1989*b*. Metamorphism and crustal stacking in the North Indian Plate, North Pakistan. *Tectonophysics*, **165**, 167–184.

TRELOAR, P. J., COWARD, M. P., WILLIAMS, M. P. & KHAN, M. A. 1989*c*. Basement cover imbrication south of the Main Mantle Thrust, North Pakistan. *In*: MALINCONICO, L. L. & LILLIE, R. J. (eds) *Tectonics of the Western Himalaya*. Geological Society of America, Special Papers, **232**, 137–152.

TRELOAR, P. J., REX, D. C., COWARD, M. P. *et al.* 1989*d*. K/Ar and Ar/Ar geochronology of the Himalayan collision in NW Pakistan: constraints on the timing of collision, deformation, metamorphism and uplift. *Tectonics*, **8**, 891–909.

TRELOAR, P. J., COWARD, M. P., CHAMBERS, A. F., IZATT, C. N. & JACKSON, K. C. 1991. Thrust geometries, interferences and rotations in the northwest Himalaya. *In*: MCCLAY, K. R. (ed.) *Thrust Tectonics*. Chapman and Hall, London, 325–342.

TRELOAR, P. J., O'BRIEN, P. J., PARRISH, R. R. & KHAN, M. A. 2003. Exhumation of early Tertiary, coesite-bearing eclogites from the Pakistan Himalaya. *Journal of the Geological Society, London*, **160**, 367–376.

VANNAY, J.-C. & GRASEMANN, B. 2001. Himalayan inverted metamorphism and syn-convergence extension as a consequence of a general shear extrusion. *Geological Magazine*, **138**, 253–276.

VINCE, K. J. 1997. *Miocene-aged extension within the Main Mantle Thrust Zone, Pakistan Himalaya.* PhD thesis, Kingston University.

VINCE, K. J. & TRELOAR, P. J. 1996. Miocene, north-vergent extensional displacements along the Main Mantle Thrust, NW Himalaya, Pakistan. *Journal of the Geological Society, London*, **153**, 677–680.

VISSERS, R. L. M., PLATT, J. P. & VAN DER WAL, D. 1995. Late orogenic extension of the Betic cordillera and the Alboran domain. *Tectonics*, **14**, 786–303.

WHEELER, J. & BUTLER, R. W. H. 1994. Criteria for identifying structures related to true crustal extension in orogens. *Journal of Structural Geology*, **16**, 1023–1027.

WILLIAMS, M. P. 1989. The geology of the Besham area, North Pakistan: deformation and imbrication in the footwall of the Main Mantle Thrust. *Geological Bulletin, University of Peshawar*, **22**, 65–82.

WINSLOW, D. M., CHAMBERLAIN, C. P. & ZEITLER, P. K. 1995. Metamorphism and melting of the lithosphere due to rapid denudation, Pakistan Himalaya. *Journal of Geology*, **103**, 395–408.

ZEILINGER, G. 2002. *Structural and geochronological study of the lowest Kohistan complex, Indus Kohistan region in Pakistan, NW Himalaya.* PhD thesis, EH Zurich.

ZEILINGER, G., BURG, J.-P., CHAUDHRY, N., DAWOOD, H. & HUSSAIN, S. 2000. Fault systems and paleo-stress tensors in the Indus Suture Zone (NW Pakistan). *Journal of Asian Earth Sciences*, **18**, 547–559.

ZEITLER, P. K. 1985. Cooling history of the NW Himalaya. *Tectonics*, **4**, 128–151.

ZHU, B., KIDD, W. S. F., ROWLEY, D. B., CURRIE, B. S. & SHAFIQUE, N. 2005. Age of initiation of the India–Asia collision in the east–central Himalaya. *Journal of Geology*, **113**, 265–285.

Constrictional extensional tectonics in the northern Oman mountains, its role in culmination development and the exhumation of the subducted Arabian continental margin

MOHAMMED AL-WARDI & ROBERT W. H. BUTLER

Institute of Geophysics and Tectonics, The University of Leeds, Leeds LS2 9JT, UK (e-mail: butler@earth.leeds.ac.uk)

Abstract: The NE margin of the Arabian continent was overthrust by 'exotic' sheets of oceanic and continental margin units (the Semail Ophiolite allochthon) in the Late Cretaceous. Although parts of this margin (Saih Hatat Massif) were deeply buried, through subduction, to depths suitable for eclogite-facies metamorphism, other parts are unmetamorphosed (Jebel Akhdar Massif). Hence an almost continuous metamorphic gradient is preserved. This forms an ideal setting within which to relate shallow and deeper-seated tectonic processes within an orogen. Structural data are presented from the Jebal Akhdar Massif, a composite antiformal structure that contains a network of structures that post-date allochthon emplacement. These include down-to-the-NNE layer-extensional shears and steeper faults. Layer-extensional shears contain open to close folds with hinge lines parallel to regional elongation directions. Larger-scale NNE-trending folds include the regional Jebel Nakhl Antiform. The same kinematic style can be traced into the exhumed high-pressure metamorphic terrane of Saih Hatat. Coeval orthogonal layer contraction and layer-thinning and elongation describes bulk constrictional 3D strain. Although this might be indicative of regional transtension, large-scale strike-slip faults, active during the extension, as predicted by general transtensional models are not evident. Consequently, it is inferred that constriction was the result of laterally varying crustal extension whereby top-to-the-NNE extension was locally combined with left-lateral shearing. Exhumation of the metamorphic series occurred under a carapace of extending allochthons, defining an elongate 'pip' of material returning to shallow crustal levels. There is, however, an imbalance between net extension and possible contraction within the Arabian continent that requires deformation within a volume of net-divergent tectonics. Thus crustal extension continued after the end of convergent tectonics in the region.

Coward (1982) was one of the first to explore the concept of extensional tectonics operating as part of a continuing compressional orogen. He suggested that major, hinterland-directed extensional faults could link kinematically onto foreland-vergent thrusts to define a wedge of extruding continental crust. His model of 'hedgehog tectonics' (Coward *et al.* 1987), where the fault-bounded wedge is plastically deformed and extended, pre-empted the modern channel-flow models for Himalayan tectonics (e.g. Jamieson *et al.* 2002). Extension within orogenic belts is now widely invoked, especially as a mechanism by which once deeply buried metamorphic rocks are returned to the Earth's surface. Many mountain belts contain high-strain zones separating metamorphic rocks, which preserve large peak metamorphic pressures, from rocks above that show no evidence of having reached these conditions. Such an apparent loss of 'barometric section' is generally interpreted as resulting from low-angle extensional shear (e.g. Jolivet *et al.* 1998). There are various competing kinematic models for the exhumation of once deeply buried tracts of continental crust within mountain belts. Wheeler *et al.* (2001) offered two options, where once subducted continental crust is exhumed either as a 'sliver' of crust open to the synorogenic surface (Fig. 1a), or as an entirely fault-bounded 'pip' (Fig. 1b). In common with many models of synorogenic exhumation of high-pressure metamorphic rocks, both of these options involve faults and shear zones that have extensional kinematics on the upper or hinterland side and contractional kinematics on the lower or foreland side of the exhuming rocks. These paired kinematic systems can be embedded within generally net-convergent systems, such as the Western Alps (Wheeler *et al.* 2001) or in areas where there is no net convergence on the plate scale (e.g. the Neogene Tyrrhenian–Apennine system, e.g. Lavecchia 1988). The driving force for these systems is the buoyancy of subducted continental crust, relative to the mantle. There

From: Ries, A. C., Butler, R. W. H. & Graham, R. H. (eds) 2007. *Deformation of the Continental Crust: The Legacy of Mike Coward*. Geological Society, London, Special Publications, **272**, 187–202.
0305-8719/07/$15

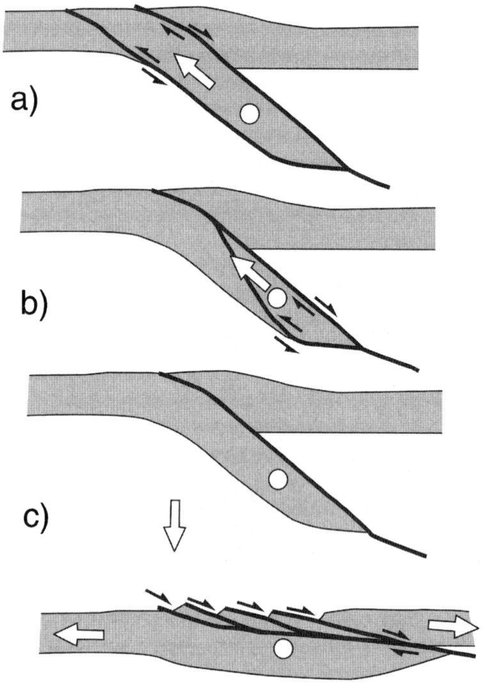

Fig. 1. Models for the exhumation of deeply buried crust (**a**) and (**b**) modified from Wheeler *et al.* (2002): (**a**) exhumation as a 'sliver' (equivalent to channel flow of Jamieson *et al.* 2002); (**b**) exhumation as a 'pip'; (**c**) exhumation by regionally divergent tectonics (in two parts). In all these models a reference point is shown within the subducted crust (circle) that represents eclogitic material subsequently exhumed to shallow crustal levels.

are other options. Where the magnitude of extensional tectonics is not matched by displacements on the underside of exhuming, once deeply buried crust (Fig. 1c), the far-field plate kinematics must have been divergent (e.g. Krabbendam & Dewey 1998). The exhumation is accomplished isostatically so the density of subducted crust is important, but it is driven by divergent tectonics.

Arguably the most dramatic example of exhumation related to truly divergent plate tectonics comes from the Caledonian chain in Norway (see review by Milnes *et al.* 1997). The ultrahigh-pressure Western Gneisses lie in the footwall to major low-angle normal faults, some of which famously carry spectacular successions of synrift sediments of Devonian age (e.g. Hornelen Basin). Devonian rifting is generally inferred to have been oblique, governed in part by major basement lineaments. Krabbendam & Dewey (1998) argued that this deformation is represented by large-scale transtensional kinematics. Transtensional models are interesting, not least because they require concurrent orthogonal layer-parallel extension and contraction (e.g. Dewey *et al.* 1998). In general, kinematic axes might be expected to be oblique to geological boundaries (e.g. as pointed out by Woodcock 1986), so transtension should be a general expectation for exhuming metamorphic terranes.

A key for testing the various tectonic models for the exhumation of specific metamorphic terranes is to trace structures from deep to shallow crustal levels and to be able to quantify the magnitude and timing of other displacements within an orogen. In many systems the exhumation of metamorphic rocks occurs well before the end of the tectonic life of a mountain belt (e.g. the Alps; Freeman *et al.* 1998). These complexities, although being an expectation of many exhumation models (e.g. Wheeler *et al.* 2001), seriously restrict further studies. Here new data are presented together with reinterpretations of the northern Oman mountains, a Late Cretaceous orogenic belt. This offers an ideal site to examine the relationship between structures at different levels within an orogen because the Arabian continental crust has not been substantially deformed on a regional scale as the orogeny progressed. The northern margin of the Arabian continent is exposed through a series of windows (Fig. 2) formed by late-stage culminations. The aim here is to present new structural data from the weakly buried parts of the orogen and link them to kinematic data and structural models for the well-studied metamorphic parts of the system. The results raise issues of the relationship between folding on a variety of scales and localized shears, especially the significance of tectonic culminations. These data show how synorogenic stratal extension and folding are kinematically related through syn- to post-orogenic crustal extension.

Geological setting

Deformation of the NE margin of the Arabian continental crust followed the Late Cretaceous obduction of the Semail Ophiolite and other far-travelled sheets of continental margin and deep-water sediments (the Hawasina Nappes and 'Oman Exotics'). South- to SW-directed emplacement of the Semail Ophiolite and the associated high-temperature metamorphic sole are dated at 93–94 Ma (Hacker *et al.* 1996). Final emplacement of the amalgamated allochthon is dated at 70–80 Ma using adjacent and overridden foredeep deposits of the Aruma Group (Robertson 1987). Subsequently, the Arabian

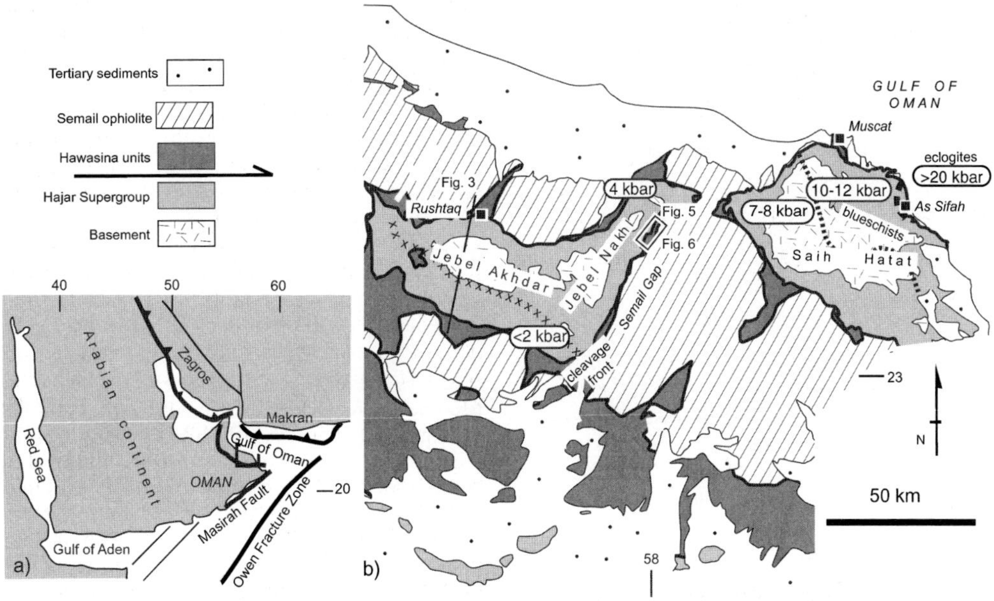

Fig. 2. (**a**) Regional setting of the northern Oman mountains in the context of Arabia. (**b**) Simplified geotectonic map of the Jebel Akhdar, Jebel Nakhl and Saih Hatat regions.

continent, below the allochthons, has been bulged up to form a series of culminations that expose the platform carbonates of the Permian–Cretaceous Hajar Supergroup together with its pre-Permian basement of the Arabian continent. The continental crust beneath the culminations is 50% thicker than under the adjacent Arabian foreland (Al-Lazki *et al.* 2002), consistent with the notion of significant contractional structures at depth. The entire complex of far-travelled nappes and deformed Arabian crust was juxtaposed and exhumed by Maastrichtian times (*c.* 67–68 Ma), as sediments of this age overlie all units and seal all the main tectonic contacts (e.g. Coleman 1981). However, the northern part of the mountains contains faults and folds that deform Maastrichtian and Palaeogene strata, indicating that deformation continued into the Tertiary (Mann *et al.* 1990), at least in part as a result of rifting and the formation of the Gulf of Oman Basin. The region is experiencing active uplift (e.g. Kusky *et al.* 2005).

Displacements on the allochthonous Semail Ophiolite and Hawasina Nappes are demonstrably of the order of several hundred kilometres (e.g. Glennie *et al.* 1974). In this regard the orogen is similar to many other parts of the Tethyan system. However, it is special because the underlying Arabian continent has, on a large scale, been only weakly deformed. Culminations of Arabian continental crust crop out as massifs (Saih Hatat in the east, Jebel Akhdar in the centre; Fig. 2b). Within these culminations the metamorphic grade gradually increases from SW to NE. The southern flank of Jebel Akhdar is essentially unmetamorphosed, whereas northeastward along the trend of Jebel Nakhl, the peak metamorphic conditions within the same stratigraphic units increase to about 200 °C and pressures of *c.* 4 kbar (Rabu *et al.* 1986).

Metamorphic rocks recording the highest burial pressures are found on the coastal fringe of the Saih Hatat Massif, near the village of As Sifah (El-Shazly *et al.* 1990; Fig. 2b). These eclogites are likely to have experienced peak pressure conditions of *c.* 20 kbar, although some workers have suggested burial to 25 kbar (Searle *et al.* 1994). The structural geology of these high-pressure rocks and their relationship to other parts of the Saih Hatat Massif have been studied recently by two groups (Miller *et al.* 2002; Searle *et al.* 2004). Nevertheless, the relationship between the As Sifah eclogites and lower-pressure rocks remains controversial, with tectonic contacts variously interpreted as thrusts or normal faults. These issues are addressed below. Both groups show the importance of a regional, NNE-trending mineral lineation and parallel sheath folds together with important detachment shears. The eclogites lie in a structural window overlain by rocks that did not experience such extreme pressures, the two domains being separated by a folded detachment surface. Moving towards the western and southern flanks of the Saih Hatat Massif, the metamorphic grade decreases markedly, through glaucophane–carpholite-bearing units (10–12 kbar) to the Fe–Mg carpholite isograd (7–8 kbar; see Jolivet *et al.* 1998, for discussion). The deformation state of these rocks is markedly lower than within the higher-pressure parts of the massif. Indeed Jolivet *et al.* (1998) argued for a largely undeformed, but exhumed, subduction channel of continental rocks from weakly buried to blueschist-facies conditions.

The timing of peak high-pressure metamorphism within the eclogites of Saih Hatat is controversial. Rb–Sr (El-Shazly *et al.* 2001) and $^{40}Ar/^{39}Ar$ cooling ages (Miller *et al.* 1999) are 82–78 Ma. These ages are broadly consistent with the stratigraphic ages for the timing of orogenesis in the northern Oman mountains as discussed above. However, Gray *et al.* (2004) reported Sm–Nd ages on high-pressure garnets from As Sifah of *c.* 110 Ma, which they interpreted as recording the timing of subduction of this tract of continental crust. It is difficult to relate these old ages to the younger ages, both of the foredeep (Aruma Group) sediments on the Arabian continent and of the oceanic lithosphere that is generally assumed to have formed the hanging wall to this subduction zone (e.g. Searle & Cox 1999, amongst many others). This oceanic lithosphere, preserved as the Semail Ophiolite, gives ages for the formation of this crust that are much younger (*c.* 80 Ma, El-Shazly *et al.* 2001). Consequently, the nature of the subduction zone that generated the high-pressure metamorphism in Saih Hatat is a matter of continuing debate (see Gray & Gregory 2004).

The structural state and history of the higher-grade parts of the Saih Hatat Massif have been variously explained in terms of simple NNE-directed extension of previously subducted crust (Jolivet *et al.* 1998), NNE extension and thrusting above a SSW-dipping intracontinental subduction zone (Miller *et al.* 2002) and thin-skinned back-thrusting and extension associated with a single, evolving NNE-dipping subduction zone (Searle *et al.* 2004). These kinematic controversies mirror the arguments surrounding the tectonic interpretation of 'retrocharriage' ('back-thrusting') structures in parts of the Western Alps (see Butler & Freeman 1996, and references therein). Further discussion of these issues is beyond the scope of this paper. Our data are concerned with rocks outside the Saih Hatat Massif.

The Saih Hatat Massif is separated from the adjacent outcrops of Arabian continental rocks (represented by the Jebel Nakhl range; Rabu *et al.* 1986) by a tectonic depression about 10 km across (Fig. 2b). Most workers believe the two culminations join at depth. Stratigraphically there is a transition from platform to slope facies in the Hajar Supergroup rocks that starts in the NE portion of Jebel Nakhl and continues into Saih Hatat (Pratt & Smewing 1990). If the assumption of structural continuity between the culminations is true, there is a simple transition both in the original geology of the continental margin and in the superimposed metamorphic state. However, across Saih Hatat the rocks become increasingly deformed so that simple stratigraphic linkages are difficult to establish. Nevertheless, the northern Oman mountains contain an excellent, reasonably continuous and little-disrupted transition down into a palaeo-subduction zone. Therefore it may be possible to relate directly the processes that operated at different levels within the underthrust continental slab without first restoring the large-scale crustal shortening structures that so commonly characterize Tethyan orogens. The studies presented here focus on the structural evolution of the Jebel Nakhl part of the Jebel Akhdar culmination (Fig. 2b).

Structural kinematics

The internal structure of the Jebel Akhdar culmination and its NE continuation (Jebel Nakhl) is remarkable for its coherence. In marked contrast to the neighbouring Saih Hatat culmination, there are no large-scale repetitions of stratigraphy. Rather the Hajar Supergroup simply youngs away from its basal unconformity with the pre-Permian basement, defining a composite upright, upward-facing antiform with a wavelength of tens of kilometres. The structural geology across the Jebel Akhdar transect is described here before considering the continuation of this massif along Jebel Nakhl. These data are part of a much larger suite that will form the subject of a companion paper in due course.

Breton *et al.* (2004) have recently reinterpreted structures, especially along the northern flank of Jebel Akhdar, in terms of NE-directed extension. That study forms the starting point for the following discussion.

Jebel Akhdar culmination

All parts of the Jebel Akhdar Massif contain extensional faults. The structures on a north–south transect, through the central part of the massif, in general comprise faults that down-throw away from the massif. Hanna (1990) interpreted these structures in terms of 'culmination collapse', essentially a process of gravity sliding from the positive topography represented by the major antiform.

On the southern flank of Jebel Akhdar, normal faults can be mapped down-section for up to 2500 m, using exposures in deep gorge sections. There is no evidence of systematic reduction in the dip of faults down-section. Nor is there any evidence for young thrust faults at the toe of the regional flank of the Jebel Akhdar Massif. Consequently, there is little to support the model of Hanna (1990) that the normal faults are driven by the local gravity potential of the massif. Collectively, the faults accommodate stratal extension on a broadly north–south axis. At some localities on the southern flank of the massif the faults deflect into bedding-parallel segments, relaying displacement along shaly horizons within the otherwise carbonate-dominated Cretaceous sediments. These shale horizons commonly contain weak pressure-solution cleavage that verges towards the north. Local bed-slip also shows this sense of shear (as shown in Fig. 3).

The northern flank of Jebel Akhdar also contains steep normal faults. The majority of these down-throw to the north and, as for the southern flank, penetrate to depth. However, the northern flank shows extensive evidence for low-angle, northward-directed extension (see also Breton *et al.* 2004). This is chiefly expressed in the interbedded shales and limestones of Cretaceous age and is manifest by linked systems of shears and detachments. In some wadi sections there is significant omission of stratigraphic units, as illustrated by the two examples shown in Figue 4.

Figure 4a shows large-scale low-angle extension (see Breton *et al.* 2004) developed through limestones of the Kahma Formation (part of the Cretaceous sequence of interbedded limestones and shales). These act as intraformational detachment faults. The slices of limestone show extensional ramp geometries, cutting off against both the footwalls and hanging walls of the detachment faults. The detachments show top-to-the-NNE shear senses. This type of geometry is also found on a bed-scale, especially within the Cretaceous limestones. A further example is shown in Figure 4b. Normal faults, developed at a high angle to bedding, branch onto bed-parallel detachments. Individual beds also show layer-parallel extension, manifest by conjugate vein arrays.

The crest of the Jebel Akhdar Massif has been deeply eroded so that the Hajar Supergroup has been lost. Consequently, it is not possible to link the structures described here for the two flanks of the antiform. Nevertheless, the top-to-the-NNE sense of shear on bedding-subparallel detachments is consistent across the massif. These structures collectively accommodate stratal extension on this SSW–NNE axis. The correlation of structures across the regional fold requires that low-angle stratal extension predates at least part of the antiform's amplification. The relative timing of the steeper faults is more equivocal. In some cases they merge into the detachments, suggesting synchronous steep and low-angle faulting. In the majority of cases the faults cross-cut all other structures, suggesting that they formed late in the local structural history.

Eastern flank of Jebel Nakhl: Wadi Dhabiah

Critical locations for choosing between models of extension that are gravity-sliding (Hanna 1990) or regional in character lie on fold limbs that are not inclined on the NNE extension

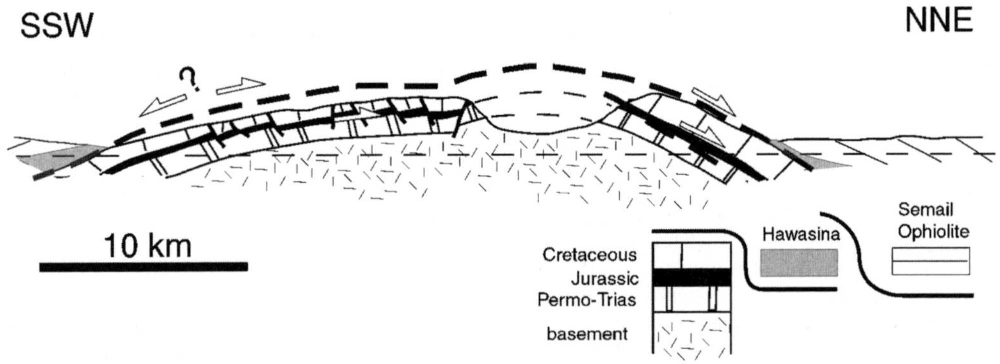

Fig. 3. Simplified structural section across Jebel Akhdar (see Fig. 2b for location and text for discussion).

a)

b)

Fig. 4. Field photograph of layer-extension structures on the northern flank of Jebel Akhdar. (**a**) Closely spaced detachment faults isolating slices of Kahma Formation limestones (Cretaceous), Wadi Sahtan (*c*. 10 km SSW of Rushtaq; Fig. 2b). (**b**) Example of bed-scale extension, within Cretaceous limestones in Wadi Beni Ghafer (*c*. 20 km east of Rushtaq; Fig. 2b). (See text for discussion.)

axis identified for central Jebel Akhdar. Data are presented here from a single transect, in Wadi Dhabiah (Fig. 5). This site lies on the east-dipping limb of the Nakhl culmination, where the large-scale structure youngs and dips eastwards, away from the Jebel Nakhl culmination. Thus if extensional structures are related to shallow-level 'culmination collapse', they should be directed towards the east.

The structural profile (Fig. 5) illustrates that the stratigraphy is disrupted by a series of east-dipping detachment faults that are subparallel to bedding. These appear to be localized along finer-grained units within the Cretaceous succession. In both the hanging walls and footwalls, beds cut out against these features with stratigraphic omission, indicating that they have accommodated stratal extension. In general, stretching lineations (Fig. 5a) on these features, defined by elongate carbonate aggregrates, together with calcite mineral lineations, plunge gently into the NE quadrant. Consequently, the detachments are characterized by gently pitching lineations (Fig. 5d), indicative of near strike-slip motion in their current orientations. Where evident, asymmetric shear criteria, chiefly extension crenulations, imply a top-to-the-NE shear sense. In a strike-slip context this is left-lateral. The detachments contain centimetre-scale buckles of foliation with generally close interlimb angles and axial surfaces subperpendicular to detachment surfaces. The hinges to these folds are variably oriented (Fig. 5b) but have a distinct cluster plunging to the SSE.

Together with detachment surfaces there are also arrays of faults, many of which are bed-confined. In these cases the faults merge and branch onto the detachment surfaces (Fig. 5). On the wadi slopes these faults show apparent downthrow, down the regional dip surface. They

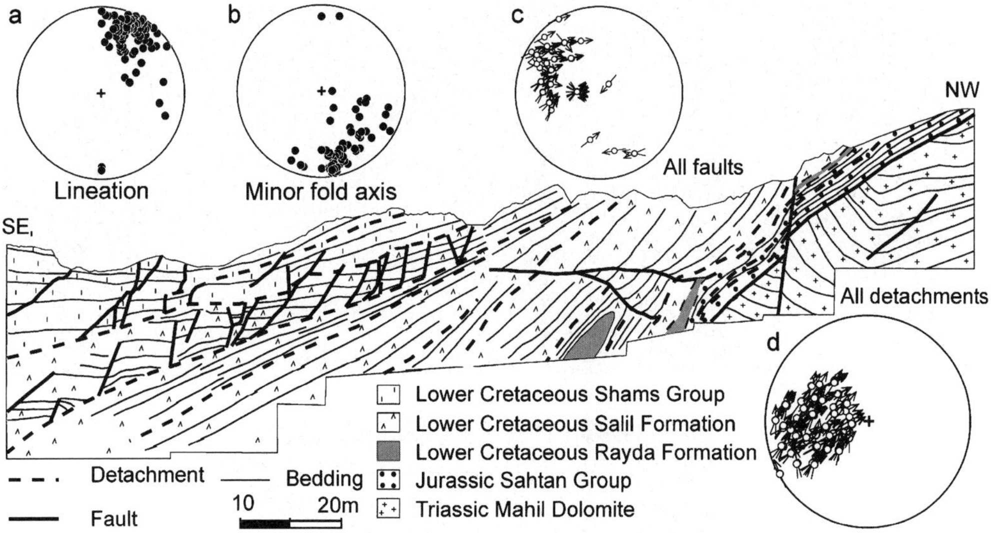

Fig. 5. Simplified structural transect as exposed on the SW wall of Wadi Dhabiah (location shown in Fig. 2b), with lower hemisphere stereoplots of structural data. (**a**) Penetrative lineations; (**b**) fold axes; (**c**) poles to faults with corresponding striations (as pitch); (**d**) poles to detachments with corresponding striation pitches.

extend stratigraphy and have clear normal-sense throws. However, when studied in three dimensions, the fault planes dip obliquely to the main bedding orientation and have obliquely pitching striations. In general, these faults appear to accommodate extension on a NE–SW axis, and are broadly compatible kinematically with the detachment surfaces onto which they branch.

The most dramatic structure to omit stratigraphy within this transect lies at the top of the Triassic Mahil Formation (Fig. 5). These rocks are dolomites and consequently display no penetrative deformation, in contrast to the Cretaceous limestones above. This partitioning of deformation is a regional feature of the entire Jebel Akhdar–Jebel Nakhl Massif. However, in Wadi Dhabiah the rocks above the Triassic dolomites are strongly disrupted. There is substantial stratigraphic omission, with the Jurassic Sahtan Group (generally 150–400 m thick), reduced to a few metres. The lower part of the Cretaceous (Salil Formation) is preserved only in a few detached fold hinges and shear-bounded pods.

The deformation style in Wadi Dhabiah (Fig. 5) is clearly not well explained by models of 'culmination collapse' (e.g. Hanna 1990). Although there is significant stratigraphic omission and normal-sense faulting, the kinematics is not directed down-dip. If the current easterly dip is removed the sense of shear is top-to-the-NNE layer extension.

Fault patterns on the eastern margin of Jebel Nakhl

Fault patterns on the eastern margin of Jebel Nakhl can be studied on the flat-irons of dipping strata between the main wadis. The faulting pattern is illustrated from a subarea shown in Figure 6 (location shown in Fig. 2b). In the study area the outcrops mainly belong to the upper part of the Hajar Supergroup (Cretaceous limestones) together with their cover of early foredeep clastic deposits (Aruma Group). Most of the faults trend ENE–WSW and NW–SE and have striations that pitch towards the massif. Taken collectively, the kinematics of these faults is complex (Fig. 6a). However, the major faults, with demonstrably large throws, have a more systematic form (Fig. 6b). These show oblique kinematics with striations chiefly pitching moderately towards the massif. When untilted by the local flank dip of the culmination, these structures appear as normal faults accommodating NE–SW extension. Thus these may be related to the stratal extension structures seen in the wadis (Fig. 5). Additionally, there are SSW-and NW-trending steep faults that contain striations that pitch away from the massif. These show mutually cross-cutting relationships and are readily explained as conjugate faults with the fault intersection plunging into the massif. The striations on these faults are variable but are generally

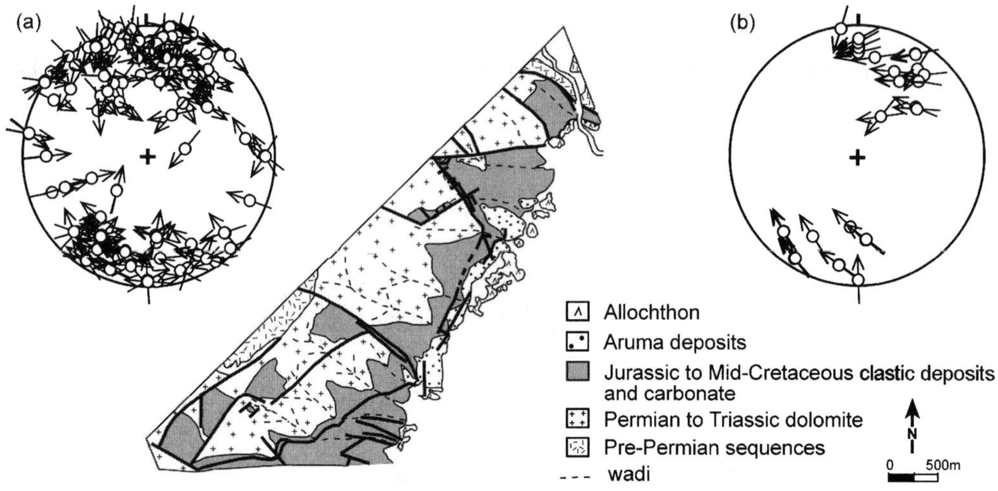

Fig. 6. Simplified geological map of the faults on the eastern flank of Jebel Nakhl (location shown in Fig. 2b). Lower hemisphere stereoplots of (**a**) poles to faults with corresponding striations (as pitch), and (**b**) the suite of faults that trend WNW–ESE with their striations. These into-the-massif pitching striations on faults are interpreted as being on tilted normal faults (Fig. 7).

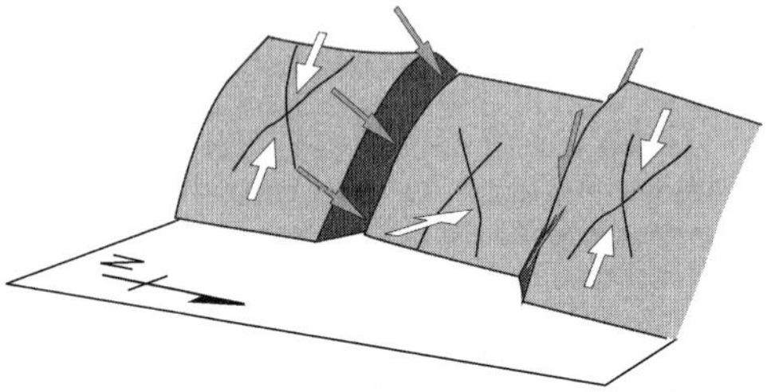

Fig. 7. Schematic block diagram illustrating the kinematics of faults on the eastern flank of Jebel Nakhl.

gently pitching. The latter are interpreted as arrays of conjugate strike-slip faults that formed at various stages of folding and the related tilting of the eastern flank of Jebel Nakhl (Fig. 7). These imply a minimum compressive stress (finite extension direction) towards the NE.

In summary, the faults on the eastern margin of Jebel Nakhl are interpreted as accommodating a combination of NNE–SSW-directed extension and NW–SE compression, represented by quasi-conjugate strike-slip faulting. Some of these fault patterns show such kinematics in the modern reference frame. Others reveal this style only when the ESE dip on the area is removed. The implication is that folding of Jebel Nakhl and faulting on its flank happened at the same time, during the same tectonic episode.

Deformation around the massif

Although data have been presented from only one transect on the eastern flank of Jebel Nakhl, our key observations are repeated elsewhere in the massif. Data from these other sites are compiled regionally in Figure 8. These data are grouped into the three main dip domains for the massif. For the eastern and NW flanks of Jebel Nakhl the dip directions are strongly oblique to the inferred regional direction of maximum extension. For the northern flank of Jebel Akhdar the dip direction broadly coincides with the stretching axis. The consistency of this axis is shown by the data. Most of the ductile extensional structures come from the lower part of the Cretaceous succession. Along with well-developed stretching lineations, this stratigraphic level also localizes bed-subparallel cleavage and fabric boudinage. Shear criteria, where present, give top-to-the-NE senses and cleavage, where asymmetric to bedding, extends layering (shear band sense) or verges NE. Thus the chief tectonic style of the Hajar Supergroup rocks, preserved beneath the allochthon of the Semail and Hawasina Nappes, is low-angle stratal extension, directed top-to-the-NE. There is no evidence of pre-extensional structures of regional extent, or of significant foreland-directed dips on the strata. Therefore the stratal extension is inferred to represent true horizontal stretching.

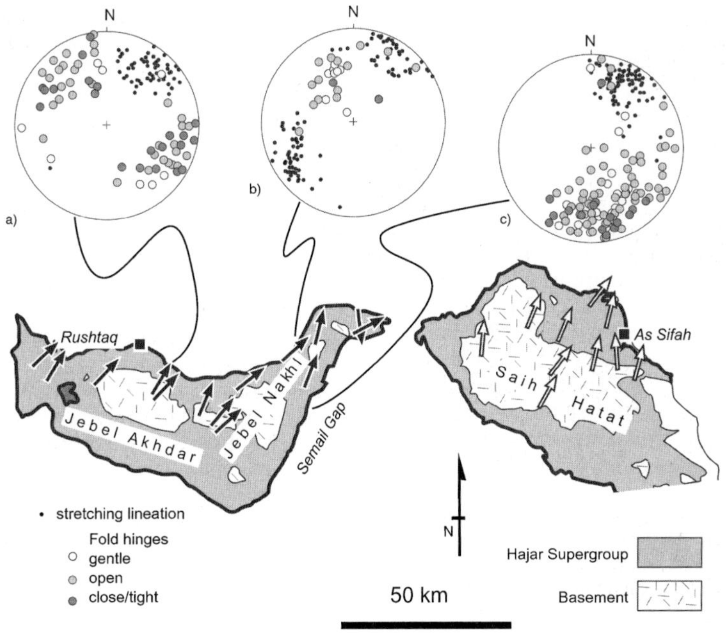

Fig. 8. Structural data (lower hemisphere stereoplots) from the Hajar Supergroup, located generally onto a map of the culmination, showing the relationships between fold hinge orientation and stretching lineation. Stretching lineation trends are summarized on the map (filled arrows, this study; open arrows summarized from Miller *et al.* 2002). (**a**) Data from the northern flank of Jebel Akhdar ($n=61$ for stretching lineation, $n=73$ for folds); (**b**) NW flank of Jebel Nakhl ($n=104$ for stretching lineation, $n=26$ for fold hinges); (**c**) the SE flank of Jebel Nakhl ($n=93$ for stretching lineation, $n=126$ for fold hinges).

Folding is widely associated with the shear fabrics described above. In Wadi Dhabiah (Fig. 5) the axes of these folds have a range of orientation from parallel to perpendicular to the gently NNE-plunging stretching lineation. There are similar ranges of fold orientation along other parts of both flanks of Jebel Nakhl (Fig. 8). On the northern flank of Jebel Akhdar (Fig. 8), the population of fold axes shows a greater concentration of orientations at a high angle to the stretching lineation.

Synkinematically rotated minor folds?

Where fold axes lie subparallel to stretching lineation, it is commonly assumed that they have been rotated into this orientation by very high simple shear strains (following the sheath fold model of Cobbold & Quinquis (1980)). For this to occur, those folds with axes that lie parallel to the lineation have formed earlier and have been more greatly distorted than those with axes at a high angle to the lineation. Breton *et al.* (2004) used this explanation for folds on the northern flank of Jebel Akhdar. To test this model fold interlimb angles are used as a proxy for distortion. Fold axes are grouped on this basis. For the sheath fold model to be applicable here, NNE-plunging fold axes should be associated with tight inter-limb angles whereas those trending WNW–ESE should be gentle. The data for the three dip domains around the culmination (Fig. 8) do not show this pattern. There is no significant relationship between interlimb angle and fold axis orientation. Consequently, we deduce that folding is not a simple result of plane strain, NE-directed simple shear. The folds are better explained as resulting from a mixture of layer-subparallel, NNE shear and nearly orthogonal layer-parallel shortening. Partitioning of these two end-member components can explain the variation in fold geometry and orientation (e.g. Dewey *et al.* 1998).

Kinematic comparisons with Saih Hatat

Deformation in Saih Hatat becomes increasingly more penetrative and ductile towards the eastern side of the culmination. This change tracks the increased peak metamorphic temperatures and pressures (Fig. 2b). Extensive kinematic studies (Jolivet *et al.* 1998; Searle *et al.* 2004; and especially Miller *et al.* 2002) all illustrate the ubiquitous NNE–SSW-trending stretching lineation (Fig. 8) and top-to-the-NE shear sense.

The Saih Hatat culmination contains widespread small- and large-scale folds with axes plunging subparallel to the stretching lineation. Again, this pattern coincides with the high-temperature parts (NE part of Jebel Nakhl) of the Jebel Akhdar culmination. Many of these folds are tight and have been explained by high-magnitude simple shear models (Miller *et al.* 2002; Searle *et al.* 2004). However, they may also be the product of non-plane strain, coeval NW–SE layer-parallel shortening.

It is striking that the kinematics of deformation within the Saih Hatat Massif is very similar to that in the neighbouring Jebel Nakhl Massif. Both show top-to-the-NNE shear, defined by strong stretching lineations. Both areas have many folds that are aligned subparallel to the stretching lineation. Although the deformation increases both in ductility and outcrop-scale complexity in tandem with the metamorphic grade, the implication is that both regions experienced the same broad style of tectonics.

Folding and the massifs

Before developing explanations for the preferential development of NNE-trending folds and NNE-trending extension, the largest scale of folding represented by the culminations themselves is discussed (Fig. 2b). These are commonly interpreted as the products of late-stage crustal shortening, presumably on SSW-directed thrusts (e.g. Hanna 1990). The variable trends of fold limbs, especially the angular changes in map pattern to accommodate Jebel Nakhl, have been used to infer the presence of complex crustal-scale thrust ramps. Crustal thickening beneath Jebel Akhdar, apart from being indicated by the >3000 m of relief, has been detected by wide-angle seismic experiments (Al-Lazki *et al.* 2002), which show thickened continental crust of up to 45 km thick beneath Jebel Akhdar. However, there are no outcrops of large-scale thrusts around the massifs, requiring these hypothetical crustal thrusts to branch up onto the base of the main allochthonous units (Hawasina and Semail nappe complex).

The structural data presented here from the flanks of Jebel Nakhl do not support the simple thrust-bend fold model outlined above (schematically illustrated in Fig. 7). The eastern limb of this anticline displays evidence for true SE–NW compression, orthogonal to the regional extension direction. In this regard it is comparable with the small-scale folds found within the massif.

The base of the Semail allochthon as an extensional detachment?

The allochthons that rim and structurally overlie the massifs of Arabian continental crust consist of the Semail Ophiolite, its metamorphic sole, and thrust sheets of oceanic and continental margin rocks, grouped here as the Hawasina units. The stacking of these sheets onto the Arabian continent has been explained in terms of simple thrust tectonic models (e.g. Searle & Cox 1999). Displacement on the base of the thrust sheet, comprising the Semail Ophiolite plus its metamorphic sole, are shown transferring downwards onto the sedimentary cover of the Hawasina units. These are in turn accreted onto the allochthon, which is then emplaced as a composite thrust sheet up onto the foredeep sediments of the Arabian continent (the Aruma Group of Robertson 1987). The frontal part of the composite allochthon comprises Hawasina rocks. In this sector of the orogen the Semail Ophiolite does not abut the foreland (Fig. 9). Consequently, a simple thrust interpretation predicts that everywhere throughout the northern Oman mountains, Hawasina units should separate rocks of the Semail Ophiolite from the rocks of the Arabian continent. The immediate footwall to the allochthon should be Aruma Group foredeep sediments. *P–T* conditions for the metamorphic sole to the Semail Ophiolite were estimated by Searle & Cox (1999) to lie between 5 and 10 kbar with temperatures of 700–900 °C. For simple thrusting models to be valid, this requires the Ophiolite Nappe sole to contain significant thicknesses (>10 km) of suboceanic mantle slices hindward of the metamorphic sole; yet, commonly, rocks of the oceanic crust form the immediate hanging wall to this sole thrust.

Figure 9 documents sites where the tectonic units are inferred here to have been removed from the allochthon zone. Although mantle rocks are found throughout the Semail Nappe, they are generally just a few kilometres thick. Furthermore, in places upper parts of the ophiolite stratigraphy lie directly against the Hawasina units. Elsewhere, ophiolite units lie on Arabian continental rocks, including directly on pre-Aruma sediments. In short, nowhere in our study area does the base of the allochthon show the geometric relationships predicted by Searle & Cox (1999). Complex thrust sequences and reimbrication do not satisfactorily explain the

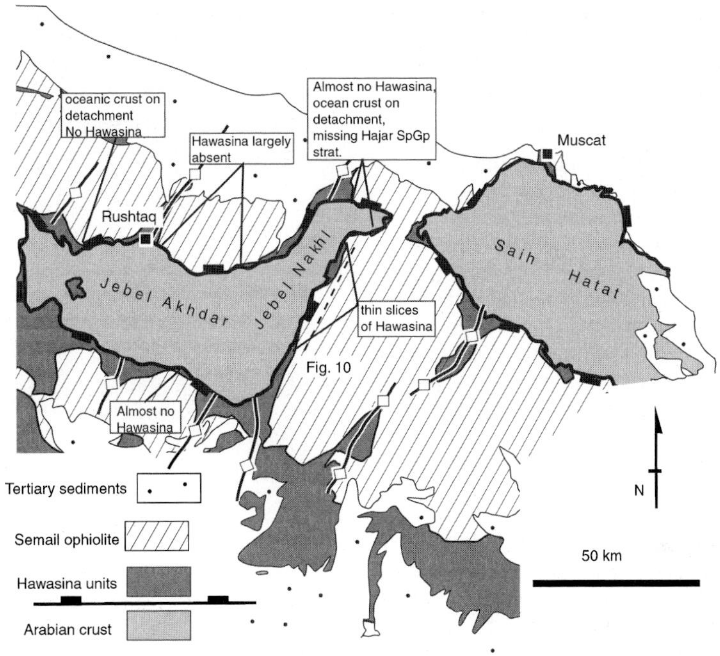

Fig. 9. Summary of structural relationships at the base of the tectonic allochthon around the northern Oman mountains. The line of the section shown in Figure 10 is indicated.

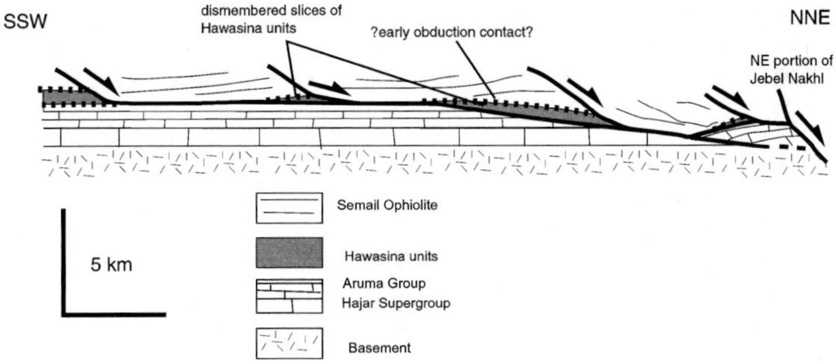

Fig. 10. Schematic section showing the structural relationships along the base of the allochthon in the vicinity of the Semail Gap. Approximate line of section is shown in Figure 9.

ubiquitous omission of units. This omission is exemplified by a transect exposed down the eastern margin of Jebel Nakhl, along the Semail Gap (Fig. 10). Here the Hawasina nappes are reduced to lenses, bounded by late shears and faults. This geometry is effectively explained by extensional faulting, dismembering the original thrust stack and reducing the thicknesses of once-continuous units to thin pods. The present tectonic contacts are provisionally interpreted as forming an array of extensional shears associated with those within the underlying Hajar Supergroup (Fig. 10).

A series of large-scale antiforms, within which the thickness of Hawasina units is preferentially preserved, are found in the allochthon around the Jebel Akhdar and Saih Hatat massifs. These folds do not continue down into the structurally underlying Arabian continental rocks, indicating that they are either detached upon, or have been truncated by, the base of the allochthons. The folds trend NNE–SSW, subparallel to the main

Nakhl fold (Fig. 9). Consequently, the main allochthon in the northern Oman mountains shows evidence for extension (of the tectonic stratigraphy) and for orthogonal compression.

Models for synchronous folding and extension: why constrictional strain?

The windows of deformed Arabian continental crust in the northern Oman mountains illustrate two apparently contradictory structural styles: NE-directed extension and vertical thinning together with NW–SE contraction. This type of deformation is clearly non-plane strain and is weakly constrictional. Constant volume constriction ($k > 1$) can readily be explained by regional transtensional strain (e.g. Dewey *et al.* 1998: Fig. 11a). Transpression, in contrast, generates oblate strains. As Dewey *et al.* (1998) pointed out, transtension is the likely outcome when maximum crustal extension directions are oriented oblique to the margins of the deforming zones. For arcuate orogens, such as the northern Oman mountain belt (Fig. 2a), some degree of kinematic obliquity is unavoidable.

Large-scale exhumation of high-pressure metamorphic rocks and concomitant crustal thinning has been explained using transtension elsewhere. A similar deformation pattern was described for the exhumation-related deformation of the ultra-high pressure eclogites of Norway's Western Gneiss Region by Krabbendam & Dewey (1997). These gneisses show strong subhorizontal elongation with synkinematic loss of barometric section (equivalent to the structural and metamorphic history described for Saih Hatat, both by Miller *et al.* (2002) and Searle *et al.* (2004)). The Western Gneisses also show constrictional finite strains and lineation-parallel folds of regional extent (Krabbendam & Dewey 1998). This pattern is similar to that found in the Jebel Nakhl area. In short, transtension, with maximum finite elongation directed on a NNE–SSW axis, provides a satisfactory explanation for the structural style in the northern Oman mountains.

An immediate question arises as to why stretching of the northern Oman orogen was oblique, as required for transtension. In the Western Gneisses of Norway, Krabbendam & Dewey (1998) argued that the kinematics of crustal extension was strongly influenced by basement-penetrating strike-slip faults. Perhaps pre-existing structures in the Arabian crust controlled extension of the northern Oman mountains. In this way, oblique extension is partitioning into a distributed transtension, together with localized strike slip. The obliquity

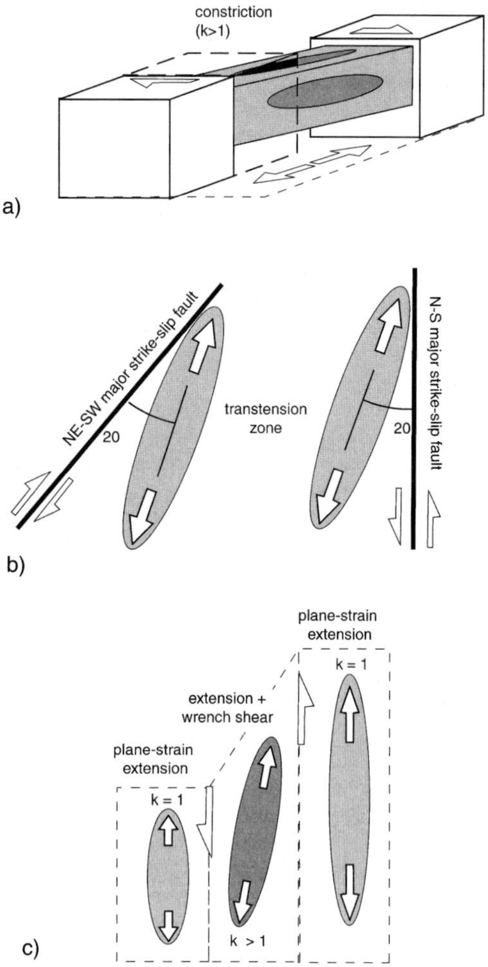

Fig. 11. Models for contraction: (**a**) the transtension model (see Dewey *et al.* 1998); (**b**) application to the geographical reference frame of the northern Oman mountains; (**c**) the differential extension model, based on Coward & Potts (1983). The last model is the one favoured here. Illustrated here in plan view, the change in map area is accommodated in three dimensions by vertical thinning.

between the direction of maximum elongation and the orientation of synchronous strike-slip faults is generally about 20° (Dewey *et al.* 1998). Consequently, for the current study in northern Oman, where finite elongation is oriented N020E, strike-slip faults are predicted to trend north–south or NE–SW (Fig. 11b). However, there are no throughgoing structures of this sense and orientation that were active after the emplacement of the main allochthons. Consequently, for strike-slip to have played a role the main faults must lie outside the present study area. Such large-scale partitioning is, however, not uncommon (see Dewey *et al.* 1998, and references therein).

During the Late Cretaceous the eastern continental margin of Arabia experienced large-scale left-lateral faulting associated with the early drift of India from its position within Gondwana (e.g. Dercourt *et al.* 1993). This deformation is recorded in Oman by the Masirah Fault (e.g. Moseley 1990; Shackleton & Ries 1990; Fig. 2a). This structure trends NE–SW and so is a possible candidate for the hypothetical strike-slip fault predicted by the transtension model. However, faults with this trend should act with a right-lateral sense to generate NNE–SSW finite elongation in adjacent belts of transtension (Fig. 11b). This is in conflict with the regional sense of shear predicted for the Arabian continental margin, although there are no published kinematic studies of the Masirah fault zone and related structures. The alternative possible fault trend is north–south with left-lateral displacement (Fig. 11b). There are no obvious candidate faults that were active in the Late Cretaceous yet identified.

Although kinematically attractive, the transtensional models for the northern Oman mountains raise as many questions as they answer. It is interesting to note that the constrictional strains appear to relate to a zone of differential exhumation: the metamorphic transition between Jebel Akhdar and Saih Hatat is strongly oblique to the inferred direction of orogenic convergence or divergence. The peak barometric conditions of the rocks in these windows can serve as proxies for the displacements associated with their exhumation. Consequently, there is far more extension associated with structures in the east (As Sifah) compared with the western side of Saih Hatat, and there is correspondingly more extension associated with the exhumation of Saih Hatat than with central Jebel Akhdar. It should be noted that Breton *et al.* (2004) interpreted the variations in metamorphic grade as simply down the dip of the palaeo-subduction zone and consequently illustrated extension on an ENE–WSW-oriented section. This is highly oblique to the regional stretching direction, which, based on the kinematic data presented here, is NNE–SSW. The spatial variations in the amount of exhumation in an ENE–WSW axis actually reflect important lateral changes in the orogen.

The consequences of differential movement in deformation zones were discussed by Coward & Potts (1983), pre-empting many of the descriptions of strain patterns in zones of oblique kinematics. They showed that strongly constrictional strains result from the superimposition of

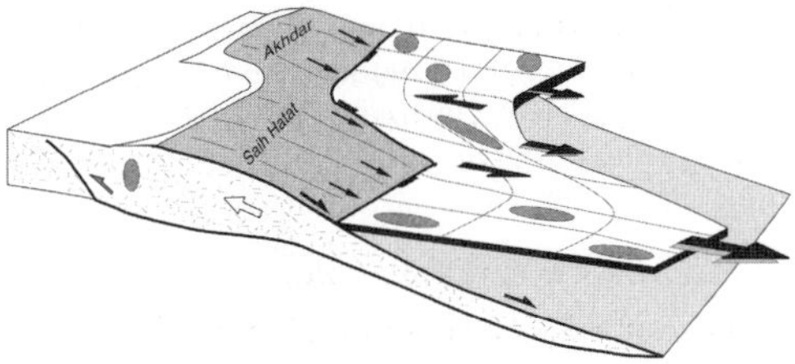

Fig. 12. Schematic model for differential late-orogenic extension in the northern Oman mountains (viewed towards the SW). The greater exhumation of the Saih Hatat Massif implies greater extensional strains in this sector of the orogen, in comparison with the Jebel Akhdar sector. The resultant differential extensional flow induced a component of wrench shear that produces local constrictional strains. In this model the geometry shows just one major detachment (and overlying stretching allochthon). In reality, the northern Oman mountain contains multiple detachments so that the patterns of extension are heterogeneous, not only laterally but also through the crust. It should be noted that only a small amount of the extension can be accommodated by crustal shortening, suggesting that the tectonic style continued as the orogen experienced plate-scale divergence.

differential shear (simple shear with a vertical shear plane) and layer extensional flow (Fig. 11c). Consequently, the displacement field associated with exhumation of the various parts of the Arabian continent will naturally generate constrictional strain. The trend of these constrictional structures in the northern Oman mountains is interesting as it parallels basement structures within the Arabian continent, influencing the location of Mesozoic faults (e.g. in the future Zagros; Sepehr & Cosgrove 2004). Within the northern Oman mountains this trend is represented by the Semail Gap (the eastern flank of Jebel Nakhl, Fig. 8) and is recorded by abrupt stratigraphic changes in the Hajar Supergroup in NE Jebel Nakhl (e.g. Pratt & Smewing 1990). Consequently, it is tentatively proposed here that the direction of extension effectively reuses the basement trends, and that these are reactivated under constriction caused by differential crustal extension. The different levels of extensional detachment (i.e. base of the allochthon, with the Hajar Supergroup, within basement) may have their own zones of differential movement that could generate disharmonic cross-fold structures.

Discussion

The key conclusion is that deformation of the Arabian continental crust that followed the obduction of the Semail and Hawasina units and concomitant partial subduction of the continental margin is characterized by NNE–SSW crustal extension and associated orthogonal constriction. Although these strains may be related to regional transtension in a geometrically and kinematically consistent model, there is little geological evidence beyond this structural study to support such a notion. The transtension model would be supported by regionally extensive strike-slip faults adjacent to the study area, either north–south, left lateral or NE–SW right-lateral structures. Consequently, an alternative model of laterally differential extensional tectonics is favoured here, based on the geometric models of Coward & Potts (1983). Not only does this model generate constriction, it also matches the kinematics on the basis of the differential exhumation of the Arabian continental crust within the northern Oman mountains. Thus the deformation can form a continuous, compatible transition from penetrative ductile strain, with its associated outcrop-scale complexity in Saih Hatat (e.g. Miller *et al.* 2002), to the more localized shears, faults and folds described here from Jebel Akhdar.

The tectonic significance of top-to-the-NNE-directed shear within the metamorphic rocks of Saih Hatat is controversial (contrast Jolivet *et al.* (1998), Miller *et al.* (2002) and Searle *et al.* (2004)). Miller *et al.* (2002) considered at least some of these structures to be back-thrusts because they repeat stratigraphy and therefore accommodated crustal shortening. In contrast, Jolivet *et al.* (1998) argued for crustal extension because the detachments omit metamorphic section, placing rocks that have not experienced eclogitic conditions on top of rocks that have. In practice, it is difficult to establish which is correct, for, although individual shear zones may repeat stratigraphy and juxtapose units that record different peak metamorphic conditions, these criteria are not, on their own, sufficiently robust to establish the crustal-scale kinematics (Wheeler & Butler 1994). The problem is one of defining where horizontal was at the time of deformation and relating this to the synkinematic barometric conditions.

The reason for studying the Oman mountains here was to evaluate the models for extensional tectonics and exhumation of high-pressure metamorphic rocks. Of the two options for the coherence of exhumed, once subducted crust proposed by Wheeler *et al.* (2001), the Oman example here is best described as a 'pip' rather than a 'sliver'. There is little evidence to support the erosion of a large panel of intermediate-grade metamorphic material such as occurs for slivers. Furthermore, a carapace of allochthonous units existed over the crest of the massifs of Arabian continental rocks. Both of the models of Wheeler *et al.* (2001: pip and sliver) predict that the crustal-scale extension described here forms merely the upper boundary of a body that is bounded on its lower side by a SSW-directed thrust system. Crustal shortening of 50% is indicated by the Moho depth beneath Jebel Akhdar (Al-Lazki *et al.* 2002), across a width of about 50 km. These values suggest about 25 km shortening, assuming approximately plane strain and a pre-existing thickness of 30 km for the crust, a result reduced for constrictional strain paths. In contrast, Breton *et al.* (2004) suggested that >100 km extension is recorded within the Arabian continent. This figure would be greatly increased by displacements along the base of the allochthonous sheets proposed here. There is thus a substantial imbalance between the amount of extension and the amount of contraction. Consequently, it is tentatively proposed that the differential extensional tectonics was active towards the end of the history of the mountain belt in Late Cretaceous time, coeval with the final period of crustal shortening but continued to initiate the rifting of the orogen and the onset of renewed subsidence in the Gulf of Oman.

We acknowledge substantial field support from Petroleum Development Oman and Sultan Qaaboos University for a postgraduate scholarship (M.A-W.). We are also indebted to S. Hanna (SQU) and J. Filbrandt (PDO) for discussions in and out of the field. I. Alsop and A. Robertson are thanked for thorough reviews, together with A. Ries for sharp editing. Yet again the seminal paper by Coward & Potts is applied to a new tectonic location. Thank you, Mike!

References

Al-Lazki, A. I., Seber, D., Sandvol, E. & Barazangi, M. 2002. A crustal transect across the Oman Mountains on the eastern margin of Arabia. *GeoArabia*, **7**, 47–78.

Breton, J-P., Béchennec, F., Le Métour, J., Moen-Maurel, L. & Razin, P. 2004. Eoalpine (Cretaceous) evolution of the Oman Tethyan continental margin: insights from a structural field study in Jabal Akhdar (Oman Mountains). *GeoArabia*, **9**, 1–18.

Butler, R. W. H. & Freeman, S. R. 1996. Can crustal extension be distinguished from thrusting in the internal parts of mountain belts? An example from the Entrelor shear zone, western Alps. *Journal of Structural Geology*, **18**, 909–923.

Cobbold, P. R. & Quinquis, H. 1980. Development of sheath folds in shear regimes. *Journal of Structural Geology*, **2**, 119–126.

COLEMAN, R. G. 1981. Tectonic setting for ophiolite obduction in Oman. *Journal of Geophysical Research*, **86**, 2497–2508.

COWARD, M. P. 1982. Surge zones in the Moine thrust zone of N.W. Scotland. *Journal of Structural Geology*, **4**, 247–256.

COWARD, M. P. & POTTS, G. J. 1983. Complex strain patterns developed at the frontal and lateral tips to shear zones and thrust zones. *Journal of Structural Geology*, **5**, 383–399.

COWARD, M. P., BUTLER, R. W. H., KNIPE, R. J. & KHAN, M. A. 1987. The tectonic history of Kohistan and its implications for Himalayan structure. *Journal of the Geological Society, London*, **144**, 377–391.

DERCOURT, J., RICOU, L. E. & VRIELYNCK, B. (eds) 1993. *Atlas Tethys Palaeogeographic Maps*. Gauthier-Villars, Paris.

DEWEY, J. F., HOLDSWORTH, R. E. & STRACHAN, R. A. 1998. Transpression and transtension zones. *In*: HOLDSWORTH, R. E., STRACHAN, R. A. & DEWEY, J. F. (eds) *Continental Transpressional and Transtensional Tectonics*. Geological Society, London, Special Publications, **135**, 1–14.

EL-SHAZLY, A. K., COLEMAN, R. G. & LIOU, J. G. 1990. Eclogites and blueschists from northeastern Oman: petrology and *P–T* evolution. *Journal of Petrology*, **31**, 629–666.

EL-SHAZLY, A. K., BRÖCKER, M., HACKER, B. & CALVERT, A. 2001. Formation and exhumation of blueschists and eclogites from NE Oman: new perspectives from Rb–Sr and $^{40}Ar/^{39}Ar$ dating. *Journal of Metamorphic Geology*, **19**, 233–248.

FREEMAN, S. R., BUTLER, R. W. H, CLIFF, R. A., INGER, S. & BARNICOAT, A. C. 1998. Deformation migration in an orogen scale shear zone array; an example from the Basal Brianconnais Thrust, Internal Franco-Italian Alps. *Geological Magazine*, **135**, 349–367

GLENNIE, K. W., HUGHES CLARKE, M. W., BOEUF, M. G., PILAAR, W. F. & REINHARDT, B. M. 1974. *Geology of the Oman Mountains*. Verhandelingen van het Koninklijk Nederlands Geologisch Mijnbouwkundig Genootschap, Amsterdam, **31**.

GRAY, D. R. & GREGORY, R. T. 2004. Comment on ‘Eoalpine (Cretaceous) evolution of the Oman Tethyan continental margin: insights from a structural field study in Jabal Akhdar (Oman Mountains)’ by Jean-Paul Breton *et al. GeoArabia*, **9**, 143–147.

GRAY, D. R., HAND, M., MAWBY, J., ARMSTRONG, R. A., MILLER, J. M. & GREGORY, R. T. 2004. Sm–Nd and zircon U–Pb ages from garnet-bearing eclogites, NE Oman: constraints on high-*P* metamorphism. *Earth and Planetary Science Letters*, **222**, 407–422.

HACKER, B. R., MOSENFELDER, J. L. & GNOS, E. 1996. Rapid emplacement of the Oman ophiolite: thermal and geochronological constraints. *Tectonics*, **15**, 1230–1247.

HANNA, S. S. 1990. The Alpine deformation of the Central Oman Mountains. *In*: ROBERTSON, A. H. F., SEARLE, M. P. & RIES, A. C. (eds) *The Geology and Tectonics of the Oman Region*. Geological Society, London, Special Publications, **49**, 341–359.

JAMIESON, R. A., BEAUMONT, C., NGUYEN, M. H. & LEE, B. 2002. Interactions of metamorphism, deformation and exhumation in large convergent orogens. *Journal of Metamorphic Geology*, **20**, 9–24.

JOLIVET, L., GOFFE, B., BOUSQUET, R., OBERHANSLI, R. & MICHARD, A. 1998. Detachments in high-pressure mountain belts, Tethyan examples. *Earth and Planetary Science Letters*, **160**, 31–47.

KRABBENDAM, M. & DEWEY, J. F. 1998. Exhumation of UHP rocks by transtension in the Western Gneiss Region, Scandinavian Caledonides. *In*: HOLDSWORTH, R. E., STRACHAN, R. A. & DEWEY, J. F. (eds) *Continental Transpressional and Transtensional Tectonics*. Geological Society, London, Special Publications, **135**, 159–181.

KUSKY, T., ROBINSON, C. & EL-BAZ, F. 2005. Tertiary–Quaternary faulting and uplift in the northern Oman Hajar mountains. *Journal of the Geological Society, London*, **162**, 871–888.

LAVECCHIA, G. 1988. The Tyrrhenian–Apennine system: structural setting and seismogenesis. *Tectonophysics*, **147**, 263–293.

MANN, A., HANNA, S. S. & NOLAN, C. 1990. The post-Campanian tectonic evolution of the central Oman Mountains: Tertiary extension of the eastern Arabian Margin. *In*: ROBERTSON, A. H. F., SEARLE, M. P. & RIES, A. C. (eds) *The Geology and Tectonics of the Oman Region*. Geological Society, London, Special Publications, **49**, 549–563.

MILLER, J. M., GRAY, D. R. & GREGORY, R. T. 1999. Geological constraints on the exhumation of a high-pressure metamorphic terrane, Oman. *In*: RING, U., BRANDON, M. T., LISTER, G. S., & WILLET, S. D. (eds) *Exhumation Processes, Normal Faulting, Ductile Flow and Erosion*. Geological Society, London, Special Publications, **154**, 241–260.

MILLER, J. M., GRAY, D. R. & GREGORY, R. T. 2002. Geometry and significance of internal windows and regional isoclinal folds in northeast Saih Hatat, Sultanate of Oman. *Journal of Structural Geology*, **24**, 359–386.

MILNES, A. G., WENNBERG, O. P., SKÅR, Ø. & KOESTLER, A. G. 1997. Contraction, extension and timing in the South Norwegian Caledonides: the Sognefjord transect. *In*: BURG, J. P. & FORD, M. (eds) *Orogeny through Time*. Geological Society, London, Special Publications, **121**, 123–148.

MOSELEY, F. 1990. The structure of Masirah Island, Oman. *In*: ROBERTSON, A. H. F., SEARLE, M. P. & RIES, A. C. (eds) *The Geology and Tectonics of the Oman Region*. Geological Society, London, Special Publications, **49**, 665–671.

PRATT, B. R. & SMEWING, J. D. 1990. Jurassic and Early Cretaceous platform margin configuration and evolution, central Oman mountains. *In*: ROBERTSON, A. H. F., SEARLE, M. P. & RIES, A. C. (eds) *The Geology and Tectonics of the Oman Region*. Geological Society, London, Special Publications, **49**, 69–88.

RABU, D., BECHENNEC, F., BEURRIER, M. & HUTIN, G. 1986. *Geological map of Nakhl, sheet NY 40-03E, scale 1:00 000, with explanatory notes.* Directorate General of Minerals, Oman Ministry of Petroleum and Minerals.

Robertson, A. H. F. 1987. The transition from a passive margin to an Upper Cretaceous foreland basin related to ophiolite emplacement in the Oman mountains. *Geological Society of America Bulletin*, **99**, 633–653.

Searle, M. P. & Cox, J. 1999. Tectonic setting, origin and obduction of the Oman ophiolite. *Geological Society of America Bulletin*, **111**, 104–122.

Searle, M. P., Waters, D. W., Martin, H. N. & Rex, D. C. 1994. Structure and metamorphism of blueschist–eclogite facies rocks from the northeastern Oman mountains. *Journal of the Geological Society, London*, **151**, 555–576.

Searle, M. P., Warren, C. J., Waters, D. J. & Parrish, R. R. 2004. Structural evolution, metamorphism and restoration of the Arabian continental margin, Saih Hatat region, Oman Mountains. *Journal of Structural Geology*, **26**, 451–473.

Sepehr, M. & Cosgrove, J. W. 2004. Structural framework of the Zagros Fold–Thrust Belt, Iran. *Marine and Petroleum Geology*, **23**, 829–843.

Shackleton, R. M. & Ries, A. C. 1990. Tectonics of the Masirah Fault Zone and eastern Oman. *In*: Robertson, A. H. F., Searle, M. P. & Ries, A. C. (eds) *The Geology and Tectonics of the Oman Region.* Geological Society, London, Special Publications, **49**, 715–724.

Wheeler, J. & Butler, R. W. H. 1994. Criteria for identifying structures related to true extension in orogens. *Journal of Structural Geology*, **16**, 1023–1027.

Wheeler, J., Reddy, S. M. & Cliff, R. A. 2001. Kinematic linkage between internal zone extension and shortening in more external units in the NW Alps. *Journal of the Geological Society, London*, **158**, 439–443.

Woodcock, N. H. 1986. The role of strike-slip fault systems at plate boundaries. *Philosophical Transactions of the Royal Society of London, Series A*, **317**, 13–29.

Co-axial horizontal stretching within extending orogens: the exhumation of HP rocks on Syros (Cyclades) revisited

CLARE E. BOND[1,2], ROBERT W. H. BUTLER[3] & JOHN E. DIXON[1]

[1]*School of GeoScience, University of Edinburgh, Grant Institute, Kings Buildings, West Mains Road, Edinburgh EH9 3JW, UK*

[2]*Present address: Department of Geographical & Earth Sciences, Gregory Building, Lilybank Gardens, University of Glasgow, Glasgow G12 8QQ, UK (e-mail: clare.bond@ges.gla.ac.uk)*

[3]*Institute of Geophysics and Tectonics, University of Leeds, Leeds LS2 9JT, UK*

Abstract: Although the role of extensional tectonics in the exhumation of high-pressure metamorphic terranes is widely established, the kinematics of such deformation remains ambiguous. This paper outlines new field data from the Attic–Cycladic blueschist belt that suggest that distributed ductile strain plays a significant role in the extension and that, consequently, the role of major detachment faults may have been over-emphasized in previous studies. The high-pressure blueschist terrane (Ermoupolis Unit) of Syros shows abundant evidence of subhorizontal extension, manifest as layer boudinage and ductile thinning without the development of significant internal detachments. The deformation approximates to pure shear stretching that was heterogeneously distributed in space and time. Minor zones of asymmetric shear are interpreted not as through-going extensional shear zones but as structures that maintain compatibility between zones of differential stretching. The progression of deformation is charted through the systematic development of increasingly lower-pressure metamorphic assemblages. However, most of the decompression (potentially from 20 kbar to 6 kbar) occurred within the blueschist stability field, as the rocks were actively extending. Heterogeneous retrogression and concomitant deformation are believed to relate to the local chemistry and availability of hydrous fluids.

The relative importance of broadly distributed, approximately pure shear deformation and strongly localized, approximately simple shear through the crust is a recurrent debate in continental tectonics. Mike Coward was at the vanguard of early attempts to explain high-deformation zones in the continental crust, chiefly in terms of simple shear, through his work on basement structures in Africa and NW Scotland. As focus shifted to basin dynamics in the 1980s, debates polarized between homogeneous rifting (sometimes called 'pure shear'; McKenzie 1978) and whole lithospheric shear zone models (e.g. Wernicke 1985). Common ground was found through the development of 'depth-dependent' stretching models (see Roberts & Yielding 1992, for review), including the heterogenous rifting model of Coward (1986). Yet the whole lithosphere shear models have retained much influence, especially in tectonic scenarios for the exhumation of high-pressure metamorphic rocks. Drawing on models from the Basin-and-Range Province that inspired Wernicke's (1985) lithospheric models, Lister *et al.* (1984) proposed that blueschists of the Attic–Cycladic belt in the Aegean had been exhumed in the footwall to major low-angle, crustal-scale normal faults. This model has since seen widespread use, not only in the Aegean but also in other parts of the Mediterranean (e.g. Jolivet *et al.* 1998) and further afield. With these continuing studies it is pertinent to examine the structural geology of these settings carefully. To what degree are the high-pressure (HP) rocks in the footwalls to large faults merely passive passengers back to upper crustal conditions, or do they contain significant distributed strains that contribute to their exhumation?

The aim here is to examine the nature of distributed deformation within an exhumed high-pressure terrane. The study area is the island of Syros, in the heart of the Attic–Cyclades blueschist terrane (Fig. 1; e.g. Bonneau *et al.* 1980). This setting was important for the early recognition of major low-angle detachment faults and their possible role in the exhumation of HP metamorphic rocks (e.g. Lister *et al.* 1984). Since then many studies have focused on the role

From: RIES, A. C., BUTLER, R. W. H. & GRAHAM, R. H. (eds) 2007. *Deformation of the Continental Crust: The Legacy of Mike Coward*. Geological Society, London, Special Publications, **272**, 203–222.
0305-8719/07/$15

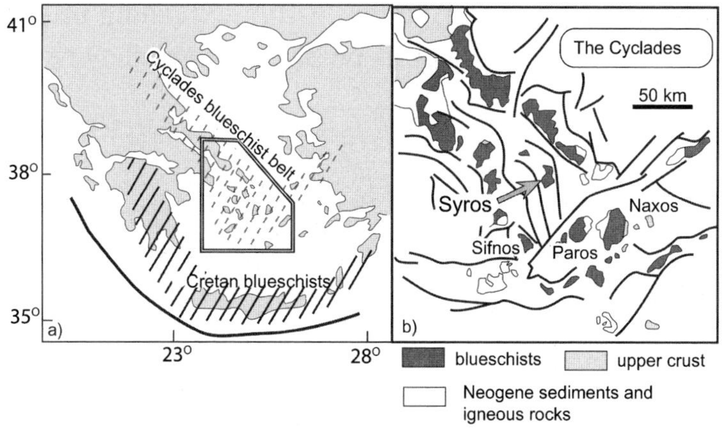

Fig. 1. (**a**) Map of the Aegean area with the high-pressure Attic–Cycladic belt (Cyclades blueschist belt) and Cretan blueschists annotated. (**b**) Map of the Cyclades, showing the location of Syros within the Cyclades chain and the orientation of major normal faults in the area. After Gautier *et al.* (1993) and Jolivet *et al.* (1998).

of the detachment faults (e.g. Jolivet *et al.* 1998). However, there is a continuing debate on the role of penetrative strain during exhumation of the HP rocks. On the basis of petrological studies, Trotet *et al.* (2001) argued for linked systems of shear zones operating at greenschist facies that overprint deformation fabrics developed under blueschist and eclogite facies. Rosenbaum *et al.* (2002) similarly argued that significant horizontal extension happened under blueschist conditions, followed by simple shear zones that operated under greenschist-facies conditions. However, this view was strongly questioned by Keiter *et al.* (2004). They argued that there is little to no penetrative deformation that has affected the rocks on Syros after peak metamorphism, and therefore exhumation must have been accommodated on a major detachment fault. Testing these different models requires integrating metamorphic and structural kinematic studies, which is the theme of this paper. A range of structural and metamorphic observations from some key sites on Syros are used to build the case for a coherent deformation model by which the high-pressure rocks have exhumed with important, but heterogeneous and partitioned, largely coaxial stretching.

The geology of Syros

Syros contains two distinct sequences of metamorphic rocks (Fig. 2). In the SE of the island, the Vari Unit consists of albitic gneisses that show no evidence of high-pressure metamorphic conditions. Trotet *et al.* (2001) considered these units to form an upper tectonic sheet, carried onto high-pressure rocks by a regionally extensive, low-angle detachment fault. The gneisses are generally believed to represent older continental basement. In contrast, the rocks beneath the detachment, termed the Ermoupolis Unit, have younger protoliths. These include metabasic units, i.e. basalts and gabbros together with tracts of serpentinite, commonly believed to be remnants of Tethyan oceanic crust (e.g. Bonneau 1984). However, most of the Ermoupolis Unit is made of highly variable metasedimentary rocks. These include pelitic schists, psammites and conglomerates together with layers of marble. The marbles are tens of metres thick and can be traced out through many kilometres through the island (Fig. 2; e.g. Ridley 1982).

In common with other high-pressure metamorphic terranes, the Attic–Cycladic blueschists are strongly retrogressed in greenschist facies. The best preserved tracts of eclogites and blueschists are found on Syros, within the Ermoupolis Unit (Dixon 1976; Dixon *et al.* 1987; Okrusch & Bröcker 1990). Peak conditions are generally estimated to lie in the upper pressure limits of the epidote–blueschist stability field, at about 20 kbar and 500 °C (e.g. Trotet *et al.* 2001). As Keiter *et al.* (2004) pointed out, there is widespread preservation of calcite pseudomorphs after aragonite (Fig. 3a) within high-pressure blueschist bodies, suggesting that, for these sites, there has been no penetrative ductile deformation below the stability field for aragonite. Keiter *et al.* (2004) placed the lower pressure limit for aragonite stability at *c.* 12 kbar for their *P–T*

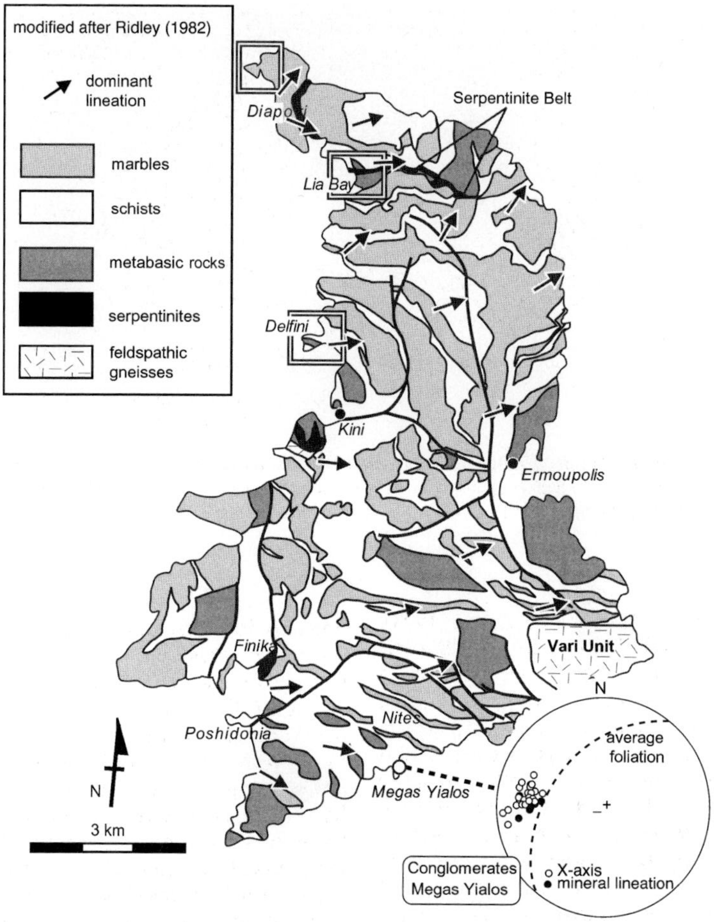

Fig. 2. Simplified geological map of Syros. After Ridley (1982). The map shows the main geological units and dominant lineation trend. The locations of sub-studies are annotated. The lower-hemisphere equal area stereonet shows a parallelism of mineral lineations with the *x*-axes of deformed clasts in a conglomerate unit at Megas Yialos.

path, so for them there was no pervasive ductile strain on Syros from pressure conditions of less than 12 kbar.

Rocks of the Ermoupolis Unit show various deformation structures. Ridley (1982) described the widespread development of a broadly east–west trending mineral lineation on the island (Fig. 2). When mineral lineations are compared with measurements of the long axis of deformed clasts (Fig. 3b) in conglomeratic parts of the metasedimentary succession (e.g. Figs 2 and 4), it is found that the lineation trend represents the true finite stretching direction for the units.

In common with earlier workers, Trotet *et al.* (2001) showed that blueschists and eclogites are patchily preserved throughout the Ermoupolis Unit. For Trotet *et al.* (op. cit.), the different degrees of preservation of blueschists in the Attic–Cyclades reflect different *P–T* paths that relate spatially to the position of deeply penetrating extensional shear zones. However, different degrees of retrogression occur on a variety of scales, from kilometres (e.g. Trotet *et al.* 2001) to hand-specimen (Fig. 3c). On the neighbouring island of Sifnos (Fig. 1), it is well established that the greenschist-facies overprint strongly relates to fluid infiltration (Schiestedt & Matthews 1987; Ganor *et al.* 1989). This also appears to be so on Syros.

The timing of key parts of the tectonometamorphic history of the Attic–Cycladic blueschists in general and of those on Syros in particular is

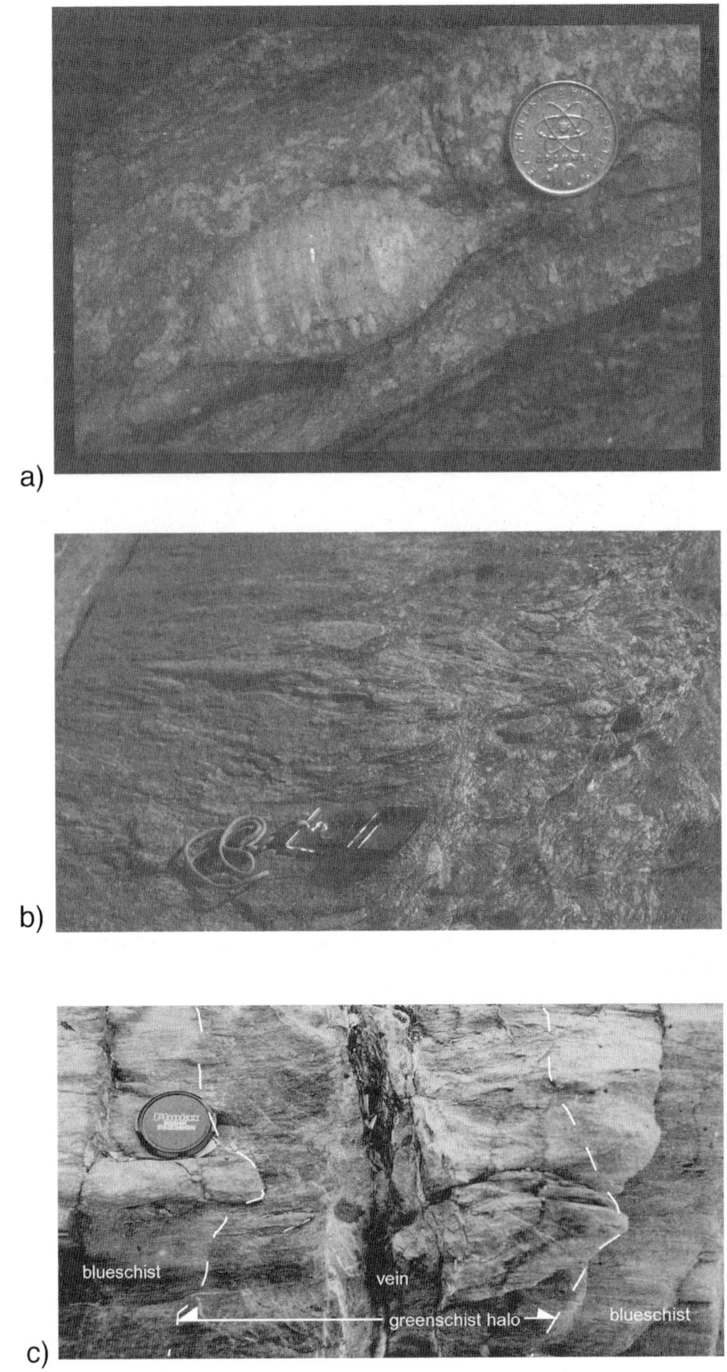

Fig. 3. Photographs of critical metamorphic and structural features seen across Syros. (**a**) Calcite pseudomorphs after aragonite, in a boudinaged marble layer. The preservation of elongate aragonite habits (now calcite) was used by Keiter *et al.* (2004) to argue against significant deformation of Syros rocks during exhumation. (**b**) Clast shapes in conglomerates at Megas Yialos. The strong elongation of clasts defines a stretching lineation that is parallel to local mineral lineations, suggesting a tectonic significance (see also Fig. 2). (**c**) Vein with greenschist 'halo'. Such examples, in which the host blueschist is retrogressed to greenschist around a vein, are common. Retrogression across the island is patchy and clearly often limited by local availability of fluid.

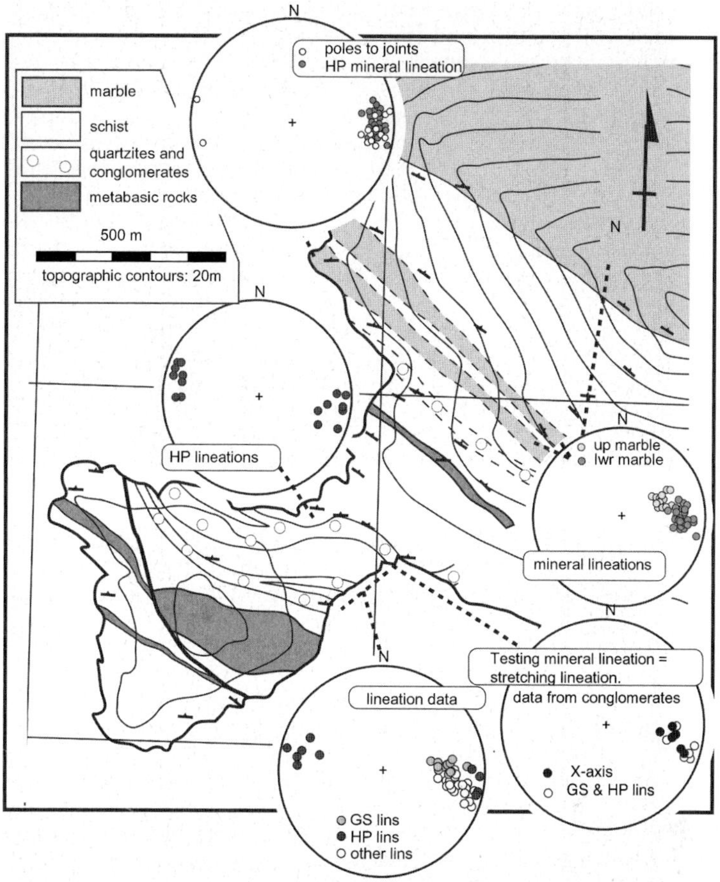

Fig. 4. Simplified geological map of the Delfini area (location shown in Fig. 2), with km^2 grid. Inset lower-hemisphere equal area stereoplots show structural data from this site. (See text for further discussion.) GS, greenschist; HP, high pressure.

highly controversial. The eclogitic meta-igneous rocks of the Ermoupolis Unit have yielded 75–80 Ma U–Pb zircon ages for omphacite, as described by Bröcker & Enders (1999), who considered these Cretaceous ages to date peak metamorphism. Other workers have presumed that they relate to the age of the sea floor (e.g. Keiter *et al.* 2004). Otherwise, much of the published geochronology for the Aegean area relies on Ar–Ar and Rb–Sr white mica ages that give an Eocene age (*c.* 53–40 Ma) for peak metamorphism and an Oligocene–Miocene age (*c.* 25–18 Ma) for greenschist-facies metamorphism (Bröcker *et al.* 2004). However, as Bröcker *et al.* (2004) pointed out, many of the Ar–Ar cooling ages are older than the Rb–Sr white mica ages for the same rocks, a good indicator of contamination by 'excess' radiogenic argon. Yet Bröcker *et al.* also identified significant discrepancies in the Rb–Sr mica geochronology suggesting important disequilibria on the sample scale. These isotopic issues mirror the conclusions of the metamorphic studies, that fluid infiltration plays a key role in the record of deformation and metamorphic processes.

Structure studies

Overview of sites

Figure 2 shows the location of the structural sites presented and summarizes the geology of the island. There is some dispute about the distribution of HP rocks across the island. Traditionally the best-preserved blueschist and eclogite outcrops are considered to lie in the northern part of Syros, north of Kambos. However, HP rocks also exist throughout the island, preserved in pods surrounded by, and interleaved with, greenschist-facies rocks. To understand the deformation relationships, observations made at Delfini are described first, where both blueschist and greenschist mineral assemblages coexist. These are then compared with those at Diapori in the acclaimed 'northern blueschist zone' and in the Kambos–Lia Bay area, described by Trotet *et al.* (2001) as a tectonic discontinuity between blueschist and greenschist assemblages. Finally, a zone of pervasive greenschist deformation at Poshidonia was examined.

Delfini

The geology of the Delfini area (Fig. 4), in common with the rest of the Syros, is made up of a coherent sequence of marbles, schists and metabasites, together with local layers of quartzites and conglomerates. The lithologies are variably retrogressed, with metabasites preserving HP assemblages of sodic-pyroxene, garnet, glaucophane and epidote, to epidote, chlorite, albite and calcite. Schist assemblages range from epidote–glaucophane–garnet–quartz schist, to epidote–chlorite–quartz schist, and finally to albite–chlorite–quartz schist (referred to here as 'epidote-blueschist', 'epidote-greenschist', and 'greenschist', respectively). The mineral assemblages of actual layers is dependent on local chemistry.

The interlayered lithologies form a continuous sequence, with no change in metamorphic grade across lithological contacts and no evidence for major tectonic breaks. There is a single mapped fault line that shows no evidence of a large displacement and across which there is no change in metamorphic grade. Consequently, it is suggested that the area has deformed as a coherent body throughout the described deformation history. Deformation is mainly defined by symmetrical boudinage of layers in both the schist and metabasite, with occasional asymmetrical shears. Figure 4 summarizes mineral lineation data, x-axes of deformed clasts in a conglomerate layer, and poles to joints in the marble. HP mineral lineations, defined by preferred orientation of glaucophane, are parallel to the greenschist mineral lineation, defined by albite and chlorite, and trend east–west. The lineation direction at Delfini is parallel to the x-axes of clasts in the conglomerate horizon, as demonstrated at Megas Yialos (Fig. 2).

In HP metabasic layers, early intrafolial folds are extended and sheared by layer-parallel flattening. Boudinaged layers containing sodic-pyroxene and garnet are preserved adjacent to sheared glaucophane–garnet schists that are also boudinaged. This interlayering of compositional and metamorphic facies variations is common and fractured boudin necks often contain chlorite- and albite-bearing veins (Fig. 5a). Observations suggest progressive deformation during decompression within single horizons and localization of deformation between different layers under different *P–T* conditions.

Epidote-blueschist layers show conjugate shears of glaucophane and quartz forming over several centimetres, extending an earlier layer-parallel foliation in an east–west direction (Fig. 5b). These epidote-blueschist layers, 30 cm wide, are symmetrically boudinaged on a metre length-scale and are bounded by zones of partial greenschist-facies retrogression. The greenschist retrogression and boudinage are spatially associated; the retrogression was probably controlled by fluid infiltration in the zones of intense deformation along the boudin margins. The boudins fracture the more competent epidote-blueschist and are mineralized with albite, chlorite, quartz and oxide (Fig. 5c). Individual lithological layers show deformation and associated metamorphic mineral growth at a range of grades.

In areas of greenschist-facies metamorphism, the albite content of the rock increases towards boudin necks and around albite and chlorite ($\pm$ calcite, oxide and quartz) segregations in boudinaged zones. The fabric in the greenschist-facies rocks wraps round the segregations and east–west-oriented mineral lineations are found on foliation surfaces (Fig. 5d). In many areas albite porphyroblasts overgrow the greenschist fabric and suggest a static overprint of the blueschist fabric by mimetic greenschist minerals. However, greenschist minerals wrap around segregations of albite and chlorite, and localized zones of deformation show flattening of albite porphyroblasts, wrapped by chlorite and mica. These observations indicate that deformation continued into the greenschist-facies stability field. It is likely that albite growth was associated with fluid infiltration and deformation (e.g. Watkins 1983; Barnicoat 1988). However, the authors believe that albite porphyroblast growth played an important role in essentially pinning deformation during growth, thereby promoting strain partitioning, most probably into adjacent areas of fluid infiltration and active retrogressive recrystallization.

The marbles at Delfini are broadly continuous. The more massive units have acted rigidly, but thinner layers have boudinaged within the schists. Some of the marbles have internal heterogeneities, with interlayering of calcitic and dolomitic horizons. Dolomitic horizons have acted more competently than those rich in calcite and

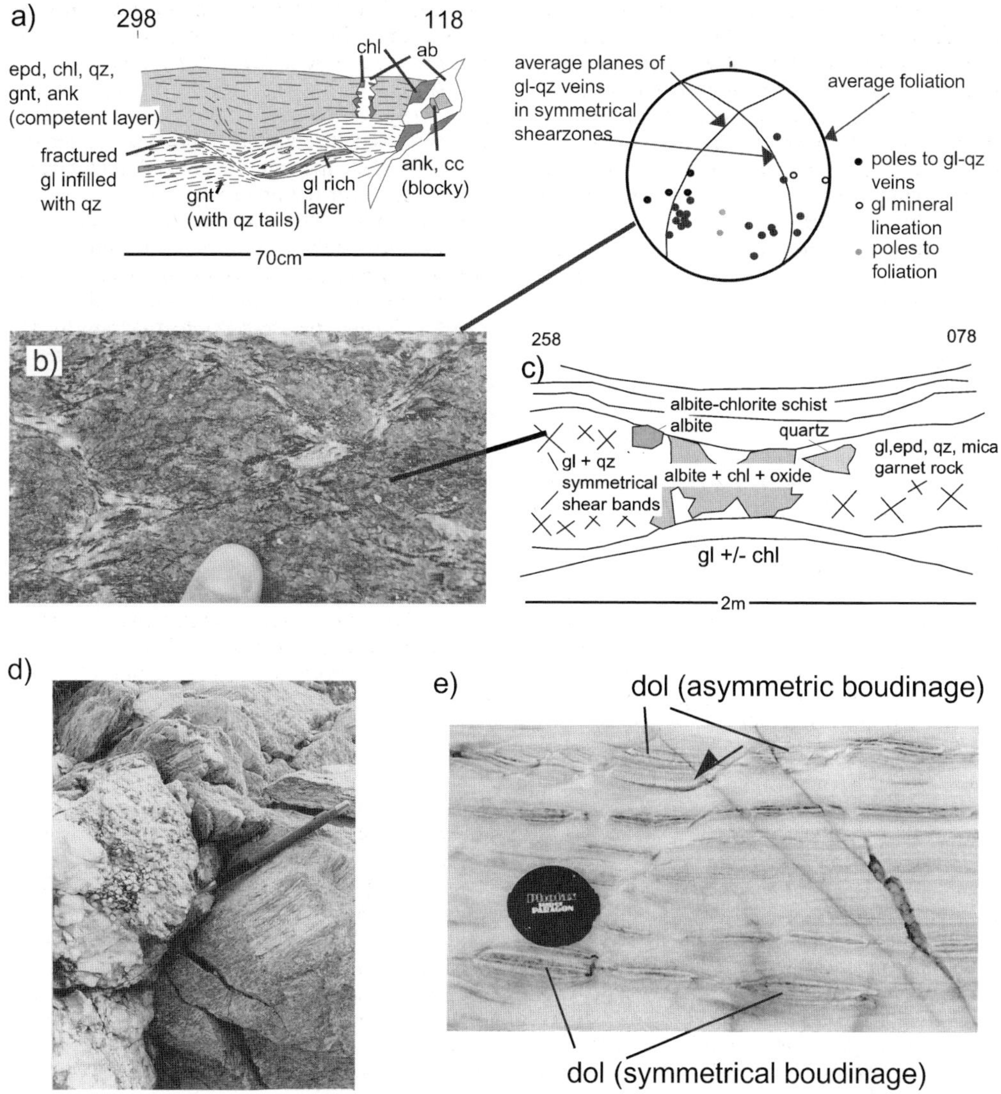

Fig. 5. Field photographs and sketches from the Delfini area. (**a**) Field sketch of boudinaged compositionally different layers, the latest increment of strain has resulted in fracture and infilling with greenschist mineral assemblages. (**b**) Stretched clots of epidote and glaucophane with glaucophane and quartz growth in extensional shears. Glaucophane needles define the extension direction, as shown in the lower-hemisphere equal area stereonet. (**c**) Field sketch of a boudinaged layer of epidote–glaucophane rock with greenschist mineral growth in boudin necks. The line from (**b**) marks the approximate location of that photograph, showing continuous extension and boudinage during different episodes of mineral growth. (**d**) Albite mineral lineations (parallel to the pencil) adjacent to a greenschist vein. (**e**) Dolomite and calcite banded marble. The dolomite layers (darker in the photograph) have acted more competently than the calcite and are boudinaged both asymmetrically (top to the east) and symmetrically. Mineral abbreviations: epd, epidote; chl, chlorite; qz, quartz; ank, ankerite; gl, glaucophane; ab, albite; cc, calcite; dol, dolomite.

have fractured and boudinaged, often showing asymmetrical, top-to-the-east, shears (Fig. 5e). Poles to extensional fractures in the marble are oriented east–west (Fig. 4), implying an east–west-oriented extension direction parallel to that defined by HP ductile structures. In the thinnest marbles, discrete fractures can be traced laterally into ductile shears in the schists.

In summary, all units show evidence for layer extension. With the exception of the marble layers, which are compositionally homogeneous, all units display a down-pressure metamorphic history. HP mineral assemblages define layer extension, overprinted in turn by epidote-blueschist and greenschist assemblages in the same kinematic framework. It might be argued that this kinematic regime continued into shallow crustal levels accommodated by the extensional fractures in the marble. As the observations in the present study include fractures linking to shears in adjacent units, we interpret that the deformation kinematics, brittle or ductile, are determined by strain rate rather than a reduction in temperature and the wholesale relocation of the units across some form of discrete 'brittle–ductile transition'.

Diapori

Traditionally, the Diapori area (Fig. 2) on the northern tip of the island has been described as the best area for the preservation of HP mineral assemblages (Ridley 1982; Dixon *et al.* 1987; Keiter *et al.* 2004). There are three mappable metasedimentary units: (1) marble containing thin layers of dolomite, but mainly grey and cream calcite; (2) conglomerate containing deformed clasts of calcite, quartz and metabasite; (3) quartz, graphite, chlorite schist containing thin marble and quartz layers (Fig. 6). These are

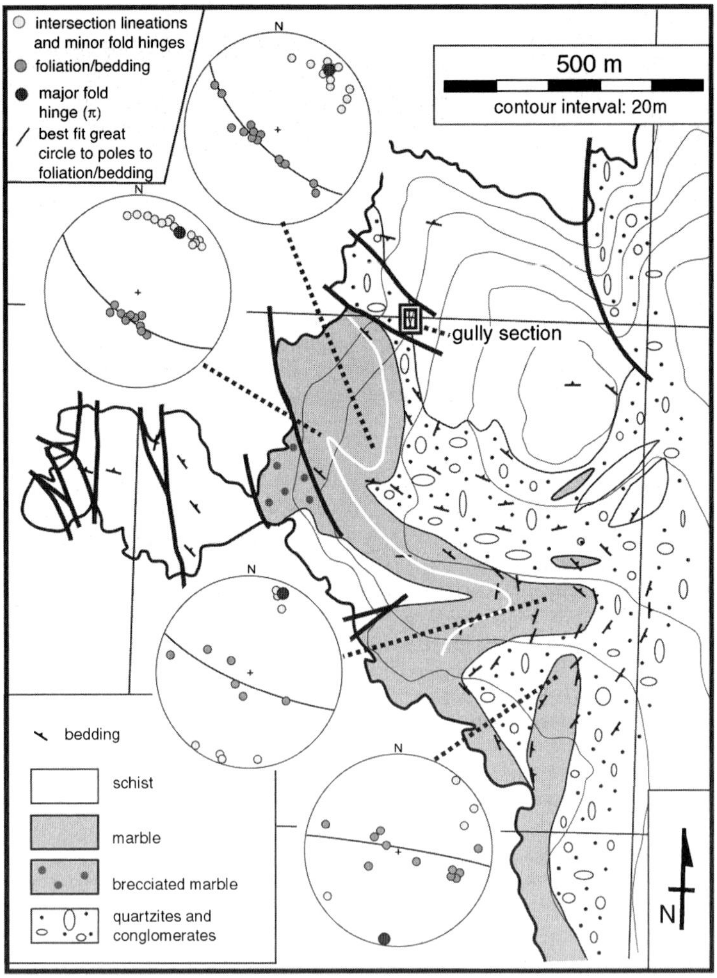

Fig. 6. Simplified geological map of the Diapori area (location shown in Fig. 2), with km^2 grid. The main area of study is marked as 'gully section'. Lower-hemisphere equal area stereonets show the trends of large folds in the marble.

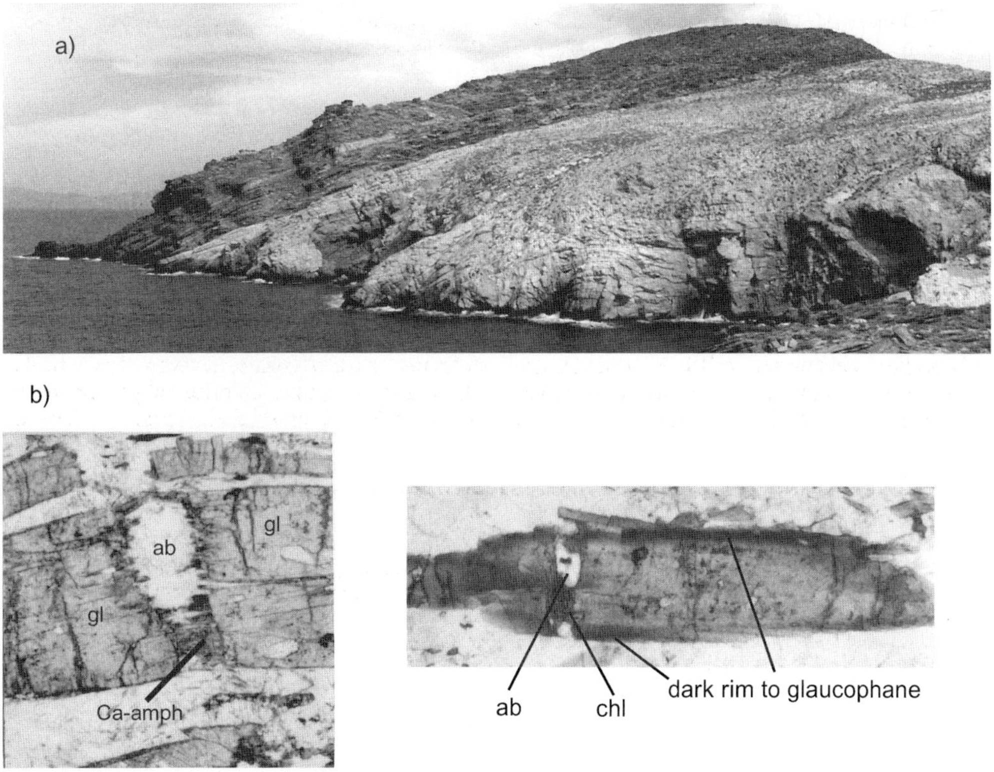

Fig. 7. Photographs of key features at Diapori. (**a**) Field photograph, from the sea looking NE, of the folds at Diapori, picked out by the main marble units. (**b**) Thin-section photographs of boudinaged glaucophane (gl) crystals, showing zoning (dark rim, pale core) and growth of calcic-amphibole (Ca-amph), albite (ab) and chlorite (chl) in fractures. Field of view in both photomicrographs *c.* 3 mm.

deformed by a series of large folds, clearly picked out by the marble beds (Fig. 7; Ridley 1982; Keitler *et al.* 2004). Folds on a map and outcrop scale are weakly curvilinear, but hinge lines are dispersed around the stretching lineation and axial surfaces are parallel to the regional flattening plane. As Keiter *et al.* (2004) pointed out, these major folds certainly existed during HP metamorphism. However, they may have had an earlier history inherited from early collision tectonics.

The observations presented here are concentrated on structures in the conglomerate and a thin layer (4–6 m thick) of retrogressed albite, chlorite schist that crops out directly above the conglomerate (Fig. 8). These lithologies were chosen for their mineral heterogeneities and evidence for retrogressive overprint, with which to deduce the relative pressure and temperature (*P–T*) constraints of deformation. Structures in the two lithologies are compared with the regional fold structures in the marble as annotated in Figure 6. The large-scale regional folds in the marble and minor parasitic folds on their limbs have hinge lines oriented NE–SW (Fig. 6). In the schist, the fold axial plane orientations vary from foliation-parallel to subhorizontal to upright. However, fold hinge lines show a constant NE–SW orientation in the schist and conglomerate, parallel to those observed in the marble (Fig. 9).

The thin schist layer (Fig. 8) is variably retrogressed and layers of glaucophane-rich material (1–2 cm wide) are preserved adjacent to retrogressed greenschist. Retrogression of the schist to greenschist-facies mineral assemblages is associated with minor zones of deformation and fluid infiltration. Albite and chlorite veins are common in the schist layer; some are foliation parallel, but most contain extensional mineral fibres and trend north–south to NW–SE, accommodating east–west to NE–SW extension (Fig. 9). The veins are surrounded by metasomatic alteration haloes, common across Syros. The haloes

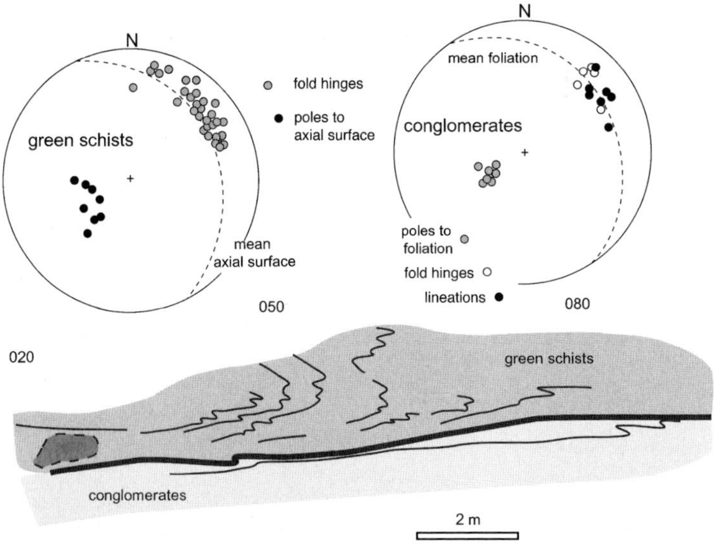

Fig. 8. Field sketch of the boundary between the greenschist and conglomeratic unit in the gully area (location shown in Fig. 6). Lower-hemisphere equal area stereonets summarize some of the main structural features.

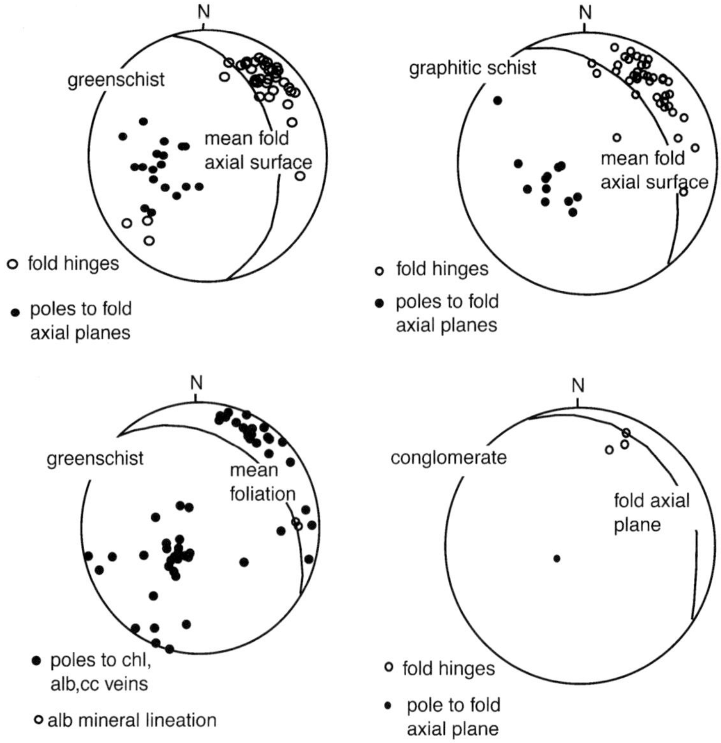

Fig. 9. Stereonets (lower-hemisphere equal area) of structural data from the Diapori area, from the conglomerate, the greenschist in the gully area (location shown in Fig. 6) and from the graphitic schist.

contain albite porphyroblasts that grow over a folded, earlier, glaucophane fabric. Elsewhere in the horizon, micro-fabrics are extensional. Glaucophane crystals, zoned with pale blue cores and dark rims, are micro-boudinaged. Glaucophane crystals fracture perpendicular to their long axes, which are generally aligned east–west on foliation surfaces. The glaucophane is partially altered to chlorite along the fractures.

The conglomerate has a matrix of calcite, quartz, mica and glaucophane. Glaucophane crystals are partially retrogressed to chlorite and albite and preserve similar micro-boudinage fabrics to those observed in the schist above. Large glaucophane crystals, readily observed on foliation surfaces in the conglomerate, trend NE–SW to east–west, parallel to fold hinge lines and intersection lineations (Fig. 9). As in the schist, the glaucophane crystals are zoned with pale blue cores and dark rims. Locally a fine outer rim of blue–green amphibole is observed (Fig. 7b). Blue–green amphibole also grows from some of the fractured, micro-boudinaged, surfaces within glaucophane. In other cases the boudin necks are filled by albite and chlorite with the glaucophane partially replaced by chlorite.

Zoned glaucophane (pale core and dark rim), in both the schist and the conglomerate, is indicative of solid solution transition towards the blue amphibole riebeckitic end-member. As noted by Brown (1974) and Maruyama *et al.* (1986), such a transition increases the stability of blue amphibole to lower pressures. Maruyama *et al.* (1986) and Liou *et al.* (1987) described a sliding reaction

$$\text{Gl-Rieb}_{ss} + \text{Epd}_{ss} + \text{Qz} + H_2O \rightarrow \text{Act}_{ss} + \text{Ab} + \text{Chl}_{ss} + \text{Mt/Hem}$$

in which decompression through the blueschist–greenschist transition produces an increasingly riebeckitic amphibole that is eventually replaced by actinolite, as defining the boundary between the blueschist-facies and greenschist-facies stability fields.

The observation of glaucophane in the schist and conglomerate suggests that boudinage occurred at the lower end of the blueschist stability field and into that of greenschist. Grain-scale electron probe analyses of blue amphibole compositions across Syros, using the Evans (1990) calibration, suggest a 3 kbar difference in the pressure conditions between initial and final growth of single crystals. From estimates of peak metamorphism of 20–14 kbar, blue amphibole is apparently stable on Syros, given appropriate compositions of fluid and Fe, to between 9 and 6 kbar.

For the Diapori area there is evidence for significant deformation during blueschist-facies, and potentially earlier, metamorphism and that the main folds developed under these conditions, as suggested by Keitler *et al.* (2004). However, there is a widespread greenschist overprint and this is associated with extensional boudinage of glaucophane at the blueschist to greenschist transition and greenschist veining. Unlike Keiter *et al.* (2004), the authors believe that the folds were strongly modified during decompression, albeit only weakly into greenschist facies. It is interesting however, to note that the HP structures at Diapori are consistent with broadly east–west to NE–SW extension at a range of metamorphic grades, as deduced for the Delfini area and elsewhere in the island.

Serpentinite Belt (Kambos–Lia Bay)

The structures of northern Syros are separated from the rest of the island by a mappable tectonic break (Ridley 1982), referred to here as the Serpentinite Belt. The best rock exposure is in the west, in the Kambos–Lia Bay area (Fig. 10). Here, boudinage has resulted in entrainment of surrounding layers, and large 'knockers' of metabasite are found within the serpentinite. Boudinage is documented in a marble band near Kambos village, where the boudin axes in the marble trend north–south, accommodating east–west extension (Fig. 10). Calcite crystals in the marble band have elongate habits and are interpreted as pseudomorphs after aragonite, implying that deformation of the marble band into boudins occurred before the aragonite–calcite transition, as calcite crystal growth has mimicked an aragonite crystal habit within the boudins. Based on the pressure estimate of Keiter *et al.* (2004), this boudinage must therefore have taken place at pressures greater than *c.* 12 kbar.

Further evidence for boudinage of marble bands at high pressures is found on the northern side of Lia Bay. Here the marble is in direct contact with the serpentinite and is isoclinally folded and boudinaged. The marble contains an impure schistose layer preserving a HP assemblage of pyroxene, glaucophane, mica, epidote, ankerite and chlorite. These pyroxene-rich layers are inferred to be the product of metasomatic reaction between serpentine and calcareous schist. They have a pervasive layer-parallel HP fabric that has formed under peak conditions and then been bent into boudin necks and ruptured while still in the stability field of omphacitic pyroxene. The schistose layer is boudinaged and fractured (Fig. 11a). Extension is approximately parallel to the strike of the foliation, NE–SW (Fig. 10).

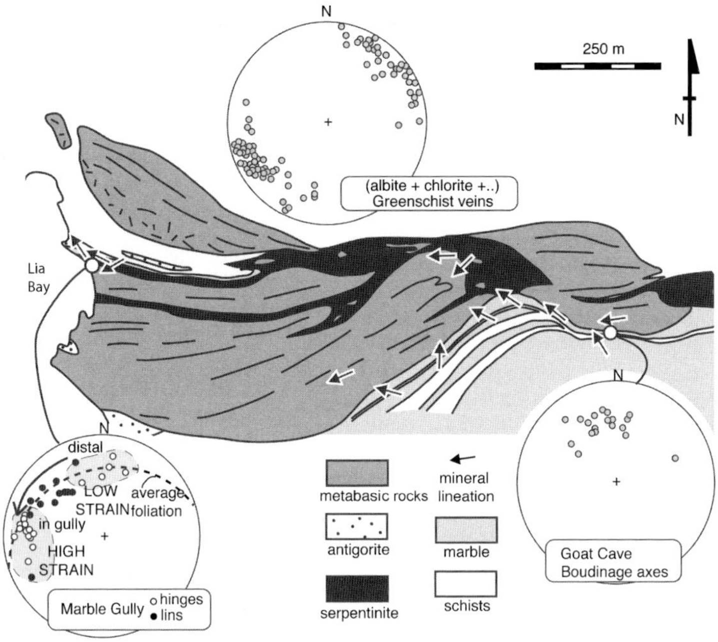

Fig. 10. Simplified geological map of the Serpentinite Belt in the Kambos–Lia Bay area, after Dixon (1969) (location shown in Fig. 2). Stereonets (lower-hemisphere equal area) summarize the main structural findings, including the reorientation of fold hinge lines and mineral lineations in the Lia Bay area as the serpentinite is approached.

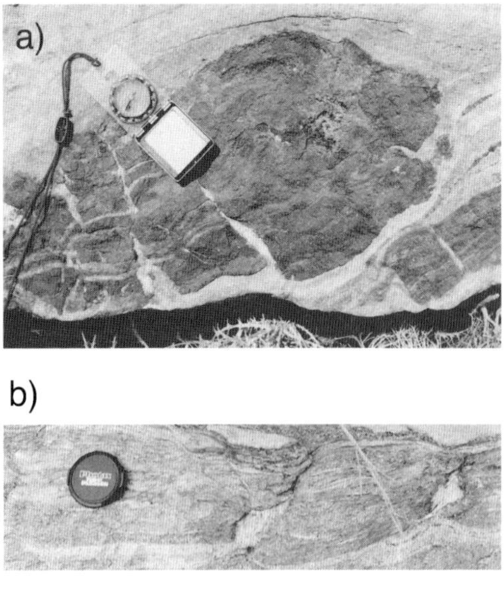

Fig. 11. Field photographs from the Kambos–Lia Bay area. (**a**) Boudinaged layer, containing epidote, sodic-pyroxene and ankerite, within a marble band. (**b**) Quartz–glaucophane shears and 'pop-aparts' in schist layer next to serpentinite.

Evidence for a link between the structures observed in the lithologies surrounding the serpentinite and the anastomosing deformation fabric in the serpentinite is seen in an adjacent schist horizon, where shear zones in the schist continue down into the serpentinite. Shear bands show top-to-the-east asymmetry. Extensional glaucophane and quartz veins are also seen in this schist horizon, accommodating extensional strain within the glaucophane stability field (Fig. 11b). Within the schist layers there is evidence for reorientation of existing structures to accommodate broadly east–west-directed extensional strain, concentrated in the serpentinite. Fold axial planes and intrafolial folds trend east–west near the contact with the serpentinite. Northwards away from the contact, fold hinge lines and lineations trend north–south and change systematically in orientation as they approach the contact. This feature is here interpreted as a progressive deformation gradient, with reorientation of fabrics towards the high-strain serpentinite zone (Fig. 10). In the metabasite boudins and schist horizons, extensional veins containing greenschist-mineral assemblages record NE–SW to east–west extension directions (Fig. 10), suggesting a continuation of the high-pressure extension direction into the greenschist-facies stability field.

Trotet *et al.* (2001) interpreted the Serpentinite Belt as a major fault zone, with a large displacement, separating the preserved HP blueschist-facies assemblages to the north from retrogressed greenschist assemblages to the south. However, there is no evidence for a sharp metamorphic contact across the belt. Structural observations in the present study suggest that both the hanging wall and footwall to the Serpentinite Belt were acting under the same deformation conditions, i.e. layer-parallel east–west oriented extension within the HP blueschist stability field and into greenschist facies, with deformation concentrated in the serpentinite. The Serpentinite Belt area shows evidence for high-pressure boudinage of marble horizons, with an east–west oriented extension direction. Mineral lineations and fold axial plane orientations are reoriented into alignment with the extension direction as the Serpentinite Belt is approached. As the area was exhumed the formation of greenschist veins in metabasite and schist horizons shows that the extension direction was kinematically the same within the greenschist-facies stability field.

Poshidonia and Nites

Throughout much of Syros the final metamorphic texture to be developed was the widespread growth of albite porphyroblasts. This textural 'event' may have served to strengthen the deforming rocks, effectively terminating strain. This late growth of albite makes the demonstration of substantial strains under greenschist facies somewhat equivocal. However, there are sites where porphyroblast growth is limited by continuing dynamic recrystallization, presumably in area of high strain rates, thereby providing unambiguous evidence for significant deformation, defined by dynamically recystallized chlorite, albite and quartz (i.e. under greenschist-facies conditions). A strongly deformed tract of greenschist-facies rock crops out on the southern edge of a serpentinite band between the villages of Finika and Poshidonia (Fig. 2). It is distinctively striped green and white on foliation surfaces and is both folded and flattened to form an L–S tectonite. Thin-section observations (Fig. 12a) revealed a fine-grained banded rock, with bands 1–2 mm wide, containing albite and chlorite and chlorite, calcite and epidote. Ductile extensional fabrics are defined by chlorite shear fabrics around albite crystals. The extensional shears are symmetrical with flattening parallel to the foliation and the extension direction. The linear fabric, defined by mineral lineations and rodded fold hinges, trends NE–SW (Fig. 12b). Albite and chlorite extensional veins occur perpendicular to the extension direction, with chlorite and albite growth from the wall rock (Fig. 12c).

Further evidence of widespread NE–SW to east–west extension throughout the Ermoupolis Unit, under greenschist-facies conditions, comes from vein arrays. Greenschist veins are common across the island and are commonly seen in boudin necks. One example is presented here, from the hillside above Nites village (location shown in Fig. 2). Here a calcite-rich layer has been boudinaged (Fig. 13). Chlorite–albite–quartz (i.e. greenschist) veins form in the boudin necks. Simple line-length measurements of vein apertures indicate 6% extension. However, the marble band has been thinned in a ductile fashion, drawn out into pods. Qualitative estimates of extension of the marble by this means are of the order of 50%.

Structural summary

The structural studies document ductile layer extension along NE–SW to east–west axes. This axial direction is defined by elongate clasts in deformed conglomerates and is perpendicular to boudin axes, extension veins and related fractures. The dominant expression of this strain is generally symmetrical layer boudinage, which occurs on scales from tens of metres (thick marble bands) down to the grain scale. Although asymmetric shear bands are found, these are concentrated along lithological boundaries and probably record local shears in zones of heterogeneous stretching. Early formed folds are strongly modified by this strain so that hinge lines trend towards parallelism with the regional stretching direction. There is no significant distinction in the deformation kinematics between structures developed under epidote blueschist conditions and those under lower burial (greenschist-facies) conditions. Consequently, it is deduced that there has been widespread distributed stretching that accompanied exhumation of the Syros blueschists. Both the strain and preservation of metamorphic history is heterogeneous over length scales of tens of metres to millimetres. There are no through-going tectonic surfaces across which there are abrupt metamorphic breaks within the Ermoupolis Unit (see Trotet *et al.* 2001). Even the major Serpentinite Belt fails to juxtapose different metamorphic units.

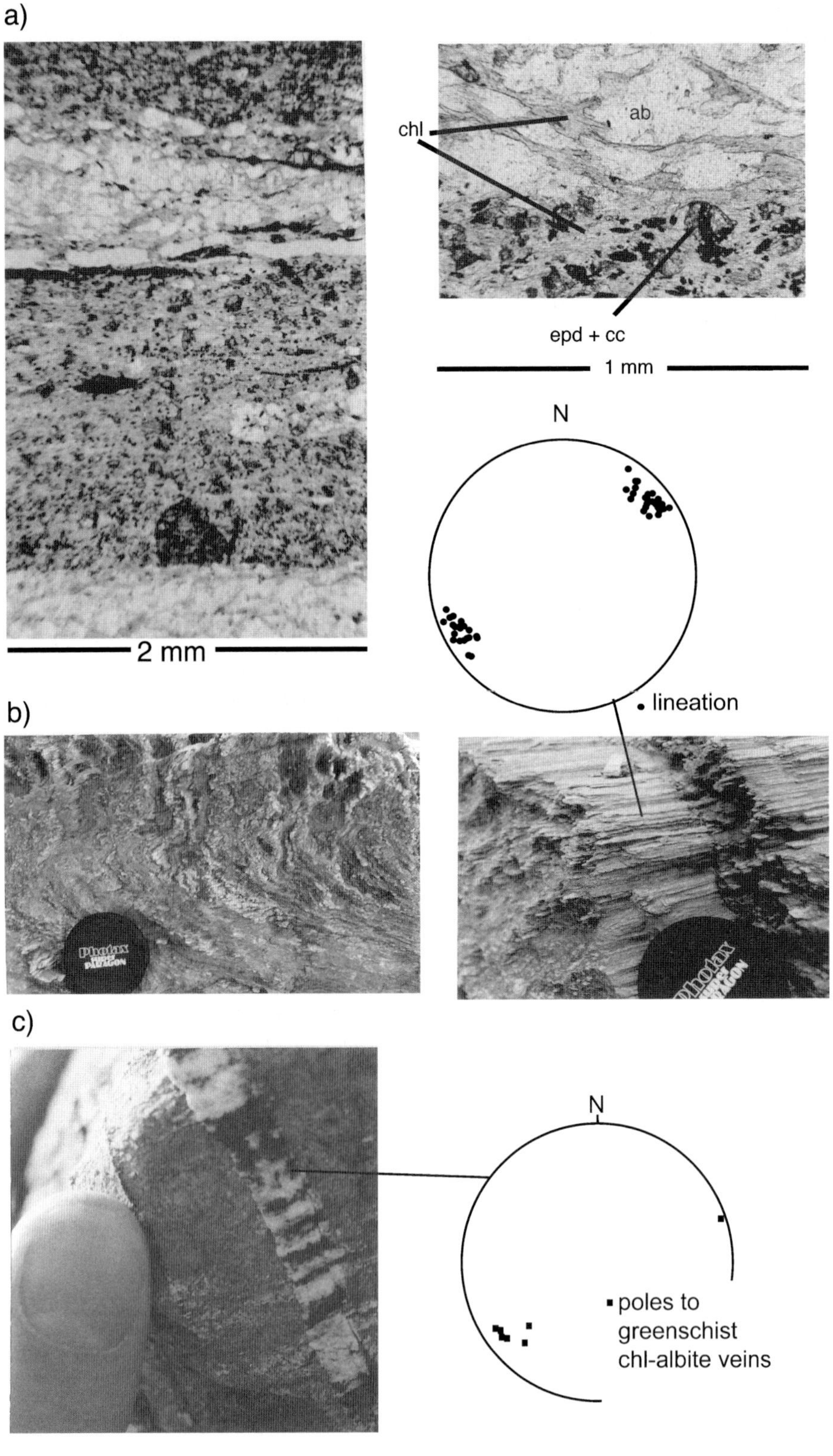
a)
chl
ab
epd + cc
1 mm
2 mm
N
• lineation
b)
c)
N
▪ poles to
greenschist
chl-albite veins

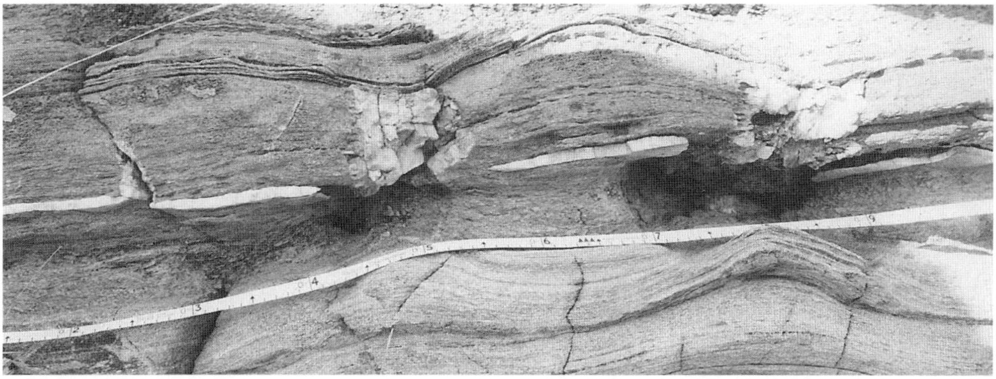

Fig. 13. Field photograph of the boudinaged layer on the Nites hillside. Greenschist minerals grow in boudin necks.

Metamorphic history of exhumation and deformation

The Attic–Cycladic blueschists are generally assumed to have been exhumed by extensional deformation processes, especially as there are insufficient detrital sediments in the area that might otherwise have recorded erosional unroofing. Consequently, the history of decompression within the blueschists offers a proxy for the tectonic thinning of the crust. The estimates of peak metamorphism for Syros range from 14 to 20 kbar. It is likely that the peak pressure conditions approached the top of this range with the growth of omphacite, preserved in metabasic units. The lower edge of the blueschist-facies stability field is dependent on the composition of blue amphibole, but could extend to pressures as low as 6 kbar, based on blue amphibole compositions from Syros, using the calibration of Evans (1990; Fig. 14). This suggests a potential decompression of 14 kbar within the blueschist-facies stability field on Syros, a significant proportion of the total decompression (a maximum of 20 kbar) during exhumation to present outcrop. Only the final part of the ductile deformation, recorded in the Ermoupolis Unit, occurred under greenschist-facies conditions.

There is a tendency to divide the tectonic history of the Attic–Cycladic belt on the basis of distinct metamorphic events (e.g. M_1 = blueschist; M_2 = greenschist; Gupta & Bickle 2004). The present case study shows that such a division is misleading as there is tectonic continuity throughout the history of decompression. A pressure–temperature–timing–deformation (*P–T–t–d*) history would help to elucidate the observations of the present study further. However, the currently available dates for the area are controversial, because of the probability of contamination with ‘excess’ radiogenic argon (e.g. Bröcker *et al.* 2004). A targeted dating study of the deformation fabrics described here would help to determine their continuity through time and to resolve the question of whether the high-pressure fabrics described in this study are part of a continuous history of layer-parallel extensional tectonics and exhumation or orogenic, their parallelism to extensional exhumation fabrics being purely coincidentally. However, it is also important to understand why the preservation of high-pressure parts of the exhumation path and the generation of high strain zones under greenschist facies is so heterogeneous.

Gupta & Bickle (2004) pointed out that the quartzofeldspathic basement rocks of the Cyclades rarely show high-pressure metamorphic assemblages but preserve older parageneses, in part because they failed to react during subduction. Gupta & Bickle reasoned that this failure and concomitant preservation of original textures, allied to an absence of subduction-related deformation, reflects a paucity of hydrous fluids during the prograde metamorphic history of the basement. A similar explanation can be applied

Fig. 12. Photographs of greenschist deformation at Poshidonia. (**a**) Thin-section photographs of layering: epidote (epd), calcite (cc) and chlorite (chl); and albite (ab) and chlorite (chl), within the deformed greenschist. Symmetrical shears are seen outlined by chlorite around albite crystals. (**b**) Field photographs of the L–S tectonite formed and the rodding of fold hinge lines. The stereonet (lower-hemisphere equal area) shows the orientation of the lineation. (**c**) Photograph of greenschist vein, growth is perpendicular to the lineation.

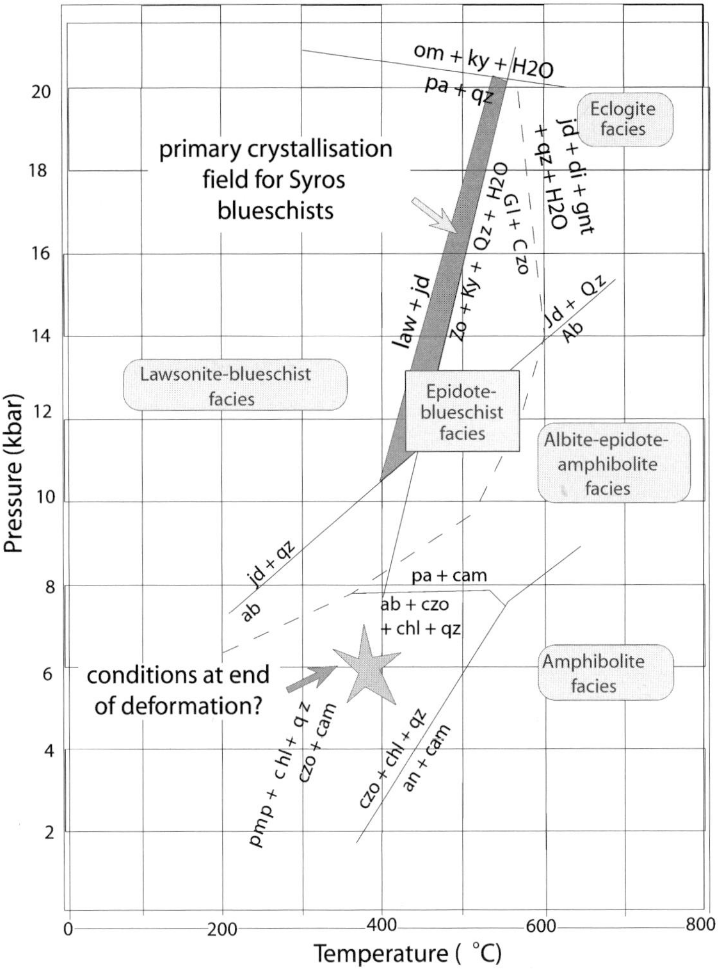

Fig. 14. Summary *P–T* diagram, after Evans (1990) showing the stability field for peak metamorphism and the conditions at the end of ductile deformation. Mineral abbreviations: om, omphacite; ky, kyanite; pa, paragonite; qz, quartz; gl, glaucophane; law, lawsonite; jd, jadeite; zois, zoisite; di, diopside; gnt, garnet; ab, albite; czo, clinozoisite; cam, calcic-amphibole; chl, chlorite; an, anorthite; pmp, pumpellyite.

to the exhumation path followed by schists and meta-igneous rocks of Syros. The growth of chloritic greenschist-facies assemblages at the expense of glaucophane blueschist-facies assemblages requires the addition of hydrous fluids (e.g. Schliestedt & Matthews 1987). Evidence for fluid-controlled retrogressive reactions on Syros are seen in blueschists as greenschist haloes around veins, at both a macro- and micro-scale. Consequently, a model is proposed here whereby the localization and progression of deformation during exhumation is limited by the availability of hydrous fluids with appropriate compositions (Fig. 15).

In this model, early exhumation can progress while the rocks are near their peak burial conditions of pressure, temperature and fluid composition. However, as horizontal extensional deformation continues, the rocks move down-pressure. Sodic amphibole in synkinematically recrystallized blueschist-facies rocks shows a tendency for compositions to alter towards the riebeckite blue amphibole end-member. Some examples also show a slight increase in Ca^{2+} composition at the edge of the blue amphibole, and a decrease in Na^{2+}, a change to calcic amphibole. As the reaction towards riebeckite is controlled by the bulk-rock Fe^{3+}/Al ratio (and to a lesser

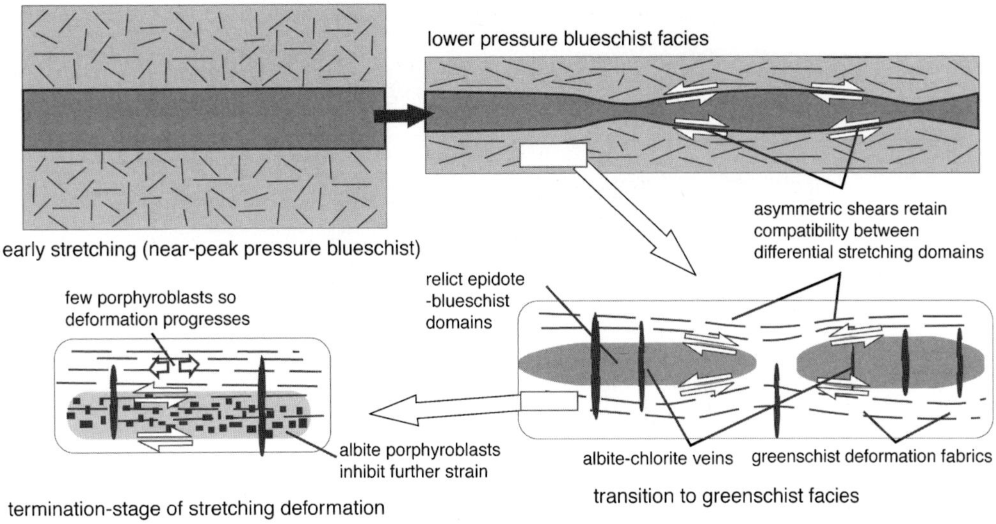

Fig. 15. Summary diagram of the structural evolution during exhumation.

extent the Fe^{2+}/Mg ratio) the ability of blue amphibole to recrystallize dynamically, will be sensitive to both fluid and bulk-rock chemistry, this may be the reason why observations of zoned glaucophane crystals are not more widely observed across Syros. Areas receiving the appropriate fluids would deform progressively down-pressure. Other areas remain essentially rigid, preserving the earlier structures intact. Fluid ingress can be limited to discrete fractures, now preserved as veins. These commonly have retrogression haloes of greenschist-facies minerals (chlorite, actinolite, albite). Although multiple cracking episodes can be identified within greenschist veins, there is no evidence for deformation localization in the greenschist haloes around veins. Only on the Delfini Peninsula does it appear that retrogressive reaction, associated with fluid infiltration, and localized deformation may be intrinsically linked. In this instance 'weaker' retrogressed greenschist layers wrap around more competent glaucophane–epidote blueschist layers that are boudinaged on a metre length scale.

In the above account the action of metamorphic reactions is to promote deformation. Of course some reactions are hardening. The growth of albite porphyroblasts at the expense of phyllosilicates is one such example. It is proposed here that porphyroblast growth has tended to pin deformation. Consequently, there are few sites (e.g. Delfini, Poshidonia) where ductile deformation has progressed after the local growth of albite porphyroblasts. The problem is that substantial secondary recrystallization (manifest as porphyroblast growth) can overprint the deformation microstructures. It is suggested here that this is part of the reason why some previous workers have undervalued the role of deformation under greenschist-facies conditions on Syros.

Discussion

The present study of structure and metamorphism of Syros reveals a kinematically linked history of ductile layer extension that accompanied the exhumation of this part of the Attic–Cycladic blueschist belt. The key conclusion is that this extension is widely distributed and, at the scale of observation, has largely symmetrical kinematics. In agreement with Rosenbaum *et al.* (2002), it was found that boudinage accommodated extension within the eclogitic-blueschist and epidote-blueschist stability fields, but it is suggested that this deformation could have played a significant role in exhumation and was not necessarily confined to deep levels in the orogenic belt. The present study showed that kinematically consistent extensional deformation was occurring during the blueschist to greenschist transition, evidenced by solid solution within boudinaged glaucophane crystals to increasingly riebeckitic compositions and the growth of actinolite into extensional fractures. Extensional greenschist veins continue the extensional regime into the greenschist-facies stability field.

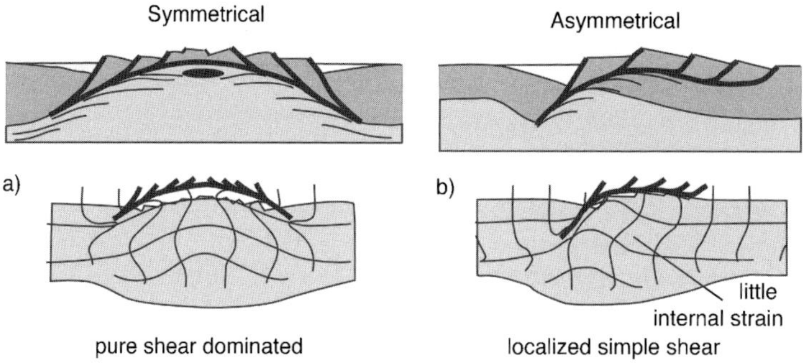

Fig. 16. Models for the extension of thickened continental crust (after Malavieille 1993).

This study also supports the observations of Keiter *et al.* (2004) that there is significant strain preserved within blueschist-facies mineral assemblages, with little modification at lower pressures and temperatures. Furthermore, there is significant boudinage and distributed layer extension that occurred within the aragonite stability field (above *c.* 12 kbar). However, much of the layer extension records the early part of the exhumation-related deformation, it retains kinematic coherence with structures developed under progressively lower-pressure conditions. Inspection of the stability field for blueschists (Fig. 14) reveals that substantial decompression can be achieved before the onset of greenschist facies and hence it is suggested that important parts of the exhumation path, and its related deformation, potentially have been misinterpreted as being burial related. This comment applies to Syros (see Keiter *et al.* 2004), possibly elsewhere within the Attic–Cycladic belt, and to other high-pressure terranes.

On a larger scale from that of Syros it appears that the crust of the Attic–Cyclades has experienced substantial vertical thinning by dominantly co-axial means. However, this strain was heterogeneously distributed in space and time, requiring local zones of non-co-axial strain, as evidenced by local zones of systematically asymmetric shear sense. The distribution of high-pressure relicts within the Ermoupolis Unit of Syros does not reflect juxtaposition by through-going major detachments but a heterogeneous metamorphic overprint through the decompression history. The sole exception to this is the tectonic contact between the Ermoupolis Unit and the tectonically overlying Vari Unit. Although this did not form part of the present study it clearly is important, potentially forming part of a detachment fault in the upper crust of the Attic–Cyclades (e.g. Lister *et al.* 1984). Despite the observations of the present study clearly suggesting that significant amounts of layer-parallel extension accommodated exhumation, the wider context of these observations and their relation to large-scale detachment structures in the region is obviously important.

Malavieille (1993) proposed two end-member models for the stretching of previously thickened continental crust (Fig. 16). In his symmetrical model (Fig. 16a) upper crustal faulting passes down, via a zone of detachment, into a wide zone of broadly subhorizontal, pure-shear stretching. This geometry contrasts with Malavieille's asymmetric model (Fig. 16b) where upper crustal faults combine onto a single master detachment that passes downwards onto a simple shear zone, deeper in the crust. In this case the deeper crust is largely undeformed. As Ring & Reischmann (2002) pointed out, with reference to Aegean blueschists, asymmetric models with low-angle detachments require very high fault slip rates to exhume high-pressure rocks faster than they can heat up. If strain through the crust is distributed more widely (Fig. 16a) then individual parts of the structure need only accommodate moderate strain rates. In any event, it is 'symmetrical', pure-shear-dominated configuration (Malavieille 1993; Fig. 16b) that provides a better description of the crustal-scale deformation.

Assuming constant density for the now-removed overburden and kilometre-scale homogeneous stretching of a ductile crust beneath a fault-dominated upper crust (e.g. Fig. 16a), the decompression history of the Ermoupolis Unit (Fig. 15) may be used to deduce the strain history of the crust. A stretching factor (β) of 3.3 is needed to deliver the total potential exhumation (from 20 kbar to 6 kbar). Of this, about 40% of the exhumation happened within the aragonite stability field ($c > 12$ kbar; Keiter *et al.* 2004). Much of the rest of the extension occurred under general epidote blueschist-facies conditions; only the last 30% crustal extension needed to have occurred under greenschist-facies metamorphism. Clearly, pure-shear extension alone cannot have brought the Syros rocks to the surface (without infinite strain). Presumably, much of the last 6 kbar of overburden pressure was removed by localized extensional faulting. In this study the low-angle detachments within the Attic–Cycladic belt are shown to be the transition zone between distributed ductile stretching at depth and upper crustal faulting. A complete understanding of the modes of crustal extension requires knowledge both of the faults and of the ductile crust below.

This study forms part of the PhD researches of C.E.B., supervised by J. E. Dixon and M. B. Holness in Edinburgh. A Natural Environment Research Council studentship is acknowledged. We thank S. Reddy and S. Mazzoli for thought-provoking reviews, although the authors take full responsibility for the views expressed here. The use of structural approaches and the relationship to crustal-scale processes were inspired by the insightful studies of continental extensional tectonics by Mike Coward. Mike never worked in the Aegean but would have enjoyed the sea food!

Mineral abbreviations

Gl, glaucophane and all blue amphibole, unless specifically expressed; Rieb, riebeckite; Epd, epidote-group minerals; Qz, quartz; Act, actinolite; Ab, albite; Chl, chlorite; Mt, magnetite; Hem, hematite; SS, solid solution.

References

BARNICOAT, A. C. 1988. The mechanisms of veining and retrograde alteration of alpine eclogites. *Journal of Metamorphic Geology*, **6**, 545–558.

BONNEAU, M. 1984. Correlation of the Hellenide nappes in the south-east Aegean and their tectonic reconstruction. *In*: DIXON, J. E. & ROBERTSON, A. H. F. (eds) *The Geological Evolution of the Eastern Mediterranean.* Geological Society, London. Special Publications, **17**, 517–527.

BONNEAU, M., BLAKE M. C., GEYSSANT, J., KIENAST, J. R., LEPVRIER, C., MALUSKI, H. & PAPANIKOLAOU, D. 1980. Tectonic significance of the blueschist units of the Cycladic belt (Hellenides, Greece) – The example of the island of Syros. *Comptes Rendus Hebdomadairies des séances de l academie des sciences serie D 290*, 23, 1463–1466.

BRÖCKER, M. & ENDERS, M. 1999. U–Pb zircon geochronology of unusual eclogite-facies rocks from Syros and Tinos (Cyclades, Greece). *Geological Magazine*, **136**, 111–118.

BRÖCKER, M., BIELING, D., HACKER, B. & GANS, P. 2004. High-Si phengite records the time of greenschist facies overprinting: implications for models suggesting mega-detachments in the Aegean Sea. *Journal of Metamorphic Geology*, **22**, 427–442.

BROWN, E. H. 1974. Comparison of the mineralogy and phase relations of blueschists for the North Cascades, Washington and greenschists from Otago, New Zealand. *Geological Society of America Bulletin*, **85**, 333–344.

COWARD, M. P. 1986. Heterogeneous stretching, simple shear and basin development. *Earth and Planetary Science Letters*, **80**, 325–336.

DIXON, J. E. 1969. *The metamorphic rocks of Syros, Greece*. PhD thesis, University of Cambridge.

DIXON, J. E. 1976. Glaucophane schists of Syros, Greece. *Bulletin de la Societé Géologique de France*, **7**, 280.

DIXON, J. E., FEENSTRA, A., JANSEN, J. B. H., KREULEN, R., RIDLEY, J., SALEMINK, J. & SCHUILING, R. D. 1987. Excursion guide to the field trip on Seriphos, Syros and Naxos. *In*: HELGESON, H. C. (ed.) *Chemical Transport in Metasomatic Processes*. NATO ASI Series, **218**, 467–518.

EVANS, B. W. 1990. Phase relations of epidote-blueschist. *Lithos*, **25**, 3–23.

GANOR, J., MATTHEWS, A. & PALDOR, N. 1989. Constraints on effective diffusivity during oxygen isotope exchange at a marble–schist contact, Sifnos (Cyclades), Greece. *Earth and Planetary Science Letters*, **94**, 208–216.

GAUTIER, P., BRUN, J-P. & JOLIVET, L. 1993. Structure and kinematics of upper Cenozoic extensional detachment on Naxos and Paros (Cyclades Islands, Greece). *Tectonics*, **12**, 1180–1194.

GUPTA, S. & BICKLE, M. J. 2004. Ductile shearing, hydrous fluid channeling and high-pressure metamorphism along the basement–cover contact on Sikinos, Cyclades, Greece. *In*: ALSOP, G. I., HOLDSWORTH, R. E., MCCAFFREY, K. J. W. & HAND, M. (eds) *Flow Processes in Faults and Shear Zones.* Geological Society, London, Special Publications, **224**, 161–175.

JOLIVET, L., GOFFÉ, B., BOUSQUET, R., OBERHANSLI, R. & MICHARD, A. 1998. Detachments in high-pressure mountain belts, Tethyan examples. *Earth and Planetary Science Letters*, **160**, 31–47.

KEITER, M., PIEPJOHN, K., BALLHAUS, C., LAGOS, M. & BODE, M. 2004. Structural development of high-pressure metamorphic rocks on Syros island (Cyclades, Greece). *Journal of Structural Geology*, **26**, 1433–1455.

LIOU, J. G., MARUYANA, S. & CHO, S. 1987. Very low-grade metamorphism of volcanic and volcaniclastic rocks: mineral assemblages and mineral facies. *In*: FREY, M. (ed.) *Low Temperature Metamorphism.* Blackie, Glasgow, 59–113.

LISTER, G. S., BANGA, G. & FEENSTRA, A. 1984. Metamorphic core complexes of Cordilleran type in the Cyclades, Aegean Sea, Greece. *Geology*, **12**, 221–225.

MALAVIEILLE, J. 1993. Late orogenic extension in mountain belts: insights from the Basin and Range and the late Palaeozoic Variscan belt. *Tectonics*, **12**, 1115–1130.

MARUYAMA, S., CHO, M. & LIOU, J. G. 1986. Experimental investigations of blueschist–greenschist transition equilibria: pressure dependence of Al_2O_3

contents in sodic amphiboles—a new geobarometer. In: Evans, B. W. & Brown, E. H. (eds) *Blueschists and Eclogites*. Geological Society of America Memoirs, **164**, 1–16.

McKenzie, D. P. 1978. Some remarks on the development of sedimentary basins. *Earth and Planetary Science Letters*, **40**, 25–32.

Okrusch, M. & Bröcker, M. 1990. Eclogite associated with high-grade blueschists in the Cyclades archipelago, Greece; a review. *European Journal of Mineralogy*, **2**, 451–478.

Ridley, J. R. 1982. Arcuate lineation trends in a deep level ductile thrust belt, Syros, Greece. *Tectonophysics*, **88**, 347–360.

Ring, U. & Reischmann, T. 2002. The weak and superfast Cretan detachment, Greece: exhumation at subduction rates in extruding wedges. *Journal of the Geological Society, London*, **159**, 225–228.

Roberts, A. M. & Yielding, G. 1992. Continental extension tectonics. *In*: Hancock, P. L. (ed.) *Continental Deformation*. Pergamon, Oxford, 223–250.

Rosenbaum, G., Avigad, D. & Sanchez-Gomez, M. 2002. Coaxial flattening at deep levels of orogenic belts: evidence from blueschists and eclogites on Syros and Sifos (Cyclades, Greece). *Journal of Structural Geology*, **24**, 1451–1462.

Schiestedt, M. & Matthews, A. 1987. Transformation of blueschist to greenschist facies rocks as a consequence of fluid infiltration, Sifnos (Cyclades), Greece. *Contributions to Mineralogy and Petrology*, **97**, 237–250.

Trotet, F., Jolivet, L. & Vidal, O. 2001. Tectono-metamorphic evolution of Syros and Sifnos islands (Cyclades, Greece). *Tectonophysics*, **338**, 179–206.

Watkins, K. P. 1983. Petrogenesis of Dalradian albite porphyroblast schist. *Journal of the Geological Society, London*, **140**, 601–618.

Wernicke, B. 1985. Uniform normal-sense simple shear of the continental lithosphere. *Canadian Journal of Earth Sciences*, **22**, 108–125.

Geometry and evolution of the Mesoproterozoic Irumide Belt of Zambia

MICHAEL C. DALY

BP Exploration, St James's Square, London SW1Y 4PD, UK (e-mail: dalym@bp.com)

Abstract: The Irumide Belt of eastern Zambia is one of a number of complex Proterozoic orogenic belts found in the African continent. The belt lies along the southeastern flank of the Tanzania–Bangweulu Craton and to the NW of the Mozambique Belt of East Africa. The dominant tectonic features of the belt are ductile shear zones, thrusts and folds related to a Mesoproterozoic, NW–SE crustal shortening event, and late-tectonic granite emplacement. Later tightening of Irumide structures and localized deformation of granites is also widespread. The timing of post-Irumide deformation is poorly constrained but is believed to be a mix of Pan–African and Late Palaeozoic reactivation and thermal reworking. This complex history is recently overprinted by significant Tertiary rifting. The Irumide deformation is evident in three tectonic zones stretching from the NW foreland of Mporokoso to the SE hinterland of Lundazi: (1) the NW-facing basement shear zones and associated cover deformation of the Luongo Fold Belt; (2) the Foreland Fold Belt of large upright folds defined by the kilometre-thick quartzite ridges of the Irumi, Shiwa Ngandu and Isoka hills; (3) an intensely deformed Internal Zone of basement and granite gneisses folded into major domes and associated tight synclines. Post-tectonic granites intrude the last of these zones and define an end to the Irumide deformation. The linking of these three zones is based on geometric, kinematic and geochronological evidence. The main Irumide deformation and metamorphism is believed to have occurred between 1100–950 Ma with a metamorphic peak between 1050 and 1000 Ma. Termination of Irumide deformation is dated by the emplacement of the post-tectonic granite and K/Ar biotite and hornblende closure dates of *c.* 950 Ma. Similar K/Ar dates from the Luongo shear zone indicate biotite closure and cooling during the period 1020–950 Ma. Together with parallel kinematic indicators, this supports a coeval development and tectonic link between the Irumide Belt and the Luongo Fold Belt. The intracontinental Irumide Belt deformation was driven by an accretionary collisional margin, to the SE of the present-day Irumide Belt, in southern Malawi and Mozambique. This accretionary margin is today represented by arc and island-arc magmatism and the complex terranes of the Mozambique Belt of East Central Africa.

The tectonic evolution of the Irumide Belt was originally discussed by Ackermann (1950, 1960), who described a major zone of vertical structures in the hinterland of the orogen. Fitches (1971), working in the northern part of the Irumide Belt, also focused on the vertical character of Irumide deformation. These observations were used by Shackleton (1973) and Kroner (1977) to support the contention that the Irumide Belt was formed through orogenic processes characterized by vertical tectonics involving minimal shortening.

Over the last 30 years a comprehensive mapping campaign of the Irumide Belt has been conducted by the Geological Survey of Zambia. This work has described much of the detailed stratigraphy and structure of the Belt. On the basis of this mapping, Daly (1986*a*,*b*) interpreted the tectonic and thermal evolution of the Irumide Belt to be characterized by closure of a marine basin through NW–SE shortening. This deformation is expressed as NW-directed thrusts and shear zones, SE-directed back-thrusts and late-orogenic granite emplacement. Ackermann's (1960) zone of vertical structure separates the dominantly NW-facing structures from SE facing structures and has been mapped as a zone of structural divergence running the length of the orogen (Fig. 1).

On the basis of U/Pb, K/Ar and Ar/Ar dates (Daly 1986a), late-tectonic granite emplacement and biotite closure occurred between 1020 and 950 Ma. The major Irumide deformation and coeval metamorphism was therefore interpreted to have occurred in the period 1100–950 Ma (Daly 1986*a*). Shenk & Appel (2001) and De Waele *et al.* (2003), on the basis of U–Pb ages, defined a more precise 1050–1000 Ma range for Irumide metamorphism. Johnson *et al.* (2005) supported this timing, on the basis of a comprehensive review of the U–Pb zircon database of Central Africa.

Daly (1986*a*,*b*) interpreted the Irumide Orogeny as closure of a continental marine basin as a result of accretionary, collisional tectonics occurring at a plate margin to the SE of the present-day Irumide Belt (Fig. 1). Johnson *et al.*

From: Ries, A. C., Butler, R. W. H. & Graham, R. H. (eds) 2007. *Deformation of the Continental Crust: The Legacy of Mike Coward.* Geological Society, London, Special Publications, **272**, 223–230.

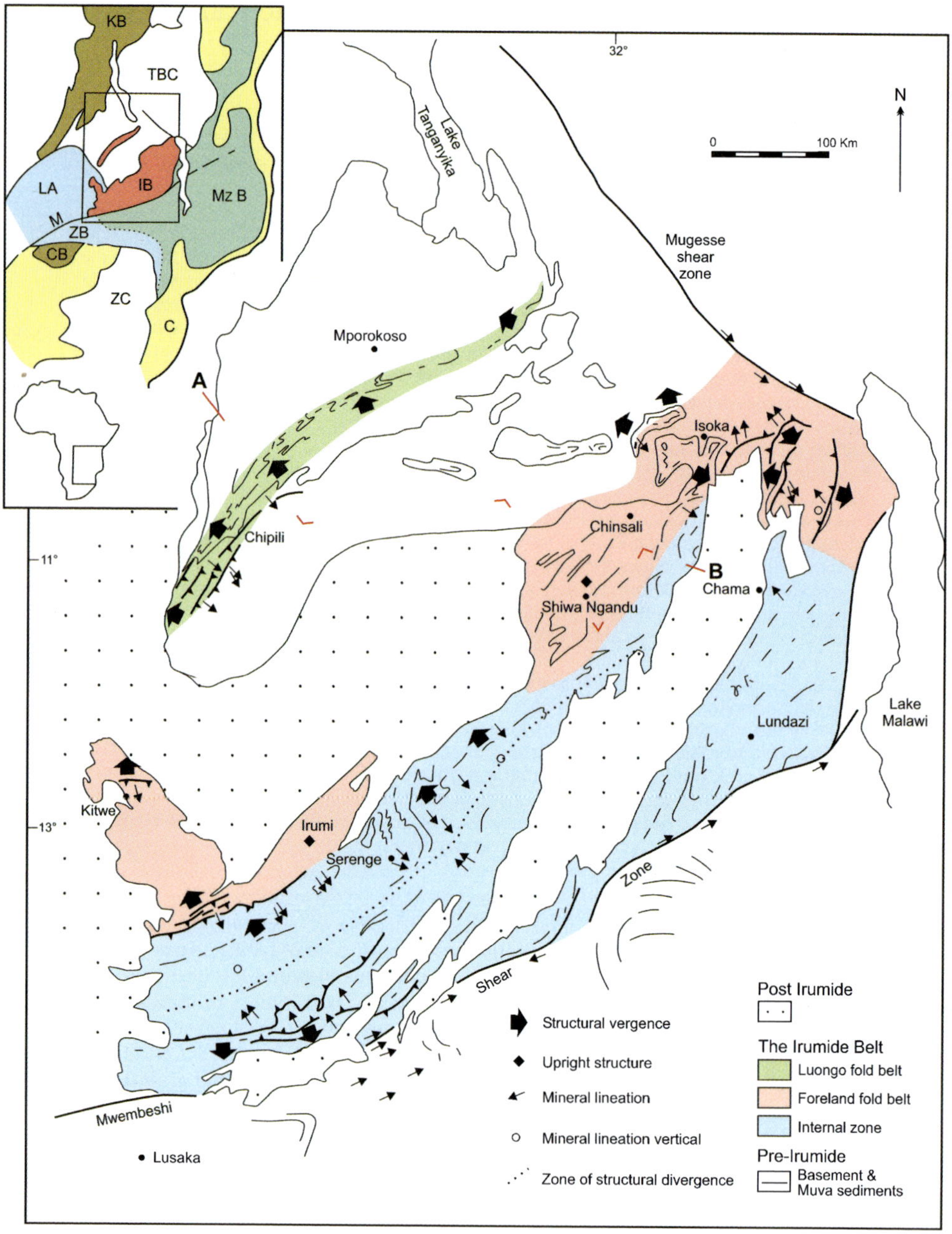

Fig. 1. Tectonic map of northern Zambia showing the location and geometry of the Irumide tectonic zones described in the text: the Luongo Fold Belt, the Foreland Fold Belt and the Internal Zone. Also shown are selected field observations of structural vergence and mineral lineation, highlighting the regional consistency of these kinematic indicators. The zone of vertical structure, described by Ackermann (1950, 1960), is shown as a zone of structural divergence across which the sense of structural vergence changes. Also, the different ENE lineation orientation associated with the Mwembeshi shear zone and its easterly extension should be noted. This is believed to be related to Lufilian Arc and Zambezi Belt deformation, overprinting Irumide structures (Coward & Daly 1983; Daly 1986c). The inset map shows the location of the Irumide Belt in Central Africa, on the southeastern flank of the Tanzanian–Bangweulu Craton and the northwestern margin of the Mozambique Belt. IB, Irumide Belt; TBC, Tanzania–Bangweulu Craton (including the Ubendian Belt); MzB, Mozambique Belt; KB, Kibaran Belt; LA, Lufilian Arc; ZB, Zambezi Belt; CB, Choma Kilomo Block; ZC, Zimbabwe Craton; M, Mwembeshi Zone; C, Cover Rocks.

(2005) supported this interpretation, postulating a series of terrane accretions to the SE of the Mwembeshi Shear Zone (Fig. 1). The Mesoproterozoic collision of these terranes formed the southern Mozambique Belt and drove the continental deformation that resulted in the Irumide tectonics described in this paper.

The subsequent evolution of the Irumide Belt was dominated by the Pan-African Zambezi and Lufilian deformational events. Coward & Daly (1984) put these in a plate tectonic context. They postulated a major Pan-African collisional boundary to the south of the Irumide Belt, between the Zimbabwe–Kaapvaal Craton and the Congo (Tanzania-Bangweulu) Craton, along the Damaran–Lufilian–Zambezi belts. Deformation and metamorphism, associated with these Pan-African belts, is in part overprinted and reworked the earlier Irumide structure.

Irumide tectonic framework

The geometry and kinematics of Irumide tectonics are manifest in three distinct tectonic zones. All three zones contain sediments and metasediments of the Palaeoproterozoic Muva Supergroup (Daly & Unrug 1982), deposited throughout central and northern Zambia. Muva Supergroup sediments are preserved as two distinct basins, the Mporokoso Basin to the NW, and the Irumide Basin to the SE, with scattered, isolated outliers between them (Fig. 1). These basins were developed above granites and volcanic rocks of the Bangweulu Block and on the southeastern flank of the Tanzania–Bangweulu Craton (present-day coordinates).

The Muva Supergroup deposition has been dated at *c.* 1880 Ma (De Waele & Fitzsimmons 2004) and it comprises the quartzite-dominated, post-Eburnian, pre-Irumide sedimentary rocks of central and northern Zambia. Detrital zircon studies (Fitzsimmons & Hulscher 2005) indicate an origin for the Muva sediments from the Congo Craton, with a provenance age spectrum ranging from 3000 to 1800 Ma.

The sediments of the Mporokoso Basin are dominantly fluviatile (Unrug 1982). They are separated from the main Irumide Belt by undeformed basement. The Irumide Basin is characterized by a southeastward progression from craton to basin of fluvio-marine to marine sediments (Daly & Unrug 1982).

The closure, deformation and metamorphism of the Irumide Basin and coeval deformation of the Mporokoso Basin are defined as the Irumide Orogeny. The kilometre thick quartzites, characteristic of the Muva Supergroup, define the trends of the dominant Irumide structures and also show the impact of late-tectonic Irumide granite emplacement. These structures, their geometry, kinematics and age, are discussed in three major zones below.

The Luongo Fold Belt: basement–cover relationships and timing

The Luongo Fold Belt (Fig. 1) comprises an arcuate basement shear zone and folded quartzite cover rocks of the Mporokoso Group (Daly 1986a). The fold belt is separated from the main Irumide Belt by the largely undeformed granites of the Bangweulu Block basement.

The basement shear zone and folded belt are best developed in the south, near Mansa (Thieme 1970) and Chipili, where sheared, mylonitic volcanic rocks can be traced laterally and vertically into sheared, mylonitic quartzite of the Mporokoso Group (Daly 1986*a*). The deformed sediments at the southeasterly basement–Mporokoso Group contact are strongly overturned to the NW and have a well-developed, SE-plunging, quartz stretching fabric (Fig. 1). Elsewhere, away from the basement–cover shear zone, this relationship is a marked subhorizontal unconformity, occasionally marked by conglomerate.

Where intensely deformed, both the basement granites and volcanic rocks are characterized by a SE-plunging extension lineation. Above, and to the NW of this basement shear zone, the overlying Mporokoso Group quartzites are folded and thrust and occasionally overturned to the NW or NNW. These observations indicate that the Luongo Fold Belt originated from NW-directed basement displacement climbing into the sedimentary cover.

The timing of the NW-directed displacement and shear zone formation is constrained by dates derived from biotites in deformed basement granites and volcanic rocks. The biotites from the shear zones yield K/Ar dates of *c.* 1000 Ma, whereas biotites from undeformed basement yield dates of 1850 Ma (Daly 1986*a*). The latter dates are in line with the estimated age of the granites themselves (Brewer *et al.* 1979).

The Foreland Fold Belt: Irumi, Shiwa Ngandu and Isoka

The Irumide Belt is separated from the Luongo folds by an area of undeformed to weakly deformed, Eburnian-age basement of Bangweulu granites, volcanic rocks and overlying, subhorizontal Muva Supergroup sediments. This undeformed foreland passes southeastwards into the Foreland Fold Belt of Muva sediments, defined by major ridges of folded quartzite. This folded zone is developed in the Irumi Hills in the south and the Shiwa Ngandu and Isoka areas in the northern Irumide Belt. The quartzites define spectacular upright folds, traceable for tens of kilometres.

This foreland structure is best developed in the Shiwa Ngandu area (Fig. 1). The folds are dominantly large scale, upright, box-like structures with steep to vertical, intensely deformed limbs. Although basement structuring may be influential in the formation of these huge structures, no basement is exposed within the fold belt. The absence of basement exposure led Daly (1986a) to interpret the fold belt as having developed above a major detachment surface of pelitic sediments. However, at the margin of this foreland belt, at Isoka (Fig. 1), the structures clearly follow major basement-involved folds and thrusts. From this it is concluded that both detachment- and basement-rooted deformational processes are active along the foreland of the belt.

The quartzite-dominated sediments of the foreland folds pass southeastwards into the high-grade metamorphic Irumide hinterland. The hinterland is characterized by intensely deformed basement gneisses and granites and remnant, highly recrystallized, quartzites and metapelites.

Direct dating of the deformation of the Foreland Fold Belt has not been achieved. The sediments and folds post-date the *c.* 1880 Ma deposition of the Muva Supergroup (De Waele & Fitzsimmons 2004) and its Eburnian basement. An interbedded rhyolite has been dated at 1820 Ma (De Waele *et al.* 2003). The main trend of the structures is cut by the late-tectonic Irumide granites.

The Irumide Internal Zone: sheared gneisses and quartzites

The Irumide Belt Internal Zone is characterized by intensely deformed and metamorphosed basement gneisses and granites with well-developed L/S mineral fabrics. These basement rocks are interleaved with quartzites believed to be a high-grade part of the Muva Supergroup of the foreland. Together they are folded into large domal structures with steep flanks. The domes in turn are intruded by late-tectonic granite. Figure 2a is a cartoon showing the evolution of this structural relationship. The field expression is shown in the sketch map of the Mutangoshi Dome (Daly 1995) from the northern Irumide Belt (Fig. 2b).

The gneissic fabric and mineral lineation are interpreted as a product of simple shear during a thrust event that deformed and interleaved the basement with the cover of the Muva sediments (Fig. 2a). The linear fabrics associated with this deformation have a dominantly NW–SE trend regionally, and can be seen to be clearly folded by later, broad fold structures with tight synclines. This relationship is well displayed in the Mutangoshi Dome where a gneissic L/S deformation fabric is folded across the domal axis (Fig. 2b).

The kinematics of this deformation was driven by NW-directed ductile displacement of the basement and associated cover. Extension lineations throughout the belt indicate that this ductile deformation had an approximately NW–SE-directed tectonic transport direction, which is compatible with the kinematics of the Luongo and Foreland Fold Belts.

High-temperature, low-pressure metamorphism was coeval with the Irumide deformation (Daly 1986*a*). The metamorphism has yielded U–Pb ages of 1046 ± 3 Ma (Schenk & Appel 2001) and 1020 ± 7 Ma (De Waele *et al.* 2004).

The Irumide Granites; a late-tectonic event

Late-tectonic granite emplacement characterizes the Internal Zone of the northern Irumide Belt. The granites cut the intense gneissic metamorphic fabrics discussed above and invade the quartzites. They are interpreted to mark the end of the major 'Irumide' deformation. Post-granite deformation is localized and characterized by steep NE- to ENE-trending shear zones believed to represent Pan-African lateral displacements (Daly 1986*a*).

U/Pb zircon analysis (Daly 1986a) dated the late-orogenic granite emplacement at 970 Ma. This interpretation has been supported by the work of De Waele *et al.* (2003, 2004*b*) based on their sensitive high-resolution ion microprobe data on zircons. In further support of a *c.* 970 Ma end to Irumide tectonics, K–Ar and Ar/Ar closure dates from granites and basement gneisses within the Irumide Belt indicate that the Irumide Belt had cooled to below 300 °C by 1000–950 Ma (Daly 1986*a*).

The age of the Irumide Orogeny

Cahen *et al.* (1984) argued that the Irumide metamorphism occurred at 1355 ± 28 Ma. However, Daly (1986*a*), on the basis of the U/Pb date on zircons from a late-orogenic granite, and an orogenic transect of K/Ar dates (Fig. 3), concluded that the Irumide deformation and associated metamorphism was significantly younger, in the range 1100–1000 Ma.

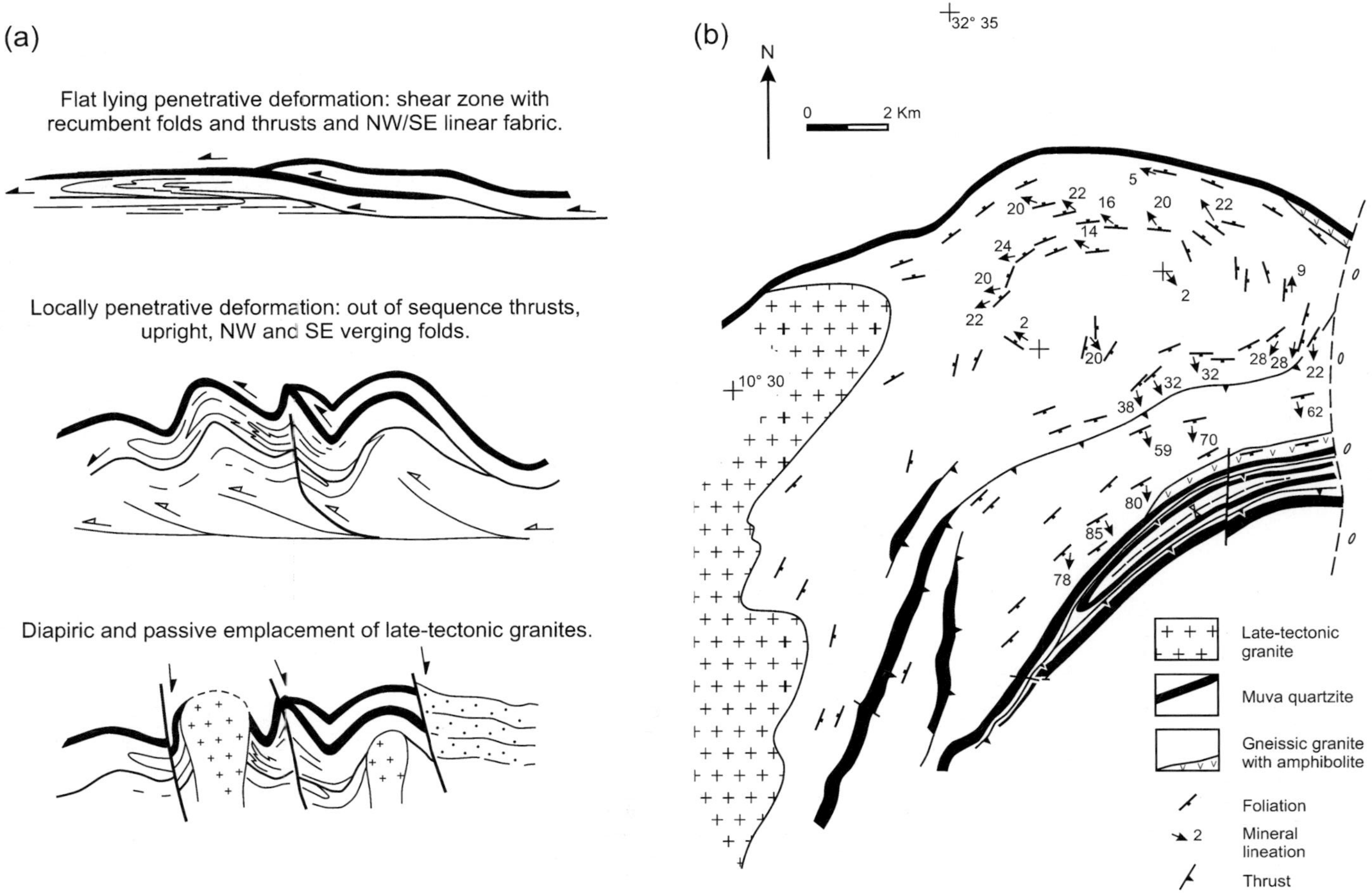

Fig. 2. (**a**) Schematic summary of the Irumide structural sequence showing basement–cover thrusting placing Irumide deformed basement gneisses over Muva quartzites and metasediments, subsequent folding of the thrust sequence, and late-tectonic granite emplacement. (**b**) Map of the Mutangoshi Dome showing the same features: intensely deformed granite gneisses, imbricated Muva quartzite within the gneiss and the tight marginal syncline of Muva quartzite defining the southern margin to the dome. The strong L/S fabric in the gneissic granite shows the mineral lineation to be clearly folded around the domal structure.

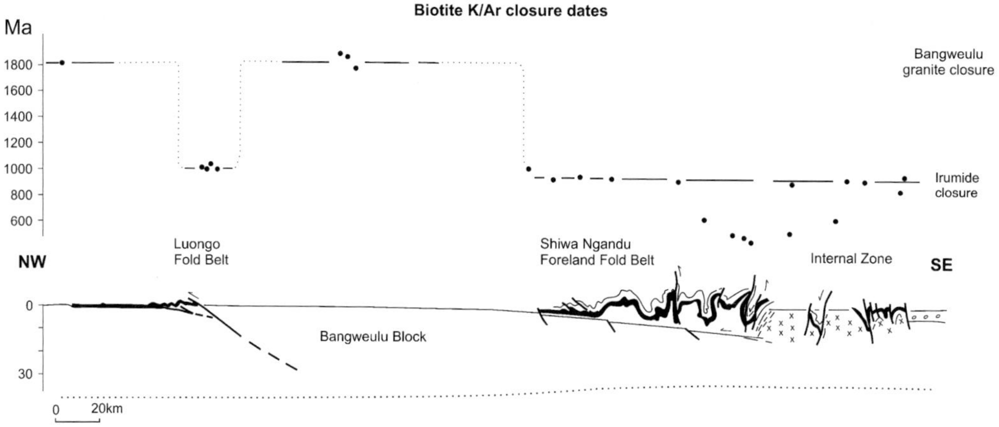

Fig. 3. A composite sketch cross-section of the northern Irumide Belt showing the Bangweulu Craton, the basement-rooted thrusts generating the Luongo Fold Belt, the large upright fold structures of the Foreland Fold Belt of the Shiwa Ngandu area, and the Internal Zone intensely intruded by granite. The approximate line of section is shown as A-B in Figure 1. Above the section, K/Ar closure dates are shown projected onto the line of section (after Daly 1986a). The closure dates, recording cooling below *c.* 300 °C, show three distinct distributions, one correlating with the *c.* 1800 Ma cooling of the Bangweulu Block granites and volcanic rocks; a second correlating with the *c.* 1000–950 Ma cooling of the Luongo metamorphism and Irumide metamorphism and late-tectonic granite emplacement. The third distribution of dates *c.* 600 Ma is interpreted to represent the Pan-African thermal reworking of the area.

On the basis of K/Ar closure dates, Daly (1986*a*) concluded that post-orogenic cooling was widely established by *c.* 950 Ma. Biotite K/Ar dates from the Luongo basement shear zone of *c.* 1000 Ma were also taken to support a broadly coeval post-deformational cooling. De Waele *et al.* (2003, 2004) and Johnson *et al.* (2005), on the basis of their precise dating methodology, came to similar conclusions. They concluded that peak Irumide metamorphism was *c.* 1020 Ma, associated with widespread late-tectonic magmatism in the period 1050–950 Ma.

A schematic tectonic cross-section through the northern Irumide Belt is shown in Figure 3 with the K/Ar closure dates from biotite superimposed (Daly 1986*a*). The figure defines distinct distributions of closure dates at *c.* 1800 Ma; *c.* 1020–950 Ma and *c.* 600 Ma. These distributions define the date at which biotite cooled below *c.* 300 °C along the line of section.

The distribution at *c.* 1800 Ma represents the closure dates of the Bangweulu Granite and volcanic rocks that are the basement to the Muva sediments and, in part, protolith to reworked Irumide gneisses. The second distribution at *c.* 1000–950 Ma, represents closure dates associated with cooling post-Irumide deformation, metamorphism and late-tectonic granite emplacement. The similarity of closure ages and kinematics between the Luongo and Irumide deformation links them chronologically and tectonically (Fig. 1 & 3). The younger distribution of dates, of *c.* 600 Ma, is interpreted to represent Ar loss as a result of later Pan-African and Late Palaeozoic thermal reworking.

Conclusions

This review of the Irumide Belt describes the geometry, kinematics and timing of a period of Mesoproterozoic tectonic activity in Central Africa. The deformation is recorded in basement and in the folded and thrust sediments of the Muva Supergroup. These mature quartzite-dominated sediments were deposited over a large area of the southeastern flank of the Bangweulu–Tanzania Craton and characterize the pre-Irumide Muva Basin. Today they occur as the distinct Mporokoso and Irumide basins.

The intense Irumide deformation was a result of NW–SE shortening and basin closure. Folds and thrusts dominantly verge to the NW in the Foreland and northwestern Internal Zone. The core of the belt is characterized by steep upright structures, whilst to the SE of this the structural vergence is dominantly southeasterly. The zone of structural divergence, where vergence switches, can be mapped the length of the orogen.

The timing of this intense Irumide deformation is constrained to a metamorphic peak in the range 1050–1000 Ma. Late-tectonic granite emplacement occurred between 1050–950 Ma. Metamorphic cooling and K–Ar closure of biotite occurred regionally in the period 1020–950 Ma. The precise impact of the later Pan-African event (Kennedy 1964) and Late Palaeozoic and Tertiary rifting episodes remains uncertain.

These observations and interpretations indicate that the Irumide Belt represents the dramatic deformation and closure of a Paleoproterozoic marine basin developed along the flank of the Tanzania–Bangweulu Craton. This deformation had crustal-scale impact that extended many kilometres into the cratonic foreland in the form of the Luongo shear zone and folds. Both basement and cover were involved in the Irumide deformation and, to a large degree, the pre-existing basin structure dictated the orogenic geometry that is today the Irumide Belt. The Irumide deformation was succeeded by a late-tectonic granite emplacement event, particularly in the northern Irumide Belt. Driving this deformation was an accretionary plate margin located to the SE (present-day coordinates) of the Irumide belt in the Mozambique Belt of Malawi and Mozambique.

Subsequent structural and thermal reworking of the Irumide Belt occurred during the Zambezi and Lufilian Pan-African orogenic events. In addition, Late Palaeozoic and Tertiary rift events further modified the Irumide Belt.

My generalities on the evolution of the Irumide Belt strive for the clarity Mike Coward brought to thinking about African tectonics. They are based on a multitude of field observations, collected during many miles of foot safaris in the Muchinga Mountains and High Plateau of Zambia. Together with imperfect isotope and mineral analyses they are a basic geological foundation for an understanding of the evolution of the Irumide Belt; an essential database for any geological and tectonic interpretation. Mike's gift, which he shared with all who were committed to geometric rigour based on direct field observation, was to make geology and tectonics inspiringly simple to understand, coherent in the largest frames, and constantly progressing. The author would like to acknowledge the two referees whose comments helped to considerably improve this manuscript, and BP Plc, which supported the production of the figures.

References

ACKERMANN, E. 1950. Ein neuer Faltengurtel in Nordrhodesien und seine tektonische Stellung im afrikanischen Grundgebirge. *Geologisches Rundschau*, **38**, 24–39.

ACKERMANN, E. 1960. Strukturen im Untergrundeines intrakratonischen Doppelorogens (Irumidien Nordrhodesien). *Geologisches Rundschau*, **50**, 538–53.

BREWER, M. S., HASLAM, H. W., DARBYSHIRE, P. F. P. & DAVIS, A. E. 1979. *Rb–Sr age Determinations in the Bangweulu Block, Luapula Province, Zambia.* Institute of Geological Sciences, London, Report, **79/5**.

CAHEN, L., SNELLING, N. J., DELHAL, J. & LEDENT, D. 1984. *The Geochronology and Evolution of Africa.* Oxford University Press, Oxford.

COWARD, M. P. & DALY, M. C. 1984. Crustal lineaments and shear zones in Africa. *Precambrian Research*, **24**, 27–45.

DALY, M. C. 1986*a*. *The tectonic and thermal evolution of the Irumide Belt, Zambia.* PhD thesis, University of Leeds.

Daly, M. C. 1986*b*. The intracratonic Irumide Belt of Zambia and its bearing on collision orogeny during the Proterozoic of Africa. *In*: COWARD, M. P. & RIES, A. C. (eds) *Collision Tectonics*. Geological Society, London, Special Publications, **19**, 321–328.

DALY, M. C. 1986*c*. Crustal shear zones and thrust belts: their geometry and continuity in central Africa. *Philosophical Transactions of the Royal Society of London*, **317**, 111–128.

DALY, M. C. 1995. The geology of the Mulilansolo Mission – Isoka area: explanation of Degree Sheet 1032 NW and NE Quarters. Report of the Geological Survey of Zambia, **92**.

DALY, M. C. & UNRUG, R. 1982. The Muva Supergroup, northern Zambia. *Transactions of the Geological Society of South Africa*, **85**, 155–65.

DE WAELE, B. & FITZSIMMONS, I. C. W. 2004. The age and detrital fingerprint of the Muva Supergroup, northern Zambia: molassic deposition to the southwest of the Ubendian belt. *Abstracts, Geoscience Africa 2004, Johannesburg*, 162–63.

DE WAELE, B., WINGATE, M. T. D., FITZSIMMONS, I. C. W. & MAPANI, B. S. E. 2003. Untying the Kibaran knot: a reassessment of Mesoproterozoic correlations in southern Africa based on SHRIMP U–Pb data from the Irumide Belt. *Geology*, **31**, 509–512.

DE WAELE, B., FITZSIMMONS, I. C. W. WINGATE, M. T. D., MAPANI, B. S. E. & TEMBO, F. 2004. A U–Pb SHRIMP geochronological database for the Irumide Belt of Zambia: from Palaeoproterozoic sedimentation to late Mesoproterozoic magmatism. *Abstracts, 32nd International Geological Congress, Florence, Italy*, 870–871.

FITCHES, W. R. 1971. Sedimentation and tectonics at the northern end of the Irumide Belt, N Malawi and Zambia. *Geologische Rundschau*, **60**, 589–619.

FITZSIMMONS, I. C. W. & HULSCHER, B. 2005. Out of Africa: detrital zircon provenance of Central Madagascar and Neoproterozoic terrane transfer across the Mozambique Ocean. *Terra Nova*, **17**, 224–35.

JOHNSON, S. P., RIVERS, T. & DE WAELE, B. 2005. A review of Mesoproterozoic to early Palaeozoic magmatic and tectonothermal history of south–central Africa: implications for Rodinia and Gondwana. *Journal of the Geological Society, London*, **161**, 433–450.

KENNEDY, W. Q. 1964. *The differentiation of Africa during the Pan-African Thermo-tectonic episode.*

Annual Report of the African Research Institute, Leeds, **8**.

KRONER, A. 1977. The Precambrian geotectonic evolution of Africa; plate accretion versus plate destruction. *Precambrian Research*, **4**, 163–213.

SHACKLETON, R. M. 1973. Correlation of structures across Precambrian orogenic belts in Africa. *In*: Tarling, D. H. & Runcorn, S. K. (eds) *Implications of continental Drift to the Earth Sciences*. Academic Press, London.

SHENK, V. & APPEL, P. 2001. Anti-clockwise *P–T* path during ultrahigh-temperature (UHT) metamorphism at *ca*. 1050 Ma in the Irumide Belt of Eastern Zambia. *Berichte der Deutschen Mineralogischen Gesellschaft, Beihefte zum European Journal of Mineralogy*, **13**, 161.

THIEME, J. G. 1970. *The geology of the Mansa area: explanation of Degree Sheet 1128, parts of NW Quarter and NE Quarter*. Report of the Geological Survey of Zambia, **26**.

UNRUG, R. 1982. The mid-Proterozoic Mporokoso Group of northern Zambia: stratigraphy, sedimentation and regional position. *Precambrian Research*, **24**, 99–121.

Tectonic evolution of the South Tethyan ocean: evidence from the Eastern Taurus Mountains (Elazığ region, SE Turkey)

A. H. F. ROBERTSON[1], O. PARLAK[2], T. RÍZAOĞLU[2], Ü. ÜNLÜGENÇ[2], N. İNAN[3], K. TASLI[3] & T. USTAÖMER[4]

[1]*Grant Institute of Earth Science, School of GeoSciences, West Mains Road, Edinburgh EH9 3JW, UK (e-mail: Robertson@ed.ac.uk)*

[2]*Department of Geological Engineering, Çukurova University, 01330, Balcalı, Adana, Turkey*

[3]*Department of Geological Engineering, Mersin University, Mersin 33343, Turkey*

[4]*Department of Geological Engineering, Istanbul University, 34310-Avcılar, Istanbul, Turkey*

Abstract: Geological information from the Eastern Taurus Mountains, part of the Tethyan (South Neotethyan) suture zone exposed in the Elazığ region, is used here to test existing tectonic hypotheses and to develop a new tectonic model. Five main tectonic stages are identified: (1) Mid–Late Triassic rifting–spreading of Southern Neotethys; (2) Late Cretaceous northward subduction–accretion of ophiolites and arc-related units; (3) Mid-Eocene subduction-related extension; (4) Early–Mid-Miocene collision and southward thrusting over the Arabian Foreland; (6) Plio-Quaternary, post-collisional left-lateral tectonic escape. During the Late Cretaceous (*c.* 90 Ma) northward intra-oceanic subduction generated regionally extensive oceanic lithosphere as the İspendere, Kömürhan, Guleman and Killan ophiolites of supra-subduction zone type. A northward-dipping subduction zone was activated along the northern margin of the ocean basin (Keban Platform), followed by accretion of Upper Cretaceous ophiolites in latest Cretaceous time. As subduction continued the accreted ophiolites and overriding northern margin (Keban Platform) were intruded by calc-alkaline plutons, still during latest Cretaceous time. The northern margin was covered by shallow-marine mixed clastic–carbonate sediments in latest Cretaceous–Early Palaeogene time. Northward subduction during the Mid-Eocene was accompanied by extension of the northern continental margin, generating large fault-bounded, extensional basins that were infilled with shallow- to deep-water sediments and subduction-influenced volcanic rocks (Maden Group). Thick debris flows ('olistostromes') accumulated along the oceanward edge of the active margin. The partly assembled allochthon finally collided with the Arabian continental margin to the south during Early–Mid-Miocene time in response to oblique convergence; the entire thrust stack was then emplaced southwards over the downflexed Arabian Foreland. Left-lateral strike-slip (tectonic escape) along the East Anatolian Fault Zone ensued.

The Taurus Mountain chain, extending for >1500 km across southern Turkey to Iran, is onc of the most important orogenic belts for the study of tectonic processes. The Eastern Taurus Mountains specifically document a complete plate-tectonic cycle beginning with continental rifting, proceeding to sea-floor spreading and culminating in continental collision. The Taurides reflect the evolution of part of the Tethys ocean, which formerly separated Gondwana from Eurasia (Fig. 1). This orogen is characteristic of many of the Mesozoic–Early Cenozoic Tethyan mountain belts of Eurasia, including the Alps (Coward *et al.* 1989), the Mediterranean region (Şengör 1984), and the Early Palaeozoic Iapetus orogen of the circum-Atlantic region (Dewey 1982). These settings differ from Cordilleran-type orogens that have not experienced continental collision (e.g. Western USA). The regional-scale Tethyan-type mountain chains are also more 'typical' of mountain-forming processes than the enormous Himalayan–Tibet orogen (Coward *et al.* 1987), which stands out as a rare, if not unique, setting in Earth history.

The Taurus Mountains have the added advantage of excellent exposure of a relatively young orogen at a high structural level, and relative accessibility. They have been regionally mapped by the Turkish Petroleum Company (TPAO) and the Mineral Research and Exploration Institute (MTA, Ankara). Research over several decades has advanced sufficiently to allow alternative tectonic models to be tested

From: RIES, A. C., BUTLER, R. W. H. & GRAHAM, R. H. (eds) 2007. *Deformation of the Continental Crust: The Legacy of Mike Coward.* Geological Society, London, Special Publications, **272**, 231–270.

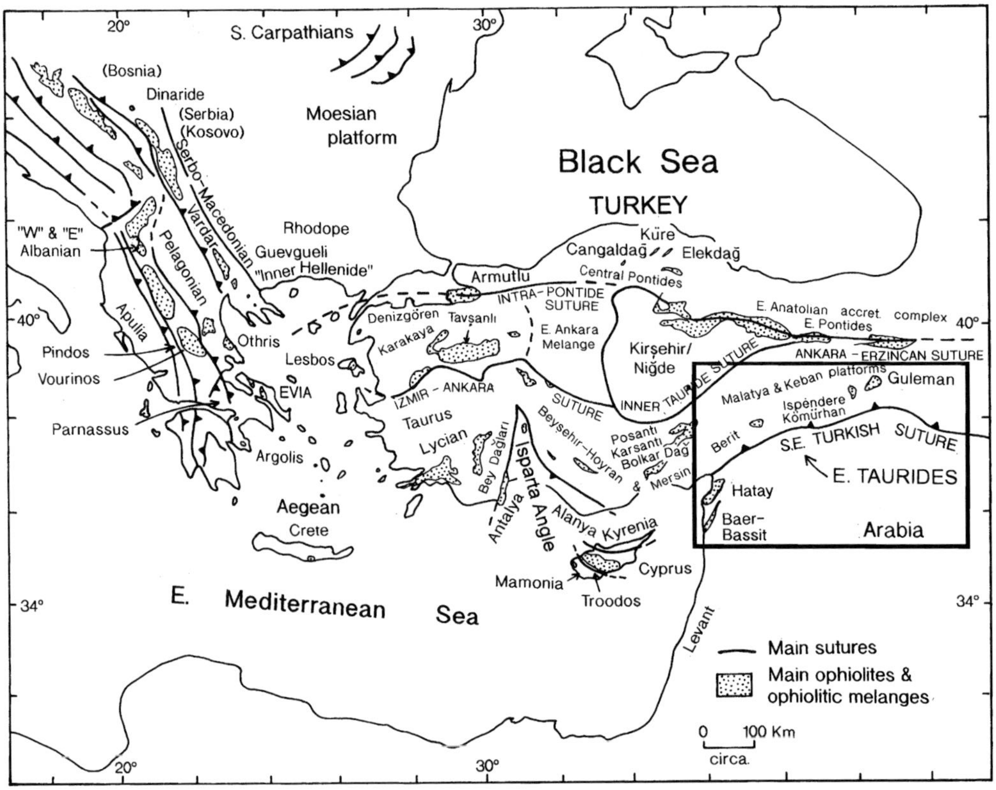

Fig. 1. Outline tectonic map of the Eastern Mediterranean region showing the main sutures and the location of the SE Turkish suture zone in eastern Turkey.

based on focused fieldwork in critical areas, as reported here.

The Tethyan evolution of the Eastern Tauride region began with rifting in the Triassic (Fig. 2a) and ended with continental collision in the Miocene. Further west, the Taurides are still in a pre-collisional stage, as remnants of the Tethys ocean still remain in the Eastern Mediterranean region to the south (Robertson 1998, 2000).

During the Triassic, one or several micro-continents rifted from Gondwana and drifted northwards opening a Mesozoic ocean basin, commonly known as the Southern Neotethys (Şengör & Yılmaz 1981; Robertson & Dixon 1984). This oceanic basin was associated with the genesis and emplacement of ophiolites during the Late Cretaceous, followed by closure during Miocene time (Fig. 2b and c).

Neotethys, as defined here, refers to several oceanic basins of Mesozoic–Early Cenozoic age in the Eastern Mediterranean region that opened following partial closure of an older ocean, termed Palaeotethys (Robertson & Dixon 1984; Robertson *et al.* 2004*b*). The Eastern Taurides form an east–west-trending linear mountain chain, of which the area discussed here, around Elazığ, in the centre of the belt (Fig. 3) can be considered as representative.

Our understanding of the Eastern Taurides in terms of modern plate-tectonic processes effectively began with the work of Robert Hall, Roger Mason and colleagues from University College London (Hall 1976). This was based on a PhD study of a small remote area, near Mutki, in the southern part of the Bitlis Massif (east of our main study area). This demonstrated the existence of Upper Cretaceous ophiolitic mélange and blueschists, which were attributed to sea-floor spreading and northward subduction of a Tethyan ocean. In contrast, utilizing regional mapping by the Turkish Petroleum Company (Perinçek 1979, 1980; Perinçek & Özkaya 1981), Şengör & Yılmaz (1981) then proposed a contrasting model involving southward subduction and back-arc basin formation along the northern margin of Gondwana. Based on an integrated

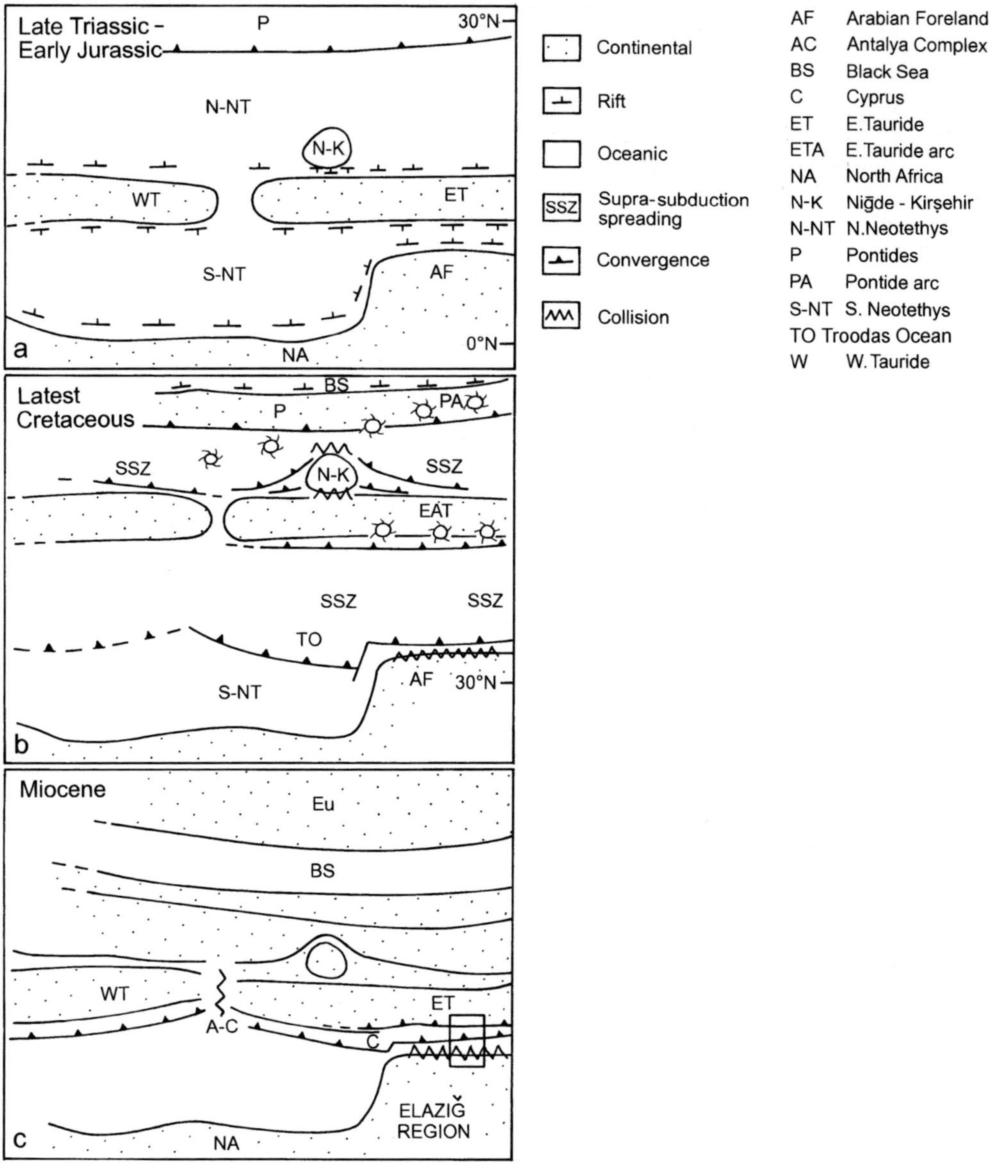

Fig. 2. Diagrammatic palaeo-tectonic sketch maps of the Mesozoic Tethys (Neotethys) in the Turkish region, indicating the setting of the study area in SE Turkey (Elazığ area). (**a**) Late Triassic–Early Jurassic; (**b**) latest Cretaceous; (**c**) Miocene. Based on Robertson (1998, 2002). Several Neotethyan basins opened in the Triassic (**a**), reached their maximum width in the Late Jurassic–Early Cretaceous, then progressively closed (**b**, **c**).

study of the thrust front in the central part of the Eastern Taurides (Maden area), Aktaş & Robertson (1984) next put forward a tectonic model involving northward subduction of a Mesozoic Tethyan ocean, with collision in either latest Cretaceous or Mid-Cenozoic time, the latter option being favoured. Utilizing mapping by MTA (e.g. Yazgan 1984) and regional tectono-stratigraphic studies (Fontaine 1981; Fourcade *et al.* 1991), it was suggested that these large Cretaceous ophiolites in the region were formed not in a southerly Neotethyan oceanic basin, but instead within a more northerly oceanic basin located closer to Eurasia. The ophiolites were

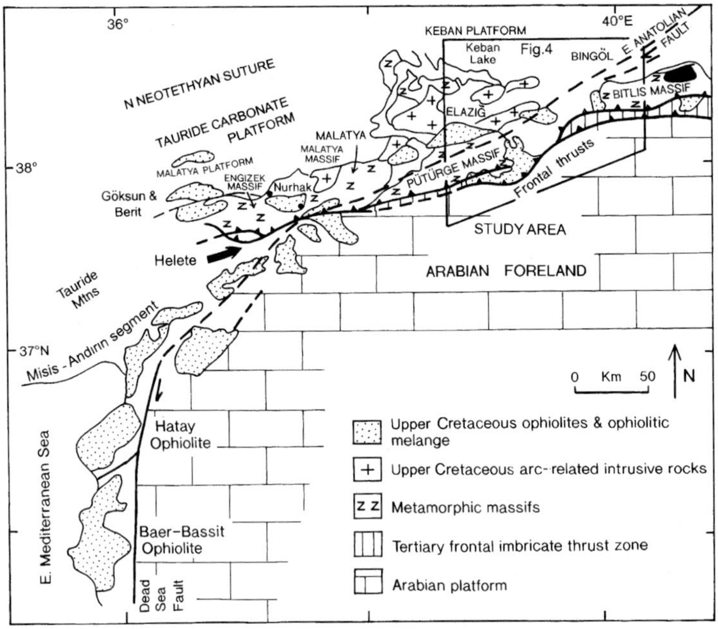

Fig. 3. Outline structural map of the SE Turkish suture zone, discussed in this paper (Elazığ area). Modified from Robertson *et al.* (2006).

emplaced by thrusting hundreds of kilometres southwards in latest Cretaceous time (Michard *et al.* 1984; Yazgan 1984). It was also believed by these workers that the Tethyan ocean in this region was complely closed by latest Cretaceous time.

Based on a study of the younger syn-post collisional sedimentary and volcanic rocks of eastern Anatolia, Dewey *et al.* (1986) clarified the timing of final closure of the Southern Neotethyan oceanic basin in SE Turkey as Early–Middle Miocene. This was followed by post-collisional left-lateral tectonic escape of Anatolia, bounded by the North and East Anatolian transform faults (Şengör *et al.* 1985). However, some geologists continued to believe that final Tethyan closure took place associated with the ophiolite emplacement in latest Cretaceous time (Beyarslan & Bingöl 2000).

Based on detailed studies of PhD-sized study areas in the western part of the Eastern Taurides, geologists from Istanbul Technical University elaborated on the concept of a Southern Neotethys that opened in the Early Mesozoic, then finally closed by Mid-Miocene time (Yılmaz 1991, 1993; Yılmaz *et al.* 1993).

Currently, the main focus of research is on the origin and emplacement of the Late Cretaceous ophiolites (Parlak *et al.* 2001, 2004; Robertson *et al.* 2006) and on the tectonic evolution of the suture zone and thrust belt.

The main tectonic models that have been proposed are summarized in Figure 4. Northward subduction is now generally assumed. There is nowadays also a near consensus that the ophiolites formed in a southerly Mesozoic oceanic basin. However, important questions and controversies remain, notably the timing of final continental break-up of the Southern Neotethys, the setting of genesis and emplacement of the ophiolites, the palaeo-tectonic setting of large metamorphic units, and the timing and mode of ocean closure and collision. The present study addresses some of these outstanding questions, utilizing evidence mainly from the well-exposed Elazığ area in the central part of the Eastern Taurides (Fig. 3), and concludes with a new tectonic model. We will show that any effective model depends critically on taking full account of the entire database of sedimentary, igneous and metamorphic rocks and their structural development within a well-defined time framework. In the discussion below we highlight the contribution of each tectonic unit to the overall tectonic evolution of the orogen. However, no attempt is made to discuss the Eastern Taurides as a whole and, in particular, the extreme east of the belt, which has received little modern study, is excluded.

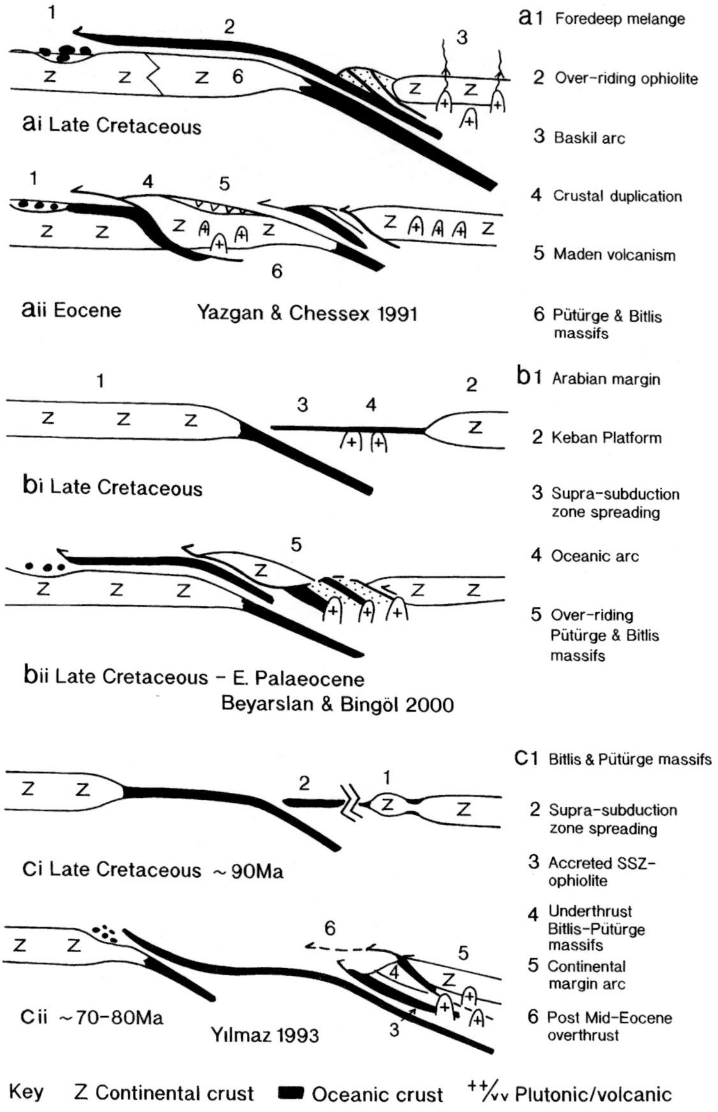

Fig. 4. Previous tectonic models for the evolution of the SE Turkish suture zone. (**ai–aii**) Late Cretaceous collision followed by Miocene thick-skinned rethrusting; (**bi–bii**) northward subduction followed by Late Cretaceous continental collision; (**ci–cii**) northward subduction, followed by re-thrusting of the Pütürge and Bitlis metamorphic massifs from the northern margin to a southerly position in post Mid-Eocene time, exposing ophiolitic and other rocks to the north of this unit.

Regional tectonostratigraphy

A broad north–south transect of the central part of the Eastern Taurus Mountains (Elazığ area) is considered here (Figs 5 and 6). The area begins in the north with a large Mesozoic carbonate platform, the Keban Platform, which is interpreted as part of the northern continental margin of the Mesozoic Southern Neotethys. Moving southwards and structurally downwards, various magmatic, metamorphic and sedimentary units are crossed, until the Arabian Foreland is reached.

(1) *Keban Platform.* This is a low-grade-metamorphosed carbonate platform of Late Palaeozoic–Early Mesozoic age, cut by granitic

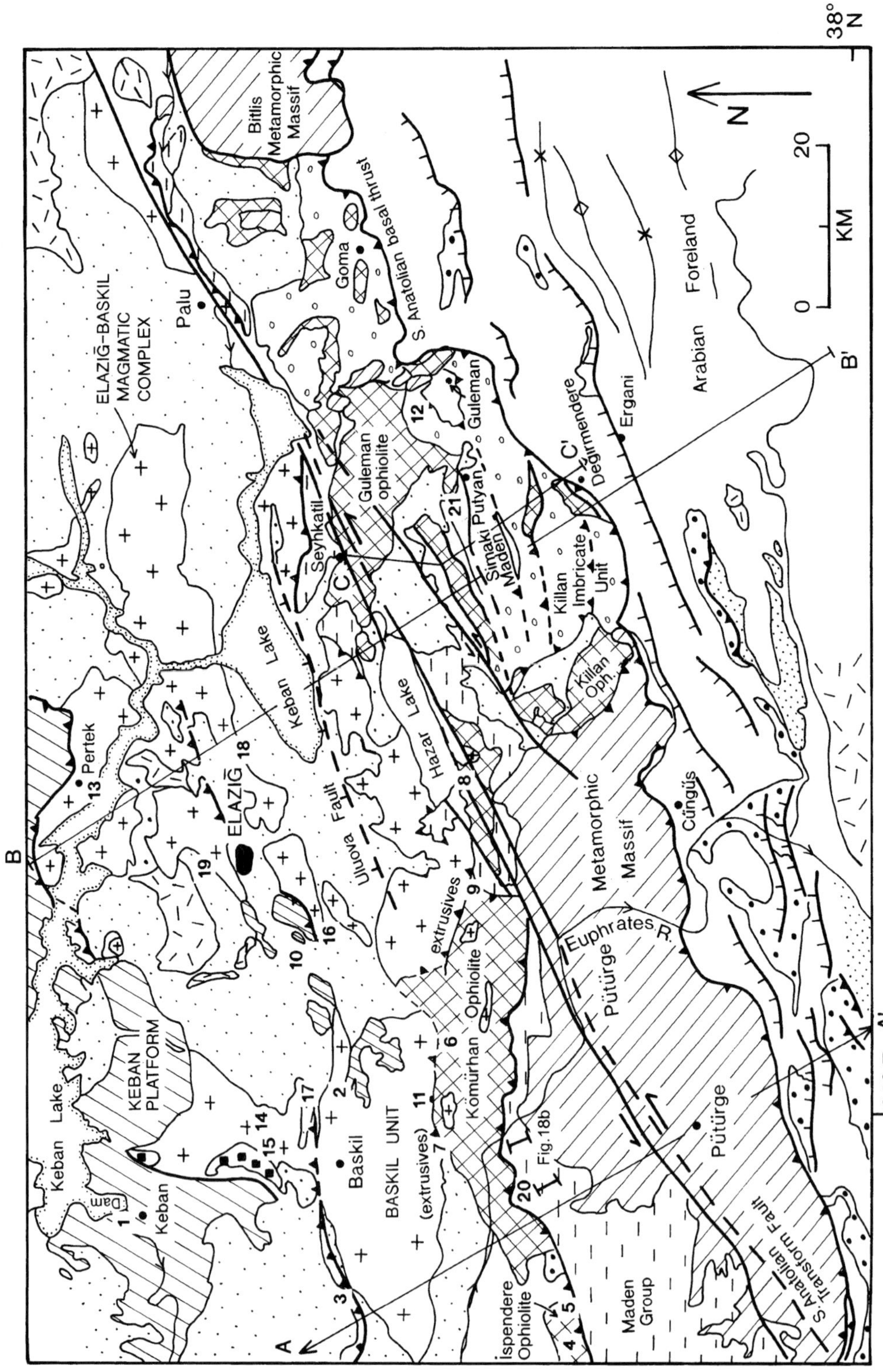
ELAZIĞ-BASKIL MAGMATIC COMPLEX
Bitlis Metamorphic Massif
S. Anatolian basal thrust
Palu
Goma
Guleman ophiolite
Guleman
Seyhkatil
Simaki
Maden
Putyan
Degirmendere
Ergani
Killan Imbricate Unit
Killan Oph.
Arabian Foreland
KM
0
20
N
38° N
B
B'
C
C'
Pertek
Keban Lake
Hazar Lake
ELAZIĞ
Uluova Fault
extrusives
Ophiolite
Metamorphic Massif
Çüngüş
Euphrates R.
Pütürge
KEBAN PLATFORM
Keban Lake
Keban
Dam
Baskil
BASKIL UNIT
(extrusives)
Kömürhan
Fig.18b
Ispendere Ophiolite
Maden Group
S. Anatolian Transform Fault
A
A'
39° E

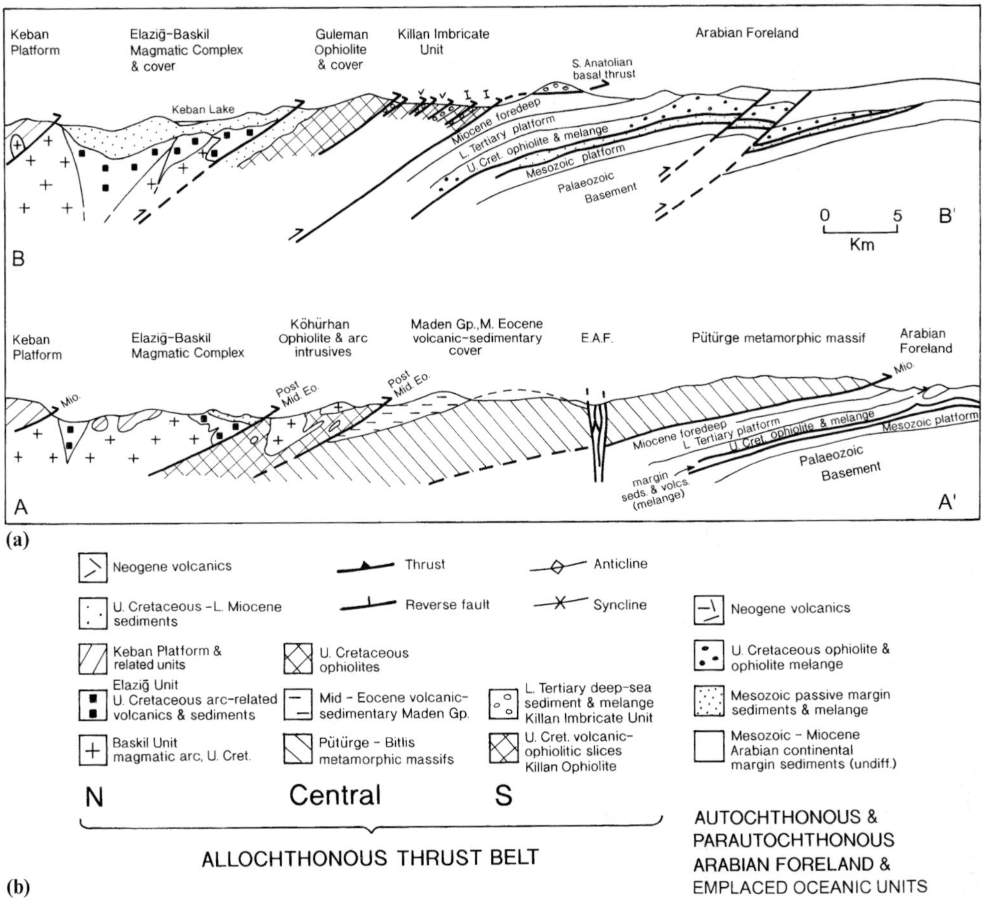

Fig. 6. (**a**) Generalized cross-sections of the Eastern Tauride Mountains in the region discussed in this paper. Modified from Yazgan and Chessex (1991). (**b**) The key to (**a**) and to Figure 5. EAF, East Anatolian Fault.

intrusions (Baskil Unit) and overlain by Cenozoic unmetamorphosed sedimentary rocks (Fig. 7).

(2) *Elazığ–Baskil Magmatic Complex*. This is an assemblage of Upper Cretaceous tholeiitic extrusive igneous rocks and related volcanic–sedimentary rocks (Elazığ Unit), cut by calc-alkaline intrusive rocks (Baskil Unit). The Elazığ–Baskil Magmatic Complex is overlain by sedimentary rocks of latest Cretaceous to Cenozoic age (Fig. 7).

(3) *Upper Cretaceous ophiolites*. From west to east, these are the İspendere Ophiolite, the Kömürhan Ophiolite (Kömürhan meta-ophiolite of Yazgan 1984) and the Guleman Ophiolite. The ophiolites are overlain by non-marine to shallow-marine, mixed clastic–carbonate sedimentary rocks of latest Cretaceous–Early Cenozoic age

Fig. 5. Simplified geological map of the area of the Eastern Tauride Mountains discussed here. The regional mapping was originally mainly carried out by the Turkish Petroleum Company (TPAO) and the Mineral Research and Exploration Institute (MTA). The main geographical features and geological units are labelled on the map. Additional places mentioned in the text are numbered: 1, Keban Dam; 2, Hamuşağı, south of Baskil; 3, Laçan; 4, Yukarı İspendere; 5, Kapıkaya Dam; 6, Fodul, near Yalındamlar; 7, Kömürhan Bridge; 8, Sivrice, Hazar Lake; 9, Karadağ; 10, Baskil road; 11, Kerik (Kömürhan Bridge–Pütürge road); 12, Aslantaş, 13, Pertek and Çaybağı; 14, Karataş Tepe; 15, Orta Mah.; 16, Badempınar; 17, Sarıgül; 18, Hasretdağ; 19, Harput; 20, road towards Malatya; 21, Putyan.

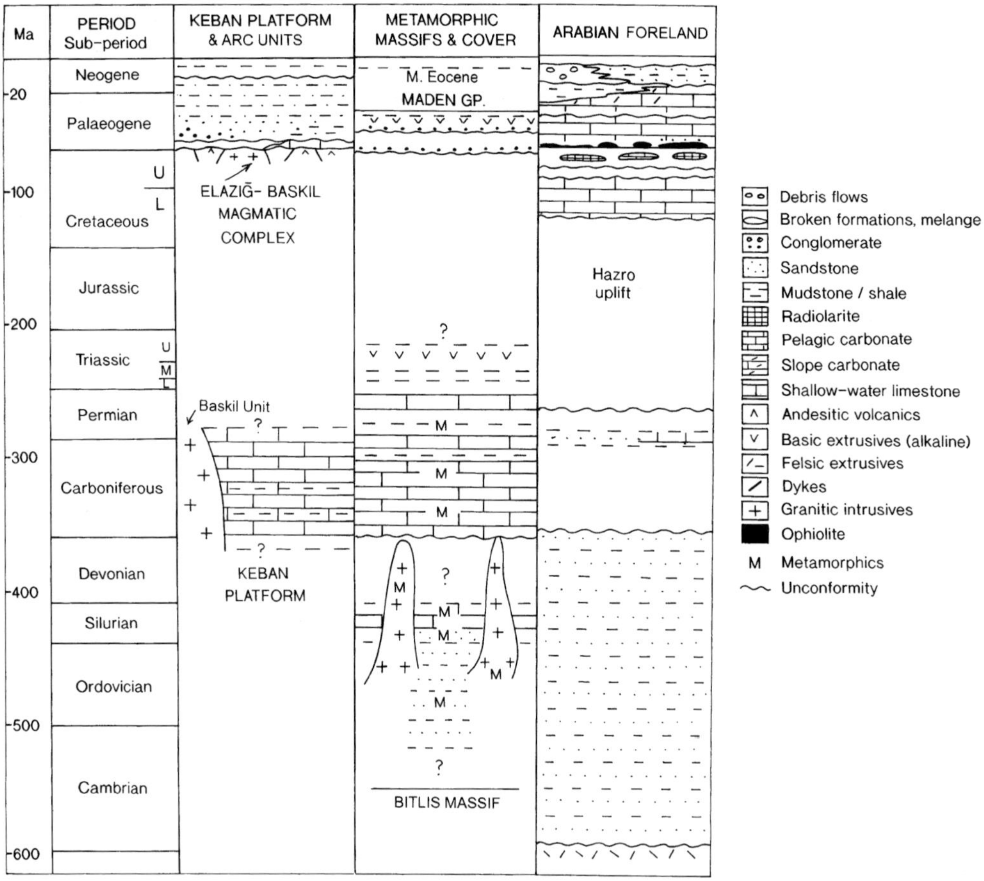

Fig. 7. Summary of the stratigraphy of the main continental-type units exposed in the region studied. (See text for data sources and literature citations.) Logs of the ophiolitic units are given in Figure 11.

(Figs 5 and 6). Dismembered ophiolitic rocks (Killan Ophiolite) are also present in the frontal part of the thrust belt.

(4) *Pütürge and Bitlis metamorphic massifs.* These units are located in the southern, structurally lower parts of the thrust belt, and exhibit 'basement' and 'cover' units that were metamorphosed in latest Cretaceous time (Figs 5 and 6). The Bitlis Massif is overlain by unmetamorphosed sediments of latest Cretaceous age. The metamorphic massifs were exhumed by the Middle Eocene and overlain by the volcanic–sedimentary Maden Group (Maden Complex; Fig. 6).

(5) *Killan Imbricate Unit.* This tectonically assembled unit forms the structurally lowest, frontal part of the thrust belt. It is most widely exposed between the Pütürge and Bitlis metamorphic massifs (Fig. 5b). This unit includes slices of Upper Cretaceous ophiolitic rocks (Killan Ophiolite) and Eocene deep-water pelagic or hemipelagic sediments (Maden Group) (Aktaş & Robertson 1984, 1990).

(6) *Arabian Foreland.* This comprises a Palaeozoic–Mesozoic succession overlying a Precambrian basement (Fig. 6). The platform was overthrust from the north by ophiolitic and related units during latest Cretaceous (Campanian–Maastrichtian) time, and was then unconformably overlain by an uppermost Cretaceous–Palaeogene non-marine to shallow-marine succession (Fig. 7). This was followed by the deposition of Lower Miocene turbidites that accumulated in a foredeep related to final southward emplacement of the thrust belt in Mid-Miocene time (Baştuğ 1980; Aktas & Robertson 1984; Dewey *et al.* 1986; Yılmaz 1993).

Each of the above units is discussed and interpreted in more detail below.

Pütürge and Bitlis metamorphic massifs

The Bitlis and Pütürge metamorphic massifs dominate the structurally lower, southerly part of the Neotethyan suture (Figs 5 and 6) and are widely exposed in the SE and SW of the region studied. Here, we are mainly concerned with the Triassic and later tectonic development. However, the Palaeozoic setting is also relevant as it allows a comparison with the stratigraphy of the northern margin (Keban Platform) and the southern margin (Arabian Foreland) of the Southern Neotethys, and this then sheds light on the palaeogeography and the palaeo-tectonic setting.

Bitlis Massif

The Bitlis Massif (Figs 3 and 7) is extensively exposed over several hundred kilometres along the Eastern Tauride thrust belt from the study area to beyond the border with Iran. Only the extreme west of the Bitlis Massif lies within our present study area. However, below we include a summary of salient features based mainly on the literature (Hall 1976; Perinçek 1979; Perinçek & Özkaya 1981; Çağlayan *et al.* 1984; Göncüoğlu & Turhan 1984; Helvacı & Griffin 1984).

The metamorphic country rocks ('basement') are mainly isoclinally folded biotite–muscovite schists and gneisses with occasional dark lenses of amphibolitic rocks. The schists and gneisses are locally kyanite-bearing, and lenses and blocks of eclogitic rocks have been reported locally. The metamorphic rocks are intruded by several elongate metagranitic bodies. Dykes of similar composition intrude the metamorphic country rocks. The granites show ductile deformation, with the development of a planar foliation, S–C tectonites and mineral stretching lineation (P. A. Ustaömer & T. Ustaömer, pers. com.).

The metamorphic basement units are overlain unconformably by quartzites and schists, with interlayered metacarbonates in the stratigraphically higher levels of the succession (Meydan Formation of Göncüoğlu & Turhan 1984). Fossils collected from the metacarbonates have yielded Givetian–Frasnian ages (Mid-Late Devonian). Higher in the succession, felsic metatuffs are possibly Carboniferous in age (Çeşme Formation). These sediments are reported to contain blocks of metacarbonates (dolomites), calcschists and actinolitic schists. Göncüoğlu & Turan (1984) considered that the granites were intruded up to, and including, units of probable Carboniferous age, although current work suggests that the granites may be of pre-Hercynian age (P. A. Ustaömer & T. Ustaömer, pers. com.). A local unconformity was reported at the base of the overlying unit, of Early Permian age (Çıkrık Formation), associated with a metaconglomerate (Göncüoğlu & Turhan 1984), but no major break in the succession appears to exist at this level. The succession continues upwards into thick-bedded, recrystallized limestones, calcschists and graphitic schist (Çıkrık Limestone), with Upper Permian fossils (Fig. 7). These metasediments are conformably overlain by thick-bedded metalimestones (Tutu Formation) of Triassic age. In some other areas (western Bitlis Massif) the succession includes Middle–Upper Triassic metavolcanic rocks and sediments, including alkali basalts, volcaniclastic deposits, shales and radiolarian sediments (Perinçek 1979, 1980, 1990; Perinçek & Özkaya 1981). Phyllites, shales and metavolcaniclastic sediments at the highest preserved levels of the succession remain undated (?Triassic or later Mesozoic).

In the south, the uppermost levels of the Bitlis Massif are overlain tectonically by ophiolitic rocks (Hall 1976; Çağlayan *et al.* 1984; Göncüoğlu & Turhan 1984). The contact is a zone of intense mylonitization, as exposed along the southern front of the metamorphic massif (e.g. near Mutki; Hall 1976). Ophiolites are also exposed along the northern margin of the Bitlis Massif, south of Lake Van, where they are mapped as being separated from the Bitlis Massif by the Middle Eocene volcanic–sedimentary Maden Group (i.e. the Maden Complex of Perinçek 1979). The ophiolitic rocks exposed in the south (e.g. Mutki area), are mainly sheared serpentinite and ophiolitic mélange, associated with blocks of radiolarian chert, metabasalt, volcanic breccia, recrystallized limestone, glaucophane-bearing greenschists and local eclogites (Hall 1976). Micritic limestones locally contain *Globotruncana* sp., indicating a Late Cretaceous age. The HP–LT metamorphism took place prior to deposition of Upper Maastrichtian cover sediments (Hall 1976; Perinçek 1979). The unconformably overlying unit (Kinzu Formation) begins with debris-flow deposits ('wildflysch'), passing upwards into sandstone–shale alternations with occasional micritic limestone interbeds that have yielded Upper Maastrichtian microfossils. The clasts and blocks were derived from ophiolitic and metamorphic 'basement rocks'.

The Upper Cretaceous facies are unconformably overlain, above a basal red conglomerate, by pelagic or hemipelagic limestones, limestone–shale alternations and sandstones, of Mid–Late Eocene age (Kızılağaç Formation). Poorly dated volcanic rocks (andesites and tuffs), interbedded with polymict conglomerates occur above this (Salhan Volcanics). These units correlate with Lower–Middle Eocene volcanic rocks and pelagic or hemipelagic limestones (Baykan Group) that are extensively exposed south of Lake Van, and also with the Middle Eocene volcanic–sedimentary Maden Group (Maden Complex).

Interpretation of the Bitlis Massif

For the discussion that follows the main point to note is that the Bitlis Massif exhibits Triassic rifting followed by deformation and HP–LT metamorphism in an active margin setting during Late Cretaceous time. This was followed by an Eocene volcanic–sedimentary succession that is considered to relate to the later stage of subduction and back-arc basin formation during mid-Cenozoic time. The Bitlis Massif was finally thrust southwards over the Arabian Foreland during the Early Miocene. The Mesozoic palaeogeographical setting of the Bitlis Massif is controversial and the additional information on the pre-Triassic 'basement' is mainly included here as it helps with comparisons, both with the Arabian Foreland to the south and the Tauride margin (Keban Platform) to the north, as discussed later in the paper.

Pütürge Metamorphic Massif

The Pütürge Massif occupies much of the southern part of the present study area (Figs 5 and 6). Regional mapping around Pütürge village (Fig. 5) indicates that the metamorphic outcrop there comprises lower and upper metamorphic units (Yılmaz 1971; Erdem & Bingöl 1995; Yılmaz *et al.* 1993). These two units are separated by a phyllitic shear zone that is interpreted as a deformed unconformity (Bingöl 1984; Yazgan 1984). The lower unit comprises augen gneiss, biotite schist and amphibolitic schist, cut by granitic gneiss, with amphibolite–prasinite veins. The upper unit includes muscovite-, staurolite-, garnet- and kyanite-bearing schists, overlain by thicker and more extensive calcschists and marble, with magnetite layers (Erdem & Bingöl 1995). The intervening shear zone (>50–100 m thick) includes chlorite–pyrophyllite–diaspore assemblages (Yazgan & Chessex 1991). The core and cover units were metamorphosed to amphibolite facies, apparently during the Late Cretaceous (Bingöl 1984; Yazgan & Chessex 1991). In addition, small tourmaline leucogranite intrusions were reported locally (Yazgan & Chessex 1991).

The Pütürge Massif can be correlated with the Bitlis Massif, although the metamorphic grade of the Pütürge Massif may be somewhat higher, as the succession appears to be more recrystallized and less age dating from fossils is available. The cross-cutting granitic rocks in the Pütürge Massif could be of Precambrian age (P.A. Ustaömer & T. Ustaömer, pers. com), and the overlying marls and calcschists may be of Permian age, extending into the Mesozoic, as in the Bitlis Massif. The metacarbonates include graphitic schists that have been correlated with similar organic-rich facies in the Keban Platform (Yılmaz 1993; Yılmaz *et al.* 1993). The reported shear zone between the upper and lower units might record Early Mesozoic rifting but more evidence is needed.

Structural work in the east of the Pütürge Massif (Hazar Lake area; Fig. 5) has demonstrated the effects of regional folding (D_1), with fold axes striking NE–SW. Muscovite, biotite and amphibole have yielded calculated K/Ar ages of mainly 85–72 Ma (Campanian–Maastrichtian) (Yazgan 1984). The D_1 deformation was reported to be associated with a prominent NNW-trending stretching lineation. Later deformation (D_2) caused upright SE-verging folding associated with low-grade metamorphism (Hempton 1984, 1985). In general, regional metamorphism took place under amphibolite- to lower greenschist-facies conditions.

The Pütürge Massif therefore follows a very similar structural history to that outlined for the Bitlis Massif above. The information on the pre-Triassic lithologies is again useful to compare with the stratigraphy of the Arabian margin and Tauride units and so shed light on the palaeotectonic setting of the Bitlis and Pütürge massifs.

Keban Platform

The Keban Platform forms a regional-scale thrust sheet above Upper Cretaceous ophiolitic and arc-related rocks exposed to the south (Figs 5, 6 and 8). For example, NW of Elazığ, a large thrust sheet of metamorphosed Keban Platform rocks overlies unmetamorphosed Upper Cretaceous magmatic rocks of the Elazığ–Baskil Magmatic Complex. Prominent hills of metacarbonate rocks are surrounded by soft-weathering lithologies. The thrust is subhorizontal, to gently northward dipping. Northwest of Baskil (Fig. 5), the Keban Platform, locally south dipping, is exposed as a mountainous ridge (near Laçan; Fig. 5, location 3). Marbles of the Keban

Platform are structurally underlain by uppermost Cretaceous volcanic–sedimentary rocks of the Elazığ Unit, with a moderately inclined (35°), NW-dipping thrust contact. In this area, thrust contacts are also exposed locally in areas that were intruded by granitic rocks (Fig. 9a). This thrust is segmented, with nearly north–south transpressional segments. To the north, the Keban Platform is structurally overlain by the Munzur Dağ, which is another major Mesozoic carbonate platform unit located further north (Özgül 1981).

The stratigraphic succession in the Keban Platform, several kilometres thick, is dominated by low-grade (greenschist-facies) metasediments (Fig. 7). Lithologies are mainly marbles, schists and black phyllites, with rare metaconglomerates and amphibolites (Bingöl 1984; Yazgan 1984; Akgül 1987; Asutay 1988; Turan & Bingöl 1991; Yılmaz 1993; Yılmaz *et al.* 1993). A mainly Permo-Carboniferous age was inferred, based on *Glomospira* and *Ammodiscus* (Kipman 1981), possibly extending into the Early Triassic (Özgül 1981).

The contact between the Keban Platform and the underlying Cretaceous ophiolitic and arc-related units (see below) is generally a thrust, as mapped SW of Elazığ (Yazgan 1984; Yazgan & Chessex 1991; Beyarslan & Bingöl 2000; Fig. 5). However, cross-cutting dioritic to granitic intrusive rocks were reported by Yazgan & Chessex (1991). Skarn zones are present between the Upper Cretaceous magmatic rocks and the Keban metamorphic rocks (Yazgan & Chessex 1991). In places, the intrusions are associated with magnetite mineralization (e.g. SE of Aşvan village, near Keban Dam). Also, contact-metamorphosed hornfelses and skarns are well exposed (e.g. NW of Birivan; also known as Ulupınar). A marble–microsynenite contact near Keban is associated with well-known silver–lead mineralization (Yazgan & Chessex 1991).

Where widely exposed near, and to the north of, Keban Dam (Fig. 5, location 1), the Keban Platform is cut by numerous large granitic, granodioritic and minor gabbroic intrusions, together with dykes of mainly intermediate composition (Yazgan 1984). The Keban metamorphic rocks are also widely exposed further west, e.g. adjacent to the Elazığ-Keban dam road, where they comprise an east-dipping succession of mainly well-bedded, dark marble with subordinate intercalations of black phyllite. Cross-cutting plutonic rocks in this area include spectacular orbicular gabbro (Fig. 10d).

To the east of the Baskil area (e.g. near Hamuşağı; Fig. 5, location 2), well-bedded marbles of the Keban Platform are cut by intrusive rocks of the Baskil Unit (locally diorite cut by quartz-monzonite). Dioritic intrusive rocks include blocks of bedded marble (metres to tens of metres in size), interpreted as xenoliths of the Keban metamorphic rocks within a pluton of the Baskil Unit (Figs 9b,c and 10b). In places, the diorite and marble are cut by altered subvertical basic dykes, up to 3 m wide (Fig. 9d). The intrusive rocks and larger marble exposures are locally separated by a low-angle shear zone (traceable >200 m laterally). This shows that the primary magmatic contacts were later deformed.

The Keban Platform is interpreted as a shallow-marine carbonate platform, although its exact age and basement–cover relations are unclear because of limited exposure. During Mesozoic time the Keban Platform is commonly viewed as having been contiguous with the Munzur carbonate platform to the north, and with the Malatya carbonate platform to the west (e.g. Michard *et al.* 1984; Fig. 8). However, these platform units might instead have formed separate palaeogeographical units (Şengör & Yılmaz 1981; Robertson & Dixon 1984; Fig. 8c and d). The Keban Platform is cut by Upper Cretaceous arc-related plutonic rocks termed the Baskil Unit

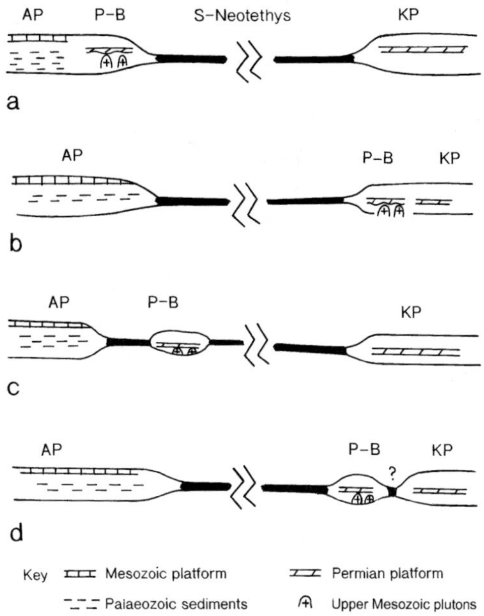

Fig. 8. Alternative possible settings of the Pütürge and Bitlis massifs. (**a**) in the south along the Arabian margin (e.g. Yazgan & Chessex 1991); (**b**) in the north along the Tauride margin (e.g. Yılmaz 1993); (**c**) as microcontinents adjacent to the Arabian margin (e.g. Şengör & Yılmaz 1981; Robertson & Dixon 1984; present study); (**d**) near the northern margin, possibly as marginal rift blocks. AP, Arabian Platform; P-B, Pütürge and Bitlis massifs; KP, Keban Platform. (See text for discussion.)

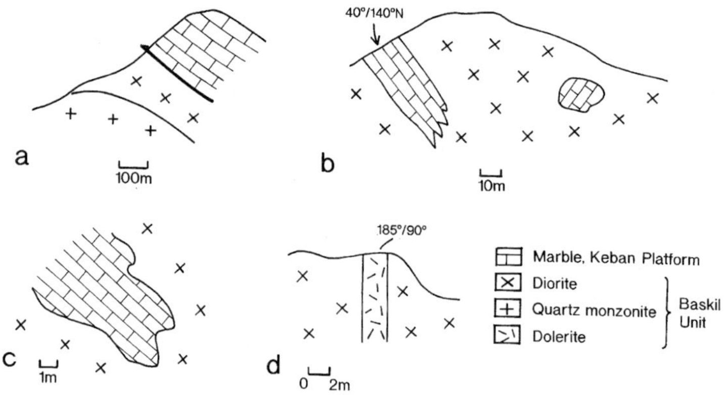

Fig. 9. Field sketches of the Baskil Unit (Elazığ–Baskil Magmatic Complex) in the Baskil area: (**a**) showing metamorphic rocks (Keban Platform) thrust over plutonic rocks of the Baskil Unit; (**b**) marble blocks from the Keban Platform metamorphic rocks forming xenoliths within the plutonic rocks of the Baskil Unit; (**c**) individual marble xenolith within the Baskil Unit; (**d**) dolerite dyke cutting a Baskil Unit pluton.

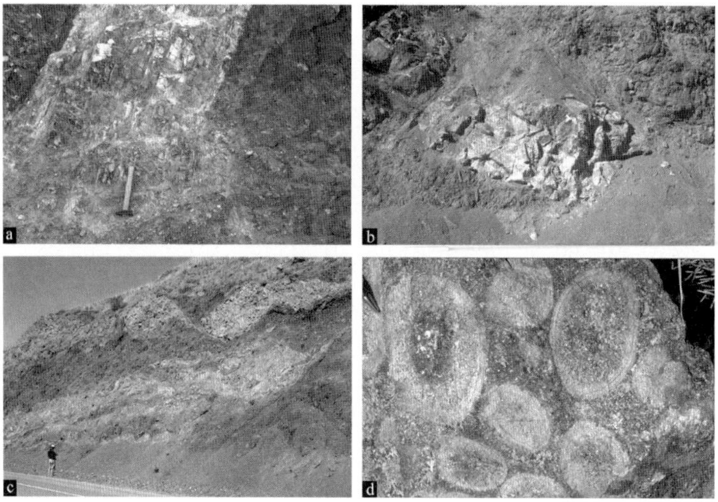

Fig. 10. Field photographs: (**a**) aplitic dyke cutting diorite of the Baskil arc unit, near Baskil; (**b**) xenolith of marble correlated with the Keban Platform within gabbro of the Baskil arc unit, near Baskil; (**c**) intermediate–silicic volcanic rocks and volcaniclastic debris flows cut by extensional faults, Elazığ Unit, near Kömürhan Bridge; (**d**) orbicular gabbro cutting the Keban Platform, near Sarıgül.

(Bingöl 1984; Michard *et al.* 1984; Yazgan 1984). Regional metamorphism probably took place in latest Cretaceous time, as the Lower Cenozoic cover sediments are unmetamorphosed.

An important question therefore is whether, during Mesozoic time, the successions in the Bitlis and Pütürge massifs were located along the Arabian margin to the south (Fig. 8a), adjacent to the Keban Platform to the north (Fig. 8b), or formed one (or several) microcontinents within the Southern Neotethys (Fig. 8c and d). The pre-Triassic platform-type successions of the Bitlis and Pütürge massifs can be generally correlated with the Arabian Foreland (e.g. Hazro Inlier) (Çağlayan *et al.* 1984). However, similar pre-rift lithologies could well have existed along the northerly (conjugate) Tauride margin (Keban Platform). Also, the Arabian Platform succession differs from the Keban Platform as it lacks intrusive or extrusive rocks (Fig. 7). In addition, these two units are everywhere separated by the basal thrust of the Tauride allochthon.

Similar (pre-rift) Permian black shales are exposed in the Pütürge–Bitlis massifs and in the Keban Platform suggesting that these units might have been located together along the northern margin of the ocean basin (Yılmaz 1993; Yılmaz *et al.* 1993; Fig. 8b). However, the Keban Platform is now located at the top of the thrust stack whereas the Bitlis and Pütürge massifs are near the base, precluding any obvious palaeogeographical correlation. The possibility that the Bitlis and Pütürge massifs formed microcontinents within the Southern Neotethys (Şengör & Yılmaz 1981; Robertson & Dixon 1984; Fig. 8c and d) is consistent with the field evidence but difficult to prove in view of their metamorphic state and the absence of unmetamorphosed rift–passive margin units. In addition, the Bitis–Pütürge massifs could conceivably represent exotic terranes but supporting field evidence of large-scale pre-Pliocene strike-slip is currently lacking, especially as all the major tectonic contacts we have so far observed are of low-angle type.

Upper Cretaceous ophiolites

Several large ophiolitic units were originally mapped as part of the regionally extensive Yüksekova Complex (Perinçek 1979, 1980), for which the type area is located in the far east of the Eastern Taurides (outside the present study area), not far from the border with Iran. The Yüksekova Complex was mapped as a wide range of volcanic and sedimentary rocks of Campanian–Early Maastrichtian age, together with ophiolitic and granitic rocks. More recently, most workers have distinguished and named individual components of the Yüksekova Complex, including ophiolitic and magmatic arc-type rocks. Individual ophiolitic bodies have been given regional names to facilitate description and interpretation (e.g. Michard *et al.* 1984; Yazgan 1984; Yazgan & Chessex 1991).

Three main ophiolitic units, which vary in tectonostratigraphy and structural setting, are present in the Elazığ area: the İspendere, Kömürhan and Guleman ophiolites (Figs 5 and 11). In addition, the strongly dismembered Killan Ophiolite is present at a low structural level near the thrust front (see below). Yazgan & Chessex (1991) distinguished between the İspendere and Guleman ophiolites, which are unmetamorphosed, and the 'Kömürhan metaophiolite', which is partially metamorphosed to amphibolite facies and, in places, has undergone ductile deformation.

İspendere Ophiolite

This unit, located in the far SW of the area studied (Figs 5 and 11), comprises a relatively intact ophiolite, with layered ultramafic rocks, layered and isotropic gabbro, well-preserved sheeted dykes and extensive basaltic–andesitic extrusive rocks, locally cut by granitic intrusions (Beyarslan & Bingöl 1991, 2000; Yazgan &

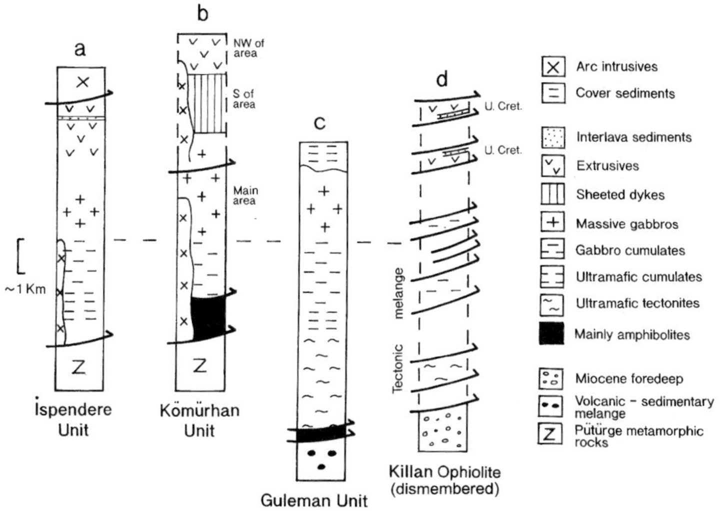

Fig. 11. Generalized logs of the Upper Cretaceous ophiolites in the area studied. (For data see sources and discussion see the text.)

Chessex 1991). The deeper part of the pseudostratigraphy, well exposed in the west (at Yukarı İspendere; Fig. 5, location 4), exposes layered ultramafic rocks, locally cut by wehrlites, but with no evidence of a preserved tectonite (depleted mantle) unit beneath. The ultramafic cumulates are characterized by plagioclase wehrlite and wehrlite. The mafic cumulates are dominated by troctolite and gabbro. Higher parts of the ophiolite succession are exposed further east (near Kapıkaya Dam; Fig. 5, location 5), where layered gabbros are cut by isolated basic dykes (<1 m thick) with well-developed chilled margins. Above come massive gabbros, with isolated diabase dykes and subhorizontal dolerite dykelets. A sheeted dyke complex is made up of diabase and quartzmicrodiorite dykes, as seen near Kapıkaya Dam. An extrusive succession exposed further east between Kapıkaya Dam and Erenli includes basalts and more fractionated volcanic rocks. A representative chemical plot of the basalt (Fig. 12) illustrates a subduction-influenced character, as indicated by the negative Nb anomaly. The succession includes thick volcaniclastic debris flows, with clasts of volcanic rocks up to 1 m in size. This succession was dated as Late Campanian–Early Maastrichtian based on the presence of planktonic Foraminifera within interbedded pelagic sediments (Yazgan & Chessex 1991).

Kömürhan Ophiolite

The laterally extensive Kömürhan Ophiolite (Fig. 5) is critical as, unlike the other ophiolites, its contacts are well exposed, both with the Pütürge Massif to the south and with the Elazığ–Baskil Magmatic Complex to the north. In the south, the ophiolite is thrust over the Middle Eocene volcanic–sedimentary Maden Group, whereas in the north it is either intruded by the Upper Cretaceous Elazığ–Baskil Magmatic Complex, or unconformably overlain by Middle–Upper Eocene sediments (Kırkgeçit Formation; see below). Petrographic descriptions, supported by geochemical evidence, are reported elsewhere (Rızaoğlu 2006; Rızaoğlu *et al.* 2006), and only features directly relevant to the tectonic setting are summarized here.

The Kömürhan Ophiolite (Fig. 11) is dominated by serpentinized tectonite, together with layered ultramafic rocks, layered gabbro, isotropic gabbro, sheeted dykes and volcanic–sedimentary units. In addition, the plutonic sequence is locally cut by calc-alkaline plutonic rocks that are correlated with the uppermost Cretaceous arc-related Baskil Unit (see below). Biotite from quartz-bearing leucodiorites has yielded ages of 85 ± 3 Ma. Also, muscovite from a trondhjemitic granophyre gave an age of

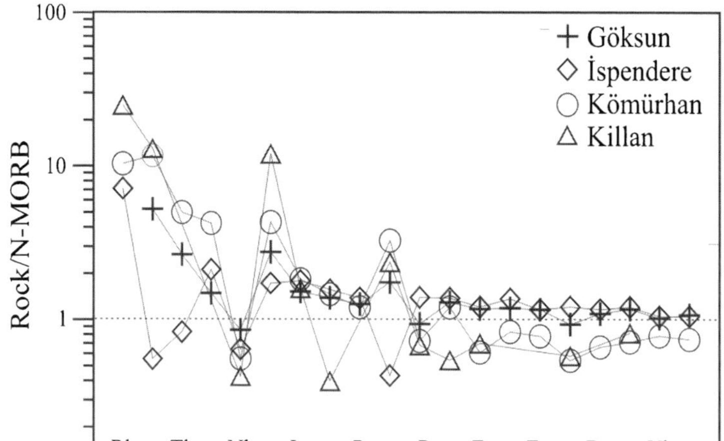

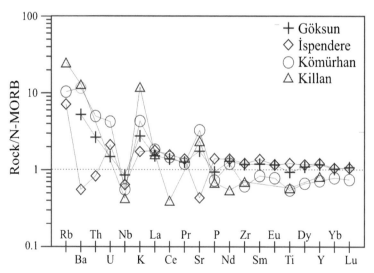

Fig. 12. Mid-oceanic ridge basalt (MORB)-normalized geochemical plots of extrusive igneous rocks from the Upper Cretaceous ophiolites (O. Parlak unpubl. data). The plots indicate that these ophiolites are likely to have formed in an SSZ-type setting. One representative sample is included from the Göksun Ophiolite (also known as the North Berit Ophiolite) further west in the zone of Upper Cretaceous ophiolitic rocks. Diagram from Sun & McDonough 1989.

78.5 ± 2.5 Ma. In addition, intrusive granodiorites were dated at 75 ± 2.4 Ma and 75.4 ± 2.5 Ma, respectively (Yazgan & Chessex 1991).

The layered ultramafic rocks are mainly wehrlites and pyroxenite. Wehrlitic intrusions are observed within layered gabbro (e.g. near Kömürhan Bridge; Fig. 5, location 7). These intrusions cut the primary layering at a high angle. The layered gabbros are dominated by olivine gabbro, normal gabbro and amphibole gabbro (e.g. Karadağ; Fig. 5, location 9). Isotropic gabbro is intensely deformed, as seen near Fodul (Fig. 5, location 6) and to the west of Hazar Lake (near Sivrice; Fig. 5, location 8). The gabbro is cut by occasional moderately inclined north–south-trending dykes (Beyarslan & Bingöl 2000).

Good exposures of sheeted dykes are exposed in the Hazar Lake area (e.g. at Kamerziyareti Tepe). Individual sheeted dykes range in thickness from 15 cm to 100 cm. Many of the dykes lack clear chilled margins (Rızaoğlu 2006; Rızaoğlu *et al.* 2006), suggesting that the dykes were intruded into still-hot rock. An overlying volcanic–sedimentary unit (*c.* 750 m thick; Fig. 11) mainly comprises tholeiitic basaltic pillow lavas, volcanic breccia, massive lava flows, intermediate to felsic lavas, volcanic debris flows, turbiditic volcaniclastic sandstones, tuffs and pelagic limestone. A typical succession is exposed along the Baskil–Kuşsarayı (Elazığ) road (Rızaoğlu *et al.* 2006; Fig. 5; location 10). Local hydrothermal sulphide mineralization is reported from the volcanic rocks (Bölücek *et al.* 2004).

The upper ophiolite levels experienced low-grade metamorphism, commensurate with sea-floor hydrothermal alteration, e.g. in the east, near Hazar Lake (Hempton 1984, 1985). In contrast, the lower levels of the plutonic sequence are dominated by foliated metagabbros (Yazgan & Chessex 1991; Rızaoğlu *et al.* 2006; e.g. near Kömürhan Bridge; Fig. 5, location 7). Associated ophiolitic harzburgites are underlain structurally by a relatively thin (i.e. 150–200 m) unit of amphibolites (Yazgan & Chessex 1991). These rocks exhibit a subduction-influenced chemistry (Rızaoğlu *et al.* 2006) (Fig. 12) and may have formed in response to intra-oceanic slicing of hot, young suprasubduction-zone (SSZ)-type oceanic crust, possibly as a type of metamorphic sole. The amphibolites have yielded K/Ar ages ranging from 127 ± 14 Ma to 89.5 ± 5 Ma, the latter age being more consistent with the regional setting of Upper Cretaceous ophiolite genesis and emplacement.

To the south, the Kömürhan Ophiolite overlies the Pütürge Metamorphic Massif with a thrust contact, dipping at 40°N, as seen south of Kerik (Fig. 5, location 11). In the SE (on the Kömürhan Bridge–Pütürge road), the base of the overlying Kömürhan Ophiolite comprises sheared, serpentinized layered cumulates. Further north, the Upper Cretaceous volcanic rocks (Elazığ Unit) of the Elazığ–Baskil Magmatic Complex structurally overlie the Kömürhan Ophiolite, with a similar angle of dip to the north. These units are intruded by calc-alkaline plutonic rocks.

Pervasive extensional shearing is present within the Pütürge Massif, the Kömürhan Ophiolite and the Elazığ Magmatic Complex, focused within several hundred metres of the thrust contact (e.g. near Kömürhan Bridge). These units exhibit strong normal faulting and boudinage, indicating down-to-the-NE extension.

South of Kömürhan Bridge (Fig. 5, location 7), near the thrust contact with the overlying Elazığ–Baskil Magmatic Complex, the Kömürhan Ophiolite is deformed by a high-strain zone, which exhibits north–south transport lineations (340°). Well-developed shear bands indicate top-to-the-NE, to top-to-the-ENE extension. Rotated crystals in ophiolitic gabbros indicate a similar extension direction, as do late-stage brittle normal faults. Southwards from the contact, layered gabbros dip southwestward and show a persistent top-to-the-NE shear (Fig. 13b), which becomes gradually weaker structurally upwards. Shear zones, up to 10 m thick, are also seen further south within layered gabbros of the Kömürhan Ophiolite. In addition, the ophiolite and small granitic intrusions are cut by down-to-the-north brittle shears in this area. Just north of the thrust contact volcanic–sedimentary rocks of the Elazığ Magmatic Complex (Elazığ Unit; see below) and overlying limestones are cut by numerous extensional faults. The limestones were dated as Middle Eocene based on large Foraminifera present (Sample 154; Fig. 14h; Appendix). The timing of the extension (one or several phases?) is not well constrained; it post-dates emplacement of the ophiolites and arc rocks in the latest Cretaceous but pre-dates the emplacement of the Elazig–Baskil Magmatic Complex over the Kömürhan Ophiolite (i.e. Late Eocene or pre-Oligocene; Perinçek 1979). The extension probably relates to regional exhumation that took place prior to, or, during the opening of the Maden extensional basin in Mid-Eocene time (see below).

Guleman Ophiolite

The unmetamorphosed, relatively undeformed Guleman Ophiolite (Fig. 11c) is exposed over a

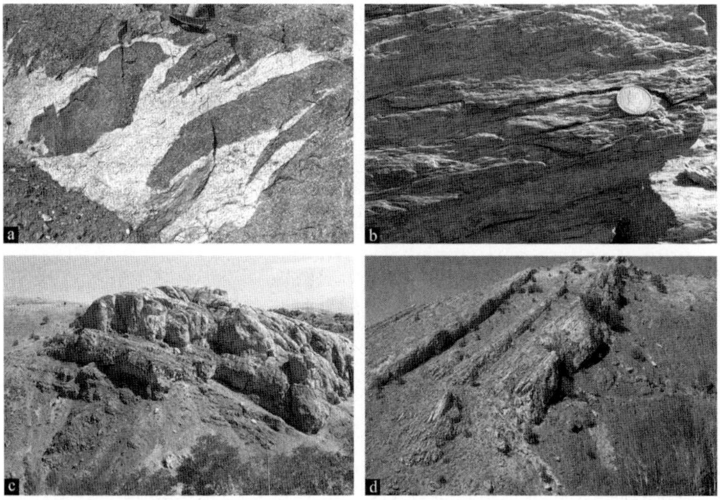

Fig. 13. Field photographs. (**a**) Plagiogranite (pale) intruding gabbro within a broad ductile shear zone; Baskil arc unit, near Baskil; (**b**) sheared gabbro showing top-to-the-north C–S fabric, possibly related to mid-Tertiary exhumation; Kömürhan Ophiolite, near Kömürhan bridge; (**c**) Maastrichtian shallow-marine limestone (Harami Formation) conformably overlying Upper Cretaceous volcanic–sedimentary facies (Elazığ Unit); near Elazığ; (**d**) Middle Eocene Limestone (Seske Formation) unconformably overlying Late Cretaceous Elazığ volcanic–sedimentary unit; NE of Baskil.

large area, SE of Hazar Lake (*c.* 200 km^2; Fig. 5). The ophiolite is locally underlain in the east by amphibolites that could represent a type of metamorphic sole, similar to the amphibolites associated with the Kömürhan Ophiolite, although these rocks were previously correlated with the internal stratigraphy of the Bitlis Massif (Yazgan & Chessex 1991). The sequence is dominated by harzburgite (ultramafic tectonite), with some dunite, passing upwards into layered cumulates composed of dunite, wehrlite, clinopyroxenite, troctolite, olivine gabbro, normal gabbro, quartz gabbro and quartz diorite (Özkan & Öztunalı 1984). The total thickness of the ultramafic rocks is estimated as 1800 m, and that of the gabbros as 1000 m. The cumulate rocks exhibit structures and textures indicative of crystal segregation, including magmatic layering, cross-bedding, slumping and synsedimentary faulting (Özkan & Öztunalı 1984). The crystallization order of the cumulate rocks is characterized by chromite–olivine–clinopyroxene–plagioclase–hornblende and quartz, as in many other Eastern Mediterranean ophiolites (Parlak *et al.* 2000). In addition, small exposures of massive gabbros are present, but no preserved sheeted dykes or extrusive rocks are known.

The Guleman Ophiolite is unconformably overlain by a well-exposed sedimentary succession of Maastrichtian–Palaeocene age, known as the Hazar Group (Perinçek 1979). For example, where well exposed near Aslantaş village (Fig. 5, location 12), coarse-grained ophiolite-derived conglomerates (included with the Ceffan Formation by Aktaş & Robertson (1984, 1990)) pass depositionally upwards into shallow-marine mudstones and sandstones (Simaki Formation) and then into neritic carbonates (Gehroz Formation).

Interpretation of the ophiolites

The ophiolites are widely interpreted as preserved fragments of a regionally extensive Late Cretaceous SSZ-type ophiolite (part of the 'Yüksekova Complex' of Perinçek 1979) that formed within the Southern Neotethys above a northward-dipping subduction zone (Aktaş & Robertson 1984; Yazgan 1984; Yazgan & Chessex 1991; Yılmaz 1991; Beyarslan & Bingöl 2000; Parlak *et al.* 2001, 2004; Robertson 2002; Robertson *et al.* 2004*a*, 2006).

These ophiolites are inferred to be of Late Cretaceous age, based on the presence of Campanian–Maastrichtian pelagic carbonates within the volcanic–sedimentary unit, although the primary crystallization age is not yet radiometrically dated. The original stratigraphy is restored as a complete ophiolite with mantle tectonite, layered and massive gabbros, sheeted dykes and a thick (up to 750 m) extrusive and

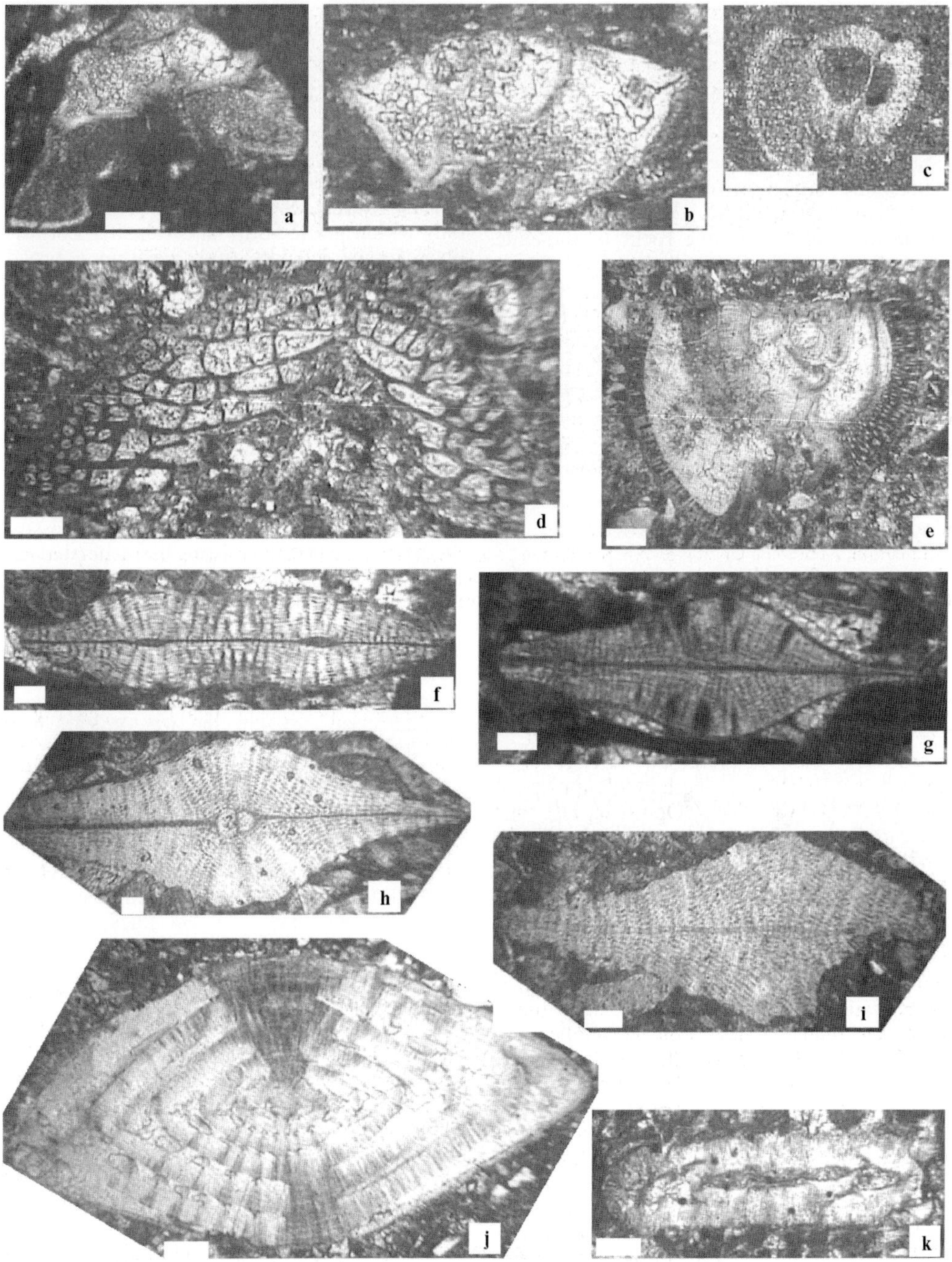

Fig. 14. Photomicrographs of selected age-significant microfossils from the Killan Imbricate Unit (**a–c**, **i**, **k**) and the Baskil area (**d–h**, **j**). (See the Appendix for a full listing of taxa identified and the locations of samples.) (**a**) *Contusotruncana contusa* (Cushman), Upper Maastrichtian, sample 220c. (**b**) *Globotruncanita stuarti* (de Lapparent), Upper Maastrichtian, Sample 220c. (**c**) *Acarinina bullbrooki* (Bolli), Middle Eocene, Sample 213a. (**d**) *Fabiania cassis* (Oppenheim); Sample 183b). (**e**) *Eorupertia magna* (le Calvez), Lutetian, Sample 183b. (**f**) *Asterocyclina* sp., Lutetian, Sample 154. (**g**) *Discocyclina scalaris* (Schlumberger); Sample 183b). (**h**) *Discocyclina seunesi* Douville, Lutetian, Sample 154. (**i**) *Orbitoclypeus ramaraoi* (Samanta), Ilerdian, Sample 214. (**j**) *Nummulites striatus* (Bruguiere), Lutetian, sample 183b. (**k**) *Assilina* cf. *yvettae* Schaub, Thanetian–Ilerdian, Sample 210. Scale bars represent 0.2 mm.

volcaniclastic sedimentary succession. Whole-rock and mineral chemistry of the extrusive and intrusive rocks (e.g. from the İspendere and Kömürhan ophiolites), provides additional evidence that the ophiolites formed in an intra-oceanic SSZ-type setting (O. Parlak, unpubl. data). Taken as a whole, the extrusive–sedimentary sequences of the Guleman and Kömürhan ophiolites comprise basic–intermediate–silicic volcanic rocks of tholeiitic composition, together with silicic tuffs, volcaniclastic turbidites and debris flows. This evidence suggests that the SSZ-type ophiolite evolved into an incipient intra-oceanic arc. The İspendere and Kömürhan ophiolites (but not the Guleman Ophiolite) are cut by calc-alkaline intrusive rocks. Similar rocks are much more extensively developed within the Elazığ–Baskil Magmatic Complex to the north, as discussed below.

Upper Cretaceous arc-related rocks

The arc-related rocks are represented by the Elazığ–Baskil Magmatic Complex in the area studied (Figs 5 and 6). This unit is dominated by basic–intermediate to silicic tholeiitic extrusive rocks (termed the Elazığ Unit), and calc-alkaline intrusive rocks (termed the Baskil Unit). The intrusive rocks were variously termed the Baskil Magmatic Rocks (Aktaş & Robertson 1984; Yazgan 1984), the Elazığ Volcanic Complex (Hempton 1984, 1985) or the Elazığ Granitoids (Beyarslan & Bingöl 2000; Turan & Bingöl, 1989, 1991), and they were included within the Yüksekova Complex by Perinçek (1979). Similar intrusive rocks are present further west in the Göksun–Afşin area (Parlak 2006).

Intrusive Baskil Unit

This unit is widely exposed north of Keban Lake, where it is regionally overthrust by the Keban Platform (Figs 5 and 9a). However, as noted above, primary magmatic contacts are preserved in some areas (e.g. east of Baskil). Sanidine from granitic rocks has yielded K–Ar ages of 76 ± 2.45 Ma and 78 ± 2.5 Ma (Yazgan & Chessex 1991).

An area north of Baskil, mapped in detail (Rızaoğlu *et al.* 2006), is dominated by large exposures of silicic intrusive rocks, interpreted as one or several plutons, composed of massive granite, granodiorite, quartz-monzonite, tonalite, quartz-diorite and diorite (e.g. Karataş Tepe; Fig. 5, location 14). In general, the more silicic plutons are cut by more basic dykes (Rızaoğlu 2006; Rızaoğlu *et al.* 2006). Numerous partially assimilated xenoliths of dark country rock (mainly <20 cm in size) are present. The granodiorite is locally cut by swarms of basic dykes, generally north–south – trending (mostly <0.6 m wide; Fig. 9d). There are also small aplitic veins and dykes (Fig. 10a). Microdiorites and granophyres are interpreted as hypabyssal magmatic rocks. Aplitic and dolerite dykes intrude the coarser-grained plutonic bodies at all structural levels, whereas rhyolitic dykes are seen only within granodiorite and tonalite. Locally, plagiogranite intrudes gabbro within a broad ductile shear zone (Fig. 13a).

Volcanic–sedimentary Elazığ Unit

Volcanic–sedimentary lithologies (Elazığ Unit) form the country rock of the intrusive Baskil Unit, either as large intact exposures or as local screens between individual intrusive bodies. Where well exposed (e.g. near Kömürhan Bridge; Fig. 5, location 7), the volcanic–sedimentary succession is composed of interbedded massive to crudely stratified lithologies, estimated as >500 m thick (Figs 10c and 15a). Massive basaltic or andesitic sheet flows predominate, mainly <20 m thick, and columnar-jointed dacites are also rarely present. Basic–intermediate pillow lavas locally include red jasper within the pillow interstices. Basaltic to andesitic lava breccias contain clasts <0.4 m in size. Volcanigenic debris flows (<30 m thick) are dominated by basaltic or andesitic clasts (<30 cm in size), in a poorly sorted volcaniclastic matrix. Very coarse, well-bedded intervals of volcaniclastic conglomerates and sandstones are also present. Sandstones occasionally contain volcanic clasts (<20 cm). Fine to medium-grained volcaniclastic sandstones (beds <15 cm thick) are well

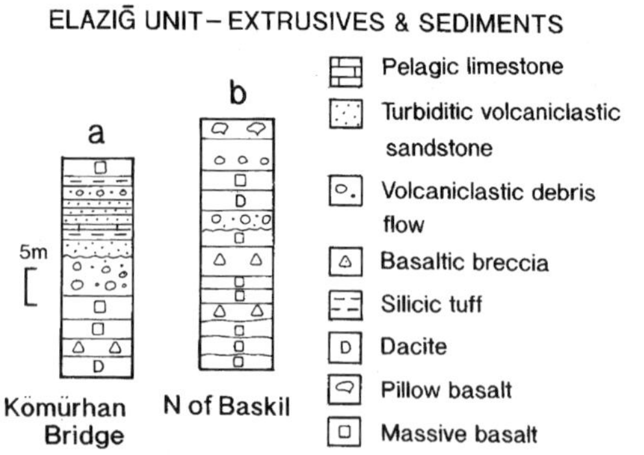

Fig. 15. Generalized logs of the volcanic–sedimentary successions from the Upper Cretaceous Elazığ–Baskil Magmatic Complex; (**a**) is dated as Late Campanian–Early Maastrichtian (Yazgan 1984). These units were regarded as 'synorogenic flysch' (Michard *et al.* 1984; Yazgan 1984), but are here interpreted as part of a volcanic-arc succession.

graded, with reddish coloured impure hemipelagic micrite near the top of individual beds. The succession includes mudstones, commonly reddish, interbedded with volcanigenic sandstones and pelagic carbonates (beds <10 cm thick). Thin (<1 m) lenses of pink pelagic limestones contain *Globotrunca* sp., indicating a Late Cretaceous age. Occasional interbeds of pale grey, finely laminated siliceous tuffs are present, in units 1–2 m thick. The relative abundance of the main lithologies is estimated as 50% lava breccia, 25% sheet flows, 25% volcaniclastic sandstone, 1% pelagic carbonate and 1% pillow lavas. However, the relative abundances of these lithologies vary between outcrops.

North of Baskil town, similar volcanic–sedimentary lithologies (Fig. 15b) are exposed between granitic intrusions, where they were previously mapped as 'synorogenic flysch' and dated as Late Campanian–Early Maastrichtian, utilizing planktic Foraminifera (Michard *et al.* 1984; Yazgan & Chessex 1991; east of Orta Mah.; Fig 5, location 15). Elsewhere (e.g. NNE of Elazığ) small exposures of the volcanic–sedimentary unit are dominated by basic–intermediate lavas, cut by occasional basic–silicic dykes. The volcanic–sedimentary unit also crops out widely further east, near Hazar Lake (Fig. 5), where it includes basaltic, andesitic and silicic lava flows, pyroclastic deposits and volcaniclastic sediments, cut by minor intrusions (e.g. silicic dykes and domes) (Beyarslan & Bingöl 2000). The volcanic rocks pass upwards into a volcanic–sedimentary succession of Campanian–Maastrichtian age.

Interpretation of the igneous–sedimentary unit

In most previous interpretations the volcanic–sedimentary Elazığ Unit was seen as representing an extrusive equivalent of the Baskil intrusive rocks in which volcanic rocks and sediments overlie the plutonic rocks. In this interpretation, the plutonic rocks were overlain first by pillow lavas, cut by rare intermediate to felsic dykes, and then by pyroclastic and volcaniclastic sediments of Campanian–Maastrichtian age (Yazgan 1984; Yazgan & Chessex 1991; Beyarslan & Bingöl 1996, 2000). However, this interpretation is unlikely for several reasons: (1) the volcanic rocks are basic to acidic and tholeiitic, whereas the intrusive rocks are intermediate–acidic and calc-alkaline; (2) no upward gradation between a high-level volcanic–sedimentary unit and deeper-level intrusive units is observed; instead the calc-alkaline plutons cut the volcanic rocks and sediments; (3) the intrusions cut both the volcanic–sedimentary unit and the directly structurally overlying Keban Platform in some places (e.g. east of Baskil), showing that no overlying volcanic–sedimentary unit existed at the time of intrusion; (4) similar volcanic–sedimentary lithologies form the uppermost levels of the İspendere and Kömürhan ophiolites further south, and comparable lithologies are associated with Upper Cretaceous ophiolites e.g. the Berit (Göksun) Ophiolite, further west in the Tauride thrust belt (Parlak *et al.* 2004; Robertson *et al.* 2006).

The volcanic–sedimentary Elazığ Unit is thus interpreted as the upper part of a Late Cretaceous ophiolitic assemblage that included basic, intermediate and silicic extrusive rocks and dykes, all of tholeiitic composition. The lower plutonic units are rarely, if ever, exposed but may be correlated with the Kömürhan Ophiolite further south.

During formation of the volcanic–sedimentary unit in Campanian–Maastrichtian time the ocean floor was clearly highly irregular, presumably related to construction of small volcanic edifices, coupled with frequent mass wasting to form debris flows and volcaniclastic turbidites. The background sediment was pelagic carbonate, without terrigenous input.

The granitic intrusive rocks form part of the same igneous complex as the Late Cretaceous calc-alkaline intrusions cutting the Keban Platform to the north and have been interpreted as an I-type continental margin arc related to northward subduction (Yazgan 1984; Yazgan & Chessex 1991; Beyarslan & Bingöl 1996, 2000). The ophiolitic basement of the volcanic–sedimentary unit, together with the Kömürhan and İspendere ophiolites in the Elazığ region, were emplaced beneath the Keban Platform and then mutually intruded by calc-alkaline granitic rocks during latest Cretaceous time.

Uppermost Cretaceous–Cenozoic cover sequence

The uppermost Cretaceous–Lower Cenozoic cover sequences constrain the palaeoenvironments and the timing of important compressional and extensional events affecting the suture zone.

Maastrichtian slope carbonates

The Elazığ–Baskil Magmatic Complex in the Elazığ area is depositionally overlain by shallow-marine limestones (Harami Formation; Fig. 13c), which contain neritic fossils of Late Campanian–Maastrichtian age (Aksoy *et al.*

1996, 1999). The contact was assumed to be an angular unconformity (Perinçek 1979). However, recent work indicates that the contact is transitional, at least locally. Shallow-marine carbonate deposition began during the later stages of genesis of the volcanic–sedimentary Elazığ Unit. Deposition began in a slope setting and continued after magmatism ended in a shallow-water setting, as seen *c.* 10 km SW of Elazığ (near Badempınar; Fig. 5, location 16) (Aksoy *et al.* 1999). This observation is critical in establishing that this part of the Elazığ–Baskil Magmatic Unit reached its present position in the Late Cretaceous. There is no possibility that the Elazığ–Baskil Magmatic Unit was ever thrust beneath the Keban Platform and later exhumed, as implied by some tectonic models (see below). The uppermost Cretaceous thrust front between the Elazığ–Baskil Magmatic Unit and the Keban Platform was evidently close to its present position by Maastrichtian time. This is consistent with the existence of calc-alkaline plutons stitching this thrust contact.

Lower Palaeocene coarse clastic sediments

Elsewhere, in the west of the area, around Baskil town, the basal sediments are conglomeratic (Lower Palaeocene Kuşçular Formation), passing southwards into red sandstones and mudstones (Fig. 16b). South of Keban, in the Baskil area, the Elazığ–Baskil Magmatic Complex is unconformably overlain by a thick unit (600 m) of Lower Palaeocene coarse clastic rocks, mainly conglomerates, dominated by clasts mainly derived from the Keban Platform. Further SW (e.g. at Sarıgül; Fig. 5, location 17), the igneous complex is unconformably overlain by a distinctive basal unit (*c.* 25 m thick) that is composed of well-sorted and well-rounded, clast-supported conglomerates. The clasts are mainly marble, with subordinate volcanic and intrusive igneous clasts. Upwards, a calcareous matrix becomes more abundant, followed by a sharp sedimentary transition (*c.* 10 cm) to rubbly limestones and marls containing *Nummulites* sp. (Upper Palaeocene–Lower Eocene Seske Formation; Perinçek 1979). The Lower Palaeocene conglomerates were eroded from the overriding Keban Platform to the north and alluvial fans prograded into a playa lake (Aksoy *et al.* 1996).

Another area located further west (*c.* 17 km west of Baskil) illustrates a marked local facies variation within the uppermost Cretaceous–Palaeocene cover sediments. In the south, the basal sediments are uppermost Cretaceous carbonates (Harami Formation) that then pass upwards into Lower Palaeocene coarse clastic deposits (Kuşçular Formation). In contrast, *c.* 7 km further north the Harami Formation is absent and the Upper Cretaceous magmatic rocks are unconformably overlain by Lower Palaeocene coarse clastic rocks (Turan & Türkmen 1996). Such relationships reflect the

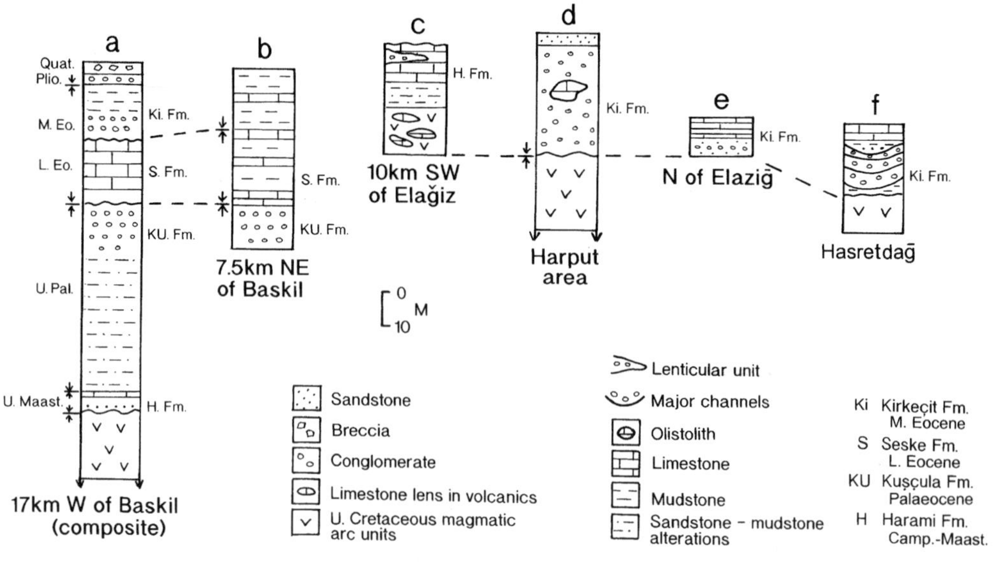

Fig. 16. Summary of the uppermost Cretaceous–Lower Cenozoic successions overlying the various allochthonous rocks emplaced in latest Cretaceous time. Data sources are specified in the text.

prevalence of marine conditions in the south, whereas the Keban Platform to the north was emergent and eroding during latest Cretaceous–Early Palaeocene time.

Upper Palaeocene–Lower Eocene shelf limestones

The Lower Palaeocene coarse clastic deposits are, in turn, abruptly overlain by mainly shallow-marine limestones of Late Palaeocene–Early Eocene age (Seske Formation; Perinçek 1979; Türkmen *et al.* 2001), marking a regional marine transgression (Fig. 16a). This calcareous unit is extensively exposed west of Malatya city (Fig. 3). A representative succession is exposed in the west of the area studied on the crest of a hill (NW of Baskil, near Laçan; Fig 5, location 3). A thin (<25 m thick) basal conglomerate (Kuşçular Formation), exposed above the Baskil Magmatic Complex there, contains large sub-rounded to sub-angular clasts (<0.8 m in size), mainly marble with subordinate schist and rare volcanic clasts (Fig. 13d). These conglomerates are directly overlain by white limestones that belong to the Seske Formation (>80 m thick). In general, marginal clastic environments dominated in the north, whereas coral-algal reefs developed further south and SW, reflecting open-marine conditions in this area (Türkmen *et al.* 2001).

Middle–Upper Eocene clastic rocks

During Middle to Late Eocene time there was a switch from mainly carbonates to deposition of variable shallow, to relatively deep-marine clastic sediments, known as the Kırkgeçit Formation (Avşar 1983; Türkmen *et al.* 2001). North of Keban Lake (Pertek area), this unit directly overlies and seals a regional north–dipping thrust contact between the Keban Platform, above and the Elazığ–Baskil Magmatic Complex, below (Fig. 5, location 13).

In the east, the Middle–Upper Eocene clastic unit unconformably overlies both the Keban metamorphic rocks and the Elazığ–Baskil magmatic rocks. For example, at Hasretdağ, NE of Elazığ (Fig. 5, location 18, and Fig. 16f) the Upper Cretaceous volcanic–sedimentary Elazığ Unit is unconformably overlain by shallow-marine clastic sediments of the Kırkgeçit Formation. The base of the succession is an irregular erosion surface, infilled with conglomerates. Above this, a spectacular series of palaeochannels is exposed (Türkmen & Essen 1997; Cronin *et al.* 2000). An argillaceous succession, *c.* 80 m thick, is interspersed with six discrete channelized clastic units that have prograded southwards, based on palaeocurrent evidence. The channelized units include debris-flow conglomerates, with clasts of Upper Cretaceous magmatic rocks and rare clasts of Upper Cretaceous shallow-marine limestone (derived from the Harami Formation). Inter-channel mudstones include trace fossils (e.g. *Paleodictyon; Zoophycus*), indicating a shallow-water setting. The succession passes upward into finer-grained sediments, interpreted as slope facies (Cronin *et al.* 2000).

Facies variation during the Middle Eocene was even more marked further west (e.g. around Baskil; Fig. 16a), where Upper Cretaceous magmatic rocks are unconformably overlain by conglomerates, sandy limestones, marls and limestones of Middle–Late Eocene age (Kırkgeçit Formation; Asutay 1988). Crudely stratified basal conglomerates include clasts (<25 cm in size) of basalt, granodiorite and nummulitic limestone. Recent work (Türkmen *et al.* 2001) has revealed a transition from a mainly carbonate to a dominantly terrigenous clastic depositional setting. West of Baskil, Middle–Upper Eocene clastic rocks (Kırkgeçit Formation) variably overlie Maastrichtian or Lower Cenozoic sedimentary units in different local areas. Rubbly bedded bioclastic limestones from one area are packed with large benthic Foraminifera, dated during this study as Lutetian (Middle Eocene) (Sample 154, Fig. 14f and g; Appendix). Further west in the Baskil area, pale grey, bioturbated, muddy carbonates are interbedded with thin- to medium-bedded, graded siliciclastic sandstones that may be storm deposits. The marls contain an abundant fauna including pectens, echinoids, bivalves, corals and calcareous algae. The marls contain Lutetian large Foraminifera (Samples 183a–c; Fig. 14e and j; Appendix), and are overthrust by volcanigenic facies of the Upper Cretaceous Elazığ–Baskil Magmatic Complex.

The Middle–Upper Eocene clastic sediments (Kırkgeçit Formation) mainly accumulated in a peripheral rift basin (Fig. 17), bounded by an active extensional fault in the south, known as the Uluova Fault (Fig. 5). From north to south, a range of marginal, to slope, to basin plain settings developed during Middle–Late Eocene time (Özgül & Kerey 1996). The basin was bordered to the north by an ENE–WSW-trending tract of marginal shelf carbonates. In response to intense extensional faulting, large limestone blocks were locally shed from the underlying calcareous succession into small fault-controlled slope basins (effectively slope canyons) near the northern margin of the rift basin (e.g. near Harput, north of Elazığ; Fig. 5, location 17, and Fig. 16d; Türkmen & Essen 1997).

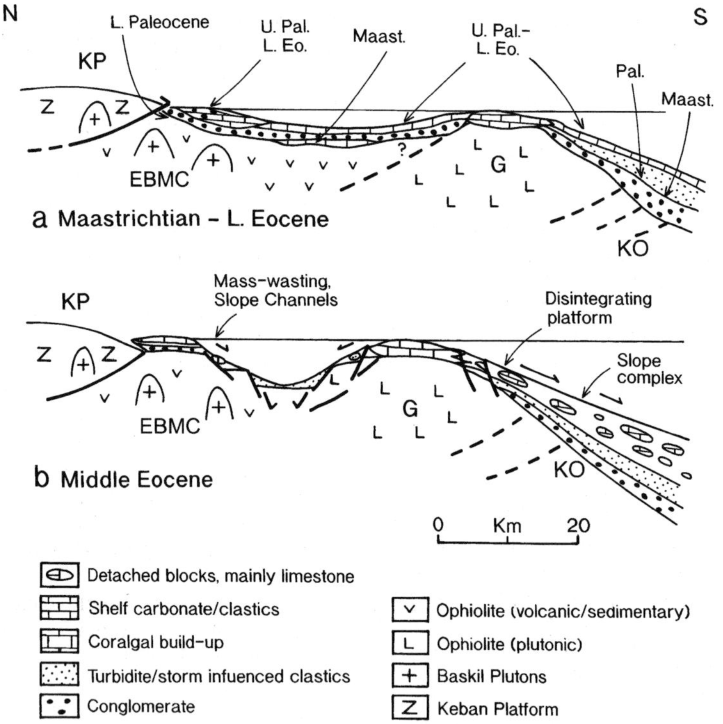

Fig. 17. Interpretation of the tectonic setting of the uppermost Cretaceous to Mid-Cenozoic sedimentary cover of the north Tauride margin (Keban Platform): (**a**) Maastrichtian–Lower Eocene facies overlie an accretionary complex; (**b**) Middle Eocene crustal extension possibly related to roll-back of the north-dipping subduction zone to the south. KO, Killan Ophiolite, KP, Keban Platform; G, Guleman Ophiolite; EBMC, Elazığ-Baskil Magmatic Complex. (See text for discussion.)

Oligocene–Lower Miocene neritic carbonates

Shallow-marine carbonates are locally exposed in the west and NW of the area, following deformation and erosion (Aksoy *et al.* 1996). West of Baskil these Miocene sediments are locally involved in thrusting (Yazgan 1984).

Tectonic implications of the sedimentary cover

The uppermost Cretaceous volcanic–sedimentary Elazığ Unit is overlain by Maastrichtian shallow-marine carbonates (Harami Formation), without any major unconformity or evidence of deep erosion. Both the Upper Cretaceous Elazığ–Baskil Magmatic Complex and the Keban Platform are unconformably overlain by Maastrichtian–Eocene mainly shallow-marine sediments, estimated to be up to 1.5 km thick (Fig. 17a). In the north, the Lower Palaeocene clastic sediments are interpreted as alluvial fans shed from the overriding Keban metamorphic thrust sheet during Early Palaeocene time (Aksoy *et al.* 1996). However, there is no evidence that these clastic sediments were actually overthrust by the Keban Platform. Thrusting apparently ended, then the clastic sediment were supplied from the, by then static, thrust front. Further south (Elazığ area), NW–SE-trending extensional palaeofaults became active during Middle Eocene time (Fig. 17b), creating the accommodation space necessary for the accumulation of channelized sediments (e.g. Hasretdağ) and basinal sediments further south.

The tectonic setting switched to compressional after Middle Eocene (pre-Oligocene) time (Perinçek 1979; Yılmaz 1993), triggering the inversion of extensional faults, regional uplift and thrusting. Further thrusting and open folding took place in pre-Pliocene time. The entire area was later dissected by high-angle faults associated with the South East Anatolian Transform Fault during Plio-Quaternary time (Fig. 5).

Middle Eocene Maden Group

The Pütürge Massif is unconformably overlain by a regionally important volcanic–sedimentary unit of Middle Eocene (Ypresian–Lutetian) age. To the east of the study area a similar unit covers the northern margin of the Bitlis Massif (Çağlayan *et al.* 1984; Göncüoğlu & Turhan 1984), and is also present to the west of the area studied in the Afşin–Elbistan and Berit areas (Perinçek & Kozlu 1984; Yılmaz *et al.* 1993; Robertson *et al.* 2006). All of these exposures were assigned to a regionally important unit known as the Maden Complex by Perinçek (1979, 1980). The term Maden Complex was applied by Rigo di Righi & Cortesini (1964) to a structurally complex unit in the southern part of the Tauride thrust belt, near Maden town, to the east of the Pütürge metamorphic massif (Fig. 5). There is a continuing debate (Yiğitbaş & Yılmaz 1996*a*) concerning the definition and significance of the 'Maden Complex'. This was variously interpreted in different areas as an intact stratigraphic succession (Perinçek & Kozlu 1984; Robertson *et al.* 2006), as a 'coloured' mélange (Hempton 1984, 1985), or as a thrust-imbricated succession (Aktaş & Robertson 1984; Yazgan & Chessex 1991; Fig. 5, location 20, and Fig. 18a; Yıldırım & Yılmaz 1991). In the area studied, a stratigraphic succession does indeed exist, although variably thrust imbricated. For this reason the conventional stratigraphic term Maden Group is adopted here.

Two successions were studied in the north-eastern part of the Pütürge Massif (Fig. 5). The more easterly succession (Fig. 18a) is well exposed along the road from Pütürge to Kömürhan Dam. The contact with the Pütürge metamorphic rocks (locally mica schists) is an irregular unconformity, dipping NW at *c.* 40°. A basal breccia contains angular clasts of metamorphic rocks (<25 cm in size), cemented by a red hematitic gritty matrix (Fig. 19a). This is followed by a fining-upward succession (mainly schistose) of coarse, then finer-grained sandstone (60–80 m). There is then a prominent volcanic interval, mainly andesite (*c.* 50 m), flow-banded rhyolite (*c.* 60–200 m thick) and fissile siliceous tuff (*c.* 6 m). Above comes a trail of elongate fossiliferous carbonate blocks. Individual blocks (up to 3 m × 5 m in size) are composed of grey marble, locally rich in *Nummulites* sp. and other large Foraminifera, dated as Lutetian (Sample 206a–c; Appendix). These limestone blocks are set within volcanigenic debris flows, with clasts up to 20 cm in size. The larger limestone blocks pass laterally into limestone debris flows composed of lithologically similar limestone blocks (up to 0.9 m × 0.2 m in size). A trail of limestone blocks can be traced up to 400 m along strike. The zone of limestone blocks is followed, up-sequence (northwards) by a thick succession (*c.* >1 km thick) that is dominated by schistose andesitic extrusive rocks, with subordinate metasedimentary intercalations. Most individual andesite flows are <5 m thick. Subordinate metasedimentary intercalations include volcaniclastic sandstones, shales, debris-flow deposits, silty and tuffaceous limestones (individually <4 m thick), pale siliceous shale (interpreted as silicic tuff), reddish shales and recrystallized red ribbon cherts. The succession commonly shows evidence of top-to-the-south shearing, marked by brittle folds, folded quartz veins, C–S fabrics and small (<10 cm) thrust duplexes. The upper contact of the Maden Group in this area is a thrust, dipping at *c.* 40° north. The layering in the overlying Kömürhan Ophiolite (layered gabbro) dips at a similar angle (*c.* 35 °N), suggesting that the intervening thrust was originally gently inclined (<10°).

The second, more deformed, north-dipping (*c.* 35°) unit was studied further west (near Kesrik, SE of Malatya; Fig. 5), although the base of the succession was not accessible. Also, the succession there was too deformed to usefully log. The higher part of the unit (*c.* 350 m thick) is dominated by greenschist-metamorphosed mudstones, andesites and andesitic breccias, with purple mudstone intercalations. Most of the succession is too sheared and metamorphosed to distinguish primary volcanic and volcanic–sedimentary features. However, the uppermost several hundred metres of the succession comprise volcanigenic debris flows, including flattened andesite clasts (<30 cm long), set in a green volcanigenic matrix. Locally, clasts (<10 cm in size) include pale silicic extrusive rocks. Intercalations of matrix-supported debris-flow deposits, several metres thick with flattened pebbles (<8 cm in size), pass depositionally upward into volcaniclastic sandstones. Several green volcanigenic units contain rare intercalations of purple schistose mudstone (up to 6 m thick). Subordinate flows of flattened pillow lavas show well-developed tension gashes. The succession also exhibits numerous small duplex structures indicating top-to-the-south shearing.

Samples of unfractionated meta-extrusive rocks were collected for chemical analysis by X-ray fluorescence (Table 1) from the higher levels of both of the above units (Nos 184–190 from the eastern locality and 202–215 from the western locality). When plotted on standard geochemical discrimination plots (Fig. 20a–e), the samples are seen to be of basaltic andesitic to andesitic composition (Fig. 20a). They mainly

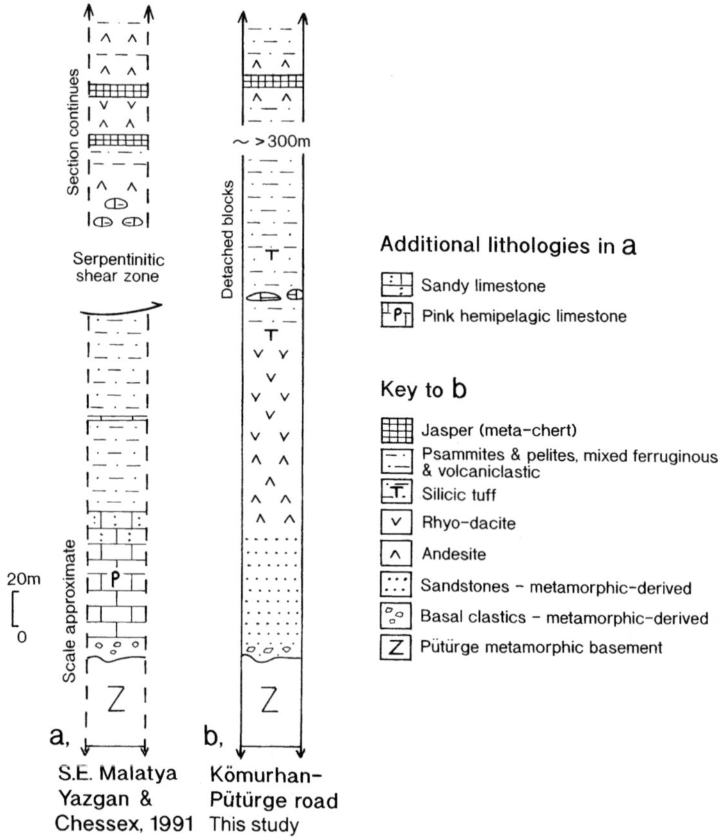

Fig. 18. Generalized logs of two representative successions of the Middle Eocene Maden Group unconformably overlying the Pütürge Metamorphic Massif: (**a**) from Yazgan & Chessex (1991); (**b**) this work.

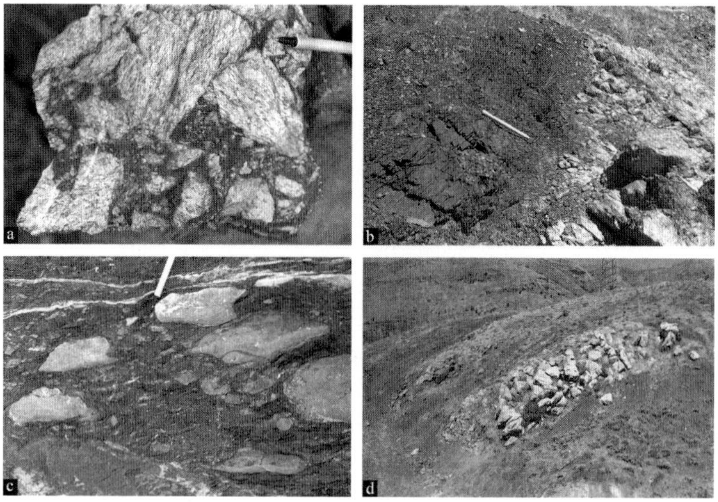

Fig. 19. Field photographs. (**a**) basal breccias of the Middle Eocene Maden Group unconformably overlying the Pütürge metamorphic complex, near Pütürge; (**b**) basal sediment of the Eocene Maden Group unconformably overlying Upper Cretaceous gabbros of the Killan Ophiolite, Killan Imbricate Unit, south of Maden town; (**c**) limestone-rich debris flows near the base of the Middle Eocene Maden Group, Killan Imbricate Unit, south of Maden town; (**d**) block of pelagic limestone within the Maden Group, east of Maden town.

Table 1. *Geochemical data for the basic extrusive rocks from the Maden Group*

	1 T/02/184	2 T/02/186	3 T/02/188	4 T/02/190	5 T/02/193	6 T/02/200	7 T/02/202A	8 T/02/203	9 T/02/207	10 T/02/209	11 T/02/215
SiO_2	52.07	46.49	50.93	51.17	48.8	68.01	51.64	47.49	49.15	50.59	50.55
TiO_2	1.14	1.51	0.87	1.38	1.07	1.04	2.13	0.81	0.85	1.39	0.79
MnO	0.2	0.18	0.14	0.2	0.19	0.03	0.1	0.15	0.14	0.18	0.12
Al_2O_3	16.35	18.68	17.34	18.4	14.47	13.89	14.03	16.81	16.5	14.66	18.61
Fe_2O_3*	11.69	11.84	8.43	10.99	9.33	5.4	12.98	8.45	14.51	9.58	7.03
MgO	6.19	8.48	6.49	5.09	12.34	3.03	9.21	7.25	5.6	5.82	5.54
CaO	4.65	3.27	7.52	3.42	5.88	0.42	1.9	8.44	3.34	8.2	6.91
Na_2O	4.31	4.58	4.78	5.56	3.73	4.45	3.77	3.94	4.5	5.35	4.94
K_2O	0.12	0.32	0.5	0.35	0.18	1.7	0.43	0.06	0.02	0.29	1.08
P_2O_5	0.17	0.22	0.13	0.21	0.08	0.21	0.34	0.16	0.08	0.11	0.17
LOI	3.32	4.51	2.94	3.23	3.65	1.93	3.65	6.62	5.53	3.68	4.12
Total	100.2	100.07	100.08	99.99	99.71	100.1	100.18	100.19	100.21	99.84	99.85
La	9	6	6	8	2	39	19	10	6	2	11
Ce	21	19	14	19	4	76	42	20	9	9	23
Nd	13	12	10	14	5	34	24	12	4	7	13
Nb	3	4	2	4	1	14	15	2	3	2	3
Zr	92	117	69	123	75	271	218	80	45	67	78
Y	28	36	20	38	23	30	37	19	24	26	22
Sr	233	182	295	135	66	40	31	325	76	141	545
Rb	1	2	6	5	2	60	21	1	0	4	12
Zn	113	134	72	122	78	156	55	77	139	95	81
Cu	37	79	62	87	87	26	19	51	45	73	57
Ni	7	30	85	15	375	31	50	119	20	64	97
Cr	9	15	157	11	718	123	63	333	8	110	244
V	324	430	239	319	189	141	238	192	370	308	255
Ba	34	65	87	112	74	367	52	25	22	30	459
Sc	34	32	35	30	30	18	39	21	34	41	34

*Total Fe given as Fe_2O_3.
Major elements in weight-percent oxide; trace elements in parts per million.
The rocks were analysed by X-ray fluorescence at the School of GeoSciences, University of Edinburgh. Analysis was carried out as specified by Fitton *et al.* (1998).
LOI, loss on ignition. (See text for explanation.)

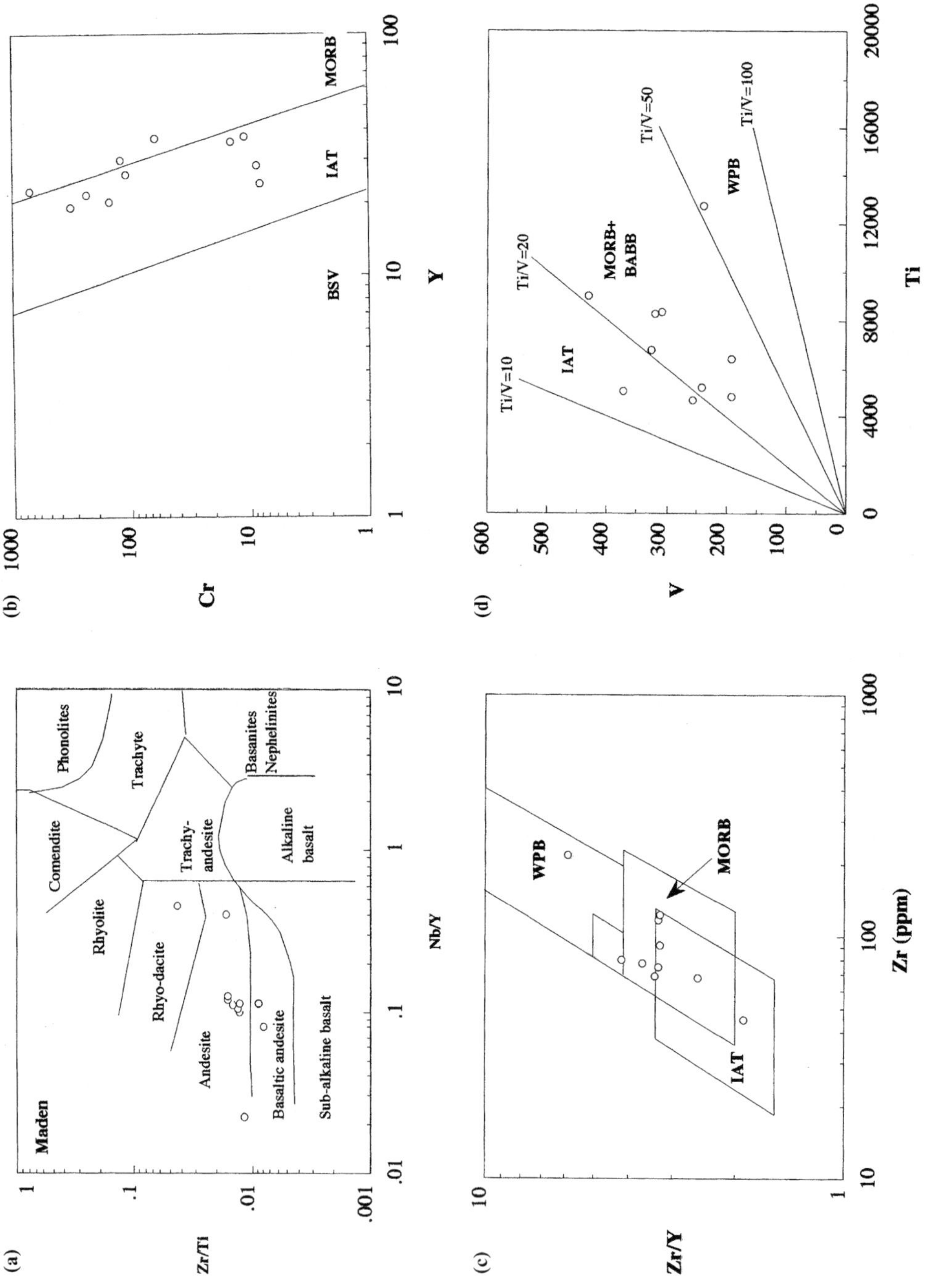

Fig. 20. For caption see p. 257 opposite.

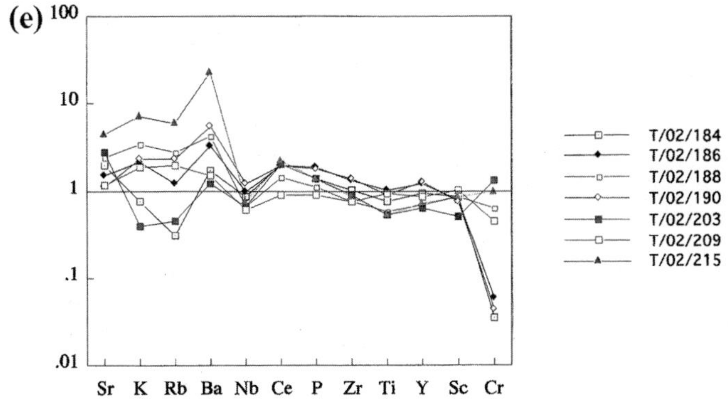

Fig. 20. Plots of chemical analyses of extrusive rocks from the Middle Eocene Maden Group. (**a**) Zr/Ti v. Nb/Y (from Winchester & Floyd 1977). (Note the basaltic andesite to andesitic composition.) (**b**) Cr v. Y. The samples lie within the island-arc tholeiitic (IAT) and mid-ocean ridge basalt fields (from Pearce 1982) (BSV; boninite series volcanism). (**c**) Zr/Y v. Zr. The samples fall in the same compositional groups, with one sample in the within-plate basalt field (from Pearce & Norry 1979). (**d**) V v. Ti. This plot suggests affinities with mainly island-arc and mid-ocean ridge or back-arc basin (BABB; back-arc basin basalt) settings (from Shervais 1982). (e) MORB-normalized 'spider' plots. All the samples show a negative Nb anomaly, suggestive of a subduction influence (from Sun & McDonough 1989).

plot in the combined or overlapping island-arc tholeiites and mid-ocean ridge basalt (MORB) field (Fig. 20b and c), but one lies in the within-plate basalt (WPB) field. The V/Ti plot is suggestive of a back-arc basin setting (Fig. 20d). All of the samples show a negative Nb anomaly on MORB-normalized 'spider' plots (Fig. 20e), suggestive of a subduction influence.

Interpretation of the Middle Eocene volcanic–sedimentary unit

The Middle Eocene Maden Group was previously interpreted in several different ways. First, it was seen as an immature island arc (Erdoğan 1975). Second, the magmatism was seen as being generated along a zone of 'intra-crustal subduction' (Michard *et al.* 1984; Yazgan 1984). In this interpretation, frictional heating along a deep-seated shear zone in a post-collisional setting favoured crustal melting and uprise of magmas (Yazgan & Chessex 1991). Third, the Maden rocks in the frontal thrust zone, south of the Bitlis Massif, were interpreted as a pull-apart basin related to oblique subduction in a setting of incipient collision (Aktaş & Robertson 1990). Finally, the Maden unit rocks was interpreted as a back-arc basin related to northward subduction (Hempton 1984, 1985; Yiğitbaş & Yılmaz 1991, 1996*a*; Yılmaz *et al.* 1993; Fig. 6a).

In the present study a distinction is drawn between the Middle Eocene Maden-type units that unconformably overlie the northern margins of the Pütürge and Bitlis massifs and contrasting volcanic rocks and sediments of the same age preserved in a structurally low position near the thrust front (Killan Imbricate Unit; see below). The overall setting of the Maden Group above the metamorphic massifs is inferred to be a rift developed above a north-dipping subduction zone, within the northern, active margin of the Southern Neotethys during its later stages of closure; hence the combined SSZ and WPB characteristics of the volcanic rocks. However, there is little evidence that this volcanism took place behind a well-developed volcanic arc, which is absent from the preserved frontal portion of the allochthon (see below).

The volcanic–sedimentary facies covering the Pütürge and Bitlis massifs document an east–west-trending, subsiding extensional basin in Middle Eocene time. Initial marine transgression, with locally derived clastic deposition, and shallow-marine carbonate deposition was followed by basic–intermediate–silicic volcanism. The presence of siliceous tuff implies volcanism in shallow water, or on land, at least initially. Extensional collapse and deepening ensued, marked by supply of limestone blocks ('olistoliths') into deeper water. The extensional basin later gradually filled with mainly andesitic volcanic rocks and volcaniclastic gravity flows, including matrix-supported breccia-conglomerates and volcanigenic muds. The siliceous radiolarian sediments are indicative of an unrestricted, relatively deep-water open-marine setting. The rift basin later closed, resulting in thrust imbrication, especially in the higher levels. The Maden Group

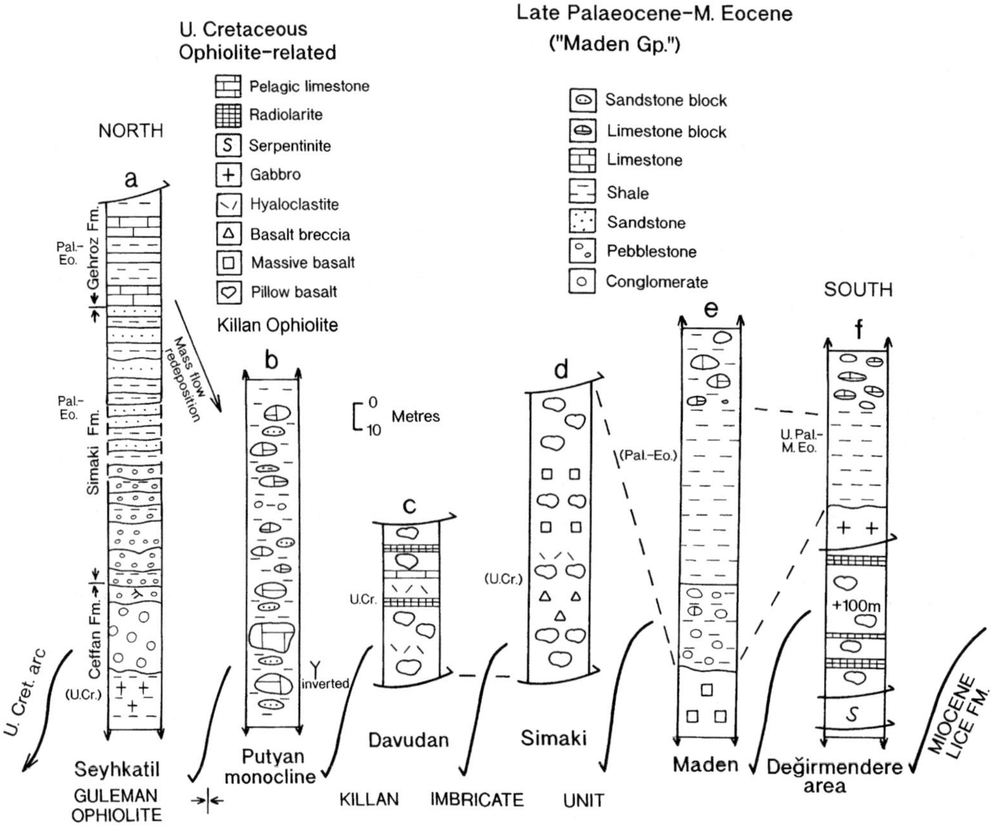

Fig. 21. Summary logs of the Killan Imbricate Unit. Data sources: Aktaş & Robertson (1984, 1990). (See text for discussion.)

covering the Pütürge Massif was then overthrust, southwards, by the Kömürhan Ophiolite, probably giving rise to the greenschist-facies metamorphism affecting the Maden Group. The timing of this thrusting is likely to be pre-Oligocene in view of the absence of preserved Oligocene sediments in the Maden Group and evidence of thrusting of this age reported from the wider region (Perinçek 1979; Yılmaz 1993).

Uppermost Cretaceous–Lower Cenozoic frontal slice complex

A regionally important imbricate slice complex comprising slices and blocks of ophiolitic and various sedimentary rocks distinguishes the southerly, structurally lowest, part of the allochthon (Figs 5 and 6). This unit was traditionally included within the Upper Cretaceous Yüksekova Complex and the Middle Eocene Maden Complex (Perinçek 1979, 1980) but was later formalized as the Killan Imbricate Unit by Aktaş & Robertson (1984), as it shows distinct features. The type area of the Killan Imbricate Unit is located between the Pütürge and Bitlis massifs. However, the term has also been applied to the frontal imbricate zone more regionally (Yazgan & Chessex 1991). This includes the southern margin of the Bitlis Massif to the east (e.g. Lice area; Aktaş & Robertson 1984), and the southern margin of the Malatya–Pütürge Massif further west (e.g. Helete area; Yıldırım & Yılmaz 1991; Robertson *et al.* 2006).

In the type area, the Killan Imbricate Unit structurally underlies the Pütürge Massif in the west, whereas to the east it is separated from the Bitlis metamorphic massif by a zone of high-angle faulting (Fig. 5). In the north, the Killan Imbricate Unit is structurally overlain by the Guleman Ophiolite, whereas in the south it structurally overlies the Miocene Arabian Foreland (Perinçek 1979). The contact zone between the Guleman Ophiolite and the Killan Imbricate Unit (e.g. near Putyan; Fig. 5, location 21) is marked by spectacular zone of detached sedimentary blocks derived from the uppermost Cretaceous–Lower Cenozoic succession exposed to the north (Hazar Group; Fig. 21a and b; Aktaş & Robertson 1984). During this study, large Foraminifera of Thanetian–Late Palaeocene age were determined within large limestone blocks (Sample 214; Fig. 14i; Appendix).

The Killan Imbricate Unit comprises several large tectonic slices, with an apparent structural thickness of > 17 km (Aktaş & Robertson 1984). The most southerly of these slices (Fig. 21f) comprises a dismembered Upper Cretaceous ophiolitic unit (Killan Ophiolite); this is unconformably overlain by Middle Eocene deep-water sediments, including detached blocks and slices of mainly pelagic carbonates and extrusive rocks (Fig. 19c). The contact between the ophiolite and the sediments is well exposed south of Maden town, by the main road (near Değirmendere). There, ophiolitic gabbro is cut by occasional altered dykes and overlain, above an irregular erosional surface, by a thin (< 10 m) interval of debris-flow deposits (up to several metres thick), including numerous gabbro clasts (< 0.6 m in size). This is followed by blocks ('olistoliths') and lenses (detached 'rafts') of pelagic and hemipelagic limestone, set within hemipelagic carbonates and tuffaceous mudstones. These limestones clasts contain large Foraminifera of Thanetian or Ilerdian age (Palaeocene–Early Eocene) age (Sample 210; Fig. 14k; Appendix). The number and size of exotic blocks and sheets increases upwards (Fig. 21f).

A second major slice, further north (Fig. 21e), includes a major unit of Upper Cretaceous ophiolitic rocks (Killan Ophiolite), mainly tholeiitic lavas. These lavas are interbedded with Upper Cretaceous radiolarites and pelagic carbonates. The economic Maden copper sulphide mine is located within this unit. Deformed, brecciated ophiolitic gabbros are unconformably overlain by chocolate brown mudstones, rich in hydrothermal epidote (0.5 km south of the Maden Mine towers). Exotic blocks of pelagic and hemipelagic limestone appear above this, within several tens of metres of the base of the cover succession. These limestones contain Foraminifera of Middle Eocene age (Sample 213a and b; Fig. 14c and d; Appendix). In the vicinity, north-dipping massive ophiolitic lavas are directly overlain by debris flows, dominated by lava clasts (up to 2.8 in size), set in a reddish matrix; for example, 300 m along the road to Alacakaca (Guleman) from the main Maden road. Local horizons are rich in clasts of pink pelagic limestone (up to 2 m × 3 m in size). Other debris flows at the base of the Eocene succession are polymict, with a mixture of basaltic and pelagic limestone clasts (Fig. 19d). The succession then passes upwards into chocolate brown, locally tuffaceous mudstones with scattered exotic limestone blocks and lenses, estimated as *c.* 500 m thick. The exotic pelagic carbonates are homogeneous, lack interbedded argillaceous or tuffaceous sediments, and exhibit sharp, sheared margins. Higher in the unit, a volcanic–sedimentary unit comprises disrupted blocks and dismembered slices of andesite, pelagic carbonate, shale, tuff and volcaniclastic sediments, with an aggregate thickness estimated at 6 km (Fig. 21d). Blocks of sheared and brecciated vesicular andesite become more abundant upwards.

Units further north again (Fig. 21c) include massive basalt, pillow basalt, lava breccia, volcaniclastic sandstone and red radiolarian chert; for example, as exposed along the Hazar Lake–Maden main road (and near Davudan). Tholeiitic basalts include pyroxene–plagioclase-phyric and aphyric varieties, with common epidote alteration. Volcaniclastic intercalations (up to 50 m thick) are locally observed. There are also several slices, or intercalations (up to 10 m thick), of pink or grey pelagic limestone and red radiolarian chert. The cherts were previously dated as Late Cretaceous utilizing Radiolaria (Aktaş & Robertson 1984) and during this study associated pelagic carbonates were identified as Late Maastrichtian in age, based on the presence of planktic Foraminifera (Samples 220a–c; Fig. 14a and b; Appendix).

Laterally equivalent units

Beneath the adjacent Pütürge and Bitlis metamorphic massifs, lithological equivalents of the Killan Imbricate Unit are restricted to small slices of mainly serpentinite above the basal thrust. Comparable Middle Eocene units are more extensively exposed outside the present study area, including beneath the Bitlis Massif to the east (e.g. in the Lice area; Baştuğ 1980; Aktaş & Robertson 1984, 1990) and beneath the Malatya Metamorphic Massif to the west (Perinçek & Kozlu 1984; Yıldırım & Yılmaz 1991; Robertson *et al.* 2006; Fig. 5).

In the east (Lice area), an elongate volcanic–sedimentary slice, up to several hundred metres thick, comprises interbedded basic–intermediate composition extrusive rocks and turbiditic sandstones, depositionally overlain by Middle Eocene pelagic carbonates. The sandstones contain abundant terrigenous metamorphic material, probably derived from the structurally overlying Bitlis Massif. Basalts analysed from this area are of high-Al composition and generally show 'enriched' stable element patterns without a detectable subduction component (Aktaş & Robertson 1990).

West of the study area (near Helete; Fig. 5) another elongate thrust sheet (*c.* 20 km long × 200 m thick; Yıldırım & Yılmaz 1991) includes ophiolitic material and tholeiitic volcanic rocks (Helete–Savrun unit), depositionally overlain by Middle Eocene pelagic carbonates (Robertson *et al.* 2006). These volcanic rocks show a marked chemical subduction influence (Yıldırım & Yılmaz 1991; Robertson *et al.* 2006).

Interpretation of the frontal imbricates

The Upper Cretaceous Killan Ophiolite is interpreted as the southerly part (trailing edge) of a regionally extensive ophiolite sheet, including the İspendere, Kömürhan and Guleman ophiolites that docked along the northern ocean basin margin, beneath the Keban Platform in latest Cretaceous time. The Killan Ophiolite, as exposed in several tectonic slices, was dismembered and emplaced in latest Cretaceous time but was not then exposed and eroded, as ophiolitic extrusive rocks are preserved, unlike the Guleman Ophiolite to the north. The Upper Cretaceous ophiolitic extrusive rocks in each of the Killan imbricates are mainly subduction-influenced tholeiites (Aktaş & Robertson 1984, 1990). An additional thrust sheet of alkaline WPB-type extrusive rocks near the structural base of the imbricate stack further east (Goma-type extrusive rocks; Aktaş & Robertson 1984, 1990) could represent fragments of seamounts accreted from the Southern Neotethys.

Several of the slices of Killan ophiolitic rocks are unconformably overlain by a thick 'volcanic–sedimentary unit' of mainly Middle Eocene age, including thick debris flows ('olistostromes') (Maden Group of Aktaş & Robertson 1984). Much of this material was derived from the north. To the north, the emplaced Guleman Ophiolite was deeply eroded and transgressed by Maastrichtian–Palaeocene clastic sediments (Ceffan and Simaki formations) and carbonate sediments (Gehroz Formation; Fig. 21a) of the Hazar Group. Along its southern margin this sedimentary cover of the Guleman Ophiolite became unstable and partially slid southwards, as detached blocks and slide sheets during Middle Eocene time. A thick wedge of hemipelagic and redeposited background carbonates and exotic limestone blocks thereby accumulated along the northern margin of a deep-water basin to the south. Two interpretations of this large-scale mass flow and redeposition are as follows. Aktaş & Robertson (1984) envisaged mass wasting of mainly carbonate sediments (Gehroz Formation) into an active subduction trench to the south, within a forearc setting (Fig. 22a). Alternatively, the collapse of the margin and mass wasting reflects a discrete pulse of extension

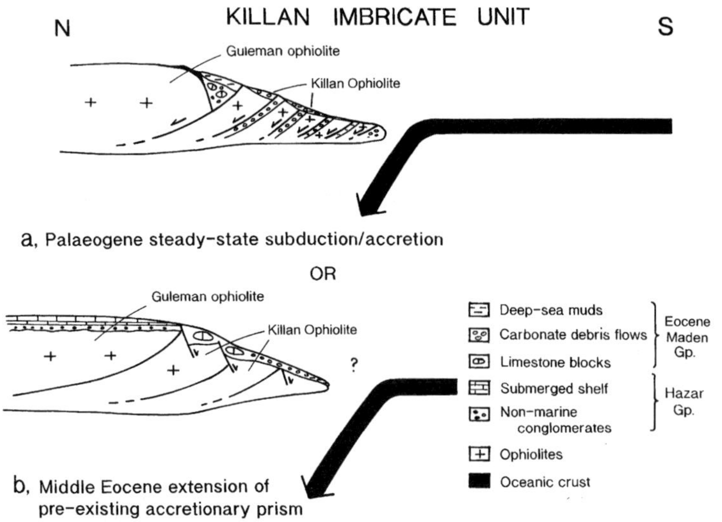

Fig. 22. Alternative tectonic models for the uppermost Cretaceous–Lower Cenozoic Killan Imbricate Unit. (**a**) Steady-state subduction–accretion (Aktaş & Robertson 1984); (**b**) initial accretion of ophiolitic rocks during latest Cretaceous time, followed by extension related to subduction slab roll-back during Mid-Eocene time. (**b**) is favoured here.

along the active margin during Mid-Eocene time (Fig. 22b). The Middle Eocene basin later collapsed and was accreted to the base of the accretionary wedge, probably at the same time as deformation of the 'back-arc' Maden Basin to the north (pre-Oligocene?). In the regional context the second option is preferred.

The location of the type area of the Killan Imbricate Unit between the Bitlis and Pütürge metamorphic massifs could be interpreted in several different ways. First, it could reflect Mesozoic palaeogeography, whereby an oceanic connection separated two microcontinents, represented by the Bitlis and Pütürge massifs. This could have created an embayment, facilitating the accretion of the Upper Cretaceous Killan Ophiolite in latest Cretaceous time. In this model, oceanic crust to the east and west was mainly subducted, apart from small ophiolitic slices preserved within the frontal imbricate zone (e.g. beneath the Bitlis Massif). An alternative is that the localized presence of the thick Killan Imbricate Unit reflects subduction zone dynamics and differential exposure along an originally linear thrust front (rather than palaeogeography). For example, subduction erosion, or strike-slip could have removed frontal accreted material. Also, tectonic exhumation of the Bitlis and Pütürge massifs in latest Cretaceous–Middle Eocene time (see below) might have been discontinuous, creating areas where metamorphic rocks are not exposed at the surface, but where thick accretionary material such as the Killan Imbricate Unit remained.

Regionally, the Middle Eocene basin further east (e.g. Lice unit) was interpreted as an extensional pull-apart basin related to oblique northward subduction during Middle Eocene time (Aktaş & Robertson 1984, 1990). The Middle Eocene basin further west (i.e. Helete unit) can be interpreted as part of an extensional basin formed above a subduction zone (Robertson *et al.* 2006), rather than an accreted oceanic arc (see Yılmaz 1993). An overall setting of oblique subduction is inferred here resulting in segmentation of the active margin, with different areas undergoing accretion, transtension, or incipient arc volcanism, comparable with the setting of the modern Andaman Sea region (e.g. Curray *et al.* 1979).

Arabian Foreland

The Tauride thrust belt is underlain by the Arabian Foreland, which forms part of the autochthonous Arabian (African) Plate to the south. Sedimentary successions (Fig. 7) shed light on the history of the Southern Neotethyan continental margin, especially its Mesozoic rift–passive margin stage and suturing during Miocene time.

The Arabian Foreland succession includes a complete stratigraphy, as exposed south of the thrust front in the Derik area near the Syrian border. This begins with felsic igneous rocks of presumed Precambrian age and associated clastic sediments. These are unconformably overlain by a mixed volcaniclastic–siliciclastic–carbonate succession, of assumed Cambrian age. Overlying largely clastic sediments of Ordovician age pass into mainly shales (locally bituminous) of Late Ordovician–Devonian age. The succession is interrupted by a Carboniferous unconformity, followed by further shallow-marine to paralic sediments. The Palaeozoic succession, *c.* 2.5 km thick, records deposition on a stable shelf near the edge of Gondwana (Rigo di Righi & Cortesini 1964; Perinçek 1979, 1981; Yılmaz 1991, 1993).

Mesozoic deposition began with shelf-type siliciclastic sediments of Early Triassic age, followed by a depositional hiatus from Late Triassic–Early Cretaceous (Barremian) time (e.g. in the Hazro inlier; Fontaine 1981). The development of reef facies, of Barremian–Turonian age, was followed by emergence and a hiatus during Coniacian–Santonian time. The shelf then subsided, creating a linear basin that infilled with siliciclastic turbidites (Kastel Formation). Deposition in this basin ended in the Early Campanian (Altıner 1989). This was followed by southward emplacement of Mesozoic slope units, in the form of broken formation and mélange (Hezan Unit) during Late Campanian–Early Maastrichtian time. The slope units include Middle Triassic dolomitic carbonates, Ladinian pelagic carbonates and Lower Norian volcanigenic sediments (Fourcade *et al.* 1991). Ocean-derived units include Tithonian–Berriasian pelagic carbonates (Konak Formation; Perinçek 1979; Altıner 1989), abundant dismembered ophiolitic units (e.g. Koçali Ophiolite) and related pelagic sediments.

The ophiolitic allochthon was transgressed by shallow-marine carbonates of Late Maastrichtian age, as seen all along the Arabian margin from Oman to Hatay in southern Turkey (Robertson 1987; Yılmaz 1993). Shallow-marine deposition was interrupted by a tilting event in the Early Eocene. Facies trends (Antak and Gercüş formations) point to uplift in the north (Rigo de Righi & Cortesini 1964). Transgressive shallow-marine carbonate deposition followed during Middle Eocene–Oligocene time across a wide area (Midyat Formation; Baştuğ 1980).

Facies become more basinal southwards, including siliceous limestones, and are overlain by evaporites and chalky marls in the north (towards the foothills structure belt). After a low-angle unconformity the succession passes into Lower Miocene turbiditic clastic sediments, which range from coarser grained in the north (Çüngüş Formation), to finer grained further south (Lice Formation; Perinçek 1979; Baştuğ 1980). In addition, poorly dated debris-flow deposits ('wildflysch') were entrained beneath the South Anatolian sole thrust.

Events affecting the Arabian Foreland

The Mesozoic succession records rifting that probably took place during Mid–Late Triassic time. Further extension possibly affected this area during Late Jurassic–Early Cretaceous time, and was followed by passive margin subsidence. The marginal slope succession, dating from Triassic time, can be reconstructed from volcanic and sedimentary rocks that were emplaced southwards onto the Arabian margin in latest Cretaceous time. For example, margin-related volcanic rocks and sediments (Hezan Unit) include Upper Jurassic–Lower Cretaceous pelagic carbonates and associated radiolarites that are preserved as blocks in the Besni Olistostrome, beneath the Koçali Ophiolite in SE Turkey.

The onset of regional convergence within the Southern Neotethys during Turonian time triggered flexural upwarping of the Arabian margin, extending from the Eastern Mediterranean to Oman (Robertson 1987; Yılmaz 1993). The emplaced margin-type units (Hezan Unit) are interpreted as a subduction–accretion complex that was overridden by an ophiolite of SSZ type (Koçali Ophiolite). The ophiolites and ophiolitic mélange correlate with ophiolites and related continental margin units of the Hatay and Baer–Bassit regions that were emplaced onto the Arabian Foreland further west (Delaloye & Wagner 1984; Delaune-Mayère 1984; Al-Riyami *et al.* 2002; Al-Riyami & Robertson 2002). During southward thrusting, the Arabian margin was flexurally loaded by the advancing accretionary wedge, including ophiolites. This culminated in collapse, followed by emplacement of the continental margin and oceanic units.

Palaeogene time recorded the re-establishment of a north-facing passive margin, from Late Maastrichtian time onwards. Tilting in the Early Eocene could record renewed northward subduction. This was followed by subsidence of the margin, possibly accentuated by the pull (i.e. negative buoyancy) of the downgoing oceanic plate (Robertson *et al.* 2004). The margin collapsed during the Miocene as the Southern Neotethys finally closed. Debris-flow deposits were shed from the advancing thrust front (Midyat Formation), passing southwards into deeper-water turbidites (Lice Formation). Prior to Mid-Miocene time, the southern part of the foredeep was overthrust by the northern part of foredeep and finally by the overriding Tauride allochthon along the South Anatolian basal thrust. Related to this collision, the Arabian Platform was locally reverse-faulted and folded within a marginal zone of deformation.

Discussion: remaining problematic issues

Ophiolites north and south of the Bitlis–Pütürge units

The ophiolitic rocks are mainly exposed to the north of the Pütürge and Bitlis metamorphic massifs (i.e. İspendere, Kömürhan, Guleman), but also occur as smaller thrust slices and ophiolitic mélange beneath the metamorphic massifs (e.g. Killan Imbricate Unit). Several explanations for this apparent duplication of ophiolites have been suggested.

(1) *Regional overthrusting.* The ophiolites represent a single regional-scale thrust sheet that was emplaced southwards over the Arabian margin, including the Pütürge and Bitlis units, related to continental collision in latest Cretaceous time (Michard *et al.* 1984; Yazgan 1984; Yazgan & Chessex 1991; Fig. 4ai). In this model, the emplacement was followed by crustal-scale rethrusting of the Arabian Foreland and the emplaced ophiolites after Middle Eocene time (Fig. 4aii). However, there is no evidence that the Arabian margin experienced continental collision until Early–Middle Miocene time.

(2) *Strike-slip.* Duplication of the ophiolites occurred as the result of 'terrane dispersal', related to oblique convergence and collision (Aktaş & Robertson 1990). The Bitlis–Pütürge massifs with their already accreted ophiolites might have been juxtaposed with the Keban Platform and its accreted ophiolites by regional-scale (hundreds of kilometres) strike-slip. However, this is unlikely as the tectonostratigraphy of the metamorphic massifs and the ophiolites–arc units differs between the northerly and southerly belts, and major (pre-Pliocene) strike-slip faults have not yet been mapped.

(3) *Crustal-scale out-of-sequence thrusting.* During latest Cretaceous time the ophiolites were accreted beneath the Bitlis–Pütürge massifs that then formed part of the southern margin of a much larger northerly continental margin unit, including the Keban Platform (Fig. 4ci). This

was followed by crustal-scale (out-of-sequence) thrusting after Middle Eocene time, which detached the Bitlis–Pütürge unit from the Keban unit and inserted the ophiolites–arc rocks between them (Yılmaz 1991, 1993; Fig. 4cii). In another version, crustal-scale rethrusting instead occurred during inferred continental collision in latest Cretaceous time (Beyarslan & Bingöl 2000; Fig. 4bi and ii). However, there is no evidence of such large-scale duplication of the tectonostratigraphy, either during Late Cretaceous or post-Mid-Eocene time in the study area or elsewhere in the Eastern Taurides.

(4) *Palaeogeography.* The Bitlis and Püturge massifs represent one, or several, microcontinents that were rifted during opening of the Southern Neotethys (Şengör & Yılmaz 1981; Robertson & Dixon 1984; Fig. 8c). This model best fits the structural evidence but needs to be tested by more fieldwork, especially in the far east of the region.

One or several spreading centres?

How can the near-simultaneous accretion of ophiolites to the Keban Platform (northern margin) and their southward emplacement over the Arabian margin in latest Cretaceous time be explained (see Robertson 2006)? This is explicable if the Southern Neotethyan Ocean was effectively closed by latest Cretaceous time (Yazgan & Chessex 1991; Beyarslan & Bingöl 2000; Fig. 4a and b), but apparently is inconsistent with the predominant view that continental collision did not take place until Early–Middle Miocene time (Dewey *et al.* 1986; Yılmaz 1991, 1993; Robertson 1998, 2000). The Africa–Eurasia convergence path necessitates an oceanic separation between Africa and Eurasia extending into Cenozoic time (Livermore & Smith 1984). The Northern Neotethys in the region was closed by Early Cenozoic time (Yılmaz *et al.* 1997; Okay & Şahintürk 1997; Rice *et al.* 2006) and cannot have accounted for this oceanic separation. The existence of a wide Black Sea to the north, subducting southwards during Late Cretaceous–Early Cenozoic time has been suggested based on igneous geochemical data (Bektaş *et al.* 1999), but as yet there is little supporting regional evidence. Assuming that a relatively wide (hundreds of kilometres) Southern Neotethys did indeed survive into Cenozoic time in SE Turkey, it is then difficult to envisage the near-simultaneous emplacement, along both margins, of ophiolites, both of SSZ type, without invoking the existence of more than one spreading centre. The implication is thus that more than one SSZ spreading centre existed, one located to the north and another to the south of the inferred Bitlis–Pütürge microcontinents; further work on this aspect is needed.

Summary and conclusions: an integrated tectonic model

Taking all the evidence discussed above, the Tauride thrust belt can be restored as a series of time slices (Fig. 23).

Triassic

The Southern Neotethys rifted to form an east–west-trending basin along the northern margin of Gondwana during Mid–Late Triassic time. Rifting was accompanied by eruption of alkaline basalts within the Pütürge and Bitlis massifs, coupled with subsidence and onset of deep-water deposition. Spreading probably began in Late Triassic–Early Jurassic time. The Bitlis and Pütürge massifs are tentatively restored as microcontinents within the Southern Neotethys.

Jurassic–Cretaceous

Passive margins were constructed, represented by the Keban Platform in the north and the Arabian Foreland in the south. Little sedimentation is preserved on the distal margins dating from this time. The Pütürge and Bitlis massifs possibly then existed as submerged microcontinental units. The Arabian margin apparently experienced uplift during Late Jurassic–Early Cretaceous time, possibly related to thermally induced uplift along the margins of the Southern Neotethys, as seen in the Levant region (Fig. 23a).

Late Cretaceous c. *90 Ma*

Northward intra-oceanic subduction began, possibly directly outboard of the Keban Platform, and the ophiolites (İspendere, Kömürhan, Guleman and Killan) formed above a northward-dipping subduction zone (Fig. 23b). Related to regional plate convergence, northward underthrusting–subduction was also initiated beneath the northern margin, presumably consuming MOR-type oceanic crust until the young (buoyant) spreading centre, represented by the SSZ-type ophiolites, arrived at the trench and was accreted. Northward subduction then continued beneath the accreted SSZ-type ophiolites and the Keban Platform, giving rise to the latest Cretaceous arc magmatism that cuts both the accreted ophiolite (Kömürhan

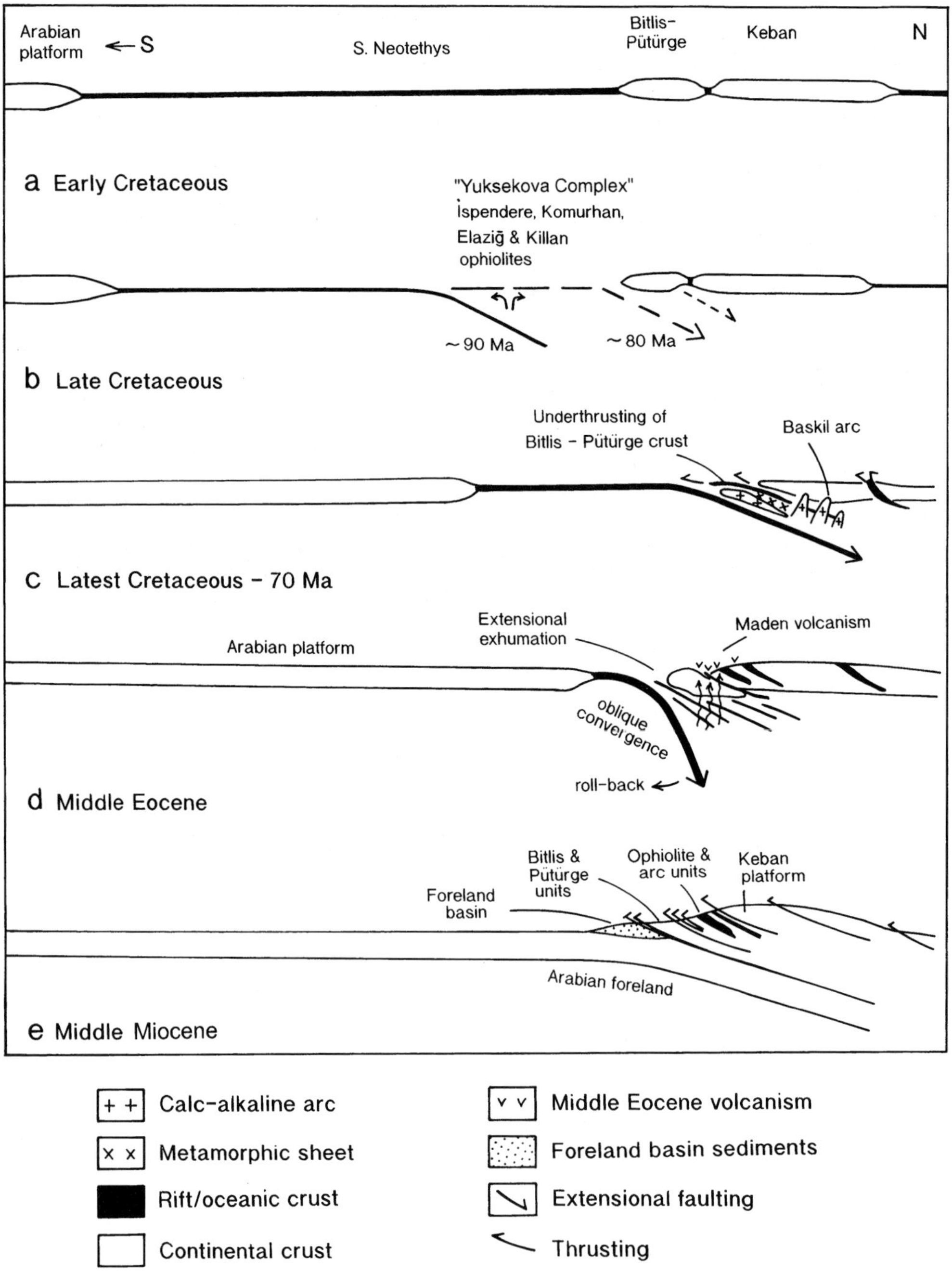

Fig. 23. Tectonic evolution of the Tauride thrust belt in SE Turkey in time slices. (See text for discussion.)

Ophiolite) and the Keban Platform to the north ('Baskil arc'). The collision of the oceanic spreading centre was perhaps preceded by subduction erosion, resulting in the destruction of the former passive margin of the Tauride (Keban) Platform. The units thrust furthest beneath the forearc (i.e. Elazığ Unit, Kömürhan and İspendere ophiolites) were intruded by calc-alkaline plutonic rocks in a fore-arc setting. Further south, the Guleman Ophiolite was accreted to the margin, uplifted and partially eroded. The Killan Ophiolite, in the most southerly position, was also accreted but remained submerged along the northerly active margin.

The Pütürge and Bitlis metamorphic units, representing previously thinned continental crust (rift-related) were underplated beneath the northern margin (Keban Platform), related to northward subduction during latest Cretaceous time. The subduction also gave rise to the HP–LT blueschist and eclogite metamorphism of Upper Cretaceous metapelagic sediments and volcanic rocks, as documented near the southern margin of the Bitlis Massif (Hall 1976). The blueschists and eclogites probably represent oceanic material that was subducted and then rapidly exhumed by latest Cretaceous time.

Exhumation of the Bitlis Massif took place, at least partially, during latest Cretaceous time, as overlying uppermost Cretaceous debris flows include clasts and blocks of metamorphic rocks. However, it seems likely that parts of the massifs remained buried beneath the forearc, as a regional Lower Cenozoic sedimentary cover is nowhere present. Final exhumation of the metamorphic massifs was probably triggered by regional extension that took place during Early–Mid-Eocene time.

Palaeogene

Regional plate convergence paused or slowed (Livermore & Smith 1984) and there is little evidence of subduction during this time. The northern margin of the remnant oceanic basin was partially emergent and eroded. Later, it was submerged and covered by a southward-deepening marginal, to deeper marine succession during Early Palaeocene–Early Eocene time. The margin topography was subdued with a strong eustatic sea-level control on transgressions and regressions. Passive margin conditions were re-established along the Arabian margin.

Middle Eocene

Northward subduction resumed and the cold, remnant oceanic slab 'rolled back' southwards, resulting in crustal extension of the northern margin (Fig. 23d). In the far north, marginal successions deepened southwards into a non-volcanic rift basin. Related to this extension, the by then exhumed Pütürge and Bitlis massifs rifted and were partially infilled with subduction-influenced extrusive rocks, deep-water volcanogenic muds, tuffs and minor siliceous sediments (Maden Group). Carbonate rocks slid from the basin margins as exotic blocks. Extension-related collapse gave rise to large-scale debris flows ('olistostromes'), as exposed between the Pütürge and Bitlis massifs (Maden Group) and elsewhere along the thrust front. The inferred roll-back was coupled with minor amounts of subduction-influenced volcanism within a frontal extensional basin (e.g. Helete Unit in the west), but there is little evidence that a substantial arc edifice developed, either in this area or elsewhere along the active margin. Convergence was probably oblique. This is suggested by the presence of chemically enriched volcanic rocks erupted in an inferred pull-apart basin along the southern margin of the Bitlis Massif (Lice area; Aktaş & Robertson 1984), and an inferred regional-scale diachroneity in the pattern of volcanism along the active margin (Yiğitbaş & Yılmaz 1996*b*; Elmas & Yılmaz 2003). The active margin experienced a pulse of compression, probably in Late Eocene time. This could relate to the final suturing of a northerly Neotethyan oceanic basin in central Anatolia to the NW (Şengör & Yılmaz 1981; Clark & Robertson 2005). This collision may have triggered the collapse the Middle Eocene basin (Maden Group) and initiated a final phase of oblique subduction, trench roll-back and diachronous collision.

Oligocene

Regional northward subduction is assumed to have been active during this time although there is little direct evidence of this from the study area. This part of the active margin experienced subduction erosion, or strike-slip removal of accreted material, or simply overthrusting during the collision that ensued. Further west along the thrust front mélange units were being accreted during this time (Misis–Andırın Complex; Robertson *et al.* 2004*a*).

Miocene–Recent

The, by then, assembled thrust belt progressively collided with the Arabian passive margin during Early–Mid-Miocene time. The existing thrust stack was further shortened by internal southward thrusting, as seen in the Baskil area where platform and arc units are locally thrust over Miocene shallow-marine sediments. Diachronous collision is documented from sedimentary patterns along the Arabian Foreland further west (Misis–Andırın segment; Derman *et al.* 1996; Robertson *et al.* 2004*a*). The Arabian Foreland was flexurally downwarped and finally overridden by Mid-Miocene time (Fig. 23e). The entire thrust stack was emplaced southward over the

Miocene foredeep along the South Anatolian sole thrust. The foreland was deformed, with folding and reverse faulting during this event. Suture tightening affected the thrust belt in Late Miocene time.

By Late Miocene time the Southern Neotethys in this region was completely closed, coupled with crustal thickening. Little further shortening took place and, during Plio-Quaternary time, there was a switch to left-lateral strike-slip and 'tectonic escape' along the East Anatolian Transform Fault, which transects the study area (Şengör *et al.* 1985).

We thank D. James for assistance with chemical analysis by X-ray fluorescence, D. Baty for assistance with drafting the figures, and Y. Cooper for producing digital images. Helpful reviews of the manuscript were provided by D. Perinçek and S. Can Genç. The editors, A. Ries and R. Butler, also made helpful suggestions.

Appendix: Fossil identifications and localities.

(See text for explanation)

154 (B1) Lutetian (Middle Eocene); limestone from Şituşağı, 15 km east of Baskil. Grid reference: Malatya K41 680686
Discocyclina seunesi Douville
Discocyclina scalaris (Schlumberger)
Nummulites striatus (Bruguiere)
Assilina placentula (Deshayes)
Operculina sp.
Ranikothalia sp.
Rotalia sp.
Textularia sp.
Miliolidae

163 (B9) Lutetian (Middle Eocene); limestone from near Kömürhan Bridge
Grid reference: Malatya K41 672663
Asterigerina rotula Kaufmann
Gyroidina subangulata (Plummer)
Eponides sp.
Cibicides sp.
Coralline algae

181 (B18) Thanetian (Upper Palaeocene); Calcareous sandstone from 0.9 km SW of Mirimümin Mah. (*c.* 16 km east of Baskil)
Grid reference: Malatya K41 664672
Lenticulina sp.
Nodosaria sp.
Globigerina sp

183a (B19) Lutetian (Middle Eocene); first limestone sample from near Arapuçağı (*c.* 20 km W of Baskil)
Grid reference: Malatya 141 857452
Eorupertia magna (le Calvez)
Asterigerina rotula Kaufmann
Gypsina linearis (Hanzawa)
Nummulites sp.
Orbitoides sp.
Ophthalmidium sp.
Textularia sp.

183b Lutetian (Middle Eocene); second limestone sample from near Arapuşağı (*c.* 20 km west of Baskil)
Fabiania cassis (Oppenheim)
Eorupertia magna (le Calvez)
Gypsina marianensis Hanzawa
Orbitolites complanatus Lamarck
Nummulites striatus (Bruguiere)
Ophthalmidium sp.
Indeterminate alga and bryozoa

183c Lutetian (Middle Eocene); third limestone sample from near Arapuçağı, (*c.* 20 km W of Baskil)
Eorupertia magna (le Calvez)
Gypsina linearis (Hanzawa)
Orbitolites sp.
Fabiania sp.

206a (B27) Lutetian (Middle Eocene); first sample of recrystallized limestone, 1 km SW of Çakçak Dağı (11 km south of main road)
Grid reference: Malatya L41 857452
Nummulites cf. *burdigalensis* (de la Harpe)
Assilina cf. *placentula* (Deshayes)
Assilina cf. *tenuimarginata* Heim

206b (B27) Eocene; second sample of recrystallized limestone, 1 km SW of Çakçak Dağı (11 km south of main road)
Nummulites sp.
Echinoid debris

206c (B27) Lutetian (Middle Eocene); third sample of recrystallized limestone, 1 km SW of Çakçak Dağı (11 km south of main road)
Nummulites cf. *striatus* (Bruguiere)
Assilina sp.

210 (B28) Thanetian–Ilerdian (Upper Palaeocene–Lower Eocene); recrystallized limestone from an exotic block, Killan Imbricate Group, by Değirmendere, 5 km SSE of Maden (Ergani)
Grid reference: Elazığ L43 440618
Assilina cf. *yvettae* Schaub
Ranikothalia cf. *sindensis* (Davies)
Discocyclina sp.

213a (B30) Middle Eocene; first sample of pelagic limestone just east of Maden on road to Karatop (Killan)
Grid reference: Elazığ L43 598493
Acarinina bullbrooki (Bolli)
Globigerina sp.

213b (B30) Middle Eocene; second sample of pelagic limestone just east of Maden on road to Karatop (Killan).
Acarinina cf. *topilensis* (Cushman)
Globigerina sp.

213c (B30) Eocene; third sample of pelagic limestone just east of Maden on road to Karatop (Killan)
Morozovella sp.
Globigerina sp.

214 (B31) Ilerdian (Lower Eocene); limestone from exotic block in olistostrome, from directly west of Arslantaşı; near base of Killan Imbricate Unit
Grid reference: Elazığ L43 620541
Discocyclina seunesi Douville
Orbitoclypeus ramaraoi (Samanta)
Rotalia trochidiformis Lamarck
Gypsina linearis (Hanzawa)
Mississippina binkhorsti (Reuss)
Operculina sp.
Gypsina sp.
Anomalina sp.
Asterocyclina sp.
Algae:
Amphiroa propria (Lemoine)
Archaeolithothamnium johnsoni Mastrorilli
Distichoplax biserialis (Dietrich)
Bryozoa

220a (B36) Upper Maastrichtian; first sample of pelagic limestone from main road section, *c.* 9 km NW of Maden (Ergani)
Grid reference Elazığ L43 537573
Contusotruncana contusa (Cushman)
Planomalina sp.
Pseudotextularia sp.

220b (B36) Upper Maastrichtian; second sample of pelagic limestone from main road section, *c.* 9 km NW of Maden (Ergani)
Contusotruncana contusa (Cushman)
Globotruncanita stuarti (de Lapparent)
Pseudotextularia sp.

220c (B36) Upper Maastrichtian; third sample of pelagic limestone from main road section, *c.* 9 km NW of Maden (Ergani)
Contusotruncana contusa (Cushman)
Globotruncanita stuarti (de Lapparent)
Heterohelicidae
Planomalina sp.

References

AKGÜL, B. 1987. *Keban yöresi metamorfik kayaçlarının petrografik incelenmesi. (Petrographic investigation of metamorphic rocks in Keban region.)* MSc thesis, Firat University, Elazığ.

AKSOY, E., TURAN, M., TÜRKMEN, I. & ÖZKUL, M. 1996. Tertiary evolution of the Elazığ Basin, E Turkey. *In*: KORKMAZ, S. & AKÇAY, M. (eds) *Jeoloji Mühendisliği Bölümü 30 yıl Sempozyum Bildirileri.* KTÜ, Trabzon, 293–310.

AKSOY, E., TÜRKMEN, I., TURAN, M. & MERIÇ, E. 1999. New findings on stratigraphic position and depositional environment of Harami Formation (Upper Campanian–Maastrichtian), south of Elazığ. *Bulletin of Turkish Association of Petroleum Geologists*, **11**(1), 1–15.

AKTAŞ, G. & ROBERTSON, A. H. F. 1984. The Maden Complex, SE Turkey: evolution of a Neotethyan continental margin. *In*: DIXON, J. E. & ROBERTSON, A. H. F. (eds) *The Geological Evolution of the Eastern Mediterranean.* Geological Society, London, Special Publications, **17**, 375–402.

AKTAŞ, G. & ROBERTSON, A. H. F. 1990. Tectonic evolution of the Tethys suture zone in S.E. Turkey: evidence from the petrology and geochemistry of Late Cretaceous and Middle Eocene Extrusives. *In*: MOORES, E. M., PANAYIOTOU, A. & XENOPHONTOS, C. (eds) *Ophiolites–Oceanic Crustal Analogues. Proceedings International. Symposium 'Troodos 1987'.* Geological Survey Department, Nicosia, 311–329.

AL-RIYAMI, K. & ROBERTSON, A. H. F. 2002. Mesozoic sedimentary and magmatic evolution of the Arabian continental margin, northern Syria: evidence from the Baer–Bassit Mélange. *Geological Magazine*, **139**, 395–420.

AL-RIYAMI, K., ROBERTSON, A. H. F., XENOPHONTOS, C., DANELIAN, T. & DIXON, J. E. 2002. Origin and emplacement of the Late Cretaceous Baer–Bassit ophiolite and its metamorphic sole in NW Syria, *Lithos*. **65**, 225–260.

ALTINER, D. 1989. An example for the tectonic evolution of the Arabian Platform margin (SE Anatolia) during Mesozoic and some criticisms of the previously suggested models. *In*: ŞENGÖR, A. M. C. (ed.) *Tectonic Evolution of Tethyan Regions.* Kluwer, Dordrecht, 117–129.

ASUTAY, H. J. 1988. Baskil (Elazığ) çevresinin jeolojisi ve Baskil magmatitlerinon petrolojisi (Geology of the Baskil region and petrology of the Baskil magmatics.) *Bulletin of Mineral Research and Exploration Institute of Turkey (MTA)*, Ankara, **107**, 48–72.

AVŞAR, N. 1983. *Elazığ yakın kuzeybatısında stratigrafik ve mikropaleontolojik araştırmalar. (Stratigraphical and micropaleontological investigations in NW part of Elazig.)* PhD thesis, Fırat University, Elazığ.

BAŞTUĞ, M. C. 1980. *Sedimentation, Deformation and Melange Emplacement in the Lice Basin, Dicle–Karabeğan Area.* Phd thesis, Middle East Technical University, Ankara.

BEKTAŞ, O., ŞEN, C., ATÈCÈ, Y. & KÖPRÜBAŞI, H. 1999. Migration of Upper Cretaceous subduction-related volcanism towards the back-arc basin of the Eastern Pontides. *Geological Journal*, **34**, 95–106.

BEYARSLAN, M. & BİNGÖL, A. F. 1991. Petrographical features of the İspendere ophiolite, Kale–Malatya (Turkey). *Geosound*, **19**, 59–68.

BEYARSLAN, M. & BİNGÖL, A. F. 1996. The geochemistry and petrology of Elazığ magmatics. *In*: KORKMAZ, S. & AKÇAY, M. (eds) *30th Annual Symposium Proceedings*, Karadeniz Teknik Üniversitesi, Trabzon, 208–224.

BEYARSLAN, M. & BİNGÖL, A. F. 2000. Petrology of a supra-subduction zone ophiolite (Elazığ, Turkey). *Canadian Journal of Earth Sciences*, **37**, 1411–1424.

BİNGÖL, A. F. 1984. Geology of the Elazığ area in the Eastern Taurus region. *In*: TEKELİ, O. & GÖNCÜOĞLU, M. C. (eds) *Geology of the Taurus Belt, Proceedings of International Symposium.* Mineral Research and Exploration Institute of Turkey (MTA), Ankara, 209–217.

BÖLÜCEK, C., AKGÜL, M. & TÜRKMEN, I. 2004. Volcanism, sedimentation and massive sulphide mineralization in a Late Cretaceous arc-related basin, Eastern Taurides, Turkey. *Journal of Asian Earth Sciences*, **24**, 349–360.

ÇAĞLAYAN, M. A., ÜNAL, R. N., ŞENGÜN, M. & YURTSEVER, A. 1984. Structural setting of Bitlis Massif. *In*: TEKELİ, O. & GÖNCÜOĞLU, M. C. (eds) *Geology of the Taurus Belt, Proceedings of International Symposium.* Mineral Research and Exploration Institute of Turkey (MTA), Ankara, 245–255.

CLARK, M. & ROBERTSON, A. H. F. 2005. Uppermost Cretaceous–Lower Tertiary Ulukışla Basin: sedimentary evolution of part of a unified basin complex within an evolving Neotethyan suture zone. *Sedimentary Geology*, **173**, 15–31.

COWARD, M. P., BUTLER, R. W. H., KHAN, M. A. & KNIPE, R. J. 1987. The tectonic history of Kohistan and its implications for Himalayan structure. *Journal of the Geological Society, London*, **144**, 377–391.

COWARD, M. P., DIETRICH, D. & PARK, G. G. (eds) 1989. *Alpine Tectonics*. Geological Society, London, Special Publications, **45**.

CRONIN, B. T., HARTLEY, A. J., ÇELİK, H., HURST, A., TÜRKMEN, I. & KEREY, E. 2000. Equilibrium profile development in graded deep-water slopes: Eocene, Eastern Turkey. *Journal of the Geological Society, London*, **157**, 943–955.

CURRAY, J. R., MOORE, D. G., LAWYER, L. A., EMMEL, F. T., RAITT, R. W., NENRY, M. & KIECKHEFER, P. W. (eds) 1979. *Geological and Geophysical Investigations of Continental Margins.* American Association of Petroleum Geologists, Memoirs, **29**, 189–198.

DELALOYE, M. & WAGNER, J.-J. 1984. Ophiolites and volcanic activity near the western edge of the Arabian plate. *In*: DIXON, J. E. & ROBERTSON, A. H. F. (eds) *The Geological Evolution of the Eastern Mediterranean.* Geological Society, London, Special Publications, **17**, 225–233.

DELAUNE-MAYÈRE, M. 1984. Evolution of a Mesozoic passive continental margin: Baer–Bassit (NW Syria). *In*: DIXON, J. E. & ROBERTSON, A. H. F. (eds) *The Geological Evolution of the Eastern Mediterranean.* Geological Society, London, Special Publications, **17**, 151–160.

DERMAN, A. S., AKDAĞ, K., GÜL, M. A. & YENİAY, G. 1996. Relationshiop between sedimentation and tectonics in the Maraş Miocene basin. *In*: *Turkish Association of Petroleum Geologists, 11th Petroleum Congress, Ankara*, 91–102.

DEWEY, J. F. 1982. Plate tectonics and the evolution of the British Isles. *Journal of the Geological Society, London*, **139**, 389–412.

DEWEY, J. F., HEMPTON, M. R., KIDD, W. S. F., ŞAROĞLU, F. & ŞENGÖR, A. M. C. 1986. Shortening of continental lithosphere: the neotectonics of Eastern Anatolia—a young collision zone. *In*: COWARD, M. P. & RIES, A. C. (eds) *Collision Tectonics.* Geological Society, London, Special Publications, **19**, 3–36.

ELMAS, A. & YILMAZ, Y. 2003. Development of an oblique subduction zone—tectonic evolution of the Tethys suture zone in Southeast Turkey. *International Geology Review*, **45**, 827–840.

ERDEM, E. & BİNGÖL, A. F. 1995. Pütürge (Malatya) metamorfitlerinin petrografik özellikleri (Petrographical features of the Pütürge (Malatya) metamorphics.) *Journal of Engineering Faculty, Firat University (Fırat Üniversitesi Mühendislik Fakültesi Dergisi)*, **7**, 73–8.5.

ERDOĞAN, T. 1975. Gölbaşı yöresinin jeolojisi. (Geology of the Gölbaşı region.) Turkish Petroleum Company Field Group Report, Ankara, **229**.

FITTON, J. G., SAUNDERS, A. D., LARSON, L. M., HARDARSON, B. S. & NORRY, M. S. 1998. Volcanic rocks of the southeast Greenland margin. *In*: SAUNDERS, A. D., LARSEN, H. C. & WISE, S. W., JR (eds) *Proceedings of the Ocean Drilling Program, Scientific Results, 152*, Ocean Drilling Project, College Station, TX, 321–350.

FONTAINE, J. K. 1981. *La plate-forme arabe et sa marge passive au Mésozoique: l'exemple d'Hazro SE de la Turquie*. Thèse 3e cycle, Université Paris XI.

FOURCADE, E., DERCOURT, J., GUNAY, Y. *et al.* 1991. Stratigraphie et paléogéographie de la marge septentrionale de la plate-forme arabe au Mesozoique (Turquie de Sud-East). *Bulletin de la Societé Géologique de France*, **161**, 27–41.

GÖNCÜOĞLU, M. & TURHAN, N. 1984. Geology of the Bitlis metamorphic belt. *In*: TEKELİ, O. & GÖNCÜOĞLU, M. C. (eds) *Geology of the Taurus Belt, Proceedings of International Symposium.* Mineral Research and Exploration Institute of Turkey (MTA), Ankara, 237–244.

HALL, R. 1976. Ophiolite emplacement and the evolution of the Taurus suture zone, South-east Turkey. *Geological Society of America Bulletin*, **87**, 1078–1088.

HELVACI, C. & GRIFFIN, W. L. 1984. Rb–Sr geochronology of the Bitlis Massif, Avnik (Bingöl) area, SE Turkey. *In*: DIXON, J. E. & ROBERTSON, A. H. F. (eds) *The Geological Evolution of the Eastern Mediterranean.* Geological Society, London, Special Publications, **17**, 403–415.

HEMPTON, M. 1984. Results of detailed mapping near Lake Hazar Eastern Taurus mountains). *In*: TEKELİ, O. & GÖNCÜOĞLU, M. C. (eds) *Geology of the Taurus Belt, Proceedings of International Symposium.* Mineral Research and Exploration Institute of Turkey (MTA), Ankara, 223–228.

HEMPTON, M. R. 1985. Structure and deformation history of the Bitlis suture near Lake Hazar, SE

Turkey. *Geologial Society of America Bulletin*, **96**, 223–243.

KİPMAN, E. 1981. Kebanın jeolojisi ve Keban Şariyajı (Geology of Keban and the Keban Thrust.) *İstanbul Üniversitesi, Yerbilimleri Dergisi*, **75**(1–2), 75–81.

LIVERMORE, R. A. & SMITH, A. G. 1984. Some boundary conditions for the evolution of the Mediterranean region. *In*: STANLEY, D. J. & WEZEL, F.-C. (eds) *Geological Evolution of the Mediterranean Basin*. Springer, Berlin, 83–100.

MICHARD, A., WHITECHURCH, H., RICOU, L.-E., MONTIGNY, R. & YAZGAN, E. 1984. Tauric subduction (Malatya–Elazığ provinces) and its bearing on tectonics of the Tethyan realm in Turkey. *In*: DIXON, J. E. & ROBERTSON, A. H. F. (eds) *The Geological Evolution of the Eastern Mediterranean*. Geological Society, London, Special Publications, **17**, 361–374.

OKAY, A. I., & ŞAHİNTÜRK, O. 1997. Geology of the Eastern Pontides. *In*: ROBINSON, A. (ed.) *Regional and Petroleum Geology of the Black Sea and Surrounding Region*. American Association of Petroleum Geologists, Memoirs, **68**, 291–311.

ÖZGÜL, N. 1981. *Munzur Dağının Jeolojisi. (Geology of the Munzur Dağ.)* MTA Report, Ankara, **6995**.

ÖZGÜL, M. & KEREY, İ. E. 1996. Deep-sea shelf facies analysis (Kırkgeçit Formation) *Turkish Journal of Earth Sciences*, **5**, 57–70.

ÖZKAN, Y. Z. & ÖZTUNALI, O. 1984. Petrology of the magmatic rocks of Guleman Ophiolite. *In*: TEKELI, O. & GÖNCÜOĞLU, M. C. (eds) *Geology of the Taurus Belt, Proceedings of International Symposium*. Mineral Research and Exploration Institute of Turkey (MTA), Ankara, 285–293.

PARLAK, O. 2006. Geodynamic significance of granitoid magmatism in southeast Anatolia: geochemical and geochronological evidence from the Göksun–Afşin (Kahranmanmaraş, Turkey) region. *International Journal of Earth Sciences* (in press).

PARLAK, O., HOECK, V. & DELALOYE, M. 2000. Suprasubduction zone origin of the Pozantı–Karsantı ophiolite (S. Turkey) deduced from whole rock and mineral chemistry of the gabbro cumulates. *In*: BOZKURT, E., WINCHESTER, J. A. & PIPER, J. D. (eds) T*ectonics and Magmatism in Turkey and the Surrounding Area*. Geological Society, London, Special Publications, **173**, 219–234.

PARLAK, O., KOZLU, H., DELALOYE, M. & HÖCK, V. 2001. Tectonic setting of the Yüksekova ophiolite and its relation to the Baskil magmatic arc within the southeast Anatolian orogeny. *Fourth International Turkish Geology Symposium, Cukurova University, Adana, Turkey*, Abstract 333.

PARLAK, O., HOECK, V., KOZLU, H. & DELALOYE, M. 2004 . Oceanic crust generation in an island are tectonic setting, SE Anatolian orogenic belt (Turkey). *Geological Magazine*, **141**, 583–603.

PEARCE, J. A. 1982. Trace element characteristics of lavas from destructive plate margins. *In*: THORPE, R. S. (ed.), *Andesites*. John Wiley & Sons, UK.

PEARCE, J. A. & NORRY, M. J. 1979. Petrogenetic implications of Ti, Zr, Y and Nb variations in volcanic rocks. *Contributions to Mineralogy and Petrology*, **69**, 33–47.

PERİNÇEK, D. 1979. *The Geology of Hazro–Korudağ–Çüngüş–Maden–Ergani–Hazar–Elazığ–Malatya Area*. Special Publication of the Geological Society of Turkey, Ankara.

PERİNÇEK, D. 1980. Bitlis Metamorfitlerinde volkanitli Triyas. (Volcanic-bearing Triassic in Bitlis metamorphics.) *Turkiye Jeoloji Kurumu Bülteni (Bulletin of the Geological Society of Turkey)*, **C23**, 201–211.

PERİNÇEK, D. 1990. Hakkari ili ve dolayının stratigrafisi, Hakkari Province, Southeast Turkey). (Stratigraphy of Hakkari city and surrounding.) *Turkish Petroleum Society Bulletin*, **2**, 21–68.

PERİNÇEK, D. & KOZLU, H. 1984. Stratigraphical and structural relations of the units in the Afşin–Elbistan–Doğanşehir region (Eastern Taurus). *In*: TEKELİ, O. & GÖNCÜOĞLU, M. C. (eds) *Geology of the Taurus Belt. Proceedings of International Symposium*. MTA, Ankara, 181–198.

PERİNÇEK, D. & ÖZKAYA, I. 1981. Tectonic evolution of the northern margin of the Arabian plate. Yerbilimleri, *Bulletin of the Institute of Earth Sciences of Hacettepe University*, **8**, 91–101.

RICE, A., ROBERTSON, A. H. F. & USTAÖMER, T. 2006. Late Cretaceous–Early Cenozoic tectonic evolution of the Eurasian active margin in the Central and Eastern Pontides, northern Turkey. *In*: ROBERTSON, A. H. F. & MOUNTRAKIS, D. (eds) *Tectonic Development of the Eastern Mediterranean Region*, Geological Society, London, Special Publications, **260**, 413–445.

RIGO DE RIGHI, M. & CORTESINI, A. 1964. Gravity tectonics in foothills structure belt of SE Turkey. *AAPG Bulletin*, **48**, 1911–1937.

RIZAOĞLU, T. 2006. *Petrography and geochemistry of the tectonomagmatic units between Baskil–Sivrice (Elazığ)*. PhD thesis, Çukurova University (in Turkish).

RIZAOĞLU, T., PARLAK, O., HOECK, V. & İŞLER, F. 2006. Nature and significance of Late Cretaceous ophiolitic rocks and their relation to the Baskil granitic intrusions of the Elazığ region, SE Turkey. *In*: ROBERTSON, A. H. F. & MOUNTRAKIS, D. (eds) *Tectonic Development of the Eastern Mediterranean Region*. Geological Society, London, Special Publications, **260**, 327–350.

ROBERTSON, A. H. F. 1987. The transition from a passive margin to an Upper Cretaceous foreland basin related to ophiolite emplacement in the Oman Mountains. *Geological Society of America Bulletin*, **99**, 633–653.

ROBERTSON, A. H. F. 1998. Mesozoic–Tertiary tectonic evolution of the Easternmost Mediterranean area; integration of marine and land evidence. *In*: ROBERTSON, A. H. F., EMEIS, K. C., RICHTER, K.-C. & CAMERLENGHI, A. (eds) *Proceeding of the Ocean Drilling Program, Scientific Results*, 160, 723–782.

ROBERTSON, A. H. F. 2000. Mesozoic–Tertiary tectonic–sedimentary evolution of a south Tethyan oceanic basin and its margins in southern Turkey. *In*: BOZKURT, E., WINCHESTER, J. A. & PIPER, J. D. (eds) *Tectonics and Magmatism in Turkey and the Surrounding Area*. Geological Society, London, Special Publications, **173**, 43–82.

ROBERTSON, A. H. F. 2002. Overview of the genesis and emplacement of Mesozoic ophiolites in the Eastern Mediterranean Tethyan region. *Lithos*, **65**, 1–67.

ROBERTSON, A. H. F. 2006. Contrasting modes of ophiolite emplacement in the Eastern Mediterranean region. *In*: GEE, D. & R. A. STEPHENSON (eds) *European Lithosphere Dynamics*. Geological Society of London, Memoirs, **32**, 233–256.

ROBERTSON, A. H. F. & DIXON, J. E. 1984. Introduction: aspects of the geological evolution of the Eastern Mediterranean. *In*: DIXON, J. E. & ROBERTSON, A. H. F. (eds) *The Geological Evolution of the Eastern Mediterranean*. Geological Society, London, Special Publications, **17**, 1–74.

ROBERTSON, A. H. F., ÜNLÜGENÇ, U., İNAN, N. & TASLI, K. 2004*a*. Misis–Andırın Complex: mélange formation related to closure and collision of the South-Tethys in S Turkey. *Journal of Asian Earth Sciences*, **22**, 413–453.

ROBERTSON, A. H. F., USTAÖMER, T., PICKETT, E. A., COLLINS, A. S., ANDREW, T. & DIXON, J. E. 2004*b*. Testing models of Late Palaeozoic–Early Mesozoic orogeny in Western Turkey: support for an evolving open-Tethys model. *Journal of the Geological Society, London*, **161**, 501–511.

ROBERTSON, A. H. F., USTAÖMER, T., ÜNLÜGENÇ, Ü. C., PARLAK, O., TAŞLI, K. & İNAN, N. 2006. The Berit transect of the Tauride thrust belt, S Turkey: Late Cretaceous–Early Tertiary accretionary and collisional processes related to the South-Neotethys. *Journal of Asian Earth Sciences*, **27**, 108–145.

ŞENGÖR, A. M. C., 1984. The Cimmeride Orogenic System and the Tectonics of Eurasia. Geological Society of America, Special Paper, **195.**

ŞENGÖR, A. M. C. & YILMAZ, Y. 1981. Tethyan evolution of Turkey: a plate tectonic approach. *Tectonophysics*, **75**, 181–241.

ŞENGÖR, A. M. C., GÖRÜR, N. & ŞAROĞLU, F. 1985. Strike-slip deformation basin formation and sedimentation. *In*: BIDDLE, K. T. & CHRISTIE-BLICK, N. (eds) *Strike–slip Deformation, Basin Formation and Sedimentation*. Society of Economic Paleontolgists and Mineralogists, Special Publications, **37**, 227–264.

SHERVAIS, J. W. 1982. Ti-V plots and the petrogenesis of modern and ophiolitic lavas. *Earth and Planetary Science Letters*, **59**, 101–118.

SUN, S. S. & MCDONOUGH, W. F. 1989. Chemical and isotopic systematics of oceanic basalts: implications for mantle composition and processes. *In*: SAUNDERS, A. D. & NORRY, M. J. (eds) *Magmatism in the Ocean Basins*. Geological Society, London Special Publications, **42**, 313–347.

TURAN, M. & BİNGÖL, A. F. 1989. Kovancılar–Baskil (Elazığ) arası bölgenin tektonostratigrafik özellikleri, (Tectonostratigraphical features of Kovancılar–Baskil (Elaziğ) region.) *Proceedings of Ahmet Acar Symposium*. Çukurova University, Adana, Turkey, 213–227.

TURAN, M. & BİNGÖL, A. F. 1991. Tectonostratigraphic characteristics of the region between Kovancılar-Baskil, Elazığ, Tukey. *In*: YETİŞ, C (ed.) *Proceedings of Ahmet Acar Geology Symposium*. Çukurova University, Adana, Turkey, 213–227.

TURAN, M. & TÜRKMEN, I. 1996. Stratigraphy and sedimentology of the Kuşçular Formation (Lower Paleocene) to the west of Elazığ, Turkey. *Turkish Journal of Earth Sciences*, **5**, 109–121.

TÜRKMEN, I. & ESSEN, N. 1997. Facies aspects of shelf, canyon, and basin plain complex: Kirkeçit Formation (Middle Eocene–Oligocene), Elazığ vicinity. Türkiye. *Fırat University Bulletin (Elazığ)*, 1979, 107–123.

TÜRKMEN, I., İNCEÖZ, M., AKSOY, E. & KAYA, M. 2001. New findings on Eocene stratigraphy and palaeogeography of Elazığ area. *Yerbilimleri*, **24**, 81–95.

WINCHESTER, J. A. & FLOYD, P. A. 1977. Geochemical discrimination of different magma series and their differentiation products using immobile elements. *Chemical Geology*, **20**, 325–343.

YAZGAN, E. 1984. Geodynamic evolution of the Eastern Taurus region. *In*: TEKELİ, O. & GÖNCÜOĞLU, M. C. (eds) *Geology of the Taurus Belt. Proceedings of International Symposium.* Mineral Research and Exploration Institute of Turkey (MTA), Ankara, 199–208.

YAZGAN, E. & CHESSEX, R. 1991. Geology and tectonic evolution of Southeastern Taurus in the region of Malatya. *Turkish Association of Petroleum Geologists Bulletin*, **3**, 1–42.

YİĞİTBAŞ, E. & YILMAZ, Y. 1996*a*. New evidence and solution to the Maden complex controversy of the southeast Anatolian orogenic belt (Turkey). *Geologische Rundschau*, **85**, 250–263.

YİĞİTBAŞ, E. & YILMAZ, Y. 1996*b*. Post-Late Cretaceous strike-slip tectonics and its implications for the Southeastern Anatolian orogen, Turkey. *International Geological Review*, **38**, 818–831.

YILDIRIM, M. & YILMAZ, Y. 1991. Güneydoğu Anadolu Orojenik Kuşağının Ekaylı Zonu. (Accretionary zone of the southeast Anatolian orogenic belt.) *Turkish Association of Petroleum Geologists Bulletin*, **3**, 57–73.

YILMAZ, O. 1971. *Étude pétrographique et géochronologique de la région de Cacas*. PhD thesis, Université de Grenoble.

YILMAZ, Y. 1991. Allochthonous terranes in the Tethyan Middle East: Anatolia and the surrounding regions. *In*: DEWEY, J. F., GASS, I. G., CURRY, G. B., HARRIS, N. B. W. & ŞENGÖR, A. M. C. (eds) *Allochthonous Terranes*. Cambridge University Press, Cambridge, 155–168.

YILMAZ, Y. 1993. New evidence and model on the evolution of the southeast Anatolian orogen. *Geological Society of America Bulletin*, **105**, 251–271.

YILMAZ, Y., YİĞİTBAŞ, E. & GENÇ, Ş. C. 1993. Ophiolitic and metamorphic assemblages of southeast Anatolia and their significance in the geological evolution of the orogenic belt. *Publication of Istanbul Teknik Universitesi Maden Fakultesi*, **12**, 1280–1297.

YILMAZ, Y., TÜYSÜZ, O., YİĞİTBAŞ, E., GENÇ, Ş. C. & ŞENGÖR, A. M. C. 1997. Geology and tectonic evolution of the Pontides. *In*: ROBINSON, A. G. (ed.) *Regional and Petroleum Geology of the Black Sea and Surrounding Region*. American Association of Petroleum Geologists, Memoirs, **68**, 183–226.

Dynamics of the Polish and Eastern Slovakian parts of the Carpathian accretionary wedge: insights from palaeostress analyses

M. NEMČOK[1], T. DILOV[2], M. WOJTASZEK[3], L. LUDHOVÁ[4], R. A. KLECKER[5], W. J. SERCOMBE[5] & M. P. COWARD[6]

[1]*EGI, University of Utah, 423 Wakara Way, Suite 300, Salt Lake City, UT 84108, USA (e-mail: mnemcok@egi.utah.edu)*

[2]*Department of Geoenvironmental Sciences, Graduate School of Science, Tohoku University, Aobayama, Aoba-ku, Sendai-shi, 980-8578 Japan*

[3]*Institute of Geological Sciences, Jagiellonian University, Oleandry 2A, PL-30-063 Krakow, Poland*

[4]*Department of Geology and Palaeontology, Faculty of Natural Sciences, Comenius University, Mlynská dolina, SK-842 15 Bratislava, Slovak Republic*

[5]*Amoco Prod. Co., P.O. Box. 4381, Houston, TX 77210, USA*

[6]*Ries–Coward Associates Ltd., 70 Grosvenor Road, Caversham, Reading RG4 5ES, UK*

Abstract: The arcuate Outer Carpathian accretionary wedge formed in front of the East Alpine–Carpathian–Pannonian (ALCAPA) megablock during the Eocene–Sarmatian. The wedge accreted sediments of the subducting remnants of the Carpathian Flysch Basin, a large oceanic tract left in front of the Alpine orogen. The palaeostress data for the orogenic hinterland (particularly the data related to the Early Miocene extension that was expanding towards the NE), combined with coeval subduction-related volcanism that was expanding towards the NE, indicate that the uneven roll-back of the subduction zone was the main mechanism controlling the development of the northern West Carpathian arc. The palaeostress data for the Tertiary accretionary wedge from the same time period are characterized by outward-fanning σ_1 trajectories that changed gradually during the wedge development. In contrast, the palaeostress data for the hinterland are characterized by preferred-directional stress events that changed abruptly during the wedge development. These palaeostress results are in accordance with the behaviour of the wedge and the hinterland, as the wedge behaved as a weak continuum and the hinterland behaved as a block mosaic with weak boundaries. The fault traces of the northern West Carpathian arc converge to both ends of the arc and suggest that the pre-existing basin was the factor that controlled the arc location. These fault trace patterns are asymmetric, indicating a slightly oblique overall convergence in a NE–SW direction. In accordance with this convergence, the palaeostress data for the accretionary wedge indicate that the western part of the wedge, which is characterized by NW–SE-oriented maximum principal compressional stress σ_1, was undergoing sinistral transpression. Meanwhile, the eastern part, which is characterized by NE–SW-oriented σ_1, was undergoing compression. Apparently, the dynamics of the accretionary wedge was further influenced by the shape of an elongated NE–SW-trending ALCAPA megablock, which was located behind the wedge and advanced in the direction of the general Early Miocene convergence during the most pronounced stages of the wedge development. This megablock served as the local indenter, as its strength surpassed that of the accretionary wedge located to its front. Further dynamic complexities were added because of the complex shape of the Magura Unit, which was located in the most proximal portion of the wedge and was stronger than the units in front of it. Wedge outcrops indicate that the large-scale shortening, which is characterized by the development of detachments and ramps, was preceded by an initial layer-parallel shortening. This is indicated by scaly fabrics and minor reverse faults that rotated into locked positions during the later accretion. Several outcrops with a wedge detachment fault indicate that there was a relatively low amount of friction during its development. The décollement zone is several hundred metres thick and shows evidence of transient fluid flow that was driven by pressure gradients. This is documented by frequent hydrofracturing, sandstone dykes and fibrous veins that opened against the weight of the whole wedge, all of which indicate cycles of higher pore fluid pressures that lowered the basal friction.

From: RIES, A. C., BUTLER, R. W. H. & GRAHAM, R. H. (eds) 2007. *Deformation of the Continental Crust: The Legacy of Mike Coward.* Geological Society, London, Special Publications, **272**, 271–302.
0305-8719/07/$15

Three major mechanisms have been proposed for the energy budget of orogens: (1) gravity spreading (e.g. Elliott 1976); (2) push from the rear (e.g. Chapple 1978; Davis *et al.* 1983; Stockmal 1983); (3) basal pull (Silver & Reed 1988; Barr & Dahlen 1989; Willett *et al.* 1993). Each mechanism generates a distinctive stress field, thereby implying different dynamics for the resultant orogenic belts, as documented by analogue material modelling (Macedo & Marshak 1999; Storti *et al.* 2000).

The field studies of arcuate orogens such as the Cretaceous–Quaternary South Carpathians, the Oligocene–Miocene Betic Chain, the Cretaceous–Palaeogene Sankiang–Yunnan–Malaya fold belt, the Miocene Mogok belt, the Cretaceous–Quaternary Hellenides and the Cretaceous–Quaternary Carpathian arc have indicated that certain combinations of major mechanisms can result in the development of arcuate orogenic belts. The development models of these belts vary between three distinct cases: (1) the oroclinal bending of the straight mountain belt (e.g. Ratschbacher *et al.* 1993*a*); (2) the gravitational spreading of the overthickened orogenic lithosphere (e.g. England 1983; Platt 1986; Dewey 1988; England & Houseman 1988; Coward 1994*a*); (3) the back-arc spreading of a thrust zone as a result of the uneven roll-back of a subduction zone (Angelier 1978; Burchfiel & Royden 1982).

The amount of curvature varies significantly between these arcuate orogenic belts (see Macedo & Marshak 1999), which probably indicates that not all of the three development cases can bring the orogen to its extreme curvature. The development case that results in extreme curvature can be found by studying an orogen that achieved extreme curvature, for example, the Carpathian arc in Central Europe, which has a curvature of 330° and was chosen as the study area for this paper.

If the Carpathian arc was developed by oroclinal bending, it should have recorded a stress field characterized by outward-fanning σ_1 trajectories, which is a typical result for a push from behind. This stress record should be present in both the orogen and its foreland. If the arc was developed by spreading of the overthickened lithosphere, it should have recorded a gravity-dominated stress field that controls polydirectional material flow into low-energy areas. This stress record should be present in the orogen but not in its foreland. If the Carpathian arc was developed by back-arc spreading, it should have recorded a stress field characterized by a narrow zone of frontal compression and a wide zone of internal extension. Again, this stress record should be present in the orogen but not in its foreland. The goal of this paper is to identify one of these three development models in the Carpathian arc. However, a suitable method of reaching the goal must first be discussed.

Typically, the arcuate belts have been studied using incremental strain data from regions such as the Western Himalayas (Treloar & Coward 1991) and the Western Alps (Spencer 1992; Coward 1994*b*). Some belts have been studied using palaeomagnetic methods; for example, the Betic Chain (e.g. Allerton 1994; Platt *et al.* 1995) and the Appalachians (Gray & Stamatakos 1997). Others have been studied using analogue material modelling; for example, the Appalachians, the Apennines, the Argentinean Andes, the Carpathians, the Hellenides, the Lesser Antilles arc system, the Southern Alps of New Zealand and the Sulaiman Range (Koons 1990; Ratschbacher *et al.* 1991; Marshak *et al.* 1992; Macedo & Marshak 1999; Storti *et al.* 2000; Marques & Cobbold 2002).

The interpretation of incremental strain data from ductile terrains (e.g. Shackleton & Ries 1984; Shackleton 1986; Ellis & Watkinson 1987) often experienced difficulties with overprinting, missing units and genetic problems that could be solved only with a very detailed study. A more suitable approach for this study utilizes palaeostress techniques, which gave successful results in the case of the Taiwan thrust belt (Angelier *et al.* 1986; Barrier & Angelier 1986), in which the interpreted stress field, characterized by outward-fanning σ_1 trajectories, was attributed to a push from behind, as documented by analogue material modelling (Huchon *et al.* 1986).

Typically, the interpretation of palaeomagnetic data was used to distinguish between rotational and non-rotational trend lines in the structural architectures of orogenic belts (e.g. Gray & Stamatakos 1997), so as to decide whether or not arcuate belts started with curved thrusts, and thereby differentiate between the three development cases.

The analogue material modelling was generally used to test whether the interpretations of palaeomagnetic and structural data are physically sound.

The best method for reaching the goal of this paper is a combination of palaeostress, palaeomagnetic and analogue material modelling methods. This choice of methods further justifies the choice of the study area, which contains the northern West Carpathians of Poland and eastern Slovakia (Fig. 1), for several reasons. First, the analogue material model for this arcuate orogen has already been made by

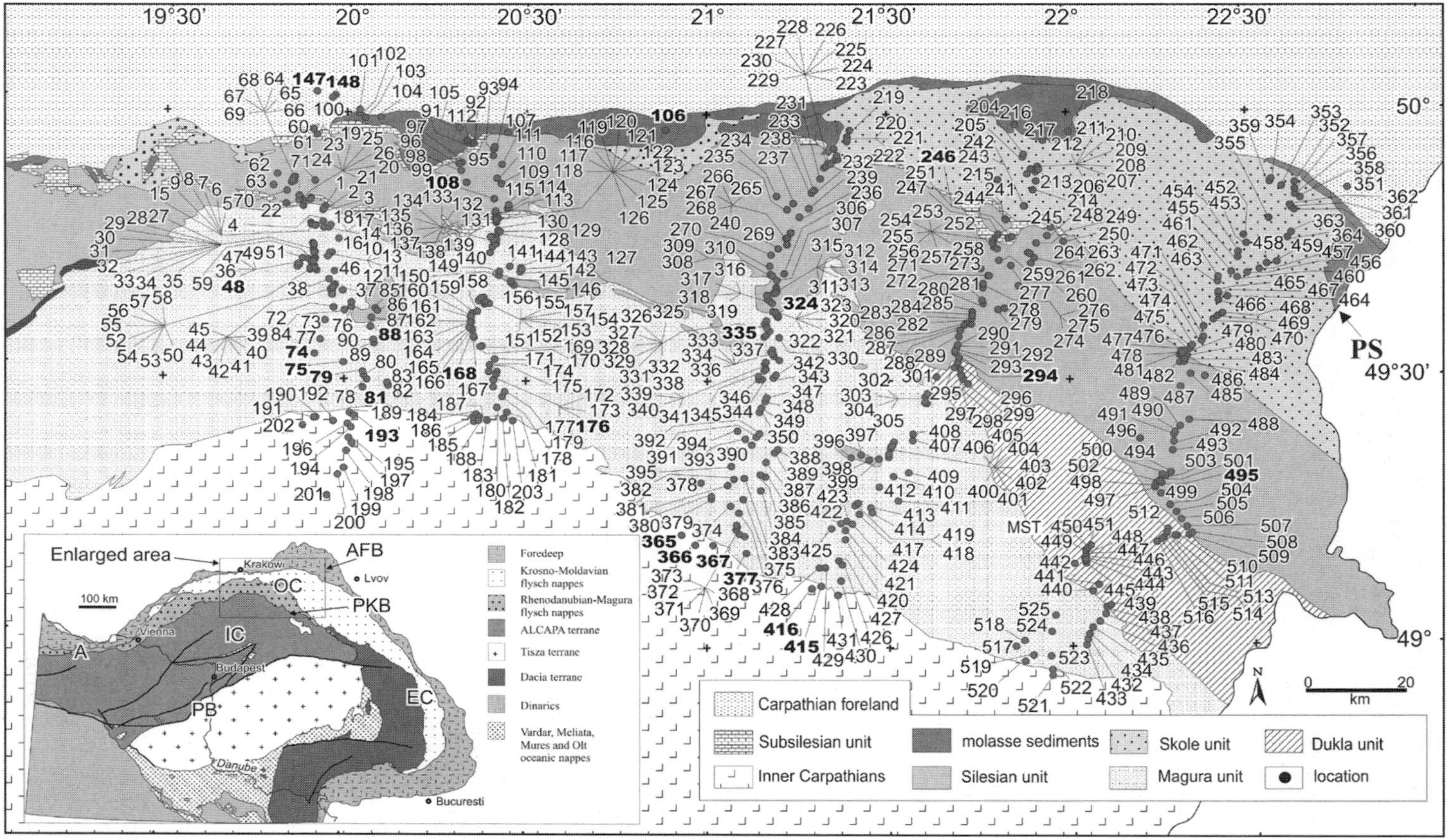

Fig. 1. Map of the Outer West Carpathian accretionary wedge, between longitude E19° and E23° and with locations of new kinematic studies. Numbers in bold indicate outcrops with polyphase structural data. The remaining outcrops have monophase data. More detailed descriptions of outcrop data can be found at http://www.geolsoc.org.uk/sup18268. A hard copy can be obtained from the Society Library. PS, Przemyśl Sigmoid. The inset shows the Carpathians. AFB, autochthonous Miocene molasse sediments of the foreland basin; OC, Outer Carpathians; IC, Inner Carpathians; EC, Eastern Carpathians; PKB, Pieniny Klippen Belt; A, Alps; PB, Pannonian Basin. The inset also shows the location of megablocks in the Inner Carpathians–Pannonian Basin. It should be noted that internal and external boundaries of the Krosno–Moldavian and Rhenodanubian–Magura flysch nappes converge at both ends of the West Carpathians located between the Alps and the East Carpathians.

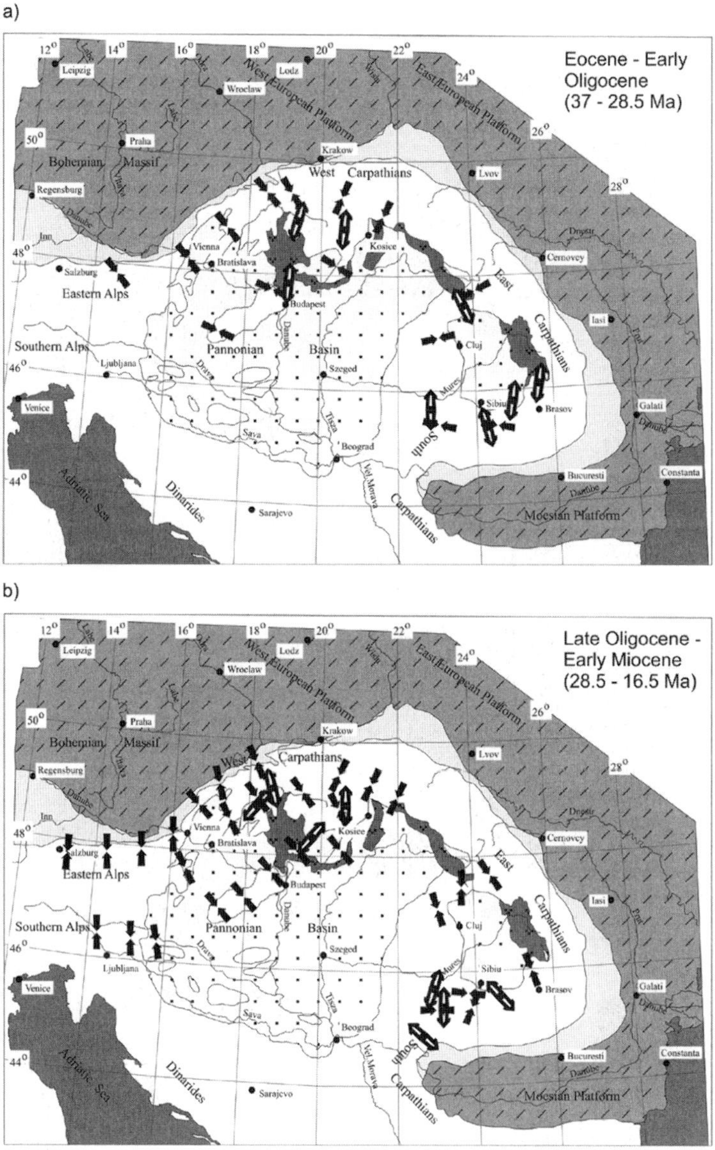

Fig. 2. Palaeostress directions in the Carpathian–Pannonian region gathered from existing literature for: (**a**) Eocene–Early Oligocene; (**b**) Late Oligocene–Early Miocene; (**c**) early Badenian; (**d**) middle Badenian; (**e**) late Badenian–Sarmatian; (**f**) early Pannonian; (**g**) late Pannonian; (**h**) present. The directions in (**a**)–(**g**) represent the average values of stress states calculated by stress inversion techniques in research papers, or compiled in syntheses (Bada 1999; Fodor *et al.* 1999). The stress states were calculated in the Alps (Decker & Jarnik 1992; Decker *et al.* 1993, 1994; Kurz *et al.* 1993; Linzer *et al.* 1995, 1997; Nemes *et al.* 1995; Nemes 1996; Peresson & Decker 1997*a*), in the broader Pannonian Basin region (Bergerat *et al.* 1983; Bergerat 1989; Csontos *et al.* 1991; Tari 1991; Csontos & Bergerat 1992; Fodor *et al.*, 1992, 1994; Márton & Fodor 1995; Benkovics 1997; Bada 1999; Györfi *et al.* 1999), in the West Carpathians (Kováč *et al.* 1989*a*, 1990, 1993, 1995; Nemčok *et al.* 1989, 1998*a*,*b*, 2000*c*; Fodor *et al.* 1990, 1995; Marko *et al.* 1990, 1991; Nemčok & Lexa 1990; Nemčok & Nemčok 1990, 1994; Nemčok 1991, 1993; Kováč & Hók 1993; Ratschbacher *et al.* 1993*b*; Vass *et al.* 1993; Fodor 1995; Sperner 1996; Sperner *et al.* 2002), in the East and South Carpathians (Ratschbacher *et al.* 1993*a*; Hippolyte & Sandulescu 1996; Linzer 1996; Morley 1996; Moser & Frisch 1996; Matenco *et al.* 1997; Zweigel 1997; Linzer *et al.* 1998) and in the Transylvanian Basin (Huismans *et al.* 1997).

c)

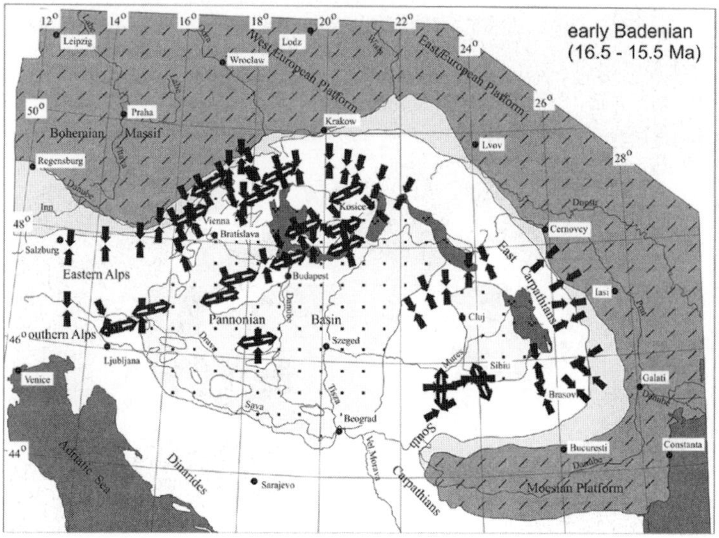

d)

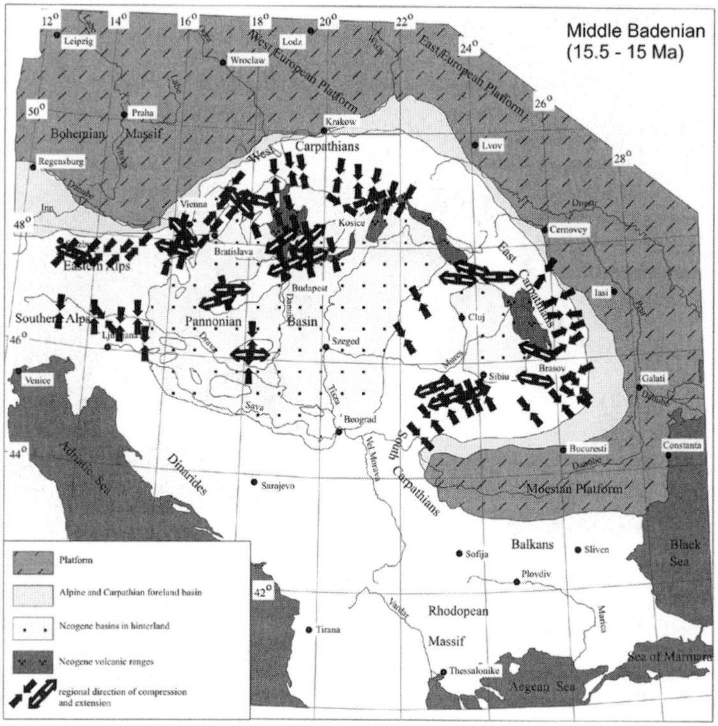

Fig. 2. Continued

e)

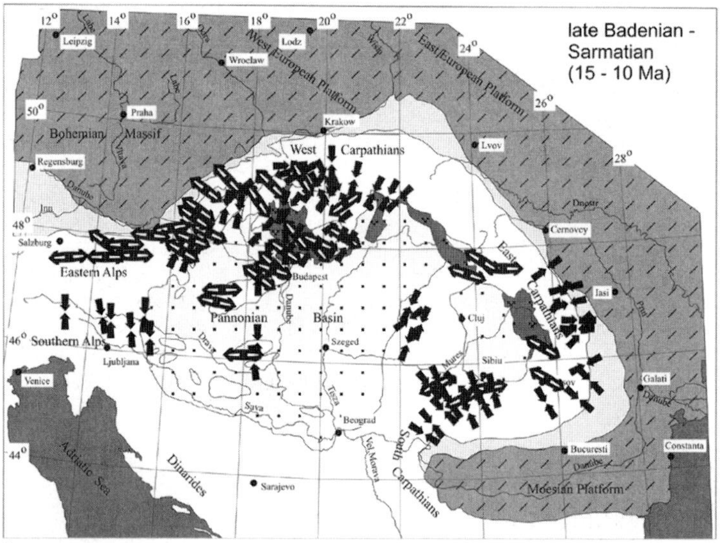

f)

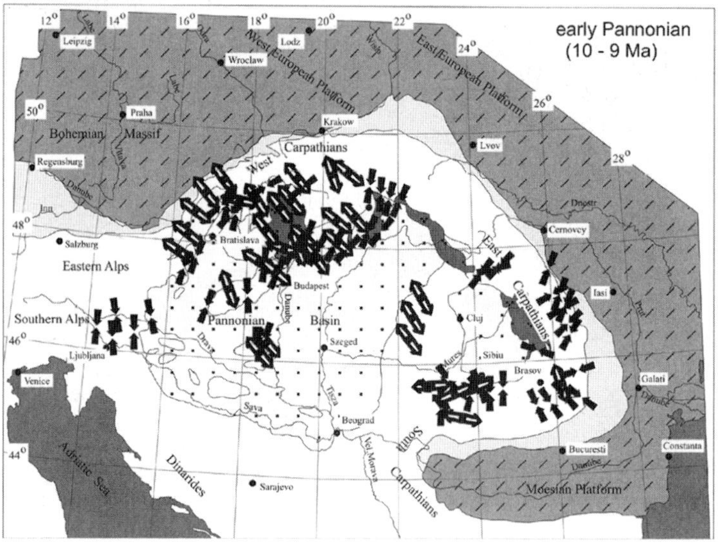

Fig. 2. Continued
The regional direction of compression is based on stress states calculated from thrust or strike-slip regimes and the regional direction of extension is taken from stress states calculated from normal fault regimes. The principal horizontal stress direction map for the present, (**h**), is modified from the World Stress Map Project (1997). Data come from earthquake focal mechanisms, overcoring and bore-hole breakout studies. The boundary conditions modelled by a finite-element approach (Bada 1999) that fit the data are shown. They indicate a fixed or slightly deforming Bohemian Massif, an active convergence in the Brasov region, a fixed Moesian Platform, an active deformation at the Dinaric front and a rotating Adriatic (Apulian) microplate.
M, Mecsek Mountains; R, Rechnitz metamorphic core complex; T, Transdanubian Central Range;
TB, Transylvanian Basin; VB, Vienna Basin.

g)

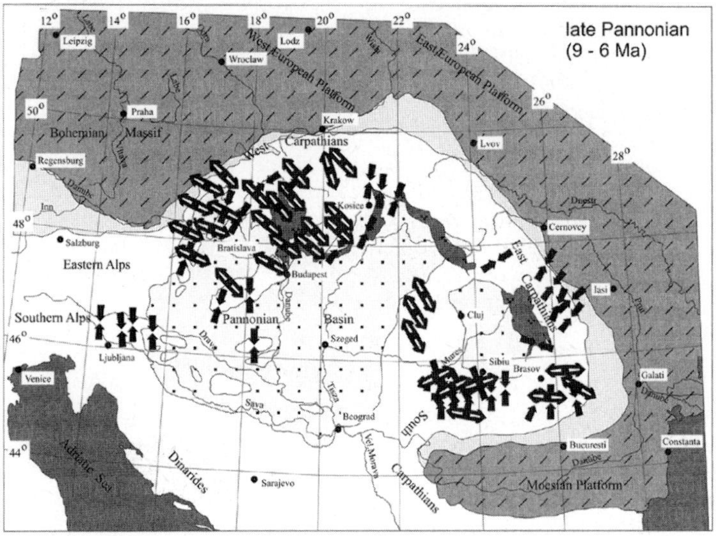

h)

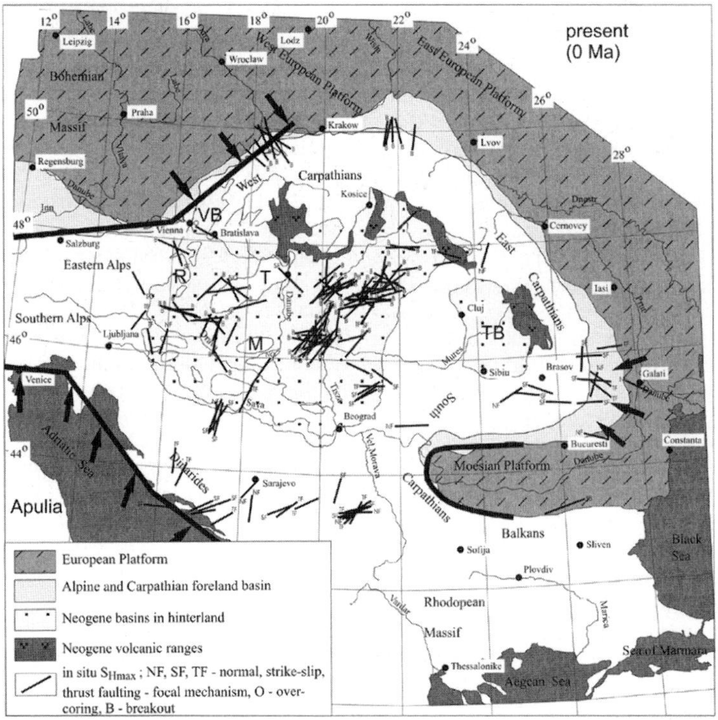

Fig. 2. Continued

Macedo & Marshak (1999). Next, the dynamics of the study area's hinterland portion can be interpreted from a large amount of recent palaeostress studies (e.g. Bergerat 1989; Nemčok *et al.* 1989; Csontos *et al.* 1991; Fig. 2) and a reasonable amount of palaeomagnetic data (e.g. Tari 1991; Fodor 1995; Márton & Fodor 1995; Grabowski & Nemčok 1999).

The dynamics of the study area's accretionary wedge portion, apart from the sparse data produced by Nemčok & Nemčok (1994) and Decker *et al.* (1997), requires original work, as does the incomplete database of palaeomagnetically determined rotation data.

Study area

The study area (Fig. 1) covers the western portion of the Cretaceous–Quaternary Carpathian arc, which has a NE–SW trend near Vienna, an east–west trend in northern Slovakia and Poland, a NW–SE to north–south trend in Ukraine and NE Romania, and an east–west trend in SW Romania. The earthquake focal mechanisms in eastern Romania indicate the last active segment of the subduction zone. The subducting slab is subvertical as it sinks under its own weight.

The Carpathians comprise several zones (Fig. 1): (1) the foreland basin with molasse sediments; (2) the Tertiary accretionary wedge, which is called the Outer Carpathians or the Flysch Belt; (3) the Pieniny Klippen Belt, which occupies the contact between the wedge and the orogenic hinterland; (4) the orogenic hinterland, which is formed by the Inner Carpathians and the Pannonian Basin and is characterized by the occurrence of subduction-related volcanic rocks and intense crustal stretching.

The Miocene molasse sediments were deposited on the Variscan basement of the East European Platform (e.g. Oszczypko & Ślączka 1985, 1989; Kováč *et al.* 1989*b*), which dips under the Tertiary accretionary wedge. The wedge accreted Lower Cretaceous–Lower Miocene sediments (e.g. Poprawa & Nemčok 1989). It is traditionally divided into outer units, such as the Skole, the Subsilesian, the Silesian and the Dukla Units, comprising the Krosno-Moldavian flysch nappes, and the internal units of the Rhenodanubian–Magura flysch nappes. An example of these internal units would be the Magura Unit, which has a different development history from the outer units, including a different detachment horizon, different timing of shortening and stronger mechanic stratigraphy. The Pieniny Klippen Belt (e.g. Andrusov *et al.* 1973) contains Triassic–Oligocene rocks as well as remnants of ophiolites. Apart from volcanic rocks (Pécskay *et al.* 1995), the orogenic hinterland is represented by Palaeogene, Neogene and Quaternary basins that have been superimposed on the older Inner Carpathians (e.g. Csontos *et al.* 1992). When the fill of these basins is stripped off (Fig. 1), the orogenic hinterland can be divided into two megablocks; the East Alpine–Carpathian–Pannonian (ALCAPA) megablock and the Tisza–Dacia megablock, which are characterized by separate movements during the development of the Carpathian arc (e.g. Csontos 1995).

Applied methods

Structural data (Fig. 1), including meso-scale folds, faults and extensional veins, have been used to gain a better understanding of the displacement history of each thrust sheet of the accretionary wedge, as well as to calculate palaeostress states. To exclude local complexities, such as local stress perturbations in fault zones, kinematic data were recorded away from the large-scale fault zones.

The stress calculation from meso-scale kinematic data was made using the computer programs of Sperner *et al.* (1993), Hardcastle & Hills (1991), Nemčok & Lislc (1995) and Nemčok *et al.* (1999*a*). The first program is based on the study by Turner (1953), who constructed compression (*P*) and extension (*T*) axes lying in the plane, comprising the fault-plane normal and striation vectors. The *P* axis is inclined at 45° to the fault plane and the *T* axis is perpendicular to the *P* axis. This method was used for datasets including fewer than four fault-striae readings and its broad-brush results are inferior to results calculated from well-populated datasets. The second to fourth programs were used for at least four faults with determined displacement sense. The second program was used only for monophase fault-striae data. These programs tested a large variety of stress configurations against the fault population from each location. Each stress tensor caused certain reactivation of faults (i.e. it resulted in calculated displacement vectors). Calculated displacement vectors were compared with the measured striations after each test cycle. The stress tensor compatible with the fault population was accepted as the stress configuration that was responsible for their activity. It has the form of a reduced stress tensor (Angelier 1989) and provides orientations of principal stresses and the ratio of their magnitudes.

Polyphase locations provided cross-cutting fault-striae data, allowing for the determination of the relative sequence of tectonic events represented by calculated stress regimes. However, establishing a chronological sequence of stress regimes was difficult, because the accretionary wedge *sensu stricto* is deeply eroded and its outcrops range in stratigraphy from Valanginian to Oligocene, transitioning to Lower Miocene, as compared with the Eocene–Sarmatian development of the wedge (e.g. Nemčok *et al.* 2000*c*). A lack of Eggenburgian–Sarmatian outcrops, with the exception of upper Badenian location 106, proved to be the main obstacle in turning the relative stress regime sequence into a chronological one.

The palaeomagnetic declination data were taken from available literature (Koráb *et al.* 1981; Krs *et al.* 1982, 1991) and the measurements were made at nine locations in cooperation with E. Márton (e.g. Márton 1997; Márton *et al.* 1997, 1999, 2000; Nemčok *et al.* 2000*b*; Zuchiewicz *et al.* 2000). New sampling was carried out to verify the quality of the previous work and to focus on missing key locations and stratigraphies. To exclude local complexities, such as complex palaeomagnetic signals, only massive shale and marl layers were used for palaeomagnetic sampling. The palaeomagnetic data provided constraints on the body rotation, allowing for a distinction between the rotated fault-striae data controlled by unperturbed stress regimes and the unrotated fault-striae data controlled by perturbed stress regimes (see Nemčok 1993; Márton & Fodor 1995).

Dynamic data from the Carpathian hinterland

This section describes the existing data on the dynamics of the Inner Carpathians, which are located behind the Tertiary accretionary wedge (see Fig. 1 for location). Local geographical names are labelled in Figures 1 and 2. These data were taken from studies referred to in Figure 2, located on a set of maps in Figure 2 and synthesized in the following text.

The determined Late Eocene (40 Ma) stress field (Fig. 2) of the northwestern side of the ALCAPA microplate has NW–SE-oriented compression and subvertical extension (e.g. Nemčok & Nemčok 1994; Fodor 1995). Syndepositional palaeostresses from the Priabonian sediments of central ALCAPA have a NW–SE and NE–SW compression and extension, respectively (e.g. Fodor *et al.* 1992, 1994; Kováč & Hók 1993; Bada 1999). Roughly, the east–west-oriented compression was determined from the Upper Eocene sediments in the southern part of ALCAPA (Fodor *et al.* 1999). Stress configurations derived from the northeastern part of ALCAPA have a north–south to NE–SW compression (Nemčok & Nemčok 1994). Determined stress tensors from the East Carpathians, the South Carpathians and the Transylvanian Basin are scarce and different workers have produced contradictory results for several reasons. First, the area contains the oldest portion of the stratigraphic section, which requires the largest amount of filtering to be done out of younger data. Next, the area has an incomplete stratigraphic section and a lack of robust datasets. Lastly, there has been an inappropriate use of palaeostress programs that were designed only for monophase data in simple structural settings (e.g. Angelier & Goguel 1979; Angelier *et al.* 1982; Sperner *et al.* 1993). Results include NE–SW (Moser & Frisch 1996; Matenco *et al.* 1997; Linzer *et al.* 1998) and east–west compressions in the South Carpathians, ENE–NE-directed compression in the northern Transylvanian Basin (Gyorfi *et al.* 1999) and north–south extension in the Transylvanian Basin (Huismans *et al.* 1997).

The determined Oligocene (35–30 Ma) stress field (Fig. 2) of the northwestern side of ALCAPA has a NW–SE and a NE–SW compression and extension, respectively (e.g. Marko *et al.* 1990, 1991; Kováč & Hók 1993; Nemčok & Nemčok 1994; Fodor 1995). Roughly, east–west compression was inferred from the dextral offset of the Oligocene basins along the southeastern side of ALCAPA (Csontos *et al.* 1992). A NW–SE- and NE–SW-oriented compression and extension was calculated (Fodor *et al.* 1992, 1994; Kováč & Hók 1993; Bada 1999) from the central parts of ALCAPA. Stress configurations from the northeastern parts of ALCAPA have a north–south to NE–SW compression (Nemčok & Nemčok 1994). Stress tensors from the South Carpathians have NE–SW compression (Moser & Frisch 1996; Linzer *et al.* 1998), a NW–SE first-order extension (Matenco *et al.* 1997) or east–west-oriented compression (Ratschbacher *et al.* 1993*a*). Stress tensors from the northern Transylvanian Basin have NNW–SSE compression (Gyorfi *et al.* 1999) or NW–SE compression (Huismans *et al.* 1997).

The reconstructed Early Miocene (22–20 Ma) stress field (Fig. 2) of the northern and central parts of ALCAPA has a NW–SE and NE–SW compression and extension, respectively (e.g. Kováč *et al.* 1989; Nemčok *et al.* 1989*a*; Fodor *et al.* 1990, 1992, 1994; Kováč & Hók 1993; Vass *et al.* 1993; Sperner 1996). Inferred and calculated stresses of the southeastern and northeastern sides of ALCAPA have a west–east and north–south to NE–SW compression, respectively (Csontos *et al.* 1992; Nemčok & Nemčok

1994; Kováč *et al.* 1995). Stresses were inferred from the dextral offset of the Early Miocene basins by Csontos *et al.* (1992). In southern and central ALCAPA, the sinistral transpressive activity of faults, driven by NW–NNW-directed compression, finished by Ottnangian times (Bada 1999). Stress tensors from the South Carpathians have a NE–SW to NNE–SSW compression (Moser & Frisch 1996; Linzer *et al.* 1998), a NW–SE first-order extension (Matenco *et al.* 1997) or an east–west-oriented compression (Ratschbacher *et al.* 1993*a*). Stress tensors from the northern Transylvanian Basin have NNW–SSE compression (Gyorfi *et al.* 1999) or NNE–SSW compression (Huismans *et al.* 1997).

Rift initiation inside the Pannonian Basin occurred in Eggenburgian–Ottnangian time (Pécskay *et al.* 1995; Horváth & Tari 1999). The Pannonian Basin region is characterized by NE–SW to ENE–WSW extension since late Ottnangian times (e.g. Fodor 1995). Pull-apart basins opened in the intra-Carpathian region during the Karpatian–middle Badenian (17.5–15 Ma) (Fig. 2) and were controlled by a north–south and west–east compression and extension, respectively (e.g. Bergerat 1989; Nemčok *et al.* 1989; Csontos *et al.* 1991). The Rechnitz metamorphic core complex was uplifted in Karpatian times as a result of to major NE–SW and minor NW–SE extension dated by fission tracks (Dunkl 1992; Dunkl & Demény 1997), which drove low-angle normal faults (Tari *et al.* 1999). The Ottnangian–Karpatian (19–16.5 Ma) stress regime, with NW–SE compression in the area of the Transdanubian Central Range, changed to the Badenian–Sarmatian (16.5–11.5 Ma) stress regime with north–south compression and the Pannonian (11.5–6.2 Ma) stress regime with NE–SW compression (Csontos *et al.* 1991; Tari 1991). North–south compression changed to NE–SW compression in various West Carpathian blocks during the middle–late Badenian (15.5–13.6 Ma) (Nemčok *et al.* 1989; Fodor *et al.* 1990; Nemčok & Lexa 1990). This stress rotation finished in central ALCAPA during the Sarmatian (13.6–11.5 Ma) (Bada 1999). Ottnangian–early Badenian sinistral transtension, driven by NW–SE compression and NE–SW extension, was reported from central ALCAPA (Márton & Fodor 1995). Karpatian–Badenian transtension driven by north–south compression and west–east extension was present in southern ALCAPA (Benkovics 1997). NW–SE compression was determined for flysch units along western ALCAPA, changing direction from NW to north, then to NE during the Karpatian–Badenian (e.g. Nemčok 1993; Fodor *et al.* 1995). It was calculated that the extension in ALCAPA advanced from its centre towards its margins during the Karpatian–middle Badenian (Nemčok *et al.* 1998*a*).

The northern East Carpathians were characterized by west to WNW compression and the southern East Carpathians by NW to NNW compression during the Early Miocene–Sarmatian (e.g. Zweigel 1997).

The Badenian–Pannonian period (Fig. 2) was the time of the intra-Carpathian basin and stress rearrangement, during which a very prominent west–east to WNW–ESE regional extension started occurring in different times and places during the end-Badenian–Sarmatian (e.g. Bergerat 1989; Fodor *et al.* 1990; Nemčok & Lexa 1990; Csontos *et al.* 1991; Bada 1999). A comparison of the calculated ratios of principal stress magnitudes of the progressively younger stresses from the Middle Slovakian volcanic region indicates a progression towards a $\sigma_1 \approx \sigma_2 >> \sigma_3$ type of stress field (Nemčok *et al.* 2000*a*). Karpatian–early Badenian sinistral strike-slip faults in the Vienna Basin area were reactivated as normal faults during the Middle Miocene (e.g. Nemčok *et al.* 1989; Nemčok 1993; Fodor 1995).

The Middle Miocene stress field determined in the South Carpathians had a NW–SE compression (e.g. Ratschbacher *et al.* 1993*a*; Girbacea 1997; Matenco *et al.* 1997). The Middle Miocene compression in the East Carpathians varied between NE–SW and NW–SE orientation in the northern and southern parts, respectively (Linzer 1996; Girbacea 1997; Zweigel 1997). The Transylvanian Basin was controlled by east–west extension during the Sarmatian (Huismans *et al.* 1997).

The boundary between ALCAPA and Tisza–Dacia has been controlled by NE–SW compression and NW–SE extension since the late Badenian (Gyorfi *et al.* 1999).

From the end of the Badenian to the Pannonian (13.6–11.5 Ma) (Fig. 2), the intra-Carpathian basins experienced a regionally consistent east–west to ESE–WNW extension (e.g. Bergerat 1989; Nemčok 1993). The South Carpathians were characterized by north–south to NNE–SSW compression (e.g. Ratschbacher *et al.* 1993*a*) or NW–SE compression (Girbacea 1997).

Later, during the Pannonian (11.5–6.2 Ma), the Carpathian stress configuration changed to a stress configuration similar to the present-day one (Fig. 2), as determined in the Vienna Basin, southern and northern Hungary, and central Slovakia (Fodor *et al.* 1990; Csontos *et al.* 1991; Benkovics 1997; Nemčok *et al.* 1998*a*). Since the early Pannonian, the time period was characterized by a short-term intra-Pannonian Basin inversion event and Pliocene–Quaternary inversion (Bada 1999 and references therein). The timing of the short-term event is largely mismatched; for example: (1) Sarmatian–Pontian (9–5.3 Ma) for the entire region, which was driven by east–west compression (Peresson & Decker 1997*b*) and was proven by numerical modelling to be physically unrealistic (see Bada 1999); (2) early Pannonian for the Central Hungarian Fault Zone (which forms the south-eastern ALCAPA boundary) or Mecsek Mts, which and was driven by north–south compression (Benkovics 1997; Csontos & Nagymarosy 1998); (3) late Pannonian for the Middle Slovakian basins, which was driven by north–south compression (Nemčok *et al.* 2000*a*).

The described calculated Pannonian stress regimes suffer from the sparsity of outcrops. The Post-Pannonian stress regimes inferred from 2D seismic data suffer from a lack of 3D interpretation.

Between the East and South Carpathians, an early Pannonian NW–SE compression later replaced by north–south compression was determined (e.g. Hippolyte & Sandulescu 1996).

To summarize this section, the Cenozoic dynamics of the Carpathian hinterland was characterized by distinct stress events, which frequently resulted from the interaction between microplates advancing behind the developing accretionary wedge.

Kinematic data from the accretionary wedge

This section describes the new data on the development of the Outer Carpathians, gathered from locations situated in the Tertiary accretionary wedge (see Fig. 1 for location). The data comprise folds and extensional veins, which are described later along with the σ_1 and σ_3 stress orientations derived from them. They also include fault-striae data from 169 locations shown in Figure 3. Figure 3a–e shows the fault-striae populations, where: (1) the whole dataset contains fewer than four fault-striae readings with similar controlling stress regimes, as determined by the method of Sperner *et al.* (1993); (2) the whole dataset suitable for other stress methods contains fewer than four outliers; (3) the whole dataset contains fault-striae readings related to several stress regimes. It was assumed that the first two categories of data were controlled by one tectonic event, the first category carrying just approximate value. Using fault categories described by Bott (1959), these data from monophase locations document that in 14% of the outcrops, the rocks were deformed predominantly by reverse faults, 19% were deformed by a combination of reverse and strike-slip faults, 14% were deformed by normal faults and the remaining 53% were deformed by strike-slip faults.

The polyphase locations were predominantly deformed by oblique- and strike-slip faulting. Figure 3f shows the fault-striae data from this dataset from selected outcrops, which were deformed by several deformational events.

The majority of minor faults in the Magura Unit (Fig. 1) and some faults in other units are lined by calcite fibres. These structures are formed by the steady growth of calcite during small increments of fault slip by a crack-and-seal mechanism (Ramsay 1980), which is slow enough to allow a diffusive mass transfer of these shear fibres by repeated fracturing, an infinitesimal amount of movement and calcite growth, infilling the rupture in the optical continuity with the fractured crystal. These fibres are generally subparallel to the existing striation, although we have found these fibres to be grown at an acute angle to the fault wall-rock in several instances.

The data from creek and road cuts display arrays of meso-scale faults with displacement ranging from a few centimetres to a few metres and show cross-cutting relationships, both among themselves and with striations on each fault plane, allowing the determination of the deformation history. Shear sense was determined from minor structures, including the lower-order shears (e.g. Petit 1987), shear fibres (e.g. Hancock 1985) and frictional structures (e.g. Dżułyński & Kotlarczyk 1965). Among the observed thrusts, both foreland-vergent and hinterland-vergent thrusts are present at outcrop. Older thrusts have formed in subhorizontally dipping sediments, thereby accommodating initial horizontal shortening. They have been subsequently folded and sometimes rotated to steep and locked positions. There are slickensides that have developed along the bedding planes. Some shale horizons contain a weak pressure solution cleavage. The largest proportion of internal slickensides of thrust sheets is formed by meso-scale strike-slip faults.

Gently dipping fault planes are included in the younger generation of thrusts from outcrops. These faults were not affected by any significant rotation. Part of this meso-scale fault population located inside the thrust sheets is subparallel to the thrust sheet defining large-scale thrusts and has the same vergence. The thrust sheets include large-scale folds and meso-scale thrusts developed inside the damage zones of thrust-sheet defining thrusts. Thrust-sheet bounding thrusts have displacements of the order of hundreds or thousands of metres.

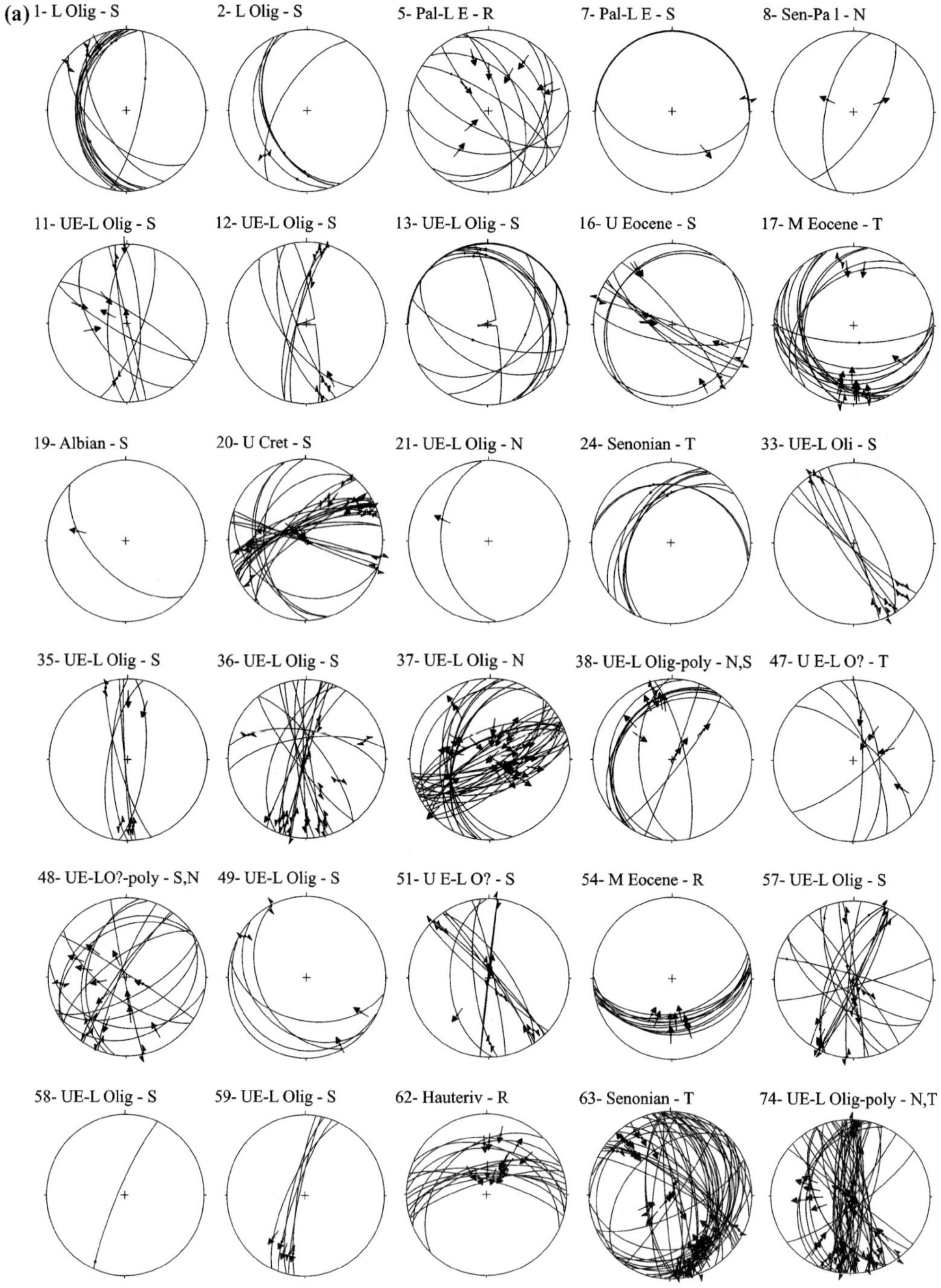

Fig. 3. Great circle diagrams of all fault-striae populations (**a**–**e**) and selected polyphase populations (**f**) at outcrops located in Figure 1. The stresses controlling these populations are listed online at http://www. geolsoc.org.uk/sup18257. A hard copy can be obtained from the Society Library. Code above each diagram contains location number, stratigraphic age of deformed rocks, indication 'poly' in the case of polyphase fault-striae dataset, and type of the controlling stress regime (R, reverse faulting; N, normal faulting; S, strike-slip faulting; T, transpressional stress). The separated monophase datasets in (**f**) are numbered, including the location number and the number of the monophase dataset.

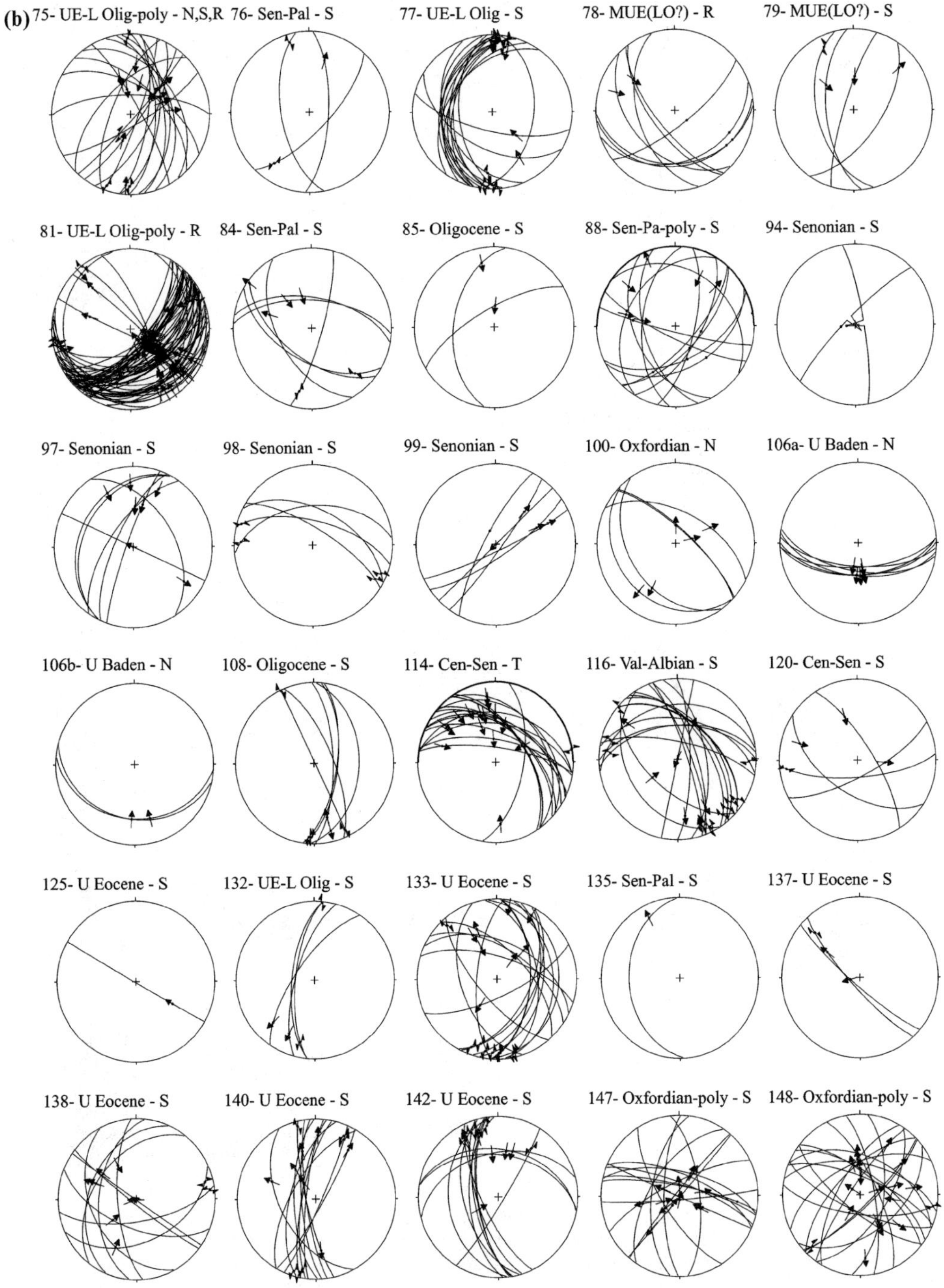

Fig. 3. Continued

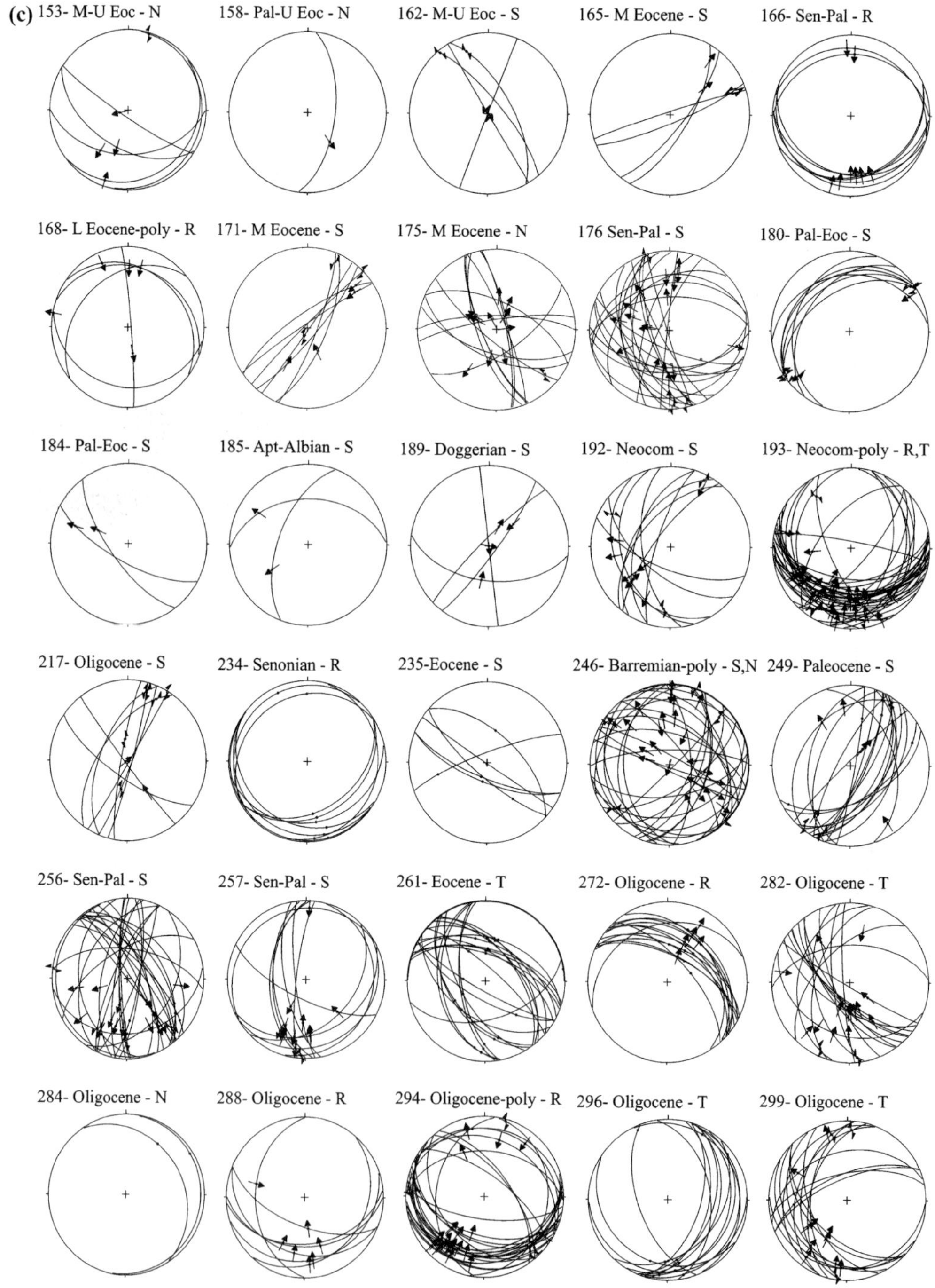

Fig. 3. Continued

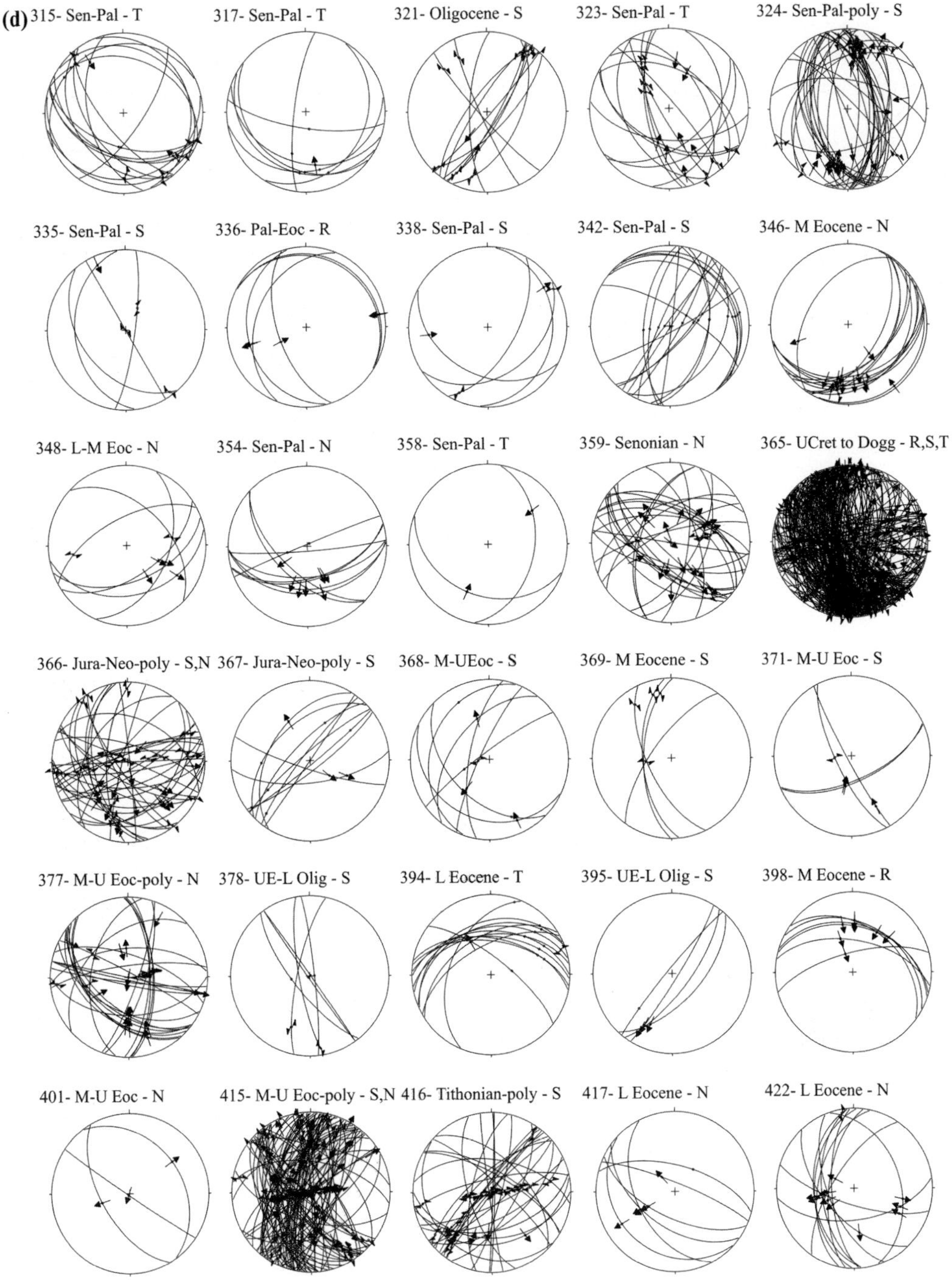

Fig. 3. Continued

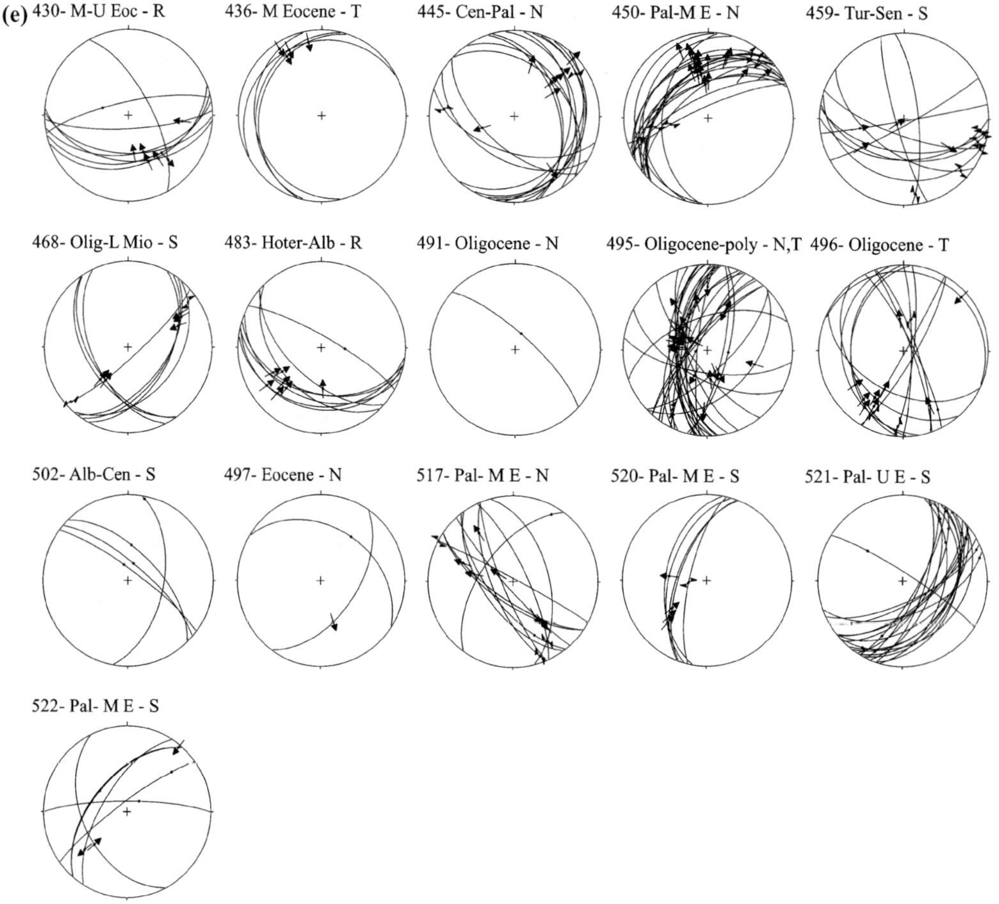

Fig. 3. Continued

Although décollements and major ramps are represented as discrete planes in balanced cross-sections through the study area (e.g. Roure *et al.* 1993; Roca *et al.* 1995; Nemčok *et al.* 2001), they contain zones of fault breccia or gouge that are several tens to hundreds of metres thick in studied outcrops. Each zone shows evidence of repeated cataclasis and calcite cementation. Some of these zones contain just a fault gouge, or a fault gouge with rounded or angular clasts. The Magura sole thrust zone is usually several hundred metres thick. Its breccia zone usually contains clasts representing footwall lithologies, whereas hanging-wall lithologies are present only in the uppermost part of the zone. Clasts and fault gouge contain multiple generations of veining with random orientations. These observations are consistent with a history of relatively large slip increments followed by stress build-up and cycles of fluid overpressure, prior to rupture (e.g. Sibson 1989, 1994; Knipe *et al.* 1991; Knipe 1993). Blocks of various sandstones, siltstones, cherts and marlstones are contained within a clay matrix, which is frequently intensely sheared and microfolded. The described large-displacement faults are usually accompanied by deformation zones on both sides, which mostly contain meso-scale faults and fractures. Outcrops indicate that more competent layers have accommodated folding through a flexural slip along their bedding planes. These surfaces are identified by striations, minor fault gouge seams or shear fibre development.

The earlier studies of the main Carpathian décollement recognized either subhorizontally oriented tensile fractures, filled by vertical mineral fibres grown against the weight of the whole thrust wedge (Nemčok *et al.* 1999*b*, 2000*c*), or randomly oriented and cross-cutting veins (Nemčok *et al.* 2000*c*), both indicating pore-fluid overpressure along the décollement. Another indicator of the pore-fluid overpressure in the accretionary wedge is the injection of sandstone dykes. The observed dykes are probably confined

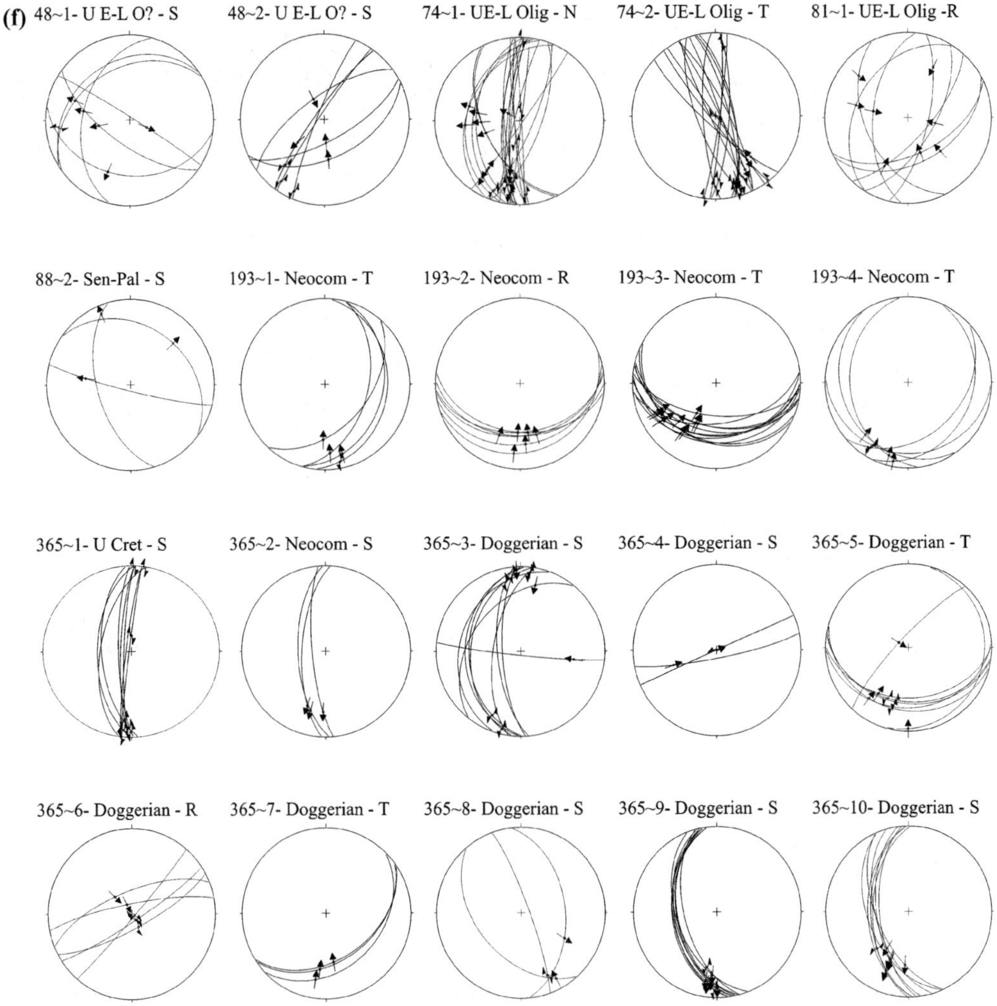

Fig. 3. Continued

to the northeastern, thickest part of the accretionary wedge, as indicated by their presence at the outcrop of the Krosno beds of the Skole Unit at location 205, the outcrop of Zlín beds of the Magura Unit at location 404 and the outcrop of Menilitic beds of the Skole Unit at location 463 (see Fig. 1 for location). There are several vertical dykes of coarse sandstone within the massive sandstone at location 205. One of these dykes is about 30 cm thick and its top is preserved at this outcrop. Its fill contains carbonaceous plant fragments, which allow for the determination of the upward direction of flow inside the column. In the uppermost parts of the dyke, these pieces made a set of concave surfaces parallel to the dyke top. In the remaining part of the dyke, these surfaces are parallel to the dyke walls. The flow pattern inferred from these contours indicates that the largest flow rate was in the centre of the sandstone dyke.

Principal stress orientations

σ_3 orientations from extensional veins

The distribution of calcite vein measurements indicates that 87% of the veins occur in well-cemented Magura facies (Fig. 4), whereas the remaining units did not undergo much veining. Most of the veins are of the stretched variety (Ramsay & Huber 1983) and were interpreted as having been opened roughly perpendicularly to their walls. Few of them contain fibres, allowing for the exact determination of the opening vectors. Veins in the Magura unit are located either along the main thrusts, where they were

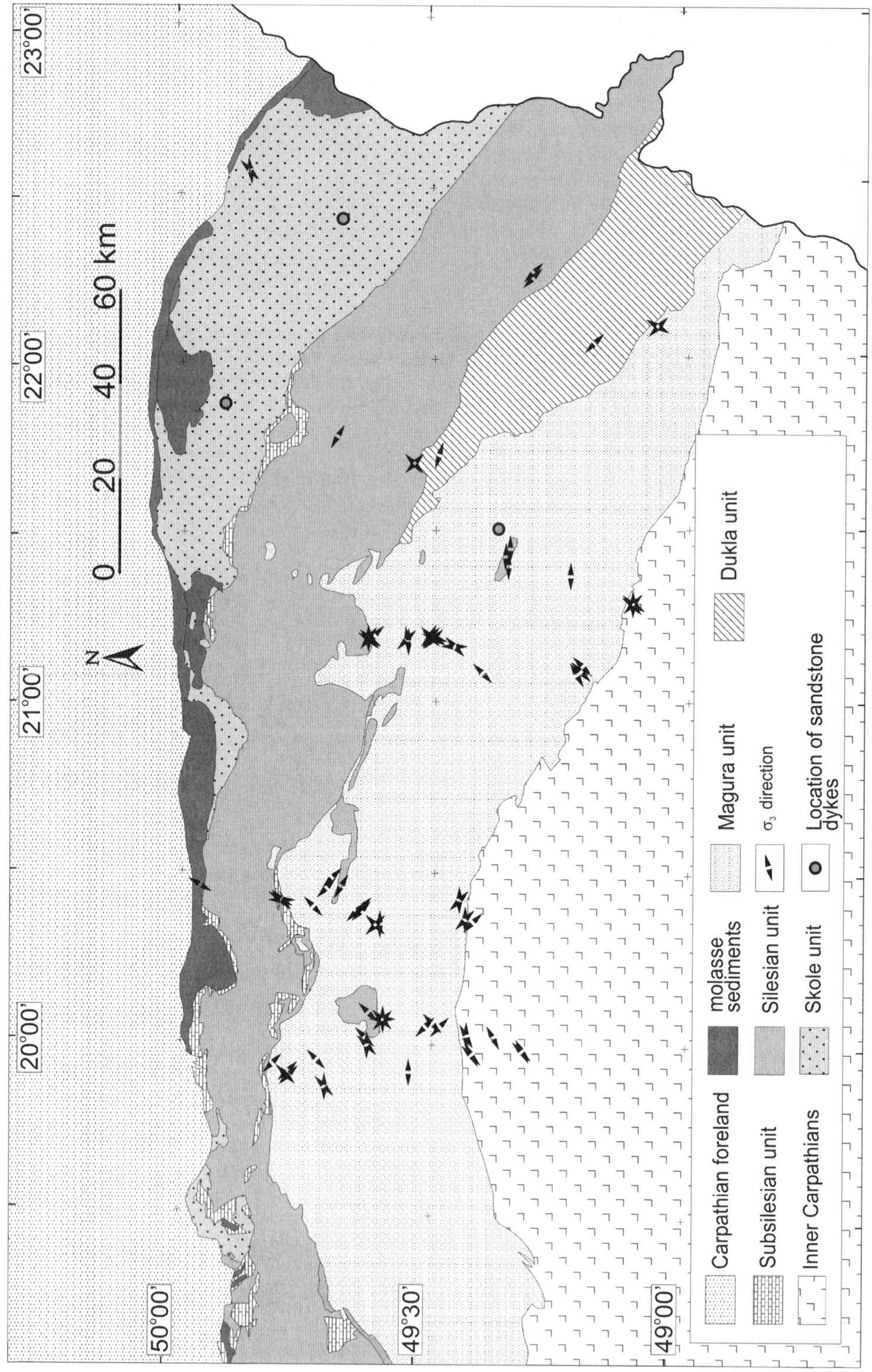

Fig. 4. Map of the Outer West Carpathian accretionary wedge from Figure 1, with σ_3 directions determined from extensional veins. Further explanation is given in the text.

opened in all directions, or inside thrust sheets, where they have a more regionally consistent opening direction pattern. Nineteen per cent of the latter veins were opened in the direction parallel to shortening: NNW–SSE to north–south in the west and NNE–SSW to NE–SW in the east, which is related either to flexure associated with folding or to the initial gravitational collapse of structures developed by shortening. Thirty-eight percent of the data indicate the orogen strike-parallel stretching in front of the Magura unit, ENE–WSW in the west and NW–SE in the east. This pattern seems to be rotated in the vicinity of the Przemyśl Sigmoid (Fig. 1). The extension directions, determined from the veins in regions of tectonic windows, always indicate that the extension was oblique to the direction of the local shortening, which indicates a strike-slip component of the deformation.

σ_1 orientations from folds

Measured meso-scale folds were formed by both fault-propagation and fault-bend folding. The frequent slickensides, formed along the bedding planes, indicate that the shortening vector was roughly perpendicular to the fold axes. This observation was used as justification for the rough determination of the maximum compressional stress σ_1 orientation as perpendicular to fold axes (Fig. 5). This rough determination needs to be used cautiously, because the assumption does not hold for transpressional folds or folds associated with strike-slip faults.

The overall system of interpreted σ_1 vectors indicates a fan pattern inside the accretionary wedge as well as in front of the thick Inner Carpathians, which were developed during pre-Tertiary time. On average, σ_1 vectors have NNW–SSE orientations along profile 1 from west to east in Figure 1, north–south orientations along profile 2, and NNE–SSW to NE–SW orientations along profiles 3–5. A relatively simple σ_1 pattern is present in front of the Magura Unit along profiles 3–5. Disturbances are present only in areas next to geometric complexities along the main thrusts. A more complex σ_1 pattern is determined from the Magura Unit, where complexities are located along major thrusts, bounding either the Magura Unit or its internal thrust sheets.

σ_1 and σ_3 orientations from faults

The principal stress directions σ_1 and σ_3 calculated from reverse, strike-slip, oblique-slip and normal faulting data are shown in Figure 6. The complete stress directions with the ratio of their magnitudes, in cases where they can be calculated, are available online at http://www.geolsoc.org.uk/sup18257. A hard copy can be obtained from the Society Library. The age of deformed rocks at each outcrop is listed in Figure 3. The diagrams in Figure 3 indicate a 26% success rate in finding data at outcrops, which is 136 out of 525. A total of 110 outcrops were deformed by a monophase fault-striae dataset. To map the reliability of the data from 'monophase outcrops', it needs to be said that 18% include fewer than four readings and 30% include 4–6 readings. Fortunately, the distribution of locations with less numerous datasets (Fig. 3) is scattered, allowing locations with robust datasets to make up for locations with minor datasets in local areas. What is surprising is the small amount of outcrops deformed by polyphase fault-striae datasets, only 25 out of 136, and a mere five of them (Fig. 3f) have robust datasets. The small amount of polyphase outcrops is not a search artefact, because the amount of 525 visited outcrops where we could find some structural data is rather robust and already represents a selection from the total, which is several times larger than that. The rare occurrence of robust polyphase locations is further highlighted by the fact that out of five polyphase locations shown in Figure 3f, two of them contain separated monophase subsets, which contain fewer than four fault-striae readings.

The calculated stress states from outcrops can be roughly divided into four basic stress regimes: thrusting (12%), transpressional (14%), normal faulting (18%) and strike-slip faulting (56%) regimes (Fig. 3).

Both thrusting and transpressional stress regimes have been calculated from the outcrops, which are located in the close vicinity of large-scale faults such as the contact between the Inner Carpathians with the Tertiary accretionary wedge, the Magura Unit sole thrust, the Silesian unit sole thrust, the Carpathian frontal thrust, faults bounding tectonic windows and faults at the contacts of major sub-units (compare Figs 1 and 3). These outcrops are homogeneously distributed over the study area.

Strike-slip stress regimes have been calculated from a majority of the outcrops. Apart from being located in the vicinity of several large-scale strike-slip faults, strike-slip faults represent the internal fault-striae data from thrust sheets (compare Figs 1 and 3). The number of outcrops with strike-slip stress regimes is largest in the west. It progressively decreases to the east, in accordance with the decreasing proportion of the well-cemented Magura unit length to the total wedge length in the cross-section through the Tertiary accretionary wedge.

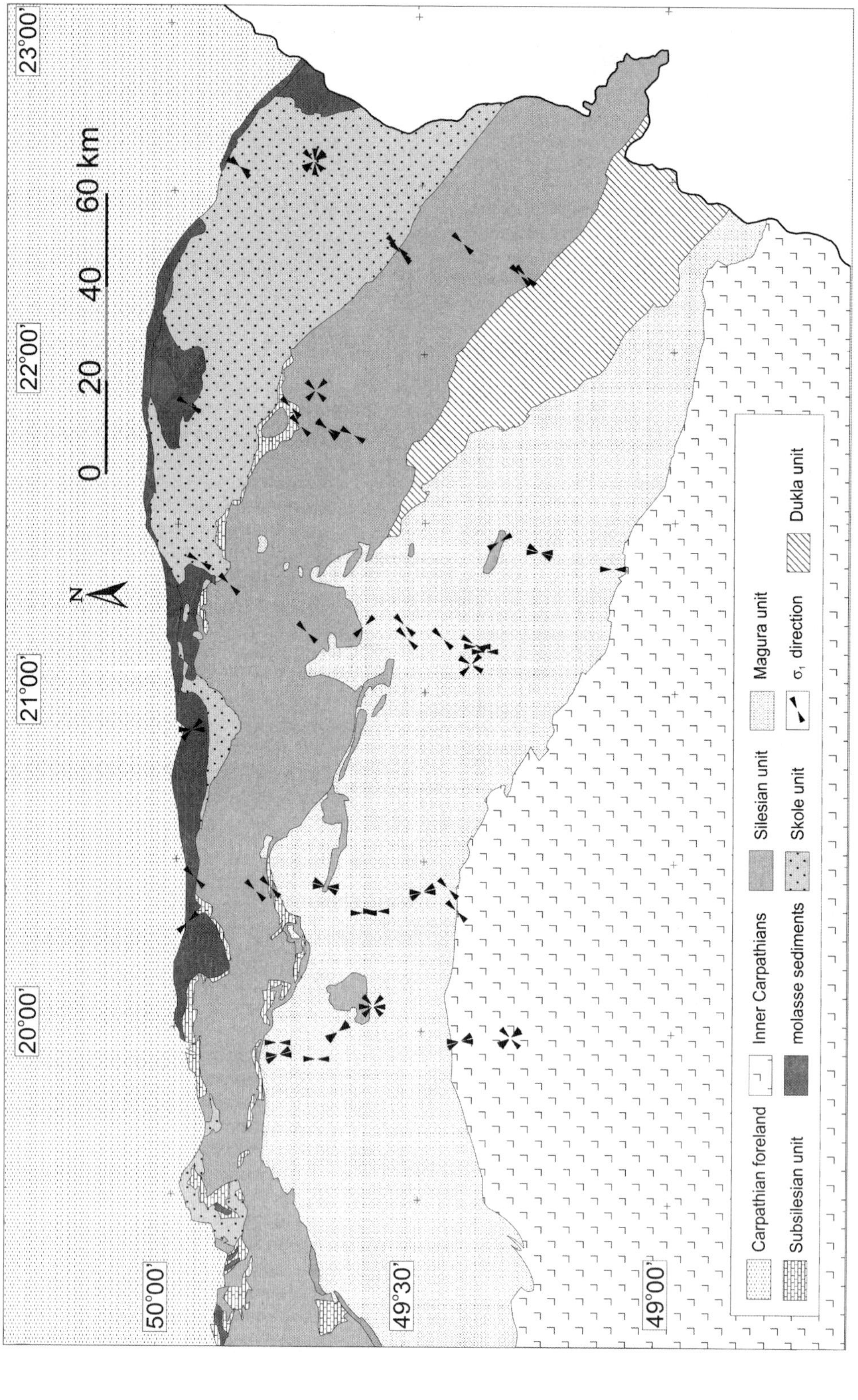

Fig. 5. Map of the Outer West Carpathian accretionary wedge from Figure 1, with σ_1 directions determined from folds. Further explanation is given in the text.

Normal faulting stress regimes have been calculated from the outcrops located in the most mountainous rear portion of the wedge, as well as at the frontal anticlines of main units and at the wedge front (compare Figs 1 and 3).

The outcrops with data relating to several successive stress regimes are located inside the Pieniny Klippen Belt, which is located just behind the Tertiary accretionary wedge (compare Figs 1 and 3) in the very rear of the accretionary wedge, at the geometrical complexities of several major unit contacts and in front of the wedge. Most of the stress regimes are located either in the Pieniny Klippen Belt or in the most western part of the accretionary wedge, where the amount of partitioning between thrusting and strike-slip faulting is the largest in the study area, as known from pre-existing studies (e.g. Nemčok *et al.* 1998*b*).

σ_1 vectors associated with thrust, strike-slip and transpressional stress regimes show a fan-like pattern inside the accretionary wedge (Fig. 6), as in the case of the rough estimation from folds (Fig. 5). σ_1 directions progressively change from NNW–SSE in the west to NE–SW in the east. However, there are local exceptions to this pattern. For example, locations 354, 359 and 459 indicate about 40° of local clockwise stress rotation in the NW vicinity of the Przemyśl Sigmoid (Fig. 1). Further exceptions are locations 193, 365, 366, 367 and 416, which reside in the Pieniny Klippen Belt, a contact zone between the Inner Carpathians and the Tertiary accretionary wedge. These locations indicate multiple reactivations of this highly deformed zone by various kinds of stress events (Fig. 3f). Exceptions are also present in the far west, where calculated stress events indicate local stress perturbations along sinistral strike-slip faults zones, calculated at outcrops such as 20, 88, 116, 120, 133, 165 and 180 (compare Figs 1 and 3). Some of these zones document small areas of pure thrusting, such as locations 5, 81 and 106, or have a local sinistral transpressional character, demonstrated by locations 17, 114, 315, 317 and 323 (compare Figs 1 and 3). As a result of the increased rotational deformation along these zones, 73% of the polyphase outcrops from the accretionary wedge reside in the west. Their stress regimes include multiple thrust, transpressional and strike-slip events, or a combination of strike-slip and transpressional events with extensional events (compare Figs 1 and 3). The sinistral body rotation in the west is also documented by older and younger stress regimes at location 108, characterized by NW–SE- and NNE–SSW-trending σ_1 vectors, respectively. The NW–SE vectors were calculated from rotated fault-striae data.

σ_3 vectors associated with normal-faulting stress regimes have been determined from 26 outcrops. With the exception of the NNE–SSW extension, σ_3 vectors are calculated from normal faults that occasionally post-dated the shortening, as indicated by the relative event succession from locations 38 and 106. The NNE–SSW extension is different in that it was calculated from outcrops 100, 147 and 148, which were located in the foreland deformed by Early Cretaceous rifting that pre-dates the accretionary wedge development. All observed normal faults were meso-scale. No evidence of large-scale normal fault propagation or reactivation of the synorogenic faults has been found.

The majority of the normal-faulting stress regimes are confined to the more proximal and mountainous parts of the accretionary wedge (Fig. 6), which formed large morphological gradients after the shortening. There are, however, eight exceptions. One such exception is location 106, which is formed by a large recumbent fold located above the detachment formed in the incompetent upper Badenian shale and evaporites. This location may represent a case where the syncontractional extension reacts to the friction reduction along the detachment and lack of lateral constraints, as known from Algeria and the Northern Apennines (Meyer *et al.* 1990; Bonini *et al.* 2002).

To summarize this section, the Cenozoic dynamics of the Tertiary accretionary wedge was characterized by a long-lasting orogenic stress regime, which underwent gradual changes in the western portion of the study area. It was subsequently replaced by a weak extension.

Palaeomagnetic data

The successful sampling of massive shale or marl from thrust sheets was a result of frequent disintegration of samples along the scaly fabrics. The sites at which the collection of samples was possible are shown in Figure 7 and listed in Table 1. Four to 12 samples were initially taken from 14 locations, but samples from five locations failed in thermal demagnetization, as they had too strong a present magnetic signal and the matching test had too large a scatter of results (E. Márton, pers. com.). The most reliable results came from locations Pl 47–57, Pl 64–71 and Pl 72–83 (where the numbers indicate the number of samples taken at each location). Locations Pl 8–19, Pl 20–27, Pl 40–46, Pl 58–63, Pl 84–90 and Pl 100–108 would require more samples for precisely determined declination and inclination. These results can only be regarded as indications.

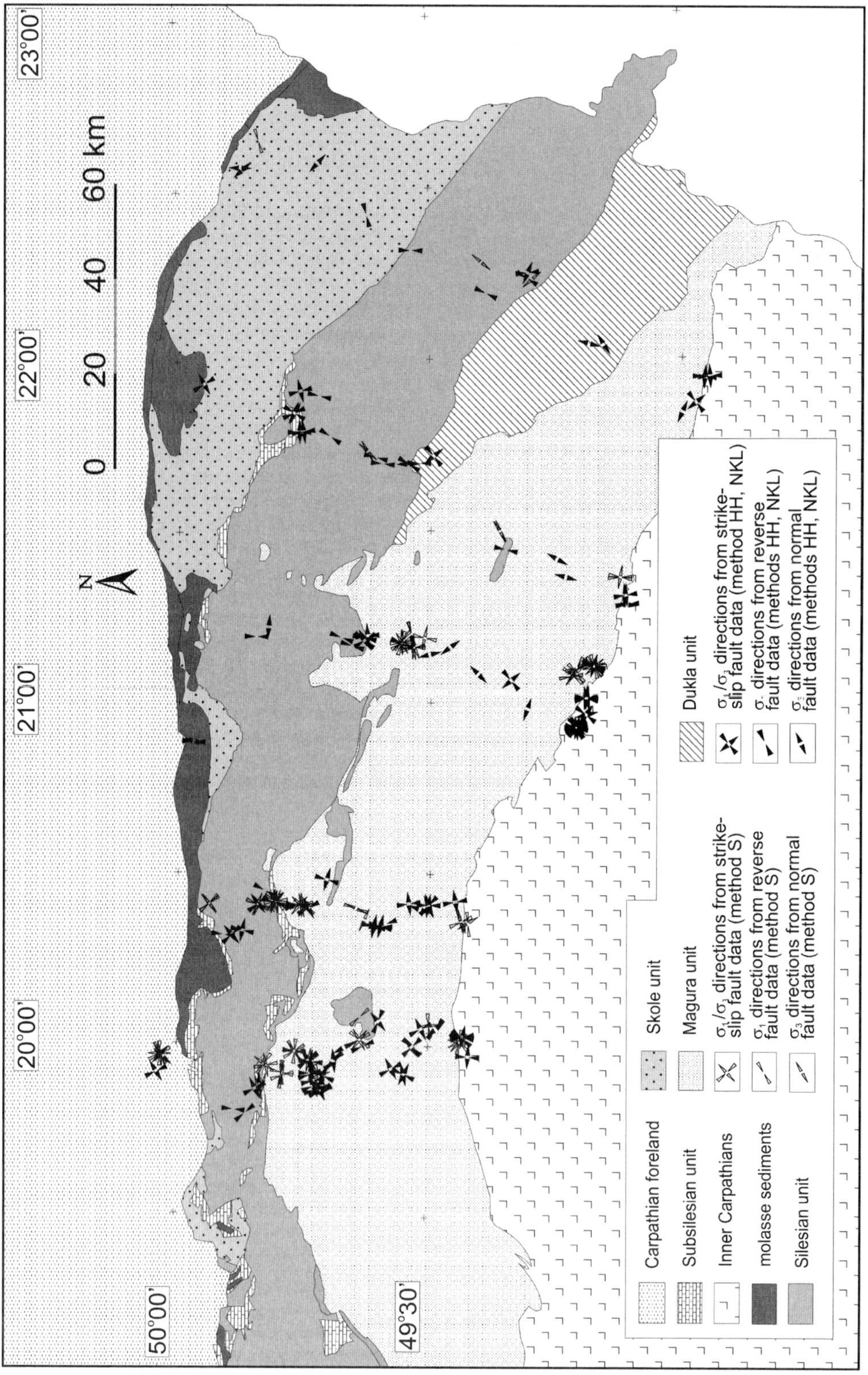
23°00'
22°00'
21°00'
20°00'
50°00'
49°30'
0 20 40 60 km
N
Carpathian foreland
Subsilesian unit
Inner Carpathians
molasse sediments
Silesian unit
Skole unit
Magura unit
σ1/σ3 directions from strike-slip fault data (method S)
σ1 directions from reverse fault data (method S)
σ3 directions from normal fault data (method S)
Dukla unit
σ1/σ3 directions from strike-slip fault data (method HH, NKL)
σ1 directions from reverse fault data (methods HH, NKL)
σ3 directions from normal fault data (methods HH, NKL)

The most reliable results show that the mass rotation in the western part of the Magura Unit was up to 90° counterclockwise since the Late Eocene, which is in accordance with the results from the Central Carpathian Palaeogene (Podhale) Basin and earlier studies in the orogenic hinterland (e.g. Túnyi & Gross 1995; Márton & Márton 1996; Márton *et al.* 1996, 1999; Túnyi & Márton 1996; Grabowski & Nemčok 1999, and references therein), but is larger than the results (60°) from the Palaeocene–Middle Eocene facies of the Magura Unit, further to the east (Krs *et al.* 1991).

The rock mass in front of the Magura Unit rotated counterclockwise in the western part, with the declination value becoming progressively smaller from the Cretaceous (43–64°) to the Neogene (20°), as indicated by the present data in conjunction with the data of Krs *et al.* (1982), which came from the area west of our region. The combination of these data with the data of Koráb *et al.* (1981), located in the easternmost Silesian Unit of our region, further indicates a progressive decrease in the counterclockwise rotation of the declination along the orogen strike, from west (64°) to east (25°), for the same stratigraphy for the units in front of the Magura Unit.

It needs to be emphasized that the interpreted rotations have only preliminary character, because the quality of the early determinations inside the wedge (Koráb *et al.* 1981; Krs *et al.* 1982, 1991) may be questionable (E. Márton, pers. com.) and the new data require further precision and completion.

Discussion

The main goal of this discussion is to select the development model of the Carpathian arc from the three possibilities outlined in the introduction, as follows.

(1) If the Carpathian arc was developed by oroclinal bending, it should have recorded a stress field characterized by outward-fanning σ_1 trajectories, which is a typical result for a push from behind. This stress record should be present in both the orogen and its foreland.

Although the determined stress field in the accretionary wedge is characterized by a system of outward-fanning subhorizontal σ_1 trajectories (Figs 5 and 6), this stress type is not present in the orogenic hinterland (Fig. 2) and therefore characterizes a rather narrow frontal zone of the orogen. This stress field type is also absent in the orogenic foreland (see Bergerat 1987), which lacks the expected stress record typical for the region around the outer arc of the fold. Therefore, the oroclinal bending model can be ruled out.

(2) If the Carpathian arc was developed by a spreading of the overthickened lithosphere, it should have recorded a gravity-dominated stress field that controls the polydirectional material flow into low-energy areas. This stress record should be present in the orogen but not in the foreland.

The new stress results from the accretionary wedge do not indicate any distinct gravity collapse (Fig. 6), apart from a tenuous initiation in the most proximal part, indicating that the accretionary wedge formed a narrow compressional zone in front of the intensively stretched hinterland (Fig. 2). The studies of extension timing in the hinterland have demonstrated that the extension was progressively expanding to a more northeasterly region of the ALCAPA megablock during the Miocene (e.g. Nemčok *et al.* 1998*a*), which is in accordance with subduction roll-back in a similar direction. Furthermore, the roll-back is indicated by subduction-related volcanism that becomes progressively younger in the northeasterly direction inside the ALCAPA megablock (see Nemčok *et al.* 1998*c*, and references therein). Therefore, the gravity spreading model can be ruled out as well.

(3) If the Carpathian arc was developed by back-arc spreading, it should have recorded a stress field characterized by a narrow zone of frontal compression and a wide zone of internal extension. This stress record should be present in the orogen but not in the foreland.

When the data for the hinterland and the accretionary wedge are compared (Figs 2 and 4–6) it is shown that the orogen was characterized by a relatively narrow frontal zone of compression and a broad internal zone of extension, especially during the time period after there was some northeastward expansion of the extensional conditions in the hinterland during the Miocene. The ALCAPA megablock was affected by subduction-related volcanism, which migrated towards the NE with time, along with the subduction roll-back. Perhaps the best indication that the subduction roll-back ran obliquely to the

Fig. 6. Map of the Outer West Carpathian accretionary wedge from Figure 1, with σ_3 and σ_1 directions determined from fault-striae data. Method S is the computer program of Sperner *et al.* (1993), method HH is from Hardcastle & Hills (1991); method NKL is from Nemčok & Lisle (1995) or Nemčok *et al.* (1999*a*). Further explanation is given in the text.

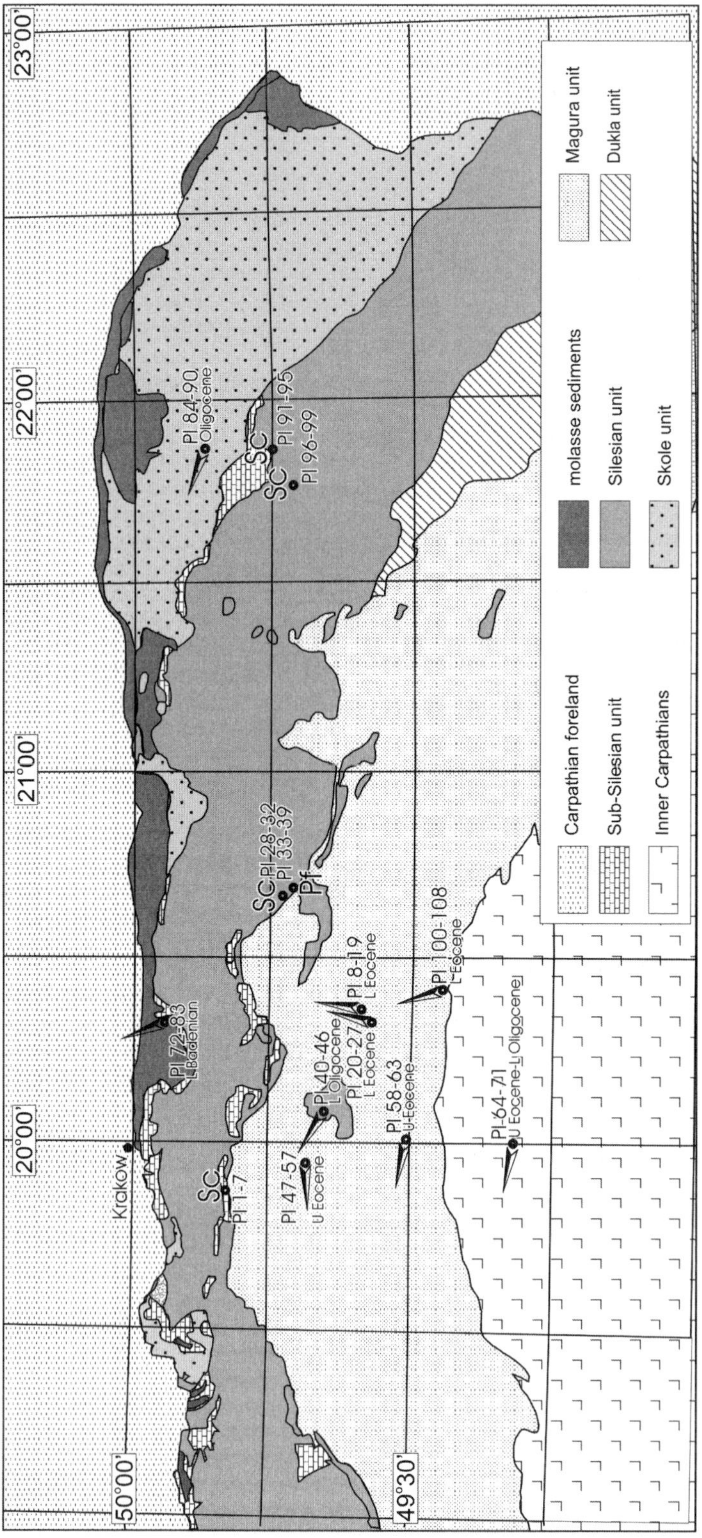

Fig. 7. Map of the Outer West Carpathian accretionary wedge from Figure 1, with determined palaeomagnetic declinations. The numeric codes at the locations indicate the number of analysed samples.

Table 1. *A list of palaeomagnetic results (according to Márton 1997; Márton* et al. *1997, 2000; Nemčok* et al. *2000*b*).*

Location	No/No	$D°$	$I°$	k	$\alpha_{95}°$	$D_c°$	$I_c°$	Cleaning	Dip	Rock age
Pl 1–7	Large scatter									
Pl 8–19	08/12	030	−60	22	12	008	−35	AF 220–350 TH 350–420	167/32	Early Eocene
Pl 20–27	06/08	014	−26	22	14	014	26	TH 250–400	162/60	Early Eocene
Pl 28–32	Large scatter									
Pl 33–39	Strong present field									
Pl 40–46	05/07	315	70	18	18	009	68	TH 250	064/18	Oligocene
		303	−17	06	32	302	−08	TH 400–450		
Pl 47–57	10/11	304	46	18	12	267	61	TH 250–375	168/30	Late Eocene
Pl 58–63	04/06	125	−50	06	42	102	−25	TH 350–375	244/37	Late Eocene
Pl 64–71	07/08	286	58	24	13	282	55	TH 300–375	249/04	Late Eoc–Olig
Pl 72–83	09/12	318	54	15	14	340	58		074/15	Badenian
Pl 84–90	02/07	≈290	43	–	–	≈290	25	TH 300	268/18	Oligocene
Pl 91–95	Large scatter									
Pl 96–99	Failed									
Pl 100–108	05/09	154	−30	41	12	164	−10	TH 300–400	352/25	Early Eocene
	08/09	153	−32	15	15					

No./No. indicates the ratio of used and collected samples. $D°$ and $I°$ are the mean palaeomagnetic declination and inclination before tilt correction; $D_c°$ and $I_c°$ are the declination and inclination after tilt correction; $\alpha_{95}°$ and k are the statistical parameters. Tilt corrections are made with the use of local bedding. Thermal demagnetization (TH) was used. AF, alternating field. Samples from locations Pl 1–7, 28–32, 33–39, 91–95 and 96–99 failed to provide results, either because of the large scatter of results, or because a strong magnetic field was present. The results with no statistical parameters or $\alpha_{95}° > 20$ must be regarded as mere indications. The location of samples is shown in Figure 7.

orogen strike and controlled the stress field in the Carpathians is stress changes in the regions behind the ceased subduction segment. These stress changes were reacting to neighbouring segments with subduction that was still active, and that was was ceasing in an easterly direction along the Carpathian arc (see Nemčok 1993). All of the aforementioned points indicate that the back-arc spreading model is the best candidate for the Carpathian arc development.

However, several complexities in the dynamics and kinematics of the study area must still be discussed, as they do not precisely fit the dynamics and kinematics that are typical for the back-arc stretching development model.

The first complexity is that the West Carpathians lack a prominent retrowedge. Analogue material modelling (Malavieille 1984; Storti *et al.* 2000) and numerical modelling (Willett *et al.* 1993) have shown that basal pull has a tendency to develop doubly vergent wedges, which are characterized by an initial high-velocity thrusting in the retrowedge and a high-frequency–low-displacement thrusting in the prowedge, followed by a low-frequency–high-displacement thrusting in the prowedge and a low-velocity thrusting in the retrowedge. Although the retrowedge has yet to be described as a significant structural element in the West Carpathians, recent studies have described a retrowedge located to the south of the Pieniny Klippen Belt in Slovakia (e.g. Sperner *et al.* 2002, and references therein). It is possible that the insignificant development of the retrowedge in the West Carpathians is caused by a slightly oblique convergence.

The strike-slip component of the displacement in the western region of the West Carpathian accretionary wedge (Fig. 1) is indicated by kinematic data for locations in the rear portion of the accretionary wedge (compare Figs 1 and 3). If paleomagnetic declination data are to indicate similar results, there must be a progressively lower amount of counterclockwise rotation in the wedge from west to east, as well as towards younger time periods. The available data for the western portion of the wedge indicate a post Late Eocene counterclockwise rotation of about 90° for the Magura Unit and about 64° for the units located in front of the Magura Unit. Over time, the 64° value decreases to 20°, which is a decrease characteristic of the post early Badenian time, and then finally decreases to 0°, which is a decrease characteristic of the late Badenian time. The along-strike decrease of the rotation value in the wedge for the same stratigraphy is indicated by a post Late Eocene counterclockwise rotation of 25° in the east, instead of a rotation of 64° in the west. It must be emphasized that this interpretation of the palaeomagnetic data is far from conclusive. The quality of earlier results (Koráb *et al.* 1981; Krs *et al.* 1982; 1991) may be questionable (Márton, pers. com.) and the new data (Fig. 7, Table 1) are not robust enough to prove or disprove this trend. Therefore, for the results to be conclusive, more locations with palaeomagnetic declination data and further precision for locations Pl 8–19, Pl 20–27, Pl 40–46, Pl 58–63, Pl 84–90 and Pl 100–108 are needed.

The second complexity is that the determined stress field for the accretionary wedge (Figs 4–6) is similar to the development model dominated by push from behind. The determined stress field in the accretionary wedge is characterized by a system of outward-fanning subhorizontal σ_1 trajectories, which point towards an indentation effect that must be discussed.

Large-scale indentation can be ruled out, because the thrust fault traces in the arcuate accretionary wedge do not converge in the apex of the wedge (Fig. 1), as shown by the analogue material modelling for indenter-controlled orogenic salients (see Macedo & Marshak 1999), but rather they converge at salient end points instead. In fact, this type of convergence implies that there was pre-existing basin control in the location of the West Carpathian arc, which would require that the deep basin location coincides with the orogenic apex location. The existence of Early Cretaceous horsts and younger intra-basinal sources in the sedimentary record of the West Carpathian accretionary wedge (e.g. Książkiewicz 1960; Roure *et al.* 1993, 1994; Oszczypko & Oszczypko-Clowes 2002) and their absence in the sedimentary record of the East Carpathian accretionary wedge (e.g. Stefanescu & Melinte 1996) indicate the progressive deepening of the remnant Carpathian Flysch Basin from the NW to the SE (see also Ryłko & Adam 2005). This deepening is in accordance with the apex location being controlled by the deepest part of the basin.

In contrast, smaller-scale indentation is likely, because rather than being homogeneous, the orogenic hinterland is composed of megablocks (Fig. 1) that underwent separate movements during the development of the accretionary wedge (see Csontos *et al.* 1992). Their strength is superior to the strength of the wedge, because of the crustal thickness contrast between the hinterland and the accretionary wedge. This makes them good candidates for local indenters. These indenters are capable of affecting the deformation of the surrounding wedge, as suggested by the analogue material studies applied to the Argentinean Andes (Marques & Cobbold 2000).

It should be noted that palaeostress data indicate noticeably different dynamics for the accretionary wedge and the orogenic hinterland. whereas the dynamics of the hinterland can be described as a system of distinct tectonic events, characterized by relatively quick transitions and relatively consistent stress regimes typical for each event (Fig. 2), the accretionary wedge dynamics are characterized as though they were more stable than those of the hinterland and were undergoing slow gradual changes (Fig. 6).

It seems as though hinterland stress has been influenced by a complex stress transfer through a system of Inner Carpathian microplates (Fig. 1). The best example of this complexity is the Sarmatian docking of the ALCAPA microplate, which previously moved toward the NE, and the coeval accelerated eastward movement of the Tisza–Dacia microplate, which caused a roughly east–west-trending extension inside the ALCAPA microplate. The timing of the docking can be inferred from balanced cross-sections that are located in front of ALCAPA (e.g. Nemčok *et al.* 1999*b*, and references therein), and the timing of the accelerated Tisza–Dacia movement can be inferred from the timing and magnitude of the magnetic declination rotations (Panaiotu *et al.* 1998). The ALCAPA stress regime for this time period is shown in Figure 2.

A weak mechanical continuum seems to represent the accretionary wedge located between the foreland and the Inner Carpathians. As has been discussed above, the combined structural (Figs 2 and 4–6) and palaeomagnetic results (Fig. 7, Table 1) indicate that there is progressively less body rotation from west to east in the study area. The large scatter of the σ_1 directions in the west (Fig. 6) can be attributed to the fact that the stresses have been calculated from the data at outcrops, which (1) underwent various amounts of sinistral body rotation and (2) were originally controlled by stress with a certain amount of σ_1 deflection, depending on the proportion of strike-slip to thrust components in the western portion of the study area. The eastern portion, which lacks the strike-slip component, is characterized by a relatively consistent synorogenic σ_1 pattern (Fig. 6).

The difference between the dynamics in the western and eastern portions of the accretionary wedge accounts for the third complexity, which is the highly asymmetric orogenic salient of the study area (Fig. 1). This complexity is a result of the NE–SW convergence, which is oblique to the strike of the northern West Carpathians. The asymmetry is best expressed by the internal fault patterns of the wedge, which are characterized by thrust faults that are parallel to the leading edge of the eastern limb of the arc that trends at a large angle to the northeasterly transport direction. The asymmetry is also expressed by the sinistral strike-slip fault systems that are parallel to the western limb of the arc that parallels the transport direction. A similar geometric situation is known from the Pennsylvanian Salient of the Appalachians, as well as from the Sulaiman Range in Pakistan, both of which were generated by oblique convergence (see Macedo & Marshak 1999).

Conclusions

(1) Meso-structural data indicate an initial horizontal shortening, followed by a large-scale development of detachments, ramps and folds.

(2) The main faults are zones that are several tens to hundreds of metres thick, composed of fault breccia or gouge. Each zone shows evidence of repeated cataclasis and calcite cementation. Both the clasts and the fault gouge contain multiple generations of veining of random orientations, indicating that there were episodes of fluid overpressure prior to rupture. Fluid overpressure is indicated by subhorizontal veins with vertically grown mineral fibres along the frontal part of the main décollement and the presence of sandstone dykes. The dykes are confined to the northeastern, thicker portion of the wedge.

(3) Most of the veining inside the thrust sheets was developed in the now well-cemented sediments of the Magura Unit. A significant portion of the structural data indicates orogen-strike-parallel stretching rather than gravitational collapse.

(4) The arcuate Carpathian orogen is best explained by the back-arc stretching development model. This model best explains the coexistence of the narrow frontal zone of compression with the wide internal zone of extension expanding in a northeasterly direction. It also explains the northeasterly younging of subduction-related volcanism and the stress changes in the segments behind ceased subduction that reacted to northeasterly subduction roll-back in neighbouring segments with active subduction, which was ceasing in an easterly direction along the Carpathian arc.

(5) The stress patterns of the accretionary wedge and the orogenic hinterland differed from each other. The fan-shaped and gradually changing stress patterns in the wedge compared with the preferred-directional and abruptly changing stress patterns in the hinterland probably reflect their rheological differences. The hinterland was characterized by having a mosaic of blocks with weak boundaries, whereas the wedge behaved as a weak continuum.

(6) σ_1 trajectories that were calculated from fault-striae data in the accretionary wedge have an overall fan-shaped pattern, which indicates local indentation effects caused by the strength contrasts between the accretionary wedge and the blocks of the orogenic hinterland. A comparison of the thrust fault traces converging to the ends of the arcuate orogen with trace convergence patterns in analogue material models indicates that there was a pre-existing basin effect at the location of the Carpathian arc.

(7) The northern West Carpathian arc is asymmetric. The eastern part is characterized by thrust faults parallel to the leading edge of the arc in this region, and the western part is characterized by sinistral strike-slip fault systems that are parallel to the western limb of the arc, which indicates that the arc was formed by oblique NE–SW-trending convergence.

This study was undertaken within the framework of the EUROPROBE–PANCARDI group projects. The work of M.N., M.W., L.L. and M.P.C. was carried out with the financial support of the Amoco Prod. Co., Houston, and later with the support of the Alexander von Humboldt Fund and the Slovak Geological. Survey Project MŻhP-513-96. T.D. thanks L. Ratschbacher for support. The authors are grateful to numerous scientists of the PANCARDI group for discussions. E. Márton and A. Tokarski are acknowledged for their palaeomagnetic work. The authors are grateful to E. Márton for the data discussion during their work on the paper and permission to publish the results of the joint study. The authors thank J. Grabowski for his friendly review. The authors wish to thank M.P.C., who did not see the final result.

References

ALLERTON, S. 1994. Vertical axis rotation associated with folding and thrusting: an example from the eastern Subbetic zone of southern Spain. *Geology*, **22**, 1039–1042.

ANDRUSOV, D., BYSTRICKÝ, J. & FUSÁN, O. 1973. *Outline of the Structure of the West Carpathians. Guidebook for Excursion, 10th Congress of the Carpatho-Balkan Geologic Association.* GÚDŠ, Bratislava, 5–44.

ANGELIER, J. 1978. Tectonic evolution of the Hellenic Arc since the Late Miocene. *Tectonophysics*, **49**, 23–36.

ANGELIER, J. 1989. From orientation to magnitudes in paleostress determinations using fault-slip data. *Journal of Structural Geology*, **11**, 37–50.

ANGELIER, J. & GOGUEL, J. 1979. Sur une méthode simple de détermination des axes principaux des constraintes pour une population de failles. *Comptes Rendusde l'Académie des Sciences, Série D*, **288**, 307–310.

ANGELIER, J., TARANTOLA, A., VALETTE, B. & MANOUSSIS, S. 1982. Inversion of field data in fault tectonics to obtain the regional stress. I. Single phase fault populations, a new method of computing the stress tensor. *Geophysical Journal of the Royal Astronomical Society*, **69**, 607–621.

ANGELIER, J., BARRIER, E. & CHU, H. T. 1986. Plate collision and paleostress trajectories in a fold–thrust belt: the foothills of Taiwan. *Tectonophysics*, **125**, 161–178.

BADA, G. 1999. *Cenozoic stress field evolution in the Pannonian Basin and surrounding orogens. Inferences from kinematic indicators and finite element modelling*. PhD thesis, Vrije Universiteit, Amsterdam.

BARR, T. D. & DAHLEN, F. A. 1989. Brittle frictional mountain building; 2, Thermal structure and heat budget. *Journal of Geophysical Research*, **94**, 3923–3947.

BARRIER, E. & ANGELIER, J. 1986. Active collision in Eastern Taiwan: the Coastal Range. *Tectonophysics*, **125**, 39–72.

BENKOVICS, L. 1997. *Etude structurale et géodynamique des Monts Buda, Mecsek et Villany*. PhD thesis, University of Flandres–Artois, Lille.

BERGERAT, F. 1987. Stress fields in the European Platform at the time of Africa–Eurasia collision. *Tectonics*, **6**, 99–132.

BERGERAT, F. 1989. From pull-apart to the rifting process: the deformation of the Pannonian Basin. *Tectonophysics*, **157**, 271–280.

BERGERAT, F., GEYSANT, J. & LEPVRIER, C. 1983. Etude de la fracturation dans le bassin pannonien, mécanismes et étapes de sa création. *Annales de la Societe Géologique du Nord*, **103**, 265–272.

BONINI, M., SOKOUTIS, D., MULUGETA, G. & KATRIVANOS, E. 2002. Modelling hanging wall accommodation above rigid thrust ramps. *Journal of Structural Geology*, **22**, 1165–1179.

BOTT, M. H. P. 1959. The mechanics of oblique–slip faulting. *Geological Magazine*, **96**, 109–117.

BURCHFIEL, B. C. & ROYDEN, L. H. 1982. Carpathian foreland fold and thrust belt and its relation to Pannonian and other basins. *AAPG Bulletin*, **66**, 1179–1195.

CHAPPLE, W. M. 1978. Mechanics of thin-skinned fold-and-thrust belts. *Geological Society of America Bulletin*, **93**, 1189–1198.

COWARD, M. P. 1994*a*. Continental tectonics. *In*: HANCOCK, P. L. (ed.) *Continental Deformation*. Pergamon, Tarrytown, NY, 264–288.

COWARD, M. P. 1994*b*. Inversion tectonics. *In*: HANCOCK, P. L. (ed.) *Continental Deformation*. Pergamon, Tarrytown, NY, 289–304.

CSONTOS, L. 1995. Tertiary tectonic evolution of the Intra-Carpathian area: a review. *Acta Vulcanologica*, **7**, 1–13.

CSONTOS, L. & BERGERAT, F. 1992. Reevaluation of the Neogene brittle tectonics of the Mecsek–Villany area (SW Hungary). *Annales Universitatis Scientiarum Budapestinensis de Rolando Eotvos Nominatae, Sectio Geologica*, **29**, 3–12.

CSONTOS, L. & NAGYMAROSY, A. 1998. The Mid–Hungarian line, a zone of repeated tectonic inversions. *Tectonophysics*, **297**, 51–71.

CSONTOS, L., TARI, G., BERGERAT, F. & FODOR, L. 1991. Evolution of the stress fields in the Carpatho-Pannonian area during the Neogene. *Tectonophysics*, **199**, 73–91.

CSONTOS, L., NAGYMAROSY, A., HORVÁTH, F. & KOVÁČ, M. 1992. Tertiary evolution of the intracarpathian area: a model. *Tectonophysics*, **208**, 221–241.

DAVIS, D., SUPPE, J. & DAHLEN, F. A. 1983. Mechanics of fold and thrust belts and accretionary wedges. *Journal of Geophysical Research*, **88**, 1153–1172.

DECKER, K. & JARNIK, M. 1992. Structural analysis of the Late Cretaceous Gosau Group of Rigaus, Fahrenberg and Nussensee (Northern Calcareous Alps, Salzburg, Upper Austria), Tertiary deformation during lateral extrusion illustrated. *Mitteilungen der Gesellschaft der Geologie- und Bergbaustudenten in Oesterreich*, **38**, 93–106.

DECKER, K., MESCHEDE, M. & RING, U. 1993. Fault slip analysis along the northern margin of the Eastern Alps (Molasse, Helvetic nappes, North and South Penninic flysch, and the Northern Calcareous Alps). *Tectonophysics*, **223**, 291–312.

DECKER, K., PERESSON, H. & FAUPL, P. 1994. Die miozane Tektonik der ostlichen Kalkalpen, Kinematik, Palaospannungen und Deformationsaufteilung wahrend der 'lateralen Extrusion' der Zentralalpen. *Jahrbuch der Geologischen Bundensanstalt*, **137**, 5–18.

DECKER, K. NESCIERUK, P., REITER, F., RUBINKIEWICZ, J., RYLKO, W. & TOKARSKI, A. 1997. Heteroaxial shortening, strike-slip faulting and displacement transfer in the Polish Carpathians. *Przeglad Geologiczny*, **45**, 1070–1071.

DEWEY, J. F. 1988. Extensional collapse of orogens. *Tectonics*, **7**, 1123–1139.

DUNKL, I. 1992. Final episodes of the cooling history of eastern termination of the Alps. *In*: NEUBAUER, F. (ed.) *The Eastern Central Alps of Austria. ALCAPA 1992 Meeting Field Trip Guidebook*. IGP/KFU, Graz, 137–139.

DUNKL, I. & DEMÉNY, A. 1997. Exhumation of the Rechnitz Window at the border of the Eastern Alps and Pannonian basin during Neogene extension. *Tectonophysics*, **272**, 197–211.

DŻUŁYŃSKI, S. & KOTLARCZYK, J. 1965. Tectoglyphs on slickensided surface. *Bulletin of the Polish Academy of Sciences, Earth Sciences*, **2**, 149–154.

ELLIOTT, D. 1976. The motion of thrust sheets. *Journal of Geophysical Research*, **81**, 949–963.

ELLIS, M. & WATKINSON, A. J. 1987. Orogen-parallel extension and oblique tectonics: the relation between stretching lineations and relative plate motions. *Geology*, **15**, 1022–1026.

ENGLAND, P. C. 1983. Some numerical investigations of large-scale continental deformation. *In*: HSU, K. J. (ed.) *Mountain Building Processes*. Academic Press, London, 129–139.

ENGLAND, P. C. & HOUSEMAN, G. A. 1988. The mechanics of the Tibetan Plateau. *Philosophical Transactions of the Royal Society of London*, Series A, **326**, 301–320.

FODOR, L. 1995. From transpression to transtension: Oligocene–Miocene structural evolution of the Vienna basin and the East Alpine–Western Carpathians junction. *Tectonophysics*, **242**, 151–182.

FODOR, L., MARKO, F. & NEMČOK, M. 1990. Evolution microtectonique et paleochamps de contraintes du Bassin de Vienne. *Geodinamica Acta*, **4**, 147–158.

FODOR, L., CSONTOS, L., BADA, G. & BENKOVICS, L. 1999. Tertiary tectonic evolution of the Pannonian basin system and neighbouring orogens, a new synthesis of paleostress data. *In*: DURAND, B. JOLIVET, L. HORVÁTH, F. & SERANNE, M. (eds) *The Mediterranean Basins, Tertiary Extension within the Alpine Orogen*. Geological Society, London, Special Publications, **156**, 295–334.

FODOR, L., FRANCŮ, J., KREJČÍ, O. & STRÁNÍK, Z. 1995. Paleogeographic and tectonic evolution of the Carpathian flysch belt of the southern Moravia (Czech Republic). *In*: *Proceedings of the XV Carpatho-Balkanian Geologic Congress*. Special Publication of the Geological Society of Greece, **40/1**, 31–33.

FODOR, L., MAGYARI, A., FOGARASI, A. & PALOTÁS, K. 1994. Tertiary tectonics and Late Paleogene sedimentation in the Buda Hills, Hungary. A new interpretation of the Buda line. *Földtani Kozlony*, **124**, 129–305.

FODOR, L., MAGYARI, A., KÁZMER, M. & FOGARASI, A. 1992. Gravity flow dominated sedimentation on the Buda paleoslope (Hungary). Record of the Late Eocene continental escape of the Bakony unit. *Geologische Rundschau*, **81**, 695–716.

GIRBACEA, R. 1997. *The Pliocene to recent tectonic evolution of the Eastern Carpathians (Romania)*. PhD thesis, University of Tübingen.

GRABOWSKI, J. & NEMČOK, M. 1999. Summary of paleomagnetic data from the central West Carpathians of Poland and Slovakia: evidence for the Late Cretaceous–Early Tertiary transpression. *Physics and Chemistry of the Earth*, **24**, 681–685.

GRAY, M. B. & Stamatakos, J. 1997. New model for evolution of fold and thrust belt curvature based on integrated structural and paleomagnetic results from the Pennsylvania salient. *Geology*, **25**, 1067–1070.

GYORFI, I., CSONTOS, L. & NAGYMAROSY, A. 1999. Early Tertiary structural evolution of the border zone between the Pannonian and Transylvanian basins. *In*: DURAND, B., JOLIVET, L., HORVÁTH, F. & SERANNE, M. (eds) *The Mediterranean Basins, Tertiary Extension within the Alpine Orogen*. Geological Society, London, Special Publications, **156**, 251–267.

HANCOCK, P. L. 1985. Brittle microtectonics: principles and practice. *Journal of Structural Geology*, **7**(3–4), 437–457.

HARDCASTLE, K. C. & HILLS, L. S. 1991. BRUTE3 and SELECT: Quickbasic 4 programs for determination of stress tensor configurations and separation of heterogeneous populations of fault-slip data. *Computers and Geosciences*, **17**, 23–43.

HIPPOLYTE, J. C. & SANDULESCU, M. 1996. Paleostress characterization of the 'Wallachian Phase' in its type area (southeastern Carpathians, Romania). *Tectonophysics*, **263**, 235–248.

HORVÁTH, F. & TARI, G. 1999. IBS Pannonian Basin project, a review of the main results and their bearings on hydrocarbon exploration. *In*: DURAND, B., JOLIVET, L., HORVÁTH, F. & SERANNE, M. (eds) *The Mediterranean Basins, Tertiary Extension within the Alpine Orogen*. Geological Society, London, Special Publications, **156**, 195–213.

HUCHON, P., BARRIER, E., BREMAECKER, J.-C. & ANGELIER, J. 1986. Collision and stress trajectories in Taiwan: a finite-element model. *Tectonophysics*, **125**, 179–191.

HUISMANS, R. S., BERTOTTI, G., CIULAVU, D., SANDERS, C. A. E., CLOETINGH, S. & DINU, C. 1997. Structural evolution of the Transylvanian Basin (Romania), a sedimentary basin in the bend zone of the Carpathians. *Tectonophysics*, **272**, 249–268.

KNIPE, R. J. 1993. The influence of fault zone processes and diagenesis on fluid flow. In: Horbury A.D. & Robinson, A. (eds) *Diagenesis and Basin Development*. American Association of Petroleum Geologists Studies in Geology, **36**, 135–151.

KNIPE, R. J., AGAR, S. M. & PRIOR, D. J. 1991. The microstructural evolution of fluid flow paths in semi-lithified sediments from subduction complex. *Philosophical Transactions of the Royal Society of London*, **335**, 261–273.

KOONS, P. O. 1990. The two-sided orogen: collision and erosion from the sand box to the Southern Alps, New Zealand. *Geology*, **18**, 679–682.

KORÁB, T., KRS, M., KRSOVÁ, M. & PAGÁČ, P. 1981. Palaeomagnetic investigations of Albian(?)–Paleocene to Lower Oligocene sediments from the Dukla unit, East Slovakian Flysch, Czechoslovakia. *Západné Karpaty, Séria Geológia*, **7**, 127–149.

KOVÁČ, P. & HÓK, J. 1993. The Central Slovak Fault System—Field evidence of a strike-slip. *Geologica Carpathica*, **44**, 155–159.

KOVÁČ, M., BARÁTH, I., HOLICKÝ, I., MARKO, F. & TÚNYI, I. 1989*a*. Basin opening in the lower Miocene strike-slip zone in the SW part of the Western Carpathians. *Geologica Carpathica*, **40**, 37–62.

KOVÁČ, M., CÍCHA, I., KRYSTEK, I., SLĄCZKA, A., STRÁNÍK, Z., OSZCZYPKO, N. & VASS, D. 1989*b*. *Palinspastic maps of the Western Carpathian Neogene, scale 1:1 000 000*. Geological Survey, Prague.

KOVÁČ, M., MARKO, F. & NEMČOK, M. 1990. Neogene history of intramontane basins in the western part of the Carpathians. *Rivista Italiana di Paleontologia e Stratigrafia*, **96**, 381–404.

KOVÁČ, M., MARKO, F. & NEMČOK, M. 1993. Neogene structural evolution and basin opening in the Western Carpathians. *Geophysical Transactions*, **37**, 297–309.

KOVÁČ, M., KOVÁČ, P., MARKO, F., KAROLI, S. & JANOČKO, J. 1995. The East Slovakian Basin—a complex back-arc basin. *Tectonophysics*, **252**, 453–466.

KRS, M., MUŠKA, P. & PAGÁČ, P. 1982. Review of paleomagnetic investigations in the West Carpathians of Czechoslovakia. *Geologické Práce, Správy*, **78**, 39–58.

KRS, M., KRSOVÁ, M., CHVOJKA, R. & POTFAJ, M. 1991. Palaeo-magnetic investigations of the flysch belt in the Orava region, Magura unit, Czechoslovak Western Carpathians. *Geologické Práce, Správy*, **92**, 125–151.

KSIĄŻKIEWICZ, M. 1960. Description of the paleogeography of the Polish Flysch Carpathians. *Prace Institutu Geologicznego*, **33**, 209–231 (in Polish).

KURZ, W., NEUBAUER, F., GENSER, H. & HORNER, H. 1993. Sequence of Tertiary brittle deformations in the eastern Tauern Window (Eastern Alps). *Mitteilungen der Österreichischen Geologischen Gesselschaft*, **86**, 153–164.

LINZER, H. G. 1996. Kinematics of retreating subduction along the Carpathian arc, Romania. *Geology*, **24**, 167–170.

LINZER, H. G., RATSCHBACHER, L. & FRISCH, W. 1995. Transpressional collision structures in the upper crust, the fold–thrust belt of the Northern Calcareous Alps. *Tectonophysics*, **242**, 41–61.

LINZER, H. G., MOSER, F., Nemes, F., Ratschbacher, L. & Sperner, B. 1997. Build-up and dismembering of a classical fold–thrust belt, from non-cylindrical stacking to lateral extrusion in the eastern Alps. *Tectonophysics*, **272**, 97–124.

LINZER, H. G., FRISCH, W., ZWEIGEL, P., GIRBACEA, R., HANN, H. P. & Moser, F. 1998. Kinematic evolution of the Romanian Carpathians. *Tectonophysics*, **297**, 133–156.

MACEDO, J. & MARSHAK, S. 1999. Controls on the geometry of fold–thrust belt salients. *Geological Society of America Bulletin*, **111**, 1808–1822.

MALAVIEILLE, J. 1984. Experimental model for imbricated thrusts: comparison with thrust-belts. *Bulletin de la Société Géologique de France*, **26**, 129–138.

MARKO, F., KOVÁČ, M., FODOR, L. & ŠUTOVSKÁ, K. 1990. Deformations and kinematics of a Miocene shear zone in the northern part of the Little Carpathians (Buková furrow, Hrabník Formation). *Mineralia Slovaca*, **22**, 399–410 (in Slovak).

MARKO, F., FODOR, L. & KOVÁČ, M. 1991. Miocene strike-slip faulting and block rotation in Brezovské Karpaty Mts. *Mineralia Slovaca*, **23**, 201–213.

MARQUES, F. O. & COBBOLD, P. R. 2002. Topography as a major factor in the development of arcuate thrust belts: insights from sandbox experiments. *Tectonophysics*, **348**, 247–268.

MARSHAK, S., WILKERSON, M. S. & HSUI, A. T. 1992. Generation of curved fold–thrust belts: insight from simple physical and analytical models. *In*: MCCLAY, K. R. (ed.) *Thrust Tectonics*. Chapman & Hall, London, 83–92.

MÁRTON, E. 1997. Tertiary paleomagnetism in the northern part of the PANCARDI region. *Przegląd Geologiczny*, **45**, 1090.

MÁRTON, E. & FODOR, L. 1995. Combination of paleomagnetic and stress data—a case study from North Hungary. *Tectonophysics*, **242**, 99–114.

MÁRTON, E. & MÁRTON, P. 1996. Large scale rotations in North Hungary during Neogene as indicated by paleomagnetic data. *In*: MORRIS, A. & TARLING, D. H. (eds) *Palaeomagnetism and Tectonics of the Mediterranean Region*. Geological Society, London, Special Publications, **105**, 155–173.

MÁRTON, E., VASS, D. & TUNYI, I., 1996. Rotation of the south Slovak Paleogene amd Lower Miocene rocks indicated by paleomagnetic data. *Geologica Carpathica*, **47**, 31–41.

MÁRTON, E., NEMČOK, M. & TOKARSKI, A. K. 1997. *Preliminary paleomagnetic results from Carpathians in Poland (Carpathian Foredeep, Outer Carpathians and Podhale Flysch)*. Instytut Nauk Geologicznych, PAN, Osrodek Badawczy w Krakowie oraz Galicia T. Group, 'Pierwsze Karpackie Warsztsty Paleomagnetyczne', Kraków.

MÁRTON, E., MASTELLA, L. & TOKARSKI, A. K. 1999. Large counterclockwise rotation of the Inner West Carpathian Paleogene flysch—evidence from paleomagnetic investigations of the Podhale Flysch (Poland). *Physics and Chemistry of the Earth*, **24**, 645–649.

MÁRTON, E., TOKARSKI, A. K. & NEMČOK, M. 2000. Paleomagnetic constraints for the accretion of the tectonic units at the stable European margin, north of the western Carpathians. *Geophysical Research Abstracts*, **2**, 2000.

MATENCO, L., BERTOTTI, G., DINU, C. & CLOETINGH, S. 1997. Tertiary tectonic evolution of the external South Carpathians and the adjacent Moesian platform (Romania). *Tectonics*, **16**, 896–911.

MEYER, B., AVOUAC, J. P., TAPPONNIER, P. & MEGHRAOUI, M. 1990. Topographic measurements of the southwestern segment of the El Asnam fault zone and mechanical interpretation of the relationship between reverse and normal faults. *Bulletin de la Société Géologique de France, Huitième Série*, **6**, 447–456 (in French).

MORLEY, C. K. 1996. Models for relative motion of crustal blocks within Carpathian region, based on restorations of the outer Carpathian thrust front. *Tectonics*, **15**, 885–904.

MOSER, F. & FRISCH, W. 1996. Tertiary deformation in the Southern Carpathians—structural analysis of a brittle deformation. *In*: *TSK 6 Symposium Erweitere Kurzfassungen*. Facultas-Universitatsverlag, Vienna, 280–282.

NEMČOK, M. 1991. Structural deformation analyses in both Flysch and Pieniny Klippen Units along the Vlára River Valley. *Geologické Práce, Správy*, **93**, 55–61 (in Slovak).

NEMČOK, M. 1993. Transition from convergence to escape: field evidence from the West Carpathians. *Tectonophysics*, **217**, 117–142.

NEMČOK, M. & LEXA, J. 1990. Evolution of the basin and range structure around the Ziar mountain range. *Geologica Carpathica*, **41**, 229–258.

NEMČOK, M. & LISLE, R. J. 1995. A stress inversion procedure for polyphase fault/slip data sets. *Journal of Structural Geology*, **17**, 1445–1453.

NEMČOK, J. & NEMČOK, M. 1990. Significance of movement vectors in the Vihorlat–Cirocha fault system. *In*: SÝKORA, M., JABLONSKÝ, J. & SAMUEL, O. (eds) *Sedimentologické problémy Západných Karpát*. Gúdš, Bratislava, 89–106 (in Slovak).

NEMČOK, M. & NEMČOK, J. 1994. Late Cretaceous deformation of the Pieniny Klippen Belt, West Carpathians. *Tectonophysics*, **239**, 81–109.

NEMČOK, M., MARKO, F., KOVÁČ, M. & FODOR, L. 1989. Neogene tectonics and paleostress changes in the Czechoslovakian part of the Vienna Basin. *Jahrbuch der Geologischen Bundesanstalt*, **132**(2), 443–458.

NEMČOK, M., HÓK, J., KOVÁČ, P., *et al.* 1998*a*. Tertiary extension development and extension/compression interplay in the West Carpathian mountain belt. Tectonophysics, **290**, 137–167.

NEMČOK, M., HOUGHTON, J. J. & COWARD, M. P. 1998*b*. Strain partitioning along the western margin of the Carpathians. *Tectonophysics*, **292**, 119–143.

NEMČOK, M., POSPÍŠIL, L., LEXA, J. & DONELICK, R. A. 1998*c*. Tertiary subduction and slab break-off model of the Carpathian–Pannonian region. *Tectonophysics*, **295**, 307–340.

NEMČOK, M., KOVÁČ, D. & LISLE, R. J. 1999*a*. Stress inversion procedure for polyphase calcite twin and fault/slip data sets. *Journal of Structural Geology*, **21**, 597–611.

NEMČOK, M., COWARD, M. P., SERCOMBE, W. J. & KLECKER, R. A. 1999*b*. Structure of the West Carpathian accretionary wedge: insights from cross section construction and sandbox validation. *Physics and Chemistry of the Earth*, **24**, 659–665.

NEMČOK, M., KONEČNÝ, P. & Lexa, O. 2000*a*. Calculations of tectonic, magmatic and residual stress in the Štiavnica Stratovolcano, Western Carpathians, implications for mineral precipitation paths. *Geologica Carpathica*, **51**, 19–36.

NEMČOK, M., DILOV, T., MÁRTON, E., *et al.* 2000*b*. Tertiary development of the Polish part of the Carpathian accretionary wedge: insights from deformed balanced cross sections, paleostress and paleomagnetic analyses. *Vijesti Hrvatskogo Geoloskog Drustva, PANCARDI 2000 Special Issue*, **37**(3), 90.

NEMČOK, M., NEMČOK, J., WOJTASZEK, M., *et al.* 2000*c*. Results of 2D balancing along 20° and 21° longitude and pseudo-3D in the Smilno tectonic window: implications for shortening mechanisms of the West Carpathian accretionary wedge. *Geologica Carpathica*, **51**, 281–300.

NEMČOK, M., NEMČOK, J., WOJTASZEK, M., *et al.* 2001. Reconstruction of Cretaceous rifts incorporated in the Outer West Carpathian wedge by balancing. *Marine and Petroleum Geology*, **18**, 39–64.

NEMES, F. 1996. *Kinematics of the Periadriatic fault in the Eastern Alps—Evidences from structural analysis, fission track dating and basin modeling*. PhD thesis, University of Salzburg.

NEMES, F., PAVLIK, W. & MOSER, M. 1995. Geologie und Tektonik im Salzachtal (Steiermark). Kinematik und Palaospanungen entlang des Enstal–Mariazell Blattverschiebungsystems in den Nordlichen Kalkalpen. *Jahrbuch der Geologischen Bundensanstalt*, **138**, 349–367.

OSZCZYPKO, N. & OSZCZYPKO-CLOWES, M. A. 2002. Newly discovered Early Miocene deposits in the Nowy Sącz area (Magura Nappe, Polish Outer Carpathians). *Geological Quarterly*, **46**, 117–133.

OSZCZYPKO, N. & SLĄCZKA, A. 1985. An attempt to palinspastic reconstruction of Neogene basins in the Carpathian foredeep. *Annales Societatis Geologorum Poloniae*, **55**, 55–75.

OSZCZYPKO, N. & SLĄCZKA, A. 1989. The evolution of the Miocene basin in the Polish Outer Carpathians and their foreland. *Geologica Carpathica*, **40**, 23–36.

PANAIOTU, C., PANAIOTU, C. E., PÉCSKAY, Z. & ROSU, E. 1998. Fast clockwise rotation in the eastern PANCARDI region during middle Miocene, (Abstract). *Annales Geophysicae*, **16**, 113.

PÉCSKAY, Z., LEXA, J., SZAKÁCS, A., *et al.* 1995. Space and time distribution of Neogene–Quaternary volcanism in the Carpatho-Pannonian region. *Acta Vulcanologica*, **7**, 15–28.

PERESSON, H. & DECKER, K. 1997*a*. The Tertiary dynamics of the northern Eastern Alps (Austria), changing paleostresses in a collisional plate boundary. *Tectonophysics*, **272**, 125–157.

PERESSON, H. & DECKER, K. 1997*b*. Far-field effects of Late Miocene subduction in the Eastern Carpathians, E–W compression and inversion of structures in the Alpine–Carpathian–Pannonian region. *Tectonics*, **16**, 38–56.

PETIT, J. P. 1987. Criteria for the sense of movement on fault surfaces in brittle rocks. *Journal of Structural Geology*, **9**, 597–608.

PLATT, J. P. 1986. Dynamics of orogenic wedges and the uplift of high-pressure metamorphic rocks. *Geological Society of America Bulletin*, **97**, 1037–1053.

PLATT, J., ALLERTON, S., KIRKER, A. & PLATZMAN, E. 1995. Origin of the western Subbetic arc (southern Spain): paleomagnetic and structural evidence. *Journal of Structural Geology*, **17**, 765–775.

POPRAWA, D. & NEMČOK, J. (eds) 1989. *Geological Atlas of the Western Outer Carpathians and their Foreland*. PIG, Warsaw; GÚDŠ, Bratislava; ÚÚG, Prague.

RAMSAY, J. G. 1980. Shear zone geometry: a review. *Journal of Structural Geology*, **2**, 83–99.

RAMSAY, J. G. & HUBER, M. I. 1983. *The Techniques of Modern Structural Geology, Volume 1: Strain Analysis*. Academic Press, London.

RATSCHBACHER, L., MERLE, O., DAVY, P. & COBBOLD, P. 1991. Lateral extrusion in the Eastern Alps, Part 1, Boundary conditions and experiments scaled for gravity. *Tectonics*, **10**, 245–256.

RATSCHBACHER, L., LINZER, H. G., MOSER, F., STRUSIEWICZ, R. O., BEDELEAN, H., HAR, N. & MOGOS, P. A. 1993*a*. Cretaceous to Miocene thrusting and wrenching along the central south Carpathians due to corner effect during collision and orocline formation. *Tectonics*, **12**, 855–873.

RATSCHBACHER, L., FRISCH, W., LINZER, H. G., *et al.* 1993*b*. The Pieniny Klippen Belt in the Western Carpathians of northeastern Slovakia, structural evidence for transpression. *Tectonophysics*, **226**, 471–483.

ROCA, E., BESSEREAU, G., JAWOR, E., KOTARBA, M. & ROURE, F. 1995. Pre-Neogene evolution of the Western Carpathians: constraints from the Bochnia–Tatra Mountains section (Polish Western Carpathians). *Tectonics*, **14**, 855–873.

ROURE, F., ROCA, E. & SASSI, W. 1993. The Neogene evolution of the outer Carpathian flysch units (Poland, Ukraine and Romania): kinematics of a foreland/fold-and-thrust belt system. *Sedimentary Geology*, **86**, 177–201.

ROURE, F., KUŚMIEREK, J., BESSEREAU, G., ROCA, E. & STRZETELSKI, W. 1994. Initial thickness variations and basement–cover relationship in the Western Outer Carpathians (SE Poland). *In*: ROURE, F., ELLOUZ, N., SHEIN, V. S. & SKVORTSOV, I. (eds) *Geodynamic Evolution of Sedimentary Basins, International Symposium, Moscow*. Technip, Paris, 255–279.

RYLKO, W. & ADAM, T. 2005. Basement structure below the West Carpathian–East Carpathian orogen junction; eastern Poland, north-eastern Slovakia and western Ukraine. *Geologica Carpathica*, **56**, 29–40.

SHACKLETON, R. M. 1986. Precambrian collision tectonics in Africa. *In*: COWARD, M. P. & RIES, A. C. (eds) *Collision Tectonics*. Geological Society, London, Special Publications, **19**, 329–349.

SHACKLETON, R. M. & RIES, A. C. 1984. The relation between regionally consistent stretching lineations and plate motions. *Journal of Structural Geology*, **6**, 111–120.

SIBSON, R. H. 1989. Earthquake faulting as a structural process. *Journal of Structural Geology*, **11**, 1–14.

SIBSON, R. H. 1994. Crustal stress, faulting and fluid flow. *In*: PARNELL, J. (ed.) *Geofluids; Origin, Migration and Evolution of Fluids in Sedimentary Basins*. Geological Society, London, Special Publications, **78**, 69–84.

SILVER, E. A. & REED, D. L. 1988. Back thrusting in accretionary wedges. *Journal of Geophysical Research*, **93**, 3116–3126.

SPENCER, S. 1992. A kinematic analysis incorporating incremental strain data for the frontal Pennine zones of the western French Alps. *Tectonophysics*, **206**, 285–305.

SPERNER, B. 1996. *Computer programs for the kinematic analysis of brittle deformation structures and the Tertiary tectonic evolution of the Western Carpathians (Slovakia)*. PhD thesis, University of Tuebingen.

SPERNER, B., RATSCHBACHER, L. & OTT, R. 1993. Fault-striae analysis: a Turbo Pascal program package for graphical presentation and reduced stress tensor calculation. *Computers and Geosciences*, **19**, 1361–1388.

SPERNER, B., RATSCHBACHER, L. & NEMČOK, M. 2002. Interplay between subduction rollback and lateral extrusion, tectonics of the Western Carpathians. *Tectonics*, **21**, 1051–1075.

STEFANESCU, M. & MELINTE, M. 1996. Cretaceous–Early Miocene subsidence and the related source and reservoir rocks in the Moldavids. *In*: WESSELY, G. & LIEBL, W. (eds) *Oil and Gas in Alpidic Thrustbelts and Basins of Central and Eastern Europe*. EAGE Special Publications, **5**, 197–200.

STOCKMAL, G. S. 1983. Modeling of large-scale accretionary wedge deformation. *Journal of Geophysical Research*, **88**, 8271–8287.

STORTI, F., SALVINI, F. & MCCLAY, K. R. 2000. Synchronous and velocity-partitioned thrusting and thrust polarity reversal in experimentally produced, doubly-vergent thrust wedges: implications for natural orogens. *Tectonics*, **19**, 378–396.

TARI, G. 1991. Multiple Miocene block rotation in the Bakony Mountains, Transdanubian Central Range, Hungary. *Tectonophysics*, **199**, 93–108.

TARI, G., DOVÉNYI, P., DUNKL, I., *et al.* 1999. Lithospheric structure of the Pannonian basin derived from seismic, gravity and geothermal data. *In*: DURAND, B., JOLIVET, L., HORVÁTH, F. & SERANNE, M. (eds) *The Mediterranean Basins, Tertiary Extension within the Alpine Orogen*. Geological Society, London, Special Publications, **156**, 215–250.

TRELOAR, P. J. & COWARD, M. P. 1991. Indian Plate motion and shape: constraints on the geometry of the Himalayan Orogen. *Tectonophysics*, **191**, 189–198.

TÚNYI, I. & GROSS, P. 1995. Paleomagnetic investigation of the Podtatranská group (Inner Carpathian Paleogene). Physical rock properties and their use in geophysics, geology and ecology. *VI Sborník referátů*, Czech Academy of Sciences, Ostrava, 122–127 (in Slovak).

TÚNYI, I. & MÁRTON, E. 1996. Indications for large Tertiary rotation in the Carpathian–Northern Pannonian region outside the North Hungarian Paleogene Basin. *Geologica Carpathica*, **47**, 43–49.

TURNER, F. J. 1953. Nature and dynamic interpretation of deformation lamellae in calcite of three marbles. *American Journal of Science*, **251**, 276–298.

VASS, D., HÓK, J., KOVÁČ, P. & ELEČKO, M. 1993. The Paleogene and Neogene tectonic events of the Southern Slovakia depressions in the light of the stress-field analyses. *Mineralia Slovaca*, **25**, 79–92 (in Slovak).

WILLETT, S. D., BEAUMONT, C. & FULLSACK, P. 1993. Mechanical model for the tectonics of doubly vergent compressional orogens. *Geology*, **21**, 371–374.

WORLD STRESS MAP PROJECT 1997. World Wide Web address: http://www-wsm.physik.uni-karlsruhe.de.

ZUCHIEWICZ, W., TOKARSKI, A. K., JAROSIŃSKI, M. & MÁRTON, E. 2000. Neotectonic evolution of the Polish Outer Carpathians in the light of structural, geomorphic, break-out and palaeomagnetic data. *Vijesti Hrvatskogo Geoloskog Drustva, PANCARDI 2000 Special Issue*, **37**(3), 132.

ZWEIGEL, P. 1997. *The Tertiary tectonic evolution of the Eastern Carpathians (Romania), orogenic arc formation in response to microplate movements*. PhD thesis, University of Tübingen.

Strike-slip deformation within the Colombian Andes

JORGE ACOSTA[1,2], FRANCISCO VELANDIA[3], JAIRO OSORIO[3], LIDIA LONERGAN[2] & HÉCTOR MORA[3]

[1]*EXGEO-CGG, Maracaibo, Venezuela (e-mail: jeaco1@hotmail.com)*

[2]*Department of Earth Science and Engineering, Imperial College, Royal School of Mines, Prince Consort Road, London SW7 2BP, UK*

[3]*Ingeominas, Diagonal 53# 34–53, Bogotá, Colombia*

Abstract: The Colombian Andes are characterized by a dominant NE structural trend, which is offset by ENE-trending right-lateral and NW-trending left-lateral structures. NE-trending faults are either dip-slip or oblique thrusts, generated as a result of a transpressive regime active since at least Palaeogene times. NW-trending faults are considered to be reactivated pre-Cretaceous extensional structures. Right-lateral shear on ENE-trending faults has resulted from oblique convergence between the Nazca Plate and the Northern Andes. Major changes in the geometry of the oblique-plate convergence between the Nazca and South American plates have generated the northward 'escape' of the Northern Andes and stress–strain partitioning within the mountain belt. These strike-slip structures have exerted important controls on sedimentation, source-rock distribution, fluid flow and ore mineralization during Cenozoic times. The interpretation of the Northern Andes as a mountain belt affected by strike-slip deformation provides a structural context in which to reassess the exploration plays.

The Colombian Andes have been interpreted as an assemblage of terraines that have been accreted to South America with a dominant NNE structural trend (Etayo-Serna *et al.* 1983; López & Barrero 2003). This interpretation has led to the assumption of plane strain deformation, orthogonal to the strike of the main structures, which, in Colombia, is almost parallel to the continental margin (Fig. 1). For this reason, the Colombian Andes have been described as a classical fold and thrust belt (Mojica & Franco 1990; Schamel 1991; Cooper *et al.* 1995). However, oblique ENE and NW strike-slip deformation has been recognised in the region (Feininger 1970; Boinet *et al.* 1986; Diederix *et al.* 1987; Cuervo 1995; Velandia & Komuro 1998; Montes 2001; Ujueta 2001; Branquet *et al.* 2002; Acosta *et al.* 2004) and the importance of these structures in the evolution of the belt has, for the most part, been neglected. In this paper, a variety of geological, geophysical, geodetic and geodynamic information has been integrated to examine the origin and evolution and of some of these strike-slip fault systems within the Colombian Andes.

Regional setting

The Andean Belt from northern Colombia to Ecuador is divided into three mountain ranges (cordilleras), which merge near 1°N latitude. Each of these cordilleras has a different composition and evolution as a result of different tectonic processes that have affected the region since Mesozoic times. The Central Cordillera originated in response to Triassic subduction and consequent volcanic and igneous activity (Barrero *et al.* 1969; Barrero & Vesga 1976; Bartok *et al.* 1981). Triassic and Jurassic backarc rifting generated a predominantly NE–SW structural trend that influenced the sedimentation in the adjacent Magdalena Valley and Eastern Cordillera. The Western Cordillera is composed of oceanic crust and deformed deep marine sediments, representing an accretionary complex established in the Late Cretaceous (de Freitas *et al.* 1997). The Eastern Cordillera represents the inversion of thick Mesozoic and Tertiary sedimentary basins (see Taboada *et al.* 2000).

Eastward subduction of the Nazca Plate beneath the Northern Andes occurs at *c.* 60 mm a^{-1} (Trenkamp *et al.* 2002) along the western margin of Ecuador and Colombia (Fig. 1). Additionally, north of latitude 8°N, the Caribbean Plate is moving ESE at an average velocity of 20 mm a^{-1} (Trenkamp *et al.* 2002). As a result of the oblique convergence of both the Nazca and the Caribbean Plates with the Northern Andes, the Andean block (Fig. 1) is moving northeastwards relative to the South American Plate (Pennington 1981; Kellogg *et al.* 1985;

From: RIES, A. C., BUTLER, R. W. H. & GRAHAM, R. H. (eds) 2007. *Deformation of the Continental Crust: The Legacy of Mike Coward*. Geological Society, London, Special Publications, **272**, 303–319.

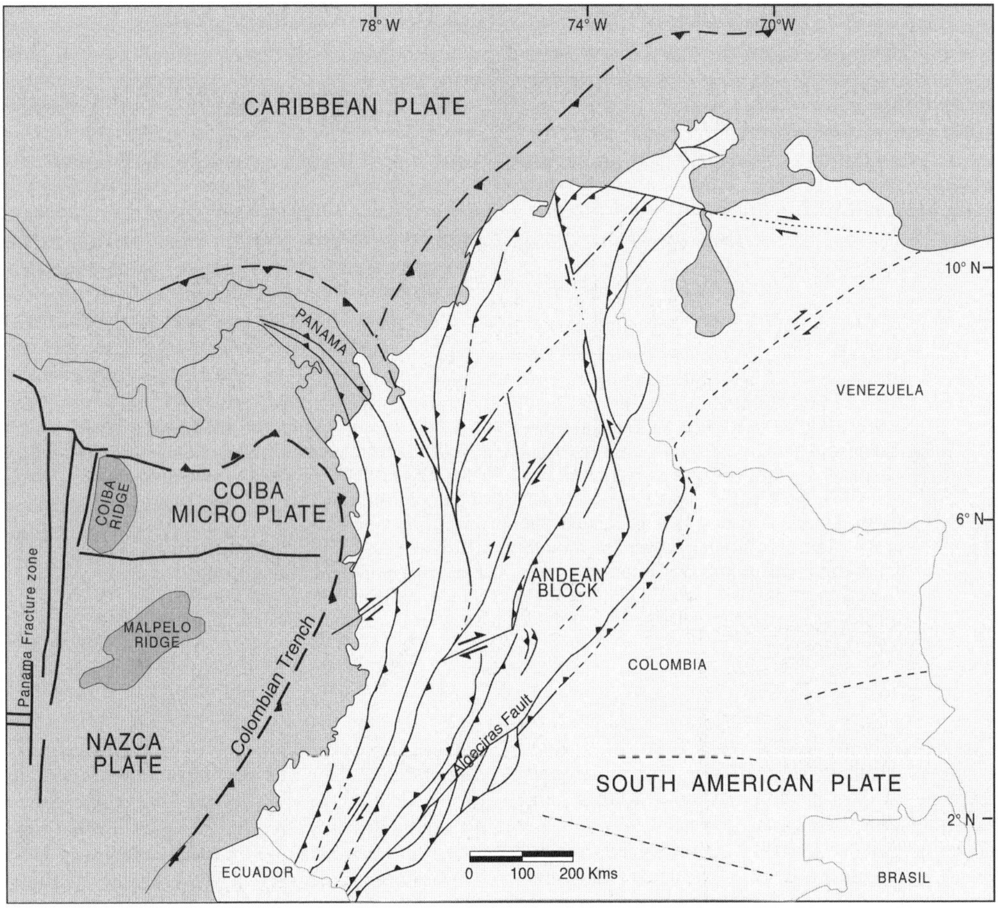

Fig. 1. Tectonic setting of the Colombian Andes.

Freymueller *et al.* 1993; Kellogg & Vega 1995; Mann 1995; Trenkamp *et al.* 2002).

Within the Andean Block, NE- and NW-trending thrust faults are offset by ENE-trending right-lateral and NW trending left-lateral strike-slip faults. Whereas some researchers consider these structures as local accommodation structures around folds and thrusts (Camargo 1995; Cooper *et al.* 1995; Branquet *et al.* 1999*a*,*b*; Corredor 2003), in this paper it is argued that they are regionally significant and represent a transpressive regime affecting the entire Northern Andes.

The Algeciras Fault system

The Algeciras Fault system occurs in the central part of the Eastern Cordillera in SW Colombia and continues southward for more than 800 km into Ecuador and the Gulf of Guayaquil (Velandia *et al.* 2005) (Fig. 1). Features of neotectonic activity have been identified along straight segments of the Algeciras Fault, which are associated with right-lateral slip (Chorowicz *et al.* 1996; Vergara 1996; Velandia & Komuro 1998). These features include synthetic and antithetic Riedel faults, principal displacement zones (PDZ), pull-apart basins (such as lazy-S shaped releasing bends, extensive and rhomboidal-shaped and releasing sidestep basins) and minor folds, located oblique to the main trace of the fault system (Fig. 2). The generation and boundaries of the pull-apart basins are dominated by transverse NW basement faults (e.g. the Sibundoy Basin). Strike-slip indicators mainly concentrate along ENE segments, whereas associated thrust faults occur along NE-trending segments. Changes in the orientation of these

Fig. 2. The Algeciras Fault system (after Velandia *et al.* 2005). Inset images are Landsat TM 5 scenes.

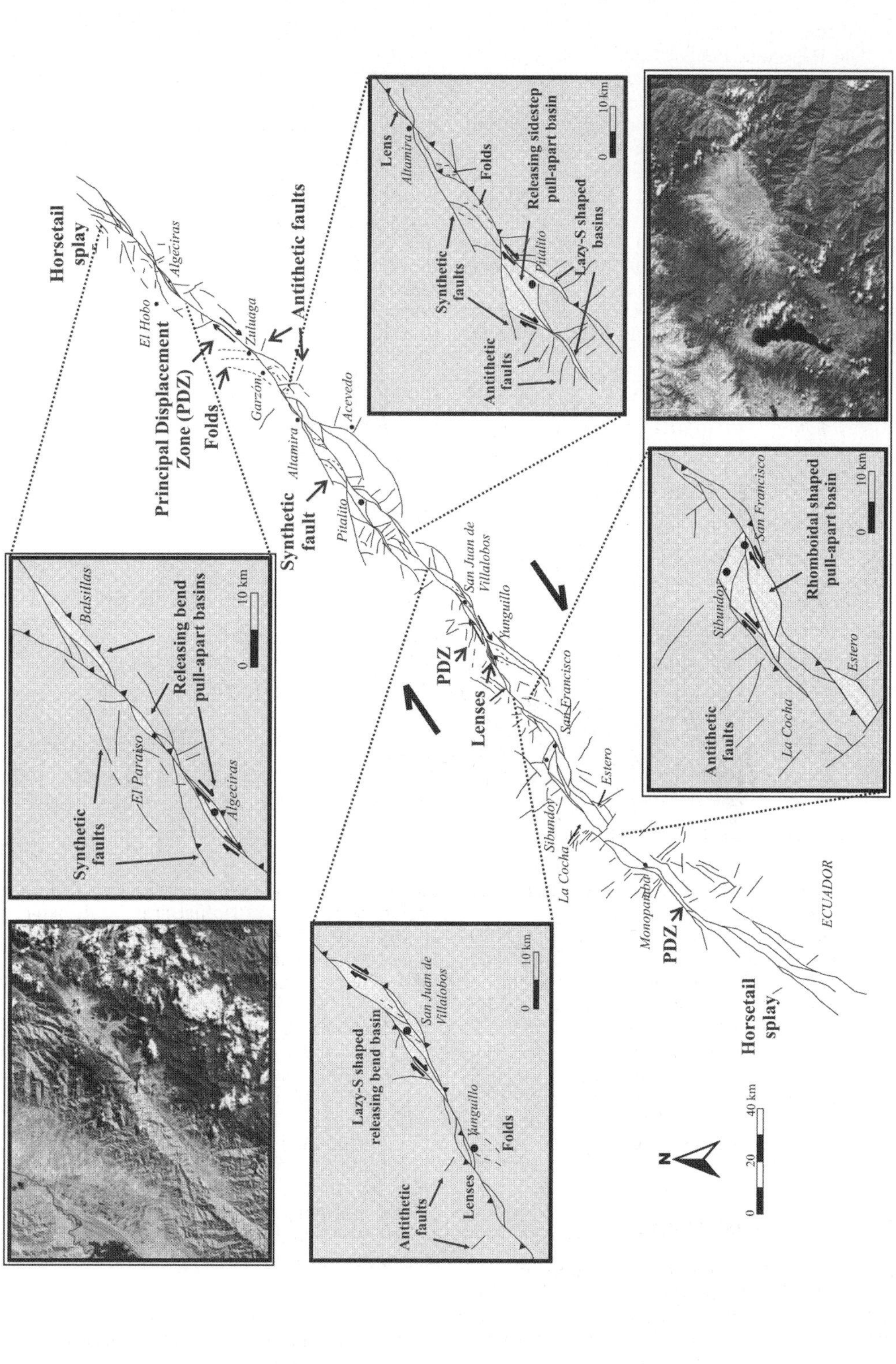
Horsetail splay
Algeciras
El Hobo
Principal Displacement Zone (PDZ)
Folds
Zuluaga
Garzón
Antithetic faults
Acevedo
Altamira
Synthetic fault
Pitalito
San Juan de Villalobos
Yunguillo
PDZ
Lenses
San Francisco
Estero
Sibundoy
La Cocha
Monopamba
PDZ
ECUADOR
Horsetail splay
N
0 20 40 km
Balsillas
Releasing bend pull-apart basins
El Paraiso
Synthetic faults
Algeciras
0 10 km
Lens
Altamira
Folds
Releasing sidestep pull-apart basin
Synthetic faults
Pitalito
Lazy-S shaped basins
Antithetic faults
0 10 km
San Francisco
Rhomboidal shaped pull-apart basin
Sibundoy
Estero
Antithetic faults
La Cocha
0 10 km
Lazy-S shaped releasing bend basin
San Juan de Villalobos
Yunguillo
Folds
Antithetic faults
Lenses
0 10 km

segments are also controlled by NW-trending structures.

The Algeciras Fault system is classified as a right-lateral strike-slip complex structure, with an important vertical component in which sedimentary cover and basement rocks are involved. Velandia *et al.* (2005) describe this fault as a zone of simple shear, caused by the oblique convergence between the Nazca Plate and the Northern Andes. It marks the boundary of the neotectonic transpressive regime in the Northern Andes which begins in Ecuador and continues into Colombia and Venezuela.

The Quetame Massif, which lies at the northern end of the Algeciras Fault system, is interpreted as a major transpressional structure, whereas active volcanism along the Colombian–Ecuadorian border at the southern end of the Algeciras Fault System indicates transtension.

Upper Magdalena Valley

The Upper Magdalena Valley is an intermontane basin that lies between the Eastern and Central Cordilleras. It has been divided into the Girardot and Neiva sub-basins, which are separated by the Natagaima Uplift (Beltrán & Gallo 1979; Corrigan 1979). As shown in Figures 3 and 4, the Neiva sub-basin exhibits three structural styles, as follows.

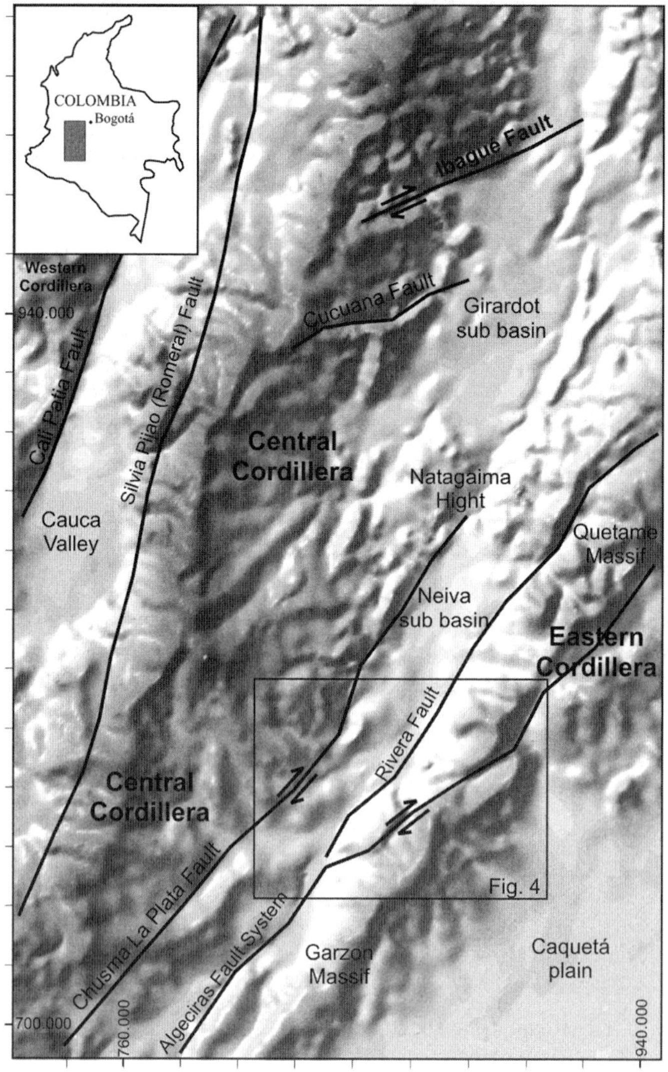

Fig. 3. Digital topographic model (DEM) of the Upper Magdalena Valley with main structural elements.

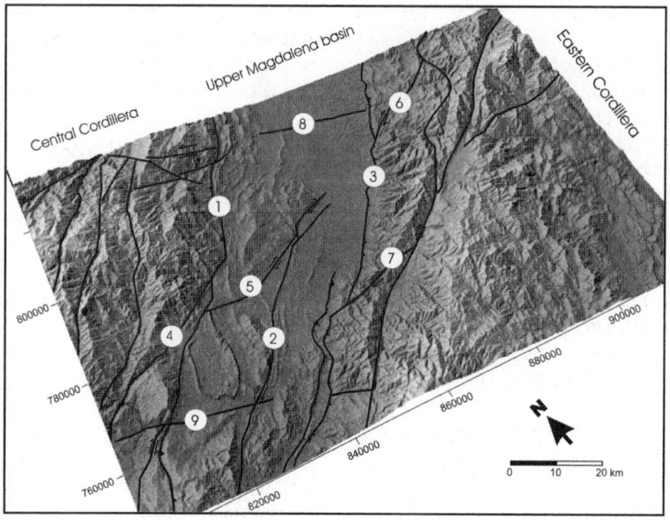

Fig. 4. DEM of Neiva sub-basin with major faults. 1, Chusma Fault; 2, El Agrado-Dina Fault; 3, Rivera Fault; 4, La Plata Fault; 5, Santa Helena Fault; 6, Platanillal Fault; 7, El Hobo Fault; 8, Neiva Fault; 9, Paso de Bobo Fault.

(1) NNE-trending thrusts carry pre-Cretaceous crystalline and Lower Cretaceous rocks over Cenozoic strata (Chusma, El Agrado–Dina and Rivera faults, Fig. 4). According to Butler & Schamel (1987), the Chusma Fault is a pre-existing basement structure that was reactivated during the Late Eocene–Early Oligocene. The El Agrado–Dina Fault is a thrust fault associated with the Chusma Fault, which, along with other minor thrust faults, forms an east-verging imbricate fan system. The west-verging Rivera Fault constitutes the boundary of the Eastern Cordillera with the Magdalena Valley.

(2) ENE-trending, right-lateral strike-slip steep faults form a left-stepping array (e.g. La Plata, Santa Helena, Platanillal and Hobo faults, Fig. 4) that affects pre-Cretaceous basement to Neogene rocks (Fig. 4). Drag folds, observed next to some of these faults, demonstrate the strike-slip nature of the structures (e.g the Santa Helena Fault). Some of these faults are lateral ramps for the north and NE reactivated faults of the Central Cordillera foothills (e.g. Chusma–La Plata system, Butler & Schamel 1987). However, the ENE-trending system continues along the Neiva sub-basin under Quaternary deposits and even affects the Eastern Cordillera (Figs 3 and 4). A large number of active neotectonic features occur along these faults.

(3) NW-trending, left-lateral strike-slip steep faults involve pre-Cretaceous basement to Neogene rocks (Neiva and Paso de Bobo faults, Fig. 4). Some workers (e.g. Renzoni 1994; Velandia 2001) have shown that these faults have been active since at least Early Cretaceous times and controlled Cretaceous and Cenozoic sedimentation along the Upper Magdalena Basin. In addition, Neogene to Quaternary basic volcanic rocks, at the junction of these NW-trending faults and NE-trending structures (Velandia 2001), indicate that the structures are still active.

Central Cordillera and Middle Magdalena Valley

The central part of the Central Cordillera comprises igneous and metamorphic rocks affected by a NE-trending system (Palestina Fault), an ENE system (Ibagué Fault), a NW system (Arma Fault) and an arcuate fault system that bounds the cordillera to the west (Romeral Fault system) (Fig. 5). This last system is a suture zone along which oceanic crust collided obliquely with a continental margin, 65–49 Ma ago (Barrero *et al.* 1969).

The Palestina Fault system is a N30°E-trending right-lateral zone that cuts through the Central Cordillera (Fig. 5) and is assumed to have developed as a result of the oblique collision of the oceanic crust during the Late Cretaceous (Feininger 1970). Strike-slip deformation along this system, (1) generated the San Lucas Serrania, a transpressive duplex located at the northern end, (2) caused an over-step where dragging and right-lateral displacement of basement faults

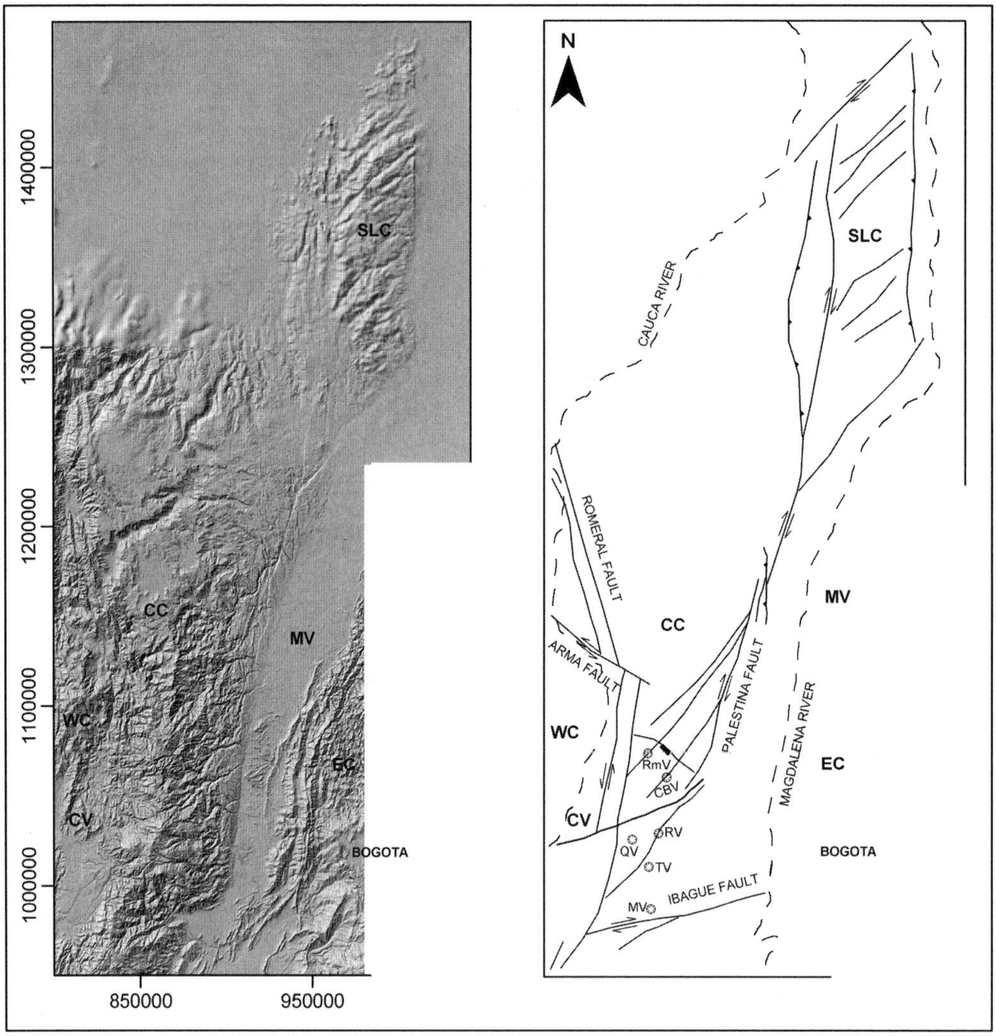

Fig. 5. DEM and map of main faults and volcanos of the Central Cordillera (CC) and Middle Magdalena Valley (MV). SLC, San Lucas Serranía; RmV Romerales Volcano; CBV, Cerro Bravo Volcano; RV, Ruiz Volcano; QV, Quindio Volcano; TV, Tolima Volcano; MV, Machin Volcano; WC, Western Cordillera; CV, Cauca Valley; EC, Eastern Cordillera.

occurred on the central part, and (3) created oblique right-lateral and normal faults that are active and control the Quaternary magmatism at the southern end of the system (Fig 5). In addition, an analysis of the magmatic rocks in this region during the present study showed that it has migrated from north to south since the Eocene. Similarly, reactivation of NW-trending faults during this time has affected the horsetail structure of the Palestina Fault system and therefore migration of magmatism and reactivation of NW-trending faults is closely related. Hence the emplacement of the volcanic bodies in this part of the Central Cordillera contrasts with that observed at the Colombia–Ecuador border.

The Ibagué Fault system right-laterally offsets the Central Cordillera by 25 km (Figs 5 & 6) (Montes *et al.* 2005). This N70°E-trending system is a left-stepping array that can be traced through the Central Cordillera from the Cauca Valley to the Magdalena Valley; it may continue

Fig. 6. Neotectonic map of the Ibagué Fault.

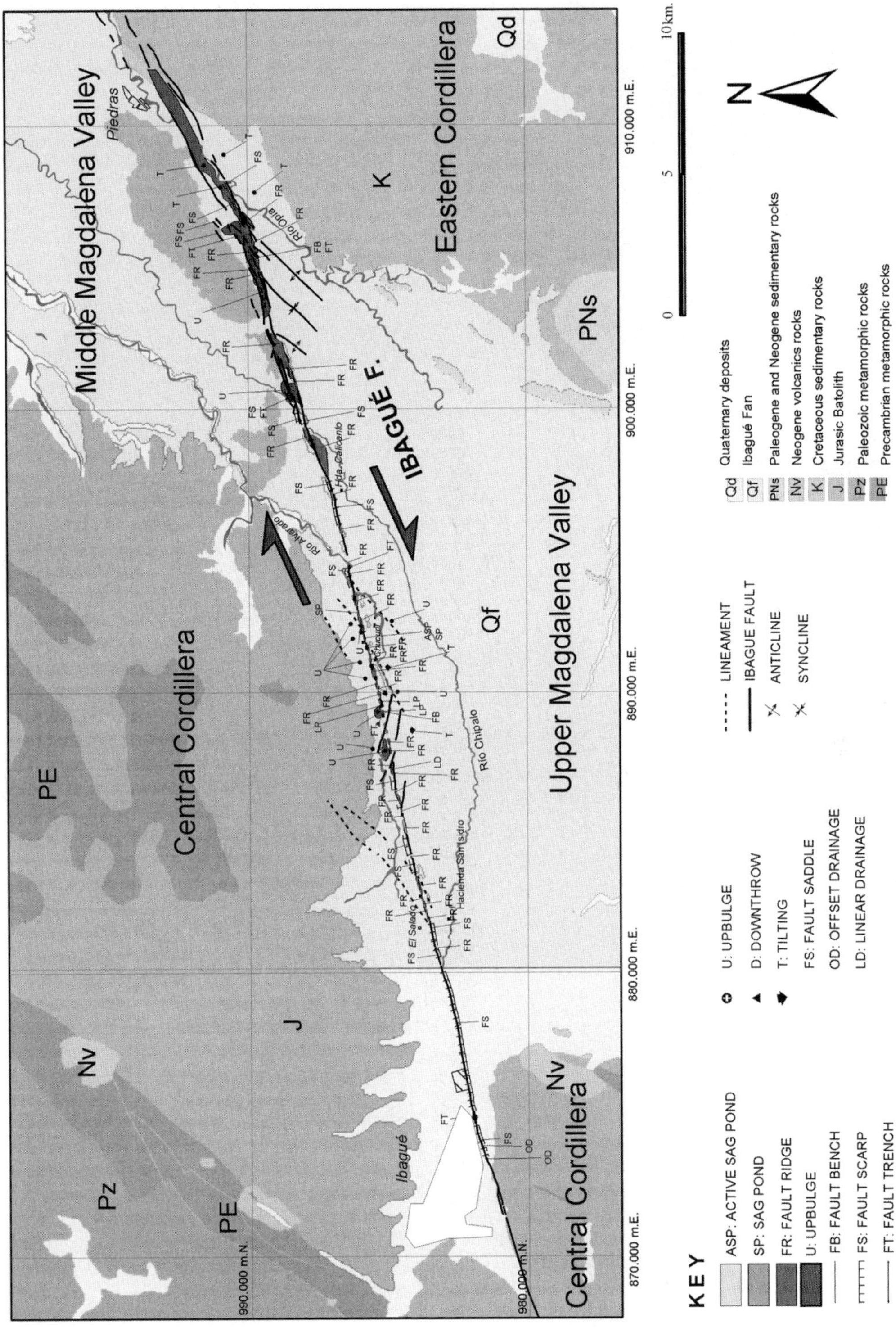
Middle Magdalena Valley
Eastern Cordillera
Central Cordillera
Upper Magdalena Valley
IBAGUÉ F.
Ibagué
Piedras
Río Opia
Río Alvarado
Río Chipalo
Hacienda San Isidro
El Salado
PE
Pz
Nv
J
K
Qf
Qd
PNs
990.000 m.N.
980.000 m.N.
870.000 m.E.
880.000 m.E.
890.000 m.E.
900.000 m.E.
910.000 m.E.
0
5
10km.
N
KEY
ASP: ACTIVE SAG POND
SP: SAG POND
FR: FAULT RIDGE
U: UPBULGE
FB: FAULT BENCH
FS: FAULT SCARP
FT: FAULT TRENCH
U: UPBULGE
D: DOWNTHROW
T: TILTING
FS: FAULT SADDLE
OD: OFFSET DRAINAGE
LD: LINEAR DRAINAGE
LINEAMENT
IBAGUE FAULT
ANTICLINE
SYNCLINE
Qd Quaternary deposits
Qf Ibagué Fan
PNs Paleogene and Neogene sedimentary rocks
Nv Neogene volcanics rocks
K Cretaceous sedimentary rocks
J Jurasic Batolith
Pz Paleozoic metamorphic rocks
PE Precambrian metamorphic rocks

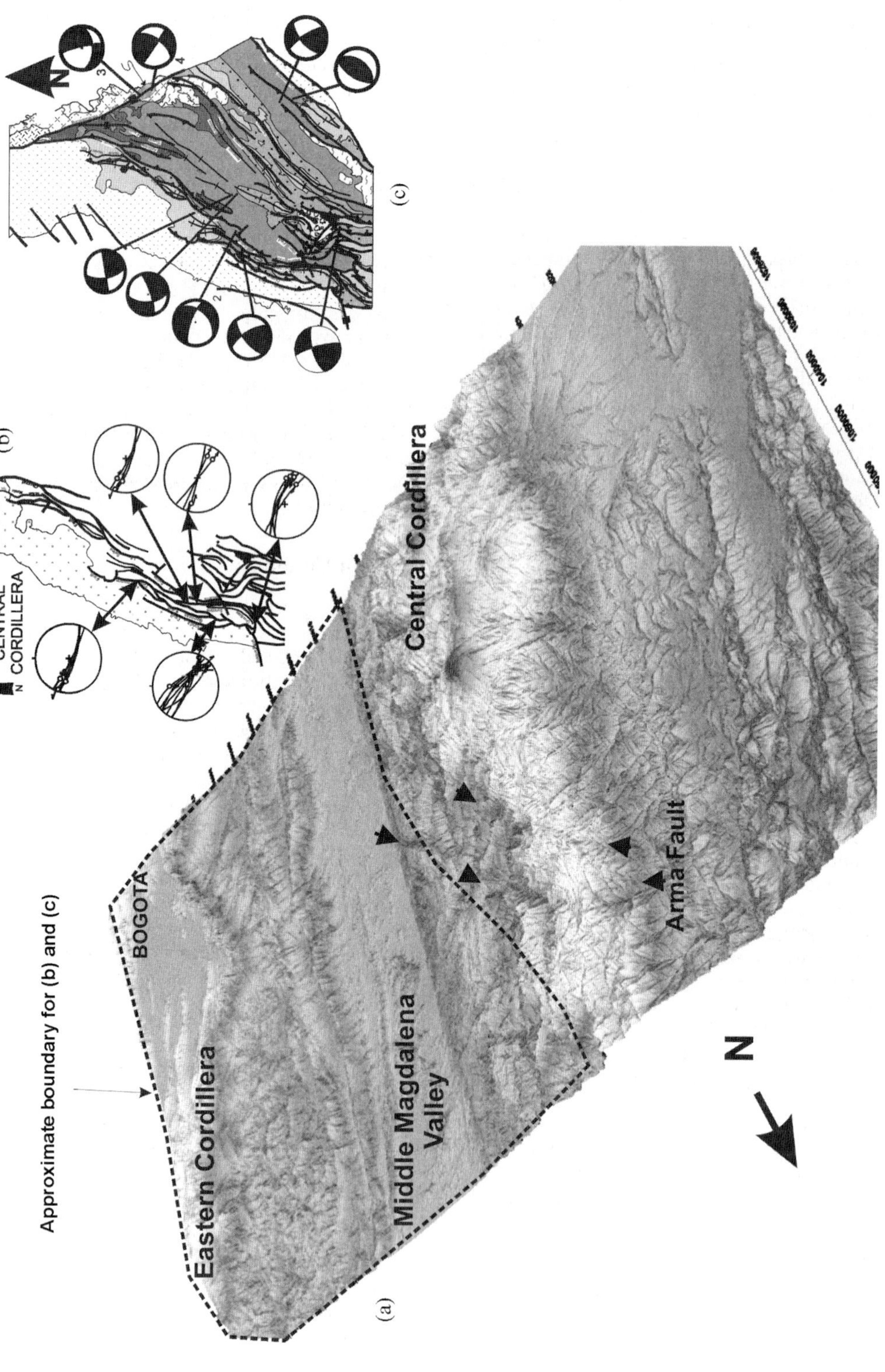

Approximate boundary for (b) and (c)
BOGOTA
Eastern Cordillera
Middle Magdalena Valley
Central Cordillera
Arma Fault
N
(a)
CENTRAL CORDILLERA
N
(b)
(c)

into the Eastern Cordillera as the Viani Fault. The main strand of the fault is a succession of shutter ridges, pull-apart basins and synthetic faults within the Ibagué Fan (Fig. 6).

Palaeoseismological studies along the main strand of the Ibagué Fan indicate an average strike-slip rate of 0.77 mm a^{-1} for the last 15 Ka (Montes *et al.* 2006). Assuming a constant slip rate of 0.77 mm a^{-1}, would imply that the Ibagué Fault has been active from Late Eocene to Early Oligocene times to account for the 25 km of lateral displacement along the Central Cordillera. However, Montes *et al.* (2006) also determined strike-slip rates as high as 3.8 mm a^{-1} for the Ibagué Fault, which, if constant over geological time, would indicate that activity on the fault was much more recent (Middle to Late Miocene). In this study, it is assumed that the average of the strike-slip rates reported by Montes *et al.* (2006) is probably the valid number to use and that the Ibagué Fault became active in the Middle to Late Oligocene.

NW-trending faults cut basement rocks of the Central Cordillera and Upper Magdalena Valley (Fig. 7). These faults are continuous from the western foothills through the Central Cordillera to the eastern foothills. The main structure of this system is the Arma Fault, which is an oblique normal, left-lateral fault. Gold-bearing igneous dykes are found only along the NW-trending faults (Lozano & Murillo 1983).

A set of NE-trending, steeply dipping predominantly normal left-lateral faults have also been identified in the western foothills of the Eastern Cordillera and Middle Magdalena Valley, which affect Neogene to Quaternary sediments (Acosta *et al.* 2004). The NW-trending structures are clearly related to focal mechanisms at depths of 24–40 km (Fig. 7), and confirm the reactivation of the NW–SE-trending faults, as previously proposed by several workers in regional studies of the Northern Andes (Acosta 1983; Gómez 1991; Ujueta 2001; Velandia & De Bermoudes 2002).

The Bucaramanga–Santa Marta Fault has a relatively straight trace to the north of the Middle Magdalena Valley (Campbell 1968; Boinet *et al.* 1986). The deformation zone of this N30°W-trending, left-lateral strike-slip fault can be traced for *c.* 500 km through northern Colombia (Fig. 8) The fault zone is defined by a set of approximately parallel faults that splay from, and rejoin, the main fault strand within a 10 km wide strip. A set of NW-trending low to moderately dipping thrust faults, striking subparallel to the main strand, also occur within the fault zone.

Fig. 7. (**a**) Digital Elevation Model of central Colombia, (**b**) stereonet plot of Neogene and Quaternary faults, (**c**) shallow focal mechanism solutions in the western foothills of the Eastern Cordillera and Middle Magdalena Valley (b and c modified from A costa *et al.* 2004).

Seismic profiles, perpendicular to the main structures on the western block of the Bucaramanga Fault (Fig. 8), show typical elements of many thrust belts around the world, including basin inversion, thin-skinned thrusting and decoupling of the post-rift cover, out-of-sequence thrusting and thick-skinned basement involved thrusting. However, in this study features typical of strike-slip movement, associated with the Bucaramanga Fault, have also been observed: (1) complex unconformities; (2) large structural changes along strike such as non-cylindrical folding of the detachment level; (3) change from open to isoclinal folding along the axis of the detachment, showing non-planar deformation.

Eastern Cordillera

The core of the Eastern Cordillera is formed by metamorphic and sedimentary rocks of Palaeozoic age and igneous extrusive and intrusive rocks of Jurassic age. Longitudinal and transverse tectonic controls have exposed a thick sequence of Cretaceous sediments of differing facies and thickness in the axial zone of the cordillera. Cenozoic and unconsolidated Quaternary deposits partially cover the region, making it difficult to follow some of the structures.

Strike-slip faulting in the axial zone of the Eastern Cordillera has been identified by several workers, who proposed that these structures are regionally related to subvertical or high-angle faults at depth (Kammer & Mojica 1996; Taboada *et al.* 2000; Sarmiento 2002). De Freitas *et al.* (1997) supported this interpretation, but additionally proposed that the NW-trending structures represent rift cross-faults.

The Bucaramanga Fault system ends to the south in the axial zone of the Eastern Cordillera, in a compressional duplex structure that shows the left-lateral movement of the system (Fig. 9) (Velandia 2005). NE-trending right-lateral faults merge with the duplex to the south generating an arcuate complex structural pattern in the region.

In the Paipa geothermal area, NW- and ENE-trending strike-slip structures have also been identified (Fig. 9). Right-lateral displacement along the ENE-trending faults, which affects the sedimentary sequence, was determined by striae

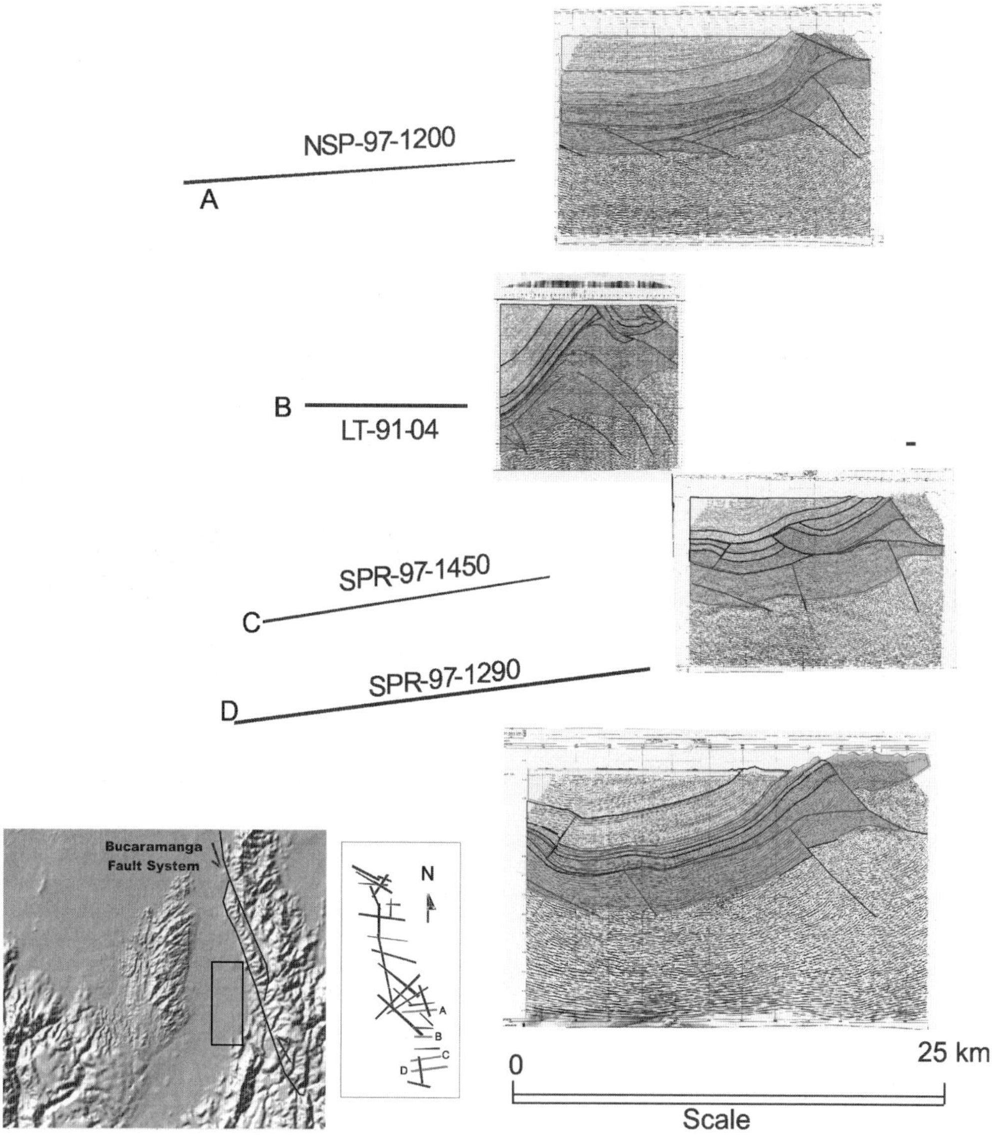

Fig. 8. Interpreted seismic profiles across the Bucaramanga Fault, Seismic data courtesy of Ecopetrol. Vertical scale in two-way travel time, to 5 seconds for sections A, B, and C; and 6 seconds for section D.

along the fault surfaces. These ENE-trending faults offset NE thrusts and are in concordance with the ENE strike-slip faults observed in the Central Cordillera (e.g. Ibagué Fault), and therefore are interpreted as a younger fault system rather than lateral ramps associated with the thrusts.

NW-trending left-lateral shear zones, which occur to the SE, are associated with a Neogene volcanic body that is the thermal source of the Paipa geothermal field. Regionally, the trace of the shear zone continues to the SE, where another volcanic body and the Iza geothermal system occur (Velandia 2005). These faults are interpreted as pre-existing extensional basement structures that were reactivated during the Andean tectonic phase and facilitated the magma emplacement.

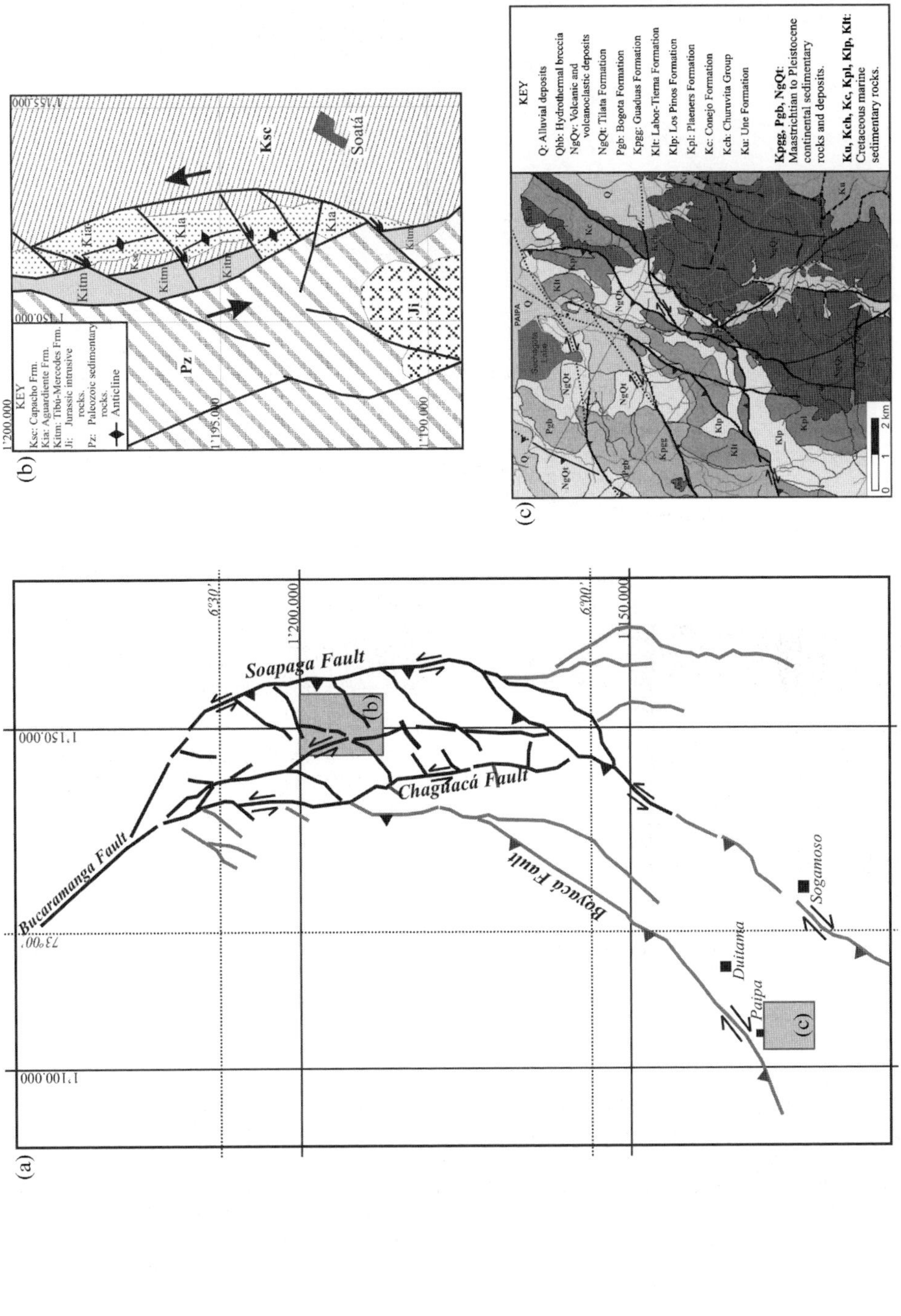

Fig. 9. **(a)** Transpressive duplex at the south end of the Bucaramanga Fault, **(b)** local structures within the duplex, **(c)** geological map of the Paipa geothermal field.

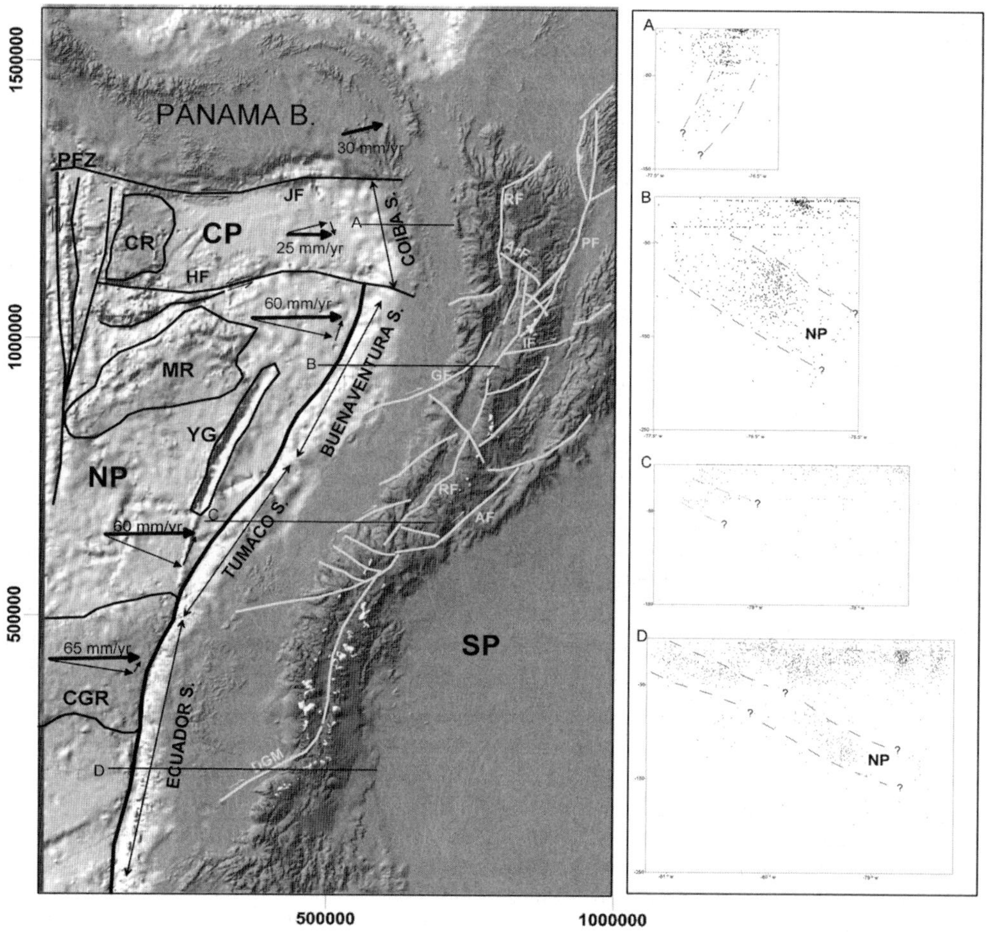

Fig. 10. Tectonic map of the Nazca plate and Northern Andes. CGR, Carnegie Ridge; NP, Nazca Plate; YG, Yaquina Graben; MR, Malpelo Ridge; HF, Hey Fault; CR, Coiba Ridge; CP, Coiba Microplate; JF Jordan Fault, SP, South American Plate; RF, Romeral Fault; PF, Palestina Fault; ArF, Arma Fault; IF, Ibagué Fault; GF, Garrapatas Fault; AF, Algeciras Fault; DGM, Dolores-Guayaquil Megashear. The seismicity plotted in profiles A, B, C and D illustrates the dip of the subducting slab. Vertical scale of A and C is 150 km; B and D is 250 km. Seismic data from Ingeominas earthquake catalogue.

Partitioning within the Colombian Andes

NW-trending strike-slip deformation within the Colombian Andes is interpreted to be associated with pre-existing basement structures. However, some other questions arise, such as: what controls the ENE-trending strike-slip deformation, the timing of the deformation and the relationship between the NW-, NE- and ENE-trending strike-slip structures? To answer these questions, the changes in the dynamics and geometry of the subducting Nazca Plate under South America took place are considered.

The subduction zone of the Nazca Plate, under the Northern Andes, is affected by erosional and accretionary processes within the coupling zone. Submarine topographic anomalies, such as the Carnegie Ridge, the Yaquina Graben and other fossil ridges, have led to a segmentation of the subduction zone. Additionally, the geometrical relationship between the convergence vector and the shape of the trench has led to strain partitioning resulting from the fact that the convergence vector can be divided into two vectors, as proposed by Toro & Osorio (2002): (1) a vector orthogonal to the trench, indicated by the deformation within the coupling zone (Fig. 10), which favours shortening and inversion of NE-trending structures within the continent; (2) a vector parallel to the trench, which is transferred into the continent, generating new ENE-trending shear structures and facilitating the reactivation of NW-trending pre-existing faults.

As a result, four distinct segments can be identified along the Nazca subduction zone in Northern South America (Orozco 2004), as follows.

(1) In the Ecuador segment, between the Gulf of Guayaquil and Esmeraldas in northern Ecuador (Fig. 10), the convergence vector is almost orthogonal to the trench, leading to a minimum of strain partitioning, as shown by the generation and reactivation of shortening structures that dominate the Andean Cordillera in Ecuador. ENE-trending strike-slip structures are present in the southern part of the segment along the Dolores–Guayaquil Megashear (Dumont & Benítez 1996). Volcanic bodies to the north of the Dolores–Guayaquil Megashear and absence of deep seismicity are the main tectonic processes within this segment. The lack of deep seismicity was used by Gutscher *et al.* (1999) to propose a flat slab under Ecuador. However, the volcanism seems contradictory to this hypothesis, but it could occur as a result of the volume compensation in a transtensional zone, related to major ENE-trending systems (e.g Algeciras Fault system).

(2) In the Tumaco Segment, between Manta (Ecuador) and the mouth of the Patia River (Fig. 10), the convergence vector is 60° oblique to the trench, favouring the transfer of displacement and deformation to the continent. ENE-trending right-lateral strike-slip faults developed within the continent, such as those in the Upper Magdalena Valley and along the Algeciras Fault system. This segment represents a huge rupture zone along the trench where subduction earthquakes of magnitude M_w 8.8 (1906), M_w 7.9 (1942) and M_w 7.8 (1958) have been recorded. However, the scarcity of deep seismic activity makes it difficult to trace the subduction slab under the continent. Parallelism and changes in direction of the volcanic belt at the Colombia–Ecuador border and the trench at the same latitude suggest that the geometry of the subduction zone changed.

(3) The Buenaventura Segment, between the Garrapatas and Hey faults to the south and north, respectively (Fig. 10), is characterized by accretion in the coupling zone (Cediel *et al.* 2004), shallow and deep seismicity, and the presence of a volcanic arc. The convergence vector is semi-orthogonal to the trench (80°), leading to the generation of ENE-trending right-lateral strike-slip faults within the continent, such as the Garrapatas and Ibague faults systems.

(4) The Coiba Segment lies between the Hey and Jordan faults forming the Coiba Microplate (Pennington 1981) (Fig. 10). This microplate was a part of the Nazca Plate, from which it split about 8 Ma ago to release the displacement of the Cocos and Nazca plates (Sayares & Charvis 2003). As a result, the Panama Fracture Zone and the Hey and Jordan faults were formed.

Currently the neighbouring Nazca Plate (to the south) and Panama Block (to the north) are moving faster (60 mm a^{-1} and 30 mm a^{-1}, respectively) eastward than the Coiba Microplate which is moving at 25 mm a^{-1} (Mora 1995), hence making the subduction process less probable in the region. The absence of deep seismicity and volcanism in the Coiba Segment is consistent with these observations. Stress is directly transferred to the continent because of the orthogonal convergence of the block, generating shortening in the Baudo Serrania.

The effect of the orthogonal convergence of the Coiba Microplate and the convergence vector of the Panama Block generates a SE-trending main stress direction within the continent, allowing tensional and left-lateral shear along pre-existing NW-, north- and NE-trending structures.

Global Positioning System data

GPS data collected from 1994 to 2003 within the North Andean Block and plotted with respect to South America confirm that part of the convergence vector is transferred to the continent, as expressed by Trenkamp *et al.* (2002), with values of displacement that reach 21 mm a^{-1} with an azimuth ranging from 58° to 89°. An elastic locking and aseismic slip imply a slip interface that is locked by enough friction to permit part of the Nazca Plate velocity to be transferred to the overriding South America Plate with the plate still sliding into the mantle with part of the original plate velocity (Trenkamp *et al.* 2002). The deformation caused by these vectors can be interpreted as: (1) continental elastic–plastic deformation, part of which will be recovered in an elastic slip event, such as an earthquake, on the subduction zone and part of which permanently deforms the Andean crust; (2) active tectonic faulting oblique to the trench, where the deformation is homogeneously distributed in simple shear zones, as proposed by Folgera *et al.* (2002).

Results from GPS data obtained before, and after, the 1999 earthquake, plus the ENE-trending strike-slip faulting indicate that both deformation mechanisms are simultaneously acting in the Colombian Andes. Therefore, either transpressional or transtensional systems will be developed, and wide continental areas will be affected by rotational shear.

In addition, there is a possible visco-elastic overprinting deformation on a subset of those vectors between 2° and 4°N (White *et al.* 2003). However, the visco-elastic part is not the main signal that is being observed. Visco-elastic processes are longer wavelength and elastic processes are shorter wavelength phenomena. In other words, when an earthquake occurs, the elastic effect is generally over in a year or two but visco-elastic processes continue for decades or centuries.

Timing and relationship between structures

Tectono-stratigraphic studies of Colombia have demonstrated the existence of pre-Cretaceous rifting which gave rise to NE-trending normal faults and NW-trending cross-fault systems (Cooper *et al.* 1995; Acosta 2002). At the end of the Mesozoic (66 Ma), the Caribbean Plate relative motion changed in the west from northeastward to eastward and began to underthrust northern South America (Mattson 1984). This drove the oblique accretion of the Western Cordillera along the Romeral Fault from 68 to 49 Ma (Barrero *et al.* 1969), causing uplift and erosion in the Central Cordillera (Cooper *et al.* 1995).

As a result of the oblique collision of the oceanic crust during the Late Cretaceous, strike-slip systems, such as the Palestina Fault, were active (Feininger 1970). It is therefore assumed that simple shear deformation occurred within the Northern Andes during this time, as proposed by Tikoff & Teyssier (1994) and Teyssier *et al.* (1995).

The Farallon–Phoenix Plate separated into the Nazca and Cocos plates at about 27 Ma, increasing the convergence rate between the Nazca and South American plates (Mattson 1984). This event coincided with the initiation of the Ibague Fault system and the other ENE-trending right-lateral strike-slip fault systems within the Northern Andes. Additionally, NW-trending left-lateral strike-slip fault systems started to be reactivated almost at the same time, suggesting that the convergence angle, although oblique, became more orthogonal than it had been previously.

The change in the convergence angle, the rheological heterogeneities within the region and the action of the newly formed ENE-trending right-lateral strike-slip faults have facilitated the continuous differential reactivation of pre-existing basement faults since the Oligocene. Some NE-trending basement structures, such as the Chusma Fault, inverted as oblique thrusts by taking advantage of the partition generated by ENE-trending structures that acted as lateral ramps. NW-trending rift cross-faults, reactivated as oblique left-lateral normal faults together with the ENE-trending right-lateral faults, acted as barriers for the Cenozoic sedimentation in the inter-montane valleys.

The accretion of the arcuate Panama Block in the northwestern corner of Colombia (Duque-Caro 1990), combined with the generation of the Coiba Microplate as a result of the formation of the Panama fracture zone and Hey and Jordan faults, was responsible for the major episode of Miocene deformation in the Colombian Andes. This last major event in the region led to a present-day maximum horizontal stress directions of 112° and 138° (Castillo & Mojica 1990). In addition, Acosta *et al.* (2004), based on measurement of kinematic data, earthquake focal mechanisms and borehole breakout data, inferred a NW-trending principal incremental strain axis (shortening axis) for the region at the present, which may have extended back to the Late Neogene, as no significant changes to plate movement directions are thought to have occurred since 11 Ma (e.g. Daly 1989).

Therefore, the NW-trending incremental strain is parallel or subparallel to the NW-trending pre-existing faults. This favours their reactivation and opening as tension faults, along which hydrothermal fluids and Neogene magmas have risen.

Implications for mineral and hydrocarbon exploration

The different rheological properties of the rocks on either side of these strike-slip structures and their different thicknesses exert a pronounced control on the structural style. On one side tight complex structures are developed, whereas on the other wide and simple folds are formed as is observed in the Upper Magdalena Valley. This pattern could affect the petroleum system if strike-slip fault systems act as migration pathways.

The ENE- and NW-trending strike-slip faults are associated with two different processes that might be either favourable or damaging for the structural trapping of hydrocarbons. Continuous reactivation of pre-existing basement faults plus the generation of new strike-slip structures enhances fracturing that is accompanied by infilling of fluids, some of which generate hydrothermal–sedimentary deposits; for example, the occurrence of emeralds as proposed by Branquet *et al.* (1999*a*), and ore mineral deposits, as suggested by Lozano & Murillo

(1983). Major concentrations of minerals, hydrothermal fluids and volcanism (especially cinder cones) are usually associated with the junction of the NE-, NW- and ENE-trending systems.

The continuous deformation process has also led to damage of pre-existing ore mineral deposits. The enhanced heat flow arising from hydrothermal fluid circulation along the strike-slip fault systems may have made organic hydrocarbons overmature. Emplacement of magma can occur, as in the Paipa and Iza geothermal fields in the Eastern Cordillera, affecting sedimentary sequences and emplacing porphyritic bodies along shear zones in the Central Cordillera, which can destroy any previously ore-enriched sedimentary sequences.

Conclusions

Stress and strain partitioning within the Northern Andes is due to the oblique convergence vector of the Nazca Plate and to the changes in the geometry of the coupling zone, which induce a transpressive regime in the region. This partitioning was expressed during Early Cenozoic times along transcurrent fault systems, subparallel to the margin (e.g. Palestina Fault system), and then along ENE-trending right-lateral structures, such as the Ibagué Fault, since the Late Palaeogene.

This partitioning also favoured the inversion of pre-existing NE-trending faults as oblique structures and the reactivation of pre-existing NW-trending faults as left-lateral structures. A conjugate movement with a right-lateral sense of motion and partitioning along left-lateral strike-slip faults led to a counterclockwise rotation of the Andean Block and northward expulsion of the whole block.

The existence of strike-slip deformation along the Colombian mountain belt is favourable for the occurrence of ore-mineral deposits and provides a new structural style that should be considered in the of assessment hydrocarbon exploration plays.

We thank P. Cobbold and an anonymous reviewer for helpful comments, Douglas Hamilton for help with the English, A. Rees and R. Graham for editorial revisions, and Ingeominas for permission to publish DEM data. This research was inspired by discussions with Mike Coward while J. Acosta conducted his PhD under Mike's supervision.

References

ACOSTA, C. E. 1983. *In*: Cadré, R. (ed.) Geodynamics of Ecuador, *Geodynamics of the Eastern Pacific Region, Caribbean and Scotia Arcs*. Geodynamic Series, American Geophysical Union, **9**, 53–63.

ACOSTA, J. 2002. *Structure, Tectonics and 3D models of the Western foothills of the Eastern Cordillera and Middle Magdalena Valley, Colombia*. Publicación Geológica Especial Ingeominas, **25**.

ACOSTA, J., LONERGAN, L. & COWARD, M. P. 2004. Oblique transpression in the western thrust front of the Colombian Eastern Cordillera. *Journal of South American Earth Sciences*, **17**, 181–194.

BARRERO, D. & VESGA, C. J. 1976. *Mapa Geológico del Cuadrángulo K-9, Armero y Mitad Sur del J-9, La Dorada. Escala 1:100 000*. Ingeominas, Bogotá.

BARRERO, D., ALVAREZ, J. & KASSEM, T. 1969. Actividad ignea y tectónica en la Cordillera Central durante el Meso-Cenozoico. *Boletín Geológico Ingeominas*, **17**, 145–173.

BARTOK, P., REIJERS, T. & JUHASZ, I. 1981. Lower Cretaceous Cogollo Group, Maracaibo Basin, Venezuela: sedimentology, diagenesis and petrophysics. *AAPG Bulletin*, **65**, 1110–1134.

BELTRÁN, N. & GALLO, J. 1979. The geology of the Neiva Sub-basin, Upper Magdalena Basin, southern portion. *In*: GEOTEC (ed.) *Geological Field-trips Colombia 1959–1978*. Colombian Society of Petroleum Geologists and Geophysicists, 253–257.

BOINET, T., BOURGOIS, J., MENDOZA, H. & VARGAS, R. 1986. La Falla de Bucaramanga (Colombia): Su función durante la Orogenia Andina. *Geología Norandina*, **11**, 3–10.

BRANQUET, Y., CHEILLETZ, A., GIULIANI, G., LAUMONIER, B. & BLANCO, O. 1999*a*. Fluidized hydrothermal breccia in dilatant faults during thrusting: the Colombian emerald deposits. *In*: MCCAFFREY, K., LONERGAN, L. & WILKINSON, J. (eds) *Fractures, Fluid Flow and Mineralization*. Geological Society, London, Special Publications, **155**, 183–195.

BRANQUET, Y., LAUMONIER, B., CHEILLETZ, A. & GIULIANI, G. 1999*b*. Emeralds in the Eastern Cordillera of Colombia: two tectonic settings for one mineralization. *Geology*, **27**, 597–600.

BRANQUET, Y., CHEILLETZ, A., COBBOLD, P. R., BABY, P., LAUMONIER, B. & GIULIANI, G. 2002. Andean deformation and rift inversion, eastern edge of Cordillera Oriental (Guateque Medina area), Colombia. *Journal of South American Earth Sciences*, **15**, 391–407.

BUTLER, K. & SCHAMEL, S. 1987. Structure along the eastern margin of the Central Cordillera, Upper Magdalena Valley, Colombia. *Journal of South American Earth Sciences*, **1**(1), 109–120.

CAMARGO, G. 1995. Elementos estructurales del área de la Sabana de Bogotá y Alrededores. *VI Congreso Colombiano del Petróleo, Bogotá*, **8**.

CAMPBELL, C. 1968. The Santa Marta Wrench fault of Colombia and its regional setting. *Fourth Caribbean Geological Conference, Trinidad*, 247–261.

CASTILLO, J. & MOJICA, J. 1990. Determinación de la Orientación de Esfuerzos Actuales a partir de Deformaciones Tectónicas ('Breakouts') en algunos Pozos Petroleros de los Llanos Orientales y del Valle Medio del Magdalena, Colombia. *Geologia Colombiana*, **17**, 123–132.

CEDIEL, F., SHAW, R. & CÁCERES, C. 2004. Tectonic assembly of the North Andean block. *In*: BARTOLINI, C., BUFLER, R. T. & BLICKWEDE, J. (eds) *The Circum Gulf of Mexico and the Caribbean: Hydrocarbon Habitats, Basin Formations and Plate Tectonics.* American Association of Petroleum Geologists, Memoirs, **79**, 815–848.

CHOROWICZ, J., CHOTIN, P. & GUILLANDE, R. 1996. The Garzon fault: active southwestern boundary of the Caribbean plate in Colombia. *Geologische Rundschau*, **85**, 172–179.

COOPER, M. A., ADDISON, T., ALVAREZ, R. *et al.* 1995. Basin development and tectonic history of the Llanos Basin, Eastern Cordillera, and the Middle Magdalena valley, Colombia. *AAPG Bulletin*, **79**, 1421–1443.

CORREDOR, F. 2003. Seismic strain rates and distributed continental deformation in the Northern Andes and three-dimensional seismotectonics of northwestern South America. *Tectonophysics*, **372**, 147–166.

CORRIGAN, H. 1979. Guide book to the Geology of the Upper Magdalena basin (Northern Portion). *In*: GEOTEC (ed.) *Geological Field-trips Colombia 1959–1978*. Colombian Society of Petroleum Geologists and Geophysists, 221–149.

CUERVO, E. 1995. Armazón rombohédrica de la geología colombiana — un modelo de evolución tectónica. *VI Congreso Colombiano del Petróleo, Memorias*, I, 71–84.

DALY, M. 1989. Correlation between Nazca/Farallon plate kinematics and forearc evolution in Ecuador. *Tectonics*, **8**, 769–790.

DE FREITAS, M., FRONCOLIN, J. B. L. & COBBOLD, P. R. 1997. The structure of the Axial Zone of the Cordillera Oriental, Colombia. *VI Simposio Bolivariano 'Exploración petrolera en las cuencas subandinas'.* Asociación Colombiana de Geólogos y Geofísicos del Petróleo, Memorias, **II**, 38–41.

DIEDERIX, H., GOMEZ, H., KHOBZI, J. & SINGER, A. 1987. Indicios neotectónicos de la Falla Ibagué en el sector Ibagué–Piedras, departamento de Tolima, Colombia. *Revista CIAF*, **11**, 242–252.

DUMONT, J. & BENÍTEZ, S. 1996. Neotectonics of the coastal region of Ecuador: a new pluridisciplinary research Project. *Third International Symposium on Andean Geodynamics (ISAG), St. Malo*, ORSTOM, Paris, 175–178.

DUQUE-CARO, H. 1990. The Choco block in the northwestern corner of South America: Structural, tectonostratigraphic, and paleogeographic implications. *Journal of South American Earth Sciences*, **3**, 71–84.

ETAYO-SERNA, F., BARRERO, D., LOZANO, H. *et al.* 1983. *Mapa de Terrenos geológicos de Colombia.* Ingeominas Publicación Geológica Especial, **14–1**, 1–235.

FEININGER, T. 1970. The Palestina Fault, Colombia. *Geological Society of America Bulletin*, **81**, 1201–1216.

FOLGUERA, A., RAMOS, V. & MELNIK, D. 2002. Partición de la deformación en la zona del arco volcánico de los Andes neuquinos (36–39°S) en los últimos 30 millones de años. *Revista Geológica de Chile*, **29**, 151–165.

FREYMUELLER, J., KELLOGG, J. & VEGA, V. 1993. Plate motions in the North Andean region. *Journal of Geophysical Research*, **98**, 21853–21863.

GÓMEZ, H. 1991. La Paleomegacizalla Transversal de Colombia, base de un Nuevo Esquema Geotectónico. *Revista CIAF*, **12**(1), 49–61.

GUTSCHER, M. A., MALAVIEILLE, J., LALLEMAND, S. & COLLOT, J. 1999. Tectonic segmentation on the North Andean margin: impact of the Carnegie Ridge collision. *Earth and Planetary Science Letters*, **168**, 255–270.

KAMMER, A. & MOJICA, J. 1996. Una comparación de la tectónica de basamento de las cordilleras Central y Oriental. *Geología Colombiana*, **20**, 93–106.

KELLOGG, J. & VEGA, V. 1995. Tectonic development of Panama, Costa Rica and the Colombian Andes: constraints from Global Positioning System geodetic studies and gravity. *In*: MANN, P. (ed.) *Geologic and Tectonic Development of the Caribbean Plate Boundary in Southern Central America.* Geological Society of America, Special Papers, **295**, 75–90.

KELLOGG, J., OGUJIOFOR, I. & KANSAKAR, D. 1985. Cenozoic tectonics of the Panama and North Andes blocks. *6th Latinoamerican Geological Congress.* Ingeominas, Bogotá, Memoir, **I**, 40–59.

LÓPEZ, E. & BARRERO, D. 2003. Transectas regionales de la corteza superior de Colombia. *VIII Simposio Bolivariano — Exploración Petrolera en las Cuencas Subandinas.* Asociación Colombiana de Geólogos y Geofísicos del Petróleo, Memoria, **I**, 279–289.

LOZANO, H. & MURILLO, A. 1983. Grandes fallas NW–SE Norte de Suramerica y sus implicaciones en la geología y mineralizaciones de oro y plata en la Cordillera Central de Colombia. *10ª Conferencia Geológica del Caribe. Memoria.*

MANN, P. (ed.). 1995. *Geologic and Tectonic Development of the Caribbean Plate Boundary in Southern Central America.* Geological Society of America, Special Papers, **295**, preface.

MATTSON, P. 1984. Caribbean structural breaks and plate movements. *In*: BONINT, W. E. (ed.) *The Caribbean–South American Plate Boundary and Regional Tectonics.* Geological Society of America, Memoirs, **162**, 131–151.

MOJICA, J. & FRANCO, R. 1990. Estructura y evolución tectónica del Valle Medio y Superior del Magdalena. *Geología Colombiana*, **17**, 41–64.

MONTES, C. 2001. *Three dimensional structure and kinematics of the Piedras–Girardot foldbelt in the northern Andes of Colombia.* PhD dissertation, University of Tennessee, Knoxville.

MONTES, N., VELANDIA, F., OSORIO, J., AUDEMARD, F. & DIEDERIX, H. 2005. Interpretación morfotectónica de la Falla Ibagué para su caracterización paleosismológica. *Boletín de Geología, Universidad Industrial de Santander*, **27**(44), 93–112.

MONTES, N., OSORIO, J., VELANDIA, F., ACOSTA, J., NUÑEZ, A., DIEDERIX, H. & AUDEMARD, F. 2006. Paleosismología de la Falla Ibagué. Unpublished internal report, Ingeominas, Bogotá, Colombia.

MORA, H. 1995. Resultados de GPS en el sector Colombiano. *In*: *Seminario de Sismotectónica del borde Llanero.* Ingeominas, Bogotá, 53–66.

OROZCO, L. A. 2004. Definición de provincias sismotectónicas y bloques de deformación actual para Colombia. Ingeominas-Universidad de Caldas. Unpublished Ingeominas internal report.

PENNINGTON, W. D. 1981. Subduction of Eastern Panamá Basin and Seísmotectonics of Northwestern South America. *Journal of Geophysical Research*, **86**(B11), 10753–10770.

RENZONI, G. 1994. *Catálogo de las unidades litoestratigráficas de Colombia. Caballos (Formación).* Ingeominas, Bogotá.

SAYARES, V. & CHARVIS, P. 2003. Crustal thickness constraints on the geodynamic evolution of the Galapagos Volcanic Province. *Earth and Planetary Science Letters*, **214**, 545–559.

SARMIENTO, L. 2002. *Mezosoic rifting and Cenozoic basin inversion history of the Eastern Cordillera, Colombian Andes. Inferences from tectonic models.* PhD thesis, University of Amsterdam.

SCHAMEL, S. 1991. Middle and Upper Magdalena Basins, Colombia. *In*: BIDDLE, T. (ed.) *Active Margins.* American Association of Petroleum Geologists, Memoirs, **52**, 283–301.

TABOADA, A., RIVERA, L., FUENZALIDA, A. *et al.* 2000. Geodynamics of the northern Andes: subductions and intracontinental deformation (Colombia). *Tectonics*, **19**(5), 787–813.

TEYSSIER, C., TIKOFF, B. & MARKLEY, M. 1995. Oblique plate motion and continental tectonics. *Geology*, **23**(5), 447–450.

TIKOFF, B. & TEYSSIER, C. 1994. Strain modeling of displacement field partitioning in transpressional orogens. *Journal of Structural Geology*, **16**(11), 1575–1588.

TORO, A. & OSORIO, J. 2002. Determinación de los tensores de esfuerzo actuales para el segmento norte de los Andes, calculados a partir de mecanismos focales de sismos mayores. *In*: *Memoirs of the 5th International Symposium on Andean Geodynamics.* Paris, 249–252.

TRENKAMP, R., KELLOG, J. N., FREYMULLER, J. T. & MORA, H. P. 2002. Wide plate margin deformation, southern Central America and northwestern South America, CASA GPS observations. *Journal of South American Earth Sciences*, **15**, 157–171.

UJUETA, J. G. 2001. Lineamientos de Dirección NO–SE y NNE–SSO a NE–SO en el Centro Occidente Colombiano y en el Ecuador. *Geología Colombiana*, **26**, 5–27.

VELANDIA, F. 2001. Fallas transversales de basamento en el Departamento del Huila, Valle Superior del Magdalena, Colombia. *11th Latinoamerican Geological Congress, Montevideo, Uruguay, Memoir*; paper 33.

VELANDIA, F. 2005. Interpretación de transcurrencia de las fallas Soapaga y Boyacá a partir de imágenes Landsat TM. *Boletín de Geología, Universidad sIndustrial de Santander*, **27**, 81–92.

VELANDIA, F. & DE BERMOUDES, O. 2002. Fallas Longitudinales y Transversales en la Sabana de Bogotá, Colombia. *Boletín de Geología, Universidad Industrial de Santander*, **24**, 37–48.

VELANDIA, F. & KOMURO, H. 1998. Análisis de lineamientos geológicos a partir de imágenes SAR de un área al SW de Colombia, Andes del Norte. *10th Latinoamerican Geological Congress, Abstracts Memoir*, **3**, 369.

VELANDIA, F., ACOSTA, J., TERRAZA, R. & VILLEGAS, H. 2005. The current tectonic motion of the Northern Andes along the Algeciras Fault System in SW Colombia. *Tectonophysics*, **399**, 313–329.

VERGARA, H. 1996. Rasgos y actividad neotectónica de la Falla de Algeciras. *VII Congreso Colombiano de Geología*, Memorias, **I**, 491–500.

WHITE, S. M., TRENKAMP, R. & KELLOGG, J. N. 2003. Recent crustal deformation and the earthquake cycle along the Ecuador–Colombia subduction zone. *Earth and Planetary Science Letters*, **216**, 231–242.

Distribution, timing, and causes of Andean deformation across South America

PETER R. COBBOLD[1], EDUARDO A. ROSSELLO[1,2], PIERRICK ROPERCH[1,3], CÉSAR ARRIAGADA[1,4], LUIS A. GÓMEZ[1,5] & CLAUDIO LIMA[1,6]

[1]*Géosciences-Rennes (UMR6118 du CNRS), Université de Rennes 1, 35042 Rennes Cedex, France (e-mail: peter.cobbold@univ-rennes1.fr)*

[2]*CONICET y Departamento de Ciencias Geológicas, Universidad de Buenos Aires, Buenos Aires, Argentina*

[3]*IRD (UR154–LMTG), 14 rue Edouard Belin, 31400 Toulouse France*

[4]*Departamento de Geología, Universidad de Chile, Casilla 13518, Correo 21, Santiago, Chile*

[5]*Ecopetrol, Bogotá, Colombia*

[6]*CENPES, Petrobras, Rio de Janeiro, Brazil*

Abstract: The Andean Orogeny in South America has lasted over 100 Ma. It comprises the Peruvian, Incaic and Quechuan phases. The Nazca and South American plates have been converging at varying rates since the Palaeocene. The active tectonics of South America are relatively clear, from seismological and Global Positioning System (GPS) data. Horizontal shortening is responsible for a thick crust and high topography in the Andes, as well as in SE Brazil and Patagonia. We have integrated available data and have compiled four fault maps at the scale of South America, for the mid-Cretaceous, Late Cretaceous, Palaeogene and Neogene periods. Andean compression has been widespread since the Aptian. The continental margins have registered more deformation than the interior. For the Peruvian phase, not enough information is available to establish a tectonic context. During the Incaic phase, strike-slip faulting was common. During the Quechuan phase, crustal thickening has been the dominant mode of deformation. To investigate the mechanics of deformation, we have carried out 10 properly scaled experiments on physical models of the lithosphere, containing various plates. The dominant response to plate motion was subduction of oceanic lithosphere beneath continental South America. However, the model continent also deformed internally, especially at the margins and initial weaknesses.

The Andes extend for about 7000 km along the west coast of South America (Fig. 1). At this convergent plate margin, the Nazca Plate and other oceanic plates subduct beneath the continental part of the South American Plate. The most notable topographic features of the Andes are: (1) several peaks over 6000 m; (2) a wide central plateau (Altiplano–Puna); (3) strong bends to north and south of the plateau; (4) belts trending east–west at the northern and southern edges of South America. The last are transcurrent boundaries, where continental South America abuts oceanic micro-plates (Caribbean in the north, Scotia in the south).

The main cause of high altitude in the Andes is a thick crust. The Moho is abnormally deep beneath the Andes, reaching 70 km beneath the Altiplano (Wigger *et al.* 1994; Yuan *et al.* 2002). Elsewhere across South America, except on the continental shelf, the Moho is at normal or near-normal depth. Abnormal crustal thickness in the Andes is mainly due to east–west shortening, in response to rapid convergence at the Pacific margin. Magmatism is a secondary contributor to crustal thickness.

The average width and elevation of the Andes varies along strike, as does the amount of shortening. This variation correlates with changes in the dip and perhaps in the buoyancy of the subducting oceanic plates (Jordan *et al.* 1983; Gutscher *et al.* 2000; Gutscher 2002). Which is the cause and which is the consequence? How does the structural style vary along strike? Does it change gradually or suddenly? Does it correlate with oroclinal bending of the mountain belt (Isacks 1988)?

Further questions are about timing. Since when has shortening accumulated? Is it relatively

From: Ries, A. C., Butler, R. W. H. & Graham, R. H. (eds) 2007. *Deformation of the Continental Crust: The Legacy of Mike Coward.* Geological Society, London, Special Publications, **272**, 321–343.
0305-8719/07/$15

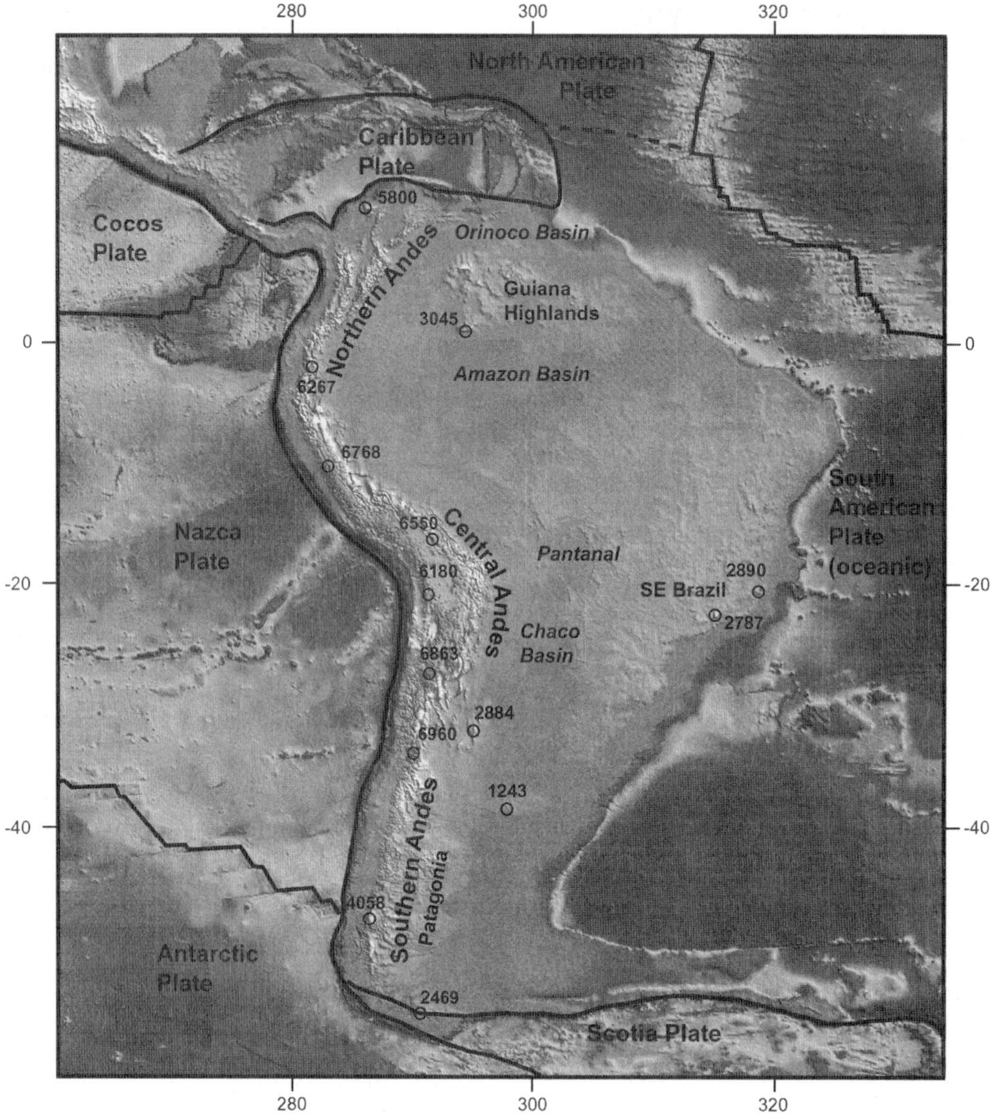

Fig. 1. Current topography of South America and surrounding tectonic plates. Spot heights are in metres. (Notice altitudes over 6000 m in Andes; close to 3000 m in Guiana Highlands and SE Brazil; and over 1000 m in Patagonia.) Background is shaded relief map of South America and surrounding ocean floor. This is not a map projection, but a 2D plot of latitude v. longitude.

recent, or does Andean deformation have a long history? Did it go through phases of increased activity?

A closer look at the topography of South America will show that high altitudes also occur well outside the Andes (Fig. 1). Over much of Patagonia, altitudes reach 1000 m. In the province of Buenos Aires, basement blocks reach 1243 m. In SE Brazil, a plateau rises eastward, reaching nearly 3000 m near the coast. The Guiana Highlands do reach 3000 m. Correspondingly, the Moho is anomalously deep in these areas, reaching 43 km beneath SE Brazil (see references given by Cobbold *et al.* 2001) and 46 km beneath the Guiana Plateau (Schmitz *et al.* 2002). Between the highlands are large depressions, almost at sea level. What causes such anomalous values of altitude and crustal thickness? Could it be Andean compression? Why do the anomalies occur in specific places?

The current paper follows the outline of a previous talk (Cobbold *et al.* 1996). However, it includes more data. We consider first the plate-tectonic context of South America. Next we summarize the active deformation, according to recent geophysical and geological investigations. Then we discuss the history of deformation. We consider areas where the quality of exposure is good at the surface, or where the petroleum industry has acquired subsurface data. The best constraints on the style and timing of deformation come from sedimentary basins, where strata have accumulated over long periods of time and ages are unequivocal. Two outstanding but neglected examples are the Atacama Basin of northern Chile and the Neuquén Basin of western Argentina. Good data also come from the passive margin of SE Brazil and from the Eastern Cordillera of Colombia. On the strength of these and other data, we have compiled new fault maps for Andean deformation at the scale of South America. Finally, we have resorted to physical modelling, as a way of explaining some of our observations.

Plate tectonics

The South American Plate is partly continental and partly oceanic (Fig. 1). On all sides, except in Central America, the surrounding plates are oceanic. Currently, the Nazca, Cocos and Caribbean plates all subduct beneath continental South America. Since the Late Cretaceous, this scenario has not changed very much, except that the Nazca and Cocos plates appeared at 23.4 Ma, by splitting of the Farallon Plate (see Tebbins & Cande 1997), and that the ridges between adjacent oceanic plates have migrated northwards with respect to South America (Nürnberg & Müller 1991). A more significant complication has been collision with Central America, which started in the Miocene. Almost certainly, the main causes of Andean Orogeny were, and continue to be, rapid convergence between the Nazca and South American plates and thermal weakening of the crust above the subduction zone (Isacks 1988). At the Caribbean and Scotian margins, convergence and transcurrent motions have introduced significant local complexities. However, there is no evidence that any continent, other than Central America, has collided with South America since the Late Cretaceous.

A factor that is less easy to take into account is plate motion with respect to an underlying fixed mantle. Silver *et al.* (1998) have suggested that westward motion of South America induces a significant drag at the base of the lithosphere and therefore modifies the balance of horizontal forces. However, the possible consequences of this model for Andean Orogeny remain to be explored.

Convergence at the Pacific margin was faster than usual during the Eocene and late Miocene and this may explain the Incaic and Quechua phases of the Andean Orogeny (Pardo-Casas & Molnar 1987; Somoza 1998). Unfortunately, plate reconstructions are less precise for earlier periods, because oceanic crust of that age has been subducted and its magnetic anomalies are not available for study (Nürnberg & Müller 1991).

Current deformation

Stress

The World Stress Map is a global compilation of contemporary tectonic stress data. The stress maps are available online (Reinecker *et al.* 2004) and show the orientation of the greatest horizontal compressive stress (S_H). The data come from focal mechanisms of earthquakes, borehole breakouts and other reliable sources. For South America, the data come mainly from seismically active areas, including the Andes but also Brazil (Fig. 2). Unfortunately, data are sparse for Patagonia, although the area is seismically active.

In general, seismic activity is more widespread than the World Stress Map would suggest. This is because many earthquakes have not yielded reliable fault plane solutions. In South America, seismic activity is especially widespread, not only over the highlands, but also over many of the sedimentary basins and even the continental margins. Thus almost the entire continent is actively deforming in one way or another.

According to the World Stress Map, South America is dominantly undergoing thrust faulting, as a result of horizontal compression. Overall, S_H is close to east–west and this would appear to reflect rapid convergence at the Pacific margin. However, in the NW and SE corners of South America, respectively, S_H trends NW–SE and NE–SW. These directions are compatible with strike-slip faulting at the northern and southern continental margins, and also with continuing collision of Central America (Pennington 1981). On a more local scale, in the forearc of the Andes and on their eastern slopes, S_H tends to be perpendicular to the main topographic scarps. Thus gravitational forces may contribute to the local state of horizontal compression.

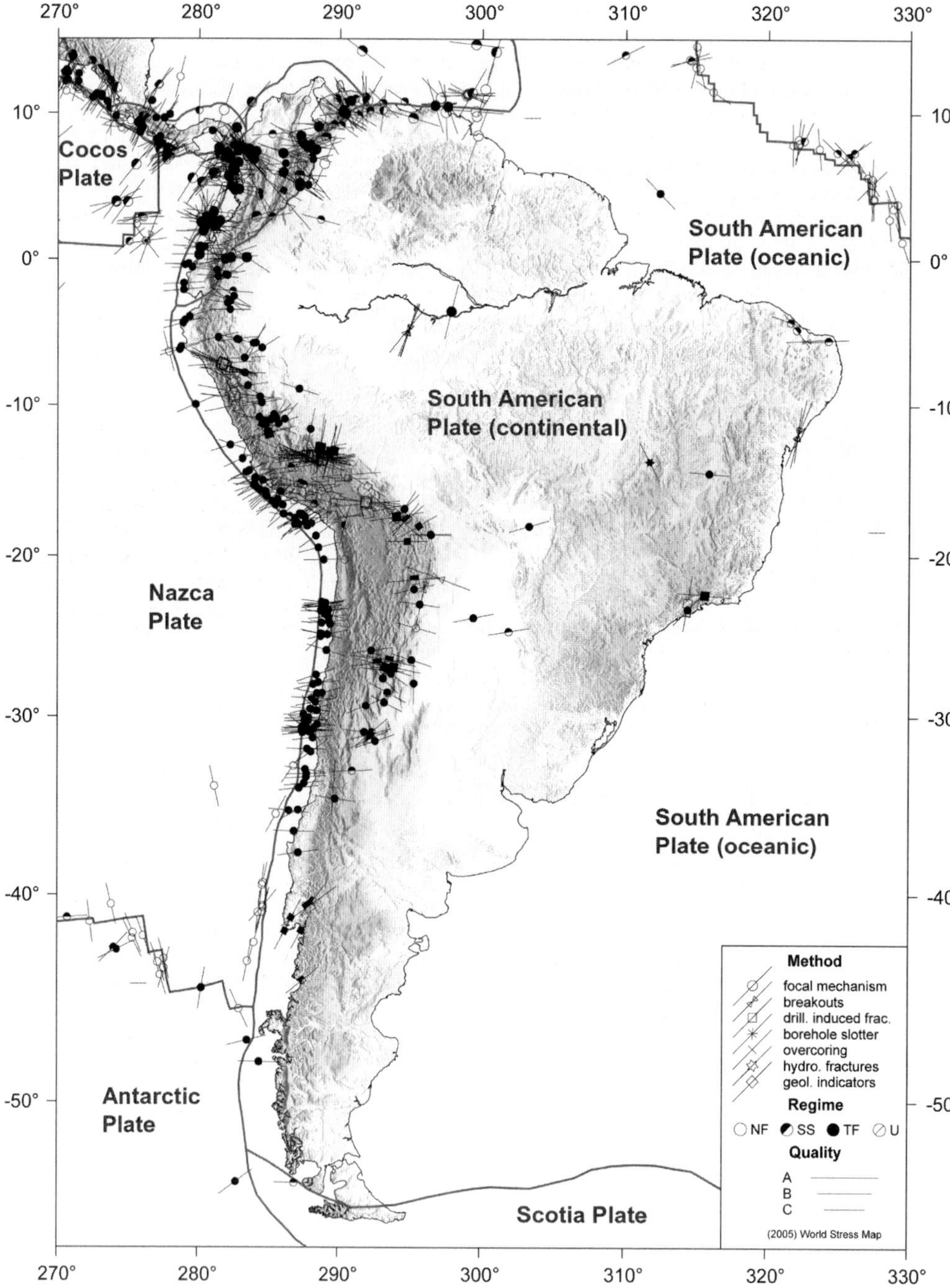

Fig. 2. Current stress in South America (World Stress Map, 2004 release, Reinecker *et al.* 2004). (Notice thrust faults (TF) over much of continent, strike-slip faults (SS) at northern and southern margins and normal faults (NF) in high Andes of Peru. Other faults are unclassified (U). Map projection is Mercator.

Thrust faulting also occurs in the highlands of SE Brazil and the Amazon Basin. Although not in the same database, data are available at regional scale for SE Brazil, including the offshore continental margin, where focal mechanisms indicate thrust faulting (Assumpção 1998). Thus it is reasonable to infer that at least part of the currently abnormal crustal thickness of SE Brazil is due to recent shortening and thickening (Cobbold *et al.* 2001).

Strike-slip faulting is common in NW South America, near the transcurrent boundary of the Caribbean Plate. Normal faulting occurs at the eastern end of this boundary. Normal faulting is also common in the high Andes of northern Peru, where S_H trends more nearly east–west.

GPS velocities

The Global Positioning System (GPS) has allowed measurements to be made of changes in position (displacements) over a period of several years. Where there is a displacement gradient, the problem is to know how much of the strain is elastic and how much is non-elastic or permanent.

The first data for South America, although subject to error, seemed to indicate that the Central Andes were shortening horizontally, whereas the foreland was not (Norabuena *et al.* 1998). Updated results, part of SNAPP (South America–Nazca Plate motion Project; World Wide Web Address: http://www.earth.northwestern.edu/research/snapp.html), are similar (Fig. 3). Like S_H in the World Stress Map (Fig. 2), GPS velocity vectors trend broadly east–west (Fig. 3). However, recent surveys seem to indicate that only a small portion of the GPS signal is due to permanent deformation (O. Heidbach, pers. comm.). Following major earthquakes at Antofagasta (1995) and Arequipa (June 2001), a large part of the strain recovered and was presumably elastic. Thus longer-term observations would appear to be necessary.

A separate dataset is available for the NW corner of South America (Trenkamp *et al.* 2002). Relative to stable South America, the NW corner is moving to the NE, causing a combination of shortening and strike-slip motion.

Palaeomagnetic data

Palaeomagnetic data have shown that the curvature of the Central Andes is mainly due to deformation; in other words, that it is an orocline (Randall 1998, and references therein; Coutand *et al.* 1999*b*; Roperch *et al.* 2000; Lamb 2001; Arriagada *et al.* 2003; Gilder *et al.* 2003; Rousse *et al.* 2003; Richards *et al.* 2004). This is an important fact, which helps us to understand how deformation has accumulated in the highest and widest part of the Andes. Because the curvature of the Andes coincides with that of the coastline, it may be that oroclinal bending is responsible for both features.

We have synthesized the available data in the form of four maps (Fig. 4), showing the amount of rotation for rocks in four age groups: Neogene, Palaeogene, Mesozoic and Palaeozoic. A simple pattern emerges, in which rotations are clockwise in the southern part of the central Andes and counter-clockwise in the northern part. We infer that (1) oroclinal bending has occurred since the Cretaceous, and (2) the older the rocks, the larger is the amount of rotation. In other words, oroclinal bending has accumulated progressively since the Cretaceous.

For the modern forearc of northern Chile and southern Peru, the palaeomagnetic data show that most of the rotation occurred before the Neogene, and probably in the Eocene (Arriagada *et al.* 2003). If further data bear out this conclusion, it has to be accepted that the Central Andes have a long history and that Neogene deformation is no more than a final, and perhaps small, fraction of it.

Fault maps

We have compiled four diagrammatic maps, summarizing the style and timing of deformation across continental South America (Figs 5–8). The maps have not been compiled accurately using, for example, a geographical information system. Instead they are schematic, and should be considered as illustrations or reviews of current knowledge.

The maps are labelled (1) mid-Cretaceous, (2) Late Cretaceous, (3) Palaeogene, and (4) Neogene. For the purposes of this paper, these names will be used informally, to represent (1) the Aptian to Albian, (2) the Cenomanian to Maastrichtian, (3) the Palaeocene to Oligocene, and (4) the Miocene to Recent. The last three maps encompass the Peruvian, Incaic and Quechua phases of Andean Orogeny, as defined by Steinmann (1929). In his view, these phases were relatively well-defined and separate events. However, there is some evidence that compressional basins have been forming intermittently since the Late Cretaceous (Noblet *et al.* 1996).

The quality and abundance of our fault data are not even. On the Neogene map, fault traces are relatively abundant in the highlands, where outcrop is of good quality, and in the

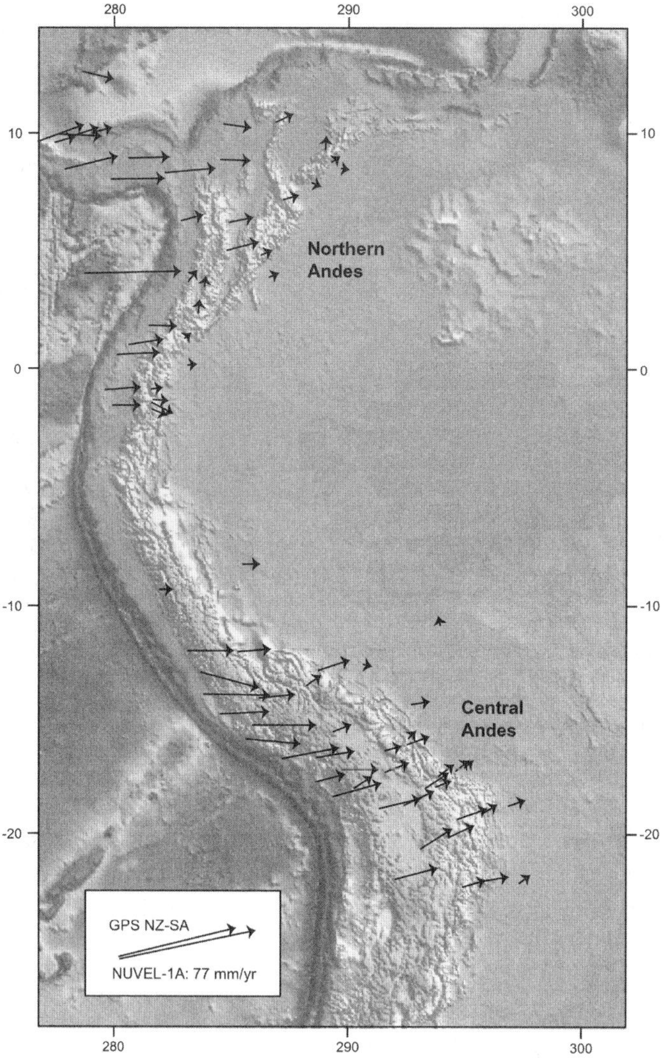

Fig. 3. Current GPS velocities in Central and Northern Andes. Reference values (bottom left) are for velocity of Nazca Plate with respect to South America, according to GPS measurements and plate model NUVEL-1A. Background is shaded relief map of South America and surrounding ocean floor. This is not a map projection, but a 2D plot of latitude v. longitude.

sedimentary basins, where petroleum exploration has been active (Fig. 5). On the other three maps, fault traces are sparse. However, that does not necessarily mean that pre-Neogene deformation was less intense. An absence of data may simply reflect the age of the rocks. In the foreland, old rocks have subsided beneath more recent sediment. In the mountains, they have undergone uplift and exhumation. In general, the older the deformation, the poorer is the remaining evidence.

Neogene (Fig. 5)

On the Neogene map, reverse faults dominate. Most of them are in the Andes, where they tend to coincide with current topographic scarps. We infer that the mountains have been through a period of uplift in the Neogene, as a result of crustal shortening and thickening.

(1) In the Central Andes, the dominant fault vergence is eastward in the eastern Sub-Andes, and westward on the western sides of the Eastern

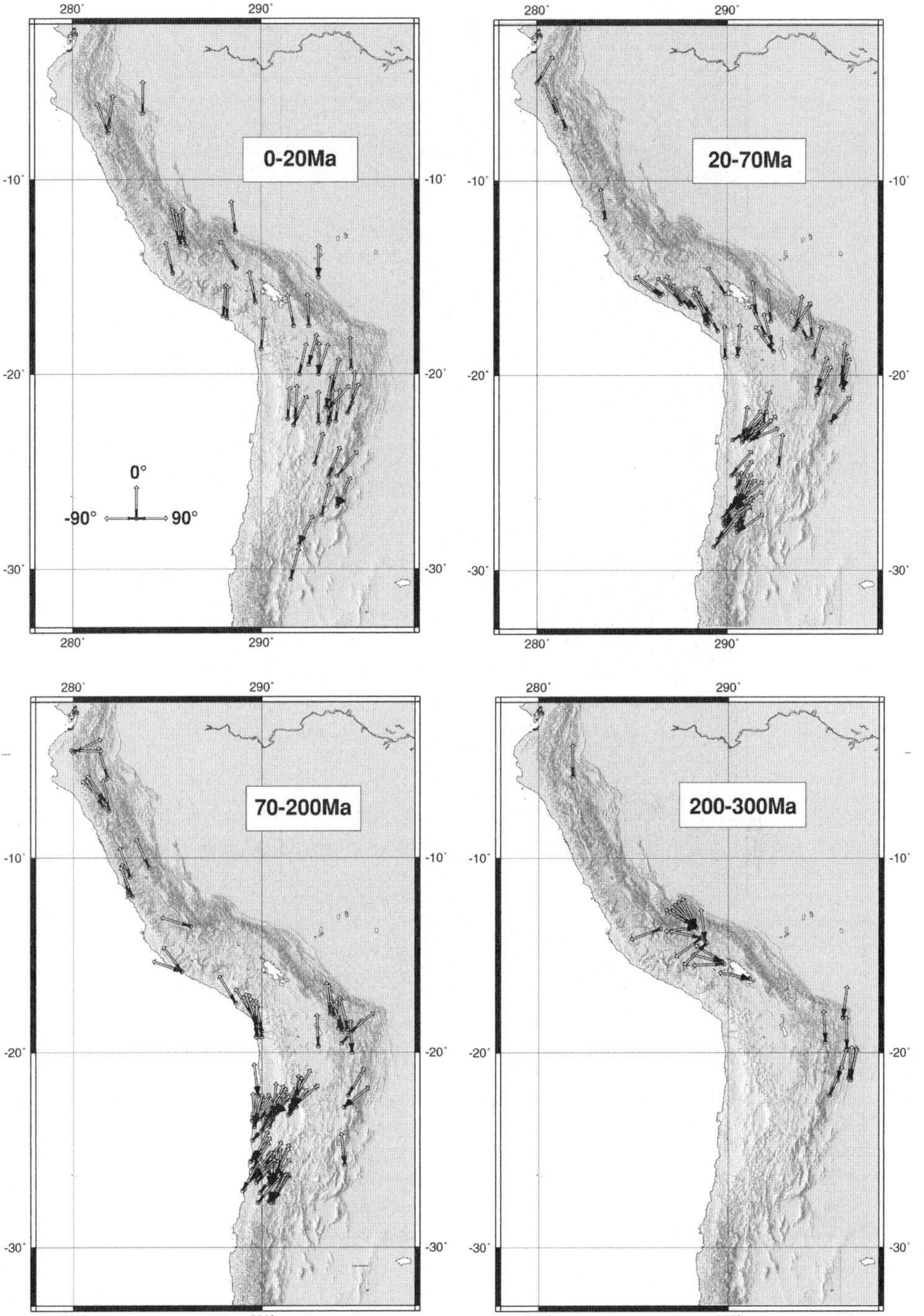

Fig. 4. Tectonic rotations in Central and Peruvian Andes. Data are from Randall (1998) and more recent publications (Coutand *et al.* 1999; Roperch *et al.* 2000; Lamb 2001; Arriagada *et al.* 2003; Gilder *et al.* 2003; Rousse *et al.* 2003; Richards *et al.* 2004). Rotations (open arrows) and their error ranges (black triangular sectors) are with respect to current north. Senses of rotation (clockwise in south, counter-clockwise in north) may explain trends of Andes and coastline. For Mesozoic and Cenozoic host rocks, magnitude of rotation increases with age (in Ma, white boxes). This is not a map projection, but a 2D plot of latitude v. longitude.

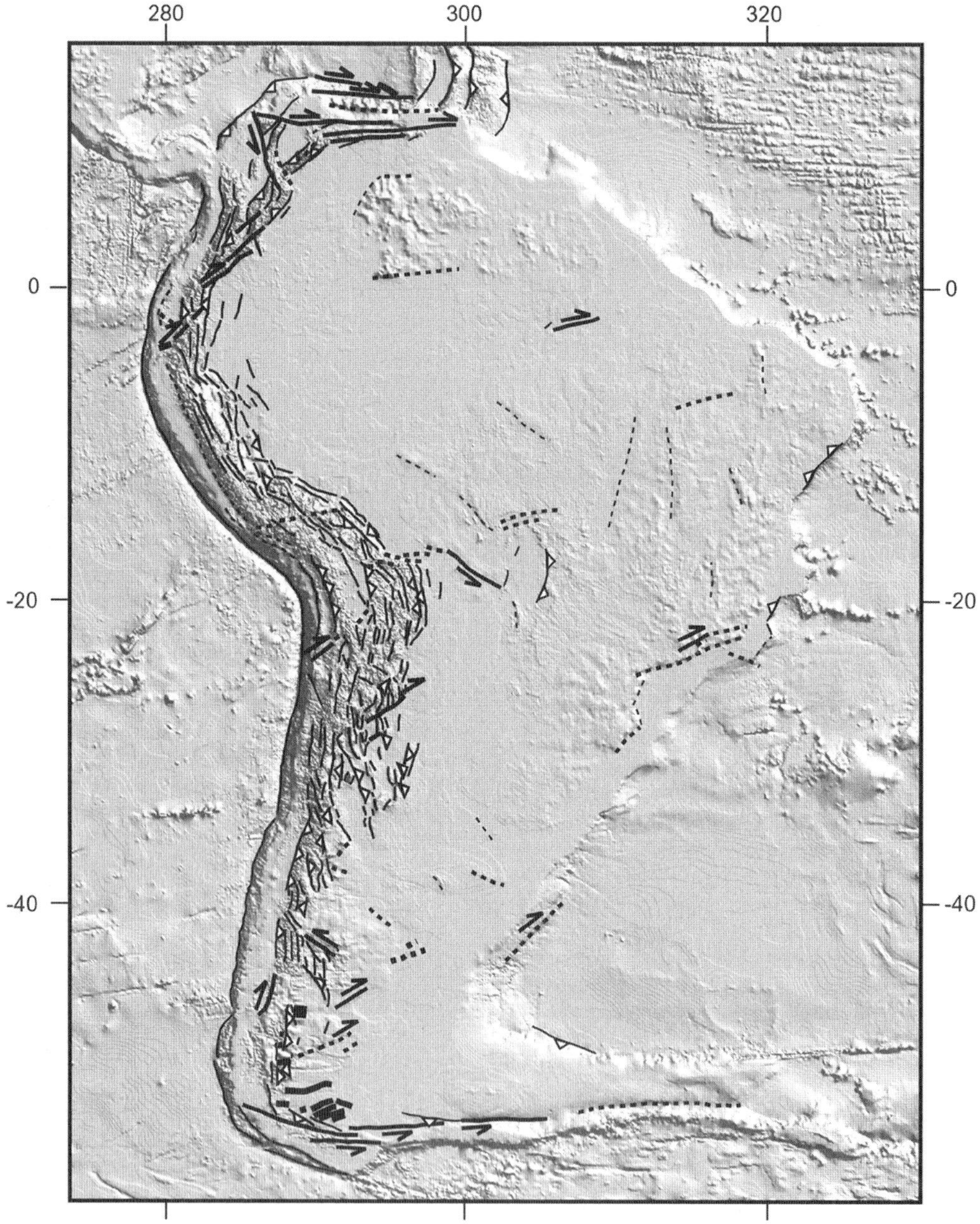

Fig. 5. Neogene faults. Fault categories are (1) dominantly reverse (fine lines, triangles pointing down dip), (2) dominantly strike-slip (bolder lines, arrows indicating sense) and (3) dominantly normal (boldest lines). Dashed lines indicate less confidence than continuous lines. (For sources of data, see text.) Background is shaded relief map of South America and surrounding ocean floor. This is not a map projection, but a 2D plot of latitude v. longitude.

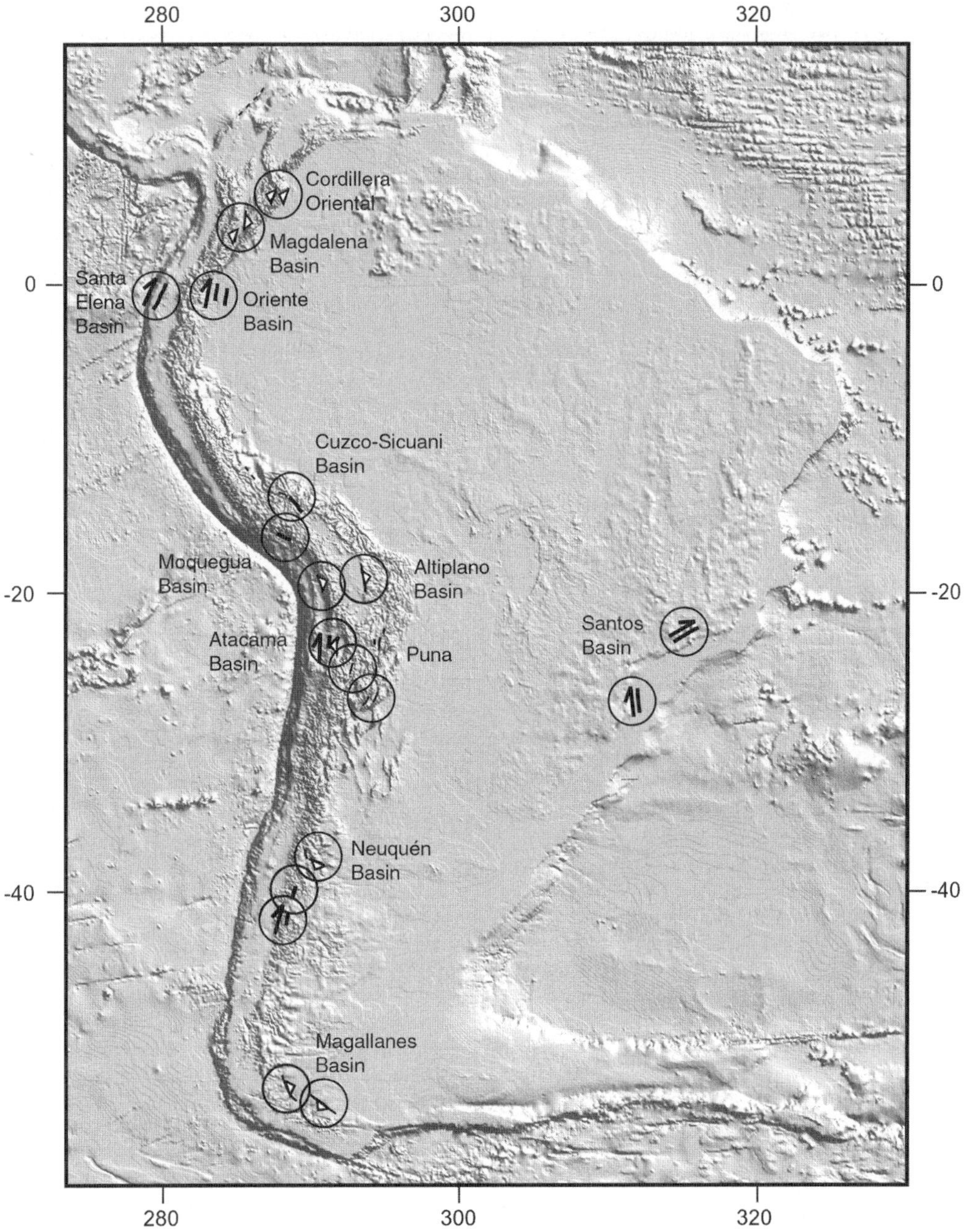

Fig. 6. Palaeogene faults. Circles draw attention to documented localities. Fault categories are (1) dominantly reverse (fine lines, triangles pointing down dip), (2) dominantly strike-slip (bolder lines, arrows indicating sense) and (3) dominantly normal (boldest lines). Dashed lines indicate less confidence than continuous lines. (For sources of data, see text.) Background is shaded relief map of South America and surrounding ocean floor. This is not a map projection, but a 2D plot of latitude v. longitude.

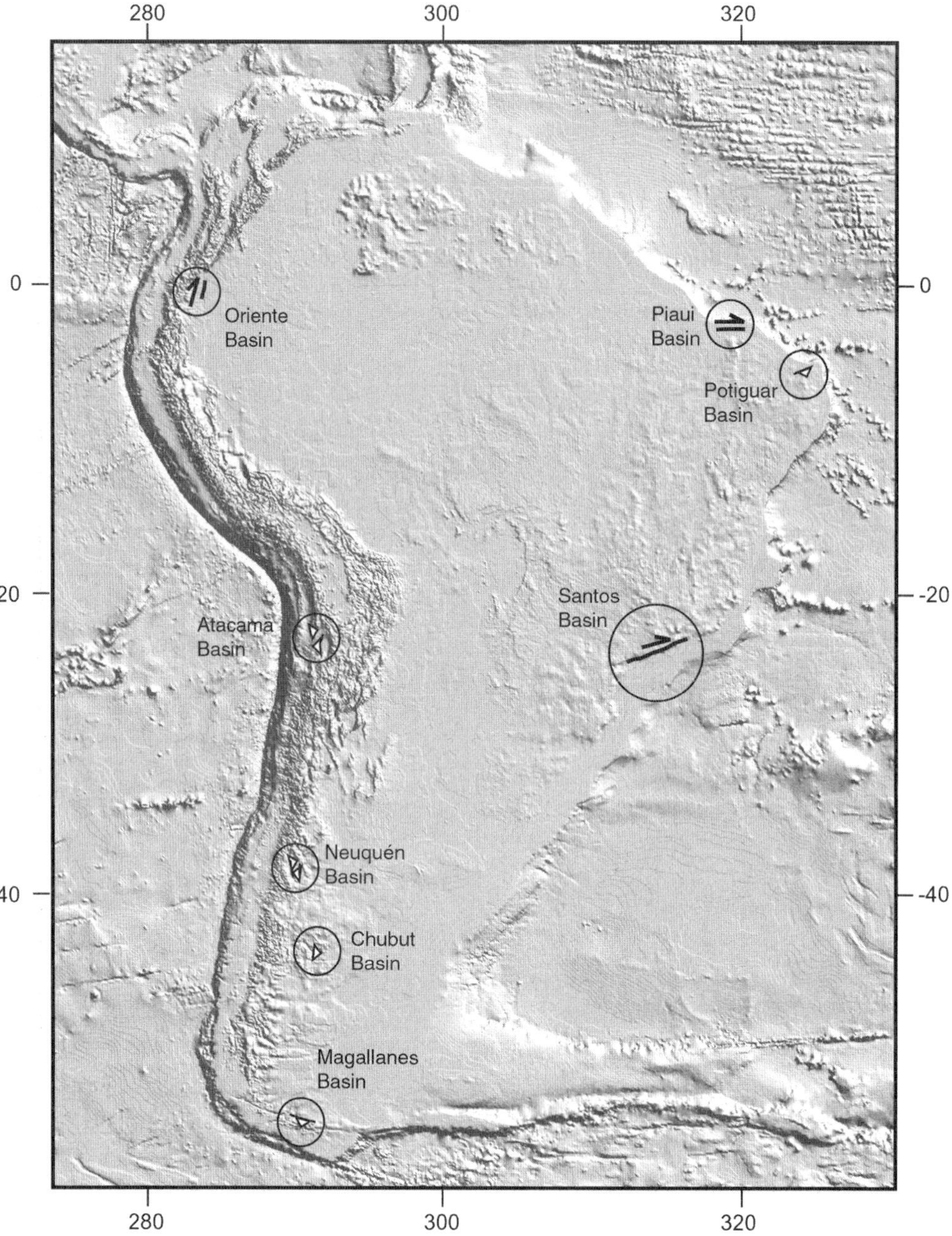

Fig. 7. Late Cretaceous faults. Circles draw attention to documented localities. Fault categories are (1) dominantly reverse (fine lines, triangles pointing down dip), (2) dominantly strike-slip (bolder lines, arrows indicating sense) and (3) dominantly normal (boldest lines). Dashed lines indicate less confidence than continuous lines. (For sources of data, see text.) Background is shaded relief map of South America and surrounding ocean floor. This is not a map projection, but a 2D plot of latitude v. longitude.

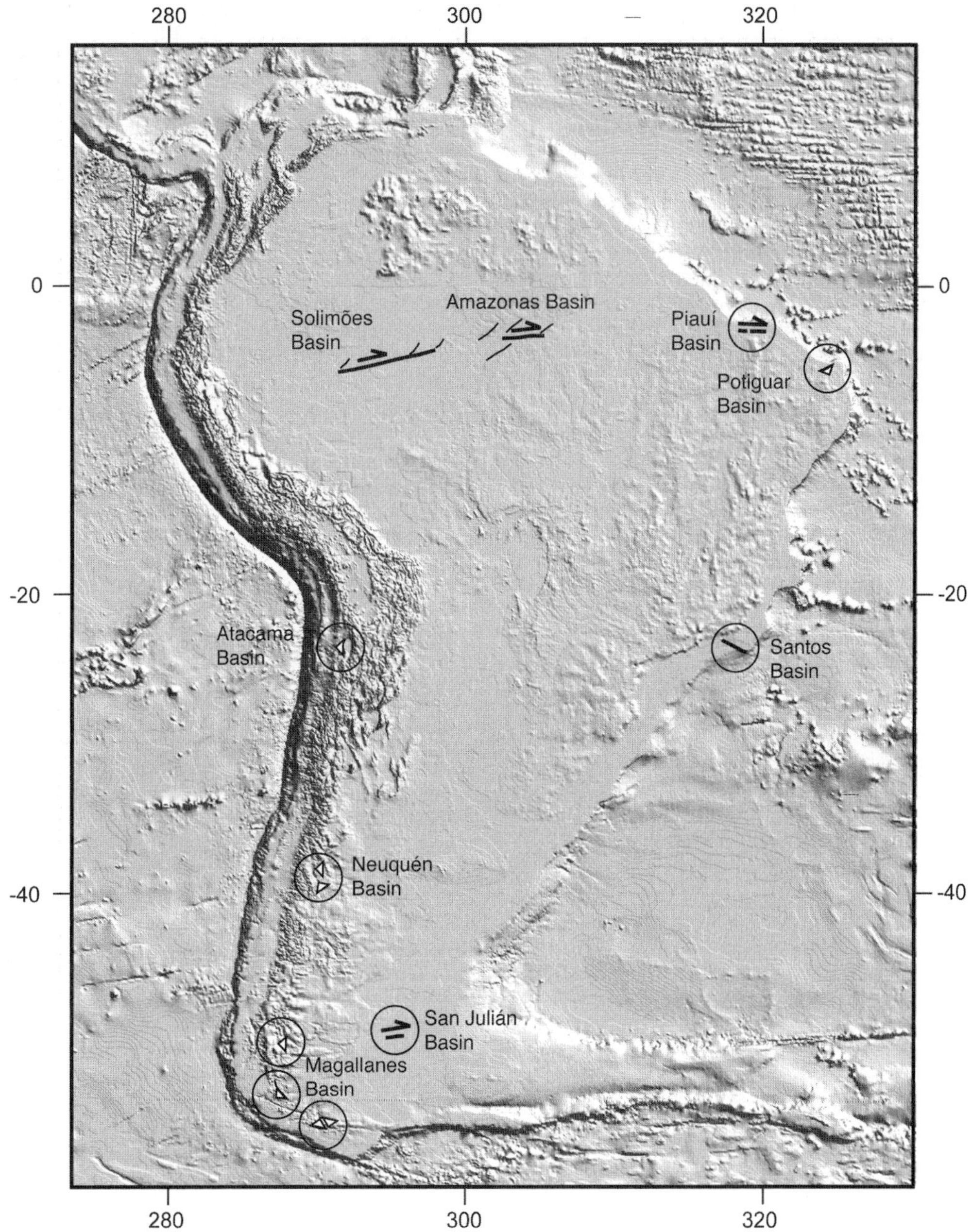

Fig. 8. Mid-Cretaceous faults. Circles draw attention to documented localities. Fault categories are (1) dominantly reverse (fine lines, triangles pointing down dip), (2) dominantly strike-slip (bolder lines, arrows indicating sense) and (3) dominantly normal (boldest lines). Dashed lines indicate less confidence than continuous lines. (For sources of data, see text.) Background is shaded relief map of South America and surrounding ocean floor. This is not a map projection, but a plot of latitude v. longitude.

Cordillera (Allmendinger *et al.* 1997; Baby *et al.* 1997; Müller *et al.* 2002; Echavarria *et al.* 2003) and Western Cordillera (Muñoz & Charrier 1996). Thus the Eastern Cordillera is the surface expression of a large crustal pop-up. Between the Eastern and Western cordilleras is the Altiplano Basin, which went through a late stage of development in the Neogene (Lamb & Hoke 1997; Lamb *et al.* 1997; Rochat *et al.* 1999). The main reverse faults of the Central Andes are deep-seated, but they branch upward into thin-skinned structures, especially in the Sub-Andes. The westward vergence of the Eastern Cordillera is inherited from the Late Palaeozoic, when crustal thickening was also active (Müller *et al.* 2002). Cleaved Ordovician slates are overlain unconformably by Cretaceous redbeds, which themselves were deformed in Palaeogene and Neogene times. Also inherited in part, from the shape of a Palaeozoic basin, is the arcuate form of the Sub-Andes (Baby *et al.* 1996).

(2) Across the high plateau (Puna) of NW Argentina, reverse faults lie between alternating ranges and basins (Allmendinger *et al.* 1997; Coutand *et al.* 2001).

(3) Reverse faults also bound most of the uplifted basement blocks in the Pampean ranges of NW Argentina (Allmendinger *et al.* 1983; Jordan & Allmendinger 1986; de Urreiztieta *et al.* 1996). Again, the dominant vergence is westward. In the southern ranges, the reverse faults have formed by reactivation of Early Cretaceous rift basins (Schmidt *et al.* 1995; Webster *et al.* 2004).

(4) In Peru and Ecuador, reverse faults are the main structural features of the cordilleras and Sub-Andes (Mathalone & Montoya 1995; Steinmann *et al.* 1999; Gil Rodríguez *et al.* 2001; Hermoza *et al.* 2005).

(5) Reverse faults are common beneath Neogene strata of the retro-arc foreland basin in Ecuador (Baby *et al.* 1999) and northern Peru (Gil Rodríguez *et al.* 2001), where they have formed by right-lateral transpressional reactivation of Mesozoic normal faults.

(6) The High Andes of west–central Argentina and central Chile are mainly due to reverse faulting of Neogene age (Ramos *et al.* 1996).

(7) Reverse faults occur in and around the Pantanal Basin of western Brazil (Milani *et al.* 1990), near the geographical centre of South America.

(8) The Guiana highlands are seismically active and the crust is thick, but whether or not this is due to Neogene shortening remains something of a mystery.

(9) The cordilleras of Colombia and Venezuela are mainly crustal pop-ups, which have formed by reactivation of Mesozoic rift basins, in a context of right-lateral transpression (Colletta *et al.* 1990, 1997; Taboada *et al.* 2000; Branquet *et al.* 2002).

(10) Transpression also explains the recent altitudes and scarps on the Atlantic margin of Brazil (Cobbold *et al.* 2001). Active fault traces line the Taubaté Rift and the River Paraíba do Sul, as far as the coast. In the Taubaté Rift, Neogene wrenching has folded and faulted Oligocene lacustrine strata.

(11) In Patagonia, reverse and strike-slip faults of Neogene age have been described in the Andes (Ramos 1989; Cembrano *et al.* 1996; Diraison *et al.* 1998), and recent faults are visible on published geological maps and satellite images of the foreland.

(12) Strike-slip faults prevail at the southern and northern edges of South America, which are transcurrent plate boundaries. At the northern edge the motion is right-lateral (Kellogg *et al.* 1985; Trenkamp *et al.* 2002), whereas at the southern edge it is left-lateral (Cunningham 1993; Diraison *et al.* 2000).

(13) In the Amazon Basin of Brazil, Neogene strike-slip faulting has reactivated a Palaeozoic rift (Mossman *et al.* 1984). The faults trend east–west as far as the margin, where they run into seismically active oceanic fracture zones.

(14) Normal faults along the Magellan Strait indicate that the island of Tierra del Fuego has been separating from mainland Patagonia and that the principal compression is NE–SW (Diraison *et al.* 1997, 2000). Normal faults also occur to the north, as far as Lago General Carrera in Chile, where they coincide with the subducted East Chile Rise (Lagabrielle *et al.* 2004).

(15) The Gulf of Guayaquil is a pull-apart basin, containing some 5000 m of Plio-Pleistocene strata (Deniaud *et al.* 1999). Normal faults, reverse faults and strike-slip faults form a horsetail splay at the SW end of the Dolores–Guayaquil Megashear, which coincides with a sharp bend in the Andes and adjacent coastline.

Palaeogene (Fig. 6)

(1) In the Central Andes, reverse faults of Palaeogene age were active in the forearc of Peru (Noblet *et al.* 1996) and northern Chile (Arriagada *et al.* 2002, 2006), in the Altiplano Basin and Cordillera Oriental of Bolivia (Lamb & Hoke 1997; Lamb *et al.* 1997; Müller *et al.* 2002), and in several intramontane basins of the high plateau (Puna) of NW Argentina (Coutand *et al.* 2001; Carrapa *et al.* 2005). Horton (2005) has identified a formerly widespread foredeep, in which middle Eocene to Oligocene strata accumulated during a period of significant shortening to the west. Such a distribution indicates that

the Andes have propagated eastward since the Palaeocene (McQuarrie *et al.* 2005).

(2) In the Western Cordillera of central Peru, the Incaic phase of deformation resulted in folds and reverse faults, which are overlain in regional unconformity by well-dated Eocene strata and volcanic rocks (Steinmann 1929; Noble *et al.* 1979, 1990).

(3) Reverse faults of Palaeogene age were active in the Oriente Basin of Ecuador (Christophoul *et al.* 2002), in the Eastern Cordillera of Colombia (Julivert 1963; De Freitas *et al.* 1997; Gómez 2003), and in the adjacent Magdalena Valley (Schamel 1991; Laumonier *et al.* 1996; Gómez *et al.* 2003).

(4) In Patagonia, there was thrusting and strike-slip faulting in the foothills of the Neuquén Basin (Cobbold & Rossello 2003) and in the Magallanes foreland basin (Ramos 1989; Alvarez-Marrón *et al.* 1993; Diraison *et al.* 2000; Ghiglione & Ramos 2005).

(5) In SE Brazil, older structures underwent transpressional reactivation in the Palaeogene (Cobbold *et al.* 2001).

Late Cretaceous (Fig. 7)

(1) In the Central Andes, reverse faults of Late Cretaceous age controlled subsidence of a foreland basin, now the Atacama Basin in the forearc of northern Chile (Arriagada *et al.* 2002, 2006; Mpodozis *et al.* 2005). Reverse faults also appeared in the Copiapó area, inverting earlier Mesozoic rifts (Mpodozis & Allmendinger 1993).

(2) Reverse faults were active in the Oriente Basin of Ecuador (Baby *et al.* 1999).

(3) In the Neuquén Basin of northern Patagonia, thrusting led to regional subsidence in a continental foreland basin, where redbeds accumulated (Cobbold & Rossello 2003). The same association occurs further south, in the Chubut Basin.

(4) In the southernmost Andes, thrust tectonics caused regional subsidence in the Magallanes foreland basin and simultaneous uplift of metamorphic rocks in Cordillera Darwin (Dalziel & Palmer 1979; Nelson *et al.* 1980; Winslow 1982; Klepeis 1994; Coutand *et al.* 1999*a*; Diraison *et al.* 2000; Ghiglione & Ramos 2005).

(5) In SE Brazil, the coastal ranges underwent uplift and exhumation (Cobbold *et al.* 2001).

(6) On the Atlantic margin of NE Brazil, there were phases of transpressional deformation in the Piauí Basin (Zalán *et al.* 1985) and in the Potiguar Basin.

Mid-Cretaceous (Fig. 8)

Although for many years the mid-Cretaceous was seen as a period of rifting or passive subsidence, evidence is accumulating for an onset of compressional deformation in the Aptian.

(1) Growth strata from the Neuquén Basin (Cobbold & Rossello 2003) and the Atacama Basin (Arriagada *et al.* 2002, 2006; Mpodozis *et al.* 2005) point clearly to a context of shortening and thickening. In both basins, transitional evaporites and continental redbeds overlie marine strata that accumulated in a rift setting during the Jurassic and Early Cretaceous.

(2) In what is now the Coastal Range of central Chile, ductile shortening occurred during the mid-Cretaceous (Arancibia 2004).

(3) In the Magallanes Basin, the earliest phase of uplift, erosion and formation of a foreland basin was of mid-Cretaceous age (Winslow 1982; Diraison *et al.* 2000).

(4) In the San Julián Basin, offshore southern Patagonia, an Early Cretaceous rift basin became strongly inverted, folded and faulted under Aptian transpression (Homovc & Constantini 2001).

(5) The same can be said for SE and NE Brazil, where compressional reactivation of the continental margin started shortly after the formation of an Aptian break-up unconformity (Cobbold *et al.* 2001; Meisling *et al.* 2001).

(6) The Amazon Basin, which formed in a rift setting during the Palaeozoic, went through a phase of strong wrenching (Szatmari 1983), sometime between the Early Jurassic and the Cenomanian, but most probably in the mid-Cretaceous. Right-lateral wrenching acted along the Amazon Basin (Caputo 1991), while, in the nascent Equatorial Atlantic, Africa was pulling away in a right-lateral sense from South America. The wrenching was responsible for strike-slip faults, reverse faults, and large folds, which uplifted the Precambrian basement. Redbeds of Albian to Cenomanian age are unconformable upon it.

Summary

The amount of available data decreases according to its geological age, but otherwise the four fault maps are broadly similar.

(1) All show reverse faulting in the Central Andes.

(2) All show reverse faulting in Patagonia.

(3) All show compressional or transpressional reactivation in SE Brazil.

(4) All show strike-slip faulting in the southernmost Andes.

(5) Two of them show strike-slip faulting in the northernmost Andes.

(6) Two of them show strike-slip reactivation of the Amazon rift.

(7) Two of them show compressional reactivation in NE Brazil.

The most obvious differences are as follows.

(1) Neogene deformation is strongest in the Central Andes.

(2) Palaeogene deformation is prevalent in the Northern, Central and Southern Andes.

(3) Cretaceous deformation appears to be prevalent in southern, eastern and central South America (as far north as Ecuador).

The last statement should be qualified, because it may reflect the availability of data. Otherwise, one is struck by the almost ubiquitous nature of compressional deformation throughout South America since the mid-Cretaceous. This makes sense, in that the mid-Cretaceous was a period of plate reorganization, following the opening of the South Atlantic (Nürnberg & Müller 1991). Ever since then, one would expect ridge push to have been active in the South Atlantic, as well as in the Pacific, keeping South America in a state of generalized compression.

Because the four fault maps are for periods when faulting appears to have been unusually active, the intervening periods remain somewhat of a mystery. One such period is the Oligocene. It has been suggested that the Oligocene was a time of normal faulting in SW South America (Jordan *et al.* 2001; Pananont *et al.* 2004). This is a subject of intense interest and debate.

That compression caused shortening and thickening in the Andes is understandable, if a high heat flow was responsible for softening, but why did deformation occur repeatedly in other areas, such as SE Brazil or the Amazon Basin? Was it simply that these areas were crustal weaknesses, prone to reactivation, or did they respond to stress concentrations, resulting from conditions at the irregular boundaries of South America?

Physical models

To obtain some insights into the mechanics of deformation at the scale of South America, 10 experiments on physical models were carried out at Géosciences-Rennes in 1992 and 1994. They followed earlier work during which limited subduction of oceanic lithosphere had been observed in physical models (Pinet & Cobbold 1992; Pubellier & Cobbold 1996) and they served as a template for experiments on subduction that were performed later at Géosciences-Rennes (Faccenna *et al.* 1996). However, the work on South America was not published at the time, because it seemed premature. Here two of the experiments are described (Figs 9 and 10). We do not pretend that they reproduce faithfully what has occurred in South America, but we believe that they provide some insights into potential mechanisms of deformation at continental scale.

The model materials were (1) heavy sand (quartz sand from Fontainebleau, France), for the brittle oceanic crust; (2) light sand (a mixture of quartz sand and ethyl cellulose), for the brittle continental crust; (3) light silicone putty (Gomme GS1R, manufactured by Rhône-Poulenc), for the ductile continental crust; (4) heavy silicone (a mixture of light silicone and powdered galena), for the mantle lithosphere; (5) clear honey for the asthenosphere (Table 1). The models were properly scaled for gravitational forces (Table 2). The model ratio of length was 10^7. For further details of scaling and of the experimental technique, the reader may consult earlier publications (Davy & Cobbold 1988, 1991; Pinet & Cobbold 1992; Pubellier & Cobbold 1996).

The models were constructed and deformed within a square box, 110 cm wide and 30 cm deep. First, the box was filled with honey. Next, a layer of heavy silicone was floated onto it. Then, a patch of light silicone was added, to represent ductile continental crust. Finally, a layer of light or heavy sand completed the layering. A travelling trough poured the sand in thin layers of uniform thickness and a mask was used to obtain the required shape of the model continent.

To obtain transform boundaries within oceanic crust, the sand was siphoned off along narrow strips, so that the heavy silicone rose to the surface along them. To initiate subduction zones, thin strips of powdered bismuth sulphide were added at the surface.

Deformation was imposed by one or more mobile plates, which travelled horizontally at steady preset speeds, without touching the bottom of the box.

Experiment 1 (Fig. 9)

The objectives of this experiment were two. Would rapid subduction of oceanic lithosphere cause shortening of an adjacent continent? Would initial weaknesses within the continent lead to heterogeneous shortening?

For simplicity, the continent was initially rectangular and homogeneous, except for an initial zone of weakness, oblique to the margin, where sand was thinner (1 mm). The zone of weakness was meant to represent a pre-existing structure, such as one of the Mesozoic rifts of South America.

To encourage subduction, a thin strip of powdered bismuth sulphide was added to the free upper surface, at the edge of the oceanic lithosphere. Being heavy, the bismuth sulphide mimicked in a simple way the increase in weight

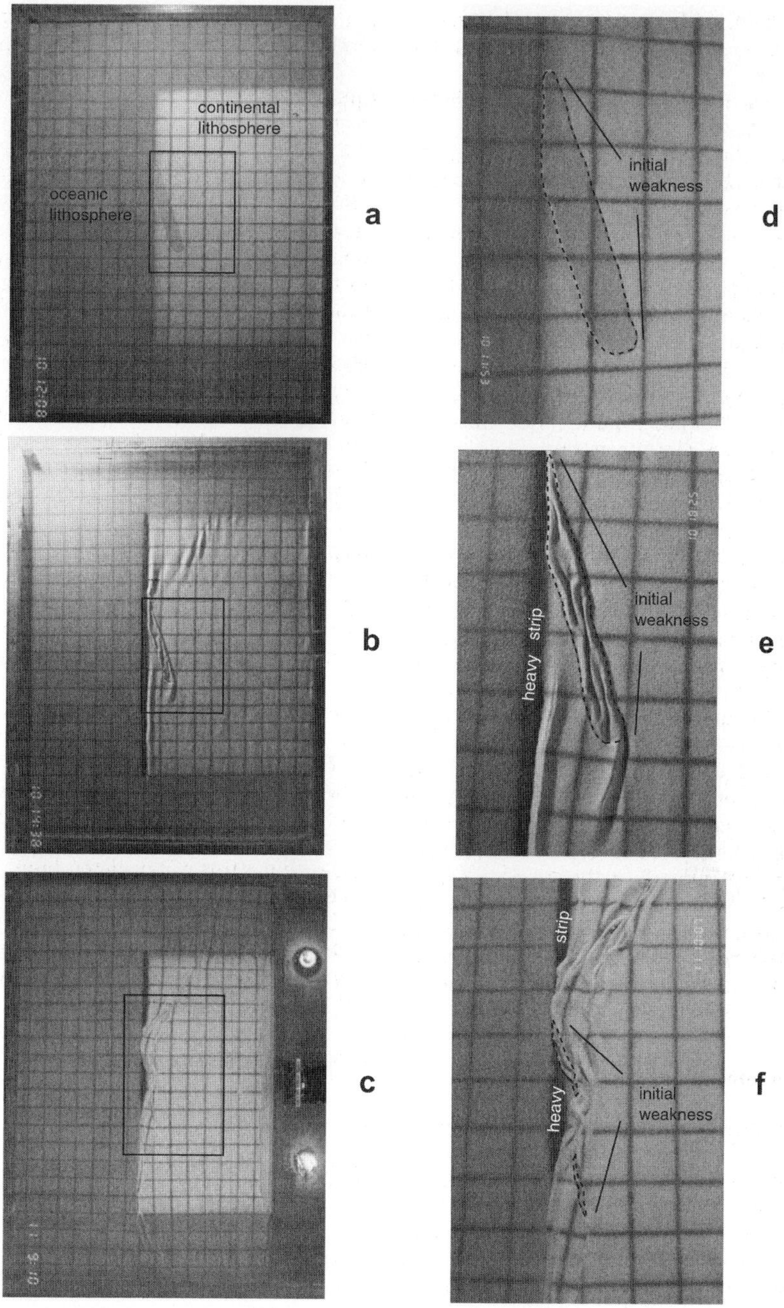

Fig. 9. Physical model of subduction and oroclinal bending. Photographs show the upper surface of the model, before deformation (**a**), after 2 h (**b**), and after 21.5 h (**c**). Initial spacing of grid lines (dark) was 5 cm. The continent (pale) was initially rectangular and homogeneous, except for an oblique zone of weakness (darker, dashed outline). Subduction of oceanic lithosphere (grey) was stimulated by adding a heavy strip of powdered bismuth sulphide (black) at the western edge of the continent. A single piston (right), advancing at 5 mm h^{-1}, caused compression and rapid subduction. Close-up views (**d**)–(**f**) of rectangular boxes shown in (**a**)–(**c**) show progressive deformation of the initial weakness and consequent oroclinal bending of the continental margin. The heavy strip underwent variable amount of subduction. The experiment was performed at Géosciences-Rennes on 10 June 1992 by E.A.R. and P.R.C.

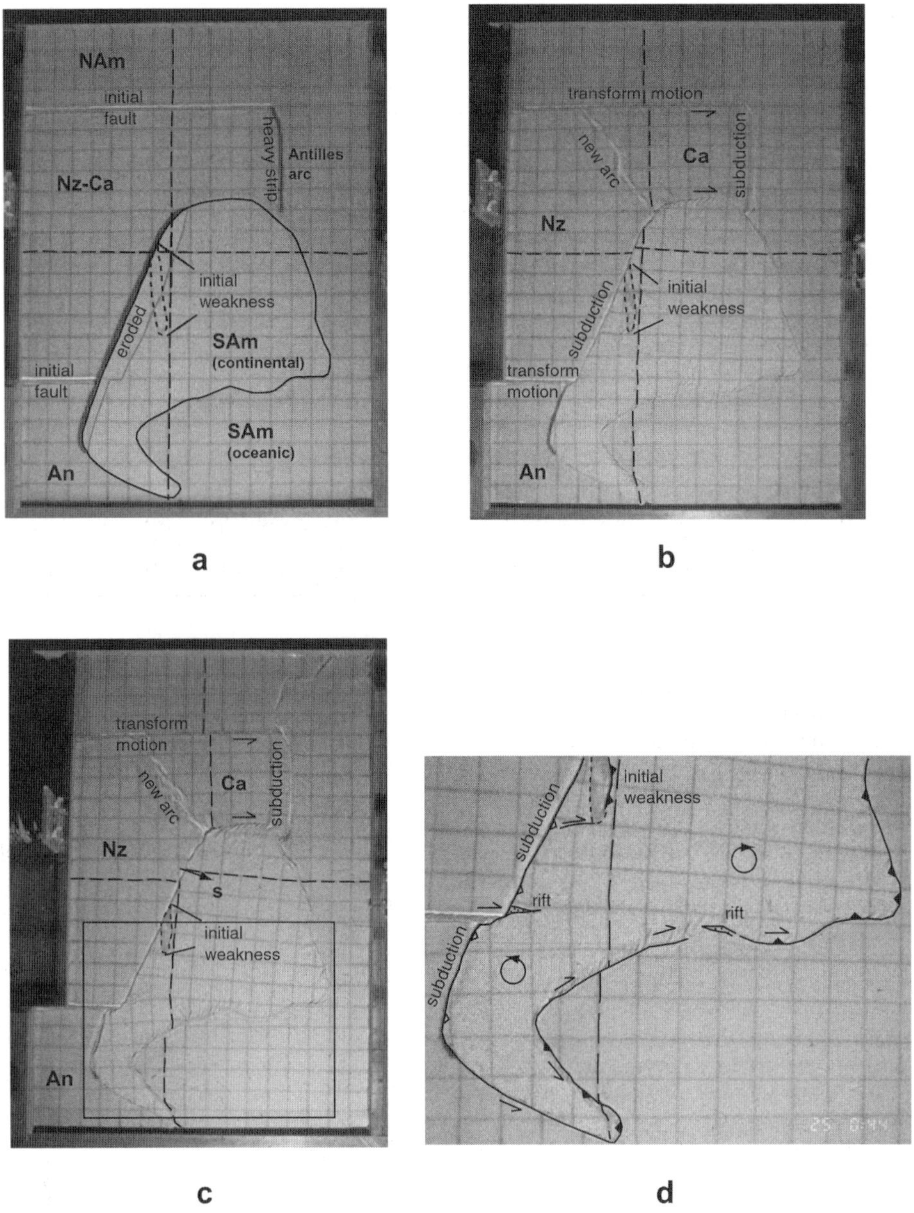

Fig. 10. Physical model of plate tectonics around South America. Photographs show upper surface of model, before deformation (**a**), after 6 h of deformation (**b**), and after 14 h (**c**). Initial spacing of grid lines (dark) was 5 cm. Reinforced markers (dashed lines) are for better interpretation. The continent (bottom centre) had the shape of South America (SAm) and was homogeneous, except for an initial weakness (dotted outline). Subduction of oceanic lithosphere was stimulated by adding heavy strips of powdered bismuth sulphide (black) at the western edge of continent and along the Antilles arc (**a**). Initial faults were made by siphoning off sand. One piston (top left), advancing at 5 mm h^{-1}, pushed the Nazca–Caribbean Plate (Nz-Ca) and North American Plate (NAm) eastward, but not the Antarctic Plate (An). A second piston (right) pushed all plates westward at 2.5 mm h^{-1}. Subducting Nazca Plate reached 7 cm under South America (continuous-line arrow, **c**). The edge of the continent became eroded (about 5 cm) by subduction (**a**). Transform motions accumulated on initial faults. Close-up (**d**) of the rectangular box in (**c**) shows details of deformation. Northern and southern parts of continental South America rotated clockwise and counter-clockwise, respectively. The experiment was performed at Géosciences-Rennes on 24 June 1994 by C.L., E.A.R. and P.R.C.

Table 1. *Physical properties of model materials*

Material	Density (g cm^{-3})	Viscosity (Pa s)	Cohesion (Pa)	Internal friction (deg.)	Thickness of continent (mm)	Thickness of ocean (mm)
Light sand	1.2		0	45	2	0
Heavy sand	1.5		50	45	0	3
Light silicone	1.16	10000			2	0
Heavy silicone	1.35	50000			4	4
Honey	1.37	100			200	200

Table 2. *Characteristic values and scaling*

System	Length (m)	Thickness (m)	Density (kg m^{-3})	Stress (Pa)	Viscosity (Pa s)	Strain rate (s^{-1})	Time (s)	Velocity (m s^{-1})
Nature	750E+04 (7500 km)	300E+02 (30 km)	300E+01	900E+06 (900 MPa)	100E+20	900E−16	111E+11 (0.35 Ma)	270E−11 (8.5 cm a^{-1})
Model	750E−03 (75 cm)	300E−05 (3 mm)	150E+01	450E−01 (45 Pa)	100E+02	450E−05	222E−00 (3.7 min)	135E-07 (5 mm h^{-1})
Ratio	100E+05	100E+05	200E−02	200E+05	100E+16	200E−13	500E+08	200E−06

that results from cooling and ageing of an oceanic lithosphere in nature.

Compression was applied at the eastern side of the continent (right, Fig. 9) by a plate sliding horizontally at 5 mm h^{-1}. Because of friction at lateral boundaries, the compressive stress was almost certainly greatest next to the piston. The plate velocity was much greater than the rate of rollback of the slab under its own weight. The experiment lasted 21.5 h (equivalent to 122 Ma in nature).

In the first stages of deformation, a thrust fault formed at the continental margin and the oceanic lithosphere started to subduct. However, after 2 h, subduction became irregular and the continent deformed (Fig. 9b). In particular, the initial weakness shortened and thickened (Fig. 9e). Another zone of deformation, marked by en echelon folds and thrusts, formed across the NW corner of the continent. Where the continent shortened, the oceanic plate subducted less. To north and south of the continent, subduction zones formed within the oceanic lithosphere.

As deformation accumulated in the zone of initial weakness, a large block to the south of it rotated clockwise, whereas areas to the north of it bent in oroclinal fashion (Fig. 9e and f). The final result was an asymmetrically sinuous margin, much like the west coast of South America. All this time, the adjacent oceanic lithosphere subducted, but did not deform internally, except by bending.

In conclusion, subduction initiated at the margin between continental and oceanic lithospheres, even though the greatest compression was on the other side of the continent. Rapid subduction resulted in deformation next to the convergent margin. The pattern of deformation reflected the mechanical heterogeneity of the continent. Large blocks rotated by slipping on the subduction zone, and the margin became asymmetrically curved.

Experiment 2 (Fig. 10)

The objective of this experiment was to investigate how a more realistic plate configuration might influence the pattern of continental deformation.

Initially, the continent had the true current shape of South America and it was homogeneous, except for an initial zone of weakness, oblique to the margin, where the sand was thinner (1 mm). As in the previous experiment, this zone of weakness was designed to represent a pre-existing structure, such as one of the Mesozoic rifts of South America. The surrounding oceanic lithosphere was divided into plates. The boundaries between them were created artificially.

To nucleate subduction, two thin strips of powdered bismuth sulphide were added to the free upper surface, (1) at the edge of the oceanic lithosphere, next to the western margin of the continent, and (2) across the oceanic lithosphere, to the north of the continent. The latter represented the convergent boundary (Antilles subduction zone) between the Caribbean and South American plates.

Two other faults were created within the oceanic lithosphere by siphoning off the sand, so that the underlying silicone rose to the surface. The faults represented the boundaries between (1) the Caribbean and North American plates and (2) the Nazca and Antarctic plates. The Nazca and Caribbean plates initially formed a single plate.

A rigid western sidewall pushed the Nazca–Caribbean Plate, and the strip to the north of it, at a velocity of 5 mm h^{-1} (equivalent to 8.5 cm a^{-1} in nature). The direction of motion was at about 80° to the continental margin (as occurs in South America today). This action simulated ridge push from the East Pacific Rise. Simultaneously, a rigid eastern sidewall pushed all the plates westward at a velocity of 2.5 mm h^{-1}, simulating ridge push from the Mid-Atlantic Rise. The experiment lasted 14 h (equivalent to 80 Ma in nature). As in the previous experiment, the plate velocities were greater than the rate of rollback of the slab under its own weight. Because of low shear strength, the artificial faults behaved as transform boundaries. Between them, compressive stress was probably almost uniform across the moving Nazca–Caribbean Plate.

In the first stages of deformation, thrust faults formed at the western margin of the continent and to the north of it. Immediately, the advancing oceanic lithosphere subducted. Bridging the gap between subduction zones, a transcurrent fault formed at the northern margin of the continent. After 2 h, a zone of thrusting and high topography, resembling Central America, appeared spontaneously within the moving oceanic plates. Subduction continued in the Antilles zone, but at about half the rate of subduction at the main convergent margin. By the end of the experiment, the Nazca Plate had subducted about 7 cm (arrow, Fig. 10d), or 700 km in nature. To this should be added about 5 cm (500 km in nature) of subduction-erosion at the edge of the continent.

The grids show that the northern and central parts of the continent rotated clockwise by about 10° with respect to the surrounding oceanic plates. In contrast, the southern part (Patagonia) rotated counter-clockwise. The clockwise rotation of the northern and southern parts probably resulted from (1) rapid advance of the Nazca and Caribbean plates, relative to the Antarctic Plate, and (2) frictional drag at the northern boundary. The counter-clockwise rotation of the southern part may have been due to drag at its southern boundary. The relative rotation between continental and oceanic parts of South America resulted in deformation along the continental margins. In particular, there was shortening and thickening along the SE margin, and rifting at the western margin next to the triple junction (Fig. 10d).

Horizontal compression was responsible for more generalized deformation at the continental margins. Because the eastern margins were oblique to the greatest stress, they took up strike-slip motion, right-lateral at the SE margin, and left-lateral at the NW margin. The wrenching resulted in en echelon folds and reverse faults. Between zones of wrenching, the two eastern apices of the continent thrust over the adjacent oceanic lithosphere. At the western margin, next to the subduction zone, the zone of initial weakness took up some shortening, although less so than in the previous experiment. Elsewhere, the continent suffered little internal deformation.

Discussion

The fault maps presented here show that compressional deformation in continental South America has accumulated primarily in the Andes, but also at other locations around the margins, especially SE Brazil and Patagonia. Moreover, deformation has been recurrent in these areas. This is not surprising, because the plate configuration and general directions of motion around continental South America have not changed greatly since the mid-Cretaceous. Mechanically speaking, the boundary conditions have remained relatively stable. Minor changes in the direction and speed of plate motions can account for variations in the rate of deformation and in structural style (the phases of Steinmann 1929).

Experiment 2, which had stable boundary conditions, also showed recurrent deformation along certain segments of the continental margin. In particular, it showed (1) strike-slip deformation at the northern and southern margins of the continent, as well as the SE and NW margins, and (2) thrusting around the eastern coastal promontories of Brazil and southern Patagonia. The former is easily understood in terms of east–west compression and lateral friction. In contrast, the latter results from wholesale rotation of northern and southern parts of the continent. Such a complex motion has not been suggested before for the real South America, but it might explain the shortening and topography of the coastal mountains of SE Brazil and the Maurice Ewing Bank (south of the Falkland Islands).

In Experiment 1, where the boundary conditions were highly simplified, an internal weakness led to a sinuous margin, involving large rotations of crustal blocks. This provides an explanation for the Bolivian orocline, where rotations have accumulated since the Cretaceous, in a large Palaeozoic foreland basin, next to a Mesozoic rift in the south.

Thus the main cause of oroclinal bending and other variations in structural style along the Andes may be mechanical heterogeneity within the continent, rather than variations in the subducting slab. Indeed, the importance of palaeogeography and pre-existing faults has been emphasized before, for example for NW Argentina (Allmendinger *et al.* 1983; Grier *et al.* 1991; Kley *et al.* 2005), Bolivia (Baby *et al.* 1996), Peru (Gil Rodríguez *et al.* 2001), and the Andes in general (Cobbold *et al.* 1996; Kley *et al.* 1999; Jacques 2003). Probably, the subject deserves more widespread recognition and further study. Typically, a continent is more heterogeneous than an oceanic lithosphere. The former is older and has inherited weaknesses, whereas the latter is younger and more uniform, as a result of consolidation at mid-oceanic ridges.

Conclusions

(1) Compressional deformation is widespread in continental South America, especially at the margins, and it has been accumulating since the mid-Cretaceous.

(2) According to geophysical data (topography, crustal thickness, GPS velocities, seismic activity, stress maps), shortening and thickening are continuing in the Andes, as well as in SE Brazil.

(3) From geological data, we have compiled maps for mid-Cretaceous, Late Cretaceous, Palaeogene and Neogene faulting. At all periods, faulting was dominant in the Andes, but it also occurred at northern and southern transcurrent boundaries, on the Atlantic margin, in Patagonia, and even in the Amazon Basin.

(4) Because deformation was recurrent at these localities, we infer that it was mainly due to reactivation of crustal weaknesses, and to special conditions on the boundaries of South America.

(5) Our physical models may provide some explanation of the above processes. The dominant response to plate motion was subduction of oceanic lithosphere beneath continental South America. However, the continent also deformed internally, especially at the margins.

(6) In one experiment, a zone of initial weakness next to the convergent margin shortened preferentially, causing large rotations of adjacent blocks and generating curvature of the margin. Such a process may help to explain the development of the Bolivian orocline.

(7) In another experiment, where the model continent had a broadly triangular shape, resembling South America, the oblique NE and SW margins deformed in strike-slip mode, the eastern apices of the continent thrust over the adjacent oceanic lithosphere, and large parts of the continent rotated, causing reverse faulting at the SE margin. Such motions may explain the complexities of deformation at the scale of South America.

P.R.C. first gave a talk on this subject in 1996, at a meeting in St. Malo. M. Coward encouraged us to publish the results. South America was among his many interests. In 1969, he and P.R.C. took part in a memorable 9 month field campaign to the Andes (Imperial College Andean Volcanoes Project). Over the following years, we had many enthusiastic discussions about South America. We thank O. Heidbach of the World Stress Map project for useful remarks and for permission to publish Figure 2. The constructive comments of the reviewers, A. Tankard and P. Baby, resulted in a better manuscript.

References

Allmendinger, R. W., Ramos, V. A., Jordan, T. E., Palma, M. & Isacks, B. L. 1983. Paleogeography and Andean structural geometry, northwest Argentina. *Tectonics*, **2**, 1–16.

Allmendinger, R. W., Jordan, T. E., Kay, S. M. & Isacks, B. L. 1997. The evolution of the Altiplano–Puna plateau of the Central Andes. *Annual Review of Earth and Planetary Sciences*, **25**, 139–174.

Alvarez-Marrón, J., McClay, K. R., Harambour, S., Rojas, L. & Skarmeta, J. 1993. Geometry and evolution of the frontal part of the Magallanes foreland thrust and fold belt (Vicuña Area), Tierra del Fuego, Southern Chile. *AAPG Bulletin*, **77**, 1904–1921.

Arancibia, G. 2004. Mid-Cretaceous crustal shortening: evidence from a regional-scale ductile shear zone in the Coastal Range of central Chile (32°S). *Journal of South American Earth Sciences*, **17**, 209–226.

Arriagada, C., Cobbold, P., Mpodozis, C. & Roperch, P. 2002. Cretaceous to Paleogene compressional tectonics during deposition of the Purilactis Group, Salar de Atacama. *Fifth International Symposium on Andean Geodynamics, Toulouse, Extended Abstracts.* IRD Editions, Paris, 41–44.

Arriagada, C., Roperch, P., Mpodozis, C., Dupond-Nivet, G., Cobbold, P. R., Chauvin, A. & Cortés, J. 2003. Paleogene clockwise tectonic rotations in the forearc of central Andes, Antofogasta region, northern Chile. *Journal of Geophysical Research*, **108**(B1), 2002, doi:10.1029/2001JB001598.

ARRIAGADA, C., COBBOLD, P. R. & ROPERCH, P. 2006. The Salar de Atacama basin: a record of Cretareous to Paleogene Compresional tectonics in the Central Andes. *Tectonics* **25**, TC1008, doi:10.1029/2004TC001770.

ASSUMPÇÃO, M. 1998. Seismicity and stresses in the Brazilian passive margin. *Bulletin of the Seismological Society of America*, **88**, 160–169.

BABY, P., SPECHT, M., OLLER, J., MONTEMURRO, G., COLLETTA, B. & LETOUZEY, J. 1996. The Boomerang–Chapare transfer zone (Recent Oil Discovery Trend in Bolivia): structural interpretation and experimental approach. *In*: ROURE, F., ELLOUZ, N., SHEIN, V. S. & SKVORTSOV, I. (eds) *Geodynamic Evolution of Sedimentary Basins.* Technip, Paris, 203–218.

BABY, P., ROCHAT, P., MASCLE, G. & HÉRAIL, G. 1997. Neogene shortening contribution to crustal thickening in the back arc of the Central Andes. *Geology*, **25**, 883–886.

BABY, P., RIVADENEIRA, M., CHRISTOPHOUL, F. & BARRAGÁN, R. 1999. Style and timing of deformation in the Oriente Basin of Ecuador. *Fourth International Symposium on Andean Geodynamics, Göttingen, Extended Abstracts.* IRD Editions, Paris, 68–72.

BRANQUET, Y., CHEILLETZ, A., COBBOLD, P. R., BABY, P., LAUMONIER, B. & GIULIANI, G. 2002. Andean deformation and rift inversion, eastern edge of Cordillera Oriental (Guateque–Medina area), Colombia. *Journal of South American Earth Sciences*, **15**, 391–407.

CAPUTO, M. V. 1991. Solimões megashear: intraplate tectonics in northwestern Brazil. *Geology*, **19**, 246–249.

CARRAPA, B., ADELMANN, D., HILLEY, G. E., MORTIMER, E., SOBEL, E. R. & STRECKER, M. R. 2005. Oligocene range uplift and development of plateau morphology in the southern central Andes. *Tectonics*, **24**, TC4011, doi:10.1029/2004TC001762.

CEMBRANO, J., HERVÉ, F. & LAVENU, A. 1996. The Liquiñe Ofqui fault zone: a long-lived intra-arc fault system in southern Chile. *Tectonophysics*, **259**, 55–66.

CHRISTOPHOUL, F., BABY, P. & DÁVILA, C. 2002. Stratigraphic responses to a major tectonic event in a foreland basin: the Ecuadorian Oriente Basin from Eocene to Oligocene times. *Tectonophysics*, **345**, 281–298.

COBBOLD, P. R. & ROSSELLO, E. A. 2003. Aptian to recent compressional deformation, foothills of the Neuquén Basin, Argentina. *Marine and Petroleum Geology*, **20**, 429–443.

COBBOLD, P. R., SZATMARI, P., LIMA, C. & ROSSELLO, E. A. 1996. Cenozoic deformation across South America: continent-wide data and analogue models. *Third International Symposium on Andean Geodynamics, St. Malo, Extended Abstracts*, ORSTOM, Paris, 21–24.

COBBOLD, P.R., MEISLING, K. & MOUNT, V. S. 2001. Reactivation of an obliquely rifted margin, Campos and Santos basins, southeastern Brazil. *AAPG Bulletin*, **85**, 1925–1944.

COLLETTA, B., HÉBRARD, F., LETOUZEY, J., WERNER, P. & RUDKIEWICZ, J.-L. 1990. Tectonic style and crustal structure of the Eastern Cordillera (Colombia) from a balanced cross-section. *In*: LETOUZEY, J. (ed.) *Petroleum and Tectonics in Mobile Belts.* Technip, Paris, 81–100.

COLLETTA, B., ROURE, F., DE TONI, B., LOUREIRO, D., PASSALACQUA, H. & GOU, Y. 1997. Tectonic inheritance, crustal architecture, and contrasting structural styles in the Venezuelan Andes. *Tectonics*, **16**, 777–794.

COUTAND, I., DIRAISON, M., COBBOLD, P. R., GAPAIS, D., ROSSELLO, E. A. & MILLER, M. 1999*a*. Structure and kinematics of a foothills transect, Lago Viedma, southern Andes (49°30′S). *Journal of South American Earth Sciences*, **12**, 1–15.

COUTAND, I., ROPERCH, P., CHAUVIN, A., COBBOLD, P. R. & GAUTIER, P. 1999*b*. Vertical axis rotations across the Puna plateau (northwestern Argentina) from paleomagnetic analysis of Cretaceous and Cenozoic rocks. *Journal of Geophysical Research*, **104**, 22965–22984.

COUTAND, I., COBBOLD, P. R., DE URREIZTIETA, M. *et al.* 2001. Style and history of Andean deformation, Puna plateau, northwestern Argentina. *Tectonics*, **20**, 210–234.

CUNNINGHAM, W. D. 1993. Strike-slip faults in the southernmost Andes and the development of the Patagonian orocline. *Tectonics*, **12**, 169–186.

DALZIEL, I. W. D. & PALMER, F. K. 1979. Progressive deformation and orogenic uplift at the southern extremity of the Andes. *Geological Society of America Bulletin*, **90**, 259–280.

DAVY, P. & COBBOLD, P. R. 1988. Indentation tectonics in nature and experiment. 1. Experiments scaled for gravity. *Bulletin of the Geological Institutions of Uppsala, New Series*, **14**, 129–141.

DAVY, P. & COBBOLD, P. R. 1991. Experiments on shortening of a 4-layer model of the continental lithosphere. *Tectonophysics*, **188**, 1–25.

DE FREITAS, M., FRANÇOLIN, J. B. M. & COBBOLD, P. R. 1997. The structure of the Axial Zone of the Cordillera Oriental, Colombia. *VI Simposio Bolivariano, Memorias, Tomo II.* Asociación Colombiana de Geólogos y Geofísicos del Petróleo, Bogotá, 38–41.

DENIAUD, Y., BABY, P., BASILE, C., ORDÓÑEZ, M., MONTENEGRO, G. & MASCLE, G. 1999. Ouverture et évolution tectono-sédimentaire du golfe de Guayaquil: bassin d'avant-arc néogène et quaternaire du Sud des Andes équatoriennes. *Comptes Rendus de l'Académie des Sciences, Série IIA*, **328**, 181–187.

DE URREIZTIETA, M., GAPAIS, D., LE CORRE, C., COBBOLD, P. R. & ROSSELLO, E. 1996. Cenozoic dextral transpression and basin development at the southern edge of the Puna Plateau, northwestern Argentina. *Tectonophysics*, **254**, 17–39.

DIRAISON, M., COBBOLD, P. R., GAPAIS, D. & ROSSELLO, E. A. 1997. Magellan Strait: part of a Neogene rift system. *Geology*, **25**, 703–706.

DIRAISON, M., COBBOLD, P. R., ROSSELLO, E. A. & AMOS, A. J. 1998. Neogene dextral transpression due to oblique convergence across the Andes of northwestern Patagonia, Argentina. *Journal of South American Earth Sciences*, **11**, 519–532.

DIRAISON, M., COBBOLD, P. R., GAPAIS, D., ROSSELLO, E. A. & LE CORRE, C. 2000. Cenozoic crustal thickening, wrenching and rifting in the foothills of the southernmost Andes. *Tectonophysics*, **316**, 91–119.

ECHAVARRIA, L., HERNÁNDEZ, R., ALLMENDINGER, R. & REYNOLDS, J. 2003. Subandean thrust and fold belt of northwestern Argentina: geometry and timing of the Andean evolution. *AAPG Bulletin*, **87**, 965–985.

FACCENNA, C., DAVY, P., BRUN, J.-P., FUNICIELLO, R., GIARDINI, D., MATTEI, M. & NALPAS, T. 1996. The dynamics of back-arc extension: an experimental approach to the opening of the Tyrrhenian Sea. *Geophysical Journal International*, **126**, 781–795.

GHIGLIONE, M. & RAMOS, V. 2005. Progression of deformation and sedimentation in the southernmost Andes. *Tectonophysics*, **405**, 25–46.

GILDER, S., ROUSSE, S., FARBER, D., MCNULTY, B., SEMPERE, T., TORRES, V. & PALACIOS, O. 2003. Post-Middle Oligocene origin of paleomagnetic rotations in the Upper Permian to Lower Jurassic rocks from northern and southern Peru. *Earth and Planetary Science Letters*, **210**, 233–248.

GIL RODRÍGUEZ, W., BABY, P. & BALLARD, J.-F. 2001. Structure et contrôle paléogéographique de la zone subandine péruvienne. *Comptes Rendus de l'Académie des Sciences, Série IIA*, **333**, 741–748.

GÓMEZ, E., JORDAN, T., ALLMENDINGER, R., HEGARTY, K., KELLY, S. & HEIZLER, M. 2003. Controls on architecture of the Late Cretaceous to Cenozoic southern Middle Magdalena Valley basin, Colombia. *Geological Society of America Bulletin*, **115**, 131–147.

GÓMEZ, L. A. 2003. *Evolution tectonique, systèmes pétroliers et prospectivité de la Vallée Moyenne du Magdalena et de la Cordillère Orientale, Colombie*. PhD thesis, Université de Rennes 1.

GRIER, M. E., SALFITY, J. A. & ALLMENDINGER, R. W. 1991. Andean reactivation of the Cretaceous Salta rift, northwestern Argentina. *Journal of South American Earth Sciences*, **4**, 351–372.

GUTSCHER, M.-A. 2002. Andean subduction styles and their effect on thermal structure and interplate coupling. *Journal of South American Earth Sciences*, **15**, 3–10.

GUTSCHER, M.-A., SPAKMAN, W., BIJWAARD, H. & ENGDAHL, E. R. 2000. Geodynamics of flat subduction: seismicity and tomographic constraints from the Andean margin. *Tectonics*, **19**, 814–833.

HERMOZA, W., BRUSSET, S., BABY, P., GIL, W., RODDAZ, M., GUERRERO, N. & MOLANDO, B. 2005. The Huallaga foreland basin evolution: thrust propagation in a deltaic environment, northern Peruvian Andes. *Journal of South American Earth Sciences*, **19**, 21–34.

HOMOVC, J. F. & CONSTANTINI, L. 2001. Hydrocarbon exploration potential within intraplate shear-related depocenters: Deseado and San Julián basins, southern Argentina. *AAPG Bulletin*, **85**, 1795–1816.

HORTON, B. K. 2005. Revised deformation history of the central Andes: inferences from Cenozoic foredeep and intermontane basins of the Eastern Cordillera, Bolivia. *Tectonics*, **24**, TC3011, doi: 10.1029/2003TC001619.

ISACKS, B. 1988. Uplift of the central Andean plateau and bending of the Bolivian orocline. *Journal of Geophysical Research*, **93**, 3211–3231.

JACQUES, J. M. 2003. A tectonostratigraphic synthesis of the Sub-Andean basins: implications for the geotectonic segmentation of the Andean Belt. *Journal of the Geological Society, London*, **160**, 687–701.

JORDAN, T. E. & ALLMENDINGER, R. W. 1986. The Sierras Pampeanas of Argentina: a modern analogue of Rocky Mountain foreland deformation. *American Journal of Science*, **286**, 737–764.

JORDAN, T. E., ISACKS, B. L., ALLMENDINGER, R. W., BREWER, J. A., RAMOS, V. A. & ANDO, C. A. 1983. Andean tectonics related to geometry of subducted Nazca plate. *Geological Society of America Bulletin*, **94**, 341–361.

JORDAN, T. E., BURNS, W. M., VEIGA, R., PÁNGARO, F., COPELAND, P., KELLEY, S. & MPODOZIS, C. 2001. Extension and basin formation in the southern Andes caused by increased convergence rate: a mid-Cenozoic trigger for the Andes. *Tectonics*, **20**, 308–324.

JULIVERT, M. 1963. Los rasgos tectónicos de la Sabana de Bogotá y los mecanismos de deformación de las estructuras. *Boletín de Geología, Universidad Industrial de Santander*, **13–14**, 5–102.

KELLOGG, J. N., OGUJIOFOR, I. J. & KANSAKAR, D. R. 1985. Cenozoic tectonics of the Panama and North Andes blocks. *VI Latin American Geological Congress, Bogotá, Colombia, Memoirs*, **1**, 40–59.

KLEPEIS, K. A. 1994. Relationship between uplift of the metamorphic core of the southernmost Andes and shortening in the Magallanes foreland fold and thrust belt, Tierra del Fuego, Chile. *Tectonics*, **13**, 882–904.

KLEY, J., MONALDI, C. R. & SALFITY, J. A. 1999. Along-strike segmentation of the Andean foreland: causes and consequences. *Tectonophysics*, **301**, 75–94.

KLEY, J., ROSSELLO, E. A., MONALDI, C. R. & HABIGHORST, B. 2005. Seismic and field evidence for selective inversion of Cretaceous normal faults, Salta rift, northwest Argentina. *Tectonophysics*, **399**, 155–172.

LAGABRIELLE, Y., SUÁREZ, M., ROSSELLO, E. A., HÉRAIL, G., MARTINOD, J., RÉGNIER, M. & DE LA CRUZ, R. 2004. Neogene to Quaternary tectonic evolution of the Patagonian Andes at the latitude of the Chile Triple Junction. *Tectonophysics*, **385**, 211–241.

LAMB, S. 2001. Vertical axis rotation in the Bolivian orocline, South America 1. Paleomagnetic analysis of Cretaceous and Cenozoic rocks. *Journal of Geophysical Research*, **106**, 26605–26632.

LAMB, S. H. & HOKE, L. 1997. Origin of the high plateau in the Central Andes, Bolivia, South America. *Tectonics*, **16**, 623–649.

LAMB, S., HOKE, L., KENNAN, L. & DEWEY, J. 1997. Cenozoic evolution of the Central Andes in Bolivia and northern Chile. *In*: BURG, J.-P. & FORD, M. (eds) *Orogeny Through Time*. Geological Society, London, Special Publications, **121**, 237–264.

LAUMONIER, B., BRANQUET, Y., LOPÈS, B., CHEILLETZ, A., GIULIANI, G. & RUEDA, F. 1996. Mise en évidence d'une tectonique compressive Eocène–Oligocène dans l'Ouest de la Cordillère Orientale de Colombie, d'après la structure en duplex des gisements d'émeraude de Muzo et de Coscuez. *Comptes Rendus de l'Académie des Sciences, Série IIA*, **323**, 705–712.

Mathalone, J. M. P. & Montoya, M.R. 1995. Petroleum geology of the Sub-Andean basins of Peru. *In*: Tankard, A. J., Suárez, S. R. & Welsink, H. J. (eds) *Petroleum Basins of South America*. American Association of Petroleum Geologists, Memoirs, **62**, 423–444.

McQuarrie, N., Horton, B. K., Zandt, G., Beck, S. & DeCelles, P. G. 2005. Lithospheric evolution of the Andean fold–thrust belt, Bolivia, and the origin of the central Andean plateau. *Tectonophysics*, **399**, 15–37.

Meisling, K., Cobbold, P. R. & Mount, V. S. 2001. Segmentation of an obliquely rifted margin, Campos and Santos basins, southeastern Brazil. *AAPG Bulletin*, **85**, 1903–1924.

Milani, E. J., Kinoshita, E. M., De Araújo, L. M. & Da Cruz Cunha, P. R. 1990. Bacía do Paraná: posibilidades petrolíferas da calha central. *Boletim de Geociências da Petrobràs*, **4**, 21–34.

Mossman, R., Falkenheim, F. U. H., Gonçalves, A. & Nepomuceno Filho, F. 1984. Oil and gas potential of the Amazon Paleozoic basins. *In*: Halbouty, M. T. (ed.) *Future Petroleum Provinces of the World*. American Association of Petroleum Geologists, Memoirs, **40**, 207–247.

Mpodozis, C. & Allmendinger, R. W. 1993. Extensional tectonics, Cretaceous Andes, northern Chile. *Geological Society of America Bulletin*, **105**, 1462–1477.

Mpodozis, C., Arriagada, C., Basso, M., Roperch, P., Cobbold, P. & Reich, M. 2005. Late Mesozoic to Paleogene stratigraphy of the Salar de Atacama basin, Antofagasta, Northern Chile: Implications for the tectonic evolution of the Central Andes. *Tectonophysics*, **399**, 125–154.

Müller, J. P., Kley, J. & Jacobshagen, V. 2002. Structure and Cenozoic kinematics of the Eastern Cordillera, southern Bolivia (21°S). *Tectonics*, **21**(5), 1037, doi:10.1029/2001TC001340.

Muñoz, N. & Charrier, R. 1996. Uplift of the western border of the Altiplano on a west-vergent thrust system, Northern Chile. *Journal of South American Earth Sciences*, **9**, 171–181.

Nelson, E. P., Dalziel, I. W. D. & Milnes, A. G. 1980. Structural geology of the Cordillera Darwin – collisional-style orogenesis in the southernmost Chilean Andes. *Eclogae Geologicae Helveticae*, **73**, 727–751.

Noble, D. C., McKee, E. & Mégard, F. 1979. Early Tertiary 'Incaic' tectonism, uplift, and volcanic activity, Andes of central Peru. *Geological Society of America Bulletin*, **90**, 903–907.

Noble, D. C., McKee, E., Mouier, T. & Mégard, F. 1990. Cenozoic stratigraphy, magmatic activity, compressive deformation, and uplift in northern Peru. *Geological Society of America Bulletin*, **102**, 1105–1113.

Noblet, C., Lavenu, A. & Marocco, R. 1996. Concept of continuum as opposed to periodic tectonism in the Andes. *Tectonophysics*, **255**, 65–78.

Norabuena, E. O., Leffler, G. L., Mao, A. *et al.* 1998. Space geodetic observations of Nazca–South America convergence across the central Andes. *Science*, **279**, 358–362.

Nürnberg, D. & Müller, D. 1991. The tectonic evolution of the South Atlantic from Late Jurassic to Present. *Tectonophysics*, **191**, 27–53.

Pananont, P., Mpodozis, C., Blanco, N., Jordan, T. E. & Brown, L. D. 2004. Cenozoic evolution of the northwestern Salar de Atacama Basin, northern Chile. *Tectonics*, **23**, TC6007, doi:10.1029/2003TC001595.

Pardo-Casas, F. & Molnar, P. 1987. Relative motion of the Nazca (Farallon) and South American plates since Late Cretaceous time. *Tectonics*, **6**, 233–248.

Pennington, W. D. 1981. Subduction of the eastern Panama Basin and seismotectonics of northwestern South America. *Journal of Geophysical Research*, **86**, 10753–10770.

Pinet, N. & Cobbold, P. R. 1992. Experimental insights into the partitioning of motion within zones of oblique subduction. *Tectonophysics*, **206**, 371–388.

Pubellier, M. & Cobbold, P. R. 1996. Analogue models for the transpressional docking of volcanic arcs in the Western Pacific. *Tectonophysics*, **253**, 33–52.

Ramos, V. A. 1989. Andean foothills structures in northern Magallanes basin, Argentina. *AAPG Bulletin*, **73**, 887–903.

Ramos, V. A., Cegarra, M. & Cristallini, E. 1996. Cenozoic tectonics of the High Andes of west–central Argentina (30–36°S latitude). *Tectonophysics*, **259**, 185–200.

Randall, D. E. 1998. A new Jurassic–Recent apparent polar wander path for South America and a review of central Andean tectonic models. *Tectonophysics*, **299**, 49–74.

Reinecker, J., Heidbach, O., Tingay, M., Connolly, P. & Müller, B. 2004. The 2004 release of the World Stress Map. World Wide Web Address: http://www.world-stress-map.org/

Richards, D. R., Butler, R. F. & Sempere, T. 2004. Vertical-axis rotations determined from paleomagnetism of Mesozoic and Cenozoic strata of the Bolivian Andes. *Journal of Geophysical Research*, **109**, B07104, doi:10.1029/2004JB002977.

Rochat, P., Hérail, G., Baby, P. & Mascle, G. 1999. Bilan crustal et contrôle de la dynamique érosive et sédimentaire sur les mécanismes de formation de l'Altiplano. *Comptes Rendus de l'Académie des Sciences, Série IIA*, **328**, 189–195.

Roperch, P., Fornari, M., Hérail, G. & Parraguez, G. V. 2000. Tectonic rotations within the Bolivian Altiplano: implications for the geodynamic evolution of the central Andes during the late Tertiary. *Journal of Geophysical Research*, **105**, 795–820.

Rousse, S., Gilder, S., Farber, D., McNulty, B., Patriat, P. & Torres, V. R. 2003. Paleomagnetic tracking of mountain building in the Peruvian

Andes since 10 Ma. *Tectonics*, **22**, 1048, doi:10.1029/2003TC001508.

SCHAMEL, S. 1991. Middle and Upper Magdalena basins, Colombia. *In*: BIDDLE, T. (ed.) *Active Margins*. American Association of Petroleum Geologists, Memoirs, **52**, 283–301.

SCHMIDT, C. J., ASTINI, R. A., COSTA, C. H., GARDINI, C. E. & KRAEMER, P. E. 1995. Cretaceous rifting, alluvial fan sedimentation, and Neogene inversion, southern Sierras Pampeanas, Argentina. *In*: TANKARD, A. J., SUÁREZ S. R. & WELSINK, H. J. (eds) *Petroleum Basins of South America*. American Association of Petroleum Geologists, Memoirs, **62**, 341–358.

SCHMITZ, M., CHALBAUD, D., CASTILLO, J. & IZARRA, C. 2002. The crustal structure of the Guyana Shield, Venezuela, from seismic refraction and gravity data. *Tectonophysics*, **345**, 103–118.

SILVER, P. G., RUSSO, R. M. & LITHGOW-BERTELLONI, C. 1998. Coupling of South American and African plate motion and plate deformation. *Science*, **279**, 60–63.

SOMOZA, R. 1998. Updated Nazca (Farallon)–South America relative motions during the last 40 My: implications for mountain building in the central Andean region. *Journal of South American Earth Sciences*, **11**, 211–215.

STEINMANN, G. 1929. *Geologie von Peru*. Karl Winter, Heidelberg.

STEINMANN, M., HUNGERBÜHLER, D., SEWARD, D. & WINKLER, W. 1999. Neogene tectonic evolution and exhumation of the southern Ecuadorian Andes: a combined stratigraphy and fission-track approach. *Tectonophysics*, **307**, 255–276.

SZATMARI, P. 1983. Amazon rift and Pisco-Juruá fault: Their relation to the separation of North America from Gondwana. *Geology*, **11**, 300–304.

TABOADA, A., RIVERA, L. A., FUENZALIDA, A. *et al.* 2000. Geodynamics of the Northern Andes: subductions and intracontinental deformation (Colombia). *Tectonics*, **19**, 787–813.

TEBBINS, S. F. & CANDE, S. C. 1997. Southeast Pacific tectonic evolution from Early Oligocene to Present. *Journal of Geophysical Research*, **102**, 12061–12084.

TRENKAMP, R., KELLOGG, J. N., FREYMUELLER, J. T. & MORA, H. P. 2002. Wide plate margin deformation, southern Central America and northwestern South America, CASA GPS observations. *Journal of South American Earth Sciences*, **15**, 157–171.

WEBSTER, R. E., CHEBLI, G. A. & FISCHER, J. F. 2004. General Levalle basin, Argentina: a frontier Lower Cretaceous rift basin. *AAPG Bulletin*, **88**, 627–652.

WIGGER, P. J., SCHMITZ, M., ARANEDA, M. *et al.* 1994. Variation in the crustal structure of the Southern Central Andes deduced from seismic refraction investigations. *In*: REUTTER, K.-J., SCHEUBER, E. & WIGGER, P. J. (eds) *Tectonics of the Southern Central Andes. Structure and Evolution of an Active Continental Margin.* Springer, Berlin, 23–48.

WINSLOW, M. A. 1982. The structural evolution of the Magallanes Basin and neotectonics in the southernmost Andes. *In*: CRADDOCK, C. (ed.) *Antarctic Geoscience*. University of Wisconsin Press, Madison, 143–154.

YUAN, X., SOBOLEV, S. V. & KIND, R. 2002. Moho topography in the Central Andes and its geodynamic implications. *Earth and Planetary Science Letters*, **199**, 389–402.

ZALÁN, P. V., NELSON, E. P., WARME, J. E. & DAVIS, T. L. 1985. The Piauí Basin: Rifting and wrenching in an Equatorial Atlantic transform basin. *In*: BIDDLE, K. T. & CHRISTIE-BLICK, N. (eds) *Strike-slip Deformation, Basin Formation and Sedimentation*. Society of Economic Paleontologists and Mineralogists, Special Publications, **37**, 177–192.

Geology and tectonics of the South Atlantic Brazilian salt basins

IAN DAVISON

Earthmoves Ltd, Chartley House, 38–42 Upper Park Road, Camberley GU15 2EF, UK
(e-mail: i.davison@earthmoves.co.uk)

Abstract: This paper first reviews the salt basins and depositional ages in the South Atlantic salt province. This comprises a series of salt basins separated by basement highs, deep graben (that never dried up), later volcanic highs and subaerial ocean spreading ridges. Initial halite and anhydrite deposition occurred first in the Sergipe–Alagoas Basin of NE Brazil at *c.* 124.8 Ma, and was closely followed by deposition in the Kwanza Basin, Angola between 124.5 and 121 Ma. The later potassium–magnesium-rich salts were deposited in the Sergipe–Alagoas and Gabon–Congo basins before 114.5 Ma. The age of the main Santos–Campos salt is not known precisely, but the latest anhydrites deposited on the southern margin of the Santos Basin post-date volcanic rocks dated at 113.2 Ma. The paper then compares the salt tectonics of the wide Campos–Santos Basin segment with the narrow South Bahia basins segment. Sediment loading in the Santos Basin produced a landward-dipping base salt, which led to the development of counter-regional faults, and inhibited downslope sliding, and enhanced later contractional effects caused by either gravity spreading or regional tectonic compression. Folding occurred in simultaneous pulses across the Santos Basin, suggesting that regional tectonic compression occurred. The narrow salt basins of South Bahia have a steeply dipping base salt horizon (4°) and pronounced folding, which initiates at the oceanward pinch-out of the salt and propagates back up the slope. The topographic highs, above fold anticlines, are rapidly eroded on narrow margin slopes, which allows the folds to grow more easily to large amplitudes at the top salt horizon.

The South Atlantic salt province comprises a series of basins that are separated by: (1) deep rifts that never dried up (Jacuipe Basin); (2) basement highs where no salt was deposited (Florianópolis High, Ascension Fracture Zone); or (3) post-salt volcanic highs (Royal Charlotte and Abrolhos) (Fig. 1). These basins contain some of the largest oilfields (Marlim Complex, *c.* 10×10^9 barrels) discovered worldwide in the last 20 years, and salt tectonics controlled the configuration of many of the producing reservoirs. This paper reviews the tectonic and depositional history of the South Atlantic salt basins, and then illustrates the differing structural styles along the southern and central Brazilian Atlantic margin. Salt tectonic styles of a broad margin are compared with those of a narrow steeper margins where less sediment has been deposited.

South Atlantic salt deposition

Distribution of the Brazilian salt basins

The Brazilian salt province is separated into at least three original salt basins (Ceará, Sergipe–Alagoas, and the South Bahia–Espírito Santo–Campos–Santos Basin). The southern end of the Santos Basin is bounded by the Florianópolis High, which was a basement high during the Barremian to early Aptian period. Thin anhydrite deposits overlie Precambrian basement or 113.2 Ma age volcanic rocks in this area (Dias *et al.* 1994). The South Bahia basins (Cumuruxatiba, Jequitinhonha and Camamu) are separated from the Espírito Santo Basin by the Abrolhos Volcanic High which was erupted and intruded during Palaeocene times (Sobreira & Szatmari 2000) (Fig. 2). The Sergipe–Alagoas Basin is separated from the Camamu Basin by the Jacuípe Basin, which is interpreted to have been a deep sediment-starved graben during deposition of the salt that may never have dried up (Fig. 1). Salt has not been penetrated in the deeper part of the Sergipe–Alagoas Basin (>1000 m) and seismic data also suggest the absence of salt structures. This contrasts with the Gabon salt basin which extends out to near the ocean–continent crustal boundary. The Sergipe–Alagoas Basin is bounded to the north by the Ascension Fracture Zone, which is assumed to have been a basement high during the Aptian. Farther north, the Ceará Salt Basin contains thin Aptian salt of the Paracuru Formation (Fig. 1). Halite is up to several metres thick in wells CES-42 and CES-46 (Regali 1989). This is the only recorded Aptian halite along both sides of the Equatorial Atlantic margin, although Aptian anhydrite has also been recognized in the Barreirinhas Basin of Brazil (Azevedo 1991) and in the interior Araripe Basin (Fig. 1).

From: RIES, A. C., BUTLER, R. W. H. & GRAHAM, R. H. (eds) 2007. *Deformation of the Continental Crust: The Legacy of Mike Coward*. Geological Society, London, Special Publications, **272**, 345–359.

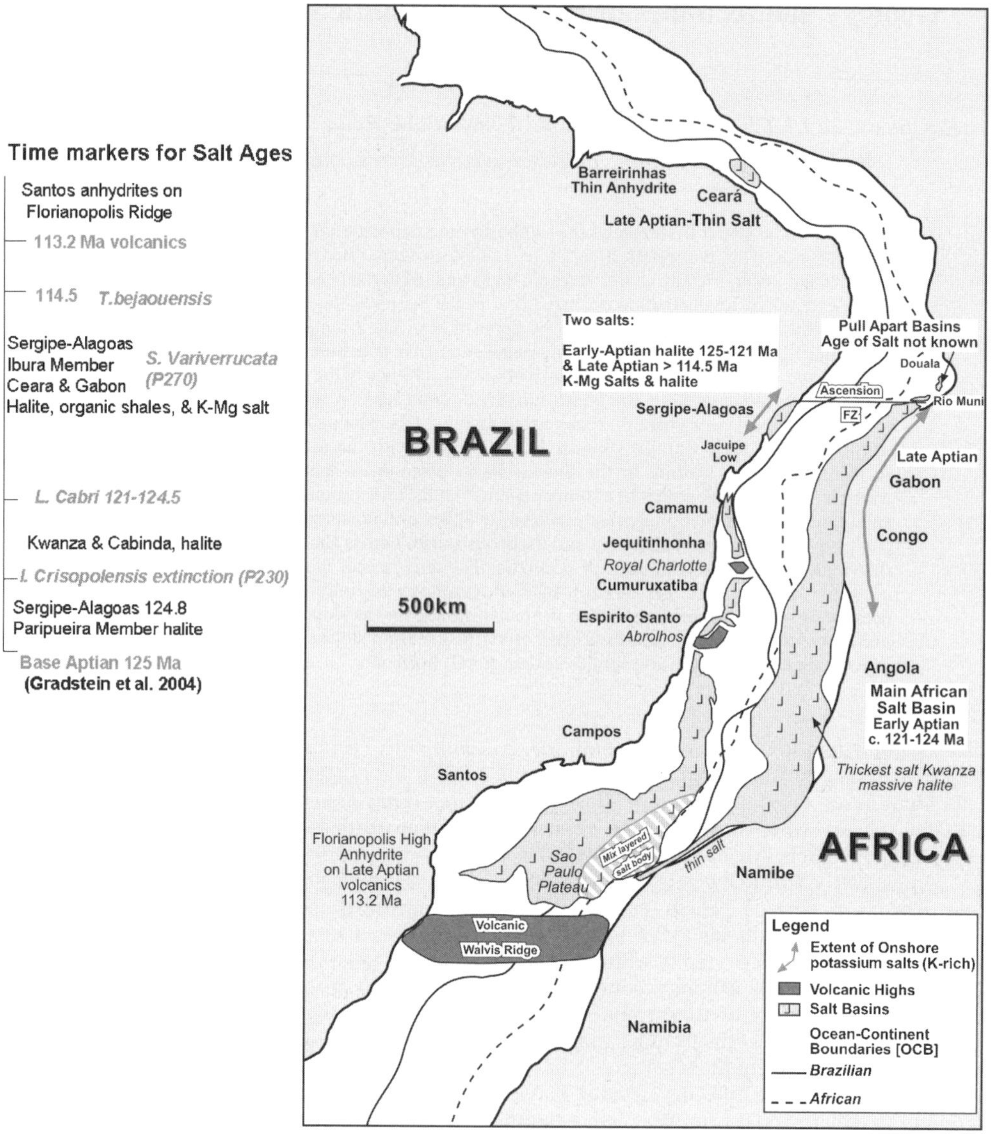

Fig. 1. Map of the South Atlantic salt province. Salt Basin outlines compiled by author.

Age and nature of Brazilian evaporite sequences

Depositional age estimates of the evaporites differ along the Brazilian margin and are summarized below (and in Fig. 1).

The salt in the Sergipe–Alagoas Basin of NE Brazil occurs in two separate intervals in the Maceió Formation (Paripueira Member) and the Muribeca Formation (Ibura Member) of Aptian age (Uesugui 1987; Feijó 1994). The Paripueira Member was deposited during palynological zones P-230 (*Inaperturopollenites crisopolensis*) to P-260 (*Inaperturopollenites turbatus*). It consists of halite beds interbedded with shales and is *c.* 100 m in thickness. This salt is estimated to have deposited around 124.8 Ma (R. Wynne-Jones, pers. comm.) The later Ibura Member of the Sergipe–Alagoas Basin is restricted to the upper part of P-270 zone (*Sergipea variverrucata*) (Uesugui 1987) onshore and on the shallow shelf. The overlying Riachuelo Formation contains

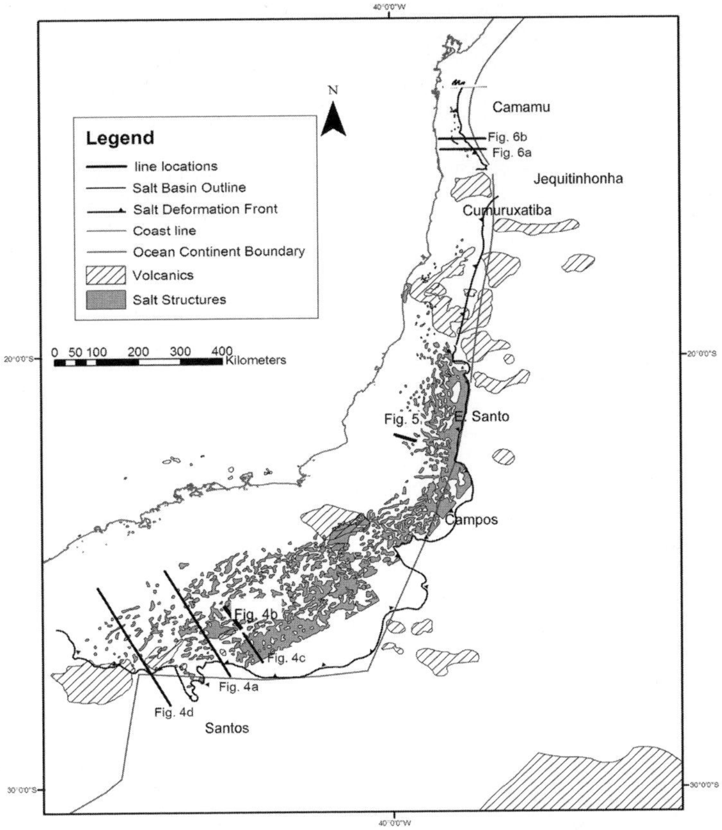

Fig. 2. Map of the southern Brazilian Atlantic margin salt basins showing location of the cross-sections in this study. Salt structures in Santos and Campos from Jamieson *et al.* (2002), and in Cumuruxatiba, Jequitinhonha and Camamu from Cainelli & Mohriak (1998) and the author's own work.

late Aptian planktonic Foraminifera (*Ticinella bejaouaensis*) and ammonites dated at 114.5 Ma (Koutsoukos *et al.* 1993). The Ibura salt in the Sergipe–Alagoas Basin was deposited in a sabkha environment with coarse clastic fan deposits occurring on the borders of the basin in half-grabens, adjacent to major normal faults. Bituminous black shales occur interbedded with the halite, dolomite and algal limestones, and these are an important hydrocarbon source rock in the northern basins of Brazil. The Ibura salt is a $MgSO_4$-free potassium mineral deposit formed of stacked cycles of halite, carnallite and sylvite up to 800 m in thickness. Several of these cycles contain >10 m thick units of primary tachyhydrite ($CaMg_2Cl_6.12H_2O$; Meister & Aurich 1972; Wardlaw 1972; Wardlaw & Nicholls 1972; Borchert 1977).

Farther south in the Santos Basin, on the Florianópolis High, anhydrite and carbonates of the Ariri Formation lie unconformably above the Curumim Volcanic series in well 1-SCS-3, which has been dated at 113.2±0.1 Ma (Dias *et al.* 1994). The age of the main salt of the Espírito Santo, Campos and Santos basins is not known, but is thought to be coeval as this is a single continuous salt basin (Fig. 2).

The thin halite of the Mundaú and Icaraí sub-basins is an isolated occurrence along the Equatorial margin in Ceará and is also assigned to the P-270 zone of late Aptian age (Regali 1989).

African salt basins

The West African Salt Basin is separated into at least three basins: Douala, Rio Muni and the main Gabon–Congo–Angola Salt Basin (Fig. 1). A structural high may have been created along the Ascension Fracture Zone during the Aptian, which separated Rio Muni from the main West African Salt Basin to the south. The Rio Muni salt has lacustrine–continental strata above it (Dailly 2000), whereas the main Gabon–Angola Salt Basin is immediately followed by fully marine Albian carbonates (R. Bate pers. comm.).

The salt in Gabon and Congo does not include $MgSO_4$ salts and contains thick tachyhydrite units (de Ruiter 1979). The salt in Gabon is particularly rich in carnallite, with beds up to 400 m thick, which produce strong seismic reflections within the evaporite interval. Interbedded carnallite, halite and thin black shale layers are also present in the shallow part of the Congo Basin (Belmonte *et al.* 1965). Bischofite and tachyhydrite occur at the top of some evaporite cycles and are considered to be original sedimentary deposits, which are extremely rare worldwide except in the conjugate Sergipe–Alagoas (Wardlaw & Nicholls 1972; Borchert 1977) and Gabon–Congo basins (Teisserenc & Villemin 1990). The most extensive and thickest potassium salt deposits are present onshore in the coastal Kouilou region of Congo, where 10 evaporite intervals are recognized with a cumulative thickness of potassium minerals of more than 100 m (Belmonte *et al.* 1965). These salt deposits were exploited in the Holle Mine area for several years, but this was abandoned as a result of flooding from an aquifer (Warren 1999).

The significance of the $MgSO_4$-free salt is that it cannot have formed from evaporation of normal seawater, yet the deposits appear to be of primary sedimentary origin. The chloride minerals sylvite, carnallite, tachyhydrite and bischofite are diagnostic of brines enriched in $CaCl_2$, probably by hydrothermal water–rock interaction. The most prolific rock host would be basalt, altered to spilitic greenstone, where albitization releases Ca into brine and chloritization absorbs Mg from brine (Hardie 1990; Jackson *et al.* 2000), and a mid-ocean ridge spreading centre was probably developed during the later salt deposition.

The African salt basins are believed to have be partially separated from the Brazilian salt basins by subaerial mid-ocean ridge spreading centres, with the salt onlapping and thinning onto the ridge (Jackson *et al.* 2000). Evaporation drawdown may have taken the local sea level down well below the present-day level (*c.* 3 km) during the early Aptian to expose the spreading centre. Seaward-dipping reflectors occur sporadically along both margins outboard, and possibly underneath, the seaward edge of the salt, and provide possible evidence for subaerial spreading (see example from Santos Basin, Fig. 4d; Jackson *et al.* 2000; Henry *et al.* 2004). Plate reconstruction work carried out by the author also suggests that ocean spreading had already commenced before the late Aptian salt was deposited, as 200 km of separation of the two continents is predicted at that time (http://www.earthmoves.co.uk/products/south_atlantic/index.html).

The salt in the Doula sub-basin, which is the most northern salt basin on the African side, is poorly known (Fig. 1). The current interpretation of the oceanic–continental crust boundary in this area suggests that the salt is located on ocean crust (Meyers *et al.* 1996). However, the salt may have been allochthonous and originally deposited higher on the shelf then flowed basinward, as it appears to have done in southern Rio Muni in Block K of Equatorial Guinea.

Ages of African salt basins

In Angola, the top of the salt is estimated to have been deposited before 121–124.5 Ma, based on the age range of early Aptian planktonic Foraminifera *Leupoldina cabri* found above the salt in a confidential well in one of the shelfal blocks in Angola and in the DSDP-364 well, which was suspended above the frontal allochthonous salt massif (Caron 1978; R. Wynn Jones pers. comm.). (It should be noted that the Aptian stage lasts from 125 Ma to 112 Ma; Gradstein *et al.* (2004)). The Kwanza salt post-dates the extinction of *Inaperturopollenites crisopolensis* and is therefore slightly younger than the Paripueira Member of the Sergipe–Alagoas Basin.

The evaporites in Gabon are thought to be the equivalent of the later Ibura Member (121–114.5 Ma, Uesugui 1987), and the Gabon and Sergipe basins were probably a single basin at that time. However, no evaporites equivalent to the older Paripueira Member of Sergipe–Alagoas (124.8 Ma) have been identified in Gabon (Doyle *et al.* 1982). It is not clear where the change in age of the salt between Angola and Gabon occurs and it is not clear whether the salt is diachronous within a single basin.

Salt Tectonics in the Greater Campos–Santos–Espírito Santo Basin

Faulting controls on salt deposition

Large normal faults are present in both the Campos and Santos basins, which offset the base Aptian salt by up to 2 km (Figs 3 & 5). The pre-salt sag phase strata and salt thickness change dramatically across the fault shown in Figure 5, but there is no evidence of fanning of the sag-phase reflectors into the fault, which suggests that a fault scarp already existed before deposition of the salt. Variations in salt thickness and facies are controlled by faulting, with thin salt (<1 km) present over highs and thicker salt (<2) in lows. Large normal faults (>2 km throw) offsetting the base and top salt have also been identified in the Sergipe–Alagoas Basin. Localized pods of salt are restricted to the downthrown side of the fault, suggesting that a large surface topography was present, where salt infilled the lows (e.g. Figueiredo 1985), but it is still not clear whether later faulting in the Sergipe–Algoas Basin occurred during the Aptian after the salt was deposited, or fault scarps existed before the salt was deposited.

Salt basin geometry

The Santos Basin is the widest salt basin in the South Atlantic, of up to 500 km width from the Santos Hinge Line to the frontal edge of the salt. The salt basin narrows to 150 km wide in the Espírito Santo Basin (Fig. 2). The Santos–Campos–Espírito Santo Basin (S–C–ES Basin) contains the largest oil and gas fields in the South Atlantic and has been the subject of several important papers on salt tectonics (e.g. Cobbold & Szatmari 1991; Demercian *et al.* 1993; Cobbold *et al.* 1995; Mohriak *et al.* 1995; Fiduk *et al.* 2004). Most of the hydrocarbon fields are combination structural–stratigraphic traps, created by movement of the salt in Cretaceous and Tertiary turbidite sandstone reservoirs.

The large rift flank uplift created the Serra do Mar Mountains, adjacent to the Santos and Campos basins, which rise to over 2.2 km above sea level (Fig. 3). This topography developed during the synrift stage and made a contribution to the differential gravitational stress affecting the salt basin. The flanking mountains and the palaeotopography of the sea bed during the Cretaceous created a differential stress of up to *c.* 100 MPa, which produced downslope sliding and frontal toe compression in the salt and overlying strata (Fig. 3). The amount of differential stress occurring at the leading edge of the salt can be estimated by using Archimedes' Principle and measuring the maximum height of the freeboard between sea bed on oceanic crust and above the frontal allochthonous salt massif (Fig. 3). The freeboard is up to 600 m in the NE Santos Basin (Mohriak 1988) and 1400 m in the Kwanza Basin (Marton *et al.* 2000), and this is approximately equivalent to a differential stress of 6 MPa and 14 MPa, respectively (using a density difference between seawater and salt or sediment of 1000 kg m^{-3} and assuming zero strength of the sediment; Fig. 3). Hence, the frontal stress is

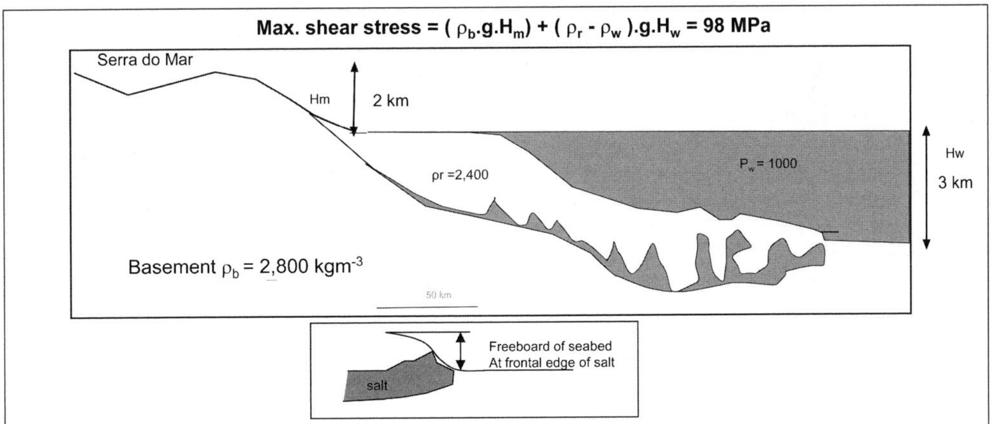

Basin Name	Freeboard on frontal salt structure/ m	Reference
Kwanza	750 m-1500 m	Marton et al. 2000
Campos	300-712 m	Earthmoves 2005
N. Santos	600m	Mohriak 1988

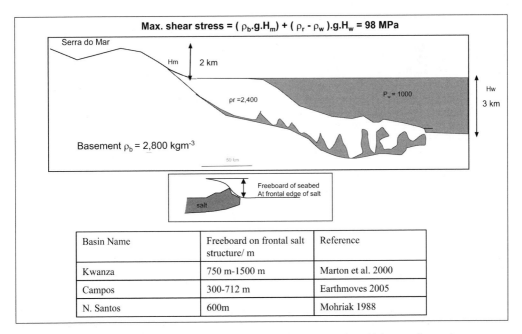

Fig. 3. Force balance on the Santos continental margin indicating topography, which created a maximum differential stress of *c.* 100 MPa, causing downslope compression on the continental margin. The allochthonous salt sheet has a freeboard up to 710 m which was produced by a compressional stress of at least 7 MPa. Inset table showing freeboard of frontal salt structures in the South Atlantic.

much less than that predicted from the margin topography. This is probably due to stress dissipation as a result of present-day folding and slip along the salt décollement.

The sedimentary loading of the Santos Basin has created a downwarp of the regional base salt horizon, which has subsided 4.5 km below the regional Early Cretaceous position to create a landward dip of *c.* 1.7° (Fig. 4a). The sediment loading occurred in Late Cretaceous times, so the landward base salt dip has created an effective physical buttress since that time. The landward dip of base salt inhibited downslope sliding of overlying sedimentary strata, and promoted counter-regional faulting caused by lateral salt expulsion in front of the prograding sediment wedge (see also Ings *et al.* 2004). Landward dip of base salt has also helped to cause a large amount of contractional folding and thrusting from Late Cretaceous through to Tertiary times (Cobbold *et al.* 1995; Cobbold 2004). Analysis of the sedimentary stratal growth patterns in the synclines between salt-cored anticlines indicates that at least one phase of contraction occurred in a simultaneous pulse across the outer half of the Santos salt basin over a 300 km wide zone. This contractional event is tentatively correlated with an end-Maastrichtian erosional unconformity in the shallow shelf area (Pereira & Macedo 1990). Stresses were so high in the outer Santos Basin salt sheet that major thrust faulting occurred, which repeated and thickened the evaporite sequence to as much as 4.5 km in thickness (Fig. 4c).

In the Campos and Espírito Santo basins the base salt dips oceanward or is almost flat, and downslope sliding has produced mainly regional seaward-dipping listric faults that sole out in the Aptian salt. Counter regional faults are less important, and the compressional folding is less marked than it is in the Santos Basin.

In the outer central and northern part of the Santos Basin the salt interval is a strongly reflective interbedded sequence which is believed to be a halite–anhydrite–clastic sediment sequence of Aptian age strata (Fig. 4b; Mohriak *et al.* 2004). The uppermost seismic reflection of this layered sequence is particularly strong and has been called the enigmatic reflector (Mohriak *et al.* 2004). This is probably an anhydrite layer, and most of the salt diapirs appear to be capped by this reflector (Fig. 4b). Thick halite occurs near the base of the evaporite sequence, and has been intruded into the overlying mixed evaporite–clastic layered sequence (Fig. 4b). Outside the fold cores the layered sequence is clearly imaged (Fig. 4b). However, these layered rocks are tightly folded in the cores of the anticlines and the steeply dipping beds are non-reflective, giving the impression that the folds have massive halite cores (Fig. 4b). The strongly anisotropic anhydrite–halite–clastic layers enhance fold amplification and some folds grew into ptygmatic shapes.

Frontal edge of the salt

The ocean–continent transition zone lies slightly inboard of the salt basin, where salt has been deposited on either normal oceanic crust or seaward-dipping reflectors (SDRs). The salt has been overthrust *c.* 20 km over oceanic crust in the Santos Basin, but in some areas it is difficult to locate a sharp ocean–continent transition and it is not clear whether the outer 50–100 km part of the Santos Basin salt lies on oceanic or continental crust. The seismic reflection data are inconclusive, because the crust below the frontal salt massif is poorly imaged over a 50 km wide zone. The gravity signature is also very transitional in this area and an abrupt density change does not occur at the ocean–continent transition.

Salt tectonics in the Jequitinhonha and Camamu basins of South Bahia

The topographic slope is much steeper in the Jequitinhonha and Camamu basins than it is farther south. The maximum width of the salt basin reaches *c.* 70 km in the South Bahia basins. In the central portion of the Jequitinhonha Basin the present-day sea bed has a 3.1° dip from the landward edge to the seaward edge of the salt, representing a total relief of 3400 m (Fig. 6).

(a)

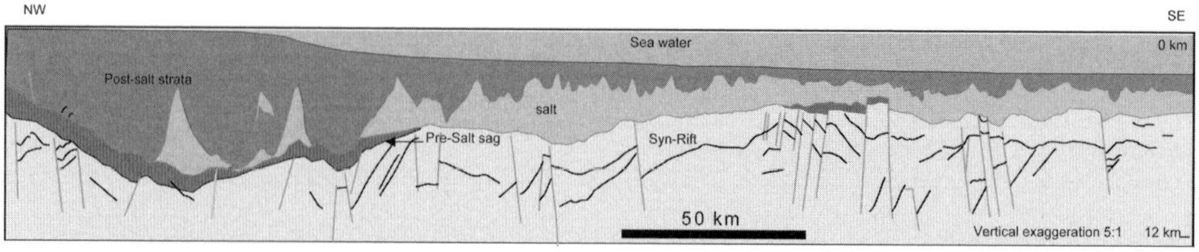

Fig. 4. (**a**) Regional cross-section through the Santos Basin showing the landward dip of the base salt caused by sedimentary loading.

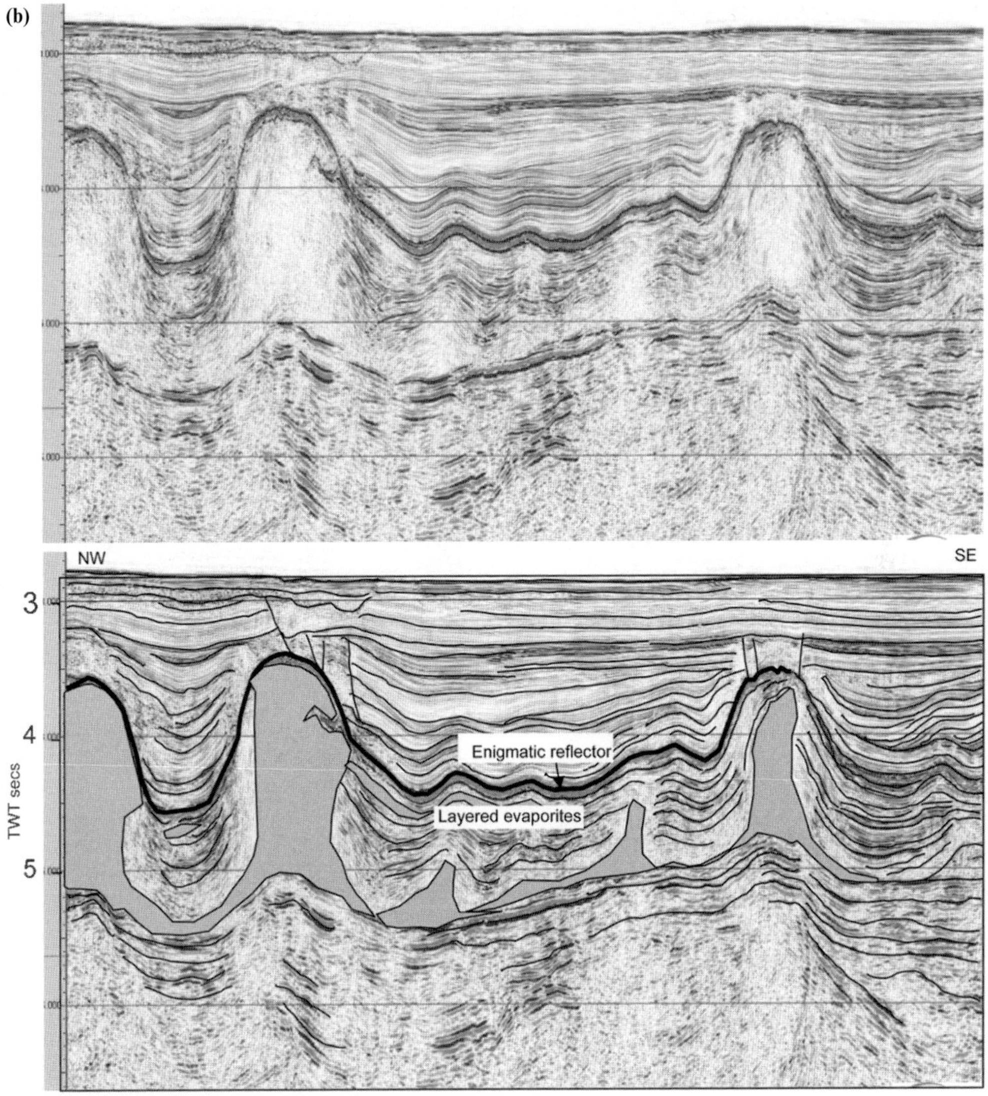

Fig. 4. (**b**) Close-up of the layered evaporite–clastic sequence in the central and northern Santos Basin, showing a lower halite section that intrudes through the upper layered part of the evaporite sequence. The evaporites are capped by the very strong reflector, informally known as the enigmatic reflector (Mohriak *et al.* 2004), which is believed to be an anhydrite layer capping the evaporite sequence. TWT, two-way travel time.

This has created a large gravitational component of downslope sliding, generating a maximum differential stress of 40 MPa (with an assumed sediment density of 2200 kg m^{-3}). A very large extensional listric fault formed at the landward edge of the salt basin, which produced a mega-rollover anticline that is *c.* 10 km wide. Early turbidite sandstone reservoirs may be trapped in the hanging wall of this fold (Fig. 6a and b).

The rest of the salt basin is dominated by folding. The geometry of growth strata around the folds indicates that they grew as a result of downslope gravity spreading with compression occurring at the leading edge of the salt because of salt pinch-out. The fold-growth strata suggest that the folds propagated backwards up the slope from the frontal salt pinch-out (Fig. 6a), with the earliest initiation of folds in the deepest water.

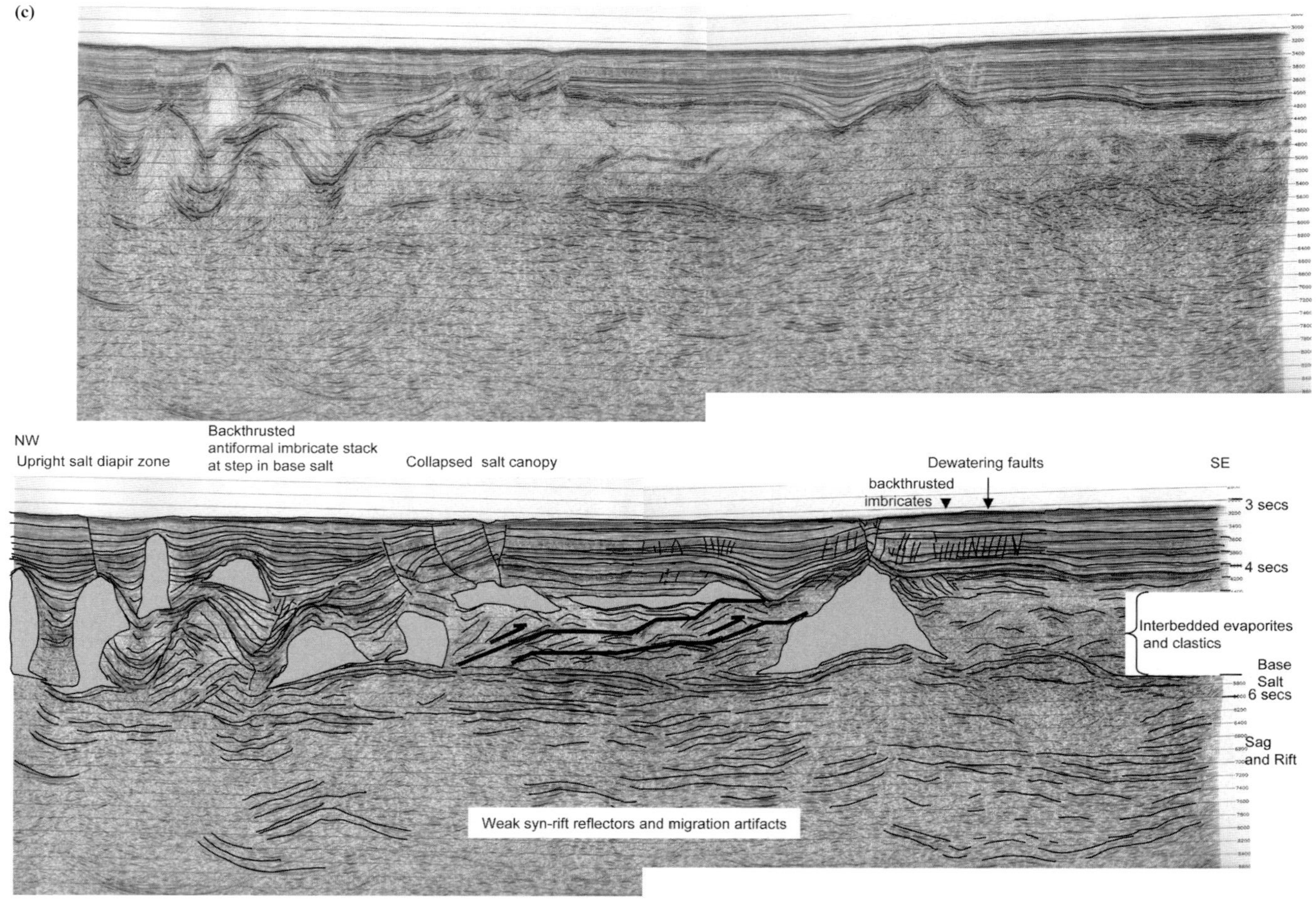

Fig. 4. (**c**) Allochthonous salt massif in the Central Santos Basin. Ramp-flat thrusted sedimentary strata are highlighted in the line drawing. The thrusted evaporite clastic imbricate fan reaches up to 4. 5 km in thickness. Allochthonous salt sheets cap the salt massif and internal ramp-flat geometry and folded imbricate fans occur where there is a step in base salt.

(d)

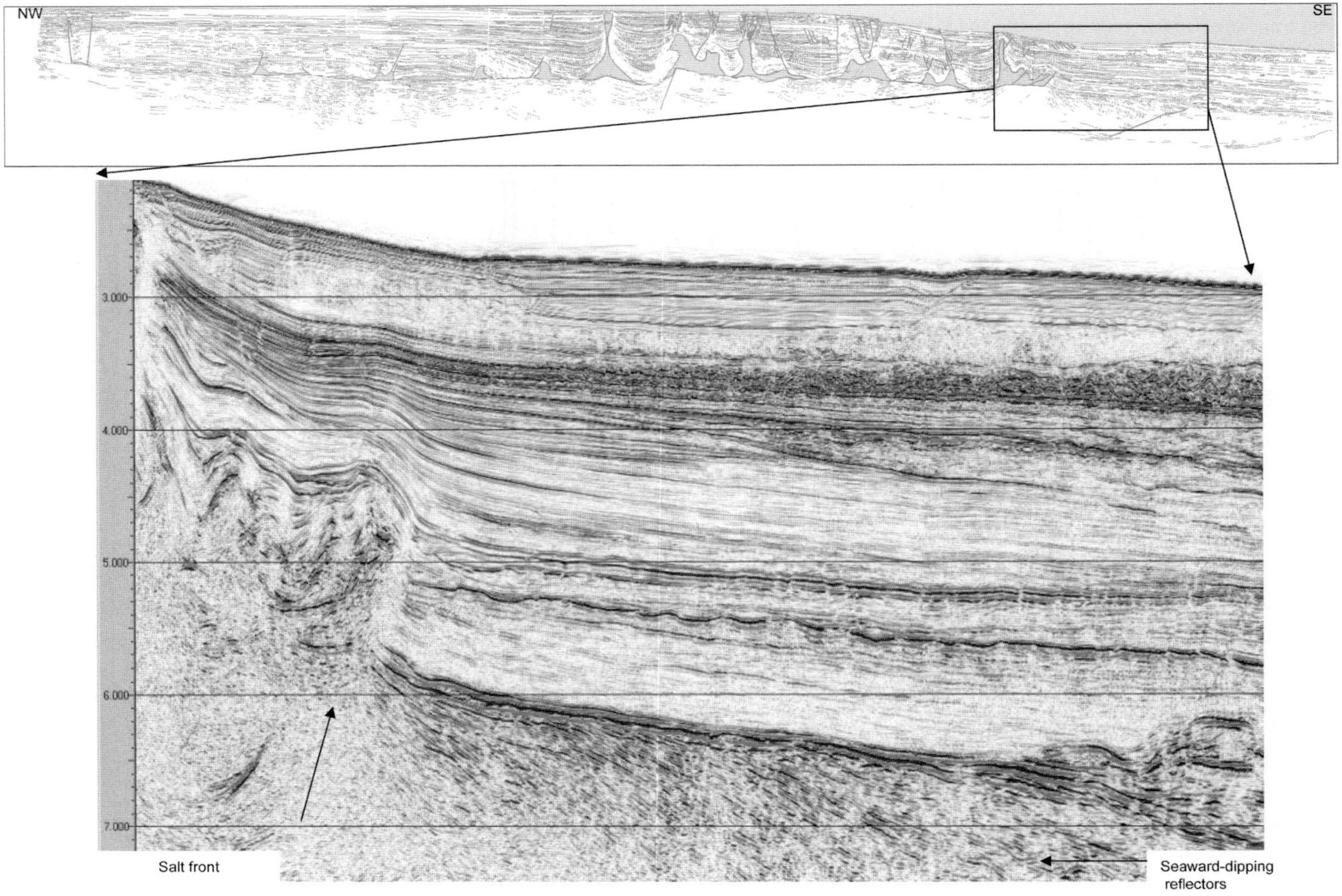

Fig. 4. (**d**) Regional cross-section through the southern Santos Basin. Close-up showing the thrust frontal edge of the salt with seaward-dipping reflectors (SDRs) interpreted to be subaerial basaltic lavas that have caused a dam, with salt found only to the landward side of the SDRs. Seismic line locations are shown in Figure 2.

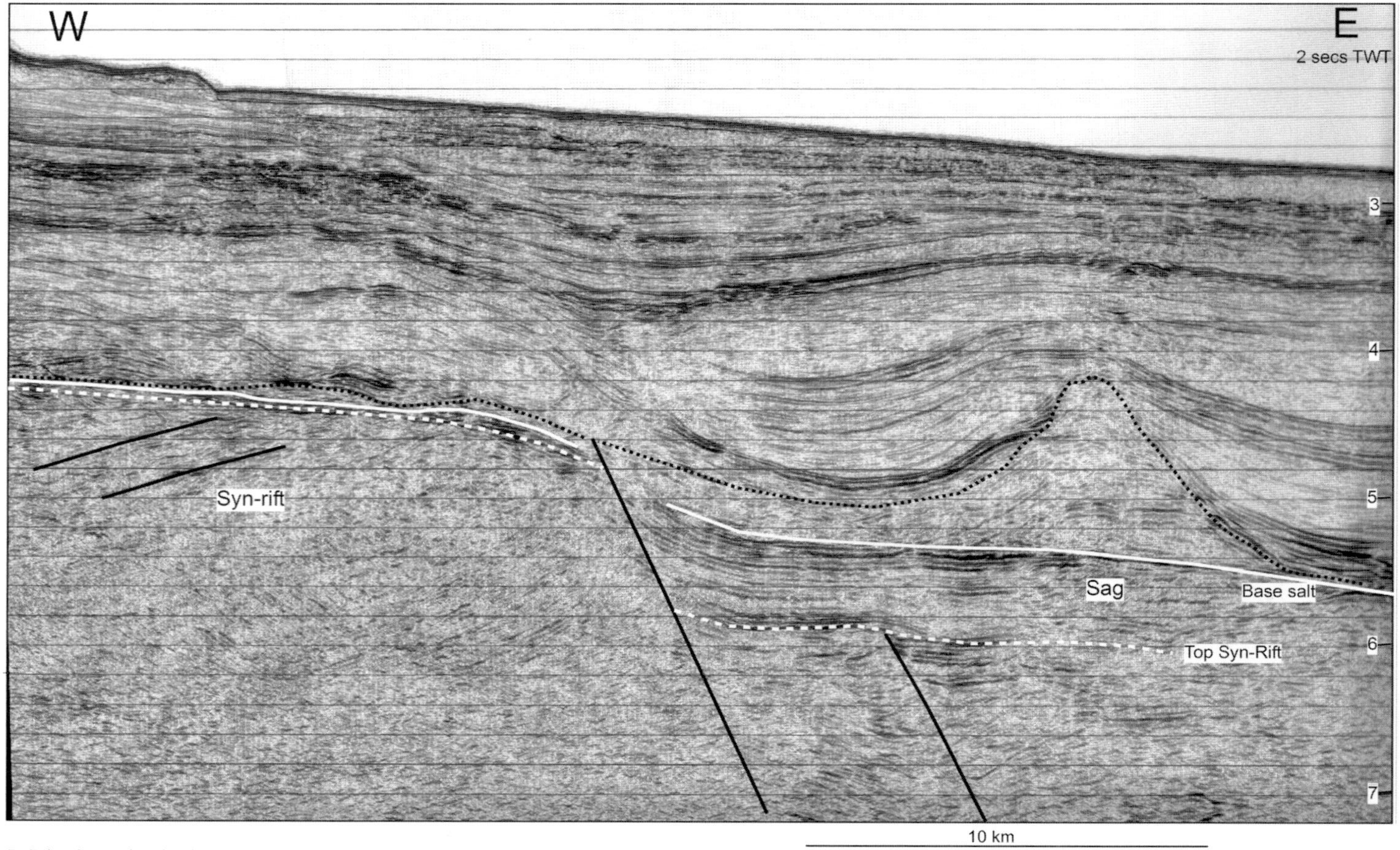

Fig. 5. Seismic section in the Campos Basin showing a large normal fault offsetting the top of the synrift sequence by *c.* 1.8 km, and base salt by 1.5 km. The top of the salt is difficult to determine in the hanging wall, but the interpretation shown here suggests that the top salt is not displaced by a fault, but is flexed downward in the same way as the overlying Cretaceous stratal reflectors. This suggests that the fault scarp was present during the sag phase and deposition of the salt. Location of seismic line is shown in Figure 2.

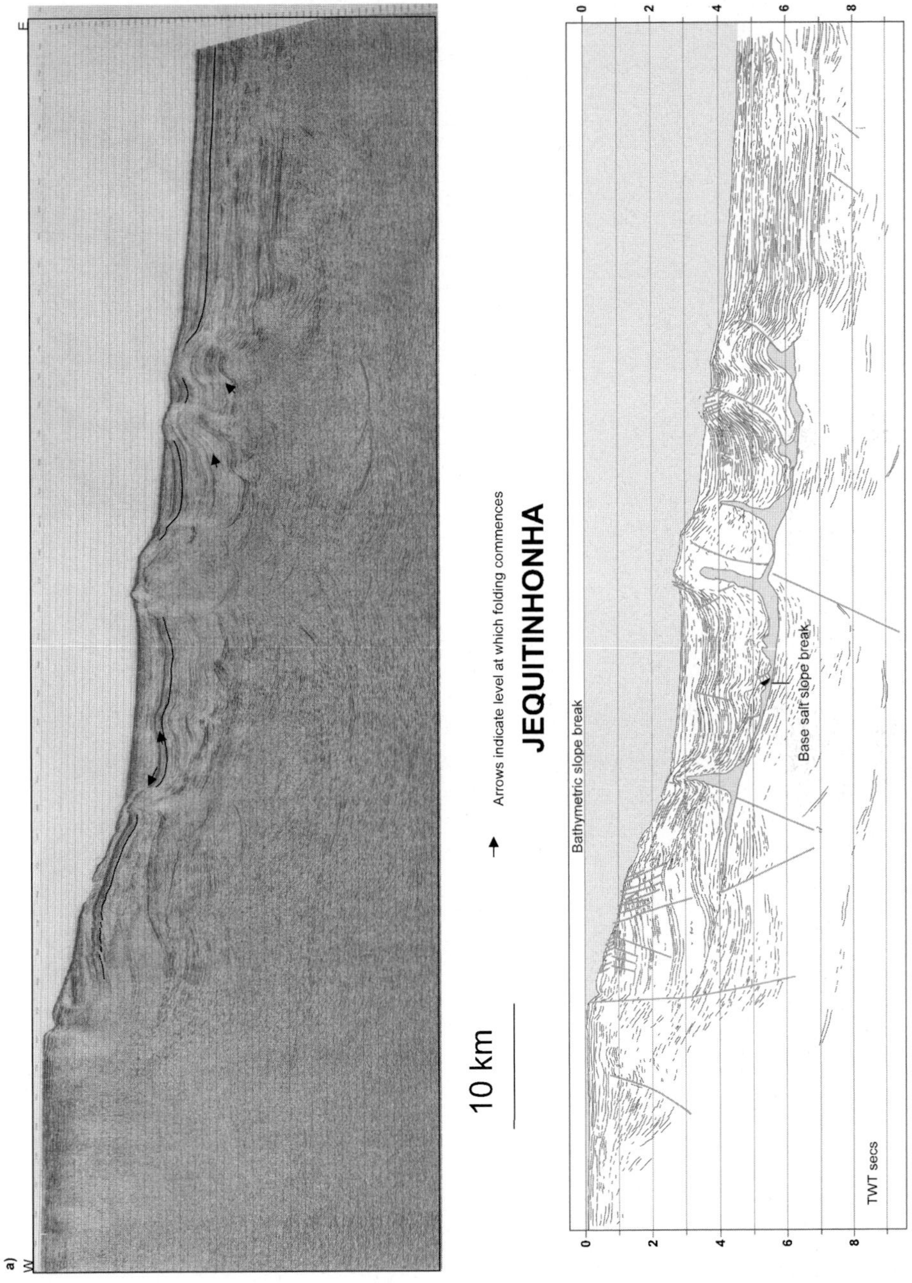

Fig. 6. (**a**, and **b**) Cross-sections through the Jequitinhonha Salt Basin. The sea bed is folded as a result of gravitational spreading of the post-salt section, which is pinned at the leading edge of the salt basin where the salt pinches out. Contractional folding is enhanced because of the high rate of erosion on the shelf which thins the sediment cover above the salt during the folding process. Location of seismic lines is shown in Figure 2.

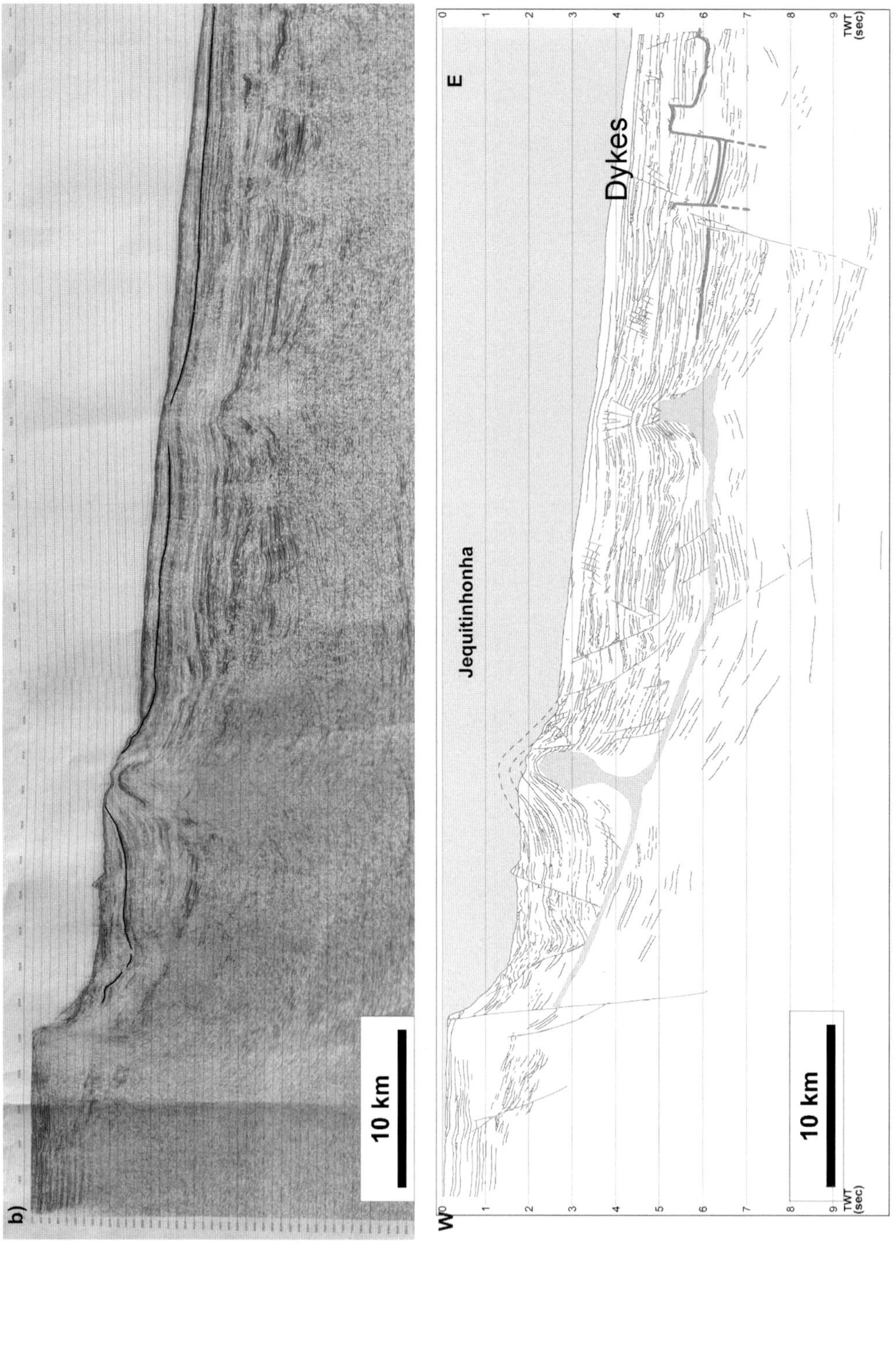
b)
10 km
W
E
Jequitinhonha
Dykes
10 km
TWT (sec)

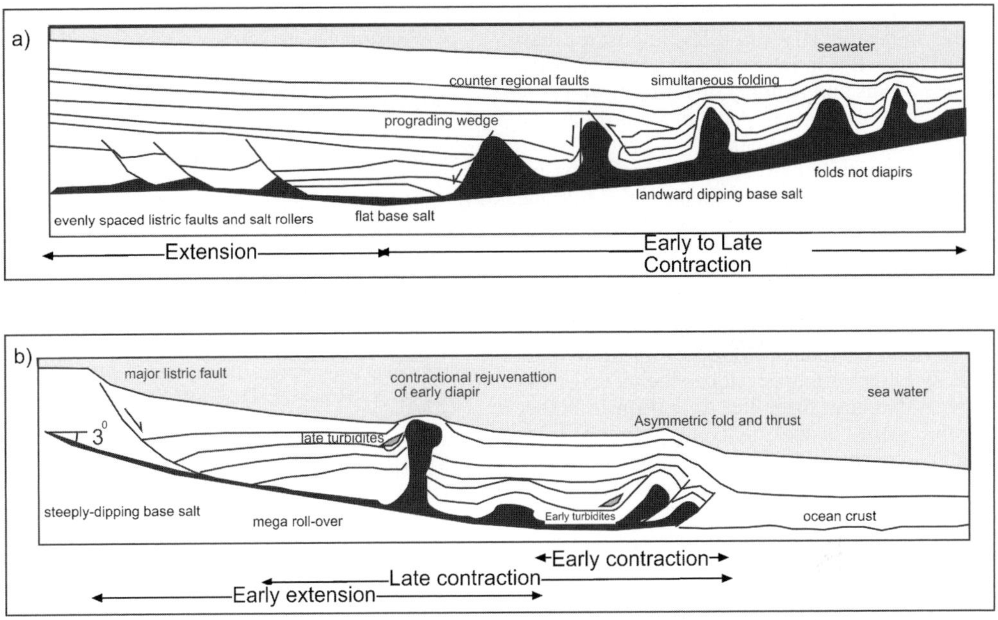

Fig. 7. Summary of the different styles of salt tectonics on the Brazilian margin. (**a**) Broad margin with flat and landward-dipping base salt horizon. Folding and counter-regional fault development are favoured on broad margins. (**b**) Narrow basin with a relatively steep oceanward-dipping base salt horizon. The salt pinch-out causes compression to propagate back up the slope and later turbidites may be trapped behind the folds.

This is the opposite sense to the usual forward-propagation of mountain fold and thrust belts. The folds that are currently the most active are highest up the continental slope, although all the folds in the section (Fig. 6b) have created sea-bed topographic relief and are still active. Erosion has removed up to 0.75 km of strata from the crest of the major folds (Fig. 6b). Rapid erosion allows the roof of the fold to uplift more easily, and the salt-cored anticline continued to create a large fold amplitude defined at top salt horizon. This positive feedback effect makes this a 'fold factory' with a physical environment ideal for growing folds with large compressive stress, low-viscosity salt layers that fill fold cores, and high erosion rates on the fold crests.

Conclusions

The Brazilian and African salt basins developed diachronously in the Aptian, and individual basins were separated by basement highs and lows. The oldest salt in the South Atlantic is thought to be the Sergipe–Algoas Paripuiera salt dated at *c*. 124.8 Ma, followed by the Kwanza Basin salt at 121–124.5 Ma, and then the Ibura Member and Gabon salt (114.5–121 Ma). The age of initiation of the main Santos–Campos salt basin is not known but the latest evaporite deposition appears to be latest Aptian (*c*. 112–113 Ma). It is still not clear whether the salt is diachronous within basins, or between basins or both. The original salt thickness and distribution were partly controlled by normal faulting, with thin salt deposited on pre-salt highs. The outer part of the salt basin is interpreted to lie on oceanic crust with the mid-ocean ridge spreading centre exposed subaerially as a result of evaporitic drawdown. A limited amount (*c*. 20 km) of overthrusting of the salt onto oceanic crust has occurred.

In the Santos Basin, a large sediment load was applied in Cretaceous times, which pushed the base salt horizon down so that it dipped landward over a large part of the basin (Fig. 7). This impeded downslope regional listric faults from forming, and counter-regional faults and upright diapirs and contraction folds are more dominant in the outer part of the basin. Numerical modelling also indicates a similar relationship with landward-dipping base salt (Ings *et al.* 2004). Contractional deformation is more pronounced in the Santos Basin, as the landward dip of the base salt caused a buttressing effect during later compressive events. One regional compressive event has been identified near the end of the Maastrichtian. Sediment loading in the

Espírito Santo and Campos basins occurred mainly in the Tertiary and is less important than in the Santos Basin. Base salt dips gently seaward in these basins and regional down-to-basin listric faults are better developed, and contractional deformation is less important.

The Jequitinhonha and Camamu basins exhibit pronounced contractional folding, because a larger gravitational component developed as a result of the steep topography on these margins (Fig. 6). The first folds formed at the leading edge of the salt and early turbidite reservoirs may have been trapped in the outer part of the basin on the landward side of these folds (Fig. 7). Later folding developed higher up on the slope so that later turbidites were trapped higher on the slope behind actively growing folds (Fig.7). The early folds in deep water were also active at this time, but they grew less quickly, as there was less erosion of the fold crests in deep water. Very large salt-cored folds (2 km amplitude) developed on narrow margins as the crests of the folds were rapidly eroded which facilitated folding. These folds developed on the continental slope, where extension would normally be expected.

I wish to thank the late Mike Coward for his inspiration in my early research years working on Precambian mobile belts in Africa, which ultimately led to me working on the tectonics of the South Atlantic. I would like to thank R. Wynn Jones for useful discussions on the age of the salt in the South Atlantic. G. Tari and J. Turner made useful comments on this paper.

References

Azevedo, R. P. 1991. *Tectonic evolution of Brazilian equatorial continental margin basins*. PhD thesis, Imperial College, University of London.

Belmonte, Y., Hirtz, P. & Wenger, R. 1965. The salt basins of the Gabon and the Congo (Brazzaville). *In*: Kennedy, W. Q. (ed.) *Salt Basins around Africa*. Institute of Petroleum, London, 55–78.

Borchert, H. 1977. On the formation of Lower Cretaceous potassium salts and tachyhydrite in the Sergipe basin (Brazil) with some remarks on similar occurrences in West Africa (Gabon, Angola etc.). *In*: Klemm, D. D. & Schneider, H. J. (eds) *Time and Strata Bound Ore Deposits*. Springer, Berlin, 94–111.

Cainelli, C. & Mohriak, W. U. 1998. Geology of Atlantic Eastern Brazilian Basins. *American Association of Petroleum Geologists, International Conference and Exhibition, Rio de Janeiro, 12–13 November, Short Course Notes, Geology of the Atlantic Eastern Brazilian Basins.*

Caron, M. 1978. Cretaceous planktonic foraminifers from DSDP Leg 40, southeastern Atlantic Ocean. *In*: Bolli, H. M., Ryan, W. B. F., McNight, B. K. et al. (eds) *Initial Reports of the Deep Sea Drilling Project*, **40**. US Government Printing Office Washington, DC, 651–678.

Cobbold, P. R. 2004. Style and timing of Andean deformation, reactivation and inversion at the scale of South America (abstract). *Continental Tectonics: Discussion Meeting in Memory of the Life and Work of Mike Coward, Geological Society, London, 27–28 May 2004.*

Cobbold, P. R. & Szatmari, P. 1991. Radial gravitational gliding on passive margins. *Tectonophysics*, **188**, 249–289.

Cobbold, P. R., Szatmari, P., Demercian, L. S., Coelho, D. & Rossello, E. A. 1995. Seismic and experimental evidence for thin-skinned horizontal shortening by convergent radial gliding on evaporites, deep-water Santos Basin, Brazil. *In*: Jackson, M. P. A., Roberts, D. G. & Snelson, S. (eds) *Salt Tectonics: a Global Perspective.* American Association of Petroleum Geologists, Memoirs, **65**, 305–322.

Dailly, P. 2000. Tectonic and stratigraphic development of the Rio Muni Basin, Equatorial Guinea, the role of transform zones in Atlantic Basin Evolution. *In*: Mohriak, W. & Talwani, M. (eds) *Atlantic Rifts and Continental Margins.* Geophysical Monograph, American Geophysical Union, **115**, 105–128.

Demercian, S., Szatmari, P., Cobbold, P. & Coelho, D. F. 1993. Style and pattern of salt diapirs due to thin-skinned gravitational gliding, Campos and Santos basins, offshore Brazil. *Tectonophysics*, **228**, 393–344.

De Ruiter, P. A. C. 1979. The Gabon and Congo basins salt deposits. *Economic Geology*, **74**, 419–431.

Dias, J. L., Sad, A. R. E., Fontana, R. L. & Feijo, F. J. 1994. Bacia de Pelotas. *Boletim Geociências da Petrobrás*, **8**, 235–246.

Doyle, J. A., Jardine, S. & Doernkamp, A. 1982. *Afropollis*; a new genus of early angiosperm pollen, with notes on the Cretaceous palynostratigraphy and paleoenvironments of northern Gondwana. *Bulletin des Centres de Recherches Exploration–Production Elf-Aquitaine*, **6**, 39–117.

Earthmoves LTD 2005. *Digital Atlas of the South Atlantic*. Multiclient Confidential Report

Feijo, F. J. 1994. Bacias de Sergipe e Alagoas. *Boletim Geociências de Petrobrás*, **8**, 149–162.

Fiduk, C., Brush, E. R., Anderson, L. E., Gibbs, P. B. & Rowan, M. G. 2004. Salt, deformation, magmatism and hydrocarbon prospectivity in the Espírito Santo Basin, Offshore Brazil. *GCSSEPM Bob F. Perkins 24th Annual Research Conference, 5–8 December 2004, Houston, TX*, CD-ROM, 640–668.

Figueiredo, A. M. F. 1985. Geologia das Bacias Brasileiras. *WEC Schlumberger Symposium.* Schlumberger, Rio de Janeiro, 1–37.

Gradstein, F. M., Ogg, J. G. & Smith, A. G. 2004. *A Geologic Time Scale 2004*. Cambridge University Press, Cambridge.

Hardie, L. A. 1990. The roles of rifting and hydrothermal $CaCl_2$ brines in the origin of potash evaporites: an hypothesis. *American Journal of Science*, **290**, 43–106.

HENRY, S., DANFORTH, A., VENTRAKAMAN, S. & WILLACY, C. 2004. PSDM- subsalt imaging reveals new insights into petroleum systems and plays in Angola–Congo–Gabon (abstract). *Petroleum Exploration Society Great Britain–Houston Geological Society Joint Africa Symposium, London, 7–8 September, 2004.*

INGS, S., BEAUMONT, C. & LYKKE, G. 2004. Numerical modelling of salt tectonics on passive continental margins: preliminary assessment of the effects of sediment loading, buoyancy, margin tilt and isostasy. *GCSSEPM Bob F. Perkins 24th Annual Research Conference, 5–8 December 2004, Houston, TX*, CD-ROM, 36–68.

JACKSON, M. P. A., CRAMEZ, C. & FONCK, J.-M. 2000. Role of subaerial volcanic rocks and mantle plumes in creation of South Atlantic margins: implications for salt tectonics and source rocks. *Marine and Petroleum Geology*, **17**, 477–498.

JAMIESON, G., FAINSTEIN, R., HANNAN, A., BILES, N., SHELANDER, D. & KRUEGER, A. 2002. Regional seismic interpretation mapping, offshore southeastern Brazil (extended abstract). *SEG International Exposition and 72nd Annual Meeting, Salt Lake City, UT, 6–11 October.*

KOUTSOUKOS, E. A., DESTRO, N., AZAMBUJA FILHO, N. C. & SPADINI, A. R. 1993. Upper Aptian–Lower Coniacian carbonate sequences in the Sergipe Basin, northeastern Brazil. *In*: SIMO, J. A. T., SCOTT, R. W. & MASSE, J. P. (eds) *Cretaceous Carbonate Platforms.* American Association of Petroleum Geologists, Memoirs, **56**, 127–144.

MARTON, L. G., TARI, G. C. & LEHMANN, C. T. 2000. Evolution of the Angolan passive margin, West Africa, with emphasis on post-salt structural styles. *In*: MOHRIAK, W. U. & TALWANI, M. (eds) *Atlantic Rifts and Continental Margins.* Geophysical Monograph, American Geophysical Union, **115**, 129–149.

MEISTER, E. M. & AURICH, N. 1972. Geologic outline and oil fields of Sergipe Basin. *AAPG Bulletin*, **56**, 1034–1047.

MEYERS, J. B., ROSENDAHL, B. R., GROSCHEL-BECKER, H., AUSTIN, J. A., JR & RONA, P. A. 1996. Deep penetrating MCS imaging of the rift-to-drift transition offshore Douala and North Gabon Basins, West Africa. *Marine and Petroleum Geology*, **13**, 791–835.

MOHRIAK, W. U. 1988. *The tectonic evolution of the Campos Basin, offshore Brazil.* PhD thesis, Oxford University.

MOHRIAK, W. U., MACEDO, J. M., CASTELLANI, R. T. *et al.* 1995. Salt tectonics and structural styles in the deep water province of the Cabo Frio region, Rio de Janeiro, Brazil. *In*: JACKSON, M. P. A., ROBERTS, D. G. & SNELSON, S. (eds) *Salt Tectonics: a Global Perspective.* American Association of Petroleum Geologists, Memoirs, **65**, 273–304.

MOHRIAK, W. U., BIASSUSI, A. S. & FERNANDEZ, B. 2004. Salt tectonic domains and structural provinces: analogies between the South Atlantic and the Gulf of Mexico. *GCSSEPM Annual Bob Perkins 24th Annual Research Conference, 5–8 December 2004, Houston, TX*, 551–587.

PEREIRA, M. J. & MACEDO, J. M. 1990. A Bacia de Santos: perspectivas de uma nova provincia petrolifera na plataforma continental sudeste brasileira. *Boletim Geociências da Petrobrás*, **4**, 3–12.

REGALI, M. S. P. 1989. A idade dos evaporitos da plataforma continental do Ceará, Brasil, e sua relação com os outros evaporitos das bacias nordestinas. *Boletim de Instituto de Geociências, Universidade de São Paulo, Publicação Especial*, **7**, 139–143.

SOBREIRA, J. F. F. & SZATMARI, P. 2000. New Ar–Ar ages for the Abrolhos volcanic rocks, East Brazilian margin. *31st International Geological Congress, Rio de Janeiro, Brazil, August 6–17* Abstracts volume, CD-ROM.

TEISSERENC, P. & VILLEMIN, J. 1990. Sedimentary basins of Gabon—geology and oil systems. *In*: Edward, J. D. & Santogrossi, P. A. (eds) *Divergent/Passive Margin Basins.* American Association of Petroleum Geologists, Memoirs, **48**, 117–201.

UESUGUI, N. 1987. Posição estratigráfica dos evaporitos da Bacia de Sergipe–Alagoas. *Revista Brasileira da Geociências*, **17**, 131–134.

WARDLAW, N. C. 1972. Unusual marine evaporites with salts of calcium and magnesium chloride in Cretaceous basins of Sergipe, Brazil. *Economic Geology*, **67**, 156–168.

WARDLAW, N. C. & NICHOLLS, G. D. 1972. Cretaceous evaporites of Brazil and West Africa and their bearing on the theory of continental separation. *International Geological Congress, 24th Meeting*, Section 6, 43–55.

WARREN, J. 1999. *Evaporites.* Blackwell Science, Oxford.

Salt tectonics in the North Sea Basin: a structural style template for seismic interpreters

S. A. STEWART

BP Azerbaijan, Chertsey Road, Sunbury on Thames TW16 7LN, UK
(e-mail: stewarsa1@bp.com)

Abstract: The North Sea Basin contains a widespread Permian salt layer that reached a depositional thickness of *c.* 1 km in the basin centre. This layer profoundly affected structural style of the post-salt succession and the basin can be divided into structural domains on this basis. In combination with regional 3D seismic data and several thousand wells this makes the North Sea a natural laboratory for salt tectonics. Four principal structural domains are illustrated here. (1) Minibasin subsidence and salt wall growth on the West Central Shelf in the Late Permian to Triassic. This area was exhumed and differentially eroded prior to Jurassic rifting, creating palaeogeomorphology analogous to the present-day Paradox Basin, Utah. (2) Regional tilt during the Mesozoic and Cenozoic led to basin-scale gravity sliding with updip detached extensional faults and downdip compressional structures, similar to gravity sliding in the circum-Atlantic salt basins. (3) Jurassic rifting propagated across the salt basin, displaying spatial variation in extensional fault style, partly as a function of salt layer thickness. (4) North Sea salt thickness was not sufficient for salt canopy development but there are two suites of minor intrusions: cylindrical, passive diapirs with associated fault and fracture patterns in the central North Sea, and sills where Permian salt from reactive diapirs intruded along thin Triassic salt layers in the southern North Sea. Cretaceous to Palaeogene regional shortening affected all these domains, resulting in a variety of reactivation styles that do not fit within commonly used definitions of inversion tectonics. The North Sea salt tectonic domains form the basis of a matrix approach to salt structure initiating and driving mechanisms, and a mechanostratigraphic scheme for tectonic structure classification.

The North Sea Basin has a widespread layer of Permian salt that affected the structural style of rifting and inversion in the Mesozoic and Cenozoic. The UK sector alone has produced some 20 billion barrels of oil and 60 trillion standard cubic feet of gas to date (BP 2005). Petroleum industry investment has generated a database of over 3000 wells and 100 000 km^2 of 3D seismic data (Fig. 1), plus basin-wide coverage of 2D seismic data. The combination of data coverage and variety of salt-related structural styles in the North Sea Basin means this is a convenient place to study salt tectonics. Salt tectonics publications have been generated here since the earliest data acquisition (e.g. Trusheim 1960; Brunstrom & Walmsley 1969; Lohmann 1972; Jenyon 1985; Stewart & Coward 1995). The Permian salts are stratigraphic elements of the Zechstein Supergroup (Taylor 1998). Additional context is provided in reviews of North Sea geological setting and tectonostratigraphy by Ziegler & Van Hoorn (1989) and Glennie & Underhill (1998).

Subdivision of the North Sea Basin according to salt tectonic style reveals large domains with internally consistent structural history and style (Fig. 2). Several of these domains are described here with the intent of illustrating the role of salt in modifying rift system architecture in a basin where seismic and well data are good quality and salt structures are not complicated by large canopies. The case studies illustrate several aspects of salt tectonics: (1) minibasin evolution in an intracratonic rift; (2) gravity sliding; (3) mechanical stratigraphic control on structural style; (4) salt intrusions and associated faults and fractures; (5) inversion tectonics in a salt basin.

Minibasin evolution and exhumation: West Central Shelf

The West Central Shelf area of the central North Sea preserves a large area of kilometre-scale minibasins (also described as 'pods' and 'rafts') that evolved prior to Jurassic rifting, in the Permian to Triassic. On the basement highs outside the main rift trend (West Central Shelf, Jæren High), these minibasins are not overprinted by Jurassic rifting (Fig. 2). The minibasins on these highs are also well imaged by seismic data. Fluctuating base level from the Late Triassic onwards led to differential erosion of the minibasins and intervening salt walls on these basement highs, giving an idea of the impact of this type of salt

From: RIES, A. C., BUTLER, R. W. H. & GRAHAM, R. H. (eds) 2007. *Deformation of the Continental Crust: The Legacy of Mike Coward.* Geological Society, London, Special Publications, **272**, 361–396.
0305-8719/07/$15

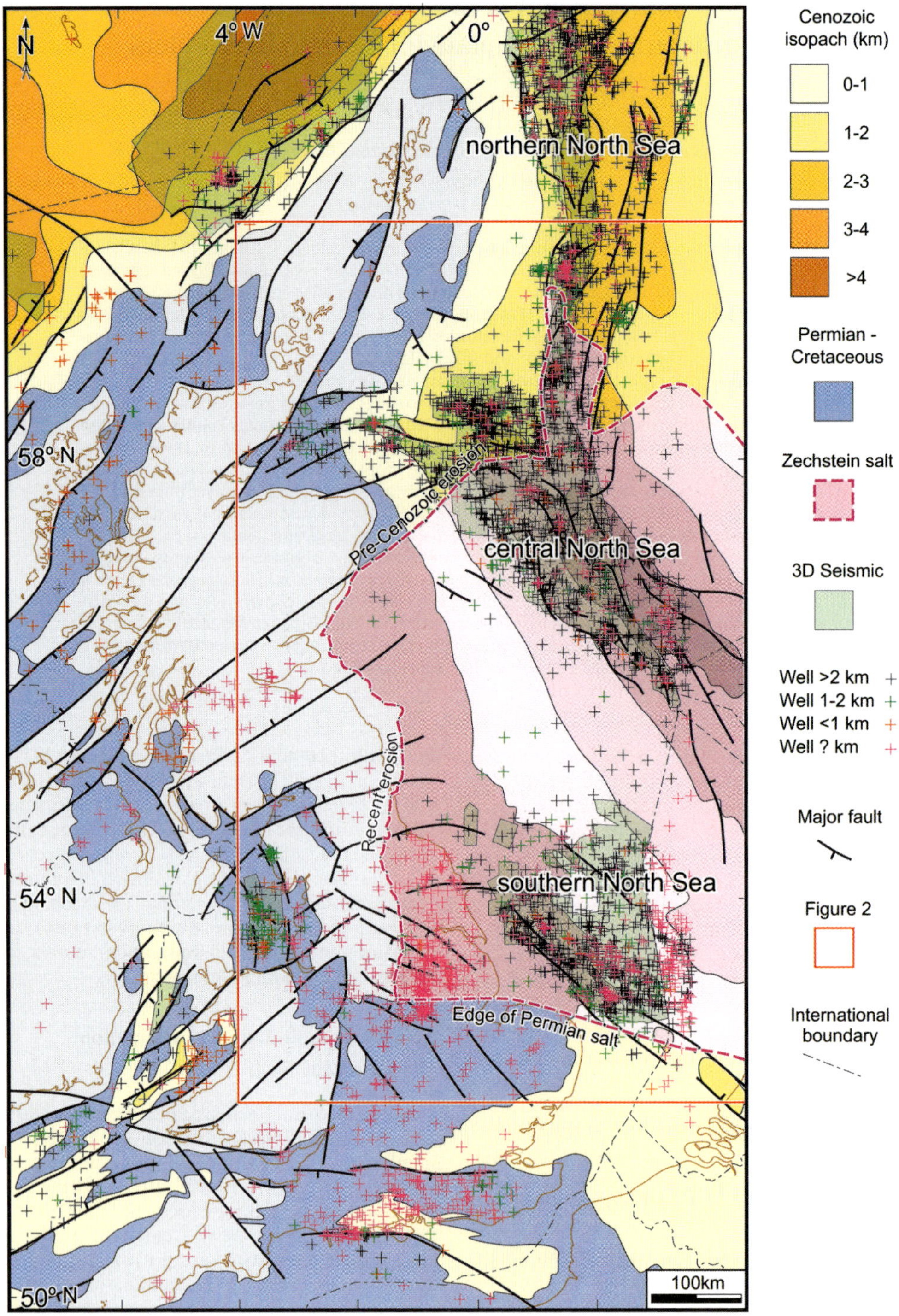

Fig. 1. Geology of the UK and western parts of the North Sea Basin highlighting the distribution of Permian salt (Zechstein Supergroup), 3D seismic coverage, well data and regional subdivisions of the North Sea. Also shown are isopachs of Cenozoic sediments indicating the variation in depth of burial of pre-Cenozoic sediments. Cenozoic isopachs change hue laterally where salt is present.

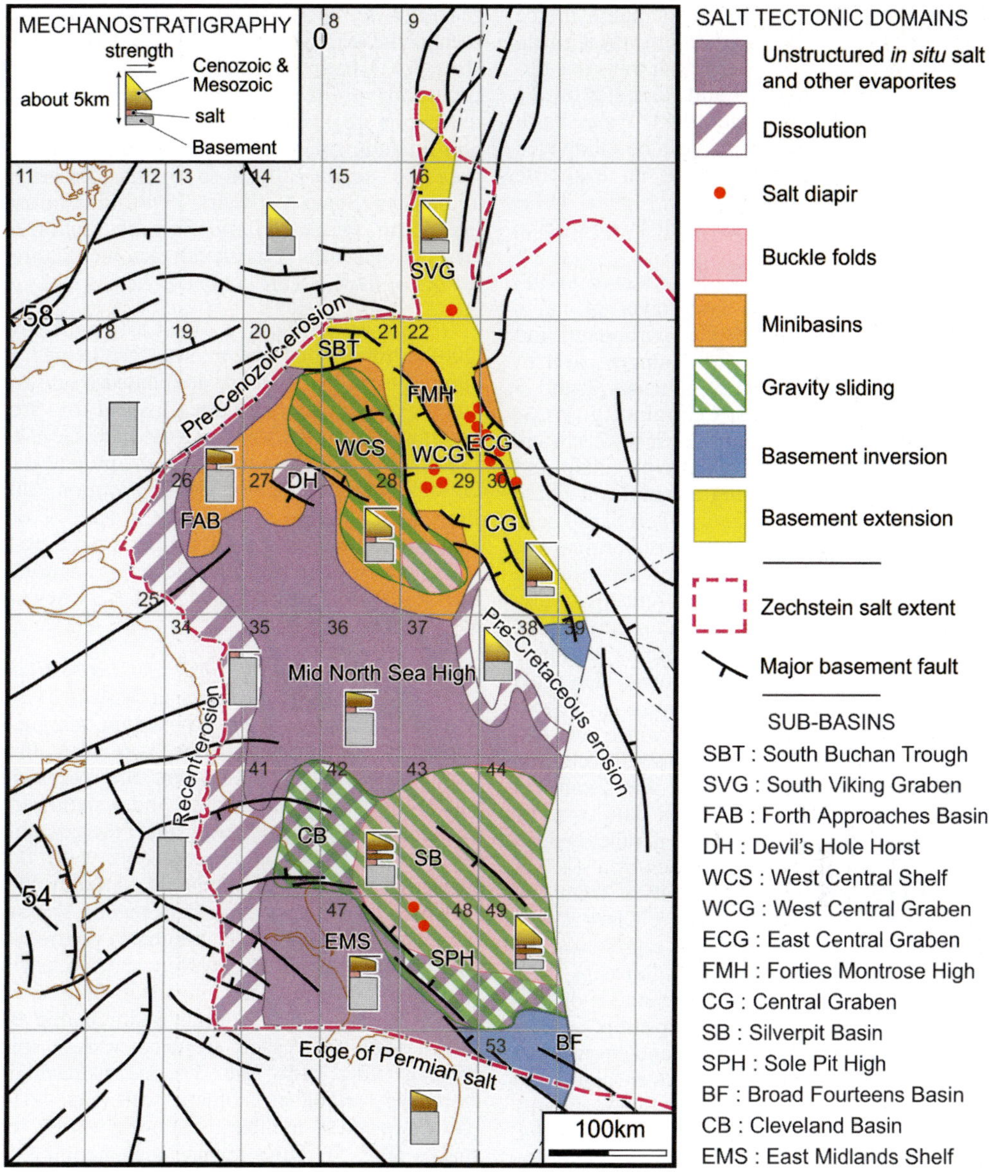

Fig. 2. Structural domains in the UK North Sea Basin based on salt tectonic styles. Basement is sub-salt (Early Permian and older). Zones of gravity sliding are shown as overprint on other domains. Mechanostratigraphic motifs show approximate depth and thickness of salt by structural domain. Degrees of latitude and longitude define boxes that are numbered as 'quadrants' in the UK offshore licensing system; quadrant numbers are shown.

tectonics on accommodation space evolution and subsequent sedimentation. Late Jurassic palaeotopography in these differentially eroded areas was reminiscent of the present-day Paradox Basin, Utah (Baars & Doelling 1987) and the South Oman Salt Basin during the Carboniferous (Heward 1990).

Permian marginal facies and minibasins

Zechstein evaporite distribution in the North Permian Basin (NPB, broadly coincident with the CNS) is less well documented than in the South Permian Basin, which spans the southern North Sea. The Zechstein sequence originally consisted of over a kilometre of halite in the basin centre, now downfaulted into the Central Graben (Smith *et al.* 1993). The salt thins to laterally equivalent carbonates and sulphates on the NPB margins (Clark *et al.* 1998). From basin margin to centre the Zechstein can be subdivided into seismic facies zones based on evaporite stratigraphy (Fig. 3; Clark *et al.* 1998). These Zechstein facies zones are associated with specific salt tectonic styles.

Zechstein zones 2 and 3 of Clark *et al.* (1998) consist of a significant basal layer of halite passing up into parallel-bedded carbonates and sulphates that dominate the younger parts of the sequence. A large area of zones 2 and 3 type Zechstein in the West Central Shelf (WCS) is characterized by complex intra-Zechstein sequence architectures (Fig. 4) with onlap and erosional surfaces recording a significant phase of salt redistribution in the late Permian (Clark *et al.* 1998). Throughout the area of Permian salt tectonics the entire Zechstein interval consists of kilometre-scale 'pods' of stacked reflective packages separated by seismically unreflective salt walls (Fig. 4). The term 'minibasin' is used here to describe these pods of sediments deposited during salt withdrawal (e.g. Rowan & Weimer 1998) and is distinct from 'raft', which refers to a sediment package that pre-dates salt tectonics. Isochores of sequences within the Zechstein minibasins mapped on 3D seismic data typically reveal a history of an early parallel-bedded package, 120–150 m thick, overlain by a stack of blob-like depocentres that are offset from one another through time (Stewart & Clark 1999). Although the differential load represented by onlapping sequences in the minibasins may well have been the principal mechanism driving minibasin subsidence to completion, evenly loaded, horizontally bedded salt and cover layers are not prone to spontaneous cover failure and salt redistribution in spite of buoyancy instability of the salt layer (Jackson & Vendeville 1994; Waltham 1997). Candidates for the initiating mechanism are differential loading by marginal clastic sedimentary systems, and thin-skinned extension (Vendeville & Jackson 1992; Koyi 1996).

Triassic minibasins and rafts

The Early Triassic was characterized by a syndepositional phase of salt tectonics in many parts of the North Permian Basin, resulting in a widespread array of kilometre-scale minibasins separated by salt walls (Smith *et al.* 1993). Apparent onlap fill geometry is often a seismic artefact resulting from multiple reflections generated by overlying relatively flat reflectors such as the sea bed, Chalk and Base Cretaceous. However, where geological and/or geophysical conditions are favourable, real intra-Triassic reflections are observed; these can be steeply dipping, including parallel, divergent and onlapping packages similar to those in the Zechstein minibasins (Stewart & Clark 1999). In contrast, the South Permian Basin Triassic section is largely isopachous. Triassic salt tectonics in three sectors of the CNS are compared here.

Forth Approaches Basin (FAB). Cartwright *et al.* (2001) showed that the internal geometries of minibasins in this area are dominated by downlapping clinoform structures typical of prograding sedimentary wedges (Koyi 1996; Ge *et al.* 1997). The FAB lies adjacent to the present-day Grampian Highlands (Fig. 3). Exploration wells show higher net to gross near the base of the Triassic section than wells further to the east, consistent with early Triassic progradational fluvial systems in this part of the CNS (Stewart & Clark 1999).

Platforms: West Central Shelf and Jæren High. Patterns of Triassic subsidence in these areas are related to Zechstein facies. Above thin, marginal Zechstein the Triassic isopach is also thin (commonly 100–300 m). Where the Zechstein succession is a mixture of salt and a significant proportion of marginal beds, the Triassic minibasins are tabular in cross-section, with flat bases. Isopachs show moderate variation (0–600 m), with the maximum thickness of Triassic sediment in any particular minibasin controlled by the amount of salt within the Zechstein sequence, and they are elongate in plan view. Where the Zechstein isopach is dominated by salt, Triassic minibasins are deep, with steeply dipping sides, and the Triassic isopach is extremely variable at kilometre scale (Fig. 4). In plan view these minibasins show a variety of shapes (Fig. 5). Three-dimensional mapping of the salt and Triassic isochores shows that the minibasins are generally similar in scale and shape to the Permian minibasins already described. In contrast to the FAB, the minibasins on the platforms began to subside after the deposition of a significant thickness of Triassic sediment; there is typically 300–1000 m of parallel-bedded, pre-tectonic sediment. It is difficult to tell whether regional thickness variation in the pre-tectonic sequence is due to a large-scale influence on accommodation space such as regional tilt, or due to diachronous onset of salt tectonics. The Triassic minibasins on the West Central Shelf are also pockmarked by curious hundred

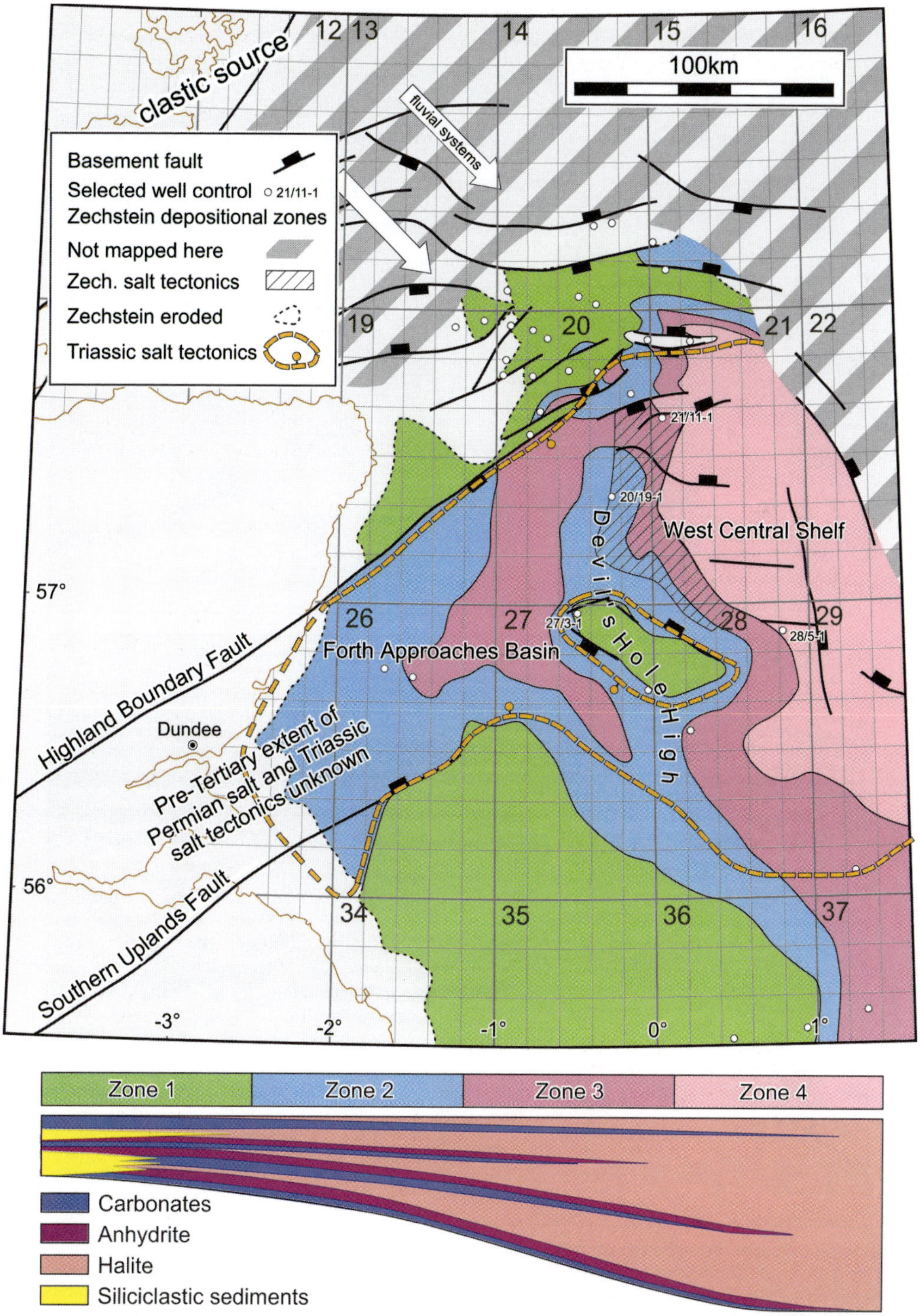

Fig. 3. Map of Zechstein seismic facies in the central UK North Sea and environs, based on mapping seismic reflectivity tied to key wells (after Clark *et al.* 1998). Sketch section showing relative proportions of lithologies and basis of Zechstein zonation.

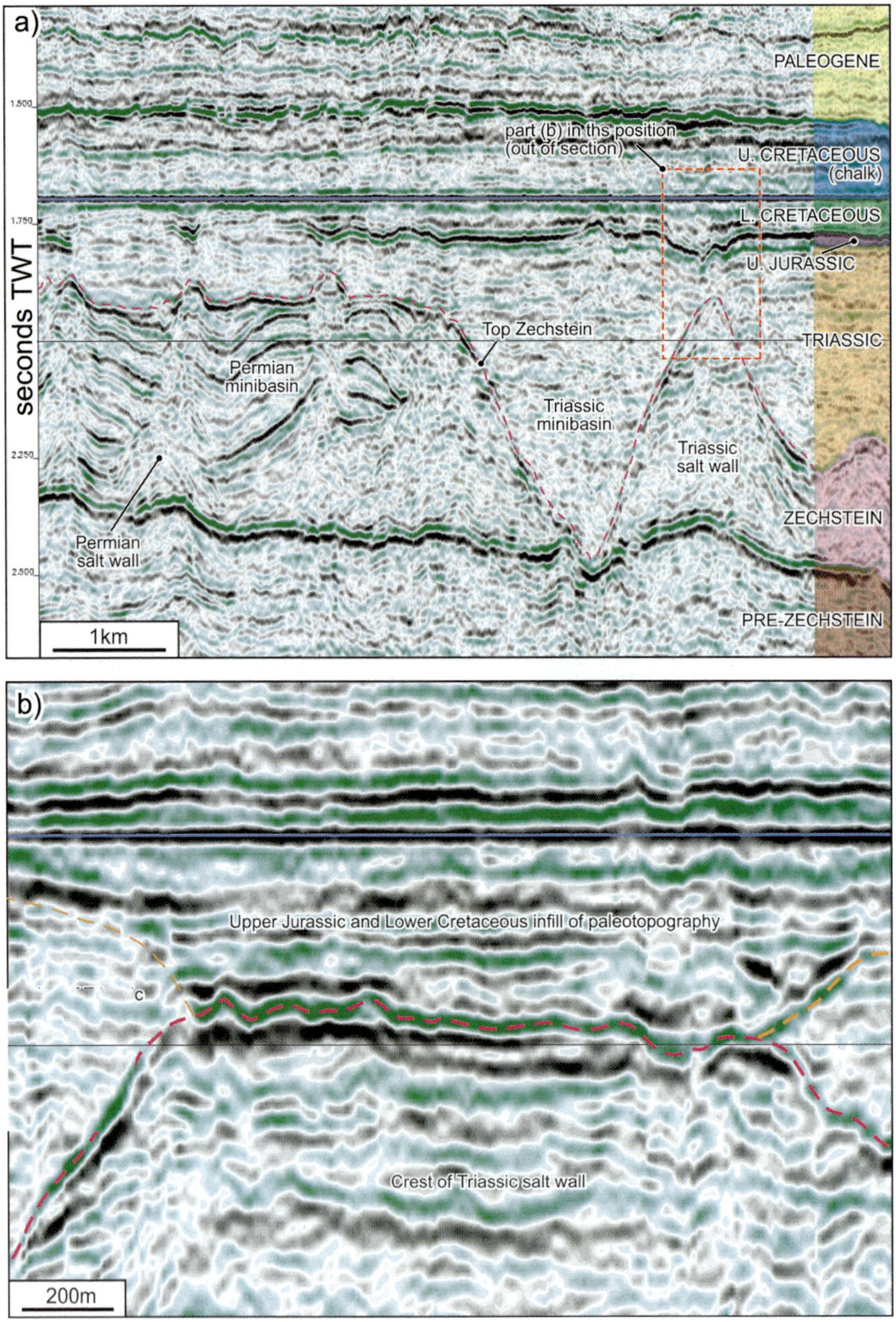

Fig. 4. Seismic sections through Permian and Triassic minibasins. Three-dimensional time-migrated data. Sections flattened on Cretaceous markers for clearer display of Mesozoic structure. (**a**) Permian minibasins within an isopachous Zechstein megasequence on left (west) are formed in zones 2/3 Zechstein seismic facies, Block 21/11 area. On the right-hand side is a distinct domain of Triassic minibasins that have subsided into zone 4 (mainly halite) Zechstein seismic facies. Base Zechstein structure below the Triassic minibasins and salt walls is largely velocity push down and pull up. Top Zechstein interpreted across section. TWT, two-way travel time. (**b**) View of crest of salt wall in analogous position to box highlighted in (**a**). Interpretation controlled by wells; 2 × vertical exaggeration. Upper Jurassic and Lower Cretaceous sequences and onlap the sides of a differentially eroded palaeovalley.

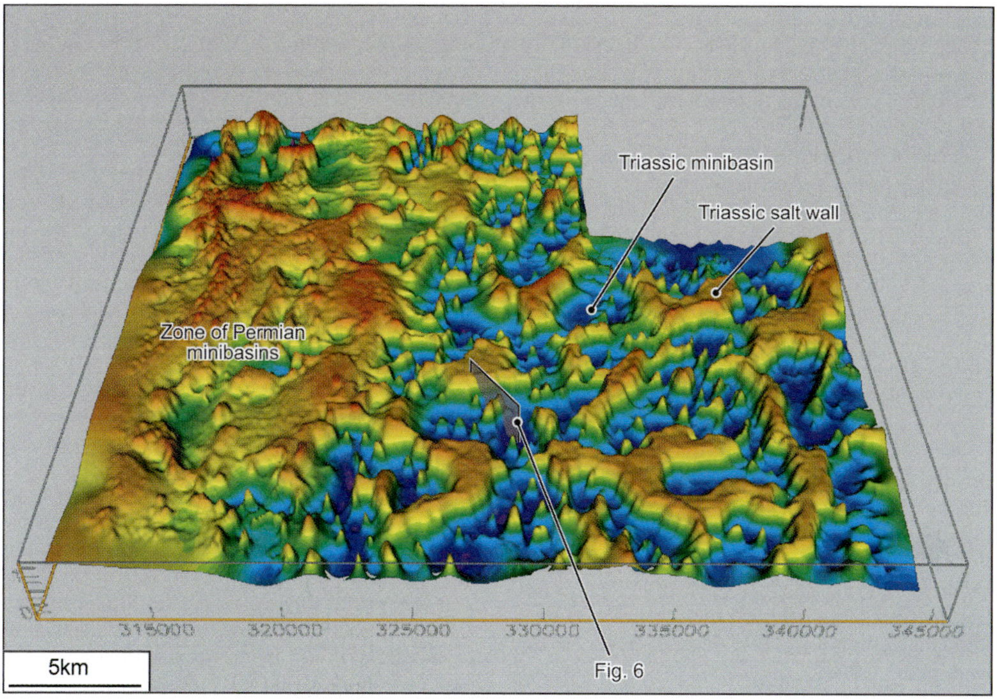

Fig. 5. View of western part of Quadrant 21, looking north. Surface is a 'minibasin map' produced by calculation of the Triassic vertical thickness as a proportion of the combined Triassic plus Zechstein intervals. This map does not differentiate the intra-Zechstein minibasins. The Triassic minibasins are pockmarked by numerous salt pillars with 100 m–1 km diameter and fairly regular spacing.

metre-scale hollows at top Triassic level that are underlain by slim salt chimneys. These are early Triassic dissolution collapse structures that were passively injected with salt as the minibasins subsided (Clark *et al.* 1999).

Graben: West Central Graben, East Central Graben, Fisher Bank Basin. Penge *et al.* (1993, 1999) reviewed 'raft tectonics' in the Central Graben area. The main contrast between the graben and the adjacent platforms is that the rafting (i.e. post-depositional gravity gliding) occurred during the Jurassic, and there is less evidence for minibasin development in the graben during the Triassic. Conformable deposition generally continued from Late Triassic to Late Jurassic. There are, however, local examples of thick Skagerrak sequences resting on salt walls between minibasins, usually above basement fault footwall highs within the Central Graben (Dickinson 1996). The Triassic–Jurassic sequences were sliced into detached fault blocks by basement fault systems associated with the main Late Jurassic extension phase in the Central Graben (Penge *et al.* 1993, 1999; Stewart 1993). The raft tectonics appear to be the result of gravity sliding on the fault block topography induced by basement faulting. In spite of the presence of 1 km thick salt in the Central Graben (Smith *et al.* 1993), accommodation space represented by the accumulation and preservation of thick, parallel-bedded Skagerrak sands (whilst the adjacent platforms were being subject to erosion) was being generated by some mechanism other than salt redistribution.

Regional model for CNS Triassic salt tectonics

The contrast between styles of Triassic deposition in the Central Graben and adjacent platforms is similar to that observed between rifts and adjacent rift flanks in analogue models of thick-skinned extension in the presence of salt layers (e.g. Nalpas & Brun 1993; Jackson & Vendeville 1994): (1) within a symmetrical graben, the cover is folded into a box-shaped syncline and extension in the core of this fold is suppressed; (2) cover stretching in the form of local detached, thin-skinned systems occurs to balance basement extension above the rift flanks and on the adjacent platforms; (3) Basement subsidence creates accommodation space in the graben relative to the adjacent platforms.

Triassic basement extension has been demonstrated in salt-free areas adjacent to the CNS such as the Danish sector, Viking Graben and Moray Firth (Steel & Ryseth 1990; Cartwright 1991; Underhill 1991; Roberts *et al.* 1995; Færseth 1996), and several workers have asserted that a significant amount of Triassic basement extension occurred in the CNS (Ziegler & Van Hoorn 1989; Høiland *et al.* 1993; Roberts *et al.* 1993; Smith *et al.* 1993). Combining these observations with thick-skinned analogue models, a pulse of Middle Triassic basement extension, probably modest in magnitude relative to Jurassic extension, is offered here as the underlying mechanism that simultaneously caused (1) thin-skinned extension (initiating minibasin subsidence) on the CNS platforms, and (2) enhanced accommodation space in the Central Graben, allowing the conformable deposition of Middle to Upper Triassic Skagerrak fluvial sediments on top of Smith Bank shales. These tectonics occurred against a backdrop of differential loading around the basin margin initiated and driven by sediment input from adjacent highlands.

Exhumation and reburial of minibasin system

The minibasin and salt wall system on the West Central Shelf (Fig. 5) was exhumed and differentially eroded in the mid to Late Triassic; subsequent sand deposition occurred on salt highs rather than in the minibasins (Wakefield *et al.* 1993).

Salt wall crests between the minibasins are overstepped by sediments ranging from Triassic (Skagerrak Fm) to Jurassic (Fulmar Fm) sands, indicating that they were exposed episodically from the Triassic to Late Jurassic (Stewart *et al.* 1999). Upward flow and extrusion of salt was presumably most active when minibasins were subsiding in the Triassic; top salt may have formed positive features like those seen today in the Middle East (Jackson *et al.* 1990; Davison *et al.* 1996). Dissolved Permian salt from active diapirs and glaciers in the CNS during the Triassic may have been the source of Middle Triassic salt in the Southern Permian Basin, which was blanketed with up to 100 m of halite (Röt Halite and Muschelkalk Halite Members). A published approximation of the original CNS Zechstein isopach (Smith *et al.* 1993) and the quantity of 30% loss suggested by Bishop *et al.* (1995) leads to an estimate of *c.* 9000 km^3 of Zechstein halite dissolution in the UK. Published SNS Triassic isopachs define a similar volume, indicating that *c.* 3000 km^3 of halite was deposited in the UK sector alone (Cameron *et al.* 1992).

On the West Central Shelf truncation of intra-Triassic seismic reflectors at top Triassic level is common, and well control demonstrates the presence of cap rock below Skagerrak sands on top of inter-minibasin Zechstein salt walls (Fig. 4; Stewart *et al.* 1999). The distribution of Fulmar Formation shallow marine sands that marked Late Jurassic transgression was determined by the topography of the transgressed surface. Analogous differentially eroded minibasin systems show that exposed crests of salt highs can erode faster than the crests of adjacent minibasins, for example, the Paradox Basin, Utah (Stewart *et al.* 1999) and South Oman Salt Basin (Heward 1990). Some salt highs are completely surrounded by low hills (minibasins) and therefore less prone to fluvial erosion, but a mechanism of dissolution and reprecipitation driven by aeolian erosion following rainfall may also have removed halite (Fig. 6; Kendall & Harwood 1996; Talbot & Allen 1996). Well control of the Jurassic isopach on highs such as the WCS shows that the topographic relief between salt valley floors and minibasin hill summits during the Late Jurassic transgression was of the order of tens of metres (Fig. 4b). Accommodation space for the transgressive sedimentary systems was a function of the connectivity of a given salt valley to the shallow marine shelf and the local preservation potential represented by embayment shape and depth of the valley floor below the lowest point on the surrounding valley wall (Fig. 6).

Gravity sliding: West Central Shelf and southern North Sea

Various extensional fault systems, that detach on the Zechstein salt, have been described in the North Sea (Petersen *et al.* 1992; Gatliff *et al.* 1994; Bishop *et al.* 1995; Stewart 1996; Huuse 1999). The most extensive are peripheral fault systems hundreds of kilometres in length around the west margins of the southern and central North Sea (Fig. 7; Stewart 1996; Stewart & Clark 1999). These fault systems are Mesozoic to Cenozoic in age and are analogous to extensional systems in updip domains of the circum-Atlantic salt basins, where there is kinematic linkage between thin-skinned extension and downdip thin-skinned compressional structures (Rowan *et al.* 2004). In the North Sea, gravity and

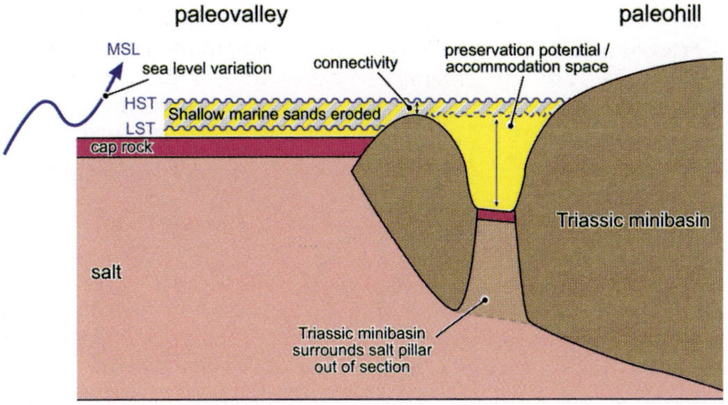

Fig. 6. Schematic section through margin of Triassic minibasin (see Fig. 5) showing interaction of sea level with topography-controlled accommodation space (3D view of accommodation space can be obtained by inverting the Triassic proportion map in Figs 4 & 5; Stewart *et al.* 1999). Sequence architectures of the Triassic and Jurassic are not discussed here (see Stewart & Clark 1999; Stewart *et al.* 1999). HST, highstand systems tract; LST, lowstand systems tract.

Zechstein salt played the roles of driving force and regional detachment, respectively. At a large scale the detached extensional systems trend parallel to present-day top basement strike (Fig. 7).

Central North Sea peripheral fault system

A detached, Cenozoic, arcuate fault system encircles the West Central Shelf, on the west side of the CNS (Fig. 7). It consists of en echelon faults in a system *c.* 200 km long and 30–60 km wide; the largest individual faults are up to 15 km in length, with heaves approaching 1 km. The faults invariably root upon inter-minibasin Triassic salt highs (Fig. 8a). The northern termination of the system coincides with the north limit of the West Central Shelf, which drops sharply across major basement faults into the South Buchan Trough. From this northerly termination, the fault system trends southwards and swings anticlockwise, eventually trending east–west at the southeasterly termination of the system in Quadrant 29. Most of the faults dip eastwards towards the Central Graben. Fault system timing is constrained by offset of deltaic sediments of the Dornoch Formation, which are Late Palaeocene to Early Eocene in age (Galloway *et al.* 1993; Gatliff *et al.* 1994), and displacement of the base Miocene is very rare.

This thin-skinned extension is largely balanced by compression of the inter-minibasin salt highs in the downdip portion of the WCS. Compression of suitably oriented salt walls and overlying sediment created salt-cored structural closures (Fig. 8a; Glennie & Armstrong 1991; Eggink *et al.* 1996). These salt highs are similar to those that form the roots of extensional faults updip. A component of compression may have leaked across into the Central Graben and been accommodated by lateral compaction of the thick Cenozoic siliciclastic section and reactivation of passive diapirs within it. For much of its length the peripheral system around the central North Sea lies on the break in slope between the relatively flat Forth Approaches Basin area and the easterly dipping WCS. The boundary between autochthonous and allochthonous cover domains also occurs above inflections in basement slope in other salt basins (Cobbold & Szatmari 1991).

Southern North Sea peripheral fault system

A Mesozoic peripheral extensional system encircles the southern North Sea basin (Fig. 7; Allen *et al.* 1994), and has been ascribed to thin-skinned gravity-driven sliding of the cover into the basin (Fig. 8b; Stewart & Coward 1995; Stewart 1996). Extension was reactivated on parts of this system in the Cenozoic. There are significant differences between salt tectonics in the southern and central North Sea. No minibasins developed in the southern North Sea at any stage. Basement (sub-salt) faulting was pervasive but cut through the Permian salt only on the basin margin and in the Central Graben, so the linkage of regional extension and shortening events from basement to cover becomes clear only when considered at a basin scale (Stewart & Coward 1995). The main regional tectonic events

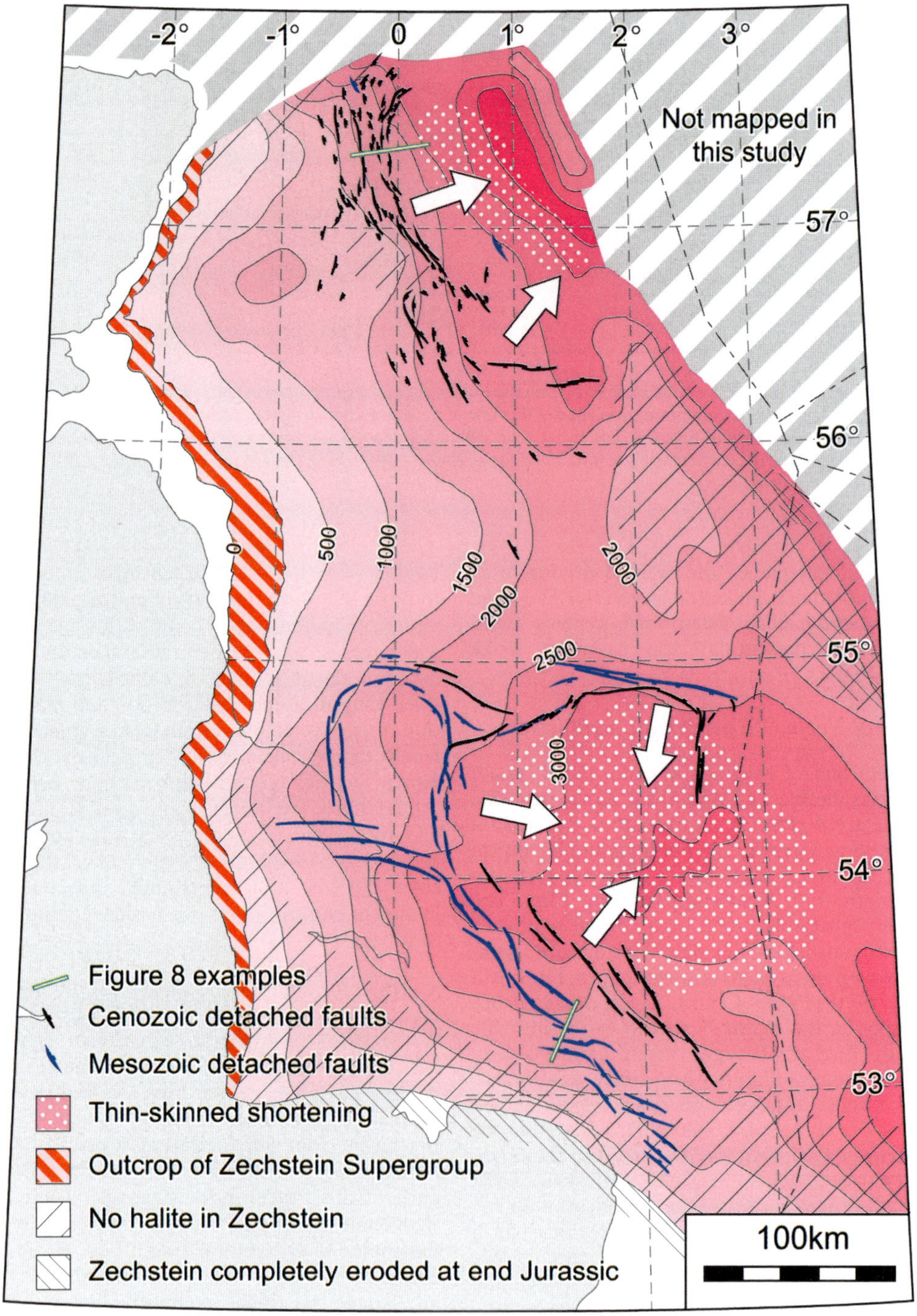

Fig. 7. Peripheral extensional fault systems in the central and southern North Sea, superimposed on present-day structure of base Zechstein (depth in metres) to show regional tilt and curvature of the detachment. Regional structure of Zechstein deepening towards the Central Graben is largely due to Cenozoic basin subsidence (see Fig. 1). Large arrows show the direction of detached slip based on fault trends and regional seismic lines that show linkage between extension and compressional structural domains. Central North Sea fault system is mostly Cenozoic. Southern North Sea fault system has Mesozoic and Cenozoic components.

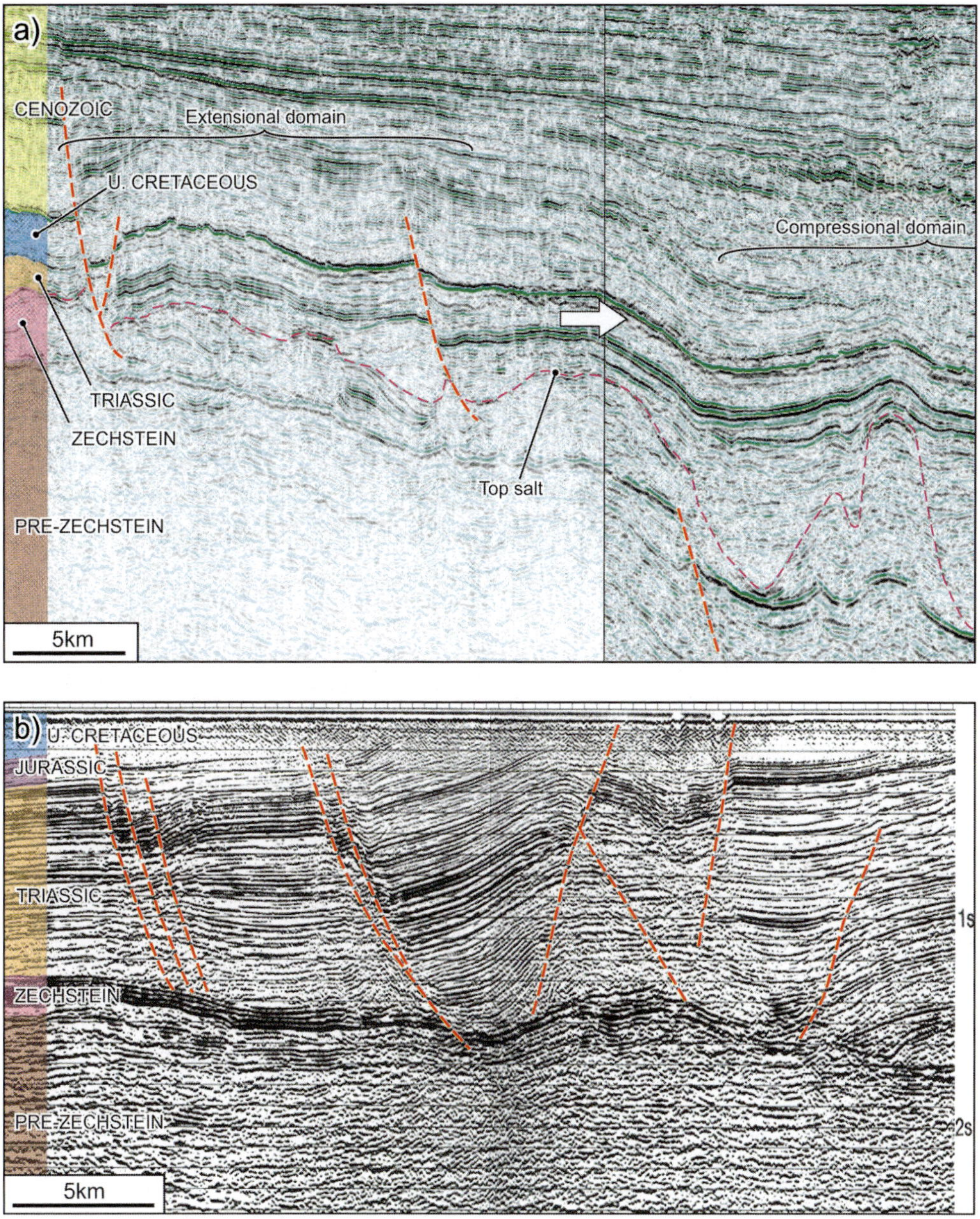

Fig. 8. Seismic sections across North Sea peripheral graben systems. Two-dimensional time-migrated seismic data; 3 × vertical exaggeration. Locations are shown in Figure 7. (**a**) Central North Sea system in Blocks 20/20, 21/16 area. Reflectors within the Zechstein are seismic facies zones 2 and 3 (see Fig. 3). Updip extension and part of downdip compressional domains are both visible in this section. Vertical exaggeration *c.* 6 ×. (**b**) Southern North Sea Mesozoic system on East Midlands Shelf. Regional pin line is Zechstein pinchout to west; sliding was to the east, basinwards.

were extension in the Mesozoic and compression in the Cenozoic (Badley *et al.* 1989; Hooper *et al.* 1995; Huyghe & Mugnier 1995; Stewart & Coward 1995).

The peripheral fault system is best preserved in the west and north of the southern North Sea basin, where it overlies subsalt gasfields, providing overburden complexity that challenges seismic imaging and depth conversion (e.g. Lappin *et al.* 2003; Sarginson 2003). The Mesozoic fault system passes northwestwards beyond the outcrop limit of the Cenozoic and Chalk and there are no constraints on Cenozoic reactivation in this area. The fault system trends southeastwards along the crest of the Sole Pit High, which contains a trend of fault-bound Cenozoic outliers (Van Hoorn 1987; Walker & Cooper 1987; Stewart & Bailey 1996). Several workers have demonstrated the effect of Triassic salt layers in addition to the Zechstein salt upon the geometry of these extensional fault systems (Walker & Cooper 1987; Hooper & More 1995). The relatively thin Triassic salts typically lead to ramp-flat geometries of faults that ultimately detach on Permian salt (e.g. Stewart & Bailey 1996). A separate role of Triassic salt in contributing to the formation of local salt sills is examined below. Triassic salts were removed by pre-Cretaceous erosion in the NE of the southern North Sea.

Influence of salt on rift geometry: Viking Graben to Central Graben

Extensional faults with kilometre-scale displacement that characterize the northern North Sea and Moray Firth also cut through the middle of the central North Sea to form the Central Graben. A comparison of fault styles, as the trend of these basement faults is followed along strike from the north into the Central Graben, shows the modification of fault geometry as the basement faults cut through a progressively thicker salt layer. The basement fault strands that bound the Central Graben are up to 20 km in length with maximum displacements of the order of 3 km. The relationship between basement faults and cover sediments in the CNS is locally complicated by the salt layer having been previously structured into a series of walls and lows (Erratt 1993; Stewart *et al.* 1996; Stewart & Clark 1999).

The degree of linkage between basement and cover structures is proportional to the ratio of detachment thickness to basement fault displacement (Koyi *et al.* 1993). This ratio can vary both spatially as a result of salt thickness and fault displacement variations, and temporally as a result of fault growth (Koyi *et al.* 1993; Stewart *et al.* 1996). Various salt thickness–fault displacement scenarios and resulting half-graben geometries based on central North Sea examples are depicted in Figure 9.

The 'thin' detachment example is relevant to graben near the edge of the North Permian Basin, such as the Buchan Graben and South Viking Graben. During the first increments of basement fault displacement the ratio of salt thickness to basement fault displacement is high, therefore the earliest cover fault can be offset from the location of the basement structure, usually towards the footwall of the basement fault (Fig. 9; Koyi *et al.* 1993; Jackson & Vendeville 1994). As basement fault throw increases, vertical linkage through the salt layer becomes firmer and new cover fault strands root directly onto the basement fault scarp, creating a continuous fault plane linking basement and cover. A key effect of basement fault displacement in salt basins is rotation of both the hanging-wall dip slope and basement fault scarp (via footwall fault block rotation). This can result in local gravity slip systems within fault-bound subbasins, with features such as a pronounced drag fold and hanging-wall syncline adjacent to the basement fault scarp (e.g. Fig. 10b). If the salt were originally several hundred metres thick or more, salt flow from hanging wall to footwall affects the partitioning of fault displacement between hanging-wall subsidence and footwall uplift, relative to base level (e.g. Jackson & Talbot 1994; Quirk *et al.* 1998). This results in a different distribution of accommodation space, particularly in the hanging wall, from that expected by the application of conventional models of extensional faulting (e.g. Gawthorpe & Hurst 1993). This effect can also be viewed in the extensional faults that root on the salt highs of the Paradox Basin.

The influence of thick, initially unstructured salt on the upward linkage of growing basement

Fig. 9. A 2D view of the variety in style of fault linkage through a salt layer, with variation in pre-rift salt thickness. This is based on serial sections following the North Sea rift system southwards from the Viking Graben into the Central Graben. (**a**) Where salt is absent, 'classic' half-graben geometries evolve. (**b**) Where salt is thin (tens of metres or less) a complex cover fault terrace array evolves above the basement scarp. With continuing extension and basement fault block rotation, a salt weld forms on the basement fault scarp and late detached antithetic cover faults accommodate basement extension. (**c**) Where a thick salt layer is present, early cover rafts separated by salt diapirs are draped across the evolving basement topography. (**d**) Over much of the central North Sea, salt is already structured by a Triassic phase of minibasin subsidence, many of the minibasins being already grounded and the salt fully redistributed at the onset of Jurassic basement rifting. Lateral slip of the minibasins as the basement fault blocks on which they rest rotate causes reactivation of the salt diapirs as actively rising or falling, depending on the position on a given dip slope.

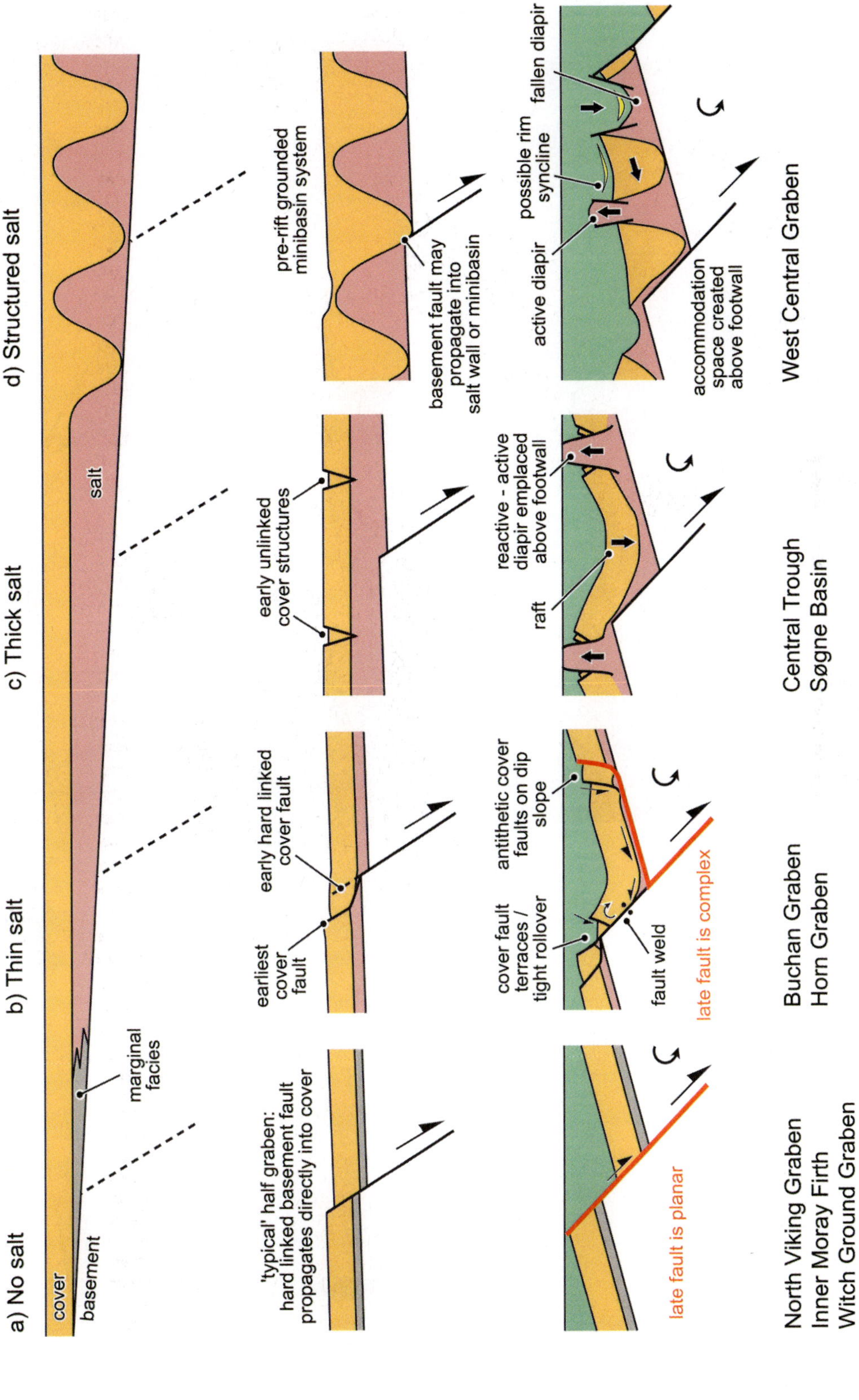
a) No salt
b) Thin salt
c) Thick salt
d) Structured salt
cover
basement
marginal facies
salt
'typical' half graben: hard linked basement fault propagates directly into cover
earliest cover fault
early hard linked cover fault
early unlinked cover structures
pre-rift grounded minibasin system
basement fault may propagate into salt wall or minibasin
late fault is planar
cover fault terraces / tight rollover
fault weld
antithetic cover faults on dip slope
late fault is complex
raft
reactive - active diapir emplaced above footwall
active diapir
possible rim syncline
fallen diapir
accommodation space created above footwall
North Viking Graben
Inner Moray Firth
Witch Ground Graben
Buchan Graben
Horn Graben
Central Trough
Søgne Basin
West Central Graben

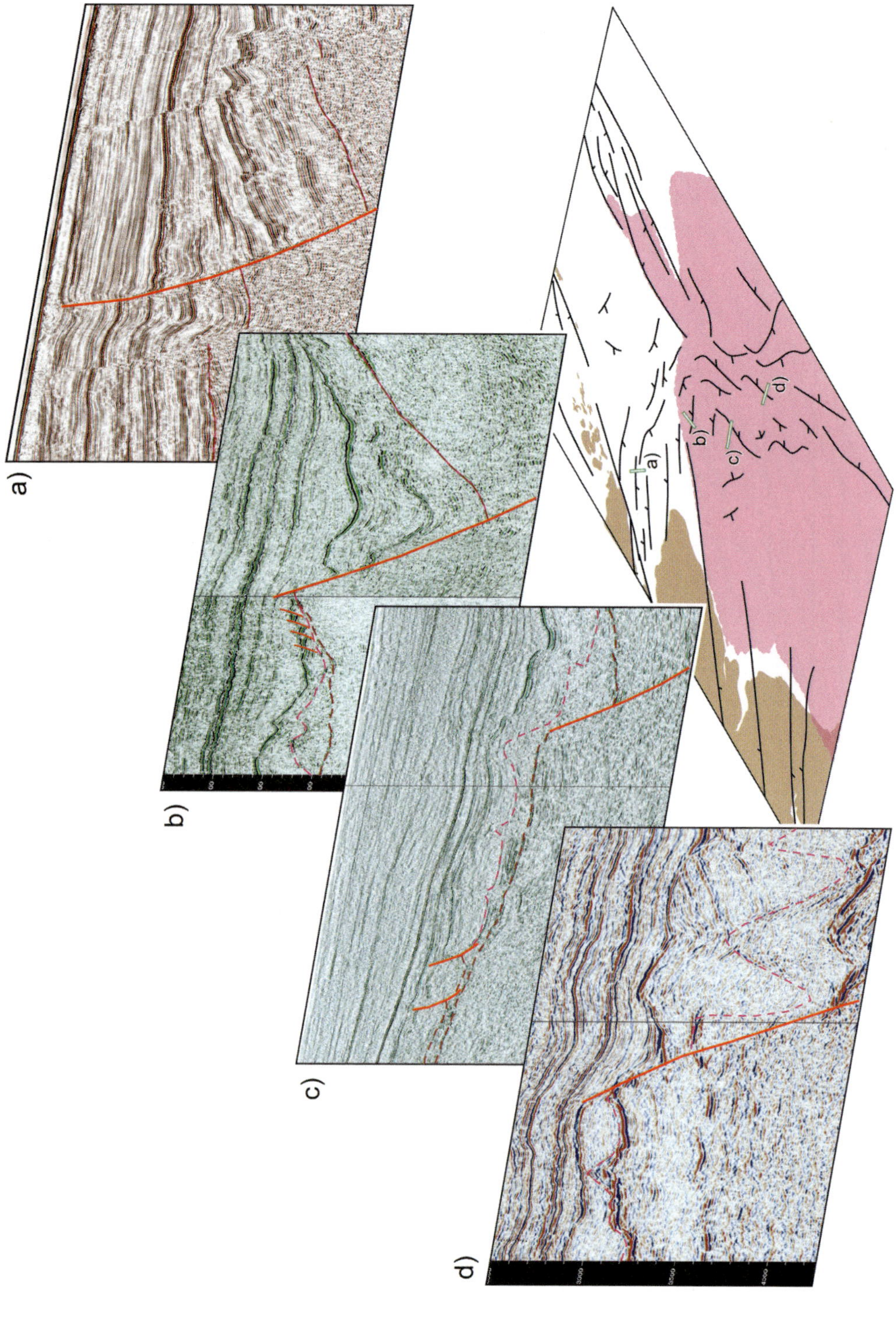
a)
b)
c)
d)

fault systems (Fig. 9) has been extensively modelled (Koyi *et al.* 1993; Nalpas & Brun 1993; Jackson & Vendeville 1994). An important feature of this scenario is that diapirs are emplaced by reactive diapirism within the cover sediments at specific locations, relative to the basement faults. After being emplaced in this way they can grow while the basin subsides, by drainage of salt from its source layer, until that source runs out or is pinched off by compression (Rowan *et al.* 2003). Sub-basins within the central North Sea, such as the Aalborg, Central Trough, Fisher Bank and Søgne basins, show features obtained in these models; for example, large diapirs perched on dip slopes and above basement faults (Roberts *et al.* 1990; Koyi & Petersen 1993; Sundsbø & Megson 1993). Spatial variation in degree of linkage on the Ula–Gyda Fault Zone and Revfallet Fault has been illustrated by Stewart (1993) and Pascoe *et al.* (1999).

Triassic salt structures locally found themselves within the Jurassic rift system and were reactivated to give a variety of salt structure styles (Fig. 9d; Erratt 1993; Gowers *et al.* 1993). In some places the basement fault propagates upwards into a salt wall whereas in others it propagates into a minibasin. A feature of a grounded minibasin system is that salt wall growth or diapirism can be rejuvenated only under the influence of lateral compression, which is likely to occur only in the hanging-wall lows as minibasins slide laterally towards one another or the basement fault scarp buttress. The spatial variation in cover–basement structure relationship is more complicated than that depicted in Figure 9 because of 3D variation in dip at top basement as a result of variations in displacement on elements of the basement fault array (Roberts *et al.* 1990). Figure 11 depicts one of the simplest geometrical scenarios in a basement fault array; two segments overlapping to give a relay zone. In addition to regular half-graben, there are major relay ramps and zones where the footwall dips away from, or at right angles to, rather than towards the basement fault scarps. These features give important components of detachment dip out of section with respect to the dip direction of the main basement fault structures. Salt-enhanced accommodation space above basement relay ramps is particularly significant as relay zones are often the sediment input points on graben margins (Gawthorpe & Hurst 1993). Examples from the margins of the Central Graben are thick Upper Jurassic sands of the Curlew and Fulmar Fields (Johnson *et al.* 1986; Eneyok *et al.* 2004). The majority of the detached extensional faults arising from slip of the rift topography trend at high angles, or are antithetic to, the basement faults (see Clausen & Korstgård 1996). It has also been shown that the geometry of detached cover faults varies with location on a slope and the magnitude of detachment dip (Maudit *et al.* 1997). These parameters vary with time in evolving basement rift systems.

Upper Jurassic structural styles in the Central Graben can be interpreted with this sort of geometrical toolkit in mind (Fig. 9). The structure of any given section and therefore the relationship between salt and the Upper Jurassic sand fairways reflects the interaction of (1) linked or balanced basement and cover structures, (2) unlinked cover slip systems with extensional and compressional elements arising from rotated hanging-wall dip slopes and confined within basement fault-defined basins. Both families of structure locally reactivate (3) pre-rift salt wall–minibasin systems.

Isopachs of the Upper Jurassic Kimmeridge Clay Formation and Lower Cretaceous Cromer Knoll Group in the Central Graben are dominated by salt redistribution effects rather than basement extension. Salt redistribution as a result of thin-skinned slip in the Central Graben might be expected to continue into the Volgian and beyond, as there is no reason to believe that the perched thin-skinned systems should have stabilized the moment basement faulting ceased, as the factors governing the strain rate and finite strain are different for the basement faults and cover slip systems. Continued thin-skinned tectonics controlled accommodation space, which received Upper Jurassic and Lower Cretaceous

Fig. 10. Seismic examples showing variation in fault linkage from basement to cover through Zechstein salt. (**a**) Moray Firth example, north of the Central North Sea. Here the Zechstein is very thin, with no halite. There is no significant mechanical variation separating basement from cover and the faults are planar through the whole section. (**b**) Example from the Buchan Trough area (Block 21/1), on the north margin of the central North Sea. The Zechstein is thin on the right-hand side (north) and thickens southwards with increasing amounts of halite. Cover has detached on the thin Zechstein in the main graben and formed a symmetrical hanging-wall syncline (see example (**a**)). (**c**) Case of basement fault in thicker halite. The basement fault has not propagated through the Zechstein but there is offset extension above the basement footwall and compression above the basement hanging wall (see Jackson & Vendeville 1994). (**d**) Bounding fault of the East Central Graben cutting Triassic minibasins and salt walls. Thickness variation of the Triassic across this fault shows that the Jurassic rift is a reactivation of Triassic extension in this area.

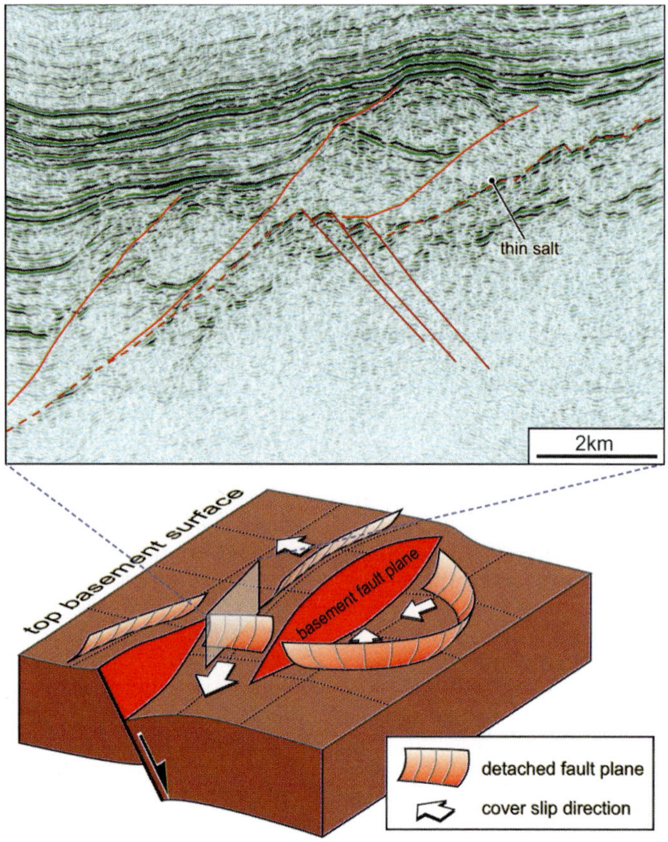

Fig. 11. The basement faults that define the Central Graben are segmented at tens of kilometres scale. This sets up local sub-basins and ramps that have counter-regional dip and produce localized gravity slip domains. This example is from Block 30/12 area. Seismic line is 2 × vertically exaggerated. Top and Base Zechstein are annotated on the seismic data as in previous figures. The basement ramp is cut by an antithetic fault zone, but the cover is broken into low-angle faults defining blocks that are slipping down into the basin. One of these blocks contains the Fulmar oilfield in Upper Jurassic sands.

turbidites shed from the adjacent platforms, adding an element of differential loading and leading to isopachs whose form is controlled more by salt redistribution than basement faulting (Fig. 9; Høiland *et al.* 1993; Richards *et al.* 1993; Carruthers *et al.* 1996).

Salt intrusions: diapirs; Central Graben and southern North Sea

There are a small number of well-developed passive diapirs fossilized in the thick Cenozoic sediments of the Central Graben (Figs 2 and 12; Davison *et al.* 2000). Their location is controlled by basement faults as described above, and their subsequent growth is by passive diapirism (Rowan *et al.* 2003). They are circular in plan view, and reach structural elevations of up to 2 km above the base Cenozoic, although none reach the present sea bed. Seismic imaging of these diapirs is good enough to show minor faults in the adjacent and overlying Cenozoic sediments. This allows description of the faults associated with passive diapirism from the perspective of segmentation of siliciclastic reservoirs at these structural levels, thus assisting seismic interpretation and structural model building in areas of poor seismic imaging.

Fault patterns associated with passive diapirs

A question can be posed: are fault patterns predictable in areas that remain poorly imaged by

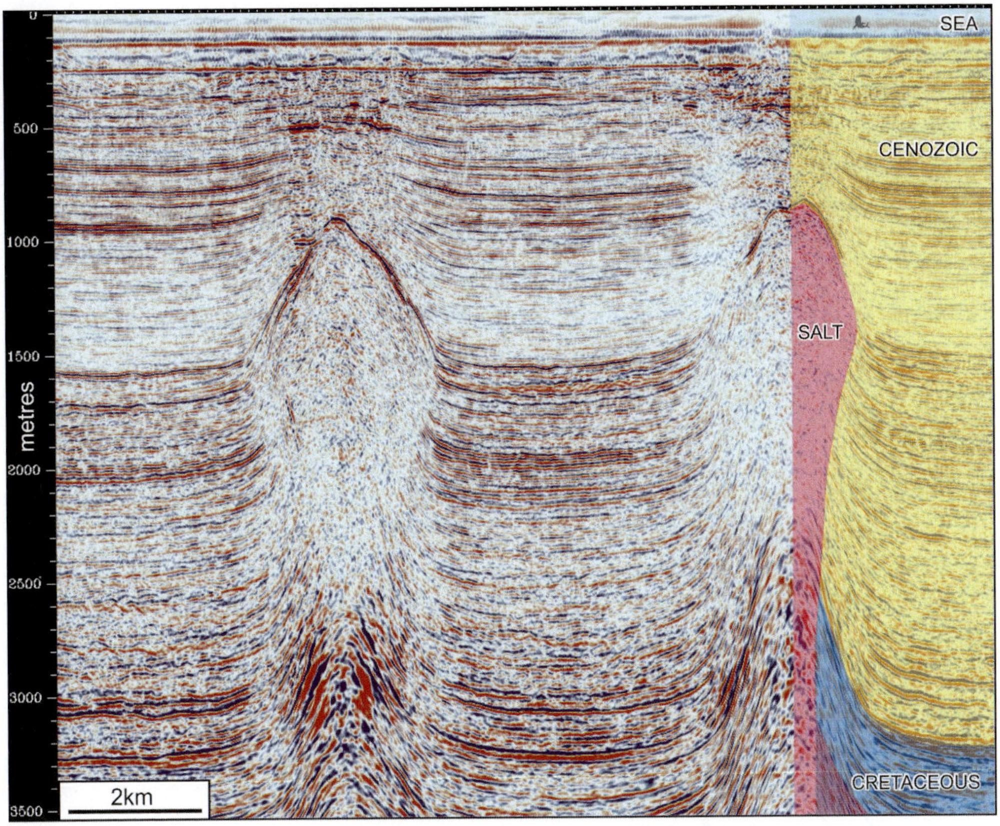

Fig. 12. Typical appearance of teardrop-shaped salt diapirs in Cenozoic sediments in the East Central Graben. Vertical scale is approximately in metres. Bright seismic amplitudes directly above diapirs are hydrocarbons that have leaked up diapir flanks and through roof seals.

seismic data, under salt overhangs for instance? Conversely, what do high-quality maps of fault patterns reveal, if anything, about the adjacent diapir? Reviews of the geometry and emplacement of salt (Jackson 1995), shale (Brown 1990) and igneous (Clemens 1998) diapirs tend not to focus on map-view patterns of faults around intrusions, although these patterns have been investigated in modelling studies (e.g. Withjack & Scheiner 1982; Walter & Troll 2001). Cross-disciplinary literature indicates that radial faults are generally associated with doming (Fig. 13a and b; e.g. Squyres *et al.* 1992; Davison *et al.* 2000) and concentric extensional faults are most commonly associated with basin subsidence (Fig. 13c; Branney 1995; Malthe-Sørenssen *et al.* 1999). Analogue models of cyclic doming and deflation support this relationship (Squyres *et al.* 1992; Walter & Troll 2001). An exception is a minor downfaulted apical cone occasionally seen above domes in experiment and nature (Alsop 1996; Davison *et al.* 2000). Radial extensional faults also occur where diapirs perturb regional polygonal fault sets (Davison *et al.* 2000). Concentric reverse faults are rare and characterize uplift caused by relatively rapid, forceful intrusion (Schultz-Ela *et al.* 1993).

There have been decades of debate on how salt diapirs are actually emplaced, and what assumptions should be made about the mechanical parameters of the intruded sediments (Jackson 1995). Currently accepted models do not have significant elements of forceful intrusion, instead favouring 'downbuilding' of adjacent sediments around an emergent or shallow diapir crest that becomes buried when salt supplies run out (Rowan *et al.* 2003). Diapirism continues until the salt supply runs out, then the diapir is buried. This sets up three structural domains around the diapir. These are summarized along with structural elements in Figure 14.

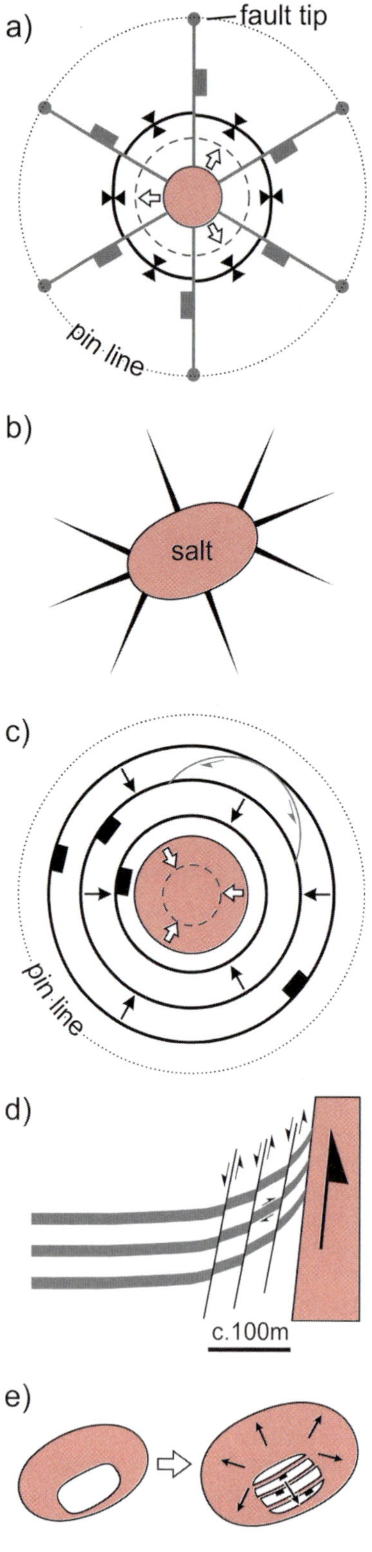

Structural domains of passive diapirs

Reservoirs associated with cylindrical salt diapirs can be segmented by radial faults, concentric faults, both or neither (Davison *et al.* 2000). Strata around cylindrical diapirs can be divided into three structural domains with characteristic fault styles.

(1) Roof zone between the present-day depositional surface and the crest of a buried, inactive diapir. This zone is characterized by doming, radial faults and, occasionally, conical graben. Doming is usually caused by differential compaction and increases with depth.

(2) A steeply dipping sheath of strata surrounds the diapir, recording near-surface diapir growth in poorly lithified sediments. These contain early gravity slumps and late concentric extensional faults within *c.* 100 m of the salt (Alsop *et al.* 2000; Davison *et al.* 2000). Regional layer-bound polygonal fault systems form radial faults within approximately one diapir radius; the only significant radial faulting mechanism below the roof zone.

(3) Diapir root zone of strata whose structural architecture records the diapirs' initiating mechanism, typically rim synclines or graben associated with reactive diapirism that detach on the salt source layer. Concentric faults have been found only in root zone rim synclines and sheared sheath strata.

The roof zone contains a differential compaction dome that decreases in amplitude upwards from top salt to the present depositional surface. Being a non-cylindrical surface, dome growth must be accommodated by penetrative strain (e.g. Lisle 1994). That strain is manifest as radial faults in zones that are sufficiently compacted to deform by brittle failure at the scale of seismic resolution. Radial faults show up as low-angle

Fig. 13. Radial and concentric fault patterns and kinematics associated with diapirs that are circular in plan view. All sketches are plan views except (**d**). Driving mechanism is salt flow and area change of the diapir in cross-section. Volume and line length balance assumed. (**a**) Expansion of central zone forces concentric fold and circumferential extension accommodated by radial faults. (**b**) Radial fault clustering at each end of elliptical hole or intrusion. (**c**) Contraction of central zone allows concentric, inward-facing extensional faults. Secondary, non-concentric structures accommodate circumferential contraction. (**d**) Sheared sediments close to diapir margin (vertical section, after Alsop *et al.* 2000, fig. 9c). These faults are subparallel to the salt–sediment interface (i.e. concentric in plan view). (**e**) Inflation or gravity spreading of diapir roof and fragments of overlying sediments.

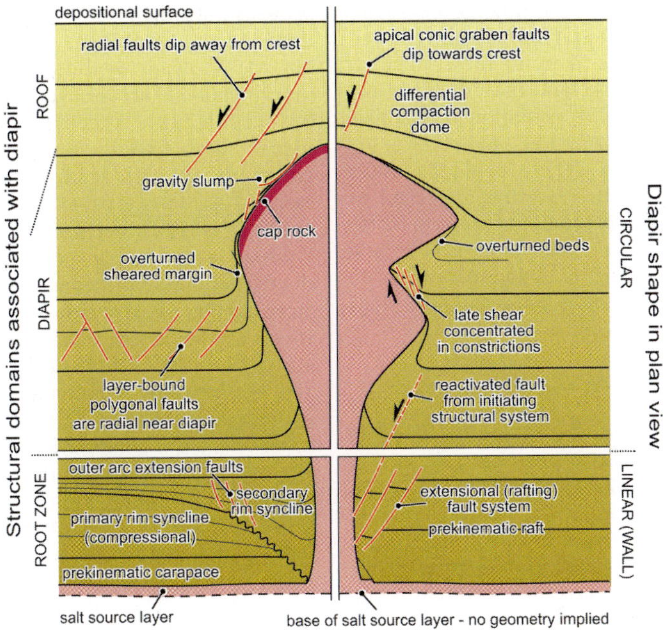

Fig. 14. Summary of structures in three structural domains of a fossil diapir, representing suites of structural elements to consider when interpreting seismic data in poor image quality areas near salt diapirs. No exhumation events are shown. Diagram is exploded to show different diapir initiation and shape scenarios, and associated structures in adjacent and roof domain strata. No scale is shown, but diapirs are typically 1–2 km in diameter. Relative proportions of root domain, diapir and roof sketched here are chosen for clarity, not significance.

extensional faults facing away from the diapir central axis in seismic sections. Less common is a conjugate strain accommodation feature in domed strata; a minor, downward-tapering conic graben reminiscent of an igloo chimney directly above the diapir crest. Reverse faults, dipping towards the diapir axis, are relatively rare, and are associated with diapir reactivation (Schultz-Ela *et al.* 1993). Repetition or inversion of stratigraphy also occurs via gravity slumping of the strata adjacent to the salt.

Adjacent sediments, in the 'diapir domain' are folded upwards and terminate against the salt at low structural cutoff angles (Fig. 14). Where the salt–sediment interface is overhanging these strata are steeply dipping or overturned. Seismic-scale radial faults expected from the kinematics of these units are rare, presumably because most of the folding occurred at or near the depositional surface when the sediments were freshly deposited and unlithified. Within a zone *c.* 100 m from the salt–sediment interface, the steeply dipping sediments sheathing the diapir are sheared by extensional, concentric faults as a function of interface orientation, relative to salt flow direction and the amount of differential compaction (Fig. 13d; Alsop 1996; Alsop *et al.* 2000). This is the only type of concentric fault found by this study to exist adjacent to a salt diapir between the root zone and roof zone. The steeply dipping sheath units can also contain repeat sequences in right-way-up or overturned gravity slides preserved on the diapir crest. Layers that are regionally prone to polygonal faulting usually organize into radial faults within about one diapir radius (Davison *et al.* 2000). This is the most likely cause of radial faulting adjacent to a diapir. These can be predicted in poorly imaged areas using estimated positions of the bounding surfaces of the polygonally faulted layer and diapir wall. Reactivated deep structures, such as extensional faults that played a role in diapir initiation, may propagate upwards into the strata, adjacent to a diapir, but should be visible outside areas of poor imaging. Reactivated deep structures are likely to give asymmetric rather than radial reservoir segmentation close to the salt–sediment interface.

The lowest domain ('root domain') contains the connection of a diapir to its source layer. Strata in this zone are likely to preserve structures that record the mechanism of diapir initiation. Two main types of initiation mechanism and characteristic structural geometries are included in Figure 14. There could be linear extensional fault trends recording detached or basement-linked raft tectonics (e.g. central North Sea), or rim synclines recording growth and deflation of a salt-cored anticline, possibly with extensional faults trending along the fold hinge (e.g. southern North Sea).

Central Graben passive diapir examples

Some 15 salt diapirs, circular rather than linear in plan view, are fossilized in the Cenozoic section that overlies the Central Graben (Davison *et al.* 2000; Birch & Haynes 2003; Rank-Friend & Elders 2004). Seismic sections of salt diapirs are shown in Figure 15. Figure 15a shows the top of a North Sea diapir, with roof zone strata diverging from the apex. Top salt is marked by a number of concordant reflections. This cap rock zone is a now-deformed exposure of top salt, consisting of a mixture of insoluble evaporites and condensed roof domain strata. The diapir apex is bounded by curved faults that offset the cap rock and force rollover folds in adjacent strata. These are interpreted here as a minor late pulse of active diapirism caused by tectonic compression. Strata above the crest are downfaulted by a subtle graben. A horizontal slice of seismic data shows that the graben is ring-shaped, and radial faults are also present (Fig. 15f).

The diapir in Figure 15b is dominated by a phase of increasing, then decreasing salt flow rate relative to sedimentation rate, resulting in a biconic, 'teardrop' form. Rotated sequences thin onto the conical crest and are also preserved down the flanks of the downward pointing cone. Connection to the source layer is not clearly imaged, a common problem in the seismic interpretation of tall diapirs, because of the challenge of acquisition and processing seismic reflection data in areas of complex velocity structure (Muerdter & Ratcliffe 2001). There are no clearly resolvable faults in the drag folds adjacent to this diapir. The diapir crest is *c.* 1000 m below sea bed and the structure appears to have been extinct since burial. It is not clear whether the lowest 500 m of roof domain strata onlap the diapir, recording significant sea bed topography, or whether strata condense onto the diapir crest.

The seismic section in Figure 15c is tangential to the widest part of a diapir to obtain a clearer image of the adjacent strata. The diapir crest projects onto the section at approximately two-thirds height. Roof domain strata are once again domed, showing well-developed radial faults (interpreted and arrowed). The diapir adjacent to this section has a 'teardrop' form, so the amplitude of drag folding caused by passive diapir growth decays with depth as the diapir becomes more distant from the line of section. This folding can be seen in dip direction in Figures 12 and 15b. Folding in something akin to a strike section shows that line lengthening that has been accommodated by a stretching mechanism whose effects are below the imaging resolution of seismic reflection data, for example, pre-lithification ductile stretching (Maltman 1994). Polygonal faults are present throughout the strata occupied by this diaper, a good indication that the steeply dipping flanking strata of this structure are segmented by radial faults. Figure 15d shows detail of a roof domain whose structural amplitude becomes more pronounced with depth, a signature of differential compaction.

Southern North Sea collapsed anticline diapirs

The southern North Sea is characterized by salt-cored buckle folds that began to grow in the Mesozoic under the influence of gravity sliding, and amplified in the Palaeogene as a result of regional shortening (Stewart & Coward 1995, 1996). Most of these structures are preserved today as detached buckle folds cored by salt pillows, but occasionally the fold crests are pierced by diapirs. Diapirs in this structural setting were the subject of classic work on salt tectonics (Trusheim 1960). A question remained for some time regarding how salt in the cores of these anticlines actually pierced the overlying units to form an intrusive structure. Stewart & Coward (1995) offered two suggestions: the anticline crests could be thinned by extensional faulting and in turn intruded by reactive diapirism, or the crests of high-amplitude folds could simply be eroded to expose the salt (Fig. 16). Seismic examples suggest that the latter mechanism accounts for initiation of many diapirs associated with collapsed anticlines in the southern North Sea and South Permian Basin, the key evidence being erosional truncation of the anticline limbs recorded at the top of the primary rim syncline sequence (Fig. 17; Cameron *et al.* 1992; Sørensen 1998).

Once the salt is breached, it can drain the pillow that cores the anticline, leading to collapse of the fold limbs, unfolding the original structure and creating space for growth of a synkinematic

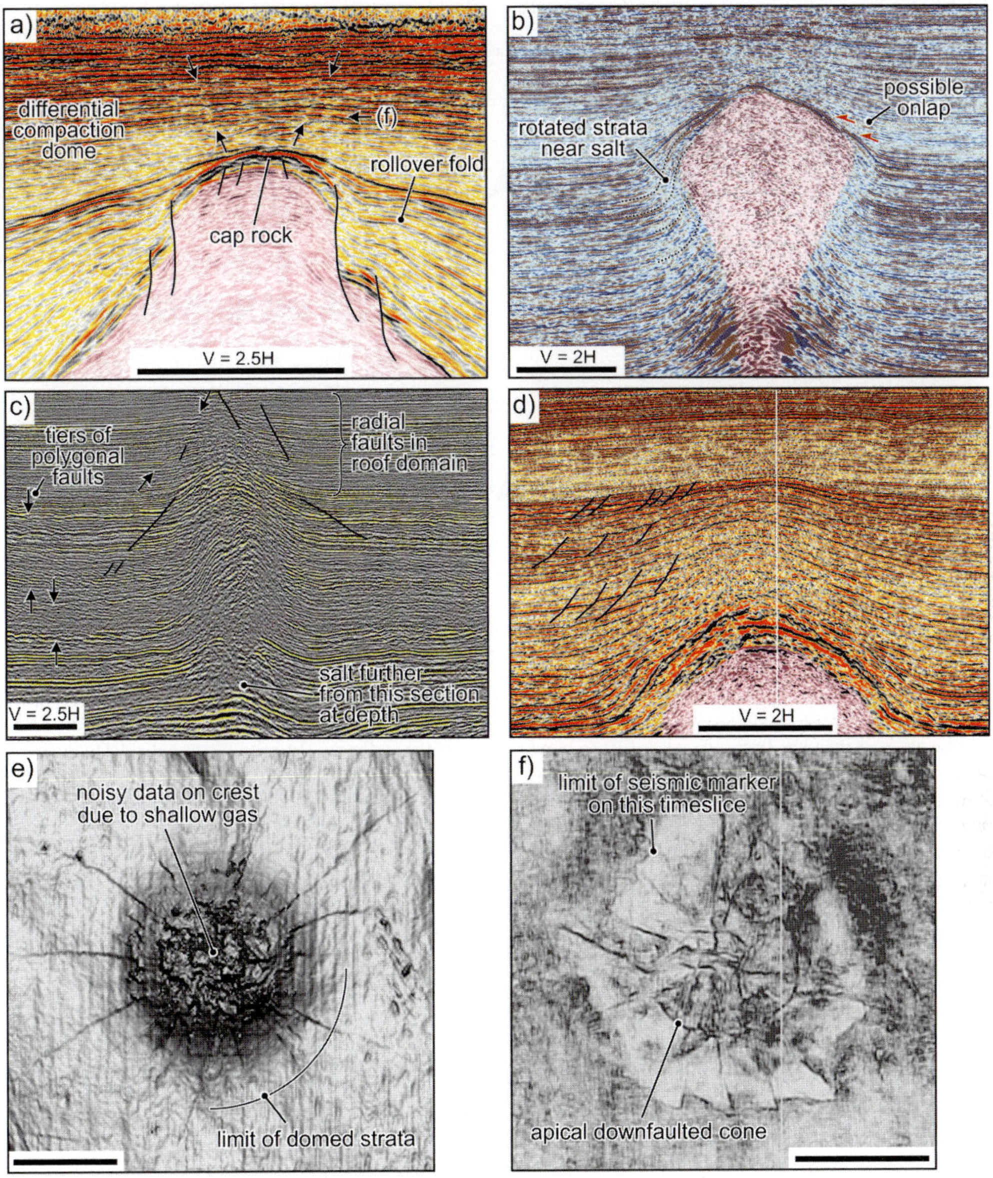

Fig. 15. Seismic examples of diapirs and associated fracture patterns from the central North Sea in vertical and plan view sections. All seismic volumes are 3D, all scale bars 1 km, vertical exaggeration *n* labelled as V = *n*H, salt interpretation shaded pink. (**a**) View of to diapir crest, North Sea. Location of timeslice (**f**) is shown. (**b**) North Sea diapir. (**c**) Section tangential to the widest part of North Sea diapir. (**d**) Tiers of radial faults in North Sea diapir roof domain. (**e**) Radial faults in domed sediments above salt diapir, North Sea (dip magnitude of mapped surface shaded). (**f**) Radial faults and crestal conic graben, coherence slice, section in (**a**).

sequence that thickens into the central diapir (Fig. 16; Vendeville 2002). Fold collapse could lead to increase in line length in the line of section, which is presumably accommodated by growth of adjacent folds. The eroded anticline limbs that thin to the centre and the collapse sequence that thickens to the centre were termed primary and secondary rim synclines, respectively, by Trusheim (1960). This mechanism of diapir initiation contrasts with the extensional

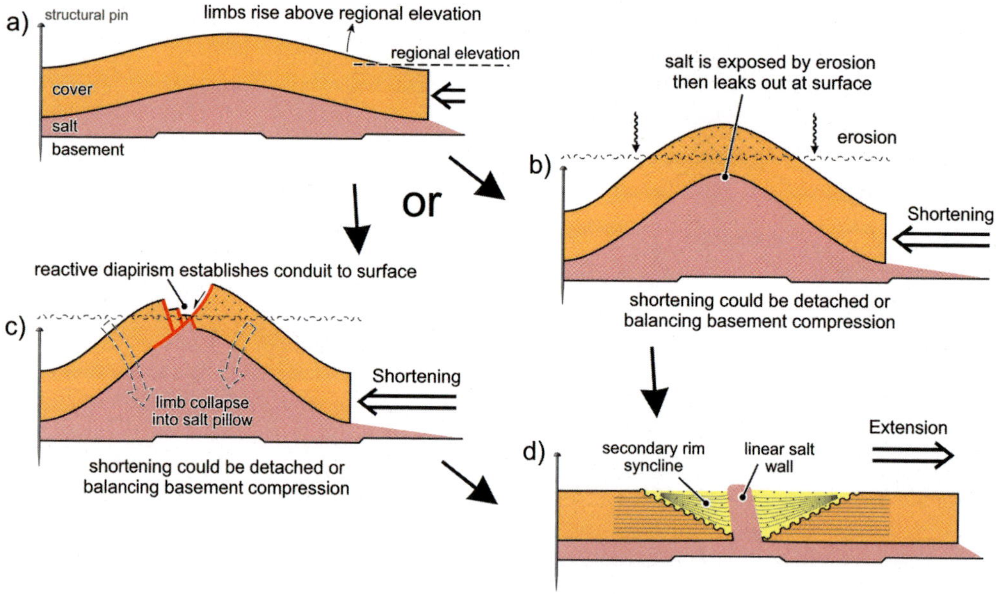

Fig. 16. Breached anticline collapse model of salt wall emplacement, based upon examples in the southern North Sea. This depiction is a thin-skinned detachment fold (e.g. southern North Sea in the Mesozoic), but the detachment fold could equally grow to balance shortening on sub-salt compressional structures (e.g. southern North Sea in the Palaeogene). (**a**) Anticline amplifies as a result of thin- or thick-skinned shortening. Then either (**b**) erosion of crest of anticline exposes salt, or (**c**) reactive diapirism intrudes crestal collapse fault zone, or some combination of the two. Then, (**d**) salt is free to bleed off to surface, deflating the salt pillow in the detachment fold core and allowing the limbs to collapse. The growth sequence thickening to the central salt conduit is a 'secondary rim syncline' (Trusheim 1960). It should be noted that the salt intrusion formed in this way will be elongate or linear in plan view, depending on the geometry of the breach.

context of reactive diapirism seen in many other salt basins (e.g. Vendeville & Jackson 1992) and produces an alternative structural architecture that could be preserved in the root zones of passive diapirs at high structural levels (Fig. 14).

Salt intrusions: sills; Southern North Sea

Salt sills can originate by a number of mechanisms in various geological settings, from emplacement within thrust sheets (Velaj *et al.* 1999) to kilometre-scale immiscible mixing of salt and siliciclastic sediments driven by massive differential loading of thick salt (e.g. Rowan *et al.* 1999). The margins of passive diapirs can include overhangs or wings as a result of variations in relative rates of salt extrusion and background sedimentation (Koyi 1998; Rowan *et al.* 2003). These wings could also be classified as sills. But most common in the North Sea are salt sills created by a different mechanism again: delamination of parts of the supra-Zechstein strata on thin autochthonous Triassic salts, made possible by intrusion of Zechstein salt (Stewart *et al.* 1996; Baldschuhn *et al.* 1998). Sills are absent from much of the North Permian Basin portion of the North Sea because Triassic salts are not present. Delamination occurs in a number of geological settings, from crustal scale (e.g. Bird 1979) and kilometre-scale magmatic stoping (e.g. Yoshinobu *et al.* 2003) to metre-scale intra-Zechstein salt flow around rafts of interbedded anhydrite and dolomite (e.g. Jenyon 1989).

As the sills always occur at the same stratigraphic level as autochthonous Triassic salts (i.e. within the Triton Anhydritic and Dudgeon Saliferous Formations and their lateral equivalents), the sills are most easily recognized by anomalous intra-Triassic salt thickness in wells or on seismic data (e.g. Fig. 18b). Triassic salts reach a maximum depositional thickness of *c.* 150 m in the UK southern North Sea sector (Cameron *et al.* 1992). Three-dimensional mapping in the vicinity of a thickness anomaly in excess of 150 m (e.g. Fig. 18) invariably reveals the presence of a steep salt structure linking

Inversion tectonics in salt basin: Central Graben and West Central Shelf

The idea of tectonic 'inversion' is used widely but not necessarily consistently in published work and by commercial geoscientists. A consensus definition was reached by Cooper *et al.* (1989), which required that (1) the inverted basin originated by extensional faulting; (2) it has recognizable synrift or passive infill sequence; (3) the same extensional faults are reactivated, leading to hanging-wall uplift. This definition excludes some scenarios where uplift has followed subsidence and other situations where at best, relative uplift or subsidence can be identified. Rather than become entangled in the semantics of that definition, some examples are offered here (Fig. 22), to illustrate the variety of relative uplift types in the North Sea salt basins and how they might be distinguished from one another.

The example shown in Figure 22a has no recognizable syn-rift or passive infill, yet the post-rift is clearly elevated above the regional level defined in the footwall. Figure 22b, from the south margin of the central North Sea, shows transpressional inversion of a graben with thin salt. It also highlights one of the issues with defining 'regional' elevation datum levels. Here the regional datum levels at shallow structural level are tilted, reflecting larger-scale, regional structure. In the contractional gravity slip domain of the West Central Shelf (Fig. 22c), the salt highs have been compressed between minibasins to accommodate updip extension (see Figs 7 and 8). Jurassic thick sequences on top of the salt are folded into anticlines (see Fig. 4b). Figure 22d shows anticlinal highs cored by Triassic minibasins in the central North Sea. These are drape folds caused by differential compaction of the thicker Jurassic and Lower Cretaceous sequences on the adjacent salt highs, possibly combined with subjacent dissolution by formation water flowing through Permian sands at base salt. Three-dimensional mapping in this area shows that the salt has not drained out of section. Without well control, which is abundant, there may be temptation to swap the units interpreted as salt and minibasins.

These examples define a framework for structural highs (Fig. 23). Differential compaction (leading to drape) is a ubiquitous process that may be locally overprinted by tectonic uplift (giving 'inversion'; Fig. 23). In this framework, two structures that are identical at post-rift structural level may have contrasting deeper stratigraphy, with potentially punishing implications for exploration drilling. For example, the salt-cored high in Figure 23b (e.g. Kittiwake Field) is a similar Cenozoic structure to that in Figure 23d (e.g. Triton Field), but wells drilling to the pre-Cenozoic below Triton would not find the Jurassic fairway that underlies the Cenozoic reservoirs of the Kittiwake Field. With no prior information, regional elevation datum levels would be difficult to use as a tool to distinguish which of these sections qualified as inversion. Although representatives of each situation depicted in Figure 23 have been described as inversion, only Figure 23a meets the criteria of Cooper *et al.* (1989). Given that compression will preferentially shorten salt structures, giving uplift of what ever lies on top of the salt, a basin or otherwise, there is a case for the definition of inversion to be relaxed to include thick depositional sequences on salt highs that are uplifted relative to local datum levels (e.g. Fig. 23b). An alternative approach is to recognize that inversion structures are a subset of tectonic reactivation structures (Holdsworth *et al.* 1997). Reactivation was defined by Holdworth *et al.* (1997) as 'the accommodation of geologically separable displacement events (intervals >1 Myr) along pre-existing structures'. Either way, it can be surprisingly difficult to separate tectonic from compactional structures; North Sea experience suggests that one should keep an open mind until all available data have been explored for evidence of thick- or thin-skinned tectonic influence.

North Sea examples as basis for structural classification systems

Initiation and driving mechanisms for the evolution of salt structures have been the subject of an enormous amount of publications (reviews by Jackson & Talbot 1994; Jackson 1995). What has emerged from these decades of research is that a wide variety of processes (with the exception of 'spontaneous halokinesis') can initiate and drive, or give way to, a different process that drives salt structure evolution. Stewart & Clark (1999) offered a summary of these mechanisms based on North Sea work (Fig. 24). Also shown in Figure 24 is an indication of modifications arising from exhumation then reburial of the salt basin. Not shown is the rich subset of structures produced when a large siliciclastic load mobilizes a thick salt layer, as seen in the Gulf of Mexico canopy and minibasin system (Rowan *et al.* 1999). Reactivation (e.g. inversion) is not shown. When viewed from the perspective of Figure 24, it could be suggested that structural processes known as 'salt tectonics' can alternatively be thought of as subsets of standard tectonic processes (compression, extension, or strike-slip) or

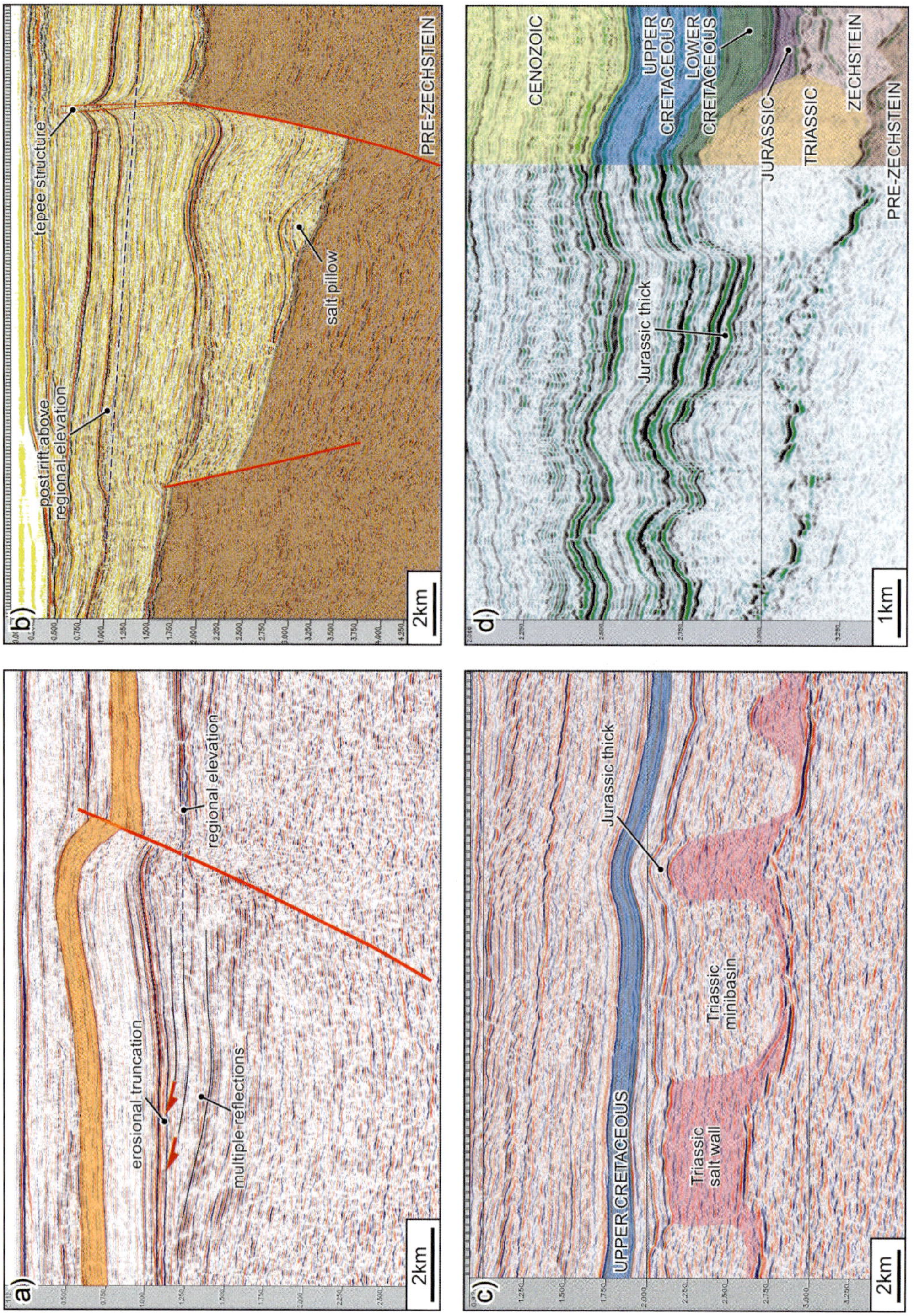
a)
erosional truncation
multiple reflections
regional elevation
2km
b)
post-rift above regional elevation
tepee structure
salt pillow
PRE-ZECHSTEIN
2km
c)
UPPER CRETACEOUS
Jurassic thick
Triassic salt wall
Triassic minibasin
2km
d)
CENOZOIC
UPPER CRETACEOUS
LOWER CRETACEOUS
JURASSIC
TRIASSIC
ZECHSTEIN
PRE-ZECHSTEIN
Jurassic thick
1km

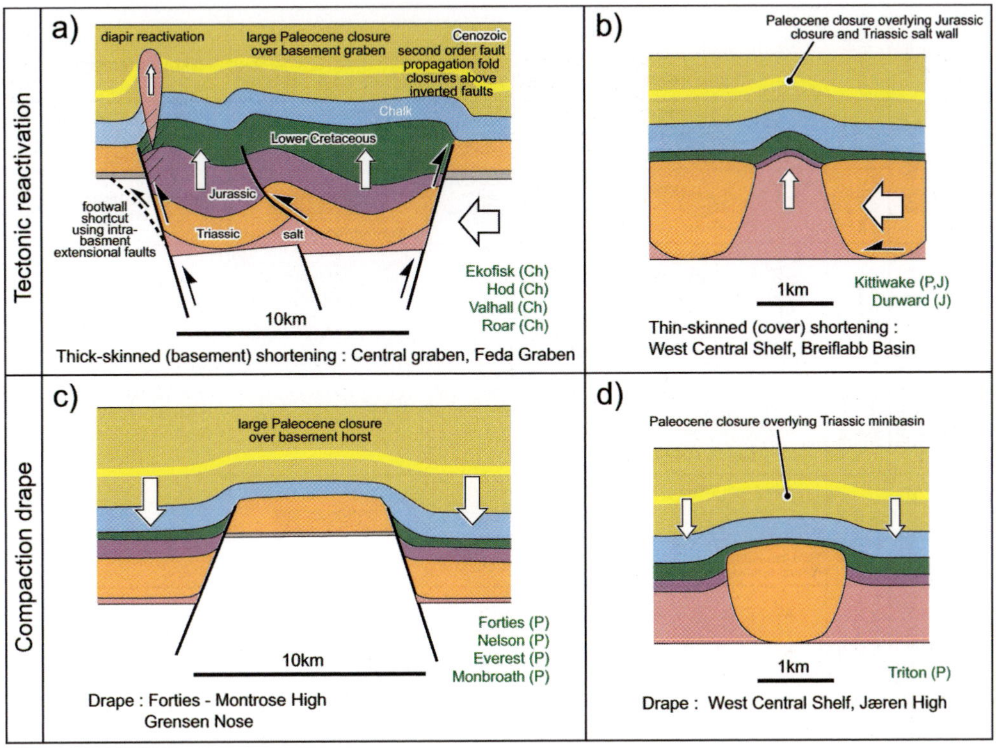

Fig. 23. Relationships between fold closures, basement structures and salt structures from central North Sea examples. Episodes of differential erosion and tectonic reactivation ('inversion') separate the major hydrocarbon fairways in the basin (Jurassic and Cenozoic). Presence of a late (post-Jurassic) closure indicates little about the underlying geology. (**a**) Basement shortening across a Jurassic graben gives large closures above the graben fill (see Fig. 22b) and in hanging-wall anticlines above the reactivated faults, which contain large Chalk oilfields. (**b**) Detached shortening compresses Triassic salt walls and uplifts overlying strata, giving stacked closures in Jurassic and Palaeocene units (see Figs 8b and 22c). Without tectonic reactivation overprint, a background signature of differential compaction creates Cretaceous and Cenozoic closures, offset from the thickest Jurassic and lower Cretaceous sequences (**c**,**d**). Seismic example of (**d**) in Figure 22d. Examples of Central North Sea hydrocarbon fields are annotated on each case, noting the reservoir: P, Palaeogene; Ch, Chalk; J, Jurassic.

differential loading scenarios. This idea is developed further in Figure 25, where salt structures are central to the construction of a paradigm for structural styles in sedimentary basins.

Figure 25 is based on the notion that structural style is a product of a given type of tectonics (e.g. extension) imposed on a given mechanostratigraphy. End-member mechanostratigraphies give contrasting structural styles in a given tectonic setting (compare the results of propagating an extensional fault through a homogeneous, mechanically strong layer versus a

Fig. 22. Seismic examples of structures around the North Sea that have all been described as 'inversion', but do not necessarily fit within published definition of inversion tectonics. (**a**) Half-graben where hanging-wall pre-rift section, partially obscured by multiples, subcrops post-rift. Post-rift is uplifted above regional elevation datum levels. No halite in Zechstein in this area. (**b**) Graben with tens to hundreds of metres of Zechstein salt. An anticline cored by a salt pillow formed as a result of gravity slip during extension (see Fig. 9). Inversion has lifted the post-rift section above regional level in the area of the graben. Strike-slip tepee structure above the graben-bounding faults suggests that the inversion was transpressional. (**c**) Triassic minibasins and salt walls, West Central Shelf. The salt highs are reactivated as the cores of Cenozoic anticlines. (**d**) Grounded Triassic minibasins in the Jæren High area. In contrast to (**c**), the salt and overlying thick Jurassic sequence are in structural lows. The post-Cretaceous highs here are cored by Triassic strata.

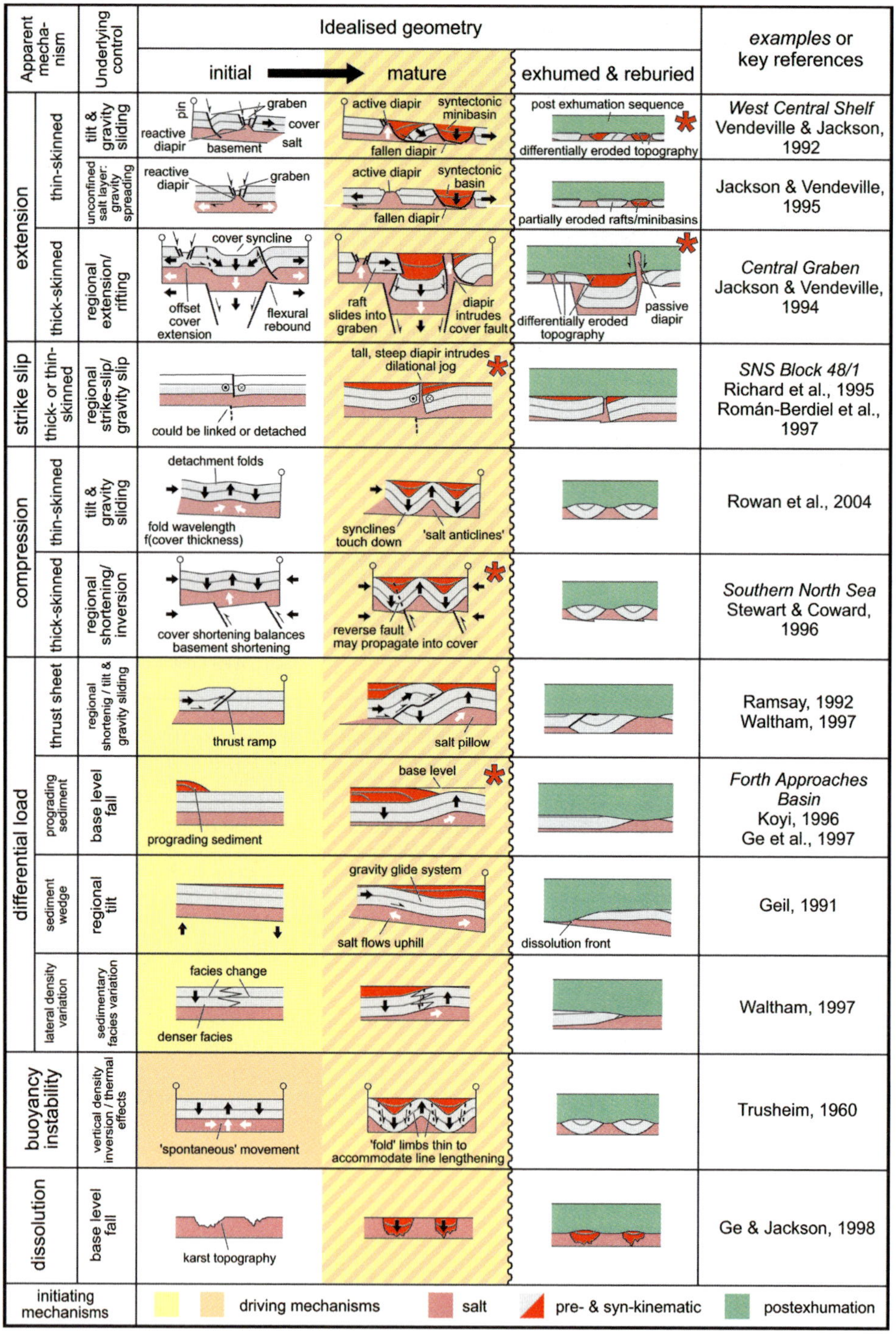

Fig. 24. Review of initiating and driving mechanisms of salt tectonics. Starred examples are from the North Sea. Progression from initial to mature structure colour is shaded to indicate that the triggering mechanism (e.g. extension) may be different from the mechanism that drives salt tectonics (e.g. differential loading). Scenarios arising from exhumation and reburial are also shown, based in part on North Sea examples, to emphasize unconformity geometries in salt basins.

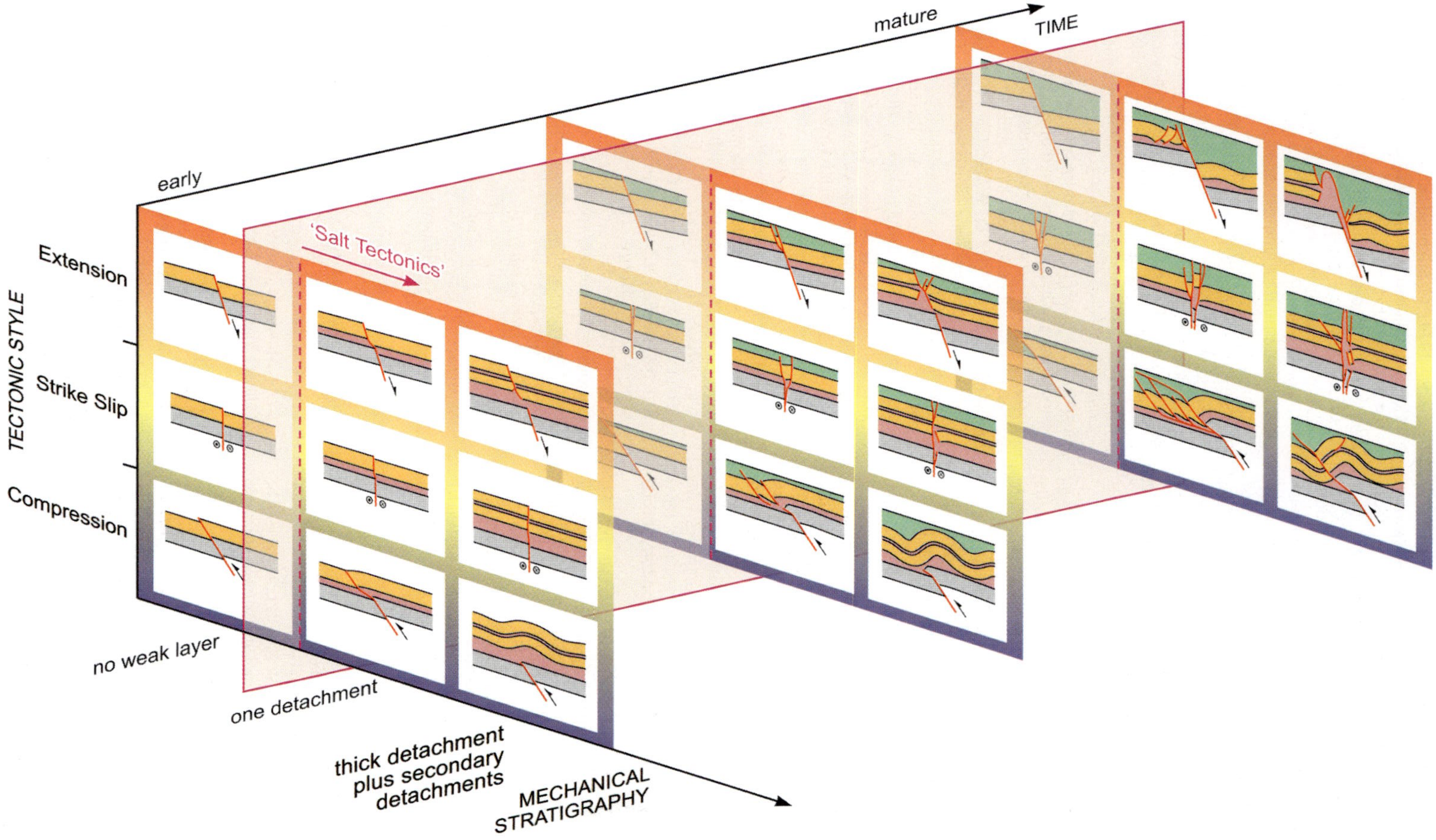

Fig. 25. 'Structural style matrix' concept that defines salt tectonics as an extra dimension to extensional, compressional and strike-slip tectonics. For each regular tectonic setting, a spectrum of styles can occur reflecting mechanostratigraphic complexity (e.g. whether salt is present). This could also represent spatial variation in a basin. Another dimension annotated here is time, recognizing that ongoing tectonics modifies the initial style, and sedimentation may also be continuing.

multilayer that includes a weak layer (Figs 9 and 25)). A fully populated matrix would be impossible to construct because of the range in possible mechanostratigraphies, combined with extra dimensions needed to represent time-dependent evolution of mechanical properties (e.g. compaction), tectonic reactivation, exhumation and reburial. Unravelling the unique combination of mechanisms that led to present-day structure in a given field area is the key role of the mapper or seismic interpreter. Figures 24 and 25 are attempts to visualize structural style toolkits that might assist the challenge.

This paper includes much published work and contributions from co-workers past and present at Amerada Hess Ltd and BP, and in academia. Reviews by A. Roberts and M. Huuse improved the manuscript. The principal acknowledgement goes to Mike Coward, for getting me started. The views expressed here are solely those of the author and not necessarily those of BP.

References

ALLEN, M. R., GRIFFITHS, P. A., CRAIG, J., FITCHES, W. R. & WHITTINGTON, R. J. 1994. Halokinetic initiation of Mesozoic tectonics in the southern North Sea: a regional model. *Geological Magazine*, **131**, 559–561.

ALSOP, G. I. 1996. Physical modelling of fold and fracture geometries associated with salt diapirism. *In*: ALSOP, G. I., BLUNDELL, D. J. & DAVISON, I. (eds) *Salt Tectonics*. Geological Society, London, Special Publications, **100**, 227–241.

ALSOP, G. I., BROWN, J. P., DAVISON, I. & GIBLING, M. R. 2000. The geometry of drag zones adjacent to salt diapirs. *Journal of the Geological Society, London*, **157**, 1019–1029.

BAARS, D. L. & DOELLING, H. H. 1987. Moab salt-intruded anticline, east–central Utah. *In*: BEUS, S. S. (ed.) *Rocky Mountain Section of the Geological Society of America. Centennial Field Guide Volume*, **2**, 275–280.

BADLEY, M. E., PRICE, J. D. & BACKSHALL, L. C. 1989. Inversion, reactivated faults and related structures: seismic examples from the southern North Sea. *In*: COOPER, M. A. & WILLIAMS, G. D. (eds) *Inversion Tectonics*. Geological Society, London, Special Publications, **44**, 201–219.

BALDSCHUHN, R., FRISCH, U. & KOCKEL, F. 1998. The 'salt wedge', a new type of salt structure in compressional tectonic regimes. *Zeitschrift der Deutschen Geologischen Gesellschaft*, **149**, 59–69.

BALDSCHUHN, R., BINOT, F., FLEIG, S. & KOCKEL, F. 2001. *Geotektonischer Atlas von Nordwest-Deutschland und dem deutschen Nordsee-Sektor*. Schweizerbart, Stuttgart.

BIRCH, P. & HAYNES, J. 2003. The Pierce Field, Blocks 23/22a, 23/27, UK North Sea. *In*: GLUYAS, J. G. & HICHENS, H. M. (eds) *United Kingdom Oil and Gas Fields, Commemorative Millenium Volume*. Geological Society, London, Memoirs, **20**, 647–659.

BIRD, P. 1979. Continental delamination and the Colorado Plateau. *Journal of Geophysical Research*, **84**, 7561–7571.

BISHOP, D. J., BUCHANAN, P. G. & BISHOP, C. J. 1995. Gravity-driven thin-skinned extension above Zechstein Group evaporites in the Western Central North Sea: an application of computer-aided section restoration techniques. *Marine and Petroleum Geology*, **12**, 115–135.

BP 2005. *Statistical Review of World Energy 2005*. World Wide Web Address: http://www.bp.com/genericsection.do?categoryId=92&contentId=7005893.

BRANNEY, M. J. 1995. Downsag and extension at calderas: new perspectives on collapse geometries from ice-melt, mining and volcanic subsidence. *Bulletin of Volcanology*, **57**, 303–318.

BROWN, K. M. 1990. The nature and hydrogeologic significance of mud diapirs and diatremes for accretionary systems. *Journal of Geophysical Research–Solid Earth and Planets*, **95**, 8969–8982.

BRUNSTROM, R. G. W. & WALMSLEY, P. J. 1969. Permian evaporites in the North Sea Basin. *AAPG Bulletin*, **53**, 870–883.

CAMERON, T. D. J., CROSBY, A., BALSON, P. S., JEFFREY, D. H., LOTT, G. K., BULAT, J. & HARRISON, D. J. 1992. *United Kingdom Offshore Regional Report: the Geology of the Southern North Sea*. HMSO for the British Geological Survey, London.

CARRUTHERS, A., MCKIE, T., PRICE, J., DYER, R., WILLIAMS, G. & WATSON, P. 1996. The application of sequence stratigraphy to the understanding of Late Jurassic turbidite plays in the Central North Sea, UKCS. *In*: HURST, A., JOHNSON, H. D., BURLEY, S. D., CANHAM, A. C. & MACKERTICH, D. S. (eds) *Geology of the Humber Group: Central Graben and Moray Firth, UKCS*. Geological Society, London, Special Publications, **114**, 29–45.

CARTWRIGHT, J., STEWART, S. A. & CLARK, J. 2001. Salt dissolution and salt-related deformation of the Forth Approaches Basin, UK North Sea. *Marine and Petroleum Geology*, **18**, 757–778.

CARTWRIGHT, J. A. 1991. The kinematic evolution of the Coffee Soil Fault. *In*: ROBERTS, A. M., YIELDING, G. & FREEMAN, B. (eds) *The Geometry of Normal Faults*. Geological Society, London, Special Publications, **56**, 29–40.

CLARK, J. A., STEWART, S. A. & CARTWRIGHT, J. A. 1998. Evolution of the NW margin of the North Permian Basin, UK North Sea. *Journal of the Geological Society, London*, **155**, 663–676.

CLARK, J. A., CARTWRIGHT, J. A. & STEWART, S. A. 1999. Mesozoic dissolution tectonics on the West Central Shelf, UK Central North Sea. *Marine and Petroleum Geology*, **16**, 283–300.

CLAUSEN, O. R. & KORSTGÅRD, J. A. 1996. Planar detaching faults in the southern Horn Graben, Danish North Sea. *Marine and Petroleum Geology*, **13**, 537–548.

CLEMENS, J. D. 1998. Observations on the origins and ascent mechanisms of granitic magmas. *Journal of the Geological Society, London*, **155**, 843–851.

COBBOLD, P. R. & SZATMARI, P. 1991. Radial gravitational gliding on passive margins. *Tectonophysics*, **188**, 249–289.

COOPER, M. A., WILLIAMS, G. D., DE GRACIANSKY, P. C. *et al.* 1989. Inversion tectonics—a discussion. *In*: COOPER, M. A. & WILLIAMS, G. D. (eds) *Inversion Tectonics*. Geological Society, London, Special Publications, **44**, 335–347.

DAVISON, I., BOSENCE, D., ALSOP, G. I. & AL-AAWAH, M. H. 1996. Deformation and sedimentation around active Miocene salt diapirs on the Tihama Plain, northwest Yemen. *In*: ALSOP, G. I., BLUNDELL, D. & DAVISON, I. (eds) *Salt Tectonics*. Geological Society, London, Special Publications, **100**, 23–40.

DAVISON, I., ALSOP, I., BIRCH, P. *et al.* 2000. Geometry and late-stage structural evolution of Central Graben salt diapirs, North Sea. *Marine and Petroleum Geology*, **17**, 499–522.

DICKINSON, B. 1996. The Puffin field: the appraisal of a complex HP–HT gas–condensate accumulation. *In*: HURST, A., JOHNSON, H. D., BURLEY, S. D., CANHAM, A. C. & MACKERTICH, D. S. (eds) *Geology of the Humber Group: Central Graben and Moray Firth, UKCS*. Geological Society, London, Special Publications, **114**, 299–327.

EGGINK, J. W., RIEGSTRA, D. E. & SUZANNE, P. 1996. Using 3D seismic to understand the structural evolution of the UK Central North Sea. *Petroleum Geoscience*, **2**, 83–96.

ENEYOK, G., BUSSINK, P. & MAAN, A. 2004. The Curlew Field, Block 29/7, UK North Sea. *In*: GLUYAS, J. G. & HICHENS, H. M. (eds) *UK Oil and Gas Fields, Commemorative Millennium Volume*. Geological Society, London, Memoirs, **20**, 509–522.

ERRATT, D. 1993. Relationships between basement faulting, salt withdrawal and Late Jurassic rifting, UK Central North Sea. *In*: PARKER, J. R. (ed.) *Petroleum Geology of Northwest Europe: Proceedings of the 4th Conference*. Geological Society, London, 1211–1219.

FÆRSETH, R. B. 1996. Interaction of Permo-Triassic and Jurassic extensional fault-blocks during the development of the northern North Sea. *Journal of the Geological Society, London*, **153**, 931–944.

GALLOWAY, W. E., GARBER, J. L., LIU, X. & SLOAN, B. J. 1993. Sequence stratigraphic and depositional framework of the Cenozoic fill, Central and northern North Sea basin. *In*: PARKER, J. R. (ed.) *Petroleum Geology of Northwest Europe: Proceedings of the 4th Conference*. Geological Society, London, 33–43.

GATLIFF, R. W., RICHARDS, P. C., SMITH, K. *et al.* 1994. *United Kingdom Offshore Regional Report: the Geology of the Central North Sea*. HMSO for the British Geological Survey, London.

GAWTHORPE, R. L. & HURST, J. M. 1993. Transfer zones in extensional basins: their structural style and influence on drainage development and stratigraphy. *Journal of the Geological Society, London*, **150**, 1137–1152.

GE, H. & JACKSON, M. P. A. 1998. Physical modelling of structures formed by salt withdrawal: implications for deformation caused by salt dissolution. *AAPG Bulletin*, **81**, 228–250.

GE, H., JACKSON, M. P. A. & VENDEVILLE, B. C. 1997. Kinematics and dynamics of salt tectonics driven by propagation. *AAPG Bulletin*, **81**, 398–423.

GEIL, K. 1991. The development of salt structures in Denmark and adjacent areas: the role of basin floor dip and differential pressure. *First Break*, **9**, 467.

GLENNIE, K. W. & ARMSTRONG, L. A. 1991. The Kittiwake Field, Block 21/18, UK North Sea. *In*: ABBOTTS, I. L. (ed.) *United Kingdom Oil and Gas Fields, 25 Years Commemorative Volume*. Geological Society, London, Memoirs, **14**, 339–345.

GLENNIE, K. W. & UNDERHILL, J. R. 1998. Origin, development and evolution of structural styles. *In*: GLENNIE, K. W. (ed.) *Petroleum Geology of the North Sea*, 4th edn. Blackwell Science, Oxford, 42–84.

GOWERS, M. B., HOLTAR, E. & SWENSSON, E. 1993. The structure of the Norwegian Central Trough (Central Graben area). *In*: PARKER, J. R. (ed.) *Petroleum Geology of Northwest Europe: Proceedings of the 4th Conference*. Geological Society, London, 1245–1254.

HEWARD, A. P. 1990. Salt removal and sedimentation in Southern Oman. *In*: ROBERTSON, A. H. F., SEARLE, M. P. & RIES, A. C. (eds) The Geology and Tectonics of the Oman Region. Geological Society, London, Special Publications, **49**, 637–652.

HØILAND, O., KRISTENSEN, J. & MONSEN, T. 1993. Mesozoic evolution of the Jæren High area, Norwegian Central North Sea. *In*: PARKER, J. R. (ed.) *Petroleum Geology of Northwest Europe: Proceedings of the 4th Conference*. The Geological Society, London, 1189–1195.

HOLDSWORTH, R. E., BUTLER, C. A. & ROBERTS, A. M. 1997. The recognition of reactivation during continental deformation. *Journal of the Geological Society, London*, **154**, 73–78.

HOOPER, R. J. & MORE, C. 1995. Evaluation of salt-related overburden structures in the U.K. southern North Sea. *In*: JACKSON, M. P. A., ROBERTS, D. G. & SNELSON, S. (eds) *Salt Tectonics: a Global Perspective*. American Association of Petroleum Geologists, Memoirs, **65**, 251–259.

HOOPER, R. J., SIANG GOH, L. & DEWEY, F. 1995. The inversion history of the northeastern margin of the Broad Fourteens Basin. *In*: BUCHANAN, J. G. & BUCHANAN, P. G. (eds) *Basin Inversion*. Geological Society, London, Special Publications, **88**, 307–317.

HUUSE, M. 1999. Detailed morphology of the Top Chalk surface in the eastern Danish North Sea. *Petroleum Geoscience*, **5**, 303–314.

HUYGHE, P. & MUGNIER, J.-L. 1995. A comparison of inverted basins of the southern North Sea and inverted structures of the external Alps. *In*: BUCHANAN, J. G. & BUCHANAN, P. G. (eds) *Basin Inversion*. Geological Society, London, Special Publications, **88**, 339–353.

JACKSON, M. P. A. 1995. Retrospective salt tectonics. *In*: JACKSON, M. P. A., ROBERTS, D. G. & SNELSON, S. (eds) *Salt Tectonics: a Global Perspective*. American Association of Petroleum Geologists, Memoirs, **65**, 1–28.

JACKSON, M. P. A. & TALBOT, C. J. 1994. Advances in salt tectonics. *In*: HANCOCK, P. L. (ed.) *Continental Deformation*. Pergamon, Oxford, 159–179.

JACKSON, M. P. A. & VENDEVILLE, B. C. 1994. Regional extension as a geologic trigger for diapirism. *Geological Society of America Bulletin*, **106**, 57–73.

JACKSON, M. P. A. & VENDEVILLE, B. C. 1995. Origin of minibasins by multidirectional extension above a spreading lobe of allochthonous salt. *In*: TRAVIS, C. J., VENDEVILLE, B. C., HARRISON, H., PEEL, F. J., HUDEC, M. R. & PERKINS, B. F. (eds) *Salt, Sediment and Hydrocarbons, GCSSEPM Foundation 16th Annual Research Conference*, 135.

JACKSON, M. P. A., CORNELIUS, R. R., CRAIG, C. H., GANSSER, A., STÖCKLIN, J. & TALBOT, C. J. 1990. *Salt Diapirs of the Great Kavir, Central Iran*. Geological Society of America, Memoirs, **177**.

JENYON, M. K. 1985. Basin-edge diapirism and updip salt flow in Zechstein of Southern North Sea. *AAPG Bulletin*, **69**, 53–64.

JENYON, M. K. 1989. Plastic flow and contraflow in superposed Zechstein salt sequences. *Journal of Petroleum Geology*, **12**, 477–486.

JOHNSON, H. D., MACKAY, T. A. & STEWART, D. J. 1986. The Fulmar oil field (central North Sea): geological aspects of its discovery, appraisal and development. *Marine and Petroleum Geology*, **3**, 99–125.

KENDALL, A. C. & HARWOOD, G. M. 1996. Marine evaporites: arid shorelines and basins. *In*: READING, H. G. (ed.) *Sedimentary Environments: Processes, Facies and Stratigraphy*, 3rd edn. Blackwell Science, Oxford, 281–324.

KOYI, H. 1996. Salt flow by aggrading and prograding overburdens. *In*: ALSOP, G. I., BLUNDELL, D. J. & DAVISON, I. (eds) *Salt Tectonics*. Geological Society, London, Special Publications, **100**, 243–258.

KOYI, H. 1998. The shaping of salt diapirs. *Journal of Structural Geology*, **20**, 321–338.

KOYI, H. & PETERSEN, K. 1993. Influence of basement faults on the development of salt structures in the Danish Basin. *Marine and Petroleum Geology*, **10**, 82–94.

KOYI, H., JENYON, M. K. & PETERSEN, K. 1993. The effect of basement faulting on diapirism. *Journal of Petroleum Geology*, **16**, 285–312.

LAPPIN, M., HENDRY, D. J. & SAIKIA, I. A. 2003. The Guinevere Field, Block 48/17b, UK North Sea. *In*: GLUYAS, J. G. & HICHENS, H. M. (eds) *United Kingdom Oil and Gas Fields, Commemorative Millenium Volume*. Geological Society, London, Memoirs, **20**, 723–730.

LISLE, R. J. 1994. Detection of zones of abnormal strains in structures using Gaussian curvature analysis. *AAPG Bulletin*, **78**, 1811–1819.

LOHMANN, H. H. 1972. Salt dissolution in subsurface of British North Sea as interpreted from seismograms. *AAPG Bulletin*, **56**, 161–168.

MALTHE-SØRENSSEN, A., WALMANN, T., JAMTVEIT, B., FEDER, J. & JØSSANG, T. 1999. Simulation and characterization of fracture patterns in glaciers. *Journal of Geophysical Research–Solid Earth*, **104**, 23157–23174.

MALTMAN, A. 1994. Prelithification deformation. *In*: HANCOCK, P. L. (ed.) *Continental Deformation*. Pergamon, Oxford, 143–158.

MAUDIT, T., GAULLIER, V., BRUN, J-P. & GUERIN, G. 1997. On the asymmetry of turtle-back growth anticlines. *Marine and Petroleum Geology*, **14**, 763–771.

MUERDTER, D. & RATCLIFF, D. 2001. Understanding subsalt illumination through ray-trace modeling, Part 3: Salt ridges and furrows, and the impact of acquisition orientation. *Leading Edge*, **20**, 803–816.

NALPAS, T. & BRUN, J.-P. 1993. Salt flow and diapirism related to extension at crustal scale. *Tectonophysics*, **228**, 349–362.

PASCOE, R., HOOPER, R. J., STORHAUG, K. & HARPER, H. 1999. Evolution of extensional styles at the southern termination of the Nordland Ridge, mid-Norway: a response to variations in coupling above Triassic salt. *In*: FLEET, A. J. & BOLDY, S. A. R. (eds) *Petroleum Geology of Northwest Europe: Proceedings of the 5th Conference*. Geological Society, London, 83–90.

PENGE, J., TAYLOR, B., HUCKERBY, J. A. & MUNNS, J. W. 1993. Extension and salt tectonics in the East Central Graben. *In*: PARKER, J. R. (ed.) *Petroleum Geology of Northwest Europe: Proceedings of the 4th Conference*. The Geological Society, London, 1197–1209.

PENGE, J., TAYLOR, B. & MUNNS, J. 1999. Rift–raft tectonics: examples of gravitational sliding structures from the Zechstein basins of northwest Europe. *In*: FLEET, A. J. & BOLDY, S. A. R. (eds) *Petroleum Geology of Northwest Europe: Proceedings of the 5th Conference*. Geological Society, London, 201–213.

PETERSEN, K., CLAUSEN, O. R. & KORSTGÅRD, J. A. 1992. Evolution of a salt-related listric growth fault near the D-1 well, block 5605, Danish North Sea: displacement history and salt kinematics. *Journal of Structural Geology*, **14**, 565–577.

QUIRK, D. G., D'LEMOS, R. S., MULLIGAN, S. & RABTI, B. M. R. 1998. Insights into the collection and emplacement of granitic magma based on 3D seismic images of normal fault-related salt structures. *Terra Nova*, **10**, 268–279.

RAMSAY, J. G. 1992. Some geometrical problems of ramp-flat thrust models. *In*: MCCLAY, K. R. (ed.) *Thrust Tectonics*. Chapman & Hall, London, 191–200.

RANK-FRIEND, M. & ELDERS, C. 2004. The evolution and growth of Central Graben salt structures, Salt Dome Province, Danish North Sea. *In*: DAVIES, R. J., CARTWRIGHT, J. A., STEWART, S. A., LAPPIN, M. & UNDERHILL, J. R. (eds) *3D Seismic Technology: Application to the Exploration of Sedimentary Basins*. Geological Society, London, Memoirs, **29**, 149–163.

RICHARD, P. D., NAYLOR, M. A. & KOOPMAN, A. 1995. Experimental models of strike-slip tectonics. *Petroleum Geoscience*, **1**, 71–80.

RICHARDS, P. C., LOTT, G. K., JOHNSON, H., KNOX, R. W.O'B. & RIDING, J. B. 1993. Jurassic of the Central and Northern North Sea. *In*: KNOX, R.W.O'B. & CORDEY, W. G. (eds) *Lithostratigraphic Nomenclature of the UK North Sea*. British Geological Survey, Keyworth.

ROBERTS, A. M., PRICE, J. D. & SVAVA OLSEN, T. 1990. Late Jurassic half-graben control on the siting and structure of hydrocarbon accumulations: UK/Norwegian Central Graben. *In*: Hardman, R. F. P. & Brooks, J. (eds) *Tectonic Events Responsible for Britain's Oil and Gas Reserves*. Geological Society, London, Special Publications, **55**, 229–257.

ROBERTS, A. M., YIELDING, G., KUSZNIR, N. J., WALKER, I. & DORN-LOPEZ, D. 1993. Mesozoic extension in the North Sea: constraints from flexural backstripping, forward modelling and fault populations. *In*: PARKER, J. R. (ed.) *Petroleum Geology of Northwest Europe: Proceedings of the 4th Conference*. Geological Society, London, 1123–1136.

ROBERTS, A. M., YIELDING, G., KUSZNIR, N. J., WALKER, I. M. & DORN-LOPEZ, D. 1995. Quantitative analysis of Triassic extension in the northern Viking Graben. *Journal of the Geological Society, London*, **152**, 15–26.

ROMÁN-BERDIEL, T., GAPAIS, D. & BRUN, J.-P. 1997. Granite intrusion along strike-slip zones in experiment and nature. *American Journal of Science*, **297**, 651–678.

ROWAN, M. G. & WEIMER, P. 1998. Salt–sediment interaction, Northern Green Canyon and Ewing Bank (offshore Louisiana), Northern Gulf of Mexico. *AAPG Bulletin*, **82**, 1896–1924.

ROWAN, M. G., JACKSON, M. P. A. & TRUDGILL, B. D. 1999. Salt-related fault families and fault welds in the northern Gulf of Mexico. *AAPG Bulletin*, **83**, 1454–1484.

ROWAN, M. G., LAWTON, T. F., GILES, K. A. & RATLIFF, R. A. 2003. Near-salt deformation in La Popa basin, Mexico, and the northern Gulf of Mexico: a general model for passive diapirism. *AAPG Bulletin*, **87**, 733–756.

ROWAN, M. G., PEEL, F. J. & VENDEVILLE, B. C. 2004. Gravity-driven fold belts on passive margins. *In*: MCCLAY, K. (ed.) *Thrust Tectonics and Hydrocarbon Systems*. American Association of Petroleum Geologists, Memoirs, **82**, 157–182.

SARGINSON, M. J. 2003. The Barque Field, Blocks 48/13a, 48/14, UK North Sea. *In*: GLUYAS, J. G. & HICHENS, H. M. (eds) *United Kingdom Oil and Gas Fields, Commemorative Millenium Volume*. Geological Society, London, Memoirs, **20**, 663–670.

SCHULTZ-ELA, D. D., JACKSON, M. P. A. & VENDEVILLE, B. C. 1993. Mechanics of active salt diapirism. *Tectonophysics*, **228**, 275–312.

SMITH, R. I., HODGSON, N. & FULTON, M. 1993. Salt control on Triassic reservoir distribution, UKCS Central North Sea. *In*: PARKER, J. R. (ed.) *Petroleum Geology of Northwest Europe: Proceedings of the 4th Conference*. Geological Society, London, 547–557.

SØRENSEN, K. 1998. The salt pillow to diapir transition: evidence from unroofing unconformities in the Norwegian–Danish Basin. *Petroleum Geoscience*, **4**, 193–202.

SQUYRES, S. W., JANES, D. M., BAER, G., BINDSCHADLER, D. L., SCHUBERT, G., SHARPTON, V. L. & STOFAN, E. R. 1992. The morphology and evolution of coronae on Venus. *Journal of Geophysical Research—Planets*, **97**, 13611–13634.

STEEL, R. & RYSETH, A. 1990. The Triassic–early Jurassic succession in the northern North Sea: megasequence stratigraphy and intra-Triassic tectonics. *In*: HARDMAN, R. F. P. & BROOKS, J. (eds) *Tectonic Events Responsible for Britain's Oil and Gas Reserves*. Geological Society, London, Special Publications, **55**, 139–168.

STEWART, I. J. 1993. Structural controls in the Late Jurassic age shelf system, Ula trend, Norwegian North Sea. *In*: PARKER, J. R. (ed.) *Petroleum Geology of Northwest Europe: Proceedings of the 4th Conference*. Geological Society, London, 469–483.

STEWART, S. A. 1996. Tertiary extensional fault systems on the western margin of the North Sea Basin. *Petroleum Geoscience*, **2**, 167–176.

STEWART, S. A. & BAILEY, H. W. 1996. The Flamborough Tertiary outlier, UK southern North Sea. *Journal of the Geological Society, London*, **153**, 163–173.

STEWART, S. A. & CLARK, J. A. 1999. Impact of salt on the structure of the Central North Sea hydrocarbon fairways. *In*: FLEET, A. J. & BOLDY, S. A. R. (eds) *Petroleum Geology of Northwest Europe: Proceedings of the 5th Conference*. Geological Society, London, 179–200.

STEWART, S. A. & COWARD, M. P. 1995. Synthesis of salt tectonics in the southern North Sea, UK. *Marine and Petroleum Geology*, **12**, 457–475.

STEWART, S. A. & COWARD, M. P. 1996. Genetic interpretation and mapping of salt structures. *First Break*, **14**, 135–141.

STEWART, S. A., HARVEY, M. J., OTTO, S. C. & WESTON, P. J. 1996. Influence of salt on fault geometry: examples from the UK salt basins. *In*: ALSOP, G. I., BLUNDELL, D. J. & DAVISON, I. (eds) *Salt Tectonics*. Geological Society, London, Special Publications, **100**, 175–202.

STEWART, S. A., FRASER, S. I., CARTWRIGHT, J. A., CLARK, J. A. & JOHNSON, H. D. 1999. Controls on Upper Jurassic sediment distribution in the Durward–Dauntless area, UK Blocks 21/11, 21/16. *In*: FLEET, A. J. & BOLDY, S. A. R. (eds) *Petroleum Geology of Northwest Europe: Proceedings of the 5th Conference*. Geological Society, London, 879–896.

SUNDSBØ, G. O. & MEGSON, J. B. 1993. Structural styles in the Danish Central Graben. *In*: PARKER, J. R. (ed.) *Petroleum Geology of Northwest Europe: Proceedings of the 4th Conference*. Geological Society, London, 1255–1267.

TALBOT, M. R. & ALLEN, P. A. 1996. Lakes. *In*: READING, H. G. (ed.) *Sedimentary Environments: Processes, Facies and Stratigraphy*, 3rd edn. Blackwell Science, Oxford, 83–124.

TAYLOR, J. C. M. 1998. Upper Permian-Zechstein. *In*: GLENNIE, K. W. (ed.) *Petroleum Geology of the North Sea*, 4th edn. Blackwell Science, Oxford, 174–211.

TRUSHEIM, F. 1960. Mechanism of salt migration in northern Germany. *AAPG Bulletin*, **44**, 1519–1540.

UNDERHILL, J. R. 1991. Implications of Mesozoic–Recent basin development in the western Inner Moray Firth, UK. *Marine and Petroleum Geology*, **8**, 359–369.

VAN HOORN, B. 1987. Structural evolution, timing and tectonic style of the Sole Pit inversion. *Tectonophysics*, **137**, 239–284.

VELAJ, T., DAVISON, I., SERJANI, A. & ALSOP, I. 1999. Thrust tectonics and the role of evaporites in the Ionian zone of the Albanides. *AAPG Bulletin*, **83**, 1408–1425.

VENDEVILLE, B. C. 2002. A new interpretation of Trusheim's classic model of salt-diapir growth. *Transactions, Gulf Coast Association of Geological Societies*, **52**, 943–952.

VENDEVILLE, B. C. & JACKSON, M. P. A. 1992. The rise of diapirs during thin-skinned extension. *Marine and Petroleum Geology*, **9**, 331–353.

WAKEFIELD, L. L., DROSTE, H., GILES, M. R. & JANSSEN, R. 1993. Late Jurassic plays along the western margin of the Central Graben. *In*: PARKER, J. R. (ed.) *Petroleum Geology of Northwest Europe: Proceedings of the 4th Conference*. Geological Society, London, 459–468.

WALKER, I. M. & COOPER, W. G. 1987. The structural and stratigraphic evolution of the northeast margin of the Sole Pit Basin. *In*: BROOKS, J. & GLENNIE, K. (eds) *Petroleum Geology of North West Europe*. Graham & Trotman, London, 263–275.

WALTER, T. R. & TROLL, V. R. 2001. Formation of caldera periphery faults: an experimental study. *Bulletin of Volcanology*, **63**, 191–203.

WALTHAM, D. 1997. Why does salt start to move? *Tectonophysics*, **282**, 117–128.

WITHJACK, M. O. & SCHEINER, C. 1982. Fault patterns associated with domes- an experimental and analytical study. *AAPG Bulletin*, **66**, 302–316.

YOSHINOBU, A. S., FOWLER, T. K., PATERSON, S. R., LLAMBIAS, E., TICKYJ, H. & SATO, A. M. 2003. A view from the roof: magmatic stoping in the shallow crust, Chita pluton, Argentina. *Journal of Structural Geology*, **25**, 1037–1048.

ZIEGLER, P. A. & VAN HOORN, B. 1989. Evolution of the North Sea rift system. *In*: TANKARD, A. J. & BALKWILL, H. R. (eds) *Extensional Tectonics and Stratigraphy of the North Atlantic Margins*. American Association of Petroleum Geologists, Memoirs, **46**, 471–500.

Analogue models of basin inversion by transpression: role of structural heterogeneity

LUCA MATTIONI[1,2], WILLIAM SASSI[1,3] & JEAN-PAUL CALLOT[1]

[1]*Institut Français du Pétrole, Rueil-Malmaison, 92852, France (e-mail: william@mve.com)*

[2]*Present address: Becip Franlab, Rueil-Malmaison, 92500, France*

[3]*Present address: Midland Valley Exploration, Glasgow G2 2HG, UK*

Abstract: The process of faulting within a crustal-scale rift basin, subjected to transpression, is simulated in a series of small-scale experiments using sand and silicone layers. The structural scenario involved three stages: (1) extension; (2) sedimentation; (3) coeval shortening and strike-slip motion. A sandpack, placed above a basal silicone layer, was submitted to extension and produced a system of horst and grabens. Following the extension phase, the resulting surface topography was covered with silicone material, thus introducing a potential décollement between the pre- and post-rift sediments. These latter strata were made of sand. After sedimentation, deformation by transpression was applied using the same amount of shortening and an increasing strike-slip displacement in the different experiments. The strain partitioning increased with the amount of horizontal shear, and strike-slip faults developed at the more advanced stages of transpression. Two phases of faulting were observed before the horst and graben faults could be reactivated. The first phase was characterized by conjugate reverse faults, striking parallel to the rift-bounding faults, compatible with a stress regime in compression. A second phase of faulting was recognized at the end of transpression, leading to the generation of Riedel R-type strike-slip faults. The stress regimes responsible for the kinematics of fault generation and reactivation were interpreted using the Coulomb failure criterion and assumed a friction angle of 30° for the undisturbed sand. The reactivation of the steep normal faults in the horst and graben occurred only after a large strike-slip displacement. The general sequence of fault generation and reactivation suggested a temporal change in the stress regime. This change was caused by the permutation of the minimum and the intermediate principal stress axes and also by a progressive rotation, in the horizontal plane, of the axis of the maximum compressive stress. The spatial variation of the stress regime was also strongly controlled by the geometry of the interbedded silicone layer. A regular and undeformed post-rift silicone layer introduced a more efficient mechanical decoupling between the post-rift cover and the stretched basin. In summary, when a pre-existing graben was present, there was a succession of two distinct 'tectonic phases', whereas without a rift, the resulting fault kinematics reflected a single stress state and one tectonic phase.

According to numerous field observations and seismic studies, the factors controlling the structural style of basin inversion include: (1) the strike and dip of the earlier faults; (2) the type of normal faults (listric or planar); (3) the geometry of the basin before inversion; (4) the time interval since extension; (5) the amount of compression relative to extension. In the last decade, the importance of the role of a pre-existing architecture in controlling the subsequent structure of a foreland fold and thrust belt is being increasingly appreciated (Gillcrist *et al.* 1987; Butler 1989; Hayward & Graham 1989; Letouzey 1990; Ziegler *et al.* 1995; Coward 1996; Roure & Colletta 1996; Mazzoli *et al.* 2001). In the Variscan foreland of the British Isles, for example, the sedimentary basins, which formed during the extensional phase, were affected by a late Westphalian mild to strong inversion when the stress field became compressive (Corfield *et al.* 1996). In the southern Apennine chain of Italy, the complex palaeogeographical architecture of the southern continental margin of Neotethys, formed during Mesozoic extension, controlled the genesis and style of deformation during Neogene compression (see Mattioni 2001 and references therein; Mazzoli *et al.* 2001).

Analogue experiments reveal in detail the 3D structural evolution of a specific model (e.g. Mandl 1988; Richard & Cobbold 1989, 1990; Colletta *et al.* 1991; Richard *et al.* 1995; Mattioni *et al.* 2004). Furthermore, in small-scale models, boundary conditions can be set according to the needs of the experimenter and, by doing this, the individual influence of different parameters on geological processes can be better investigated and understood. Many previous experiments on fault reactivation processes have studied

From: Ries, A. C., Butler, R. W. H. & Graham, R. H. (eds) 2007. *Deformation of the Continental Crust: The Legacy of Mike Coward*. Geological Society, London, Special Publications, **272**, 397–417.
0305-8719/07/$15

only the orthogonal compression of elementary extensional fault patterns, such as reactivation of a simple listric normal fault or tilted blocks (e.g. McClay 1989, 1996; Buchanan & McClay 1991; McClay & Buchanan 1992; Mitra 1993; Eisenstadt & Withjack 1995; Roure & Colletta 1996). Experiments with pre-cut planar discontinuities, introduced within the sand cake, have been performed by Sassi *et al.* (1993) and, more recently, by Viola *et al.* (2004). Overall, these studies illustrate how the reactivation is strongly controlled by the orientation of the old faults, relative to the stress field. Experiments simulating oblique shortening (transpression) were performed by Schreurs & Colletta (1998) and McClay *et al.* (2004). They imposed an oblique shear component at the base of the model over its entire width, the aim being to simulate oblique deformation of a model driven by distributed basal flow. These experiments showed how older faults should determine to a large extent the subsequent fault pattern and evolution. This has been described also by Schreurs (2004). In experiments where an extensional phase was followed by compression, Brun & Nalpas (1996) noted that reactivation of extensional normal faults is possible with oblique compression (i.e. when the angle between compression and the trend of pre-existing faults is less than 45°). Nalpas *et al.* (1995) and Dubois *et al.* (2002) demonstrated that fault reactivation is difficult when the post-rift fill is thick, whereas it is much easier if the overburden is thin.

The objective of the experiments was to improve understanding of the control exerted by inherited faults during basin inversion by transpression. Inherited faults represent zones of mechanical heterogeneity when their cohesive strength and friction coefficient values are lower or greater than those of the intact rocks (Sibson 1974, 1985; Jaeger & Cook 1979). Extension produces several fault-bounded horsts and interposed troughs. This architecture may induce a complex mechanical behaviour and have a strong impact on subsequent structural development of the basin. Of particular interest is the genesis and development of new structures versus the reutilization of structural weaknesses. For this, the study focused on evolving structures for different ratios between the velocity vectors of compression and strike-slip, as well as on the role of an intra-basin décollement. Experimental observations are discussed in the light of a static mechanical analysis to link the fault generation and/or reactivation pattern to the applied stress regime.

Analogue models of transpression tectonics

Experimental set-up and procedure

The experimental set-up consisted of a wooden box with two free sides (Fig. 1). The other two sides of the box comprised two sliding backstops attached to two basal plates that moved by means of computer-controlled stepper motor, allowing the deformation to be localized at a velocity discontinuity near the central part of the model (Malavielle 1984; Allemand *et al.* 1989). One of the basal plates was able to slide in and out of the plane of the section to simulate strike-slip deformation. Thus, oblique shortening (i.e. transpression) could be achieved by combining the basal strike-slip shear component and a transverse shortening. For all the experiments described, the strike-slip component of oblique deformation was arbitrarily chosen to be of sinistral sense. For practical reasons the north direction within the models is taken as indicated in Figure 1.

The original configuration of each model (i.e. before extension) is shown in Figure 1a. The base of each analogue model consisted of a silicone layer, 1 cm thick, which was placed directly over the plates. Sand and a thin level of glass powder were poured on top of the silicone layer to produce a 2.5 cm thick stratified sand–glass powder pack. The interlayered level of glass powder acted as a stratigraphic marker, thus allowing the identification of structures on cross-sections during the deformation.

Five analogue experiments were designed to study the process of tectonic faulting in the context of the two successive tectonic phases: a first phase of uniform extension (rift event) and a second phase that was an inversion event of kinematically controlled transpression. To demonstrate the control exerted by the pre-existing graben, a first experiment (T0) was performed in which transpression was applied to an undisturbed system of horizontal sand and silicone layers.

Four experiments (herein referred to as T1, T2, T3 and T4) were run in two steps: first, a symmetrical extensional deformation phase was imposed on the model, the direction of extension being perpendicular to the longitudinal edges of the sandbox. At the end of extension, the stretched model was filled by a thin level (0.5 cm) of silicone that draped the irregular horst-and-graben topography (Fig. 1b), so that also the resulting geometry of the silicone bed was irregular. Finally, a sand–glass powder cake, 1 cm thick, was placed above this level. Experiment T4 differed from the others in that, after extension,

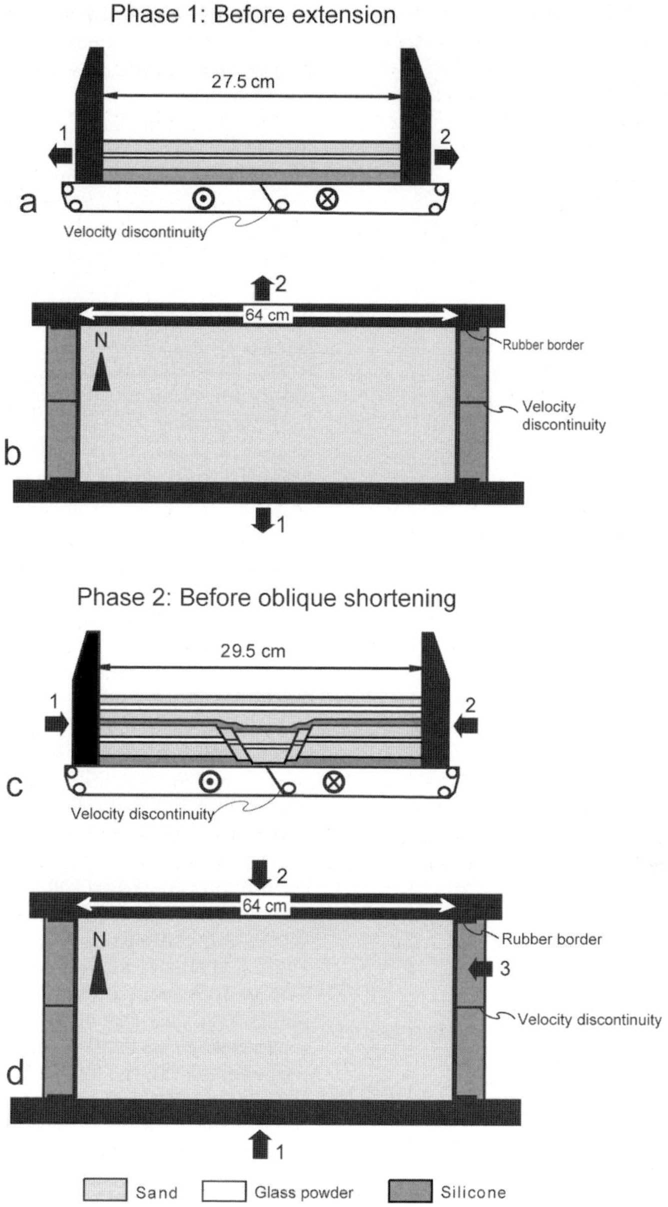

Fig. 1. Schematic representation of the experimental apparatus and original configuration of each model before extension (Phase 1), and before oblique shortening (Phase 2). (**a**) and (**c**) are schematic cross-sections through the model, whereas (**b**) and (**d**) show a schematic top view. Black arrows 1, 2 and 3 indicate sense of movement of the computer-controlled stepper motors.

the resulting graben and adjacent undisturbed domains were first covered by sand, such that the silicone was placed above a flat-lying topography. Most of the experiments were repeated at least twice and the results were reproducible.

Table 1 summarizes the boundary conditions and the values of the main parameters that were adopted in each experiment. Table 1 shows that from one transpression experiment to the next, the shortening strain rate was always 2 cm h^{-1},

Table 1. *Values of parameters and boundary conditions*

	Extensional phase		Compressional phase						
Experiment number	Duration of extension (min)	Velocity of extension (cm h^{-1})	Thickness of the interlayered ductile layer (PDMS) (cm)	Duration of experiment (min)	Velocity of compression (cm h^{-1})	Velocity of basal plate (cm h^{-1}) (cm)	Total applied shear displacement	Final width of the model (cm)	Maximum longitudinal shortening (%)
T0	No extension		0.5	180	2	1	3	23.5	20
T1	30	4	0.5	180	2	1	3	23.5	20
T2	30	4	0.5	180	2	2	6	23.5	19
T3	30	4	0.5	180	2	3	9	23.5	19
T4	30	4	0.5	180	2	3	9	23.5	19

whereas the basal strike-slip shear component was varied to investigate its influence on fault genesis and pattern, as well as on fault reactivation processes.

The extension phase was induced with a displacement vector direction perpendicular to the longitudinal sidewalls using a velocity of 4 cm h^{-1} (e.g. 2 cm h^{-1} on each motor). After 2 cm of displacement, all the models displayed a highly structured basin, roughly organized in two asymmetric rifts, separated by a large horst. The width of the graben, and the associated horst blocks, varied considerably along strike, passing from a few to tens of millimetres. The extensional deformation was mostly localized along the main faults bounding the two graben. These structures showed a planar shape with a dip angle ranging from 60° to 70° and a strike perpendicular to the extension direction, which meet at the brittle–ductile interface. Locally, the deformation was more heterogeneous and was accommodated along several minor faults that affected the sedimentary fill within the two graben. These structures varied greatly in their length and associated displacement; some of these structures showed lateral terminations, so that the resulting fault-bounded blocks also varied in size. Before transpression, the width of all models was 29.5 cm, and the longitudinal dimension was 64 cm and was parallel to the shear component of deformation (Fig. 1).

Our experiments were analysed by X-ray computerized tomography, a non-destructive technique that generated cross-sectional images through the models (Hounsfield 1973; Mandl 1988; Richard *et al.* 1989; Colletta *et al.* 1991). The analysis and interpretation of the experiments were carried out by means of: (1) images representing vertical sections of the model, perpendicular to the longitudinal sidewalls of the box (i.e. parallel to the direction of extension); (2) images representing horizontal sections through the model and line-drawings; (3) surface pictures at different stages of the deformation; (4) 3D reconstruction of fault zones, as well as of several surfaces within the models, at different stages of deformation. For the analysis of surface pictures, a square grid of coloured sand markers was finely traced onto the uppermost surface.

Materials and scaling

In the experiments, sedimentary brittle rocks were simulated with sand, which has a low/negligible cohesion, an angle of internal friction of 30°, and a density ranging from 1400 to 1600 kg m^{-3}. The ductile behaviour of weak layers within the brittle upper crust was simulated by silicone putty (PDMS) layers. The latter behaves nearly as a Newtonian fluid, with a density of 0.97 g cm^{-3} and a viscosity of 2.5×10^4 Pa s at room temperatures and strain rates below 3×10^{-3} s^{-1}.

The models were scaled for length, viscosity and time, following the basic principles, discussed by Hubbert (1937) and Ramberg (1981), applied at basin scale (the upper 7 km of the crust). The length ratio between models and natural examples was 10^{-5} (1 cm in the model represented 1 km in nature), the viscosity ratio was 2×10^{-15} (based on a viscosity of 10^{19} Pa s as a maximum value for evaporites), and the time ratio was 4×10^{-10}. It is important to keep in mind that the role of some geological parameters (e.g. temperature gradient, erosion, among others) could not be taken in account. However, this oversimplification was considered not to affect the conclusions as the aim was to provide only insights on the role of specific parameters during basin inversion by transpression.

Model results

For all experiments, Table 2 gives the orientation of the faults produced or reactivated, in chronological order. The newly formed reverse faults, which cut through the ancient graben structures, the newly formed strike-slip faults and the reactivated normal faults were distinguishable in the acquired images of the experiments.

Transpression inside an undisturbed horizontal brittle–ductile layered system

Experiment T0. Fig. 2 shows the development of the thrusting in cross-section (Fig. 2a) and the fault pattern at the end of the experiment in map view, on a slice below the upper décollement level (Fig. 2b). Three main thrust faults were initiated during the early stages of oblique shortening, with a strike direction at around N120° and a dip angle varying from 31° to 35° (Table 2). Horizontal slices through the model (Fig. 2b) indicate that the thrust faults were arranged in a dextral-stepping en echelon pattern. As deformation increases, the faults grew in length and displacement. Increasing oblique shortening led to an overlapping configuration of these thrusts. At this stage, further lateral propagation of their tips appeared to be inhibited by the interaction of stress fields around the overlapping fault segments and relay structures. The latter were oriented roughly N040° and show an oblique (sinistral) reverse sense of movement.

A source of structural complexity in this transpression experiment came from the rheological contrast between the ductile silicone and the brittle sand. Within the upper brittle layer, the decoupling effect of the upper silicone layer did not permit the localization of the deformation in the central part of the model, and the model was first deformed by bulk shearing distributed over a large area. The onset of discrete brittle failure took place at advanced stages of deformation, when several east–west-oriented thrusts and pop-ups developed nearby the edges of the sandbox (Fig. 2a). Some of these (for example, those in the right side of the model of Fig. 2a) are in line with the thrusts that formed in the lower sand layer; others (those on the left side of the model) are due to boundary effects. In the final configuration, after 20% of longitudinal shortening (Fig. 2), the deformation within the upper brittle layer was completely decoupled from its substratum, and was accommodated by a large fold; the fold hinge was roughly in the middle of the model, above the underlying thrust fault.

Transpression inside a horst-and-graben system

Experiment T1 (Fig. 3a–c). During the early phase of transpression, the pre-existing normal faults were gently tilted from 64° to 71° (Fig. 3a), as a result of horizontal shortening. No reactivation was detected along such pre-existing features. As the oblique compression continued, three thrusts were initiated within the lower rifted layer; they rooted at the base of the rifted area, at the boundary between viscous and Coulomb materials. The dip of the thrusts ranged from 25° to 28°, with a strike parallel to faults of the first generation (Fig. 3b). As they reached the overlying layer of silicone their dip decreased. Some of these thrust faults propagated through the rifted zone and cut the pre-existing normal faults. The latter were passively transported along the reverse fault (Fig. 3a).

Within the post-rift sequence, oblique shortening was accommodated by two main thrusts that were initiated at low angles (*c.* 28°) and propagated roughly parallel to the underlying basin margins (Fig. 3a). As already observed within the lower brittle layer, lateral rheological variation, which occurred at the edges of the graben between viscous (i.e. the interlayer silicone bed) and granular material (the sand of the post-rift fill), seemed to control the nucleation and subsequent propagation of these thrusts. These are conjugate and caused extrusion of the post-rift basin fill (Fig. 3a). No

Table 2. *Orientation values of faults produced in each experiment, within both the lower and upper brittle layers*

Experiment	Basement			Cover		
	Dip direction (deg)	Dip (deg)	Nature	Dip direction (deg)	Dip (deg)	Nature
T0	221	34	Reverse fault	Conjugate east–west Reverse faults		
	134	48	Reverse fault	Other structures are due to edge effects		
	130	52	Reverse fault			
	198	34	Reverse fault			
	201	38	Reverse fault			
	195	22	Reverse fault			
T1	5	27	Reverse fault	183	27	Reverse fault
	357	26	Reverse fault	178	29	Reverse fault
	3	29	Reverse fault	183	28	Reverse fault
T2	0	33	Reverse fault	0	24	Reverse fault
	168	29	Reverse fault	0	29	Reverse fault
	190	26	Reverse fault	184	28	Reverse fault
	130	70	Strike-slip (R-type) fault	313	73	Strike-slip (R-type) fault
	310	66	Strike-slip (R-type) fault	308	75	Strike-slip (R-type) fault
	340	50	Oblique thrust fault	128	70	Strike-slip (R-type) fault
T3	180	28	Reverse fault	180	28	Reverse fault
	3	30	Reverse fault	178	38	Reverse fault
	178	29	Reverse fault	183	26	Reverse fault
	163	78	Strike-slip (R-type) fault	0	28	Reverse fault
	165	84	Strike-slip (R-type) fault	2	27	Reverse fault
	168	85	Strike-slip (R-type) fault	155	70	Strike-slip (R-type) fault
	165	58	Strike-slip (R-type) fault	153	75	Strike-slip (R-type) fault
	150	45	Strike-slip (R-type) fault	148	78	Strike-slip (R-type) fault
	180	70	Reactivated fault	160	77	Strike-slip (R-type) fault
	165	65	Reactivated fault	162	77	Strike-slip (R-type) fault
	171	68	Reactivated fault	0	75	Strike-slip (Y-type) fault
				355	73	Strike-slip (Y-type) fault
				352	68	Strike-slip (Y-type) fault
				307	73	Strike-slip (R'-type) fault

Table 2. *Continued*

Experiment	Basement			Cover		
	Dip direction (deg)	Dip (deg)	Nature	Dip direction (deg)	Dip (deg)	Nature
T4	2	28	Reverse fault	331	84	Strike-slip (R-type) fault
	180	30	Reverse fault	146	86	Strike-slip (R-type) fault
	323	84	Strike slip (R-type) fault	151	84	Strike-slip (R-type) fault
	320	83	Strike slip (R-type) fault	323	86	Strike-slip (R-type) fault
	153	78	Strike slip (R-type) fault	155	87	Strike-slip (R-type) fault
	184	66	Reactivated fault	328	86	Strike-slip (R-type) fault
	176	68	Reactivated fault	147	85	Strike-slip (R-type) fault
				150	87	Strike-slip (R-type) fault
				184	48	Reverse fault
				3	10	Reverse fault

Newly formed reverse faults cutting through the ancient graben structures, newly formed strike-slip faults and the reactivated pre-existing normal faults are distinguished. (See the text for further explanation.)

strike-slip fault developed. Instead, the two reverse faults accommodated the strike-slip component of deformation, which became sinistral reverse faults. Other thrusts developed, within the cover but close to the sidewalls (Fig. 3c), and are considered as boundary effects.

In the final configuration (Fig. 3b and c), transpressional deformation was strongly localized within the lower and upper brittle layers, in the inherited rift. In contrast, the adjacent domains, within the lower brittle layer, were only weakly affected by the deformation during oblique shortening. Another important feature is that all the induced transpression was taken up by thrust faults within the lower and upper brittle layers. Strike-slip faults were absent. The newly formed structures were parallel to the trend of the pre-existing normal faults, then oblique to the direction of transpression (Fig. 3b and c).

Experiment T2 (Figs 4a, b; and 5). In the early stages of transpression, several thrust faults developed within the lower brittle layer, their dips varying between 28° and 32° (Fig. 4a). Although more complex, all the thrusts in the lower brittle layer were parallel to the trend of the pre-existing normal faults (Fig. 4b). Except for the 'northernmost' thrust, all the others were initiated at the base of the stretched area; that is, where an important rheological difference occurred. Some of these propagated through the basin, thus cutting the pre-existing normal faults (Fig. 4a). These latter were first steepened, then cut and subsequently passively translated in the thrust hanging wall. As in the previous experiment, it is noteworthy that normal faults did not show any evidence of reactivation. As transpression continued, early reverse faults remained active and also accommodated the strike-slip component of the deformation, thus becoming sinistral oblique-slip reverse faults. At more advanced stages of deformation, new sinistral strike-slip faults (synthetic Riedel shears, R) formed (Fig. 4a). Their strike orientation was around N040°, and they were arranged in a dextral-stepping en-echelon pattern. They were subvertical towards the top, but curved at depth and branched into earlier formed thrust faults. At the end of the experiment (Fig. 4b), the newly formed strike-slip faults had cut across the stretched area, and the pre-existing faults were offset and sinistrally displaced.

Within the upper brittle layer, two main thrusts, with opposite vergence, formed first at the edges of the graben; the latter were roughly parallel to the margins of the underlying rifted area (Fig. 4a). Their dip varied from 29° to 32°. Also in this experiment, the post-rift basin fill

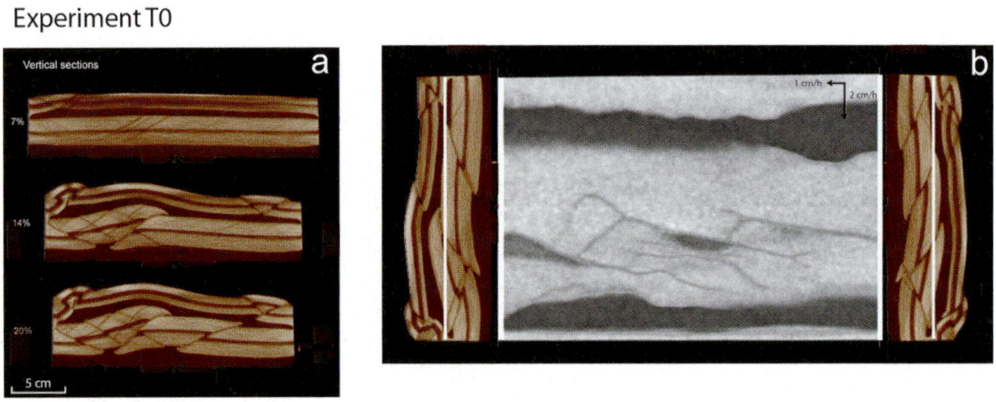

Fig. 2. Experiment T0. (**a**) Vertical section through the central part of the model showing the fault evolution at three consecutive stages of transpression. (**b**) Horizontal slice through the model at the end of the deformation. Location of the horizontal section within the model is shown in accompanying vertical sections (one at each end).

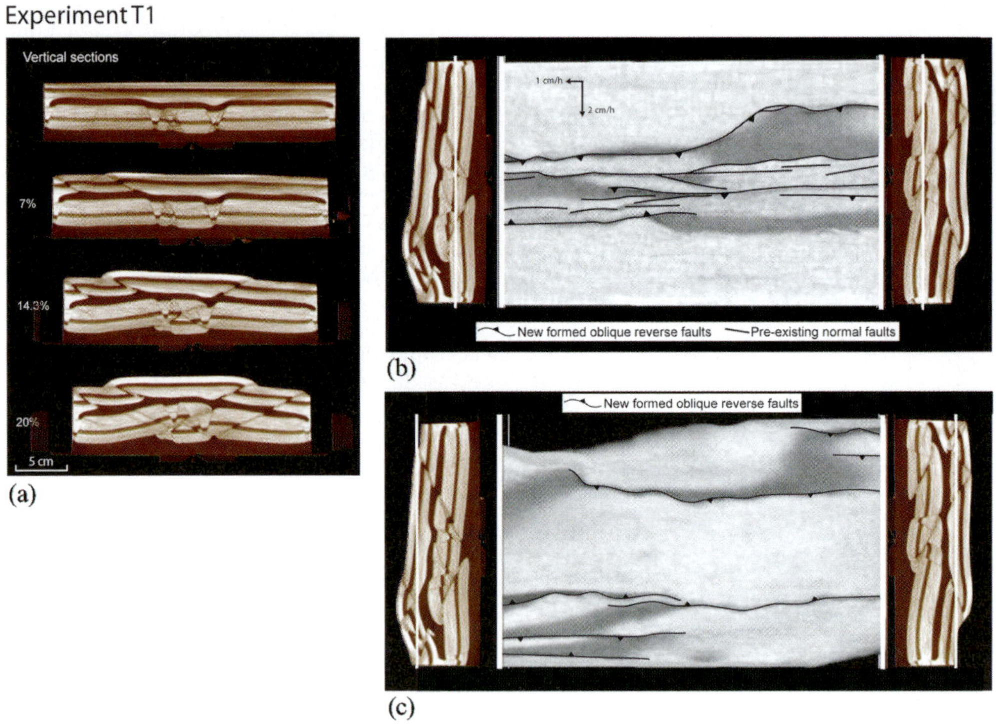

Fig. 3. Experiment T1. (**a**) Vertical section through the central part of the model showing deformation at four consecutive stages of transpression. (**b**) Horizontal slice within the lower brittle layer of the model at the end of the deformation. Its position within the model is shown in accompanying vertical sections. (**c**) Horizontal section within the upper brittle layer of the model at the end of the experiment. Its location is shown in accompanying vertical sections.

was extruded and emplaced onto adjacent and more external domains. After increasing deformation (Fig. 5), slip along the two thrust faults became oblique (sinistral reverse). At more advanced stages of transpression, the deformation was partitioned onto several synthetic Riedel type (R) structures, that developed with a strike of roughly N040° and a sinistral offset. In

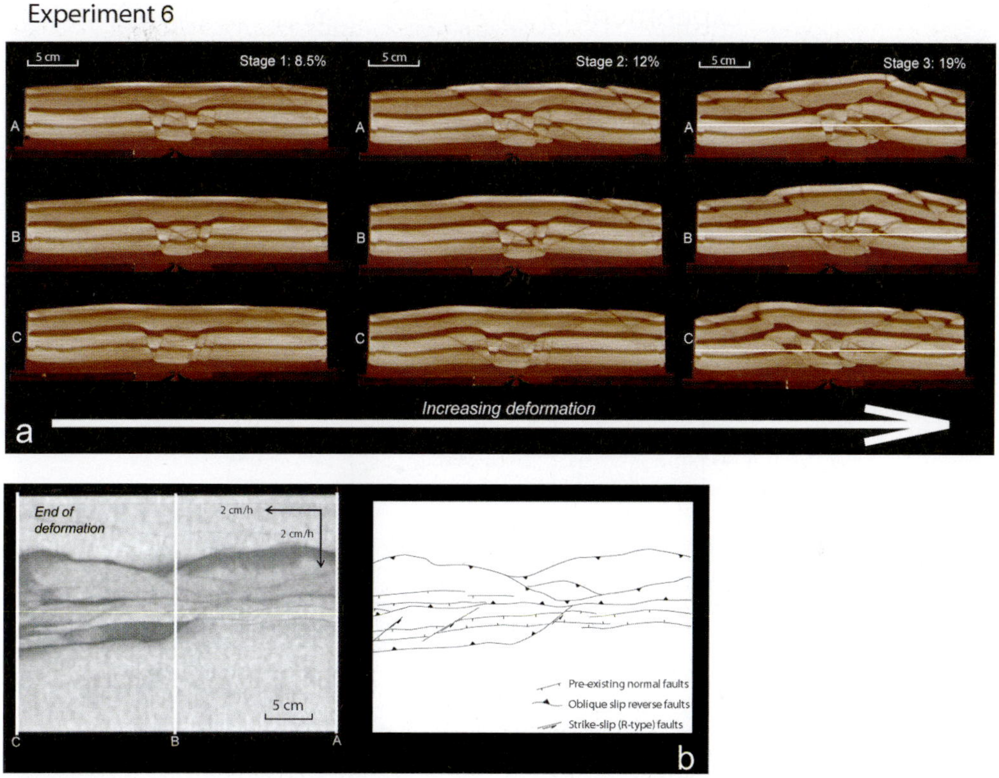

Fig. 4. Experiment T2. (**a**) Vertical sections (A, B, and C) showing faults at three consecutive stages of transpression. Their location is shown in Figure 4b (for the lower brittle layer) and in Figure 5 (for the surface). (**b**) Horizontal slice through the lower brittle layer of the model showing the complex fault pattern at the end of the experiment. Its position within the model is shown by a white line in stage 3 of Fig. 4a.

surface view, they were confined between the two main reverse faults (Fig. 5); in cross-section, they were subvertical and rooted into the interlayered silicone. As they approached the two confining oblique reverse faults, they branched into them.

Experiment T3 (Figs 6a, b, 7 and 8). The history of this model is well described by three vertical cross-sections (Fig. 6a). Several thrust faults formed in the early stages of transpression. They were initiated at the base of the rift; that is, where the silicone and brittle sand were in lateral contact. Their dips varied from 29° to 38° (Table 2), and they were roughly parallel to the rift edges (Fig. 6b). After increasing deformation, they propagated through the stretched area and the pre-existing normal faults were cut and passively translated in the thrust hanging wall. The intermediate stages of the experiment showed that further deformation was accommodated by several strike-slip faults (R-type synthetic faults), which were arranged in a dextral-stepping en echelon pattern. Their strike varied from N060° to N073°; they were subvertical towards the top, curved at depth and branched with earlier formed thrust faults. As they propagated within the rifted area, they cut across the pre-existing north-dipping, normal faults and when they approached the favourably oriented older normal structures (i.e. dipping to the south), they bent into them, used a small segment of the existing low-cohesion planes, and then left with an 'exit' direction that is the same as the 'entry'. In detail (Fig. 7), these small segments of normal faults, reused by the newly formed strike-slip faults, were also partially reactivated with a dip-slip reverse (or at least oblique reverse) sense of movement. As shown in Stage 3 of Figure 6, and in the detail of Figure 7, the amount of such reactivation was large enough to

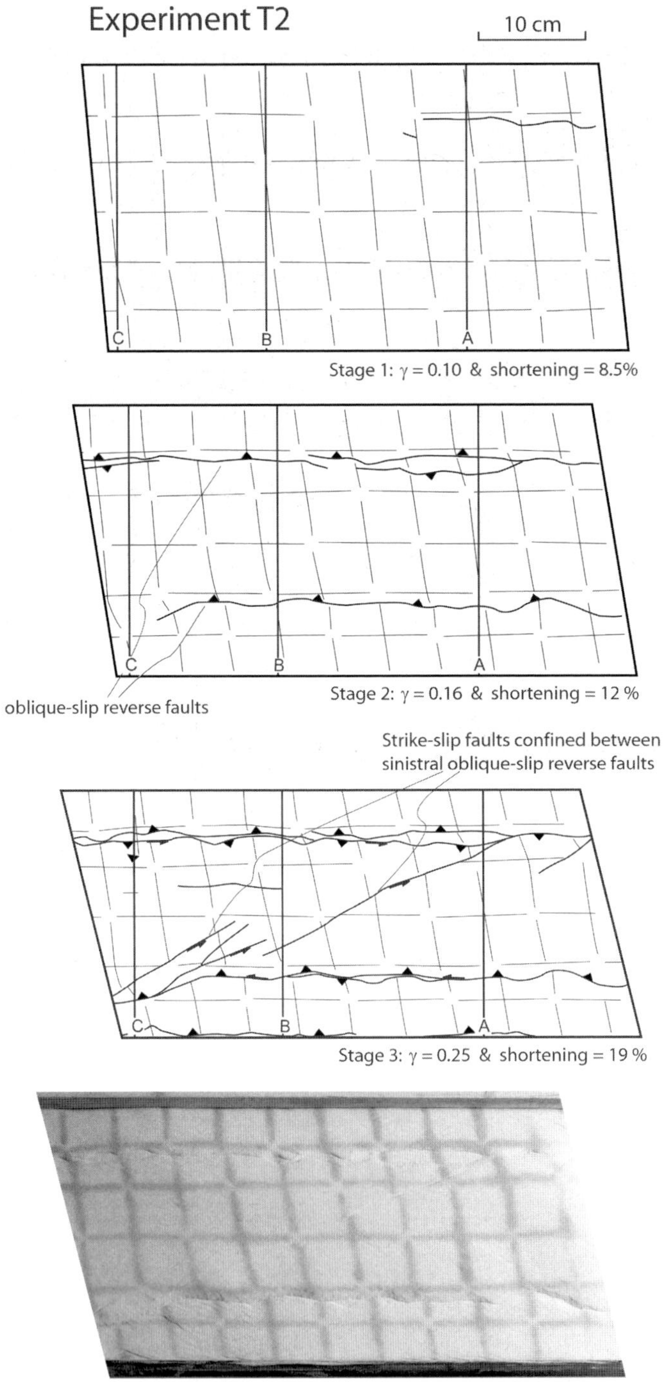

Fig. 5. Experiment T2. Line drawings after photographs of surface, representing three consecutive stages of transpression. Lines A, B and C represent the location of vertical sections of Figure 4a. The accompanying photograph is representative of the end of the experiment. (See the text for further explanation.)

Experiment T3

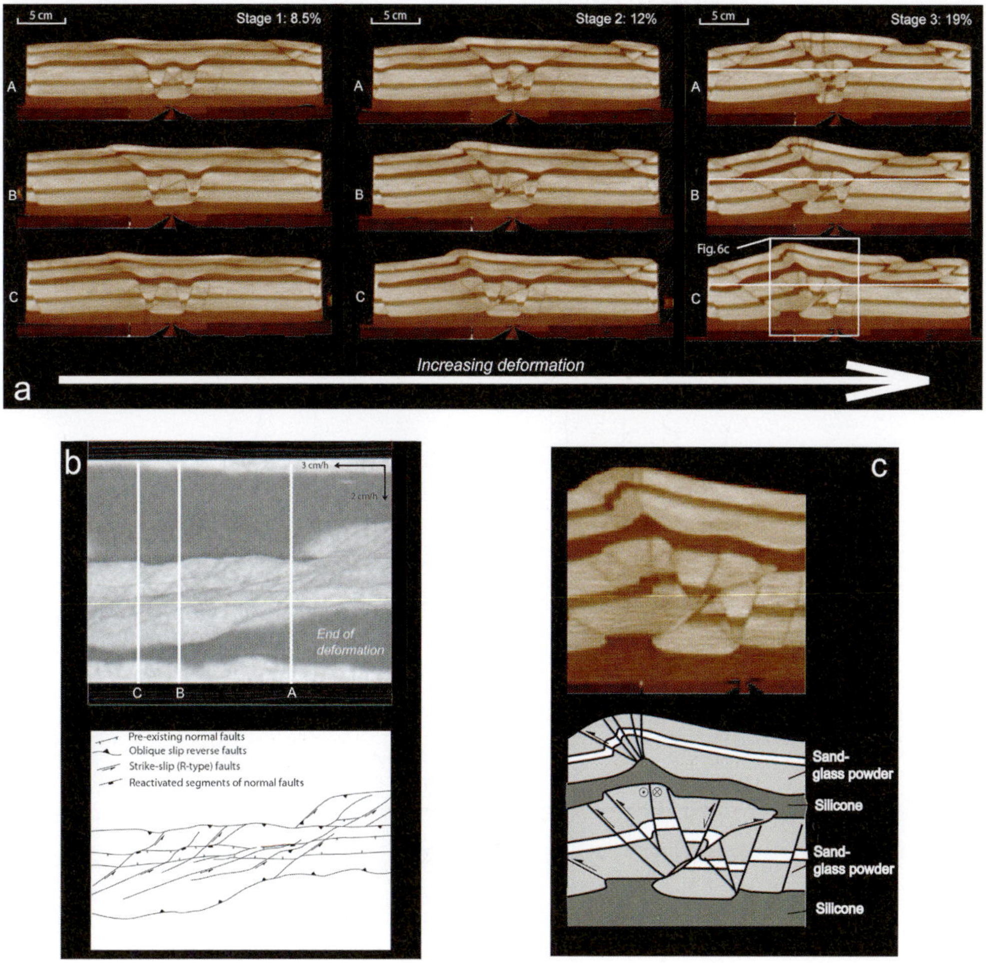

Fig. 6. Experiment T3. (**a**) Vertical sections (A, B, and C) showing faults at three consecutive stages of transpression. Their position within the lower brittle layer is shown in Figure 6b. (**b**) Horizontal slice through the lower brittle layer of the model, showing the fault pattern at the end of the experiment. The position of the horizontal section within the model is indicated by a white line in stage 3 of Figure 6a. (**c**) Enlargement of inset in section C of stage 3.

allow the recovery of the original pre-extension topography.

Within the post-rift sequence, in the early phases of oblique shortening (Stage 1 of Fig. 6; Fig. 7), two main structures, with opposite vergence were initiated roughly parallel to the underlying basin margins and with a low angle of dip (*c*. 28°). In vertical sections, they nucleated at the base of the brittle sand and accommodated a dip-slip reverse sense of displacement.

At more advanced stages of transpression, the strain became distributed onto several en echelon synthetic Riedel type (R) structures, whose surface strike was between N058° and N065° (Table 2). Their right-stepped arrangement was consistent with sinistral shearing. They were between the two main reverse faults; these were therefore active and accommodated part of the strike-slip component of the deformation so that, with increasing deformation, they became sinistral oblique-slip reverse faults. The R-type strike-slip faults started to develop close to the main oblique faults and, with increasing displacement, also propagated in the middle part

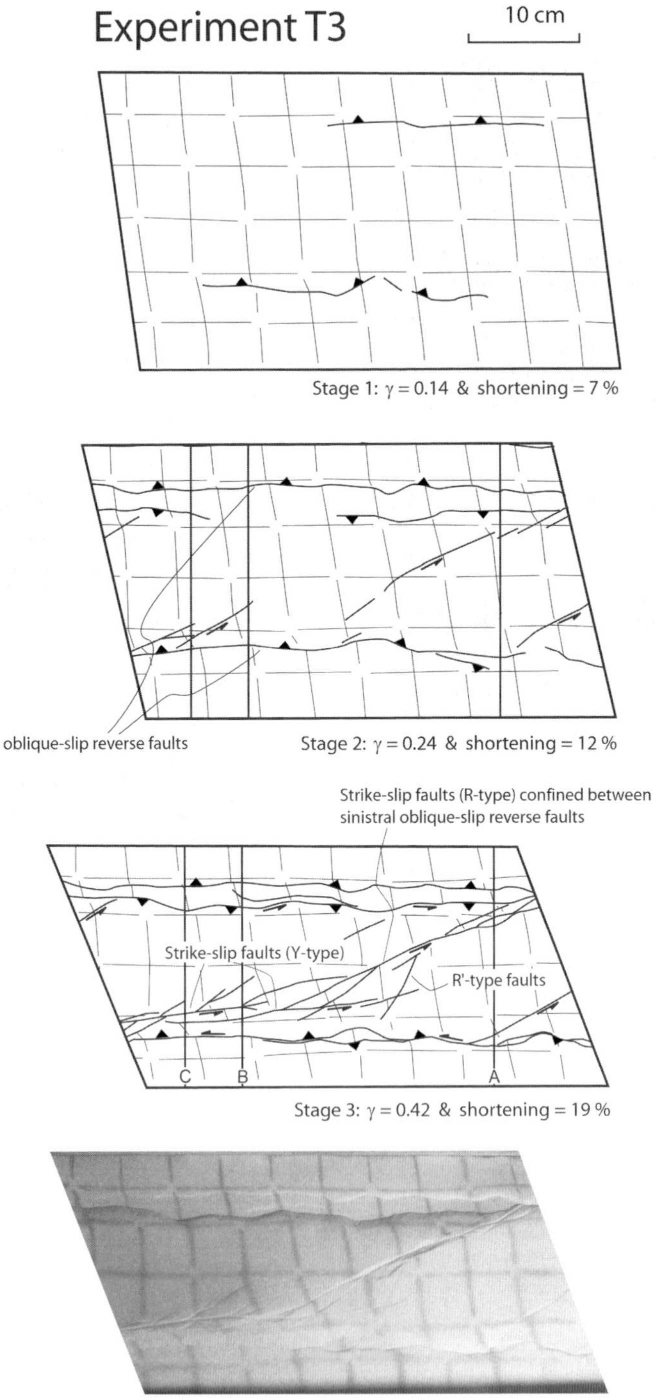

Fig. 7. Experiment T3. Line drawings after photographs of surface showing three consecutive stages of transpression. Lines A, B and C show the position of vertical sections of Figure 6a. The accompanying photograph is representative of the end of the experiment. (See the text for further explanation.)

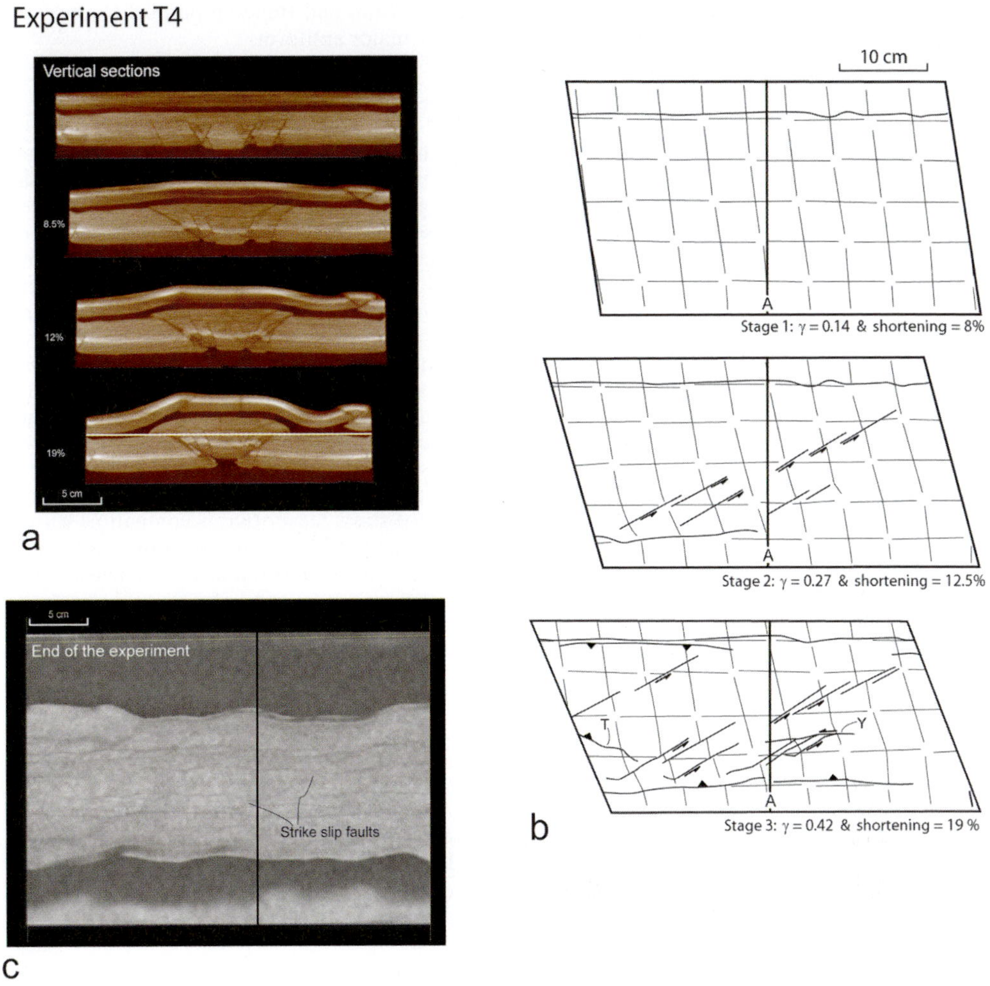

Fig. 8. Experiment T4. (**a**) Vertical section showing the fault evolution at three consecutive stages of transpression. Its position within the model is shown in (**b**) and (**c**). (**b**) Line drawings after surface photographs at three stages of oblique shortening. (**c**) Horizontal slice through the lower brittle layer of the model showing the fault pattern at the end of the experiment. (See the text for further explanation.)

of the model. In cross-section (Fig. 6), these faults were subvertical and extended down to the interbedded silicone. As they approached the two main oblique reverse faults, they branched into them. With further deformation, lower angle sinistral faults (Y in Fig. 7) formed with an east–west strike direction. They developed mainly in the overlap area between adjacent dextral-stepping faults and linked into, or in some cases cut, the earlier formed R-type faults. This resulted in a complex pattern of anastomosing shear zones, including shear lenses and blocks. At very late stages of transpression, a few high-angle strike-slip faults (R′ in Stage 3 of Fig. 7) also formed.

Experiment T4 (Fig. 8a and b). This experiment differed from the others. After extension, the resulting rifted area was covered by a thin layer of sand. This led to a flat-lying topography, above which the interbedded silicone was placed. Thus, the latter was even and subhorizontal. This configuration has been of particular importance, as it allowed the effective role exerted by the original geometry of an interlayered silicone level onto fault genesis and pattern during transpression to be deciphered.

Within the lower brittle layer, the deformation is very similar to that of the previous experiment. In fact, two main low-angle (*c.* 28°) faults developed at the edges of the rifted area and ran roughly parallel to the trend of the pre-existing normal faults. They nucleated at the base of the brittle sand and, at very early stages of deformation, accommodated a dip-slip reverse sense of displacement. Furthermore, several low-angle faults splayed upwards from the tip of each individual pre-existing normal fault. Increasing deformation led to the generation of several R-type synthetic strike-slip faults, which were organized in a dextral-stepping en echelon pattern. Their strike varied from N060° to N073°; as they propagated within the rifted area, they bent into the pre-existing normal faults, dipping to the south, reusing and reactivating some small segments of them. The final stage of the deformation, represented by three vertical sections through the model illustrated in Figure 8a, showed that the two main sinistral oblique reverse faults, at the edges of the lower brittle layer stretched area, produced a pronounced positive inversion of sedimentary fill of the basin, which was gradually emplaced onto the adjacent and poorly deformed domains.

Within the upper brittle layer, a regular and subhorizontal silicone level at the base of the post-rift sequence led to a fault evolution that was markedly different from that of the previous experiments (Fig. 8). The onset of discrete brittle failure took place only at advanced stages of deformation, and the model was first deformed by bulk shearing distributed over a large area, as can be seen from the distortion of the sand markers. Increasing deformation resulted in the development of a more pervasive system of faults. These were several en echelon synthetic Riedel type (R) structures, oriented roughly N60° (Table 2), and whose right-stepped arrangement is consistent with a sinistral shearing. As deformation proceeded, lower angle sinistral faults (Y in Fig. 8) developed with a roughly east–west strike. At very advanced stages of deformation, gently dipping reverse faults (T in Fig. 8), with dips of 30–50°, formed with a surface strike at a high angle to earlier formed R-type faults. Vertical sections at the end of experiment (Fig. 8b) showed a general folding of the cover, forced by the progressive positive inversion of the sedimentary fill within the underlying brittle layer. This broad and double-verging forced fold had a large flat top and flanks, dipping 27°, and was parallel to the trend of the underlying graben system (i.e. east–west). They were locally offset by several minor break-thrusts, developed in the later stages of deformation and trending parallel to the flanks of the major antiform.

Interpretation

In this section the fault kinematics observed within the upper and lower brittle layers of sand and glass powder in each model are examined to assess how: (1) the pre-existing graben and horst structures, and (2) the mechanical decoupling by ductile layers can control the internal stress regimes and the style of the deformation during a transpressive tectonic phase.

In the experiments the displacement vector on faults cannot be determined accurately and thus it is not possible to numerically compute a mean reduced stress tensor from a given fault-slip dataset (in the sense of Carey & Brunier 1974). However, it is easy to define graphically a reduced stress tensor that is compatible with the fault generation or reactivation patterns. A reduced stress tensor indicates a tensor of the form

$$D = \sigma_{ij}$$

where $\sigma_{ij} = \sigma_{ji}$ (with i and j being 1, 2 or 3) and

$$\sigma^2_{11} + \sigma^2_{22} + \sigma^2_{33} + \sigma^2_{12} + \sigma^2_{13} + \sigma^2_{23} = 1. \qquad (1)$$

D defines a 'normalized stress deviator' and is homothetic to the total stress tensor T by the relationship

$$T = \alpha I + \beta D$$

where I is the identity and α and β are two real scalar coefficients.

Here the convention is that the compressive stress is negative in sign, and σ_1 is the 'maximum' compressive principal stress (with respect to magnitude, i.e. absolute value). Therefore the principal stresses are $\sigma_1 < \sigma_2 < \sigma_3$ and the anisotropy of the reduced stress tensor is measured by the ratio

$$R = (\sigma_2 - \sigma_1)/(\sigma_3 - \sigma_1) \qquad (2)$$

where $\sigma_3 \neq \sigma_1$.

For the undisturbed sand, the Coulomb failure criterion with a friction angle value of 30° (i.e. an internal friction coefficient of 0.57 and no cohesion) explains the observed dip angles of newly formed faults in many sandbox experiments when the mean stress tensor is known. It is well known that these mechanical parameters are difficult to determine experimentally (see discussion by Krantz 1991, and Mourgues &

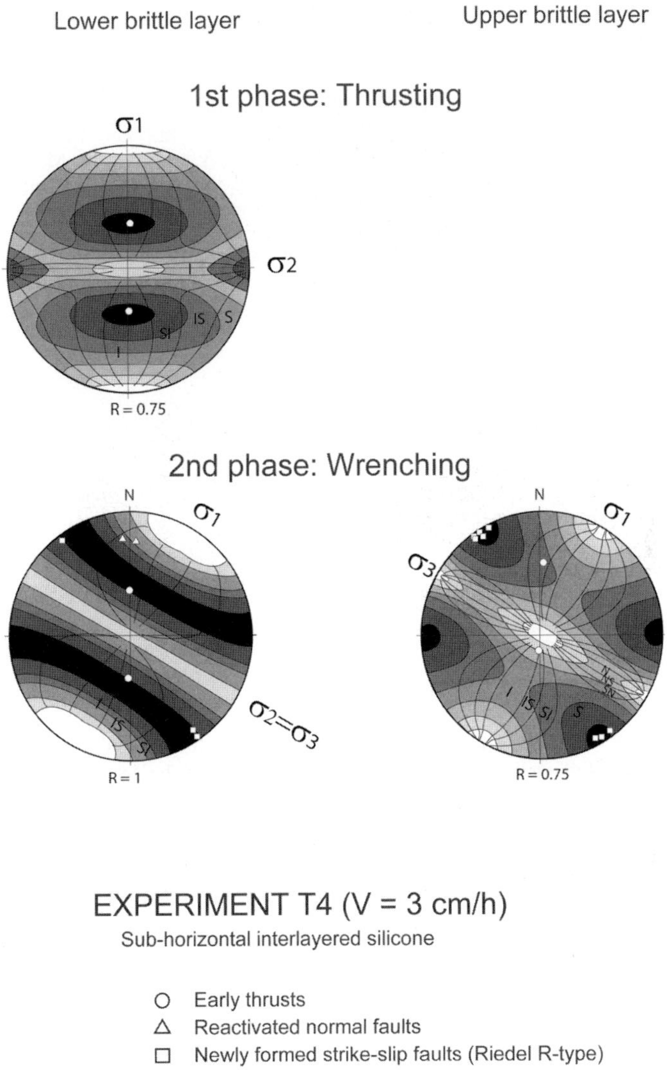

Fig. 12. Mean stress tensors explaining the observed sequence of faulting in the lower and upper brittle layers of experiment T4 (see Table 2 for fault orientation data and text for explanation).

the strike-slip velocity is high, small segments of pre-existing normal faults are reactivated with a reverse sense of displacement.

This general sequence of fault generation–reactivation suggests a change in the stress regime with time. This change is caused by the switching of the minimum and intermediate principal stress axes and also by progressive rotation of the axis of the maximum compressive stress in the horizontal plane. This axis initially trends north–south and progressively rotates towards NE–SW, the angle depending on the velocity of the applied simple shear and on the friction coefficient of the sand.

If there is no pre-existing basin, no change in the stress regime occurs through time. In experiment T0, only one generation of structures developed. A single generation of structures was produced in the upper brittle layer of experiment T4, when the post-rift silicone layer was deposited as a subhorizontal and regular stratum. In this experiment, there is a clear spatial partitioning of the fault generation–reactivation pattern with a two-phase (compression, then strike-slip) stress regime in the stretched lower brittle layer and a single strike-slip stress regime in the 'post-rift' cover.

The main controls investigated in the experiments were the pre-existing fault architecture and the amount of strike-slip. The most important factor controlling the stress regime through time was the orientation of the pre-existing faults with respect to the applied simple shear component of the transpression. The shape of the decoupling layers is also fundamental because the geometry of the interbedded silicone layer influences the stress distribution, and a regular and undeformed post-rift silicone layer introduces mechanical decoupling between the post-rift cover and the stretched basin.

This series of experiments demonstrated important consequences for stress–strain relationships and apparent tectonic phases generated during a single inversion–transpression event. Pre-existing rift basins controlled the structural style, the formation and reactivation of faults, and the variation of the stress state through time. Future work should test the influence of pre-existing rifts that lie oblique to the imposed direction of simple shear.

We thank P. Cobbold, R. Butler, A. Ries and R. Graham for improving the quality of the manuscript with their valuable comments and suggestions. Constructive comments and discussions were also exchanged with I. Moretti and G. Schreurs. Ms C. Fichen, J. M. Mengus and D. Pillot are thanked for their assistance in building the models and processing of the CT-images. L. M. was in part financially supported by a grant (D.R. n. 293, 13/02/2002) from the University of Camerino (Italy) which is gratefully acknowledged.

References

ALLEMAND, P., BRUN, J.-P., DAVY, P. & VAN DEN DRIESSCHE, J. 1989. Symétrie et asymmétrie des rifts et mécanismes d'amincissiment de la lithosphère. *Bulletin de la Société Géologique de France*, **3**, 445–451.

BRUN, J. P. & NALPAS, T. 1996. Graben inversion in nature and experiments. *Tectonics*, **15**(2), 677–687.

BUCHANAN, P. G. & MCCLAY, K. R. 1991. Sandbox experiments of inverted listric and planar fault systems. *Tectonophysics*, **188**, 97–115.

BUTLER, R. W. H. 1989. The influence of pre-existing basin structure on thrust system evolution in the Western Alps. *In*: COOPER, M. A. & WILLIAMS, G. D. (eds) *Inversion Tectonics*. Geological Society, London, Special Publications, **44**, 105–122.

CAREY, E. & BRUNIER, B. 1974. Analyse théorique et numérique d'un modèle mécanique élémentaire appliqué à l'étude d'une population de failles. *Comptes Rendus de l'Académie des Sciences*, **279**, 891–894.

COLLETTA, B., BALÉ, P., BALLARD, J. F., LETOUZEY, J. & PINEDO, R. 1991. Computerized X-ray tomography analysis of sandbox models: examples of thin-skinned thrust systems. *Geology*, **19**, 1063–1067.

CORFIELD, S. M., GAWTHORPE, R. L., Gage, M., Fraser, A. J. & Besly, B. M. 1996. Inversion tectonics of the Variscan foreland of the British Isles. *Journal of the Geological Society, London*, **153**, 17–32.

COWARD, M. P. 1996. Balancing sections through inverted basins. *In*: BUCHANAN, P. G. & NIEUWLAND, D. A. (eds) *Modern Developments in Structural Interpretation, Validation and Modelling*. Geological Society, London, Special Publications, **99**, 51–77.

DUBOIS, A., ODONNE, F., MASSONNAT, G., LEBOURG, T. & FABRE, R. 2002. Analogue modelling of fault reactivation: tectonic inversion and oblique remobilisation of grabens. *Journal of Structural Geology*, **24**, 1741–1752.

EISENSTADT, G. & WITHJACK, M. A. 1995. Estimating inversion: results from clay models. *In*: BUCHANAN, J. G. & BUCHANAN, P. G. (eds) *Basin Inversion*. Geological Society, London, Special Publications, **88**, 119–136.

GILLCRIST, R., COWARD, M. P. & MUGNIER, J. L. 1987. Structural inversion and its controls: examples from the Alpine foreland and French Alps. *Geodinamica Acta*, **1**, 5–34.

HAYWARD, A. B. & GRAHAM, R. H. 1989. Some geometrical characteristics of inversion. *In*: COOPER, M. A. & WILLIAMS, G. D. (eds) *Inversion Tectonics*. Geological Society, London, Special Publications, **44**, 17–39.

HOUNSFIELD, G. N. 1973. Computerized transverse axial scanning (tomography). *British Journal of Radiology*, **46**, 1016–1022.

HUBBERT, M. K. 1937. Theory of scale models as applied to the study of geologic structures. *Geological Society of America Bulletin*, **48**, 1459–1520.

JAEGER, J. C. & COOK, N. G. W. 1979. *Fundamentals of Rocks Mechanics*, 3rd edn. Chapman & Hall, London.

KRANTZ, R. W. 1991. Measurements of friction coefficients and cohesion for faulting and fault reactivation in laboratory models using sand and sand mixtures. *Tectonophysics*, **188**, 203–207.

LETOUZEY, J. 1990. Fault reactivation, inversion and fold-thrust belt. *In*: Letouzey, J. (ed.) *Petroleum and Tectonics in Mobile Belts*. Technip, Paris, 101–128.

MALAVIEILLE, J. 1984. Modélisation expérimentale des chevauchements imbriqués: application aux chaînes des montagnes. *Bulletin de la Société Geologique de France*, **26**, 129–138.

MANDL, G. 1988. *Mechanisms of Tectonic Faulting*. Elsevier, Amsterdam.

MATTIONI, L. 2001. *Definizione dell'assetto geologico-strutturale dell'Appennino lucano ed implicazioni sull'evoluzione tettonica della catena sud-appenninica.* PhD thesis, University of Camerino.

MATTIONI, L., LE POURHIET, L. & MORETTI, I. 2004. Extension through a heterogeneous crust. The case of Gulf of Corinth (Greece). Part I: Analogue modelling. *Bollettino di Geofisica Teorica ed Applicata*, **45**, 237–241.

Mazzoli, S., Barkham, S., Cello, G., Gambini, R., Mattioni, L., Shiner, P. & Tondi, E. 2001. Reconstruction of the continental margin architecture deformed in the contraction of the Lagonegro Basin, southern Apennines, Italy. *Journal of the Geological Society, London*, **158**, 309–319.

McClay, K. R. 1989. Analogue models of inversion tectonics. *In*: Cooper, M. A. & Williams, G. D. (eds) *Inversion Tectonics*. Geological Society, London, Special Publications, **44**, 41–62.

McClay, K. R. 1996. Recent advances in analogue modelling: uses in section interpretation and validation. *In*: Buchanan, P. G. & Nieuwland, D. A. (eds) *Modern Developments in Structural Interpretation, Validation and Modelling*. Geological Society, London, Special Publications, **99**, 201–225.

McClay, K. R. & Buchanan, P. G. 1992. Thrust faults in inverted extensional basins. *In*: McClay, K. R. (ed.) *Thrust Tectonics*. Chapman & Hall, London, 93–104.

McClay, K. R., Whitehouse, P. S., Dooley, T., & Richards, M. 2004. 3D evolution of fold and thrust belts formed by oblique convergence. *Marine and Petroleum Geology*, **21**, 857–877.

Mitra, S. 1993. Geometry and kinematic evolution of inversion structures. *AAPG Bulletin*, **77**, 1159–1191.

Mourgues, R. & Cobbold, P. R. 2003. Some tectonic consequences of fluid overpressures and seepage forces as demonstrated by sandbox modelling. *Tectonophysics*, **376**, 75–97.

Nalpas, T., Le Douaran, S., Brun, J. P., Unternehr, P. & Richert, J. P. 1995. Inversion of the Broad Fourteens Basin (offshore Netherlands), a small-scale model investigation. *Sedimentary Geology*, **95**, 237–250.

Ramberg, H. 1981. *Gravity, Deformation and the Earth's Crust*. Academic Press, New York.

Richard, P. & Cobbold, P. R. 1989. Structures en fleur positives et décrochements crustaux: modélisation analogique et interprétation mécanique. *Comptes Rendus de l'Académie des Sciences, Série II*, **308**, 553–560.

Richard, P. & Cobbold, P. 1990. Experimental insights into partitioning of fault motions in continental convergent wrench zones. *Annales Tectonicae*, **4**, 35–44.

Richard, P., Ballard, J. F., Colletta, B. & Cobbold, P. 1989. Naissance et évolution de failles au-dessus d'un décrochement de socle: modélisation analogique et tomographie. *Comptes Rendus de l'Académie des Sciences, Série II*, **309**, 2111–2118.

Richard, P., Naylor, M. A. & Koopman, A. 1995. Experimental models of strike-slip tectonics. *Petroleum Geoscience*, **1**, 71–80.

Roure, F. & Colletta, B. 1996. Cenozoic inversion structures in the foreland of the Pyrenees and Alps. *In*: Ziegler, P. A. & Horvath, F. (eds) *Peri-Tethys Memoir 2: Structure and Prospects of Alpine Basins and Forelands*. Mémoires du Museum National d'Histoire Naturelle, **170**, 173–209.

Sassi, W., Colletta, B., Balé, P. & Paquereau, T. 1993. Modelling of structural complexity in sedimentary basins: the role of pre-existing faults in thrust tectonics. *Tectonophysics*, **226**, 97–112.

Schreurs, G. 2004. 3D Analogue modelling of basin inversion: the effect of distributed wrenching or transpression on pre-existing grabens. *Bollettino di Geofisica Teorica ed Applicata*, **45**, 264–268.

Schreurs, G. & Colletta, B. 1998. Analogue modelling of faulting in zones of continental transpression and transtension. *In*: Holdsworth, R. E., Strachan, R. A. & Dewey, J. F. (eds) *Continental Transpressional and Transtensional Tectonics*. Geological Society, London, Special Publications, **135**, 59–79.

Sibson, R. H. 1974. Frictional constraints on thrust, wrench, and normal faults. *Nature*, **249**, 542–544.

Sibson, R. H. 1985. A note on fault reactivation. *Journal of Structural Geology*, **7**, 751–754.

Viola, G., Odonne, F. & Mancktelow, N. S. 2004. Analogue modelling of reverse fault reactivation in strike-slip and transpressive regimes: application to the Giudicarie fault system, Italian Eastern Alps. *Journal of Structural Geology*, **36**, 401–418.

Ziegler, P. A., Cloetingh, S. & van Wees, J. D. 1995. Dynamics of intra-plate compressional deformation: the Alpine foreland and other examples. *Tectonophysics*, **252**, 7–59.

The role of major fault zones in controlling the geometry and spatial organization of structures in the Zagros Fold–Thrust Belt

M. SEPEHR[1] & J. W. COSGROVE[2]

[1]*Geology Department, NIOC Exploration, Yaghma Alley, Jomhouri-e Islami Avenue, Tehran, Iran, (e-mail: zagrosftb@gmail.com)*

[2]*Department of Earth Science and Engineering, Royal School of Mines, Imperial College, Prince Consort Road, London SW7 2BP, UK*

Abstract: The present-day morphology of the Zagros Fold–Thrust Belt is dominated by magnificent exposures of NW–SE-trending folds. This mountain belt is also characterized by a series of belt-parallel and belt-oblique (transfer) fault zones. Not all the fault zones have a clear exposure at the surface because of the presence of thick incompetent overlying sedimentary successions, but they can be identified from a study of the present-day seismicity of the belt and by the spatial organization of the overlying folds. The folds are not often cross-cut by the faults but plunge towards, or are deflected and end against, these blind transfer fault zones. As a result, shortening is accommodated by different fold trains on either side of the fault. This decoupling in turn causes the step-like offset of the major, belt-parallel thrust zones and the related topographic elements. These offsets occur on all scales, from regional (e.g. across the Kazerun and Izeh fault zones) to local. These transfer faults–lateral ramps may be influenced by pre-existing structures or by facies boundaries, which in particular influenced the Zagros Basin in the Cretaceous. In addition to controlling sedimentation and the compartmentalization of deformation, these fault zones also act as paths of fluid migration, as indicated by the present-day concentration of oil seepages and thermal or sulphur springs.

The geometry of fold–thrust belts, and the stepping and termination of fault zones along strike, have been widely discussed (e.g. Ries & Shackleton 1976; Marshak & Wilkerson 1992; Macedo & Marshak 1999; Marshak 2004). Termination and displacement between segments of thrust faults take place along transfer faults or lateral ramps (Dahlstrom 1969, 1970; McClay 1991). Macedo & Marshak (1999) suggested that the segmentation of fold–thrust belts along strike develops in response to a number of tectonic situations, including sedimentary thickness variations along and across the belt, the strength and pinch-out of detachments (change of detachment horizons along strike) and the interaction with foreland obstacles, such as inherited basement structures. As a result, the surface expression of belt-parallel fault zones is characterized by frontal ramps, offset by lateral or oblique-lateral ramps (transfer faults). The lateral and oblique ramps allow different amounts of belt-normal shortening to occur along the strike of a fold–thrust belt, leading to a step-like geometry of the belt when viewed in plan. Recognition and understanding of transfer faults, which are very common within fold–thrust belts such as Rocky Mountains (Dahlstrom 1970; Fermor 1999; Bégin & Spratt 2002; Dixon & Spratt 2004), are important as they control the evolution and partitioning of deformation.

The Zagros Fold–Thrust Belt lies on the northeastern margin of the Arabian Plate and is dominated by impressive exposures of NW–SE trending folds (Fig. 1). Despite the excellent exposures of the folds in the Zagros Belt, few fault zones are exposed at the surface. The geomorphology and seismicity of the belt has been used to identify some of these blind fault zones (Berberian 1981, 1995). However, because the presence of some of the proposed fault zones is doubtful, the term ‘flexure’ (Falcon 1961, 1969) is still used in Zagros literature. In this paper the influence of blind faults on the morphology and spatial organization of folds at the surface is discussed. A study of the geometry and organization of folds has allowed blind faults to be detected. The method has been tested by studying folds above blind faults, known to exist from seismicity data, and has been used to determine previously undetected and seismically inactive faults. Some of the fault zones that define the boundaries of the Dezful Embayment, a geological depression in the central part of the Zagros Mountain Belt (the major hydrocarbon province

From: RIES, A. C., BUTLER, R. W. H. & GRAHAM, R. H. (eds) 2007. *Deformation of the Continental Crust: The Legacy of Mike Coward*. Geological Society, London, Special Publications, **272**, 419–436.
0305-8719/07/$15

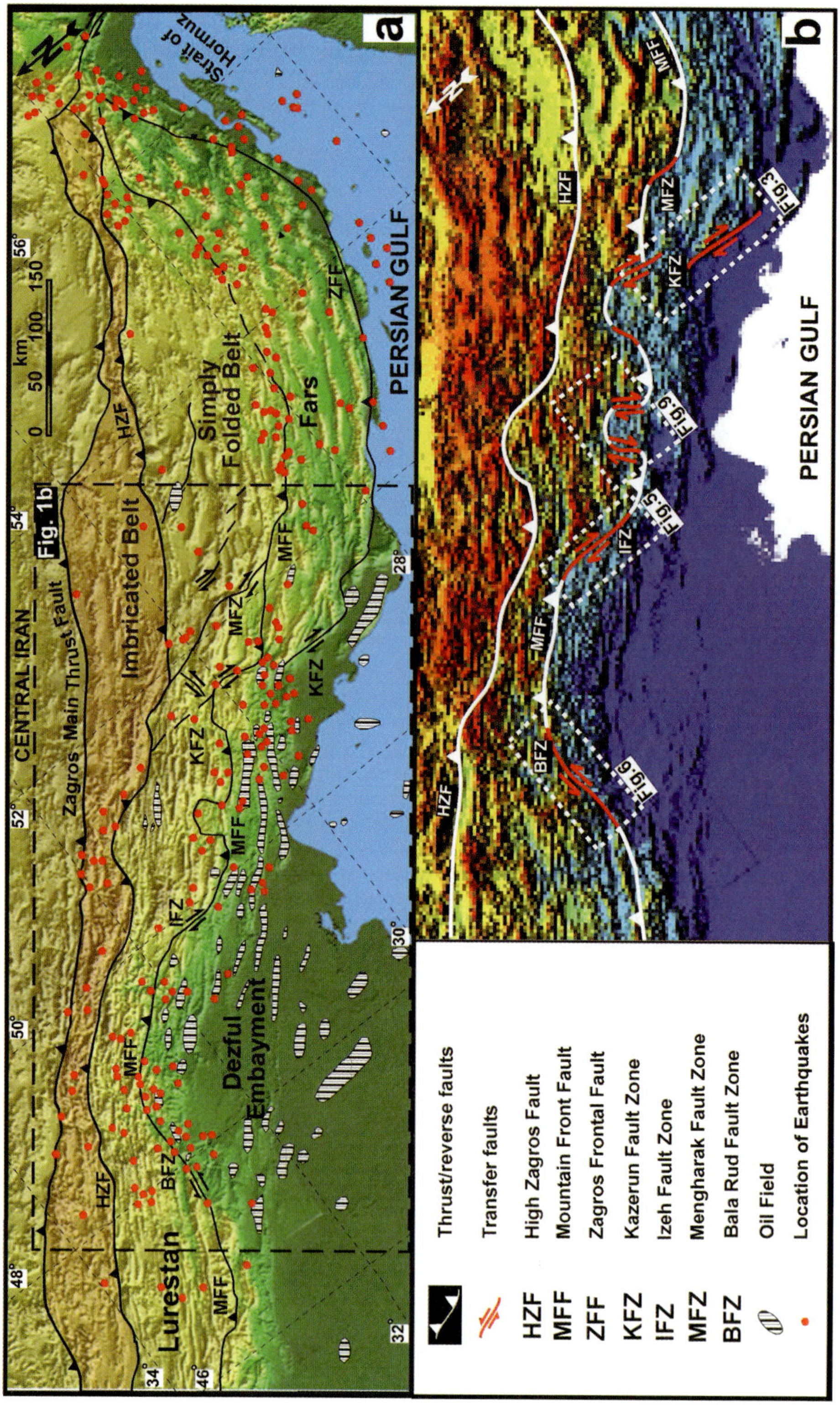

Fig. 1. (**a**) Topography relief and structural map of the Iranian sector of the Zagros Fold–Thrust Belt showing the location of the major fault zones, which coincide with the zone of high seismicity (modified from Ni & Barazangi 1986) and distribution of oilfields. (**b**) A 1 km digital elevation model of the central part of the Zagros Mountain Belt, showing the step-like topography along the Mountain Front Fault.

of the Zagros); (Fig. 1), are discussed. The fault zones include the east–west-trending Bala Rud Fault Zone to the NW, the NW–SE-trending Mountain Front Fault to the NE and the north–south-trending Kazerun Fault Zone to the SE (Fig. 1). The faulted boundaries of the embayment are examined, to gain a better understanding of their role in basin evolution and consequently hydrocarbon generation, migration and entrapment within the Dezful Embayment and the surrounding region. Some of these fault zones cause the step-like geometry (sinuosity) that characterizes the mountain belt, and particularly the mountain front fault zones, when viewed in plan (Fig. 1). These fault zones appear to act as transfer faults that accommodate the offsets (contrast position) of the Zagros deformation fronts. It is observed that these transfer faults rarely intersect the NW–SE-trending anticlines.

Tectonic setting

The Zagros Fold–Thrust Belt contains 8–14 km thick Cambrian–Recent succession, which lie on a Precambrian basement. These sediments were deposited on a platform that was relatively stable from the Cambrian until the collision between the Arabian and Iranian plates in the Tertiary (Takin 1972; Falcon 1974; Berberian & King 1981; Beydoun *et al.* 1992). Shortening across the Zagros Fold–Thrust Belt in the cover, which is estimated to be 30–85 km (Falcon 1974; Blanc *et al.* 2003; McQuarrie 2004), occurred by thrusting and folding above various décollement horizons (Table 1). In contrast, shortening in the basement occurs dominantly by faulting. It is thought that NW–SE-trending Permo-Triassic normal faults in the basement (the result of Permo-Triassic spreading of the Neo-Tethys Ocean to the NE of the Arabian Plate) were reactivated as reverse faults during the Late Tertiary collision (Jackson 1980; Berberian 1981; Jackson & Fitch 1981). The thick Cambrian Hormuz Salt, at the base of the sedimentary succession, and other evaporite horizons (e.g. the Dashtak and Gachsaran formations) within the succession (Berberian 1981; Sepehr & Cosgrove 2004; Talebian & Jackson 2004), prevented these basement faults from rupturing the cover rocks and reaching the surface. As a result of these decoupling horizons, the deformation in the basement and the sedimentary cover occurred independently.

The position of the suture zone between the Arabian and Iranian plates is a matter of debate (Alavi 1994); it has traditionally been defined by the NW–SE-trending fault zone known as the Zagros Main Thrust Fault (Fig. 1); (e.g. Stocklin 1974). To the SW of the suture and within the Zagros Belt, a series of major fault zones, which are either parallel or oblique to the folded belt, divide the Zagros Belt into different structural regions along and across the belt. The structural zones parallel to the belt are the Imbricated and the Simply Folded Belts (Fig. 1). The Simply Folded Belt itself is divided into three structural zones laterally. These are, from NW to SE, the Lurestan, Dezful Embayment and Fars regions (Fig. 1).

Major fault zones of the Zagros Belt

The major fault zones linked to the Zagros collision fall into two categories: (1) belt-parallel fault zones (thrust faults); (2) belt-oblique fault zones (transfer faults). The present morphotectonic features of the Zagros Belt have been significantly influenced by these two fault sets, which were generated or reactivated during the shortening linked to the continental collision in the Tertiary.

Belt-parallel fault zones

The belt-parallel fault zones consist of NW–SE-trending faults parallel to the belt and include pre-existing normal faults, which have been inverted as a result of Tertiary collision between the Arabian and Iranian plates. They are

Table 1. *Major detachment horizons in the Zagros Fold–Thrust Belt*

Geological Province	Main Detachment	Age	Lithology
Dezful embayment	Gachsaran	Lower Miocene	Evaporite
Lurestan	Garau	Lower Cretaceous	Shale
Simply folded Belt NE	Kazhdumi	Lower Cretaceous	Shale
of the Dezful Embayment	Dashtak	Triassic	Evaporite
Fars	Hormuz	Cambrian	Salt

dominantly zones of segmented reverse faults or thrusts and their activity has produced linear zones of uplift that has resulted in the formation of a stepped topographic profile across the fold–thrust belt, downstepping to the SW. These fault zones have been identified on the basis of the present morphotectonics and seismicity of the belt (Berberian 1995). Most of them can be detected on the topography relief map of the belt (Fig. 1). The three most important fault zones are the High Zagros, the Mountain Front and the Zagros Frontal faults.

The High Zagros Fault. This is the best exposed fault zone in the Zagros Belt. It separates the Imbricated Belt or High Zagros Thrust Belt (an intensely deformed zone) to the NE from the Folded or Simply Folded Belt to the SW (Fig. 1). The High Zagros Fault has up to 6 km of vertical displacement (Berberian 1995). The area NE of the High Zagros Fault, which corresponds to the Imbricated Belt, was also a positive feature (a horst) before, and during, the Permo-Triassic (Koop 1978; Szabo & Kheradpir 1978). Early Tertiary movement of the High Zagros Fault separated the piggy-back basin, with flysch-type sediments in the hanging wall to the NE, from the marine marls in the footwall to the SW (Sherkati & Letouzey 2004). The hanging wall of the fault has remained an uplifted block and has been the source of most detritus since the Miocene.

The Mountain Front Fault. This is a major topographic front which trends parallel to the belt. It coincides approximately both with the 1500 m topographic contour and with the zone of current seismicity (Fig. 1a) along the belt (Jackson & McKenzie 1984; Ni & Barazangi 1986; Talebian & Jackson 2004), which is the result of faulting at a depth of 10–20 km (Talebian & Jackson 2004). This fault zone subdivides the Simply Folded Belt and has influenced sedimentation in the Zagros Foreland Basin since the Early Tertiary (Sepehr & Cosgrove 2004; Sherkati & Letouzey 2004). The exposed anticlines to the NE of the Mountain Front Fault are tight fold and are associated with several detachment horizons. In contrast, to the SW in the Dezful Embayment, those folds that host hydrocarbons are buried beneath the Lower Miocene evaporite (Gachsaran Formation); (Table 1), and are themselves extensively folded. Major and minor apparent left- and right-stepping offsets occur along the Mountain Front Fault (Fig. 1b), and these are discussed in the following sections.

The Zagros Frontal Fault. This front, also known as the 'Zagros Foredeep Fault' (Berberian 1995), separates the present alluvial basin of the Zagros Belt from the Simply Folded Belt (Fig. 1). It partly controls the morphology of the Persian Gulf and is marked by relatively long linear anticlines in the Lurestan, Dezful Embayment and Fars regions. These elongate folds are mostly associated with thrust faults and display a change in orientation in the Fars region from NW–SE to ENE–WSW, when traced SE towards the Strait of Hormuz (Fig. 1). Seismically, this front is not as active as the Mountain Front Fault (Talebian & Jackson 2004); (Fig. 1).

Belt-oblique fault zones

Belt-oblique fault zones consist of N–S and NNE–SSW-trending faults (the Arabian Trend) and E–W faults with the Arabian trend generated the N–S trending structural traps in Saudi Arabia and in the northwestern part of the Persian Gulf (Mina *et al.* 1967; Murris 1980). The formation of these fault zones may date back to the Palaeozoic but there was certainly a major pulse of activity along them during the Cretaceous (Sepehr & Cosgrove 2004; Sherkati & Letouzey 2004). These fault zones include the Kazerun and Izeh fault zones, which were reactivated in the Cretaceous, with peak activity corresponding to the time of obduction of ophiolites in the Neyriz area of the Fars region (Sepehr 2001; Sherkati & Letouzey 2004). A series of palaeo-highs formed in the Dezful Embayment and further south in the Persian Gulf as a result of movement along these fault zones (Fig. 2a). Their activity caused major thickness and facies variations of the Cretaceous sediments within the Dezful Embayment and Persian Gulf (Fig. 2a and b). This is illustrated in Figure 2b and in particular in the Gachsaran 2 well (located on one of these palaeo-highs), where the upper part of the Sarvak, the entire Ilam and most of the Gurpi formations are missing.

The present step-like geometry of the frontal part of the Mountain Front Fault Zone in the central part of the Zagros Belt is shown by a number of transfer fault zones (Fig. 1b). These include the Bala Rud, Izeh and Kazerun fault zones. These fault zones coincide with zones of high seismicity and major topographic relief (Fig. 1a and b). Folds commonly plunge towards, and end against these the blind fault zones (i.e. the faults do not cross-cut the anticlines). These are characteristic features of the boundaries of the Dezful Embayment, which are transverse to the belt. In addition to indicating the location of blind transfer faults it is suggested in this paper that such terminations indicate that these faults were active simultaneously with folding.

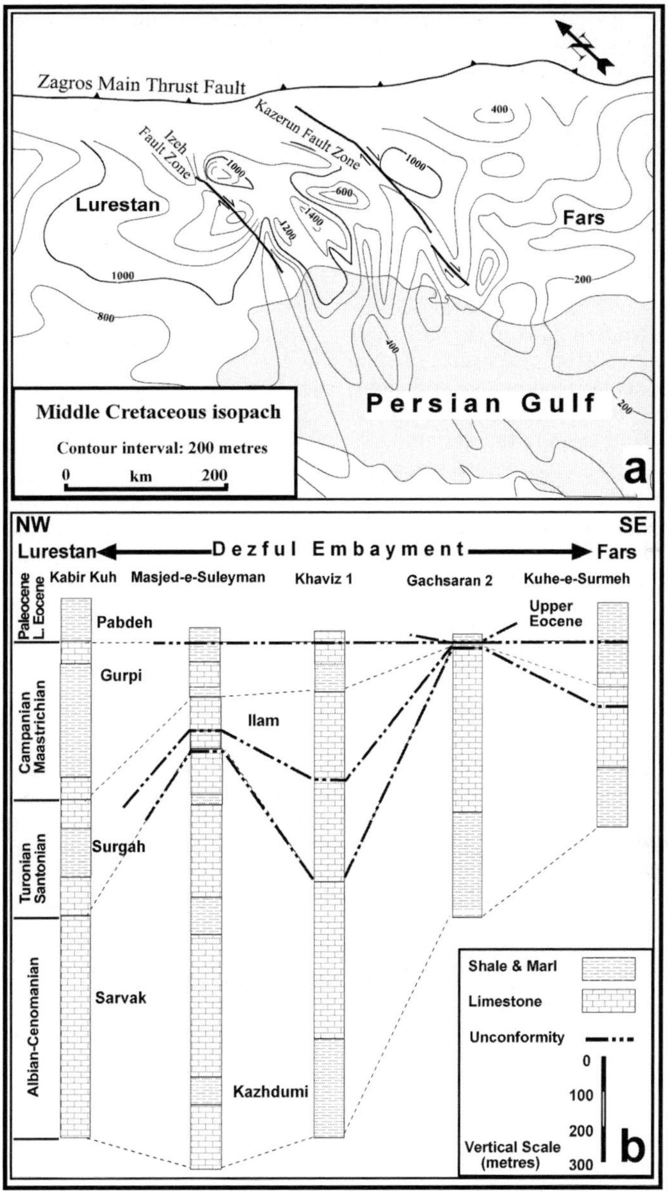

Fig. 2. (**a**) Middle Cretaceous isopach map, illustrating a significant thickness variation in the central part of the Zagros Basin in an area that coincides with the Kazerun and Izeh fault zones (modified from Koop & Stoneley 1982). (**b**) Cretaceous correlation chart showing a significant thickness variation and sedimentary gaps along the belt in the central part of the Zagros (modified from Setudehnia 1978).

The Kazerun Fault Zone. This fault zone trends N–S and is expressed at the surface by a transverse valley, *c.* 300 km long, extending from the High Zagros Fault in the north to the Persian Gulf coast in the south (Fig. 1). It consists of four segments that are termed, from north to south, the Sisakht, Yasuj, Kamarij and Burazjan segments (Sepehr 2001; Sepehr & Cosgrove 2005). All but the Yasuj segment act as transfer faults or lateral ramps, which link the different segments of the Zagros deformation fronts, that is, the High Zagros and Mountain Front faults (Figs 1 and 3). The Kamarij and Burazjan segments, which define the southeastern boundary of the Dezful Embayment, are characterized by a major downthrow to the west and also by the termination of folds against them (Fig. 3). The Kamarij Fault terminates in a thrust fault (a segment of the Mountain Front Fault) to the south along the Sarbalesh Anticline (Figs 3 and 4a). The Cambrian Hormuz Salt intruded along the Kamarij segment and its withdrawal led to the collapse of the western flank of the Sarbalesh Anticline (Fig. 4a). Surface exposure of this fault is marked by subhorizontal lineation along a steeply inclined (65° dipping) fault plane (Fig. 4b). The foreland basin to the west and SW of this anticline contains huge thicknesses of the Mid–Upper Miocene sediments. These beds have been dragged into vertical and overturned against the thrust fault to the SW of the Sarbalesh Anticline (Fig. 4c and d). Wedging of these sediments (Fig. 4c) and a progressive unconformity reported along both the lateral and frontal part of the fault zone is the result of syntectonic sedimentation (Sepehr & Cosgrove 2005). This model is used here to explain the other boundaries of the Dezful Embayment, which all have similar characteristics.

The Kazerun Fault Zone is seismically active and the majority of moderate-sized earthquakes along this fault zone occur close to the junction with the Mountain Front Fault (Fig. 1a). The fault-plane solutions of the earthquakes suggest that strike-slip movement took place along the fault at an estimated depth of 4–10 km, with an estimated average error of ± 3 km (Baker *et al.* 1993; Maggi *et al.* 2000; Talebian & Jackson 2004). The depth of the basement is estimated to be just under 10 km (Motiei 1995) in this part of the Zagros, indicating that most of the fault zones are within the sedimentary cover and not in the basement.

The overall mechanics of a fold–thrust belt is significantly affected by the presence or absence of salt (Davis & Engelder 1985). The Hormuz Salt, which separates the Precambrian metamorphic basement from the cover in the Fars region, is regarded as the main detachment in the region (Talbot & Alavi 1996; Bahrudi & Koyi 2003); (Table 1). More than 100 diapirs emerge at the surface to the east of the Kazerun Fault in the Fars region. In contrast, no trace of the Hormuz Salt has been found to the west of the Kazerun Fault (i.e. in the Dezful Embayment). As a result of the presence of the Hormuz Salt to the east, the folded belt has migrated about 80–100 km further SW than in the Dezful Embayment region (Figs 1 and 3). The Burazjan segment of the Kazerun Fault, which has a left-stepping arrangement of about 20 km without overlap with the Kamrij segment, acts as an oblique-lateral ramp, decoupling the deformation to the west from that in the Fars region to the east (Figs 1 and 3). As the result of right-lateral strike-slip movement on the underlying fault, anticlines along the Kamarij segment have been strongly deflected or have an orientation that is subparallel to the trace of the fault (typical of en echelon folds); (Fig. 3). The Kazerun Fault Zone is the site of several Hormuz salt diapirs and several thermal and sulphur-rich springs, particularly along the Burazjan segment (Fig. 3).

The Izeh Fault Zone. This is another north–south-trending structure to the west of the Kazerun Fault (Fig. 1). An apparent right-lateral displacement of the Mountain Front Fault and a zone of high seismicity occur along this fault (Fig. 1a). This fault zone divides the Simply Folded Belt of the Zagros to the NE of the Dezful Embayment, which is known as the Izeh Zone (Motiei 1995; Sherkati & Letouzey 2004), into two subzones with very intense folding and thrusting to the west compared with the east. The present morphology of the Izeh Fault is very similar to the Kamarij and Burazjan segments of the Kazerun Fault Zone. The anticlines to the east of the fault zone end against it and are not cut, or displaced, by the fault (Fig. 5). The present authors consider that the fault acted as a lateral ramp linking two segments of the Mountain Front Fault, one to the SW of the Mangasht Anticline and the other to the SW of the Bangestan Anticline (Fig. 5). The Izeh Fault Zone appears to have been active along with the Kazerun Fault during the Mid-Cretaceous (Fig. 2a) and it separates the shallow basin of the Fars from the Lurestan Basin. The latter includes the northwestern part of the Dezful Embayment and is mainly associated with deeper sedimentary facies. The change in facies of Eocene sediments, between the Jahrum Formation to the east and Shahbazan Formation to the west of the fault zone (Motiei 1993), indicates that the Izeh Fault Zone remained active into the Tertiary.

The Bala Rud Fault Zone. This is an east–west-trending belt of flexuring and faulting, which represents the northwestern limit of the Dezful Embayment (Figs 1 and 6). Pattinson & Takin (1971) estimated a vertical displacement of about 3–5 km, downthrow to the south occurred across this fault zone. The major zone of current seismicity, which is concentrated along the NW–SE-trending Mountain Front Fault, abruptly changes its orientation to east–west and follows

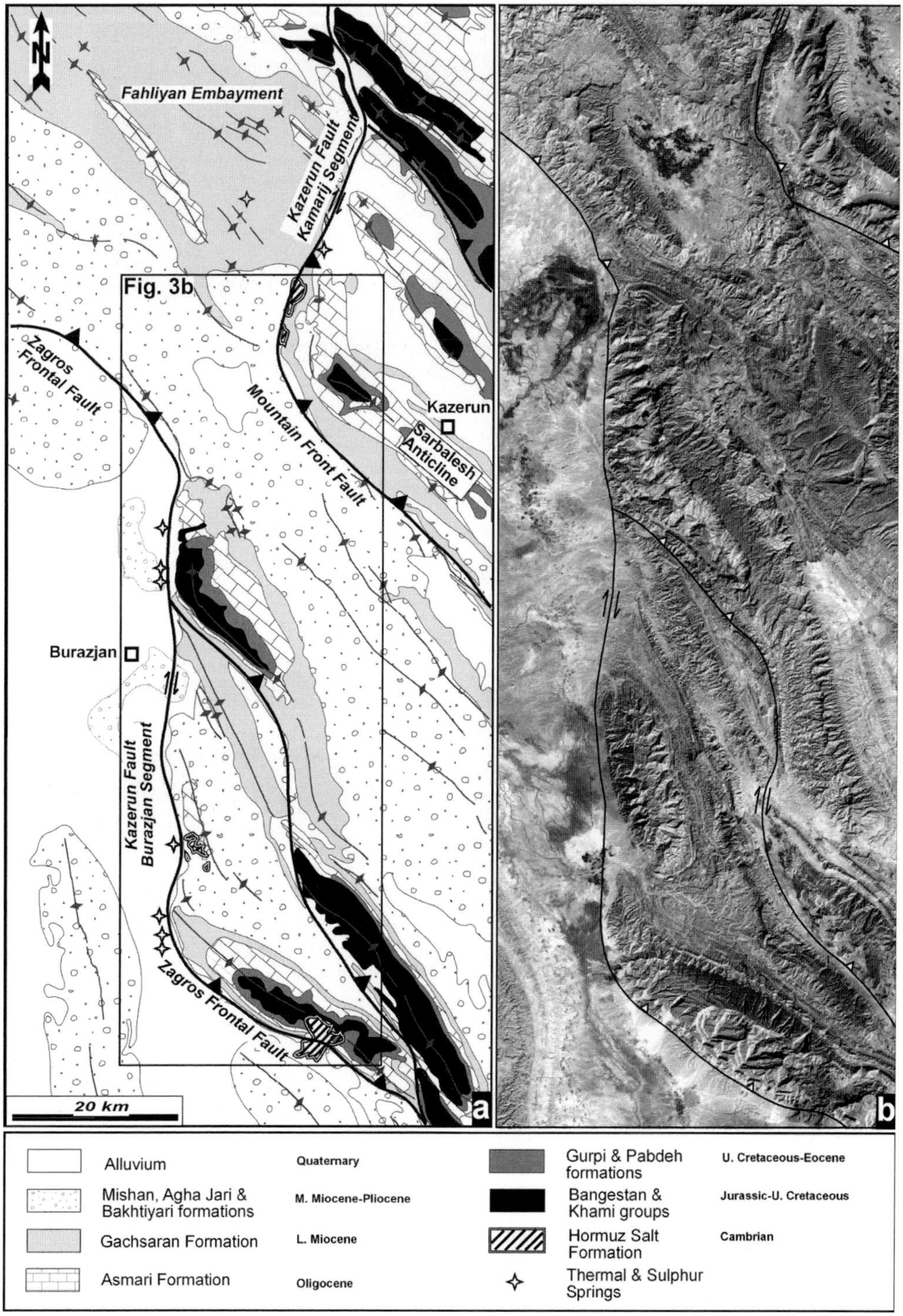

Fig. 3. (**a**) Geological map of the southern segments of the Kazerun Fault Zone (modified from IOOC 1969; McQuillan 1975), showing the spatial arrangement of anticlines along the fault zone (see Fig. 1b for the location). (**b**) TM satellite image of the Burazgan and part of Kamarij segments of the Kazerun Fault Zone, as highlighted in Figure 5a.

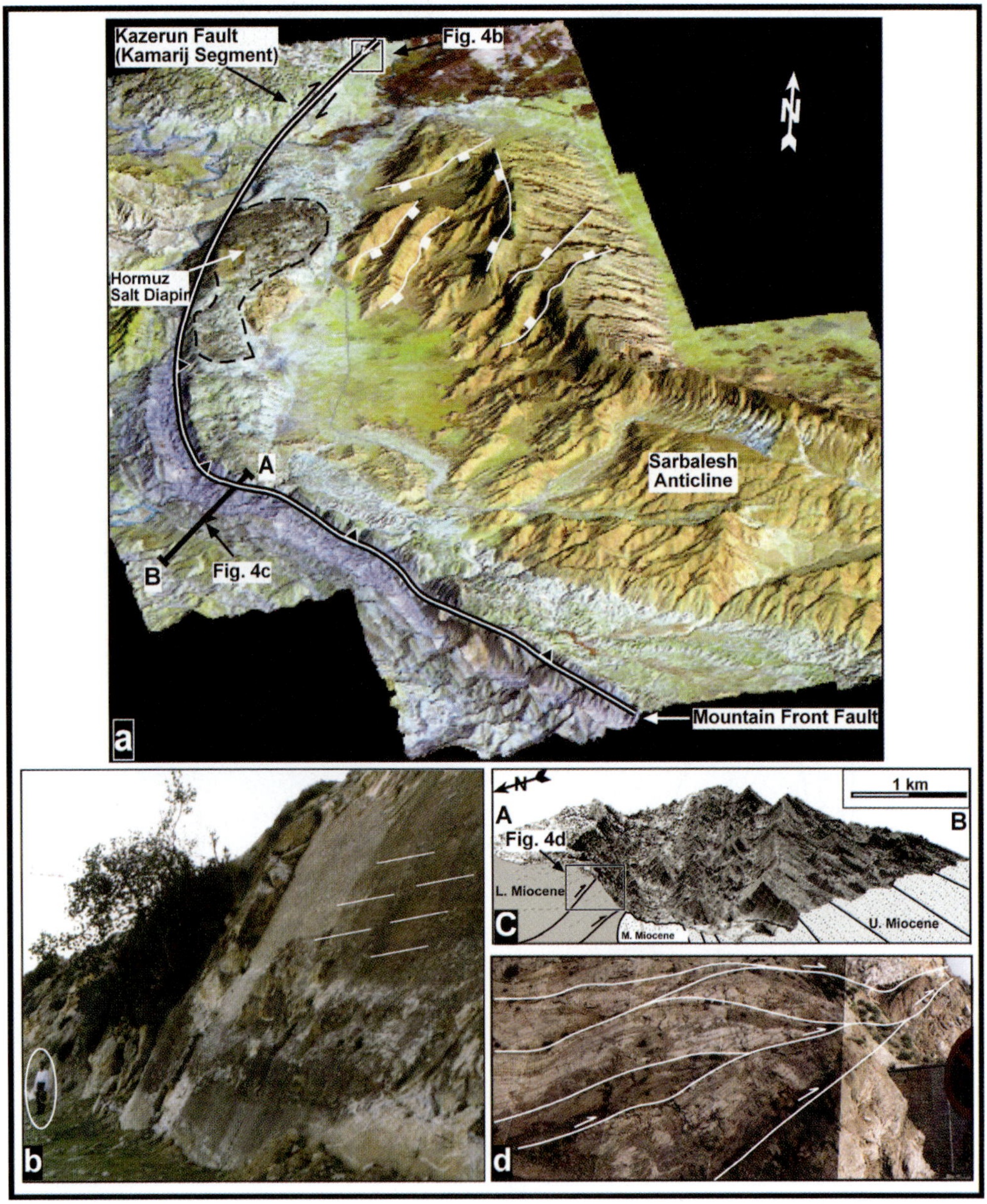

Fig. 4. (**a**) A 3D perspective view of the Sarbalesh Anticline, showing the termination of the Kamarij segment into a thrust fault in the southwestern part of the anticline. The location of Figure 4b and c are highlighted in this image. (**b**) Photograph of the Kazerun Fault scarp (Kamarij segment) with a north–south-trending subhorizontal lineation. (**c**) Digital elevation model and cross-section across the thrust fault (Mountain Front Fault), SW of the Sarbalesh Anticline, showing the bedding dip variation of foreland basin sediments in the footwall. (**d**) A close-up of series of low-angle thrust faults to the SW of the Sarbalesh Anticline as highlighted in (**c**).

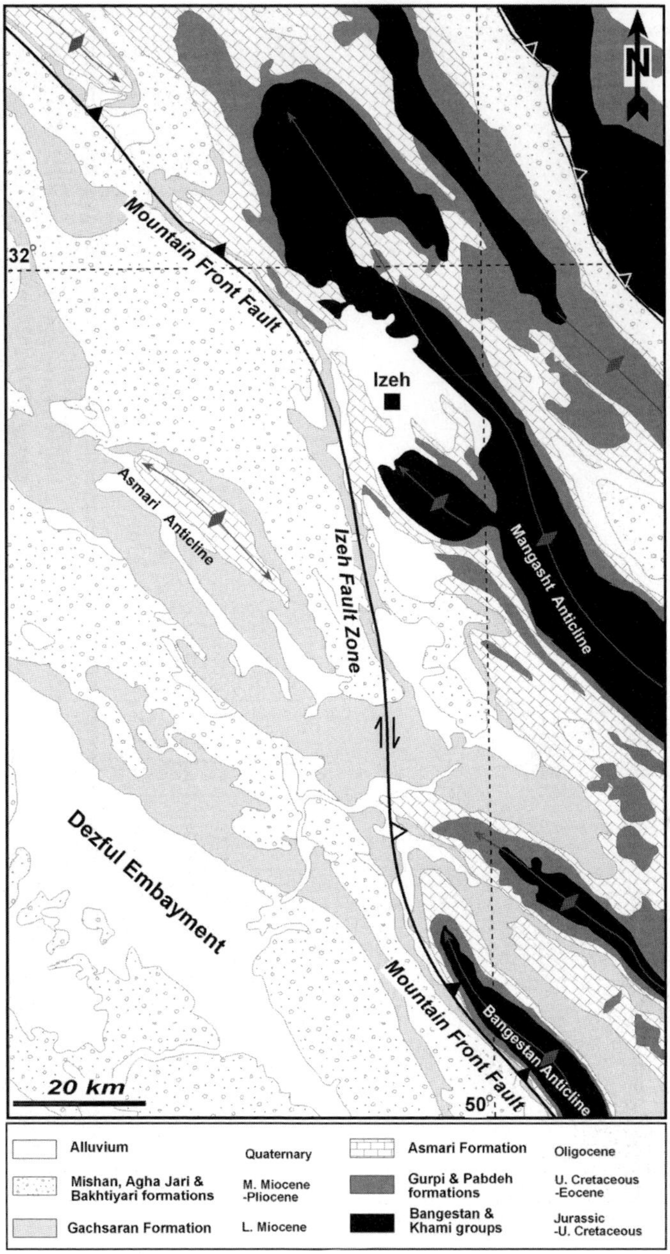

Fig. 5. Geological map of the northeastern part of the Dezful Embayment along the Izeh Fault Zone (modified from IOOC 1969), showing the termination of anticlines against the fault. (See Fig. 1b for the location.)

the Bala Rud Fault Zone (Fig. 1a). All the anticlines to the north of this fault zone plunge towards the fault (Fig. 6), and to the south in the Dezful Embayment the anticlines are hidden beneath a thick sequence of Miocene sediments. Despite the fact that the fault zone is not exposed at the surface, the presence of en echelon folds above the fault zone is an indication that left-lateral displacement has taken place along the fault. This sense of movement is supported by

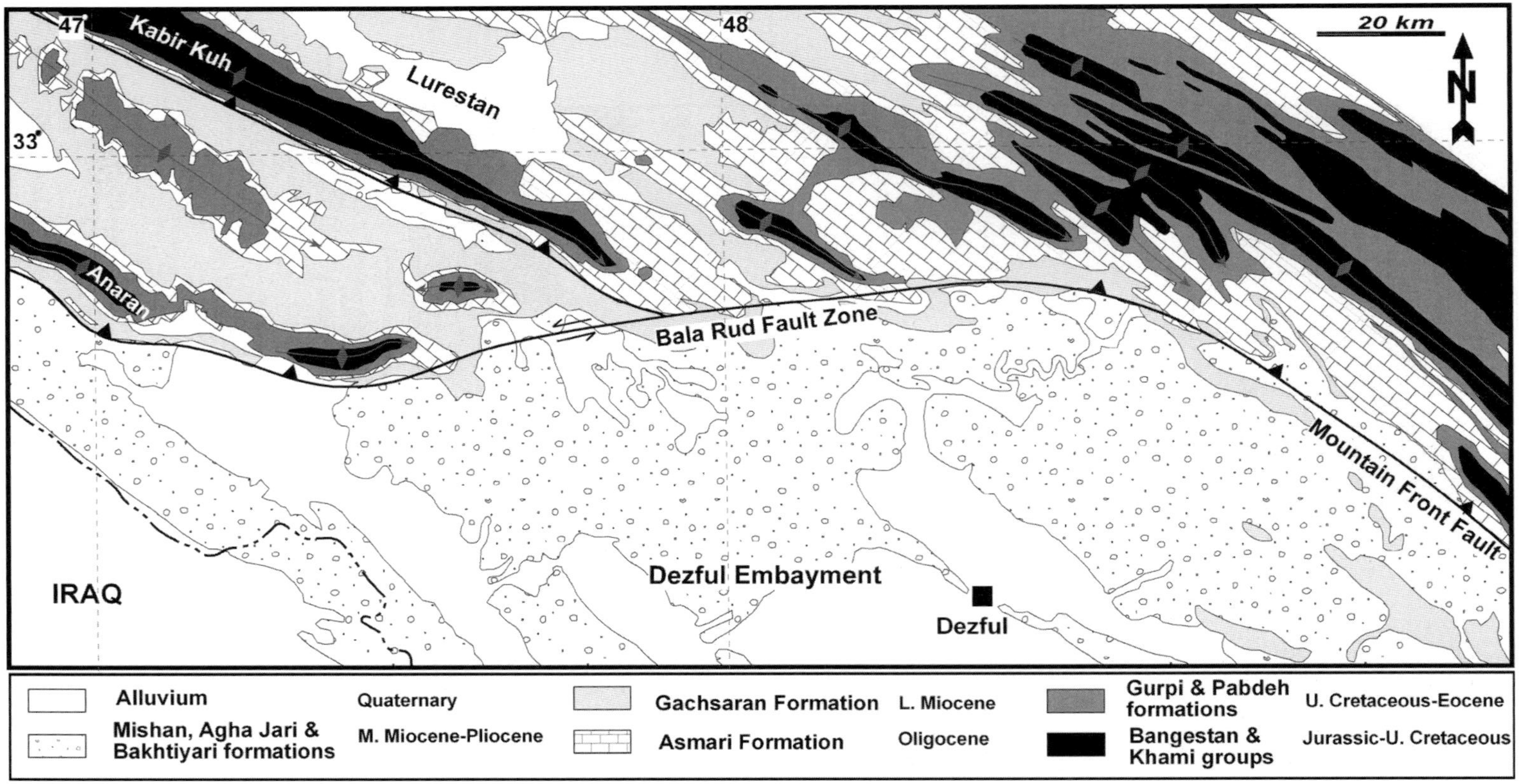

Fig. 6. Geological map of the northwestern corner of the Dezful Embayment (modified from IOOC 1969), showing the termination of anticlines against the Bala Rud Fault Zone. (See Fig. 1b for the location.)

one of the fault-plane solutions presented by Talebian & Jackson (2004). Their work also shows that some of the deepest earthquakes occurred in the northwestern corner of the Dezful Embayment, where the sedimentary cover is known to be very thick. The Bala Rud Fault Zone acts as a lateral ramp linking two segments of the Mountain Front Fault, one to the NE of the Dezful Embayment and the other to the SW of the Lurestan region (Figs 1 and 6), and has very similar characteristics to the Kazerun and Izeh fault zones. This fault zone has had a major influence on Zagros sedimentation since the Late Cretaceous (Pattinson & Takin 1971) and separated the Lurestan and Dezful basins during the deposition of the Upper Cretaceous sediments. The isopach of the Asmari Formation (Oligocene), and also the distribution of the Kalhur Member (Lower Miocene evaporite), coincides with, and was controlled by, the east–west trend of the Bala Rud Fault Zone, the NW–SE trend of the Mountain Front Fault zones in the Dezful Embayment and the NW–SE trend of the Kabir Kuh Anticline in the Lurestan Region (Fig. 6, see also Sepehr & Cosgrove 2004, fig. 9). This is an indication of synchronous activity along the Mountain Front and Bala Rud fault zones during Oligocene–Early Miocene times.

The Mengharak Fault Zone. This structure and the Sabzpushan and Sarvestan fault zones (Berberian 1995) are NNW–SSE-trending fault zones that lie to the east of the Kazerun Fault in the Fars region (Fig. 1). Although the Mengharak Fault Zone is a belt-oblique fault zone, it has different characteristics compared with the Izeh and Kazerun fault zones. No major vertical displacement occurred across the fault and the anticlines do not terminate against it (Fig. 7). The fault displaces the Dadenjan Anticline in a right-lateral sense for some 10 km (Fig. 7) and terminates at a segment of the Mountain Front Fault to the SE.

Transfer faults and the spatial organization of folds in the Zagros Belt

Buckle folds in the upper crust typically have the shape of a pericline (an elongate dome) with an aspect ratio (half-wavelength to axial length ratio) of between 1:5 and 1:10. When viewed in plan, these folds are generally offset from each other and form an interdigitating arrangement of overlapping folds. This spatial organization and geometry characterizes buckle folds on all scales (see Price & Cosgrove 1990; Cosgrove & Ameen 2000). In contrast, fault-related folds

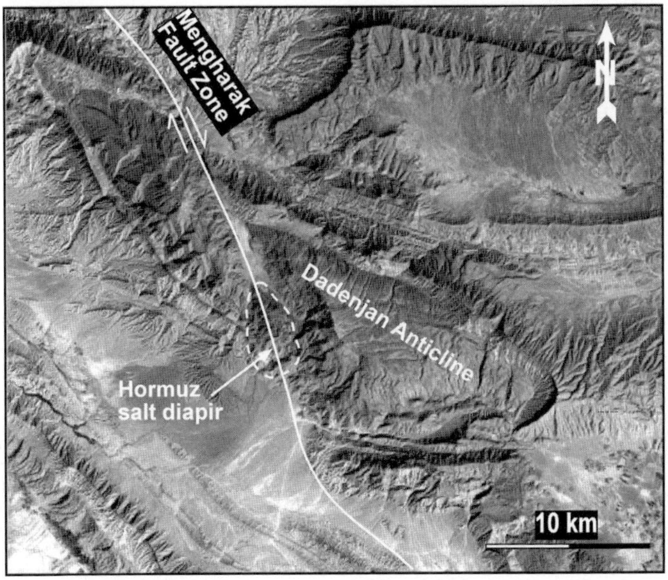

Fig. 7. Satellite image showing the right-lateral displacement of the Dadenjan Anticline by the Mengharak Fault Zone (see Fig. 1).

(i.e. fault-propagation or fault-bend folds) commonly have a higher aspect ratio, determined by the strike length of the underlying fault. Wilkerson *et al.* (2002) summarized the mechanisms and factors that cause the termination of fault-related folds as: (1) the loss of slip on the underlying frontal fault ramp; (2) the change in fault geometry laterally (lateral or oblique ramps) as the fault climbs to a shallower detachment; (3) a combination of the two mechanisms, in which terminations may be influenced by pre-existing structures or a facies boundary. A thrust fault and its associated folds may form segments and the linkage between the segments formed by transfer faults (lateral ramp or tear fault). As illustrated in Figure 8, the overlying folds associated with segmented thrust faults have opposed plunges and terminate against buried transfer faults. Dixon & Spratt (2004) ran a series of physical models consisting of two frontal ramp segments linked by a lateral ramp or tear fault. Their models illustrate the development of opposite-facing folds, which terminate laterally against the transfer fault. Their models also show that the frontal ramp and its associated folds propagate along strike and across the transverse structures.

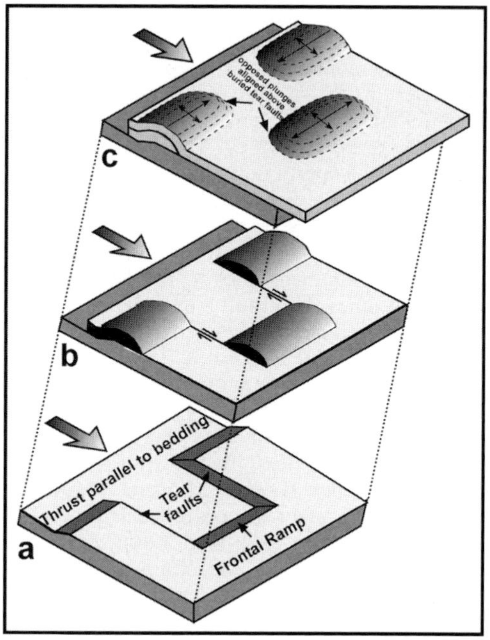

Fig. 8. Schematic diagrams illustrating (**a**) the geometry of footwall boundary associated with frontal and lateral ramps (tear faults), (**b**) bedding surface in the lower part of thrust sheet, and (**c**) bedding surface and opposed plunging folds that form above buried transfer faults (after Dahlstrom 1970; Dixon & Spratt 2004).

As was noted earlier within the Zagros Belt folds terminate against the lateral (transverse) boundaries of the Dezful Embayment (e.g. along the Kazerun, Izeh and Bala Rud fault zones); (Figs 3, 5, 6 and 9). Such fold organization can be used to recognize smaller-scale subsurface transfer faults. Two small embayments have formed in the NE of the Dezful Embayment between the Izeh and Kazerun fault zones (Figs 1, 3 and 9). These embayments, which are here called the Dehdasht Embayment (to the NW) and Fahliyan Embayment (to the SE), represent a continuation of the Dezful Embayment and are formed as a result of further segmentation of the Mountain Front Fault (Figs 1, 9 and 10a). The northeastern boundary of the Dehdasht Embayment is defined by the Kuh-e Siah Anticline, which represents the position of the Mountain Front Fault (Figs 9 and 10a, b). It is suggested here that the linkage between this front and its lateral equivalent along the Bangestan and Mish structures, to the NW and SE of this embayment, respectively, probably relate to the subsurface presence of transfer fault zones that are blind (see Fig. 8). These faults do not crop out, because of the very thick incompetent unit of the Lower Miocene evaporites of the Gachsaran Formation. Anticlines such as the Mish, Khami and Lar to the east and the Bangestan to the west plunge towards, and terminate abruptly against, these transfer faults (Figs 9 and 10a, c). This resulted in the incorporation of the Khaviz Anticline in the frontal part into the embayment area, which exposes the Asmari Formation (Fig. 9). As can be seen on the geological map and satellite image (Figs 9 and 10a), this anticline is constrained between the transfer faults that bound the Dehdasht Embayment, and is isolated from the neighbouring structures. This has allowed shortening to be accommodated by different fold trains on either side of these transfer faults. This fold, however, propagates along strike and across the transfer faults and has some overlap with the Bangestan Anticline. This is a characteristic feature associated with transfer faults shown in physical models by Dixon & Spratt (2004), where two frontal ramps propagate along strike and pass their initial terminations against the transfer faults. These faults most probably root to the same detachment horizon on which the folds were formed.

This characteristic fold pattern has also been used in other areas to detect buried lateral ramps. For example, such a pattern was recognized in

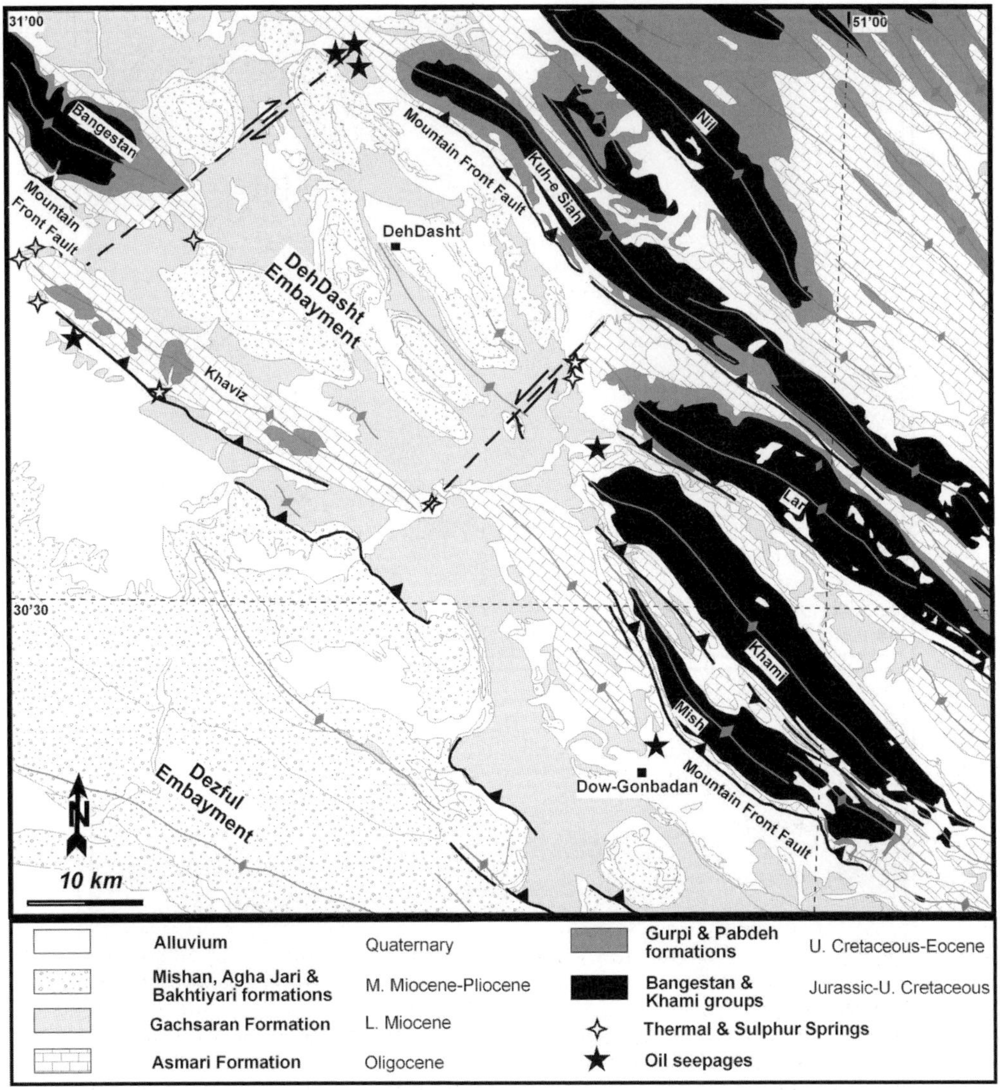

Fig. 9. Geological map of the northeastern corner of the Dezful Embayment (modified from Evers 1977), showing the overall geometry of the Dehdashst Embayment, its associated transfer faults and localization of fluid along the these fault zones. (See Fig. 1b for the location.)

the Canadian Rocky Mountains (Fig. 8), and also in central Pennsylvania by Pohn & Coleman (1990), who used seismic evidence to confirm the presence of the faults. The generation of these lateral ramps appears to be the result of the termination or pinch-out of detachments caused by the Mid-Cretaceous activity of pre-existing north–south-trending fault zones, between the Kazerun and Izeh fault zones (Sepehr & Cosgrove 2004; Sherkati & Letouzey 2004). The effect of these pre-existing fault zones on the basin architecture of the central part of the Zagros Belt is illustrated in Figure 2. As noted earlier major thickness and facies variations are linked to palaeohighs in the Khaviz area (see Fig. 2b), which is located in the Dehdasht area, and the Gachsaran structure to the SE (Fig. 2b). These palaeohighs can also be seen on the basement map of the Zagros Belt (Morris 1977; Motiei 1995).

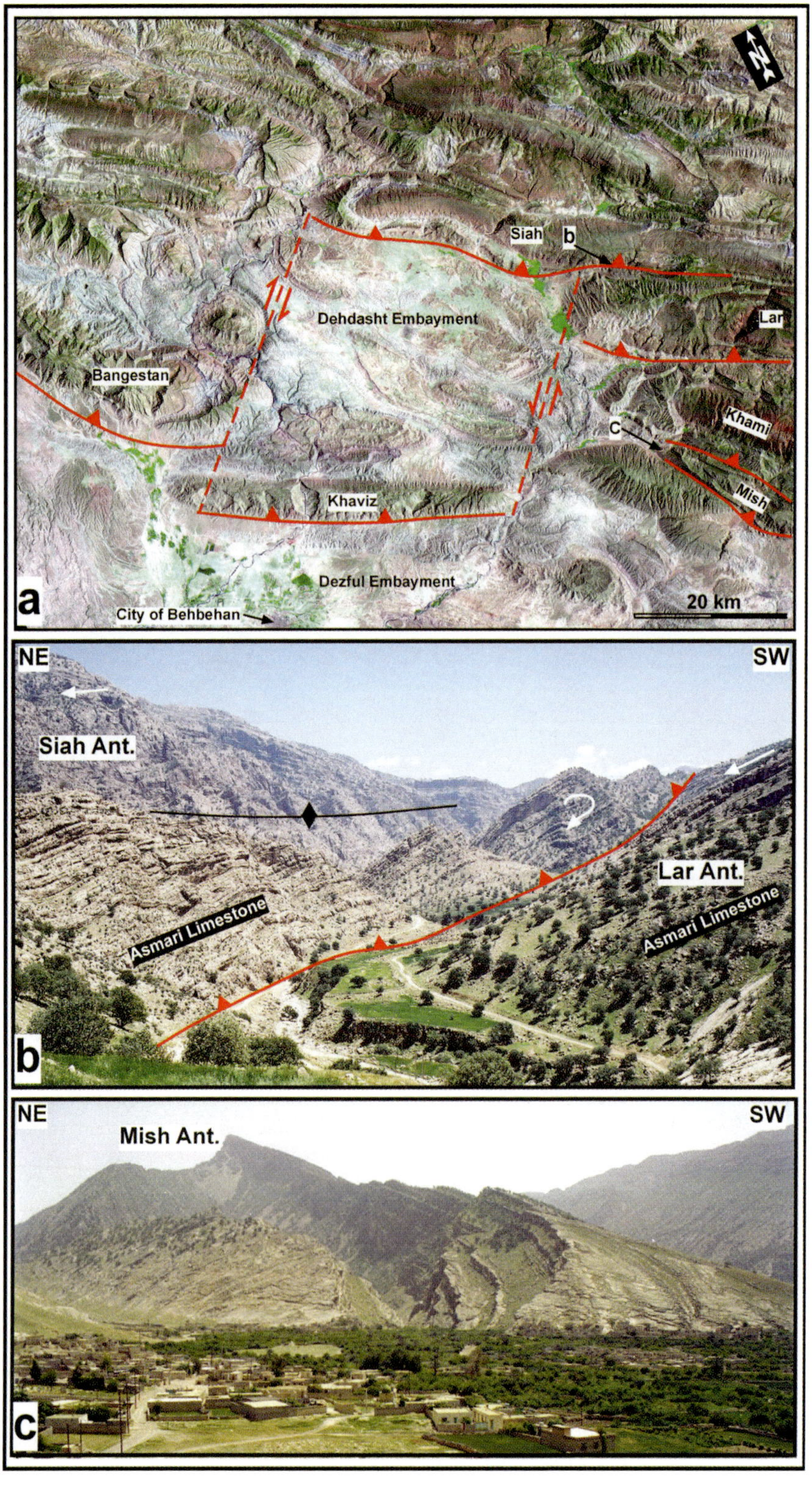
N
Siah
b
Lar
Dehdasht Embayment
Bangestan
Khami
C
Mish
Khaviz
Dezful Embayment
a
20 km
City of Behbehan
NE
SW
Siah Ant.
Lar Ant.
Asmari Limestone
Asmari Limestone
b
NE
SW
Mish Ant.
c

It is important to have a good understanding of subsurface (blind) transfer fault systems, because, in addition to the compartmentalization of deformation, the structural evolution of these structures in turn affects fluid migration pathways and trapping potential. A concentration of thermal or sulphur springs and oil seeps occurs along the transfer fault zones in the Dehdasht Embayment, mainly at the junction between lateral and frontal ramps (Fig. 9). This phenomenon is also observed along the Kazerun Fault Zone (Fig. 3a).

Structural evolution of the Zagros Belt

The Zagros Foreland Basin has been associated with the development of important thrust fronts since the continental collision between the Arabian and Iranian plates in the Tertiary (Fig. 1). The foreland-directed propagation, lateral extent and the present geometry of these thrust fronts has been determined by the rheological profile of the cover rocks as well as basin geometry. Based on the above discussion, the following tectonic model for the evolution of the Zagros Basin is proposed (Fig. 11). The Kazerun Fault Zone was probably active during the Cambrian, when it formed the western limit of the rheologically important Hormuz Salt Formation (Fig. 11a). Extensional events, linked to the opening of the Neo-Tethys, affected the sedimentation and the basin geometry of Zagros during the Permo-Triassic and produced a series of grabens and half-grabens with a similar trend to the present-day folded belt (Fig. 11b); (see also Sepehr & Cosgrove 2004, fig. 5). This event, which probably affected the entire Zagros Basin, was more pronounced to the west of the Kazerun Fault, where the Hormuz Salt is absent. In the Fars region, however, the basin geometry would be expected to be less complex because the basement structures were decoupled from the cover rocks by a 2–3 km thickness of the Hormuz Salt. Examination of the Cretaceous isopach maps of the Zagros (Fig. 2a), suggests that the basin geometries in the central part of the Zagros are strongly influenced by the north–south-trending structures (i.e. between the Izeh and

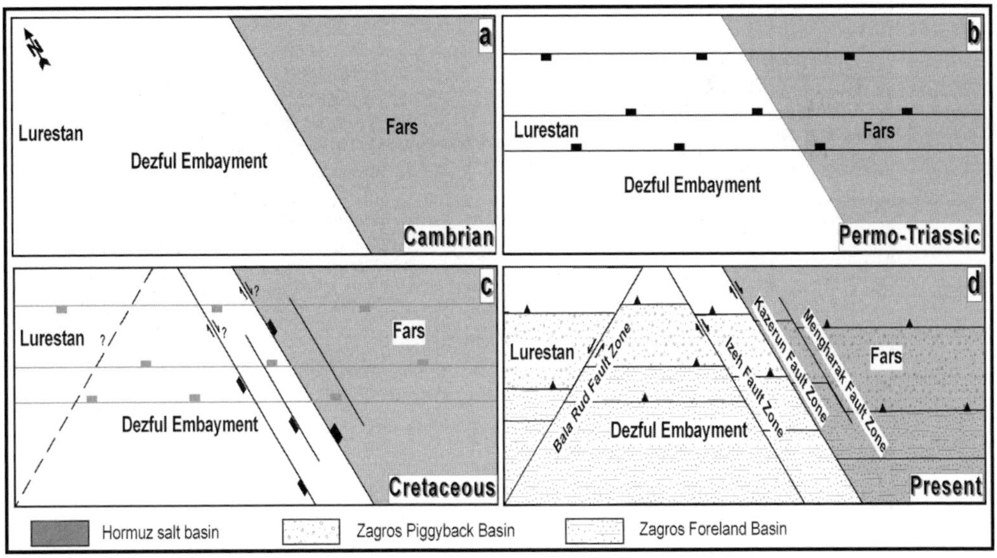

Fig. 11. Schematic diagram illustrating the proposed structural evolution model for the Zagros Belt in map view.

Fig. 10. (**a**) TM satellite image of the Dehdasht Embayment and its associated structures (b and c represent the location of (**b**) and (**c**)) (**b**) Photograph, looking SE, demonstrating the thrusting of overturned beds of Asmari Formation (Oligocene) of the Siah Anticline over the same formation on the northeastern flank of the Lar Anticline. (**c**) Photograph showing the northwestward plunging of the Mish Anticline towards the Dehdasht Embayment.

Kazerun fault zones). These fault zones caused lateral thickness and facies changes (Fig. 2b) and also probably cut and displaced the pre-existing Permo-Triassic faulted blocks (Fig. 11c). It is therefore suggested here that the present geometry, the style of deformation and formation of transfer fault zones within the Zagros Fold–Thrust Belt, particularly those that define the Dezful Embayment boundaries (Figs 1 and 11d), have been largely determined by the pre-collisional basin geometry and the intimately related variations in the rheological profile of the cover rocks.

Conclusions

The present geometry of the Zagros Fold–Thrust Belt is defined by major belt-parallel and belt-oblique fault zones. Some of these are the result of reactivation of pre-existing faults and others are formed on the major detachment horizons in the cover succession. Although these fault zones are not generally exposed at the surface, the geometry and spatial organization of folds indicate that the majority of the belt-oblique fault zones, which form the lateral boundaries of the Dezful Embayment, are lateral ramps or transfer faults. These transfer faults link various segments of the major belt-parallel fault zones, such as the Mountain Front Fault. Folds in the cover rocks above these buried fault zones either terminate or are deflected against the fault zones, or are arranged in an en echelon pattern along them, but folds are not cross-cut by the faults. This suggests that the fault zones were active boundaries since the start of folding, and that the deformation on either side of them occurred by the development of two independent fold domains. A similar pattern of structures has been found in relatively small-scale embayments in the northeastern boundary of the Dezful Embayment. The lateral boundaries of these embayments are also associated with (smaller-scale) transfer faults. These transfer faults are marked at the surface by a number of thermal springs and oil seepages. This is an indication of their importance as a pathway for migration of fluids.

References

ALAVI, M. 1994. Tectonics of the Zagros orogenic belt of Iran: new data and interpretations. *Tectonophysics*, **229**, 211–238.

BAHRUDI, A. & KOYI, H. 2003. Effect of spatial distribution of Hormuz salt on deformation style in the Zagros fold and thrust belt: an analogue modelling approach. *Journal of the Geological Society, London*, **160**, 719–733.

BAKER, C., JACKSON, J. & PRIESTLEY, K. 1993. Earthquakes on the Kazerun Line in the Zagros Mountains of Iran: strike-slip faulting within a fold-and-thrust belt. *Geophysics Journal International*, **115**, 41–61.

BÉGIN, N. J. & SPRATT, D. A. 2002. Role of transverse faulting in along-strike termination of Limestone Mountain Culmination, Rocky Mountain thrust and fold belt, Alberta. *Journal of Structural Geology*, **24**, 689–707.

BERBERIAN, M. 1981. Active faulting and tectonics of Iran. *In*: GUPTA, H. K. & DELANY, F. M. (eds) *Zagros–Hindu Kush–Himalaya Geodynamic Evolution*. American Geophysical Union, Geodynamics Series, **3**, 33–69.

BERBERIAN, M. 1995. Master 'blind' thrust faults hidden under the Zagros folds: active basement tectonics and surface morphotectonics. *Tectonophysics*, **241**, 193–224.

BERBERIAN, M. & KING, G. C. P. 1981. Towards the paleogeography and tectonic evolution of Iran. *Canadian Journal of the Earth Sciences*, **18**, 210–265.

BEYDOUN, Z. R., HUGHES CLARKE, M. W. & STONELEY, R. 1992. Petroleum in the Zagros basin: a Late Tertiary foreland basin overprinted onto the outer edge of a vast hydrocarbon-rich Palaeozoic-Mesozoic passive margin shelf. *In*: MACQUEEN, R. W. & LECKIE, D. A. (eds) *Foreland Basins and Foldbelts*. American Association of Petroleum Geologists, Memoirs, **55**, 309–339.

BLANC, E. J.-P., ALLEN, M. B., INGER, S. & HASSANI, H. 2003. Structural style in the Zagros Simple Folded Zone, Iran. *Journal of the Geological Society, London*, **160**, 401–412.

COSGROVE, J. W. & AMEEN, M. S. 2000. A comparison of the geometry, spatial organisation and fracture patterns associated with forced folds and buckle folds. *In*: COSGROVE, J. W. & AMEEN, M. S. (eds) *Forced Folds and Fractures*. Geological Society, London, Special Publications, **169**, 7–21.

DAHLSTROM, C. D. A. 1969. Balanced cross sections. *Canadian Journal of Earth Sciences*, **6**, 743–757.

DAHLSTROM, C. D. A. 1970. Structural geology in the eastern margin of the Canadian Rocky Mountains. *Bulletin of Canadian Petroleum Geology*, **18**, 332–406.

DAVIS, D. M. & ENGELDER, T. 1985. The role of salt in fold and thrust belts. *Tectonophysics*, **119**, 67–88.

DIXON, J. M. & SPRATT, D. A. 2004. Deformation at lateral ramps and tear faults-Centrifuge models and examples from the Canadian Rocky Mountain Foothills. *In*: MCCLAY, K. R. (ed.) *Thrust tectonics and hydrocarbon systems*. American Association of Petroleum Geologists, Memoirs, **82**, 239–258.

EVERS, H. J. 1977. *Geological Compilation Map of Behbehan*, scale 1:250 000. National Iranian Oil Company, Tehran.

FALCON, N. L. 1961. Major earth-flexuring in the Zagros Mountains of southwest Iran. *Quarterly Journal of the Geological Society of London*, **117**(4), 367–376.

FALCON, N. L. 1969. Problem of the relationship between surface structures and deep displacement illustrated by the Zagros range. *In*: KENT, P., SATTERWAITE, G. & SPENCER, A. (eds) *Time and Place in Orogeny*. Geological Society, London, Special Publications, **2**, 9–22.

FALCON, N. L. 1974. Southern Iran: Zagros mountains. *In*: SPENCER, A. (ed.) *Mesozoic–Cenozoic Orogenic Belts*. Geological Society, London, Special Publications, **4**, 199–211.

FERMOR, P. 1999. Aspects of the three-dimensional structure of the Alberta Foothills and Front Ranges. *Geological Society of America Bulletin*, **111**, 317–346.

IOOC 1969. *Geological Map of South-West Iran*. IOOC Geological and Exploration Division, Tehran.

JACKSON, J. A. 1980. Reactivation of basement faults and crustal shortening in orogenic belts. *Nature*, **283**, 343–346.

JACKSON, J. A. & FITCH, T. 1981. Basement faulting and the focal depths of the larger earthquakes in the Zagros Mountains (Iran). *Geophysical Journal of the Royal Astronomical Society*, **64**, 561–586.

JACKSON, J. A. & MCKENZIE, D. P. 1984. Active tectonics of the Alpine–Himalayan Belt between Western Turkey and Pakistan. *Geophysical Journal of the Royal Astronomical Society*, **77**, 185–284.

KOOP, W. J. 1978. *The Palaeostructural History of Southwest Iran and its Effect on Hydrocarbon Generation and Entrapment*. National Iranian Oil Company, Report 1292 (unpublished).

KOOP, W. J. & STONELEY, R. 1982. Subsidence history of the Middle East Zagros Basin, Permian to Recent. *Philosophical Transactions of the Royal Society of London, Series A*, **305**, 149–168.

MACEDO, J. & MARSHAK, S. 1999. Controls on the geometry of fold-thrust belt salients. *Geological Society of America Bulletin*, **111**, 1808–1822.

MAGGI, A., JACKSON, J. A., PRIESTLEY, K., & BAKER, C. 2000. A re-assessment of focal depth distributions in southern Iran, the Tien Shan and northern India: do earthquakes really occur in the continental mantle? *Geophysical Journal International*, **143**, 629–661.

MARSHAK, S., 2004. Salients, recesses, arcs, oroclines, and syntaxes-A review of ideas concerning the formation of map-view curves in fold–thrust belts. *In*: MCCLAY, K. R. (ed.) *Thrust Tectonics and Hydrocarbon Systems*. American Association of Petroleum Geologists, Memoirs, **82**, 131–156.

MARSHAK, S. & WILKERSON, M. S. 1992. Effect of overburden thickness on thrust belt geometry and development. *Tectonics*, **11**, 560–566.

MCCLAY, K. R. 1991. Glossary of thrust tectonics terms. *In:* MCCLAY, K. R. (ed.) *Thrust Tectonics*. Chapman & Hall, London, 419–433.

MCQUARRIE, N. 2004. Crustal scale geometry of the Zagros fold–thrust belt, Iran. *Journal of Structural Geology*, **26**, 519–535.

MCQUILLAN, H. 1975. *Geological Compilation Map of Kharg–Ganaveh–Kazerun*, scale 1:250 000. National Iranian Oil Company, Tehran.

MINA, P., RAZAGHNIA, M. T. & PARAN, Y. 1967. Geological and geophysical studies and exploratory drilling of the Iranian continental shelf, Persian Gulf. *Proceedings of the 7th World Petroleum Congress, Mexico*, 870–903.

MORRIS, P. 1977. Basement structure as suggested by aeromagnetic surveys in SW Iran. *Second Geological Symposium of Iran*. Internal Report, Iranian Petroleum Institute, Tehran.

MOTIEI, H. 1993. Stratigraphy of Zagros. *In*: HUSHMANDZADEH, A. (ed.) *Treatise on the Geology of Iran*. Geological Survey of Iran Publications.

MOTIEI, H. 1995. Petroleum geology of Zagros. *In*: HUSHMANDZADEH, A. (ed.) *Treatise on the Geology of Iran*. Geological Survey of Iran Publications.

MURRIS, R. J. 1980. Middle East stratigraphic evolution and oil habitat. *AAPG Bulletin*, **64**, 598–617.

NI, J. & BARAZANGI, M. 1986. Seismotectonics of the Zagros continental collision zone and a comparison with the Himalayas. *Journal of Geophysical Research*, **91**, 8205–8218.

PATTINSON, R. & TAKIN, M. 1971. *Geological significance of the Dezful Embayment boundaries*. National Iranian Oil Company Report, **1166** (unpublished).

POHN, H. A. & COLEMAN, J. L., JR 1990. Fold patterns, lateral ramps and seismicity in central Pennsylvania. *Tectonophysics*, **186**, 133–149.

PRICE, N. J. & COSGROVE, J. W. 1990. *Analysis of Geological Structures*. Cambridge University Press, Cambridge.

RIES, A. C. & SHACKLETON, R. M. 1976. Patterns of the strain variation in arcuate fold belts. *Philosophical Transactions of the Royal Society of London, Series A*, **283**, 281–288.

SEPEHR, M. 2001. *The tectonic significance of the Kazerun Fault Zone, Zagros Fold–Thrust Belt, Iran.* PhD thesis, Imperial College, University of London.

SEPEHR, M. & COSGROVE, J. W. 2004. Structural framework of the Zagros Fold–Thrust Belt, Iran. *Marine and Petroleum Geology*, **21**, 829–843.

SEPEHR, M. & COSGROVE, J. W. 2005. The role of the Kazerun Fault Zone in the formation and deformation of the Zagros Fold–Thrust Belt, Iran. *Tectonics*, **24**, doi:10.1029/2004TC001725.

SETUDEHNIA, A. 1978. The Mesozoic sequence in southwest Iran and adjacent area. *Journal of Petroleum Geology*, **1**, 3–42.

SHERKATI, S. & LETOUZEY, J. 2004. Variation of structural style and basin evolution in the central Zagros (Izeh zone and Dezful Embayment), Iran. *Marine and Petroleum Geology*, **21**, 535–554.

STOCKLIN, J. 1974. Possible ancient continental margins in Iran. *In*: BURK, C. A. & DRAKE, C. L. (eds) *The Geology of Continental Margins*. Springer, New York, 873–887.

SZABO, F. & KHERADPIR, A. 1978. Permian and Triassic stratigraphy, Zagros basin, southwest Iran. *Journal of Petroleum Geology*, **1**, 57–82.

TAKIN, M. 1972. Iranian geology and continental drift in the Middle East. *Nature*, **235**, 147–150.

TALBOT, C. J. & ALAVI, M. 1996. The past of a future syntaxis across the Zagros. *In*: ALSOP, G. I., BLUNDELL, D. J. & DAVISON, I. (eds) *Salt Tectonics.* Geological Society, London, Special Publications, **100**, 89–110.

TALEBIAN, M. & JACKSON, J. 2004. A reappraisal of earthquake focal mechanisms and active shortening in the Zagros Mountains of Iran. *Geophysical Journal International*, **156**, 506–526.

WILKERSON, M. S., APOTRIA, T. & FARID, T. 2002. Interpreting the geological map expression of contractional fault-related fold termination: lateral/oblique ramps versus displacement gradients. *Journal of Structural Geology*, **24**, 593–607.

Analysis of a mesoscopic duplex in SW Tuscany, Italy: implications for thrust system development during positive tectonic inversion

GIULIO CASINI, FRANCESCO ANTONIO DECANDIA & ENRICO TAVARNELLI

Dipartimento di Scienze della Terra, Università di Siena, Via Laterina 8, I-53100, Siena, Italy (e-mail: casini14@unisi.it)

Abstract: The advances in the field of inversion tectonics, pioneered by Mike Coward and co-workers, have shown that many thrust belts originated at the expense of pre-orogenic rift basins that originally had complex extensional architectures. These architectures are reflected by significant lateral thickness and facies changes within the deformed stratigraphic sequences. Although these changes are widely documented from the restoration of balanced sections across thrust fans, they are significantly less well documented from restoration of duplex structures. As a consequence, most available duplex models assume layer-cake stratigraphic sequences. In this contribution a peculiar mesoscopic duplex is described. This structure developed across a single irregular, previously extended quartzite layer of the Arenarie di Poggio al Carpino Formation (Upper Permian–Lower Triassic), during the Late Tertiary orogenic event that led to development of the Apennine chain. Through comparison of the analysed duplex with macroscopic analogues, it is proposed that similar structures may occur on a wide variety of scales, in the Apennines as well as in other orogenic belts.

Contractional deformation at convergent lithospheric plate boundaries and within orogenic belts is mainly accommodated by thrust systems and related folds. Thrust systems are generally grouped into two broad, end-member categories: thrust fans and duplex structures (Boyer & Elliott 1982; Mitra 1986). The former occur mainly in the frontal parts of orogenic belts (Morley 1986; Vann *et al.* 1986), whereas the latter tend to be confined to the more internal zones. Thrust systems are important in transferring orogenic contraction from deep to shallow crustal levels towards undeformed forelands (Dahlstrom 1970; Boyer & Elliott 1982; Coward & Butler 1985; Butler 1986).

Extensive research in the field of inversion tectonics during the last three decades has shown that many thrust belts originated at the expense of pre-existing rift basins with complex extensional architectures. The pioneering investigation carried out by Mike Coward and co-workers in the Western Alps (Gillcrist *et al.* 1987; Coward 1994, and references therein) has influenced the research of a generation of structural geologists (e.g. see Butler 1989; Williams *et al.* 1989; Bond & McClay 1995; Corfield *et al.* 1996). It illustrates that pre-orogenic extensional deformation largely controls the geometry and evolution of thrust systems (for reviews, see also Coward 1994, 1996). These relationships are widely shown in balanced sections across thrust fans, but they are less well documented for duplex structures, which generally restore to layer-cake stratigraphic successions (e.g. see Boyer & Elliott 1982; Diegel 1986). The paucity of this documentation, with only rare published examples (e.g. see Tanner 1992), makes it difficult to evaluate the role of structural inheritance during duplex formation. In this paper an exceptionally well-exposed mesoscopic duplex of Late Tertiary age, which propagated across a precursor boudinage structure inherited from an episode of Mesozoic extension, is described. The duplex crops out in a deep fluvial gorge in SW Tuscany, in the innermost parts of the northern Apennines of Italy.

Geological setting

The northern Apennines of Italy are an arcuate fold-and-thrust belt that developed as a result of east-directed imbrication of several tectonic units onto the African (i.e. Adria) foreland plate during the Alpine orogenesis (Boccaletti *et al.* 1980). The imbricated tectonic units, differentiated since Late Palaeozoic time, originated from various palaeogeographical domains (Boccaletti *et al.* 1980). Differentiation of the palaeogeographical domains continued during the rifting stage that culminated, in Jurassic time, with the opening of the Tethys Ocean, and with drifting of the African and European plates in the Jurassic–Cretaceous time interval (Bernoulli 1967; D'Argenio & Alvarez 1980). From Late

From: Ries, A. C., Butler, R. W. H. & Graham, R. H. (eds) 2007. *Deformation of the Continental Crust: The Legacy of Mike Coward.* Geological Society, London, Special Publications, **272**, 437–446.
0305-8719/07/$15

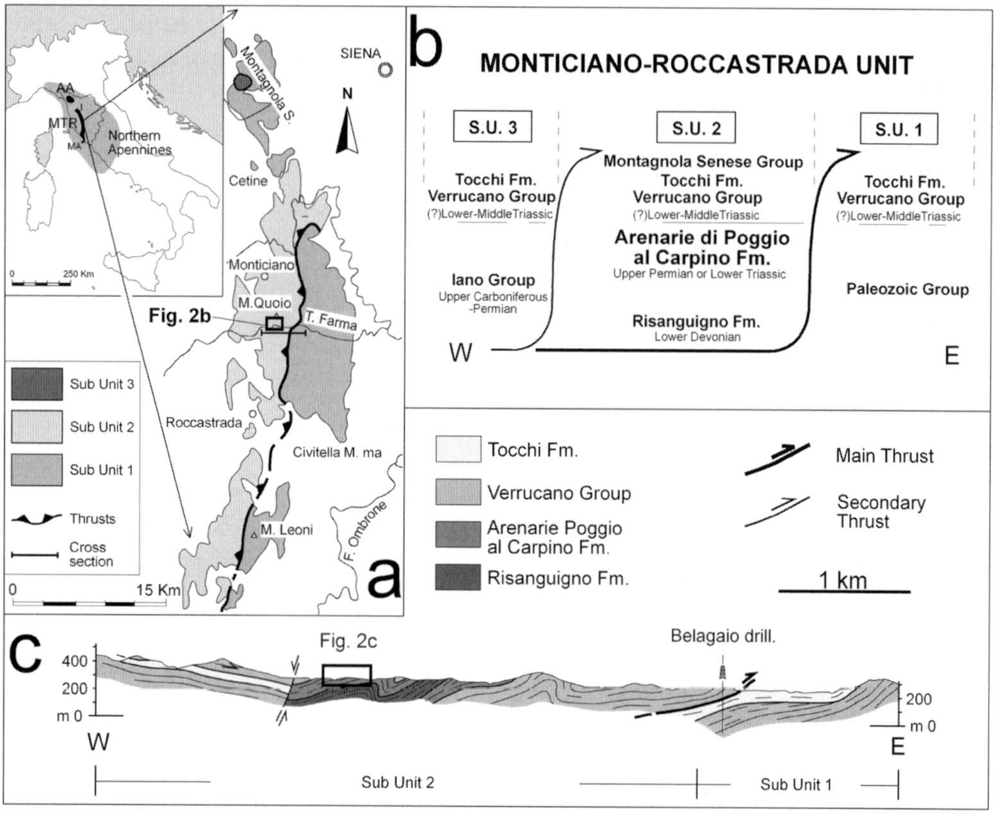

Fig. 1. The Tuscan Metamorphic Complex in the northern Apennines of Italy, with location of the Mid-Tuscan Ridge (MTR), the Alpi Apuane (AA), Iano (I) and Monte Argentario (MA). (**a**) Tectonic sketch map of the Mid-Tuscan Ridge: the main sub-units 1, 2 and 3 are shown. (**b**) Schematic stratigraphic relationships within the tectonic sub-units 1, 2 and 3 of the Monticiano–Roccastrada Unit. (**c**) General cross-section along the Farma River valley (Location shown in (**a**)).

Cretaceous time onwards (Decandia & Elter 1972; Abbate *et al.* 1994, and references therein), following a general reversal of the relative plate motion, the Tethys Ocean was subducted, and the European and Adria continental margins eventually collided in the Late Oligocene. The palaeogeographical domains located on the Adria continental margin were affected by shortening, with development of the main thrust-bounded tectonic units. Stacking of the tectonic pile produced important duplications within the palaeogeographical domain of Tuscany, and these relationships are still visible in the Alpi Apuane Zone. Here a passive margin sedimentary sequence was thickened by a regionally important duplex, which developed in Late Oligocene time under greenschist-facies conditions (the Tuscan Metamorphic Complex; Carmignani & Kligfield 1990). From Early Miocene time onwards, the northern Apennines experienced late- and post-orogenic extension, with the development of low-angle and high-angle normal faults that dismembered the fold-and-thrust architecture of the belt, and also modified the original contractional geometry of the Alpi Apuane duplex (Carmignani *et al.* 1994).

The Tuscan Metamorphic Complex may be traced south of the Alpi Apuane. It occurs within the Mid-Tuscan Ridge, a prominent arcuate morpho-geological feature that extends for over 120 km from Iano, in the north, to Mt. Argentario, in the south (Fig. 1a). This feature is mainly flanked by Neogene marine sediments, which represent the infill of post-orogenic extensional graben. The Palaeozoic–Triassic successions exposed in the Mid-Tuscan Ridge were deposited in the Tuscan palaeogeographical domain, and were later incorporated in the Monticiano–Roccastrada Unit (Fig. 1a), a thrust-bounded tectonic slice that experienced low-grade regional metamorphism (Franceschelli *et al.* 1986). Three distinct minor thrust sheets are

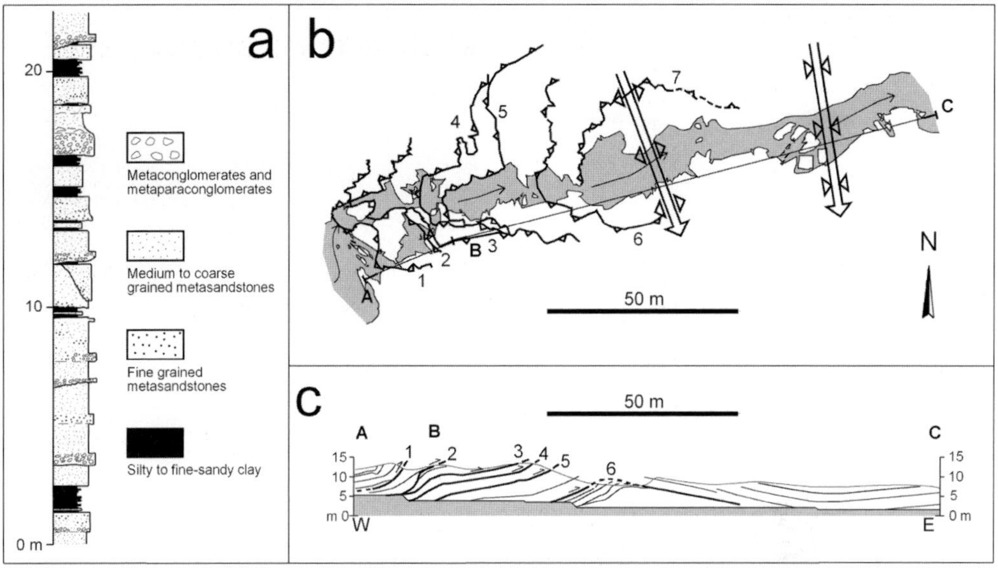

Fig. 2. Stratigraphic and structural features of the Arenarie di Poggio al Carpino Formation along the Farma River. (**a**) General stratigraphic column (modified from Cirilli *et al.* 2001). (**b**) Structural map showing the main thrust contacts (1–7) and the location of the Canaloni duplex (7). (**c**) General cross-section (trace ABC in (**b**) modified from Casini 2003).

recognized within the Monticiano–Roccastrada Unit, namely the Iano, Monte Quoio–Montagnola Senese and Monte Leoni–Farma sub-units (Lazzarotto *et al.* 2003, and references therein; Fig. 1b). The stratigraphic succession of the Monticiano–Roccastrada Unit comprises marine deposits of Devonian–Carboniferous age, neritic to brackish deposits of Permo-Triassic age, and fluvial–deltaic deposits of Triassic age (Lazzarotto *et al.* 2003). In particular, the Permo-Triassic sequence involved in the Monte Quoio–Montagnola Senese sub-unit is represented by the Arenarie di Monte Argentario Formation (Cirilli *et al.* 2002), and by the Arenarie di Poggio al Carpino Formation (Cocozza *et al.* 1978). The latter consists of alternating quartzites and phyllites, which originated from sediments that were deposited within a shallow-marine environment (Engelbrecht 1997*a*,*b*, 2000). Based on its palynological content, the Arenarie di Poggio al Carpino Formation has been attributed to the Late Permian–Early Triassic (Lazzarotto *et al.* 2003; Spina *et al.* 2001).

Structural features of the Arenarie di Poggio al Carpino Fm along the Farma River

The Arenarie di Poggio al Carpino Formation is well exposed *c.* 5 km to the south of Monticiano, in a gorge cut by the Farma River (Fig. 1a and c). The main stratigraphic features were described in detail by Engelbrecht (1997*a*,*b*, 2000) and by Cirilli *et al.* (2001). In this outcrop, the formation consists of a *c.* 25 m thick sequence of metaconglomerates and quartzites locally associated with dark grey and black phyllites (Fig. 2a; Cirilli *et al.* 2001). The coarse quartzite layers are not laterally continuous, but rather display abrupt facies and thickness changes that correspond to braided channels (Fig. 3a). Very often the quartzites and metaconglomerates, arranged in layers up to 5 m thick, are observed to terminate laterally over *c.* 10 m horizontal distance (Fig. 3b). The overall architecture is indicative of a deltaic–fluvial environment (Engelbrecht 1997*a*,*b*, 2000; Cirilli *et al.* 2001).

A detailed 1:100 scale mapping of a *c.* 4500 m^2 wide area in locality 'I Canaloni' (Casini 2003; Fig. 2b) made it possible to accurately define the structural geometry of the deformed Arenarie di Poggio al Carpino Formation. The earliest recognized fabric is a well-developed, bedding-parallel foliation, which has the features of a coarsely spaced stylolitic cleavage within the quartzite layers, and becomes a penetrative schistosity within the phyllites. This foliation is systematically associated with development of boudinage structure that affects the most

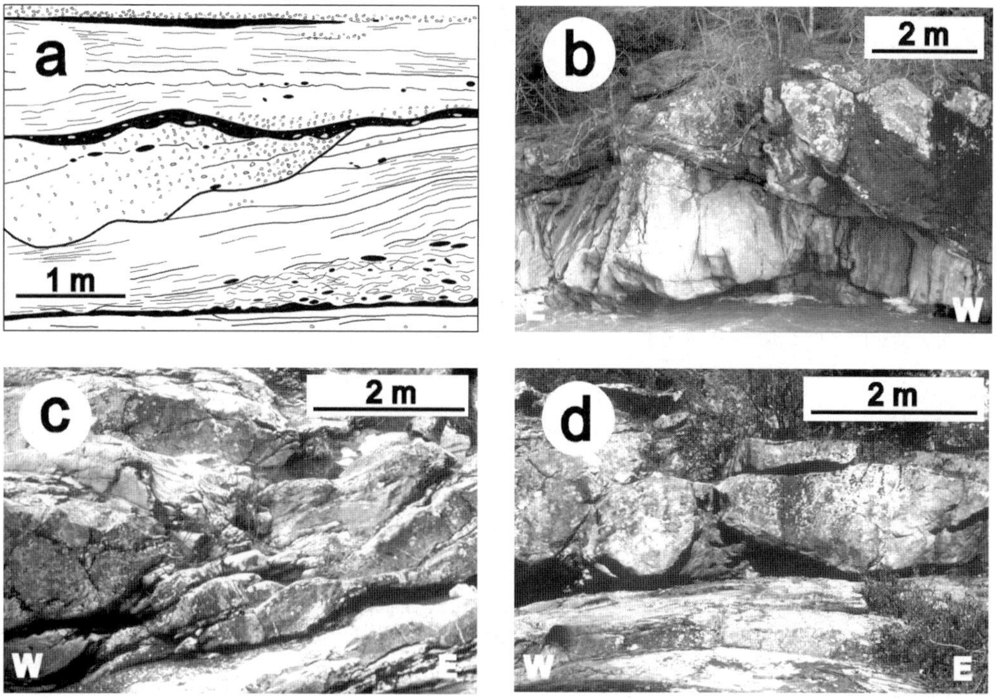

Fig. 3. Depositional and deformational features of the Arenarie di Poggio al Carpino Formation at I Canaloni. (**a**) Braided channel (modified from Engelbrecht 1997*a*). (**b**) Lateral termination of a quartzite layer. (**c**) Bedding-parallel boudinage structure, outlined by bedding-normal quartz veins. (**d**) Antiformally folded boudin pairs (location shown in Fig. 4).

competent quartzite layers, often exaggerating their depositional lateral thickness changes (Fig. 3c). In most cases the necks of the boudins are truncated by centimetre-scale bedding-normal, quartz-rich tensile Mode I veins (Fig. 3c). The close relationship of a ubiquitous bedding-parallel foliation and of boudinage structures indicates that the Arenarie di Poggio al Carpino Formation experienced extensional deformation after deposition (Casini 2003). The lack of precise stratigraphic constraints makes it difficult to define the age of this extensional episode. A Mesozoic, probably Triassic, age is proposed because of the structural relationships that will be described in this paper, and because of regional considerations that will be discussed below.

The extensional fabrics described above are overprinted by thrusts and related folds. The main macroscopic structure consists of an apparently simple fold train, dominated by an east-verging fold pair with wavelength of *c*. 90 m (Fig. 2c). In detail, however, the overall structure is more complex. The apparently simple folds form a complicated antiform–synform system. The main fabrics and their overprinting relationships in the limb and hinge regions of the folds indicate a polyphase deformation history, produced during distinct contractional tectonic events (Casini 2003). The complete dataset collected during the detailed structural survey is not reported here, and will be presented elsewhere. The present paper focuses on the geometry and kinematics of the duplex. The available stratigraphic data inferred from the regional literature (e.g. Carmignani *et al.* 2001, and references therein) indicate that the contractional deformation occurred during the Oligocene–Miocene.

In summary, therefore, the structural architecture of the Arenarie di Poggio al Carpino Formation exposed along the Farma River reveals a complex deformation history, characterized by a switch from Early Mesozoic extension to Late Tertiary contraction. This sequence of events reflects an episode of positive tectonic inversion (terminology after Williams *et al.* 1989).

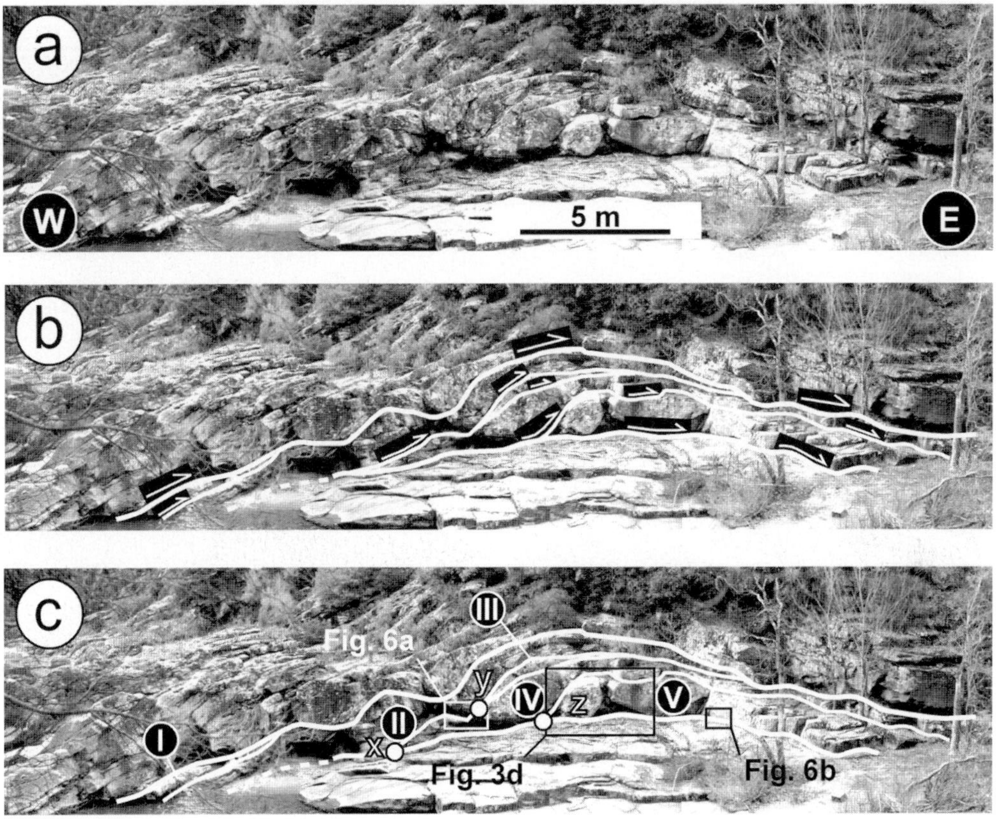

Fig. 4. The Canaloni duplex (location shown in Fig. 2b). (**a**) General view. (**b**) Thrust system trajectories. (**c**) Location of the five principal thrust-bounded horses, I–V, and of the related trailing branch points x, y and z. The location of details discussed in the text is indicated.

A mesoscopic duplex at 'I Canaloni'

A fortuitous combination of excellent, almost continuous exposure and a good vertical relief along the northern bank of the Farma River (Fig. 2b), makes it possible to define the 3D geometry of the macroscopic antiform–synform system of Figure 2c. Here one quartzite layer of the Arenarie di Poggio al Carpino Formation, with an original thickness ranging from 30 cm to 1 m, is intensely duplicated by a mesoscopic, metric-scale duplex (Fig. 4). The structure consists of a roof thrust and a floor thrust, located within metapelites, connected by minor link thrust splays that isolate five thrust-bounded horses (I–V in Fig. 4c). The distribution of bedding surfaces across the duplex defines a NW–SE-trending, moderately SW-plunging antiform (Fig. 4a and b). The antiform affects not only the roof thrust, as in an antiformal stack (Boyer & Elliott 1982), but also the floor thrust and the connecting splays. This indicates a complex deformation history, characterized by the late antiformal folding of a pre-existing, simpler duplex structure. The recognized position of the trailing branch points from which individual connecting splays emanate (Fig. 4c), and a systematic westerly dip of individual thrust-bounded horses, suggest that the thrust system originated as a west (i.e. hinterland-dipping) duplex, that was later folded round the antiform. The dip of the thrust-bounded horses, II–IV, decreases gradually from west to east (Fig. 4), a feature that suggests that the duplex was formed according to a piggy-back thrusting sequence, with new horses detached from the footwall of previously emplaced horses (Butler 1987).

The floor and roof thrust surfaces, and the connecting thrust splays, all display abundant quartz-rich mineral cluster lineations, which make it possible to define the average direction of tectonic transport (Fig. 5). The mean transport

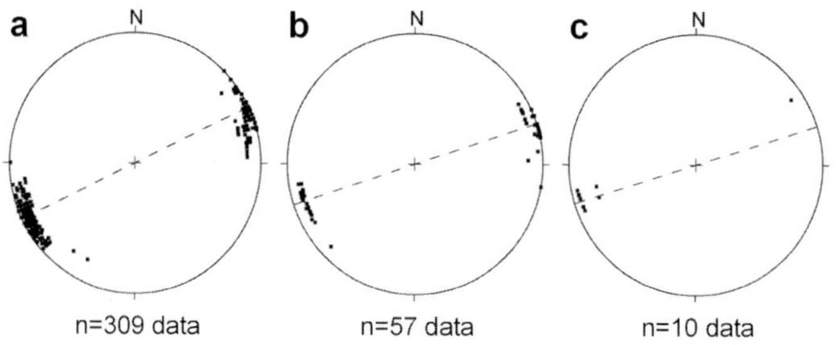

Fig. 5. Orientation data for kinematic indicators within the Canaloni duplex (equal area projection, lower hemisphere). (**a**) Data from the floor thrusts (inferred direction of tectonic transport N064°E). (**b**) Data from the connecting splays (inferred direction of tectonic transport N072°E). (**c**) Data from the roof thrusts (inferred direction of tectonic transport N070°E).

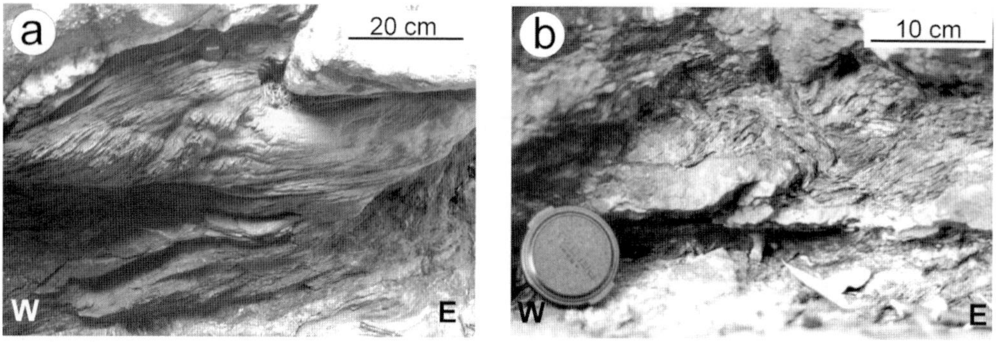

Fig. 6. Features of minor folds along the main detachments within the Canaloni duplex. (**a**) Asymmetric fold pair with axial-plane schistosity deflected at a trailing branch point (location shown in Fig. 4). (**b**) East-verging anticline along the floor thrust (location shown in Fig. 4).

direction, inferred from mineral lineations measured along the floor thrust (Fig. 5a), the connecting splays (Fig. 5b) and the roof thrust (Fig. 5c), ranges from N064E to N072E, indicating internal consistency through the duplex structure. The lineations are always associated with slickenlines, whose steps indicate top-to-the-east displacements. The floor thrust is located within a phyllite horizon, whose thickness ranges from 30 to 250 cm. Centimetre-scale layers of quartzites, intercalated within the phyllites, are often affected by minor, east-verging folds (Fig. 6b) whose formation was accompanied by development of a finely spaced axial-planar schistosity. This is deflected at, or in the vicinity of, the trailing branch points of the connecting splay thrusts (Fig. 6a). The footwall and hanging-wall cut-off points of thrust-bounded horses are often ornamented by steeply west-dipping, or subvertical, Mode I tensile quartz veins, structures that formed during the extensional event that preceded the development of the duplex.

Restoration of the Canaloni duplex

A possible kinematic model for the Canaloni duplex is illustrated in Figure 7. The Arenarie di Poggio al Carpino Formation was deposited during the Late Permian–Early Triassic in a fluvio-deltaic environment. The deformed quartzite layer corresponds to a system of delta channels, and much of the lateral thickness variation within the channels was inherited during deposition (Fig. 7a). Boudins were formed at the expense of the previously undeformed bed (Fig. 7b) during Mesozoic, probably Triassic, time. This deformation largely resulted in accentuation and amplification of the original, depositional lateral thickness changes. Boudinage was accompanied by development of mesoscopic fabrics, such as a pervasive bedding-parallel foliation

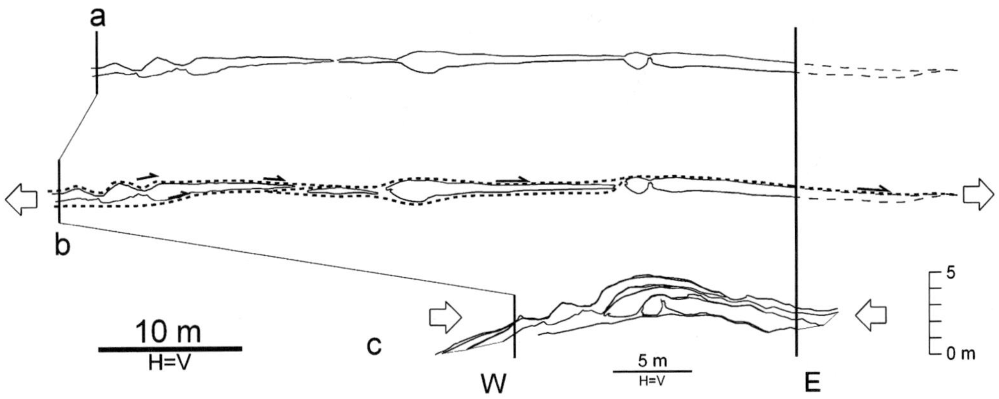

Fig. 7. Balanced cross-section and restored templates of the Canaloni duplex (a–c in time). The dashed lines in (**b**) indicate the trajectories of future thrust propagation. It should be noted that the location of the main thrust ramps in the restored template coincides with the main boudin necks.

and bedding-normal Mode I tensile veins, especially abundant at boudin necks. During the Oligocene–Miocene, the previously extended strata experienced contractional deformation, and the westernmost boudins were telescoped onto their adjacent undeformed counterparts. The progressive eastwards migration of the contractional front led to development of an imbricate structure with the features of a hinterland-dipping duplex. Further contraction, probably induced by the upward propagation of a deeper thrust, resulted in antiformal refolding of the hinterland-dipping duplex. The final shape of the investigated structure thus mimics that of an antiformal stack duplex (Fig. 7c).

Sequential restoration of the Canaloni duplex makes it possible to evaluate the amount of both pre-orogenic extension and orogenic contraction experienced by the deformed quartzite bed (Fig. 7). The initial length of the bed between the chosen pin and loose lines is *c.* 46 m (Fig. 7a). The bed is extended by boudinage by *c.* 3 m (Fig. 7b). Thrust propagation across the previously extended bed led to the development of a hinterland-dipping duplex, which accommodated *c.* 30 m of horizontal contraction (Fig. 7c).

In addition to quantitative estimates, restoration of the Canaloni duplex also provides some insights into the process of duplex formation. It has been extensively shown that thrust ramps in imbricate systems are nucleated by perturbations along the main glide horizons or décollements (e.g. Knipe 1985). In the study of the Canaloni duplex, an obvious perturbation or mechanical anisotropy is represented by the boudinage structure inherited from pre-orogenic extension. The trace of propagating thrusts across the restored quartzite bed indicates that thrust ramps systematically occur at boudin necks (Fig. 7b). As a result, the final duplex geometry is dictated by both position and spacing of individual boudins in the pre-thrusting template. There is also locally some indication that the thrust ramp propagation process was not always completed within the duplex. The best example is found in the lowermost horse (IV of Fig. 4c). Here the boudins, separated by a tight neck, are antiformally folded, and the westernmost boudin is tilted counterclockwise by *c.* 30° (Fig. 3d), suggesting that the thrust ramp failed to propagate through the boudin neck.

Implications for Apennine tectonics

The recognition of bedding-parallel extension within the Arenarie di Poggio al Carpino Formation poses the question of the age of this deformation. In the absence of radiometric data, the boudinage and related vein–foliation features could be ascribed to post-orogenic extension, which locally developed under low-grade metamorphic conditions in southern Tuscany during the evolution of the Apennine–Tyrrhenian system (Franceschelli *et al.* 1986). However, this interpretation is not consistent with the fact that the investigated extensional structures are systematically overprinted by orogenic contraction. The Arenarie di Poggio al Carpino Formation was stratigraphically covered by a *c.* 6000 m thick sequence of Mesozoic and Tertiary sediments after deposition (Carmignani *et al.* 2001), under conditions that would favour the development of low-grade structures. The widespread occurrence of synsedimentary normal faults within the rocks of the Verrucano Group

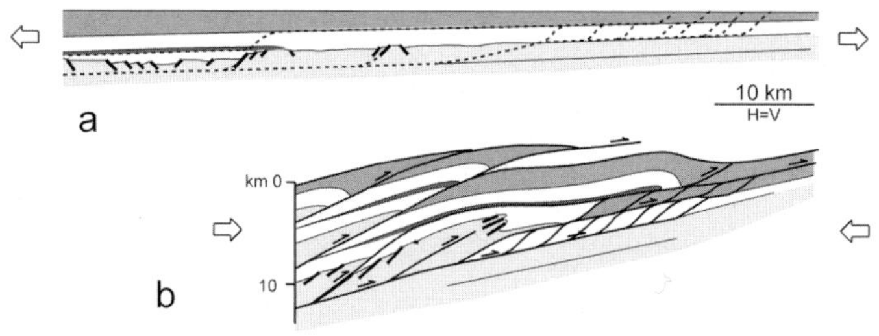

Fig. 8. Schematic illustration (a–b in time) of the development of the Alpi Apuane metamorphic complex (modified from Carmignani & Kligfield 1990). The normal faults in the restored template were inferred from the stratigraphic record. It is proposed that this is an example of a macroscopic duplex developed across a pre-thrusting normal fault array.

and overlying Mesozoic formations (Cirilli *et al.* 2001) suggests that the extensional deformations described in the Arenarie di Poggio al Carpino Formation can be referred to a pre-thrusting event of Mesozoic, probably Triassic, age.

The results of this investigation in southern Tuscany may have important implications for an understanding of the geometry and kinematic evolution of larger imbricates in the Apennine belt. The largest duplex in the northern Apennines occurs in the Alpi Apuane region of northwestern Tuscany, and its evolution was interpreted as resulting from imbrication of a previously extended stratigraphic sequence (Carmignani & Kligfield 1990, fig. 8). This inference largely relies on the recognition within individual horses of local stratigraphic variations related to synsedimentary normal faults of Mesozoic age (Fig. 8a). The documented influence of inherited extension during development of the mesoscopic duplex at I Canaloni suggests that the structure of the Alpi Apuane metamorphic complex is, in fact, that of a macroscopic duplex, whose thrust ramps were probably controlled by the inferred, pre-orogenic synsedimentary normal faults (Fig. 8b).

The recognition of the Canaloni duplex, which involves a previously extended layer, has a more general implication for the description of the architecture of the Apennine belt, whose deep structure is poorly constrained. Deep boreholes for geothermal research, abundant in southern Tuscany, indicate that the basement rocks underlying the sedimentary cover are imbricated, defining a 'Complesso a Scaglie' (Tectonic Wedge Complex; Pandeli *et al.* 1991). The Tectonic Wedge Complex is floored by a common sole thrust located at the top of the crystalline basement, and is roofed by an upper thrust located at the base of the unmetamorphosed sedimentary cover. The sole and roof thrusts are linked by minor splays that isolate several slices or horses largely consisting of metasediments. This thrust system, of Late Tertiary age (Boccaletti *et al.* 1980), propagated across an array of pre-orogenic extensional structures, well documented within the Mesozoic–Cenozoic stratigraphic succession. Because of a remarkable analogy in deformation history with the mesoscopic Canaloni duplex, the Tectonic Wedge Complex represents a duplex of regional extent that affected a previously extended succession.

Conclusions

Conventional models assume that thrust structures mainly result from telescoping of layer-cake stratigraphic sequences (e.g. Boyer & Elliott 1982; Diegel 1986). However, most orogenic belts were formed at the expense of pre-existing rift basins or passive margins, whose extensional structures profoundly influence the kinematic evolution and final geometry of superimposed thrust systems (e.g. see Williams *et al.* 1989; Coward 1994). This structural inheritance, widely reported by Mike Coward and co-workers (e.g. see Gillcrist *et al.* 1987), has been subsequently illustrated in many regions that experienced positive inversion (e.g. the Pyrenees, Bond & McClay 1996; the British Isles, Corfield *et al.* 1996). A common feature to these inverted settings is that pre-orogenic normal faults appear to have largely controlled the geometry and evolution of thrust fans (e.g. see Butler 1989). On the other hand, there is surprisingly little information available on structural controls by pre-orogenic extensional structures during the development of duplex structures (e.g. see Tanner 1992).

Placed in this context, the mesoscopic Canaloni duplex provides an original example to illustrate how, in regions that have experienced positive tectonic inversion, the geometry and evolution of duplexes are influenced by precursor extensional structures within their restored templates. The common tectonic histories of the Canaloni duplex and of other, larger imbricates in the Apennines, such as the Alpi Apuane Metamorphic Complex or the Tuscan Wedge Complex, suggest that these latter structures are, in fact, macroscopic and regional analogues, respectively. Based on this inference, we propose that duplex development across pre-thrusting extensional faults represents an important process in accommodating orogenic contraction during positive tectonic inversion. The resulting structures are thus probably a very common deformation feature in other parts of the Apennines, as well as in many other orogenic belts.

The research presented in this paper has been greatly influenced by the seminal work of Mike Coward, pioneer in the fields of continental deformation and inversion tectonics. Fieldwork was financially supported through a MIUR-COFIN 2003 project on 'Inherited structures and their influence and evolution on the construction of fold-and-thrust belts' (fund to F.A.D.). The constructive reviews by R. Graham and R. Butler, and the editorial comments by A. Ries, are gratefully acknowledged.

References

ABBATE, E., BORTOLOTTI, V., PASSERINI, P., PRINCIPI, G. & TREVES, B. 1994. Oceanisation processes and sedimentary evolution of the Northern Apennine ophiolite suite: a discussion. *Memorie della Società Geologica Italiana*, **48**, 117–136.

BERNOULLI, D. 1967. Probleme der Sedimentation im Jura Westgriechenlands und des zentralen Apennin. *Verhandlungen der Naturforschenden Gesellschaft in Basel*, **78**, 35–54.

BOCCALETTI, M., COLI, M., DECANDIA, F. A., GIANNINI, E. & LAZZAROTTO, A. 1980. Evoluzione dell'Appennino settentrionale secondo un nuovo modello strutturale. *Memorie della Società Geologica Italiana*, **21**, 359–373.

BOND, R. M. G. & MCCLAY, K. R. 1995. Inversion of a Lower Cretaceous extensional basin, south central Pyrenees, Spain. *In*: BUCHANAN, J. G. & BUCHANAN, P. G. (eds) *Basin Inversion*. Geological Society, London, Special Publications, **88**, 415–431.

BOYER, S. E. & ELLIOTT, D. 1982. Thrust systems. *AAPG Bulletin*, **66**, 239–267.

BUTLER, R. W. H. 1986. Thrust tectonics, deep structure and crustal subduction in the Alps and Himalayas. *Journal of the Geological Society, London*, **143**, 857–873.

BUTLER, R. W. H. 1987. Thrust sequences. *Journal of the Geological Society, London*, **144**, 619–634.

BUTLER, R. W. H. 1989. The influence of pre-existing basin structure on thrust system evolution in the Western Alps. *In*: COOPER, M. A. & WILLIAMS, G. D. (eds) *Inversion Tectonics*. Geological Society, London, Special Publications, **44**, 105–122.

CARMIGNANI, L. & KLIGFIELD, R. 1990. Crustal extension in the northern Apennines: the transition from compression to extension in the Alpi Apuane core complex. *Tectonics*, **9**, 1275–1303.

CARMIGNANI, L., DECANDIA, F. A., FANTOZZI, P. L., LAZZAROTTO, A., LIOTTA, D. & MECCHERI, M. 1994. Tertiary extensional tectonics in Tuscany (Northern Apennines, Italy). *Tectonophysics*, **238**, 295–315.

CARMIGNANI, L., DECANDIA, F. A., DISPERATI, L. *et al.* 2001. Inner Northern Apennines. *In*: VAI, G. B. & MARTINI, I. P. (eds) *Anatomy of an Orogen: the Apennines and Adjacent Mediterranean Basins*. Kluwer, Dordrecht, 197–214.

CASINI, G. 2003. *Analisi strutturale della Formazione delle Arenarie di Poggio al Carpino in località 'I Canaloni' (T. Farma—Province di Siena e Grosseto)*. MSc Thesis, University of Siena.

CIRILLI, S., DECANDIA, F. A., LAZZAROTTO, A. & SPINA, A. 2001. I Canaloni: The Poggio al Carpino sandstones. *In*: DECANDIA, F. A., LAZZAROTTO, A., SANDRELLI, F., SPINA, A., CIRILLI, S., PANDELI, E. & ALDINUCCI, M. (eds) *Stratigraphic-Structural Evolution of the Late Palaeozoic-Triassic Sequences of Southern Tuscany (Northern Apennines)*. Dipartimento di scienze della Terra, Università di Siena, 30 April–7 May, 2001, Field Trip Guidebook, 46–48.

CIRILLI, S., DECANDIA, F. A., LAZZAROTTO, A., PANDELI, E., RETTORI, R, & SANDRELLI, F. 2002. Stratigraphy and deopositional environment of the Mt. Argentario sandstones (Southern Tuscany, Italy). *Bollettino della Società Geologica Italiana*, Volume Speciale, **1**, 489–498.

COCOZZA, T., COSTANTINI, A., Lazzarotto, A. & SANDRELLI, F. 1978. Continental Permian in Southern Tuscany (Italy). *In*: TONGIORGI, M. (ed.) *Report on Tuscan Paleozoic Basement*. CNR International Report of the 'Progetto Finalizzato Energetica-Sottoprogetto Energia Geotermica', 35–49.

CORFIELD, S. M., GAWTHORPE, R. L., GAGE, M., FRASER, A. J. & BESLY, B. M. 1996. Inversion tectonics of the Variscan foreland of the British Isles. *Journal of the Geological Society, London*, **153**, 17–32.

COWARD, M. P. 1994. Inversion tectonics. *In*: HANCOCK, P. R. (ed.) *Continental Deformation*. Pergamon, Oxford, 289–304.

COWARD, M. P. 1996. Balancing sections through inverted basins. *In*: BUCHANAN, P. G. & NIEUWLAND, D. A. (eds) *Modern Developments in Structural Interpretation, Validation and Modelling*. Geological Society, London, Special Publications, **99**, 51–77.

COWARD, M. P. & BUTLER, R. W. H. 1985. Thrust tectonics and the deep structure of the Pakistan Himalaya. *Geology*, **13**, 417–420.

DAHLSTROM, C. D. A. 1970. Structural geology in the eastern margin of the Canadian Rocky Mountains. *Canadian Petroleum Geologists Bulletin*, **18**, 322–406.

D'ARGENIO, B. & ALVAREZ, W. 1980. Stratigraphic evidence for crustal thickness changes on the southern Tethyan margin during the Alpine cycle. *Geological Society of America Bulletin*, **91**, 681–689.

DECANDIA, F. A. & ELTER, P. 1972. La zona ofiolitifera del Bracco nel settore compreso tra Levanto e Monte Zatta (Liguria Orientale). *Memorie della Società Geologica Italiana*, **11**, 503–530.

DIEGEL, F. A. 1986. Topological constraints on imbricate thrust networks, examples from the Mountain City window, Tennessee, U.S.A. *Journal of Structural Geology*, **8**, 269–280.

ENGELBRECHT, H. 1997*a*. *Zur Geologie der zone von Monticiano–Roccastrada (Suedtoskana, Italien)*. PhD thesis, University of Munich.

ENGELBRECHT, H., 1997*b*. From Upper Palaeozoic extensional basin fill to late Alpine low grade metamorphic core complex: preliminary note on the sedimentary and tectonic development of the Monticiano–Roccastrada Zone (MRZ; Southern Tuscany, Italy). *Zeitschrift der Deutschen Geologischen Gesellschaft*, **148**, 523–546.

ENGELBRECHT, H. 2000. Deposition of tempestites in the Eastern Rheic Strait: evidence from the Upper Palaeozoic of Southern Tuscany. *Facies*, **43**, 103–122.

FRANCESCHELLI, M., LEONI, L., MEMMI, I. & PUXEDDU, M. 1986. Regional distribution of Al-silicates and metamorphic zonation in the low-grade Verrucano metasediments from the Northern Apennines, Italy. *Journal of Metamorphic Geology*, **4**, 309–321.

GILLCRIST, R., COWARD, M. P. & MUGNIER J. 1987. Structural inversion and its controls: examples from the Alpine foreland and the French Alps. *Geodinamica Acta*, **1**, 5–34.

KNIPE, R. J. 1985. Footwall geometry and the rheology of thrust sheets. *Journal of Structural Geology*, **7**, 1–10.

LAZZAROTTO, A., ALDINUCCI, M., CIRILLI, S. *et al.* 2003. Stratigraphic correlation of the Upper Palaeozoic–Triassic successions in southern Tuscany, Italy. *Bollettino della Società Geologica Italiana*, Volume Speciale, **2**, 25–35.

MITRA, S. 1986. Duplex structures and imbricate thrust systems: geometry, structural position, and hydrocarbon potential. *AAPG Bulletin*, **70**, 1087–1112.

MORLEY, C. K. 1986. A classification of thrust fronts. *AAPG Bulletin*, **70**, 12–25.

PANDELI, E., BERTINI, G. & CASTELLUCCI, P. 1991. The Tectonic Wedges Complex of the Larderello area (southern Tuscany—Italy). *Bollettino della Società Geologica Italiana*, **110**, 621–629.

SPINA, A., CIRILLI, S., DECANDIA, F. A. & LAZZAROTTO, A. 2001. Palynological data from the Arenarie di Poggiop al Carpino Fm. (Southern Tuscany, Italy). *In*: DECANDIA, F. A., LAZZAROTTO, A., SANDRELLI, F., SPINA, A., CIRILLI, S., PANDELI, E. & ALDINUCCI, M. (eds) *Stratigraphic and Structural Evolution of the Late Carboniferous to Triassic Continental and Marine Successions in Tuscany (Italy): Regional Reports and General Correlation, 30 April–7 May, 2001, Abstracts Volume*, Dipartimento dï Science della Terra, Università di Siena, 65–66.

TANNER, P. W. G. 1992. Morphology and geometry of duplexes formed during flexural-slip folding. *Journal of Structural Geology*, **14**, 1173–1192.

VANN, I. R., GRAHAM, R. H. & HAYWARD, A. B. 1986. The structure of mountain fronts. *Journal of Structural Geology*, **8**, 215–227.

WILLIAMS, G. D., POWELL, C. M. & COOPER, M. A. 1989. Geometry and kinematics of inversion tectonics. *In*: COOPER, M. A. & WILLIAMS, G. D. (eds) *Inversion Tectonics*. Geological Society, London, Special Publications, **44**, 3–15.

Structural style and hydrocarbon prospectivity in fold and thrust belts: a global review

MARK COOPER

EnCana Corporation, 150 9th Avenue SW, Calgary, Alberta, Canada, T2P 2S5 (e-mail: mark.cooper@encana.com)

Abstract: A statistical analysis of reserves in fold and thrust belts, grouped by their geological attributes, indicates which of the world's fold and thrust belts are the most prolific hydrocarbon provinces. The Zagros Fold Belt contains 49% of reserves in fold and thrust belts and has been isolated during the analysis to avoid bias. Excluding the Zagros Fold Belt, most of the reserves are in thin-skinned fold and thrust belts that have no salt detachment or salt seal, are partially buried by syn- or post-orogenic sediments, are sourced by Cretaceous source rocks and underwent their last phase of deformation during the Tertiary. A significant observation is that the six most richly endowed fold and thrust belts have no common set of geological attributes, implying that these fold belts all have different structural characteristics. The implication is that deformation style is a not critical factor for the hydrocarbon endowment of fold and thrust belts; other elements of the petroleum system must be more significant. Other fold and thrust belts may share the structural attributes but the resource-rich fold belts overwhelmingly dominate the total reserves in that group of fold belts. There is nothing intrinsic in fold and thrust belts that differentiates them from other oil- and gas-rich provinces other than the prolific development of potential hydrocarbon traps. Many of the prolific, proven fold and thrust belts still have significant remaining exploration potential as a result of politically challenging access and remote locations.

This paper developed from a review of the geological characteristics of fold and thrust belts that contain hydrocarbons. The primary data source for this study is the International Exploration and Production Database marketed by IHS, which contains data on production and reserves for gas, oil and condensate on all producing and discovered fields around the world, excluding onshore North America. This is the most complete dataset available but it must be appreciated that the data are of variable quality. These data have been supplemented by information from the US Geological Survey World Petroleum assessments where they are available (USGS 2000). Information on the geological characteristics of the fold belts in this review has been derived from published literature.

The purpose of the paper is to analyse statistically the geological characteristics of hydrocarbon-productive fold and thrust belts. There have been few previous attempts to undertake this type of analysis (Graham *et al.* 1997) and most reviews of hydrocarbon potential are limited in geographical scope (e.g. Picha 1996; Brookfield & Hashmat 2001). The analysis presented here focused on a few selected key parameters that could potentially affect hydrocarbon prospectivity and reserves distribution.

The review of geological characteristics focused on structural style observations such as whether the fold belt is thick or thin skinned, presence of a salt detachment, the presence of a salt seal and syn-orogenic burial. The depth to detachment and the thickness of the competent beam involved in the deformation were also noted but not analysed in detail because of the variable quality of the data for these factors. Time elements, such as the age of onset of the last deformation phase in the fold and thrust belt and the depositional age of the source rock, were also recorded and analysed. There are many other factors that could have been considered (e.g. pre-existing basement structures, source rock characteristics and age of source maturation). These other factors are also important but were beyond the scope of the dataset for this paper.

In this assessment a fold belt is considered to be any hydrocarbon province that is dominated by compressional tectonics resulting from plate convergence. Fold belts that have their origins as the contractional toes to extensional systems on continental margins have been excluded. These fold belts have become important hydrocarbon provinces as exploration drilling has moved out into deep-water continental margins (e.g. the deep-water Gulf of Mexico, deep-water Niger Delta and Brazil). This decision was taken because the fundamental tectonic driving mechanism is different from that in a convergent margin fold belt even though the geometric

From: Ries, A. C., Butler, R. W. H. & Graham, R. H. (eds) 2007. *Deformation of the Continental Crust: The Legacy of Mike Coward.* Geological Society, London, Special Publications, **272**, 447–472.

characteristics are obviously very similar (Rowan *et al.* 2004).

The IHS dataset includes reserves information for discovered fields. It takes no account of the yet-to-find potential of the basins. The dataset was extracted from the IHS database in March 2004 and was then edited to remove all fields that were not located in fold and thrust belts.

Importance of fold and thrust belts as hydrocarbon provinces

Based on the IHS field reserves data, 14% of the world's discovered reserves are in fold and thrust belts developed at convergent plate boundaries, a significant proportion of the global reserve base. This percentage appears to be largely independent of hydrocarbon phase (Fig. 1a). The split of oil, gas and condensate indicates that the percentage of oil (59%) in fold and thrust belts is very similar to the percentage of oil (54%) in all global reserves (Fig. 1b). The conclusion is that the oil:gas:condensate ratio is roughly the same in fold and thrust belts as it is for all global petroleum reserves. One of the difficulties in undertaking a statistical analysis of fold belts is that the dataset is dominated by the Zagros Fold Belt of Iran, Iraq, Syria and Turkey, which accounts for 49% of all the established reserves in the fold belts around the world.

The USGS global assessment of resources in 2000 concluded that fold and thrust belts amounted to 15% of the global total of undiscovered resources (USGS 2000). The implication is that as known fold and thrust belt reserves constitute 14% of global reserves, the yet-to-find is almost identically proportioned based on the tectonic setting. The conclusion is that fold and thrust belts represent an absolutely average sample of global hydrocarbon resources, there is nothing statistically distinctive about fold and thrust belts; they are oil prone because they are a very good sample of an oil-prone world.

Hydrocarbon discoveries in fold and thrust belts date back to the earliest days of oil exploration in the late 19th and early 20th centuries. The primary reason for these discoveries was that early drilling tended to focus on structurally simple anticlines that could be mapped using the surface geology, which mimicked the subsurface

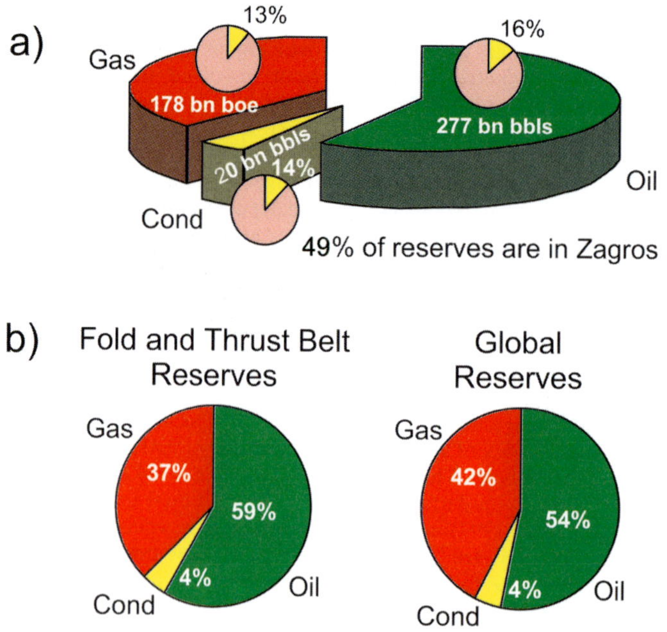

Fig. 1. (**a**) Distribution of hydrocarbon type in fold and thrust belts; total volumes are indicated on the pie chart segments. The yellow segments of the smaller pie charts indicate the proportions of global reserves in fold and thrust belts for each hydrocarbon type with the actual percentage labelled. (**b**) Comparison of hydrocarbon type split between fold and thrust belts and all global reserves.

structure at the reservoir level. This ultimately led to the discovery of super-giant oilfields in the Zagros Fold Belt of Iran and Iraq, such as Kirkuk, in the early decades of the 20th century. However, 80% of the giant fields were discovered after 1950 because of the challenges of exploring in structurally complex terrain. For example, in Wyoming the first discovery was in 1900, but it was not until the late 1970s that the first giant field (Whitney Canyon–Carter Creek) was discovered (Lamerson 1982). Structural complexity is a major problem when exploring many fold and thrust belts because the surface structural expression is commonly decoupled from the subsurface structural geometry at the reservoir level. Seismic imaging and ability to accurately map complex subsurface structures are therefore the keys to exploration. The reasons for geophysical exploration and field mapping are obvious, but structural and tectonic analysis can also improve risk assessment. Detailed structural analysis allows identification of prevalent geometric patterns of faulting and folding. Dahlstrom (1970), Boyer & Elliott (1982) and Suppe (1983) used structural analysis to establish general rules of structural cross-section interpretation. These rules, when combined with field and geophysical data, can tightly constrain the location, shape, and size of structural traps (e.g. Cooper *et al.* 2004).

The Alberta foothills provide a well-documented example of how the evolution of structural models has affected exploration success over several generations (Gallup 1975; Ower 1975; Stockmal *et al.* 2001). Other examples are the Papua New Guinea fold and thrust belt (Hobson 1986; Hill 1991; Hill *et al.* 2004) and the Dagestan fold and thrust belt (Sobornov 1994). Revisions of structural model paradigms still continue to yield exploration success even in mature fold and thrust belts (e.g. in the Utah overthrust belt; Moulton & Pinnell 2005). The common progression in the exploration of most fold and thrust belts is from the exploration of the simpler, near-surface structures to the deeper, more complex, sub-thrust structures, which in many cases hold the larger prizes (e.g. the Alberta foothills; Gallup 1975; Ower 1975; Stockmal *et al.* 2001).

Fold and thrust belts included in this review

The 55 fold and thrust belts included in this review are shown in Figure 2 and Table 1. The reserves data in the IHS database are organized

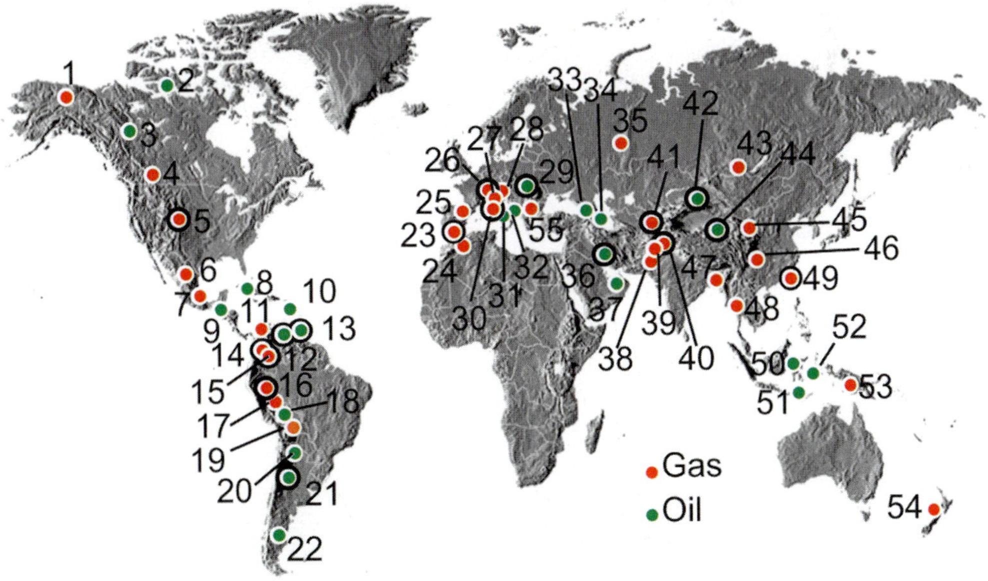

Fig. 2. Location map of fold and thrust belts included in this study. Each fold and thrust belt is labelled with a reference number that is included in Table 1. The locations are colour coded by the predominant hydrocarbon type, and those symbols that are outlined in black indicate fold and thrust belts that Mike Coward worked on during his career.

Table 1. *Summary of data for fold and thrust belts*

Fold belt	Country	Orogen	Thin or thick skinned	Buried	Salt seal	Salt detachment	Salt detachment age	Onset of last deformation	Competent beam (km)	Depth to detachment (km)	Source age	No. of belt in Fig. 2	Oil + Condensate (mm bbl)	Gas (mm boe)	Total reserve (mm boe)	Oil or Gas	Maturity index
Altun Shan FB	China	Himalayan	Thick	No	Partial	No		Pliocene			Oligo-Miocene	44	664	554	1218	O	
Arctic FB	Canada	Arctic	Thin	No	No	No		Palaeocene			Palaeocene	2	3	0	3	O	
Assam FB	Bangladesh, India, Myanmar	Himalayan	Thin	No	No	No		Miocene	0	> 5	Palaeocene	47	135	345	480	G	48
Atlas FB	Algeria, Italy	Atlas	Both	No	No	Yes	Trias	Miocene		10	Silurian	24	94	107	201	G	
Balkan FB	Bulgaria	Alpine	Thin	No	No	No		Eocene			Jurassic	55	0	0	0	G	
Banggai FB	Indonesia	Banda Arc	Thin	No	No	No		Early Jur			Oligo-Miocene	50	33	929	963	G	
Beni FB	Bolivia	Andean	Thin	No	No	No		Miocene	> 3	> 5	Devonian	18	7	2	8	O	
Betic FB	Spain	Alpine	Thin	No	No	Yes	Trias	Miocene	0–1		Late Miocene	23	0	0	0	G	
Brooks Range	USA	Rockies	Thin	No	No	No		Early Cret			Jurassic	1	0	0	0	G	
Carpathian FB	Poland, Ukraine, Czech R., Romania, Austria, Slovakia	Alpine	Thin	Partial	No	Partial		Miocene	1	> 2	Oligocene	29	5643	1785	7428	O	31
Caucasus FB	Azerbaijan, Uzbekistan, Kazakhstan, Russia	Caucasus	Thick	Part/Yes	No	No		Miocene	2	6	Oligocene & Trias–Jurassic	34	26954	13973	40927	O	60
Chaco FB	Argentina, Bolivia	Andean	Thin	No	No	No		Miocene	1	5	Middle Dev	19	2033	12034	14067	G	55
Cuban FB	Cuba	Cuban	Thin	Yes	No	Yes	Jur	Miocene	1	5	Late Jurassic	8	378	10	388	O	67
Cuyo FB	Argentina	Andean	Thick	No	No	No		Miocene	> 3	> 10	Late Triassic	20	1673	80	1752	O	
Dagestan FB	Russia	Caucasus	Thick	Partial	Partial	No		Miocene	2	6	Oligocene	33	3897	1386	5283	O	51
Dinarides	Albania	Alpine	Thin	Yes	No	Yes	Trias	Pliocene	1–4	> 5	Mio-Pliocene	32	592	228	820	O	
Eastern Alps	Austria	Alpine	Thin	Yes	Yes	Yes	Trias	Eocene	1–4	> 2	Oligocene	28	6	41	47	G	
Eastern Cordilllera	Colombia	Andean	Thick/ Thin	No/Yes	No	No		Miocene	0		Late Cret	14	7	9	16	G	24
Gissar FB	Uzbekistan, Tajikistan	Himalayan	Both/ Thick	No	No/Part	No/Part		Miocene	1	10	Early Jurassic	41	1113	1347	2459	G	
Guajira Prism	Colombia	Andean	Thin	Yes	No	No		Miocene			Unknown	11	0	67	67	G	
Jura FB	France	Alpine	Thin	No	No	Yes	Trias	Miocene	1	3	Late Carb	26	0	1	1	G	
Kirthar FB	Pakistan	Himalayan	Thin	No	No	No		Palaeocene	> 5	10	Early Cret	38	0	278	278	G	
Llanos Foothills	Colombia, Venezuela	Andean	Both/ Thin	No	No	No		Miocene			Late Cret	15	2512	1275	3788	O	37
Loei-Phetchabun FB	Thailand	Himalayan	Thick	No	No	No		Late Cret	2	5–10	Triassic	48	1	180	181	G	
Madre de Dios FB	Peru	Andean	Thin	No	No	No		Miocene	2	> 5	Devonian	17	937	2879	3816	G	
Malargue–Agrio FB	Argentina	Andean	Both	No	No	No		Miocene	1	5	Late Jurassic	21	481	242	723	O	71
Maturin FB	Venezuela	Andean	Thin	Yes	No	No		Miocene	2	5	Late Cret	12	22612	17370	39982	O	28
NE Caribbean FB	Barbados	Caribbean	Thin	No	No	No		Pliocene			Eocene	10	13	4	18	O	
New Zealand	New Zealand	New Zealand	Both	Yes/No	No	No		Tertiary			Late Cret	54	36	108	144	G	
Northern Apennines	Italy	Alpine	Thin	Partial	No	Partial		Miocene	2		Plio-Pleist	30	105	1841	1946	G	

Table 1. *Continued*

Fold belt	Country	Orogen	Thin or thick skinned	Buried	Salt seal	Salt detach-ment	Salt detach-ment age	Onset of last deformation	Comp-etent beam (km)	Depth to detach-ment (km)	Source age	No. of belt in Fig. 2	Oil + Cond-ensate (mm bbl)	Gas (mm boe)	Total resevre (mm boe)	Oil or Gas	Mat-urity index
Northern Rockies FB	Canada	Rockies	Thin	No	No	No		Palaeocene			Cambrian	3	235	29	264	O	
Oman FB	Oman	Zagros	Thick	Yes	No	No		Miocene			Late Precamb	37	6	5	11	O	15
Papuan FB	Papua New Guinea	New Guinean	Both	No	No	No		Miocene	0	5	Jurassic	53	770	2245	3015	G	
Potwar FB	Pakistan	Himalayan	Thin	No	No	Yes	EoCamb	Palaeocene	3	3–5	Palaeocene	40	401	390	791	G	
Pyrenees	France, Spain	Alpine	Thin	No	No	Yes	Trias	Eocene	1	> 3	Late Jurassic	26	641	1921	2562	G	
Qilian Shan FB	China	Himalayan	Thick	No	No	No		Jurassic			Early Palaeoz	45	0	22	22	G	
Reforma FB	Mexico	Mexican	Thin	Partial	No	Yes	Callov	Palaeocene	1–4	5–6	Middle Cret	9	50765	10641	61406	O	
Rockies FB	Canada	Rockies	Thin	No	Yes	No		Palaeocene			Early Carb	4	1100	936	2036	G	13
San Bernardo FB	Argentina	Andean	Thick	No	No	No		Miocene	> 3	> 10	Early Cret	22	4637	984	5621	O	46
Sayan-Tuva FB	Russia	East Siberian	Thick	Yes	Yes	No		Jurassic		> 10	Late Precamb	43	267	6540	6807	G	61
Seram FB	Indonesia	Banda Arc	Thick	No	No	No		Miocene			Late Triassic	50	21	1	22	O	
Sierra Madre Orientale	Mexico	Mexican	Thin	No	No	Yes	Trias	Campanian	> 5	> 5	Late Jurassic	6	2	58	60	G	
Southern Alps	Italy	Alpine	Thin	Yes	Yes	Yes	Trias	Eocene	1–4	> 2	Late Triassic	27	29	163	192	G	
Southern Apennines	Italy	Alpine	Thin	Partial	No	Partial		Miocene	2		Late Triassic	31	906	531	1437	O	
Sulaiman FB	Pakistan	Himalayan	Thin	No	No	No		Palaeocene	1	> 5	Early Cret	39	32	2819	2852	G	
Taiwan FB	Taiwan	Taiwan	Thin	No	No	No		Pliocene			Unknown	49	50	443	493	G	
Tien Shan FB	China	Himalayan	Thick	Yes/Part	No/Yes	No		Oligocene	3-5	> 10	Late Permian	42	11214	2576	13789	O	69
Timor FB	East Timor	Banda Arc	Thick	No	No	No		Miocene			Late Triassic	51	0	0	0	O	
Trinidad FB	Trinidad and Tobago	Caribbean	Thin	No	No	No		Pliocene	3	3–5	Late Cret	13	2520	567	3087	O	47
Ucayali FB	Peru	Andean	Thick	No	No	No		Miocene	1	> 10	Late Triassic	16	57	64	120	G	
Ural FB	Russia	Urals	Thin	No	Yes	No		Permian	4	4	Late Dev	35	817	2894	3711	G	4
Utah Wyoming FB	USA	Rockies	Thin	No	Yes	No		Palaeocene			Middle Cret	5	600	3167	3767	G	
Veracruz FB	Mexico	Mexican	Thin	Partial	No	Yes		Late Cret	5	5	Late Cret	7	130	242	372	G	
Yunan Guizhou FB	China	Himalayan	Thin	No	Yes	No		Tertiary		> 5	Late Triassic	46	0	2820	2820	G	50
Zagros FB	Iran, Iraq, Syria, Turkey	Zagros	Both	Partial	Yes	No/Part		Pliocene	3	8	Middle Cret	36	152170	80338	232508	O	24

FB, fold belt. Stratigraphic ages are abbreviated as necessary; mm boe, million barrels oil equivalent; mm bbl, million barrels.

Table 2. *Key fold belt references*

Fold belt	References	Fold belt	References
Altun Shan Fold Belt	Gu & Di 1989; Qinmin & Coward 1990; Jin *et al.* 2002	New Zealand	Knox 1982; Pilaar & Wakefield 1984; Collier & Johnston 1990
Arctic Fold Belt	Harrison & Bally 1988	Northern Apennines	Mattavelli *et al.* 1993; Zappaterra 1994; Coward *et al.* 1999
Assam Fold Belt	Bastia *et al.* 1993; Mallick *et al.* 1997; Kent *et al.* 2002	Northern Rockies Fold Belt	Yose *et al.* 2001
Atlas Fold Belt	Beauchamp *et al.* 1996, 1999	Oman Fold Belt	Grantham *et al.* 1987; Robertson *et al.* 1990; Mount *et al.* 1998
Balkan Fold Belt	Karagjuleva & Cankov 1974; Foose & Manheim 1975	Papuan Fold Belt	Hill *et al.* 2004
Banggai Fold Belt	Shaw & Packham 1992	Potwar Fold Belt	Khan *et al.* 1986; Pennock *et al.* 1989; Dolan 1990
Beni Fold Belt	Illich *et al.* 1984; Baby *et al.* 1995	Pyrenees	Espitalie & Drouet 1992; Bourrouilh *et al.* 1995; Le Vot *et al.* 1996
Betic Fold Belt	Blankenship 1992	Qilian Shan Fold Belt	Chen *et al.* 1987; Guo & Zhang 1989; Ulmishek 1992
Brooks Range	Hubbard *et al.* 1987; ANWR Assessment Team US Geological Survey 1998; Cole *et al.* 1998	Reforma Fold Belt	Peterson 1983; Gonzalez-Garcia & Holguin-Quinones 1991; Santiago & Baro 1992
Carpathian Thrust Belt	Roure *et al.* 1993; Krejci *et al.* 1996; Slaczka 1996	Rockies Fold Belt	Bally *et al.* 1966; Cooper 2000; Stockmal *et al.* 2001
Caucasus Fold Belt	Ulmishek 1990, 2001; Abrams & Narimanov 1997	San Bernardo Fold Belt	Homovc *et al.* 1995; Peroni *et al.* 1995
Chaco Fold Belt	Dunn *et al.* 1995; Moretti *et al.* 1996	Sayan-Tuva Fold Belt	Kontorovich *et al.* 1990
Cuban Fold Belt	Ball *et al.* 1985; Echevarria-Rodriguez *et al.* 1991; Campos *et al.* 1996	Seram Fold Belt	Courteney *et al.* 1988; Sykora 2000
Cuyo Fold Belt	Villar & Puettmann 1990; Dellape & Hegedus 1995; Uliana *et al.* 1995	Sierra Madre Orientale	Gonzalez-Garcia & Holguin-Quinones 1991; Marrett & Aranda 1999; Eguiluz 2001
Dagestan Fold Belt	Sobornov 1994	Southern Alps	Roeder 1992; Anelli *et al.* 1996
Dinarides	Zappaterra 1994; Velaj *et al.* 1999	Southern Apennines	Pieri & Mattavelli 1986; Bally *et al.* 1988; Zappaterra 1994
Eastern Alps	Muller *et al.* 1988; Ortner & Sachsenhofer 1996; Zimmer & Wessely 1996	Sulaiman Fold Belt	Raza *et al.* 1989; Dolan 1990; Jadoon *et al.* 1994
Eastern Cordilllera	Kronman *et al.* 1995; Reyes *et al.* 2000	Taiwan Fold Belt	Suppe 1980, 1981
Gissar Fold Belt	Brookfield & Hashmat 1978; Khain *et al.* 1991	Tien Shan Fold Belt	Wang *et al.* 1992; Li *et al.* 1996; Gao & Ye 1997
Guajira Prism	Ruiz *et al.* 2000	Timor Fold Belt	Charlton *et al.* 1991; Shaw & Packham 1992
Jura Fold Belt	Laubscher 1962; Mascle 1994	Trinidad Fold Belt	Persad 1985; Rohr 1991; Requejo *et al.* 1994
Kirthar Fold Belt	Dolan 1990; Robinson *et al.* 1999; Schelling 1999	Ucayali Fold Belt	Illich *et al.* 1985; Mathalone & Montoya 1995
Llanos Foothills	Cazier *et al.* 1995; Cooper *et al.* 1995; Drozd & Piggott 1996	Ural Fold Belt	Masters & Peterson 1981; Dikenshteyn 1986; Ulmishek 1988
Loei-Phetchabun Fold Belt	Cooper *et al.* 1989; Sattayarak *et al.* 1989	Utah Wyoming Fold Belt	Lamerson 1982; Warner 1982
Madre de Dios Fold Belt	Mathalone & Montoya 1995; Moretti *et al.* 1996	Veracruz Fold Belt	Moran-Zenteno 1994; Jennette *et al.* 2003
Malargue–Agrio Fold Belt	Mello *et al.* 1994; Urien & Zambrano 1994; Manceda & Figueroa 1995	Yunan Guizhou Fold Belt	Chen *et al.* 1994; Ryder *et al.* 1994
Maturin Fold Belt	Talukdar *et al.* 1988; Roure *et al.* 1994; Parnaud *et al.* 1995	Zagros Fold Belt	Bordenave & Burwood 1990; Beydoun *et al.* 1992; Berberian 1995
NE Caribbean Fold Belt	Speed *et al.* 1991; Babaie *et al.* 1992; Wallace *et al.* 2003		

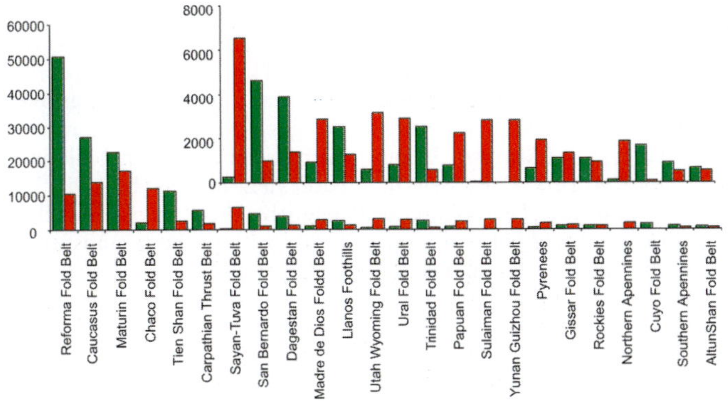

Fig. 3. Graph of the distribution of hydrocarbon reserves in fold and thrust belts, in order of decreasing total reserves. Green, oil and condensate in mm bbl; red, gas in mm boe. The Zagros Fold Belt is excluded from the chart; the inset chart represents the fold belts vertically below at a larger scale.

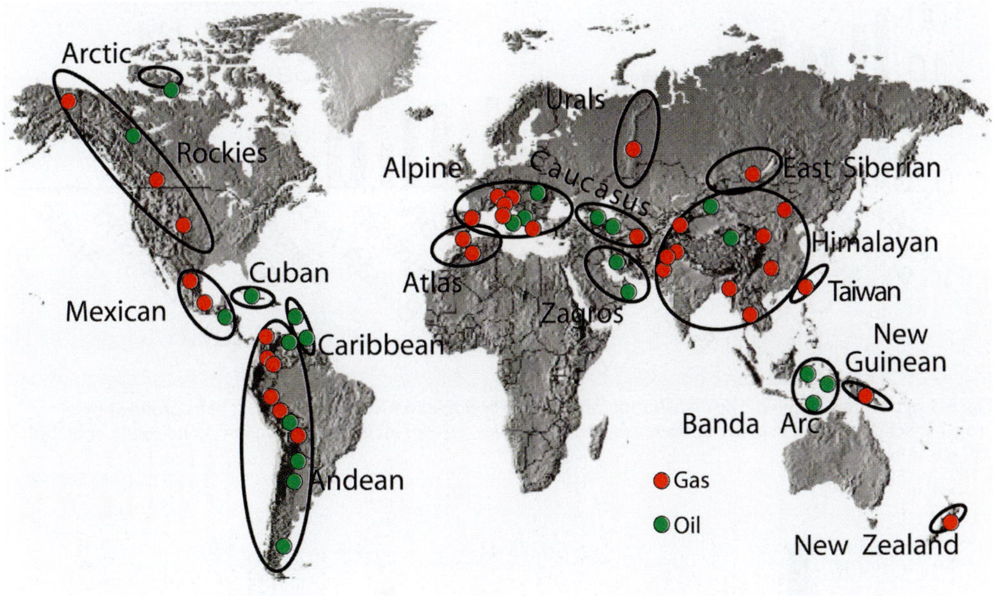

Fig. 4. Location map of orogenic belt groupings for the fold and thrust belts included in this study (Table 1).

by basin and sub-basin but not by fold belt. The dataset had to be carefully reviewed and edited to extract only fields that are within fold belts and to assign each field to the appropriate fold belt. The initial dataset of nearly 22 000 fields was reduced to just over 2900 fields. The key references for the geological attributes of each fold belt are listed in Table 2. In several cases an attribute has been recorded as partial (Table 1), which means that it is present only over a portion of the (sub)basin area. In addition, many of the fold and thrust belts span a number of (sub)basins that may have different attributes; in such cases the reserves in that (sub)basin have been appropriately attributed and the fold belt noted as having a mixture of characteristic factors (Table 1). Those fold and thrust belts that Mike Coward worked on during his career are highlighted in Figure 2, which illustrates the extent of his influence in shaping the understanding of many of these fold and thrust belts.

The database includes 37 fold and thrust belts that contain giant fields (>250 million barrels of oil equivalent mm boe); 25 of the fold and thrust belts have reserves of more than 1 billion barrels of oil equivalent (bn boe) and 16 have reserves of more than 3 bn boe (Fig. 3 and Table 1). The fold belts which lie in the last category include the Zagros Fold Belt (one of the world's most prolific hydrocarbon provinces) the Maturin Basin of East Venezuela, the Reforma Fold Belt in Mexico, the Caucasus and the Tien Shan in China (Fig. 3). The thrust and fold belts with the largest total reserves are mostly dominated by oil, with the notable exception of the Chaco Fold Belt (Fig. 3 and Table 1).

The fold and thrust belts can be conveniently grouped into the orogenic systems within which they are located (Fig. 4); this allows for the analysis of the established reserves in the orogenic belts. The orogenic belts are ranked by total reserves in Figure 5; the graphs show the split of oil, gas and condensate expressed in billions of barrels (bn bbl) or billions of barrels of oil equivalent for gas (bn boe). The dataset is dominated by the Zagros Fold Belt, which accounts for 49% of all the established reserves in the fold belts around the world and has four times the reserves of the next largest orogenic belt, the Andean Orogen. This strongly skews any observations and conclusions drawn from the analysis of the reserves data and for this reason the

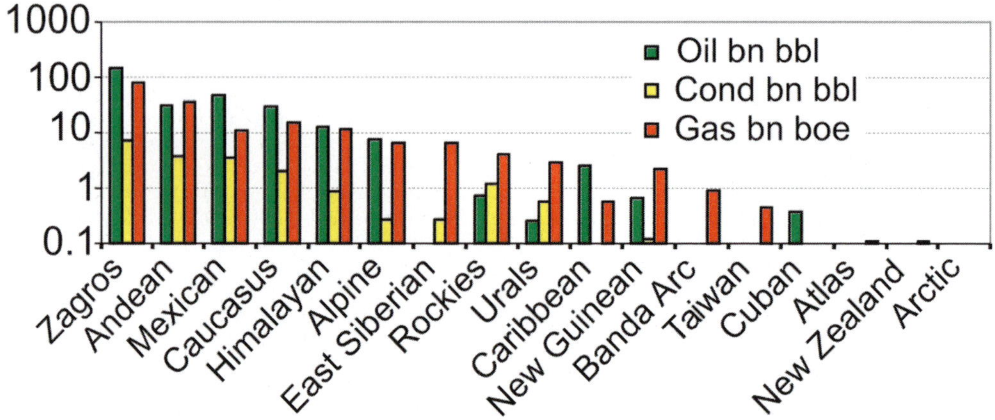

Fig. 5. Logarithmic graph of the distribution of hydrocarbon reserves in fold and thrust belts grouped by orogenic belt (Table 1), in order of decreasing total reserves. Green, oil in bn bbls; yellow, condensate in bn bbl; red, gas in bn boe.

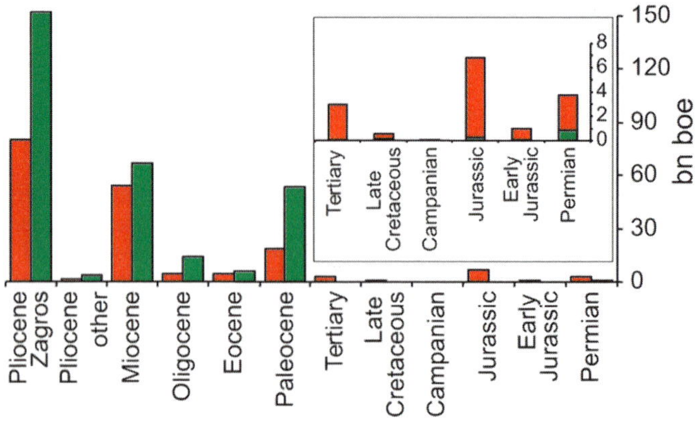

Fig. 6. Graph of the distribution of hydrocarbon reserves in fold and thrust belts grouped by the age of onset of the last phase of deformation (Table 1). Green, oil and condensate in bn bbl; red, gas in bn boe. The inset chart shows the older ages of deformation at a larger scale.

Zagros Fold Belt has been isolated on subsequent graphs. Oil is the dominant hydrocarbon type in the six orogenic belts with the largest reserves; the exception is the Andean Orogen, where gas is slightly more significant.

Analysis of fold and thrust belt reserves

Reserves by age of deformation

The reserves can be analysed by the age of the onset of the last phase of deformation in the fold and thrust belt (Fig. 6); any earlier deformation phases are ignored. This shows the Pliocene age deformation of the Zagros Fold Belt to be dominant. The Miocene and Palaeocene are the second and third most important times of hydrocarbon-rich fold and thrust belt development. All other times of fold and thrust belt last phase deformation are volumetrically insignificant by comparison. Clearly the preservation potential of a fold and thrust belt is enhanced when it is relatively young, but as the age of deformation becomes progressively greater, there is more chance of the fold and thrust belt being uplifted and eroded (e.g. the Appalachian fold and thrust belt) or buried to uneconomic depths beneath a later passive margin (e.g. the Variscan fold and thrust belt beneath the European Atlantic margin).

With the exception of the Urals and Sayan-Tuva fold belts, all of the 16 provinces with >3 bn boe had their last phase of deformation in the Tertiary. The age of the last phase of deformation is important when considering the likelihood of post-charge modification of traps and potential seal failure. It is therefore not surprising that both the Ural and Sayan-Tuva fold belts have salt seals that have helped to maintain trap integrity over lengthy periods of geological time. The inset graph of fold and thrust belts with pre-Tertiary ages of deformation shows that they are strongly gas dominated (Fig. 6). This is not a surprise, as the greater the age of deformation, the more likely it is that the source rock will have entered the gas window as a result of post-orogenic burial.

Source rock age in fold and thrust belts

The age of the primary source rock in each of the fold and thrust belts has also been analysed. Cretaceous source rocks, which also source the Zagros Fold Belt, account for nearly 75% of all fold and thrust belt reserves (Fig. 7). Even with the Zagros Fold Belt excluded, Cretaceous source rocks are still the volumetrically most significant and have an oil:gas ratio of 70:30. The next most significant source rocks are the Oligocene (dominantly oil), the Devonian (primarily gas), the Jurassic (oil:gas ratio 50:50) and the Permian (oil dominant). Not surprisingly, the pre-Mesozoic source rocks tend to have produced more gas than oil reserves, which does not necessarily imply any correlation with the type of source rock. It probably has more to do with the greater likelihood of being more thermally mature as a result of greater burial since deposition. The geographical distribution of source rock ages in fold and thrust belts are shown in Figure 8.

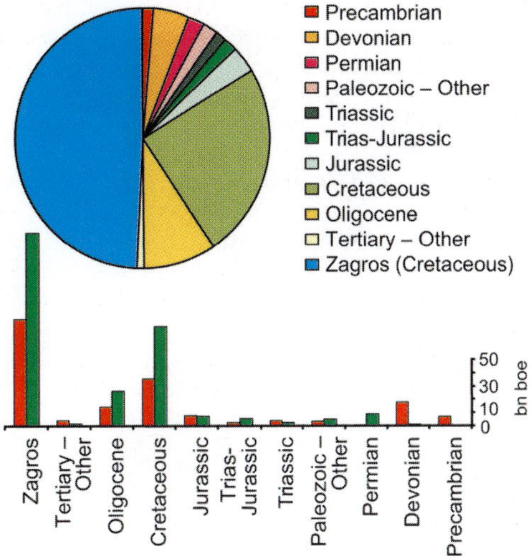

Fig. 7. Graphs of the distribution of hydrocarbon reserves in fold and thrust belts grouped by the age of the source rock (Table 1). The pie chart shows the total reserves for each grouping of source rock age. The other graph shows the distribution of hydrocarbon type for each grouping of source rock age. Green, oil and condensate in bn bbl; red, gas in bn boe.

Reserves by deformation style

Deformation style strongly influences the distribution of reserves within fold and thrust belts. The parameters captured in the summary table (Table 1) that influence deformation style include whether the fold and thrust belt is thin or thick skinned, the presence of a salt seal, the presence of a salt detachment and whether the fold and thrust belt is buried or not.

Giant fields are often hosted by simple structures in fold and thrust belts. The key factors in determining the likelihood of their existence

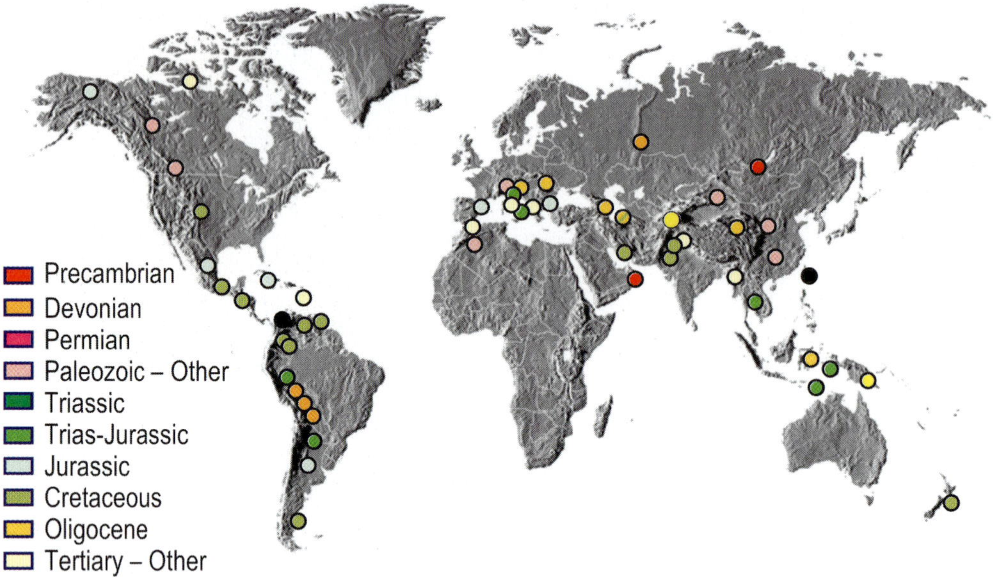

Fig. 8. Map showing the distribution of the age of the source rock in fold and thrust belts reviewed (Table 1). Where more than one age of source rocks is a significant contributor both colours are shown on the symbol as diagonal stripes.

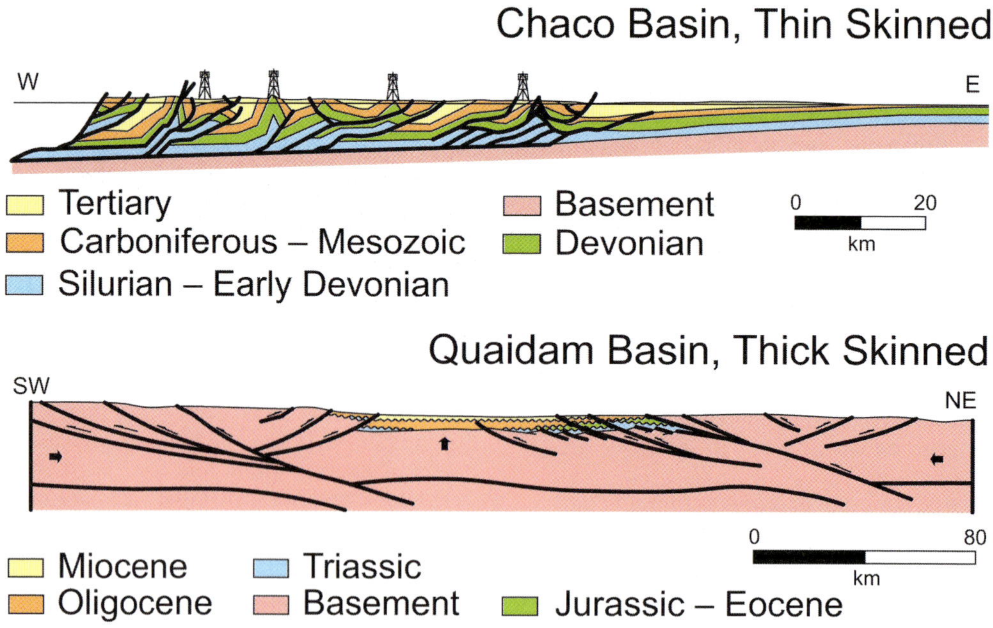

Fig. 9. Cross-sections through examples of thin- and thick-skinned fold and thrust belts to illustrate characteristic geometries. The thin-skinned Chaco Basin section is modified from Moretti *et al.* (1996); the thick-skinned Quaidam Basin section from the Altun Shan fold belt is modified from Qinmin & Coward (1990).

include the presence of a thick competent unit (e.g. >2 km of carbonate) in the hanging wall, thus encouraging simple box folds (e.g. the Zagros Fold Belt), and the depth to detachment for the system. These data have been captured in Table 1 but have not been analysed in detail.

Thin-skinned, thick-skinned or both thin- and thick-skinned. For the analysis of the thin- or thick-skinned style of deformation the dominant style of the productive structures has been considered, as opposed to considering the style of all structures in the fold and thrust belt. The deformation is considered to be thick skinned if it involves a significant thickness of the crust (Coward 1983), which usually implies that the basal detachment is within crystalline basement (Cooper 1996). Figure 9 shows type examples of thin- and thick-skinned deformation in fold and thrust belts.

Thin-skinned deformation accounts for *c.* 60% of reserves in fold and thrust belts excluding the Zagros Fold Belt (Fig. 10). The Zagros Fold Belt shows both thick- and thin-skinned deformation, based on the recent work of Blanc *et al.* (2003). The thick-skinned fold and thrust belts have a slightly higher oil:gas ratio in comparison with thin-skinned fold and thrust belts, but neither differs significantly from the overall oil:gas ratio in fold and thrust belts (Fig. 1). The geographical distribution of thin-skinned, thick-skinned and mixed fold and thrust belts is shown in Figure 11.

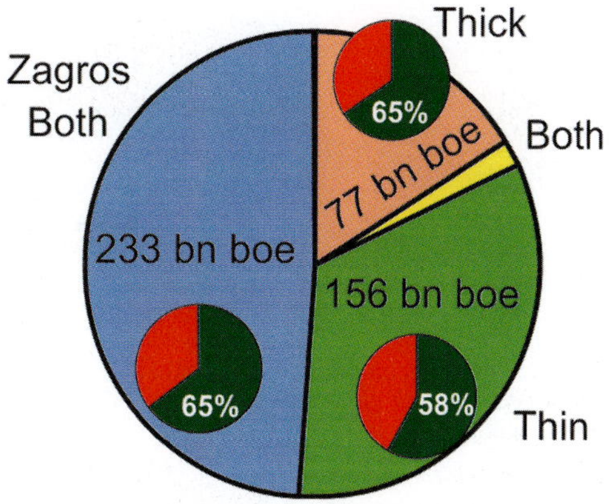

Fig. 10. Graph of the distribution of hydrocarbon reserves in fold and thrust belts grouped by thin- or thick-skinned deformation style (Table 1). The pie chart shows the total reserves for each grouping of deformation style; total volumes are labeled on the pie chart segments. The smaller pie charts indicate the proportions of oil and condensate to gas for each deformation style with the percentage of oil and condensate labelled. Green, oil and condensate; red, gas.

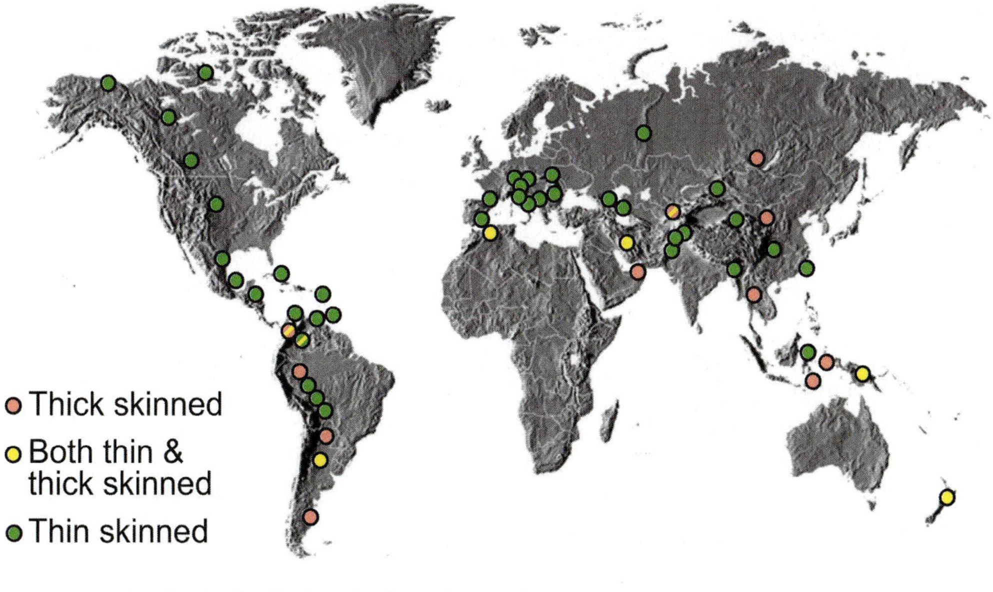

Fig. 11. Map showing the distribution of deformation style in the fold and thrust belts reviewed (Table 1). Where more than one deformation style is present the symbol shows diagonally striped colours representing the two deformation styles.

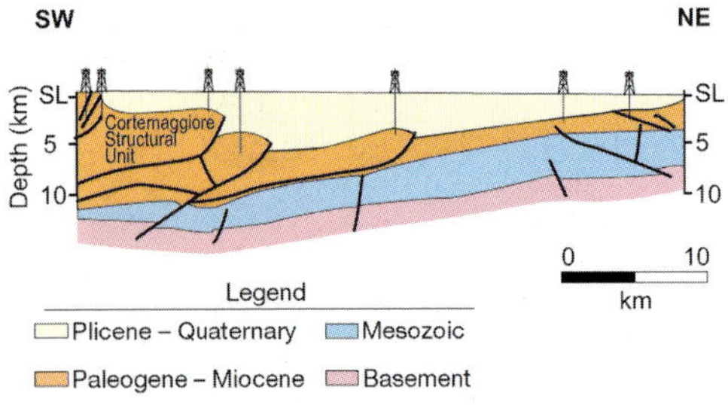

Fig. 12. Cross-section through the Northern Apennines, an example of a buried fold and thrust belt; modified from Pieri (1992).

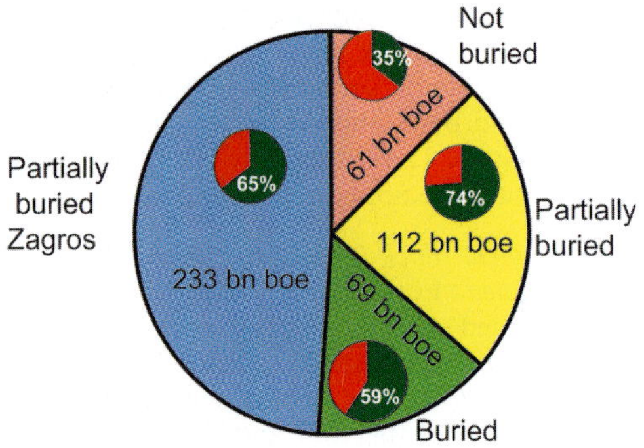

Fig. 13. Graph of the distribution of hydrocarbon reserves in fold and thrust belts grouped by burial state (Table 1). The pie chart shows the total reserves for each grouping of burial state; total volumes are labeled on the pie chart segments. The smaller pie charts indicate the proportions of oil and condensate to gas for each burial state with the percentage of oil and condensate labelled. Green, oil and condensate; red, gas.

Burial of fold belts. Another aspect of geometry and deformation history and style that was examined is whether or not the fold and thrust belt has been buried by either syn- or post-depositional sediments, exemplified by the Northern Apennines (Fig. 12). Normally, thrusting is associated with elevation and the simple structures of the frontal zones form last and will post-date the significant loading and hydrocarbon generation. Burial, however, encourages maturation of the source after trap formation if the source was either immature or early mature during the deformation.

Partially buried fold and thrust belts dominate the reserves distribution even when the partially buried Zagros Fold Belt is excluded from consideration (Fig. 13). Oil is the most important hydrocarbon type in partially buried fold and thrust belts (Fig. 3). Fold and thrust belts, that are buried, are strongly dominated by oil, and those that are not buried are dominated by gas (Fig. 13). The geographical distribution of the different classes of burial by sediment in fold and thrust belts is shown in Figure 14.

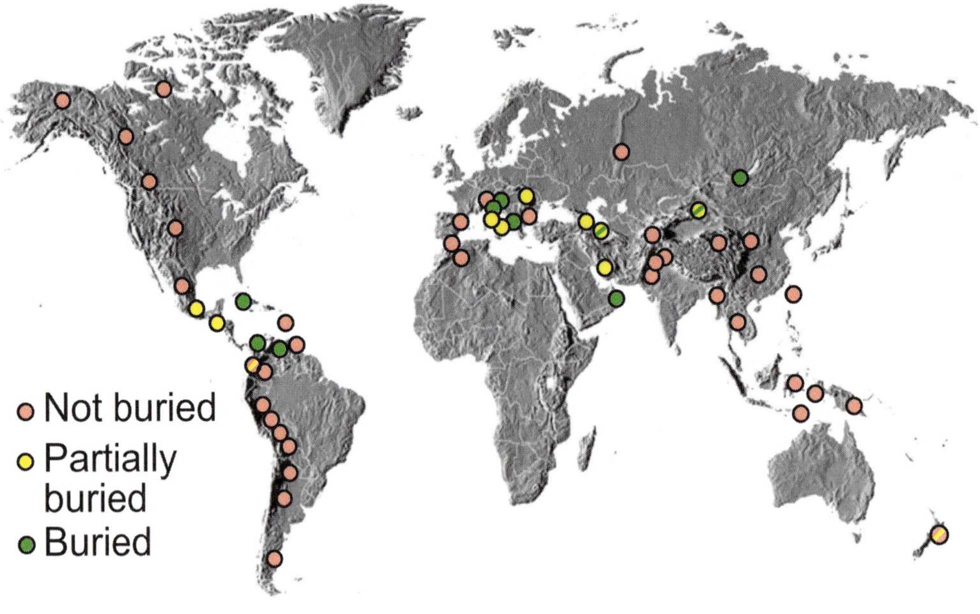

Fig. 14. Map showing the distribution of burial state in the fold and thrust belts reviewed (Table 1). Where more than one burial state is present the symbol shows diagonally striped colours representing the two burial states.

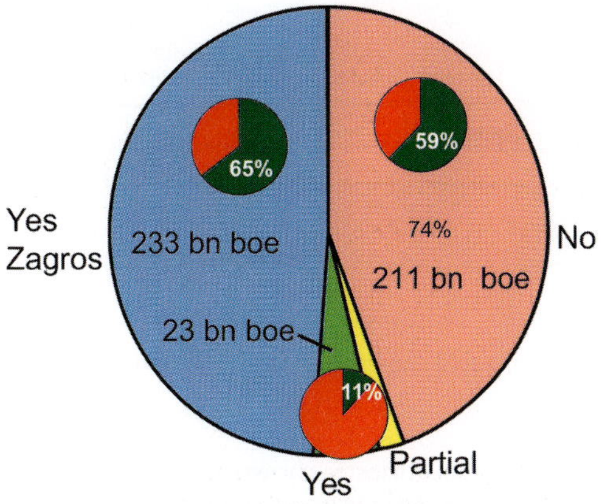

Fig. 15. Graph of the distribution of hydrocarbon reserves in fold and thrust belts grouped by presence of salt seal (Table 1). The pie chart shows the total reserves for each grouping of seal type; total volumes are labelled on the pie chart segments. The smaller pie charts indicate the proportions of oil and condensate to gas for each seal type with the percentage of oil and condensate labelled. Green, oil and condensate; red, gas.

Salt Seals in fold and thrust belts. The presence of a salt top seal in fold and thrust belts is not significant in the reserves distribution, with the notable exception of the Zagros Fold Belt, which is oil dominant (Fig. 15). The other fold and thrust belts that have salt top seals are very strongly gas-prone, which is possibly due to the effectiveness of the salt seal in retaining a gas charge, and the majority have a Palaeogene or earlier final phase of deformation. In fold and thrust belts with no salt seal, oil is the dominant hydrocarbon type (Fig. 15). The geographical distribution of salt seals in fold and thrust belts is shown in Figure 16.

Salt detachments in fold and thrust belts. The presence of a salt detachment in a fold and thrust belt has a strong influence on the deformation style, tending to favour thin-skinned structures as a result of the efficiency of the detachment (Fig. 17). The Zagros Fold Belt is problematic in this analysis, as a recent paper (Blanc *et al.* 2003) suggested that the Vendian–Cambrian Hormuz Salt is present only in the SE part of the Zagros Fold Belt, which is less petroliferous (Fig. 18). Fold and thrust belts with no salt detachment dominate the reserves, excluding the Zagros Fold Belt; in fold and thrust belts with no salt detachment the oil:gas ratio is *c.* 50:50, in contrast to fold and thrust belts with a salt detachment, where the oil:gas ratio is about 80:20 (Fig. 18). This could perhaps be due to the salt detachment inhibiting the migration of gas from secondary deeper and more mature source rock horizons beneath the salt detachment into the traps located above the detachment. The geographical

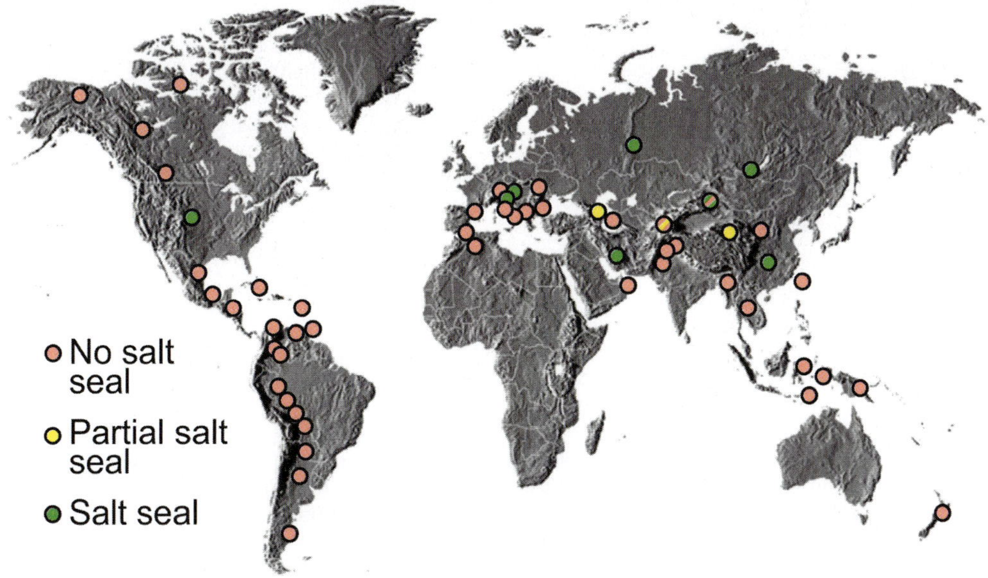

Fig. 16. Map showing the distribution of seal type in the fold and thrust belts reviewed (Table 1). Where more than one seal type is present the symbol shows diagonally striped colours representing the two seal types.

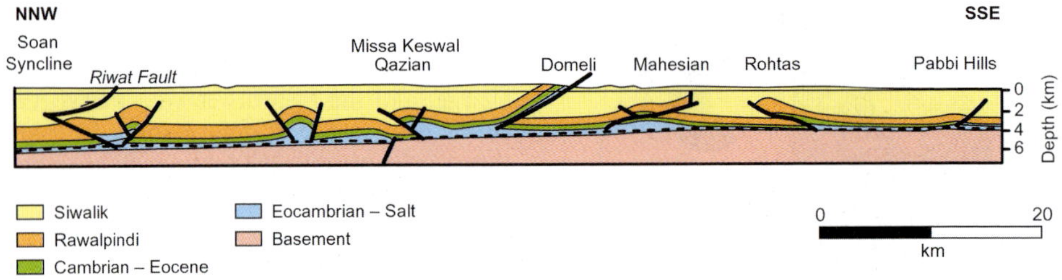

Fig. 17. Cross-section through the Potwar Fold Belt, an example of a fold and thrust belt with a salt detachment; modified from Pennock *et al.* (1989).

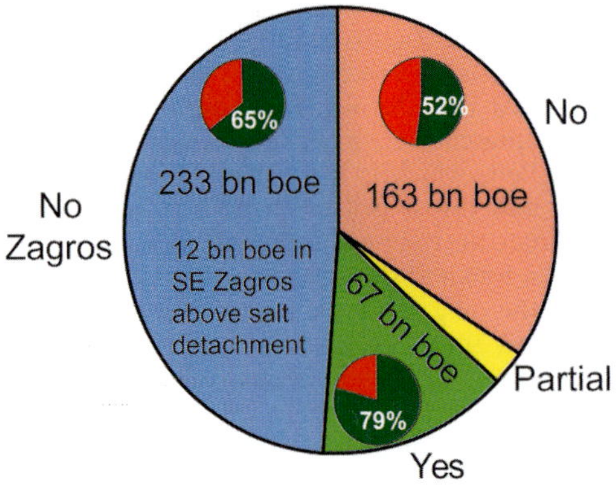

Fig. 18. Graph of the distribution of hydrocarbon reserves in fold and thrust belts grouped by presence of salt detachment (Table 1). The pie chart shows the total reserves for each grouping of detachment type; total volumes are labelled on the pie chart segments. The smaller pie charts indicate the proportions of oil and condensate to gas for each detachment type with the percentage of oil and condensate labelled. Green, oil and condensate; red, gas.

distribution of salt detachments in fold and thrust belts is shown in Figure 19.

Reserves distribution based on deformation style. The four factors discussed above in this section all contribute to the deformation styles observed in fold and thrust belts. A classification of fold and thrust belts based on these four factors has been developed and the fold and thrust belts reviewed have been assigned to the appropriate classification category. The classification uses the factors in the following sequence and coded by a single letter as indicated in parentheses, thick- or thin-skinned (K, thick; T, thin; B, both), burial (Y, yes; N, no; P, partial), salt seal (Y, yes; N, no; P, partial) and salt detachment (Y, yes; N, no; P, partial). The reserves distribution is shown in Table 3 and geographical distribution of the different categories is shown in Figure 20. The Zagros Fold Belt is dominated by oil and is both thick- and thin-skinned, partially buried, has a salt seal and no salt detachment and thus has the classification code of BPYN.

Other categories that favour significant oil reserves are fold and thrust belts that are:

- thin-skinned (T), partially buried (P), no salt seal (N), salt detachment (Y) (TPNY 50.9 bn bbls); >99% of these reserves are in the Reforma Fold Belt (Table 1);
- thin-skinned (T), buried (Y), no salt seal (N), no salt detachment (N) (TYNN 22.6 bn bbls); >99% of these reserves are in the Maturin Fold Belt (Table 1);
- thick-skinned (K), partially buried(P), no salt seal (N), no salt detachment (N) (KPNN 18.8 bn bbls); all of these reserves are in a part of the Caucasus Fold Belt (Tables 1 and 3);
- thick-skinned (K), buried (Y), no salt seal (N), no salt detachment (N) (KYNN 17.2 bn bbls); reserves are in parts of the Caucasus and Tien Shan Fold Belts (Tables 1 and 3).

Significant gas reserves are found in the following fold and thrust belt types:

- thin-skinned (T), unburied (N), no salt seal (N), no salt detachment (N) (TNNN 20.5 bn boe); >60% of these reserves are in the Chaco Fold Belt (Table 1);
- thin-skinned (T), buried (Y), no salt seal (N), no salt detachment (N) (TYNN 17.4 bn boe); >99% of these reserves are in the Maturin Fold Belt (Table 1);
- thick-skinned (K), partially buried (P), no salt seal (N), no salt detachment (N) (KPNN 11.0 bn boe); all of these reserves are in a part of the Caucasus Fold Belt (Tables 1 and 3);
- thin-skinned (T), partially buried (P), no salt seal (N), salt detachment (Y) (TPNY 10.9 bn boe); >99% of these reserves are in the Reforma Fold Belt (Table 1).

Clearly, the categories that favour large oil reserves also favour large gas reserves and in terms of total reserves the top four categories excluding the Zagros Fold Belt are as follows.

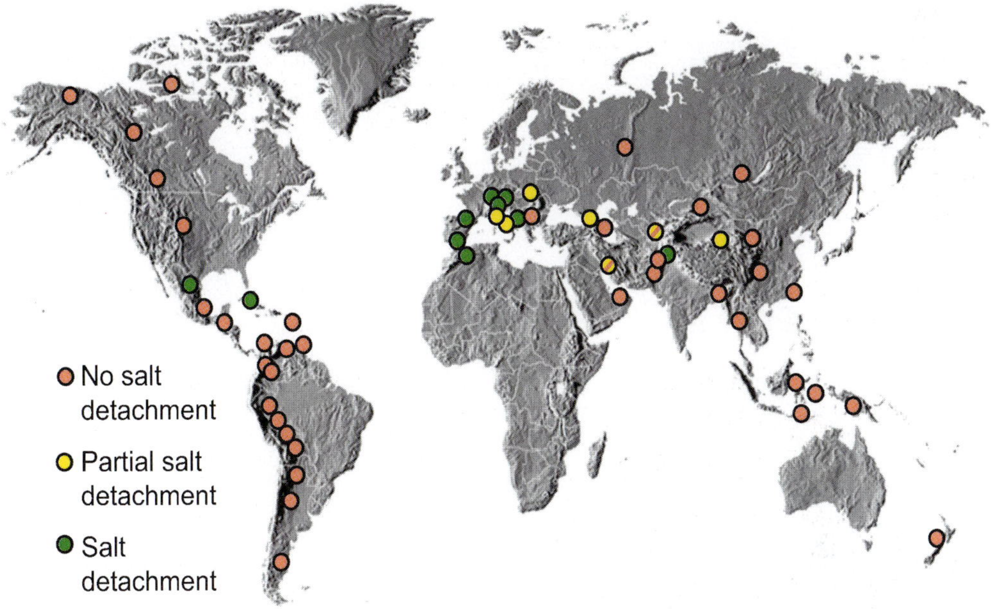

Fig. 19. Map showing the distribution of detachment type in the fold and thrust belts reviewed (Table 1). Where more than one detachment type is present the symbol shows diagonally striped colours representing the two detachment types.

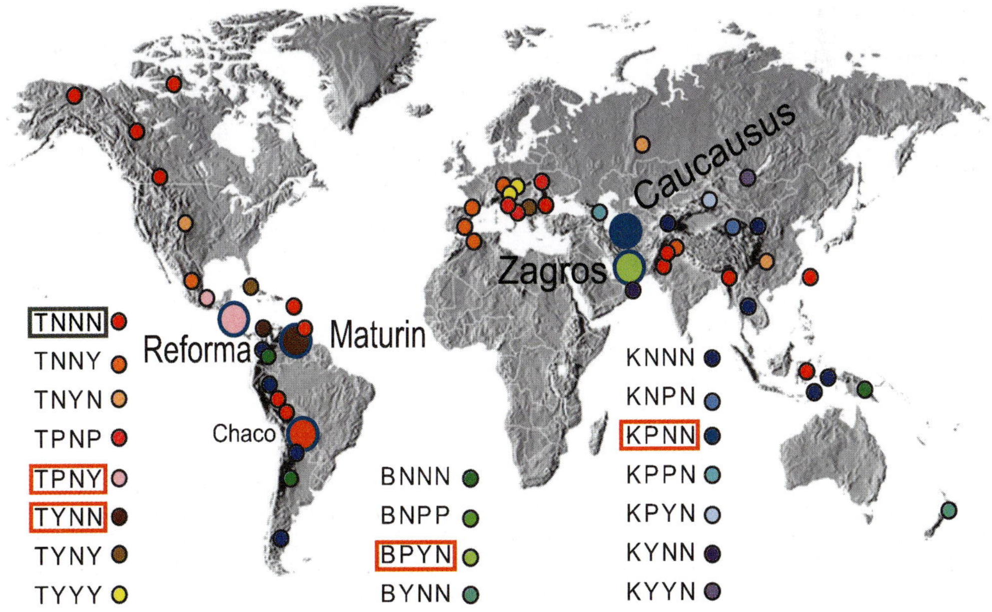

Fig. 20. Map showing the distribution of deformation style in the fold and thrust belts reviewed (Table 3). Where more than one deformation style is present the symbol shows only the colour of the predominant deformation style.

Table 3. *Classification of deformation style*

Thick or thin skinned	Burial	Salt seal	Salt detachment	Fold belts	Type code	Oil & condensate recoverable (mm bbl)	Gas recoverable (mm boe)
Thick & thin skinned	Unburied	No salt seal	No salt detachment	Llanos (part), Malargue–Agrio, Papuan, New Zealand (part)	BNNN	3763	3802
Thick & thin skinned	Unburied	No salt seal	Salt detachment	Atlas	BNNY	94	107
Thick & thin skinned	Unburied	Partial salt seal	Partial salt detachment	Gissar (part)	BNPP	244	1072
Thick & thin skinned	Partially buried	Salt seal	No salt detachment	Zagros	BPYN	152170	80338
Thick & thin skinned	Buried	No salt seal	No salt detachment	New Zealand (part)	BYNN	36	68
Thick skinned	Unburied	No salt seal	No salt detachment	Cuyo, E Cordillera (part), San Bernado, Ucayali, Seram, Timor, Gissar (part), Loei Phetchabun, Qilian Shan	KNNN	7263	1606
Thick skinned	Unburied	Partial salt seal	No salt detachment	Altun Shan	KNPN	664	554
Thick skinned	Partially buried	No salt seal	No salt detachment	Caucasus (part)	KPNN	18821	11002
Thick skinned	Partially buried	Partial salt seal	No salt detachment	Dagestan	KPPN	3897	1386
Thick skinned	Partially buried	Salt seal	No salt detachment	Tien Shan (part)	KPYN	2104	1995
Thick skinned	Buried	No salt seal	No salt detachment	Caucasus (part), Tien Shan (part), Oman	KYNN	17249	3556
Thick skinned	Buried	Salt seal	No salt detachment	Sayan-Tuva	KYYN	267	6540
Thin skinned	Unburied	No salt seal	No salt detachment	Balkan, Beni, Chaco, Madre de Dios, Llanos (part), Arctic, Banggai, NE Caribbean, Trinidad, Assam, Kirthar, Sulaiman, N Rockies, Rockies (Can), Taiwan	TNNN	5998	20532
Thin skinned	Unburied	No salt seal	Salt detachment	Betic, Jura, Pyrenees, Potwar, Sierra Madre Orientale	TNNY	1044	2374
Thin skinned	Unburied	Salt seal	No salt detachment	Yunan Guizhou, Utah–Wyoming, Urals	TNYN	2517	9614
Thin skinned	Partially buried	No salt seal	Partial salt detachment	Carpathians, N Apennines, S Apennines	TPNP	6653	4158
Thin skinned	Partially buried	No salt seal	Salt detachment	Reforma, Veracruz	TPNY	50895	10883
Thin skinned	Buried	No salt seal	No salt detachment	Guajira, Maturin, E Cordillera (part)	TYNN	22612	17445
Thin skinned	Buried	No salt seal	Salt detachment	Dinarides, Hellenides, Cuban	TYNY	970	238
Thin skinned	Buried	Salt seal	Salt detachment	E Alps, S Alps	TYYY	35	203

• thin-skinned (T), partially buried (P), no salt seal (N), salt detachment (Y) (TPNY 61.8 bn boe); >99% of these reserves are in the Reforma Fold belt (Table 1);

• thin-skinned (T), buried (Y), no salt seal (N), no salt detachment (N) (TYNN 40.1 bn boe); >99% of these reserves are in the Maturin Fold Belt (Table 1). It should be noted that this deformation style would also include the fold and thrust belts that develop as the contractional toes to extensional systems on continental margins. These fold belts have become important hydrocarbon provinces (e.g. the deep-water Gulf of Mexico, deep-water Niger Delta and Brazil), but were excluded from this review as discussed above.

• thin-skinned (T), unburied (N), no salt seal (N), no salt detachment (N) (TNNN 30.3 bn boe); 47% of these reserves are in the Chaco Fold Belt (Table 1).

• thick-skinned (K), partially buried (P), no salt seal (N), no salt detachment (N) (KPNN 29.8 bn boe); all of these reserves are in a part of the Caucasus Fold Belt (Tables 1 and 3).

This provides some insights into the types of fold and thrust belt that should be explored if significant reserves or a particular hydrocarbon type are desired. One constant factor is that, except for the Zagros Fold Belt, a salt seal does not appear to be necessary for significant reserves to be present. What is particularly striking is that in most of the categories discussed above, there is one fold and thrust belt that dominates the reserves in the category. The only exception is the TNNN category, where, although the Chaco Fold Belt accounts for a high proportion of the reserves, a number of other fold belts also contribute significant reserves (Table 3). The data suggest that, based on deformation style, prolific hydrocarbons occur in fold belts that are thin-skinned with no salt detachment or salt seal. Whether or not the thin-skinned fold and thrust belt is buried does not appear to be a critical factor.

A key observation from this analysis is that the six most richly endowed fold and thrust belts have no common set of deformation style attributes. The conclusion is that deformation style attributes are not critical factors in controlling the hydrocarbon endowment of fold and thrust belts and that the non-structural elements of the petroleum system are more important in determining hydrocarbon endowment.

Gas- and oil-prone thrust belts

The characteristics of gas- or oil-prone fold and thrust belts are based on total gas and oil reserves rather than the number of fold and thrust belts dominated by each hydrocarbon type. Whether a fold and thrust belt is thin- or thick-skinned does not appear to be a critical factor in determining the dominant hydrocarbon type; however, the other factors described above definitely are.

• Gas-prone fold and thrust belts are characterized by a pre-Palaeogene age of the last deformation phase, Palaeozoic source rocks, a salt seal, no salt detachment and are not at present buried by syn- or post-orogenic sediment.

• Oil-prone fold and thrust belts are characterized by a Cenozoic age of the last deformation phase, post-Jurassic source rocks; no salt seal (excepting the Zagros Fold Belt), a salt detachment and are currently buried or partially buried by syn- or post-orogenic sediment.

This very clear distinction provides a potential tool for the exploration of fold and thrust belts where a particular hydrocarbon type is the goal of the exploration programme. In the author's opinion the most important factor is the age of the last deformation.

Exploring petroleum systems in fold and thrust belts

The area of a fold and thrust belt that is most prospective for hydrocarbons is the external foothills belt between the leading thrust of the internal zone and the limit of thrusting in the foreland basin, whether emergent or buried. Commercial quantities of oil and gas have been discovered in almost 50 fold and thrust belts (Table 1). Predictably, fields are aligned parallel to the structural trend. Structural traps are usually present throughout the belt, yet hydrocarbon reserves tend to be located in a fairly discrete zone within the thrust belt. In many cases the productive region is a band along the external fringe of the thrust belt. This is because normally the generation and expulsion front moves ahead of the deformation front and the normal asymmetry of the basin encourages migration into the foreland. As a result, there is a stronger possibility of the frontal thrust creating a giant field (>250 mm boe) than for structures that are further back from the thrust front.

Toward the hinterland (internal region of the orogenic belt), the reservoir horizons tend to be breached and flushed, older source rocks may be overmature, and younger source rocks, present in the clastic foredeep, may be absent. Toward the foreland (external region of the orogenic belt) of the productive trend, the reservoir horizons tend to be depositionally thinner, the source rocks may be immature, the young source rocks may overlie the reservoir, and the structural traps may be small or absent.

Thrust belts have long been considered difficult areas in which to explore for hydrocarbons. One of the reasons for this view is the difficulty of predicting subsurface structure. However, the key risk in many fold and thrust belts is whether trap formation predated hydrocarbon generation. Many of the hydrocarbons generated end up in the foreland in stratigraphic traps, in tar belts and within old structures buried beneath the foreland basin sediments. This problem is summarized below.

• Thrust systems elevate rocks above their regional elevation, thus potentially removing the source rocks from the generating window (A in Fig. 21).

• If the source is intra-thrust sheet then only at the trailing edges will the source be still at regional elevation and capable of generating hydrocarbons. The available fetch will depend on thrust sheet size and will be degraded as displacement increases because less source volume will still be at regional elevation (B and B′ in Fig. 21).

• If the source is in the roof sequence the same problems as for intra-horse sourcing apply and communication with the reservoir may be difficult to achieve (C in Fig. 21).

• If the source is in the footwall similar problems apply but in addition migration pathways will be limited by the availability of across-fault juxtapositions of reservoir and source (D in Fig. 21).

• The system will work if subsequent burial of the thrust belt, by syn-orogenic sediments, puts the entire system, including source and traps, in the maturity window. In this case, traps predate the generation and migration of hydrocarbons.

• The system will work if the thrusting is synchronous with, or shortly post-dated rapid burial by, foreland basin sediment. The loading effect of the thrust belt creates the accommodation space in the foreland basin, which is then progressively cannibalized by the prograding thrust system. In this case, the structures develop as the source rocks are in the maturity window; much of the early charge may migrate into the foreland basin but the later charge is trapped.

• The system will work if the thrusting is responsible for pushing the source into the generation window (E in Fig. 21).

Despite having potential source and reservoir rocks several of the fold and thrust belts included in this review have only modest resource endowments (Table 1), probably because of problems with the timing of maturation and structuration. The really prolific fold and thrust belts, with >10 bn boe of reserves (Zagros, Reforma, Maturin, Caucasus, Chaco and Tien Shan), all have world-class source rocks. A good rule of thumb is that one discovery in a particular structural zone of a fold and thrust belt mitigates the primary risk, timing of maturation and migration in relation to trap formation, and normally there will be a number of other accumulations.

Future potential in fold and thrust belts

To assess the future potential of fold and thrust belts, the data in the USGS 2000 World Petroleum Assessment were used (USGS 2000). Unfortunately, this assessment covers only selected hydrocarbon provinces and thus does not provide a complete dataset of yet-to-find (YTF) resource estimates. For those fold and thrust belts where an assessment did exist, a maturity index was calculated, which is the

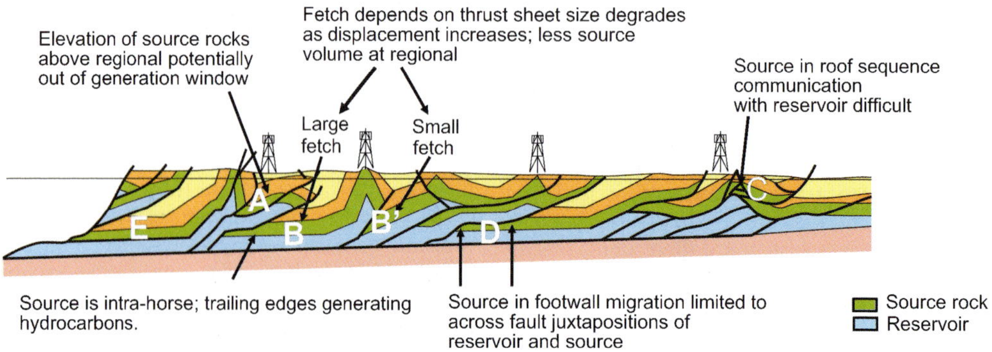

Fig. 21. Cross-section based on Figure 9 annotated to illustrate different configurations of structural geometry and source rock position (see text for discussion).

YTF % of the sum of the discovered reserves and the YTF; the higher this number is the less mature the exploration of the fold and thrust belt (Table 1). All fold and thrust belts that have a yet-to-find resource estimate of >2 bn boe were compiled into Table 4. Two fold and thrust belts were added to Table 4 for which no YTF numbers were available from the USGS but which are believed to offer significant additional resource potential. The location of the fold and thrust belts is shown on the world map (Fig. 22). Many of the thrust belts in Table 4 remain relatively poorly explored for a number of reasons that include remote location (Gissar, Tien Shan) and limited or lack of access for international oil companies (Zagros, Reforma).

The advent of technology that allows production in ultra-deep water over the last 20 years has driven exploration of the fold and thrust belts that develop as the contractional toes of extensional systems on passive margins (Rowan *et al.* 2004). Some of these systems host significant reserves; for example, the Gulf of Mexico fold belts, the toe of the Niger Delta and deep-water Brazil. These and other similar areas still offer significant undiscovered resource potential.

Conclusions

This paper presents a statistical summary of reserves in fold and thrust belts based primarily on an IHS dataset of reserves for discovered fields to which a number of geological attributes have been added (Table 1). This provides a powerful summary dataset of the key geological characteristics of the fold belts included in the review, which has been used to interrogate the IHS dataset. The analysis of the data has identified which of the world's fold and thrust belts are the most prolific hydrocarbon provinces and the attributes of these provinces. The most prolific fold and thrust belt is the Zagros Fold Belt, which accounts for 49% of all reserves in fold and thrust belts, and the Zagros Fold Belt has, as a result, been isolated during the analysis to avoid skewing the other conclusions.

Fold and thrust belts represent an average sample of the world's hydrocarbon resources and have a virtually identical oil:gas:condensate ratio to the global resource endowment. Fold and thrust belts are oil prone (59% oil) because they are an almost perfect representation of an oil-prone world. Excluding the Zagros Fold Belt, most of the reserves are contained in fold and thrust belts that are thin-skinned, have no salt detachment or salt seal, are partially buried by syn- or post-orogenic sediments, are sourced by Cretaceous source rocks and underwent the last phase of deformation during the Tertiary. The particularly telling observation, however, is that the top six most richly endowed fold and thrust belts have no common set of structural

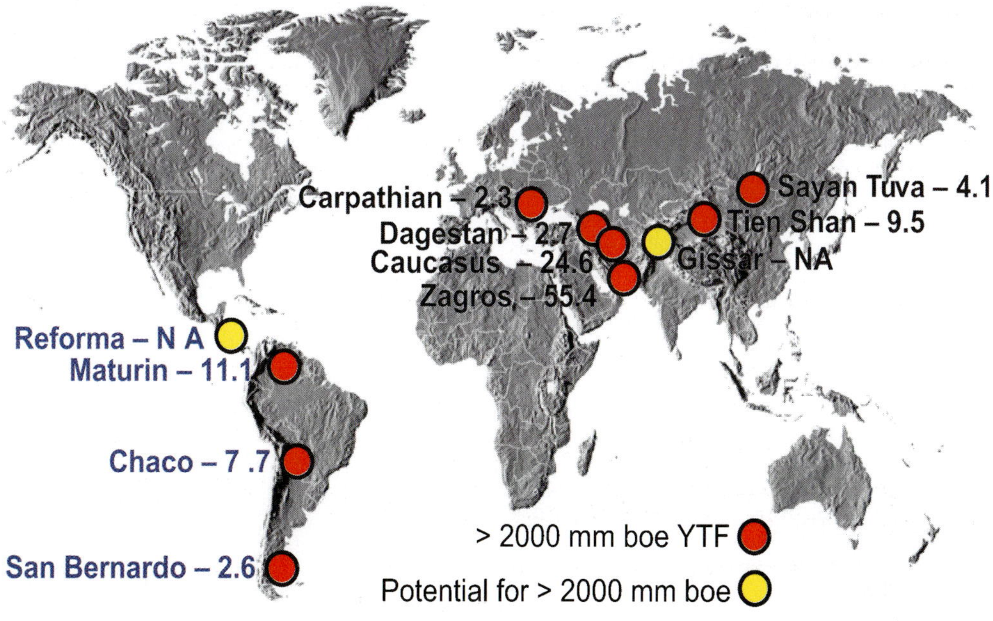

Fig. 22. Map of fold and thrust belts that offer >2000 mm boe of yet-to-find (YTF) resources (Table 4). NA, not applicable.

Table 4. *Future potential of fold and thrust belts*

Fold belt	Oil + condensate (mm bbl)	Gas (mm boe)	Total (mm boe)	Oil or gas	Maturity index	YTF (mm boe)
Zagros Fold Belt	152170	80338	232508	O	24	55452
Caucasus Fold Belt	26954	13973	40927	O	60	24578
Maturin Fold Belt	22612	17370	39982	O	28	11084
Tien Shan Fold Belt	11214	2576	13789	O	69	9484
Chaco Fold Belt	2033	12034	14067	G	55	7669
Sayan-Tuva Fold Belt	267	6540	6807	G	61	4138
Dagestan Fold Belt	3897	1386	5283	O	51	2717
San Bernardo Fold Belt	4637	984	5621	O	46	2577
Carpathian Thrust Belt	5643	1785	7428	O	31	2280
Gissar Fold Belt	1113	1347	2459	G	n.a.	n.a.
Reforma Fold Belt	50765	10641	61406	O	n.a.	n.a.

YTF, yet-to-find; n.a., not applicable.

attributes. The top six also fall into an attribute set that may also be shared with other fold and thrust belts but within which they dominate, making up >90% of the reserves within the attribute set. This implies that the resource-rich fold and thrust belts all have a unique combination of characteristics that is not necessarily repeatable in others. This also implies that structural attributes are not the critical factor controlling the distribution of hydrocarbon reserves in fold and thrust belts. If the structural attributes of fold and thrust belts are not critical factors in resource endowment then what are the critical factors? In common with other prolific petroleum provinces, these are the presence of a world-class source rock and the presence of a regionally effective reservoir–seal couplet. The Zagros Fold Belt illustrates this perfectly; the most prolific fold and thrust belt is essentially the deformed NE margin of the Arabian Basin, the world's most prolific petroleum province, with which it shares many petroleum system elements. Thus there is nothing intrinsic in fold and thrust belts that differentiates them from other oil- and gas-rich provinces other than the prolific development of potential hydrocarbon traps. The very distinctive characteristics of oil-prone and gas-prone fold and thrust belts offers a potential tool for targeting a particular hydrocarbon type.

The success or failure of hydrocarbon exploration in a fold and thrust belt is primarily controlled by the relative timing of source rock maturation, hydrocarbon migration and trap development; unless the timing is favourably configured it is unlikely that exploration will be successful. The analysis of the maturity index shows that many of the prolific fold and thrust belts still have significant remaining upside; remote location and politically challenging access have limited opportunities for this potential to be realized.

I wish to thank M. Warren and J. Squires for their valuable comments on the evolving drafts of the manuscript, M. Allen for discussions on the Zagros Fold Belt, IHS for the use of their reserves database, and EnCana Corporation for permission to publish this paper. C. Kluth is thanked for a constructive review, and F. Peel made a number of insightful comments and recommendations that substantially improved the final version of this paper.

References

Abrams, M. A. & Narimanov, A. A. 1997. Geochemical evaluation of hydrocarbons and their potential sources in the western South Caspian depression, Republic of Azerbaijan. *Marine and Petroleum Geology*, **14**, 451–468.

Anelli, M., Mattavelli, L. & Pieri, M. 1996. Structural–stratigraphic evolution of Italy and its petroleum systems. *In*: Ziegler, P. A. & Horvath, F. (eds) *Peri-Tethys, Memoir 2 : Structure and Prospects of Alpine Basins and Forelands*. Mémoires du Muséum National d'Histoire Naturelle, **170**, 455–483.

ANWR Assessment Team US Geological Survey (eds) 1998. *The Oil and Gas Resource Potential of the Arctic National Wildlife Refuge 1002 Area, Alaska*. US Geological Survey Open-File Report **98–34**.

Babaie, H. A., Speed, R. C., Larue, D. K. & Claypool, G. E. 1992. Source rock and maturation evaluation of the Barbados accretionary prism. *Marine and Petroleum Geology*, **9**, 623–632.

Baby, P., Moretti, I., Guillier, B., Limachi, R., Mendez, E., Oller, J. V. & Specht, M. 1995. Petroleum system of the northern and central Sub-Andean zone. *In*: Tankard, A. J., Suarez Soruco, R. & Welsink, H. J. (eds) *Petroleum Basins of South*

America. American Association of Petroleum Geologists, Memoirs, **62**, 445–458.

BALL, M. M., MARTIN, R. G., BOCK, W. D. *et al.* 1985. Seismic structure and stratigraphy of northern edge of Bahaman–Cuban Collision Zone. *AAPG Bulletin*, **69**, 1275–1294.

BALLY, A. W., GORDY, P. L. & STEWART, G. A. 1966. Structure, seismic data and orogenic evolution of southern Canadian Rocky Mountains. *Bulletin of Canadian Petroleum Geology*, **14**, 337–381.

BALLY, A. W., BURBI, L., COOPER, C. & GHELARDONI, R. 1988. Balanced cross sections and seismic reflection profiles across the Central Apennines. *Memorie della Società Geologica Italiana*, **35**, 257–310.

BASTIA, R., NAIK, G. C. & MOHAPATRA, P. 1993. Hydrocarbon prospects of Schuppen belt–Assam: Arakan Basin. *In*: BISWAS, S. K., DAVE, A., GARG, P., PANDEY, J., MAITHANI, A. & THOMAS, N. J. (eds) *Proceedings 2nd Seminar on Petroliferous Basins of India. K. D. Malviya Institute of Petroleum Exploration, Oil and Natural Gas Corporation Limited, Dehra Dun, 18–20 December 1991, 1 (East Coast, Andaman and Assam–Arakan Basins)*, 493–506

BEAUCHAMP, W., BARAZANGI, M., DEMNATI, A. & EL ALJI, M. 1996. Intracontinental rifting and inversion: the Missour Basin and Atlas Mountains of Morocco. *AAPG Bulletin*, **80**, 1459–1482.

BEAUCHAMP, W., ALLMENDINGER, R. W., BARAZANGI, M., DEMNATI A. & EL ALJI, M. 1999. Inversion tectonics and the evolution of the High Atlas Mountains, Morocco, based on a geological–geophysical transect. *Tectonics*, **18**(2), 163.

BERBERIAN, M. 1995. Master 'blind' thrust faults hidden under the Zagros Fold Belt fold; active basement tectonics and surface morphotectonics. *Tectonophysics*, **241**, 193–224.

BEYDOUN, Z. R., HUGHES CLARKE, M. W. & STONELEY, R. 1992. Petroleum in the Zagros Basin: a Late Tertiary foreland basin overprinted onto the outer edge of a vast hydrocarbon-rich Paleozoic–Mesozoic passive-margin shelf. *In*: MACQUEEN, R. W. & LECKIE, D. A. (eds) *Foreland Basins and Fold Belts*. American Association of Petroleum Geologists, Memoirs, **55**, 309–339.

BLANC, E. J. P., ALLEN, M. B., INGER, S. & HASSANI, H. 2003. Structural styles in the Zagros simple folded zone, Iran. *Journal of the Geological Society, London*, **160**, 401–412.

BLANKENSHIP, C. L. 1992. Structure and palaeogeography of the external Betic Cordillera, southern Spain. *Marine and Petroleum Geology*, **9**, 256–264.

BORDENAVE, M. L. & BURWOOD, R. 1990. Source rock distribution and maturation in the Zagros orogenic belt; provenance of the Asmari and Bangestan reservoir oil accumulations. *Organic Geochemistry*, **16**, 369–387.

BOURROUILH, R., RICHERT, J. P. & ZOLNAI, G. 1995. The North Pyrenean Aquitaine Basin, France: evolution and hydrocarbons. *AAPG Bulletin*, **79**, 831–853.

BOYER, S. E. & ELLIOTT, D. 1982. Thrust systems. *AAPG Bulletin*, **66**, 1196–1230.

BROOKFIELD, M. E. & HASHMAT, A. 2001. The geology and petroleum potential of the North Afghan Platform and adjacent areas (northern Afghanistan, with parts of southern Turkmenistan, Uzbekistan and Tajikistan). *Earth-Science Reviews*, **55**, 41–71.

CAMPOS, P. G., GRIMALT, J. O., BERDIE, L., LOPEZ-QUINTERO, J. O. & NAVARRETE-REYES, L. E. 1996. Organic geochemistry of Cuban oils 1: The northern geological province. *Organic Geochemistry*, **25**, 475–488.

CAZIER, E. C., HAYWARD, A. B., ESPINOSA, G., VELANDIA, J., MUGNIOT, J. F. & LEEL, W. G. 1995. Petroleum geology of the Cusiana field, Llanos Basin Foothills, Colombia. *AAPG Bulletin*, **79**, 1444–1463.

CHARLTON, T. R., BARBER, A. J. & BARKHAM, S. T. 1991. The structural evolution of the Timor collision complex, Eastern Indonesia. *Journal of Structural Geology*, **13**, 489–500.

CHEN, F., SUN, J., WANG, P., SUN, G. & LIU, J. 1987. Structural features and gas prospect of the fold thrust belt in the western margin of Ordos Basin. *Geoscience*, **1**, 103–113.

CHEN, S. F., WILSON, C. J. L., LUO, Z. L. & DENG, Q. D. 1994. The evolution of the western Sichuan Foreland Basin, southwestern China. *Journal of Southeast Asian Earth Sciences*, **10**, 159–168.

COLE, F., BIRD, K. J., MULL, C. G., WALLACE, W. K., SASSI, W., MURPHY, J. M. & LEE, M. 1998. A balanced cross section and kinematic and thermal model across the northeastern Brooks Range mountain front, Arctic National Wildlife Refuge, Alaska. *In*: ANWR Assessment Team US Geological Survey (eds) *The Oil and Gas Resource Potential of the Arctic National Wildlife Refuge, 1002 Area, Alaska*. US Geological Survey Open-File Report **98–34**.

COLLIER, R. J. & JOHNSTON, J. H. 1990. The identification of possible hydrocarbon source rocks, using biomarker geochemistry, in the Taranaki basin, New Zealand. *Journal of Southeast Asian Earth Sciences (New Zealand)*, **5**, 231–239.

COOPER, M. A. 1996. Passive-roof duplexes, and pseudo-passive-roof duplexes at mountain fronts: a review. *Bulletin of Canadian Petroleum Geology*, **44**, 410–421.

COOPER, M. A. 2000. Structural style variations in the BC Foothills. *GeoCanada 2000, Calgary, Alberta, May 2000 Convention Abstracts*, Abstract No. 466.

COOPER, M. A., HERBERT, R. & HILL, G. S. 1989. The structural evolution of Triassic intermontane basins in northern Thailand. *In*: THANASUTHIPAK, T. & OUNCHANUM, P. (eds) *Proceedings International Symposium on Intermontane Basins; Geology and Resources*. Chiang Mai University, Chiang Mai, Thailand, 231–242.

COOPER, M. A., ADDISON, F. T., ALVAREZ, R. *et al.* 1995. Basin development and tectonic history of the Llanos Basin, Eastern Cordillera, and Middle Magdalena Valley, Colombia. *AAPG Bulletin*, **79**, 1421–1443.

COOPER, M. A., BREALEY, C., FERMOR, P., GREEN, R. & MORRISON, M. 2004. Structural models of subsurface thrust-related folds in the foothills of British Columbia: case studies of sidetracked gas wells. *In*: McClay, K. R. (ed.) *Thrust Tectonics and Hydrocarbon Systems*. American Association of Petroleum Geologists, Memoirs, **82**, 579–597.

Courteney, S., Cockcroft, P., Phoa, R. S. K. & Wight, A. W. R. 1988. *Indonesia—Oil and Gas Fields Atlas, VI: Eastern Indonesia.* Indonesian Petroleum Association, Jakarta.

Coward, M. P. 1983. Thrust tectonics, thin-skinned or thick-skinned and the continuation of thrusts to deep in the crust. *Journal of Structural Geology*, **5**,113–125.

Coward, M. P., De Donatis, M., Mazzoli, S., Paltrinieri, W. & Wezel, F.-C. 1999. The frontal part of the northern Apennines foreland fold and thrust belt in the Romagna–Marche area (Italy): shallow and deep structural styles. *Tectonics*, **18**, 559–574.

Dahlstrom, C. D. A. 1970. Structural geology in the eastern margin of the Canadian Rocky Mountains. *Bulletin of Canadian Petroleum Geology*, **18**, 332–406.

Dellape, D. & Hegedus, A. 1995. Structural inversion and oil occurrence in the Cuyo Basin of Argentina. *In*: Tankard, A. J., Suarez Soruco, R. & Welsink, H. J. (eds) *Petroleum Basins of South America.* American Association of Petroleum Geologists, Memoirs, **62**, 359–368.

Dikenshteyn, G. Kh. 1986. Volga Ural oil gas province. *Petroleum Geology*, **22**, 139–154.

Dolan, P. 1990. Pakistan: a history of petroleum exploration and future potential. *In*: Brooks, J. (ed.) *Classic Petroleum Provinces*. Geological Society, London, Special Publications, **50**, 503–524.

Drozd, R. J. & Piggott, N. 1996. The geochemistry of the Cusiana field oils. *In*: Mello, M. R., Trindade, L. A. F. & Hessel, M. H. R. (eds), ALAGO Special Publication. 4th Latin American Congress on Organic Geochemistry, Bucaramanga, Colombia, October 1994, extended abstracts, 58–64.

Dunn, J., Hartshorn, K. & Hartshorn, P. 1995. Structural styles and hydrocarbon potential of the Subandean thrust belt of southern Bolivia. *In*: Tankard, A. J., Suarez Soruco, R. & Welsink, H. J. (eds) *Petroleum Basins of South America.* American Association of Petroleum Geologists, Memoirs, **62**, 523–544.

Echevarria-Rodriguez, G., Hernandez-Perez, G., Lopez-Quintero, J. O. *et al.* 1991. Oil and gas exploration in Cuba. *Journal of Petroleum Geology*, **14**, 259–274.

Eguiluz, S. 2001. Geological evolution and gas resources of the Sabinas Basin in northeastern Mexico. *In*: Bartolini, C., Buffler, R. T. & Cantu-Chafa, A. (eds) *The Western Gulf of Mexico Basin: Tectonics, Sedimentary Basins and Petroleum Systems.* American Association of Petroleum Geologists, Memoirs, **75**, 241–270.

Espitalie, J. & Drouet, S. 1992. Petroleum generation and accumulation in the Aquitaine Basin, France. *In*: Spencer, A. M. (ed.) *Generation, Accumulation and Production of Europe's Hydrocarbons; II.* European Association of Petroleum Geoscientists, Special Publications, **2**, 127–149.

Foose, R. M. & Manheim, F. 1975. Geology of Bulgaria: a review. *AAPG Bulletin*, **59**, 303–335.

Gallup, W. B. 1975. A brief history of the Turner Valley oil and gas field. *In*: Evers, H. J. & Thorpe, J. E. (eds) *Structural Geology of the Foothills between Savanna Creek and Panther River, S.W. Alberta, Canada.* Canadian Society of Petroleum Geoscientists and Canadian Society of Exploration Geophysicists Joint Convention Guidebook, 12–17.

Gao, C. & Ye, D. 1997. Petroleum geology of the Tarim Basin, northwestern China: recent advances. *Journal of Petroleum Geology*, **20**, 239–244.

Gonzalez-Garcia, R. & Holguin-Quinones, N. 1991. Geology of the source rocks of Mexico. *Proceedings of the 13th World Petroleum Congress*, Vol. 2. John Wiley & Sons, Chichester, **13**, 95–104.

Graham, R., Herbert, R. & Smart, R. 1997. Thoughts on petroleum occurrence in fold and thrust belts. *American Association of Petroleum Geologists/Asociación Mexicana de Geólogos Petroleros Research Symposium: Oil and Gas Exploration and Production in Fold and Thrust Belts, Abstracts*, 23–26 February 1997, Veracruz, Mexico (unpaginated).

Grantham, P. J., Lijmbach, G. W. M., Posthuma, J., Hughes Clarke, M. W. & Willink, R. J. 1987. Origin of crude oils in Oman. *Journal of Petroleum Geology*, **11**, 61–80.

Gu, S. & Di, H. 1989. Mechanism of formation of the Qaidam Basin and its control on petroleum. *In*: Zhu, X. (ed.) *Chinese Sedimentary Basins.* Elsevier, Amsterdam, 45–51.

Guo, Z. & Zhang, J. 1989. A discussion on the oil and gas potential of the structural belt in the western margin of the Ordos Massif viewed from the thrust nappe tectonics. *Acta Petrolei Sinica (Shiyou Xuebao)*, **10**, 31–38.

Harrison, J. C. & Bally, A. W. 1988. Cross-sections of the Parry Islands fold belt on Melville Island, Canadian Arctic Islands: implications for the timing and kinematic history of some thin-skinned décollement systems. *Bulletin of Canadian Petroleum Geology*, **36**, 311–332

Hill, K. C. 1991. Structure of the Papuan Fold Belt, Papua New Guinea. *AAPG Bulletin*, **75**, 857–872.

Hill, K. C., Keetley, J. C., Kendrick, R. D. & Sutriyono, E. 2004. Structural and hydrocarbon potential of the New Guinea Fold Belt, a review. *In*: McClay, K. R. (ed.) *Thrust Tectonics and Hydrocarbon Systems.* American Association of Petroleum Geologists, Memoirs, **82**, 494–514.

Hobson, D. M. 1986. A thin skinned model for the Papuan thrust belt and some implications for hydrocarbon exploration. *Australian Petroleum Production and Exploration Association Journal*, **26**, 214–224.

Homovc, J. F., Conforto, G. A., Lafourcade, P. A. & Chelotti, L. A. 1995. Fold belt in the San Jorge Basin, Argentina; an example of tectonic inversion. *In*: Buchanan, J. G. & Buchanan, P. G. (eds) *Basin Inversion.* Geological Society, London, Special Publications, **88**, 235–248.

HUBBARD, R. J., EDRICH, S. & RATTEY, R. P. 1987. Geologic evolution and hydrocarbon habitat of the 'Arctic Alaska Microplate'. *In*: TAILLEUR, I. & WEIMER, P. (eds) *Alaskan North Slope Geology*. Pacific Section, SEPM, Bakersfield, CA; Alaska Geological Society, Anchorage, AK, 797–830.

ILLICH, H. A., HANEY, F. R. & GRIZZLE, P. L. 1984. Geochemical significance of seep oil from the Subandino Norte, Northwest Bolivia. *Geochimica et Cosmochimica Acta*, **48**, 391–394.

ILLICH, H. A., HANEY, F. R. & PRUITT, J. D. 1985. Hydrocarbon geochemistry of oils from eastern Peru; a model of risk reduction in new exploration ventures. T*ransactions of the 4th Latin American Geological Conference*, **4**, 351–363.

JADOON, I. A. K., LAWRENCE, R. D. & LILLIE, R. J. 1994. Seismic data, geometry, evolution and shortening in the active Sulaiman fold and thrust belt of Pakistan, southwest of the Himalayas. *AAPG Bulletin*, **78**, 758–774.

JENNETTE, D., WAWRZYNIEC, T., FOUAD, K. *et al*. 2003. Traps and turbidite reservoir characteristics from a complex and evolving tectonic setting, Veracruz Basin, southeastern Mexico. *AAPG Bulletin*, **87**, 1599–1622.

JIN, Q., ZHA, M., LIU, Z., GAO, X., PENG, D. & LIN, L. 2002. Geology and geochemistry of source rocks in the Qaidam Basin, NW China. J*ournal of Petroleum Geology*, **25**, 219–238.

KARAGJULEVA, J. & CANKOV, C. 1974. Regions of Alpine folding, the Bulgarian Carpathian Balkan area, Fore Balkan. *In*: MAHEL', M. (ed.) *Tectonics of the Carpathian Balkan Regions; Explanations to the Tectonic Map of the Carpathian Balkan Regions and their Foreland*. Geological Institute of Dionyz Stur, Bratislava, 308–316.

KENT, W. N. HICKMAN, R. G. & DASGUPTA, U. 2002. Application of a ramp/flat-fault model to interpretation of the Naga thrust and possible implications for petroleum exploration along the Naga thrust front. *AAPG Bulletin*, **86**, 2023–2045.

KHAIN, V. E., SOKOLOV, B. A., KLESHCHEV, K. A. & SHEIN, V. S. 1991. Tectonic and geodynamic setting of oil and gas basins of the Soviet Union. *AAPG Bulletin*, **75**, 313–325.

KHAN, M. A., AHMED, R., RAZA, H. A. & KEMAL, A. 1986. Geology of Petroleum in Kohat-Potwar Depression, Pakistan. *AAPG Bulletin*, **70**, 396–414.

KNOX, G. J. 1982. Taranaki Basin, structural style and tectonic setting. J*ournal of Geology and Geophysics (New Zealand)*, **25**, 125–140.

KONTOROVICH, A. E., MANDEL'BAUM, M. M., SURKOV, V. S., TROFIMUK, A. A. & ZOLOTOV, A. N. 1990. Lena–Tunguska Upper Proterozoic–Palaeozoic petroleum superprovince. *In*: BROOKS, J. (ed.) *Classic Petroleum Provinces*. Geological Society, London, Special Publications, **50**, 473–489.

KREJCI, O., FRANCU, J., POELCHAU, H. S., MULLER, P. & STRANIK, Z. 1996. Tectonic evolution and oil and gas generation at the border of the North European Platform with the West Carpathians (Czech Republic). *In*: WESELY, G. & LIEBL, W. (eds) *Oil and Gas in Alpidic Thrustbelts and Basins of Central and Eastern Europe*. Special Publication of the European Association of Geoscientists and Engineers, **5**, 177–186.

KRONMAN, G. E., RUSHWORTH, S. W., JAGIELLO, K. & ALEMAN, A. 1995. Oil and gas discoveries and basin resource predictions in Latin America. *In*: TANKARD, A. J., SUAREZ SORUCO, R. & WELSINK, H. J. (eds) *Petroleum Basins of South America*, American Association of Petroleum Geologists, Memoirs, **62**, 53–61.

LAMERSON, P. R. 1982. The Fossil Basin area and its relationship to the Absaroka thrust fault system. *In*: POWERS, R. B. (ed.) *Geologic Studies of the Cordilleran Thrust Belt*. Rocky Mountain Association of Geologists, Denver, 279–340.

LAUBSCHER, H. P. 1962. Die Zwiephasenhypothese der Jurafaltung. *Eclogae Geological Helvetial*, **55**, 1–22.

LE VOT, M., BITEAU, J. J. & MASSET, J. M. 1996. The Aquitaine Basin: oil and gas production in the foreland of the Pyrenean fold-and-thrust belt. New exploration perspectives. *In*: ZIEGLER, P. A. & HORVATH, F. (eds) *Peri-Tethys, Memoir 2 : Structure and Prospects of Alpine Basins and Forelands*. Mémoires du Muséum National d'Histoire Naturelle, **170**, 159–171.

LI, D., LIANG, D., JIA, C., WANG, G., WU, Q. & HE, D. 1996. Hydrocarbon accumulations in the Tarim Basin, China. *AAPG Bulletin*, **80**, 1587–1603.

MALLICK, R. K., RAJU, S. V. & GOGOI, D. K. 1997. The Langpar–Lakadong Petroleum System, Upper Assam Basin, India. *Indian Journal of Petroleum Geology*, **6**, 1–18.

MANCEDA, R. & FIGUEROA, D. 1995. Inversion of the Mesozoic Neuquen rift in the Malargue fold and thrust belt, Mendoza, Argentina. *In*: TANKARD, A. J., SUAREZ SORUCO, R. & WELSINK, H. J. (eds) *Petroleum Basins of South America*, American Association of Petroleum Geologists, Memoirs, **62**, 369–382.

MARRETT, R. & ARANDA, M. 1999. Structure and kinematic development of the Sierra Madre oriental fold–thrust belt, Mexico. *In*: WILSON, J. L. & MARRETT, R. A. (eds) *Stratigraphy and structure of the Jurassic and Cretaceous Platform and Basin Systems of the Sierra Madre Oriental, Monterrey and Saltillo Areas, Northeastern Mexico; a Field Book and Related Papers*. South Texas Geological Society Field Guide, 69–98.

MASCLE, A. 1994. *Hydrocarbon and Petroleum Geology of France*. European Association of Petroleum Geoscientists Special Publications, **4**.

MASTERS, C. D. & PETERSON, J. A. 1981. *Assessment of Conventionally Recoverable Petroleum Resources, Volga Urals Basin, USSR*. US Geological Survey Open-File Report, **1**–**8**.

MATHALONE, J. M. P. & MONTOYA, M. 1995. Petroleum geology of the sub-Andean basins of Peru. *In*: TANKARD, A. J., SUAREZ SORUCO, R. & WELSINK, H. J. (eds) *Petroleum Basins of South America*. American Association of Petroleum Geologists, Memoirs, **62**, 423–444.

MATTAVELLI, L., PIERI, M. & GROPPI, G. 1993. Petroleum exploration in Italy: a review. *Marine and Petroleum Geology*, **10**, 410–425.

MELLO, M. R., TRINIDADE, L. A. F., RANGEL, A. V. O. *et al.* 1994. Comparative geochemical characterization of Latin American oils derived from Devonian to Miocene source rocks: a biological marker and isotope approach. *In*: MELLO, M. R., TRINDADE, L. A. F. & HESSEL, M. H. R. (eds) *ALAGO Special Publication.* Fourth Latin American Congress on Organic Geochemistry, Bucaramanga, Colombia, October 1994, *Extended Abstracts*, 109–112.

MORAN-ZENTENO, D. 1994. *The Geology of the Mexican Republic.* American Association of Petroleum Geologists, Studies in Geology, **39**.

MORETTI, I., BABY, P., MENDEZ, E. & ZUBIETA, D. 1996. Hydrocarbon generation in relation to thrusting in the Sub-Andean Zone from 18 to 22 degrees S, Bolivia. *Petroleum Geoscience*, **2**, 17–28.

MOULTON, F. C. & PINNELL, M. L. 2005. Stunning Utah oil, gas discovery focuses on Hingeline. *Oil and Gas Journal*, **103**(3), 42–49.

MOUNT, V. S., HERTIG, S., O'DONNELL, G. P. & KRANTZ, R. W. 1998. Structural styles and timing of the North Oman Mountain Deformation Front. *GeoArabia: Middle East Petroleum Geosciences*, **3**, 690–698.

MULLER, M., NIEBERDING, F. & WANNINGER, A. 1988. Tectonic styles and pressure distribution at the northern margin of the Alps between Lake Constance and the River Inn. *Geologische Rundschau*, **77**, 787–796.

ORTNER, H. & SACHSENHOFER, R. 1996. Evolution of the Lower Inn Valley Tertiary and constraints on the development of the source area. *In*: WESELY, G. & LIEBL, W. (eds) *Oil and Gas in Alpidic Thrustbelts and Basins of Central and Eastern Europe.* Special Publication of the European Association of Geoscientists and Engineers, **5**, 237–248.

OWER, J. 1975. The Moose Mountain structure, birth and death of a folded fault play. *In*: EVERS, H. J. & THORPE, J. E. (eds) *Structural Geology of the Foothills between Savanna Creek and Panther River, S.W. Alberta, Canada.* Canadian Society of Petroleum Geoscientists and Canadian Society of Exploration Geophysicists Joint Convention Guidebook, 22–29.

PARNAUD, F., GOU, Y., PASCUAL, J. C., TRUSKOWSKI, I., GALLANGO, O. & PASSALACQUA, H. 1995. Petroleum geology of the central part of the Eastern Venezuelan Basin. *In*: TANKARD, A. J., SUAREZ SORUCO, R. & WELSINK, H. J. (eds) *Petroleum Basins of South America.* American Association of Petroleum Geologists, Memoirs, **62**, 741–756.

PENNOCK, E. S., LILLIE, R. J., ZAMAN, A. S. H. & YOUSAF, M. 1989. Structural interpretation of seismic reflection data from Eastern Salt Range and Potwar Plateau, Pakistan. *AAPG Bulletin*, **73**, 841–857.

PERONI, G. O., HEGEDUS, A. G., CERDAN, J., LEGARRETA, L., ULIANA, M. A. & LAFFITTE, G. 1995. Hydrocarbon accumulation in an inverted segment of the Andean Foreland: San Bernardo belt, central Patagonia. *In*: TANKARD, A. J., SUAREZ SORUCO, R. & WELSINK, H. J. (eds) *Petroleum Basins of South America.* American Association of Petroleum Geologists, Memoirs, **62**, 403–419.

PERSAD, K. M. 1985. Outline of the geology of the Trinidad area. *Transactions of the 4th Latin American Geological Conference*, Port-of-Spain, **2**, 738–758.

PETERSON, J. A. 1983. Petroleum geology and resources of southeastern Mexico, northern Guatemala and Belize. *US Geological Survey Circular*, **760**, 1–44.

PICHA, F. J. 1996. Exploring for hydrocarbons under thrust belts—a challenging new frontier in the Carpathians and elsewhere. *AAPG Bulletin*, **80** 1547–1564.

PIERI, M. 1992. Cortemaggiore Field, Italy; Po Plain, Northern Apennines. *In*: BEAUMONT, E. A. & FOSTER, N. H. (compilers) *Structural Traps; VII.* American Association of Petroleum Geologists Treatise of Petroleum Geology, Atlas of Oil and Gas Fields, **A-25**, 99–118.

PIERI, M. & MATTAVELLI, L. 1986. Geologic framework of Italian petroleum resources. *AAPG Bulletin*, **70**, 103–130

PILAAR, W. F. H. & WAKEFIELD, L. L. 1984. Hydrocarbon generation in the Taranaki Basin, New Zealand. *In*: DEMAISON, G. & MURRIS, R. J. (eds) *Petroleum Geochemistry and Basin Evaluation.* American Association of Petroleum Geologists, Memoirs, **35**, 405–423.

QINMIN, W. & COWARD, M. P. 1990. The Chaidam Basin, NW China; formation and hydrocarbon potential. *Journal of Petroleum Geology*, **13**, 93–112.

RAZA, H. A., RIAZ, A. S., MANSHOOR, A. S. & AHMAD, J. 1989. Petroleum prospects; Sulaiman sub-basin, Pakistan. *Pakistan Journal of Hydrocarbon Research*, **1**, 21–56.

REQUEJO, A. G., WIELCHOWSKY, C. C., KLOSTERMAN, M. J. & SASSEN, R. 1994. Geochemical characterization of lithofacies and organic facies in Cretaceous organic-rich rocks from Trinidad, East Venezuela Basin. *Organic Geochemistry*, **22**, 441–459.

REYES, A., MONTENEGRO, G. & GOMEZ, P. 2000. Evolucion tectonoestratigrafica del Valle Inferior del Magdalena, Colombia. *VII Simposio Boliviariano Exploracion Petrolera en Las Cuencas Subandianas, Caracas, Venezuela, 10–13 Septiembre 2000*, PDVSA, 293–309.

ROBERTSON, A. H. F., SEARLE, M. P. & RIES, A. C. (eds) 1990. *The Geology and Tectonics of the Oman Region.* Geological Society, London, Special Publications, **49**.

ROBINSON, C. R., SMITH, M. A. & ROYLE, R. A. 1999. Organic facies in Jurassic and Cretaceous source rocks, southern Indus Basin, Pakistan. *International Journal of Coal Geology*, **39**, 205–225.

ROEDER, D. 1992. Thrusting and wedge growth, Southern Alps of Lombardia (Italy). *Tectonophysics*, **207**, 199–243.

ROHR, G. M. 1991. Exploration potential of Trinidad and Tobago. *Journal of Petroleum Geology*, **14**, 343–354.

ROURE, F., ROCA, E. & SASSI, W. 1993. The Neogene evolution of the outer Carpathian flysch units (Poland, Ukraine and Romania): kinematics of a foreland/fold-and-thrust system. *Sedimentary Geology*, **86**, 177–201.

ROURE, F., CARNEVALI, J. O., GOU, Y. & RUGGIERO, A. 1994. Geometry and kinematics of the North

Monogas thrust belt (Venezuela). *Marine and Petroleum Geology*, **11**, 347–362.

ROWAN, M. G., PEEL, F. J. & VENDEVILLE, B. C. 2004. Gravity-driven fold belts on passive margins. *In*: MCCLAY, K. R. (ed.) *Thrust Tectonics and Hydrocarbon Systems*. American Association of Petroleum Geologists, Memoirs, **82**, 157–183.

RUIZ, C., DAVIS, N., BENTHAM, P., PRICE, A. & CARVAJAL, D. 2000. Structure and tectonic evolution of the South Caribbean Basin, southern offshore Colombia: a progressive accretionary system. *VII Simposio Boliviariano Exploracion Petrolera en Las Cuencas Subandianas, Caracas, Venezuela, 10–13 Septiembre 2000*, PDVSA, 334–355.

RYDER, R., RICE, D. D., SUN, Z., ZHANG, Y., QIU, Y. & GUO, Z. 1994. *Petroleum Geology of the Sichuan Basin, China*. Report on US Geological Survey and Chinese Ministry of Geology and Mineral Resources field investigations and meetings, October 1991. US Geological Survey Open-File Report, **67**.

SANTIAGO, A. J. & BARO, A. 1992. Mexico's Giant Fields, 1978–1988 Decade. *In*: HALBOUTY, M. T. (ed.) *Giant Oil and Gas Fields of the Decade 1978–1988*. American Association of Petroleum Geologists, Memoirs, **54**, 73–99.

SATTAYARAK, N., SRIGULWONG, S. & PUM-IM, S. 1989. Petroleum potential of the Triassic pre-Khorat intermontane basin in northeastern Thailand. *In*: THANASUTHIPAK, T. & OUNCHANUM, P. (eds) *Proceedings of the International Symposium on Intermontane Basins; Geology and Resources*. Chiang Mai University, Chiang Mai, Thailand, 43–58.

SCHELLING, D. D. 1999. Frontal structural geometries and detachment tectonics of the northeastern Karachi Range, Pakistan. Himalaya and Tibet: mountain roots to mountain tops. *Geological Society of America Special Paper*, **328**, 287–302.

SHAW, R. D. & PACKHAM, G. H. 1992. The tectonic setting of sedimentary basins of Eastern Indonesia: Implications for hydrocarbon prospectivity. *Journal of the Australian Petroleum Exploration Association*, **32**, 195–213.

SLACZKA, A. 1996. Oil and Gas in the Northern Carpathians. *In*: WESELY, G. & LIEBL, W. (eds) *Oil and Gas in Alpidic Thrustbelts and Basins of Central and Eastern Europe*. Special Publication of the European Association of Geoscientists and Engineers, **5**, 187–196.

SOBORNOV, K. O. 1994. Structure and petroleum potential of the Dagestan thrust belt, northeastern Caucasus, Russia. *Bulletin of Canadian Petroleum Geology*, **42**, 352–363.

SPEED, R. C., BARKER, L. H. & PAYNE, P. L. B. 1991. Geologic and hydrocarbon evolution of Barbados. *Journal of Petroleum Geology*, **14**, 323–342.

STOCKMAL, G. S., OSADETZ, K. G., LEBEL, D. & HANNIGAN, P. K. 2001. *Structure and Hydrocarbon Occurrence, Rocky Mountain Foothills and Front Ranges, Turner Valley to Waterton Lakes—Field Trip Guidebook*. Geological Survey of Canada, Open File **4111**.

SUPPE, J. 1980. A retrodeformable cross section of northern Taiwan. *Proceedings Geological Society of China*, **23**, 46–55.

SUPPE, J. 1981. Mechanics of mountain building and metamorphism in Taiwan. Geological Society of China, Memoirs, **4**, 67–89.

SUPPE, J. 1983. Geometry and kinematics of fault-bend folding. *American Journal of Science*, **283**, 684–721.

SYKORA, J. J. 2000. The buried fold–thrust belt of Offshore Seram. *AAPG Bulletin*, **84**, 1502.

TALUKDAR, S., GALLANGO, O. & RUGGIERO, A. 1988. Generation and migration of oil in the Maturin Sub-basin, eastern Venezuelan Basin. *Organic Geochemistry*, **13**, 537–547.

ULIANA, M. A., ARTEAGA, M. E., LEGARRETA, L., CERDAN, J. J. & PERONI, G. O. 1995. Inversion structures and hydrocarbon occurrence in Argentina. *In*: BUCHANAN, J. G. & BUCHANAN, P. G. (eds) *Basin Inversion*. Geological Society, London, Special Publications, **88**, 211–233.

ULMISHEK, G. F. 1988. Upper Devonian–Tournaisian facies and oil resources of the Russian craton's eastern margin. *In*: MCMILLAN, N. J., EMBRY, A. F. & GLAN, D. J. (eds) *Devonian of the World. Proceedings 2nd International Symposium on the Devonian System; Volume I, Regional Syntheses*. Memoir of the Canadian Society of Petroleum Geologists, **14**, 527–549.

ULMISHEK, G. F. 1990. Uzen Field—U.S.S.R. Middle Caspian Basin, South Mangyshlak Region. *In*: BEAUMONT, E. A. & NORMAN, H. (compilers) *Structural Traps IV: Tectonic and Nontectonic Fold Traps, American Association of Petroleum Geologists, Special Publications TR*, 281–297.

ULMISHEK, G. F. 1992. *Geology and hydrocarbon resources of onshore basins in eastern China*. US Geological Survey Open-File Report **OF 93-41992**.

ULMISHEK, G. F. 2001. *Petroleum Geology and Resources of the Middle Caspian Basin. Former Soviety Union*. US Geological Survey Bulletin, **2201-A**.

URIEN, C. M. & Zambrano, J. J. 1994. Petroleum systems in the Neuquen Basin, Argentina. *In*: MAGOON, L. B. & DOW, W. G. (eds) *The Petroleum System—From Source to Trap*. American Association of Petroleum Geologists, Memoirs, **60**, 513–534.

USGS 2000. *US Geological Survey World Petroleum Assessment 2000—Description and Results*. USGS Digital Data Series **DDS-60** (CD ROMs).

VELAJ, T., DAVISON, I., SERJANI, A. & ALSOP, I. 1999. Thrust tectonics and the role of evaporites in the Ionian Zone of the Albanides. *AAPG Bulletin*, **83**, 1408–1425.

VILLAR, H. J. & PUETTMANN, W. 1990. Geochemical characteristics of crude oils from the Cuyo Basin, Argentina. *Organic Geochemistry*, **16**, 511–519.

WALLACE, G., MOORE, J. C. & DILEONARDO, C. G. 2003. Controls on localization and densification of a modern décollement; northern Barbados accretionary prism. *Geological Society of America Bulletin*, **115**, 288–297.

WANG, Q. & NISHIDAI, T. & COWARD, M. P. 1992. The Tarim Basin, NW China; formation and aspects of petroleum geology. *Journal of Petroleum Geology*, **15**, 5–34.

WARNER, M. A. 1982. The source and time of generation of hydrocarbons in the Fossil Basin, Western Wyoming Thrust Belt. *In*: POWERS, R. B. (ed.)

Geologic Studies of the Cordilleran Thrust Belt. Rocky Mountain Association of Geologists, Denver, 805–815.

YOSE, L. A., EIBEN, T., BROWN, S., KOMPANIK, G. S., DAVIS, T. L. & MAXWELL, S. R. 2001. 3-D Geologic model of a fractured carbonate reservoir, Norman Wells Field, NWT, Canada. *Bulletin of Canadian Petroleum Geology, Special Issue: The Devonian of Western Canada—Aspects of a Carbonate Petroleum System*, **49**, 86–116.

ZAPPATERRA, E. 1994. Source rock distribution model of the periadriatic region. *AAPG Bulletin*, **78**, 333–354.

ZIMMER, W. & WESSELY, G. 1996. Exploration results in thrust and subthrust complexes in the Alps below the Vienna Basin in Austria. *In*: WESELY, G. & LIEBL, W. (eds) *Oil and Gas in Alpidic Thrustbelts and Basins of Central and Eastern Europe*. Special Publication of the European Association of Geoscientists and Engineers, **5**, 81–108.

The impact of deformation timing on the prospectivity of the Middle Magdalena sub-thrust, Colombia

WILLIAM SASSI[1,4], ROD GRAHAM[2], RALPH GILLCRIST[3], MIKE ADAMS[2] & RAMON GOMEZ[3]

[1]*Institut Français du Pétrole, Rueil Malmaison, France*
[2]*Hess Ltd, London WCZN 6AG UK (e-mail: rod.graham@hess.com)*
[3]*Cepsa, 28042 Madrid, Spain*
[4]*Present address: Midland Valley Exploration, Glasgow G2 2HG, UK*

Abstract: Once deeply buried rocks are elevated in thrust belts, the resulting effects on reservoir evolution, source-rock maturity, hydrocarbon phase and charge history pose major problems for thrust belt exploration. To understand the geometrical evolution and burial history of thrust belts, successive structural restorations and dynamic basin modelling are needed. The forward modelling program 'Thrustpack' provides a semi-quantitative way forward, and this paper presents a 'Thrustpack' case study. The area considered is Rio Horta in the western foothills of the Colombian Eastern Cordillera, where westward-directed frontal structures break out onto the foreland basin of the Middle Magdalena Valley. A large sub-thrust anticline underlies the frontal thrusts and provides a substantial exploration lead. Following conventional models of back-thrusting and 'fish-tailing', the structure can be interpreted as entirely late, post-dating the overlying thrusts and once buried by the entire sedimentary megasequence of the Magdalena foreland basin. This would imply that the prospective section had been buried to a depth of about 12 km before uplift, and suggest a hydrocarbon graveyard, or, at best, dry gas in fractured, tight rock and potential overpressure. If the structure formed early, there is a chance of preserving both original porosity and liquid hydrocarbon in the structure, and charge risk is lessened because hydrocarbons were able to migrate into a structure that already existed. Hints from geological maps and the (generally poor quality) seismic data suggest that this is the more likely situation. It is consistent with the idea of an evolving palaeo-landscape and a mountain front with a very long history, where the structure remained relatively elevated during later sedimentation and thrusting. The modelling of these two alternative possible structural histories in 'Thrustpack' tests their viability and quantifies the hydrocarbon maturation, migration history and porosity evolution. The model in which the structure develops early presents real exploration opportunity whereas the alternative presents unacceptable exploration risk.

The effects of burial and subsequent uplift on reservoir degradation, thermal evolution and hydrocarbon charge rank with the structural complexity of thrust-related traps and imperfect seismic imagery of thrust belts as serious problems for thrust belt exploration.

Generally speaking, the most attractive targets in thrust belts are sub-thrust structures at mountain fronts. Such structures are high risk, but they are large and thus potentially high-volume traps. Rio Horta is an example, located beneath the mountain front on the east side of the Middle Magdalena Basin in Colombia, the west-directed thrust belt on the western flank of the Eastern Cordillera (Fig. 1).

There have been four previous 'Thrustpack' studies in this region. Toro *et al.* (2004) concentrated on the east-directed thrust belt on the eastern side of the Cordillera, leaving the western flank unpinned and therefore not constrained. Cortez (2004) ran geometrical models across the western margin without a pin on the eastern side. Acosta *et al.* (2003) modelled two lines close to those of Toro *et al.* (2004), with the aim of demonstrating different maturation histories, north and south of the Ibague Fault, a fundamental cross element in this area of the Magdalena Valley. One of these lines traverses the Eastern Cordillera and is pinned at both sides and therefore rigorously restored. Restrepo-Pace *et al.* (2004) specifically modelled the Rio Horta area, although not with the aim of distinguishing between structural models.

The 'problem' of mountain fronts

A well-known, but still fundamental issue at mountain fronts is that the leading structures are deformed and translated whereas the foreland is undeformed and fixed. What happens to the

From: RIES, A. C., BUTLER, R. W. H. & GRAHAM, R. H. (eds) 2007. *Deformation of the Continental Crust: The Legacy of Mike Coward.* Geological Society, London, Special Publications, **272**, 473–498.
0305-8719/07/$15

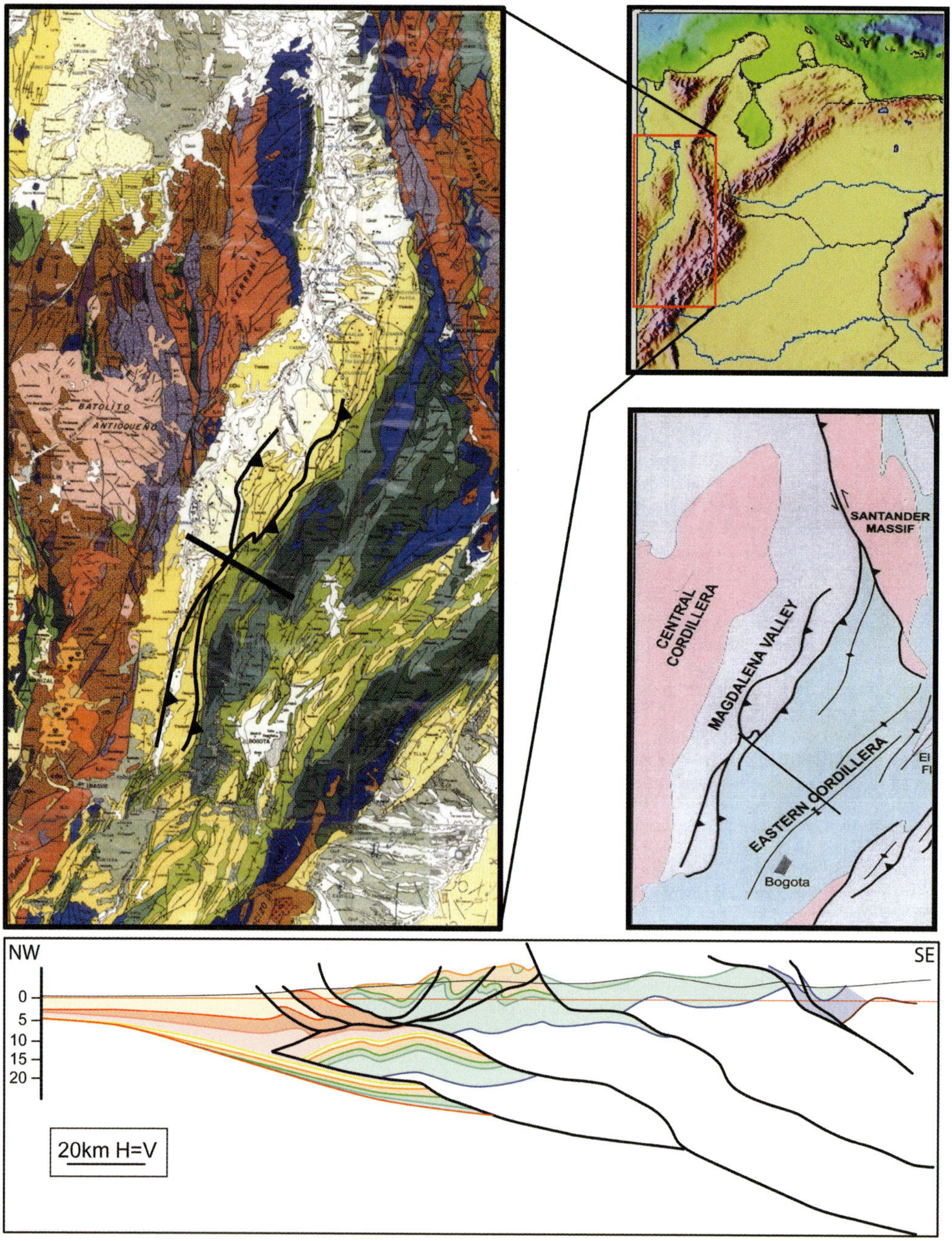

Fig. 1. Location of the Middle Magdalena Basin, the Rio Horta area and the modelled section line. Blue, Jurassic; dark green, Lower Cretareous; Light green, Upper Cretareous (including source horizon); yellow, Palaeogene; pinks and fawn, Neogene.

accumulated displacement of the thrust belt? Does it pass into the foreland? If so, how? If it does not, how is it accommodated? Vann *et al.* (1986) summarized the possible solutions to these problems, and Figure 2 is taken from that study.

If some displacement does pass into the foreland, faults in the foreland basin floor may be inverted, or bedding-parallel detachments may develop, to emerge many kilometres beyond the main mountain front, just as the folds of

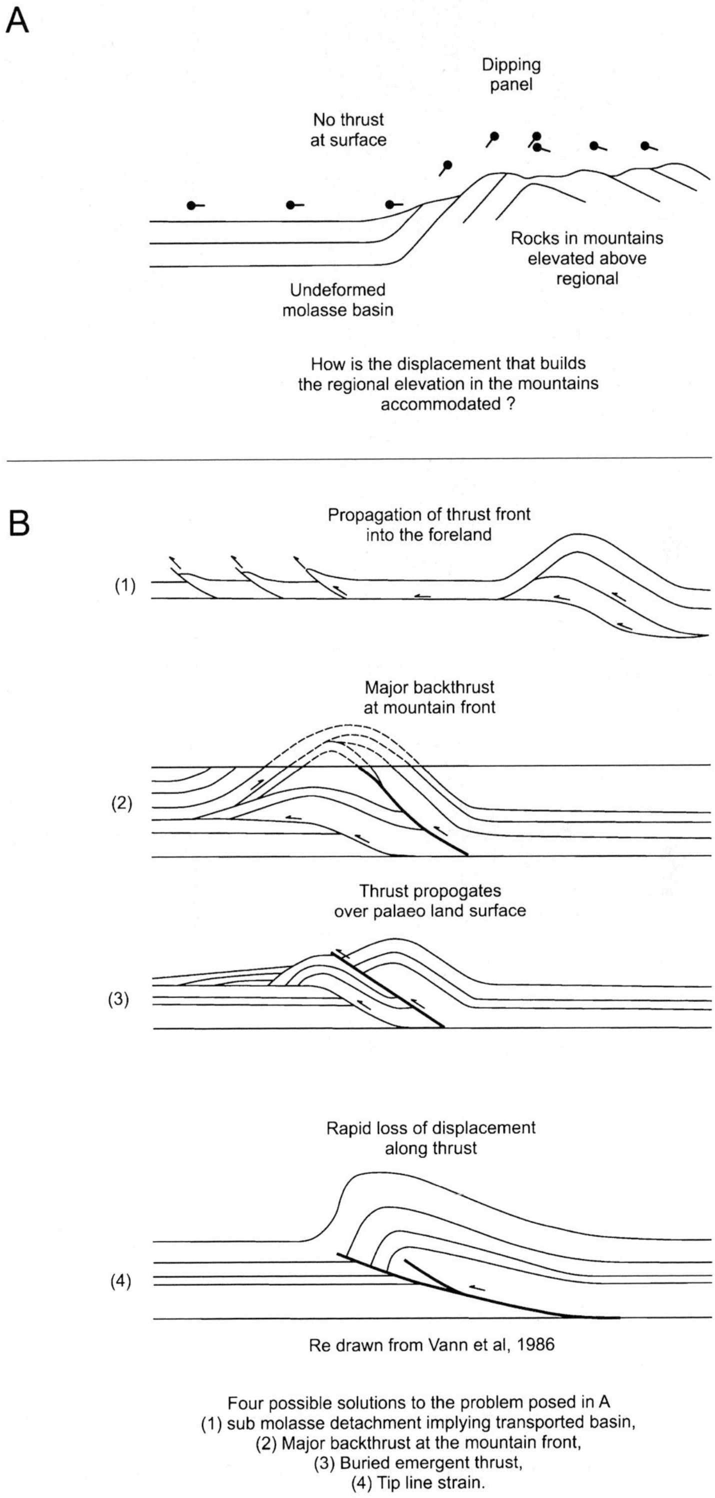

Fig. 2. The mountain front problem and its solution (after Vann *et al.* 1986).

the Jura Mountains do beyond the NE edge of the Alpine foreland basin. We should also expect a layer-parallel pervasive strain bead ahead of the mountain front, a feature that might have an effect on reservoir porosity, but is unlikely to accommodate tens of kilometres of displacement.

One common solution to the mountain front problem is the 'frontal back-thrust' or 'frontal triangle zone' hypothesis of Jones (1982). The idea is that if a wedge is driven underneath a stratal cover, then the sense of displacement at the base of the cover is in the opposite direction to that in which the wedge is driven. The wedge can be shortened without affecting the material above this 'roof thrust' except to fold it by accommodation to the wedge shape. The hypothesis is sometimes elaborated into 'fishtailing', where displacement is accommodated by back-thrusts and forward thrusts, zigzagging up through the upper section.

In some places (not Canada) the frontal back-thrust is something of a last resort hypothesis. A uniformitarian (therefore more reasonable) general view might be that thrusts always seek the topographic surface. They form eroded topography if they reach it, become progressively onlapped, and climb on. Significant progressive onlap without positive topographic expression and erosional unconformity requires that the basin subsidence (driven by the lithospheric loading of the internal thrust belt) exceeds the elevation associated with thrusting (the situation predicted here for the Rio Horta structure)

Once a mountain front thrust stack is overlain by younger undeformed sediments, then the unconformity surface is likely to represent a lithological discontinuity, which can become a slip surface. This makes the analogy of driving a wedge beneath a carpet a real possibility. Unconformities commonly become reactivated as frontal back-thrusts, although only limited displacement is now required. There are many examples; Lonergan (1993) has described a very good one from the sub-Betics of southern Spain.

'Thrustpack' methodology: structural interpretation, forward modelling of burial and uplift history

In addition to the requirements of a source rock, a seal and a reservoir, exploration in thrust belts requires an understanding of lithosphere subsidence, sedimentation and erosion in relation to faulting and folding so that we can predict the timing of hydrocarbon maturation and expulsion in relation to trap formation. Roure & Sassi (1995) described a general framework and methodology for structural and maturity studies at the regional scale along 2D geological cross-sections. The modelling methodology includes the following four steps: (1) construction of an admissible (balanced) cross-section with coherent geometry for the present day and a template that depicts the pre-deformation geometry as accurately as possible; (2) validation of the structural interpretation by a reconstruction of the major deformation stages using a kinematic forward model of deformation; (3) validation of the timing of the structural deformation by calibration of the present-day temperature (using bottom hole data) and reconstruction of the temperature history using available palaeotemperature indicators (e.g. vitrinite reflectance data, apatite fission tracks, kerogen maturity data); (4) computation of generated hydrocarbon products based on the time–temperature scenarios and on a specific compositional scheme for transformation of kerogen into hydrocarbons (Tissot *et al.* 1987; Ungerer *et al.* 1990; Rudkiewicz & Behar 1994; Rudkiewicz *et al.* 1996).

In 'Thrustpack', the principle of balanced cross-sections (Dahlstrom 1969) is an underlying assumption, and two computer algorithms are proposed to simulate the kinematics of fault-bend folding and fault-propagation folding. The tectonic deformation is constrained by area and mass conservation in the vertical plane, parallel to the direction of transport. The fault-bend folding algorithm (the 'Kink algorithm' of Suppe (1983)) was written and developed successively by Endignoux (1989), Endignoux & Mugnier (1990), Zoetemeijer & Sassi (1992) and Zoetemeijer (1993). A second algorithm, 'Foldis' (Divies & Sassi 1996; Divies 1997) was developed to simulate folding by flexural slip and rock compaction caused by burial increase (Sassi *et al.* 1998; Sassi & Rudkiewicz 1999, 2000). Additionally, a vertical shear mode can be applied as a kinematic boundary condition to simulate vertical motion such as lithospheric-scale basement subsidence and uplift (Zoetemeijer 1993; Sciamanna *et al.* 2004).

A structural sequence is built in a forward sense, starting from the initial geometry and terminating with the present-day geometry. After a few trial and error iterations, any illogicalities in the restoration become evident, and different interpretations may need to be considered. To make geological sense, and give the required series of admissible intermediate sections, parameters such as the elevation and subsidence (and their rates), shortening, sea level and palaeo-environment must all be compatible and must augment the geometrical constraints of section balancing (bed lengths, area, matching cut-offs, etc.). The total picture is thus a very powerful test of the validity of the scheme of tectonic and geometric evolution.

The generality: thermal history and generation of hydrocarbons

Coupling the heat transfer in sediments with the kinematics of thrust deformation

The first attempts to link the structural–stratigraphic changes and the thermal evolution of sedimentary basins in two dimensions were by Shi & Wang (1987), Endignoux (1989), Endignoux & Wolf (1990) and Ter Voorde (1996). The transient effects of thrust kinematics on the thermal regime were investigated by Shi & Wang (1987) for basement-involved thrusting and by Endignoux & Wolf (1990) for sedimentary overburden. In a sense, these studies were confusing because they concluded that thrusting could lead to local inversion of the thermal gradient and assumed that rapid thrust emplacement versus slow heat diffusion could generate a transient thermal regime over a long period of time. This idea was supported by Grossling (1959), Gretener (1981) and Brewer (1981). More recently, Husson & Moretti (2002) have concluded that, in general, thrust velocities are too low to maintain a transient effect by heat conduction, although this phenomenon may occur at plate boundaries when convergence rates are relatively high (i.e. >1 cm a^{-1} Brewer 1981; Gretener 1981; Jaboyedoff 1999).

To deal with the effects of thrusting, sedimentation, erosion and subsidence on the thermal evolution of a basin, a specific numerical scheme is required. In the Thrustpack program, the calculation method is based on (1) heat transfer by conduction–diffusion, and (2) a discrete separation of the geological events to compute temperature by 'instantaneous' sedimentation, erosion and/or thrusting.

For each intermediate geometry of a structural evolution (i.e. fixed geometry), the heat equation is solved using the finite-element Galerkin method (Hughes 1987; Roure & Sassi 1995; Sassi & Rudkiewicz 1999; Deville & Sassi 2006). Considering a fixed geometry, the heat governing equation is recalled here for all transfer modes except the advection–convection term related to the fluid phase in a porous medium:

$$\rho \cdot C \cdot \frac{\partial T}{\partial t} = \vec{\nabla} \bullet (k \cdot \vec{\nabla} T) + Q_c \qquad (1)$$

where ∂ is the differential operator, $\vec{\nabla}\bullet$ is the divergence operator, $\vec{\nabla}$ is the gradient operator, T is the temperature (in K), Q_c is the source term accounting for radiogenic heat production (in W m^{-3}), ρ is the bulk density of the sediment (in Kg m^{-3}), C is the sediment heat capacity (in J kg^{-1} K^{-1}), k is the thermal conductivity (in W m^{-1} K^{-1}) and t is the time.

The left hand member in equation (1) quantifies the time-dependent diffusion effect for the transient heat transfer problem. In a steady-state thermal problem this term is simply not taken into account. To compute the temperature field at a given stage of the structural evolution, a temperature or a heat flux must be defined around the surface limiting the geological cross-section as the boundary conditions. Variations in time and in space of either the surface temperature or the basal heat flux, or both, can be defined and a sensitivity analysis performed within the spectrum of possible thermal histories. In this study the boundary conditions were defined as follows: (1) on each side of the restored section there was no horizontal heat flux; (2) a fixed temperature was assigned along the surface topography; (3) along the base of the section a set of heat flux functions varying both in space and in time were successively tested. Comparison of different basal heat fluxes over time illustrates the impact of different levels of lithospheric heat contribution, but to keep the temperature fields easy to analyse, no radiogenic heat flux was considered in the Thrustpack model steps.

Two possible heat transfer solutions can be computed. These are the steady-state and the transient situations illustrated in Figure 3. The left column of Figure 3 illustrates the transient thermal regime where the temperature field owing to the displacement along faults is considered. Constant surface temperature and a constant basal heat flux were assumed. The first calculation step is called the 'solid advection of temperature. After an instantaneous 'fault jump', a thermal perturbation can be mapped and shown by the offset of the isotherms across the fault. The second calculation step quantifies the thermal relaxation toward equilibrium temperature. Equation (1) is numerically solved over the time interval that separates the new cross-section from the previous one. This time interval can be arbitrarily defined to optimize the whole computation workflow. The finite-element algorithm used for solving the transient mode is called the generalized trapezoidal approach (see Hughes 1987; Sassi & Rudkiewicz 1999).

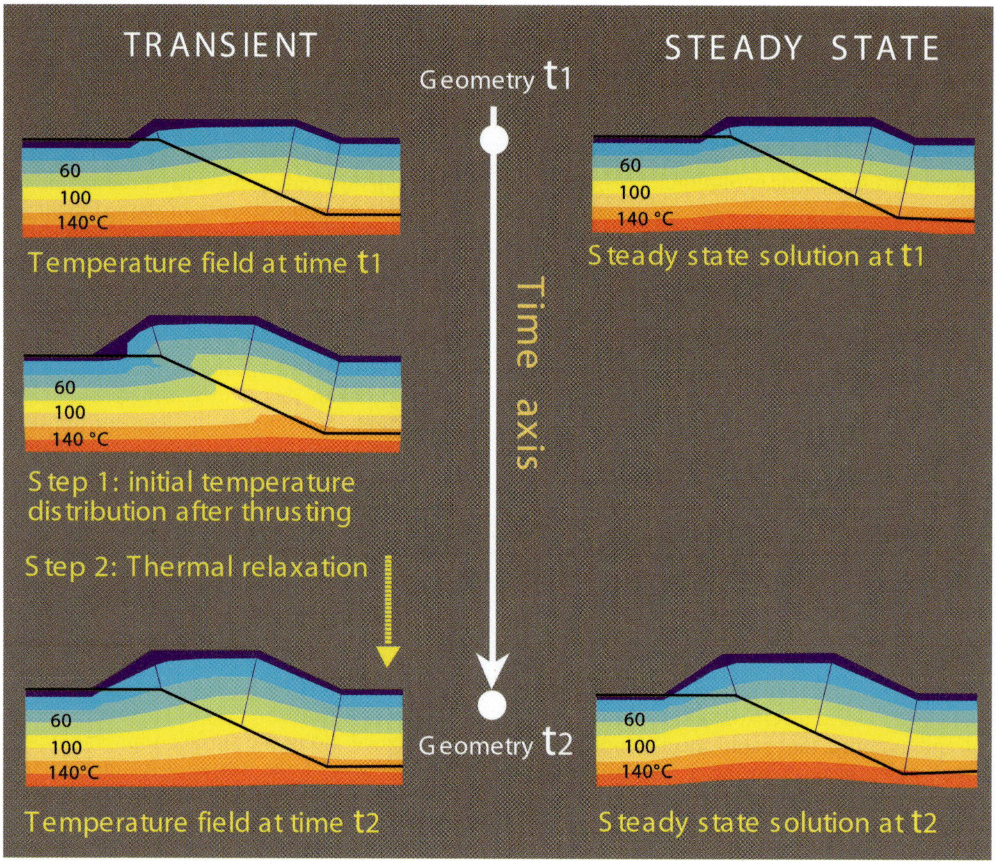

Fig. 3. Schematic representation of the transient and steady-state numerical algorithms incorporated in the Thrustpack thermal finite element code.

Transient or steady-state solution?

Thrusting and sedimentation are modelled by a series of 'fault jumps' and 'strata depositions'. This is artificial, but usually can be rationalized geologically. In this respect, it is important to determine the situations in which this numerical scheme is adequate to properly reconstruct the temperature history. This being done, the number of intermediate palinspastic cross-sections that need to be generated can be optimized. This logic is dictated by the understanding of the regional geology and the nature and physics of the heat transfer problem.

With increase of sedimentation, the temperature of the underlying rocks increases.

When thrusting takes place (Fig. 4), heat is transported by the displaced sediments, resulting in 'hotter' material being transported over relatively 'colder' rocks and leading to a decrease in temperature in the thrust hanging wall, which may be enhanced by erosion. An increase of temperature is expected in the footwall, as a result of increase in burial. For slow thrust emplacement the history curves for a point in the footwall and the hanging wall are shown in the fault-bend example of Figure 4. Whether a steady temperature profile is reached at any time in the system will depend on the relative importance of heat advection as a result of thrust kinematics, and the heat transfer by diffusion–conduction. The critical velocity of thrusting and/or the limiting rate of sedimentation for a steady-state or a transient resolution can be examined using the characteristic time for heat diffusion. Considering a single flat–ramp–flat thrust sheet, Endignoux & Wolf (1990) defined the time required to reach maximum burial for a point below a thrust ramp by the ratio

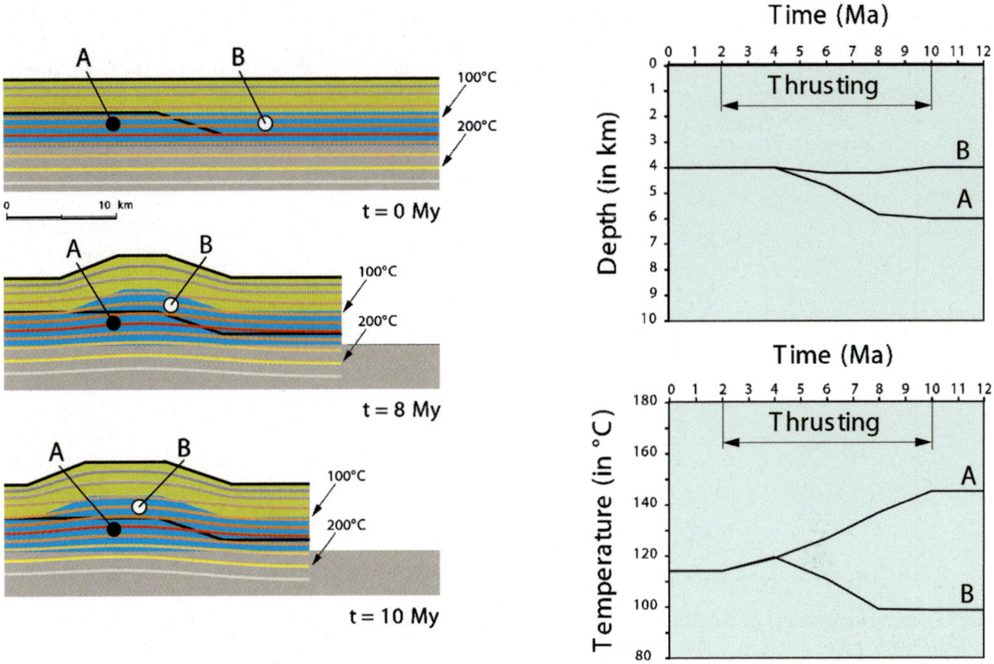

Fig. 4. The simplest example for the reconstruction of the burial and temperature history curves: the growth of a fault-bend fold thrust anticline. There is no erosion, no sedimentation, and the thrust velocity is slow enough to ensure thermal computation under steady-state mode regime.

$$t_a = \frac{H}{v \cdot \sin\theta} \tag{2}$$

where H is the thickness to thrust sheet, θ the dip angle of the thrust ramp and v (in m s^{-1}) the thrust velocity (i.e. the rate of horizontal shortening, 'v.sinθ' being the net burial velocity). Here, homogeneous rock properties of the overburden were assumed. Parameter t_a was taken as the characteristic time of thrusting and was compared with the characteristic time of thermal diffusion, which is given by

$$t_d = \frac{H^2}{K} \tag{3}$$

with K (in m^2 s^{-1}) being the thermal diffusivity of the overburden rock.

$$K = \frac{k}{\rho \cdot C} \tag{4}$$

with k representing the thermal conductivity, ρ the bulk density of the sediment and C the bulk heat capacity of the overburden rock.

In the Thrustpack program, the sediment thermal conductivity k is represented by an isotropic tensor, $k^e = kI$, where I is the identity matrix:

$$k = k_s^{(1-\phi)}\, k_w^{\phi} \tag{5}$$

where k_w is the heat conductivity of water, k_s the heat conductivity of the solid and $\phi = \phi(z)$ the porosity of the sediment.

The sediment heat capacity is also taken as an isotropic tensor and is a function of the relative water and solid content of the bulk sediment:

$$\rho C = \rho_w C_w \phi + \rho_s C_s (1 - \phi) \tag{6}$$

where ρ_w is the water density, C_w is the water heat capacity, ρ_s is the density of the solid and C_s is the heat capacity of the solid.

Then using equations (2) and (3) and by analogy with the Peclet number in fluid mechanics, Endignoux & Wolf (1990) proposed using the ratio

$$P = \frac{t_d}{t_a} = \frac{H \cdot v \cdot \sin\theta}{K} \tag{7}$$

to identify where the steady-state or the transient problem is the most appropriate to build a

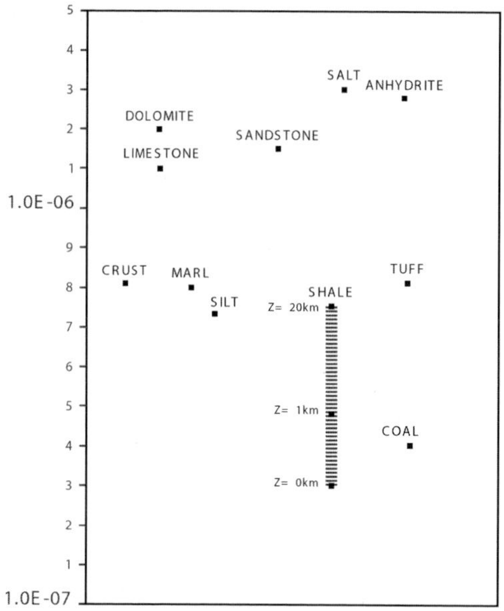

Fig. 5. Typical magnitudes of the thermal diffusivity of standard rock lithologies. For shales, the vertical bar shows the interval when water contribution through porosity is varied from the surface to a great depth.

geologically realistic temperature field reconstruction.

For most dry-rock lithologies the thermal diffusivity falls into two groups, as shown in Figure 5, with a first group with values above 1.e–6 and a second one below 1.e–6. The bulk thermal diffusivity for shale is drawn in this figure with a thick segment to show the effect of water from surface ($z=0$ km) to great depth ($z>5$km).

In Figure 6, equation (3) is plotted as a log–log diagram to highlight that for most crustal rocks lithologies, the characteristic diffusion time is actually very small, thus giving a justification for the adopted numerical scheme (the fault or strata instantaneous emplacement method of Fig. 3). In Figure 6 it is shown that the advection time should be chosen to be lower than 10 years when considering the emplacement of a 10 m layer thickness. In fact, this shows that the Peclet number is usually very small when considering burial rates from millimetres per year to a few centimetres per year, which is reasonable for many thrusts (an average over a series of seismic jumps). Heat transfer by conduction will never affect temperature gradients across a fault over a long period of time (even with a cyclicity of a 1 m jump every 10 years).

In Figure 7, the threshold velocities derived from equation (7) are plotted as a function of the thrust sheet thickness and the fault dip angle. The critical thrust velocity is about 5 mm a^{-1} when the dip of the ramp is 30° and the thrust décollement depth is 2.2 km. These curves were obtained for a thermal diffusivity of 1.2e–6 $m^2 s^{-1}$, choosing a numerical time step such that Pe = 0.02. The advection time is the time required to reach maximum burial, a numerical time step that can be defined as a fraction of the natural advection time step. During numerical tests it was found that choosing $T_a = 50T_d$, as a numerical time-step increment, is a safe option to ensure a solution with a maximum temperature deviation of less than 5 °C for the point A in Figure 4. In complex structural settings the key parameter that dictates whether a steady-state or a transient computation mode is required is the 'net burial', which varies locally and integrates both thrust emplacement and erosion or sedimentation synchronous with thrusting. When the burial rate is below the threshold curve and the time variations in the boundary conditions do not change too rapidly, a steady solution is appropriate. Nevertheless, thermal reconstruction will replicate the non-linear effect linked to the change in the structural geometry (as shown by the history curves shown in Fig. 4).

Thrustpack takes account of the porosity of the rocks, and the temperature of the fluid phase is always assumed to be at equilibrium with that of the solid phase; therefore, the short-term thermal variations brought about by the circulation of hot hydrothermal fluids are neglected though they may be important in diagenetic precesses (Holbecker 2004; Roure *et al.* 2003; Faure *et al.* 2004). Once a realistic and reasonable thermal history is achieved, the source rock maturity can be computed using geochemical models of primary cracking, secondary cracking and expulsion such as those described by Ungerer *et al.* (1988), Forbes *et al.* (1991) and Rudkiewicz & Behar (1994). In this study source rock data are limited, therefore only the transformation ratio is used to indicate source rock maturity.

Specific case study: Rio Horta

The Eastern Cordillera of Colombia is an inverted Jurassic back-arc rift with thin-skinned thrust systems at both edges, against the Llanos Foreland in the east, and against the Magdalena Valley in the west (also an asymmetric foreland basin in the area of Rio Horta; Fig. 1). Stratigraphically, a Jurassic redbed rift fill is followed by Cretaceous post-rift sag, which contains rich source rock horizons. This is the

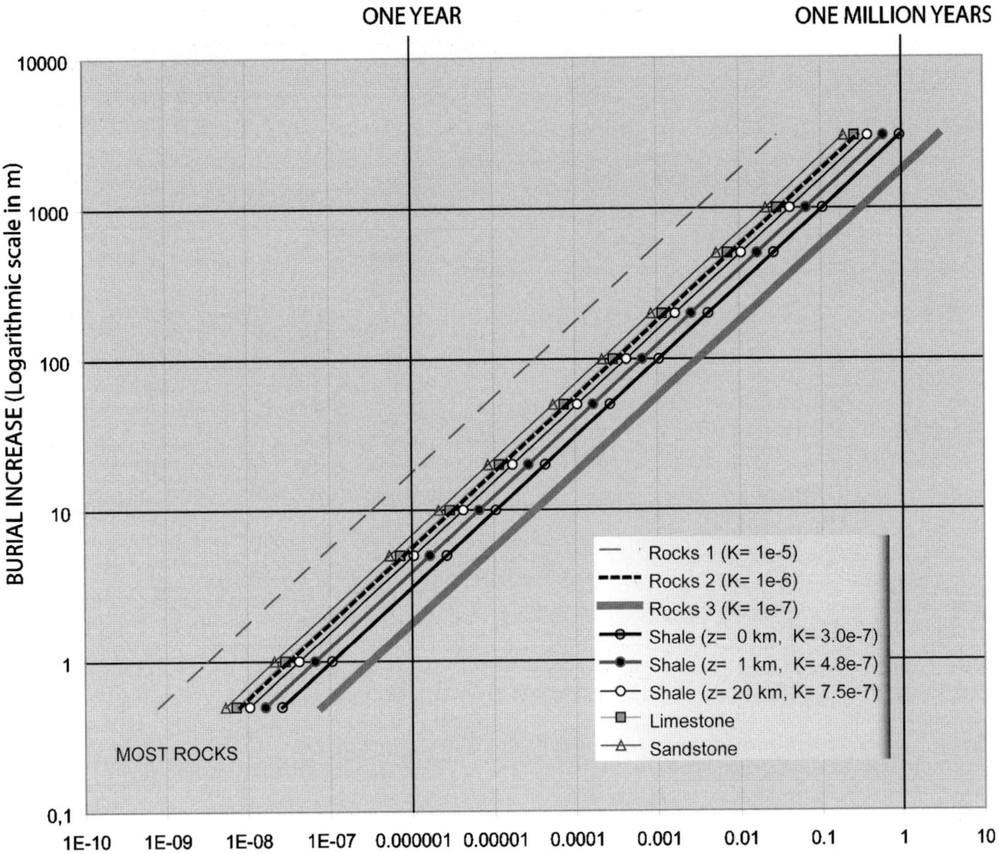

Fig. 6. Log–log diagram of the characteristic diffusion time v. 'instant emplacement' by burial for different rock material properties. Most rocks plot between the line for sandstone and that for shales at the surface.

'Villeta Formation', a type 2 source rock in conventional source rock classification, or type A in the classification of Pepper & Corvi (1994). There are three distinct Tertiary clastic foreland basin sequences separated by significant unconformities: Palaeocene (Guaduas, Umir, Lisama), Upper Eocene–Oligocene (La Paz, Esmeralda, Mugrosa, Colorado, sometimes collectively referred to as 'Gualanday') and Mio-Pliocene (Honda or Real). Different units act as reservoirs in different locations. At Rio Horta the main reservoir target (the most robust sand) is the La Paz Formation of Middle Eocene age. The stratigraphic relationships are shown in Figure 9, (adapted from Cooper *et al.* 1995). Most of these Tertiary formations were deposited during deformation events: they are the syntectonic 'molasse' of the Colombian Andes.

On the geological map, the frontal thrusts of the Cordillera (Fig. 1) carry Upper Cretaceous and Palaeogene rocks over the Mio-Pliocene 'Honda' Formation, the youngest unit of the foreland basin megasequence of the Middle Magdalena (Fig. 1). The thrust bows (salients) run out over the foreland both north and south of the core area of Rio Horta. The seismic data (Figs 10 and 11) show the Cretaceous-carrying 'master' thrust in red. Ahead of it are leading imbricates lying entirely within the Honda section (the basal detachment having climbed up-section), although these structures are not clearly apparent on the geological maps. A major anticline lies beneath these frontal structures, one of an en echelon pair. Though not particularly well imaged seismically (as is often the case in thrust belts), there are a number of critical geometrical relationships in the seismic data (Figs 10 and 11) that tell us that the structure is real and not velocity pull-up. First, the panel of reflectors that represents the leading limb of the sub-thrust

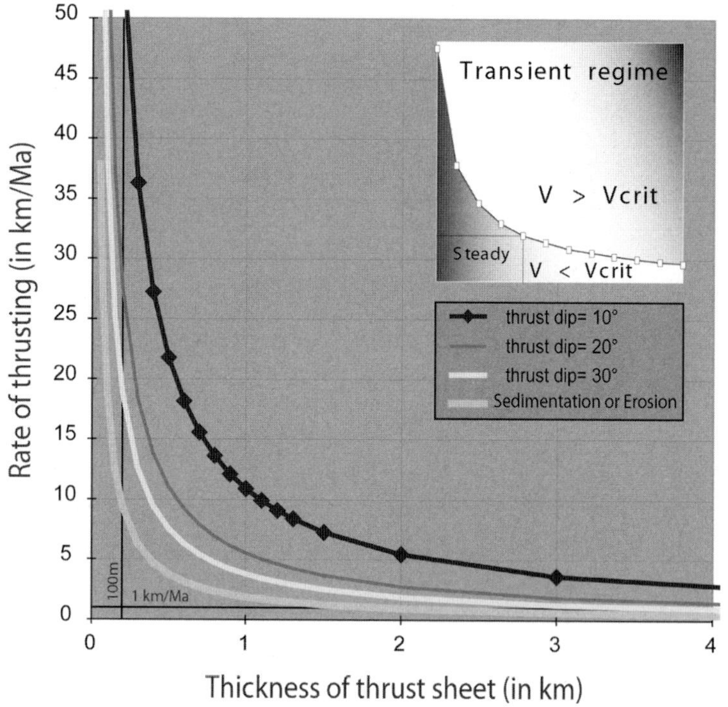

Fig. 7. Critical thrust velocity curves for several fault dip angles and assuming Pe = 0.02 (see text for explanation) (diagram modified after Endignoux & Wolf 1990).

anticline is robust; second, the amplitude is very large and the overlying thrust sheets do not have a particularly high seismic velocity: much of them are made up of the same Mio-Pliocene 'molasse' as the potential reservoir in the upper section of the prospective structure. Third, even though the data are poor, there are acceptable easterly dipping reflections in the back limb, so confidence in the back-limb dip is justified.

Well correlations in the foreland suggest that the good reflectors towards the base of the foreland-basin megasequence represent the La Paz Formation (the red pick in Figs 10 and 11). The seismic data suggest repetition of this package of reflectors, that the dips in the leading limb of the anticline are terminated at a thrust (a hanging wall cut-off), and that the matching footwall cut-off is some 15 km back down the dip of a panel of La Paz reflectors, which must therefore represent a footwall 'flat'. The recognition of this geometry is fundamental. It implies >15 km of displacement (reconstructed in the 2DMove restoration in Fig. 12) but beyond the leading edge of the structure the foreland basin megasequence is neither deformed nor translated. In this part of the Magdalena Valley, the onlapping foreland basin sediment wedge is clearly undisturbed. Where does the displacement go?

Two different explanations form the basis of the two 'Thrustpack' models that are described in this paper. The first (Model 1, Fig. 13), employs a 'palaeo-landscape' argument where, initially, the thrust carrying the Rio Horta structure defined the topographic surface. There cannot have been much topographic expression in the early stages because the seismic data do not show erosion at the crest of the Rio Horta Anticline, but the sediments of the foreland basin megasequence are assumed to have been deposited ahead of, and over, the structure. In Model 1, therefore the sub-thrust anticline is an early structure, and the overlying thrusts are later structures. In Model 2 the Rio Horta structure is assumed to have developed late (Fig. 14) after the deposition of most of the foreland basin megasequence and the emplacement of the overlying thrusts. The absence of displacement in the foreland basin ahead of the structure is explained by back-thrusting and 'fish-tailing' into the higher thrust sheets.

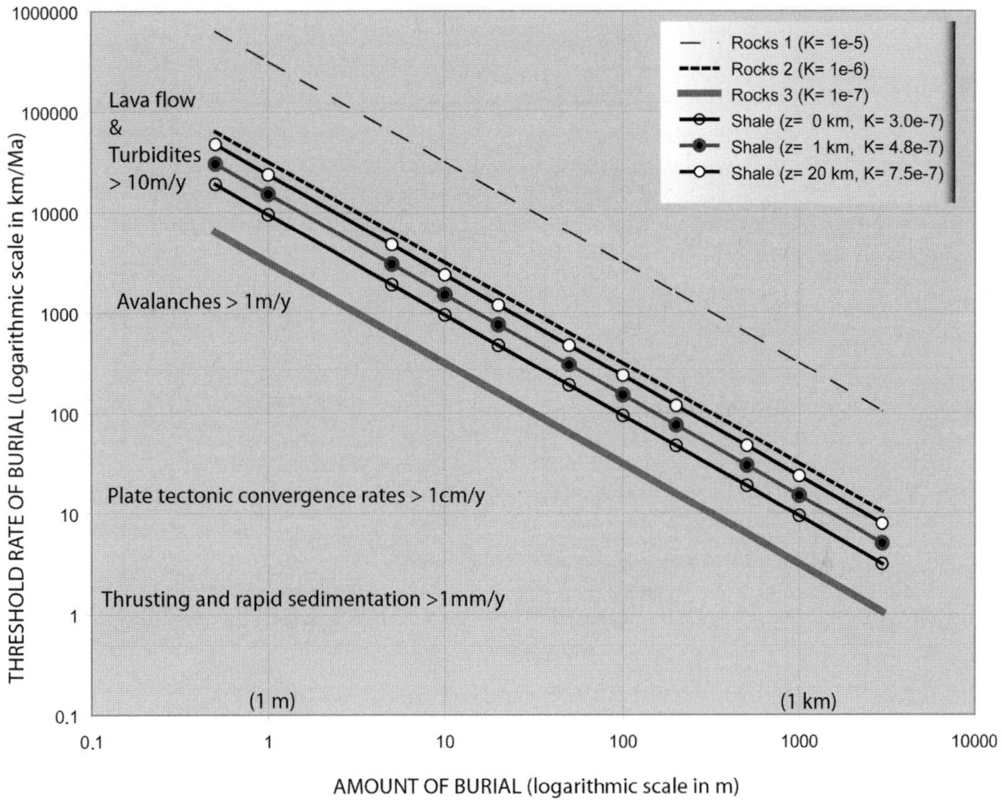

Fig. 8. Log–log diagram (Pe = 1) giving the threshold burial rate v. an instantaneous increase in depth.

The undeformed template that was re-stacked in 'Thrustpack' was a simplified version of the '2DMove' restoration (Fig. 12) of a section originally drawn by hand from seismic, map and well data. We hope to have constrained the whole geological evolution within reasonable limits in the models, and contend that there are valid reconstructions of the structural history, acceptable amounts of erosion and sedimentary thickness, valid depositional environments, an acceptable sequence of topography (evolving mountain fronts with reasonable relief through time), acceptable lithospheric configuration, and acceptable amounts and rates of uplift and subsidence.

Model 1: the Rio Horta sub-thrust anticlines as early structures in the deformation sequence

The key elements of the seismic interpretation that drive this model are as follows: (1) the La Paz Formation is folded by a large 'sub-thrust' anticline; (2) the fold lies on a thrust sheet that was emplaced during deposition of the La Paz Formation and the thrust rides over the lower part of that sequence; (3) the geometry suggests that erosion on the emerging topography was limited. No angular unconformity is visible, and the (probable) onlap of the foreland basin megasequence onto the structure (Fig. 11) indicates that the anticline was developing in a basin that was actively subsiding. The significant burial of the Rio Horta structure did not occur until the overlying far-travelled thrust sheet was emplaced above it in the Late Miocene and Pliocene. Thus, geometrically, the structure would seem to be close to maximum burial depth at present day (Fig. 15).

The cause of the subsidence is presumably the loading by more internal thrust sheets. The present-day profile from the foreland into the basin (the dip of the foreland basin floor) is rather steep, a short-wavelength foreland,

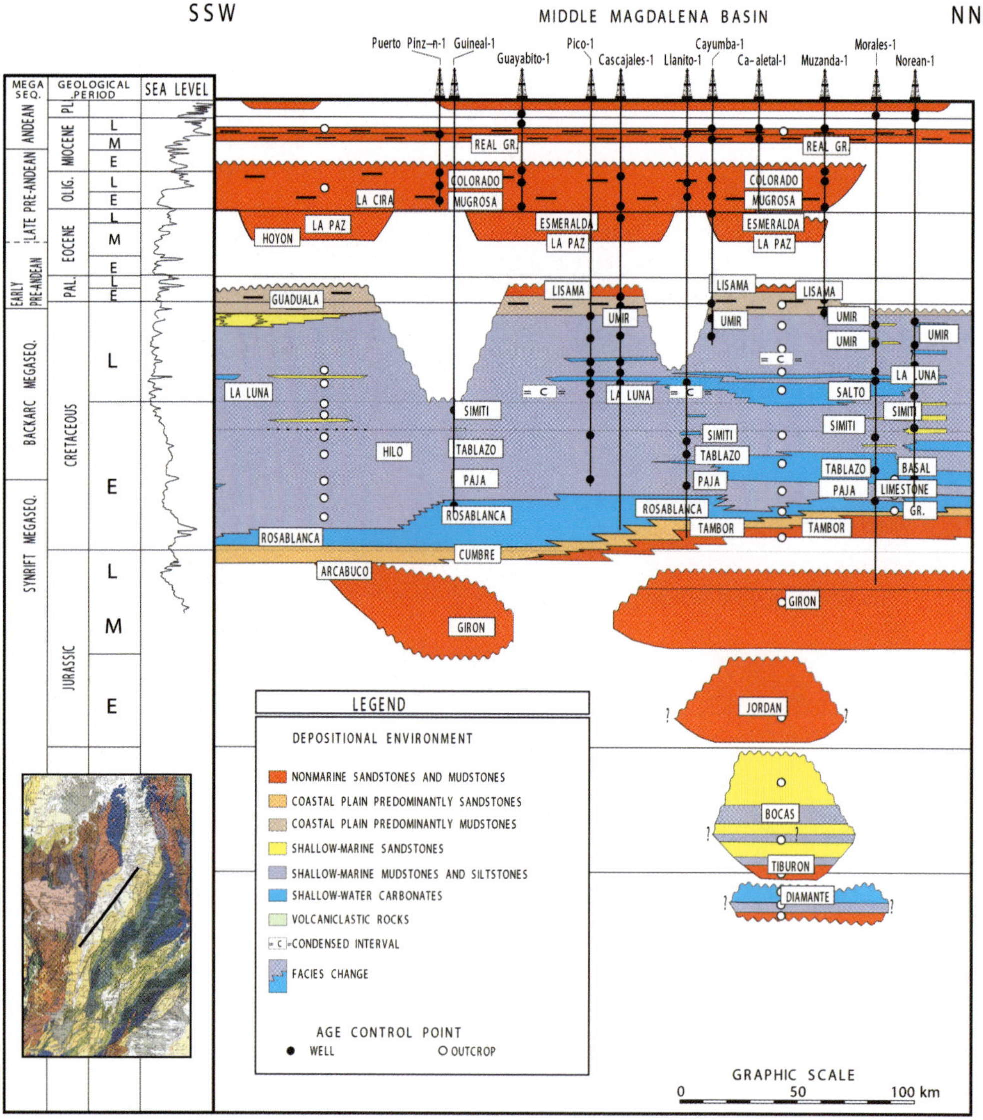

Fig. 9. Chronostratigraphy of the Magdalena Valley after Cooper *et al.* (1995); Rio Horta area is highlighted.

comparable with the profile of foreland basins developed on strongly stretched crust (Fig. 12). An analogous abrupt flexure is also required throughout the 'Thrustpack' kinematic evolution of Model 1 to maintain the balance of displacement, topographic height and sediment thickness (Figs 13 and 14). If this slope seems steeper than reasonable, it might be regarded as a negative aspect of the model.

The outcrop pattern on the geological map (Fig. 1) emphasizes the suggestion of early development that is deduced from the seismic geometry. North and south of the area of the sub-thrust anticline, the leading higher thrust imbricates break forward into the foreland basin. As a general rule, thrusts run forward where it is mechanically easy for them to do so, where there is a better detachment, or where there is no

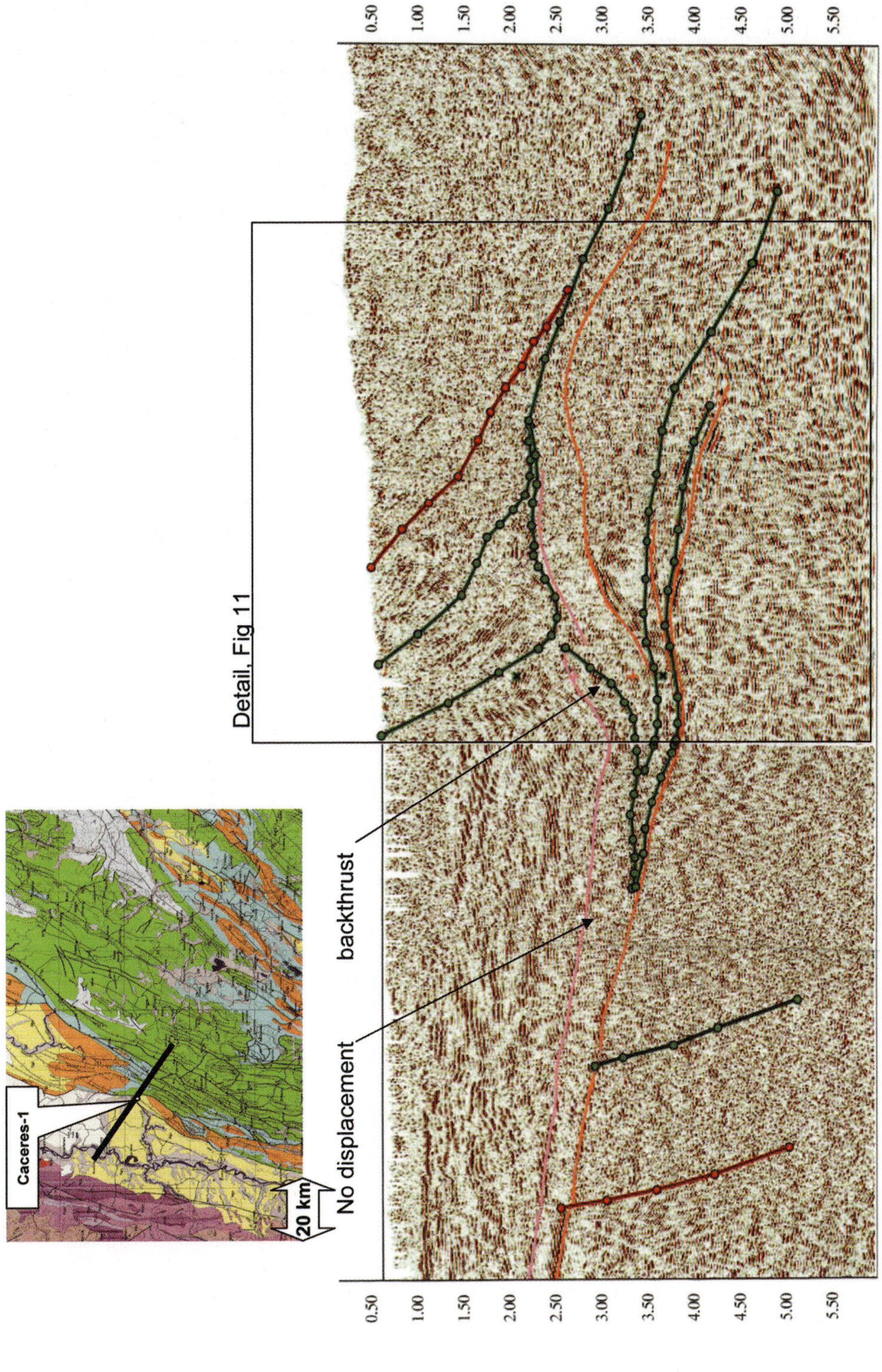

Fig. 10. Seismic line through the Rio Horta prospect structure with line-drawing of major structural elements.

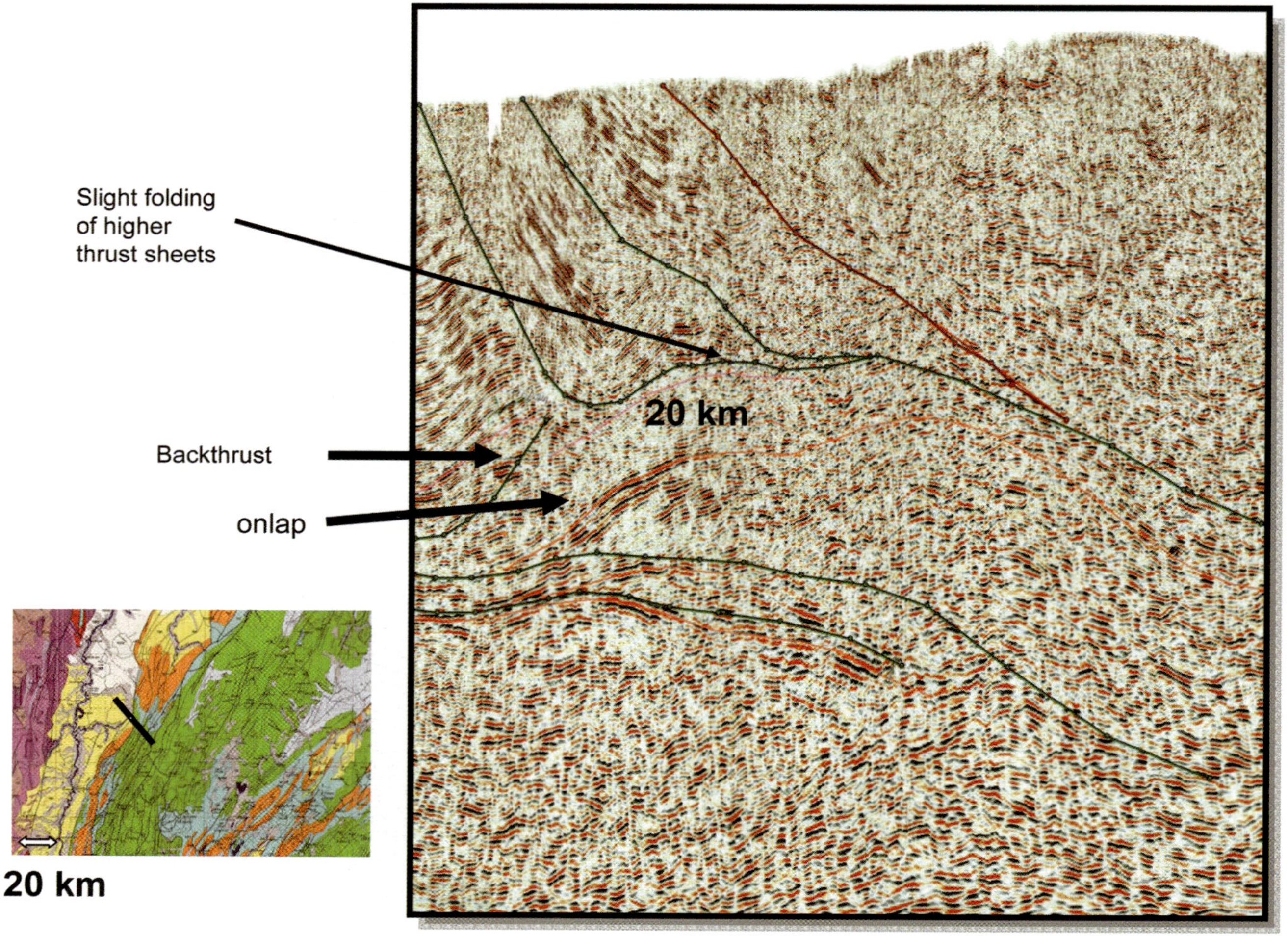

Fig. 11. Seismic line (close-up of line in Fig. 10) with line-drawing of major structural elements.

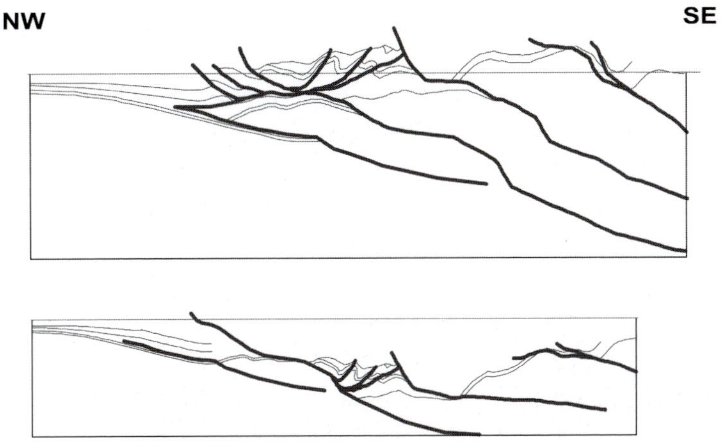

Fig. 12. Original deformed and partially restored cross-sections using 2DMove software (Midland Valley™).

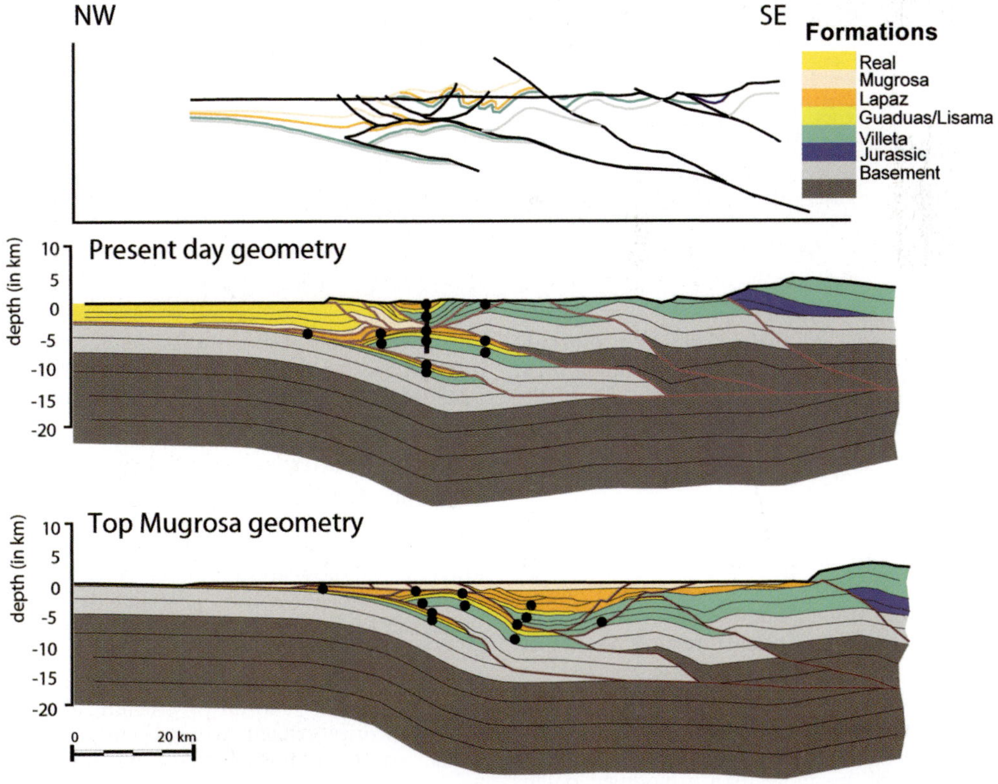

Fig. 13. Model 1: present-day geometry of the 2DMove and Thrustpack cross-sections and geometry of the intermediate cross-section at Mugrosa (Early Miocene) time. •, selected points for which the burial, temperature and maturity evolutions were analysed; some of them are aligned according to the projection of the Guineal well (in the north of the area).

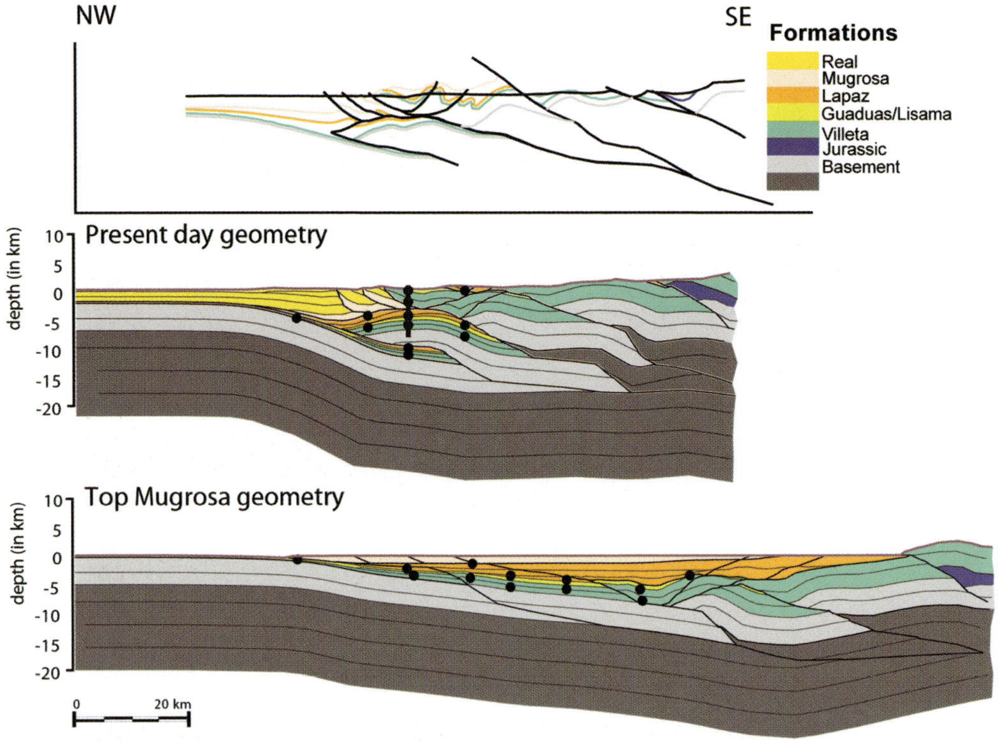

Fig. 14. Model 2: present-day geometry of the 2DMove and Thrustpack cross-sections and geometry of the intermediate cross-section at Mugrosa time. •, selected points for which the burial, temperature and maturity evolutions were analysed; some of them are aligned according to the projection of the Guineal well (in the north of the area).

obstruction. In the analogy of waves breaking on a shore on either side of a protruding rock, the waves break forward on either side of the rock and stack up in the area behind it. The 'obstruction' here would presumably be a pre-existing structure. The Rio Horta 'sub-thrust' leads are the rocks on the shore.

The Rio Horta structure does seem to gently fold the thrust sheet above it (Figs 10 and 11), and because these structures cut the youngest beds of the Honda Formation, some development of the sub-thrust structure must have taken place relatively recently. There also seems to be a back-thrust ahead of the main anticline (arrowed in Fig. 11). In Model 1, this structure is assumed to be poorly developed and without significant displacement; no more than a modified onlap, which, like the gentle folding of the overlying thrust sheets, can be attributed to slight late movement on the deep structure. In Model 2, on the other hand, considerable displacement on the back-thrust is necessary to accommodate the offset suggested by matching the hanging-wall and foot-wall cut-offs of the Rio Horta structure.

Model 2: the alternative view of the evolution of the Rio Horta system

In Model 2 (Fig. 14), it is assumed that the lower thrust sheet and the development of the sub-thrust anticline entirely post-date the higher thrust sheet, therefore, all of the 15 km displacement must be transferred onto the back-thrust (Figs 10 and 11) or be accommodated by ductile strain ahead of the sub-thrust structure. There is too much displacement to transfer into ductile strain, so there must be back-thrusting, or, because the back-thrust does not come to the surface, we must 'fish-tail' the displacement into the overriding thrust system. This is possible but seems intuitively unlikely. It should be noted that, as in Model 1, a short-wavelength foreland,

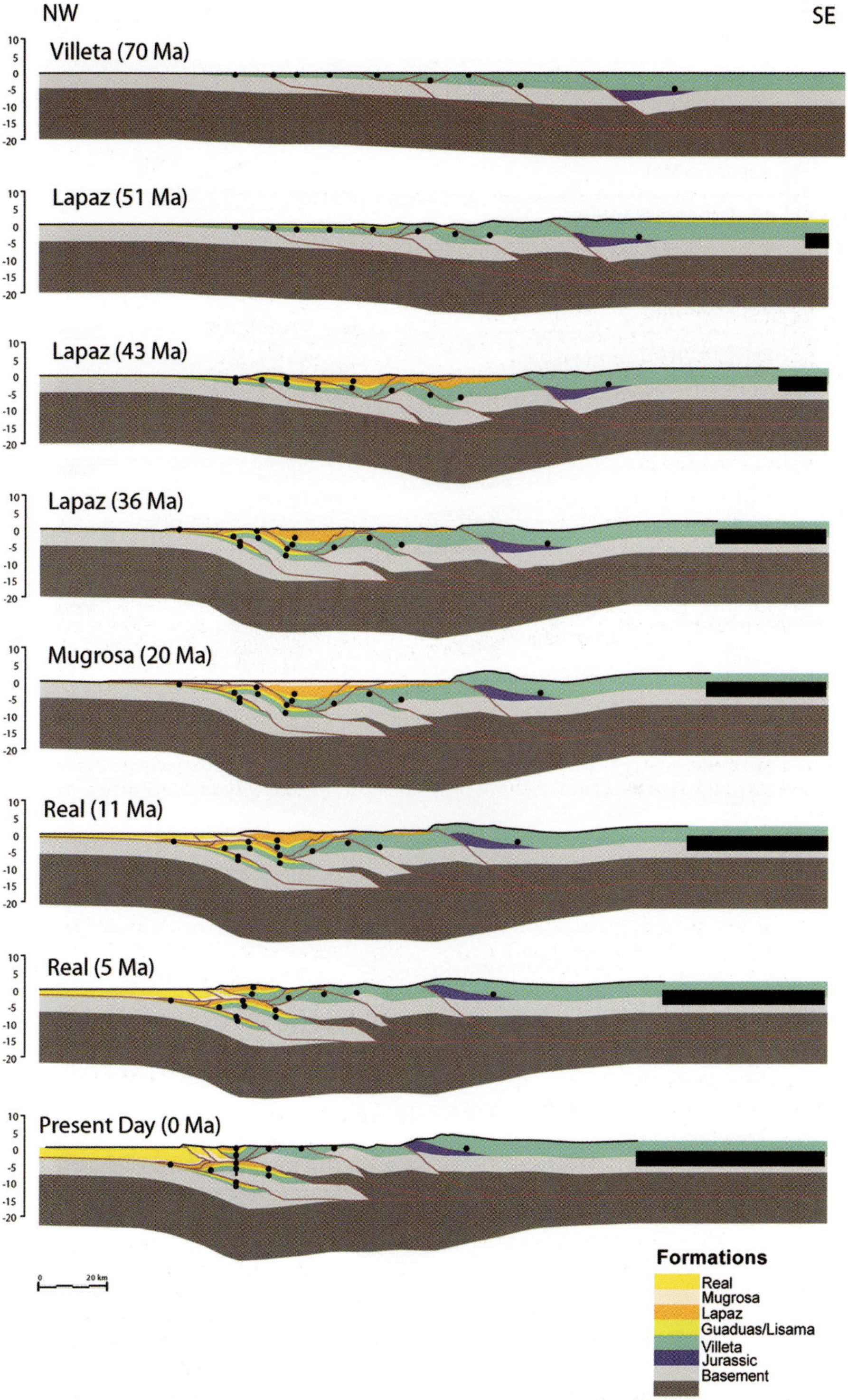

Fig. 15. Selected evolutionary stages to illustrate the structural scenario of Model 1 (eight of a total of 10 sections). •, translation of selected points since their burial time.

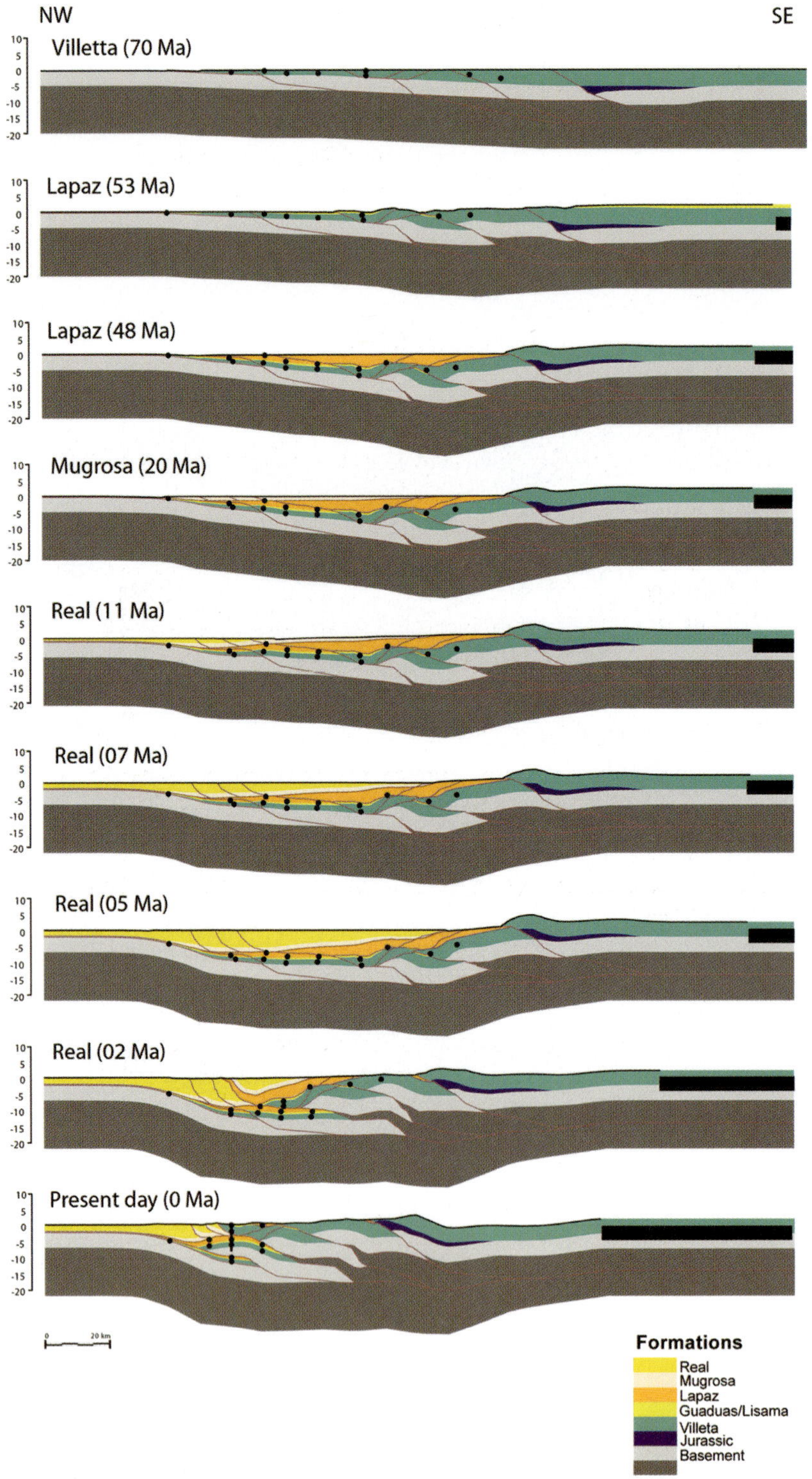

Fig. 16. Selected evolutionary stages to illustrate the structural scenario of Model 2 (nine of a total of 12 sections). •, translation of selected points since their burial time.

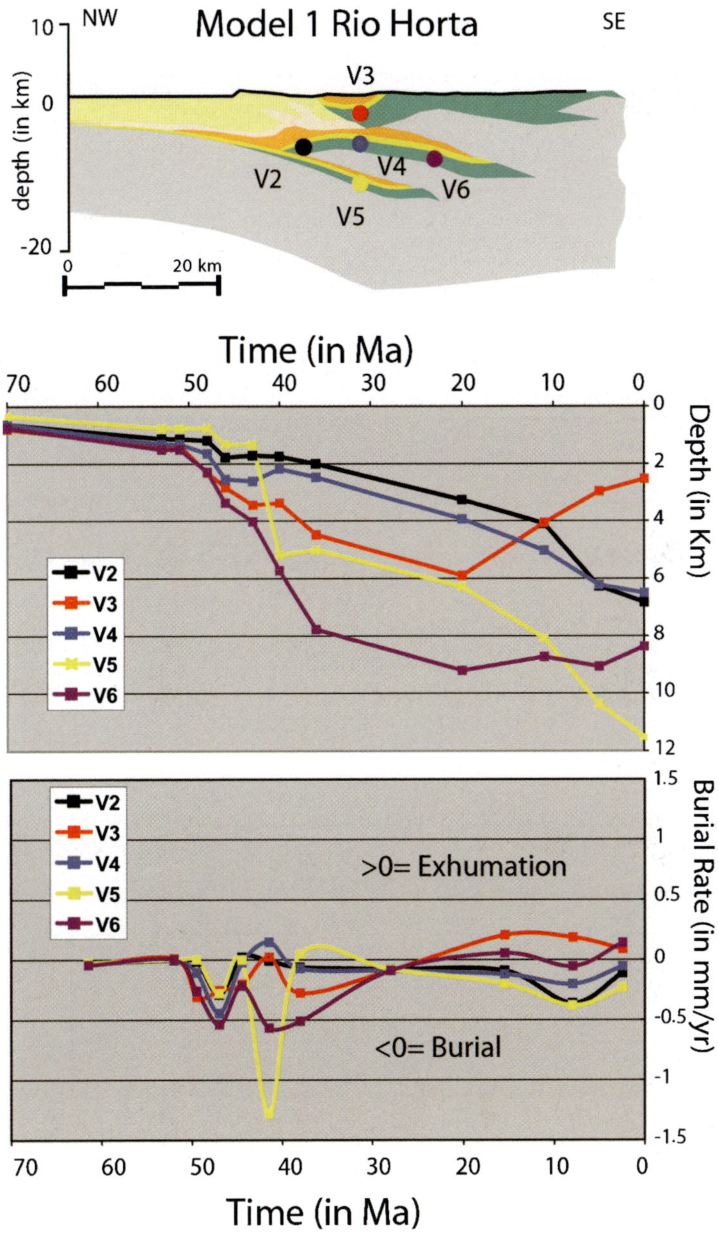

Fig. 17. Model 1: burial history and burial rate curves for selected points in the Villeta Formation (Upper Cretaceous) in different structural units.

with a steep basal dip, is required throughout the modelling stages.

Discussion and petroleum system modelling

Two snapshots from the Thrustpack sequential geometries (present day and Early Oligocene, Top Mugrosa) are shown for each of the models in Figures 13 and 14. In both models the final forward model is a reasonably good approximation of the original restored section (an essential constraint on the Thrustpack procedure). The Early Oligocene stage (Mugrosa) is chosen because the different evolution of the two models

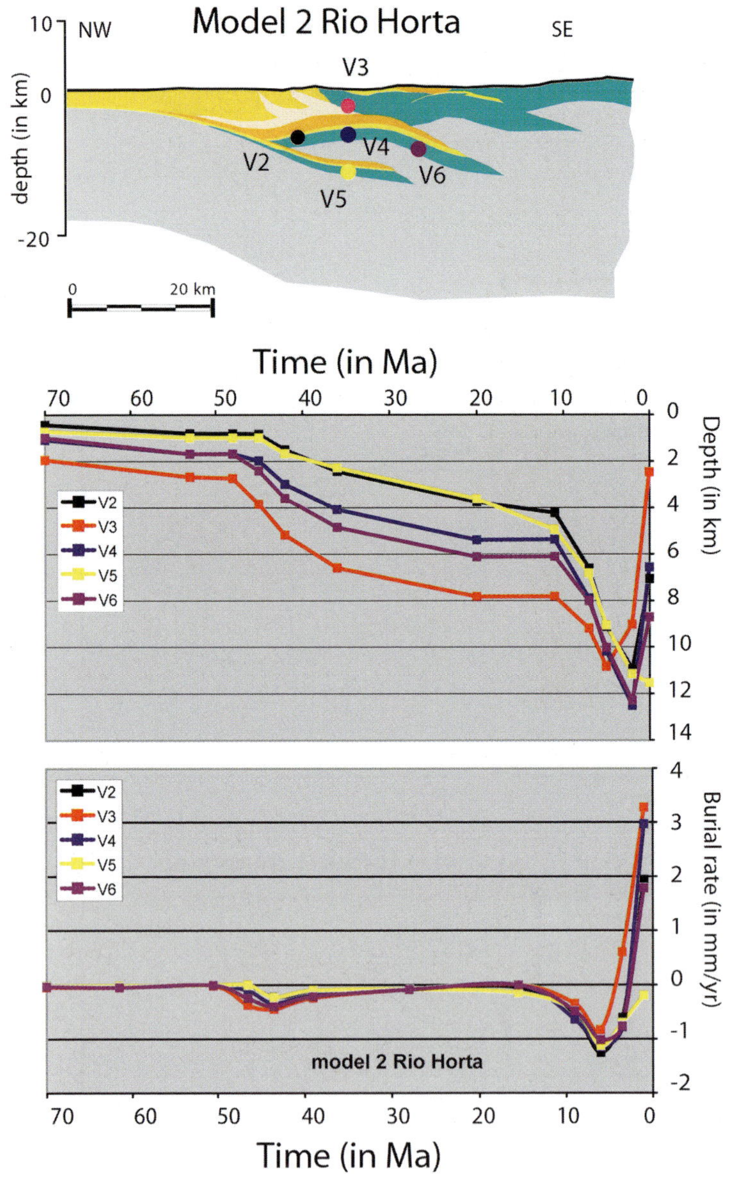

Fig. 18. Model 2: burial history and burial rate curves for selected points in the Villeta Formation in different structural units.

is most obvious at this time. In Model 1 the Rio Horta structure is almost fully developed; in Model 2 it is not yet initiated. Figures 15 and 16 show the original templates and other stages in the evolution.

Figures 17 and 18 show burial curves and burial rate curves for the Cretaceous Villeta source rock from various positions around the structure. The differences are stark. It should be noted that the subsidence rates of the selected points are reasonable (<1 mm a^{-1}), except for the recent history of Model 2, which looks slightly too fast to be real.

The computed temperature profiles from the models at the present day are shown in Figure 19. The temperature profile from the nearest well, Guineal 1, is an imperfect reference because of its structural position in a higher thrust sheet;

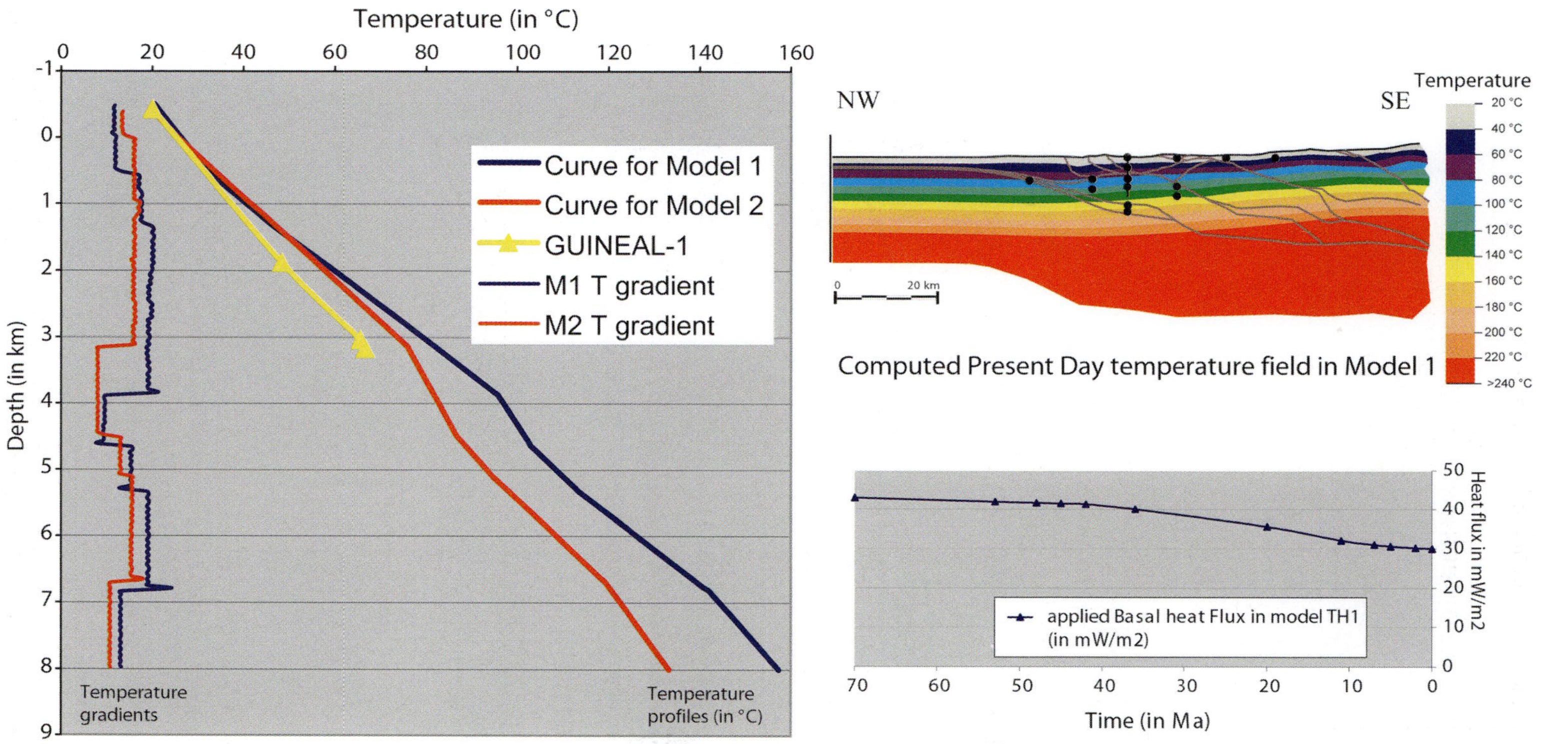

Fig. 19. Thrustpack's temperature reconstruction: calibration of thermal boundary conditions for Models 1 and 2, with downhole temperature data in Guineal 1. Cross-section shows the present-day iso-temperature lines. For this computation the surface temperature was kept constant in time and space, and a time-varying basal heat flux was applied as shown in the bottom right diagram.

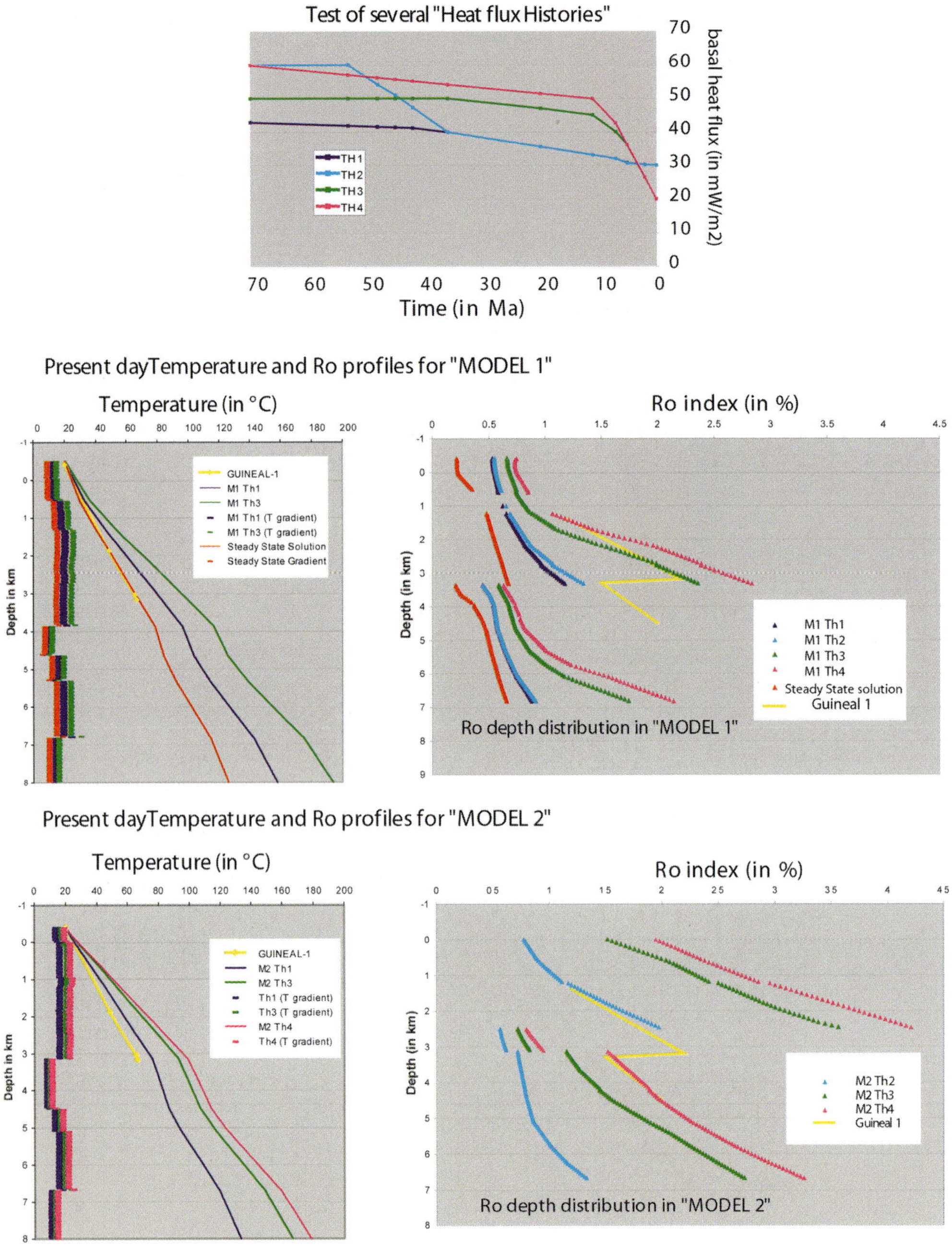

Fig. 20. Test of various thermal regimes according to different geohistories of the basal heat flux for Models 1 and 2. The variations were tested to tentatively match and compare with Thrustpack R_o results v. vitrinite reflectance data from Guineal 1.

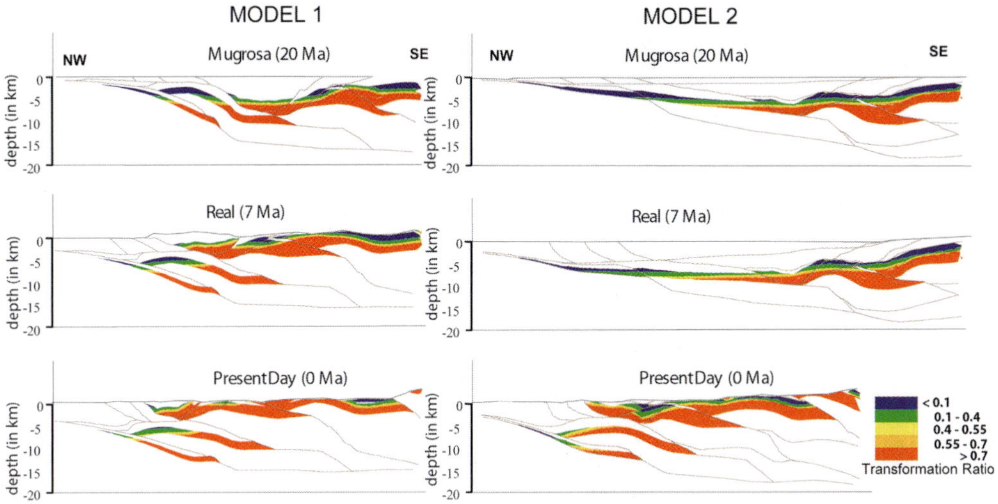

Fig. 21. Computed transformation ratio in the source rock formation of the cross-sections at three key periods for Model 1 (left column) and Model 2 (right column) resulting from the Th1 (see Figs 19 and 20) thermal scenario.

nevertheless, a good match was found using 20 °C of surface temperature and 30 mW m^{-2} of basal heat flux. Constant surface temperature and a variable basal heat flux were extrapolated back through time (Fig. 19), therefore the difference in temperature gradients between Model 1 and Model 2 is entirely due to geometry and the lithological sequence. Each change in slope along the temperature profile marks a change in the thermal properties assigned to rock type (sand and shale).

Figure 20 is an attempt to match the 'Thrustpack' predictions against the only palaeotemperature data available. These are R_o data, also from Guineal, shown as the yellow curve in the left-hand diagrams in Figure 20. The other curves in these diagrams are attempts to match the R_o profile from Thrustpack modelling using a position in the higher thrust sheet, analogous to that of Guineal (Guineal itself lies off the line of section). Different heat fluxes are used, and shown by the different coloured curves (red indicates constant geothermal gradient); for the other curves different thermal decays are assumed. None of the curves fit either Model 1 or Model 2 very well. However, in view of the level of the confidence in the other checks and balances (the geometrical correspondence of model and section and the fit with Guineal's temperature profile), we prefer to believe that the vitrinite data are unreliable.

The plots of transformation ratio and porosity evolution, derived from the two reconstructions in Thrustpack (Figs 21 and 22), are fairly self explanatory. They clearly suggest the greater prospectivity of the structure if it evolved through the sequence of Model 1, and vividly illustrate the enormous importance of the interpretation of structural geometry and structural sequence in this type of environment. Figure 21 presents the two extreme possibilities, oil mature at maximum burial at the present day versus gas mature and 10 km elevation in the last few million years.

The deep burial and late elevation in Model 2 would probably lead to a tight reservoir, fractured by late elevation. The maturity modelling predicts gas, and the rapid late elevation might suggest overpressure. The gas would occupy fracture porosity which would close up during production, something that we believe to have occurred at Opon, a gas discovery in a sub-thrust structure not far from Rio Horta, and a regional analogue for Rio Horta.

In Model 2 the maturity within the Rio Horta structure itself spans transformation ratio zones ranging from immature to gas. Downdip eastwards is a gas kitchen. Whether gas derived from here might displace oil from the Rio Horta structure must remain a matter of speculation, where the size and integrity and amplitude of the structure become significant issues.

Conclusions

Thermal evolution in a foreland fold and thrust belt system is essentially controlled by the net rate of burial of the rocks estimated by integrating thrusting, sedimentation and erosion, and by the thermal boundary conditions. In this respect,

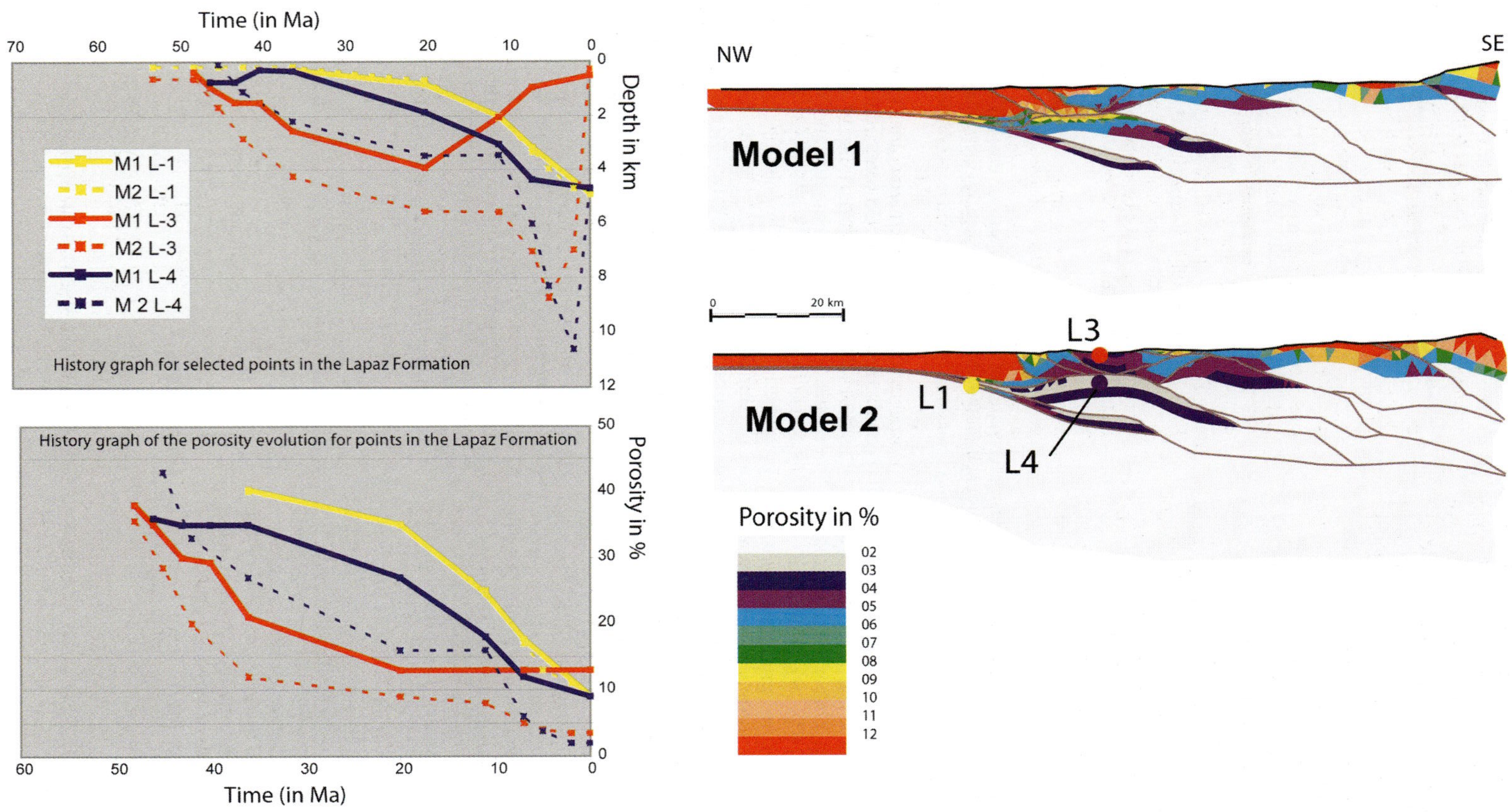

Fig. 22. Modelled present-day distribution and time variation, for selected points in the La Paz reservoir, of the sediment porosity in Model 1 compared with that in Model 2 (same porosity–depth relationships in each case; differences are due to burial path).

the magnitude of basal heat flux has a stronger effect on the computed temperature profile than the magnitude of the surface temperature. An assumption of steady state is valid where the burial rate is below the threshold rates of heat diffusion in the media (i.e. 1 < km Ma^{-1}). Faulting and thermal conduction cannot be responsible for maintaining a transient thermal regime, except in situations of very rapid burial rate.

The petroleum systems of most fold and thrust belts are much better constrained by 2D rather than 1D modelling, but it is vital to understand geometry and sequence to properly appraise their prospectivity. Thrustpack allows us to do this and to therefore better specify exploration risk. In the case of Rio Horta it is the difference between having a prospect and not having one.

We thank Ecopetrol for providing data, and in particular P. Restrepo-Pace for allowing access to his previous work in this area.

References

ACOSTA, J., GRAHAM, R. & SASSI, W. 2003. Structural interpretation and source rock maturation modelling along two distinct transects in the Upper/Middle Magdalena Basin, Colombia. *In*: *Proceedings of the VIII Simposio Bolivariano—Exploration Petrolera en las Cuencas Subandinas*, Cartagena de Indias, 1–15 Extended Abstract.

BREWER, J. 1981. Thermal effects of thrust faulting. *Earth and Planetary Science Letters*, **56**, 233–244.

COOPER, M. A., ADDISON, F. T., ALVAREZ, R., *et al.* 1995. Basin development and tectonic history of the Los Llanos basins, Eastern Cordillera and middle Magdalena Valley, Colombia. *AAPG Bulletin*, **79**(10), 1421–1443.

CORTEZ, M. 2004. *Evolution structurale du front centre occidental de la Cordillère Orientale de Colombie*. Thèse de doctorat, Université Pierre et Marie Curie, Paris VI.

DAHLSTROM, C. D. A. 1969. Balanced cross sections. *Canadian Journal of Earth Sciences*, **6**, 743–757.

DEVILLE, E. & SASSI, W. 2006. Contrasting thermal evolution of thrust systems: an analytical and modeling approach in the front of the Western Alps. *AAPG Bulletin*, **90**, 887–907.

DIVIES, R. 1997. *FOLDIS, un modèle cinématique de bassins sédimentaires par éléments discrets associant plis, failles érosion/sédimentation et compaction*. Thèse de doctorat, Université de Grenoble I.

DIVIES, R. & SASSI, W. 1996. *Méthode pour réaliser un modèle cinématique en 2D de bassins géologiques affectés par des failles*. Brevet d'enregistrement national no. 96/05 736. Rapport IFP, **43066**.

ENDIGNOUX, L. 1989. *Une modélisation numérique de l'évolution cinématique et thermique des structures chevauchantes*. Thèse de doctorat, Université Joseph-Fourier, Grenoble.

ENDIGNOUX, L. & MUGNIER, J. L. 1990. The use of forward kinematical model in the construction of a balanced cross-section. *Tectonics*, **9**, 1249–1262.

ENDIGNOUX, L. & WOLF, S. 1990. Thermal and kinematic evolution of thrust basins: 2D numerical model. *In*: LETOUZEY, J. (ed.) *Petroleum Tectonics in Mobile Belt*. Technip, Paris, 181–192.

FAURE, J. L., OSADETZ, K., BENAOUALI, Z. N., SCHNEIDER, F. & ROURE, F. 2004. Kinematic and petroleum modelling of the Alberta foothills and adjacent foreland—west of Calgary. *Oil & Gas Science and Technology—Revue de l'Institut Français du Pétrole*, **59**(1), 81–108.

FORBES, P. L., UNGERER, P. M., KUHFUSS, A. B., RIIS, F. & EGGEN, S. 1991. Compositional modeling of petroleum generation and expulsion: trial application to a local mass balance in the Smorbukk Sor Fiel, Haltenbanken Area, Norway. *AAPG Bulletin*, **75**(5), 873–893.

GRETENER, P. E. 1981. *Geothermics: Using Temperature in Hydrocarbon Exploration*. American Association of Petroleum Geologists, Education Course Note Series, **#17**.

GROSSLING, B. F. 1959. Temperature variations due to the formation of a geosyncline. *Geological Society of America Bulletin*, **70**, 1253–1281.

HOLZBECHER, E. 2004. Mathematical analysis of the effect of sedimentation and compaction on steady transport profiles in sediments. *Transport in Porous Media*, **57**, 279–296.

HUGHES, J. T. R. 1987. *The Finite Element Method. Linear Static and Dynamic Finite Element Analysis*. Prentice–Hall, Englewood Cliffs, NJ.

HUSSON, L. & MORETTI, I. 2002. Thermal regime of fold and thrust belts—an application to the Bolivian sub-Andean zone. *Tectonophysics*, **345**, 253–280.

JABOYEDOFF, M. 1999. Modèles thermiques simples de la croûte terrestre: un regard sur les Alpes. *Bulletin de la Société Vaudise des Sciences Naturells*, **86**(4), 229–271.

JONES, P. B. 1982. Oil and gas beneath east-dipping underthrust faults in the Alberta foothills. *In*: POWERS, R. B. (ed.) *Geologic Studies of the Cordilleran Thrust Belt, Vol. 1 Rocky Mountain Geology*, Denver, Co.

LONERGAN, L. 1993. Timing and kinematics of deformation in the Malaguide Complex, Internal Zone of the Betic Cordillera. *Tectonics*, **12**, 460–476.

PEPPER, A. S. & CORVI, P. J. 1994. Simple kinetic models of petroleum formation. Pt 1: oil and gas generation from kerogen. *Marine and Petroleum, Geology*, **12**(3), 291–319.

RESTREPO-PACE, P. A., COLMENARES, F., HIGUERA, C. & MAYORGA, M., 2004. A fold-and-thrust belt along the western flank of the Eastern Cordillera of Colombia—style, kinematics, and timing contraints derived from seismic data and detailed surface mapping. *In*: MCCLAY, K. R. (ed.) *Thrust Tectonics and Hydrocarbon Systems*. American Association of Petroleum Geologists, Memoirs, **82**, 598–613.

ROURE, F. & SASSI, W. 1995. Kinematics of deformation and petroleum system appraisal in Neogene foreland-and-thrust belts. *Petroleum Geosciences*, **1**, 253–269.

ROURE, F., BORDAS-LEFLOCH, N., TORO, J., *et al.* 2003. Petroleum systems and reservoir appraisal in the sub-Andean basins (eastern Venezuela and eastern Colombian foothills). *In*: BARTOLINI, C., BUFFLER, R. T. & BLICKWEDE, J. (eds) *The Circum-Gulf of Mexico and the Caribbean: Hydrocarbon Habitats, Basin Formation, and Plate Tectonics*. American Association of Petroleum Geologists, Memoirs, **79**, 750–775.

RUDKIEWICZ, J.-L. & BEHAR, F. 1994. Influence of kerogen type and TOC content on multiphase primary migration. *Organic Geochemistry*, **21**(2), 121–133.

RUDKIEWICZ, J.-L., SCHNEIDER, F., BEHAR, F., GAULIER, J.-M., WENDEBOURG, J. & SASSI, W. 1996. Challenges and achievements in basin modeling: predicting the nature and the volume of hydrocarbons. *In*: GOMEZ LUNA, M. E. & MARTINEZ CORTÉS, A. (eds) *Geoquimica Organica—5e Congreso Latino-American, Cancun*, 6–10 October 1996, Resumenes, 380.

SASSI, W. & RUDKIEWICZ, J. L. 1999. *Thrustpack version 6.2: 2-D integrated maturity studies in thrust areas*. Institut Français du Pétrole Report, **45372**.

SASSI, W. & RUDKIEWICZ, J.-L. 2000. Computer modelling of petroleum systems along regional cross-sections in foreland and fold and thrust belts (abstract). *In*: *Proceedings of the Conference on Geology and Petroleum Geology of the Mediterranean and Circum-Mediterranean Basins (European Association of Geophysicists and Engineers, Malta, 1–4 October 2000), Extended abstracts*, **C27**, 1–4.

SASSI, W., RUDKIEWICZ, J-L. & DIVIES, R. 1998. New methods for integrated modeling of deformation and petroleum generation in fold and thrust belts (abstract). *American Association of Petroleum Geologists Annual Meeting Programs*, **82**, N13 Supplement.

SCIAMANNA, S., SASSI, W., GAMBINI, R., RUDKIEWICZ, J.-L., MOSCA, F. & NICOLAI, C. 2004. Predicting hydrocarbon generation and expulsion in the Southern Apennines thrustbelt by 2D integrated structural and geochemical modelling Part I: structural and thermal evolution. *In*: SWENNEN, R., ROURE, F. & GRANATH, J. W. (eds) *Deformation, Fluid Flow and Reservoir Appraisal in Fold and Thrust Belts*. American Association of Petroleum Geologists, Hedberg Series, **1**, 51–67.

SHI, Y. & WANG, C. Y. 1987. Two-dimensional modelling of the *P–T–t* paths of regional metamorphism in simple overthrust terrains. *Geology*, **15**, 1048–1051.

SUPPE, J. 1983. Geometry and kinematics of fault-bend folding. *American Journal of Science*, **283**, 684–721.

TER VOORDE, M. 1996. *Tectonic modeling of lithospheric extension along faults, implications for thermal and mechanical structure and basin stratigraphy*. PhD thesis, Vrije Universiteit Amsterdam.

TISSOT, B. P., PELET, R. & UNGERER, Ph. 1987. Thermal history of sedimentary basins, maturation indices, and kinetics of oil and gas generation. *AAPG Bulletin*, **71**(12), 1445–1466.

TORO, J., ROURE, F., BORDAS-LEFLOCH, N., LE CORNEC-LANCE, S. & SASSI, W. 2004. Thermal and kinematic evolution of the eastern Cordillera fold and thrust belt, Colombia. *In*: SWENNEN, R., ROURE, F. & GRANATH, J. W. (eds.) *Deformation, Fluid Flow and Reservoir Appraisal in Fold and Thrust Belts*. American Association of Petroleum Geologists, Hedberg Series, **1**, 79–115.

UNGERER, Ph., BURRUS, J., DOLIGEZ, B., CHENET, P. Y. & BESSIS, F. 1990. Basin evaluation by integrated two-dimensional modelling of heat transfer, fluid flow, hydrocarbon generation, and migration. *AAPG Bulletin*, **74**(3), 309–335.

VANN, I. R., GRAHAM, R. H. & HAYWARD, A. B. 1986. The structure of mountain fronts. *Journal of Structural Geology*, **8**, 215–227.

WALTHAM, D., TABERNER, C. & DOCHERTY, C. 2000. Error estimation in decompacted subsidence curves. *AAPG Bulletin*, **84**(8), 1087–1094.

ZOETEMEIJER, R. 1993. Tectonic modelling of foreland basins. Thin skinned thrusting, syntectonic sedimentation and lithospheric flexure. PhD thesis, Vrije Universiteit, Amsterdam, 90. 906478-8, 148 pp.

ZOETEMEIJER, R., & SASSI, W. 1992. 2D reconstitution of thrust evolution using the fault-bend method. *In*: MCCLAY, K. R. (ed.) *Thrust Tectonics*. Chapman & Hall, London, 133–140.

ZOETEMEIJER, R., SASSI, W., ROURE, F. & CLOETINGH, S. 1992. Stratigraphic and kinematic modelling of thrust evolution, northern Apennines, Italy. *Geology*, **20**, 1035–1038.

The implications of fracture swarms in the Chalk of SE England on the tectonic history of the basin and their impact on fluid flow in high-porosity, low-permeability rocks

MANDEFRO BELAYNEH, STEPHAN K. MATTHÄI & JOHN W. COSGROVE

Department of Earth Science and Engineering, Royal School of Mines, Imperial College, Prince Consort Road, London SW7 2BP, UK (e-mail: m.belayneh@ic.ac.uk)

Abstract: The Upper Cretaceous (Senonian) Chalk in Kent, SE England, is considered with the aim of establishing the tectonic history of the basin in which it was deposited, based on the chronology of fractures and an understanding of the role of these fractures in controlling fluid movement in high-porosity–low-permeability sediments. The earliest brittle structures in the study area are NE–SW-striking, flint-filled shear fractures, with dips of *c.* 60°, which were formed when the maximum compression (σ_1) was vertical and were utilized as channels for fluid movement during flint filling. Flint also occurs along bedding planes, suggesting a diagenetic source. This phase was followed by the development of NW–SE-striking fracture swarms containing fractures ranging between vertical joints and steeply dipping hybrid fractures with acute dihedral angles of *c.* 40°. The absence of flint along these fractures indicates that they formed after diagenesis of the Chalk. NW–SE-striking, subvertical, regularly spaced, through-going joints then formed as a result of a NW–SE regional compression linked to the Alpine collision. The final stage in the basin history relates to the formation of bed-parallel and vertical (i.e. bed-normal), bed-restricted, systematic and unsystematic fractures associated with uplift and unloading. To model fluid flow through the fracture network present in the Chalk, a finite-element–finite-volume modelling was carried out. The fracture geometries mapped in the field were discretized using unstructured hybrid element meshes with discrete fracture representations. The permeability of fractures was calculated from the cubic law and the petrophysical properties of the rock matrix were taken from Chalk reservoirs in the North Sea. In the models, a constant pressure was applied at the top of the oil-saturated, fractured Chalk while water was injected at the base. In spite of greater density, the water preferentially displaced the oil from the fractures and migrated faster through the fracture swarms and joints than through bed-restricted fractures and the rock matrix. Almost 83% of the total flow within the model occurred through the fractures. The results of the field study, combined with those of the numerical modelling, suggest that fracture swarms have a strong impact on the movement of fluids in fractured and faulted reservoirs.

Field studies show that zones of closely spaced, highly localized fractures or joint clusters with a very small spacing are common (Segall & Pollard 1983; Odling 1997; Gillespie *et al.* 1999). They have been documented in the Upper Cretaceous Chalk of Kent (Bevan & Hancock 1986), in the Burren Limestone of County Clare, Ireland (Gillespie *et al.* 2001; Odling *et al.* 1999), the Upper Carboniferous Cove and Gordale Limestone Formations in North Yorkshire (Belayneh 2003), and from numerical models (e.g. Renshaw & Pollard 1994; Darcel *et al.* 2003; Olson 2004). These clusters of closely spaced fractures are referred to as fracture swarms and are encountered in many hydrocarbon reservoirs, where they can be important conduits for, or barriers to, hydrocarbon migration. Although fracture swarms have been widely documented in a large range of geological settings and field areas, the detailed geometry of these swarms, their mechanism(s) of formation, and particularly their impact on fluid movement are poorly understood.

Although empirical studies show a positive correlation between porosity and permeability (see Holness 1997) in sandstone and many carbonates, Chalk is an exception. Chalk reservoirs such as those in the Austin Chalk, Texas, the Valdemar Field of the Danish Central Graben and the Ekofisk Field are typically characterized by a high porosity and low permeability. For example, Jakobsen *et al.* (2004) reported porosity values ranging from 20 to 48% from the Lower Cretaceous interbedded pelagic–hemipelagic Chalk, marly Chalk and marlstone reservoirs in the Valdemar Field. The corresponding matrix permeability ranges from 0.1 to 4 mD. The Chalk in the Ekofisk Field shows average porosity of 32% and corresponding matrix permeability ranging between 0.1 and 10 mD. However, the effective permeability (defined as the combined

From: RIES, A. C., BUTLER, R. W. H. & GRAHAM, R. H. (eds) 2007. *Deformation of the Continental Crust: The Legacy of Mike Coward.* Geological Society, London, Special Publications, **272**, 499–517.
0305-8719/07/$15

permeability of the matrix and fractures) is 50 mD (see Toublanc *et al.* 2005). The relatively high effective permeability reported in the Ekofisk reservoir probably relates to the existence of well-connected fractures and faults in the vicinity of the production well(s). Thus, unless these Chalk reservoirs are fractured, oil recovery from primary porosity will be low. A knowledge of fracture orientation and density, the aperture (i.e. whether the fractures are sealed, partly sealed or open), whether the fractures are layer-restricted or through-going, or whether they occur in isolation or form swarms, is vital when attempting to understand the movement of fluids through such reservoirs and thus be in a position to improve oil recovery and enhance production.

The influence of well-connected fractures on fluid movement in reservoirs is poorly understood because of the difficulty of monitoring fluid flow in experiments and of representing thin fractures in reservoir simulations. Although open fractures represent only a small fraction of the total pore volume (Dershowitz & Miller 1984; Taylor *et al.* 1999) they have a first-order effect in controlling fluid flow. This impact is influenced by fracture aperture, the presence or absence of infill, and the ratio of fracture to matrix permeability (Nelson 1985; Sanderson & Zhang 1999; Matthäi & Belayneh 2004). Study on fluid flow through fractures is substantial, including an analytical solution for single-phase flow through fractures (ignoring the role of matrix permeability) by Zimmerman & Bodvarsson (1996), work on the role of the relative permeability between fractures and a porous matrix using single phase by Taylor *et al.* (1999); Belayneh (2003); Bogdanov *et al.* (2003) and Matthäi & Belayneh (2004), and papers on multi-phase problems by Kazemi & Gilman (1993), Geiger *et al.* (2003) and Karimi-Fard & Firozabadi (2003).

To understand fluid flow within high porosity, low permeability fractured rocks, we studied the 120 m thick Upper Cretaceous Chalk of which *c.* 20 m is extensively exposed around the coast of SE England. The studied coast lies between Minnis Bay in the west and Ramsgate in the east (Fig. 1). Similar exposures can be found at Dover and Folkestone (Middle Chalk *c.* 70 m and Upper Chalk *c.* 116 m thick), and between Eastbourne and Brighton, which provide continuous cliff sections. Three-dimensional control on fracture network geometry and orientation in the study area was provided by the wave-cut platform. The fieldwork was carried out with the objectives of: (1) determining the chronology of the fracture sets using offsets, infill, abutting relationships and other field evidence; (2) determining the orientation, joint density and spacing distributions of the fracture swarms and the background joints; (3) determining the lithological controls on fracture spacing. Having established the 3D geometries and spatial organization of the fracture swarms, an attempt was made using numerical analysis, to quantify their influence on the movement of fluids through the rock.

The type of brittle failure (shear or extensional) is determined by the differential stress, with the required conditions for shear failure and extensional failure being $\sigma_1 - \sigma_3 > 4T$ and $\sigma_1 - \sigma_3 < 4T$, respectively, where T is the tensile strength of the rock (see, e.g. Cosgrove 1995, 1997). Extensional fractures form parallel to σ_1, and normal to σ_3, and shear fractures form parallel to σ_2 as a conjugate set, *c.* 30° either side of σ_1. An examination of the Navier–Coulomb–Griffith brittle failure criteria indicates that there is a rapid transition from shear fracturing to extensional fracturing through intermediate 'hybrid' fractures, which have both extensional and shear displacements along them (Fig. 2). Hybrid fractures range in orientation between that of the shear and extensional fractures. A variety of names have been used to describe these structures including hybrid extension–shear fractures (Price & Cosgrove 1990), hybrid joints (Bahat 1991; Hancock 1994), mixed-mode fractures (Twiss & Moores 1992), transitional tensile (Suppe 1985) and transitional fractures (Van der Pluijm & Marshak 1997; Engelder 1999).

Pollard & Aydin (1988) defined joints as fractures with evidence of opening mode displacement (i.e. extensional fractures). Others have defined joints as a surface along which there has been no appreciable displacement (Price 1966; Hancock 1985). The second definition allows all three types of fractures to be classified as joints as long as the displacements are small.

In many tectonic settings, where there are no major structures such as folds and faults (e.g. in the Margate area), joints are the only widespread structure available for analysis. Hancock (1994) argued that joints are 10^2–10^5 times more abundant than faults and extremely useful in determining the tectonic history of a region. Belayneh & Cosgrove (2004) have argued that even this range underestimates the abundance of fractures compared with other tectonic structures.

Tectonic history of the study area and surrounding region

Bevan & Hancock (1986) examined fractures from a number of localities in the Upper Cretaceous and Palaeogene rocks of south England

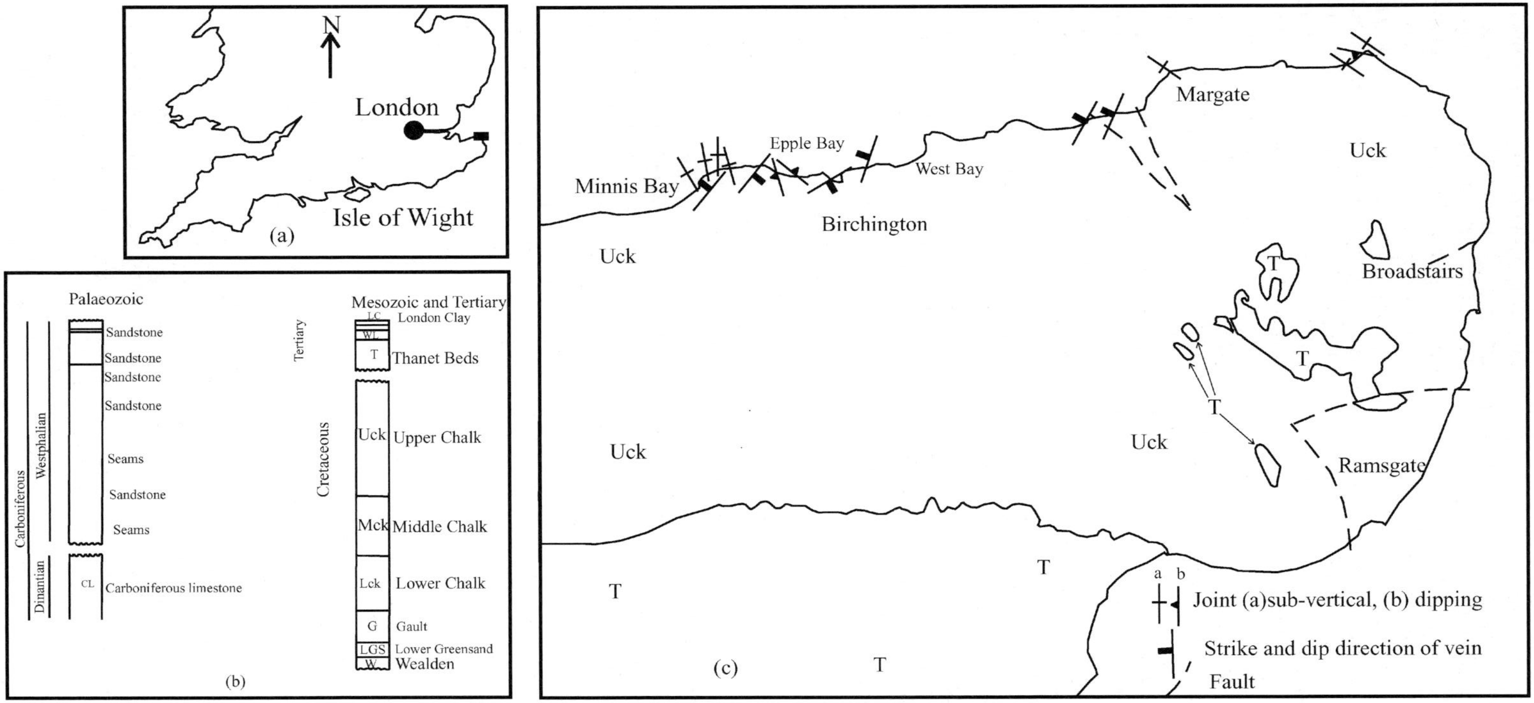

Fig. 1. (**a**) Location map of the study area; (**b**) stratigraphic log; (**c**) geology of the area showing veins, fractures and joints mapped in the area (from Shephard-Thorn 1988). Only representative measurements of strike and dips of veins, fractures and joints are shown.

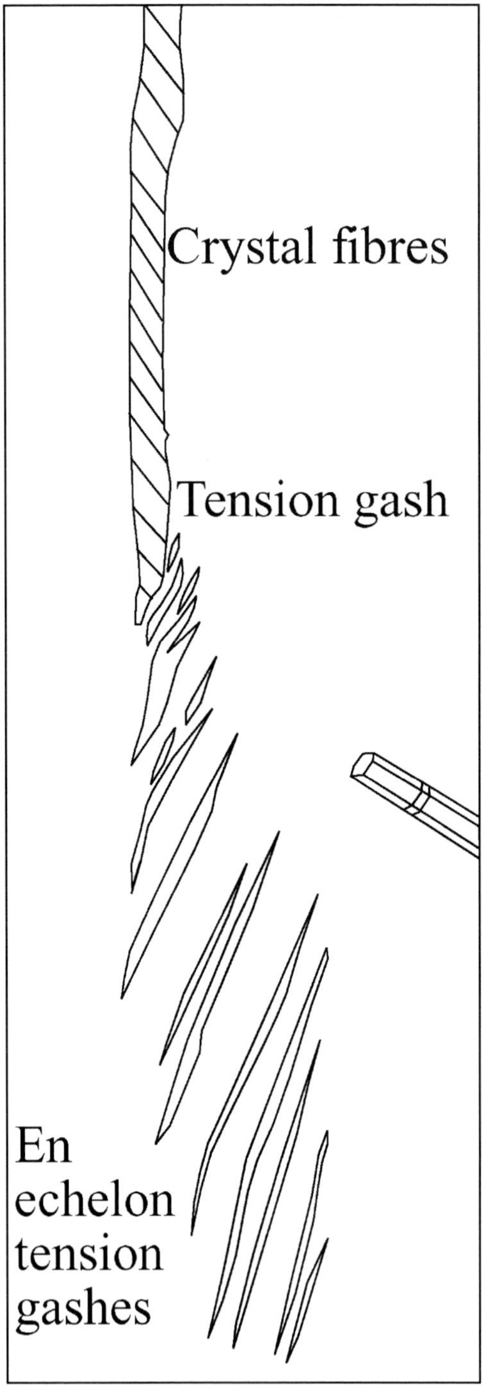

Fig. 2. Line drawing of hybrid extension and shear fracture, running laterally into a shear zone (Price & Cosgrove 1990, fig. 1.63). The eraser head of a pencil (right) is shown for scale.

and north France. They considered the NW–SE-trending extension fractures to be associated with the Alpine collision. They argued that these fractures were superimposed on, and obliquely cross-cut, the east–west-trending flexures (such as the Purbeck–Isle of Wight Monocline) and associated fracture systems linked with this folding. The monoclines represent forced folds that formed in response to reverse dip-slip movement on east–west-trending basement faults. Ameen (1988) showed that forced folds in the Purbeck – Isle of Wight Monocline occur above high-angle reverse and normal faults, and the cover accommodates faulting by rigid body rotation and internal deformation.

This internal deformation is expressed as fractures and, based on his modelling work (op. cit.) Ameen, argued that different fracture orientation and fracture types would form in different locations around these flexures. Ameen & Cosgrove (1990) carried out a kinematic analysis of the mesofractures in the Upper Cretaceous Chalk and Tertiary sandstones at Studland Bay, Dorset, which are situated on the gently dipping limb of the Purbeck–Isle of Wight Monocline, in an attempt to determine the tectonic history of the region since the Upper Cretaceous. They concluded that many of the fractures in the area were linked to the formation of the monocline. Ameen (1995) described a study of fractures in the Upper Cretaceous Chalk of the Isle of Thanet, Kent, aimed at quantifying the evolution of the major structure in the area (i.e. an east–west-trending, south-facing monoclinal forced fold). Ameen's study, which was based on both field and seismic data, showed that the forced fold was initiated by differential sedimentation and compaction associated with regional extension and the deposition of the Chalk. However, the fractures linked to the formation of the monoclines affect only the rocks in their immediate vicinity, and large areas of Chalk, including the study area, contain fracture sets linked to more regional events.

Methods

Restraining walls, 30–50 cm wide and 1–1.5 m high, have been built along most parts of the coast. Areas where the fracture swarms occur erode faster than the 'intact' Chalk and to counteract this they have been grouted above the restraining walls along most of the coast. Nevertheless, because of their susceptibility to erosion, the fracture swarms generally show a U-shaped re-entrant in the cliff face when viewed in plan. Although some difficulties were encountered in measuring the spacing of fractures within the swarms and the distance between adjacent swarms, a sufficiently extensive database was obtained to allow a basin evolution history to be established. In addition, when used in numerical analyses, these field observations allowed the significance of fracture swarms for hydrocarbon migration in reservoirs to be determined.

To carry out fluid flow simulation through the rock mass, photographs were taken of the cliff section. Fractures were traced from these photographs and then rectified. Apertures vary along the fracture planes because of the fracture roughness and processes such as weathering and dissolution or offsets at contact asperities. Fracture apertures (including bedding planes) measured on the outcrop are mostly 0.5 mm and this value is taken as an average (effective) aperture for the entire flow simulations. For values of porosity and permeability within the Chalk, measured values from the Valdemar Field of the Danish Central Graben were used. Here oil is produced from the upper Hauterivian–Aptian succession (the Tuxen and Sola Formations) comprising interlayered pelagic–hemipalegic chalks, marly chalks and marlstones. Jakobsen *et al.* (2004), based on studies of core data, estimated that the porosity of the Chalk ranges between 20 and 48% and the matrix permeability is between 10^{-16} and 4×10^{-16} m^2. The reservoir and fluid properties used in the simulation are summarized in Table 1.

These properties and geotechnical data were then used in the simulation to determine the flow through the fractures and the matrix blocks in this natural fractured system. To capture the smallest features in the model (i.e. fractures) and largest features (matrix blocks) within the domain of interest, unstructured hybrid-element meshes were employed. Unlike structured grids (e.g. finite-difference grids), this method is suited for representing the complex geometries of real geological fracture networks (see Matthäi *et al.* 2005). The 2D fracture pattern traced from the mosaic of field photographs of the cliff section was given a unit thickness and it was assumed that fracture geometry remained unchanged throughout the thickness. The numerical model incorporates all the relevant physics for discrete fracture representation, in particular the capillary transfer of fluids from matrix to adjacent fractures (Geiger *et al.* 2003; Matthäi *et al.* 2005). Flow through fractures and along bedding planes is calculated using the cubic law (Witherspoon *et al.* 1980), which predicts permeability of fractures with an aperture of 0.5 mm as 1.0416×10^{-11} m^2.

Geology and structure of the study area

The rocks exposed along the coast of SE England are Upper Cretaceous Chalk (Fig. 1b and c),

Table 1. *The reservoir and fluid properties and boundary conditions applied to the model for the numerical analysis*

Permeability			1.0×10^{-16} m^2
Porosity (%)			0.35
Total system compressibility			1.0×10^{-9} m^3 m^{-3} Pa^{-1}
Density oil (ρ_o)			800.0 kg m^{-3}
Density water (ρ_w)			1000.0 kg m^{-3}
Viscosity oil (μ_o)			2.0×10^{-3} Pa s
Viscosity water (μ_w)			1.0×10^{-3} Pa s
Initial oil saturation (S_o)			0.95
Initial water saturation (S_w)			0.05
Residual saturation water (S_{wr})			0.05
Residual saturation oil (S_{or})			0.14
Brooks–Corey parameter, λ (matrix)			2.0
Capillary entry pressure (P_d)			100 Pa
JOINT permeability			1.04×0^{-11} m^2
JOINT porosity (%)			1.0
JOINT entry pressure (P_d)			10.0 Pa
JOINT Brooks–Corey parameter, λ			0.2
JOINT residual saturation water (S_{wrj})			0.0
JOINT residual saturation oil (S_{orj})			0.0
BEDDING Brooks–Corey parameter, λ			1.0
TOP	Dirichlet	fluid pressure	1.0×10^6 Pa
BOTTOM	Neumann	fluid source	2.0×10^{-10} m^3 s^{-1}
BOTTOM	Dirichlet	saturation water	1. 0
BOTTOM	Dirichlet	saturation oil	0. 0

which is subdivided into the Lower, Middle and Upper Chalk. The Upper Chalk is the only lithology exposed along the studied coastal section in the vicinity of Margate and Ramsgate (Fig. 1). It consists mainly of smooth, massively bedded white Chalk with some nodular beds. Flint occurs throughout the formation, mostly as nodules along the bedding planes (Fig. 3a) but sometimes along cross-cutting fractures (Fig. 3b). The Chalk contains a wide variety of fossils, including fish teeth, echinoids, ammonites, gastropods, polyzoa and bivalve shells.

As noted above, the exposed thickness along the coast is *c.* 20 m and bedding is subhorizontal. Because the Upper Chalk is the only lithology exposed, the influence of lithology on fracture orientation and density cannot be considered in this study. The Chalk is in places deeply weathered and protected from sea erosion by walls. Fractographic features, such as plumose structures and twist hackle fringes, which are widely documented in carbonate beds from elsewhere and which have been successfully used to deduce the history of joint initiation, propagation and arrest, are not observed on fractures in the study area (e.g. Belayneh 2004). In addition, there are no other structures such as faults or folds, solution seams, or other kinematic indicators to assist in the task of analysing the tectonic evolution of the basin. In the absence of such major structures, we have had to rely on the fractures.

Fractures

On the basis of field observations a four-fold classification for brittle structures in the study area is proposed: (1) the earliest fractures are flint-filled shear fractures striking NE–SW and dipping *c.* 60°, either to the NW or SE; (2) the second group comprises fracture swarms made up of both vertical extensional joints and steeply dipping 'hybrid fractures', which strike NW–SE; (3) the third group comprises NW–SE-striking, high-angle to vertical, background extension joints, thought by Bevan & Hancock (1986) to have formed during the NW–SE Alpine convergence; (4) the fourth group of fractures are bed-parallel and layer-normal, bed-restricted systematic and unsystematic fractures.

Conjugate veins

The earliest structures in the study area are conjugate shear fractures with flint mineralization. These fractures are less abundant than those formed during stages 2 and 3. They strike NE–SW and dip *c.* 60° either to the NW or SE. No evidence of offset of the bedding planes across these fractures was observed. The flint has a variable width, ranging from 1 mm to a maximum of 5 cm. It is dark brown, has a glassy appearance and occurs either along the fractures, along the bedding planes or as nodules with irregular shapes in the vicinity of fractures and bedding planes (Fig. 3a and b). Close inspection of these veins shows that there are alternating changes in colour in a direction normal to the vein walls, which are approximately symmetrical about the centre. This indicates that several pulses of silica-rich fluids moved along these fractures. In addition, granulation seams, representing bands of crushed Chalk less than 1 cm thick, are commonly observed (Fig. 4a and b). They are subparallel to shear fractures and, as can be seen from Figure 4a and b, they show no observable shear displacement and are cross-cut by the later NW–SE-trending fracture swarms.

Fracture swarms

The fracture swarms, which are more commonly found west of Margate and around Broadstairs, strike NW–SE and consist of vertical extensional joints and hybrid fractures with a dihedral angle (2θ) varying between zero (for a mode 1 joint) and *c.* 40°. These fractures typically forms X or Y patterns on cliff sections. The vertical extensional joints that formed during this time are difficult to differentiate from those joints that were formed during the Alpine collision (stage 3) throughout NW Europe (e.g. Bevan & Hancock 1986), as neither are mineralized and both have more or less the same orientation. In places, fractures formed during the second event show yellowish, brownish and reddish colouring that provides evidence for fluid circulation along them. The intensity of colouring is strongest at the joint walls and gradually decreases into the intact Chalk. The width of these zones ranges from a few millimetres to a maximum of 5 mm on either side of the fracture surfaces. Some of the bedding planes are also stained and this is also probably related to fluid movement along them (Fig. 4a and b).

The fracture swarms are easily discerned in the cliffs because of their tendency to erode and weather more rapidly than the adjacent, less fractured chalk, and, consequently, they form small U-shaped re-entrants into the cliff face (Fig. 5). The spacing between individual swarm ranges from several metres to a few tens of metres, and the spacing of the fractures within the swarm ranges from a few millimetres to centimetres. The fracture swarms are made up of both steeply dipping hybrid fractures and vertical extensional

(a)

(b)

Fig. 3. (**a**) Diagenetic flint parallel to bedding in *c.* 15 m cliff section at Ramsgate; (**b**) flint-filled shear fracture. White dashed line shows the outline of the flint. Camera lens cap has a diameter of 5 cm.

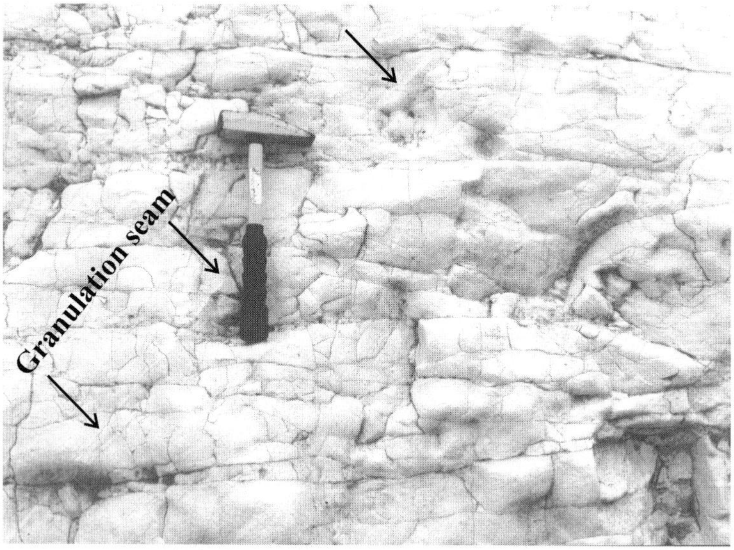

(a)

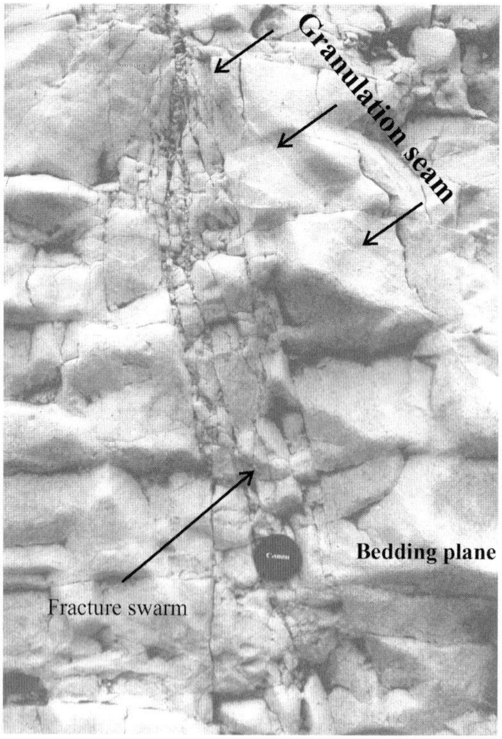

(b)

Fig. 4. Evidence of bedding and other fractures utilized for fluid movement: (**a**) stained beds and bed-parallel fractures with apertures of 0.5 mm; (**b**) zones of anastomosing interconnected fractures. Granulation seams are parallel to shear fractures and are indicated by arrows. In both cases some fractures and bedding planes show reddish and reddish brown colour, which is strongest on the walls of these discontinuities and 5 mm wide on both sides. The colouring decreases from the maximum at the wall of bedding planes and fractures as one moves into the country rock.

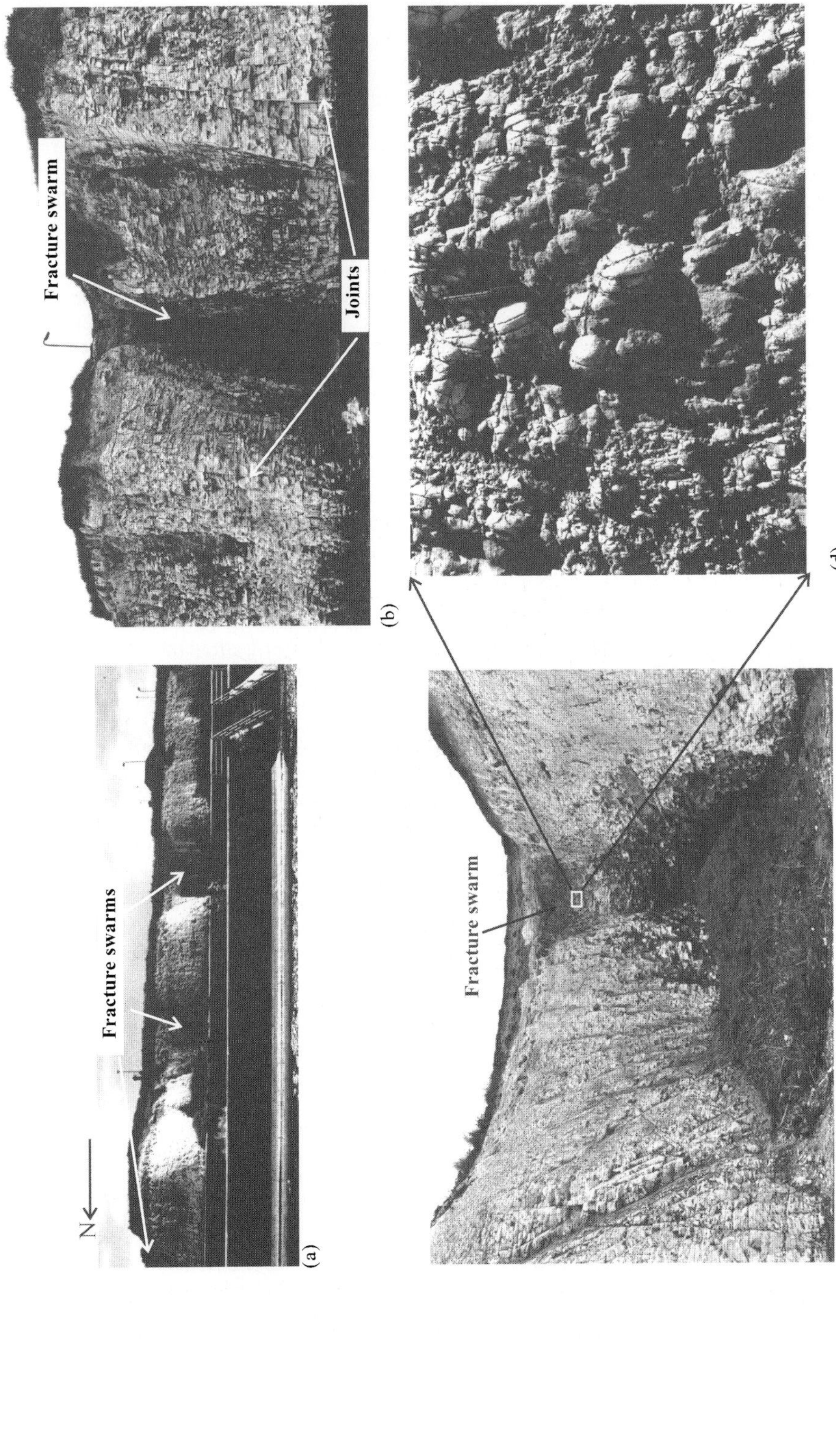

Fig. 5. Fracture swarms. **(a)** Synoptic view from offshore; **(b)** vertical joints superimposed on fracture swarms; **(c)** close-up view of individual fracture swarm made up of vertical extensional joints and hybrid fractures with low dihedral angle (i.e. 2θ *c.* 40°); **(d)** close-up view of hybrid fractures that facilitated fast weathering. The dihedral angle between the conjugate pair of the fractures is 40°.

joints. These frequently link to form an interconnected and anastomosing fracture network. The linking of these fractures created good channels for fluid flow (Fig. 5a–d).

Joints formed during the Alpine collision

NW–SE-striking vertical to steeply dipping, through-going joints cut the Chalk. The spacing ranges between 30 and 50 cm or locally is on a metre-scale. These vertical extensional joints (Fig. 6a and b) are not mineralized and have apertures of *c.* 5 mm. They have sub-planar walls and were formed during Alpine collision (e.g. Bevan & Hancock 1986).

Fractures associated with uplift and exhumation

The most common and widespread of all brittle structures in the Upper Cretaceous Chalk of Kent are fractures associated with uplift and exhumation. They consist of three varieties: (1) well-defined, bed-restricted, vertical fractures forming ladder patterns with the bedding planes; (2) bed-parallel fractures; (3) non-systematic fractures with varying orientation. There is no evidence of alteration along these fractures. They are not considered in detail in this study, which focuses on the geometry and hydraulic properties of the fracture swarms.

Numerical simulation results

The fractured Chalk shown in the photograph in Figure 7a is represented as a line drawing in Figure 7b. The lines representing the fractures were 'extruded' into Non-Uniform Rational B-Splines (NURBS) surfaces using a computeraided design program (Rhinoceros™) and discretized using tetra meshes, then converted into hybrid-element meshes as shown in Figure 7c. In this analysis the different types of fractures were grouped into families and assigned material property. All fractures were represented by surfaces of triangular and quadrilateral elements. The matrix blocks were given unique porosity and permeability values. Unknowns, such as saturation and fluid pressure, were computed at the nodes from the values applied to the model boundaries. Figure 8a shows the monitored fracture network. A constant pressure (4.67×10^4 Pa) was applied at the top of the model and a single-phase, steady-state analysis was used to analyse fluid flow along the joints and hybrid fractures that form the fracture swarms as well as along the layer-bound joints. It was found that fluid focusing (shown in red) occurs at the intersection of fractures. The fastest flow occurs along hybrid fractures (i.e. the fracture swarms) and the through-going joints, as is shown by red vectors. Almost 83% of the total flux is accounted for by these discontinuities, indicated by light-coloured zones, in which the pressure diffuses faster (Fig. 8b).

In the two-phase flow, 'water' is injected at the base of the oil-saturated model at a rate of 2×10^{-10} m^3 s^{-1}. The four sides of the model are treated as no-flow boundaries. For the large density difference between water and oil (200 kg m^{-3}) displacement should be gravity dominated. The injection rate should also be small enough for water monotonically to under-ride the oil (Table 1; Skæveland & Kleppe 1992). In the numerical experiment, as expected, water displaces the oil as it passes through the isotropic, homogeneous, unfractured region at the base of the model. For the low injection rate, it takes *c.* 14 days to displace the oil from this region. However, as soon as the water front passes into the fractured zone, water enters through the tips of the fractures and displaces oil more rapidly than in the surrounding Chalk matrix (Fig. 9a). As shown in Figure 9b, water is focused into the two fracture swarms represented in the model. The matrix block at the base is approaching its bulk irreducible saturation of oil (i.e. *c.* 0.14). Thus, oil saturation ranges from fully saturated (0.95 oil saturation; see Table 1) in the centres of the matrix blocks down to 20–40% adjacent to through-going joints and fracture swarms. In the region between the two fracture swarms and on the right-hand side of the model, oil saturation remains totally undisturbed. Figure 9c shows water breakthrough on the left-hand side of the model. Under the given boundary conditions and with the reservoir and fluid properties used in this simulation, it takes slightly over a year (*c.* 374 days) for water breakthrough to occur along the fracture swarms. The total oil saturation of the model decreases non-linearly with time (Fig. 10). After 18 months of basal injection at a constant rate and production from the top of the model, 55% of the remaining oil is in place. The resulting saturation distribution is very inhomogeneous. In spite of the gravitational forces at work, water injection does not maximize production. Counter-current and co-current imbibition processes, which govern the transfer of fluids between the fracture and adjacent matrix, are rather slow. How much oil will be recovered by this mechanism depends on several factors, including the transfer rate, the saturation of oil within the fractures, the surface area of fractures and the size of the matrix blocks.

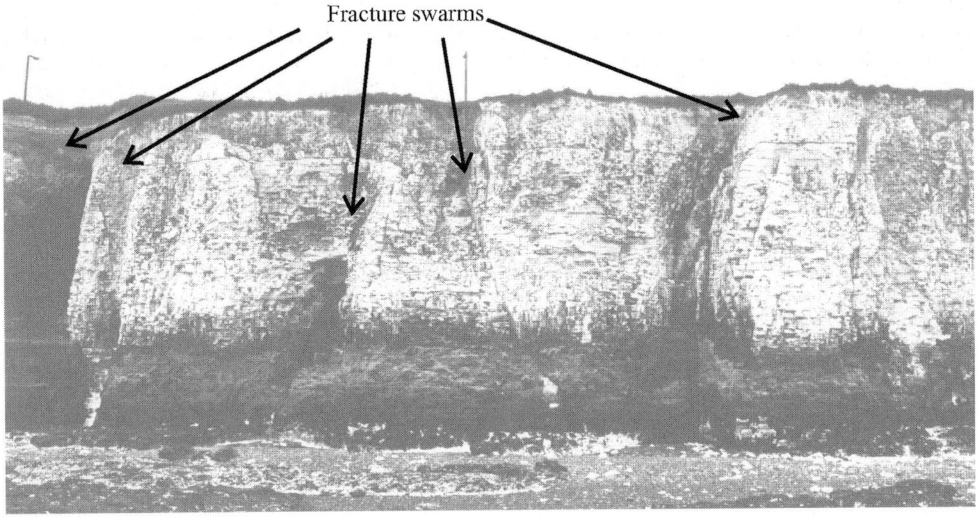

(a)

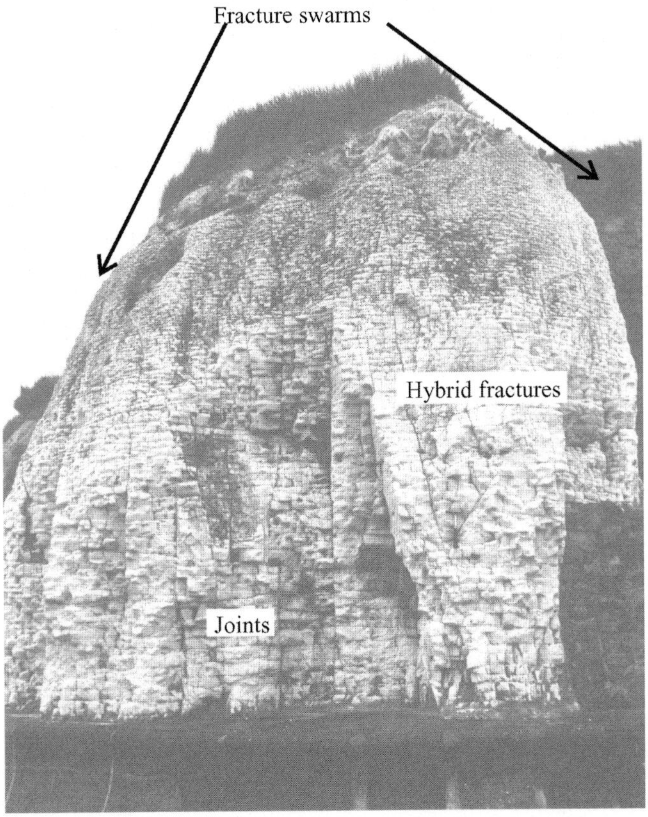

(b)

Fig. 6. (**a**) Vertical joints with zones of fracture swarms; (**b**) vertical joints with spacing of 30–50 cm. It should be noted that the receding part of the cliff lies within the zone of fracture swarms both on the right- and left-hand side of the photograph. The lamp-posts at the top-left and top-middle of (**a**) indicate scale.

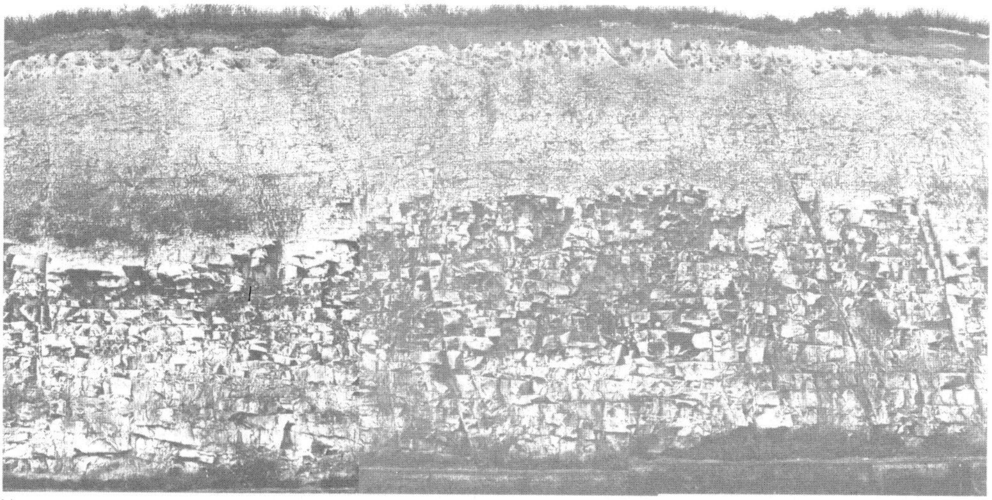

(a)

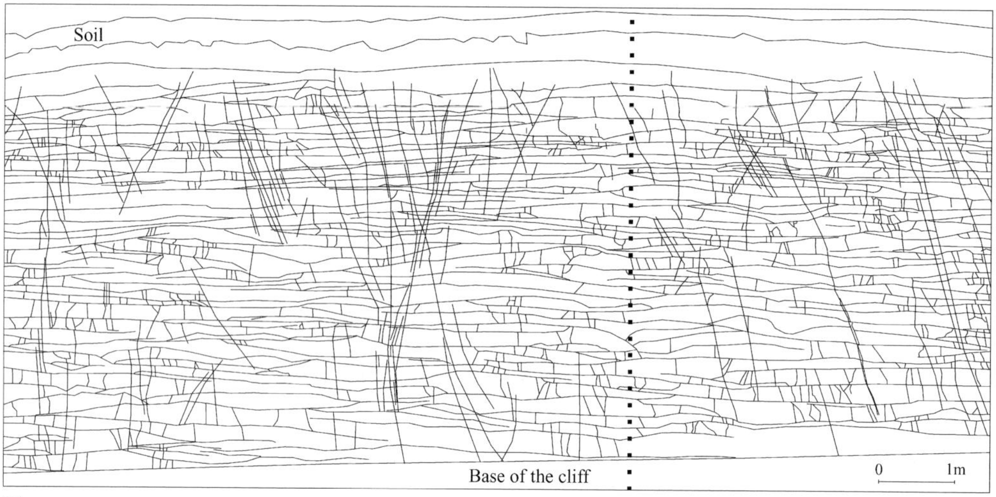

(b)

Fig. 7. (**a**) Photograph of a cliff section containing bedding planes, fracture swarms consisting of extensional and hybrid fractures, bedding and bed-parallel fractures and layer-bound and non-systematic fractures. (**b**) Line drawing of the fractures. The section shown is 13 m long and 6.3 m high. The section to the left of the dotted line was selected for meshing and numerical simulation and the model is assumed to have a thickness of 1 m.

Discussion

There are no major structures that can be used to establish the structural evolution of the study area. Fortunately, the analysis of minor structures (e.g. fractures) can give important information regarding basin evolution and the temporal variation of the magnitude and direction of the major principal stresses, as well as providing an indication of the differential stress that was operating at the time of their formation.

The principal stresses and the differential stress in a tectonically relaxed basin (i.e. one in which the sediments are affected by only the overburden stress) increase linearly with depth (Price 1966; Price & Cosgrove 1990; Cosgrove 2001). The earliest brittle structures considered in this work are flint-filled conjugate shear fractures, striking NE–SW and dipping *c.* 60° either to the NW or SE, which formed when the differential stress was $>4T$ (i.e. when the overburden stress was relatively high; σ_1). These conditions

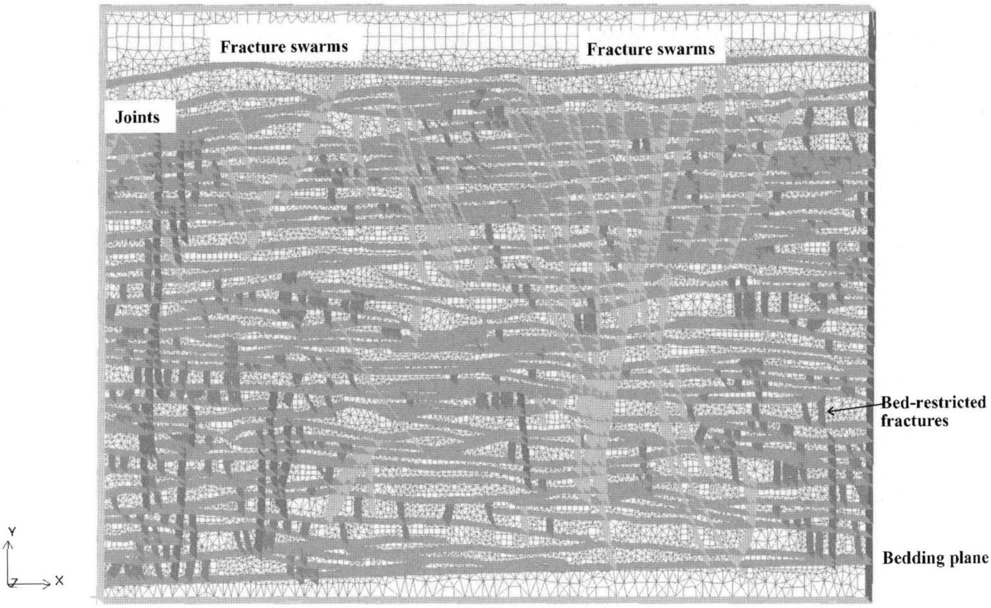

(c)

Fig. 7. (c) Poly-element type finite-element mesh of the fractured Chalk whereby fractures and matrix blocks are discretely represented and are assigned measured or estimated petrophysical properties.

probably represent a period during basin subsidence when the Chalk was buried relatively deeply. Although no shear displacement was observed on these fractures, their conjugate geometry and their orientation are those of embryonic normal faults formed in response to a stress field in which σ_1 is vertical and σ_2 and σ_3 are horizontal and oriented NE–SW and NW–SE, respectively. They are therefore interpreted as shear fractures. In addition, granulation seams locally observed along these shear fractures (Fig. 4a and b) can be used to deduce the stress conditions operating during their mode of formation. Granulation seams are thought to form under conditions of high deviatoric stress, low confining pressure (i.e. at a relatively shallow depths in the crust), and low temperature (Mitra 1988). They typically accommodate small shear offsets, which are generally less than a few millimetres in dimension (Antonellini & Aydin 1995). These fractures were later utilized for fluid circulation (i.e. flint mineralization) and may be comparable with the normal meso-faults with flint reported elsewhere in the region (see Bevan & Hancock 1986).

The next set of brittle structures to form were the NW–SE-striking hybrid fractures and associated vertical extensional joints, which together define fracture swarms. The occurrence of hybrid fractures is indicated by the low value of the dihedral angle (*c*. 40° compared with the 60° for the earlier, flint-filled NE–SW-trending shear fractures), and implies that the magnitude of the differential stress was *c*. $4T$. This reduction in differential stress, compared with the stress field operating during the formation of earliest formed fractures (the conjugate normal faults), indicates that the deformation occurred at shallower depths and that it may be related to the onset of uplift. Like group 1, these fractures are related to a vertical σ_1, but the orientations of σ_2 and σ_3 (i.e. NW–SE and NE–SW, respectively) are different. It is interesting to note that the change of the stress field from the first to the second stage has involved no rotation of the major principal stress axes but only a change in the relative magnitude of the stresses; that is, the original σ_2 became σ_3 and vice versa.

The third phase of brittle deformation was the formation of vertical NW–SE-striking extensional joints associated with the Alpine collision. These joints are comparable with the single set of vertical extension joints reported by Bevan & Hancock (1986), and the transition from hybrid fractures of stage 2 (when σ_1 was vertical) to extensional joints in stage 3 (when σ_1 was

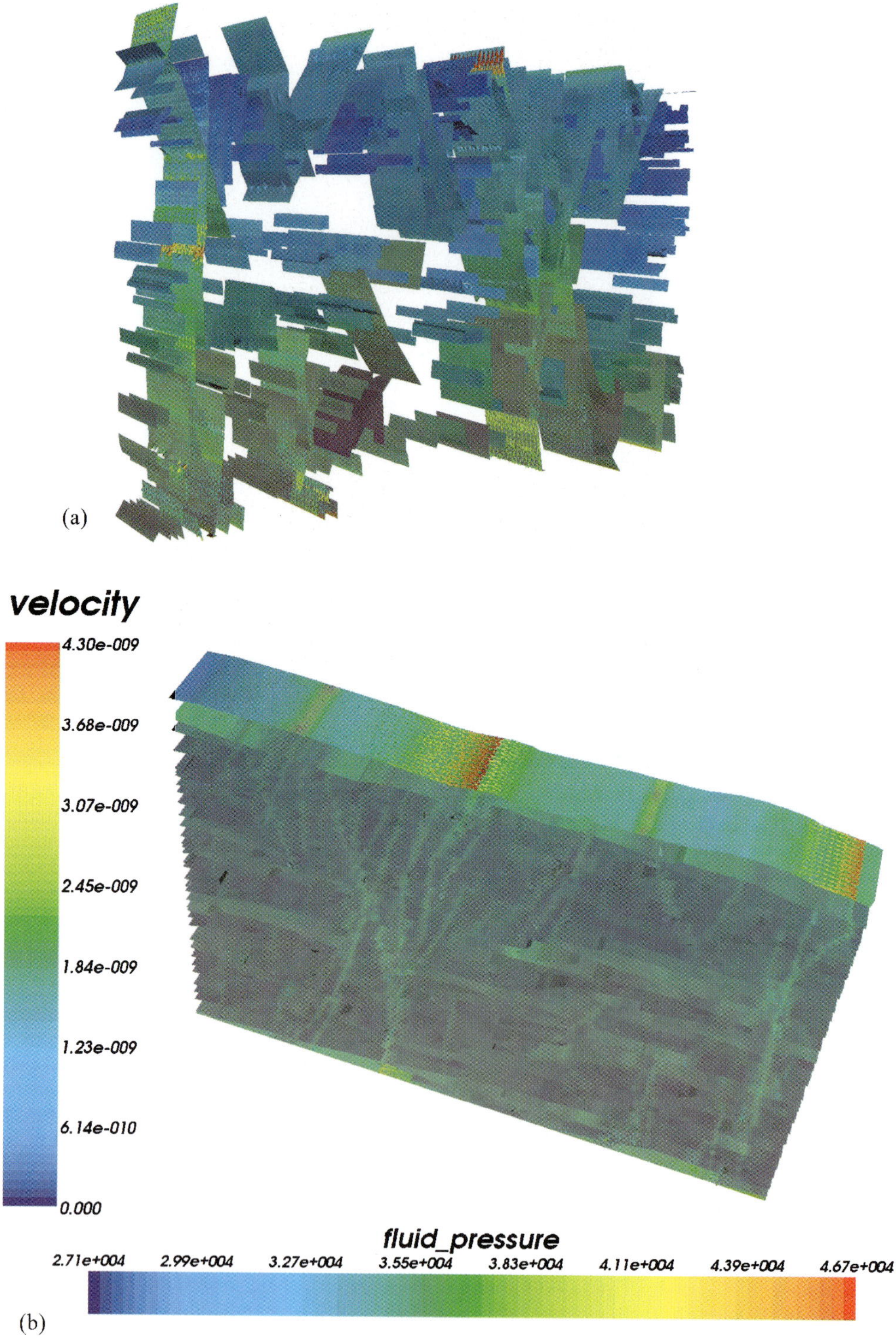

Fig. 8. (**a**) Skeleton of fractures making up the numerical model; (**b**) pressure diffusion in the entire fractured Chalk. The magnitude and direction of fluid movement along the fractures and through the matrix is represented by the arrows using a rainbow colour scheme (red for high and blue for low).

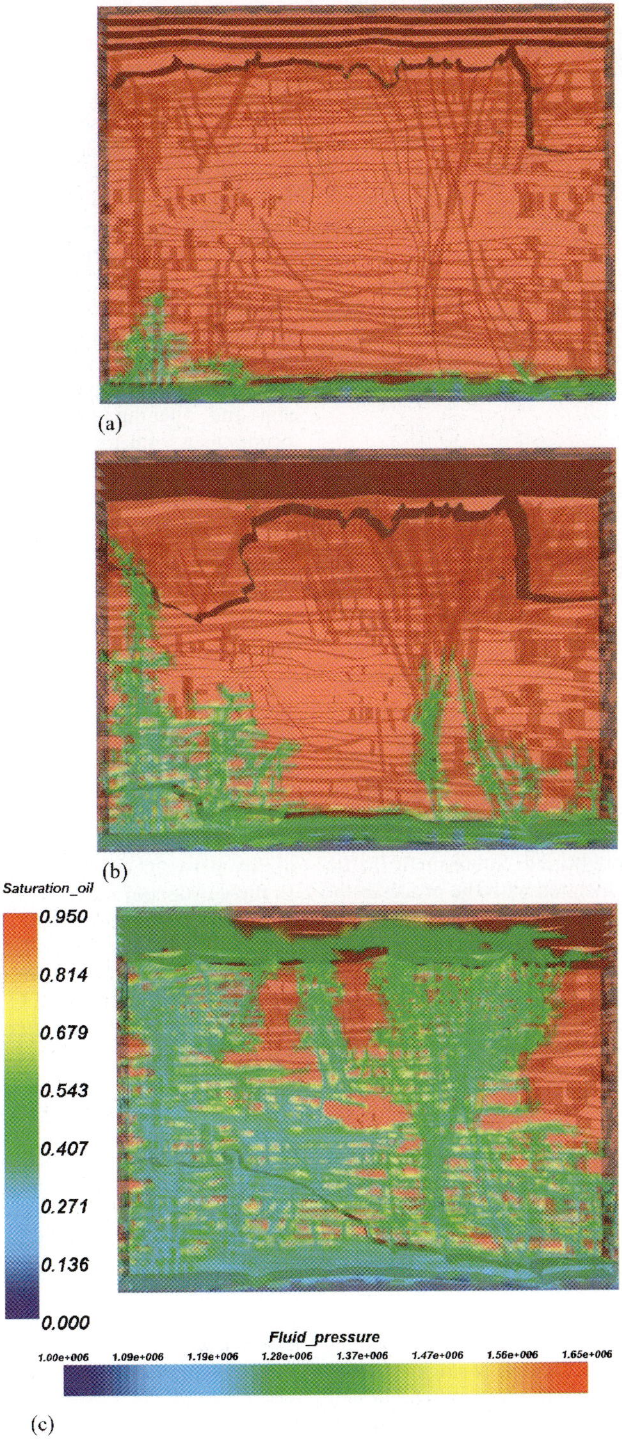

Fig. 9. (**a**) Displacement of oil by water after 57.8 days. The front moves uniformly for the first 14 days in the homogeneous isotropic chalk at the base of the model. (**b**) Movement of water predicted after 173.6 days. (**c**) Oil saturation pattern after *c*. 1.427 years. Water breakthrough has already occurred on the left-hand side of the model after 374 days.

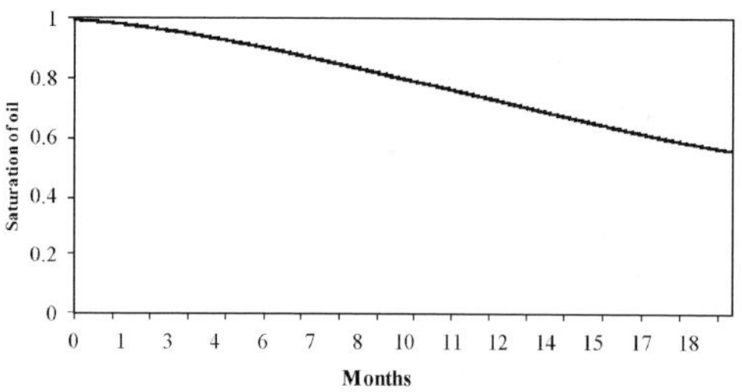

Fig. 10. Plot of oil saturation v. time for the model. Oil saturation within the model varies from 0.95 (initial saturation of oil) to 0.14 (residual saturation). (Note highly perturbed isobars within the fractured region of the model in Fig. 9a–c.)

horizontal and oriented NW–SE) reflects this change in stress regime. For the formation of vertical extensional joints, the magnitude of the differential stress must have been $<4T$. This indicates that a continued reduction in the overburden stress is linked to the further exhumation of the Chalk. The fourth and last group of fractures to form in the study area were layer-bound, systematic and unsystematic fractures probably associated with final stages of uplift and erosion of the overlying cover. We note that there is a gradual reduction in the magnitude of the differential stress associated with the stress regimes linked to the successive brittle failure events. This indicates that fractures started forming when the Chalk was deeply buried. Subsequent brittle failure events are associated with the processes of uplift and reduction of the overburden stress, probably linked to the Alpine collision.

In summary, it can be seen that the orientation of σ_1 (vertical) remained unchanged during the first two phases of brittle deformation (i.e. during the formation of the early flint-filled shear fractures and the later vertical extensional and hybrid fractures) and that σ_2 changed from NE–SW to NW–SE. This switch in the orientation of σ_2 and σ_3 was accompanied by a decrease in the magnitude of the differential stress. The formation of fracture swarms, described in the present paper, is linked to this second phase of brittle deformation and may correspond to the conjugate steeply inclined hybrid joints described by Bevan & Hancock (1986, fig. 2b). During the formation of the third suite of NW–SE-trending joints, which are vertical extensional joints, the orientation of the principal stress axes remained unchanged but the stress values changed so that σ_1 became subhorizontal trending NW–SE and σ_2 was vertical. σ_3 remained in the same orientation it had during the formation of the second suite of fractures (i.e. NE–SW). These NW–SE-trending brittle structures occur throughout southern England and northern France, and were considered by Bevan & Hancock (1986) to be related to neotectonic normal faults of the lower Rhine embayment. The last brittle deformation in the study area formed layer-restricted systematic and non-systematic fractures. These are linked to continued uplift and relaxation of the rocks and are not considered in detail in this work.

Previous studies based on field observations (Gillespie *et al.* 2001) and numerical analyses (Renshaw & Pollard 1995; Al-Mahruqi 2001) showed that when the compression acting perpendicular to bedding is only low to modest, slip and opening along the bedding interface occurs as a joint tip approaches it. This reduces the degree of stress concentration at the tip of the fracture and propagation ceases. However, if bonding exists across the bedding and/or the compressive stress acting normal to the interface is sufficiently high, any opening and slip along the interface will be inhibited and thus the propagation of fractures across the bedding will be facilitated. Multilayer (i.e. through-going) rather than single-layer (strata-bound) fractures will then form. The fractures linked to the first three episodes of deformation, including the fracture swarms, are through-going fractures.

The field study and numerical simulations of Taylor *et al.* (1999) and Matthäi & Belayneh (2004) have shown that if the contrast in permeability between the fractures and matrix is two to three orders of magnitude or greater, the fractures will have a significant effect in channelling flow and the system will behave as a dual-porosity medium. Fluid flow in the system will be dominantly through fractures. If, however, either the fractures have very small aperture and are sealed with mineral veins or other infilling such as clay smearing that significantly reduces the permeability, or if the matrix is relatively permeable, the system can be treated as single-porosity medium (i.e. the influence of the fractures on flow is small and can be ignored).

The present study has shown that the oil displacement is controlled by (1) the presence or absence of fractures, (2) the fracture pattern, and (3) fracture geometry. Oil displacement is further perturbed by viscous fingering. This process is well documented and occurs when a less viscous fluid, such as gas or water, displaces a more viscous fluid, such as oil (e.g. Blunt *et al.* 1994). The viscosity contrast between the two fluids in our experiment was two. This was sufficient to create small perturbations along the displacement front, which led to the development of fracture-guided viscous fingers. When the water entered a fractured zone the front became uneven and this unevenness was further exacerbated by viscous fingering. Furthermore, it has been demonstrated (Di Donato *et al.* 2005; Matthai *et al.* 2005) that if the rock contains fractures with varying size and orientation, the large fractures are swept first. However, the specific surface area of these larger fractures will be small, and consequently oil recovery from them is low (Fig. 10). In contrast, if the rock only contains many smaller, interconnected fractures, their specific surface area will be high, leading to a better recovery. If fracture swarms are present in the medium, they focus the flow and will compartmentalize oil-saturated regions. This will probably make it even more difficult to displace oil by water. The implication is that the occurrence of fracture swarms in a reservoir is not necessarily good news.

Conclusion

The fracture network in the Chalk of the study area is the result of successive stages in the evolution of basin history. The earliest fractures were NE–SW-striking flint-filled shear fractures, which probably formed while the Chalk was buried to considerable depth within the basin. The second episode of fracturing resulted in the formation of through-going NW–SE-striking fracture swarms. They consisted of extensional and hybrid shear extension fractures indicating a reduction in differential stress. Nevertheless, the overburden was still sufficiently large to prevent interbed slip, thus allowing the formation of through-going fractures and fracture swarms.

The Alpine collision resulted in a NW–SE-directed compression, which produced the third set of brittle structures, namely NW–SE-striking, vertical extension fractures (joints) indicating a further reduction in differential stress and the overburden stress, linked to continued uplift and erosion.

Numerical modelling of fluid flow through these networks was carried out using the detailed geometry of the fractures and fracture swarms derived from the field study together with the values of permeability and porosity assigned from offshore Chalk reservoirs. The results indicate that gravity plays a subordinate role in two-phase displacement in this heterogeneous type of medium. The water preferentially invades the fractures and by-passes the oil in the matrix blocks. It was found that the fracture swarms focused the flow and compartmentalized the model into regions of different oil saturation. Regions away from the swarms often retained most of the oil during water injection.

This work has shown how fractures are swept hierarchically starting with the through-going fractures (fracture swarms and joints) but the volume of oil recovered from them is low. Oil within the matrix blocks is withheld because of their much lower permeability and probably also because of capillary effects.

We would like to thank P. Connolly and D. Peacock for their thorough reviews of the manuscript. This paper was written while M.B. was Research Associate in the Department of Earth Science and Engineering, Imperial College, and sponsored by the ITF consortium on 'Improved Simulation of Fractured and Faulted Reservoirs'. T. Eiben is thanked for his opinion on the Ekofisk Field.

References

AL-MAHRUQI, S. A. S. 2001. *Fracture patterns and fracture propagation as a function of lithology*. Unpublished PhD thesis, Imperial College, London.

AMEEN, M. S. 1988. *Folding of layered cover due to dip-slip basement faulting*. Unpub. PhD thesis, Imperial College, London.

AMEEN, M. S. 1995. Fracture characterisation in the chalk and the evolution of the Thanet monocline, Kent, southern England. *In*: AMEEN, M. S. (ed.) *Fractography: Fracture Topography as a Tool in Fracture Mechanics and Stress Analysis*. Geological Society, London, Special Publications, **92**, 149–174.

AMEEN, M. S. & COSGROVE, J. W. 1990. A kinematic analysis of mesofractures from Studland Bay, Dorset. *Proceedings of the Geologists' Association*, **101**, 303–314.

ANTONELLINI, M. & AYDIN, A. 1995. Effects of faulting on fluid flow in porous sandstones: geometry and spatial distribution. *AAPG Bulletin*, **79**, 642–671.

BAHAT, D. 1991. *Tectonofractography*. Elsevier, Amsterdam, 354p.

BELAYNEH, M. 2003. *Analysis of natural fracture networks in massive and well-bedded carbonates and the impact of these networks on fluid flow in dual porosity modelling*. Unpub. PhD thesis, Imperial College, London.

BELAYNEH, M. 2004. Paleostress orientation inferred from surface morphology of joints on the southern margin of the Bristol Channel Basin, UK. *In*: COSGROVE, J. W. & ENGELDER, T. (eds) *The Initiation, Propagation, and Arrest of Joints and Other Fractures*. Geological Society, London, Special Publications, **231**, 241–255.

BELAYNEH, M. & COSGROVE, J. W. 2004. Fracture pattern variation around a major fold and their implication regarding fracture prediction from limited data: an example from Bristol Channel Basin. *In*: COSGROVE, J. W. & ENGELDER, T. (eds) *The Initiation, Propagation, and Arrest of Joints and Other Fractures*. Geological Society, London, Special Publications, **231**, 89–102.

BEVAN, T. G. & HANCOCK, P. L. 1986. A late Cenozoic regional mesofracture system in southern England

and northern France. *Journal of the Geological Society, London*, **143**, 355–362.

BLUNT, M. J. BARKER, J. W, RUBIN, B., MANSFIELD, M., CULVERWELL, I. D. & CHRISTIE, M. A. 1994. Predictive theory for viscous fingering in compositional displacement. *SPE Reservoir Engineering*, **9**, 73–80.

BOGDANOV, I., MOURZENKO, V. V. & THOVERT, J.-F. 2003. Effective permeability of fractured media in steady state flow. *Water Resources Research*, **39**, doi: 10.1029/2001WR000756.

COSGROVE, J. W. 1995. The expression of hydraulic fracturing in rocks ands sediments. *In*: AMEEN, M. S. (ed.) *Fractography: Fracture Topography as a Tool in Fracture Mechanics and Stress Analysis*. Geological Society, London, Special Publications, **92**, 187–196.

COSGROVE, J. W. 1997. The influence of mechanical anisotropy on the behaviour of the lower crust. *Tectonophysics*, **280**, 1–14.

COSGROVE, J. W. 2001. Hydraulic fracturing during the formation and deformation of a basin: a factor in the dewatering of low-permeability sediments. *AAPG Bulletin*, **85**, 737–748.

DARCEL, C., BOUR, O. & DAVY, P. 2003. Stereological analysis of fractal fracture networks. *Journal of Geophysical Research*, **108**, doi:10.1029/2002JB002091.

DERSHOWITZ, B. & MILLER, A. 1984. Dual porosity fracture flow and transport. *Geophysical Research Letters*, **22**, 1441–1444.

DI DONATO, G., HUIYUN, L., TAVASSOLI, Z. & BLUNT, M. J. 2005. Multi-rate transfer dual porosity modelling of gravity drainage and imbibition. *Proceedings of the SPE Reservoir Simulations Symposium, Houston, TX, 31 January – 2 February 2005*, SPE Paper 93144.

ENGELDER, T. 1999. Transitional-tensile fracture propagation: a status report. *Journal of Structural Geology*, **21**, 1049–1055.

GEIGER, S., ROBERTS, S., MATTHÄI, S. K. & ZOPPOU, C. 2003. Combined finite volume and finite element methods to simulate flow in geologic media. *ANZIAM Journal*, **44**(E), 180–201.

GILLESPIE, P. A., JOHNSTON, J. D., LORIGA, M. A., MCCAFFREY, K. J. W., WALSH, J. J. & WATTERSTON, J. 1999. Influence of layering on vein systematics in line samples. *In*: MCCAFFREY, K. J. W., LONERGAN, L. & WILKINSON, J. J. (eds) *Fractures, Fluid Flow and Mineralization*. Geological Society, London, Special Publications, **155**, 35–56.

GILLESPIE, P. A., WALSH, J. J., WATTERSON, J. BONSON, C. G. & MANZOCCHI, T. 2001. Scaling relationships of joint and vein array from the Burren, County Clare, Ireland. *Journal of Structural Geology*, **23**, 183–201.

HANCOCK, P. L. 1985. Brittle microtectonics: principles and practices. *Journal of Structural Geology*, **7**, 437–457.

HANCOCK, P. L. 1994. From joints to paleostress. *In*: ROURE, F. (ed.) *Peri-Tethyan Platforms*. Technip, Paris, 145–158.

HOLNESS, M. B. 1997. The permeability of non-deforming rock. *In*: HOLNESS, M. B. (ed.) *Deformation-Enhanced Fluid Transport in the Earth's Crust and Mantle*. Chapman & Hall, London, 9–39.

JAKOBSEN, F., INESON, J. R., KRISTENSEN, L. & STEMMERIK, L. 2004. Characterization and zonation of marly chalk reservoir: the Lower Cretaceous Valdemar Field of the Danish Central Graben. *Petroleum Geosciences*, **10**, 21–33.

KARIMI-FARD, M. & FIROZABADI, A. 2003. Numerical simulation of water injection in fractured media using the discrete-fracture model and the Galerkin method. *SPE Reservoir Evaluation and Engineering*, **6**, 117–126.

KAZEMI, H. & GILMAN, J. R. 1993. Multiphase flow in fractured petroleum reservoirs. *In*: BEAR, J., TSANG, C. F. & MARSILY, G. (eds) *Flow and Contaminant Transport in Fractured Rocks*. Academic Press, San Deigo, CA, 267–323.

MATTHÄI, S. K. M. & BELAYNEH, M. 2004. Viscous flow partitioning between fractures and permeable matrix. *Geophysical Research Letters*, **31**, L07602, doi:10.1029/2003GL019027.

MATTHÄI, S. K. M., MEZENTSEV, A. & BELAYNEH, M. 2005. Control-volume finite-element two-phase flow experiments with fractured rock represented by unstructured 3D hybrid meshes. *Proceedings of SPE Reservoir Simulation Symposium, Houston, TX, 31 January – 2 February 2005*, SPE Paper 93341.

MITRA, S. 1988. Effects of deformation mechanisms on reservoir potential in Central Appalachian Overthrust Belt. *AAPG Bulletin*, **72**, 536–554.

NELSON, R. A. 1985. *Geologic Analysis of Naturally Fractured Reservoirs*. Gulf Publishing Company, Houston, TX.

ODLING, N. 1997. Scaling and connectivity of joint systems in sandstones from western Norway. *Journal of Structural Geology*, **19**, 1257–1271.

ODLING, N. E., GILLESPIE, P., BOURGINE, B. *et al.* 1999. Variations of fracture system geometry and their implications for fluid flow in fractured hydrocarbon reservoirs. *Petroleum Geosciences*, **5**, 373–384.

OLSON, J. E. 2004. Predicting fracture swarms — the influence of sub-critical crack growth and the crack-tip process zone on joint spacing in rock. *In*: COSGROVE, J. W. & ENGELDER, T. (eds) *The Initiation, Propagation, and Arrest of Joints and Other Fractures*. Geological Society, London, Special Publications, **231**, 73–87.

POLLARD, D. D. & AYDIN, A. 1988. Progress in understanding jointing in the last century. *Geological Society of America Bulletin*, **100**, 1181–1204.

PRICE, N. J. 1966. *Fault and Joint Development in Brittle and Semi-Brittle Rocks*. Pergamon, Oxford.

PRICE, N. J. & COSGROVE, J. W. 1990. *Analysis of Geological Structures*. Cambridge University Press, Cambridge.

RENSHAW, C. E. & POLLARD, D. D. 1994. Numerical simulation of fracture set formation: a fracture mechanics model consistent with experimental observation. *Journal of Geophysical Research*, **99**, 9359–9372.

RENSHAW, C. E. & POLLARD, D. D. 1995. An experimentally verified criterion for propagation across un-bonded frictional interface in brittle, linear elastic materials. *International Journal of Rock Mechanics, Mining Science & Geomechanics Abstracts*, **32**, 237–249.

SANDERSON, D. & ZHANG, X. 1999. Critical stress localization of flow associated with deformation of well fractured rock masses, with implications for mineral deposits. *In*: MCCAFFREY, K. J. W., LONERGAN, L. & WILKINSON, J. J. (eds) *Fractures, Fluid Flow and Mineralization*. Geological Society, London, Special Publications, **155**, 69–81.

SEGALL, P. & POLLARD, D. D. 1983. Joint formation in granitic rock of the Sierra Nevada. *Geological Society of America Bulletin*, **94**, 563–575.

SHEPHARD-THORN, E. R. 1988. *Geology of the country around Ramsgate and Dover*. Memoir of the British Geological Survey, Sheets 274 and 290 (England and Wales).

SKJÆVELAND, S. M. & KLEPPE, J. (eds) 1992. *SPOR Monograph: Recent Advances in Improved Oil Recovery Methods for North Sea Sandstone Reservoirs*. Norwegian Petroleum Directorate, Stavanger.

SUPPE, J. 1985. *Principles of Structural Geology*. Prentice–Hall, Englewood Cliffs, NJ.

TAYLOR, W. L., POLLARD, D. D. & AYDIN, A. 1999. Fluid flow in discrete joint sets: field observations and numerical simulations. *Journal of Geophysical Research*, **104**, 28983–29006.

TOUBLANC, A., RENAUD, S., SYLTE, J. E., CLAUSEN, C. K., EIBEN, T. & NADLAND, G. 2005. Ekofisk Field: fracture permeability evaluation and implementation in the flow model. *Petroleum Geoscience*, **11**, 321–330.

TWISS, R. J. & MOORES, E. M. 1992. *Structural Geology*. W. H. Freeman, New York.

VAN DER PLUIJM, B. A. & MARSHAK, S. 1997. *Earth Structure: an Introduction to Structural Geology and Tectonics*. McGraw–Hill, New York.

WITHERSPOON, P. A., WANG, J. S. Y., IWAI, K. & GALE, J. E. 1980. Validity of cubic law for fluid flow in a deformable rock fracture. *Water Resources Research*, **16**, 1016–1024.

ZIMMERMAN, R. W. & BODVARSSON, G. S. 1996. Hydraulic conductivity of rock fractures. *Transport in Porous Media*, **23**, 1–30.

Au–quartz mineralization near the base of the continental seismogenic zone

RICHARD H. SIBSON

Department of Geology, University of Otago, P.O. Box 56, Dunedin, New Zealand (e-mail: rick.sibson@stonebow.otago.ac.nz)

Abstract: The base of the continental seismogenic zone is defined within individual fault zones by the transition with depth from pressure-sensitive frictional (FR) faulting to temperature-sensitive quasi-plastic (QP) ductile shearing. The depth of this FR–QP transition fluctuates principally as a consequence of variations in geothermal gradient and crustal lithology but other factors (e.g. fluid pressure level, strain rate) also play a role. For quartz-dominant and feldspar-dominant lithologies, respectively, it corresponds approximately to isotherms at 300–350 °C and *c.* 450 °C, defining an undulating transition zone in the mid-crust with a relief of the order of 5–10 km. This transition zone correlates with the greenschist-facies metamorphic environment where the bulk of mesozonal Au–quartz lodes form in mixed continuous–discontinuous shear zones. In areas of crustal convergence and thickening, where fluid release results from prograde metamorphic dehydration, especially at the greenschist–amphibolite-facies transition in the middle to deep crust, the seismogenic carapace acts as an upper crustal stress guide and low-permeability lid to overpressured metamorphic fluids migrating through shear zone conduits. Under appropriate combinations of stress and fault architecture in the brittle carapace, substantial fluid volumes may be trapped beneath this elastic lid at sufficient overpressure to generate dilatant fault–fracture meshes discharging episodically by fault–valve action following fault rupture, with permeability locally enhanced by aftershock activity distributed about the rupture zones. Topographic irregularities in the seismic–aseismic transition determine rupture nucleation sites and probably play a critical role in focusing the discharge of overpressured metamorphic fluids into the seismogenic layer. This helps to account for the observed spacing of mesozonal lode systems along transcrustal shear zones.

Gold–quartz veins are tracers of high-flux aqueous flow in the crust. Given recent laboratory-based estimates plus direct measurements of transport solubilities for Au-H-S complexes ranging from c. 10 ppb to >1 ppm under greenschist facies conditions (Stefánsson & Seward 2003; Simmons & Brown 2006), a significant gold deposit of 100 tonnes requires the focused passage of 0.1–10 km^3 of hydrothermal fluid assuming 100% efficiency of gold precipitation from the fluid. Vein textures generally show, however, that flow responsible for mineralization was episodic, occurring in a succession of high-flux pulses. Mechanisms allowing fluid redistribution in the Earth depend critically on the pressure of fluid contained in pore and/or fracture space, and its variation with depth. The level of fluid pressure, P_f, at depth z in the Earth is usefully defined in relation to the vertical stress, σ_v, by the pore-fluid factor:

$$\lambda_v = P_f/\sigma_v = P_f/\rho g z \qquad (1)$$

where ρ is rock density and g is gravitational acceleration (Hubbert & Rubey 1959).

Hydrothermal Au–quartz mineralization has two principal habitats. Epizonal gold–quartz mineralization is generally developed at depths <1–2 km in extensional–transtensional tectonic settings with concurrent felsic magmatism (Henley 1985), where large fluid volumes of predominantly meteoric water may be circulated by convective flow under hot or cold hydrostatic pressures (λ_v *c.* 0.4). In contrast, mesozonal lode gold deposits were mostly developed in compressional–transpressional settings (often related to accretion–collision complexes) through the passage of overpressured fluids ($\lambda_v \rightarrow 1.0$) at depths between 5 and 15 km, without any clear magmatic associations (Roberts 1987; Groves *et al.* 1995). Mesozonal vein systems are most extensively developed in Late Archaean granite–greenstone belts, but comparable vein assemblages are known from the Palaeozoic (e.g. Victorian Goldfield, Australia), Mesozoic (e.g. Mother Lode gold-belt of California), and Cenozoic eras (e.g. Juneau, Alaska, gold-belt of Eocene age). The mineralizing fluids are generally believed to be derived, in areas of crustal thickening, from prograde metamorphic dehydration in the middle

From: RIES, A. C., BUTLER, R. W. H. & GRAHAM, R. H. (eds) 2007. *Deformation of the Continental Crust: The Legacy of Mike Coward*. Geological Society, London, Special Publications, **272**, 519–532.
0305-8719/07/$15

to deep crust, especially at the greenschist–amphibolite-facies transition (Kerrich & Wyman 1990; Groves *et al.* 1998; McCuaig & Kerrich 1998). Though known from both sub-greenschist and high-grade metamorphic environments (crustal continuum model of Groves 1993), a large proportion (>90%) of mesozonal gold lodes (including the largest known deposits) were deposited within localized shear zones of mixed continuous–discontinuous character active in greenschist-facies metamorphic environments (McCuaig & Kerrich 1998). These structures are related to the 'semi-ductile roots' of brittle fault zones in the seismogenic upper crust and apparently form the principal conduits for fluid discharge from the lower crust.

The inference explored here is that this style of mineralization is characteristically associated with the gradational frictional–quasi-plastic (FR–QP) transition zone defining the base of the continental seismogenic zone, and that the 3D topography of this transition zone, together with the brittle architecture and stress state within the seismogenic carapace, plays a critical role in controlling the localization of inversely ponded overpressured fluids that give rise to mesozonal lode gold mineralization.

The continental seismogenic zone

The seismogenic zone outlined by background microseismicity is largely restricted to the upper half of actively deforming continental crust, defining the zone of unstable frictional faulting (Sibson 1983; Hill *et al.* 1990; Ito 1999). Larger ruptures (M > 6) commonly (though not invariably) nucleate towards its base and rupture predominantly upwards and laterally through this seismogenic layer (Fig. 1). There is, however, abundant evidence from geological studies of exhumed portions of the mid-crust that larger fault zones generally continue downwards below the seismogenic crust as localized ductile aseismic shear zones. The latter commonly range in thickness from tens of metres to kilometres.

In seismically active areas of moderate to high heat flow (60–100 mW m^{-2}), such as the extensional Basin and Range province and the predominantly strike-slip San Andreas Fault system in the western USA, the seismic–aseismic transition usually lies at depths of 10–20 km (Sibson 1984; Hill *et al.* 1990), the deeper levels commonly being associated with areas of active thrusting and crustal thickening. For the exceptionally high heat flow of the extending back-arc Taupo Volcanic Zone, New Zealand, where heat transfer through the upper crust is dominated by hydrothermal convection and averages *c.* 700 mW m^{-2}, the seismogenic zone is restricted to the top 6–8 km (Bryan *et al.* 1999). In the immediate vicinity of geothermal fields around recently intruded high-level plutons, it shallows to just a few kilometres (Muraoka *et al.* 1998). Studies in Japan and New Zealand also show

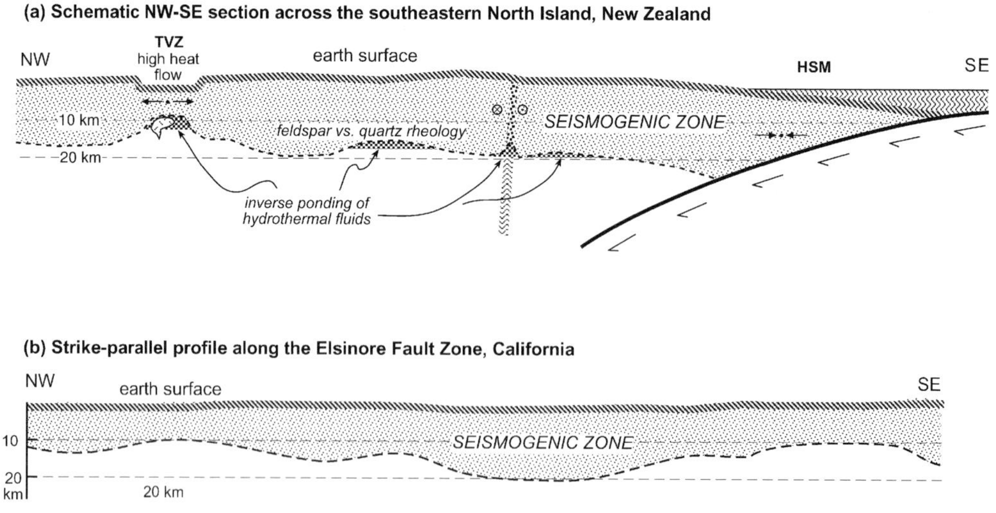

Fig. 1. Regional variations in the depth of the seismogenic zone in continental crust: (**a**) Schematic NW–SE cross-section modelled on the active Hikurangi subduction margin (HSM) and Taupo Volcanic Zone (TVZ) in the southeastern North Island of New Zealand (after Anderson & Webb 1994). (**b**) NW–SE longitudinal profile illustrating varying depth of the seismogenic zone along the Elsinore dextral strike-slip fault of southern California (after Nazareth & Hauksson 2004).

local deepening of the seismogenic zone by 5–10 km in the immediate hanging wall of subduction thrust interfaces (Anderson & Webb 1994; Hasegawa *et al.* 1994) in general accord with expectations from thermal models of subduction refrigeration (Peacock 1996).

On the basis of thermal modelling and direct drilling intercepts in geothermal areas, the gradational FR–QP transition defining the base of seismic rupturing in crustal fault zones generally corresponds to isotherms ranging from 300–350 °C in quartz-rich crust to *c.* 450 °C for feldspar-dominant rheologies, equivalent to low- to mid-greenschist-facies metamorphic conditions (Sibson 1984; Scholz 1988; Muraoka *et al.* 1998; Ito 1999; Williams *et al.* 2004). Along individual strike-slip fault zones the depth of the seismogenic zone may vary by 5–10 km. For the longitudinal depth profile along the Elsinore dextral strike-slip fault illustrated in Figure 1b, long-wavelength fluctuations in the depth of the seismic–aseismic transition correlate inversely with heat flow (Bonner *et al.* 2003; Nazareth & Hauksson 2004). More abrupt fluctuations in seismogenic depth may be caused by changes in lithology affecting rheology (Sanders & Magistrale 1997; Magistrale 2002). Such may be the case around the focal region of the 1989 M 7.1 Loma Prieta earthquake where local seismic activity deepened by about 5 km to *c.* 18 km, coincident with a sliver of high-velocity material (gabbro?) trapped within the distributed fault zone (Eberhart-Phillips & Michael 1998). Notably, the Loma Prieta rupture nucleated right at the base of this anomalously deep part of the background seismogenic zone, supporting the argument that such features may serve as locking asperities that control rupture nucleation (Sibson 1984).

It appears, therefore, that the principal factors determining the varying depth of the continental seismogenic zone are changes in geothermal gradient and crustal composition (chiefly the quartz/feldspar ratio; Fig. 2). Deepening of the seismic–aseismic transition may be caused by locally depressed heat flow or by a change from a quartz-dominant to a feldspar-dominant rheology (Sibson 1984). However, other factors such as the localized strain rate in shear zones at the FR–QP transition and the level of fluid pressure in the frictional regime of the fault zone may also play a role. Increased strain rate from local narrowing of the QP shear zone or elevated fluid pressure would both tend to deepen the seismic–aseismic transition. There is also a possibility that the base of the seismogenic zone is time-dependent through the stress–strain-rate cycle between successive large earthquake ruptures.

Overpressured fluids around the base of the seismogenic zone

Geophysical techniques can be used to image likely areas of fluid overpressuring at depth in the crust (Hyndman & Shearer 1989). In the Transverse Ranges of California, which are undergoing active north–south shortening, local bright reflective zones with polarity reversals have been imaged at 18–23 km beneath the

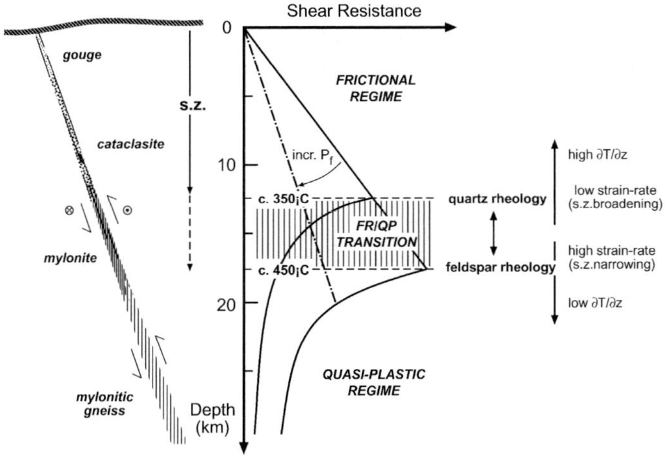

Fig. 2. Schematic cross-section of transcrustal continental fault zone and related shear strength profile illustrating the effect of lithological and physical factors (P_f, fluid pressure; $\partial T/\partial z$, geothermal gradient; strain rate) on the depth of the FR–QP transition defining the base of the seismogenic zone (s.z.).

crystalline assemblage of the San Gabriel Mountains (Ryberg & Fuis 1998). The bright reflectors define a gently dipping décollement at the base of the seismogenic zone into which seismically active thrust faults at the range-front appear to root. These reflectors have been attributed to arrays of flat-lying macroscopic extension fractures containing lithostatically overpressured fluids (Fuis *et al.* 2001). Elsewhere within the Transverse Ranges, strong seismic reflectors define the downwards continuation of seismically active thrust faults, below the seismogenic zone, at dips of 25–40° to depths of *c.* 25 km. The reflectors here are interpreted as ductile shear zones that are strongly overpressured up to the base of the seismogenic zone (Fuis *et al.* 2003).

The coincidence of strong seismic reflectors with a zone of reduced seismic velocities and low electrical resistivity also led Stern *et al.* (2001) to infer fluid overpressuring within the moderately dipping dextral-reverse Alpine Fault Zone in the South Island of New Zealand at depths below the seismogenic zone, with probable extension into an undulose décollement. On the basis of V_P and V_P/V_S anomalies, Chen *et al.* (2001) have likewise inferred the existence of near-lithostatic overpressures in the focal region of the 1999 M 7.6 Chi-Chi earthquake at *c.* 8 km depth on the Chelungpu thrust fault in the Taiwan accretionary wedge, and their post-failure extension along the rupture zone, which extended down-dip to depths of *c.* 20 km. This is an important example because it illustrates that fluid overpressuring, localized around active thrust faults, sometimes extends well into the upper crustal seismogenic zone. Tomographic studies have also been used to infer heterogeneous accumulations of fluids at subseismogenic depths in the Japanese forearc (Zhao *et al.* 2002).

There is, thus, therefore, accumulating geophysical evidence in areas of crustal convergence and thickening by reverse faulting that, at least locally, the base or lower half of the seismogenic zone is fluid overpressured towards lithostatic values (i.e. $\lambda_v \rightarrow 1.0$).

The seismogenic zone as an upper crustal stress guide

Rheological strength profiles of the crust constructed for regions undergoing prograde metamorphism with associated fluid release at depth suggest that fault strength attains a maximum towards the bottom of the frictional seismogenic zone and diminishes to very low values beneath it as fluid pressure levels approach lithostatic (Sibson & Scott 1998). In such areas, the subgreenschist brittle carapace serves as the principal load-bearing portion of the crust (Fig. 3). Deep borehole stress measurements in cratonic areas support the notion that the hydrostatically fluid-pressured portion of the upper crust is the principal load-bearing component of the lithosphere (Zoback & Townend 2001).

Measurements of present-day tectonic stress fields (principal compressive stresses $\sigma_1 > \sigma_2 > \sigma_3$) across the Earth also demonstrate the existence of remarkably uniform 'Andersonian' stress provinces over broad regions, with two of the principal stresses horizontal and the vertical

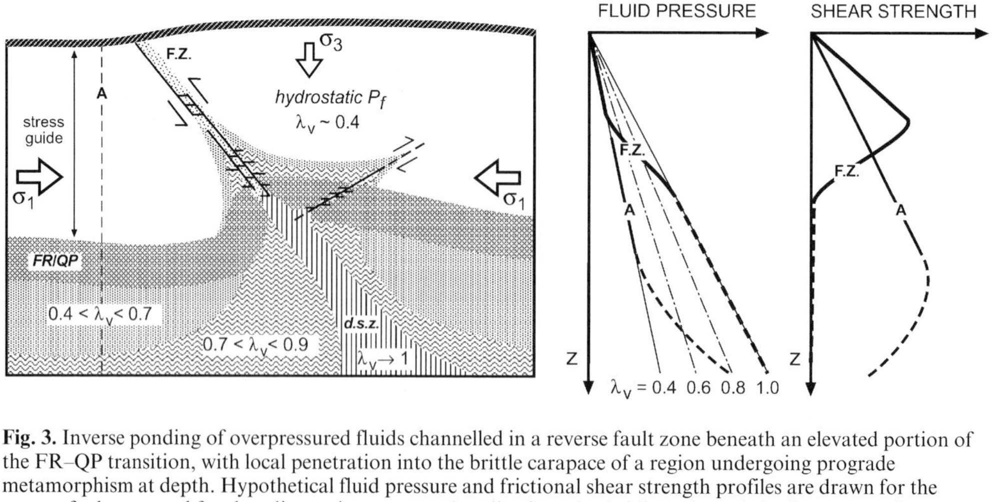

Fig. 3. Inverse ponding of overpressured fluids channelled in a reverse fault zone beneath an elevated portion of the FR–QP transition, with local penetration into the brittle carapace of a region undergoing prograde metamorphism at depth. Hypothetical fluid pressure and frictional shear strength profiles are drawn for the reverse fault zone and for the adjacent intact crust. A well-oriented subsidiary thrust is in the process of formation. F.Z., fault zone; d.s.z., ductile shear zone.

stress, σ_v, equal to σ_1 (extensional regime), σ_3 (compressional regime), or σ_2 (strike-slip regime) (Anderson 1951; Zoback 1992). However, areas of stress heterogeneity occur at the boundaries between stress provinces, and local stress heterogeneities may also arise, for example, through torsion or buckling of the 'elastic lid'. This possibility of significant stress field heterogeneity should be kept in mind throughout the following discussion on containment of overpressured fluids, which assumes simple 'Andersonian' stress fields with vertical and horizontal stress trajectories.

Mesozonal Au–quartz lodes

Most large mesozonal Au–quartz vein systems have developed in association with predominantly reverse-sense shear zones of mixed continuous–discontinuous character that were active under greenschist metamorphic conditions, broadly equivalent to the gradational FR–QP transition environment inferred at the base of the continental seismogenic zone (Roberts 1987; McCuaig & Kerrich 1998). Hosting structures are often in the vicinity of, but subordinate to, regional shear zones, which themselves tend to be only sparsely mineralized, but this is not always the case. For example, a significant proportion of the deposits within the Mother Lode gold-belt of California are hosted in the Melones Fault Zone for *c.* 200 km along strike (Knopf 1929). Within individual shear zones, mineralization generally extends for only a limited distance along strike (generally <1–2 km). Veins occupy the hosting shear zones as well as mesh structures of extensional and extensional–shear fractures interlinked by low-displacement shears developed in their wallrocks (Fig. 4). Form and style of the fracture meshes vary considerably, a key

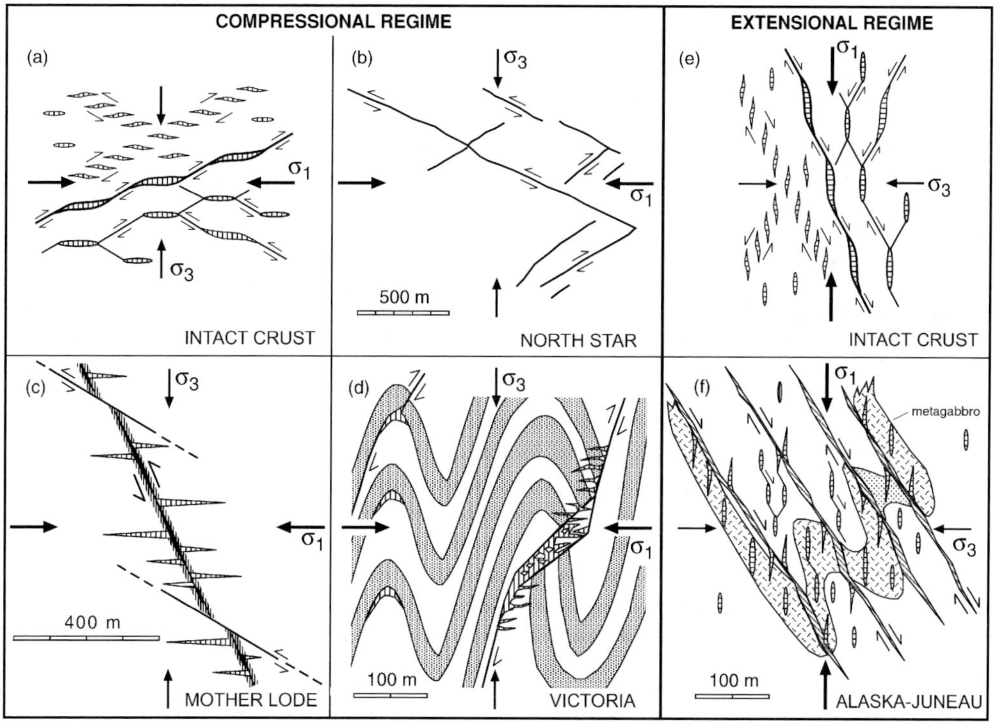

Fig. 4. Fault–fracture meshes in different settings. Compressional regime: (**a**) mesh components developing within intact crust (faults as indicated, extension fractures cross-hatched); (**b**) Au–quartz veins hosted by conjugate sets of low-displacement thrust faults disrupting a granite–greenstone assemblage, North Star Mine, Grass Valley, California (after Johnston 1940); (**c**) Carson Hill Mine, representing typical Mother Lode style with Au–quartz lodes hosted by steep reverse faults flanked by extension vein arrays, disrupted by late-stage thrusts (Julihn & Horton 1938); (**d**) Au–quartz veins in saddle reefs and dilational jogs along reverse faults, Victoria, Australia (after Cox *et al.* 1991). Extensional regime: (**e**) fault–fracture meshes forming in intact crust; (**f**) Au–quartz veins in an extensional fault–fracture mesh localized around a folded layer of relatively competent metagabbro, Juneau, Alaska (Miller *et al.* 1992).

factor being the proportion and distribution of relatively high-competence (i.e. high tensile strength) rock, which promotes extensional over shear failure (Sibson 2000).

Growth textures in the extension and extensional–shear veins commonly record histories of incremental 'crack-seal' dilation with occasional evidence for episodes of open-space filling (Boullier & Robert 1992), suggesting that the hosting fractures were locally gaping at the time of hydrothermal flow and deposition. Fault-hosted veins often exhibit ribbon texture with bands of quartz interlaminated with slivers of detached wallrock, developed subparallel to the walls (Chace 1949). It is clear that the fault–fracture meshes functioned as localized high-permeability conduits within otherwise low-permeability crust, allowing episodic rapid flow of substantial fluid volumes. Tapering of extension veins away from the shear zones also leads to the inference that the hosting shear zones themselves were the principal localized conduits for fluids overpressured to near-lithostatic values (Cox 1995), in accordance with experimental evidence for enhanced permeability in deformation zones under low effective stresses (i.e. as $P_f \rightarrow \sigma_3$) (Cox *et al.* 2001).

The structural form of the vein systems, coupled with fluid-inclusion analyses provide evidence for repeated cycling of fluid-pressure within the lithostatic–hydrostatic range (Sibson *et al.* 1988; Sibson 1990; Boullier & Robert 1992; Wilkinson & Johnston 1996; Parry 1998). This has led to the inference of cyclical fault-valve behaviour (i.e. repeated interseismic accumulation of fluid overpressure to near-lithostatic values prior to fault rupture), concentrated in a region of mixed brittle–ductile rheology around the seismic–aseismic transition (Fig. 3). Fault rupture is then followed by discharge along the enhanced permeability of the rupture zone (Sibson 1992; Cox 1995; Robert *et al.* 1995). Although described from a range of tectonic settings (e.g. Cox *et al.* 1991; Craw & Norris 1991; Miller *et al.* 1992; Robert *et al.* 1995; Nguyen *et al.* 1998; Sibson & Scott 1998; McKeagney *et al.* 2004), it is notable that mesozonal lode systems are most extensively developed in compressional–transpressional regimes in association with predominantly reverse-slip fault zones.

The factors that determine which portions of the shear zones become mineralized remain poorly understood, especially the controls that determine localization of mineralization along strike. However, it is a common circumstance for the principal lode-hosting structure, with which the fault–fracture meshes are associated, to be poorly oriented for frictional reactivation within the prevailing stress field (e.g. Sibson *et al.* 1988; Tunks *et al.* 2004), although this is not invariably the case (e.g. Nguyen *et al.* 1998). It is also not uncommon for the distributed fault–fracture meshes to be transected, at a late stage in their development, by near-barren, through-going faults that are well oriented for reactivation in the stress field. The conditions under which fault–fracture meshes form or reactivate determine the conditions for high-flux flow giving rise to mesozonal Au–quartz lodes (Sibson & Scott 1998).

Fluid containment below the seismogenic carapace

With the brittle seismogenic carapace acting as a containing lid, the architecture of mid-crustal shear zones, coupled to the 3D topography of the seismic–aseismic transition (both along individual fault zones and on a regional scale), probably play key roles in focusing the discharge of overpressured fluids from the middle to deep crust (Fig. 1). Containment of overpressured fluids in and around the base of the seismogenic zone is affected by fault architecture (which may be new-formed or inherited), and by the stress state in the overlying carapace (Sibson & Rowland 2003). In some areas the hydrostatic–lithostatic fluid pressure interface may directly coincide with the predominantly temperature-controlled FR–QP transition. Such seems likely to be the case in regions undergoing progressive crustal extension with active normal faulting, such as the Taupo Volcanic Zone, New Zealand, where convective circulation of hydrostatically pressured fluids apparently extends through the full depth of the seismogenic zone. Overpressured fluids are more easily contained, however, within compressional regimes, where they may locally penetrate upwards some distance into the FR regime, particularly along reverse fault conduits (Fig. 3), leading to a heterogeneous distribution of overpressure.

Permeability in relation to the seismic cycle

The low bulk permeabilities ($<10^{-18}\,m^2$) needed to contain overpressured fluids in the mid-crust are generally met within intact assemblages of metamorphic rock (Manning & Ingebritsen 1999). Paradoxically, the passage of the large fluid volumes needed to form mesozonal vein systems requires high permeability, at least transiently, in the hosting structures. However, flow through fault–fracture systems may itself lower permeability rapidly by hydrothermal deposition, so that there are competing processes of permeability creation and destruction within active fault zones (Parry 1998). Several factors need to be considered in relation to this critical issue of time-dependent permeability in and around active fault structures.

First, grain-scale permeability is enhanced by orders of magnitude in active shear zones as effective stresses are progressively reduced with $P_f \rightarrow \sigma_3$ (Cox *et al.* 2001). Additionally, the formation of mesh structures with gaping extension fractures, both within shear zones and extending into their wallrocks, promotes localized high flux flow but requires the tensile overpressure condition, $P_f > \sigma_3$, to be met prior to main fault failure. A final important consideration is the aftershock activity that invariably follows mainshock ruptures and probably plays a critical role in mesozonal mineralization (Micklethwaite & Cox 2004). Aftershocks are notably distributed throughout a substantial rock volume surrounding a mainshock rupture with concentrations at fault irregularities and at rupture tips (King *et al.* 1994). Such distributed fracturing allows rapid ingress of fluid into the main rupture zone from a broad region of the surrounding, overpressured rock-mass. This is likely to be especially important at the down-dip termination of dip-slip ruptures. For example, the spread of aftershocks with time in the 1997 Umbria–Marche, Italy, extensional earthquake sequence has been modelled in terms of a fluid pulse discharged from the base of the seismogenic zone (Miller *et al.* 2004). Progressive reduction of fracture permeability from hydrothermal self-sealing will probably occur throughout the aftershock period.

Conditions for activation of fault–fracture meshes

Void creation in the mid-crust through fracture dilation is inhibited by increasing overburden pressure with depth but becomes possible when fluid overpressure, P_f, counteracts the vertical stress, σ_v. At a depth z in crust with average density ρ the effective vertical stress is:

$$\sigma_v' = (\sigma_v - P_f) = \sigma_v(1 - \lambda_v) = \rho g z(1 - \lambda_v) \quad (2)$$

where g is gravitational acceleration and λ_v is the pore-fluid factor, as previously defined. A key question, therefore, is the maximum overpressure (λ_v value) that can be sustained in a particular tectonic setting. Formation or reactivation of brittle faults and fractures limits sustainable overpressure by providing drainage channels and can thus be used to define likely conditions for mesozonal mineralization.

A failure mode plot of differential stress, $(\sigma_1 - \sigma_3)$, versus effective vertical stress, σ_v' (or λ_v at 10 km depth) (Fig. 5), defines the stress–fluid-pressure conditions under which different modes of brittle failure and fault reactivation may occur in compressional ($\sigma_v = \sigma_3$) and extensional ($\sigma_v = \sigma_1$) tectonic regimes for rock with varying tensile strength, T. The two sets of failure criteria also define the limiting stress–fluid-pressure conditions for strike-slip faulting with $\sigma_v = \sigma_2$. They can be used to characterize the conditions under which high-flux flow through gaping fractures is likely to develop in the mesozonal environment (Sibson 2004*a*). The following points are apparent:

(1) The existence of a through-going cohesionless fault that is well oriented for frictional reactivation (reshear) within the prevailing stress field inhibits all other modes of brittle failure. Absence of such structures is thus a prerequisite for high-flux flow through dilatant fault–fracture meshes.

(2) Sustainable differential stress and fluid pressure are inversely related to each other: the greater the differential stress, the lower the sustainable fluid overpressure, and vice versa. Mesh formation, involving dilation of extension fractures, therefore requires differential stress to be low.

(3) At high λ_v values, mixed mode failure becomes possible in rock assemblages with varying tensile strength, leading to the formation of fault–fracture meshes.

(4) Overpressure within intact rock in extensional regimes can be limited by the formation of dilatant extensional and extensional–shear fractures at sub-lithostatic fluid-pressure levels, but supralithostatic fluid pressures are needed for development of dilatant meshes in compressional regimes (unless stress heterogeneity exists such that $\sigma_3 < \sigma_v$).

(5) Fluid overpressures approaching lithostatic values (i.e. $\lambda_v \rightarrow 1$) are much easier to sustain in compressional stress fields. Additionally, there is a stronger likelihood of high-amplitude fluid-pressure cycling from fault-valve action in compressional regimes.

High-flux flow through distributed fault–fracture meshes is therefore limited to areas under low differential stress that are devoid of through-going, low-cohesion faults that are well oriented for reactivation. Mesh activation requires a precarious balance to be maintained

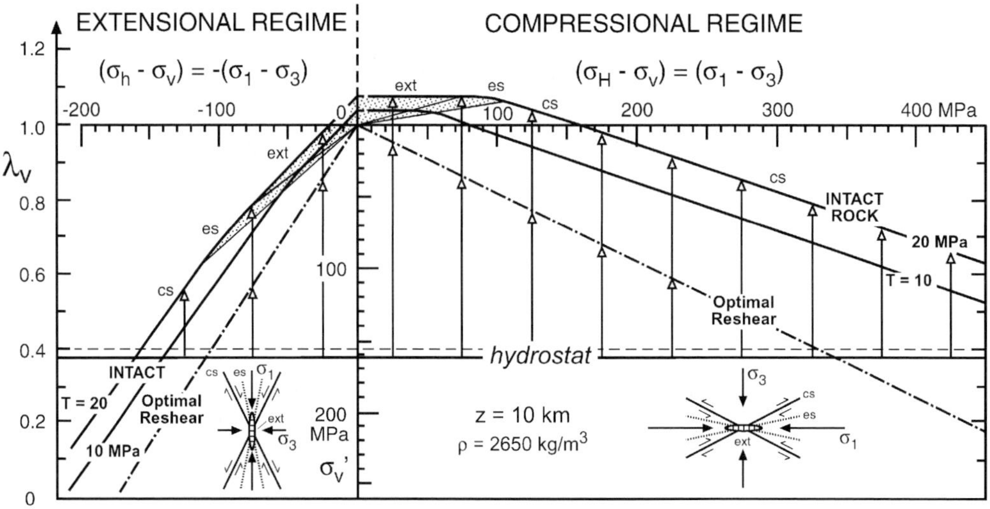

Fig. 5. Brittle failure mode plot of differential stress ($\sigma_1 - \sigma_3$) v. pore-fluid factor, λ_v, (and effective vertical stress, σ_v') at 10 km depth, defining the sustainable overpressure for compressional and extensional tectonic regimes. Failure envelopes for intact rock are constructed for internal friction, $\mu_i = 0.75$ and $T = 10$ and 20 MPa (cs, es, and ext define fields of compressional shear, extensional–shear, and extensional failure, respectively); reshear of optimally oriented faults assumes static friction, $\mu_s = 0.6$; rock density, $\rho = 2650$ kg m^{-3}. Shaded areas define fields where mesh structures incorporating gaping extension and extensional–shear fractures may develop. Hydrostatic fluid-pressure condition represented by bold line at $\lambda_v = 0.38$; open-headed arrows define sustainable overpressure above hydrostatic at particular values of differential stress for intact rock ($T = 20$ MPa), and for reshear.

between low differential stress and near-lithostatic fluid overpressure. The specialized circumstances where such flow may occur include: (1) 'intact crust' or crust reconstituted by metamorphism where fault–fracture meshes are 'self-generated' by migration of overpressured fluids (Sibson & Scott 1998); (2) regions of stress heterogeneity around fault tips or stepovers (Segall & Pollard 1980); (3) areas where existing faults have 'healed', regaining cohesive strength by hydrothermal cementation (e.g. Nguyen *et al.* 1998); (4) areas where existing fault sets are severely misoriented (i.e. oriented at >50–60° to σ_1), either through inheritance or from progressive fault 'dominoing' or comparable mechanisms (Sibson *et al.* 1988). These factors help to explain why the most extreme forms of fault-valve action, giving rise to the most extensively developed mesozonal lode systems, are best developed around steep reverse faults in compressional or transpressional regimes (Sibson 1990). High-flux flow, without formation of macroscopic fractures, remains possible as a consequence of enhanced grain-scale permeability at low effective stress in shear zones. It may also give rise to distributed mineralization, but likewise requires low effective stress ($\lambda_v \rightarrow 1$) which can only be sustained under low levels of differential stress (Fig. 5).

Tectonic settings favouring high-flux flow

Fluid-rich environments that favour high-flux valving flow through fault–fracture meshes are illustrated in Figure 6. A first, obvious tectonic setting for extreme valving action involves the compressional inversion of sedimentary basins where faults, inherited from previous extensional rifting, are poorly oriented for reactivation as reverse faults during shortening (Fig. 6a). During the transition from crustal extension to compression, the progressive increase in mean stress contributes to strong fluid overpressuring and the continued reactivation of unfavourably oriented faults (Sibson 2004b). The Santa Barbara Channel–Ventura Basin region of southern California, where fluid overpressuring to near-lithostatic levels is associated with seismically active steep reverse faults and hydrocarbon migration, represents one active setting where this style of fluid redistribution is coupled to compressional inversion.

Forearc hanging walls, which may include collision–accretion assemblages along continental margins, are particularly favoured settings for fault-valve activity because they overlie a long-lasting fluid source in the form of subducting and dewatering oceanic crust and sediment (Fig. 6b). Notably, this is the most common

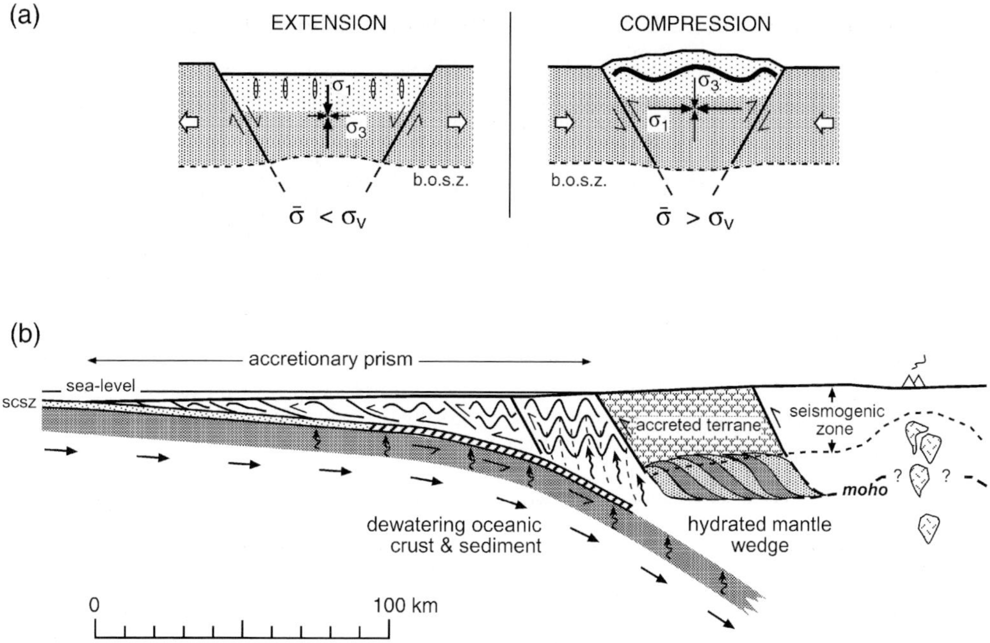

Fig. 6. Schematic representations of fluid-rich tectonic settings for mesh formation and extreme valving action. (**a**) Compressional inversion of a former rift basin with accompanying change in mean stress from less than, to greater than, the vertical stress (b.o.s.z., base of seismogenic zone). (**b**) Accretion–collision system with reverse faults progressively steepening to frictional lock-up in the hanging wall above subducting and progressively dewatering oceanic crust and sediment (scsz, subduction channel shear zone; hachured along seismogenic thrust interface responsible for major subduction thrust ruptures). Inferred intense fluid release in the hanging wall above the down-dip termination of subduction thrust ruptures is denoted by large squiggly arrows.

inferred setting for 'orogenic' (mesozonal) gold deposits (Groves *et al.* 1998). Sets of thrust faults steepen progressively within sedimentary packages undergoing progressive contraction and upright folding (Sibson & Scott 1998), and also at the margins of accreted terranes. Extreme valving action is likely to set in as the reverse faults approach frictional lock-up at dips of 50–60° but will continue only so long as the supply of lithostatically overpressured fluid is maintained.

Relevant to this latter environment are recent observations of seismic tremor activity concentrated in the depth interval 10–40 km in the hanging wall above the down-dip termination of the locked subduction thrust interface beneath Vancouver Island (Rogers & Dragert 2003; Kao *et al.* 2005). Tremor activity migrates for tens of kilometres along strike as well as upwards, and is temporally coincident with episodes of aseismic slip along the subduction interface, down-dip from locked portions of the interface (Fig. 6b). From the seismic style of the tremors and their spatial coincidence with a zone of strong seismic reflectors and high electrical conductivity in the overlying crust, there is a strong inference that they are related to the migration of overpressured fluids derived from the subducting slab. This active setting bears a remarkable resemblance to the palaeotectonic setting inferred for Central California during the early Cretaceous at the time of mineralization in the Mother Lode gold-belt (Bohlke & Kistler 1986; Elder & Cashman 1992; Ingersoll 1997).

Topography of the seismic–aseismic transition in relation to fluid discharge

Topographic variations in the base of the seismogenic zone seem likely to exert a control on metamorphic fluid discharge into the upper seismogenic crust. Spacing between adjacent peaks or troughs in the base of the seismogenic zone along the strike-slip faults of southern California, as exemplified by the depth profile for the Elsinore Fault (Fig. 1b), is typically *c.* 60 ± 20 km with a peak-to-trough spacing of 30 ± 10 km and is attributable to a combination of variations in heat flow and crustal composition along strike (Magistrale 2002; Nazareth & Hauksson 2004). This spacing is comparable with typical separations of *c.* 60 ± 10 km between clusters of mesozonal Au–quartz deposits along the major Porcupine–Destor and Larder Lake–Cadillac fault structures in the Abitibi Greenstone Belt in Quebec, with hints of a second-order characteristic spacing at *c.* 30 ± 5 km (Robert & Poulsen 2001). Clusters of mesozonal Au-quartz deposits are also typically spaced at *c.* 30–40 km along the Boulder–Lefroy and related faults in the Kalgoorlie district of the Yilgarn Craton in Western Australia (Geological Survey of Western Australia 2001).

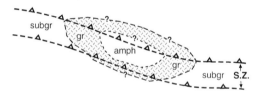

One may anticipate that locally elevated portions of the seismic–aseismic transition in areas of high geothermal gradient would promote 'inverse ponding' of buoyant hydrothermal fluids, derived from prograde metamorphism in the middle to deep crust. This is especially likely in the vicinity of reverse faults because isotherm displacement may create 'thermal antiforms' on their hanging walls (Figs 3 and 7). Conceivably, upward discharge of significant fluid volumes through the shear zone conduit could further elevate the FR–QP transition by advecting heat and promoting reaction softening (Wintsch *et al.* 1995; Imber *et al.* 2001). Such positive feedback would lead to progressive elevation of the FR–QP transition with time and increased focusing of discharge with fluids drawn in predominantly from along strike (Fig. 7). A diagnostic feature of such focusing would be local elevation of metamorphic grade and associated hydrothermal alteration around the associated major fault structure (Fig. 8). Alteration haloes associated with some of the reverse-fault hosted Victorian gold deposits (e.g. Li *et al.* 1998) could be manifestations of such 'feedback' focusing.

On the other hand, through their role as asperities, depressed portions of the seismogenic zone in areas of reduced heat flow form preferred sites for rupture nucleation, and as such may also focus valving discharge for severely misoriented faults. In these circumstances, the diagnostic feature would be an association of fault-hosted gold–quartz veins with an area of lower metamorphic grade along the major fault trace (Fig. 8). It should be noted, for example, that the large mesozonal systems of the Kalgoorlie and Boulder–Bardoc region, adjacent to the Boulder–Lefroy fault in Western Australia, are associated with an area of low greenschist assemblages and lower-temperature hydrothermal alteration, flanked by higher-temperature alteration assemblages in the surrounding granite–greenstone assemblage (Witt & Vanderhor 1998). Additionally, in the Red Lake district of Ontario,

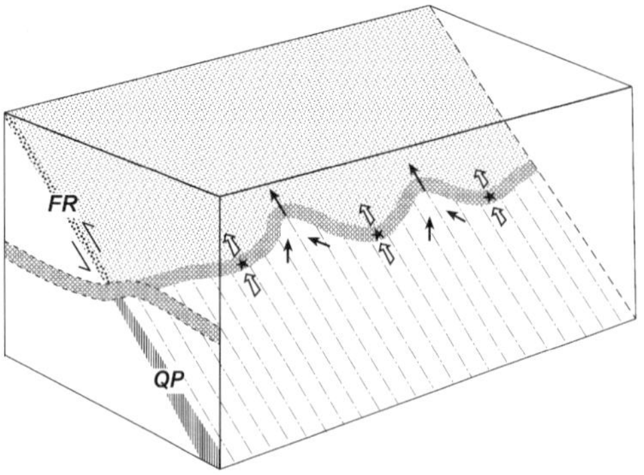

Fig. 7. Fluid focusing through local elevation of the FR–QP transition along a reverse fault, or at rupture nucleation sites (stars) located at local depressions in the base of the seismogenic zone.

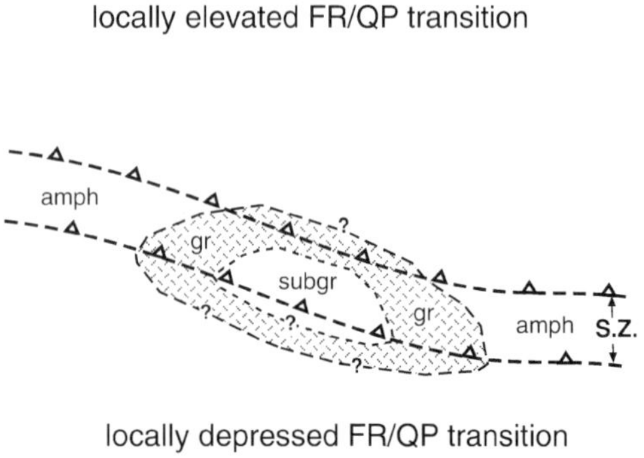

Fig. 8. Patterns of metamorphic isograds developed in fault–rock assemblages in association with local elevations and depressions of the FR–QP transition (S.Z., shear zone; amph, amphibolite-facies assemblage gr, greenschist-facies assemblage; subgr, sub-greenschist-facies assemblages; ?, uncertain extension of metamorphic assemblages beyond shear zone margins). Greenschist-facies assemblages are most likely to host Au–quartz vein systems.

Canada, mesozonal gold deposits are notably concentrated in a complex of intersecting shear zones bearing greenschist assemblages, but decrease in number beyond the greenschist–amphibolite isograd, which cuts across the shear zones at high angles (Andrews *et al.* 1986).

Thus, both peaks and troughs in the base of the seismogenic zone may contribute to fluid focusing. However, a major problem with the suggested diagnostic techniques is the need to discriminate the metamorphic assemblages that characterize the shear zones during mineralization from those developed during the peak in regional metamorphism, which, in many instances, occurs significantly earlier (Groves *et al.* 1998; McCuaig & Kerrich 1998; Witt & Vanderhor 1998). Moreover, rheological changes may also be induced by other factors. Abrupt changes in rheological behaviour may be induced by variations in bulk lithology. For example, in a low- to mid-greenschist-facies metamorphic environment, a shear zone that is fully ductile in a quartz-rich granitic terrain may become more brittle in character and susceptible to lode development as it passes into a gabbroic assemblage with feldspar-dominant rheology. Second-order controls may also arise from local variations in strain rate caused by varying degrees of shear localization, which may itself be lithologically controlled. Narrowing of shear zones should lead to faster strain rates, enhanced brittle behaviour and a stronger likelihood of lode development. There is also considerable evidence that shear zone intersections and other fault irregularities (jogs, bends, etc.) contribute significantly to fluid focusing (Andrews *et al.* 1986; Robert & Poulsen 2001; Micklethwaite & Cox 2004).

Concluding discussion

In areas of crustal convergence and thickening with active prograde metamorphism at depth, the upper crustal seismogenic zone serves as a stress guide and containing lid to overpressured metamorphic fluids. The vast majority of mesozonal Au–quartz lodes formed at temperatures of 300–450 °C, broadly coincident with the gradational FR–QP transition defining the base of this seismogenic zone. However, the development of Au–quartz lodes hosted in fault–fracture meshes, associated with valving activity on reverse faults, requires a delicate balance to be maintained between differential stress and fluid overpressure in appropriate structural settings. Peaks and troughs in the FR–QP transition, defining the base of the seismogenic zone, seem likely to play an important role controlling the localization of mesozonal lode gold systems along transcrustal fault zones.

Local highs in the FR–QP transition, allowing inverse ponding of overpressured fluids, would be expected in areas of enhanced heat flow, in areas where a lateral transition occurs from feldspar-dominant to quartz-dominant shear zone rheology, or perhaps in areas where there is a localized reduction in shear strain rate from the broadening of shear zones. In convergent settings, thermal domes may initiate from isotherm displacement along reverse faults and amplify as a consequence of progressive heat advection by hydrothermal fluids coupled to reaction softening. Depressed portions of the seismogenic zone capable of acting as mainshock nucleation sites form in thermal lows, in areas of lateral transition from quartz-dominant to feldspar-dominant shear zone rheology, or in areas of high strain rate where shear zones narrow or merge. With rupture nucleation at cold, deep 'keels' in the seismic–aseismic transition, it is also conceivable that lateral propagation of ruptures into along-strike areas of higher heat flow may provide the transient fracture permeability that sometimes allows lode gold deposits to form in shear zones active under high-greenschist- and amphibolite-facies conditions (Groves *et al.* 1998).

Concepts developed here may conceivably have application to other styles of Au-mineralization, such as that in the Archaean Witwatersrand Basin of South Africa, from which >40% of the world's mined gold has been extracted from auriferous quartz-pebble conglomerates. Debate over the origin of these deposits (pure hydrothermal v. hydrothermally remobilized placer) continues but the mineralization developed in portions of a clastic sedimentary sequence affected by low-greenschist metamorphism ($T < 350$ °C; $2.5 < P < 3.5$ kbar) (Phillips & Law 1994; Barnicoat *et al.* 1997; Frimmel 1997), suggesting an environment immediately overlying the base of the seismogenic zone. Regional structural studies have now established the role of large-scale thrust tectonics at various stages in the history of the basin (Coward *et al.* 1995) and the hosting of hydrothermal Au-mineralization by predominantly flat-lying fractures and microfractures developed in the tip zones of low-displacement thrusts (Barnicoat *et al.* 1997; Jolley *et al.* 2004). It seems likely, therefore, that this mineralization was also associated with the migration of hydrothermal fluids overpressured to near-lithostatic values, perhaps generated at the leading edge of a foreland thrust system in the manner suggested by Cello & Nur (1988). In the prevailing compressional stress field, the migrating fluids either introduced or redistributed gold into 'self-generated' distributed fault–fracture meshes developing within essentially intact rock (see Sibson 1996), allowing local high-flux flow before they coalesced into propagating thrusts. In the context of this paper, the key point is that the gold was either remobilized or introduced by migrating hydrothermal fluids overpressured to approximately lithostatic values, in association with incipient development of brittle thrust faults near the base of the palaeoseismogenic zone.

A circumstantial case has been presented associating the development of mesozonal gold–quartz lodes with trapping of overpressured fluids near the base of the seismogenic zone. The irregular topography of the seismic–aseismic transition is speculated to play a critical role in governing the upward discharge of metamorphically derived hydrothermal fluids into the upper, seismogenic crust. The situation is complicated, however, by the likelihood of heterogeneous differential stress and distribution of fluid overpressure as fault systems approach the lock-up condition needed for extreme valve activity. Much remains to be worked out concerning the details of mechanical controls on the formation of mesozonal Au–quartz lodes, in particular the relative efficacy of local highs and depressions in the FR–QP transition as focusing controls on the discharge of overpressured fluids.

Special thanks go to E. G. Charlesworth, M. Clark, D. Craw, L. Miller, H. Poulsen, L. Robb and F. Robert for education and travels in the realm of gold, and to S. F. Cox and B. Yardley for a healthy combination of scepticism and constructive criticism.

References

ANDERSON, E. M. 1951. *The Dynamics of Faulting and Dyke Formation with Application to Britain*, 2nd edn. Oliver & Boyd, Edinburgh.

ANDERSON, H. & WEBB, T. H. 1994. New Zealand seismicity: patterns revealed by the upgraded National Seismograph Network. *New Zealand Journal of Geology and Geophysics*, **37**, 477–493.

ANDREWS, A. J., HUGON, H., DUROCHER, M., CORFU, F. & LAVIGNE, M. J. 1986. The anatomy of a gold-bearing greenstone belt: Red Lake, Northwestern Ontario, Canada. *In*: MACDONALD, A. J. (ed.) *Proceedings of Gold '86: An International Symposium on the Geology of Gold Deposits*. Toronto, 2–22.

BARNICOAT, A. C., HENDERSON, I. H. C., KNIPE, R. J. *et al.* 1997. Hydrothermal gold in the Witwatersrand Basin. *Nature*, **386**, 820–824.

BOHLKE, J. K. & KISTLER, R. W. 1986. Rb–Sr, K–Ar, and stable isotope evidence for the ages and sources of fluid components of gold-bearing quartz veins in the northern Sierra Nevada Foothills metamorphic belt, California. *Economic Geology*, **81**, 296–322.

BONNER, J. L., BLACKWELL, D. D. & HERRIN, E. T. 2003. Thermal constraints on earthquake depths in California. *Bulletin of the Seismological Society of America*, **93**, 2333–2354.

BOULLIER, A.-M. & ROBERT, F. 1992. Paleoseismic events recorded in Archean gold–quartz vein networks, Val d'Or, Abitibi, Quebec, Canada. *Journal of Structural Geology*, **14**, 161–180.

BRYAN, C. J., SHERBURN, S., BIBBY, H. M., BANNISTER, S. C. & HURST, A. W. 1999. Shallow seismicity of the central Taupo Volcanic Zone, New Zealand: its distribution and nature. *New Zealand Journal of Geology and Geophysics*, **42**, 533–542.

CELLO, G. & NUR, A. 1988. Emplacement of foreland thrust systems. *Tectonics*, **7**, 261–271.

CHACE, F. M. 1949. Origin of the Bendigo saddle reefs with comments on the formation of ribbon quartz. *Economic Geology*, **44**, 561–569.

CHEN, C.-H., WANG, W.-H. & TENG, T.-L. 2001. 3D velocity structure around the source area of the 1999 Chi-Chi Taiwan earthquake before and after the mainshock. *Bulletin of the Seismological Society of America*, **91**, 1013–1027.

COWARD, M. P., SPENCER, R. M. & SPENCER, C. E. 1995. Development of the Witwatersrand basin, South Africa. *In*: COWARD, M. P. & RIES, A. C. (eds) *Early Precambrian Processes.* Geological Society, London, Special Publications, **95**, 243–269.

COX, S. F. 1995. Faulting processes at high fluid pressures: an example of fault-valve behaviour from the Wattle Gully Fault, Victoria, Australia. *Journal of Geophysical Research*, **100**, 12841–12860.

COX, S. F., WALL, V. J., ETHERIDGE, M. A. & POTTER, T. F. 1991. Deformation and metamorphic processes in the formation of mesothermal vein-hosted gold deposits–examples from the Lachlan Fold Belt in central Victoria, Australia. *Ore Geology Reviews*, **6**, 391–423.

COX, S. F., KNACKSTEDT, M. A. & BRAUN, J. 2001. Principles of structural control on permeability and fluid flow in hydrothermal systems. *Reviews in Economic Geology*, **14**, 1–24.

CRAW, D. & NORRIS, R. J. 1991. Metamorphogenic Au–W veins and regional tectonics: mineralization throughout the uplift history of the Haast Schist, New Zealand. *New Zealand Journal of Geology and Geophysics*, **34**, 373–383.

EBERHART-PHILLIPS, D. & MICHAEL, A. J. 1998. Seismotectonics of the Loma Prieta, California, region determined from three-dimensional V_p, V_p/V_s, and seismicity. *Journal of Geophysical Research*, **103**, 21099–21120.

ELDER, D. & CASHMAN, S. 1992. Tectonic control and fluid evolution in the Quartz Hill, California, lode gold deposits. *Economic Geology*, **87**, 1795–1812.

FRIMMEL, H. E. 1997. Detrital origin of hydrothermal Witwatersrand gold–a review. *Terra Nova*, **9**, 192–197.

FUIS, G. S., RYBERG, T., GODFREY, N. J., OKAYA, D. A. & MURPHY, J. M. 2001. Crustal structure and tectonics from the Los Angeles basin to the Mojave Desert, southern California. *Geology*, **29**, 15–18.

FUIS, G. S., CLAYTON, R. W., DAVIS, P. M. *et al.* 2003. Fault systems of the 1971 San Fernando and 1994 Northridge earthquakes, southern California: relocated aftershocks and seismic images from LARSE II. *Geology*, **31**, 171–174.

GEOLOGICAL SURVEY OF WESTERN AUSTRALIA 2001. *Western Australia Atlas of Mineral Deposits and Petroleum Fields, 2001*. Western Australia Geological Survey, Perth.

GROVES, D. I. 1993. The crustal continuum model for late-Archean lode gold deposits of the Yilgarn Block, Western Australia. *Mineralium Deposita*, **28**, 366–374.

GROVES, D. I., RIDLEY, J. R., BLOEM, E. M. J. *et al.* 1995. Lode-gold deposits of the Yilgarn block: products of late Archaean crustal-scale overpressured hydrothermal systems. *In*: COWARD, M. P. & RIES, A. C. (eds) *Early Precambrian Processes*. Geological Society, London, Special Publications, **95**, 155–172.

GROVES, D. I., GOLDFARB, R. J., GEBRE-MARIAM, M., HAGEMANN, S. G. & ROBERT, F. 1998. Orogenic gold deposits: a proposed classification in the context of their crustal distribution and relationship to other gold deposit types. *Ore Geology Reviews*, **13**, 7–27.

HASEGAWA, A., HORIUCHI, S. & UMINO, N. 1994. Seismic structure of the northeastern Japan convergent margin: a synthesis. *Journal of Geophysical Research*, **99**, 22295–22311.

HENLEY, R. W. 1985. The geothermal framework for epithermal deposits. *In*: BERGER, B. R. & BETHKE, P. M. (eds) *Geology and Geochemistry of Epithermal Systems*. Reviews in Economic Geology, **2**, 1–24.

HILL, D. P., EATON, J. P. & JONES, L. M. 1990. Seismicity, 1980–86. *In*: WALLACE, R. E. (ed.) *The San Andreas Fault System, California*. US Geological Survey, Professional Papers, **1515**, 115–151.

HUBBERT, M. K. & RUBEY, W. W. 1959. Role of fluid pressure in mechanics of overthrust faulting. *Geological Society of America Bulletin*, **70**, 115–166.

HYNDMAN, R. D. & SHEARER, P. M. 1989. Water in the lower continental crust: modeling magnetotelluric and seismic reflection results. *Geophysical Journal International*, **98**, 343–365.

IMBER, J., HOLDSWORTH, R. E., BUTLER, C. A. & STRACHAN, R. A. 2001. A reappraisal of the Sibson–Scholz fault model: the nature of the frictional to viscous ('brittle–ductile') transition along a long-lived, crustal-scale fault, Outer Hebrides, Scotland. *Tectonics*, **20**, 601–624.

INGERSOLL, R. V. 1997. Phanerozoic tectonic evolution of central California and environs. *International Geology Review*, **39**, 957–972

ITO, K. 1999. Seismogenic layer, reflective lower crust, surface heat flow and large inland earthquakes. *Tectonophysics*, **306**, 423–433.

JOHNSTON, W. D. 1940. *The Gold Quartz Veins of Grass Valley, California*. US Geological Survey Professional Papers, **194**.

JOLLEY, S. J., FREEMAN, S. R., BARNICOAT, A. C. *et al.* 2004. Structural controls on Witwatersrand gold mineralization. *Journal of Structural Geology*, **26**, 1067–1086.

JULIHN, C. E. & HORTON, F. W. 1938. *Mines of the Southern Mother Lode Region: Part I: Calaveras County*. US Department of the Interior Bulletin, **413**.

KAO, H., SHEN, S.-J., DRAGERT, H., ROGERS, G., CASSIDY, J. F. & RAMACHANDRAN, K. 2005. A wide depth distribution of seismic tremors along the Northern Cascadia margin. *Nature*, **436**, 841–844.

KERRICH, R. & WYMAN, D. A. 1990. The geodynamic setting of mesothermal gold deposits: an association with accretionary tectonic regimes. *Geology*, **18**, 882–885.

KING, G. C. P., STEIN, R. S. & LIN, J. 1994. Static stress changes and the triggering of earthquakes. *Bulletin of the Seismological Society of America*, **84**, 935–953.

KNOPF, A. 1929. *The Mother Lode System of California*. US Geological Survey, Professional Papers, **157**.

LI, X., KWAK, T. A. P. & BROWN, R. W. 1998. Wallrock alteration in the Bendigo gold ore field, Victoria, Australia: uses in exploration. *Ore Geology Reviews*, **13**, 381–406.

MAGISTRALE, H. 2002. Relative contribution of crustal temperature and composition to controlling the depths of earthquakes in southern California. *Geophysical Research Letters*, **29**, 10.1029GL-014375.

MANNING, C. E. & INGEBRITSEN, S. E. 1999. Permeability of continental crust: implications of geothermal data and metamorphic systems. *Reviews in Geophysics*, **37**, 127–150.

McCUAIG, T. C. & KERRICH, R. 1998. P–T–t–deformation–fluid characteristics of lode gold deposits: evidence from alteration systematics. *Ore Geology Reviews*, **12**, 381–453.

McKEAGNEY, C. J., BOULTER, C. A., JOLLY, R. J. H. & FOSTER, R. P. 2004. 3-D Mohr circle analysis of vein opening, Indirama lode-gold deposit, Zimbabwe: implications for exploration. *Journal of Structural Geology*, **26**, 1275–1291.

MICKLETHWAITE, S. & COX, S. F. 2004. Fault segment rupture, aftershock zone fluid flow, and mineralization. *Geology*, **32**, 813–816.

MILLER, L. D., BARTON, C. C., FREDERICKSEN, R. S. & BRESSLER, J. R. 1992. Structural evolution of the Alaska Juneau gold deposit, southeastern Alaska. *Canadian Journal of Earth Sciences*, **29**, 865–878.

MILLER, S. A., COLLETTINI, C., CHIARALUCE, L., COCCO, M., BARCHI, M. & KAUS, B. J. P. 2004. Aftershocks driven by a high-pressure CO_2 source at depth. *Nature*, **427**, 724–727.

MURAOKA, H., UCHIDA, T., SASADA, M. *et al.* 1998. Deep geothermal resources survey program: igneous, metamorphic, and hydrothermal processes in a well encountering 500 °C at 3729 m depth, Kakkonda, Japan. *Geothermics*, **27**, 507–5334.

NAZARETH, J. J. & HAUKSSON, E. 2004. The seismogenic thickness of the southern California crust. *Bulletin of the Seismological Society of America*, **94**, 940–960.

NGUYEN, P. T., COX, S. F., HARRIS, L. B. & POWELL, C. M. 1998. Fault-valve behaviour in optimally oriented shear zones: an example at the Revenge gold mine, Kambalda, Western Australia. *Journal of Structural Geology*, **20**, 1625–1640.

PARRY, W. T. 1998. Fault-fluid compositions from fluid-inclusion observations and solubilities of fracture-sealing minerals. *Tectonophysics*, **290**, 1–26.

PEACOCK, S. M. 1996. Thermal and petrologic structure of subduction zones. *In*: BEBOUT, G. E., SCHOLL, D. W., KIRBY, S. H. & PLATT, J. P. (eds) *Subduction–Top to Bottom*. Geophysical Monograph, American Geophysical Union, **96**, 119–133.

PHILLIPS, N. G. & LAW, J. D. M. 1994. Metamorphism of the Witwatersrand gold fields: a review. *Ore Geology Reviews*, **9**, 1–31.

ROBERT, F. & POULSEN, K. H. 2001. Vein formation and deformation in greenstone gold deposits. *Reviews in Economic Geology*, **14**, 111–155.

ROBERT, F., BOULLIER, A.-M. & FIRDAOUS, K. 1995. Gold–quartz veins in metamorphic terranes and their bearing on the role of fluids in faulting. *Journal of Geophysical Research*, **100**, 12861–12879.

ROBERTS, R. G. 1987. Ore deposit models #1–Archean lode gold deposits. *Geoscience Canada*, **14**, 37–52.

ROGERS, G. & DRAGERT, H. 2003. Episodic tremor and slip on the Cascadia subduction zone: the chatter of seismic slip. *Science*, **300**, 1942–1943.

RYBERG, T. & FUIS, G. S. 1998. The San Gabriel Mountains bright reflective zone: possible evidence of young mid-crustal thrust faulting in southern California. *Tectonophysics*, **286**, 31–46.

SANDERS, C. & MAGISTRALE, H. 1997. Segmentation of the northern San Jacinto fault zone, southern California. *Journal of Geophysical Research*, **102**, 27453–27467.

SCHOLZ, C. H. 1988. The brittle-plastic transition and the depth of seismic faulting. *Geologische Rundschau*, **77**, 319–328.

SEGALL, P. & POLLARD, D. D. 1980. Mechanics of discontinuous faults. *Journal of Geophysical Research*, **85**, 4337–4350.

SIBSON, R. H. 1983. Continental fault structure and the shallow earthquake source. *Journal of the Geological Society, London*, **140**, 741–767.

SIBSON, R. H. 1984. Roughness at the base of the seismogenic zone: contributing factors. *Journal of Geophysical Research*, **89**, 5791–5799.

SIBSON, R. H. 1990. Conditions for fault-valve behaviour. *In*: KNIPE, R. J. & RUTTER, E. H. (eds) *Deformation Mechanisms, Rheology, and Tectonics*. Geological Society, London, Special Publications, **54**, 15–28.

SIBSON, R. H. 1992. Implications of fault-valve behaviour for rupture nucleation and recurrence. *Tectonophysics*, **211**, 283–293.

SIBSON, R. H. 1996. Structural permeability of fluid-driven fault–fracture meshes. *Journal of Structural Geology*, **18**, 1031–1042.

SIBSON, R. H. 2000. A brittle failure mode plot defining conditions for high-flux flow. *Economic Geology*, **95**, 41–48.

SIBSON, R. H. 2004*a*. Controls on maximum fluid overpressure defining conditions for mesozonal mineralization. *Journal of Structural Geology*, **26**, 1127–1136.

SIBSON, R. H. 2004*b*. Frictional mechanics of seismogenic thrust systems in the upper continental crust: implications for fluid overpressures and redistribution. *In*: McClay, K. R. (ed.) *Thrust Tectonics and Hydrocarbon Systems*. American Association of Petroleum Geologists, Memoirs, **82**, 1–17.

SIBSON, R. H. & ROWLAND, J. V. 2003. Stress, fluid-pressure, and structural permeability in seismogenic crust, North Island, New Zealand. *Geophysical Journal International*, **154**, 584–594.

SIBSON, R. H. & SCOTT, J. 1998. Stress/fault controls on the containment and release of overpressured fluids: examples from gold–quartz vein systems in Juneau, Alaska, Victoria, Australia, and Otago, New Zealand. *Ore Geology Reviews*, **13**, 293–306.

SIBSON, R. H., ROBERT, F. & POULSEN, K. H. 1988. High-angle reverse faults, fluid pressure cycling, and mesothermal gold–quartz deposits. *Geology*, **16**, 551–555.

SIMMONS, S. F. & BROWN, K. L. 2006. Gold in magmatic hydrothermal solutions and the rapid formation of a giant ore deposit. *Science*, **314**, 288–291.

STEFÁNSSON, A. & SEWARD, T. M. 2004. Gold(I) complexing in aqueous sulphide solutions to 500 °C at 500 bar. *Geochimica et Cosmochimica Acta*, **68**, 4121–4143.

STERN, T., KLEFFMAN, S., OKAYA, D., SCHERWATH, M. & BANNISTER, S. 2001. Low seismic wave speeds and enhanced fluid pressure beneath the Southern Alps of New Zealand. *Geology*, **29**, 679–682.

TUNKS, A. J., SELLEY, D., ROGERS, J. R. & BRABHAM, G. 2004. Vein mineralization at the Damang Gold Mine, Ghana: controls on mineralization. *Journal of Structural Geology*, **26**, 1257–1273.

WILKINSON, J. J. & JOHNSTON, J. D. 1996. Pressure fluctuations, phase separation, and gold precipitation during seismic fracture propagation. *Geology*, **24**, 395–398.

WILLIAMS, C. F., GRUBB, F. V. & GALANAIS, S. P. 2004. Heat flow in the SAFOD pilot hole and implications for the strength of the San Andreas Fault. *Geophysical Research Letters*, **31**, L15S14, doi:10.1029/2003GL019352.

WINTSCH, R. P., CHRISTOFFERSON, R. & KRONENBURG, A. K. 1995. Fluid–rock weakening of fault zones. *Journal of Geophysical Research*, **100**, 13021–13022.

WITT, W. K. & VANDERHOR, F. 1998. Diversity within a unified model for Archean gold mineralization in the Yilgarn craton of Western Australia: an overview of the later-orogenic, structurally-controlled gold deposits. *Ore Geology Reviews*, **13**, 29–64.

ZHAO, D., MISHRA, O. P. & SANDA, R. 2002. Influence of fluids and magmas on earthquakes: seismological evidence. *Physics of the Earth and Planetary Interiors*, **132**, 249–267.

ZOBACK, M. L. 1992. First- and second-order patterns of stress in the lithosphere: the World Stress Map project. *Journal of Geophysical Research*, **97**, 11703–11728.

ZOBACK, M. D. & Townend, J. 2001. Implications of hydrostatic pore pressures and high crustal strength for the deformation of intraplate lithosphere. *Tectonophysics*, **336**, 19–30.

Structural geometry and development of the Witwatersrand Basin, South Africa

ALASTAIR BEACH[1] & RORIC SMITH[2]

[1]*Exploration Consultants Limited, 309 Reading Road, Henley on Thames RG9, 1EL, UK (e-mail: abeach@globalnet.co.uk)*

[2]*AngloGold Ashanti Exploration Australasia, Level 13 St Martins Tower, 44 St Georges Terrace, Perth, WA 6000, Australia*

Abstract: The Witwatersrand Basin is an Archaean basin situated on the Kaapvaal Craton of Southern Africa. The results presented here focus on the structural geometry and development of the basin. Detailed structural sections across the western and northwestern parts of the basin are presented, using seismic data integrated with borehole, mine and outcrop information. The structural development of the basin can be expressed in simple terms, and in a manner that is standard practice within the oil industry. There are several clearly identified stages in basin evolution. The basin was initiated as a rift during Dominion Group times (*c.* 3074 Ma), with post-rift thermal subsidence during the early part of West Rand Group times. Thermal subsidence would have been completed by late West Rand Group times (*c.* 2900 Ma). Minor volcanic interludes within the West Rand Group sequence may testify to the existence of phases of extension during West Rand Group times. Onset of compression and thrusting outside the thermal basin generated a flexural load and clastic input into the basin as it evolved from thermal sag to foreland basin during late West Rand Group times (*c.* 2950 Ma). Foreland basin development culminated in Central Rand Group times, with an increasingly coarse-grained clastic input, and thrust systems that progressively encroached on the basin margins, profoundly influencing structural styles. Thrusting was interrupted during Klipriviersberg Group times (2714 Ma) by the accumulation of basic volcanic rocks. Further thrusting occurred at the end of Klipriviersberg Group times. The basin then returned to an extensional tectonic setting during the Platberg Group rifting (2709 Ma), a major rift event across much of the area. Thermal subsidence related to this rift phase occurred during late Platberg Group times. The overprint of Platberg Group extensional faults breaks up the structural continuity of the Central and West Rand Group sediments within, and adjacent to, the basin, and it is difficult to elucidate the earlier compressional thrust–fold structures. Careful integration of seismic, borehole, mine and outcrop data allows structures from the thrusting event be recognized and more complete sections drawn. These present a larger-scale view of the structure of the basin than has previously been obtained.

The Witwatersrand Basin is an Archaean basin situated on the Kaapvaal Craton of Southern Africa. Gold has been mined in the Witwatersrand Basin for well over 100 years; it has produced about 40% of the world's mined gold, and still contains around 30% of the world's known gold reserves.This activity has generated a huge amount of geological research. It is surprising that a coherent overview of the structural and tectonic development of the basin has not been reached before. Perhaps this is in part due to the paucity of outcrop in many areas, and in part to the focused nature of many mine-based studies that have been carried out.

It is probably only with the publication of the work by Coward *et al.* (1995) and the results presented here that an overview is now being gained. Both these studies arose as part of company-generated projects, with the necessary proprietary nature and confidentiality of results attached. The initiative of both company projects was based on an acceptance that an oil exploration approach to the analysis of the whole basin could provide new insights into exploration potential for the basin. At the time the company projects were initiated, this approach was far from common or accepted in the mineral exploration industry. The biggest step forward was the acquisition of regional seismic reflection datasets across the basin as a key way of understanding basin geometry and evolution.

The results presented here focus on the structural geometry and development of the basin, and arose as part of a collaborative interdisciplinary basin analysis study carried out by Anglo American Uranium and Gold Division (now AngloGold Ashanti).

From: Ries, A. C., Butler, R. W. H. & Graham, R. H. (eds) 2007. *Deformation of the Continental Crust: The Legacy of Mike Coward.* Geological Society, London, Special Publications, **272**, 533–542.
0305-8719/07/$15

The basin has been the subject of numerous studies over many years because of its economic significance, and divergent views about the structural and tectonic development have been published. Exposure throughout the main part of the basin is generally poor, and studies have therefore been based largely on subsurface mine and borehole data. The results presented here have benefited from the interpretation of some 15 000 km of seismic reflection data acquired throughout the basin and adjacent areas by Anglo American, integrated with borehole and mine data, as well as regional stratigraphic studies.

The availability of extensive seismic reflection data has allowed a more complete understanding of the basin structure. Coward *et al.* (1995) were the first researchers to report the results of seismic interpretation across the area, and were able to present a new framework for the structural development of the basin that for the first time gave an integrated overview of structural styles throughout the basin. Their work derived from a collaborative study with Gencor, more or less at the same time as this Anglo American study was being conducted, although company confidentiality prevented any discussion between the two groups during the progress, and after the completion, of their respective investigations.

The essence of the structural framework described by Coward *et al.* (1995) is corroborated here, but the focus of this paper is on detailed structural sections across the western and north-western parts of the basin using seismic data that were not available to Coward and co-workers.

The location of the Witwatersrand Basin is shown in Figure 1, and Figure 2 summarizes the now well-known general stratigraphic sequence for the basin. The lowermost sequence, the Dominion Group, has been dated in its upper part at 3074 Ma (Robb & Meyer 1994) (Fig. 2). Coward *et al.* (1995) suggested that this group was deposited in a rift setting, although they admitted that no direct evidence (such as seismic imaging of rift geometries) was available to them. With increased quality of seismic acquisition and processing, the Anglo American study found that in several places in the western part of the

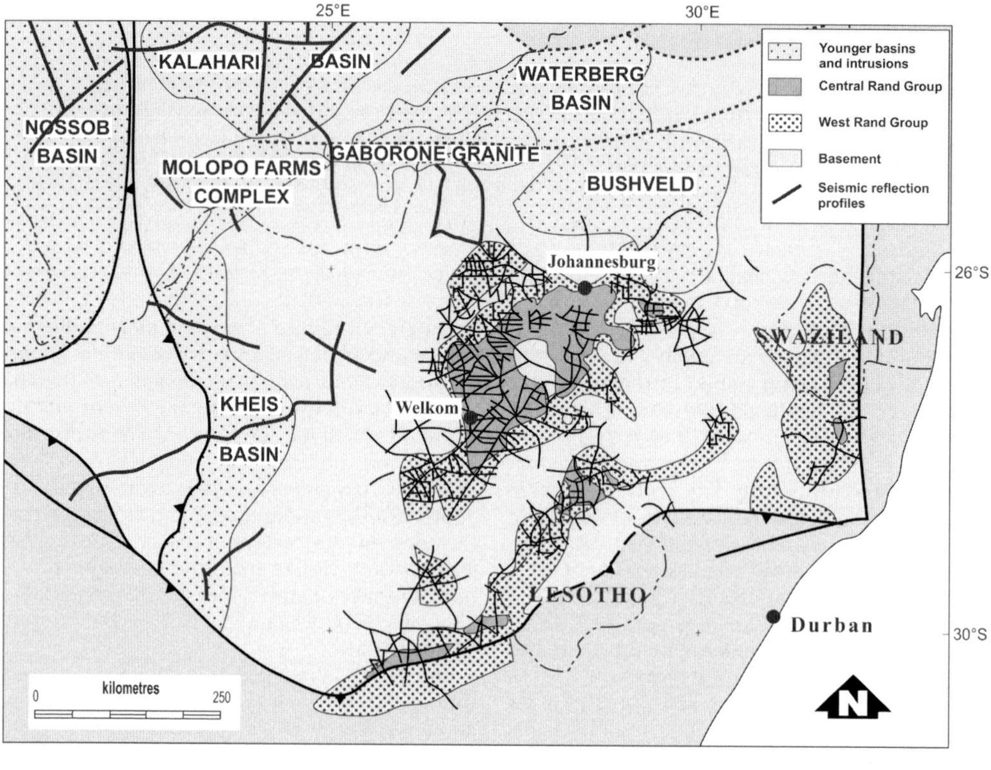

Fig. 1. Location of the Witwatersrand Basin within the Kaapvaal Craton, South Africa. Location of seismic reflection profiles available for this study are shown.

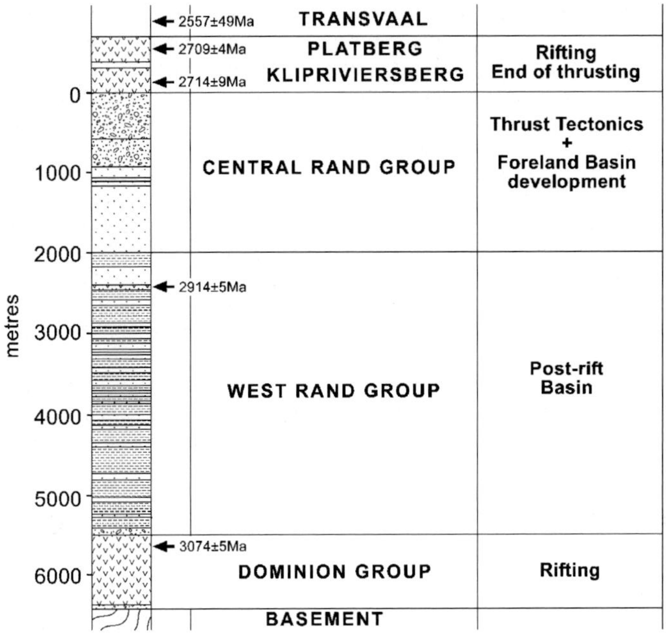

Fig. 2. Stratigraphic sequence for the Witwatersrand Basin, showing age dates available and main tectonic events.

basin, it was possible to see rift structures within the Dominion Group, thus substantiating the suggestion made by Coward *et al.* (1995).

The Dominion Group is dominated by a sequence of clastic sediments, volcaniclastic deposits and lavas, and is followed by the West Rand Group, a sequence of clastic and largely marine sediments deposited in what is interpreted here as the post-rift thermal subsidence phase of the Dominion Group rift.

In the upper part of the West Rand Group, the nature of the basin changes from a post-rift thermal sag to a foreland basin, interpreted here to be largely in response to thrusting directed from the NW. The age of the uppermost part of the West Rand Group has been determined as *c.* 2914 Ma from the Crown Lava (Robb & Meyer 1994).

The Central Rand Group represents a foreland basin fill in front of the advancing thrust system, increasingly dominated by coarse clastic sequences and alluvial-fan deposits. The overall style of the basin from Dominion Group to Central Rand Group times is illustrated schematically in Figure 3.

In the western and northwestern parts of the basin, thrust sequences were eroded, prior to deposition of the Klipriviersberg Group volcanic rocks at the base of the Ventersdorp Supergroup. These volcanic rocks have been dated at 2714 Ma (Robb & Meyer 1994). Thrusting continued after the deposition of the Klipriviersberg Group, but was quickly followed by a major phase of extensional tectonics, and the deposition of the Platberg Group of synrift to post-rift sequences, which included a considerable thickness of volcanic rocks. Platberg Group rocks have been dated at around 2709 Ma in the upper part of the volcanic sequence (Robb & Meyer 1994).

Minor compression and inversion at the end of Platberg Group times was followed by deposition of the regionally extensive Transvaal Group. An age of 2557 Ma has been obtained from the lower part of the Transvaal Group (Robb & Meyer 1994).

The dominant structural style, seen on many seismic sections within the basin and on geological sections from the gold mines, is that of extensional tectonics related to Platberg Group rifting. Within the basin, these faults are generally planar, but west of the basin margin they are generally listric in geometry, where they are interpreted to have reactivated earlier thrust faults in extension. The strong overprint of Platberg Group extensional faults breaks up the continuity of the Central and West Rand Groups

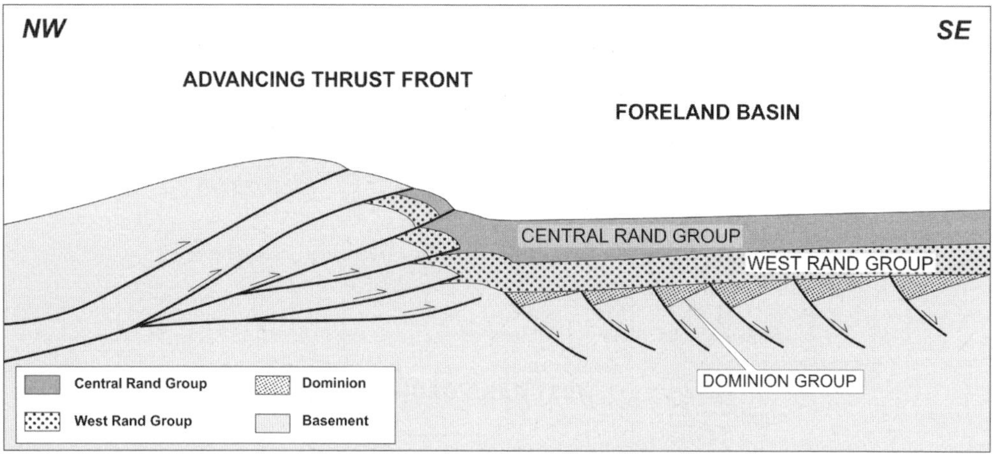

Fig. 3. Overall tectonic style for the Witwatersrand Basin, showing an early phase of Dominion Group rifting, a phase of West Rand Group post-rift thermal subsidence, and the development of a Central Rand Group foreland basin in front of an actively advancing fold and thrust belt. The effects of the later Platberg Group extension are not shown.

within and adjacent to the basin, and has made it very difficult to elucidate the earlier compressional thrust–fold structures that are late Central Rand Group in age. Only through the careful integration of seismic, borehole, mine and outcrop data can the importance of the thrusting event be recognized and more complete sections be drawn. This was the approach adopted by Coward *et al.* (1995), and a similar approach has been followed here.

Structural sections

A number of structural sections are presented here across the western margins of the basin. These have been derived from the interpretation of seismic reflection profiles using borehole ties and mine data, and where available, outcrop data. The sections are presented in order of scale, starting with a regional section and finishing with mine-scale sections. The location of the sections presented are shown in Figure 4. Platberg Group extensional faults dominate the visible structure on most sections, and tend to obscure the earlier thrust structures. Therefore, in several of the sections, the effects of Platberg Group extension have been removed. Where this has been done, it is noted in the figure caption or the text.

Figure 5 presents a regional section across the area. The section has been simplified by removing most of the younger Platberg Group extensional faults, and by rebuilding the section above the current erosional level. The approximate present-day erosion level is shown. Regional seismic data show strong reflectors that are interpreted as shear zones, deep within the basement at about 20 km current depth (not shown in Fig. 5). They climb up through the crust from west to east and emerge into the western margin of the basin, where they can be identified as thrust structures. Figure 5 shows that the present-day western margin of the basin is a thrust margin, rather than the original depositional margin of the basin, especially during West Rand Group times. It only approximates the depositional margin of the basin in late Central Rand Group times.

Near Vryburg (see Fig. 5), West Rand Group sequences are preserved, and a younger extensional Platberg Group basin is present. In the east of the section, the DeBron High is a horst block formed during Platberg Group extension, but superimposed on an earlier thrust culmination. The Leary Syncline is not a separate basin, but a structurally preserved remnant of stratigraphy.

The section shown in Figure 6 runs through the Klerksdorp–Orkney mining district, and out in a northwesterly direction across the present-day basin margin. This section shows the present-day geometry; that is, Platberg Group extensional faults have not been restored and removed.

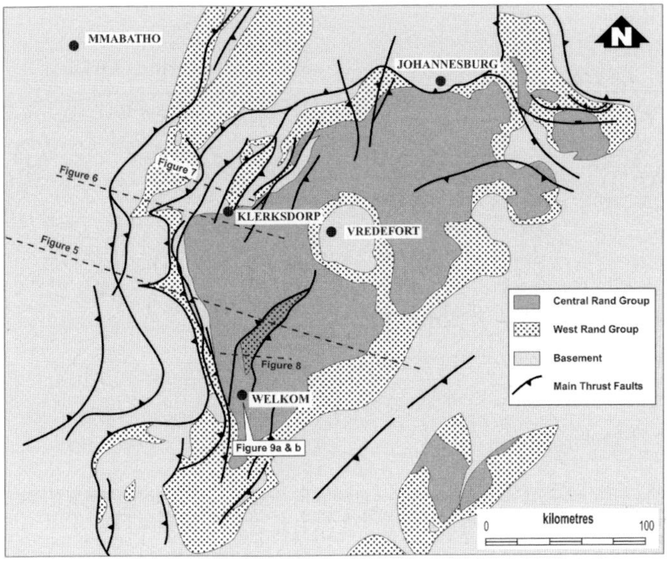

Fig. 4. Location of the structural sections presented in this paper.

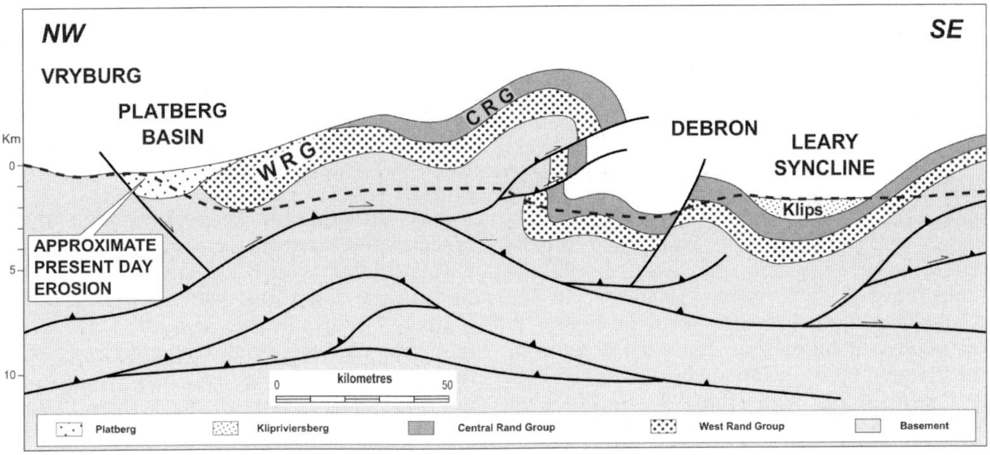

Fig. 5. Regional cross-section from Vryburg to the Leary Syncline (see Fig. 4 for location). This section omits most of the Platberg Group extension faults. Two major faults are shown, the first bounding a Platberg Group age basin near Vryburg, the second showing how the DeBron Horst is now defined as a structural high as a result of Platberg Group extension, superimposed on earlier thrusting. The overall geometry of thrust structures has been interpreted above the level of the present-day erosion across the area.

The overprint of the Platberg Group rifting structures makes it more difficult to see and understand the geometry of the earlier thrusting. Work carried out as part of this study shows that, to the west of Klerksdorp, there is an overturned fold that sits in the footwall of a major thrust that has breached the fold and placed basement over West Rand Group sediments. Field outcrops around Klerksdorp show very clearly the geometry of the frontal folds of the thrust belt (see Clendenin *et al.* 1990), and the careful integration of drilling data with the seismic interpretation in this study has allowed the thrust structures to be identified. Further west from Klerksdorp,

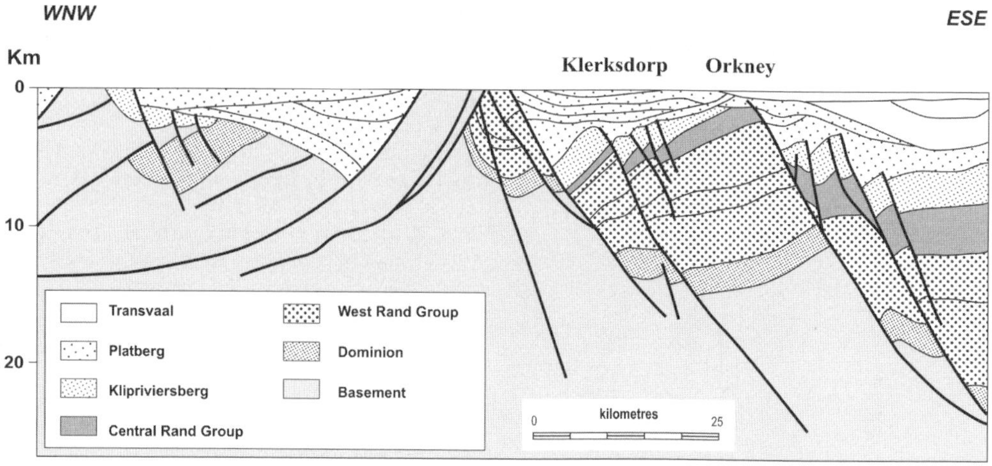

Fig. 6. Section showing the present-day geometry of a section that passes through the Klerksdorp–Orkney mining area. The section has been drawn from seismic and drill data. (For location see Fig. 4.)

a major thrust fault has been reactivated in extension and now carries an extensional Platberg Group basin in its hanging wall. Below this Platberg Group basin, a wedge of Dominion Group is preserved in the footwall of another thrust that has emplaced basement over Dominion Group.

In general, the Platberg Group extension faults to the west of the present basin margin have a listric geometry, where they are interpreted to have formed as reactivated thrusts faults, whereas within the basin itself, the faults have a more planar geometry. In the Klerksdorp–Orkney area, shown in Figure 6, the seismic interpretation shows the division of the Platberg Group sequence into synrift wedges and post-rift fill, with erosional truncation of Klipriviersberg Group and Central Rand Group sequences in uplifted footwalls. The Platberg Group extensional faults pose a major challenge to underground mining activities, as they offset the ore-bearing horizons within the Central Rand Group repeatedly across a wide range of fault throws.

The section in Figure 7 illustrates in more detail some of the thrust geometries in the Klerksdorp area. As with Figure 6, this section shows the present-day geometry without removal of the effects of Platberg Group extension. It has been drawn from two seismic reflection profiles, which do not exactly meet, hence the slight mismatch of geology at their join in the centre of the section.

Sections such as those shown in Figures 6 and 7 give a clear insight into the recognition of a structure imperative for this margin of the basin. Around Klcrksdorp, it is clear from field observations and boreholes that tie into the seismic data, that the structural style of this margin is that of a thrust and fold belt that existed prior to Platberg Group extension. This interpretation, which seems to have eluded many previous workers, was first clearly put forward by Coward *et al.* (1995).

The structure at Wilkoppies is a thrust syncline developed in the footwall of a thrust, visibly folding West Rand Group sequences at the surface. The thrust was reactivated during Platberg Group extension as a listric extensional fault, and carries a small Platberg Group basin in its hanging wall. Klipriviersberg Group volcanic rocks are preserved beneath these Platberg Group sequences, and rest directly on West Rand Group sediments. The timing of thrusting is interpreted here to be essentially late Central Rand Group–pre-Klipriviersberg Group, resulting in the erosion or non-deposition of the Central Rand Group sequence in the hanging wall of the thrust, and preservation of these relationships as a result of later extensional faulting.

At the western end of the section (Fig. 7), the Rietkull Syncline is another thrust-related fold, clearly seen in the field and in drill data, which was subsequently broken up by two east-dipping extensional faults of Platberg Group age.

Figure 8 shows a section in the Welkom area that has been partly restored to show the pre-Platberg Group geometry. Platberg Group

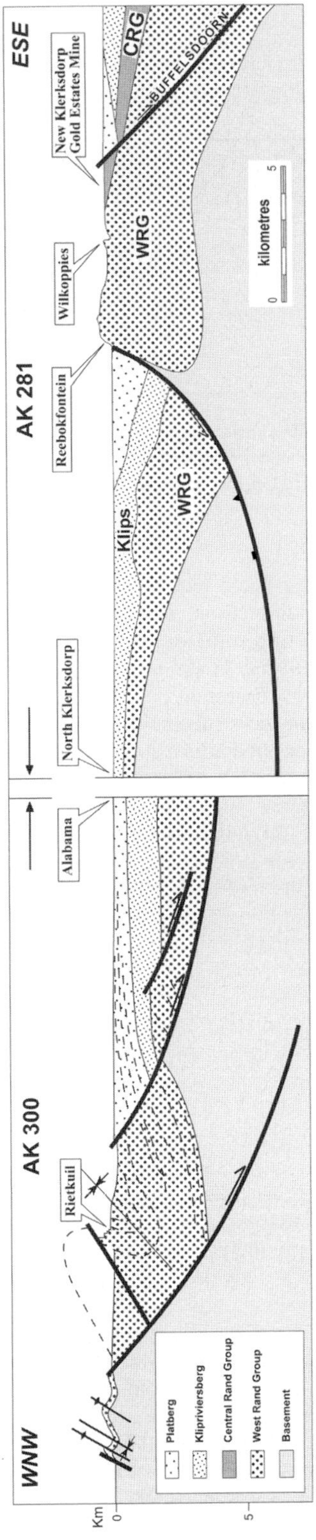

extensional faults have been restored, and eroded sequences of Klipriviersberg Group and Central Rand Group have been built back into the section.

This section clearly identifies the presence of thrust structures, those in the west verging east and those in the east verging west. Several of these thrusts were later reactivated as Platberg Group extensional structures. The section shows that thrusting occurred after the deposition of the Klipriviersberg Group volcanic rocks. However, the geometries in the western part of the section show that there was also a phase of significant thrusting in pre-Klipriviersberg Group times. The Central and West Rand Group sequences show folds and thrusts that have been eroded and truncated, prior to deposition or extrusion of the Klipriviersberg Group volcanic rocks.

The Rheedersdam Thrust is shown at the left-hand side of Figure 8, and a more detailed understanding of the geology of this area can be gained from the numerous mines in this area, near to the town of Welkom, as shown in Figure 9. Both sections shown in Figure 9 are derived from mine sections, and the effects of Platberg Group extensional faulting have been removed from both.

Figure 9a is drawn from the FSG Mine, just to the north of Welkom, and Figure 9b is from the Beisa Mine, just to the south of Welkom. Both sections show the progressive folding and overstepping of unconformities that is so typical of a thrust–foreland basin margin, in a way that has been graphically documented by Anadon *et al.* (1986) in NE Spain (see Phillips & Law 2000). The recognition of syntectonic unconformities along this part of the western margin of the Witwatersrand Basin allows the relative timing of thrusting at this location to be precisely determined.

In Figure 9a, the first principal post-thrust fold unconformity that erodes and cuts back through the structure is at the base of VS5 Elsburg; this unit is in turn overstepped and truncated by the younger Boulder Beds. In Figure 9b, the relationships are similar, but here the folding is much more intense and affects also the younger Klipriviersberg Group sequence. Thus, in this area of the basin, two episodes of thrusting can be seen; the first was late syn-Central Rand

Fig. 7. Section showing the present-day geometry through the Klerksdorp area. The section has been drawn from seismic and drill data. (For location see Fig. 4.)

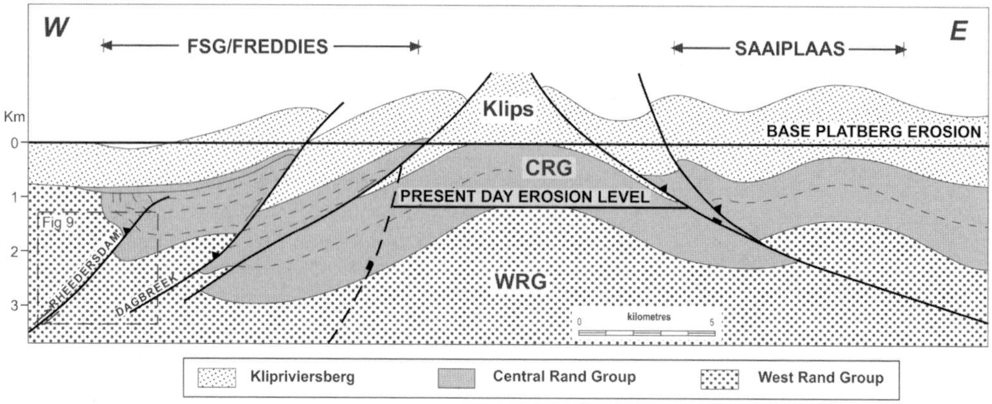

Fig. 8. Section through the Welkom area that has been partly restored to show the pre-Platberg Group geometry. Platberg Group extensional faults have been restored and eroded sequences of Klipriviersberg Group and Central Rand Group have been built back into the section. (For location see Fig. 4.)

Group in age, whereas the second was post Klipriviersberg Group in age.

Conclusion

As a result of the work presented here, it is possible to summarize the basin development, in a way that is standard practice within the oil industry, as follows.

(1) The basin was initiated as a rift during Dominion Group times.

(2) Post-rift thermal subsidence ensued over *c.* 100 Ma after rifting, during the early part of West Rand Group times.

(3) Thermal subsidence, using a simple McKenzie type model, would have been completed by late West Rand Group times, although minor volcanic interludes within the West Rand Group sequence, such as the Crown Lava, suggest some extension during West Rand Group times.

(4) The onset of compression and thrusting outside the extensive thermal basin provided a flexural load and clastic input into the basin as it evolved from thermal sag to foreland basin during late West Rand Group times.

(5) The development of the foreland basin culminated during Central Rand Group times, with an increasingly coarse-grained clastic input and thrust systems that progressively encroached on the basin margins and profoundly influenced the structural style on these margins.

(6) Thrusting was interrupted during Klipriviersberg Group times by the accumulation of basic volcanic rocks.

(7) Further thrusting occurred at the end of Klipriviersberg Group times.

(8) The basin tectonics then changed to an extensional tectonic setting with the Platberg Group rifting, a major rift event across much of the present-day basin, and across large areas of what is now basement outcrop, west of the basin.

(9) Thermal subsidence related to this rift phase occurred during late Platberg Group times.

Integrated basin studies of the Witwatersrand have also provided an overview of the relationship between gold mineralization and structure, stratigraphy and basin subsidence. The simplest view is that mineralizing fluids, driven by the late Central Rand Group thrusting event, were introduced into proximal foreland basin sequences (see Barnicoat *et al.* 1997), with major thrusts providing the fluid transport paths. These fluids interacted with hydrocarbons that had matured from source rocks, within the West Rand Group and possibly the Central Rand Group, as a result of combined thermal subsidence and thrust loading (Gray *et al.* 1998; England *et al.* 2002), the hydrocarbons having migrated up dip towards the basin margins. The thrust tectonic event thus becomes pivotal in controlling the key aspects of geology that generated a very large gold resource: fluid transport, host-rock facies, hydrocarbon generation, and gold trapping sites.

However, there is still a huge controversy over the origin of the gold. The traditional and long-standing model was that the gold had a detrital or placer origin. This view is still held by many workers, and often considered to be irrefutable (Minter 1990, 1999). In the last 20 years an increasing amount of data have

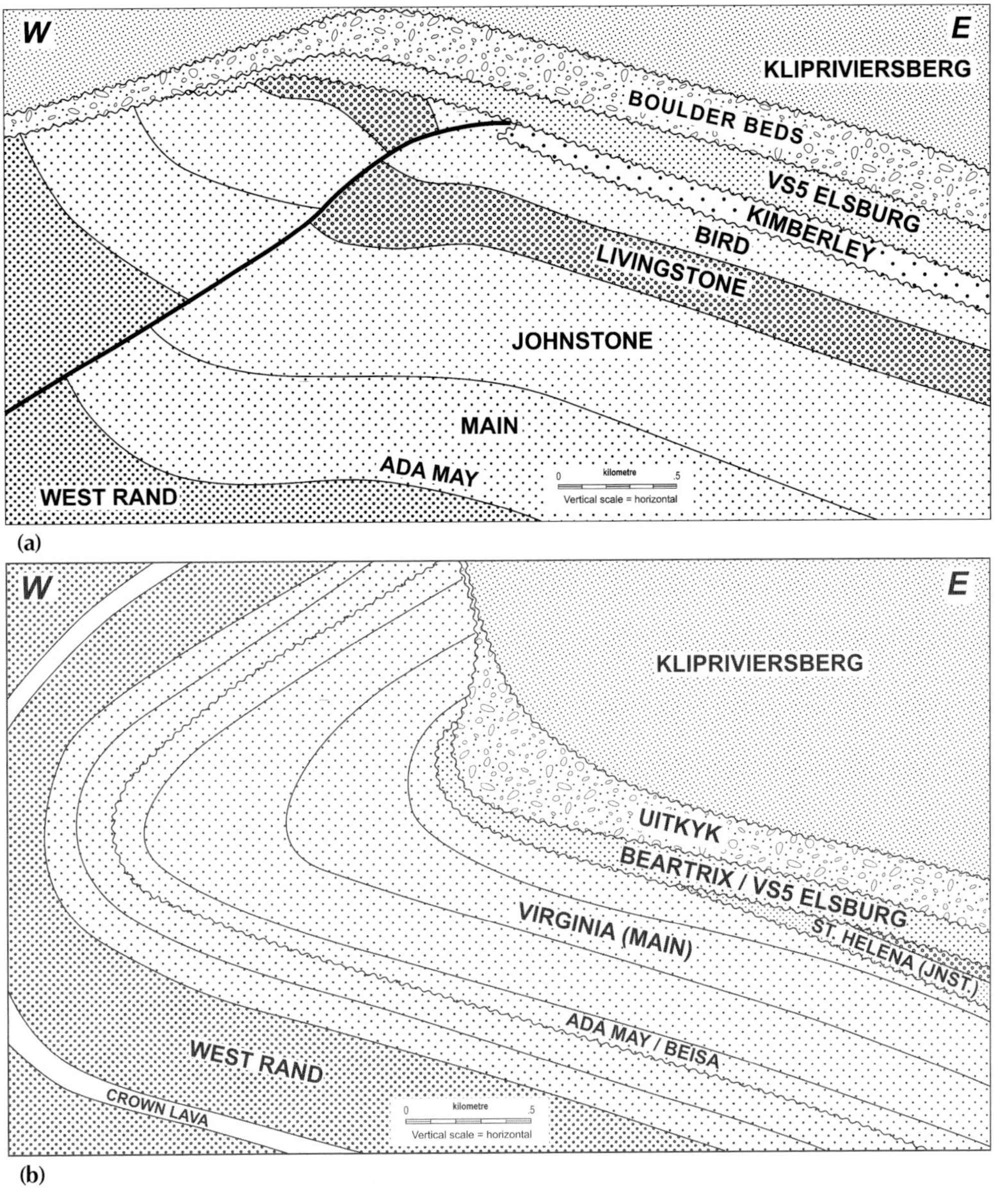

Fig. 9. (**a**) Section drawn from the FSG Mine, just to the north of Welkom (**b**) Section drawn from the Beisa Mine just to the south of Welkom. Both sections show the progressive folding and overstepping of unconformities that is typical of a thrust–foreland basin margin. The effects of Platberg Group extensional tectonics have been removed from both sections, which were drawn from subsurface mine data. (For location see Fig. 4.)

suggested that the gold had a hydrothermal origin, some of this evidence originating in the company-motivated basin analysis studies, and some through the work carried out by Phillips and co-workers (see Phillips & Law 2000 for a thorough review and discussion). The controversy remains unresolved, and recent Re–Os age determinations (Kirk *et al.* 2001) have injected new life into the controversy by suggesting that the isochrons obtained (2990 Ma) preclude the origin of gold mineralization through a hydrothermal process, as these ages predate the deposition of the Central Rand Group host rocks.

In detailed studies of the relationship between gold mineralization and small-scale structure, Jolley *et al.* (1999, 2004) presented data and interpretations that overwhelmingly support a model for the structural control of gold mineralization in fracture networks and thrust structures generated during the late Central Rand Group and post Klipriviersberg Group–pre Platberg Group thrusting events. Those workers interpreted the fracture networks, which provide a linked fluid flow pathway through the rocks, as well as sites for gold precipitation, as being generated in the tip zones of larger thrust faults deeper in the section. Given that the Platberg Group extensional faults offset the gold-bearing sequences in the Central Rand Group, the implication is that much of the gold mineralization was already in place prior to Platberg Group extension.

This paper synthesizes part of an Anglo American in-house basin analysis study undertaken between 1990 and 1993 under the auspices of the ACC Gold and Uranium Division. We are therefore grateful to Anglo American for supporting this study and for permission to publish these results. We also acknowledge the role played by M. B. Watchorn and S. R. Lawrence in managing the basin analysis project.

References

Anadon, P., Cabrera, L., Colombo, F., Marzo, M. & Riba, O. 1986. Syntectonic intraformational unconformities in alluvial fan deposits, eastern Ebro Basin margins (NE Spain). *In*: Allen, P. A. & Homewood, P. (eds) *Foreland Basins*. International Association of Sedimentologists, Special Publications, **8**, 219–228.

Barnicoat, A. C., Henderson, I. H. C., Knipe, R. J. *et al.* 1997. Hydrothermal gold in the Witwatersrand basin. *Nature*, **386**, 820–824.

Clendenin, C. W., Charlesworth, E. G. & Maske, S. 1990. Structural styles of fault inversion influencing the Witwatersrand Supergroup: examples from Oukop, northeast of Klerksdorp. *South African Journal of Geology*, **93**, 202–210.

Coward, M. P., Spencer, R. M. & Spencer, C. 1995. Development of the Witwatersrand Basin, South Africa. *In*: Coward, M. P. & Ries, A. C. (eds) *Early Precambrian Processes*. Geological Society, London, Special Publications, **95**, 243–269.

England, G. L., Rasmussen, B., Krapez, B. & Groves, D. I. 2002. Archaean oil migration in the Witwatersrand Basin of South Africa. *Journal of the Geological Society, London*, **159**, 189–201.

Gray, G. J., Lawrence, S. R., Kenyon, K. & Cornford, C. 1998. Nature and origin of 'carbon' in the Archaean Witwatersrand Basin, South Africa. *Journal of the Geological Society, London*, **155**, 39–59.

Jolley, S. J., Henderson, I. H. C., Barnicoat, A. C. & Fox, N. P. C. 1999. Thrust-fracture network and hydrothermal gold mineralisation: Witwatersrand Basin, South Africa. *In*: McCaffrey, K. J. W., Lonergan, L. & Wilkinson, J. J. (eds) *Fractures, Fluid Flow and Mineralization*. Geological Society, London, Special Publications, **155**, 153–165.

Jolley, S. J., Freeman, S. R., Barnicoat, A. C. *et al.* 2004. Structural controls on Witwatersrand gold mineralisation. *Journal of Structural Geology*, **26**, 1067–1086.

Kirk, J., Ruiz, J., Chesley, J., Titley, S. & Walshe, J. 2001. A detrital model for the origin of gold and sulphides in the Witwatersrand Basin based on Re–Os isotopes. *Geochimica et Cosmochimica Acta*, **65**, 2149–2159.

Minter, W. E. L. 1990. Paleoplacers of the Witwatersrand Basin. *Mining Engineering*, **42**, 195–199.

Minter, W. E. L. 1999. Irrefutable detrital origin of Witwatersrand gold and evidence of eolian signatures. *Economic Geology*, **94**, 665–670.

Phillips, G. N. & Law, J. D. M. 2000. Witwatersrand gold fields: geology, genesis and exploration. *In*: Hagemann, S. G. & Brown, P. E. (eds) *Gold 2000*. Reviews in Economic Geology, **13**, 439–500.

Robb, L. J. & Meyer, F. M. 1994. Geological environment and mineralization processes during the formation of Witwatersrand Au–U deposits. *XVth CMMI, Council of Mining & Metallurgical Institutes Congress*, South African Institute of Mining & Metallurgy (Johannesburg), **3**, 3–18.

Progressive evolution of a late orogenic thrust system, from duplex development to extensional reactivation and disruption: Witwatersrand Basin, South Africa

S. J. JOLLEY[1,2], G. W. STUART[1], S. R. FREEMAN[1], R. J. KNIPE[1], D. KERSHAW[3,4], E. MCALLISTER[1,5], A. C. BARNICOAT,[1,6] & R. F. TUCKER[3,7]

[1]*Rock Deformation Research Limited, School of Earth Sciences, University of Leeds, Leeds LS2 9JT, UK*

[2]*Shell UK Limited, 1 Altens Farm Road, Nigg, Aberdeen AB12 3FY, UK (e-mail: steve.jolley@shell.com)*

[3]*Avgold Limited, 56 Main Street, Johannesburg 2001, South Africa*

[4]*AngloGold, 11 Diagonal Street, Johannesburg 2001, South Africa*

[5]*A/S Norske Shell, P.O. Box 40, N-4098 Tananger, Norway*

[6]*CRC Geoscience Australia, PO Box 378, Canberra, ACT 2601, Australia*

[7]*Snowden Exploration Africa, PO Box 2613, Parklands 2121, South Africa*

Abstract: This paper examines progressive evolution of fault architectures through late orogenic compression- to post-orogenic extensional deformation in the Witwatersrand Basin, South Africa. The results indicate that rapid extrusion of mafic lavas of the lower Klipriviersberg Group formed a rigid 'lid' over the thrust front, changing its mechanical character and thereby driving a change of structural style from fold growth to passive roof duplex. Flexural tightening of folds in the core of the triangle zones at this time may have helped provide the dynamic permeability for distributed ingress of hydrothermal fluids and consequent gold mineralization. Shortly afterwards, the kinematic environment changed to become extensional. However, this study shows sharp lateral partitioning of the duration of kinematic style and structural amplification, such that thrusting and extension coexisted along strike in the upper Klipriviersberg Group. Thus the switch from thrusting to extension was progressive within the region, but locally very rapid. As the local kinematic environment became extensional, the fault system evolved progressively, with the early stages of kinematic changes being dominated by a process of reactivation by architectural scavenging, in which new extensional structures developed by selectively reusing and incorporating geometrical segments of earlier formed thrust and normal faults. Three basic stages can be identified in this evolution: broad extension above underlying detachments, involving reactivation of lateral structures; a period of intensive reactivation and kinematic reworking incorporating frontal structures; and an abandonment stage when the detailed influence of the earlier architecture diminished and the fault system developed larger through-going normal faults. The interaction of the newly developing fault system with the pre-existing architecture constitutes pre-programming of the final geometry, in which individual large faults are composed of a reticulated network of new and inherited segments. The observations are consistent with fault scale being a key control on the fault reactivation involved. This study has involved full integration of a dataset comprising 2D and 3D seismic reflection data, geological mine plans, logging of over 120 km of drill core and underground mapping in deep mine workings that pass 3 km into the seismic volume at 2–3 km depth.

Understanding the processes of late orogenic evolution often depends on unravelling the controls and interactions between thrusting, magmatism and extension. These processes can involve complex transitions from contractional to extensional regimes (Coward 1982; Law *et al.* 1986, 2004; Royden & Burchfiel 1987; Constenius 1996; Cavinato & De Celles 1999; Jolivet *et al.* 1999, and references therein). The resulting structural and kinematic framework typically includes foreland thrust systems and trailing extensional sub-basins (e.g. Hatzfeld *et al.* 1993; Eva *et al.* 1998; Hatzfeld 1999). Studies that use combinations of surface and subsurface data have documented various aspects of the geological record left by the diachronous passage

From: RIES, A. C., BUTLER, R. W. H. & GRAHAM, R. H. (eds) 2007. *Deformation of the Continental Crust: The Legacy of Mike Coward*. Geological Society, London, Special Publications, **272**, 543–569.

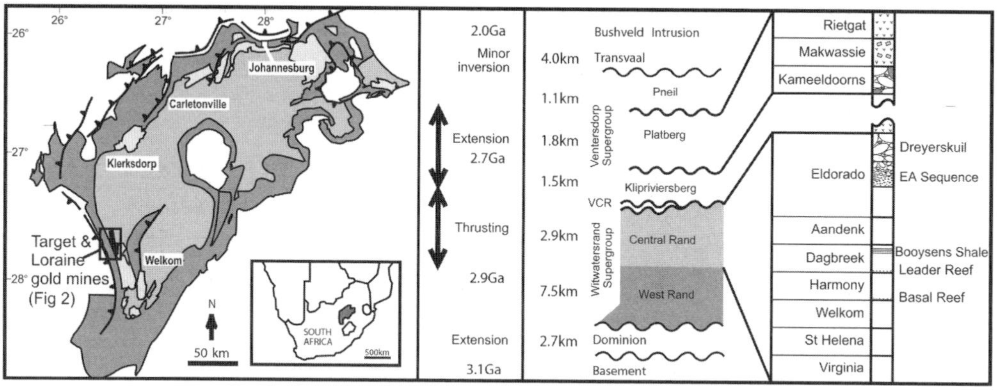

Fig. 1. Tectonostratigraphic summary of the Witwatersrand Basin and the Welkom Goldfield (map back-stripped to base Klipriviersberg Group). The Welkom Goldfield, Loraine Gold Mine and the Target 3D seismic survey are indicated. Dates and tectonic events are based on Armstrong *et al.* (1991) and Coward *et al.* (1995), respectively.

of the 'kinematic zones' of foredeep, thrust belt and extension. Extensional deformation in the foredeep is seen to be rapidly superseded by thrusts and folds, which are, in turn, disrupted by normal faulting associated with the back-arc extension (e.g. Butler *et al.* 1992; Hippolyte *et al.* 1995; D'Agostino *et al.* 1998; Scisciani *et al.* 2002). In addition to the kinematic zones, thrusting and extension may be coeval across lateral linking structures (e.g. Hippolyte *et al.* 1995). Similar work describes the post-thrusting extension, in which normal faults link into major ramps within the thrust system, and shallow down-dip into the associated thrust detachments (e.g. West 1993; Coward *et al.* 1995; Constenius 1996; Keller & Coward 1996; Mohapatra & Johnson 1998; Sue & Tricart 1999, 2002; Tavarnelli 1999; Mirabella *et al.* 2004). But how does the fault architecture evolve to accommodate this progressively changing kinematic environment?

This paper reports a detailed study of the 3D evolution, and scaling relationships involved in reworking of fault systems, from duplex development to the subsequent transition from contractional to extensional deformation. To do this, a well-constrained example of this process, within a rare fully integrated centimetre to seismic-scale dataset has been examined. The example is from the Witwatersrand Basin of South Africa, where the interaction of compressional and late extensional deformation was described at regional scale by Coward *et al.* (1995), using 2D seismic surveys and outcrop mapping at the northern basin margin. The advantage to our more detailed study is that decades of deep gold mining in the basin has generated enormous volumes of geological, geophysical, geotechnical and geochronological data, and provided remarkable 3D access to fault systems. The study area, in the SW part of the basin, is centred on the Loraine and Target gold mines on the northern edge of the Welkom Goldfield (Fig. 1). Faults interpreted within 3D seismic reflection data were visited and studied in detail at 2–3 km depth in mine workings within the seismic data volume. This study has integrated 2D and 3D seismic interpretation, 3D structural modelling, geological mine plans, drill core logging of 50 surface boreholes (equivalent to over 120 km continuous core), and the authors' underground mapping across a *c.* 1 km depth profile in Loraine Mine and in the decline tunnels that pass directly from Loraine Mine into Target Mine within the overlapping seismic data volume (Fig. 2). The study area contains a distinctive lithostratigraphy of sediments and volcanic rocks, with well-defined syndepositional growth structures and feeder dykes. This has provided a well-constrained framework that defines the progressive evolution of structural style, fault architecture, scaling and selectivity of fault reactivation.

The Witwatersrand System

The Archaean Witwatersrand Basin is situated on the ancient Kaapvaal Craton, where it overlies volcanic and sedimentary rocks of the earlier Dominion rift basin. It formed in an Andean- or Apennine-style collisional setting dominated by southeasterly verging thrust tectonics (e.g. Winter 1987; Coward *et al.* 1995). The basin fill comprised foredeep shales and quartzites of the

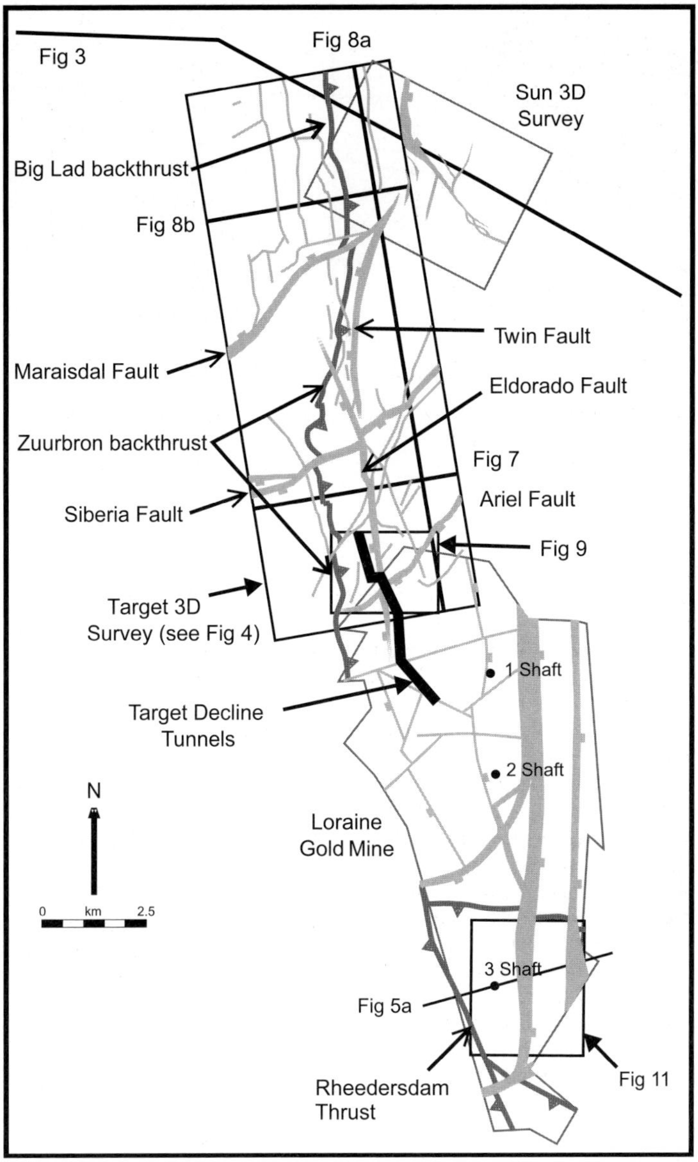

Fig. 2. Simplified map showing Loraine Gold Mine (LGM), 3D seismic surveys and Target decline tunnels. Location of 2D seismic line, seismic sections, structural sections and LGM structure maps indicated.

West Rand Group (minor volcanic rocks 2914 ± 8 Ma, Armstrong *et al.* 1991), and alluvial quartzites and conglomerates of the Central Rand Group (Fig. 1), deposited during the period *c.* 2910–2715 Ma with detritus derived in part from unroofing of nearby contemporary granitoids (Robb *et al.* 1991). The Central Rand Group conglomerates host the bulk of the basin's famous gold deposits, termed 'reefs'. These gigantic strata-bound gold deposits have traditionally been considered to be palaeoplacers (e.g. Minter 1978, 1999), although leading proponents of that model have recently begun to favour a 'modified placer' model, in which it is now 'generally agreed [that the bulk of the gold grains] are hydrothermal precipitates' (Frimmel & Minter 2002; see also Frimmel 2005). Recent Re–Os dating of gold grains by Kirk *et al.* (2001, 2002) yielded dates that are similar to the bracketed age of deposition of the Central Rand

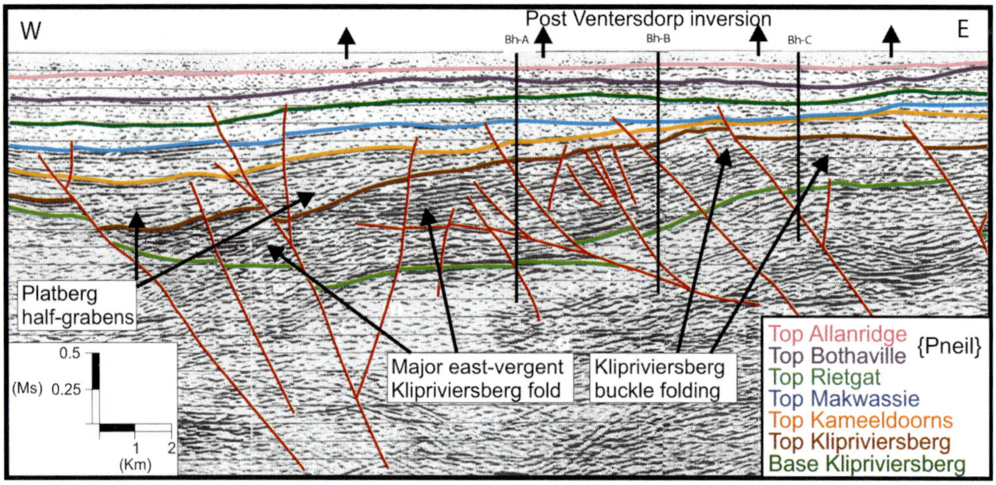

Fig. 3. Composite 2D seismic reflection line (data *c.* 1985), showing eroded major Klipriviersberg Group folds, Platberg Group half-grabens and subsequent mild post-Ventersdorp Group inversion. (See Fig. 2 for location.)

Group and therefore appear to support a (modified) placer origin for gold in the Witwatersrand Basin. However, Hannah *et al.* (2004) and Schaefer *et al.* (2004) explored alternative interpretations for these data involving the mixing of residual detrital Os-rich phases with younger gold in the analysed samples. Other recent work indicates that the ores formed after host-rock diagenesis by hydrothermal means with transport of gold in solution, prior to precipitation (e.g. Phillips & Myers 1989; Barnicoat *et al.* 1997; Fox 2002). Linked microstructural studies, mesoscale mapping and seismic interpretations show that gold grains are contained within fractures together with relict hydrocarbon and mineral assemblages resulting from synkinematic fluid flow and hydrothermal precipitation focused within thrust-fracture permeability (Jolley *et al.* 1999, 2004; Phillips & Law 2000).

Figure 3 illustrates the large-scale structural style in the north of the study area in the northern Welkom Goldfield (Fig. 2). Here, the structure consists of a broadly north–south-striking thrust–fold system, disrupted by north–south and east–west- to NE–SW-striking normal faults. The fault system can be broadly subdivided into geometrical types (thrusts, planar-normal and listric-normal; see Table 1). Extensive mining and drilling of Witwatersrand stratigraphy, along the western margin of the goldfield, shows that it is folded by a major easterly verging growth fold, which is truncated in its steep limb by the unconformable base of the Klipriviersberg Group lavas (see later discussion). Komatiitic and basaltic lavas of the lower Klipriviersberg Group (2714 ± 8 Ma, Armstrong *et al.* 1991), were extruded directly onto the end-Witwatersrand landform. Basal lavas formed local growth folds

Table 1. *The generalized fault classification for northern part of Welkom Goldfield used in this paper*

Type structure (see **Figs 1 and 3**)	Strike trend	Characteristics
Forethrusts (e.g. Rheedersdam Fault)	North–south	Easterly vergent, forming major and mesoscale duplexes
Backthrusts (e.g. Zuurbron Fault)	North–south	Westerly vergent, forming passive roof to forethrust duplexes
Planar normal faults (e.g. Siberia Fault)	NE–SW to NNE–SSW	Generally steep northerly and southerly dipping faults in two trends
Listric normal faults (e.g. Eldorado Fault)	North–south to NNW–SSE	Westerly dipping, typically listric faults that link asymptotically into earlier formed forethrusts

before being rapidly covered during the filling of the basin during the waning stages of contraction and the onset of orogenic collapse (Coward *et al.* 1995; Jolley *et al.* 2004). Late Klipriviersberg Group basalts and clastic sediments and bimodal volcanic rocks of the Platberg Group (Makwassie porphyries 2709 ± 4 Ma, Armstrong *et al.* 1991) were then deposited into grabens formed during extensional reactivation and disruption of the earlier Witwatersrand thrust system. The Pniel Group sediments and volcanic rocks were deposited in the subsequent post-rift environment. Van der Westhuizen *et al.* (1991) indicated that overall, the Ventersdorp Supergroup lavas show calc-alkaline to tholeiitic affinity, with geochemical and normalized incompatible element plot characteristics of modern continental margin arcs, in which the basalts and andesites of the Klipriviersberg Group and Pniel Group were derived from a subduction zone mantle wedge, and those of the Platberg Group were produced from an enriched lithospheric mantle source that had been modified by a subduction zone component.

The basin was affected by several phases of subsequent inversion and subsidence (Coward *et al.* 1995) but the strata that record the detail of these events have been eroded from much of the Welkom Goldfield. Permo-Triassic Karoo sandstones and shales were deposited unconformably onto Archaean Ventersdorp Supergroup strata in the present study area. However, evidence from seismic reflection data, mining and drilling activity shows that at least one phase of post-Ventersdorp Supergroup, pre-Karoo contractional deformation resulted in mild basin inversion (e.g. Fig. 3).

The following sections of the paper assess the relative timing of the fault structures within the study area, and the role of reactivation and capture in the evolution of the late orogenic fault architecture. All of the named faults and fault types discussed in this paper are plotted in Figures 2 and 4 and are listed in Table 1.

Seismic-scale geometries and timing of structural development

Thrusting and folding

In the Loraine–Target area, located in the northwestern part of the Welkom Goldfield, the folded Eldorado Formation shows upward coarsening from alluvial sandstone and conglomerate deposits to more proximal fanglomerates in the EA sequence, to diachronous polymictic conglomerates of the Dreyerskuil members (Fig. 1; Kingsley 1987; Winter 1987). Primary thinning into, and within, the steep western limb of the fold is accentuated by an array of inter- and intra-formational unconformities (Fig. 5a and 5b), which become increasingly angular down stratigraphic section to the base of the underlying Aandenk Formation. Beneath this, primary westward thinning is comparatively minor, and the older stratigraphy is folded post-depositionally into a tight syncline. Thus, although the instantaneous depositional slope was minor, the preceding depositional surfaces were progressively tilted and eroded. This fold is therefore very similar in scale, geometry and sedimentology to the syndepositional growth-folds seen in Phanerozoic thrust systems, such as the Pyrenees (e.g. Williams *et al.* 1998; Lawton *et al.* 1999).

The Basal Reef zone in the steep west limb is disrupted by east-verging, downward-facing mesoscale folds and thrusts (Fig. 6). The detachments to these mesoscale structures are erosionally truncated together with host stratigraphy against the younger Eldorado Formation. Extension and slumping of poorly lithified growth fold strata in response to material critical-taper mechanisms, produces mesoscale contractional and extensional 'soft-sediment' structures (e.g. Nigro & Renda 2004). However, the structures described here host cataclastic and phyllonitic fault rocks, requiring kilometre-scale overburden to form (Fisher & Knipe 1998). If these minor thrusts and folds were formed during development of the major fold, they would be expected to face upwards and verge to the west in its steep west limb. Thus, these minor structures formed after burial, prior to major folding, passive rotation, erosion and capping by deposition of the Eldorado Formation. Early thrust structures similar to these are associated with hydrothermal mineralization of this reef zone, prior to major folding and erosion, elsewhere in the goldfield (Jolley *et al.* 2004).

In the Loraine Mine, the Uitkyk Member at the top of the Central Rand Group is a rubbly proximal fanglomerate deposit. This grades northwards across the Target Mine area into the Dreyerskuil Member, a fanglomerate package that includes a distal quartzite facies. These quartzites become the dominant rock type further north. The base of the Klipriviersberg Group lavas represents a major density and seismic velocity boundary with the quartzitic Central Rand Group sediments (*c.* 6.5 km s^{-1} v. *c.* 5.6 km s^{-1}, respectively). This contact therefore has a strong negative reflection coefficient, producing a high-amplitude reflection. However, the thick more proximal conglomerate facies of the Dreyerskuil sequence has a higher density and

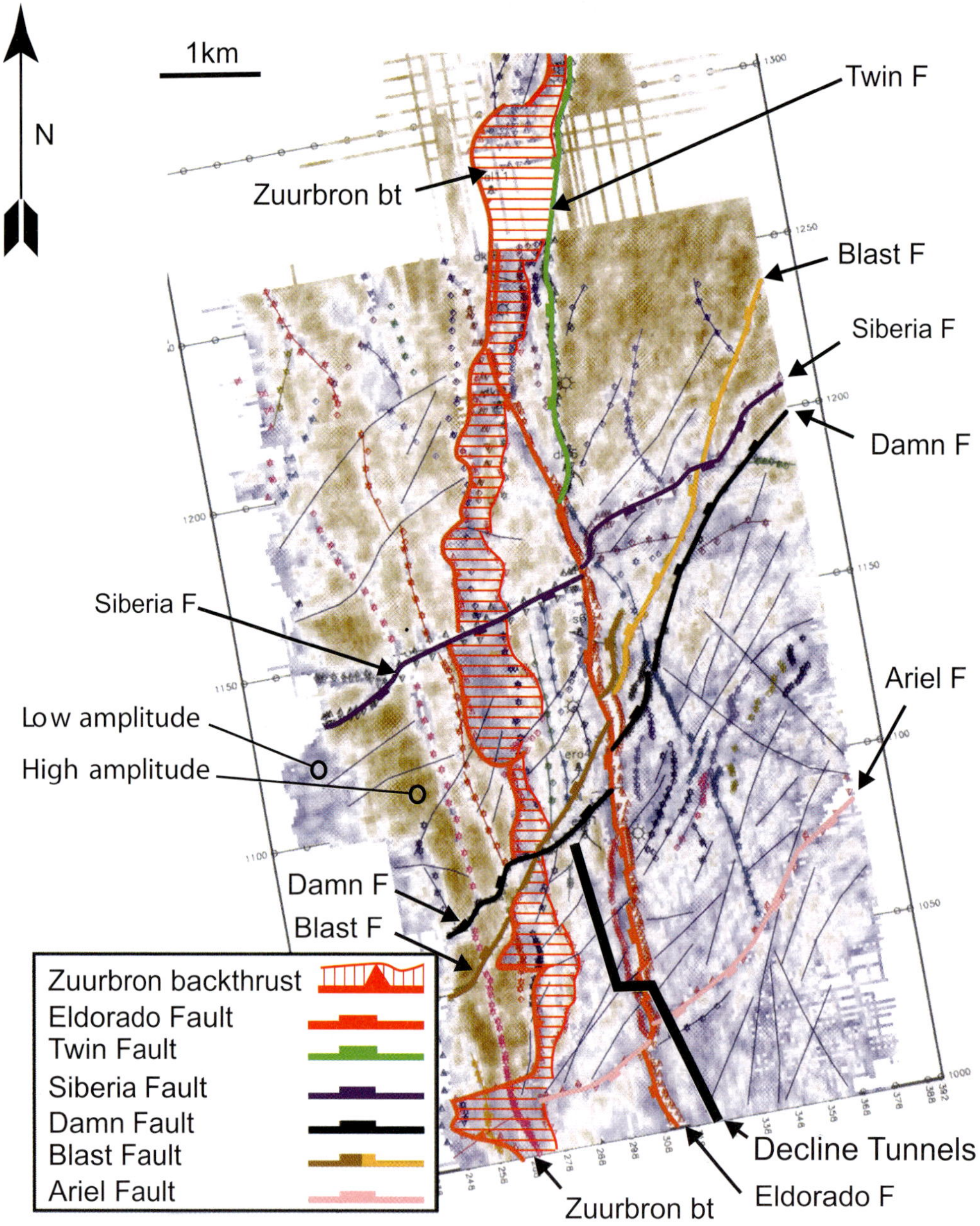

Fig. 4. Reflection amplitude display of base Klipriviersberg Group (KRG) showing fault interpretation. Cross-hatching shows the separation of KRG hangingwall and footwall cut-offs by the Zuurbron back thrust. F, fault; bt, back thrust.

velocity than either its more distal, finer-grained quartzite facies or the underlying quartzitic Central Rand Group sediments. Consequently, the dominantly conglomeratic Dreyerskuil sequence reduces the acoustic impedance contrast and therefore reduces the base Klipriviersberg Group reflection amplitude. Conversely, the base Dreyerskuil reflector is brightest where its lower sequence is composed of conglomerate-rich proximal facies. The Dreyerskuil facies types can therefore be mapped from lateral changes in amplitude, with control from geological and

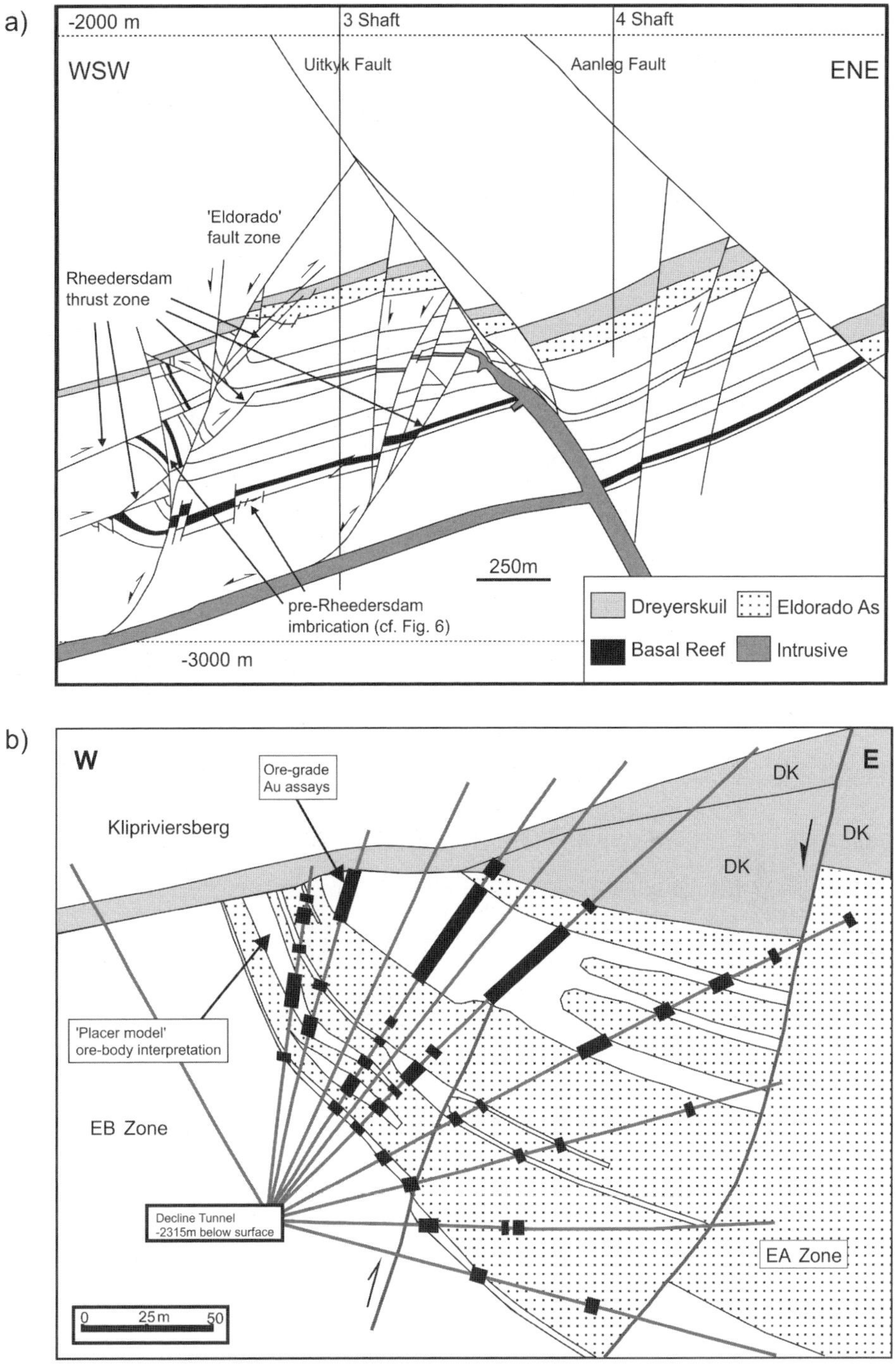

Fig. 5. (**a**) Stylized structural section through mine workings in southern Loraine Gold Mine (after mine geologists *c.* 1987; also Winter 1987). Note the Central Rand Group growth monoform with thrust mid-limb, and later normal faults that alternately reactivate and cut the thrusts. (See Fig. 2 for location; structure section.) (**b**) Fan-drilling from the northern part of the Target decline tunnels (see Fig. 2) showing stratigraphic and gold assay interpretation of the EA–Dreyerskuil (DK) growth fold sequence, and the later listric Eldorado Fault. Diagram provided by R. F. Tucker from Avgold press release.

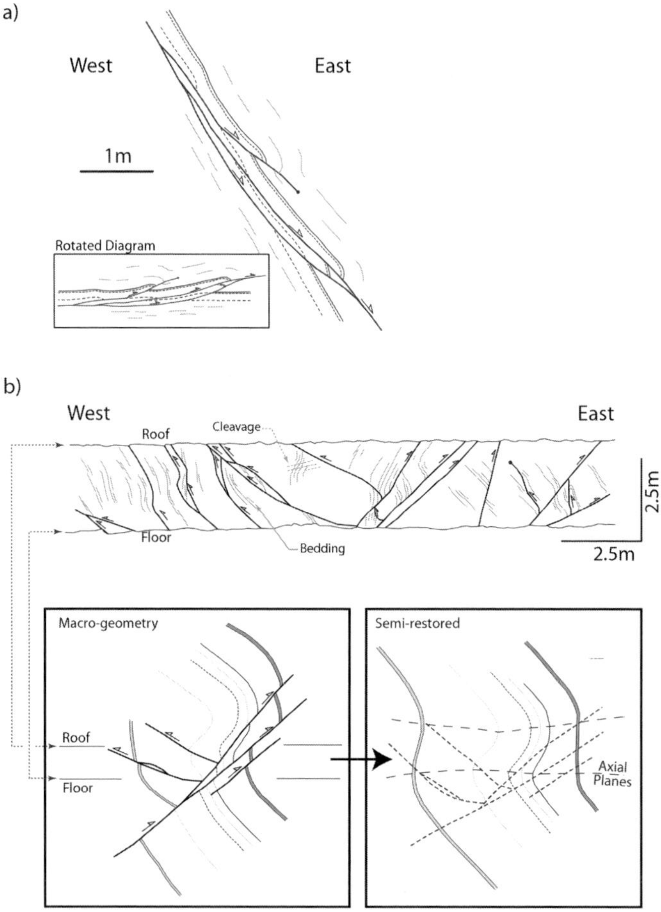

Fig. 6. Sketches of structures exposed in working faces within the 3-shaft area of Loraine Gold Mine, showing typical downward-facing, east-verging thrusts and folds in the Basal Reef within the western limb of the monoform.

geophysical borehole logs (Stuart *et al.* 2000). This amplitude mapping shows that the conglomerates are restricted to the south side of the Siberia Fault (Fig. 4), indicating that the fault was active during deposition of the Dreyerskuil sequence and contemporary rise of the synclinal steep limb to the west.

Seismic data, drilling and mine excavation shows that the steep limb of the growth fold is dislocated by easterly verging thrusts (Fig. 5; Winter 1987; Jolley *et al.* 2004). In the Loraine–Target area, some of the thrusts steepen up-dip and tip-out within the EA, Dreyerskuil or basal Klipriviersberg Group stratigraphy, and some flatten out into the stratigraphy of the eastern limb. The westerly verging Zuurbron backthrust is prominent on the seismic data, cutting the sedimentary rocks of the Central Rand Group and the lower Klipriviersberg Group lavas (Fig. 7). In the north, the base lavas steepen, into a west-vergent footwall syncline beneath the backthrust. Use of a distinctive reflector package *c.* 200 m above the basal contact as a reference datum helps to reveal growth of the lower Klipriviersberg Group lavas into this syncline, and onlapping or draping of minor folds in what is now the hanging wall of the backthrust (Fig. 7c). This structure tips-out to the south across Loraine Mine, where an array of meso-scale backthrusts and folds have been exposed in underground tunnels and chamber excavations (S.J.J., pers. obs., 1992, 1998). Together, the Rheedersdam forethrusts and the Zuurbron backthrust form a passive roof duplex, similar to

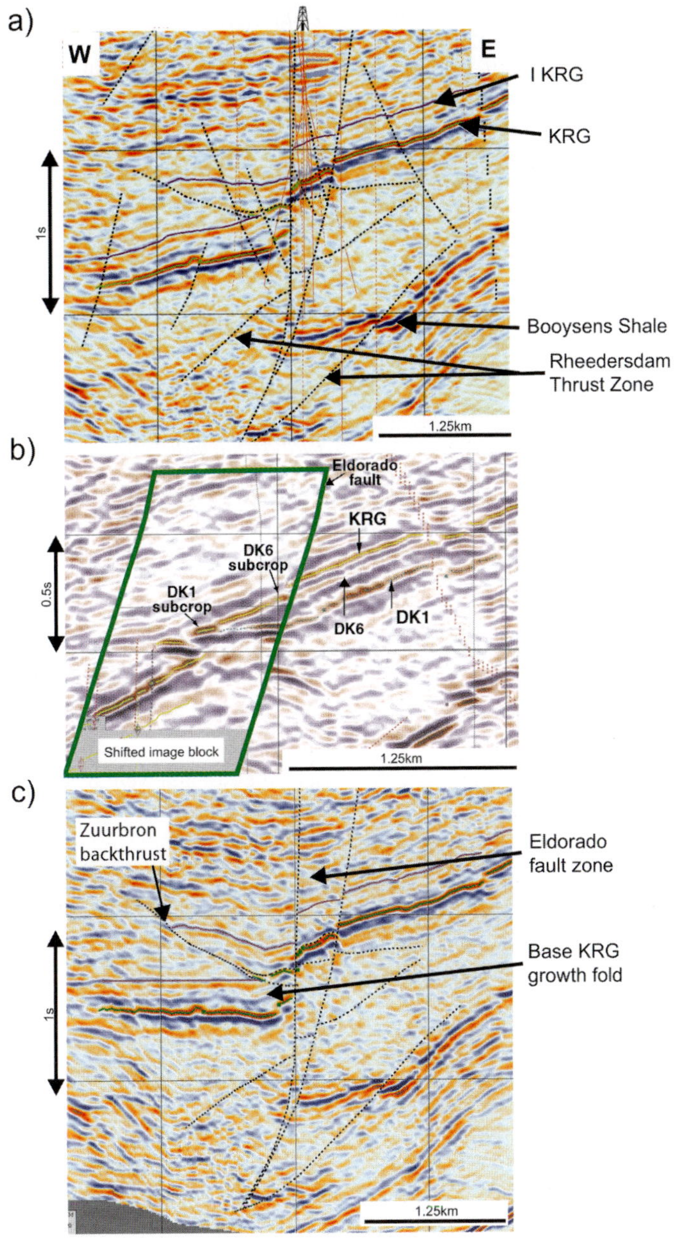

Fig. 7. (**a**) East–west seismic section from the Target 3D volume showing key faults and reflectors, with linkage between Eldorado normal fault and underlying forethrusts. (**b**) East–west seismic section from the Target 3D volume, with restoration of the Eldorado Fault emphasizing the reflection character of the base Klipriviersberg, Dreyerskuil strata and growth structure. (**c**) Flattening along intra-Klipriviersberg reflector as a datum emphasizes synkinematic contractional growth in the lower Klipriviersberg Group. KRG, base Klipriviersberg; IKRG, intra-Klipriviersberg marker; DK1, base Dreyerskuil; DK6, intra-Dreyerskuil bed. (See Fig. 2 for location.)

triangle zones that typify Phanerozoic thrust fronts (e.g. MacKay *et al.* 1996). South of the Maraisdal Fault, the Klipriversberg and Platberg reflectors are conformable; but north of the fault, the contact between the Klipriviersberg Group and the overlying Platberg Group is an angular unconformity, beneath which the Klipriviersberg Group is deformed into a large-scale monoform, representing the culmination of the duplex (Fig. 3). This indicates that the thrusting deformation was partitioned across the Maraisdal Fault, such that thrust-related structures to the north continued to amplify into the upper Klipriviersberg Group.

Extensional faulting

The seismic data were found to contain high-amplitude reflections adjacent to normal faults, which correspond to intrusive sills intersected in boreholes. These intrusive reflectors are modestly discordant and often paired, as a result of acceleration and deceleration of seismic energy across the top and basal contacts. The reflections disappear where the intrusive sills become too thin or steep to image, but the amplitude of the base Klipriviersberg reflector dims where intrusive rocks pass through it (Stuart *et al.* 2000). At Loraine Mine, these igneous bodies emanate as 'side sills' from branch lines or bends in large normal faults (Fig. 5a), and have geochemical signatures similar to upper Klipriviersberg Group and Platberg Group lavas (Owens & Jolley 1993).

The basal Klipriviersberg reflector package maintains a layer-cake thickness of *c.* 200 m across both the NE–SW-trending Siberia Fault and the NNW–SSE-trending Eldorado Fault (Fig. 7). Similarly, there is no change in thickness of the Platberg Group across either of these faults, indicating that normal movement and associated depositional growth on them took place only during extrusion of the upper Klipriviersberg Group lavas. In contrast, north of the Maraisdal Fault, the basal Platberg Group sediments grow locally into the hanging walls of some north–south-trending faults; and expand more generally towards a larger depocentre within a half-graben, west of the goldfield (Fig. 3). The lower Platberg Group sequence above this gradually thickens northwards across the Target area, but does not contain growth geometries against any faults. The upper Platberg Group sequence is essentially a layer-cake with no discernible fault-controlled thickness changes, except where it expands markedly into the hanging wall of the NE–SW-striking Maraisdal Fault (Fig. 8).

Late inversion

North of the Maraisdal Fault, 2D seismic data show modest uplift of the post-rift Pniel Group above its regional level, to the east of two large lower Platberg-age normal faults. Reactivation of a backthrust, similar to the Zuurbron backthrust, contributes to this uplift (Fig. 3). Few of the other normal faults in the Target 3D seismic data have obvious late reactivation geometries, although subtle buckling of Klipriviersberg reflectors occurs locally above parts of the Eldorado Fault.

Seismic-scale fault reactivation

Planar normal faults

The Siberia and Maraisdal faults pass steeply through the higher structural levels of the thrust system (Figs 2 and 8). However, reflection amplitude mapping described above indicates syn-Dreyerskuil movement on a precursor structure to the preserved Siberia Fault, and displacement on the Zuurbron backthrust changes across the Siberia Fault and certain locally east–west- to WNW–ESE-trending segments of similar faults (e.g. Figs 4 and 9a). This indicates that these faults originated within the earlier thrusting deformation and were then captured during propagation of normal faults with similar strike. Furthermore, although the Siberia Fault cuts, and displaces, earlier NE–SW- and NNE–SSW-trending faults, it steps trajectory along a small segment of each fault, indicating that it also captured these segments as it formed. The Ariel Fault (Figs 4 and 9a), is composed of similar discrete NE–SW- and NNE–SSW-trending segments, implying that it also captured parts of earlier NNE–SSW-trending faults. Conversely, to the west of the decline tunnels, NNE–SSW-trending structures cut the Ariel Fault, and the NNE–SSW Blast Fault cuts the NE–SW Damn Fault (Figs 4 and 9a). Clearly, the propagation and normal movement on the NE–SW and NNE–SSW-trending fault sets was broadly coeval, leading to mutual capture and cross-cutting relationships.

Listric normal faults

The Eldorado Fault throws the Siberia Fault down to the west, with a significant component of oblique left-lateral offset (Fig. 4). The Eldorado Fault transfers its remaining throw to the Twin Fault across a complex relay ramp, north of the Siberia Fault. The lower Klipriviersberg reflectors show a classic hanging-wall roll-over geometry, associated with the Eldorado

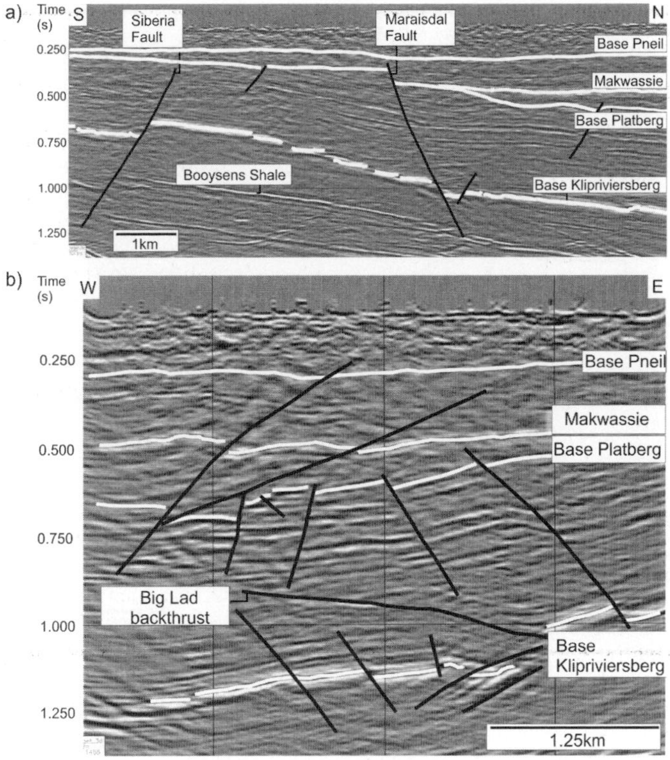

Fig. 8. (**a**) North–south seismic section from the Target 3D volume showing normal faults and Platberg Group palaeo-valleys and depositional growth packages. (**b**) East–west seismic section from the northern Target 3D volume showing Platberg Group growth packages; and Big Lad backthrust, which has experienced Platberg extensional reactivation and late post Ventersdorp contractional reactivation. (See Fig. 2 for location.)

and Twin faults. Reflector disruption and detailed borehole control tightly constrain these faults to shallow downwards to link into the underlying west-dipping forethrusts. Extensive mining and drilling activity across a *c.* 1 km depth profile in Loraine Mine shows that Eldorado-type faults alternately cut, and link into, the forethrusts (e.g. Fig. 9b). Thus the Eldorado and Twin faults are listric faults, which appear to have focused on forethrusts at different depths on either side of the Siberia Fault, cutting the backthrust and displacing the trailing edge of the triangle zone to the west. The map trace of the Eldorado Fault has a reticulated appearance caused by capture of short segments of earlier formed Siberia-type faults (Fig. 9a). Fault-horizon mapping in the seismic data shows that throw on the Eldorado Fault was compartmentalized across these structures to form a series of segments with repeated variation in throw on a 100–500 m length scale (Fig. 10).

Small fault reactivation

The aim of this section is to discuss whether the seismic interpretation presented here has characterized the fault scale range that has been reactivated, or if significant reactivation occurred in the smaller faults below the resolution of the seismic data.

Small seismic-scale faulting

As the throw on a fault diminishes, the two-way-time offset of seismic reflectors becomes increasingly difficult to map. Coherency filtering, edge detection and reflection attribute analysis can be used as the throw approaches the seismic resolution limits. One theoretical rule-of-thumb suggests that the smallest fault throws that can be imaged by seismic amplitudes are those where throw is equivalent to ¼ dominant seismic wavelength (see Townsend *et al.* 1998, for discussion). However, this ¼ wavelength measure does not

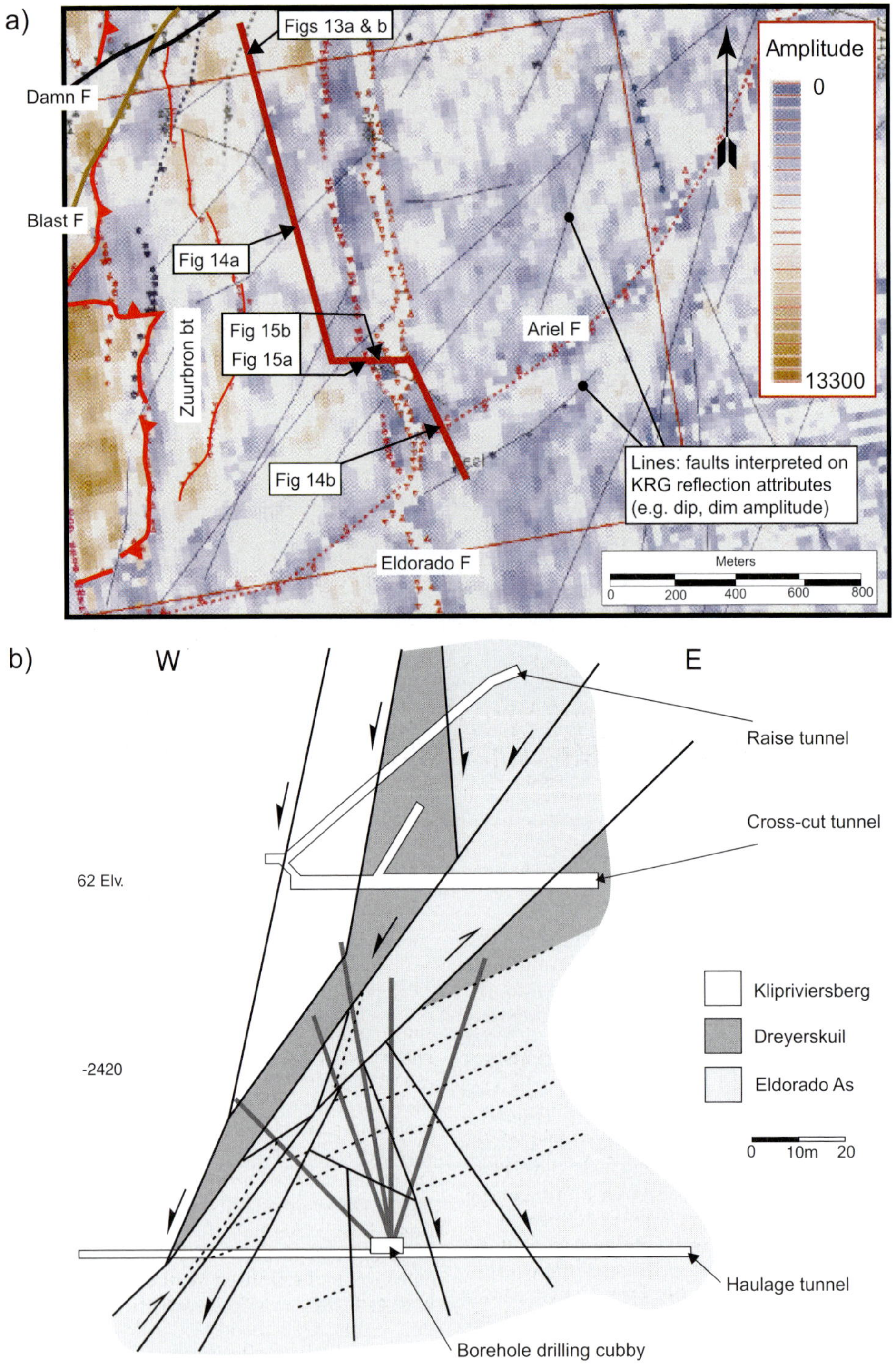

Fig. 9. (**a**) Seismic reflection amplitude map showing faults in the vicinity of the Target decline tunnels with locations of structure face maps drawn by surveying geology exposed in mine walls. (**b**) Structural interpretation through mine workings and drilling information in the northern part of Loraine Gold Mine, near Shaft 1 (Fig. 2), showing Eldorado-type normal faults linking into reactivated earlier formed forethrusts.

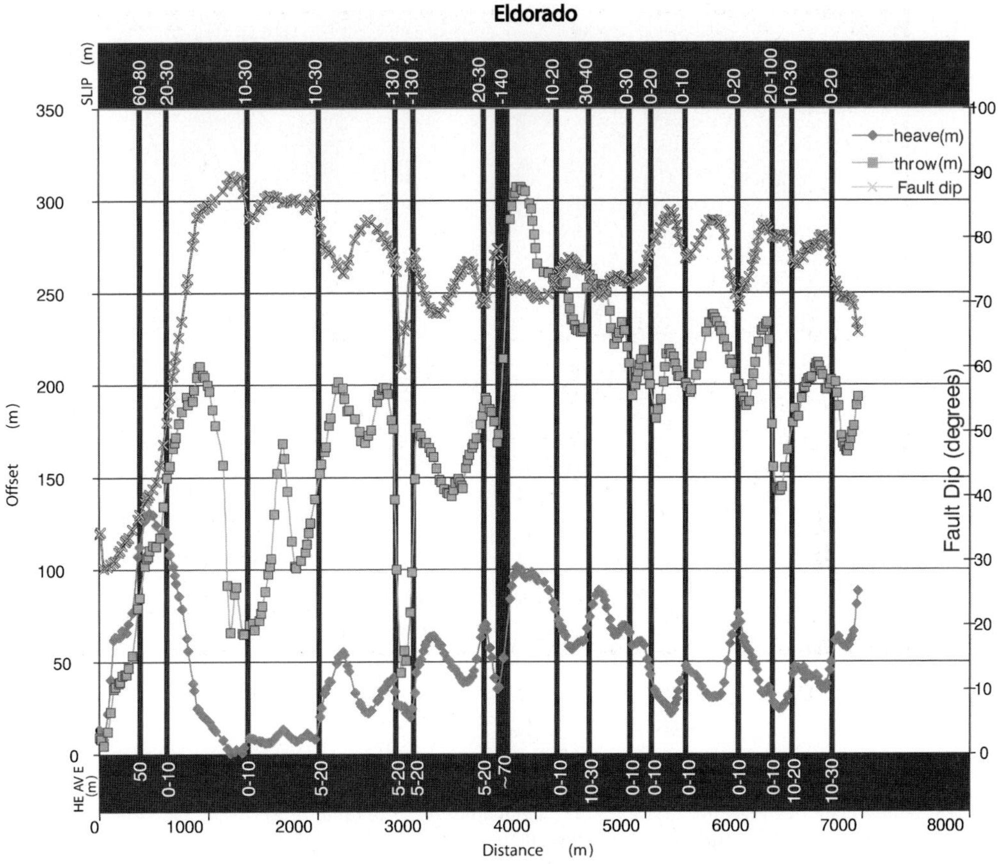

Fig. 10. Throw variation along the Eldorado Fault. (Note that throw segments are bounded by the intersection of Siberia-type faults.) The ratio of the difference between the throw minima and maxima of a segment and the length of that segment varies from 1:5 to 1:30 for each segment, and within an individual segment the rate of change of throw approaches 1:3.

take into account the strength of the acoustic impedance contrast and the range of frequency content (bandwidth) causing the reflections displaced by the fault. Modern 3D seismic acquisition and processing techniques can therefore image smaller fault throws than the 'theoretical' lower limit. In the case of the Target Mine data, it has been possible to measure the resolution of the data directly by comparing reflection attribute anomalies with real fault throws exposed in mine workings within the seismic data cube. Fan-drilling, close to one Siberia-type fault (Fig. 14a as described below), reveals only 5–10 m vertical throw of the base Dreyerskuil and Klipriviersberg contacts. Despite its small throw, this fault was imaged in the base Klipriviersberg reflector (Fig. 9; Stuart *et al.* 2000). This compares well with correlations made between base Klipriviersberg reflection attributes and faults mapped in mine workings, within a seismic survey with similar acquisition and processing characteristics in the north of the basin (6–18 m throw resolution, Gibson *et al.* 2000). It is therefore concluded that the fault maps generated from the 3D seismic data are inclusive of faults within the 10–20 m throw range (¼ wavelength rule = 25 m), and that smaller throws, in the 5–10 m range, are included where the data quality permits (Fig. 11).

Sub-seismic-scale faulting

From the above, only faults with throws over *c.* 10 m are likely to have been systematically imaged by the 3D seismic data over the whole

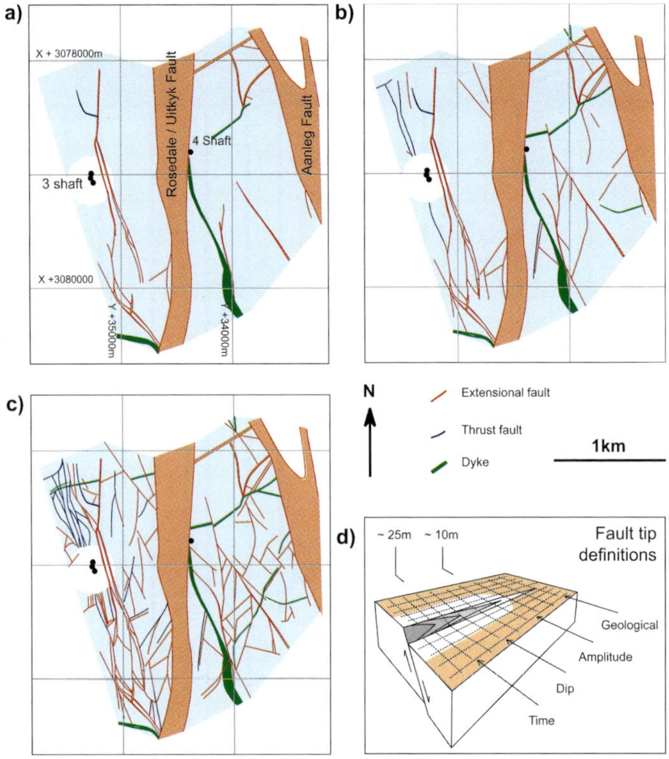

Fig. 11. Fault maps of Loraine Gold Mine 3-shaft area, constructed by collation of data from available hard-copy geological mine plans (see Fig. 2 for location.) (**a**) Fault map inclusive of fault throws over 25 m. (**b**) Fault map inclusive of fault throws down to 10 m. (**c**) Full fault map, inclusive of all fault throws down to the mine's routine geological mapping limit of *c.* 2 m. (**d**) Cartoon of seismic attribute-defined fault tips according to throw resolution of each attribute. Dotted lines are horizon interpretation.

survey area. To characterize the full fault population, representative fault maps were constructed from data in available 1:200 scale geological mine plans, which record more than 40 years excavation of the Basal Reef at Loraine Mine (Figs 2 and 11). To limit the dilution of this thin (centimetre-scale) ore with waste from the hanging wall and footwall, standard mining practice has been to restrict mining (stope) width to 2 m. Faults of less than 1–2 m throw therefore have a minimal impact on mining activity, as the thin ore zone is still contained within the stope width. Consequently, mine geologists have found it necessary and practical to routinely map only faults with larger throws. Despite this lower limit to the data, information extracted from the maps has allowed comparison in the present study of fault architectures and throw variations across the scale ranges seen in mine workings at Loraine Mine with those mapped from the seismic data.

Fault throw:length ratios

The measured throw to length ratios of thrust faults at Loraine Mine are between 1:25 and 1:100, although there is only a limited amount of relevant data on the plans (Fig. 12a). The normal fault data show a broad scatter, with up to an order of magnitude variation in length for a given throw (Fig. 12b). In the Loraine Mine 2-shaft area, 85% of the normal faults measured have a maximum throw of less than 20 m. In general, 70% of the normal faults have a throw to length ratio of 1:70 to 1:100, but those with maximum throws greater than 20 m have a much reduced ratio, averaging only 1:10. There is an edge effect in these data, where the large faults are only partially sampled by the mine plans. However, as shown in the structural map of the Loraine Mine 3-shaft area (Fig. 11), the majority of normal faults are not single isolated faults, but are linked into or bounded by other faults.

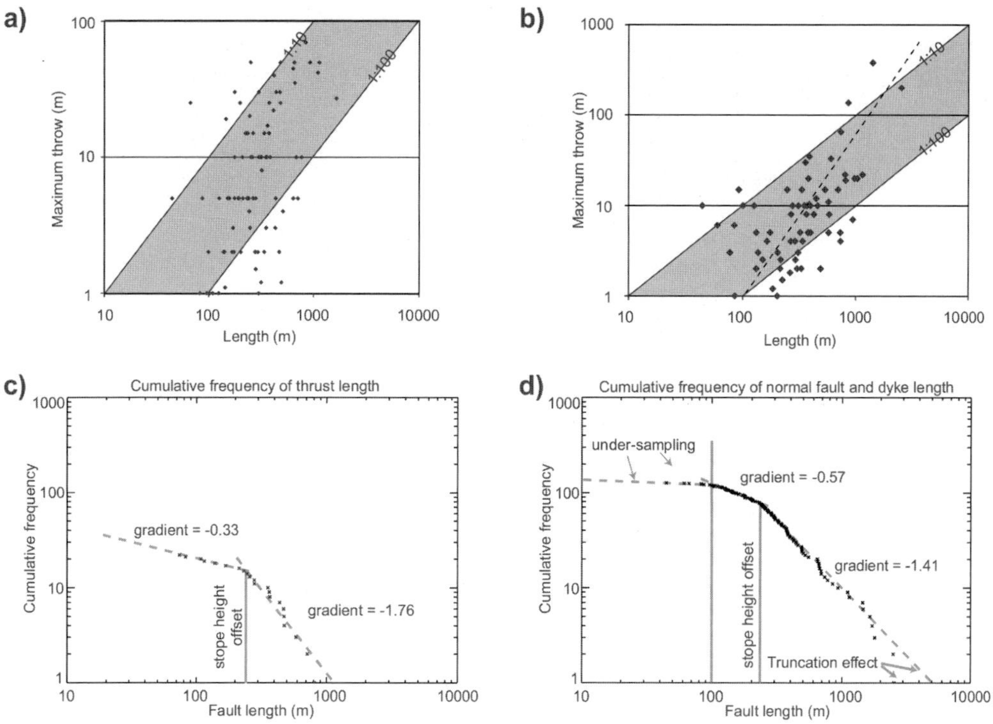

Fig. 12. Plots of fault throw and strike-length data extracted from collated Loraine Gold Mine fault maps. (**a**) Thrust fault throw:strike-length. (**b**) Normal fault throw:strike-length. (**c**) Cumulative size frequency of thrust fault population. (**d**) Cumulative size frequency of normal fault population.

Although some are splays from larger faults, with asymmetrical throw profiles, those that are bounded by other faults represent an important end-member of the throw:length population, where the maximum length is less than would be usually anticipated given their throw. As all of these anomalous faults are located between other major faults, their distribution is to some extent predictable (e.g. capture of Siberia-type faults as displacement relays in Eldorado-type faults). Consequently, the scatter and exaggerated throw to length ratio for this dataset does not reflect the geometrical arrangement of a ‘single-event’ fault system, but rather that of a reticulated fault array resulting from a complex fault interaction and capture history.

Fault scale frequency distribution

Scaling of the normal faults showed a well-defined gradient of -1.41 for faults between 220 and 2000 m long, and a well-defined gradient decrease to -0.57 below 220 m (Fig. 12d). This change correlated with fault throws of *c.* 2 m, coincident with the lower limit of consistent fault mapping at the mine. A further change in gradient occurred at a strike length of *c.* 100 m, equivalent to throws of *c.* 1 m, which would be contained within the mining width and therefore only rarely mapped. These gradient changes were therefore a product of bias in the original data collection, rather than a real scaling relationship. For fault lengths greater than 2000 m, the data deviated from a linear trend. This is a common pattern in fault population studies, and is indicative in this case of the largest faults exceeding the size of the mine and therefore extending beyond the map area characterized. The -1.41 gradient therefore appeared to be the best estimate of the true population gradient. If this gradient is extrapolated to encompass all fault sizes, it predicts a population in the mapped area equivalent to 46 faults with a length of >100 m (*c.* 1 m or more throw), cutting each 1 km^2.

Thrusts represented a relatively small proportion of the faults mapped within the shallow limb of the syncline (Fig. 11), although more thrusts have been mapped in the steep western limb.

The cumulative size frequency scaling gradient for these structures showed two distinct sections (Fig. 12c). Thrusts with a strike length of <250 m (2–4 m throw) produce a relatively shallow gradient (−0.33). This is again consistent with the *c.* 2 m stope width and lower limit of routine throw mapping. The relatively steep gradient (−1.76) for strike lengths >250 m is therefore believed to be more representative, predicting a large number of small unmapped faults. A large proportion of this 'missing' strain was probably contained within the small, bedding-subparallel thrusts that were commonly seen in the areas shown in Figure 11 (S.J.J., pers. obs. 1992). Extrapolation of the frequency–length gradient predicted that, on average, 14 thrusts >100 m (1–4 m throw) will occur in every 1 km^2. This is a sparse population when compared with that of the normal faults, even if additional mid-limb thrusting to the west is taken into account. If this is a true reflection of the geology, the normal throw bias in the preserved Loraine Mine fault throw population may be explained by normal reactivation of some of the thrusts. In this scenario, the original reverse throw on these structures has been reset to modest values or net extension. Support for this comes from the detailed mine plans, which show north–south forethrusts and normal faults transitional with each other along strike, and in some areas swarms of thrusts and normal faults mapped together in complex fault zones, sharing lateral ramps and branching into one another; this process was also directly observed in mesoscale structures underground (S.J.J., pers. obs. 1992, 1998; also Jolley *et al.* 2004).

This study indicates that similar reworked fault architectures can be seen in both the seismic data and mine plans. The largest (seismic-scale) faults in Loraine Mine have broadly north–south Eldorado trends and are cross-linked by normal faults and dykes with broadly east–west trends (e.g. Fig. 11a). The majority of the small- to sub-seismic-scale faults trend between NW–SE, NNW–SSE and NE–SW (e.g. Fig. 11b). Some sub-seismic faults form complex ladder zones, which compartmentalize displacement along individual faults and relay it between adjacent large fault segments. These smaller structures therefore clearly developed in response to movement on the seismic-scale faults. They fall into two general strike trends (NW–SE to NNW–SSE and NE–SW), to produce a rhomboidal pattern of fault-bounded compartments, *c.* 100 m × 200 m in size (Fig. 11c). They form a component of the fault system's architecture and kinematics that is not imaged by the seismic data.

Reactivation of fault damage zones

In this section the kinematic style of reactivation within fault damage zones is assessed, from data collected by mesoscale face-mapping of faults exposed in mine workings and decline tunnels within the seismic data cube (Fig. 9a). These face maps were constructed by surveying mesoscale faults and fractures with respect to an offset tape, supplemented by photographs and sketches.

Forethrusts and backthrusts

Geologists at Loraine Mine described the damage zone to a major forethrust (displacement 250–300 m), exposed during mining, as comprising: (1) a central *c.* 5 m thick high-strain zone containing bands of sericitic 'shaly' material, breccias, vein quartz and pods of exotic stratigraphy; (2) a lower-strain 10–15 m wide outer damage zones composed of bedding drag and shear-thinning, fracturing and quartz veins. The Zuurbron backthrust, encountered in the Target decline tunnels, has a similar damage zone arrangement. (1) The inner damage zone (Fig. 13a) is characterized by narrow shallow east-dipping shear zones containing phyllonites and mica-rich banded cataclasites, and more moderately east-dipping, bedding-parallel sericitic shears. Substructures include west-vergent cleavage and flat-lying quartz-bearing shear fractures, and steep faults and fractures that accommodate dilation and domino-style rotation of intervening blocks. (2) The outer damage zone (Fig. 13b), is dominated by bedding slip marked by veneers of micaceous cataclasite, and small anastomosing faults subparallel to bedding. Shallow east-dipping faults link asymptotically with some of the bed-parallel shears to form thrust horses.

The kinematic function of the backthrust damage zone appears to have been a combination of: (1) central slip across a network of thrust plane-parallel shear surfaces and cross-linking bed-parallel and secondary structures; and (2) a broader card-deck style bedding slip, linked by cross-branching thrust-plane-parallel structures in the outer damage zone. Contemporary fluid flow is shown by locally pervasive muscovite–pyrophyllite alteration. An analogy can be drawn with other anomalously mica-rich fault rocks formed in quartzitic host rocks, where phyllosilicates were precipitated and concentrated during synkinematic fluid flow and dissolution of quartz (e.g. Newman & Mitra 1993). Elsewhere in the basin, this is associated with hydrothermal gold mineralization in thrust-fracture systems (e.g. Barnicoat *et al.* 1997; Jolley *et al.* 1999,

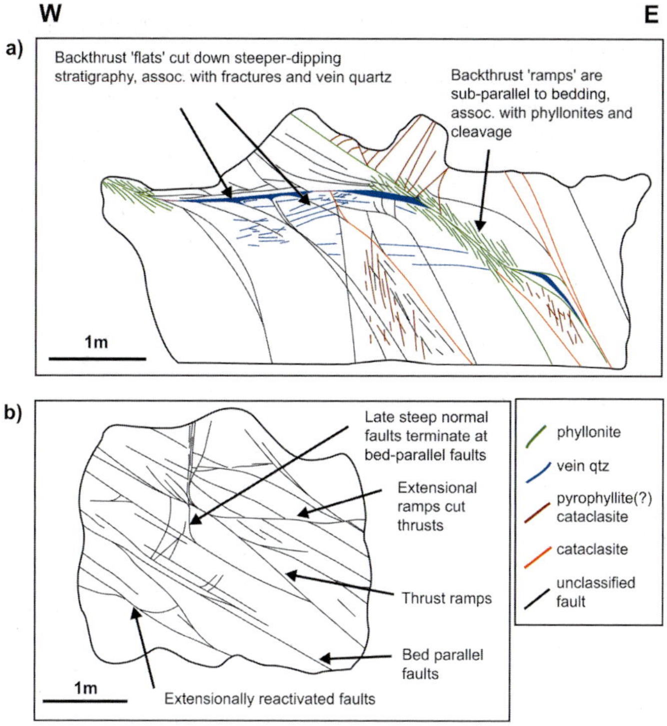

Fig. 13. Structure of Zuurbron backthrust fault damage zone, as exposed in the decline tunnel walls, constructed by surveying the structural features with respect to a datum tape stretched along the wall. This shows thrust-related substructure and nature of later extensional reactivation. (**a**) Inner damage zone. (**b**) Outer damage zone. (See Fig. 9 for location.)

2004). The thrust damage zone in Figure 13 was reworked during extensional reactivation, initially by steep to subvertical normal faults and fractures, and then by steep east-dipping cataclastic normal faults that cut bedding and alternately cut and link into thrust-plane- and bed-parallel shears. These faults were then downthrown to the east by reactivation of some of the bed-parallel shears. Collectively, these structures indicate that extension in the damage zone evolved from initial pure shear stretching to decoupling of hanging wall and footwall by selective reactivation of the thrust zone's shear planes.

Normal faults

Planar faults. Fan-drilling either side of the fault shown in Figure 14a showed oblique displacement of east-dipping stratigraphy (30–40 m strike-slip, 5–10 m vertical throw). To the SW, the base Klipriviersberg cut-off in the hanging wall to the Zuurbron backthrust jumps laterally by *c.* 50 m across this fault, suggesting that it originated as a lateral structure in the thrust system (Fig. 9a). To the NE, throw on the fault increases near its intersection with the Eldorado Fault, which bifurcates and shows a *c.* 30 m throw increase in the same location, suggesting that the fault was partly reactivated there to partition displacement on the Eldorado Fault. This movement history is recorded in the fault's damage zone: (1) the *c.* 1 m wide inner damage zone comprises anastomosing cataclastic faults and fractures between thin subplanar clay-like gouge stringers; (2) the footwall outer damage zone contains steep quartz veins, quartz-cemented breccias and cataclastic faults. In contrast, the hanging wall contains clustered arrays of interlinked cataclastic normal faults and few quartz-bearing structures. Outboard of this, an early mesoscale triangle zone is developed, in which small faults appear to be mutually cross-cutting and thrusted away from the inner damage zone. Later steep faults, developed at the periphery of the damage zone, emanate as wing cracks from the shallow structures, alternately cutting and linking to them, and a network of steep

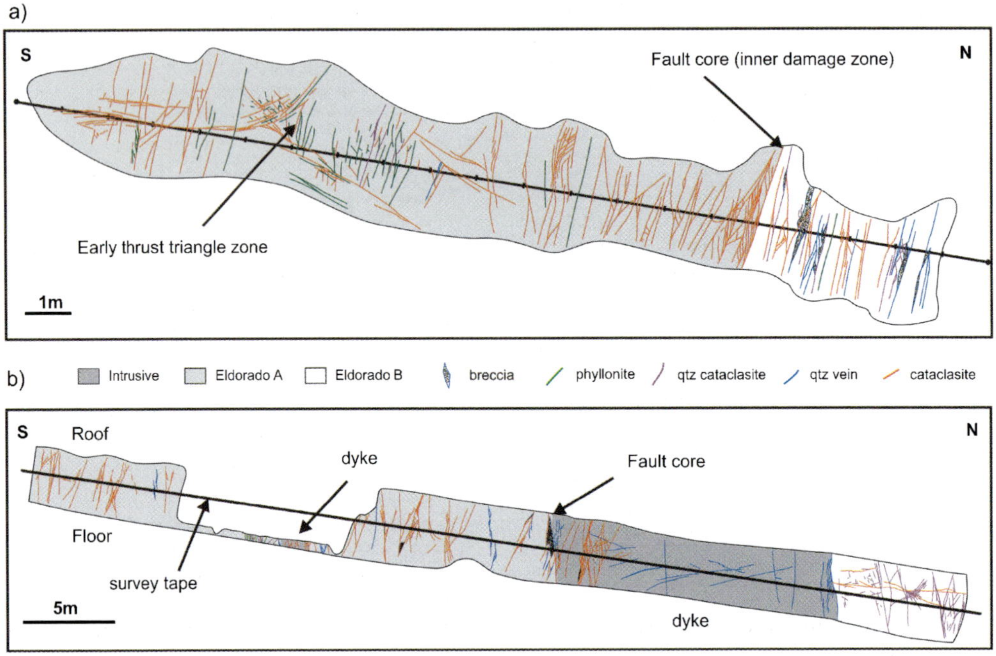

Fig. 14. Structure maps of Siberia-type normal fault damage zones, as exposed in the decline tunnel walls, constructed by surveying the structural features with respect to a datum tape stretched along the wall. This shows remnant early thrust-related substructure amongst the younger normal fault substructures. (**a**) Oblique Fault. (**b**) Ariel Fault. (See Fig. 9 for location.)

fractures and faults detach from the floor fault in the triangle zone.

In the seismic data, the Ariel Fault (Fig. 2) has *c*. 60 m throw in the footwall of the Eldorado Fault, but abruptly loses 35–40 m of this throw along a NE–SW segment in the immediate hanging wall to the Eldorado Fault. At the same place, the Eldorado Fault gains *c*. 40 m throw on the north side of the Ariel Fault. Clearly, part of the Ariel Fault was reactivated to partition displacement in the hanging wall of the Eldorado Fault. Further to the west, the strike of the Ariel Fault swings to a more east–west orientation and increases throw, suggesting a waning influence of the displacement by the Eldorado Fault. To the east, the Ariel Fault has a smooth displacement profile, indicating that it was largely unaffected. The displacement on the Zuurbron backthrust also changes across the Ariel Fault, suggesting that certain segments of the Ariel Fault originated as lateral ramps in the thrust system. This movement history is evident in the exposed damage zone, with preservation of the following features (Fig. 14b): (1) The inner damage zone is intruded by mafic igneous rock of similar composition and appearance to other known Klipriviersberg Group intrusive rocks in Loraine Mine (Owens & Jolley 1993). The southern 3 m of this dyke is intensely altered and pervaded by sericitic (rectorite?)-bearing fractures and breccias, phyllonites and quartz veins. (2) The outer damage zone consists of clusters of linked cataclastic normal faults with minor vein quartz. Deformation is concentrated on the southern side of a second subsidiary dyke, in tightly clustered ladder-like arrays of cataclastic normal faults and locally formed breccias, but without significant phyllosilicates or alteration. The nearby quartzites contain small early bedding-subparallel cataclastic thrust faults, which are offset by steeper cataclastic normal faults. These normal faults link to shallower-dipping conjugate sets of faults and fractures, which also appear in part to terminate, or detach, against the earlier thrust structures.

Listric faults. The Eldorado Fault Zone consists of two fault planes in the Target Mine decline tunnels. Exposure of the western strand is intermittently preserved between zones of geotechnical support as follows: (1) The main fault plane juxtaposes the basal EA sequence against older rocks across an intensely cleaved phyllonitic fault contact (Fig. 15a); the phyllosilicates in this fault rock apparently originate from clay-smear of adjacent lithologies (see Fisher & Knipe 1998). This is flanked by a complex linked network of steep, moderate and shallow-dipping normal faults. (2) In the outer damage zone (Fig. 15b), the strata contain early shallow west-dipping cataclastic thrust faults that form swarms of subparallel structures and small duplexes. Local cleavage vergence and stepped slickenfibres in many fault planes indicate top-to-the-east thrust displacement. Later local extensional reactivation is shown by cross-printing of the contractional structures by quartz-filled tension gashes and vein arrays, which are in turn locally cut, and offset, by late top-to-the-west extensional movement on the thrust planes. Following this, the thrusts were cut and downthrown to the east by steep east-dipping cataclastic normal faults and cross-printed by other steeper structures in the damage zone.

Progressive evolution of fault–fracture architecture

Thrusting

Meso-scale structures, associated with a mid-Central Rand Group thrusting event at Loraine Mine and other mines in the district, appear to have controlled Basal Reef mineralization (Jolley *et al.* 2004). However, the main thrust system described in this paper is a later event, which appears to have evolved progressively through the late Central Rand Group into the Klipriviersberg Group period. The key stages in this evolution are shown in Figure 16 and reviewed below:

(1) A suite of broadly NE–SW- and WNW–ESE- to NW–SE-trending early normal faults and fractures formed in the foredeep in advance of the thrust front (e.g *sensu* Hippolyte *et al.* 1995; Scisciani *et al.* 2002). Nearby, the EA and Dreyerskuil sequences were deposited syntectonically in a series of alluvial fans along the line of an end-Witwatersrand thrust front, with increasingly local control on deposition by this growth folding and the early normal structures.

(2) Forethrusts, associated with the Rheedersdam Thrust Zone, dislocated the fold's mid-limb. At this stage, at least some early normal faults were captured to form lateral ramps. Larger structures of this type (e.g. Siberia Fault) compartmentalized the gross geometry and displacement of the developing thrust system (Fig. 16a).

(3) A passive roof duplex formed during accumulation of the lower Klipriviersberg Group (Fig. 16b). This can be seen south of the Maraisdal Fault, by growth of the basal lava

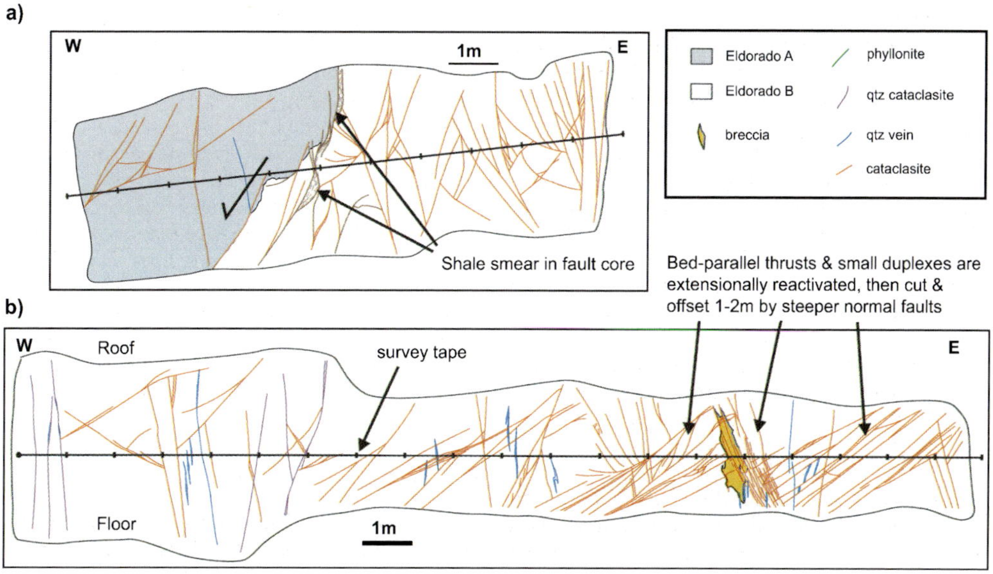

Fig. 15. Structure maps of Eldorado-type normal fault damage zones, as exposed in the decline tunnel walls, constructed by surveying the structural features with respect to a datum tape stretched along the wall. This shows reactivation and subsequent cutting of earlier thrust substructures. (See Fig. 9 for location.)

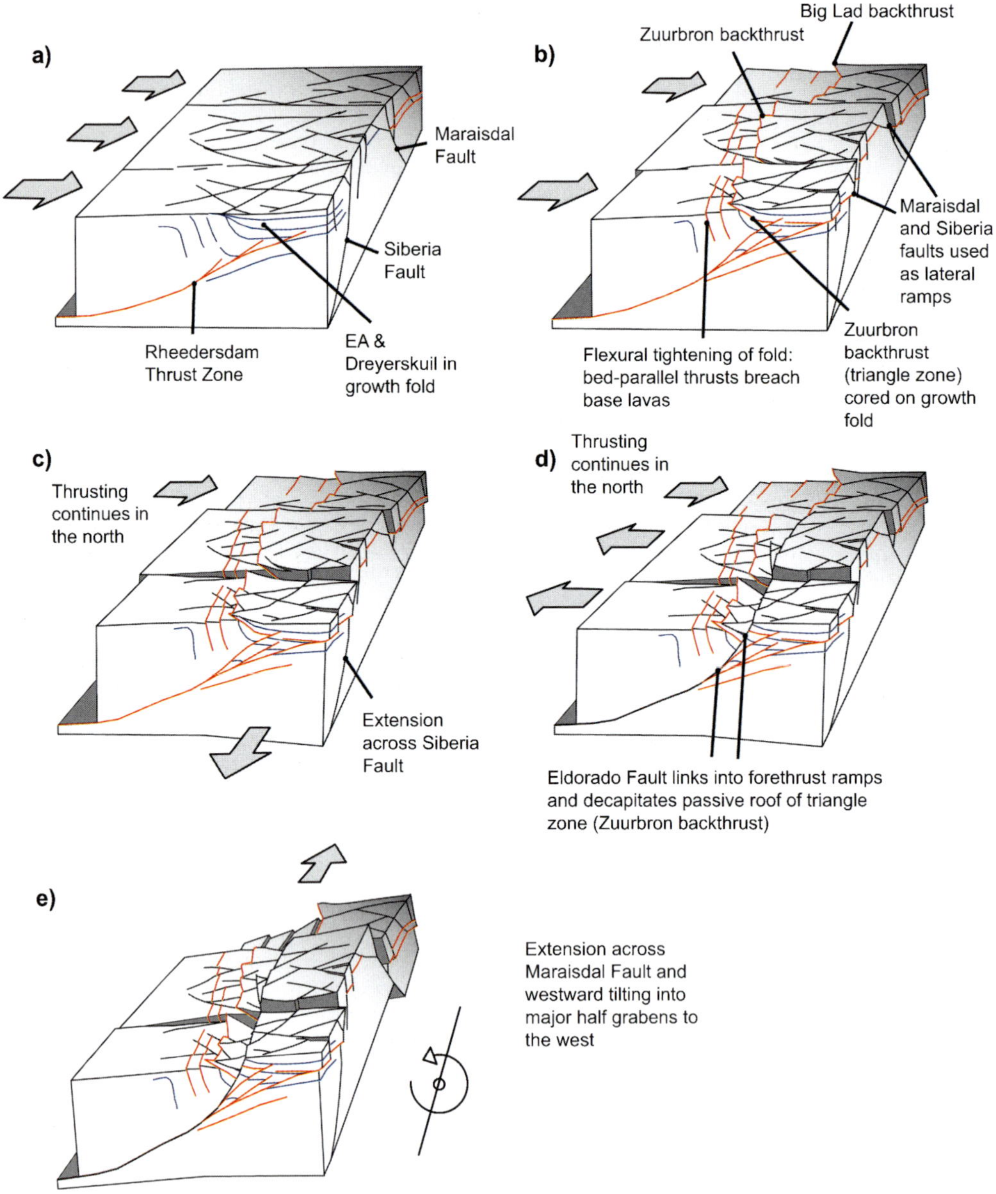

Fig. 16. Schematic block diagrams of progressive structural evolution of Target–Loraine area, northern Welkom Goldfield, back-stripped to the base Klipriviersberg Group contact. (**a**) Dreyerskuil–VCR: thrusting and folding, growth fold in EA and Dreyerskuil; early 'normal' faults exploited as local laterals; precursors to Maraisdal and Siberia faults act as key laterals in thrust system. (**b**) Lower Klipriviersberg Group: thrusting and backthrusting; growth fold focuses triangle zone; flexural tightening of fold breached base lavas; early 'normal' faults re-exploited as local laterals; precursors to Maraisdal and Siberia faults act as key laterals. (**c**) Upper Klipriviersberg Group (1): thrusting and backthrusting (north of Maraisdal); extension to south especially across the Siberia Fault; early 'normal' faults captured as extensional faults at this time. (**d**) Upper Klipriviersberg Group (2): thrusting and backthrusting continues (north of Maraisdal); extension to south switches to retro-reactivation of thrust system with dominant throw across newly formed thin-skinned Eldorado Fault and similar structures nearby; early 'normal' faults recaptured and exploited as lateral faults to Eldorado Fault system. (**e**) Platberg Group: massive extension and tilting (north of Maraisdal Fault); wholesale passive westward tilting (south of Maraisdal Fault).

sequence into a kinematically related west-vergent syncline (Fig. 7); the presence of geochemically distinct komatiitic sills within some thrust planes (see below); and the fact that the backthrust cuts the lower Klipriviersberg Group, whereas upper Klipriviersberg Group normal faults in turn cut through the backthrust and reactivate the underlying forethrusts. It appears that with the onset of Klipriviersberg Group volcanism, the mechanical character of the thrust-front changed to incorporate a rapidly thickening 'lid' of dense competent lavas, thus driving the change in structural style. Displacement across the Zuurbron backthrust varies along strike and changes suddenly as it crosses steep east–west- to WNW–ESE-trending Siberia-type faults, to give the duplex a reticulated character. It is tempting to suggest that some of the larger structures of this type (e.g. Siberia Fault) were inherited from older structural events such as the Dominion rifting or West Rand Group thrusting, whereas the smaller structures originated within the Central Rand Group rocks as early normal faults in the foredeep. Whatever their origin, it is clear that they evolved into steep lateral ramps and hanging-wall drop faults that accommodated lateral partitioning of displacement and imbricate stacking during accumulation of both the Dreyerskuil and lower Klipriviersberg Group sequences. North of the Maraisdal Fault, the thrusting deformation continued into the upper Klipriviersberg Group, indicating sharp lateral partitioning of the duration of structural amplification (Fig. 16b).

Extension

The architecture of the normal fault system also appears to have evolved progressively through three broad stages:

(1) Normal movement on planar faults is associated with synkinematic depositional growth in the upper Klipriviersberg Group. Changes in the displacement on the Zuurbron backthrust across these faults and the remnant contractional structures in their damage zones suggest that certain east–west-trending to WNW–ESE-trending segments originated as lateral thrusts. Larger structures of this type, such as the Siberia Fault, include these remnant features but cut through the higher structural levels of the thrust system and offset the duplex. The faults pass into the reflector packages of the West Rand Group beneath, indicating that the faults are probably hard-linked into underlying thrust-related detachments (see Jolley *et al.* 2004, fig. 9). The NE–SW- and NNE–SSW-trending planar faults were broadly coeval, as indicated by their mutual cross-cutting, reactivation and capture relationships (Fig. 16b and c).

(2) Oblique normal-sinistral movement on the Eldorado Fault offsets the Siberia Fault. However, synkinematic depositional growth associated with the Siberia, Eldorado and Twin faults is restricted to the upper Klipriviersberg Group. In detail, the Eldorado and Twin faults are listric faults that link asymptotically into the trailing edge of the underlying forethrust duplex. At mesoscale level, early card-deck style reactivation of small thrust-plane-parallel structures, followed by development of steeper structures, linked extensional displacement stepwise across the axis of the thrust damage zones. This achieves an overall macroscale asymptotic link between the reactivated thrust and the new steeper normal fault forming in its hanging wall. Siberia-type faults were also reworked at this time, with some captured segments acting to compartmentalize displacement along the trace of Eldorado-type faults (Fig. 16d).

(3) Movement on the Eldorado, Twin and Siberia faults was restricted to the upper Klipriviersberg Group. However, a similar fault to the west is associated with growth in the Platberg Group, and movement on the Maraisdal Fault and structures in its hanging wall began only in the upper Platberg Group. The bulk of the structure in the Loraine–Target area is contained within the hanging-wall rollover to one of these major faults, which can be seen to offset the end-Klipriviersberg landform surface with growth in basal Platberg Group sediments (Fig. 3). Clearly, these faults cut the higher structural levels of the thrust system and deactivated the associated earlier-formed parts of the normal fault system (Fig. 16e). These later structures demonstrate lateral partitioning of the onset and style of extensional faulting that it is believed formed part of the third stage of the regional fault system's development, which saw major deep-seated faults, characterized by classic growth sequence geometries, beginning to form during deposition of the lower Platberg Group.

Synkinematic gold mineralization

Some thrust planes and lateral ramps at Loraine Mine contain komatiitic and tholeiitic sheet intrusive rocks, geochemically affiliated with lower Klipriviersberg Group lavas (see Myers *et al.* 1990; Owens & Jolley 1993). In the north of the basin, similar Klipriviersberg Group dykes cut gold-hosting thrust-fracture networks that imbricate the basal lava flows (Jolley *et al.* 1999, 2004; Gibson *et al.* 2000). This suggests that the thrusting at Loraine and Target mines is of similar age to the synkinematic mineralization seen elsewhere in the basin. Smit & Scheepers (2000) and Smit *et al.* (2001) conducted scanning electron microscopy (SEM), and proton-induced X-ray emission (PIXE) analyses on samples from Dreyerskuil drill core. These techniques allow element mapping and study of the microstructural textural context of gold grains to be conducted in remarkable detail. They showed that gold grains in the Dreyerskuil Member were associated with hydrocarbon, within hydrothermal assemblages including chlorite, brannerite and uraninite, and contained within post-depositional microstructural sites such as fractures, pyrite armouring, inclusions in post-depositional pyrite, crystal crack fillings and the interface between various pyrite overgrowths. These observations are compatible with other studies using similar techniques in other 'reefs' nearby and elsewhere in the basin (e.g Barnicoat *et al.* 1997; Jolley *et al.* 1999, 2004). Although the mineralization of the EA–Dreyerskuil sequence at the Loraine and Target mines was not investigated in detail in this study, structures that may explain the link between deformation and the distribution of gold within these ores were identified. The footwall of the backthrust contains minor reverse faults with similar dip and strike trend to the folded Central Rand Group, suggesting that they originated within the plane of stratigraphy in the steep western limb. These features can be identified as linear amplitude anomalies and steps in the base Klipriviersberg seismic reflector. They appear to correlate with bed-subparallel zones of S–C fabrics and small-scale fracture arrays within Target drill cores, which show top-to-the-west shear sense and mutual cross-cutting relationships with more shallowly dipping thrust shear-fractures. Mesoscale bed-subparallel reverse faulting and local westward overturning of the base Klipriviersberg Group is also seen along certain Central Rand Group subcrops in Loraine Mine. Additionally, low-displacement low-angle forethrust–backthrust complexes are widespread within the hanging walls of larger-scale forethrust structures in the steep western limb of the major fold structure at Loraine and Target mines. Elevated gold grades over significant mining width in the folded EA and Dreyerskuil members are associated with packages of strata within panels of similar structural dip in Loraine and Target mines, and small faults and fractures are clearly common where reef packages are mineralized in drill cores from the Target area. Indeed, some sulphide-bearing fractures in the hanging wall and footwall of sheared 'reefs' sampled from mine-workings, have been seen to host sub-millimetre scale 'visible' gold grains. It is therefore suggested that flexural tightening of the fold within the core of the triangle zone resulted in subcrops breaching the base lavas contact, and synkinematic gold mineralization in, and adjacent to, the associated substructure developed during this deformation (Fig. 17; see Jolley *et al.* 1999, 2004).

Discussion

Progressive kinematic evolution and partitioning

The thrust front developed as a growth fold with a thrusted mid-limb during EA–Dreyerskuil deposition, which deformed mesoscale thrusts and folds from an earlier thrusting and mineralizing event (see Jolley *et al.* 2004). Penecontemporaneous extensional structures, developed in the foredeep, ahead of the fold (*sensu* Hippolyte *et al.* 1995; Scisciani *et al.* 2002), became incorporated as lateral ramps in the developing thrust system.

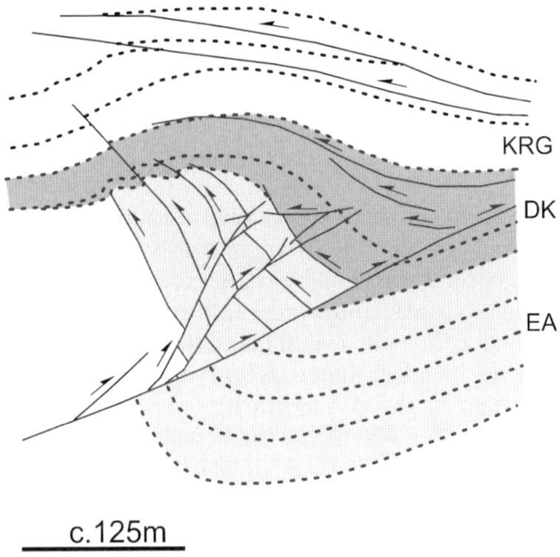

Fig. 17. Schematic illustration of mesoscale structures developed during tightening in the core of the triangle zone, including flexural shearing and thrust-fracture networks. The latter may constitute dynamic permeability pathways controlling synkinematic hydrothermal gold mineralization within the EA–Dreyerskuil sequence at Loraine and Target. KRG, Klipriviersberg Group; DK, Dreyerskuil; EA, Eldorado A series.

However, rapid extrusion of lower Klipriviersberg Group flood basalts changed the mechanical properties of the thrust front. Consequently, the thrust system evolved into a reticulated triangle zone, with displacements compartmentalized across the earlier lateral structures. It seems likely that flexural tightening of the fold, within the core of the triangle zone at this time, may have provided the dynamic fault–fracture permeability for hydrothermal fluid flow and precipitation of gold in the younger strata (see Jolley *et al.* 1999, 2004); similar deformation processes may also have occurred to some extent during the later post-Ventersdorp Group inversion event.

The subsequent Ventersdorp Group rifting was already established by earliest Platberg Group time (e.g. Coward *et al.* 1995; Jolley *et al.* 2004), although kinematic partitioning and diachroneity makes it difficult to pinpoint an exact timing of change from thrusting to extension within the Klipriviersberg reflector series. Despite this, this study clearly indicates that south of the Maraisdal Fault, the local extensional deformation history initiated during accumulation of the upper Klipriviersberg Group, shortly after the triangle zone was formed. This was first expressed by movement of conjugate planar Siberia-type faults at a range of scales, incorporating segments of earlier thrust lateral ramps. These structures probably formed in response to patchy reactivation of underlying detachment planes, analogous to distributed extensional deformation recorded above Alpine detachments (e.g. Sue & Tricart 1999, 2002). Frontal thrust ramps were then reactivated very soon afterwards (also during accumulation of the upper Klipriviersberg Group), so that new listric faults such as the Eldorado Fault broke the back of the duplex and reworked segments of Siberia-type faults as lateral ramps in the extension. The rapidity of the switch between Siberia- and Eldorado-type geometries as the dominant reactivation character implies that these structures were kinematically related. This is here interpreted to reflect the competition between displacement transfer from differential reactivation of local imbricate thrust stacks and distributed extension above underlying detachments, during the early stages of kinematic reversal. Meanwhile, north of the Maraisdal Fault, thrusting continued into late Klipriviersberg Group time, with the onset of extension in early Platberg Group time. At this time, major normal faults developed which cut through the earlier thrusts and extensional faults, such that the bulk of the seismic survey area in this study lies within the hanging-wall roll-over into a Platberg Group half-graben.

An overall rapid reversal of kinematics from thrust tectonics to active extensional graben formation is shown by the fact that it occurred during continuing extrusion within a single evolving volcanic depositional system (Klipriviersberg Group), which available dates (Armstrong *et al.* 1991; Robb *et al.* 1991) suggest may have occurred over only several million years, similar to the rapid changes seen in more modern orogens (e.g. Constenius 1996; Cavinato & De Celles 1999). However, sharp lateral partitioning of the duration of kinematic style and structural amplification is demonstrated here, such that thrusting and extension coexist along strike across the Maraisdal Fault. Thus the switch from thrusting to extension is progressive within the region, but locally very rapid.

Reactivation, fault growth and abandonment

The resolution of the 3D seismic data within this study has been calibrated by direct underground observation of faults within the seismic cube to show mapping of small faults from the seismic data to be inclusive of 10–20 m throws and some 5–10 m throws. That these faults are involved in the reactivation process is demonstrated by examining exposures of their damage zones in mine workings. However, it should be noted that the reworking of selected small-scale faults and fractures, within the damage zones, is a secondary effect that takes place to facilitate reactivation of the larger-scale feature. Small faults, exposed outboard of these damage zones, appear unaffected. Indeed, a suite of small 1–5 m throw faults in the mine plans appear unaffected by the surrounding larger-scale faults, suggesting that they are not involved in the reactivation process. Other small faults are clustered within large fault relay zones, suggesting that they are directly involved, but as newly formed secondary structures. This is analogous to development of small fault clusters in reverse reactivated normal fault relays (e.g. Kelly *et al.* 1999). The structure maps and data derived from Loraine's Mine plans and the Target seismic data show that the majority of normal faults are not single isolated faults, but are linked into, or bounded by, other faults. Consequently, the scatter and exaggerated maximum fault throw to length ratio for this dataset does not reflect the characteristics of simple 'single event' faults. Instead, the data reflect the complex interaction and capture history of the area, in which individual faults are hybrid reticulated forms.

The process of fault reactivation has generally been viewed as superimposition of a new structural regime onto an existing structural framework, usually involving a significant hiatus between events (e.g. Holdsworth *et al.* 1997). However, this paper has used an integrated well-constrained dataset, across a range of scales, to describe how a late orogenic thrust system progressively evolved to become an extensional fault system. Thus, faults formed by a combination of new segment propagation and interactive capture or reuse of pre-existing faults to form hybrid features. This involved a reactivation process (of architectural scavenging) in which pre-existing faults were reworked, in some cases several times, to perform new kinematic functions (e.g. Siberia-type normal faults captured lateral thrust structures, which were then in places subsequently recaptured as lateral structures within the Eldorado Fault Zone). Analogies to this style of kinematic reworking include reactivation of normal faults as strike-slip faults in the Sydney Basin (e.g. Peacock & Shepherd 1997), the selective reworking of basement fault arrays under transtensional conditions (e.g. Morley *et al.* 2004), and repeated alternate reworking of 'frontal' faults as thrusts and normal faults (e.g. Mirabella *et al.* 2004).

Observations in this study indicate that during the early stages of kinematic reversal the fault system was dominated by selective reactivation (architectural scavenging), but that there was a progressive reduction of the detailed influence that pre-existing structures had on the evolving extensional deformation. Similarly, in modern orogens shallow-dipping normal faults and thrust structures at higher structural levels are frequently seen to be cut shortly afterwards by larger steep normal faults (e.g. Hippolyte *et al.* 1995; D'Agostino *et al.* 1998; but see Scisciani *et al.* 2002).

Selective reactivation: fault zone weakening or fault size?

The triangle zone and the Siberia- and Eldorado-type faults were formed in rapid succession, with complex reworking patterns evident during deposition of the same Klipriviersberg Group extrusive sequence; and contemporary thrusting and extension to the north and south of the Maraisdal Fault respectively, during deposition of the upper Klipriviersberg Group. Given the rapidity of switch between Siberia- and Eldorado-type fault geometries and the repeated reworking of the fault architecture south of the Maraisdal Fault, it appears that fault orientation was a lesser restriction on fault reactivation, and also implies that all these faults formed under similar burial conditions. Indeed, the suite of fault rocks formed within all the normal fault damage zones is very similar. Consequently, as a result of the present study of the kinematics within the damage zones, it appears that the damage zone attributes, such as the zone's internal geometry (the arrangement of small-scale fault orientation distributions and clustering) and/or the geomechanical properties of the fault rocks these features contain, have influenced the detailed mechanisms by which fault damage zones were reworked and new linking faults propagated during reactivation. However, observations here suggest that fault reactivation was effectively controlled by the requirement for primary and secondary kinematic functions, and influenced by strata-mechanical juxtaposition and other geometrical considerations at many orders of magnitude larger scale. As the size of a pre-existing fault and that of other nearby larger faults (and underlying detachments) appears to be an important control on its reactivation potential, these observations are analogous to healing–reloading models of single-event fault growth (Cowie 1998; Walsh *et al.* 2001). In this sense, the 'size' of a reactivated fault refers to its whole reticulated network of newly propagated segments and incorporated pre-existing fault segments. Thus, the final geometry of such a fault is to some extent pre-programmed by the interaction of a new fault system with a pre-existing architecture. It therefore appears that the evolution of the pattern and scale of fault reactivation has been controlled to some extent by two main factors: (1) the ability of the later stress system to focus on, and resolve sufficient shear stress onto, the smaller features to exploit the weaker sections of the pre-existing fault architecture, especially in the latter stages of the evolution; (2) the strain response of the collective hanging wall to movement of major underlying detachment-scale structures.

Conclusions

(1) This paper provides a detailed study of the structural complexity associated with the transition between compressional deformation and extension associated with late orogenic evolution.

(2) It provides a detailed account of the evolution of part of the Witwatersrand Basin. This highlights the important role of rapidly extruding late orogenic volcanic rocks in changing the mechanical character of the thrust front, and thereby driving a change of structural style from fold growth to passive roof duplex.

(3) Sharp lateral partitioning of the duration of kinematic style and structural amplification took place, such that thrusting and extension initially coexisted along strike. The switch from thrusting to extension was progressive within the region, but locally very rapid.

(4) The integration of multi-scale datasets, including seismic, mine plans and underground mapping, illustrates the geometrical evolution of fault arrays, where early selective extensional reactivation follows compressional deformation. New extensional structures developed by a process of new segment propagation and 'architectural scavenging', in which certain geometrical segments of earlier formed thrust and normal faults were selectively reactivated and incorporated into the new fault arrays. Subsequent extension is accommodated on a suite of through-going faults that disaggregate the preceding fault systems.

(5) The study suggests that the rugosity of arrays of fault damage zone substructures, and the mechanical attributes of fault rocks they contain, control the detail of the reactivation and fault linkage mechanisms involved. However, the data suggest that the reactivation process is governed by scale effects.

This paper is dedicated to the memory of our former friends and colleagues in Witwatersrand studies, Mike Coward and Martin Cox. Our involvement in Witwatersrand Basin studies was particularly motivated by the insight provided by Mike Coward: his superb discussions helped with development of early ideas and work plans, and his continued interest in our progress was greatly appreciated. The study reported here is based on work conducted under contract for Avgold Limited, to whom the authors are grateful for permission to publish, granted by N. Gray and R. Tucker (our views expressed on the mechanisms of mineralization are not necessarily theirs). We thank J. McGill for help and support during data collection at Loraine and Target gold mines; A. Deiss for help collating borehole information; and W. Bradbury and G. Phillips for help drafting figures. Constructive reviews by R. Spencer, P. Cobbold, R. Butler and A. Ries helped us to improve the manuscript.

References

ARMSTRONG, R. A., COMPSTON, W., RETIEF, E. A., WILLIAMS, I. S. & WELKE, H. J. 1991. Zircon ion microprobe studies bearing on the age and evolution of the Witwatersrand triad. *Precambrian Research*, **53**, 243–266.

BARNICOAT, A. C., HENDERSON, I. H. C., KNIPE, R. J., *et al.* 1997. Hydrothermal gold mineralization in the Witwatersrand basin. *Nature*, **386**, 820–824.

BUTLER, R. W. H., GRASSO, M., & LA MANNA, F. 1992. Origin and deformation of the Neogene–Recent Maghrebian Foredeep at the Gela Nappe, SE Sicily. *Journal of the Geological Society, London*, **149**, 547–556

CAVINATO, G. P. & DE CELLES, P. G. 1999. Extensional basins in the tectonically bimodal central Apennines fold–thrust belt, Italy: response to corner flow above a subducting slab in retrograde motion. *Geology*, **27**, 955–958.

CONSTENIUS, K. N. 1996. Late Paleogene extensional collapse of the Cordilleran foreland fold and thrust belt. *Geological Society of America Bulletin*, **108**, 20–39.

COWARD, M. P. 1982. Surge zones in the Moine thrust zone of NW Scotland. *Journal of Structural Geology*, **4**, 247–256.

COWARD, M. P., SPENCER, R. M. & SPENCER, C. E. 1995. Development of the Witwatersrand Basin, South Africa. *In*: COWARD, M. P. & RIES, A. C. (eds) *Early Precambrian Processes*. Geological Society, London, Special Publications, **95**, 243–269.

COWIE, P. A. 1998. A healing–reloading feedback control on the growth rate of seismogenic faults. *Journal of Structural Geology*, **20**, 1075–1087.

D'AGOSTINO, N., CHAMOT-ROOKE, N., FUNICIELLO, R., JOLIVET, L. & SPERANZA, F. 1998. The role of pre-existing thrust faults and topography on the styles of extension in the Gran Sasso range (central Italy). *Tectonophysics*, **292**, 229–254.

EVA, E., PASTORE, S. & DEICHMANN, N. 1998. Evidence for ongoing extensional deformation in the western Swiss Alps and thrust-faulting in the southwestern Alpine foreland. *Journal of Geodynamics*, **26**, 27–43.

FISHER, Q. J. & KNIPE, R. J. 1998. Fault sealing processes in siliciclastic sediments. *In*: JONES, G., FISHER, Q. J. & KNIPE, R. J. (eds) *Faulting, Fault Sealing and Fluid Flow in Hydrocarbon Reservoirs*. Geological Society, London, Special Publications, **147**, 117–134.

FOX, N. P. C. 2002. Exploration for Witwatersrand deposits and analogues. *In*: COOKE, D. R. & PONGRATZ, J. (eds) *Giant Ore Deposits: Characteristics, Genesis and Exploration*. CODES Special Publications, **4**, 243–269.

FRIMMEL, H. E. 2005. Archaean atmospheric evolution: evidence from the Witwatersrand gold fields, South Africa. *Earth-Science Reviews*, **70**, 1–46.

FRIMMEL, H. E. & MINTER, W. E. L. 2002. Recent developments concerning the geological history and genesis of the Witwatersrand gold deposits, South Africa. *In*: MARCH, E. E., GOLDFARB, R. J. & DAY, W. C. (eds) *Global exploration 2002; integrated methods for discovery*. Society of Economic Geologists, Special Publications, **9**, 17–45.

GIBSON, M. A. S., JOLLEY, S. J. & BARNICOAT, A. C. 2000. Interpretation of the Western Ultra Deep Levels 3-D seismic survey. *Leading Edge*, **19**, 730–735.

HANNAH, J. L., STEIN, H. J., MARKEY, R. J. & SCHERSTÉN, A. 2004. Gold: a Re–Os geochronometer? *Geochimica et Cosmochimica Acta*, **68** (Suppl. 1), A773.

HATZFELD, D. 1999. The present-day tectonics of the Aegean as deduced from seismicity. *In*: DURAND, B., JOLIVET, L., HORVATH, F. & SERANNE, M. (eds) *The*

Mediterranean Basins: Tertiary Extension within the Alpine Orogen. Geological Society, London, Special Publications, **156**, 415–426.

HATZFELD, D., BESNARD, M., MAKROPOULOS, K. & HATZIDIMITRIOU, P. 1993. Microearthquake seismicity and fault-plane solutions in the southern Aegean and its geodynamic implications. *Geophysical Journal International*, **115**, 799–818.

HIPPOLYTE, J.-C., ANGELIER, J. & BARRIER, E. 1995. Compressional and extensional tectonics in an arc system: example of the Southern Appenines. *Journal of Structural Geology*, **17**, 1725–1740.

HOLDSWORTH, R. E., BUTLER, C. A. & ROBERTS, A. M. 1997. The recognition of reactivation during continental deformation. *Journal of the Geological Society, London*, **154**, 73–78.

JOLIVET, L., FRIZON DE LAMOTTE, D., MASCLE, A. & SERANNE, M. 1999. The Mediterranean basins: Tertiary extension within the Alpine orogen — an introduction. *In*: DURAND, B., JOLIVET, L., HORVATH, F. & SERANNE, M. (eds) *The Mediterranean Basins: Tertiary Extension within the Alpine Orogen*. Geological Society, London, Special Publications, **156**, 1–14.

JOLLEY, S. J., HENDERSON, I. H. C., BARNICOAT, A. C. & FOX, N. P. C. 1999. Thrust-fracture network and hydrothermal gold mineralization: Witwatersrand Basin, South Africa. *In*: MCCAFFREY, K. J. W., LONERGAN, L. & WILKINSON, J. (eds) *Fractures, Fluid Flow and Mineralization*. Geological Society, London, Special Publications, **155**, 153–165.

JOLLEY, S. J., FREEMAN, S. R., BARNICOAT, A. C., *et al.* 2004. Structural controls on Witwatersrand gold mineralisation. *Journal of Structural Geology*, **26**, 1067–1086.

KELLER, J. V. A. & COWARD, M. P. 1996. The structure and evolution of the Northern Tyrrhenian Sea. *Geological Magazine*, **133**, 1–16.

KELLY, P. G., PEACOCK, D. C. P., SANDERSON, D. J. & MCGURK, A. C. 1999. Selective reverse-reactivation of normal faults, and deformation around reverse-reactivated faults in the Mesozoic of the Somerset coast. *Journal of Structural Geology*, **21**, 493–509.

KINGSLEY, C. S. 1987. Facies changes from fluvial conglomerate to braided sandstone of the early Proterozoic Eldorado Formation, Welkom Goldfield, South Africa. *In*: ETHRIDGE, F. G., FLORES, R. M., HARVEY, M. D. & WEAVER, J. N. (eds) *Recent Developments in Fluvial Sedimentology*. Society of Economic Paleontologists and Mineralogists, Special Publications, **39**, 359–370.

KIRK, J., RUIZ, J., CHESLEY, J., TITLEY, S. & WALSHE, J. 2001. A detrital model for the origin of gold and sulfides in the Witwatersrand basin based on Re–Os isotopes. *Geochimica et Cosmochimica Acta*, **65**, 2149–2159.

KIRK, J., RUIZ, J., CHESLEY, J., WALSHE, J. & ENGLAND, G. 2002. A major Archean gold and crust-forming event in the Kaapvaal Craton, South Africa. *Science*, **297**, 1856–1858.

LAW, R. D., CASEY, M. & KNIPE, R. J. 1986. Kinematic and tectonic significance of microstructures and crystallographic fabrics within quartz mylonites from the Assynt and Eriboll regions of the Moine thrust zone, NW Scotland. *Transactions of the Royal Society of Edinburgh: Earth Sciences*, **77**, 99–126.

LAW, R. D., SEARLE, M. P. SIMPSON, R. L. 2004. Strain, temperature and vorticity of flow at top of the Greater Himalayan Slab, Everest Massif, Tibet. *Journal of the Geological Society, London*, **161**, 305–320.

LAWTON, T. F., ROCA, E. & GUIMERÀ, J. 1999. Kinematic–stratigraphic evolution of a growth syncline and its implications for tectonic development of the proximal foreland basin, southeastern Ebro basin, Catalunya, Spain. *Geological Society of America Bulletin*, **111**, 412–431.

MACKAY, P. A., VARSEK, J. L., KUBLI, T. E., DECHESNE, R. G., NEWSON, A. C. & REID, J. P. (eds) 1996. *Triangle Zones and Tectonic Wedges*. Bulletin of Canadian Petroleum Geology, Special Issue, **44**, 139–422.

MINTER, W. E. L. 1978. A sedimentological synthesis of placer gold, uranium, and pyrite concentrations in Proterozoic Witwatersrand sediments. *In*: MIALL, A. D. (ed.) *Fluvial Sedimentology*. Canadian Society of Petroleum Geologists, Memoirs, **5**, 801–829.

MINTER, W. E. L. 1999. Irrefutable detrital origin of Witwatersrand gold and evidence of aeolian signatures. *Economic Geology*, **94**, 665–670.

MIRABELLA, F., CIACCIO, M. G., BARCHI, M. R. & MERLINI, S. 2004. The Gubbio normal fault (Central Italy): geometry, displacement distribution and tectonic evolution. *Journal of Structural Geology*, **26**, 2233–2249.

MOHAPATRA, G. K. & JOHNSON, R. A. 1998. Localization of listric faults at thrust fault ramps beneath the Great Salt Lake basin, Utah: evidence from seismic imaging and finite element modelling. *Journal of Geophysical Research*, **103**, 10047–10063.

MORLEY, C. K., HARANYA, C., PHOOSONGSEE, S., KORNSAWAN, A. & WONGANAN, N. 2004. Activation of rift oblique and rift parallel pre-existing fabrics during extension and their effect on deformation style: examples from the rifts of Thailand. *Journal of Structural Geology*, **26**, 1803–1829.

MYERS, R. E., MCCARTHY, T. S., BUNYARD, M., *et al.* 1990. Geochemical stratigraphy of the Klipriviersberg Group volcanic rocks. *South African Journal of Geology*, **93**, 224–238.

NEWMAN, J. & MITRA, G. 1993. Lateral variations in mylonite zone thickness as influenced by fluid–rock interactions, Linville Falls fault, North Carolina. *Journal of Structural Geology*, **15**, 849–863.

NIGRO, F. & RENDA, P. 2004. Growth pattern of underlithified strata during thrust-related folding. *Journal of Structural Geology*, **26**, 1913–1930.

OWENS, A. C. & JOLLEY, S. J. 1993. *The geochemistry and structure of dykes and sills at Loraine Gold Mine Limited.* Anglovaal Ltd, Unpublished Report, **TEC/ACO/6**.

PEACOCK, D. C. P. & SHEPHERD, J. 1997. Reactivated faults and transfer zones in the Southern Coalfield, Sydney Basin, Australia. *Australian Journal of Earth Sciences*, **44**, 265–273.

PHILLIPS, G. N. & LAW, J. D. M. 2000. Witwatersrand gold fields: geology, genesis and exploration. *Society for Economic Geology Reviews*, **13**, 439–500.

PHILLIPS, G. N. & MYERS, R. E. 1989. The Witwatersrand Goldfields: Part I. An origin for Witwatersrand gold during metamorphism and associated alteration. *In*: KEAYS, R. R., RAMSAY, W. R. H. & GROVES, D. I. (eds) *The Geology of Gold Deposits: Perspective in 1988*. Economic Geology Monographs, **6**, 598–608.

ROBB, L. J., DAVIS, D. W. & KAMO, S. L. 1991. Chronological framework for the Witwatersrand Basin and environs: towards a time-constrained depositional model. *South African Journal of Geology*, **94**, 86–95.

ROYDEN, L. H. & BURCHFIEL, B. C. 1987. Thin-skinned north–south extension within the convergent Himalayan region: gravitational collapse of a Miocene topographic front. *In*: COWARD, M. P. DEWEY, J. D. & HANCOCK, P. L. (eds) *Continental Extensional Tectonics*. Geological Society, London, Special Publications, **28**, 611–619.

SCHAEFER, B. F., PEARSON, D. G., ROGERS, N. W. & BARNICOAT, A. C. 2004. Re–Os isotope and PGE constraints on the timing and origin of gold mineralisation in the Witwatersrand basin. *Geochimica et Cosmochimica Acta*, **68** (Suppl. 1), A773.

SCISCIANI, V., TAVARNELLI, E. & CALAMITA, F. 2002. The interaction of extensional and contractional deformations in the outer zones of the Central Apennines, Italy. *Journal of Structural Geology*, **24**, 1647–1658.

SMIT, C. M. & SCHEEPERS, R. 2000. Microstructural constraints on Au mineralization in selected areas of the Welkom goldfield, Witwatersrand basin, South Africa. *Journal of African Earth Sciences*, **31**, 71–72.

SMIT, C. M., SCHEEPERS, R. & PRZYBYLOWICZ, W. 2001. The morphology and trace element composition of pyrite from the Dreyerskuil Member at Target, Witwatersrand Basin, South Africa: implications for secondary gold mineralization. *In*: STONE, G. (ed.) *National Accelerator Centre Annual Report 2001*. National Accelerator Centre, Somerset West, South Africa.

STUART, G. W., JOLLEY, S. J., POLOMÉ, L. & TUCKER, R. F. 2000. Application of 3D seismic attribute analysis to mine planning: Target gold deposit, South Africa. *Leading Edge*, **19**, 736–742.

SUE, C. & TRICART, P. 1999. Late-Alpine brittle extension above the Frontal Pennine Thrust near Briancon, Western Alps. *Eclogae Geologicae Helvetiae*, **92**, 171–181.

SUE, C. & TRICART, P. 2002. Widespread post-nappe normal faulting in the Internal Western Alps: a new constraint on arc dynamics. *Journal of the Geological Society, London*, **159**, 61–70.

TAVARNELLI, E. 1999. Normal faults in thrust sheets: pre-orogenic extension, post-orogenic extension, or both? *Journal of Structural Geology*, **21**, 1011–1018.

TOWNSEND, C., FIRTH, I. R., WESTERMAN, R., KIRKEVOLLEN, L., HARDE, M. & TORILL, A. 1998. Small seismic-scale fault identification and mapping. *In*: JONES, G., FISHER, Q. J. & KNIPE, R. J. (eds) *Faulting, Fault Sealing and Fluid Flow in Hydrocarbon Reservoirs*. Geological Society, London, Special Publications, **147**, 1–25.

VAN DER WESTHUIZEN, W. A., DE BRUIYN, H. & MEINTJES, P. G. 1991. The Ventersdorp Supergroup: an overview. *Journal of South African Earth Sciences*, **13**, 83–105.

WALSH, J. J., CHILDS, C., MEYER, V., *et al.* 2001. Geometric controls on the evolution of normal fault systems. *In*: HOLDSWORTH, R. E., STRACHAN, R. A., MAGLOUGHLIN, J. F. & KNIPE, R. J. (eds) *The Nature and Tectonic Significance of Fault Zone Weakening*. Geological Society, London, Special Publications, **186**, 157–170.

WEST, M. W. 1993. Extensional reactivation of thrust faults accompanied by coseismic surface rupture, southwestern Wyoming and north–central Utah. *Geological Society of America Bulletin*, **105**, 1137–1150.

WILLIAMS, E. A., FORD, M., VERGÉS, J. & ARTONI, A. 1998. Alluvial gravel sedimentation in a contractional growth fold setting, Sant Llorenç de Mornys, southeastern Pyrenees. *In*: MASCLE, A., PUIGDEFÀBREGAS, C., LUTERBACHER, H. P. & FERNÀNDEZ, M. (eds) *Cenozoic Foreland Basins of Western Europe*. Geological Society, London, Special Publications, **134**, 69–106.

WINTER, H. DE LA R. 1987. A cratonic foreland model for Witwatersrand Basin development in a continental back-arc, plate-tectonic setting. *South African Journal of Geology*, **90**, 409–427.

Reactivated Palaeozoic normal faults: controls on the formation of Carlin-type gold deposits in north-central Nevada

JOHN L. MUNTEAN[1], MICHAEL P. COWARD[2] & CHARLES A. TARNOCAI[3]

[1]*Nevada Bureau of Mines and Geology, Mail Stop 178, University of Nevada, Reno, NV 89557-0088, USA (e-mail: munteanj@unr.edu)*

[2]*Ries–Coward Associates Ltd, 70 Grosvenor Road, Caversham, Reading RG4 5ES, UK*

[3]*Oro Gold Resources Ltd, Suite 1440–625 Howe Street, Vancouver, British Columbia, Canada V6C 2T6*

Abstract: Mappable surface structures control linear trends of Carlin-type gold deposits in north–central Nevada. Some of these structures probably resulted from reactivation of Palaeozoic normal faults, linked to underlying basement faults that originated during rifting of western North America during the Proterozoic. These old faults served as conduits for deep crustal hydrothermal fluids responsible for formation of Carlin-type gold deposits in the Eocene. The reactivated structures are recognized by stratigraphic and structural features. Stratigraphic features include rapid facies changes, growth fault sequences and sedimentary debris-flow breccias. Structural features resulted from inversion of the normal faults during the Late Palaeozoic Antler and subsequent orogenies. Inversion features include asymmetric hanging-wall anticlines, flower-like structures, and 'floating island' geometries. Inversion resulted in structural culminations that occur directly over the basement faults, providing an optimal setting for the formation of Carlin-type gold deposits.

North–central Nevada is one of the world's most important gold provinces. More than 6000 tonnes of gold have been produced or identified (Nevada Bureau of Mines and Geology 2004). The vast majority of the gold occurs in deposits known as Carlin-type gold deposits because of similarities to the famous Carlin gold mine. Carlin-type gold deposits are epigenetic, disseminated auriferous pyrite deposits characterized by carbonate dissolution, argillic alteration, and silicification of typically calcareous sedimentary rocks (Hofstra & Cline 2000; Cline *et al.* 2006). They formed during a short time interval in the Eocene between *c.* 42 and 36 Ma (Hofstra *et al.* 1999; Tretbar *et al.* 2000; Arehart *et al.* 2003). The alignment of ore deposits in Nevada has been recognized for many years (e.g. Roberts 1960, 1966). The Carlin and Battle Mountain–Eureka trends are the two best known alignments of Carlin-type gold deposits. The Carlin and Battle Mountain–Eureka trends have been demonstrated to correspond to gross geophysical and isotopic features (see Grauch *et al.* 2003), including gradients in basement gravity (Grauch *et al.* 1995), zones of electrical conductivity (Rodriguez 1998) and initial strontium and lead isotope ratios of Mesozoic and Tertiary igneous rocks (Wooden *et al.* 1998; Tosdal *et al.* 2000). In this paper it is argued that the Carlin and Battle Mountain–Eureka trends correspond to reactivated Palaeozoic normal fault zones that probably had their origins in the Proterozoic during rifting of the western margin of North America, as suggested by Tosdal *et al.* (2000). Mappable geological features that define the Carlin and Battle Mountain–Eureka trends and possibly new trends of Carlin-type gold deposits are described.

Rifting of the western margin of North America resulted in deposition of dominantly quartzite, and siltstone, in latest Proterozoic to earliest Cambrian times. Development of the passive margin sequence continued through the Devonian with deposition of interbedded carbonates and shales on the shelf and, to the west, silty carbonate units along the continental slope. By the end of the Devonian, at least 8–10 km of sediments were deposited (Stewart 1972, 1980; Stewart & Poole 1974; Bond *et al.* 1985; Poole *et al.* 1992). In earliest Mississippian times, deep-water siliciclastic and basaltic rocks (referred to here as the upper plate) were thrust eastward over the shelf-slope sequence (referred to here as the lower plate) along the Roberts Mountain Thrust during the Antler Orogeny (Roberts 1951; see also Poole *et al.* 1992). Subsequent compressional events in the Late Palaeozoic and Mesozoic include the Humboldt, Sonoma, Elko and Sevier orogenies (see Stewart 1980; Thorman *et al.* 1991; Burchfiel *et al.* 1992).

From: RIES, A. C., BUTLER, R. W. H. & GRAHAM, R. H. (eds) 2007. *Deformation of the Continental Crust: The Legacy of Mike Coward*. Geological Society, London, Special Publications, **272**, 571–587.

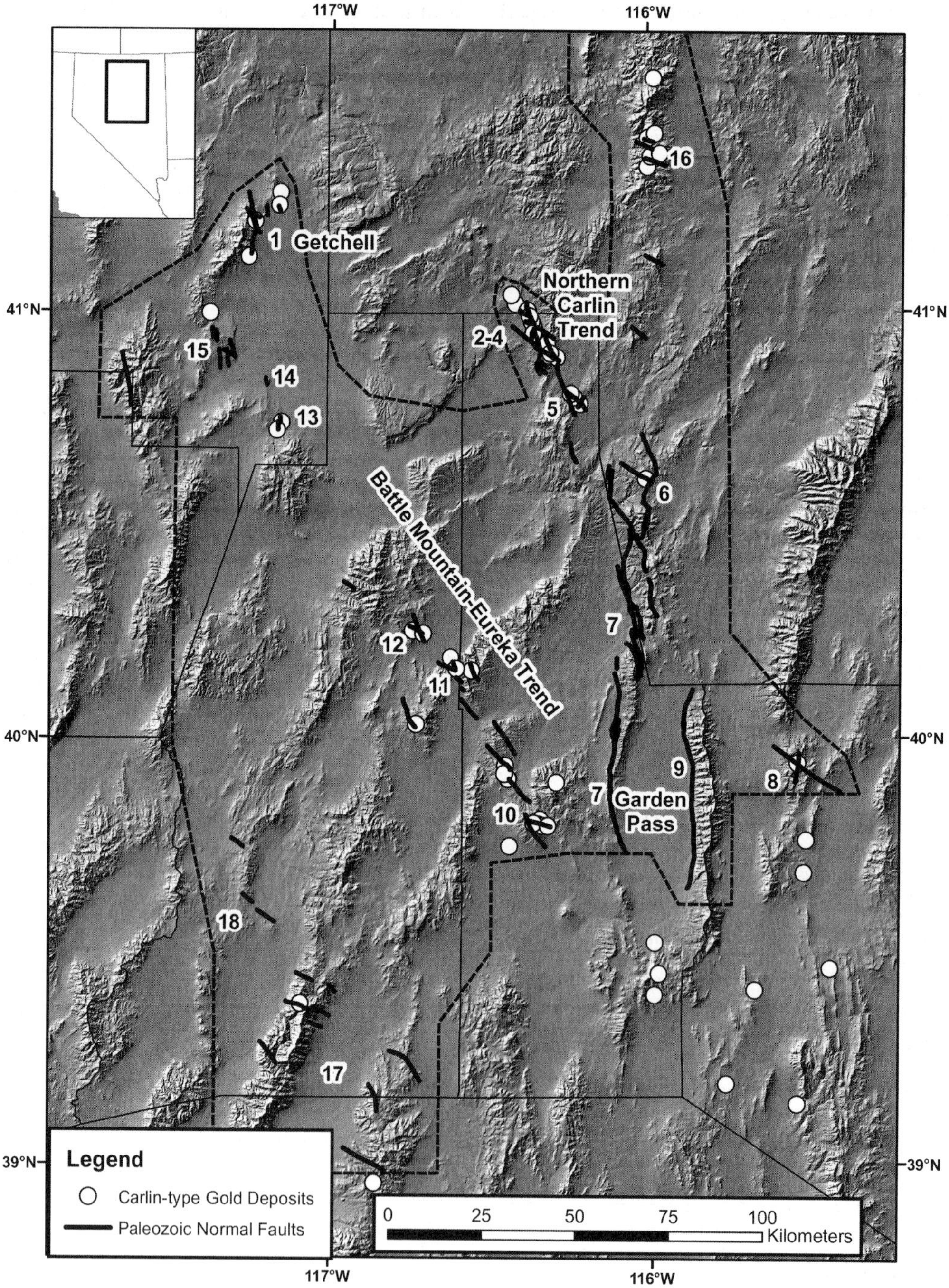

Fig. 1. Shaded relief map of north–central Nevada showing locations of Carlin-type gold deposits and Palaeozoic normal faults identified in this study. The corresponding numbers refer to the list in Table 3. The dashed line delimits the area that was analysed for this study. For reference, the continuous lines outline counties in north–central Nevada.

In the Eocene, north–central Nevada experienced an abrupt shift in tectonic activity from compression to extension and renewed magmatism (see Burchfiel *et al.* 1992; Christiansen & Yeats 1992; Cline *et al.* 2005).

Typically, 'thin-skinned' fold and thrust features that formed during the Late Palaeozoic and Mesozoic orogenies have been described in Nevada (see Stewart 1980). However, inversion of Proterozoic extensional faults during the Late Mesozoic–Early Tertiary Laramide Orogeny has been documented to the east in the Rocky Mountains (e.g. Davis 1978; Marshak *et al.* 2000). 'Thick-skinned' deformation and inversion features, which are typical of deformed cratonic margins worldwide (see Coward 1994), have been only rarely described for Nevada in the literature (e.g. Carpenter *et al.* 1993; Tosdal 2001; Cline *et al.* 2005). Yigit *et al.* (2003) suggested that Palaeozoic normal faults may have controlled gold mineralization in the Gold Bar district in Nevada. However, they interpreted fault-propagation folds and thrust faults, with imbricate splay geometries in the Gold Canyon deposit, to have developed over the tips of major low-angle thrust faults rather than by inversion of a high-angle Palaeozoic normal fault (Yigit *et al.* 2003, fig. 15). A major goal of this paper is to present evidence consistent with inversion and 'thick-skinned' deformation in several localities throughout north–central Nevada. The other goal of the paper is to present a spatial relationship between Palaeozoic normal faults and the location of Carlin-type gold deposits and argue that the faults served as the main conduits for deep auriferous hydrothermal fluids, sourced from the middle to lower crust.

Evidence for Palaeozoic normal faults in north–central Nevada

Based on analysis of published geological maps, field checks, mine visits, review of literature and local detailed mapping, evidence has been found for Palaeozoic normal faults throughout north–central Nevada (Fig. 1). In addition to typical methods of dating earliest movement on structures (offset of units of known age, stratigraphic superimposition), we identified both stratigraphic features (Table 1) and features of fault inversion (Table 2) that suggest the presence of Palaeozoic normal faults.

Features of fault inversion include characteristic fold and fault geometries that form when normal faults are reactivated during compressional orogenies, as summarized by

Table 1. *Sedimentary and stratigraphic relationships used to recognize Palaeozoic normal faults*

(1) Thickening, thinning or abrupt facies changes in Palaeozoic rocks, especially towards faults
(2) Growth fault sequences
(3) Sedimentary breccias with linear boundaries
(4) Reefs or other shallow carbonate sequences forming on the top of tilted fault blocks
(5) Syngenetic barite or sulphide occurrences in the lower plate of the Roberts Mountains Thrust
(6) Local absences of widespread stratigraphic units

Table 2. *Inversion and other structural features used to recognize Palaeozoic normal faults*

(1) Fault propagation folds: fold geometries that involve long, gently dipping backlimbs and short, steep forelimbs
(2) Monoclines
(3) Related kinematics between folds and high-angle faults
(4) 'Flower structures': radiating arrays of faults in the steep forelimb area that root on a master fault (wedge-shaped in section) and are subparallel in trend to the axial plane of the associated anticline
(5) Footwall shortcut thrust faults
(6) 'Floating-island' geometries
(7) Narrow zones of anomalously trending fold axes within a thrust terrain
(8) Refolded or non-cylindrical folded upper plate rocks
(9) Folded thrust faults
(10) Zones of upright to inclined, tight to isoclinal folds in rocks that otherwise have recumbent or open folds
(11) High-angle reverse faults
(12) Folds with anomalous vergence

Williams *et al.* (1989) and Coward (1994). The development of such geometries is schematically illustrated in Figure 2. First, normal faulting results in the formation of a synrift growth sequence (C in Fig. 2a) overlying pre-rift basement and sediments (A and B in Fig. 2a), followed by later deposition of post-rift sediments (D and E in Fig. 2a). During compression, reverse reactivation of the original normal fault causes development of an asymmetric hanging-wall anticline, which forms where hanging-wall rocks are displaced from the original normal fault onto a new higher level along a more gently dipping thrust (Fig. 2b). The synrift growth sequence is folded into a characteristic harpoon shape. The hanging wall anticline in the post-rift sediments has the characteristics of a fault propagation fold. The shortcut thrust may splay

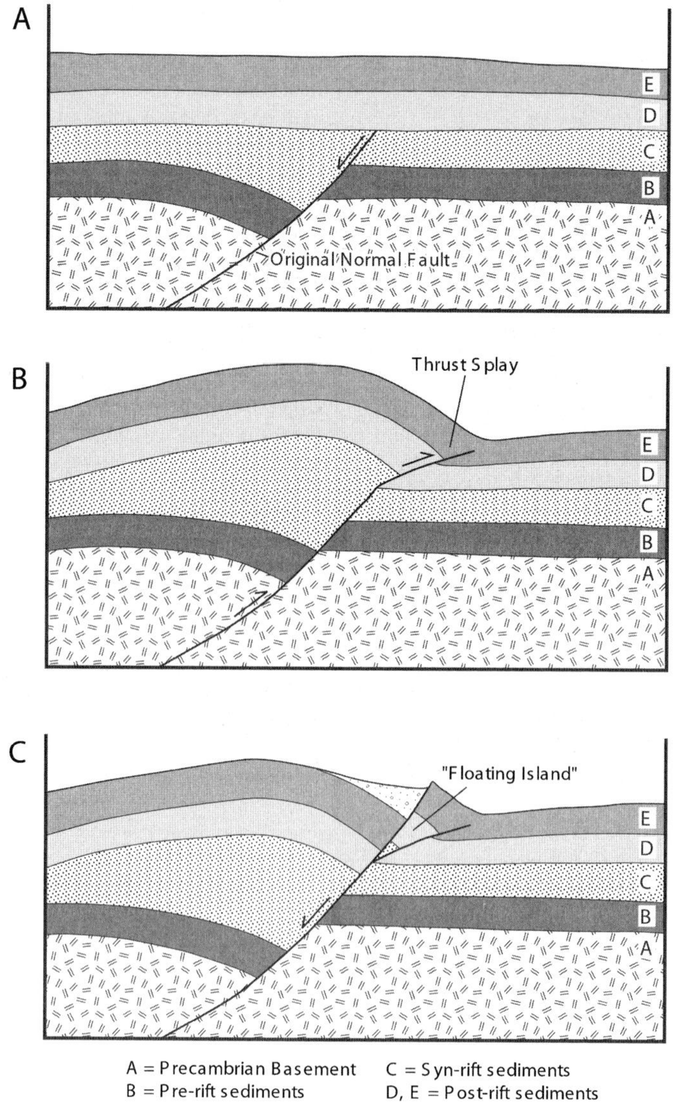

Fig. 2. Schematic cross-sections showing idealized geometries that develop during inversion of a normal fault. (**a**) Normal faulting, deposition of synrift growth sequence (C) over basement (A) and pre-rift sediments (B), and later deposition of post-rift sediments (D, E). (**b**) Inversion and formation of thrust splay and hanging-wall anticline. (**c**) Later extension and formation of 'floating island'. Modified partly from Williams *et al.* (1989).

Table 3. *Interpreted Palaeozoic and older normal faults*

Locality	Evidence	References
(1) Getchell–Twin Creeks	(1) Abrupt linear N70°W boundary to a sequence of sedimentary debris-flow breccias and basalts that were deposited along a monocline, inferred to have formed during extensional reactivation of a buried high-angle WNW-trending normal fault (2) NNW-trending faults (e.g. Getchell Fault) show local folded growth features in their hanging walls, as interpreted from seismic sections (3) Local occurrences of sedimentary exhalative sulphide occurrences (4) Conelea Anticline at Twin Creeks interpreted to be an inversion-related fault-propagation fold that was truncated during emplacement of Roberts Mountain Allochthon (5) Pennsylvanian–Permian Etchart Limestone is substantially thicker in the hanging wall of the Getchell Fault and contains abundant quartzite pebble conglomerate layers that were probably derived during fault growth from Cambrian–Ordovician quartzite in the footwall (6) Narrow zone of tight, symmetrical NNW-trending folds in the Etchart Limestone in the hanging wall of the parallel west-dipping Midway Fault	Breitt *et al.* 2005; Stenger *et al.* 1998; Placer Dome Exploration staff, Pers comm., 1999; Bloomstein *et al.* 1991; this study
(2) Carlin trend (general)	(1) Zone of anomalous fold axes: fold axes in lower and upper plate rocks trend NW within the Carlin trend and trend NE outside the Carlin trend	Evans & Theodore 1978
(3) N5°E to N35°W Post-Gen Fault System; northern Carlin trend	(1) Asymmetric anticlines with fold axes parallel to the Post-Gen Fault System, including the Tuscarora Spur and Post Anticlines; these anticlines precede emplacement of the 158 Ma Goldstrike Stock (2) Shortcut thrust, west-verging asymmetric Ernie Anticline and 'floating island' at Rodeo (3) Reverse faults (e.g. Ridge Fault) and normal faults with reverse drag features (e.g. J series faults) (4) Abundant debris-flow breccias, especially those surrounding the pillar-shaped biohermal Bootstrap Limestone forming at top of tilted fault block in footwall of Post Fault at Meikle (5) Lower plate Devonian sedimentary exhalative sulphide occurrences	Leonardson & Rahn 1996; Armstrong *et al.* 1998; Emsbo *et al.* 1999; Moore 2001; Volk *et al.* 2001; this study
(4) N60-70°W faults; northern Carlin trend	(1) Asymmetric N60–70°W anticlines (West Bazza and Betze Anticlines) (2) Betze Anticline does not involve rocks higher in the section than the lower half of the Devonian Rodeo Creek Fm (3) West Bazza flower structure (4) Abrupt facies boundary extending N60–70°W from Meikle between shelf biohermal and ooloidal limestones of the Devonian Bootstrap Limestone to the north and debris-flow breccias and laminated slope carbonates of the time-equivalent Popovich Fm to the south that strongly suggests synsedimentary Devonian faulting	Leonardson & Rahn 1996; Armstrong *et al.* 1998; Lauha 1998; Griffin 2000; Moore 2001; Bettles 2002
(5) Gold Quarry	(1) N50°W Good Hope reverse fault, interpreted here to be the result of inversion	Harlan *et al.* 2002
(6) Rain	(1) Late Mississippian to Early Pennsylvanian Tonka Fm, which is part of the post-Antler overlap sequence, was deposited on a paleosurface that bevelled different levels of the Early Mississippian Antler fold and thrust belt as well as N60–70°W-striking Early Mississippian normal faults, including the Rain Fault, that cut the fold and thrust belt; the Mississippian normal faults were inverted during late Palaeozoic(?) southward-directed shortening as steeply to moderately dipping reverse faults (2) Flower structure with radiating array of faults that results in a 'floating island' geometry	Williams *et al.* 2000; Tosdal 2001; Cline *et al.* 2005

Table 3. *Continued*

Locality	Evidence	References
(7) Piñon and Sulfur Springs Ranges	(1) Erosional removal of Devonian Devil's Gate Limestone and exhumation of the Devonian Telegraph Canyon Fm as a result of asymmetric, high-angle fault propagation folds, prior to emplacement of Roberts Mountain Allochthon (2) Presence of carbonate debris-flow breccias locally in the lower plate Devonian Telegraph Canyon Fm dolomites, near Union Pass (3) Asymmetric anticlines with N5°E–N25°W-trending fold axes that fold the Roberts Mountain thrust (4) Locally sourced angular quartzite fragments in conglomerate of the Permian Garden Valley Fn, which are in hangingwall of high-angle fault with quartzites of the Devonian Oxyoke Canyon Fm in the footwall, near Garden Pass	Carlisle & Nelson 1990; Carpenter *et al.* 1993; This study
(8) Bald Mountain	(1) WNW distribution of: (a) Mississippian Diamond Peak Fm conglomerate facies, (b) Pennsylvanian Ely Fm reef facies, (c) multiple facies transitions in the Permian Arcturas Fm, and (d) Permian Carbon Ridge platform facies, from the Diamond Mountains to the Butte Range (2) Asymmetric N50–60°W anticline along northeastern flank of NW-aligned late Jurassic Bald Mountain Stock; Cambrian–Ordovician strata in the anticline have lateral facies changes to carbonate debris-flow breccias (3) NNE-trending reverse faults	Cox & Otto 1995; Nutt *et al.* 2000; This study
(9) Diamond Range	(1) Thick Permian conglomerates are interpreted to be recording Permian extension (2) Overturned asymmetric anticline–syncline pairs	Nolan *et al.* 1971; This study
(10) Roberts Mountains	(1) Asymmetric NW-trending anticlines that fold the Roberts Mountain thrust (2) Flower structures in the steep forelimb of the NW-trending asymmetric anticline in Gold Canyon open pit (3) Transverse WNW-trending anticline associated with Gold Bar satellite gold deposits	Murphy *et al.* 1978; Yigit *et al.* 2003; This study
(11) Cortez	(1) Both WNW and NNW-trending asymmetric anticlines that fold the Roberts Mountain thrust in the hanging wall of the Cortez Fault (2) Ordovician Eureka Quartzite unconformably overlies the Cambrian Hamburg Dolomite; nearly 1000 m of Cambrian and Ordovician stratigraphy is missing (Cambrian Dunderberg and Windfall Fms, Ordovician Pogonip Group) (3) West-verging recumbent folds in Horse Canyon open pits, interpreted to be anticlines related to shortcut thrusts in the footwall of the NNW-trending Horse Canyon fault zone	Gilluly & Masursky 1965; Ross 1977; This study
(12) Pipeline–Gold Acres	(1) N15–30°W-trending asymmetric, east-verging anticline just west of the Pipeline open pit (2) N50–60°W folds in low-angle shear zone that hosts Pipeline (3) Narrow zone of tight N50–60°W folds along the northern margin of Gold Acres west of Pipeline open pit	Foo *et al.* 1996*a*,*b*; Wrucke, 1974; This study
(13) Marigold	(1) Truncation of NNW-trending high-angle normal faults by Golconda Thrust (Early Triassic) in the 8 South open pit (2) Abrupt lateral facies changes including thick hanging-wall sedimentary breccias in Pennsylvanian Edna Mtn Fm., which thin away from NNW-trending faults	Marigold mine staff, pers. comm., 1999; McGibbon & Wallace 2000
(14) Lone Tree	(1) Conglomerates of the Pennsylvanian Battle Fm with clasts of quartzite thin considerably away from Lone Tree Hill, which is composed of quartzite of the Ordovician Valmy Fm	Lone Tree mine staff, Pers. comm. 1999

Table 3. *Continued*

Locality	Evidence	References
(15) Edna Mountains	(1) Pennsylvanian Highway Limestone thins out in hanging walls away from NNW-trending faults (2) Conglomerates of the Pennsylvanian Battle Fm thin considerably toward axes of WNW-trending folds, suggesting palaeotopographic high (3) NNW-trending reverse fault that places Cambrian Preble Fm up against Ordovician Valmy Fm	Erickson & Marsh 1974*a,b*; This study
(16) Jerritt Canyon	(1) 'Floating island' in the footwall of the WNW-trending New Deep Fault in the Murray Mine (2) WNW faults are filled by 320 Ma andesite dykes (3) WNW faults interpreted as lateral ramps to SE-directed thrusting and duplexing	Hofstra *et al.* 1999; Dewitt 2001; Jones 2005
(17) Austin area (Toiyabe and Toquima ranges)	(1) WNW-trending monoclines that overprint the prominent NNE structural trend in the ranges (2) Cambrian to Early Mississippian strata and structures are cut and tilted by north-dipping normal faults and then bevelled and overlain by Pennsylvanian to Early Permian sedimentary sequences with local mafic lava flows	McKee, 1968, 1976; Smith & Miller, 1990
(18) Ravenswood (southern Shoshone Range)	(1) NW-trending asymmetric anticline and monoclines that overprint the prominent NNE structural trend in the range and fold Roberts Mountain Thrust	This study

into imbricate fans, which can be termed in a descriptive sense a 'flower structure'. Such flower structures in Nevada have commonly been attributed to strike-slip faulting (e.g. Lauha 1998; Williams *et al.* 2000). Thrusts like this can create 'floating islands' (Fig. 2c). When a later phase of normal motion along the inverted fault takes place, as during Teritary extension in Nevada. The hanging wall is dropped down and a wedge of older rocks is created between younger rocks in a triangular-shaped zone of deformation. If a footwall shortcut thrust does not form and movement of the hanging wall along the original normal fault ceases, upright to inclined, tight to isoclinal, symmetrical folds can form in the hanging wall.

Many of the inversion geometries illustrated in Figure 2 and listed in Table 2 are present in north–central Nevada and are described in this paper; namely, fault-propagation folds, flower structures and floating islands. However, none of these features are unique to inversion. As pointed out by Cooper *et al.* (1989), inversion cannot be unequivocally recognized unless folded growth sequences are present. Therefore, except for growth fault sequences, either folded or unfolded, few if any of the features in Tables 1 and 2 prove the existence of Palaeozoic normal faults. This paper does not fully document any folded growth sequences. However, it is believed that the presence of several features in Tables 1 and 2 at given localities in Figure 1 is highly suggestive of a Palaeozoic normal fault, and, at a minimum, Palaeozoic normal faults and subsequent inversion of those faults should be considered as a viable hypothesis to explain the observed features. Table 3 lists the localities numbered in Figure 1 and the corresponding, supporting evidence for Palaeozoic normal faults. Next, more detailed evidence is presented for Palaeozoic normal faults at Garden Pass, in the northern Carlin trend, and in the Getchell district.

Garden Pass

At Garden Pass (Fig. 1), a half-graben bounded by a west-dipping fault contains conglomerates, sandstones and sandy limestones of Permian age (Garden Valley Formation) (Figs 3 and 4). The Permian rocks rest on the Ordovician Vinini Formation, which is in the upper plate of the Roberts Mountain Thrust. In the footwall of the fault are Devonian dolomites and locally quartzites that are in the lower plate of the Roberts Mountain Thrust. Within the Permian rocks there is a prominent conglomerate that

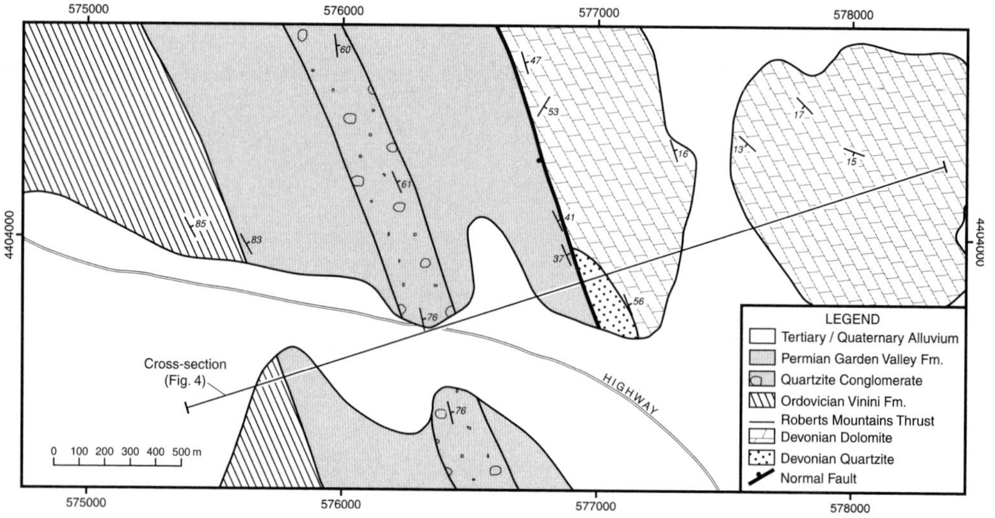

Fig. 3. Map of Garden Pass area completed during this study, showing location of cross-section in Figure 4. Coordinates are UTM metres (NAD 27, Zone 11). (See text for discussion.)

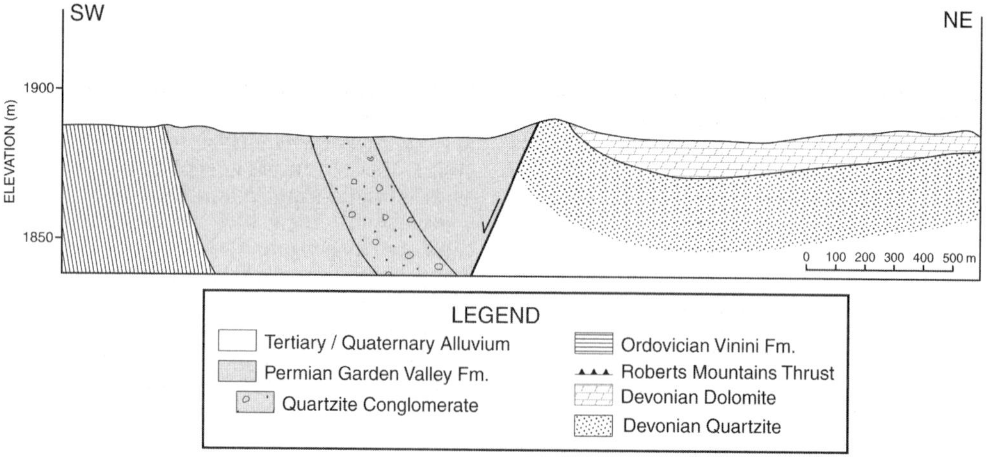

Fig. 4. Cross-section of Garden Pass area looking N15°W.

contains angular, pebble- to cobble-sized clasts of quartzite that appear to be identical to the Devonian quartzite in the footwall, strongly suggesting fault growth during the Permian. The Permian rocks were subsequently folded into a hanging-wall anticline during Mesozoic compression, as interpreted in Figure 5. There are continuations of this fault or similar faults all along the western edge of the ranges, north of Garden Valley Pass (Fig. 1).

Northern Carlin trend

First, evidence for inversion of a buried Palaeozoic (or older) normal fault zone at the scale of the entire Carlin trend (Fig. 1) comes from regional inspection of fold axes. Evans & Theodore (1978) first demonstrated that the Carlin trend corresponds to a zone of anomalously trending fold axes. Outside the Carlin trend fold axes trend mostly NNE, fairly typical

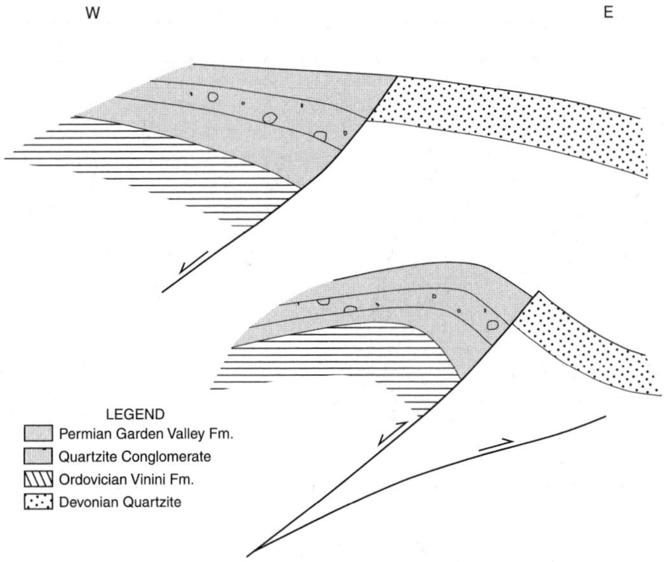

Fig. 5. Schematic cross-section of Garden Pass area, illustrating interpreted development of inversion structures at Garden Pass. Top: partially restored cross-section showing original Permian normal fault. Bottom: development of fault-propagation fold during Mesozoic inversion. See text for discussion.

of folds associated with the Antler Orogeny and subsequent compressional events. However, within the Carlin trend, in a zone <10 km wide, fold axes trend NW, parallel to the alignment of Carlin-type gold deposits.

Ample stratigraphic evidence for Palaeozoic normal faulting exists in the northern Carlin trend (Figs 1 and 6). Northwest of the Post-Betze open pit, Palaeozoic normal faulting is suggested by a rapid facies change over a distance of <800 m across a WNW-trending boundary (Armstrong *et al.* 1998; Griffin 2000; Moore 2001; Bettles 2002). Massive oolitic, fossiliferous limestones of the Devonian Bootstrap Limestone, indicative of shallow high-energy conditions, occur to the NE. To the SW, laminated muddy limestones and debris-flow breccias of the time-equivalent Popovich Formation indicate a transition to deeper water. At the Meikle Mine, a prominent pillar of Bootstrap Limestone in the footwall of the Post Fault is surrounded by carbonate debris-flow breccias (Volk *et al.* 1995). Such relationships are characteristic of reefs forming on the tops of tilted fault blocks (see Enos & Moore 1983). Gold-bearing sedimentary exhalative sulphide occurrences in the Popovich Formation (Emsbo *et al.* 1999) also suggest the presence of synsedimentary faulting.

Examples of fold geometries in the northern Carlin trend, consistent with inversion, are illustrated with cross-sections in Figure 7. At the Rodeo Mine (Fig. 7a), the N30°W-trending Ernie Anticline is a tight asymmetric west-verging fold in the hanging wall of the parallel Ernie Fault, which is a reverse fault (Baschuk 2000). The vergence is anomalous in that most folds associated with the Antler and subsequent orogenies are east-verging. The Ernie Fault can be interpreted as a footwall shortcut thrust associated with inversion of the Post Fault. The Post Fault was later reactivated in the Tertiary with a significant normal component, resulting in a 'floating island' preserved between the Ernie and Post faults. The parallel Post Anticline in the Post-Betze open pit and the Tuscarora Anticline, to the south in the Genesis open pit, are analogous to the Ernie Anticline.

At West Bazza (Fig. 7b), a series of N60–70°W-trending high- and low-angle south-dipping faults, with a characteristic radiating geometry, has been interpreted as a flower structure, related to strike-slip faulting (Lauha 1998). The geometry is interpreted here as a radiating array of shortcut thrusts. These faults have parallel-trending, asymmetric north-verging anticlines in their hanging walls. Again, as at Rodeo, there are characteristic 'floating islands', where reverse motion is preserved in the hanging wall of the lower-angle shortcut thrusts but not in the hanging wall of the original higher-angle normal

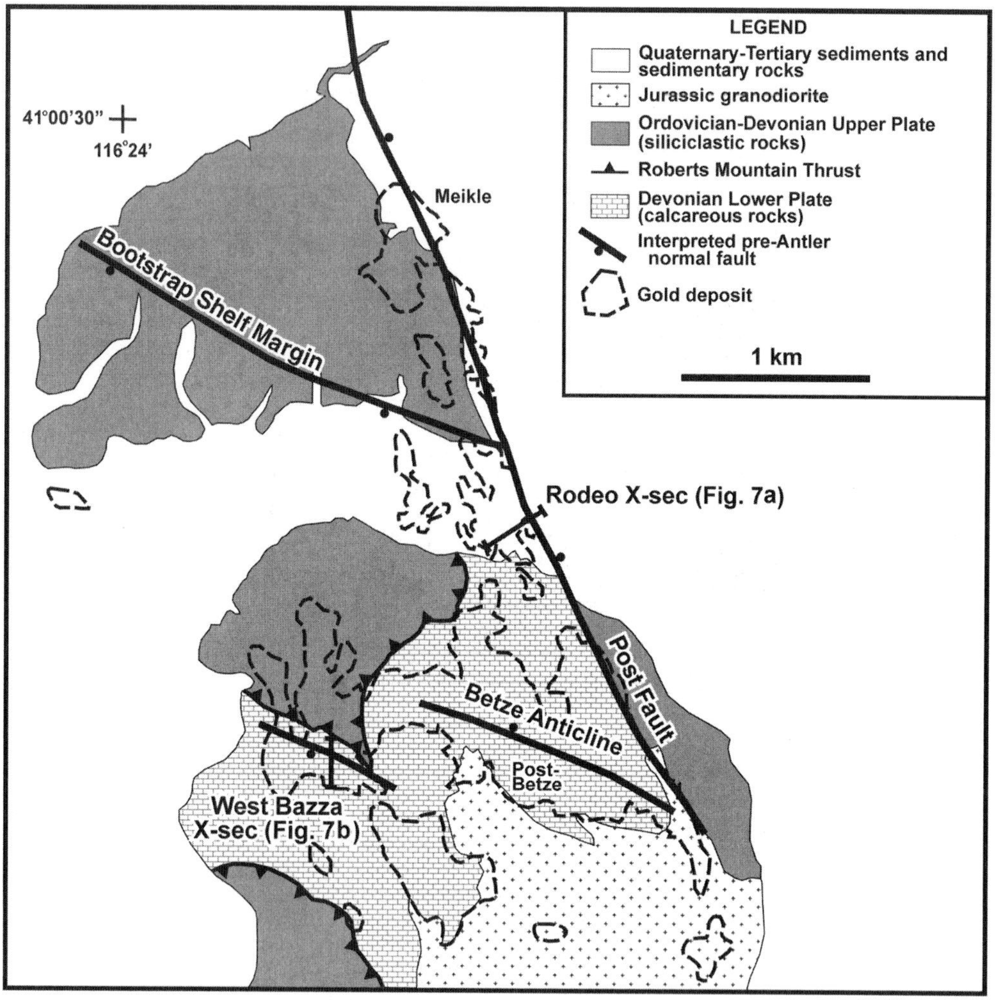

Fig. 6. Map of the northern Carlin trend, modified from Bettles (2002) and Moore (2002), showing the location of interpreted Palaeozoic normal faults and cross-sections (Fig. 7) discussed in text.

fault. The shortcut thrusts are locally intruded by Jurassic dykes, indicating that the structure is at least Jurassic in age (Lauha 1998). The flower structure in the West Bazza Pit is parallel, but with opposite vergence, to the Betze Anticline, a main ore-control in the Post-Betze open pit. The Betze Anticline has been related to the emplacement of the Jurassic Goldstrike Stock (Leonardson & Rahn 1996); however, the folds predate the Goldstrike Stock, as argued by Moore (2001). Both the West Bazza and Betze anticlines are interpreted to be related to reactivation of Palaeozoic WNW-trending faults that developed along the southern boundary of the Bootstrap Limestone shelf.

Getchell

As for the northern Carlin trend, evidence for both NNW- and WNW-trending Palaeozoic normal faults is present in the Getchell district (Figs 1 and 8). A lower sequence of pillow basalt and underlying sedimentary debris-flow breccias of Cambrian–Ordovician age has a sharp N70°W southern margin that is an important ore control to the Turquoise Ridge deposit (Fig. 8). The margin occurs along the northern limb of a monocline that is interpreted to have formed by syndepositional reactivation of an underlying north-dipping, WNW-trending Palaeozoic normal fault (Placer Dome Exploration, pers.

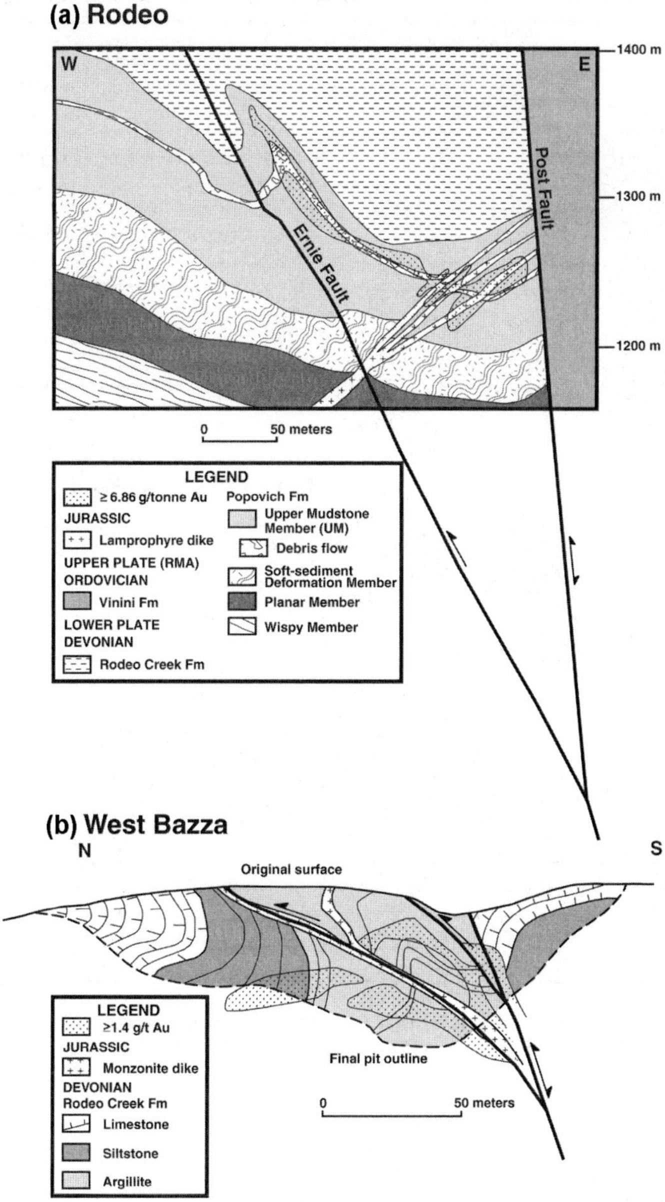

Fig. 7. Examples of inverted Palaeozoic normal faults in the northern Carlin trend. Bold lines are the interpreted inversion-related faults. (**a**) Cross-section of the Rodeo deposit looking N30°W, modified from Baschuk (2000). The Ernie Fault is interpreted to be a shortcut thrust related to inversion of the Post Fault as represented by the interpreted projections of the faults below the box enclosing the cross-section. The reverse separation on the Ernie Fault and the tight asymmetric anticline in its hanging wall should be noted; and that the top of the cross-section is *c*. 250 m below the surface. The section is based on fans of closely spaced underground core holes, which are not shown here, but were shown by Baschuk (2000). (**b**) Cross-section of the West Bazza pit looking east, modified from Lauha (1998). The radiating array of shortcut thrusts (bold lines), which shows net contraction, should be noted. The Palaeozoic normal fault, to the right, shows net extension. All of the faults have hanging wall anticlines.

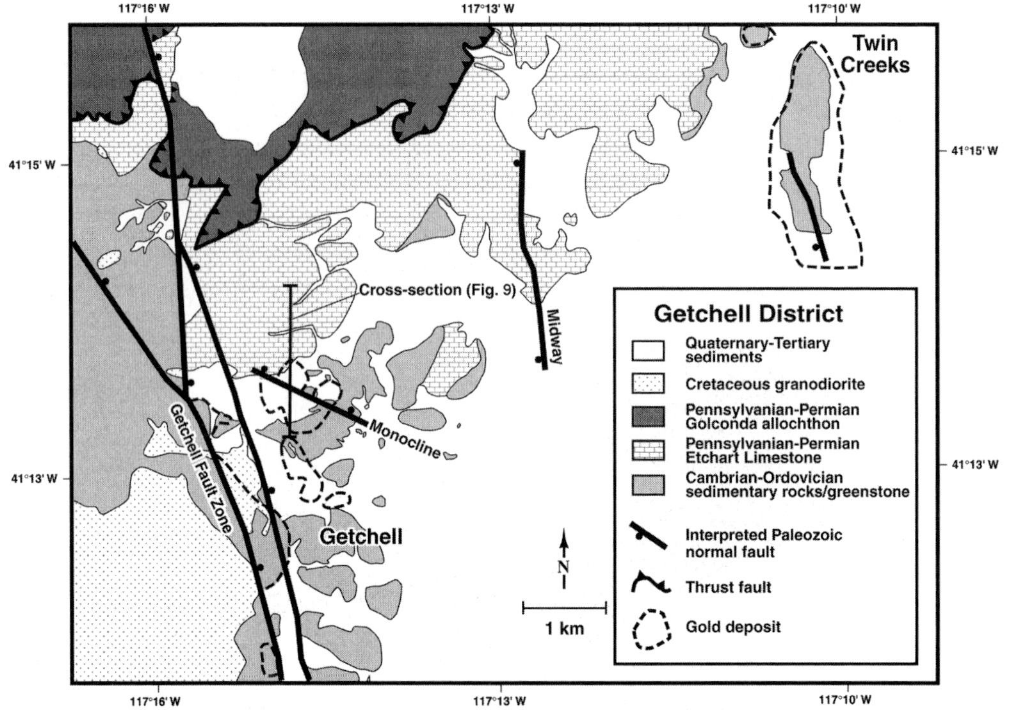

Fig. 8. Geological map of the Getchell–Twin Creeks area, based mostly on mapping by Hotz & Willden (1964) and unpublished mapping by Placer Dome geologists. The map shows location of interpreted Palaeozoic normal faults discussed in the text and the location of the cross-section shown in Figure 9.

comm., 1999; Fig. 9). In addition, folded growth sequences along east-dipping faults with NNW strikes, such as the Getchell Fault, are interpreted from seismic sections. At the Twin Creeks gold deposit, just to the east, the asymmetric NW-trending, east-verging Conelea Anticline, located in the hanging wall of the parallel Lopear Thrust (Bloomstein *et al.* 1991), is a fault-propagation fold, interpreted here to be the result of inversion of a west-dipping NNW-trending normal fault. The Conelea Anticline is truncated by what was interpreted by Breit *et al.* (2005) to be the Roberts Mountain Thrust.

Post-Antler reactivation of the Getchell Fault is evident in the Pennsylvanian–Permian Etchart Limestone. The Etchart Limestone appears to be substantially thicker east of the Getchell Fault and contains abundant interbeds of quartzite pebbles (Fig. 8). The pebbles appear to be derived from Cambrian and Ordovician quartzite located in the footwall of the Getchell Fault, suggesting that there was fault growth during deposition of the Etchart Limestone. The Etchart Limestone was broadly folded (*c.* 2 km wavelengths) along NE-trending axes during the Golconda and/or subsequent Mesozoic orogenies, but inversion is evident in a narrow zone of tight, symmetrical NNW-trending folds in the Etchart Limestone in the hanging wall of the parallel west-dipping Midway Fault (Fig. 8).

Relationship between Palaeozoic normal faults and Carlin-type deposits

Comparisons demonstrate a remarkable similarity between Carlin-type deposits in all districts in Nevada (Cline *et al.* 2005). Although isotopic differences suggest different fluid sources at some deposits, detailed studies show that all districts display broadly similar styles of mineralization and alteration over vertical scales of at least 1 km and up to 20–35 km laterally in individual districts. The large hydrothermal systems responsible for Carlin-type gold deposits are characterized by low-salinity fluids (mostly *c.* 2–3 wt% NaCl equivalent), moderate CO_2 contents (<4 mol%), high Au/Ag ratios, high Au/base metal ratios, a Au–As–Hg–Sb association, moderate temperatures (180 and 240 °C), a lack

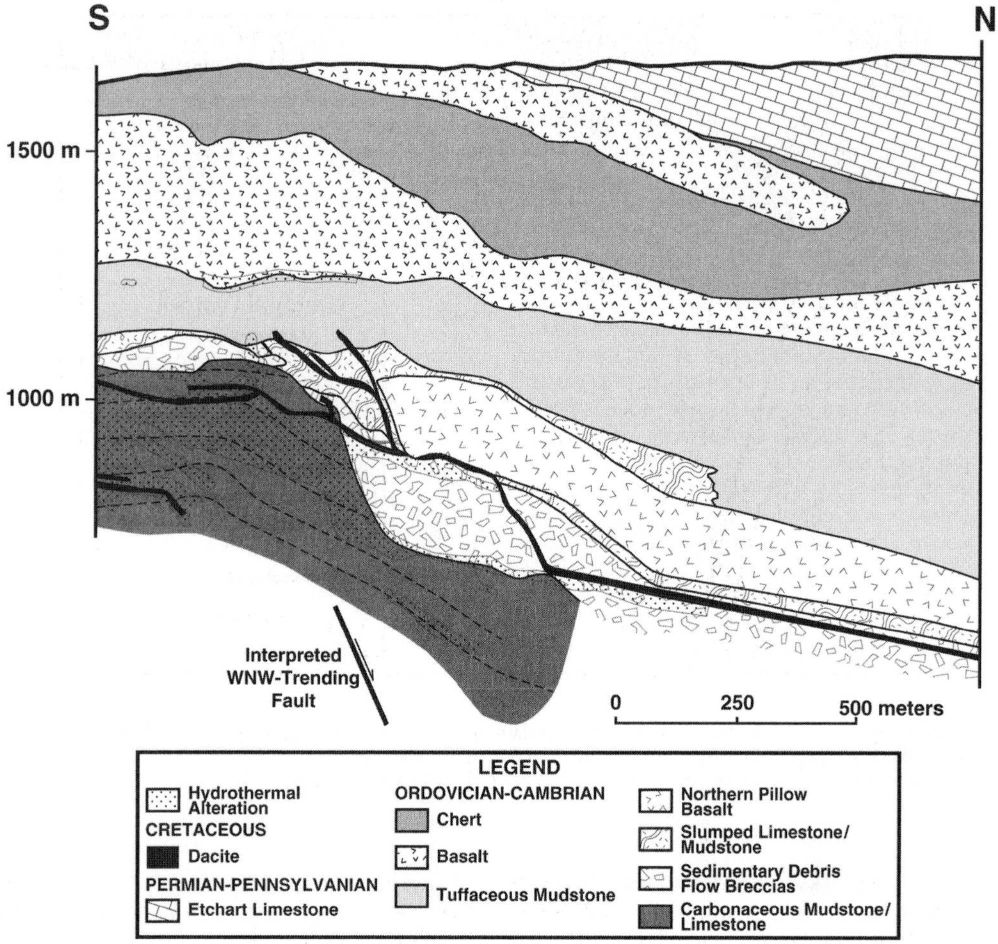

Fig. 9. North–south section (867600E) looking west through the north part of the Turquoise Ridge deposit at Getchell based on work completed during this study, showing WNW-trending monocline. As discussed in the text, the monocline is interpreted to have formed by syndepositional normal reactivation of an underlying normal fault. The monocline formed the margin to a basin that filled initially with carbonate debris-flow breccias and then with pillow basalt. The section is based on surface core holes (not shown) spaced 30 m apart.

of consistent alteration and metal zoning, and a coincidence with regional thermal events (see Hofstra & Cline 2000; Cline *et al.* 2005). These characteristics are broadly consistent with other hydrothermal systems that form other types of large 'gold-only' deposits in the world, such as orogenic gold deposits. As originally pointed out by Phillips & Powell (1993), such deposits form from a uniform ore fluid that required a large and uniform source. They suggested that deep crustal-scale processes could best generate such a fluid. Although most stable isotope data indicate exchanged meteoric waters as the main source of hydrothermal fluids, data from Getchell and the Deep Star deposit in the northern Carlin trend point towards a magmatic or metamorphic fluid source (Cline & Hofstra 2000; Heitt *et al.* 2003). The fluid source may be exchanged meteoric, magmatic or metamorphic, rather than having a local source associated with epizonal stocks and shallow convecting meteoric water, such as a porphyry-related hydrothermal system that would exhibit strong lateral zoning patterns in metals and alteration (i.e. Sillitoe & Bonham 1990). Cline *et al.* (2005) concluded that hydrothermal fluids, responsible for the formation of Carlin-type deposits, had their origins during removal of the Farallon slab below north–central Nevada in the Eocene, which promoted deep crustal melting, prograde metamorphism and devolatilization, thus generating deep, primitive fluids. In the upper crust, ore fluids were then diluted by exchanged meteoric waters, prior to depositing gold within a few kilometres of the surface.

Figure 1 shows a close spatial correlation between the proposed Palaeozoic normal faults and the location of Carlin-type gold deposits. Zones of Palaeozoic normal faults are coincident with the Carlin and Battle Mountain–Eureka trends. There is an inherent bias because this study focused on mine areas where the exposure is better and there is much more information. However, Figure 1 also shows proposed Palaeozoic normal faults well away from known mines. As shown in Figure 1 and described in Table 3, Palaeozoic normal faults that have been identified in this study mostly trend NNW (N0–30°W) and WNW (N50–70°W). Studies of rift strata and dyke swarms in the Rocky Mountains, the Colorado Plateau and the Mid-continent indicate that WNW-trending faults originally formed during a rifting event between 1.1 and 1.3 Ga, and formation of north-trending faults and reactivation of WNW-trending faults occurred between 0.7 and 0.9 Ga (Marshak *et al.* 2000; Timmons *et al.* 2001). Thorman & Ketner (1979) first pointed out evidence for N50–70°W-trending basement faults of probable Proterozoic origin in northeastern Nevada (e.g. Wells Fault) based on offset of regional stratigraphic and structural features.

The coincidence of these Proterozoic features with the Palaeozoic faults identified in this study, strongly suggests that the faults are linked at depth with basement faults, formed during continental rifting of western North America in Proterozoic times and were continually reactivated in the Early Palaeozoic during the formation of the continental margin. Such basement-penetrating, linked high-angle fault systems probably have a greater vertical extent than later faults and served as the main collecting points and conduits for deep, gold-bearing crustal fluids responsible for Carlin-type mineralization in the Eocene. Inversion of these fault systems during the Antler and subsequent orogenies commonly resulted in structural culminations, especially where NNW- and WNN-trending Palaeozoic normal faults intersect. Subsequent erosion of these culminations led to the currently observed windows of lower plate rocks. The superimposition of these structural culminations over Palaeozoic normal faults created an optimal setting for the formation of Carlin-type gold deposits.

This paper would not be possible without the support and contributions of many geologists. From Placer Dome, including the Cortez, Bald Mountain, and Turquoise Ridge mines, we would like to acknowledge J. Thorson, R. Conelea, P. Klipfel, A. Norman, R. Marcio, V. Chevillon, G. Edmondo, R. Hays, K. Balleweg, J. Hebert, T. Thompson, J. Brady, S. Thomas, D. Bahrey, K. Wood and A. Dorff. We especially acknowledge A. Jackson and E. Gonzales-Urien of Placer Dome for suggesting the study and supporting it to its completion. The mine staffs of Newmont Mining, Barrick Gold, Anglo Gold, and Glamis Gold are congratulated for graciously giving mine tours and publishing data from their properties. J.L.M. is especially grateful to Placer Dome, specifically W. Howald and G. Hall, for allowing publication of these data and concepts that were generated with his colleagues during his tenure with Placer Dome as an exploration geologist. We also thank C. Thorman and E. Nelson for their constructive reviews of the manuscript. Also, J.L.M. will be eternally indebted to Mike Coward for opening his eyes to the forest as well as the trees.

References

Arehart, G. B., Chakurian, A. M., Tretbar, D. R., Christensen, J. N., McInnes, B. A. & Donelick, R. A. 2003. Evaluation of radioisotope dating of Carlin-type deposits in the Great Basin, Western North America, and implications for deposit genesis. *Economic Geology*, **98**, 235–248.

Armstrong, A. K., Theodore, T. G., Oscarson, R. L. *et al.* 1998. Preliminary facies analysis of Silurian and Devonian autochthonous rocks that host gold along the Carlin trend, Nevada. United States. *In*: Tosdal, R. M. (ed.) *Contributions to the Gold Metallogeny of Northern Nevada.* US Geological Survey Open-File Report, **98–338**, 38–68.

Baschuk, G. J. 2000. Lithological and structural ore controls within the upper zone of Barrick's Rodeo deposit, Eureka County, Nevada. *In*: Cluer, J. K., Price, J. G., Struhsacker, E. M., Hardyman, R. F. & Morris, C. L. (eds) *Geology and Ore Deposits 2000: the Great Basin and Beyond.* Geological Society of Nevada, Reno, 989–1001.

Bettles, K. 2002. Exploration and geology, 1962 to 2002, at the Goldstrike property, Carlin trend, Nevada. *In*: Goldfarb, R. J. & Nielsen, R. L. (eds) *Integrated Methods for Discovery: Global Exploration in the Twenty-first Century.* Society of Economic Geologists Special Publications, **9**, 275–298.

Bloomstein, E. I., Massingill, G. L., Parratt, R. L. & Peltonen, D. R. 1991. Discovery, geology, and mineralization of the Rabbit Creek gold deposit, Humboldt county, Nevada. *In*: Raines, G. L., Lisle, R. E., Schafer R. W., & Wilkinson, W. H. (eds) *Geology and Ore Deposits of the Great Basin.* Geological Society of Nevada, Reno, 821–843.

BOND, G. C., CHRISTIE-BLICK, N., KOMINZ, M. A. & DEVLIN, W. J. 1985. An early Cambrian rift to post-rift transition in the Cordillera of western North America. *Nature*, **316**, 742–745.

BREIT, F. J., RESSEL, M. W., ANDERSON, S. D. & MARNIE-MUIRHEAD, E. M. 2005. Geology and gold deposits of the Twin Creeks Mine, Humboldt County, Nevada. *Field Trip Guidebook 4, Sediment-Hosted Gold Deposits of the Getchell District, Nevada. Symposium 2005 Window to the World.* Geological Society of Nevada, Reno, 77–102.

BURCHFIEL, B. C., COWAN, D. S. & DAVIS, G. A. 1992. Tectonic overview of the Cordilleran orogen in the western United States. *In*: BURCHFIEL, B. C., LIPMAN, P. W., & ZOBACK, M. L. (eds) *The Geology of North America, the Cordilleran Orogen: Conterminous U.S.* Geological Society of America Decade in North American Geology Series, **G-3**, 9–56.

CARLISLE, D. & NELSON, C. A. 1990. *Geologic Map of the Mineral Hill Quadrangle, Nevada.* Nevada Bureau of Mines and Geology Map, **97**.

CARPENTER, J. A., CARPENTER, D. G. & DOBBS, S. W. 1993. Structural analysis of the Pine Valley area, Nevada. *Nevada Petroleum Society 1993 Field Conference Guidebook*, 9–49. Nevada Petroleum Society, Inc, Reno, Nevada.

CHRISTIANSEN, R. L. & YEATS, R. S. 1992. Post-Laramide geology of the U.S. Cordilleran region. *In*: BURCHFIEL, B. C., LIPMAN, P. W. & ZOBACK, M. L. (eds) *The Geology of North America, the Cordilleran Orogen: Conterminous U.S.* Geological Society of America, Decade in North American Geology Series, **G-3**, 261–406.

CLINE, J. S. & HOFSTRA, A. H. 2000. Ore fluid evolution at the Getchell Carlin-type gold deposit, Nevada, USA. *European Journal of Mineralogy*, **12**, 195–212.

CLINE, J. S., HOFSTRA, A. H., MUNTEAN, J. L., TOSDAL, R. M. & HICKEY, K. A. 2005. Carlin-type gold deposits in Nevada: critical geologic characteristics and viable models. *In*: HEDENQUIST, J. W., THOMPSON, J. F. H., GOLDFARB, R. J. & RICHARDS, J. P. (eds) *Economic Geology 100th Anniversary Volume*. Society of Economic Geologists, inc, Littleton, Colorado, 451–484.

COOPER, M. A., WILLIAMS, G. D., DE GRACIANSKY, P. C. *et al.* 1989. Inversion tectonics — a discussion. *In*: COOPER, M. A. & WILLIAMS, G. D. (eds) *Inversion Tectonics*. Geological Society, London, Special Publications, **44**, 335–347.

COWARD, M. 1994. Inversion tectonics. *In*: HANCOCK, P. L. (ed.) *Continental Deformation*. Permagon, Oxford, 289–304.

COX, B. E. & OTTO, B. R. 1995. *Interim report for the Bald Mountain–Alligator Ridge regional geologic mapping project*. Unpublished Placer Dome US internal report.

DAVIS, G. H. 1978. Monocline fold pattern of the Colorado Plateau. *In*: MATTHEWS, V., III (ed.) *Laramide Folding Associated with Basement Block Faulting in the Western United States*. Geological Society of America, Memoirs, **151**, 215–233.

DEWITT, A. B. 2001. Structural architecture of the Jerritt Canyon district and gold deposits. *In*: SHADDRICK, D. R, ZBINDEN, E., MATHEWSON, D. C. & PRENN, C. (eds) *Regional Tectonics and Structural Control of Ore: the Major Gold Trends of Northern Nevada*. Geological Society of Nevada Special Publications, **33**, 135–145.

EMSBO, P., HUTCHINSON, R. W., HOFSTRA, A. H., VOLK, J. A., BETTLES, K. H., BASCHUK, G. J. & JOHNSON, C. A. 1999. Syngenetic Au on the Carlin trend: implications for Carlin-type deposits. *Geology*, **27**, 59–62.

ENOS, P. & MOORE, C. H. 1983. Fore-reef slope. *In*: SCHOLLE, P. A., BEBOUT, D. G. & MOORE, C. H. (eds) *Carbonate Depositional Environments.* American Association of Petroleum Geologists Memoirs, **33**, 507–538.

ERICKSON, R. L. & MARSH, S. P. 1974*a*. *Geologic Map of the Iron Point Quadrangle, Humboldt County, Nevada*. US Geological Survey Map, **GQ-1175**.

ERICKSON, R. L. & MARSH, S. P. 1974*b*. *Geologic Map of the Golconda Quadrangle, Humboldt County, Nevada*. US Geological Survey Map, **GQ-1174**.

EVANS, J. G. & THEODORE, T. G. 1978. *Deformation of the Roberts Mountains Allochthon in North–Central Nevada.* US Geological Survey, Professional Papers, **1060**.

FOO, S. T., HAYS, R. C., JR & MCCORMACK J. K. 1996*a*. Geology and mineralization of the Pipeline gold deposit, Lander county, Nevada. *In*: COYNER, A. R. & FAHEY, P. L. (eds) *Geology and Ore Deposits of the American Cordillera*. Geological Society of Nevada, Reno, 95–109.

FOO, S. T., HAYS, R. C., JR & MCCORMACK J. K. 1996*b*. Geology and mineralization of the South Pipeline gold deposit, Lander county, Nevada. *In*: COYNER, A. R. & FAHEY, P. L. (eds) *Geology and Ore Deposits of the American Cordillera*. Geological Society of Nevada, Reno, 111–121.

GILLULY, J. & MASURSKY, H. 1965. *Geology of the Cortez Quadrangle, Nevada*. US Geological Survey Bulletin, **1175**.

GRAUCH, V. J. S., JACHENS, R. C. & BLAKELY, R. J. 1995. Evidence for a basement structure related to the Cortez disseminated gold deposit trend and implications for regional exploration in Nevada. *Economic Geology*, **90**, 203–207.

GRAUCH, V. J. S., RODRIGUEZ, B. D. & WOODEN, J. L. 2003. Geophysical and isotopic constraints on crustal structure related to mineral trends in north–central Nevada and implications for tectonic history. *Economic Geology*, **98**, 269–286.

GRIFFIN, G. L. 2000. Paleogeography of late Silurian–Devonian autochthonous carbonates: implications for old faults and intrusive distribution, Goldstrike property, Nevada (abstract). *In*: CLUER, J. K., PRICE, J. G., STRUHSACKER, E. M., HARDYMAN, R. F. & MORRIS, C. L. (eds) *Geology and Ore Deposits 2000: the Great Basin and Beyond.* Geological Society of Nevada, Reno, A8.

HARLAN, J. B., HARRIS, D. A., MALLETE, P. M., NORBY, J. W., ROTA, J. C. & SAGAR, J. J. 2002. Geology and mineralization of the Maggie Creek District. *In*: THOMPSON, T. B., TEAL, L. & MEEUWIG, R. O. (eds) *Gold Deposits of the Carlin Trend.* Nevada Bureau of Mines and Geology Bulletin, **111**, 115–142.

HEITT, D. G., DUNBAR, W. W., THOMPSON, T. B. & JACKSON, R. G. 2003. Geology and geochemistry of the Deep Star gold deposit, Carlin trend, Nevada. *Economic Geology*, **98**, 1107–1136.

HOFSTRA, A. H. & CLINE, J. S. 2000, Characteristics and models for Carlin-type gold deposits. *In*: HAGEMANN, S. E. & BROWN, P. E. (eds) *Gold in 2000*. Reviews in Economic Geology, **13**, 163–220.

HOFSTRA, A. H., SNEE, L. W., RYE, R. O. *et al.* 1999. Age constraints on Jerritt Canyon and other Carlin-type gold deposits in the western United States—relationship to mid-Tertiary extension and magmatism. *Economic Geology*, **94**, 769–802.

HOTZ, P.E. & WILLDEN, R. 1964. *Geology and Mineral Deposits of the Osgood Mountains Quadrangle, Humboldt County, Nevada*. US Geological Survey, Professional Papers, **431**.

JONES, M. 2005. Jerritt Canyon district Independence Mountains, Elko County, Nevada, gold's at fault. *In:* CALICRATE, T., LEAVITT, E., O'MALLEY, P. & CRAFFORD, E. J. (eds) *Field Trip Guidebook 8, Sediment-Hosted Gold Deposits of the Independence Range, Nevada. Symposium 2005 Window to the World*. Geological Society of Nevada, Reno, 99–122.

LAUHA, E. A. 1998. The West Bazza pit and its relationship to the Screamer deposit. *In:* KIZIS, J. A. (ed.) *Shallow Expressions of Deep, High-Grade Gold Deposits*. Geological Society of Nevada Special Publications, Reno, **28**, 133–145.

LEONARDSON, R. W. & RAHN, J. E. 1996, Geology of the Betze–Post gold deposits, Eureka County, Nevada. *In*: COYNER, A. R. & FAHEY, P. L. (eds) *Geology and Ore Deposits of the American Cordillera*. Geological Society of Nevada, Reno, 61–94.

MARSHAK, S., KARLSTROM, K. & TIMMONS, J. M. 2000. Inversion of Proterozoic extensional faults: An explanation for the pattern of Laramide and Ancestral Rockies intracratonic deformation, United States. *Geology*, **28**, 735–738.

MCGIBBON, D. H. & WALLACE, A. B. 2000. Geology of the Marigold area, *In*: THEODORE, T. G. (ed.) *Geology of Pluton-related Gold Mineralization at Battle Mountain, Nevada*. Monographs in Mineral Resource Science, Center for Mineral Resources, University of Arizona, **2**, 222–240.

MCKEE, E. H. 1968. *Geologic Map of the Austin Quadrangle, Lander County, Nevada*. US Geological Survey Map, **GQ-1307.**

MCKEE, E. H. 1976. *Geology of the Northern Part of the Toquima Range, Lander, Eureka, and Nye Counties, Nevada*. US Geological Survey, Professional Papers, **931.**

MOORE, S. 2001. Ages of fault movement and stepwise development of structural fabrics on the Carlin trend. *In*: SHADDRICK, D. R., ZBINDEN, E., MATHEWSON, D. C. & PRENN, C. (eds) *Regional Tectonics and Structural Control of Ore: the major Gold Trends of Northern Nevada*. Geological Society of Nevada, Special Publications, **33**, 71–89.

MOORE, S. 2002. Geology of the northern Carlin trend (map). *In*: THOMPSON, T. B., TEAL, L. & MEEUWIG, R. O. (eds) *Gold Deposits of the Carlin Trend*. Nevada Bureau of Mines and Geology Bulletin, **111**.

MURPHY, M. A., MCKEE, E. H., WINTERER, E. L., MATTI, J. C. & DUNHAM, J. B. 1978. *Preliminary Geologic Map of the Roberts Creek Quadrangle, Nevada*. US Geological Survey Open-File Report, 78–376.

Nevada Bureau of Mines and Geology. 2004. *The Nevada Mineral Industry 2003*. Nevada Bureau of Mines and Geology, Special Publications, **MI-2003**.

NOLAN, T. B., MERRIAM, C. W. & BREW, D. A. 1971. *Geologic Map of the Eureka Quadrangle, Eureka and White Pine Counties, Nevada*. US Geological Survey Map, **I-612**.

NUTT, C. J., HOFSTRA, A. H., HART, K. S. & MORTENSEN, J. K. 2000. Structural setting and genesis of gold deposits in the Bald Mountain–Alligator Ridge area, east–central Nevada. *In*: CLUER, J. K., PRICE, J. G., STRUHSACKER, E. M., HARDYMAN, R. F. & MORRIS, C. L. (eds) *Geology and Ore Deposits 2000: the Great Basin and Beyond*. Geological Society of Nevada, Reno, 513–537.

PHILLIPS, G. N. & POWELL, R. 1993. Link between gold provinces. *Economic Geology*, **88**, 1084–1098.

POOLE, F. G., STEWART, J. H., PALMER, A. R. *et al.* 1992. Latest Precambrian to latest Devonian time: Development of a continental margin. *In*: BURCHFIEL, B. C., LIPMAN, P. W. & ZOBACK, M. L. (eds) *The Geology of North America, the Cordilleran Orogen: Conterminous U.S.* Geological Society of America, Decade in North American Geology Series, **G-3**, 9–56.

ROBERTS, R. J. 1951. *Geology of the Antler Peak Quadrangle, Nevada*. US Geological Survey Map, **GQ-10**.

ROBERTS, R. J. 1960. *Alignment of Mining Districts in North–Central Nevada*. US Geological Survey, Professional Papers, **400-B**, B17–B19.

ROBERTS, R. J. 1966. *Metallogenic Provinces and Mineral Belts in Nevada*. Nevada Bureau of Mines Report, **13**, A, 47–72.

RODRIGUEZ, B. D. 1998. Regional crustal structure beneath the Carlin trend, Nevada based on deep electrical geophysical measurements. *In*: TOSDAL, R. M. (ed.) *Contributions to the Gold Metallogeny of Northern Nevada*. US Geological Survey Open-File Report, **98–338**, 15–19.

ROSS, R. J., JR 1977. Ordovician paleogeography of the western United States. *In*: STEWART, J. H., STEVENS, C. H. & FRITSCHE, A. E. (eds) *Paleozoic Paleogeography of the Western United States*. Pacific Section, Society of Economic Paleontologists and Mineralogists, Pacific Coast Paleogeography Symposium, **1**, 19–38.

SILLITOE, R. H. & BONHAM, H. F. 1990. Sediment-hosted gold deposits: distal products of magmatic–hydrothermal systems. *Geology*, **18**, 157–161.

SMITH, D. L. & MILLER, E. L. 1990. Late Paleozoic extension in the Great Basin western United States. *Geology*, **18**, 712–715.

STENGER, D. P., KESLER, S. E., PELTONEN, D. R. & TAPPER, C. J. 1998. Deposition of gold in Carlin-type deposits: the role of sulfidation and decarbonation at Twin Creeks, Nevada. *Economic Geology*, **93**, 201–215.

STEWART, J. H. 1972. Initial deposits in the Cordilleran geosyncline: evidence of a Late Precambrian separation. *Geological Society of America Bulletin*, **83**, 1345–1360.

STEWART, J. H. 1980. *Geology of Nevada*. Nevada Bureau of Mines and Geology Special Publications, **4**.

STEWART, J. H. & POOLE, F. G. 1974. Lower Paleozoic and uppermost Precambrian Cordilleran miogeocline, Great Basin, western United States. *In*: DICKINSON, W. R. (ed.) *Tectonics and Sedimentation*. Society of Economic Paleontologist and Mineralogists, Special Publications, **22**, 28–57.

THORMAN, C. H. & KETNER, K. B. 1979. West-northwest strike-slip faults and other structures in allochthonous rocks in central and eastern Nevada and western Utah. *In*: NEWMAN, G. W. & GOODE, H. D. (eds) *Basin and Range Symposium*. Rocky Mountain Association of Geologists, 123–134.

THORMAN, C. H., KETNER, K. B., BROOKS, W. E., SNEE, L. W. & ZIMMERMAN, R. A. 1991. Late Mesozoic-Cenozoic tectonics in northeastern Nevada. *In*: RAINES, G. L., LISLE, R. E., SCHAFER R. W., & WILKINSON, W. H. (eds) *Geology and Ore Deposits of the Great Basin*, Geological Society of Nevada, Reno, 25–45.

TIMMONS, J. M., KARLSTROM, K. E., DEHLER, C. M., GEISSMAN, J. W. & HEIZLER, M. T. 2001. Proterozoic multistage (*ca.* 1.1 and 0.8 Ga) extension recorded in the Grand Canyon Supergroup and establishment of northwest- and north-trending tectonic grains in the southwestern United States. *Geological Society of America Bulletin*, **113**, 163–190.

TOSDAL, R. M. 2001. Building the structural architecture of the Carlin trend: evidence from the northern Piñon Range, northeastern Nevada. *In*: SHADDRICK, D. R, ZBINDEN, E., MATHEWSON, D. C. & PRENN, C. (eds) *Regional Tectonics and Structural Control of Ore: the major Gold Trends of Northern Nevada*. Geological Society of Nevada Special Publications, **33**, 129–134.

TOSDAL, R. M., WOODEN, J. L. & KISTLER, R. W. 2000. Geometry of the Neoproterozoic continental breakup, and implications for location of Nevada mineral belts. *In*: CLUER, J. K., PRICE, J. G., STRUHSACKER, E. M., HARDYMAN, R. F. & MORRIS, C. L. (eds) *Geology and Ore Deposits 2000: the Great Basin and Beyond*. Geological Society of Nevada, Reno, 451–466.

TRETBAR, D. R., AREHART, G. B. & CHRISTENSEN, J. N. 2000. Dating gold deposition in a Carlin-type gold deposit using Rb/Sr methods on the mineral galkhaite. *Geology*, **28**, 947–950.

VOLK, J., LAUHA, E., LEONARDSON, R. & RAHN, J. 1995. Structural geology of the Betze-Post and Meikle deposits, Elko and Eureka Counties. *In*: GREEN, S. (ed.) *Trip B—Structural Geology of the Carlin Trend, Geology and Ore Deposits of the American Cordillera: Geological Society of Nevada Field Trip Guidebook*, Geological Society of Nevada, Reno, 180–194.

VOLK, J., WEAKLY, C., PENICK, M. & LANDER, A. 2001. Structural geology of the Goldstrike property, north–central Nevada. *In*: SHADDRICK, D. R., ZBINDEN, E., MATHEWSON, D. C. & PRENN, C. (eds) *Regional Tectonics and Structural Control of Ore: The Major Gold Trends of Northern Nevada*. Geological Society of Nevada Special Publications, **33**, 361–380.

WILLIAMS, C. L., THOMPSON, T. B., POWELL, J. L. & DUNBAR, W. 2000. Gold-bearing breccias of the Rain mine, Carlin trend, Nevada, USA. *Economic Geology*, **95**, 391–404.

WILLIAMS, G. D., POWELL, C. M. & COOPER, M. A. 1989. Geometry and kinematics of inversion tectonics. *In*: COOPER, M. A. & WILLIAMS, G. D. (eds) *Inversion Tectonics*. Geological Society, London, Special Publications, **44**, 3–15.

WOODEN, J. L., KISTLER, R. W. & TOSDAL, R. M. 1998. Pb isotopic mapping of crustal structure in the northern Great Basin and relationships to Au deposit trends. *In*: TOSDAL, R. M. (ed.) *Contributions to the Gold Metallogeny of Northern Nevada*. US Geological Survey Open-File Report, **98–338**, 20–33.

WRUCKE, C. T. 1974. *Geologic Map of the Gold Acres–Tenabo Area, Shoshone Range, Lander county, Nevada*. US Geological Survey Map, **MF-647**.

YIGIT, O., NELSON, E. P., HITZMAN, M. W. & HOFSTRA, A. H. 2003. Structural controls on Carlin-type gold mineralization in the Gold Bar district, Eureka County, Nevada. *Economic Geology*, **98**, 1173–1188.

Index

Page numbers in italic, e.g. *118*, refer to figures. Page numbers in bold, e.g. **151**, signify entries in tables